Biographies of Western Photographers

Biographies of Western Photographers

A Reference Guide to Photographers
Working in the 19th Century American West

BY CARL MAUTZ

CARL MAUTZ PUBLISHING 1997

First Edition

Designed by Richard D. Moore
Edited by Rosemarie Mossinger, Cathie Leavitt and Katherine Hudson
Composed in Adobe Garamond type
Printed in the United States of America

Frontispiece: Ormsby's studio, Stockton, California. Carte-de-visite, c. 1865.
Collection of the author.

Library of Congress Catalog No. 94-077984

Cataloging-in-Publication Data

Mautz, Carl
    Biographies of western photographers : a reference guide to photographers
working in the 19th century American west / by Carl Mautz
      p. cm.
      Includes bibliographical references and index.
      ISBN 0-9621940-7-7

    1. Photographers—West (U.S.) 2. Photographers—West (U.S.)—19th
century.   I. Title.

TR139.M38 1997   770.92´2791
                                          QBI96-40141

10 9 8 7 6 5 4 3 2 1

CARL MAUTZ PUBLISHING
228 COMMERCIAL STREET, NO. 522
NEVADA CITY, CALIFORNIA 95959

CONTENTS

ACKNOWLEDGEMENTS

This book results from the efforts of several key people. Richard Moore is foremost, as his cover and page designs provide a fine delivery system for the information contained in the book. Rosemarie Mossinger spent countless hours entering data and cross-referencing information, a task that will, however, require far more hours of labor before full integration is approached. Rosemarie, Cathie Leavitt and Katherine Hudson edited the directories. Olaf is always available when I need advice and support. The "Imprints" essay was massaged by many of my collector/dealer friends, including Ken Appollo, Henry Deeks, Larry Jones, Jeremy Rowe and Olaf, but error and debatable assertions are my responsibility.

Many changes have occurred in my life since the last edition of the *Checklist of Western Photographers*, and with these changes, some notes about who was sending short lists of data about photographers to me have been misplaced, and thus I cannot thank everyone by name. I will try to be a better housekeeper in the period before the next edition.

Those whose names are in my records include Peter Palmquist, who edited an earlier version of the California directory. I compiled the California list, working to a large extent from my prior compilations, my study group of California imprints and from the published work of Peter Palmquist. David Mattison edited the British Columbia list, most of which was derived from his published work. David also edited the Klondike directory. Jeremy Rowe contributed most of the Arizona list. Richard Rudisill's list of New Mexico photographers served as the base for that state's section. Opal Harber's list continues to provide most of the information for Colorado. Mike Cirelli has for years provided raw data to David Mattison, Peter Palmquist and me, so special thanks go to him for his work on Pacific Coast photographers, particularly those in the state of Washington. Bruce Erickson provided much of the information on Hawaii, a list augmented by the research of Lynn Davis. Bradley Richards edited the Utah section. Bruce Hooper generously shared his research on Idaho photographers, which also benefited greatly from the published work of Arthur A. Hart. David Haynes compiled much of the information contained in the Texas section, which was enhanced by contributions from Larry Jones. John Graf contributed a substantial list of photographers from Wisconsin. Loren Jost's research is the basis of the Wyoming list. John Carter's Nebraska Historical Society list was essential to the Nebraska and Iowa sections. David Reeh's compilation is contained in the Oklahoma and Indian Territory lists. Tom Robinson's massive work on Oregon is the source of much of the data provided for that state, and unfortunately time constraints precluded inclusion of his updated research. Joan Schwartz and her colleagues compiled most of the list for Western Canada. Nan Lawler generously provided information on Arkansas photographers. The Kansas Historical Society provided several lists from business directories compiled by their staff on photographers working in Kansas.

Others who have contributed to this book include: Jean Rosenbloom, T. K. "Tex" Treadwell, Paula Fleming, Nicollete Bromberg, John Craig, William Allen, Tracey Baker, Bob Besom, Joanna C. Scherer, Jim Caddick, Ross Kelbaugh, Robert Lewis, Carolyn Marr, Richard Storch, Susan Williams, Jonathan McCabe, John McWilliams, Kristi Wohlschlagel and Manon Wilson.

Finally, I want to thank Robert O. Brown, who inadvertently started me on this path many years ago. I have had the pleasure of renewing my acquaintance with Bob, who continues to be an avid researcher and collector of photographers' imprints.

It has been ten years since the last edition of the Checklist of Western Photographers, a one-hundred page booklet identifying names, towns and estimated dates for photographers working in each western state, territory or province in North America above the Mexican border. The data was recorded primarily from the imprints on photographs which passed by my scrutiny or that of a colleague. In the years since 1986, thousands of additional photographers have been identified as a result of the efforts of many researchers throughout the West. Some of these efforts were self-motivated. Other projects were initiated by institutions. A loose circle of researchers have gathered occasionally and adopted a name, The Regional Photographic History Group. Based on the multiple efforts of these researchers, the amount of information has multiplied. Some states are covered by directories dedicated specifically to that state, while others are covered by unpublished compilations available on computer disk or in photocopy format from institutions. My aim in this book is to give an overview of the data available, to point interested parties toward specific sources of information, and to stimulate continued research.

Despite the massive quantity of data contained in this volume, there is much more information to be compiled, as well as many inter-relationships to be identified and integrated. This compilation is still a work-in-progress, and all additions, corrections and other comments are welcome. Dates are often educated estimates, so more precise dating information is always welcome. The fact is, however, that dating the careers of many photographers will always require some educated speculation, but that's part of the fun and mystery of the process.

The alert reader will notice that each state listing is a little different. Part of the reason is uneven editing, which is my responsibility, but some of it is a result of the source. For example, much of the data for California is based on the research of Peter Palmquist. Peter's compilation of California photographers is well-integrated; he has cross–referenced many entries to blend information from disparate sources. Work remains, of course, but Peter's information is impressive and creates an accurate picture of most California photographers' careers. On the other hand, the compilation of the Kansas Historical Society, although a yeoman effort and

very useful, is simply a recitation of business directory basics, i.e., name, place, date (similar to my Checklist from years past). Much more research is required to create the kind of integrated picture that emerges from Peter Palmquist's work. Another exemplary body of research is David Mattison's work on British Columbia photographers. My hope is that this book will push researchers in the direction of Peter and David's standard.

One might ask why one would bother with such research. Besides being a source of enjoyment and distraction from life's difficulties, can old photographs deepen one's understanding and enhance one's life? I believe they can.

The photographic image allows intimate access to a different time. Would you like to time travel? Ponder an interesting old photograph, and feel the space depicted. Do you want to experience an older culture? Look deeply into the scene and let your emotions connect with the faces, the dress, the grooming, the implements and other features. The photograph is an imprint of time transmitted by light and caught in matter. The image teaches us about the transitory nature of all things, all people and of ourselves. If you gaze into these photographs and let them stir your feelings, a sense of familiarity forms, and you get a sense of of how individuals assume their reality. Each person is shaped by his or her own history and context, and each person makes myriad assumptions about what is real and what is true, but when you realize that they are merely assumptions, they begin to seem less concrete.

The ancient Book of Ecclesiastes asserts that there is nothing new under the sun, and I think this is true and evidenced in photography. There may not have been personal computers a few years ago, but in the realm of human behavior and drama, there is nothing new under the sun. You see this in the faces of the women laced up in corsets and covered with intricate, overflowing petticoats, gowns and coats, or men with broad cravats, vests and greatcoats. One begins to see through the outward differences within this antique milieu, and revealed are the faces of friends, children one grew up with, one's parents, fellow workers and others, but in a different cultural context with its own set of assumptions, its own sense of reality. But nothing seems to have changed in the consciousness of individuals. The stories of the past are relevant to us, because we live the same stories and can empathize with those whose experience parallels ours. So while the photographs tell us of the outward differences of one age from another, in the faces and figures we can see ourselves and realize that no set of assumptions is ever permanent, and that while nothing essential changes, being in the world remains a mystery.

Whatever your motivation, be it distraction from worry, pure fun, aesthetics, cultural fascination or philosophical musing, photographs from the past are an emerging source of interest. Much work remains, however, before the historical framework in which the photographs were created is understood. This is the jigsaw puzzle which Peter Palmquist proposes as a metaphor for the endeavor:

"Whereas it is nigh impossible for a single researcher to find and record all of the world's past photographers, the job can be broken up into smaller bites, with each researcher contributing data from their region. The end result of this cooperative effort, like a completed jigsaw puzzle, provides . . . an understanding far beyond the sum of its parts."

CARL MAUTZ

PREFACE

Over the past decade and a half, compilations of information on early photographers have become more numerous. Their most common format lists people or galleries with dates and locations, while some offer biographical summaries or illustrations and quoted source material. All of them are intended to aid research by illuminating attributions, working regions, or time periods in which the images may be further studied. As each new list appears, the job of archivists and diverse photograph researchers is made easier, and many images begin to reveal their secrets more readily.

Since most previous work has come from the efforts of one or two dedicated people, the results have usually centered on specifically limited geographic areas: one country, one state, or even one city. Only lately have broader coverages appeared to answer new interests in historical photography: women photographers, daguerreotypists, and Pictorialists, for example, but even these have often been restricted geographically. In addition, a degree of frustration remains with the breaks in the trail of mobile picture makers, because the regional pieces have not all been assembled and integrated

within the mosaic. Too often researchers work in unchosen isolation from their next-door neighbors.

This present volume of *Biographies of Western Photographers* takes a needed step of logical advance upon Carl Mautz's earlier checklists as a design for heaving bridges over the gaps in careers and the gaps in communication among researchers. It offers precedent for detailed connections in the overall history of photography and encourages separated researchers to produce the missing pieces. It is an idea whose time has come. It deserves to be appreciated and helped by regionalists and collectors, by genealogists and historians, and by anyone who is concerned with early photographs. Let there be more.

RICHARD RUDISILL
Curator of Photographic History
Palace of the Governors
Museum of New Mexico
Santa Fe

PHOTOGRAPHERS' IMPRINTS
AND INFORMATION ON ANTIQUE PHOTOGRAPHS

*"Everyone who has examined cartes-de-visite and cabinet photographs has been tantalized
by the striking variety of imprints on the backs of the cards."* [1]

WILLIAM C. DARRAH

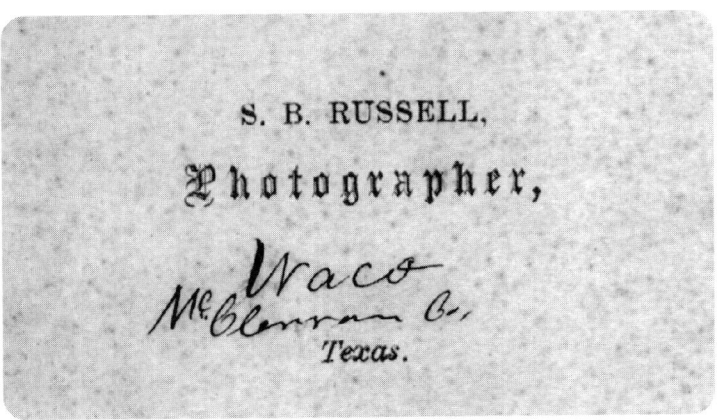

INTRODUCTION

Ken Appollo, an itinerant dealer of antique photographs, advised me many years ago to collect photographers' "imprints." He reasoned that because early book imprints had achieved substantial value in the book collecting market, "backmarks" (as known to some collectors) on photograph mounts would also become valued and collected regardless of the subject or quality of the image itself. My perceptive friend was imparting generous wisdom. This was an unexplored realm of fresh interest to the antique photography collector at an affordable price. In addition, it was a natural progression from the fascination with the image to a hunger for information about the history behind the image. Who were these photographers? Where did they learn their craft? What conditions shaped their technique? What determined where they worked, why they moved, and how they attracted business? Was photography a vocation or an avocation? Who were the operators, the colorists, the managers, and what role did the spouses, children and siblings play? The questions were endless. Answers were buried within the imprints on the image mounts themselves.

I waited ten years before taking Appollo's advice, but in 1986 I began purchasing carte-de-visite and cabinet card portraits for their imprints alone. My motivation was two-fold. First, I wanted to continue to collect information from these photographs for use in compiling biographical information for my book, *Checklist of Western Photographers*. Second, I remembered refusing to purchase a carte-de-visite portrait from Volcano, California, for $1 in 1976, because I thought the price should have been 10 cents. In 1986, I thought that should I be lucky enough to find a carte-de-visite from Volcano priced at $1, I would value it at $10. Thus, my covetous logic continued, a $10 imprint in 1986 might be worth $100 in 1996. It is now 1996, and alas, a Volcano imprint may not be worth much more than $10, rather than the $100 I had fantasized. But greed took hold. Combined with my curiosity for the information itself, I launched an imprint collection which now numbers many thousands. In the process, I contributed to Appollo's travels, during which he located a broad range of imprints, including many scarce examples, which enriched my collection many fold.

1. Half plate daguerreotype with artist's name, "Lemire," a Canadian daguerreotypist, scratched into the surface of the plate, c. 1846.

CASED IMAGES AND EARLY PAPER PRINTS

Initially, some daguerreotype artists followed the custom of painters by scratching their names into the daguerreotype plate. Daguerre, an artist himself, etched his signature in plates produced while developing the daguerreotype process. Those who produced Talbot's paper calotypes also followed the artist's tradition by imprinting their work with written signatures, often on the paper negative. The firm of W & F Langenheim of Philadelphia, for example, signed paper negatives which transferred a positive reflection of the signature onto the calotype print.

As the daguerreotype process spread, however, and portraits were produced for profit, few daguerreotypists signed their work. As the 1840s progressed, astute daguerreotype operators began imprinting their names either on the brass mat protecting the daguerreotype (the first appearing as early as 1840) or on the velvet interior side of the daguerreotype case (illustration 2). In time, the city where the studio was located, and perhaps a studio name, was also imprinted. The practice of imprinting daguerreotype cases or mats, while not uncommon, never became a general practice, however, and collecting "maker marked" daguerreotypes is a distinct specialty in today's market. Toward the end of the era of cased images era around 1860, some studio operators utilized a paper label or printed card on the reverse of the plate to display their imprint.

The practice of imprinting did not increase to any significant degree with the advent of the ambrotype or melainotype, or on the later carte-de-visite size (2½" x 4") tintype in paper envelope or folder. Carte-de-visite specialist Henry Deeks estimates that 10% of the carte-de-visite style tintypes with paper backs contained imprints.

2. Velvet cushion in a sixth plate daguerreotype case used by James M. Ford, c. 1855.

3. Engraved imprint on the mat protecting a quarter plate daguerreotype by Frederick Coombs, c. 1851.

Printed imprints of photographers' names and addresses are found on some calotype or salt print portraits, particularly by some larger studios.

Stereoviews were commercial products intended for widespread distribution, so stereoview producers often utilized imprints for advertising and to identify authorship from about 1854.

CARTE-DE-VISITE AND CABINET CARDS

The carte-de-visite migrated from its place of origin in France to America toward the end of the 1850s and became widespread at the beginning of the Civil War. Imprinting became the rule rather than the exception. One finds many carte-de-visite mounts without imprints, however, although they clearly were made in sophisticated studios. Imprinting required a card stock from a supplier and an arrangement with a printer, so gaps between the purchase of card stock and imprinting were undoubtedly common in the early years. By the 1870s, card companies offered imprinting services as part of their sales of card stock, much like companies today offer calling cards, letterhead, and the like, as services to enhance sales of paper products.

"Cartomania" was a catch word coined by the popular press to reflect the enthusiasm for cartes-de-visite. As this phenomenon evolved throughout the Civil War and post-war western migration, card mount fashions reached a point when each year new variations of colors, edge design, finishes, gilding, etc. appeared. Darrah suggests that "dating a carte-de-visite by style of card stock alone is highly accurate, usually [plus or minus] one year."[2] Appollo, however, allows a five year spread in accuracy based on carte-de-visite mount style. He has pointed out that old card stock was used by some photographers, particularly in rural areas.

4. Rubber stamp imprint of Fosnot & Hunter on the reverse of a stereoview, c. 1875.

5. Civil War carte-de-visite portrait by the Sutterly Brothers, c. 1863.

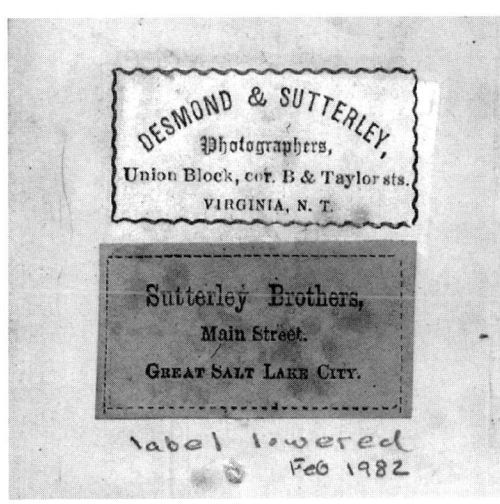

6. Reverse of illustration 5, showing a paper label imprint of the Sutterly Brothers, Great Salt Lake City, and a printed imprint of Desmond & Sutterly, Virginia, Nevada Territory. The paper label was placed over the printed label, and moved by collector/dealer Henry Deeks in 1982, according to Deeks' notes below the label, suggesting that the Sutterlys were using an obsolete mount while traveling in Utah to take photographs during the early 1860s.

7. Manuscript imprint of William M. Godfrey on the reverse of a carte-de-visite, c. 1875.

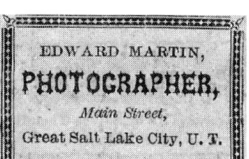

8. Paper labels with photographers' imprints on cartes-de-visite, c. early 1860s.

9. Impressed imprint by Fish Photo, Readstown, Wisconsin, on a grey mount portrait, c. 1910.

10. Rubber stamp imprint of J. Fritz on the reverse of the paper holder of a carte-de-visite size tintype.

TYPES OF IMPRINTS ON MOUNTS

Imprints on photographic mounts or tintype paper holders occur in six general categories. They can be described as follows:

1. Manuscript, i.e., hand written imprints which usually include only the photographer's name and the word "photographer" or "artist";
2. Imprinted paper labels or stamps pasted or glued on the mount, usually on the reverse, and including the photographer's name and the word "photographer" or "artist";
3. Blind stamped name of the photographer, either embossed (raised) or impressed (indented) into the card mount, often into the photographic paper itself;
4. Rubber-stamped name, address and sometimes the logo of the photographer;
5. Printed name and address of the photographer on the front or reverse of the mount. Also frequently found on the reverse are logos, patriotic or mythological symbols, information on services available such as copying, medals or awards won by the studio, prices, personal information such as masonic affiliation of the photographer, and so forth.

In addition to the imprints on mounts and holders, a sixth category exists:

6. Signatures or printed labels etched or affixed on negatives providing information within the photographic print as to the identity of the photographer or subject.

Combinations of these general forms of imprints also occur, particularly rubber stamp overprints on printed names or logos, indicating a new studio proprietor or change of studio location. Paper labels were also utilized to indicate such changes, or were sometimes attached to describe the subject of the image such as those found on the California scenic series by the Thomas Houseworth Studio. Occasionally, information is lined out and substitute information is written in.

Generally, carte-de-visite card mounts contained the photographer's imprint on the reverse of the mount, but fashion shifted, and imprints began appearing on the fronts of the mounts, clearly visible below the

11. Printed imprint with mythological motif on the reverse of a carte-de-visite by William Brown, c. 1862.

12. Imprint of Jesse Whitehurst, Richmond, Virginia, in the negative of a carte-de-visite, c. 1862.

photographic print. By the time the cabinet card era had fully arrived, imprints most often occurred on the bottom front with no imprint at all on the reverse, although throughout the era, some photographers advertised on both front and reverse. By the time an era of "grey mount" blandness eclipsed the rococo variety of late cabinet card styles around the turn-of-the-century, imprints occurred infrequently on the reverse of mounts.

Occasionally, one encounters card mounts with the imprint entirely scratched out, indicating a new studio owner without the means or intent to overprint or substitute new card stock. Scratching may imply more sinister motives, perhaps pirating or stolen mounts or images, although this notion may be more melodramatic fantasy than reality. A curious example I have witnessed was a series of cabinet card portraits of Kiowas by Will Soule. These portraits have always been collectible. Someone took the trouble to scratch out in straight lines Will Soule's name, address and other information printed on the mount. Why? My theory is that the scratching took place before communications media created widespread knowledge of Soule's images, and the obliteration of the name was a way to create ambiguity around the authorship of the photographs and allow distance between selling stolen photographs and identification of the crime involved. But who knows?

13. Printed imprint on a carte-de-visite, c. 1870, by I. H. Bonsall showing a Kansas City, Kansas, studio location with a rubber stamp overprint indicating an additional Arkansas City, Kansas, studio location.

14. Printed imprint on a carte-de-visite, c. 1875, by Pryse & Ewing, showing a change of studio location from Red Cloud, Nebraska, to Hastings, Nebraska. The change is indicated by the ink line through the name Red Cloud and the name Hastings written below.

15. Printed imprint at the bottom of a cabinet card portrait, c. 1890.

16. *Various tax stamps on cartes-de-visite, 1864-66.*

TAX STAMPS

At the height of the demand for carte-de-visite portraits during the Civil War, the federal government levied a tax on "sun pictures" beginning August 1, 1864. The law required photographers to collect a tax for each photograph sold, to affix a revenue stamp to the reverse of the photograph, and to hand cancel each stamp with name or initials and date of sale. Some larger studios were allowed to avoid the stamp requirement and report revenues by paying taxes monthly, while others simply ignored the requirement. Still others affixed only one stamp to one of several cartes-de-visite ordered (often one of a dozen). Thus, the absence of a stamp does not mean a particular image was made outside the period when revenue stamps were required. Many photographers simply made an "x" mark, while others made small dash marks on the stamps, and still others used punch or rubber stamp cancellations. Some large studios may have cancelled by the sheet by drawing a line in ink across the entire grid.

The tax required on most photographs was based on the retail price of the photograph. The following are tax rates on photographs:
2 cents on photographs selling for less than 25 cents;
3 cents on photographs selling for 25 cents to 50 cents;
5 cents on photographs selling for 50 cents to $1;
5 cents on photographs selling for each additional $1 or part thereof.

All revenue stamps issued were legal to use, and all but the "Certificate" stamp are known to have been used, because the "Certificate" stamp was sold out prior to the tax being imposed on photographs. All denominations of stamps from one cent to fifteen cents are known to have been used on photographs.

There were no revenue stamps issued entitled "Photograph," although one was designed. My small collection of tax stamped photographs reveals the following titles:
Proprietary
Bank Check
Playing Cards
Telegraph
Express
Inland Exchange

Colors of stamps vary and different stamps appear in myriad combinations. Errors and unusual perforations provide additional variety.

The requirement to affix revenue stamps to photographs was repealed and terminated on August 1, 1866, so photographs with revenue stamps date from between the start and end dates of the law, and those with dates written by hand reflect the exact day the photograph was sold.

The most common photographs with stamps affixed are cartes-de-visite. Tintypes and stereoviews are less common. Some other photograph formats have been noted with revenue stamps, but they are scarce. Another factor determining scarcity is location, because studios in urban areas appeared more conscientious about affixing stamps than those in remote locales. Photographers in California's mother lode towns, however, provided many interesting examples of small town imprints with revenue stamps.

OTHER STAMPS

Postage stamps were sometimes used as tax stamps, although this was an illegal practice. Photographs were sometimes mailed without envelopes, which could result in postage stamps being affixed to the mount and/or a postal cancellation. Thus, it might be possible to find a photograph with imprint, revenue and postal stamp, and photographer's and postal cancellations as well. If discovered, such a combination would be extremely rare.

An additional type of stamp or label sometimes found on carte-de-visite mounts are those customarily in use by booksellers or stationers, many of whom carried commercially produced photographs for sale as products. California's Lawrence & Houseworth, for example, sold cartes-de-visite and stereoviews of popular statuary and portraits of famous European personalities in their shop and affixed their stationer's stamp to the mount or impressed it with a blind stamp.

MANUSCRIPT NOTES OR IDENTIFICATIONS

Other interesting sources of information, and variations to imprint collecting, are manuscript notes, doodles and identifications of sitters. Styles of handwriting are often attractive due to the practice of good penmanship, favored in times past but largely lost to us today. The variety of information is infinite, and the following are a few examples of what can be discovered:

1. Genealogical leads provided by subject identifications open many avenues to research;
2. Notes can indicate the relationship of the photograph's subject to historical events;
3. Notes often provide clues to cultural assumptions and values prevalent during the period of the photograph format, thus reflecting cultural history;
4. Personal notes often reveal a sense of humor or reflect psychological attitudes and feelings, such as romantic longing or self-deprecation;
5. Sometimes the notes are from the photographer to an assistant with instructions for enlargements, copying or hand coloring, indicating practices among portrait photographers of the era;
6. Drawings and doodles reflect varied cultural influences and the likelihood that old photographs have served as a prime source of art paper for children.

A collectible imprint combined with an interesting manuscript identification and commentary is demonstrated in illustration 23.

First, the imprint combines both a paper label and printed matter, the latter being the words: "PHOTOGRAPHIC ARTIST." The paper label reflects the photographer's name, i.e., Joseph Haag, but Mr. Haag's name is preceded by an ampersand (&), suggesting that the label was once part of a larger label and that the first name was torn off. Turning to the index of photographers in this book, one finds Joseph Haag in Kansas with the following entry:

HAAG, JOSEPH
Active in Leavenworth, 1870–99. Partner in Ploetz & Haag, 1870–71, at 99 Shawnee; at 404 Delaware Street, 1876–80; 406 Delaware Street

17. *Paper label imprint on a carte-de-visite by H. K. Roberts, c. 1865, with two cent tax stamp(cancelled by ink slash marks) affixed and the subject identified in manuscript.*

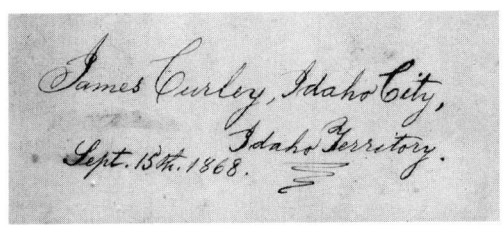

18. *Dated manuscript identification of the subject on a carte-de-visite without a photographer's imprint, c. 1860.*

19. *Reverse of a cabinet card portrait of a young girl by Rifenburg & Dowe, Reno, Nevada, c. 1885. Doodle of "Count Lemons" and identification of the author as "artist James Wilcox."*

20. Carte-de-visite portrait of "Jack," c. 1866, by C. L. Hamilton, Fort Randall, D. T.

21. Reverse of illustration 20 with the photographer's printed imprint and manuscript notes in pencil as follows: "He is a Yanktonian. He was struck by lightning & while he lay senseless & was supposed dying, he dreamed that the great final battle was fought—that the whites were victorious." Another note dates the carte-de-visite (or the lightning strike) June 7, 1866.

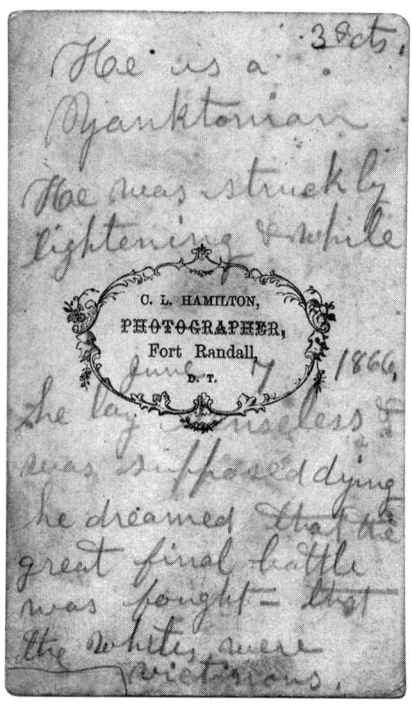

(one imprint shows 404 Delaware Street), 1882–97. Retoucher, Bauer's Studio, 1897–98; partner with John Cassella at 102 South 5th, 1899–1900, operating as Cassella & Haag. Julia Haag, listed as a photographer in Leavenworth, 1896–97, could be Joseph Haag's daughter.

Since the imprint is on a carte-de-visite mount commonly used in the 1860s, it seems likely that the label was a remnant of a partnership with Ploetz from an earlier year than accorded the partnership in my biographical entry, i.e., 1870–71, that Mr. Haag was using an earlier style carte-de-visite mount on work he was doing after 1871, or that Mr. Haag had an as yet unidentified partner prior to 1870.

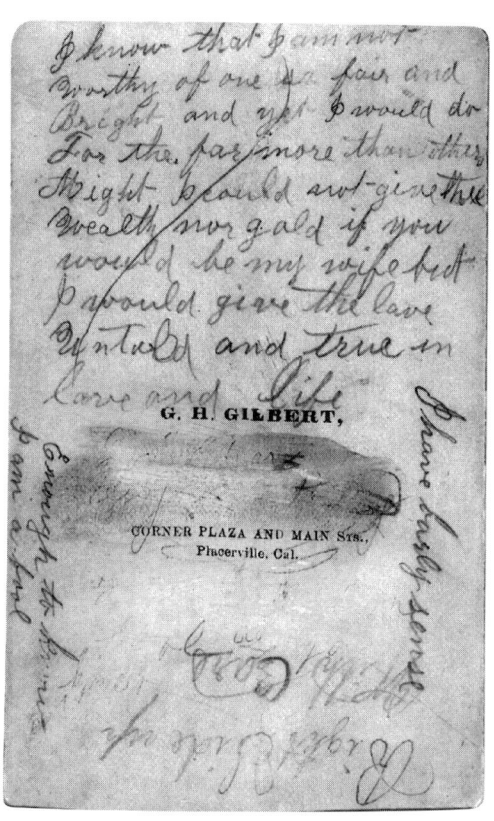

22. Carte-de-visite portrait of a young woman by G. H. Gilbert, c. 1875. The reverse contains a printed imprint and notes, with part of the notes crudely erased away (comparison with identical Gilbert imprints indicates there was no printing in the area erased). The unerased notes read, "I know that I am not worthy of one so fair and bright and yet I would do for thee far more than others might. I could not give thee wealth nor gold if you would be my wife, but I would give thee love untold and true in love and life."
In another space, a note in another hand reads, "I have barely sense enough to know I am a fool." And in perhaps yet another hand, the words appear, "Right Side up, With Care."

Turning to the manuscript writing on the card mount, the identification was made by one person, and the remainder of the information by another. The first writing identifies the subject of the portrait, "M. Legard, Aged 28 yrs, 6 months, Ti . . . ." The second hand "Ti . . ." to complete the word "Time: 1870 or 1871, Cleveland, Ohio." The second writer goes on to provide details from the life of M. Legard including an opinion that Legard was a vain and henpecked man whose wife caused him to change his name from Schuett to Legard to imply French ethnicity rather than Dutch.

The imprint and writing on this photograph provide a rich variety of information through its combination of partial, printed paper label; printed title on the mount; manuscript identification; and manuscript notes by a second hand, reflecting cultural information and psychological attitudes and feelings.

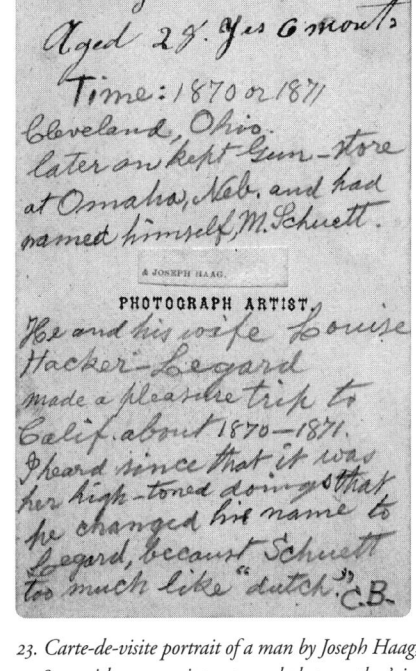

23. Carte-de-visite portrait of a man by Joseph Haag, c. 1870, with manuscript notes and photographer's imprint on a torn paper label.

TRACING CAREERS

One rewarding pursuit for the imprint collector or researcher is following the progression of photographers from location to location, particularly along routes that evolved through the expansion of the American West. Imprints also reveal the vagaries of human relationships as partners coupled, uncoupled and re-coupled in one location or another.

The Sutterly Brothers, Clement and J. K., provide an interesting example of various forms of movement and association. The following is a list of name and place identifications on printed imprints in my collection (not necessarily in chronological order):

Sutterly Bros.. . . . . Salt Lake City, U.T.
Desmond & Sutterly. . . Virginia, N.T.
Sutterly . . . . Wadsworth, Nev.
Sutterly . . . . Elko, Nev.
Sutterly & Co. . . . . Virginia, Nev.
Sutterly . . . . Virginia, Nev.
Sutterly Bros.. . . . . Virginia, N.
Sutterly Bros.. . . . . Napa City, Cal.
Sutterly & Dart. . . . . . . Traveling
                              Photographer
Sutterly . . . . Lakeport, Cal.
C. Sutterly. . . . . Traveling
                              Photographer Cal.
C. Sutterly. . . . . Ukiah, Cal.
C. Sutterly. . . . . Ione, Cal.
Sutterly . . . . Ione, Cal.
C. Sutterly. . . . . Amador County,
                              Traveling
                              Photographer

Researchers have also noted imprints for Pilliner & Sutterly in Nevada; Sutterly & Rendall; and Sutterly Brothers & Junk, Idaho City, Idaho, 1865–66.

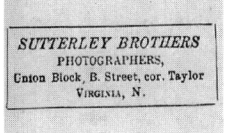

24. Various carte-de-visite and cabinet card imprints relating to the Sutterly brothers, Clement and K. J., and several of their partners, c. 1860–85.

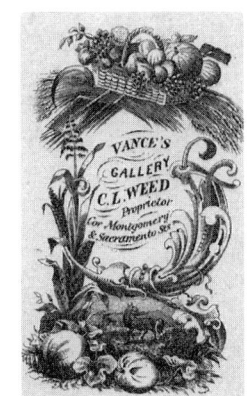

25. Printed imprint on a carte-de-visite by C. L. Weed, who bought Vance's Gallery in 1861.

26. Impressed imprint on a carte-de-visite portrait and mount by Bradley & Rulofson, SanFrancisco, c. 1875.

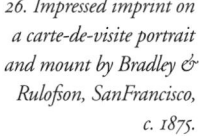

27. Printed imprint with a drawing on the reverse of a carte-de-visite by Marston, San Francisco, c. 1875.

28. Various printed imprints on cartes-de-visite by medium and small town California photographers, c. 1870–80.

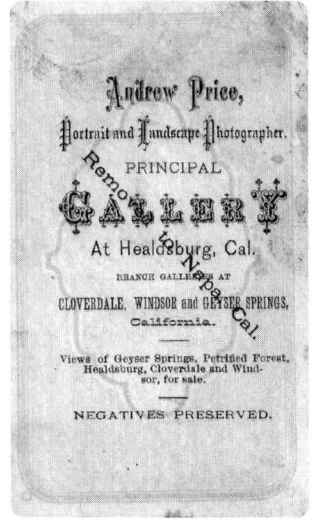

GEOGRAPHICAL LOCATION RELATED TO SCARCITY

Scarcity of imprints varies widely from place to place. Most of my experience is in collecting imprints from California, where scarce imprints have begun to be collected by a small cadre of collectors and regionalists. From my field experience, some structure can be ascribed to what is available.

California carte-de-visite imprints can be divided roughly into five categories based on the size of the town in which the studio operated, plus a "wild card" category consisting of itinerants. The meaning of town size in this context is imprecise and refers to the approximate population during the period when the photograph was produced, not the size of the town today.

My five categories of California towns during the carte-de-visite era plus the sixth for itinerants is as follows:

1. Metropolis: There was one metropolis in California during the 19th century: San Francisco. People visited this major seaport from all over the world as well as all parts of California, many taking a "likeness" home in the form of a carte-de-visite portrait. San Francisco was home to a great number of photography studios, far more than any other city in the West. The list includes major operators like William Shew, G. D. Morse, B. F. Howland, C. E. Watkins, Bradley & Rulofson, and many more. These studios produced vast quantities of photographs. San Francisco imprints are common, but within the mass of imprints available are scarce or rare imprints from short lived studios, itinerants, or from larger operators who altered imprints periodically. Vance's Gallery and its successors, first C. L. Weed and then Bradley & Rulofson, used different designs with various mythological motifs, some of which appear to be relatively scarce. I count twenty-seven distinct varieties of Vance, Weed and/or Bradley & Rulofson imprints in my collection.

2. Regional cities: These are regional, commercial hubs with many photography studios, and include Oakland, Sacramento, Stockton, San Jose, Los Angeles, etc. Imprints from the larger operators in these towns are fairly common, although some early examples are scarce.

3. Large towns: These towns were big enough to support several photography studios and produced significant quantities of imprinted photographs. Marysville, Oroville, Chico, San Diego, Santa Cruz, Placerville, Eureka, Petaluma, etc. can be included in this category. Some early examples of such imprints are scarce.

4. Medium towns: Examples are Nevada City, Dutch Flat, Napa, Watsonville, Vallejo, San Luis Obispo, Healdsburg, Visalia, Tulare City, Riverside, San Bernardino, Santa Barbara, etc. Imprints from these towns are scarce. One album, however, full of imprinted carte-de-visite photographs from one locale can create the illusion that they are less scarce than they actually are.

5. Small towns: These are the towns with truly scarce imprints, because they either had not acquired substantial populations by the end of the carte-de-visite era, such as San Rafael, Anaheim, Davisville, Pajaro, Suisun, etc., or they had expanded and drastically contracted with the vagaries of mineral discoveries, such as Howland Flat, Gold Hill, Forest City, Iowa Hill, Bodie, etc.

6. The "wild card" category covers traveling or itinerant photographers. Some were major operators seeking expanded business contacts, while others seem to have been enamored of the life-style or forced to it through necessity.

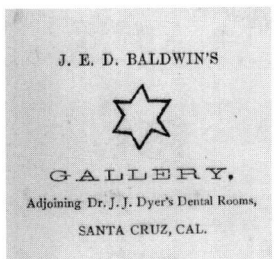

29. Various printed imprints on cartes-de-visite by medium and small town California photographers, c. 1870–80.

Among the interesting imprints in this group are those noting boldly the nature of the traveling studio. Examples of these imprints include:

Smith's California Photo Car
Abell's Art-Studio Car
E. A. Bonine, Tent Photographer, California
Rifenburg and Dowe, Portable Building
R. Rogers, Traveling Photographer,
    California
McGinley & Shubert's Flying Photograph
    Gallery, California

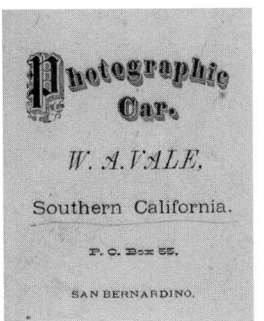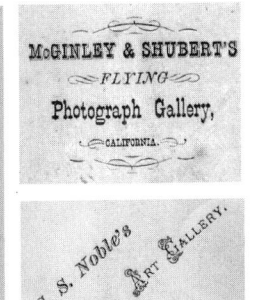

30. Various printed imprints on cartes-de-visite by traveling California photographers, c. 1860–75.

Some photographers imply their nomadic service by referring to California without specifying a city. For example:

Carl Schuman Photo, Cal.
Schuman & Bruner, Photo, Cal.
S. S. Noble's Photographic Parlors, Cal.
California Art Co.

A combination of both imprint and a manuscript identification refering to a geographic location can indicate a traveling photographer. An example from my collection is a carte-de-visite with the rubber stamp imprint: "From B. F. Steven's Photo' Gallery" and a manuscript identification written above the imprint: "Mrs. White, Grizzly Flat."

Other itinerants identify their base of operations, such as:

Boston Railroad Photo Car, Pacific Coast
    Address, Sacramento, Cal.
Elite Photo Studio, Traveling 1891,
    Permanent Address, 107 Grove Street, San Francisco

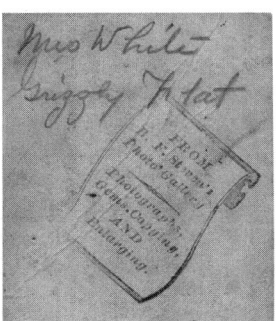

31. Rubber stamp imprint with manuscript identification on a carte-de-visite portrait of a woman by B. F. Steven, a traveling photographer working around Sonora, California, in the 1870s.

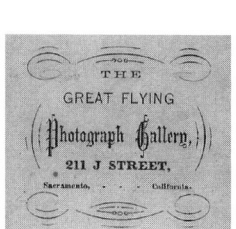

32. Printed imprints on cartes-de-visite by J. C. Kemp, a traveling California photographer, c. 1870s.

One particularly energetic entrepreneur was J. C. Kemp of Sacramento, whose traveling imprints include:

Kemp & Kluit, Traveling Photographers
J. C. Kemp Flying Photograph Gallery
Great Flying Photograph Gallery
The Great Flying Photograph Gallery
Celebrated Flying Photograph Gallery
Celebrated Great Flying Photograph Gallery (one carte-de-visite in my collection has a Virginia [City] address)
Great Celebrated Centennial Flying Photograph Gallery

There are many similar examples of traveling photographers' imprints with numerous variations for every state of the United States.

TERRITORIAL IMPRINTS

One particularly fascinating area of imprint collecting relates to the Territories of the United States. Territories that existed within the period when paper photographs were produced (generally after 1858) and the Territorial designations found on imprints in my collection are as follows:

33. Printed imprint with blanks for writing in photograph number, place (Alaska Territory) and caption on a carte-de-visite by Edweard Muybridge, from his Alaska trip in 1873.

34. Tax stamp on a carte-de-visite, c. 1865, and a rubber stamp imprint by A. & M. Stafford, successors to the photographer identified in a printed imprint as C. H. Walker, Brownsville, N. T. (Nebraska Territory).

STATE	STATEHOOD GRANTED	TERRITORIAL DESIGNATIONS
Alaska	1958	"Alaska Ter" (hand written on Muybridge's Helios carte-de-visite mount from his 1868 survey.)
Arizona	1912	A. T.
Colorado	1876	C. T.; Col. Ter'y
Dakota [N. & S.]	1889	D. T.; Dakota
Hawaii	1958	H. I.
Idaho	1890	I. T.; Idaho T.
Indian/Oklahoma	1907	I. T.; Indian Territory; O. T.
Kansas	1861	None found to date
Minnesota	1858	None found to date
Montana	1889	M. T.; Montana Ty.
Nebraska	1867	N. T., Neb. Ter.
Nevada	1864	N. T.
New Mexico	1912	None found to date
Utah	1896	U. T.
Washington	1889	W. T.; Wash. Ter.; Wash'g Ter.; Washington Ter.
Wyoming	1890	W. Ter.; Wy. Ter.

ETHNIC IMPRINTS

Another approach to imprint collecting relates to imprints with ethnic identities suggested by various factors, including or in addition to the imprint. On one hand, however, this aspect of imprint collecting seems too vague in that every name suggests some ethnic origin. English surnames are by far the most common. Dutch, German, Irish, Scottish and French are also common. Americans mixed and moved from the beginning of the nation, so the jumble of European surnames scattered throughout the West reduces the interest such imprints might have, at least to the general collector. Another important and unfortunate factor is that there were large numbers of Americans, such as African and Native Americans, whose ethnic names were eliminated en masse, thus eradicating one index to collecting antique images based on ethnic identity. Anglicizing names was common for many Europeans as well, particularly those from eastern or southern Europe.

On the other hand, there are distinct indices of ethnicity, and when two or more of these indices overlap, a collectible quality occurs similar to the collectible resonance that occurs with the appearance of the word "Territory" on an imprint. If the photographer's name and the studio's community share a history of ethnicity, interest is enhanced. If the photographer's name, location, facial features and clothing of the subject, and manuscript writing on the mount suggest an ethnic identity, or if the studio name displays ethnic pride, there is even more interest in collecting the image and its imprint.

35. *Carte-de-visite, c. 1875, without a photographer's imprint. Portrait of Johnny Adams, a Shoshone, found in an album belonging to the Bauer Family of Sacramento, California. Mr. Adams has adopted non-native clothing and hair style for this portrait, but his facial features clearly reveal that he is a Native American. The subject is identified in penciled manuscript on the reverse of the mount.*

36. *Cabinet card of "Chin Fah" [sic] by Wai Chen Hin of San Francisco, c. 1880.*

37. Printed imprint on the reverse of illustration 36.

Categories of ethnic indicators include:

1. Studio or photographer's name, such as Wai Chen Hin, a Chinese photographer in San Francisco, or Vitalini & Bianchi, also of San Francisco;
2. Studio identity, such as Flaten & Skrivseth's Norsk Atelier, August Timpe's Deutsch Photography (cover illustration), or Galeria de la Plaza Los Angeles ;
3. A branch studio in a home country such as Aune of Portland, Oregon, with a branch in Trondhjem [sic], Norway;
4. Manuscript identification on the photograph or mount, such as "Fratelli Bafio di Cesare" (brothers of the family Bafio di Cesare) written on the reverse of a cabinet card by Arnold of San Luis Obispo, a California seaport well known for its Italian population in the 19th century;
5. Ethnic appearance or costume;
6. Locations with distinct ethnic populations such as North Beach, the center of San Francisco's "Little Italy," or Honolulu, Hawaii, a crossroads of ethnic diversity including Portuguese, Japanese, Anglo American, Polynesian, etc. Some states are known for the ethnic identity of large segments of their populations, such as Wisconsin and Minnesota.

38. Carte-de-visite by Aune with printed imprint indicating studios in Norway and Oregon, c. 1890.

39. Cabinet card portrait of an Italian family in San Luis Obispo with a manuscript notation in Italian on the reverse.

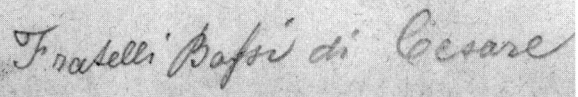

A quick look at my small collection of cabinet cards with Wisconsin imprints suggests a large German population as revealed by the following names:

Breitwisch	Koerner	Schubert
Goetz	Krueger	Spettel
Halbach	Menzel	Weigand
Hagendorff	Scharf	Wollensak

A spot count of my Minnesota cartes-de-visite totaled seventy-four different photographers on various imprints with twenty-three having Scandinavian last names, or 31% of the total.

As examples of ethnic indicators, consider the following: Illustrations 41, the front and reverse of a cabinet card dating around 1880: One can start anywhere, as there are at least four indicators of ethnicity, all of which suggest Polynesian. The indices include facial features, dress, location and the manuscript name, "Annie Kauahele."

Illustration 42 is a cabinet card portrait in my collection with the imprint, D. James Palace Car. The folks dancing in the image both wear wooden shoes and are clothed in everyday, winter garb. To me this suggests northern European ethnicity, cold weather, and farm country. Scanning the directories for states in the northern part of the west, I found D. James in Wisconsin, whose studio was in Marshfield around 1880. I concluded from this that D. James operated as a traveling photographer out of Marshfield, Wisconsin, in rural regions such as the Dakotas, Minnesota, Iowa, etc.; that the subjects of the photograph were probably of Scandinavian or German ethnicity; that they were country folk; and that at least this traveling photographer braved winter weather to ply his trade.

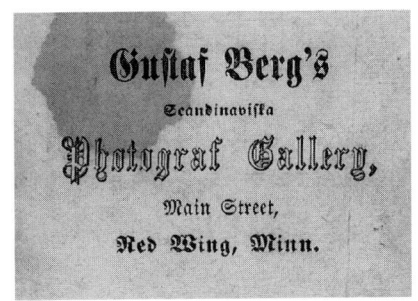

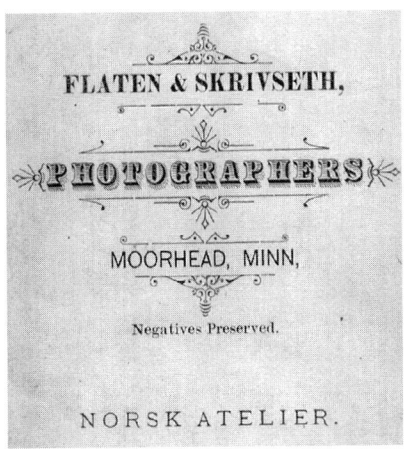

40. Printed imprints on cartes-de-visite by Minnesota photographers with Scandinavian names, c. 1870-75.

42. Cabinet card portrait of a dancing couple by D. James, a traveling photographer out of Marshfield, Wisconsin, c. 1880.

41. Cabinet card portrait of Annie Kauahele, c. 1880, by Montano of Honolulu, Hawaii, a photographer of Portuguese descent.

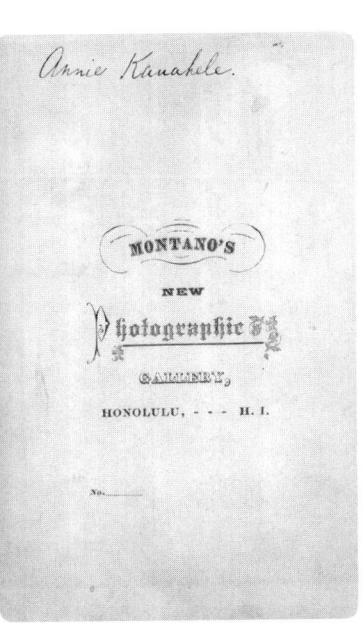

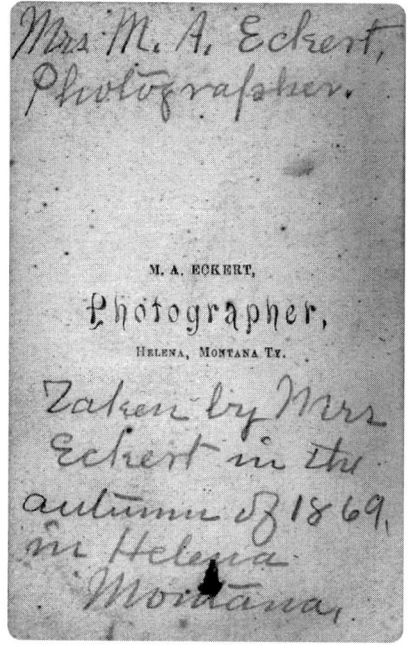

GENDER AND MARITAL STATUS

Some collectors, such as the dean of California photo-historians, Peter Palmquist, look for imprints reflecting women photographers. Most imprints clearly indicate masculine identities, as it was the men who pursued careers for the most part in the 19th century. Women, however, were integrating various occupations, and since photography was new, it provided ripe opportunities to women with inclinations toward art, business, or both.

In addition to gender identification, occasionally husband and wife identities are specified by the use of "Mr. and Mrs." Also, the marital status of women photographers is expressed by the use of Miss or Mrs. One imprint from northern California near the Oregon border, has a blank after an ampersand following the name "Wells," and the blank is filled in by hand with the word "Lady." Thus, "Wells & Lady" is the imprint for the photographer at the time the photograph was made. (One wonders what other word might be inserted instead of "Lady.")

43. Cartes-de-visite with imprints indicating women photographers, c. 1866–75, either alone or with a husband.

44. Carte-de-visite with a partially printed imprint with blanks filled in by hand, c. 1867.

VALUE

To my knowledge, no one has conducted a thorough study of imprint values. The value of imprints and other information contained on photographs depends on the interest of collectors, be they individuals or institutions. The current market relates to many factors, some enumerated below. Additional factors affecting value are novelty of subject, print quality and overall condition of mount and image. For example, a period identification in manuscript which identifies the subject of a photograph as a famous Western outlaw should greatly enhance the value of the photograph itself. The manuscript identification of the subject may also have value itself. If a signature is by a known person, it will have value on the autograph market. A period message of historic importance will have value in the market for historical documents, and any relationship to the photograph itself should enhance the value of the photograph. An imprint alone may have value to some colletors if it is from a town no longer in existence, such as Scales, California. Someone else may value a Territorial designation in an imprint, because they value artifacts or documentation from a particular Territory of the United States.

Specific values for the various types of imprints have yet to be established. Some perceptive observers, such as Connecticut dealer William L. Schaeffer, place premiums on manuscript imprints as the rarest of early photographers' imprints (e.g. illustration 48).

After manuscript imprints, embossed or impressed imprints appear to be the scarcest, although this scarcity is a relative fact, since some studios issued large numbers of embossed or impressed cartes-de-visite. For example, during the 1870s, the San Francisco firms of Bradley & Rulofson, G. D. Morse and Carleton E. Watkins all impressed their names with a blind stamp on both print and mount. In Sacramento, J. A. Todd embossed his cartes-de-visite with a blind stamp in the 1860s just below the photographic print.

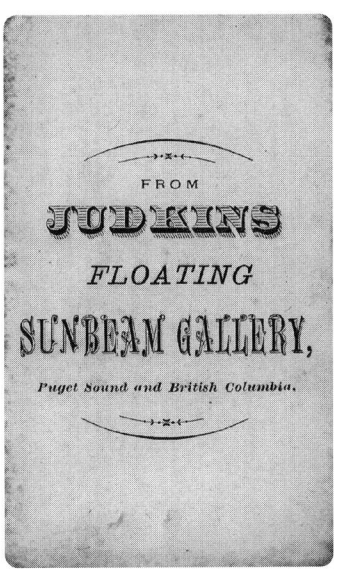

45. Territorial imprints: (left) a carte-de-visite by George D. Wakely, Colorado Territory, c. 1861;(below) a cabinet card by C. C. Stotz, El Reno, Oklahoma Territory, c. 1890.

46. Cartes-de-visite with imprints indicating traveling photographers, c. 1875-80.

47. Rubber stamp imprint with manuscript identification of the studio location on a carte-de-visite by James H. Lucas, Standing Rock, Dakota Territory, c. 1875.

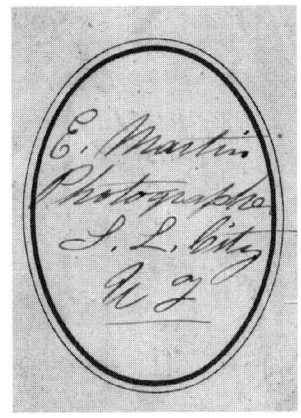

48. Manuscript imprint with printed border on a carte-de-visite by Edward Martin, Salt Lake City, Utah Territory, c. 1865.

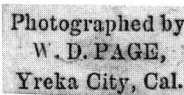

49. Paper label imprints on California cartes-de-visite, c. 1860-65.

50. Rubber stamp imprint on a carte-de-visite portrait by George Fardon when he operated in Victoria, Vancouver Island, c. 1860.

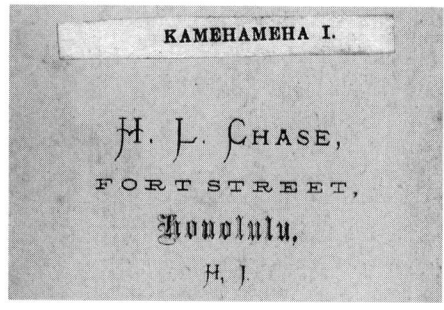

51. Carte-de-visite by H. L. Case, Honolulu, Hawaiian Islands, c. 1865, with printed photographer's imprint and a paper label describing the subject of the photograph.

I find small paper label imprints to be attractive and desirable. These paper labels appeared early in the carte-de-visite era and disappeared quickly but not entirely. California photographer William Shew used a paper label on many of his early cartes-de-visites. I have collected four different colors of Shew paper label imprints, and one blue one on the back of an ambrotype in a wall frame. Scarcer paper labels have appeared on photographs by California photographers working outside of San Francisco such as Oroville photographer E. A. Kusel, Yreka City's W. D. Page, Eureka's H. Anderson, and Sherriff of Sac. City.

Paper labels were replaced by printed and rubber stamp imprints, the latter being by far the scarcer of the two, often indicating, a more modest photographic establishment.

Overprinted imprints are often scarce and tell a story of the sale or failure of one gallery and the establishment of a new one.

Imprints appearing in the negative occurred late in the 19th century in America, so early examples are somewhat scarce, although the practice appears more common in England. I looked through thousands of my California cartes-de-visite and found not one example of a name appearing in the negative. On the other hand, I have a carte-de-visite by Jesse Whitehurst, famed Virginia daguerreotypist, with his name tastefully imprinted on the negative, and another by the major Montreal photographer, William Notman.

Regarding value, the subject, quality and condition cannot be ignored. If an imprint is rare, neither ordinary subject, substandard production quality, nor ragged condition will deter a collector from purchasing the imprint at a fair price; but should the photograph that goes with the imprint depict a fascinating subject, exhibit the highest print quality, or be in mint condition, then value appreciates according to the enhancement introduced by each such element.

All of the salient factors related to types of imprints—studio location, manuscript identification or information, tax stamps and cancellations, postal stamps and cancellations, other stamps, subject interest, image quality and overall condition—establish the value of a photograph collected for its photographer's imprint.

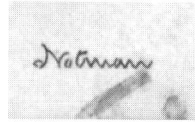

52. Carte-de-visite portrait, c. 1870, by Notman with Notman's signature in the negative.

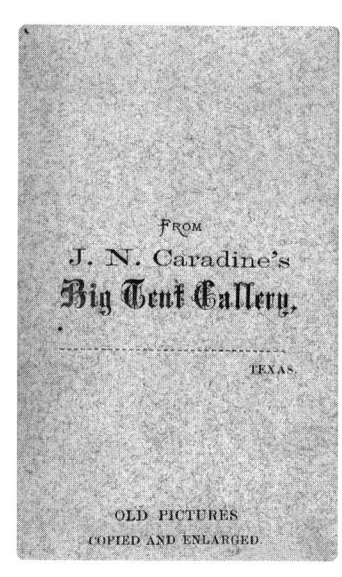

53. Carte-de-visite, c. 1880, with a printed imprint for J. N. Caradine, traveling photographer, leaving a blank after Texas for the name of the town to be filled in.

LIST OF FACTORS INFUENCING IMPRINT VALUE

A. TYPES OF IMPRINTS:
1. Manuscript
2. Blind stamp–embossed
3. Blind stamp–impressed
4. Paper label re photographer's identity
5. Rubber stamp
6. Printed
7. Photographer's identity in the negative–manuscript
8. Photographer's identity in the negative–printed
9. Combinations of any or all of the above

B. MANUSCRIPT:
1. Identification
2. Historical information
3. Cultural information
4. Personal information
5. Photographer's instructions
6. Drawings and doodles
7. Subject information in negative
8. Combinations of any or all of the above

C. TAX STAMPS:
1. Values
2. Colors
3. Titles
4. Perforation varieties
5. Errors

D. TAX STAMP CANCELLATIONS:
1. Initials
2. Dates

3. Marks
4. Hole punches
5. Rubber stamps

E. OTHER STAMPS AND CANCELLATIONS:
1. Stationer
2. Bookseller
3. Apothecary, etc.
4. Postal
5. Postal cancellation
6. Subject identification

F. GEOGRAPHICAL LOCATION:
1. Metropolis
2. Regional cities
3. Large towns
4. Medium towns
5. Small towns
6. Itinerant
7. Territorial

G. ETHNICITY, GENDER AND MARITAL STATUS:
1. Photographer's name
2. Studio identity
3. Branch studio in a home country
4. Subject identification
5. Ethnic look or dress
6. Locations with distinct ethnic population
7. Gender
8. Marital status

CONCLUSION

This system of categorization underscores the variety available in collecting antique photography. This system does not purport to be complete, nor is it expected to satisfy all collectors and researchers. It can provide structure for identifying, categorizing and valuing photographers' imprints and accompanying information. Without question, there is much more to be learned about these subjects. Undoubtedly, some photographers' imprints are much scarcer than others. Where there is scarcity, there will be the pursuit of value, and where there is information, there will be research. Each endeavor augments the other, and with each, the panorama of history becomes clearer.

1. Darrah, William C., carte-de-visite in *Nineteenth Century Photography*, W. C. Darrah, Gettysburg, Pennsylvania, 1981, p. 16.
2. Ibid, p. 15.

DATING EARLY PHOTOGRAPHS BY FORMAT AND MOUNT INFORMATION

by Jeremy Rowe

Early photographs can generally be dated by format and mount type. Notations on the mounts may provide additional information about the image, but should always be verified by other sources if possible.

Printed mount notations such as photographer's identification and title are fairly reliable, but can still provide false information. Handwritten notations are the most suspect, often being added long after the image was made by persons with only secondary knowledge. Some weight can be given to apparent period notation—in fountain pen or pencil—as opposed to ball point, but the information should be compared with other clues such as format, mount style, period of operation for identified photographers, "logic" related to events occurring near the time indicated, etc.

Dating by mount type and style provides another rough indicator for identifying images. The caveat is that many photographers, particularly in more remote areas, failed to keep up with photographic fashion and used old mounts until their stocks were exhausted.

An additional concern stems from the recent increase in interest and demand for historic photographs. The increasing activity in the photographic market has caused some forgeries to appear. In addition to simply adding incorrect notations about subject or location on the mount, more sophisticated efforts to mislead have appeared in recent years. False attributions for photographers such as Henry Buehman and Adam C. Vroman have been placed on images with rubber stamps to identify them as Arizona or Western photographs and improve marketability. Some of these images have even found their way into institutional collections to be used to "prove" the correctness of other forgeries in the marketplace.

Images have also been removed and remounted on more interesting mounts to increase value. Photographic postcards have been falsified by rubber stamping logos and stamp boxes onto vintage and contemporary photographs to make them appear to be historic images. Photographs of military subjects taken at re-enactments have also been portrayed—and sold—as vintage images. Unfortunately, as time goes on, and competition and value effect the market, the number and creativity of forgers will increase. The best protection is knowledge, either your own, or that of an expert.

Given this preface, the following information is provided to assist in verification of dating using information based on the type and style of the photographic mount.

CASED PHOTOGRAPHS

Daguerreotype	1839–1858 + or −
Ambrotype	1854–1865 + or −
Melaineotype, Ferrotype, Tintype and Panotype (leather, paper or oilcloth)	1856–1900 +

CARD MOUNTED PHOTO DESIGNATION BY SIZE

Postage stamp photographs (also Gem size tintypes)	$^{15}/16''$ x 1 $^{7}/16''$	1877
Stereograph	3½" x 7" to 5"x 7"	1850s to 1950s
Cartes-de-visite	2½" x 4"	1850s to 1900s
Kodak formats:		
circular images 2½" diameter produced by Original & #1 Kodak cameras		1888
circular images 3½" diameter produced by#2 Kodak cameras		1889
circular images 3¼" diameter produced by #3 Kodak cameras		1890
rectangular 4" x 5" images produced by#4 Kodak cameras		1890
Boudoir	5½" x 8½"	1880s
Swiss mount	6½" x 2⅘"	1890s
Cabinet card	6 ½" x 4½"	1866–1900s
Imperial mount	7" x 10"	1890s
Promenade card	7½" x 4"	1890s
Paris card	9¾" x 6¾"	1890s
Panel card	13" x 7½"	1890s

STEREOGRAPH DATING (3½" x 7")

Photographic images
    Flat mount
        Square corner–1857–70
            White, cream or gray–1857–63
            Shades of yellow–1861–70
            Red, green, blue, or lavender–1866–70
        Rounded corner, Standard size–1868–90
        Larger sizes (5"x 7")–1873–90
    Curved mount
        Buff–1879–1910
        Gray–1892–1950
        Black–1902–60
Printed images
    Black and white, or colored halftones–1898–1930

CARTES-DE-VISITES (2½″ X 4″)

In use from approximately 1860 into the 1890s.

Thin stock (.4 mm) with square corners–to c. 1870.

.5 mm stock with square or rounded corners
–c. 1870–1875.

.6 mm stock with square or rounded corners
–c. 1873–1884.

.7 mm stock with square or rounded corners
–c. 1879–1890s.

Revenue stamps were used on card mounted photographs produced between September 1, 1864 and August 1, 1866, most frequently on cartes-de-visites.

CABINET CARDS (6½″ X 4½″)

Variety of colors from–c. 1860s to c. 1910

Maroon or dark green–c. 1880s.

Gold border–pre-1885.

Scalloped edges–after mid-1880.

Impressed border and lettering–after c. 1890.

POSTCARDS

Postcards can include original photographs and copy images which can predate the card by almost 70 years. Guidelines for determining a range of dates for photographic postcard images can rely on several elements:

If postally used, the postmark indicated the latest possible date for the image.

Unused cards, or those sent in an envelope and without postmark, can use the stamp box printing to provide information about the earliest possible date for the image.

Images can include dating information printed in the image itself.

Undivided back (typically pre-1907) vs. divided back.

STAMP BOX IDENTIFICATION

ARGO (Defender Photo Supply Company)–c. 1905

ARISTO, above eagle logo–c. 1906

ARTURA, in fleur-de-lis–c. 1906

AZO (Kodak):

with corner diamonds–c. 1907

with corner triangle pointing up–c. 1906

with corner triangle pointing up and down–after 1918

with corner square–after 1926

CYKO:

in solid script–(ANSCO)–c. 1904

in open script–(ANSCO)–c. 1906

DEFENDER–c. 1910–20

DEFENDER, with diamond inside box–after 1920

KRUXO, with corner cloverleaf–c. 1907

NOKO–c. 1907

PMO–c. 1907

SOLIO–c. 1903

VELOX (Kodak):

in general–1902–1931

with corner triangle–c. 1906

with corner diamonds–c. 1907

with corner square–c. 1907

BIOGRAPHIES OF PHOTOGRAPHERS

KLONDIKE PHOTO CO.

Special thanks to David Mattison for his editing and substantial contribution to this section.

ADAMS & COMPANY
Active in Dawson, Yukon Territory, c. 1901; also known as Adams & Larkin.

ADAMS & LARKIN
Active in Dawson, Yukon Territory, c. 1901; also known as Adams & Company.

ALASKA VIEW & PHOTO COMPANY
Active in Skagway, Alaska, 1900.

ALBERTSTONE, R.
Active in Sitka, Alaska, 1890, operating the Sitka View & Portrait Company.

BARLEY, H. C.
Active in Skagway, Alaska, c. 1900.

BLISS, H. A.
Active in Yukon Territory, 1897+.

BURDON, LANCE
Active in Atlin-Quesnel section of the Yukon Telegraph Line, 1900-01.

BUSBY, EDWARD SCOTT
See British Columbia.

CALLARMAN, F. A.
Produced stereoviews in Skagway, Alaska.

CANTWELL, GEORGE C.
Active in Dawson, Yukon, 1901. Published *The Klondike, A Souvenir*, c. 1901. Also listed as George G. Cantwell.

CARLYON, FRED W.
Born in Union Grove, Wisconsin; died in Olympia, Washington. Active in Stikine River District, British Columbia, and in Wrangell, Alaska, 1898-1900+. Operated Carlyon's Studio.

CARLYON'S STUDIO
Active in Ft. Wrangell, 1898, operated by Fred W. Carlyon.

CASE & DRAPER
Partnership of W. H. Case and Herbert Draper in Lake Bennett, Alaska, 1900; also in Sitka.

CASE, W. H.
Active in Lake Bennett, Alaska, 1900; partner in Case & Draper.

CLEVELAND, V.
See British Columbia.

CRAIG, M. H.
Active in Dawson, Yukon, 1898.

CURTIS, ASAHEL
Born in Le Sueur County, Minnesota; died in Seattle, Washington. Traveling photographer in the Yukon from Seattle, Washington, 1897-1900; employed by his brother, Edward S. Curtis. See Washington.

CURTIS, EDWARD S.
Official photographer from Seattle, Washington, with Harriman Expedition in Alaska, 1899. See Washington.

DARMS, H. A.
Active c. 1903-04. Also spelled Darns.

DAWSON, GEORGE MERCER
Born in Pictou, Nova Scotia, 1849; died in Ottawa, Ontario, 1901. Active in the Yukon, 1887.

DE GROFF, EDWARD
Active in Sitka, Alaska, 1900.

DOBBS, BEVERLY BENNETT
Born in Missouri, 1868; died in Seattle, 1937. He learned photography in Lincoln, Nebraska; moved to Bellingham, Washington, operating for twenty years. Also active in New Whatcom, Washington, c. 1895. He won a gold medal at the Louisiana Purchase Exposition and photographed the Seward Peninsula of Alaska extensively.

DOODY, J.
Active in Dawson, c. 1907.

DRAPER, HERBERT
Active in Lake Bennett, Alaska, 1900; partner in Case & Draper with W. H. Case.

DUCLOS
Active in Dawson, Yukon Territory, 1895, with partner Per Edward Larss in Larss & Duclos.

EDWARDS BROTHERS
Active in Stikine River Trail, British Columbia; the Yukon, 1897-98. Partnership of Edgar Herbert and George William Edwards.

EDWARDS, EDGAR HERBERT
Partner with his brother, George William in Stikine River Trail, British Columbia; the Yukon, 1897-98.

EDWARDS, GEORGE WILLIAM
Operated as Edwards Brothers with his brother Edgar Herbert in Stikine River Trail, British Columbia; the Yukon, 1897-98.

ELLINGSON, E. O.
Active in Dawson, Yukon, c. 1910.

GARRISON, A. A.
See British Columbia.

GILLIS, A. J.

GOETZMAN
Active in Dawson, Yukon, 1900-03.

HAMACHER, E. J.
Active in Alaska, c. 1898.

HEGG, ERIC A.
Photographer from Seattle, Washington, active in Dawson, Yukon, 1898. Also known as Hegg & Company and Hegg & Larss. See Washington.

    Murray Morgan, *One Man's Gold Rush, A Klondike Album, Photographs* by
        E. A. Hegg, University of Washington Press, Seattle, 1967.
    Ethel Anderson Becker, *Klondike '98: E. A. Hegg Goldrush Album*, Binfords & Mort, Portland, Oregon, 1967.

HIRSCHFELD, ALFRED CYRIL
Born in London, England, 1866; died in San Francisco. Active in Atlin, British Columbia, 1899-1901.

HOMAN, CHARLES A.
Active in Alaska and the Yukon, 1883.

HOOPER, C. N.
Active in area, c. 1900, specific locations unknown.

HUNT, FRED G. L.
Landscape photographer in Skagway, Alaska.

JOHNSON
Active in Dawson, Yukon.

JOHNSON, ALBERT J.
Operated a studio and camera shop in Fairbanks, c. 1910-14.

JUDKINS, DAVID ROBY
Born in Chesterville, Maine, 1836; died in Santa Maria, California, 1909. Active in Skagway, Alaska, c. 1880-1909.

KAJAWARA, TAKUMA
Born in Japan, 1877; died in New York, 1960. Active in Dawson, Yukon, 1898.

KINSEY & KINSEY
Brothers Clarke and Clarence Kinsey, active in Grand Forks, Yukon Territory, 1898. See Washington.

KINSEY, CLARENCE
See Kinsey & Kinsey. See Washington.

KINSEY, CLARKE
See Kinsey & Kinsey. See Washington.

LA ROCHE, FRANK
Active in Alaska and the Yukon, 1897. Produced excellent 8″ x 10″ views of a wide range of Alaska scenes, and published a souvenir album in 1898. Made over one hundred trips to Alaska and the Yukon. See Washington and British Columbia.

LARKIN
Partner in Adams & Larkin.

LARSS & DUCLOS
Partnership of Per Edward Larss and Duclos, active in Dawson, Yukon Territory, 1895.

LARSS, PER EDWARD
Born in Tjarby, Halland County, Sweden, 1863. Original name was Larson. Active as partner in Larss & Duclos, Yukon Territory, 1895, and in British Columbia.

LOMAN BROTHERS
Active in Juneau.

MADSEN, C.
Location unknown.

MAYNARD, HANNAH HATHERLY
See British Columbia.

MAYNARD, RICHARD
View photographer active in British Columbia with his wife, Hannah. See British Columbia.

McINTIRE, DR. HUGH H.
Made rare views of the Pribilof Islands of Alaska, published by L. T. Sparhawk, Vermont.

MINTO, LADY MARY CAROLINE
Born in England, c. 1858; died 1940. Active in the Yukon, 1900.

MOORE, THOMAS V.
Photographed Fairbanks, 1880s; issued rare "Views of Alaska" series; originally from Williamsburg, Virginia.

MOOSBAUER, L.
Active in Wrangell, Skagway and Sitka, Alaska, 1890.

MUIRHEAD BROTHERS
Charles H. and Lewis Potter Muirhead, Jr. Active in the Yukon and northern British Columbia, 1899-1900+.

MUIRHEAD, CHARLES H.
Born in Scotland. Active with his brother, Lewis Potter, Jr., operating as Muirhead Brothers in the Yukon and northern British Columbia, 1899-1900+.

MUIRHEAD, LEWIS POTTER, JR.
Born in Scotland. Partner with Charles H. in Muirhead Brothers, active in the Yukon and northern British Columbia, 1899-1900+.

MUYBRIDGE, EADWEARD J.
Famous photographer from San Francisco, accompanied an expedition aboard the sidewheeler *Pacific*, 1868. See California.

NOWELL, FRANK. H.
Born February 19, 1864; died at Crystal Lake, Washington, 1950. Arrived in Alaska from North Platte, Nebraska, 1886, where he established the first dairy ranch in Alaska. Studio in Nome, c. 1900; photographed ships, scenes, Indians, and miners. Moved his studio to Seattle, 1909, and was the official photographer of the Alaska-Yukon-Pacific Exposition, 1909.

PIKE, WARBURTON MAYER
Born in England, 1861; died 1915. Active in Stikine River District, British Columbia; Cassiar District, British Columbia, and the Yukon, 1892-93.

PILLSBURY, ARTHUR C.
Born in Wareham, England, September 20, 1861; died in Bournemouth, England, October 20, 1915. Active in Wrangell, Discovery (Pine City), Alaska, and the Yukon, 1898-99. Assistant was V. Cleveland of Discovery (Pine City), British Columbia. See California.

POND, PERCY E.
Active in Juneau, Alaska, 1893-1943; partner in Winter & Pond.

PRATHER

RATTENBURY, FRANCIS MAWSON
See British Columbia.

ROBERTSON, L. E.
Active in Glenora, 1898.

ROCHE, L. A.
Traveling photographer from Seattle, Washington; in Alaska, c. 1897.

SCHALLERER, OTTO
Active in Seward, Alaska, 1900s.

SCHWATKA, FREDERICK
Born in Galena, Illinois, c. 1849; died in Portland, Oregon, 1892. Active in Alaska and the Yukon, 1883.

SITKA VIEW & PORTRAIT COMPANY
Operated by R. Albertstone in Sitka, 1890.

SMYTHE, SIDNEY ALFRED
See British Columbia.

SONICHSEU, N.
Active in Ft. Wrangell, Alaska, 1883.

STRAND, WALTER
Active in Discovery City, 1900.

VOGEE, ANTON
Born in Norway, 1866(?); died in Vancouver, British Columbia, 1950. Active in Alaska and the Yukon, 1899-1900.

W & S
Active in Lake Bennett, Alaska, 1900.

WEBSTER & STEVENS
Active in Dawson, Yukon and Nome, Alaska, 1898-99.

WINTER & POND
Partnership of Lloyd V. Winter and Percy E. Pond, active in Juneau, Alaska, 1893-1943; in the Yukon, 1898.
> Victoria Wyatt, *Images from the Inside Passage: An Alaskan Portrait by Winter & Pond*, University of Washington Press, Seattle, in association with the Alaska State Library, 1989.

WINTER, LLOYD V.
Partner in Winter & Pond; active in Juneau, Alaska, 1893-43; in the Yukon, 1898.

WOLFE
Active in Dawson, Yukon, c. 1906.

WOODSIDE, HENRY JOSEPH
Born in Arkwright, Ontario, 1858; died in Ottawa, Ontario, 1929. Active in Teslin Trail, British Columbia and the Yukon, 1898.

Buehman & Co.

Nos. 314, 314½, & 316 Congress St
UP STAIRS,
East of Post Office.
TUCSON, A. T.

Special thanks to Jeremy Rowe for his substantial contribution to this section. For more detailed reference to the photographers of Arizona, see Jeremy Rowe's Photographers in Arizona 1850-1920: A History & Directory, *Carl Mautz Publishing, 1997.*

ADDIS & PORTER
Partnership of Alfred S. Addis and Porter in Tucson, c. 1879. See Alfred S. Addis.

ADDIS, ALFRED SHEA
Possibly licensed in Leavenworth, Kansas, September 1862, and with his brother, May 1863. Probable partner with Kock at 425 Montgomery Street in San Francisco, licensed February 1865. Operated a gallery in Tucson on Myers Street, south of the Palace Hotel with a partner named Porter whom he bought out, October 1879. Also listed at the corner of Camp and Convent Streets, Church Plaza. Moved to New Mexico, 1880; active in Las Cruces, 1880; Silver City, 1881-82; Lake Valley, 1882.

ADKINS & HARRISON
Partnership of Wesley C. Adkins and Ralph T. Harrison in Phoenix, c. 1913.

ADKINS, WESLEY C.
Operated at 218 ½ West Washington, Phoenix, c. 1912. Partner with Ralph T. Harrison in Adkins & Harrison, 1913.

ALLEN, CHARLES R.
Partner of Jennings. Itinerant photographers, c. 1898. Sold 450 negatives to Albert S. Reynolds, 1899. Photographed Arizona and New Mexico with Weiner, 1889-91. Listed with partner Gommel, 1892-93; with Jennings, 1895-1900.

ALLEN, W. H.
Active in Lowell, 1909-10.

ALTENBURGH, WILLIAM
Active in Phoenix, c. 1895-97. Operated at 243 West Madison as Messinger & Altenburgh.

AMERICAN STEREOSCOPIC COMPANY
Founded in 1898. R. Y. Young photographed Petrified Forest, Clifton, Morenci, 1903-07.

AMES, F. A.
Documented the Moqui Indians for the Bureau of American Ethnology, 1887-89, and produced an album, *Photographs of Indian Reservations at Moqui.*

ANTHONY, F.
Active in Bisbee; licensed as itinerant, 1907.

ARELDSON PHOTO
Active in Clarkdale, 1915-20.

ARIZONA GALLERY
Tent gallery operated by A. M. Feldman, Tucson, c. 1901.

ARIZONA PHOTO COMPANY
Located at 27 East Adams, Phoenix, c. 1915, A. E. Hackett, proprietor.

ARIZONA PHOTO GALLERY
Operated by A. M. Feldman at studio of Stone & Jackson, Tucson, c. 1906-07.

ARIZONA PHOTOGRAPH COMPANY, INC.
One of the first multifaceted photographic partnerships in Arizona, organized c. 1903; offered studio and location photogaphers, print production and marketing. Partners were Erwin Baer, Tom Bate, W. R. Humphries, A. E. Suppinger, and Percival Armitage. Duration of the corporation unknown.

ARIZONA SOUVENIR PICTURE COMPANY
Active in Roosevelt, 1906-11.

ARIZONA TENT GALLERY
Operation of Stone & Jackson, managed by A. M. Feldman, Tucson, c. 1903-04.

ARMITAGE, PERCIVAL
Active in Prescott, 1903-15. Partner in the Arizona Photograph Company, Inc., in Prescott with Erwin Baer, Tom Bate, W. R. Humphries, and A. E. Suppinger, c. 1903. Listed as Armitage Photo Company of Humboldt, c. 1906-15. Active in the Bradshaw mining district.

ARMITAGE PHOTO COMPANY
Partnership of Percival Armitage, Erwin Baer, Tom Bate, W. R. Humphries, and A. E. Suppinger, operating in Prescott, c. 1906-15.

ATLANTIC PACIFIC VIEW AND PORTRAIT COMPANY
Active in Tucson, 1902-11. Wallace B. and Joseph C. Parker operated at Parker's, 6th and Broadway. Listed as A&PV&P Co.

AUSTIN, A. H.
Active in Solomonville, c. 1912-13.

AVELDSON
Active in Jerome, c. 1915. Photographed Jerome and the Montana Hotel fire.

BAER, ERWIN
Arrived in Prescott from St. Louis, May 1883; partner with Mitchell until his retirement, 1885. Operated a gallery in Flagstaff, c. 1887-90. Partner in the Arizona Photograph Company, Inc., in Prescott with Percival Armitage, Tom Bate, W. R. Humphries, and A. E. Suppinger, c. 1903. Listed at the Lawler or Lawrence Block, 1907-12. Also was partner with Hammaker, Haynes and Bate.

BAGNASCO, POLICARPO
Studio at 22 Camp Street, Tucson, c. 1881.

BAILEY, W.
Active in Globe, 1909-10, operating Globe Photographic Company.

BAKER, E. W.
Active in Douglas, c. 1905. Partner of L. A. Skelly on E Street between 9th and 10th. Also operated in Santa Fe, New Mexico, 1888-92.

BALLINGER, L. A.
Active in Bisbee; licensed as itinerant, c. 1904.

BAN-AP PHOTO
Active in Douglas, c. 1907.

BANNER, R.
Active in Bisbee; licensed as itinerant, c. 1904.

BARNES, WILL CROFT
Born 1858; died 1936. Active in Ft. Apache, 1880s. Stationed at Ft. Apache as corporal-telegrapher and later as sergeant. Entered U.S. Forest Service, 1907. Traveled extensively and photographed throughout the West.

BARNETT, CHARLES W.
Born in San Bernardino, California, September 29, 1858. Established a gallery, 1881, in Mesa. Moved to Phoenix, 1882, and became a partner of Rothrock, 1882-94; in Tempe, 1893; Phoenix, 1894. Also active in Hayden, c. 1884.

BARTHELMESS, CHRISTIAN
See Montana.

BATE, TOM H.
Active in Phoenix, c. 1899; Prescott, 1907-10, with his studio in the Head Building. Partnership with Erwin Baer until 1913. Partner in the Arizona Photograph Company, Inc., in Prescott with Erwin Baer, Percival Armitage, W. R. Humphries, and A. E. Suppinger, c. 1903. Also operated Bate Studio at 103 South Cortez into the 1920s.

BAUMAN, JULES
Active in Prescott, 1884-1900.

BEAMAN, E. O.
Beaman was a New York landscape photographer who became the official photographer to the U.S. Geological Survey's Powell Expedition, summer 1871, upon the recommendation of his supplier, E. & H. T. Anthony & Company. James Carleton is listed as an assistant. Beaman left the survey January 1872, and spent some time photographing the Indians of New Mexico and Arizona before returning East. After Beaman left the expedition, his assistant and Powell's cousin, Clem Powell, took over but proved unable to photograph. He was replaced by James Fennemore of the C. R. Savage Gallery in Salt Lake City. Fennemore instructed an interested member of the party, John K. Hillers, in photography, and Hillers became assistant photographer, and then took over as official photographer, 1873, when Fennemore quit due to illness.

BEARCE, E. A.
Operated the New York Gallery in Phoenix, c. 1898.

BEASLEY, A. D.
Active in Phoenix, c. 1910.

BEATTIE, J. W.
Active in Phoenix, 1895-97. Operated at Fly's Gallery on East Washington, 1895; 409 West Washington, 1897.

BEATTY, C. S. (MRS.)
Active in Prescott in 1907-11, operating gallery on Cortez Street with partner Will R. Beatty.

BEATTY, WILL R.
Active in Prescott, c. 1896-11. Partner with Mrs. C. S. Beatty 1907-11.

BECKSTEIN
Partner of Daniel Markey in Bisbee, c. 1895.

BELL, DR. WILLIAM A.
Born in Liverpool, England, c. 1830; died in Philadelphia, January 28, 1910. Operated a gallery in Philadelphia with his brother-in-law John Keen, 1848, and his own gallery, c. 1850. Later a partner of J. E. McClees and E. P. Hipple. Purchased McClees gallery, 1867. Chief photographer for the Army Medical Museum after the Civil War, photographing all of the generals and most battlefields. Reopened gallery in Philadelphia, c. 1869. Photographed along the 32nd parallel route of the Kansas Pacific Railway Survey across Arizona, 1867. Photographer on Palmer-Wright-Calhoun survey for the Union Pacific Railway, Eastern Division (Kansas-Pacific Survey) through Arizona, 1867-68. *New Tracks in North America* published in London, 1869,

contained illustrations from his photos. Took over 100 negatives during 1871-72 Powell survey. Also traveled through northern Arizona, 1872, photographing the Hopi. Official photographer for the Wheeler survey of the Grand Canyon, 1872, where he developed the idea for large panoramas. He made a panorama of the 1876 Centennial exhibition for Gutekunst using six 18″ x 22″ plates. Member of the Photographic Society of Philadelphia.

BELL, GEORGE V.
Probable itinerant listed at Box 1980, Bisbee, c.1905.

BEMIS, F. C. (MRS)
Itinerent tent gallery operator in Globe, c. 1885.

BERTOLACCI, G. T. E.
Active in Yuma, c. 1884.

BLAINE, CHARLES E.
Active in Phoenix, 1918-20.

BLAINE, CHARLES S.
Studio at 905 West Jefferson, Phoenix, 1899-1900.

BLEAK, ELLYE ELLSWORTH
Active in Mesa, 1899-1920. Operated Ellsworth Studio between Mac-Donald and Robson, c. 1915. Also listed as Ellye Irwin Ellsworth and Ellye Irwin.

BOGEN, ROBERT
Active in Glendale, c. 1919.

BOLANOS, HELIODORO
Active in Tucson; studio at 78 North Stone, 1907; in Post Office Building, 1907-10.

BONINE, ELIAS A.
Born 1843; died 1916. Active in Yuma, Pasadena, and Los Angeles. Listed as photographer in Yuma, 1881. Known for his studio portraits of Native Americans. Also active in Pickett Post, Pinal, Queen Creek, Silver King and Yuma.

BONINE, ROBERT K.
From Tyrone, Pennsylvania, a cousin of E. A. Bonine, he marketed photos of Yuma and Ehrenburg which may have been taken by R. K. or exchanged with E. A. Bonine.

BOOKSLY, A.
Active in Fredonia, c. 1912-13.

BOOTH & MILO
Partnership in Douglas c. 1919, on Florida near 11th.

BOOTH, ALBERT J.
Active in Morenci, 1911-12. Also advertised in Yuma, 1912-13.

BOROUGH, E. B.
Active in Bisbee, c. 1902. Purchased studio of Louis A. Nemeck on south side of upper Main Street.

BOSTON RAILROAD PHOTO CAR
Active in Flagstaff, 1890s.

BRANCH, JOHN W.
Active in Phoenix at 218 West Washington, 1909-10; at Hartwell Studio, 29 ½ South 2nd. Later moved to Tempe, 1912-15, on Mill between 6th and 7th; returned to Phoenix, 1919-21.

BRENNAN, M. F.
Active in Jerome, 1901-17.

BRIGHT, J. A.
Active in Wilcox, 1890s.

BROWN, M. L.
Active in Douglas. Operated on E Street between 8th and 9th, c. 1905; 449 4th, 1907-12.

BROWN, W. CALVIN
Lieutenant in the New Mexico Territorial Militia who photographed Johnson Canyon, Canyon Diablo, and Hopi area, c. 1885. Also active in Holbrook, c. 1900, as photographer for Atlantic & Pacific Railroad.

BROWN, WILLIAM HENRY
Born 1844; died in El Paso, Texas, December 19, 1886. Active in Santa Fe, New Mexico, 1866-86. Worked in partnership with his father, Nicholas Brown, until 1867. Ran a studio in Chihauhua, Mexico, 1867-69. Partner with George C. Bennett, 1880-82. Photographed Zuni Pueblos.

BRUCE, C. A.
Studio on North Montezuma, Prescott, 1900-12.

BRUENSTEINER, MAX
Stereographer active in Phoenix.

BRUUNAGE, M. J.
Active in Tucson. Studio operator for Buehman, c. 1880.

BRYANT, HENRY
Operated Quick Finish Kodak Company in Prescott, c. 1920, at 218 West Gurley.

BUCHHOLTZ, H.
Stereographer active in Tucson.

BUCK, A. J.
Traveled from Vance, Texas, to photograph Clifton, April 1897.

BUEHMAN & COMPANY
Studio operated by Henry Buehman, in Tucson c. 1881, at 105 Congress.

BUEHMAN & HARTWELL
Partnership of F. A. Hartwell and H. H. Buehman operating gallery in Tucson, c. 1880s.

BUEHMAN, HENRY H.
Born in Bremen, Germany, May 14, 1851; died in Tucson, December 20, 1912. Emigrated to San Francisco, 1868, and worked for Bradley & Rulofson. Buehman opened a studio in Visalia, California, 1869. Itinerant throughout Southwest, 1871-74. Purchased Tuscon gallery from Adolfo and Juan Rodrigo, c. 1875. He took a six week tour of Ft. Apache, Camps Bowie and Grant, and the San Carlos Reservation, December 1875; photographed San Xavier, 1876. He traveled to Camp Huachuca, Charleston, Tombstone, Ft. Bowie, Ft. Apache, Ft. Thomas, September-November 1879. At Huachuca, he took a dozen views of the camp and scenery, and views of the mines in Charleston, Tough Nut, Corbin Mills, Tombstone, Contention, Grand Central and elsewhere. Partner with F. A. Hartwell, c. 1880s, including galleries in Tucson and Phoenix, corner of Jefferson and Pima Streets; operating as Buehman & Company, Tucson, at 105 Congress Street, c. 1881; partner with George Roskruge, 1881-83; 314 and 316 Congress Street, c. 1883-84; 30 West Congress, c. 1897; Post Office Building, 1907; at 30 West Congress, 1909, listed as "H. Buehman &

Company, Photographers and Dealers in Arizona Views, Moldings and Picture Frames." Operated the Elite Studio in Post Office Building, c. 1911.

BULL
Recruited from California to run Williscraft Studio in Prescott, 1875.

BURCHARD & MELVIN
Studio on Mill Avenue, Tempe, c. 1892.

BURCHARD, JAMES EDWARD
Active in Flagstaff. Possible operator of the Flagstaff Art Gallery, c. 1887.

BURGE, J. C.
Studio on Montezuma Street, Prescott, c. 1881. Worked for Atlantic & Pacific Railroad in Prescott, June-October 1881, and June-August 1882. Moved to Globe, 1883, then to the Grand Canyon, 1884. In partnership with Hildreth in Flagstaff, 1884; Kingman, 1885, and then to New Mexico.

BURGESS, J. C.
Stereo photographer in Arizona.

BURLAN
Active in Arizona City (Yuma) and Clifton; also in Silver City, New Mexico, advertised with Harry W. Lucas.

BURT, CHARLES S.
Specific location and dates unknown.

BURTIS, GEORGE
Active in Roosevelt in 1907-08.

BURTIS, GEORGE (MRS.)
Active in Roosevelt, c. 1907.

BUSHMAN & COMPANY
Studio in Tucson.

CALIFORNIA ART GALLERY
Operated by Cicero Grime producing tintypes and stereographs in Globe, c. 1882.

CAPITAL ART GALLERY
Prescott gallery on Cortez, north of the Courthouse; owned and operated by C. A. Gentile before 1869; Francis A. Cook, 1869-74; Flanders, 1874; Williscraft, 1874; Mitchell, c. 1877-1900s(?).

CARLTON, JAMES
Assisted Beaman on photographic excursion through Northern Arizona, 1872.

CARSON, AMBROSE W.
Born in Texas, 1875. Active in Douglas, October 1906. Active in Altus and Mountain View, Oklahoma, with brother H. R. Carson, 1897-1905, and then to California prior to moving to Douglas. Operated studio with brother M. R. Carson until 1911, and then purchased Irwin studio which he operated until c. 1915 when he returned to the Douglas studio to rejoin his brother.

CARSON BROTHERS
See Ambrose W. and Hugh Ruth Carson.

CARSON, HUGH RUTH
Born in Carrol County, Arkansas, June 24, 1864; died in Prescott, Arizona, February 17, 1953. Partner in studios in Altus and Mountain View, Oklahoma, with brother Ambrose Carson, 1897-1905. Active

in Douglas at Queen Studio, 529 11th, 1907. Moved to Bisbee until 1919, then returned to the Douglas studio. Active in Bisbee and Douglas as a photographer until c. 1949.

CARSON, M. R.
Operated studio in Douglas with his brother, A. W. Carson, c. 1906-11; purchased Irwin studio, c. 1911.

CARTER, CHARLES W.
Photographed Moqui Buttes in northern Arizona. He sold his negative collection to the Bureau of Information of the Mormon Church, 1906. See Utah.

CATTON, C. W.
Active in Phoenix, c. 1881. Partner of George H. Rothrock. Several examples of Catton & Rothrock mounts with Catton's name abraded from mount indicates use by Rothrock after dissolution of the partnership.

CHASE
Assistant to C. S. Fly in Tombstone, 1880s.

CHRISTENSEN, PETER C.
Active in Glendale, c. 1915-18.

CHRISTY, ISAAC MARSHALL
Active in Phoenix, c. 1887.

CLARK, CHARLES
Traveled with C. L. White on his Projectoscope Tour showing motion pictures in Arizona, c. 1898.

CLARK, R. H.
Active in White River and known to have photographed Apache.

CLARK, ROBERT
Active in Holbrook, c. 1895.

CLAUSEN, C. H.
Active in Phoenix, 1895-97. Operated on Monroe Street, then Elite Gallery at 22 South 3rd Avenue.

CLAUSEN, C. H. (MRS.)
Affiliated with Elite Gallery at 22 South 3rd Avenue in Phoenix, c. 1898.

CLEMENT, E. L.
From Oak Park, Illinois; stereographed the Grand Canyon, 1890s.

COBB, WILLIAM HENRY
Active in Oak Creek and vicinity, 1890s.

COHEN, JOSEPH
Active in Phoenix, 1914-17, at 1st Avenue.

COLEMAN
Listed as partner in Kemp & Coleman operating in Tombstone, c. 1881.

COLEMAN, JAMES W.
Active in Jerome, c. 1895.

CONE, J. T.
Active in Williams, c. 1895.

CONKLIN, ENOCH
Stereographer for Continent Publishing Company working in Arizona. Also marketed stereographs of the Prescott area (at least one

originally D. P. Flanders image from 1874), and "Tucson & Vicinity" (original images by Henry Buehman).

COOK, FRANCIS A.
Born 1832. Arrived in Prescott, 1864, from New York at age 32. Purchased camera from Gentile and began operation, c. 1869, when he bought Gentile's studio. Partner in L. W. Worth gallery, probably on Cortez street; with Nathan P. Pierce, 1869-72; also partner with Richard M. Hargrave. Studio was also known as the Capital Art Gallery, subsequently used by other photographers such as Flanders, Williscraft and Mitchell over the next decades. Also active in Camp Verde and Phoenix, 1872. Sold gallery to Williscraft, 1874.

COOLEY, BEN D.
Active in Bisbee, c. 1909, produced photographic postcards of Bisbee floods.

COOLIDGE, DANE
Born in Natick, Massachusetts, 1873; died in Berkeley, 1940. Author, naturalist and photographer who photographed cowboys and ranch life in Arizona, Texas, and California, c. 1907-16.

COPELAND
Active in Phoenix in 1905-06; partner in Stacy & Copeland.

COREY, KATE
Born 1861; died 1958. Active in Arizona, 1904-12. New York artist and self-taught photographer who came to visit in 1904 and stayed to study. Photographed Hopis and Hopi culture, creating a body of photographs and paintings.
   Barton Wright, Marnie Gaede and Marc Gaede, *The Hopi Photographs of Kate Corey*, Chaco Press, 1986.

CORY, H. T.
   Active in Arizona, c. 1916.

COTTEN, C. W.
Active in Phoenix in 1899-1908. Operated at Elite Gallery, 22 South 3rd Avenue near Washington.

COX
Partner with Stone in Flagstaff, c. 1908; produced panoramic photographs.

COYLE, JOHN H.
Active in Bisbee, c. 1903-04. Operated on Brewery Gulch over Dunn's opposite the Post Office. Later operated in Winkelman, c. 1912-13.

COZBY, OLIVER
Active in Ft. Huachuca, 1907-10. Operated Model Photo Gallery at 102 South Stone, Tucson, c. 1912. Also known as O. Cosby.

CULP'S PHOTO STUDIO
Active in Morenci, 1909-10.

CURTIS, C. D.
Active in Williams and St. Johns, c. 1894.

CURTIS, CLINTON
Itinerant photographer in north Arizona, c. 1895.

CURTIS, EDWARD SHERIFF
See Washington.

D'HEUREUSE, RUDOLPH
French survey photographer in southern Arizona c. 1863, specifically

in the Yuma area and Ft. Mohave.

DAVENPORT, M. L.
Active in Phoenix, c. 1899, operating the Sunbeam Studio in partnership with A. F. Messenger.

DAVIDSON, ARTHUR H.
Active in Morenci in 1903-04. Publisher of "Picturesque Arizona" stereoviews of Morenci, Metcalf and vicinity.

DEPUE, OSCAR B.
Early motion picture photographer active at the Grand Canyon and the Hopi Pueblos, 1899-1900. Presented motion pictures at trading post in Canyon Diablo, 1900.

DETROIT PHOTOGRAPHIC COMPANY
Marketed numerous photomechanical postcards of Grand Canyon, Native Americans, Phoenix, and general Arizona subjects, 1900-07. See William H. Jackson in Nebraska.

DICKISON, E. (MISS)
Active in Wellton, 1909-10.

DINWIDDIE, WILLIAM
Photographed the Papago on W. J. McGee survey, 1894.

DIX, GEORGE C.
Active in Bisbee in the Schmidt Building, c. 1916. Photographed the Bisbee Exportation, 1917, and marketed photo postcard series (including approximately 50 titles) on the event.

DIXON, W. L.
Active in Poland, 1909-10.

DODGE, KATHERINE T.
Active in San Carlos, c. 1899. Photographed the Apache.

DONALDSON, M. D.
Active in Bisbee, 1911-12.

DONNELL, T. M.
Active in Phoenix, 1903-10, at 18 West Washington. Also listed in Tempe, 1907.

DOWE, D. W.
Active in Bisbee, 1897-1904. Produced *Souvenir of the Great Copper Belt In and Around Bisbee*, 1904, illustrated with photo-engravings.

DRAKE, CHARLES L.
Active in Wilcox, 1909-10.

EASTMAN
Active in Bisbee, 1904.

ELITE STUDIO
Active in Tucson, c. 19(?)-20. Located in Post Office Building until at least 1911, then at 79 North Stone Avenue, c. 1919-20. Operated by H. H. Wilcox, c. 1908; by Henry Buehman, c. 1911.

ELITE STUDIOS & GALLERY
Active in Phoenix, 1899-1908. Listed at 22 South 3rd Avenue near Washington. Operators included Mr. and Mrs. C. H. Clausen and C. W. Cotten.

ELKIN & ELKIN
Partnership operating in Phoenix, c. 1918, at 1 Cactus Way, Kunselman's old Photocraft Shop.

ELKIN, LAUREN
Operated Kunselman's old Photocraft Shop at 1 Cactus Way, Phoenix, as Elkin & Elkin, c. 1918.

ELLSWORTH, ELLYE IRWIN
Active in Mesa, 1899-1920; operated Ellsworth Studio between Mac-Donald and Robson, c. 1915, using the name Ellye Ellsworth Bleak. Also listed as Ellye Irwin.

EMANUEL
Active in Prescott, c. 1881.

EMPIE, HAL D.
Active in Safford, c. 1906. Cowboy, photographer, artist and author; produced photographic postcards of ranching and life in Arizona.

EVERETT & SON, J. E.
Active in Casa Grande, c. 1888.

EVERETT'S STUDIO
Active in Prescott, c. 1895.

FARCIOT, CHARLES O.
Born in Switzerland, 1839; died in Chino Ranch, California, 1891. Active in Tombstone and Charleston, 1879-80. Civil War veteran listed as clockmaker and engineer prior to arrival in Arizona. Traveled extensively while photographing central and southern Arizona beginning in 1879. Photographed Camp Apache, Maricopa Wells, Pinal, Silver King, McMillenville, Globe, and mining and ethnographic subjects. Active in Globe, November 1879-January 1880. Probable studio in Charleston, 1881-83. Left Arizona for Alaska on first commercial mining expedition with Ed Schieffelin of Tombstone via San Francisco. Farciot's stereographs were marketed by the studio of his brother-in-law Edouart of Edouart & Cobb, 504 Kearney Street, San Francisco, as "Arizona Views." The series may include as many as 150 titles.

FARQUAHAR, JULIUS THEO
Active in Douglas, c. 1902; Globe, c.1908. Operated the Globe Photographic Company at 162 West Bailey. Produced cabinet and larger photos, 1911-12.

FELDMAN, ALITTIER M.
Based in Tucson. Tent gallery operator, c. 1885-95.

FELDMAN, FREDERICK J.
Operated as itinerant "Traveling Photographer." Listed in Tombstone, c. 1880; Bisbee, c. 1890; Tucson, 1893, as a tintypist and operating the Arizona Gallery in a tent; in El Paso, 1895.

FENNEMORE, JAMES
Active 1870s-80s. An operator for C. R. Savage in Salt Lake, Fennemore replaced E. O. Beaman as the photographer for the Powell expedition, 1871-72. Fennemore instructed an interested member of the party, John K. Hillers, in photography, and Hillers became assistant photographer, and then took over as official photographer, 1873, when Fennemore quit due to illness.

FETTER, W. L.
Active in Flagstaff and Bisbee, 1888.

FEWKES, DR. JESSE WALTER
Chief of the Bureau of American Ethnology, 1895-1923; made prints and lantern slides of Arizona.

FLAGSTAFF ART GALLERY
Active in Flagstaff, c. 1887, possibly operated by James Edward Burchard.

FLAGSTAFF PHOTOGRAPH GALLERY
Active in Flagstaff, c. 1890, James Edward Burchard operator.

FLANDERS & PENLON
Partnership active in Prescott, 1873-74.

FLANDERS, DUDLEY P.
Born in Massachusetts, 1840. Licensed as Flanders & Tuttle Photographers, Arcata, California, 1865. Active in Eureka, California, 1866; San Francisco and Grass Valley, 1867; branch gallery in Truckee, 1868. Arrived in Arizona from Los Angeles, c. 1873, and operated with partner in Flanders & Godfrey. Formed partnership with Henri Penlon, November 1873 (Flanders & Penlon), and arrived at Ft. Mohave in December. Purchased a gallery from F. A. Cook in Prescott, offering stereographs under the title of "A Photographic Album of a Trip Through Arizona" by Flanders and Penlon. Henri Penlon passed away in Prescott February 6, 1874. Flanders moved on to Tucson in the summer 1874. Operated out of the studio of Adolpho Rodrigo on the corner of Courthouse and Maiden Lane in Tucson, July 1874. Made excursions to Fts. Bowie and Apache, San Carlos, and southeastern Arizona until September 1874. Left Tucson, October 1874, to return to Los Angeles via Yuma. Subsequently issued two versions of a stereographic series, "Scenes in Arizona," including approximately 100 images. Flanders' stereographs of Arizona were subsequently issued on the mounts of Payne, Stanton & Company of Los Angeles, Willliscraft of Prescott, and the Continent Publishing Company (whether with permission or as pirated views is not known, but prints appear to be from original negatives).

FLY & HOLFSTEAD
Active in Tucson on Fremont Street, c. 1888.

FLY, CAMILIUS S.
Born in Andrew County, Missouri, 1849; died in Tombstone, October 12, 1901. Fly came to Tombstone, 1879, with wife Mary and operated a gallery on 312 Fremont Street near the O.K. Corral. Listing: "Photographer & Lodgings, 312 Fremont, Tombstone." Photographed Tombstone and vicinity producing cartes-de-viste, cabinet cards, mounted photographs and some stereoviews. Fly also operated a gallery in Phoenix, 1893-94, at 219 East Washington. He operated a gallery at the Norton House on Upper Main Street, Bisbee, 1889-1901. Fly was known for an important series he made of Geronimo, Apache warriors, General Crook and the Indian fighters who subdued him, and the gunfighters and lawmen who made Tombstone famous. Negatives destroyed in studio fire, 1912, and warehouse fire, 1915.

Ben T. Traywick, *Camillus Sidney Fly, The Man Who Photographed History*, Red Marie's, 1985.

FLY, MARY E. (MRS.)
Active in Tombstone, 1907-12. Worked gallery with husband Camilius prior to his death, 1901. Also active in Bisbee, c. 1895, continuing as a photographer until c. 1912.

FLYING GALLERY
Studio operated by William H. Willliscraft in Prescott, c. 1876.

FONDERMAN, O.
Active in Bisbee; licensed as an itinerant, November 15, 1908.

FORBES, DR. ROBERT
Photographed Arizona vegetation and agriculture, c. 1900.

FORTIN, JASPER
Active in Phoenix, 1916-20. Operated at 716 Grand Avenue and 1100 East Van Buren.

FRAESDORF, WILLIAM
Active in Benson, c. 1907.

FUERMAN, HENRY
Active in Grand Canyon, c. 1911.

FURL, J. FRANK
Active in Phoenix, c. 1900.

GAIGE, J. G.
Died at Camp Goodwin, July 1869. Early itinerant in New Mexico and Arizona. Returned to Santa Fe, c. 1862. Licensed as photographer in Albuquerque, March 1863. Contracted with quartermaster of New Mexico Military District to photograph posts, 1865. Active at Fort Sumner where the Navajo Indian Nation was in captivity, February-March 1866. Studio at southwest corner Plaza, opposite Perea's. Advertised as "J. C. Gaige, The Photographer" in Tucson *Weekly Arizonan*, May 1869. Also listed as Gage; may be the same person as George A. Gaige.

GALBRAITH, ROY L.
Operated in Mesa, c. 1919, at 106 West 1st.

GARDNER, ALEXANDER
Born in Paisley, Scotland, October 17, 1821; died in Washington D.C., December 1882. Worked for Matthew Brady during the Civil War, and later for the Department of the Interior, Union Pacific Railway, and Union Army. With William Bell, photographed northern Arizona in vicinity of current Flagstaff during the Union Pacific Railway's Eastern Division survey of the 35th Parallel (Kansas-Pacific Survey), 1867.

GENTILE, CARLOS (CHARLES) G.
Born in Naples, Italy, 1835; died in Chicago, Illinois, 1893. Began photographic career, 1863, a year after arriving in Victoria from San Francisco. Worked on Vancouver Island and in British Columbia until 1866. In 1864 Gentile took photographs of the "Leach River Gold Flurry" that arose after he discovered traces of gold while cleaning his photographic apparatus. Gentile left British Columbia, September 1866, losing a box of his stereo negatives. He opened a gallery in San Francisco, 1867, then worked as an itinerant in the Southwest. He was a Prescott photographer prior to 1869, then sold his gallery to F. A. Cook, and is listed in the Arizona Citizen, August 19, 1871, as a traveling photographer with Governor Safford's prospecting party in the Pinal mountains. Operated a gallery in Adamsville, 1871. Exhibited paper prints and ambrotypes at the 8th Industrial Exhibition in California. Operated the Gentile Photography Gallery in Chicago, 1874-85. Gentile gained notoriety through his affiliation with Dr. Carlos Montezuma, a famous Native American doctor and Indian rights activist.

GILGANNON, DANIEL S.
Active in Morenci, 1909-12.

GILL, DE LANCEY W.
Born in Camden, South Carolina, July 1, 1859; died in Alexandria, Virginia, August 30, 1940. Illustrations editor of the U.S. Geological Survey, and from 1899, performed the same function for the Smithsonian Institution Bureau of American Ethnology. Photographer for W. J. McGee survey to study the Papagos, 1900.

GILLINGHAM, W. P.
Based in Clifton, operating a tent gallery with partner Charles Granville Johnson, c. 1888.

GLOBE PHOTOGRAPHIC COMPANY
Active in Globe, 1909-10; W. Bailey operator.

GOMMEL, G. EDWARD
Listed as partner of Charles R. Allen, c. 1892-93, location unknown.

GONZALES, LEONARDO
Active in Morenci, c. 1917.

GOTTLEIB, HARRY JOSEPH
Born in New York, 1882; died 1936. Active in Tucson, 1911-12; Tempe, 1916-19.

GRAVES, G. A.
Active in Bisbee; photographed Bisbee, C & A Smelter, Douglas, and Tombstone mines, summer 1906.

GREAT WESTERN VIEW COMPANY
Active in Bisbee, c. 1898. Operated by Lewis Jones and (?) Kennat, 1889-1900. Also active in Naco.

GREEN, W. HUGH A.
Active in Bisbee, 1909-10. Operated at 114 Tombstone Canyon. Active in Phoenix, 1911-15, at 18 West Washington.

GREGORY, A. D.
Studio operator for Buehman in Tucson, c. 1880.

GRIFFITHS, D.
Photographed Navajo reservation and vicinity, c. 1903.

GRIME, CICERO
Active in Globe, 1880-81. Listed as "Photographer, Globe" and "Cicero Grime Photographic Gallery Globe City and Pinal Arizona." He robbed a stagecoach and was nearly hanged, 1882; sentenced to Yuma Territorial Prison. Operated the California Art Gallery in Globe, ex-operator of I.C.U. Photograph Car in California. Made tintypes and stereographs.

GUEN, HUGH
Active in Bisbee, 1900-10; Phoenix, 1911-12.

GUZMAN, E. S.
Active in Douglas, c. 1919, at 752 G Avenue.

HACKETT, ARTHUR E.
Proprietor of the Arizona Photo Company in Phoenix, c. 1914.

HACKETT, H. A.
Active in Flagstaff, c. 1900. Photographer and publisher of stereographs and photographic postcards.

HADSELL, WALTER P.
Operator in Henry Buehman's studio, Tucson.

HAELSIG
Partner in Plummer & Haelsig.

HAMMAKER, H. C.
Active in Prescott, 1870s-90s.

HAMMAKER, H. L.
Active in Phoenix, c. 1897. Partner of F. A Hartwell. Also listed as H. L. Haymaker.

HAMMER, RICHARD W.
Surveyor photographer for Native American Photo Company.

HANNA, FORMAN
Born in Anson, Texas, 1882; died 1950. Active in Globe, c. 1904. Pharmacist and photographer of the pictorial style who produced a large body of work, c. 1910-47. Member of the Camera Club of New York and a Fellow of the Royal Photographic Society of London.
Forman Hanna: Pictorial Photographer of the Southwest, Northland Press, 1985.

HANSEN, H. B.
Active in Douglas, c. 1911-12.

HARGRAVE, RICHARD M.
Active in Prescott, 1872. Partner of F. A. Cook after breakup with Nathan P. Pierce. He was arrested, indicted and sentenced to hang for the murder of Ignacio Rubio in November 1872, but pardoned by the governor, June 1873, and released.

HARRIS, JOSEPH
Studio at 179 South Meyer, Tucson, c. 1920.

HARRISON, RALPH T.
Active in Phoenix, 1914-17.

HARTWELL & HAMMAKER
Partnership in Phoenix, c. 1899-1900, at 29 South 2nd Street.

HARTWELL, BYRON J.
Active in Phoenix, c. 1898.

HARTWELL, FRANCIS A.
Born in Canada, April 1852; died in Phoenix, June 1908. Active in Tucson; partner of Henry Buehman, 1880s. Active in Phoenix, c. 1889-1908, at 29 South 2nd.

HARTWELL, STEVEN
Active in Glendale, 1910.

HARTWELL'S STUDIO
Operating in Phoenix, c. 1912-13. John Branch listed as proprietor, but probably a subsequent owner.

HARVEY, FRED
Entrepreneur and publisher; photographed the Grand Canyon and vicinity.

HAWKINS, DR.
Postcard photographer in Jerome, c. 1920.

HAWKINS PHOTOGRAPHER
Active at Grand Canyon, c. 1899.

HAYMAKER, H. L.
Partner of Hartwell in in Phoenix, c. 1898, operating as Hartwell & Hammaker. Also listed individually as Hammaker.

HAYNES, WILLIS P.
Active in Tucson, 1880s.

HDRDLICKA, ALES
Smithsonian anthropologist who documented Apache and Pimas, 1905, and Pueblo, Hopi, and Navajos, 1908.

HEATH, CHARLES E.
Active in Phoenix and Tucson, 1912-25. Listed as Heath Studio.

HEATH STUDIO
Studio in Tucson, c. 1914, located in the AUOW Building, Miss Anna Hulbert, manager.

HEATH STUDIOS
Studio operated by Charles Heath, Board of Trade Building at Adams and 2nd Avenue, Phoenix, c. 1913-20.

HEGEMAN, ELIZABETH COMPTON
Active in Phoenix, c. 1897.

HEISTER, HENRY T.
Santa Fe, New Mexico, was Heister's primary location. He photographed Fort Defiance and within the Navajo reservation, 1877-78.

HEUTHEN
Operated at 271-275 South Meyer Street, Tucson, c. 1910.

HICKSON, C. L.
Active in Yuma, 1907-10. In partnership with Hickson & Quint, c. 1912.

HICKSON, J. C.
Active in Yuma, 1912-13.

HILDRETH & BURGE
Itinerant photographers based in Flagstaff gallery, 1884.

HILDRETH, JAMES
Itinerant from Utah; active in Flagstaff with J. C. Burge, 1884, traveling and operating a gallery as Hildreth & Burge. Continued independently as itinerant, c. 1886; listed in Bisbee, 1888.

HILL, W. H. (MRS.)
Active in Bisbee, c. 1910. Purchased studio from Hugh Green.

HILLERS, JOHN K.
Born in Hanover, Germany, 1843; died in Washington, D.C., 1925. Worked on J. W. Powell's second survey of the Grand Canyon. Trained in photography by survey photographer, James Fennemore of the C. R. Savage Gallery in Salt Lake City, Hillers became his assistant, then took over as official photographer when Fennemore quit due to illness, 1873. Worked with Powell through 1878. Also served as the photographer on the 1879 expedition into the Southwest for the U.S. Geological Survey. Hillers served as Chief Photographer in later surveys for the Bureau of American Ethnology of the Smithsonian Institution, retiring in 1900.

> Don D. Fowler, *Myself in the Water: The Western Photographs of John K. Hillers*, Smithsonian Institute Press, Washington and London, 1989. *"Photographed all the Best Scenery," Jack Hillers' Diary of the Powell Expedition, 1871-1875*, Don D. Fowler, ed., University of Utah Press, Salt Lake City, 1972.

HINSHAW, THOMAS E.
Traveled from Utah through Arizona with Orson Huish, 1899, making stereoviews and portraits.

HOLFSTEAD
Active in Tombstone, c. 1888; partner in Fly & Holfstead.

HOLLAND, LEON H.
Studio at 51 ½ MacDonald in Mesa, c. 1915.

HOOPES, H. E.
Traveled with A. C. Vroman from Medina, Pennsylvania, through Arizona and New Mexico, August 1903.

HORNER, HARRY H.
Itinerant operating in Tucson, c. 1891.

HORTON, J.
Active in Prescott, c. 1885.

HOUGH, WALTER
Born 1859; died 1935. Archeological researcher, c. 1898. Photographer for the Gates-U.S. National Museum survey, 1901.

HOUSEWORTH, THOMAS
Born in New York, June 21, 1828; died in San Francisco, April 13, 1915. Stereograph publisher, 1864-73; photographer, 1872-93. Made studio portraits of Yumas and Pimas as part of Arizona Indians Series. See California.

HUISH, ORSON
Traveled from Utah through Arizona with Thomas Hinshaw making stereoviews and portraits, 1899.

HULBERT, ANNA (MISS)
Manager of Heath Studio in AUOW Building, Tucson, c. 1914.

HUMPHRIES, WILFRED R.
Born in England, 1876. Partner in the Arizona Photograph Company, Inc., in Prescott with Erwin Baer, Percival Armitage, Tom Bate and A. E. Suppinger, c. 1903. Active in Bisbee from 1903; operated Humphries Photo Company at Copper Queen Hotel, c. 1904-05. Continued to visit Bisbee from El Paso, Texas, studio until c. 1909. Produced photographs and photographic and printed postcards of Bisbee and Cochise Counties.

HUNT, ORRIS P.
Parked a railroad car on a siding in Bisbee, January 1896. Advertised "The San Francisco Photograph Car domiciled near roundhouse is doing a good business at present."

HUNTER, EDWARD
Active in Flagstaff beginning c. 1887. Operator for Baer's Flagstaff gallery, 1887. Later operated Hunter's Art Parlor in Flagstaff.

IRWIN, ELLYE
Active in Mesa, 1899-1920. Operated Ellsworth Studio between MacDonald and Robson in Mesa, c. 1915. Also listed as Ellye Ellsworth Bleak and Ellye Irwin Ellsworth.

IRWIN, JOHN
Active in Bisbee, c. 1903, as partner with brothers Marvin and William.

IRWIN, MARVIN E.
Born in Lometa, Texas, 1881; died 1961. Active in Bisbee, 1904, as assistant to brothers John and William. Operated studio in Douglas, 1912-45 at 927 G Avenue.

IRWIN STUDIO
Operated by Marvin E. Irwin in Douglas, c. 1912-45; associated with Ambrose W. Carson, 1911-15.

IRWIN, WILLIAM EDWARD
Born in Red Oak, Missouri, 1871; died in Douglas, 1935. Learned photography in Indian Territory or Texas, c. 1893, operated galleries in Chickasha, Oklahoma, and Silver City, then in Bisbee, 1904-22. Listed in Post Office Building, Bisbee, c. 1905, and the Jacob Schmidt Building, Bisbee, 1907, 1909. Renovated McPhearson Building as studio, operating there 1913-22, when he opened a studio in Douglas.

IVES, LIEUTENANT JOSEPH CHRISTMAS
Expedition photographer on Colorado River expedition, 1857. May have been one of the first photographers to work in Arizona.

JACKSON, WILLIAM HENRY
Photographed the lost cities of the Southwest in Arizona and New Mexico (Hopi pueblos), 1879. Photographed in Mexico for Mexico Central Railway, 1883. Photographed Flagstaff and San Francisco Mountains, 1881. See Nebraska.

JAMES, GEORGE WHARTON
Born 1858; died 1923. Anthropologist and photographer active in Grand Canyon, Hopi pueblos, and northern Arizona, 1895-1901, producing stereographs and prints.

JARVIS, CHARLES
Active in Arizona, c. 1896; listed in St. Johns, 1907.

JENKINS, S. P.
Active in Central, c. 1905-10.

JENNINGS
Itinerant photographer and partner of Charles Allen, c. 1898. Sold 450 negatives to Albert S. Reynolds, 1899.

JENNINGS, E. M.
Active in Prescott, 1870s, possibly as late as 1890s. Advertised as photographer in Prescott, "E. M. Jennings, Photographer, Prescott. Views of the following sections of the Territory: Prescott and vicinity, all prominent mining camps, Walnut Grove Lake, Camp Verde and Vicinity, Hot Springs (Castle Creek), Flagstaff and vicinity, Natural Bridge (Tonto Basin), Apache, San Carlos and other posts, Fort Grant and vicinity, Cliff Dwellings on Beaver Creek, Walnut Canyon and Oak Creek, Tip Top and vicinity, Grand Canyon of the Colorado, Ec. Ec. [sic.]. Ask for catalogue." Also listed as M. Jennings.

JOHNSON, CHARLES GRANVILLE
Born 1832; died 1914. Active in Colorado City (Ft. Yuma), Arizona Territory, 1863-68. In La Paz, 1864, according to census. Produced Views of Arizona and the Colorado River, San Francisco, California, 1868. He took some of the earliest photographs of Arizona including the Cocopa Indians. He was living in Tombstone, 1897. Printed on photo mounts: "The Arizonian, Entered according to act of Congress in the year 1868, in the Clerk's Office of California, by Chas. G. Johnson, Photographer, San Francisco, Cal." Also published illustrated pamphlets illustrated with images of Arizona, c. 1869. Operated a tent gallery with W. P. Gillingham in Clifton, c. 1888.

JOHNSON, K. M.
Studio operated at 417 Mill Avenue, Tempe, c. 1918.

JOHNSON, N. E.
Active in Oatman, 1910-20; also active in Parker.

JONES, J. C.
Active in Clifton, c. 1899

JONES, LEWIS
Operated the Great Western View Company in Bisbeee, c. 1898; partner with Kennat; also listed in Naco.

JUDD, NEIL M.
Photographed north Arizona, 1908-09, with Scott M. Young.

KELLEY, E. W.
Active 1890s-1910s, based in Chicago, Illinois. Listed as Kelley & Chadwick Publishers; produced stereo photographs of Grand Canyon, c. 1906.

KELLEY, ROY F.
Operated Kelley Studios in Miami, Arizona, 1914-55; employed A. J. and W. T. Mullarkey as operators.

KEMP & COLEMAN
Active in Tombstone, c. 1881, operating gallery on Allen Street.

KEMP & KLUIT
Partnership active in Arizona.

KEMP, EDWARD H.
Photographed the Grand Canyon and Hopi pueblos, c. 1905. Operated in San Francisco, producing lantern slides of Snake Dance and Grand Canyon. Images published by Santa Fe Railroad. Partner of Coleman, c. 1881; partner in Kemp & Kluit.

KENNAT
Active in Bisbee, c. 1898. Operated Great Western View Company in partnership with Jones and Lewis. Also listed in Naco.

KEY & TEISMAN
Active in Bisbee; licensed as itinerant, November 1909.

KEY, W. H.
Active in Globe, c. 1909-10.

KEYS PHOTO STUDIO
Operating in Benson, c. 1909-10.

KINNEY
Active in Prescott, 1870s; listed at the Grapevine Station, 1878.

KLINE, J. W.
Active in Roosevelt.

KOLB BROTHERS
Active in Williams, c. 1901, then South Rim of the Grand Canyon. Partners Emery and Ellsworth Kolb operated a studio at the Grand Canyon producing stereographs, mounted photographs and motion pictures.

KOLB, ELLSWORTH
Active in Williams, c. 1901, then South Rim of the Grand Canyon with brother Emery. Produced stereographs of river trips through the Grand Canyon, 1906 and 1911. Made motion pictures of the Hopi Snake Dance at Walpi, 1911 and 1913.
    Ellsworth L. Kolb, *Through the Grand Canyon from Wyoming to Mexico,*
    Macmillan Company, 1938.

KOLB, EMERY
Active in Williams, c. 1901, then South Rim of the Grand Canyon with brother Ellsworth. Made motion pictures of the Hopi Snake Dance at Walpi, 1911 and 1913.

KOPPLIN, WILLIAM ERNEST
Photographer for the Santa Fe Railroad working in northern Arizona, c. 1912. Produced lantern slides of Hopi and Navajo and motion pictures of Hopi Snake Dance.

KORF, ABE M.
Active in Tempe, c. 1909-10; Phoenix, 1912-13, at 316 West Washington.

KOVARICK, ALBERT J.
Active in Ft. Grant, c. 1890.

KUNSELMAN, ELTON E.
Operated The Photocraft Shop at 1 Cactus Way, Phoenix, c. 1916-17.

LA LUNA STUDIO
Studio operated by I. K. Wilson at 146 Stone, Tucson, c. 1917-18.

LACY, W. A.
Active in Bisbee, c. 1905, on Main Street.

LANGFORD, W. L.
Douglas (Ragtown), c. 1904.

LARA, VINCENTE
Active in Nogales, c. 1912-13.

LARSON, OLAF P.
Photographer from Moscow, Idaho, who worked in Arizona, c. 1900. Photographed Bisbee, Jerome, Nogales, Phoenix and mining subjects.

LAWSON, TOM
Active in Silver King.

LONG, C. C.
Active in Phoenix, 1903-08, at 28 West Washington.

LORING
Partner with George Rothrock in Prescott, c. 1878.

LOWE, M. W.
Active in Globe, 1908-10, at 161 East Oak; in Douglas, partner with C. L. Stubbs in Queen Studio on 11th Street. Photographed 1908 Bisbee flood. Also spelled Low.

LUBKIN, WALTER
Official photographer for the construction of Roosevelt Dam c. 1907-12, operating out of Mesa.

LUCAS & BURLAN
Partnership active in Clifton, 1885.

LUCAS, HARRY W.
Active in Arizona City (Yuma), c. 1880, then in Silver City, New Mexico. Operated in Clifton as Lucas & Burlan, 1885, returning to Silver City, New Mexico, 1886.

LUMMIS, CHARLES
Photographed the Hopi, 1891. See California.

LURLEY, LUCY (MISS)
Active in Snowflake.

LYMAN, HARVEY O.
Active in Tempe, 1912-13.

MACDOUGAL, DR. DANIEL T.
Photographed deserts of Arizona for the Carnegie Desert Laboratory.

MALONE, D. T.
Active in Phoenix, c. 1915. Photographed Phoenix, Hayden and vicinity.

MARKEY, DANIEL A.
Active in Ft. Apache as partner with Myton, 1885; photographed San Carlos, late 1880s. Arrived in Bisbee as an itinerant with Backstein, c. 1895, and began operating his own studio on Upper Main Street. Listed as Markey's Studio, 1900. Also listed as C. A. Merkey.

MARKS, C. W.
Active in Morenci, c. 1895-1907.

MARMELEJO, GEORGE
Active in Bisbee, c. 1898, operating Wigwam Photo.

MARTIN, A. L.
Active in Williams, c. 1895.

MARY ANN STUDIO
Active in Winslow.

MASON, JANIE ELLIS
Wife of officer stationed at Ft. Apache; cited for photographic work in the records of the Smithsonian Museum.

MATTESON, SUMNER
Born September 15, 1867; died 1920. Traveled and photographed throughout the Southwest and visited the Hopi, 1901 and 1902.

MAUDE, FREDERICK HAMER
Photographer from Los Angeles and friend of George Warton James. Photographed the Grand Canyon and Hopi ceremonials on annual trips beginning c. 1895. See California.

MAUDLIN, WILLIAM E.
Active in Miami, Arizona, c. 1912-13.

McCULLOCH, JASPER M.
Active in Phoenix, 1912-46, as McCulloch Brothers, Inc., at 18 North 2nd Avenue.

McCULLOCH, WILLIAM PATRICK
Born 1880; died 1971. Active in Phoenix, 1912-46, as McCulloch Brothers, Inc., at 18 North 2nd Avenue.

McKENNA, WILLIAM
Active in Prescott; possible operator of Cook's Gallery in August 1874, prior to sale of the studio to Williscraft. Possibly active as late as 1877.

MEALEY, MARTIN W.
Active in Phoenix, 1897-1910. Operated Mealey's New York Photo Studio at 213 East Washington, c. 1899-1900. Studio transferred to J. A. Westburg. Operated Mealey Studio at 29 South 2nd, c. 1909-10.

MEALEY, W. P.
Active in Phoenix, c. 1898, with M. W. Mealey.

MEARNS, EDGAR A.
Born 1856; died 1916. Active in Arizona.

MELHAGEN, O. H.
Active in Bisbee, c. 1900.

MELVEN
Active in Flagstaff, c. 1895, operating as Melven Photo.

MELVIN
Partner in Burchard & Melvin operating in Tempe, c. 1892, on Mill Avenue.

MENDELEFF, COSMOS
Active at Mishongnovi and Walpi. Smithsonian ethnographer and photographer visiting Hopi pueblos, August 1885.

MERIWETHER, H. B.
Active in Globe, c. 1909, operating as H. B. Meriwether & Company.

MESSINGER & ALTENBURGH
Partnership of A. F. Messinger and William Altenburgh in Phoenix, c. 1895-98, at 243 West Madison.

MESSINGER, A. F.
Active in Phoenix in 1899-1900. Cabinet card imprint "A. F. MESSENGER, Viewest [sic]. Scenes in Phoenix and Salt River Valley, PHOENIX, ARIZONA." Listed in partnership as Messinger & Altenburgh at 243 West Madison, c. 1895- 98.

MICHAEL & SHILLCOCK
Itinerants active in Flagstaff, c. 1896.

MIDDLETON, F. W.
Purchased photographic equipment in Flagstaff 1885; produced stereographs in Holbrook, c. 1885-90.

MILLER, ANDREW
Photographer from Silver City, New Mexico. Active in Globe, c. 1886; Bisbee, 1897. Photographed Apache Indians. Killed by Yaqui Indians on August 3, 1899, in Sonora, Mexico.

MILLER, VICTOR
A cinematographer for *Pathe's Weekly* who photographed Hopi Snake Dance at Walpi, 1913. Arrested after attempting to escape with the exposed film (which was confiscated) without signing non-commercial release.

MILLER, J.
Photographed and published views of Hopi pueblos and Snake Dance, c. 1898.

MILO
Partner in Booth & Milo, operating a studio in Douglas, c. 1919, on Florida near 11th.

MISSION STUDIOS
Active in Yuma, c. 1915.

MITCHELL & BAER
Partnership of Daniel F. Mitchell and Erwin Baer in Prescott, c. 1875. Operated the Capitol Art Gallery, and used similar backdrops as Buehman & Hartwell. Photographed southwest tribes.

MITCHELL, DANIEL FRANCIS
Left San Francisco for Prescott, December 1877; partner with Erwin Baer, c. 1875; took over Williscraft's gallery, formerly known as Capital Art Gallery on Cortez Street north of the Courthouse after a trip photographing Mohave Country. Advertised Rothrock's Arizona Views for sale in his gallery.

MODEL PHOTO GALLERY
Studio operated at 102 South Stone by F. P. Sweet, 1911, and by Oliver Cozby, 1912 in Tucson.

MONTFORT, E.
Marketed photographs of Arizona and New Mexico, 1885-95.

MOON, F. W.
Active in San Carlos, 1870s. Reverse of photograph reads "F. W. Moon, photographer, Company B., 11th U.S. Infantry, San Carlos. Views of Military post, Indian life, etc. Always on hand. First class work guaranteed."

MOON, KARL E.
Born in Ohio, 1879; died 1948. Photographer for Santa Fe Railroad. Moon did most of his photograpic work among the Indians of New Mexico, Arizona and Oklahoma, but was active in Pasadena, California, 1914-48. Moon produced a monumental work entitled *Indians of the Southwest*, 1936, which included fifty atlas-folio photographic prints from his archive. Moon also painted Indian subjects, and his wife, Grace Purdie, produced extensive western illustrations for children's books and magazines.
    Haines, Robert D. Jr., *Carl Moon - Photographer & Illustrator of the American Southwest*, Argonaut Book Shop, 1982.

MOONEY, JAMES
Born 1885; died 1921. Bureau of American Ethnology researcher who photographed the Navajo in Arizona.

MOORE, SAMUEL
Active at 713 G Avenue in Douglas, c. 1912-13.

MORA, JOSEPH
Born 1876; died 1947. Trained as a graphic artist; traveled from California to Arizona, 1904. Lived on the Hopi reservation and documented ceremonial events and portraits of participants with photographs and watercolors, 1904-06.

MORRISON, R. E.
Operated at 102 South Stone, Tucson, c. 1914.

MORTIN, J.
Itinerant operating out of Prescott, c. 1884.

MOSSER, WILLIAM
Active in Phoenix, c. 1898.

MULLARKEY, A. J.
Active in Miami, Arizona; employed by Roy F. Kelley.

MULLARKEY, W. T.
Employed by Roy F. Kelley in Miami, Arizona.

MUSSEY, FRED B.
Active in Phoenix, 1898-1935. Operated Sunbeam Studio in the Gooding Building. Also in partnership with M. L. Davenport, c. 1900, at 246 West Washington.

NATIVE AMERICAN PHOTO COMPANY
Operated by surveyor and photographer Richard W. Hammer.

NEMECK, LOUIS A.
Active in Bisbee, c. 1898-1902, operating a studio on the south side of Upper Main Street.

NEPHEW, J.
Active in Bisbee, 1901-04.

NEUMAN, WILLIAM J.
Active in Nogales, c. 1906-13. Advertised as photographer and manager of Lyric Motion Picture Theater. Also spelled Newman.

NEW YORK GALLERY
Studio operated by E. A. Bearce, Phoenix, c. 1898.

NEW YORK PHOTO STUDIO
Active in Phoenix, 1897-1910. Operated by M. W. Mealey, c. 1898.

NEWMAN, WILLIAM J.
See William J. Neuman.

NEWPORT, F. T.
Active in Oracle, c. 1909.

NIMS, FRANKLIN A.
Born in Eldorado, Kansas. Active in Colorado Springs, 1870s; Arizona, 1869. Photographer with Brown-Stanton expedition down the canyon of the Colorado, 1889-90.

O'SULLIVAN, TIMOTHY
Born in Ireland; died in Statten Island, New York, January 14, 1882. Active as photographer, 1857-80. Apprenticed with Matthew Brady, and worked with Gardner in Brady's Washington D.C. Gallery, c. 1856. Worked with Brady as assistant during the Civil War, 1861; joined Gardner as a civilian photographer of the war, 1862. Worked for numerous surveys, 1867-74; In Tucson and Camp Mohave, 1871; Wheeler Survey photographer, 1871-75. Printed Wheeler Survey negatives under contract, 1875-76.

Joel Snyder, *American Frontiers: The Photographs of Timothy H. O'Sullivan, 1867-1874*, Aperture, New York, 1981.
James D. Horan, *Timothy O'Sullivan, America's Forgotton Photographer*, Bonanza Books, New York, 1966.
Rick Dingus, *The Photographic Artifacts of Timothy O'Sulivan*, University of New Mexico Press, Albuquerque, 1982.

OSBON, CALVIN
Active in California, 1900s, in Santa Rosa, San Jose and Fresno. Osborn produced stereographs and imperial cabinet cards of Flagstaff, imperial cabinet cards of Tucson and vicinity and of the Grand Canyon, 1890s. Photographed Bisbee and the Grand Canyon, 1910-17.

PARKER & PARKER
Partnership active 1873-75; father and son partners Joseph C. Parker and Francis A. Parker opened their gallery on Main Street in Yuma, 1874.

PARKER, FRANCIS A.
Co-founder of gallery with father Joseph C. Parker; active in 1874.

PARKER, JOSEPH C.
Active in 1874. Co-founder of gallery with son, Francis A. Parker. Active in Los Angeles, California, c. 1877. Returned to Arizona, 1889, with the Atlantic & Pacific Railroad and worked in Flagstaff and Winslow. Operated a photographic tent with W. B., W. D. and W. F. Parker, c. 1899-1901. Listed as a partner in Atlantic & Pacific Portrait Company, c. 1902-11.

PARKER, W. B.
Tucson, Arizona Territory c. 1903-04. Operated photographic tent with Joseph Parker; partner in Atlantic & Pacific Portrait Company, c. 1908.

PARKER, W. D.
Active in Tucson, c. 1901. Operated photographic tent with Joseph Parker, c. 1899-1901.

PARKER, W. F.
Active in Tucson, c. 1899-1900. Operated photographic tent with Joseph Parker, c. 1899-1901.

PARKERS
Operated Atlantic Pacific View and Portrait Company, 6th and Broadway, Tucson, c. 1907-08; probably W. B. and Joseph C. Parker.

PARTRIDGE, F. J.
Active in Tucson. Studio operator for Buehman, c. 1880.

PASEVITCH, JOSEPH
Active in Flagstaff, c. 1889.

PAYNE, D. R.
Photographer for 1892 border survey in Bisbee, c. 1892.

PEABODY, HENRY GREENWOOD
Photographed the Grand Canyon, 1896; Arizona Indians, 1906. Possibly continued activity in the Grand Canyon into the 1930s. See California.

PENLON, HENRI
Died in Prescott, February 6, 1874. Licensed as a photographer in Los Angeles, May 1865. Partner of D. P. Flanders during trip to Arizona, 1873. Flanders & Penlon mounts issued by Flanders for images produced throughout Arizona. Also spelled Penelon.

PEREIRA, JOSEPH
Active in Tucson, c. 1919-20, operating Pereira Studio at 136 East Congress.

PERRINE, EDWARD I.
Assistant to J. H. Coyle in Bisbee, c. 1903.

PERRY, OLIVER H.
Active in Jerome, c. 1912-13.

PETERSON, JOSEPH
Active in Snowflake, c. 1907.

PHILLIPS, FENLEY W.
Active in Hackberry, c. 1890. Photographed Grand Canyon, Williams and vicinity.

PHOTOGRAPHIC ARTIST OLD GALLERY
Active in Prescott, c. 1875, located north of Courthouse.

PIERCE, NATHAN PARDA
Born 1830; died 1911. Active in Prescott, 1869-72; partner of F. A. Cook.

POLLOCK, JEANETTE
Active in Tempe, c. 1916.

PORTER
Active in Tucson, c. 1879; partner of Alfred S. Addis.

PORTILLO, JESUS
Studio at 417 East Madison, Phoenix, c. 1918.

POWELL, CLEMENT
Assistant photographer in Powell survey, 1871; cousin of Major Powell.

PRESCOTT STUDIO
Gallery in Prescott, c. 1919-20, operated by A. J. Jennings at 119 East Gurley.

PRESTON, JOHN C.
Listed as photographer in 1870 Arizona census, age 27, originally from Alabama.

PRIOR, N. W.
Listed as artist in 1870 census, living in Williamson's Valley near Prescott; age 30, originally from Virginia.

PUTNAM & VALENTINE
Photographed the Grand Canyon, c. 1910.

QUEEN STUDIO
Operated by M. W. Lowand C. L. Stubbs in Douglas, c. 1904, on 11th Street.

QUICK FINISH KODAK COMPANY
Studio operated by Henry Bryant at 218 West Gurley in Prescott, c. 1919.

QUINT, ROY T.
Active in Yuma, c. 1912-13; partner in Hickson & Quint.

RANDALL, A. FRANK
Active in Wilcox and itinerant, 1883-88. Some overlap in negatives and prints with Ben Wittick; specific authorship uncertain. In Las Cruces, New Mexico, November 1885-May 1886.

RANDEBAUGH, J. D.
Operated a gallery in Williams, c. 1898-1907; sold out to the Kolb brothers.

RATCLIFF, C. E.
Active in Williams, c. 1920. "C. E. Ratcliff Photos and Curios, Williams."

RAUDELEAGH, OLIVER B.
Active in Williams, c. 1907.

RESLER, CALVIN A.
Active in Buckeye, c. 1914.

REYNOLDS, ALBERT S.
Photographed Bisbee, Douglas and Tucson, 1898-1901; probably an amateur.

RHODES, JOHN P.
Studio at 213 West Washington, Phoenix, c. 1892-1906.

RINCKWITZ, RICHARD L.
Active in Glendale, c. 1918.

RING, T. A.
Studio at 240 East Congress, Tucson, c. 1917.

RISDON, O. A.
Active in Clifton and Metcalf, 1907-16; also operated a studio in Bisbee, c. 1912-13.

RISDON'S STUDIO
Active in Clifton and Metcalf, c. 1907.

RISTELHEUBER (MR. & MRS.)
Active in Bisbee, c. 1902. Opened a studio in Barnaby Building offering "stamp photographs, button jewelry, copying and enlarging."

ROBINSON, H. F.
First president of Phoenix Camera Club, 1892.

RODRIGO, ADOLFO
Visited Prescott from Los Angeles, May 1870. Operated a gallery in Tucson, July 1874, at the corner of Courthouse Street and Maiden Lane. Apparently worked with Flanders during his 1874 excursion to southern Arizona; partner with Buehman who operated the gallery prior to buying him out, 1875.

ROGERS, CHARLES THOMAS
Born in Freeport, Maine, 1827; died in Bath, Maine, September 25, 1903. Daguerreotypist in Gardiner, Maine, 1853; studio in St. Louis, Missouri, 1854; sheriff of Mendocino County, California, c. 1855; miner and traveling photographer in Arizona, 1863-64. Listed in 1864 Arizona census as photographer.

ROSE, GEORGE LYMAN
Photographed petrified forest, Holbrook and Winslow, 1890. Produced stereographs of the Hopi.

ROSKRUGE, GEORGE
Active in Tucson, c. 1880s. Partner of Buehman in Buehman & Company, 1883. Also made photographs in Arizona as a surveyor for the U.S. Surveyor General, 1890.

ROTHROCK & BARNETT
Partnership of Charles Barnett and G. H. Rothrock in Phoenix, 1882-94.

ROTHROCK & CATTON
Partnership active in Phoenix, c. 1886.

ROTHROCK, GEORGE H.
Born in Jefferson City, Missouri, March 1843. Operated a gallery in Bakersfield, California, 1870-75. Active as an itinerant, 1876-78, after arriving in Yuma with Young, and alone after Young's death, 1876. Established a gallery in Prescott, January 1878, on Montezuma Street. In April 1878, formed partnership with Loring and established a studio at the News Depot, then at Loring's Bazaar. Partnership with Charles Barnett in Phoenix, 1882-94. Moved his gallery to Tempe, 1893. Rothrock and Barnett retired, and the *Arizona Miner*, May 31, 1878, lists Mitchell as having Rothrock's Arizona Views for sale in his gallery. Listed as "Rathrock [sic], photographer", Phoenix, 1882-83. Traveled to Bisbee, 1885. Partner in Rothrock & Catton, Phoenix, c. 1886. After leaving photography, Rothrock became a farmer and worked for the Arizona Canal Company.

ROWNTREE, W. A.
Active in Tucson, c. 1909, located on South Stone and Jackson. Possibly in Bisbee, 1916-17. Also listed as Rountree.

ROYAL STUDIO
Operated in Douglas, c. 1919, at 732 G Avenue.

RUSSELL, FRANK
Photographed on the Gila Reservation, 1900-02.

RUSSELL, WILLIAM F.
Studio in Phoenix, c. 1914-17, at 35 East Washington.

RYDEN & WESTBERG
Partnership in Phoenix, c. 1907.

RYDEN
Partner in Ryden & Westberg active in Phoenix, c. 1907.

SADLER, GEORGE
Listed as official photographer for the 1910 Phoenix Aero Meet.

SAMANO, RAYMOND
Active in Nogales, c. 1906-07.

SANDERS
Photographed Walnut Canyon, c. 1889.

SATO, T.
Active in Winslow, c. 1912-13.

SAVAGE, CHARLES R.
Traveled in Arizona, 1872, 1875 and 1877-79. See Utah.

SCHOLEY
Active in Arizona, c. 1882, location unknown.

SCHROEDER
Came from California, 1876; assistant to Williscraft in Prescott and Camp Verde. Possible alternate spelling of Schroeter.

SCHROETER
Active in Ft. Huachuca, 1885-90s. Also active in Bisbee and Wilcox.

SCHWEMBERGER, SIMEON
Franciscan monk working in Gallup, New Mexico, and Window Rock area, c. 1909; also worked in St. Michaels.

SCOTT, J.
Assistant to Flanders in Prescott, 1874.

SEXTON, JAMES H.
Studio in Phoenix, c. 1917, at 604 ½ West Van Buren.

SHAW, C. H.
Studio at 26 and 30 North First Avenue, Phoenix, c. 1900. Shaw photographed the Hopi Snake Dance, 1901.

SHILLCOCK
Partner in Michael & Shillcock, itinerants in Flagstaff, 1896.

SKELLEY, ELLEN B. (MRS.)
Active in Globe, c. 1907.

SKELLEY, LOTE ADISON
Active in Silver City, New Mexico, c. 1888-98. Located in Globe, c. 1896-1907.

SLADSKY, CHARLES
Studio operator for Buehman in Tucson, c. 1880.

SMITH & PEAT
Active in Bisbee; licensed as itinerants, February 14, 1907.

SMITH, ERWIN E.
Born in Honey Grove, Texas, 1886; died 1947. Photographed cattle ranch life in Texas, Arizona, Mexico and New Mexico, c. 1900s. Worked on Colonel Greene's Oregon ranch near Herford, summer 1909. Produced illustrated articles for magazines such as the *Saturday Evening Post*.

SMITH, KNIGHT A.
Active in Globe, c. 1909.

SMITH, S. D. (MRS.)
Active in Snowflake, c. 1912-13.

ST. CLAIR, EDWARD
Operated St. Clair Photogaph Gallery in Flagstaff, c. 1887-89

STACEY & COPELAND
Active in Phoenix, 1905-06.

STACEY, C. I.
Active in Phoenix, c. 1905-06.

STALEY, FRANK
Postcard photographer in Phoenix, c. 1910-15.

STELL, BERNARD
Active in Sun City.

STEPHENS, H. R.
Active in Phoenix, c. 1911. Advertised as "The Hartwell Old Photographic Studio" at 29 South 2nd.

STEVENSON, JAMES
Traveled with Powell Survey, 1879.

STEVENSON, MAXILDA COXE
Born 1850; died 1915. Wife of James Stevenson of the Powell Survey, she first visited the territory 1879, then returned and photographed the Hopi and Zuni, 1896-1909.

STONE
Partner in Stone & Cox, c. 1908, operating in Flagstaff. Produced panoramic photographs.

STONE, FRED L.
Studio at 512 North Stone in Tucson, c. 1908.

STRAND STUDIO
Active in Phoenix, c. 1919.

STUART, W. F.
Active in Flagstaff, 1900-05; El Paso, 1906-23.

STUBBS, C. L.
Operated as partner with M. W. Low in Queen Studio on 11th Street, Douglas, c. 1904.

SUFEA, FRANK
Active in Humboldt and Prescott, c. 1907.

SUNBEAM STUDIO
Operated by partners F. Mussey and M. Davenport in Phoenix, 1898-1900.

SUPPINGER, A. E.
Itinerant based in Prescott, c. 1902. Documented mining and development of the Bradshaw mountains, producing photographic and printed materials. Partner in the Arizona Photograph Company, Inc., in Prescott with Erwin Baer, Percival Armitage, Tom Bate and W. R. Humphries, c. 1903.

SWEET, F. P.
Operated Model Photo Gallery at 102 South Stone, Tucson c. 1911.

SYKES, GODFREY
Active in Tucson, c. 1910.

TABER, ISAAC W.
Operated studio in San Francisco, California, 1864-1905; marketed Grand Canyon views (possibly purchased from or produced by other photograhers). See California.

TARR, J. A.
Active in Kingman, c. 1907.

TAYLOR, GRACIE S.
Active in Bylas, dates unknown.

TAYLOR, JAMES A.
Active in Bisbee, c. 1905, on Brewery Avenue; also listed at Broadway and Brewery Avenue.

TEISMAN
Active in Bisbee; listed as partner in Key & Teisman, licensed as itinerants, November 1909.

THE PHOTOCRAFT SHOP
Studio at 1 Cactus Way, Phoenix, c. 1915, operated by G. B. Wilbur.

THOMAS, CHARLES
Listed in the census of 1864 as a photographer in Prescott, age 35, from Maine.

THWAITES, GEORGE H.
Active in Globe, c. 1907.

TIBBETS, H. C.
Produced photographic album and lantern slides of Roosevelt Dam and Apache Trail, operating out of San Francisco.

TIESMAN AND KEY
Active in Bisbee, licensed as itinerants, 1905.

TILLOTSON, FRANK H.

TISINGER, R. M.
Active in Phoenix.

TROTT, ANDREW. P.
Possibly active as an ambrotypist in Boston, Massachusetts, c. 1859-60s. Operated in Junction City, Kansas, c. 1875. Offered stereographs of Prescott and northwestern Arizona. Whether original photographer or acquired negatives through trade or purchase is yet to be determined. Identical images appear on Flanders and Mitchell mounts.

TRUAX
Active in Winslow, c. 1910.

TUCKER, C. H.
Active in Flagstaff area, c. 1890.

TUCSON PHOTO COMPANY
Operated by N. G. Wallace at 29 South Stone in Tucson, c. 1912-13.

TURLEY, LUCY (MISS)
Active in Snowflake, c. 1909.

TURNBULL, ROBERT A.
Active in Phoenix, 1909-15. Partner in Westburg & Turnbull, 1909-10, 213 East Washington.

UPDIKE, LISLE CHANDLER
Operated a number of portrait studios in Phoenix, 1906-76. Traveled throughout Arizona making photographs to sell in his studios.

VALENTINE
Partner in Putnam & Valentine. Photographed the Grand Canyon, 1910.

VAN NESS, CARL
Operated gallery at 168-180 East Washington, Phoenix, c. 1901.

VROMAN, ADAM CLARK
Visited Hopi pueblos, 1895, returning periodically during the next 10 years to photograph Hopi of northern Arizona and New Mexico. See California.

WASSON, C. L.
Photographer for International Stereograph Company; active in southern Arizona, c. 1907.

WATKINS, CARLETON
Photographed in Arizona for Southern Pacific Railroad, April 10- May 18, 1880. Images include cactus and scenics, Charleston, Tombstone, Tucson, Yuma and vicinities. Issued Arizona stereoviews as part of Watkins New Pacific Coast Series (nos. 4837- 4831). See California.

WEBSTER, LEONARD A.
Active in Ray, c. 1912-13.

WEED, WILLIAM L.
Operated Weed Art Studio at 129 South Stone, Tucson, c. 1920. Previously associated with Buehman's studio.

WENFOR, GEORGE
Active in Phoenix at Jefferson Street. Wenfor possibly misspelling of Wonfor.

WESTBURG, JOHN F.
Active in Phoenix, 1907-12. Operated Westburg Studio, superseding

Mealey Studio at 213 East Washington, c. 1908. Also partner in Ryden & Westberg, c. 1907; partner in Westburg & Turnbull, 1909-10, 213 East Washington.

WESTGARD, A. L.
Active in Ehrenberg, c. 1911.

WHITE, C. L.
Traveled with Charles Clark on his Projectoscope Tour showing motion pictures throughout Arizona c. 1898. Fell from a train in Holbrook, his legs were mangled and he died several days later from the injuries.

WIGWAM PHOTO
Operated by George Marmelejo in Bisbee, c. 1898.

WILBUR, G. B.
Operated The Photocraft Shop in Phoenix, c. 1915, at 1 Cactus Way.

WILCOX, GENERAL TIMOTHY E.
Photographed the Apaches, 1887-91.

WILCOX, H. H.
Manager of Elite Studio in Tucson, c. 1908.

WILLIAMS, JOHN RODERICK
Active in Safford, 1900-17. Also active in Globe, c. 1904. Produced views of mining and Globe area including February 1904 flood. No imprint for this photographer, but manuscript titling and credits on some mounts.

WILLIAMS, R.
Active in Pima, c. 1907.

WILLIAMS, THOMAS F.
Operated Williams Studio at 223 East Washington, Phoenix, c. 1916-17.

WILLISCRAFT, WILLIAM HAMILTON
Active in Prescott, c. 1875. Boot and shoe maker who purchased the local gallery and hired an operator to run a photograph studio making tintypes. Purchased Cook's gallery in Prescott, 1875, opened a short time, then closed until April 1876. With his assistant, Schroeder, he began using a traveling "gallery on wheels," May 5, 1876. Moved his gallery to Camp Verde, November 11, 1876. Also known as the Flying Gallery and Williscraft & Company.

WILSON, I. K.
Operated in Tucson at 146 Stone, c. 1913-17; as La Luna Studio at 146 Stone, c. 1917-19; and as Wilson Studio at 19 Stone Avenue, c. 1919-20.

WILSON, LAWRENCE (MRS.)
Active in Phoenix, 1903-17. Operated at 5 South 2nd, 1907-10; 29 West Jefferson, 1912.

WITTICK & BURGE
Brief partnership of G. B. Wittick and J. C. Burge; issued stereoviews.

WITTICK, GEORGE BEN
Born in Huntington, Pennsylvania, January 1, 1845; died August 30, 1903. Served in the Army at Ft. Snelling, Minnesota, 1861. Studio in Moline, Illinois, late 1870s. Arrived in Santa Fe, 1878. Partnerships with W. P. Bliss and R. W. Russell, c. 1880-84. Wittick moved his studio to Albuquerque, March 1881. Partner in Wittick & Burge, c. 1880s. Traveled with Matilde Coxe Stevenson on her ethnographic survey of Arizona, 1881. He traveled to Arizona on the Atlantic & Pacific Railroad, photographing Flagstaff and northern Arizona, c. 1884. Gallery in Gallup, New Mexico, 1884-1900.
   Patrick Janis Broder, *Shadows On Glass: The Indian World of Ben Wittick*, Rowman & Littlefield, 1990.

WOLPI
Active in Arizona.

WONFOR, GEORGE H.
Landscape painter from St. Louis. In Albuquerque, December 1888, as partner with W. Calvin Brown; in Las Vegas, Chloride and Las Cruces, New Mexico through January 1890. In Tucson, c. 1890, with a gallery on East Congress Street. Advertised as "George H. Wonfor Artistic Photographer."

WOOD, H. E.
Photographer with Troop F of the 1st U.S. Cavalry, Nogales, c. 1917.

WOOSTER, GEORGE N.
Active in Prescott, dates unknown.

WORTH, L. W.
Active in Prescott, c. 1869; probable partner of F. A. Cook.

YOUNG
Came to Yuma with Rothrock, 1876. They opened a tent gallery offering ambrotypes, cartes-de-visite, cabinets, and stereo views, and in March 1886, held sciopticon exhibitions. Rothrock and Young met in Phoenix, late 1876, but Young died of pneumonia soon thereafter.

YOUNG, R. Y.
Operated American Stereoscopic Company, founded 1898. Photographed the Petrified Forest, Clifton and Morenci, 1903-07. Young's photographs were published by the American Stereoscopic Company.

YOUNG, SCOTT M.
With Neil M. Judd, photographed northern Arizona, 1908-09.

AARON, SIDNEY D.
Active in Springdale, 1911. Partner in Speece & Aaron, c. 1910.

ADAMSON, OTIS & ELLA E.
Active in Springdale, 1906.

ALBERTSON
Active in Fayetteville, 1903.

ALLMAN, LOUIS P.
Active in Hot Springs, 1908.

ALVERSON
Active in Harrison, c. 1890.

ANSELBERG & BOOTH
Partnership operating in Hot Springs, 1912, between W. S. Booth and David W. Anselberg.

ANSELBERG, DAVID W.
Active in Hot Springs, c. 1917-21. Partner is Anselberg & Booth, 1912..

ATKINS, A. S.
Active in Arkadelphia, c. 1880.

ATTWATER'S PHOTO STUDIO
Active in Rogers, 1907.

BAGWELL, J. O.
Active in Helena, c. 1885.

BAKER, J. W.
Active in Rogers, 1900.

BALARD, UNIS K.
Active in Price Township, 1900.

BARDWELL, B.
Active in Rosboro, Pike County, c. 1910+.

BARDWELL, CAREY L.
Active in Rosboro, Pike County, c. 1910+.

BARKER, ALBERT W.
Active in Eureka Springs, 1892.

BARNES
Active in Winslow, c. 1910.

BEATON, C. P.
Active in Rogers, 1900.

BEATON, EVA LEWALLEN
Active in Rogers.

BECK, F. W.
Active in Eureka Springs.

BINGHAM, GEORGE H.
Active in Rogers, 1906-12.

BLACKFORD, A. W.
Active in Kingston, 1906.

BOOTH
Active in Dardanelle, c. 1895.

BOOTH, W. S.
Active in Hot Springs, c. 1908-12. Partner is Anselberg & Booth.

BOOTH, WILLIE L.
Active in Eureka Springs, 1900.

BRASWELL, J. W.
Active in Jasper, c. 1910.

BRASWELL, JAMES T.
Active in Berryville, c. 1910.

CADMAN, ALBERT W.
Active in Rogers, 1892.

CALAHAN BROTHERS
Dennis and George R. Calahan, active in Eureka Springs, c. 1888.

CALAHAN, DENNIS
Active in Eureka Springs, 1888-92. Partner in Calahan Brothers, 1888. Also spelled Callahan.

CALAHAN, GEORGE R.
Active in Eureka Springs, 1888; partner in Calahan Brothers.

CALDWELL, W. M.
Active in Mena, c. 1900.

CARDWELL, R. D.
Active in Hot Springs, 1917.

CARSON, AMANDA (MRS.)
Active in Hot Springs, 1912.

CAUDLE, ARTHUR B.
Active in Fayetteville, 1892.

CAUGHEY, ALICE
Active in Sulphur Springs, c. 1910.

CHANDLEE & CHANDLEE
Active in Eureka Springs, 1906. See Fyler & Chandlee.

CHANDLEE, JOHN
Active in Eureka Springs in partnership with William B. Fyler, 1884.

CHAPMAN & COMPANY
Active in Eureka Springs, 1906.

CHICAGO ART GALLERY
Studio of E. G. Everett in Hot Springs, c. 1885.

CLARK, A.
Active in Rogers.

CLARK, WILLIAM J.
Active in Rogers, 1906.

COOK, C. C.
Active in Ft. Smith, c. 1900.

COSAND & SARGENT
Active in Springdale, c. 1910.

CRON, A. W.
Active in Hot Springs, 1915-17.

CROUCH, JOSEPH E.
Active in Fayetteville, 1880.

CURNUTT, W. L.
Active in Compton, 1912.

DAWSON, R. W.
Active in Little Rock at the corner of 5th and Main Streets, c. 1885.

DECKER
Known as "Peg Leg," active in Leslie, c. 1907+; in Marshall, 1914.

DELUXE STUDIO
Active in Hot Springs, 1917+.

DUNLAP BROTHERS
William W. and Charles C. Dunlap, active in Fayetteville, 1904.

DUNLAP, CHARLES L.
Active in Fayetteville, 1904, partner with brother William W., operating as Dunlap Brothers.

DUNLAP, WILLIAM W.
Partner in Dunlap Brothers with Charles C., Fayetteville, 1904.

ECKLER, E. H.
Operating as Eckler's Art Studio or Eckler's Studio in Hot Springs, c. 1908.

EOFF, M. C.
Active in Kingston, 1912-13.

EVERETT, E. G.
Operating as Chicago Art Gallery in Hot Springs, c. 1885.

FARLEY, ROBERT
Active in Round Prairie Township, 1880.

FIELD, JULIAN HERMAN
Born in Waupun, Wisconsin, February 19, 1869; died in Fayetteville, Arkansas, January 14, 1936. Operated his first studio in Berlin; married his assistant, Minnie Bell Dies. Moved to Fayetteville, 1913, where he opened a portrait studio. He was known for pictorialist art images, and some were published in nationally circulating periodicals; he was also known for his book illustrations and extensive work depicting life at the Univeristy of Arkansas and around Fayetteville.

FIELD, MINNIE BELL DIES
Born March 16, 1879; died in Fayetteville, 1962. Wife of Julian Herman Field, she served as his assistant at his studio in Waupun, Wisconsin, before and after their marriage. She continued her work as a lab technician and retoucher at their Fayetteville studio. After his death, 1936, she sold from the studio's inventory of photographs.

FLESSER & VANCOUR
Active in Hot Springs, 1910.

FOWLER, WILLIAM HOWARD
Active in Rogers, 1918.

FOX, JOHN
Active in Jasper, c. 1910.

FRAZIER
Active in Springdale, c. 1910.

FURGUSON, KATIE
Active in Eureka Springs, 1900.

FYLER & CHANDLEE
Partnership of William B. Fyler and John Chandlee in Eureka Springs, 1884.

FYLER, F. F.
Active in Eureka Springs, c. 1900.

GANNER, JOHN HUDELSON
Active in Pope and Yell Counties, and in Russellville, Dardanelle, Ozark and Conway, 1900+.

GRABILL, BURCH ENOS
Born in Ohio, 1868. Active in Fayetteville, 1901-15. Known for his documentary photographs taken during his tour of duty in the Philippines. Grabill also captured much of the life around Fayetteville and published an extensive line of real photo postcards after the war. In 1915, Grabill moved to Shreveport, Louisiana, where he continued his documentary work, returning to northwest Arkansas during the summers.

GRAHAM, A. E.
Active in Green Forest, 1900.

GRAY BROTHERS
Active in Eureka Springs, c. 1914.

GRAY, LUCIEN
Active in Eureka Springs, 1906-12.

GUILLIAMS, ROBERT F.
Active in Siloam Springs, 1900-12.

GUINTER, A. J.
Active in Union Township, 1900.

HALL, B.
Active in Eureka Springs, c. 1900.

HALLY, W. H.
Active in Hot Springs, 1917.

HANSARD & HOWERTON
Partnership of John W. Hansard and James R. Howerton, active in Fayetteville, 1884.

HANSARD & LARRICK
Partnership active in Bentonville; M. Larrick.

HANSARD & OSBORN
Active in Fayetteville, 1888; J. W. Hansard and O. W. Osborn.

HANSARD, ARTHUR
Active in Bentonville, 1900-12; also active in Gentry.

HANSARD, JOHN W.
Active in Fayetteville, c. 1880-82, and also Verona, Missouri. Partner in Hansard & Howerton in Fayetteville, 1884. Known for railroad views.

HANSARD, RAPHAEL W.
Active Bentonville, 1888-92.

HAPPY HOLLOW
Active in Hot Springs, 1890s-1915. Popular studio in a miniature western town located in the resort area . Operated by Norman E. McLeod, known simply as "McLeod," an eccentric who emulated the dress and storytelling of Buffalo Bill Cody. Also known as McLeod's Happy Hollow and New Happy Hollow Studio.

HARRIS, LAURA
Active in Bentonville, 1900-12.

HATHAWAY, JOE
Active in Rogers, 1912.

HILTEBRAND, BERT
Active in Mena, 1900+.

HOEL, ROBERT
Active in Hot Springs, 1915

HOWARD, WILLIAM L.
Itinerant active in Lonoke, Faulkner and Pulsaki Counties, c. 1900+.

HOWERTON, J. R.
Active in Fayetteville, 1868-70. See Hansard & Howerton.

HUGHES, THOMAS J.
Active in Evansville, 1888.

HUNTER
Active in Siloam Springs.

IVEY, HENRY J.
Active in Fayetteville, 1906.

JOHNSON, O. R.
Active in Huntsville, 1892.

KAMPTON, WILLIAM H.
Active in Springdale Township, 1900.

KAPPEN, WILLIAM G.
Active in Eureka Springs, c. 1900.

KENNAN, GEORGE W.
Active in Springdale, 1883-86.

KENNEDY, J. F.
Active in Hot Springs, c. 1877; published stereoviews.

KETTERING'S STUDIO
Active in Fayetteville, 1908.

KILBOURN, MYRON J.
Active in Bentonville, 1912.

KINCAID, J. C.
Active in Hot Springs, 1910-12.

LARRICK, M.
Active in Genry, 1906.

LEE, EMMET
Active in Winslow, c. 1906.

LEWIS, HERBERT P.
Active in Gravette, c. 1900-06.

LEWIS, R.
Active in Gravette, 1900.

LICHLYTER, MARYMAN DENTON
Active in Springdale, c. 1910.

LINSERMIER, JOHN
Active in Gentry, 1912.

LUCAS, GRACIE
Active in Prairie Township, 1900.

MABERLY, L.
Active in Bentonville, 1900.

MARTIN, AMANDA
Active in Weddington, 1900.

MARTIN, GEORGE W.
Partner is Rosser & Martin, Eureka Springs, 1906.

MAXWELL, S. A.
Active in Hot Springs, c. 1908.

McCOLLISTER, NETTIE
Active in Eureka Springs, 1900.

McCOLLISTER, SPENCER
Active in Eureka Springs, 1892-1900; Green Forest, 1906.

McGUE & WARWICK
Active in Hot Springs, 1908.

McGUE, J. E.
Active in Hot Springs, 1915-17.

McHENRY, LOU (MRS.)
Active in Winslow, c. 1900-17. Also known as Mrs. Fred McHenry.

McLEOD, NORMAN E.
Operating "New Happy Hollow Studio" in Hot Springs, c. 1890s-1915. Also known as McLeod's Happy Hollow.

MEALOUS, FRANK
Active in Hot Springs, 1910-12.

MILLER, DANIEL
Active in Hot Springs, c. 1908.

MILLER'S STUDIO
Studio operated by Daniel Miller, c. 1908.

MILLS & SON, E. L.
Active in St. Paul, 1906.

MOORE, W. P.
Active in Eureka Springs, 1900.

MORGAN, TOM P.
Active in Rogers, c. 1910.

MORLEDGE, C. G.
Operated the Southern Photograph Company in Ft. Smith, c. 1895.

MORRISON, JAMES
Active in Prairie Grove, 1900.

MORROW, W. A.
Active in Hot Springs, 1910.

NELSON, B. H.
Active in Hot Springs, 1912.

NICHOL, W. H.
Active in Huntsville, 1906.

NICHOLS, WILLIAM H.
Active in War Eagle Township, 1900.

OSBORN, O. W.
Active in Fayetteville in patnership with J. W. Hansard, 1888.

OXFORD, C. L.
Active in Robinson Community(?), c. 1900.

PARKER & REED
Partnership in Fayetteville, 1907.

PATE, THOMAS G.
Active in Fayetteville, 1912.

PATTON, MARY
Active in Boston Township, 1900.

PENNELL
Partner in Raisor & Pennell, Eureka Springs, c. 1900.

PENSE, S. D.
Active in Eureka Springs, c. 1910.

PERNOT, H. C.
Active in Van Buren, c. 1895.

PETERS, CLAUS
Active in Green Forest, 1912.

PHELAN, LAURA J.
Active in Illinois Township, 1900.

PHILLIPS, LUTIE & ORA
Partnership in Huntsville, c. 1900.

PICKERILL, P. G.
Studio at 205 Main Street in Little Rock, c. 1890.

PLASTER, OSCAR L.
Active in Mena, 1918+.

POWELL PHOTO
Studio in Elkins, c. 1910.

RADER, J. E.
Active in Hot Springs, c. 1908.

RAISOR & PENNELL
Partnership in Eureka Springs, c. 1900.

RAISOR & WERTS
Active in Eureka Springs, c. 1900.

REDNER, H. H.
Active in Hot Springs, c. 1910.

REED
Active in Fayetteville, c. 1910. See Parker & Reed.

RICE, THAD
Active in Siloam Springs, c. 1910. See Suttle & Rice.

ROBERTS, M. E.
Active in Fallsville, 1900.

ROGERS ART STUDIO
Active in Rogers, c. 1900.

ROSSER & MARTIN
Active in Eureka Springs, 1906; Benjamin L. Rosser and George W. Martin.

ROSSER, BENJAMIN L.
Partner in Rosser & Martin, Eureka Springs, 1906; listed alone, 1912.

RUGG, D. B.
Active in Rogers.

RUTHERFORD, LOUISA
Active in Valley Township, 1900.

SARATOGA STUDIO
Operating in Hot Springs, 1912-15.

SARGENT, FRANK
Active in Springdale, 1900.

SAVE, F. W.
Active in Hot Springs, 1917.

SHAFFER, H. W.
Active in Elm Springs, 1900.

SHELTON, JOHN
Active in Van Buren Township, 1900.

SINCLAIR, JOHN J.
Active in Goodwill Township, 1900.

SNYDER, ROBERT R.
Active in Eureka Springs, 1900.

SOUTHERN PHOTOGRAPH COMPANY
Operated by C. G. Morledge in Ft. Smith, c. 1895.

SPEECE & AARON
Partnership in Springdale, c. 1910. See Sidney D. Aaron.

SPENCER, AUGUSTUS I.
Active in Siloam Springs, 1906.

STERLING, LON
Active in Hot Springs, c. 1908.

STEWART, H. L.
Active in Rogers.

STONE, DUDLEY
Active in Fayetteville, 1904-17.

STONECIPHER, JAMES A.
Active in Hot Springs, 1910-21.

STOTZ, C. C.
Active in Bentonville, 1888.

STRICKLAND, T. B.
Active in Siloam Springs, c. 1910.

SUTTLE & RICE
Partnership active in Siloam Springs, 1912. See Thad Rice.

SUTTLE, HENRY J.
Active in Siloam Springs, c. 1890-1900.

SUTTLE, JACOB H.
Active in Prairie Grove, 1906-12.

SWEENEY, HERVIE E.
Active in Goshen, 1900.

THOMPSON, GRANVILLE W.
Active in Cave Creek, 1892.

TIBBS, NATHAN J.
Active in Eureka Springs, 1888-92.

TROMATER, GEORGE W.
Active in Springdale, 1900.

VANCOUR
Partner in Flesser & Vancour, active in Hot Springs, 1910.

VANDEVER
Active in Lincoln, c. 1910.

VANKIRK, V.
Active in Rogers.

WADE PHOTO
Active in Winslow, c. 1910.

WALKER, G. W.
Active in Hot Springs, c. 1908.

WATTON, C. E.
Owner of Watton's Gallery in Fayetteville, 1899. Also listed as C. E. Walton.

WALTON, C. E.
See C. E. Watton.

WARWICK
Partner in McGue & Warwick, Hot Springs, 1908.

WATTS, H. CLAY
Active in Cave Springs.

WERTS
Partner is Raisor & Werts, Eureka Springs, c. 1900.

WHITTEN, S. R.
Active in Hot Springs, 1915.

WILCHER, W. J.
Active in Hot Springs, c. 1908.

WOOD, J. R.
Active in Hot Springs, 1917.

YOUNG (MRS.)
Active in Fayetteville c. 1880.

YOUNG, JESSIE
Active in Fayetteville, 1880.

YOUNG, S. J. (MRS.)
Active in Fayetteville, 1888-1900.

YOUNG, SARRAH L.
Active in Fayetteville, 1900. May be the same as Mrs. S. J. Young.

Special thanks to David Mattison for his substantial contribution to this section. For more detailed reference to the photographers of British Columbia, see Camera Workers: The British Columbia Photographers Directory, 1858-1900, *by David Mattison, available from the author at 2236 Kinross Avenue, Victoria, BC, Canada V8R 2N5.*

ABERDEEN, ISHBEL MARIA, LADY
Born 1857; died 1939. Published *Through Canada with a Kodak*, illustrated with her travel snapshots taken in 1891, and some professional images. Wife of Governor-General Gordon.

ADAMS & PIERCE
Partnership of E. C. Adams and W. C. Pierce in Nanaimo, 1897; Washington state, 1898(?).

ADAMS, E. C.
Employed as an artist at C. W. Bart's studio in Vancouver, 1896; partner in Adams & Pierce operating in Nanaimo, 1897; later in Washington.

AGNEW, WILLIAM BURL
Active in Victoria, 1890, 1894-95; employed by Savannah & Company as photographer, 1890, 1895; retoucher, 1894.

ALBRECHT, A. A.
Traveling photographer from Spokane, Washington; active in Sandon, c. 1895. See Washington.

ALDER COTTAGE STUDIO
Managed by T. H. Moore in Vancouver, 1897.

ALEXANDER, J. M. L.
Active in 1891; amateur who photographed the Masset church.

ALLEN, EDWARD P.
Photographer with the Field Columbian Museum (now the Field Museum of Natural History, Chicago), on expedition accompanying ethnographer, George Amos Dorsey.

ALLEN, WILLIAM RUSSELL
Active in Pilot Bay, 1894-98.

ANDERSON, HENRY
Active in Windermere, 1887; possibly an amateur.

ANDERSON, ROBERT W.
Born 1831; died after 1897(?). Established in Toronto, c. 1862, as a portrait and landscape photographer; studio known as the Pantechnetheca Gallery. Advertised "cheap and good" views and groups taken to order while visiting Vancouver.

ASHMAN, WILLIAM M.
Arrived on the Active from San Francisco; operated Gentile's Photographic Gallery in Victoria, 1867.

ATKINSON, J. B.
Active in New Westminster, 1889.

BAER, REVEREND WALTER WESLEY
Amateur photographer and promoter of the Vancouver Camera Club. He gave lantern slide shows, 1894; lived in Victoria after 1900.

BAILEY & COMPANY, C. S.
Active in Vancouver, 1887-89. Begun by Charles S. Bailey with associates Fred V. Bingham and E. Straube. Located at 133 Carrall Street, 1887-88; 227 Hastings Street, 1888-89. The company was succeeded by Bailey & Neelands.

BAILEY & NEELANDS
Partnership of Charles S. Bailey and Hamilton George Neelands operating studio in Vancouver, 1889-90.

BAILEY BROTHERS
Partnership in Vancouver and Kamloops, 1890-98, operating a gallery that dealt in books, stationery supplies and photographs. The Baileys' brother-in-law, Joseph Coupland, was also a principal in the firm. See Charles S. Bailey and William Bailey.

BAILEY, CHARLES S.
Born 1869; died 1896. Arrived in Vancouver, winter 1887-88; operated as C. S. Bailey & Company with F. V. Bingham and E. Straube until 1889, then formed a partnership with Hamilton George Neelands lasting for about a year. Bailey Brothers was formed with brother William, 1890. He visited Hawaii, January-May 1895, with E. A. Hegg, the photographer of the 1898 Klondike gold rush, and they photographed Oahu together.

BAILEY, WILLIAM
Born 1865; died 1936 or 1937. Arrived in Vancouver, December 1890, to form Bailey Brothers with brother Charles. Generally a business manager, he occasionally took photographs. He married and moved to Kamloops, 1895.

BAKER
Active in Camp McKinney, c. 1900.

BAKER, WILLIAM PEACOCK
Born 1841; died 1942. Active in Victoria at 59 ½ Government Street, 1898-1900.

BALLARD, C.
Amateur awarded a prize at the New Westminster Provincial Fair, 1893.

BALTZLY, BENJAMIN
Born 1835; died 1883. Employed by William Notman, Baltzly served as a photographer with an expedition of the Geological Survey of Canada, arriving in Victoria, July 1871, and subsequently journeyed up the Fraser and Thompson rivers as far as the Yellowhead Pass. Baltzly worked for Notman, 1870-75, and 1876-77.

BARRACLOUGH, W. H.
Active in Chilliwack, c. 1896.

BART, C. W.
Partner in Smith & Bart operating in Seattle, 1889, with D. T. Smith. Opened the Popular Photo Parlour at 55 Cordova Street, Sullivan's Block, in Vancouver by 1895. He moved to Rossland, c. 1897; located in Nelson, c. 1900, working for the Wadds Brothers.

BARTHOLE, W.
Active in Vancouver at 59 Cordova Street, 1896.

BARTLETT, L. B. (MRS.)
Active in Victoria, 1885, employed at the Elite Photo Gallery, 112 Government Street.

BASSETT, WILLIAM P.
Awarded a prize for the best collection of amateur photos at the New Westminster Provincial Fair, 1898.

BAUGEN, SIMON
He tried to establish a photo studio in the Norwegian colony at Bella Coola, 1896-97, but was unsuccessful.

BEAVER PHOTOGRAPH GALLERY
Studio in Vancouver managed by David Ferguson, next to Public Reading Room at 130 Cordova Street, 1893.

BEECHER, C. M.
Amateur and member of Vancouver Camera Club, c. 1897.

BENSON, ALFRED ROBSON
Amateur active in Nanaimo, 1860. He arrived in 1849, and served as a physician at various Hudson's Bay Company forts and towns, including Victoria and Nanaimo, 1857-62, and Vancouver, Washington. Francis G. Claudet met him at Nanaimo and utilized some of his equipment to obtain a view of Nanaimo, 1860. Mount Benson near Nanaimo was named after him, 1859.

BENSON, O. B.
Active in Nelson, May 1891; Ainsworth, possibly June 1891; Revelstoke, August 1891. May be the same as O. B. Benson of Fremont, Colorado, 1891-92.

BENTLEY, WESLEY D.
Active in Winnipeg, c. 1890s, managing the Berlin Portrait Company, 213 Rupert West. Also operated in Victoria under the same name at 32 Government Street, 1895.

BERLIN PORTRAIT COMPANY
Active in Winnipeg, c. 1890s, 213 Rupert West; managed by Wesley D. Bentley. Employed J. Nelkin, photographer. George Bentley, proprietor, Wesley D. Bentley, assistant manager, and David Feldman, artist. Operated in Victoria at 32 Government Street, 1895.

BERRY
Partner with Edward C. Brooks operating as Brooks & Berry in Victoria at 164 Johnson Street, 1890s.

BESSELL & COMPANY
Active in Vancouver, 1899-1901. Located at 534 Cordova Street, 1899; 729 Pender Street, 1899-1901. Studio managed by Mildred P. Bessell.

BESSELL, MILDRED P.
Photographer at the Edwards Brothers studio in Vancouver, 1899; managed her own studio, Bessell & Company, 1899-1901.

BEVERIDGE, ERSKINE
Born 1852(?); died 1920. Scottish photographer who visited Vancouver, Kamloops and New Westminster on his way around the world, 1885. His son published a collotype edition of his photographs.

BIGGART, PERCY A.
A photographer at the Vancouver Photo Company, 1891-92; on his own, 1895.

BINGHAM, FRED V.
Headquartered in Winnipeg, 1881-87; partner with A. B. Thom, 1884. He traveled extensively along the CPR line and described himself as the "Official Photographer C.P.R." Partner with C. S. Bailey in Vancouver, 1888, but disappeared after that.

BLACKETT, CUTHBERT
Born 1837; died 1925. Came to Canada, 1887; moved to Victoria, 1889, after two years in Winnipeg. He moved to Vancouver as worked as a clerk at Trueman & Caple, 1891, then served as their photographer during the next two years. Moved back to Victoria and worked as a laborer, and went back to photography, 1895. Also known as Bert or Burt Blackett.

BLACKIE, E. M. (MISS)
Worked in Blackie's Studio, Victoria, 1897.

BLACKIE, WILLIAM GOURLIE
Operated Blackie's Studio in Victoria at Mary Street and Esquimalt Road, 1895-99.

BLACKLIN
Partner Blacklin & Bristow operating in Victoria, 1862.

BLACKLIN & BRISTOW
Studio at Fort Street, next to Central School in Victoria, 1862.

BLAIR, WILLIAM
Artist and photographer active in Victoria, 1892-1900; studio at 60 Yates Street, 1900.

BLAKE & RODIER
Partnership of A. E. Blake and George Rodier in Victoria, 1898-99; studio at 52 Government Street.

BLAKE, A. E.
Partner in Blake & Rodier Victoria, 1898-99.

BLANC, LOUIS A.
Studio in Victoria, 1865; Richfield, 1867; Barkerville, 1868. Some of his photographs were published as engravings in the *Canadian illustrated News* by the *Cariboo Sentinel*, 1872. His main occupation was jeweler.

BLAND, FRED JOHNSON
Partner with H. Veasey in Winnepeg, 1888-89; studio in Whonnock, 1899-1900.

BLANE, H.
Probably an itinerant in Vernon, 1896; possibly the same as John Henry Blome.

BLISS, HENRY ANSON
Amateur active in Dawson, Yukon Territory, 1897-1900+. A Yukon government accountant who accompanied federal and Yukon Territory government officials to Dawson, 1897. Also known as Harry A. Bliss.

BLOME, JOHN HENRY
Active in Ashcroft, 1895-96; Clinton, the Okanagan and Nicola valleys, and as an itinerant in Canmore, 1896; in Kamloops, 1898. Blome's obituary called him "an artist of more than average ability." See California and Washington.

BLOOMFIELD, CHARLES

BOAS, FRANZ
Born 1858; died 1942. Regarded as one of the founders of modern anthropology, Boas learned photography in Berlin from Hermann Wilhelm Vogel. On his first field trip to British Columbia, he took pictures of the Cowichan people. On a later trip, 1888-89, he may have employed O. C. Hastings, also employing him at Ft. Rupert, November 1894. Boas also hired E. C. Brooks, who was photographing canneries and sawmills along the Skeena River, 1888.

BODURTHA
Active in Esquimalt and Victoria, mid to late 1860s. Imprint on carte-de-visite refers to "Bodurtha, Photographer, H.M.S. *Zealous*," a ship based at Esquimalt.

BOLT, A. E.
Active in Vancouver, 1897.

BONNEY, F. L.
Studio at Lake Front, Brooklyn, 1898-99.

BOOEN, J.O.
Itinerant in Chilliwack and other areas of British Columbia, 1895-96. See Washington.

BOORNE, WILLIAM HANSON
Born 1859; died 1945. A major photographer of Alberta, Boorne opened his studio in Calgary, 1886, with the help of his cousin, Ernest Gundry May. The studio was known as Boorne & May and branches were established at Banff and Edmonton. The Calgary headquarters failed, 1893, and Edmonton branch manager C. W. Mathers purchased the business. Boorne moved to Vancouver and was listed as a photographer for one year. Boorne visited Victoria and Vancouver, May 1890, to cover the visit of the Duke and Duchess of Connaught.

BOOTH, R. C.
Active in Vancouver at 59 or 75 Cordova Street, 1891-93.

BOREL, F. A.
Moved from Dunnville, Ontario; operated in Vancouver at White's Studio, 2 Cordova East Street, 1897.

BOVILL BROTHERS
Active in New Westminster on Columbia Street, opposite Colonial Hotel, August 1886.

BOVILL, WHEATLEY
Active in New Westminster, 1886-89. Associated with his brother William in Bovill Brothers, 1886. Partner with S. J. Thompson in Thompson & Bovill, 1887. Wheatley also worked as an architect (Bovill & Ross) and real estate agent. He was married August 1888, and may have returned to England, 1896.

BOVILL, WILLIAM
Active in New Westminster, 1886-87. Partner with his brother Wheatley in Bovill Brothers, 1886; partner in Thompson & Bovill, 1887.

BOYDEN, E. L.
Active in Nanaimo before 1886, when his studio was purchased by J. W. Sampson.

BRAND, FRED
Born in Switzerland, c. 1870-71; died 1954. Amatuer active in Port Alberni, 1898-1908.

BRIDGES, D. (MISS)
Active in Victoria, 1897, working for E. J. Eyres' Imperial Studio, 76 Yates Street.

BRISTOW
Partner in Blacklin & Bristow in Victoria, 1862, on Fort Street next to Central School.

BRITISH COLUMBIA PHOTO & FINE ART STUDIO
Studio and store in New Westminster, 1892-95, 441 Columbia Street, managed by S. J. Thompson. Also known as British Columbia Fine Art Gallery.

BROCK & COMPANY, J. A.
Studio in Vancouver, 1886-89. First established by J. A. Brock in Belleville, Ontario, c. 1882; moved to Brandon c. 1883. H. T. Devine joined partnership, 1886, opening the studio in Vancouver. The partnership was formally dissolved in November 1887, announced in April 1888.

BROCK, JOHN ALLAN
Born in Canada, 1848; died in California (?). Active in Belleville, Ontario, c. 1882; Brandon, Manitoba, c. 1883. He moved to Vancouver, 1886 and ran the studio, J. A. Brock & Company at Cordova

and Abbott Streets in partnership with H. T. Devine. Brock returned to Brandon late 1886, operating his studio there until the late 1890s. Relocated to Los Angeles, c. 1890. See California.

BROOKS & BERRY
Partnership of E. C. Brooks and Berry in Victoria, 1890s, at 164 Johnson Street.

BROOKS, EDWARD COLEY
Active in Victoria, c. 1887-91(?) at Johnson and Cook Streets and 164 Johnson Street, where he also was a partner in Brooks & Berry, c. 1890s. During 1893, he visited Kaslo for about a month. He was active in Nanaimo, c. 1892-1900, at 50 Victoria Crescent; also listed on Commercial Street, 1898. Primarily a portrait photographer, he also engaged in landscape work.

BROUNE, LOTHEAN
Active in Nicola Valley, 1890. Possibly the same as John Lothian Browne.

BROWN, F. R.
Active in Vancouver, 1892, at 413 Seymour Street.

BROWN, GEORGE HAY
Active in Victoria, 1864, on Government Street, west side near View Street. According to a newspaper article, he was "Formerly connected with Brady's extensive Photographic Galleries of New York and Washington, U.S., and recently from New Orleans, La." He worked with Edward Jacobs and Walter Ogilvie in New Orleans in the National Art Union Photograph Gallery, 1863, at 93 Camp Street. There was also a G. H. Brown, daguerreotypist, in Fredericton, New Brunswick, 1846.

BROWNE, JOHN LOTHIAN
Active in New Westminster, 1885, on Columbia Street. He moved his studio to Kamloops, 1886; partner in Reid & Browne, 1889. He moved back to New Westminster, April 1891, and opened the Sunbeam Photo and Art Company Ltd., operating until c. 1898. Located at 437 Columbia Street, 1891; 24 Sixth Street, 1893-98.

BROWNLEE, J. H.
The western agent for the *Dominion Illustrated* magazine, Brownlee accompanied W. H. Boorne to Victoria and Vancouver in British Columbia to cover the visit of the Duke and Duchess of Connaught, 1890.

BRUCE, HENRY
Born 1832; died 1910. Veteran of the Crimean War, he operated a photo studio in London before emigrating to Vancouver with the Royal Engineers, 1858. Unknown if he practiced photography in British Columbia.

BUEL, JAMES WILLIAM
Born 1849; died 1920.

BUELL, OLIVER B.
Born 1844; died 1910. Active in Great Barrington, Massachusetts, 1865; published views in New York showing military preparations for the Riel Rebellion, 1885; in Denver, Colorado, 1879. He also photographed construction work on the CPR in the Rocky Mountains, summer 1885, visiting British Columbia with Governor-General Lord Lansdowne. Photographed along the main line of the CPR, 1886. He gave lantern slide shows in Canada, 1880s, last returning to western Canada, 1905.

BURDON, LANCE
Photographed the Atlin-Quesnel section of the Yukon Telegraph line, 1900-01.

BURTON, WALTER FRANCIS
Amatuer active in Victoria at 60 Cook Street, 1897. Some of his photographs of Victoria golf courses were reproduced in *Western Recreation.*

BUSBY, EDWARD SCOTT
Born 1862(?); died 1952. A customs official who photographed a spike ceremony on the White Pass & Yukon Railroad, 1899. He appeared in E. A. Hegg's photograph of the event, and identified himself in a souvenir album published by Hegg, 1900.

BUSH, HENRY
A photographer in Germany, he settled in San Francisco as a daguerreotypist, late 1850s. He remained in photography until 1872. He visited Victoria, 1862; published a book of poetry, *The Harp of the Day*, 1865, relating his travels to British Columbia during the Cariboo gold rush.

BUTCHER & COMPANY
Studio managed by Arthur Butcher in Victoria, 1892(?)-97(?). Located at 95 Douglas Street, 1892-95; 202 Fort Street, 1897.

BUTCHER, ARTHUR
Active in Victoria, 1890-97; worked for Savannah & Company, then managed his own studio, Butcher & Company. Located at 56 Fort Street, 1891; 95 Douglas Street, 1892-95; 202 Fort Street, 1897. Name also spelled Busker, or Buskera.

BUXTON, BERTRAM H.
Amatuer active in Masset, 1882. He may have been the first tourist to photograph the Haida.

CALVERT, J.
Amateur active in Nanaimo, 1900.

CAMERON, AGNES DEANS
Born 1863; died 1912. Amatuer photographer, c. 1896-1908. A Victoria teacher, school principal and writer, she made a 10,000 mile journey with her niece Jessie Cameron Brown up the Mackenzie River to the Arctic Circle, 1908. It was published as *The New North*, 1910, illustrated with photographs taken by her and her niece.

CAMPBELL
Active in New Westminster(?), 1893, exhibiting a photographic collection.

CAMPBELL, J. F.
Active in Fairview, 1900-01.

CANFIELD, FRANCIS ORRA
Active in New Westminster, 1890-92, working for S. J. Thompson at 620 Columbia Street. He later went into teaching and retired as a principal from a New Westminster school, 1938.

CANNING, ARTHUR A.
Active in Vancouver, 1897, 634 Cordova Street, possibly working for the Edwards Brothers; in Nanaimo, 1898; Lethbridge, Alberta, 1899; Kamloops, 1900.

CAPLE & COMPANY, N.
Active in Vancouver, 1894-96; at 329 Hastings Street, 1894-96; 517 Hastings Street (Ogle Block), 1896-1900; 546 Granville Street, 1900+. Norman Caple established his own studio after his partnership with R. H. Trueman had dissolved towards the end of 1893, at the former address of C. S. Bailey & Company.

CAPLE, NORMAN
Born 1866; died 1911. Active in Vancouver, 1889-97. Partner with R. H. Trueman, c. 1890-93, operating as Trueman & Caple, 302 Cordova Street. Operated his own studio, 1894-97 as N. Caple & Company; located at at 329 Hastings Street, 1894-96; 517 Hastings Street, 1896.

Caple was married in England, 1892, to Florence Kate Le Grix Akerman (1867-1950), and the couple had four sons.

CARLYON, FRED W.
Born in Wisconsin, 1865; died in Olympia, Washington, 1956. Amateur from Wrangell, Alaska, where he operated a jewelry business; photographed in the Stikine River region during the Klondike Gold Rush, 1898.

CARPENTER & COMPANY
Active in Rossland, 1899-1903, 26 ½ Columbia Avenue; operated by W. J. Carpenter after his partnership with G. E. Millar was dissolved.

CARPENTER & MILLAR
Partnership of W. J. Carpenter and G. E. Millar, active in Rossland, 1897-99, 26 ½ Columbia Avenue.

CARPENTER, WILLIAM JEFFERSON
Partner with G. E. Millar in Carpenter & Millar, Rossland, 1897-99; 26 ½ Columbia Avenue. After the partnership dissolved, he continued the business as Carpenter & Company, 1899-1903. Active in Greenwood, 1899; Spokane, 1905-08. Moved to Vancouver, 1910-13, 303 Hastings West Street. Also known as the Carpenter Studio in Vancouver.

CARR, RICHARD
See California.

CARTMEL, JAMES
Active in Victoria(?), 1887.

CAVE, E. J.
Active in Vancouver, 1893.

CAWTHON, JAMES BROWN
Active in Victoria, 1898.

CHAMBERS, ARTHUR HYDE
Born 1852; died 1935. He may have worked as a photographer in Barcelona, Spain, c. 1888. Active in Northfield, 1892; Nanoose Bay, 1895; Victoria, 1899-1900, at 59 ½ Government Street. He sold his business to Mr. A. Bloom, May 1900, for $200. By 1902, he was in Nanaimo where he signed an agreement with E. C. Brooks to take over Brooks' photography business.

CHAPMAN, JOHN HOWARD ARTHUR
Born 1862(?); died 1942. Arrived in Victoria from England, 1890. Worked as a traveling salesman and photographer, c. 1895-1936. The Provincial Archvies of British Columbia purchased Chapman's collection, 1936. Chapman photographed many subjects and marketed them as postcards.

CHAPMAN, W.
Active in Vancouver, 1900+.

CHRISTIANSEN, KARL BRINK
Active in the Danish colony, Cape Scott, 1899-1909.

CLARK, J. H.
Active in New Westminster, c. 1890.

CLAUDET, FRANCIS GEORGE
Arrived in New Westminster from London, February 1860, the manager of the assay office and mint. An amateur whose photographs were sent to the London Exhibition of 1862, along with some specimens from the mint. Claudet returned to London, 1873.

CLAVERING, ROBERT KNOX
Active in Vancouver, 1900.

CLEVELAND, V.
Active in Discovery (Pine City), 1899, working with A. C. Pillsbury.

CLUTTERBUCK, WALTER J.
Active in Windermere and East Kootenays, 1887. An amateur, he published his exploration adventures in the B.C. *1887: A Ramble in British Columbia*, under the nom de plume, Skipper.

COLLINS, R. B.
Active in Vancouver, 1892, at 31 Carrall Street, John White's old studio. His newspaper ad claimed he had twenty years' experience in the United States and England.

CONDEROY, R. A.
Active in Vancouver, 1899, at 225 Carral Street, working for Alphonse Savard's Imperial Studio.

COOK, JAMES
Active in New Westminster, 1900-01, at Columbia Street, Hawley Block, working for E. F. Easthope & Company.

COOK, JOHN
Active in Victoria, 105 ½ Douglas Street, 1900.

COOK, T. J.
Active in Vancouver, 1898; possibly an amateur.

COOKE, J. REGINALD
Active in Vernon, 1900, working as an itinerant.

COOPER, ALEXANDER D.
Itinerant in Donald, 1891.

COOPER-COLES
Amatuer active c. 1895; member of Vancouver Camera Club.

COUGHLAN, J. A.
Active in Nanaimo, 1889, on Church Street(?).

COUGHLAN, WILLIAM P.
Active in Nanaimo, 1888-1900. Located at Church Street(?), 1889, Fitzpatrick Street(?), 1893; 26 Fitzwilliam Street(?), 1895-1900. Primarily a portrait artist, but an article in the *Nanaimo Free Press*, 1888, described a photograph he took of the ship *Northbrook* at anchor.

COWAN, THOMAS H.
Active in Rossland, 1900, 111 ½ East Columbia.

COWDEROY, WILLIAM
Born in London, England, 1882(?); died 1953. Arrived in Vancouver, 1887. Listed as a bookbinder's apprentice, 1897-98, 1900+; as a photographer, 1899. Vice president of the Wrigley Printing Company in Vancouver for nearly twenty years. He was considered one of the most outstanding bookbinders in Canada. Also known as Harry.

COWE
Active in Kelowna, 1895(?).

CRACKNELL, E. E.
Amateur active c. 1895; member of Vancouver Camera Club.

CRAIGG, J. AUGUSTUS
Active in Victoria, 1869-72. Purchased the Theatre Photographic Gallery on the west side near View Street, from George Robinson, 1869, and sold it to Stephen A. Spencer, April 1872. Craigg appears to have taken only portraits, working both outdoors and indoors.

CRAVATTE, LILLIE (MISS)
Active in Victoria, 1899, employed by George Preston, 56 Fort Street.

CROWELL & McCLURE
Active in Vancouver, 1889, visiting from San Francisco and reported to be photographing buildings and streets for a publication about the Pacific Northwest coast of the U.S. and Canada.

CROWELL, GEORGE W.
Active in Victoria, 1885, working for Peterson & Company, 112 Government Street. See California.

CUMMING BROTHERS
Active in Lillooet, 1892-95(?), managed by Robert D. and William, Jr.; specializing in views of the Fraser River and hydraulic mines.

CUMMING, ROBERT D.
Active in Lillooet, 1892-95; partner in Cumming Brothers.

CUMMING, WILLIAM, JR.
Active in Lillooet, 1892; partner in Cumming Brothers.

CURTIS, EDWARD SHERIFF
Born 1868; died 1952. He may have worked in British Columbia before 1900. Curtis had two partnerships in Seattle, 1891-97, as a portrait photographer under the names Rothi & Curtis and Curtis & Guptil. He entered a collection of his photographs in the New Westminster Provincial Fair of 1898, and traveled to Alaska, 1899, as official photographer of the E. H. Harriman expedition. His brother Asahel Curtis (1874-1941) was also a photographer and covered the Klondike gold rush, 1898-1900+; may not have visited British Columbia on his way north. See Washington.

DALLY, FREDERICK
Born in England, 1838; died in England, 1914. Active in Victoria, 1866-70. Operated his photo studio on the south side of Fort Street across the street from his former dry goods store. Had a second studio in Barkerville, 1868, destroyed by fire the same year. He sold his Victoria gallery, September 1870, to the Green Brothers, then moved to Philadelphia to study dentistry and returned to England. The Maynards acquired many of his glass negatives, 1870s-80s, which they marketed under their own imprint.

DALTON, WILLIAM TINNISWOOD
Born in England, 1854. An architect, he was active as an amateur photographer in Vancouver, 1888-1900.

DAVIS, JOSEPH
Active in New Westminster, 1869-90, on Columbia Street. Portrait and landscape photographer.

DAVIS, S. (MISS)
Active in Victoria, 1893, at John Savannah's studio, 56 Fort Street.

DAVIS, WALTER
Active in Nanaimo, 1877, operating as Nanaimo Photographic Gallery in the studio formerly owned by John King Gilbert. In Victoria, 1887, on Superior Street (?). See Washington.

DAVIS, WILLIAM H.
Born in Pennsylvania, 1858. Active in New Westminster and Victoria, 1875; Nanaimo, 1877+. See Washington.

AWSON, GEORGE MERCER
Born in Pictou, Nova Scotia, 1849; died in Ottawa, Ontario, 1901. A member of the British North American Boundary Survey, 1873-74, which traveled a short distance into the mountains beyond Waterton Lakes, Alberta. Appointed to the Geological Survey of Canada staff,

1875. His 1878 photographs and report on the Haida peoples of the Queen Charlotte Islands is a valuable ethnic work, published in 1880. Dawson became director of the Geological Survey, 1895.

DAY, MADGE (MISS)
Active in Vancouver, 1897-99; worked for John White's studio, 2 Cordova Street, 1897; for Savard's Imperial Studio, 225 Carrall Street, 1899.

DEANE, E. B.
Amateur active c. 1895; member of Vancouver Camera Club.

DESMOND, ROBERT AUXLEY
Active in Victoria, 1874-(?). Hired from the San Francisco studio of Bradley & Rulofson by S. A. Spencer of the Victoria Theatre Photographic Gallery, June-October 1874. In October, he worked for Noah Shakespeare in the gallery next door; both studios were located on Government Street, west side near View Street. See California.

DEVILLE, EDOUARD GASTON
Born in France, 1849; died in Ottawa, Ontario, 1924. Surveyor-General of Canada, 1885-1924, with the Dominion Land Survey, Deville took a camera on his 1886 inspection tour and made a number of extremely good views between Port Arthur and Victoria.

DEVINE, HARRY TORKINGTON
Born in England, 1865; died in Vancouver, 1938. Active in Vancouver, 1886-89, and 1895-97, at various locations on Cordova Street. Partner with J. A. Brock, 1886-87.

DIAMOND CITY PHOTOGALLERY
Studio in Nanaimo, 1892-95, owned and managed by John Sampson.

DICKEY, C. J.
Active in Victoria, 1892, 58 Blanshard Street(?).

DINGLE, WALTER
Born in England, 1875; died in Burnaby, 1947. Active in Chilliwack, 1897-98.

DOLAN, JAMES C.
Worked for the Elite Photo Studio in Rossland, 1897, at 112 ½ East Columbia Avenue.

DOMINION PHOTO COMPANY
Studio in Kaslo located on Front Street and managed by J. Hoag & Son, 1899. They had a studio with the same name in Nelson on Victoria Street, corner of Ward Street, 1899-1900.

DOSSETTER, EDWARD
Photographer in England, c. 1871. Active on the northwest coast, Victoria and Vancouver, 1881-90. He accompanied Dr. I. W. Powell on an inspection tour of Indian reserves, June and July 1881, and took many outstanding views and portraits.

DOUGLAS & COMPANY, A.
Active in Vancouver, 1893, upstairs at 615 Hastings, opposite the Leland Hotel, managed by A. Douglas and H. Douglas. Closed by September 1896.

DOUGLAS, A.
Born in Scotland. Active in Vancouver, 1893-96, 615 Hastings Street, Innes Block. Partner in A. Douglas & Company.

DOUGLAS H.
Active in Vancouver, 1895; another partner in A. Douglas & Company.

DRESSER, ALFRED WOODROFFE
Born in England. Amateur photographer active in Victoria before

1901(?). He was a Royal Engineer, 1897-1903; architect, 1909-11. Also spelled Woodruffe.

DRUMMOND, ARTHUR
Active in Steveston, 1892.

DUNBAR, CHARLES TROTT
Born in Rhode Island, 1861. Active in Vancouver, 1890s. A real estate agent for the Union Land Company, St. Paul, Minnesota; he may have taken photos in conjunction with real estate sales.

DUNCAN, WILLIAM
Born in England, 1823; died in Alaska, 1918. Sponsored by the Church Missionary Society in England, Duncan established Metlakatla, 1862. Several of his followers also took up photography.

DURYEA PHOTO COMPANY
Operated in Vancouver, 1818-20, by William C. Duryea.

DURYEA, WILLIAM C.
Active in Vancouver, 1908-20; operated as Duryea Photo Company, 1918-20.

DUSTERHOEFT, WILLIAM
Born in Illinois, 1878; died in Chilliwack, 1961. Amateur active 1890s-1900+.

EASTHOPE & COMPANY
Studio in New Westminster, 1899-1900, 620 Columbia Street, Hawley Block.

EASTHOPE, E. FREDERICK
Active in New Westminster, 1894-97, at 620 Columbia Street; in Vancouver, 1897-1904, at 610 Granville Street. Began work for S. J. Thompson as an assistant, then progressed to printer and photographer at Thompson's Studio. In October 1899, he opened Easthope & Company in Thompson's old studio.

EDDIE, GEORGE MARION
Active in Rossland, 1898, operating the Elite Photo Studio, 121 ½ East Columbia. Also spelled Eadie.

EDWARDS, ARTHUR N.
Amateur active in Vancouver, 1897-1900+.

EDWARDS BROTHERS
Active in Vancouver, 1891-1911. Located at 622 Cordova Street, next door to Pioneer Art Gallery, 1891-93; 534 Cordova Street, 1893-1902. Brothers George William and Edger Herbert were portrait and landscape photographers from Waterloo, Ontario. Produced a series documenting the damage to the CPR line by the Fraser River flood of 1894; George also photographed in the Klondike during the gold rush, 1898. The company continued in business, selling photographic and motion picture supplies, 1911-20.

EDWARDS, E. J.
Active in Greenwood, 1898. He was also listed in the 1900 directory under Greenwood, but no occupation was given.

EDWARDS, EDGAR HERBERT
Born in Ontario, 1870(?); died in Vancouver, 1947. Active in Vancouver, 1891-1911; partner with older brother, George William Edwards in Edwards Brothers studio.

EDWARDS, GEORGE WILLIAM
Born in Brighton, Ontario, 1867; died in Vancouver, 1944. Active in Vancouver, 1891-1911.

ELITE PHOTO GALLERY
Studio in Victoria, 1885, 112 Government Street, operated by Peterson & Crowell.

ELITE PHOTO STUDIO
Studio in Nanaimo, 1895-97, on Commercial Street, operated by Larss & Pierce, 1895; by Adams & Pierce, 1897.

ELITE PHOTO STUDIO
Studio in Rossland, 1897-98, 121 ½ East Columbia, managed successively by J. C. Dolan and G. M. Eddie.

ELLIS, ROBERT
Active in Victoria, 1898-99.

EVANS, J. R.
Active in Revelstoke, 1894, operating a portrait studio near the CPR water tank.

EVANS, THOMAS ALBERT
Active in Vancouver, 1893, as a photographer's assistant.

EVELEIGH, SYDNEY MORGAN
Amateur active in Vancouver, 1900, affiliated with the Arts and Crafts Association.

EXCELSIOR STUDIO
Studio in Vancouver, 1899; at 418 Hastings Street and Mt. Pleasant; also listed at 442 Seventh Avenue. Operated by A. and O. Risem.

EYRES, EDMUND JAMES
Born in London, England, 1834(?); died in Victoria, 1910. Active in Victoria, 1892-1900. Worked at Queen's Art Photo Studio, 1893, 59 ½ Government Street; operated the Imperial Studio, 1894-1900+, 76 Yates Street. Primarily a portrait photographer; the Colonist reported that he and E. A. Harris had invented a device for producing vignette photographs, 1897.

FARDON, GEORGE ROBINSON
Born in Birmingham, England, 1807; died in Victoria, 1886. Emigrated to New York and is believed to have followed the gold rush to California, 1849. Operated a daguerreotype studio in San Francisco, 1855-58. Moved to Victoria and continued in photography, c. 1858-72; on Government Street, 1861-63; 68 Government Street, 1863; Langley Street at Yates Street, 1863-71 or later. Primarily a portrait photographer, his clients included many early political figures, but he also practiced landscape work. He published an album of albumen print views of San Francisco, 1856, the first of its kind in North America. Very few landscape photographs of Victoria are known; some were displayed at the London International Exhibition of 1862.

FERGUSON, A. G.
Amateur active in Vancouver, c. 1897. Member of Vancouver Camera Club.

FERGUSON, DAVID
Active in Vancouver, 1893, 130 Cordova Street, operating the Beaver Photograph Gallery.

FEWSTER, E. M. (MISS)
Active in Vancouver, 1897-99, 45 Cordova Street, working for the Wadds Brothers.

FINLEY, WILLIAM BURTON
Active in New Westminster at 725 Fifth Avenue, 1898; in Nanaimo on Commercial Street with a branch in Vancouver, 1899-1900; in Kamloops, 1902-03.

FLEMING BROTHERS
Studio in Victoria, 1889-1900. Located at 61 Government Street, 1889-92; 50 ½ Government Street, 1893-1900. Operated by Edgar and Harold Fleming, the building in which the upstairs studio was located is still standing at 1014 Government Street.

FLEMING, EDGAR
Born in London, England, 1860(?); died in Victoria, 1938. Prior to emigrating to Victoria, he worked for London Stereoscopic and Photographic Company, Regent Street West, London. Active in Victoria, 1887-1900. Partner in Inchbold & Fleming, 1887-89, on Government Street; partner with his brother Harold in Fleming Brothers, 1889-1900. Primarily a portrait photographer, but also did outdoor work; he joined an expedition exploring Vancouver Island, July 1896.

FLEMING, HAROLD
Born in London, England; died in Victoria, 1934. Active in Victoria, 1889-1900; partner with brother Edgar in Fleming Brothers studio.

FLETCHER, T. J.
Active in Nanaimo, 1888; an itinerant member of the Great Eastern Photographic and Advertising Company.

FORBES-MACKIE, K.
Active in Victoria, 1894, employed by E. J. Eyres Studio, 59 ½ Government Street.

FORD, GEORGE
Possibly visited Victoria, 1858, traveling from Steilacoom where he had been taking daguerreotype portraits for six weeks (since the middle of July 1858), after moving from Olympia. Ford opened a gallery the following year in Steilacoom with E. A. Light.

FORD, LILLIAN M. (MISS)
Active in New Westminster, 1893-94, working as retoucher for S. J. Thompson at 620 Columbia Street.

FOREST, ALEXANDER
Active in Victoria, 1869, working for Frederick Dally, on Fort Street, south side near Government Street.

FOUGNER, IVER
Born in Lillehammer, Norway, 1870; died in Bella Coola, 1947. An amateur photographer, he was educated in Norway and the U.S., taught in Minnesota and then joined the first group of Norwegian immigrants to Bella Coola, 1894. He was a teacher, first secretary of the colony's governing body, and the Indian Agent, 1910-36. He may have toured the U.S. with magic lantern slides, 1896.

FOX, W. W.
Active in Lake Superior, 1890. His views were published in *Dominion Illustrated News*, August 2, 1890.

FRANCIS, E. K.
Active in Revelstoke, 1891-94. Established in Calgary, 1885, with A. M. McKinnel, operating as Francis & McKinnel. He lived in Revelstoke while working as an itinerant in the communities along the CPR line into British Columbia

FREDERICK, E. K.
Active in Vancouver, 1899, 326 Cordova Street(?).

FREEMAN, BARNABAS COURTLAND
Born 1870(?); died 1935. Active in Skidegate, 1897. A Methodist missionary stationed at Skidegate, Port Simpson and Port Essington.

FRENCH, MAY (MISS)
Active in New Westminster, 1890-92, working as retoucher for S. J. Thompson.

FRENCH, W. J.
Active in New Westminster, 1878.

FULTON, CHRISTOPHER
Active in New Westminster, 1862, Columbia Hotel; Victoria, 1862, partner with J. W. Vaughan in the Victoria Theatre Photographic Gallery. After dissolution of partnership, he worked as itinerant in the Williams Creek District, 1863, along the gold creeks of the Cariboo, in Camerontown and Richfield. Managed a billiard and bowling saloon in Camerontown, 1865-66.

GALE, MINA (MISS)
Active in Kamloops, 1891-93, operating in J. L. Browne's old studio after arriving from Orangeville, Ontario.

GARDEN, JAMES FORD
Born in Woodstock, New Brunswick, 1847; died in Vancouver, 1914. A Dominion Land Surveyor and civil engineer, he photographed in the Kamloops area, 1886, and the Lake Coquitlam area, 1887. Mayor of Vancouver, 1898-1900, and a Vancouver MLA, 1900-09.

GARDENER, R. H.
Active in Victoria, 1890, at the Windsor Hotel, 23 Government Street. Possibly an itinerant.

GARDINER, ROSWELL H.
Active in Victoria, 1888, as an itinerant; manager of the Great Eastern Photographic and Advertising Company during its Victoria tour. He later ran a studio in Portland, the Great Eastern Art Company. See California.

GARRISON, A. A.
Active in Discovery (Pine City), 1899; managed Vogee's branch gallery.

GENTILE, CHARLES G.
Born in Italy, 1835; died in Chicago, Illinois, 1893. Active in Victoria, 1863-66. Operated a portrait studio in conjunction with his store, and produced a series of landscape views of Vancouver Island and British Columbia. Accompanied Governor Frederick Seymour's party to the Cariboo country, 1865. Photographed the Alberni area and the Leech River and Sooke district during the height of the gold rush, 1864, and parts of Washington Territory, 1866. He left British Columbia, 1866, leaving Noah Shakespeare in charge of the gallery, but did not return. Studio was located on Fort Street, north side at Government on Robinson's Block, 1863-66; Government Street, west side near View Street, 1866. He was reported in San Francisco, 1867; U.S. Southwest, 1868; Santa Barbara, California, 1869; and in Chicago, late 1870s. See California and Arizona. Also listed as Carlos Gentile.

GIBSON, WILFRED
Born 1886; died 1968. Professional photographer in Victoria; son of William Hewison Gibson.

GIBSON, WILLIAM HEWISON
Born in Lancashire, England, 1861; died in Victoria, 1942. An amateur active in Victoria, 1890-1936(?) and father of professional photographer, Wilfred Gibson.

GILERT, JOHN KING
Born in Cornwall, England, 1834(?); died in Nanaimo, 1876. Active in Nanaimo, 1876, on Bastin Street next to Temperance House (hotel). The studio was leased to W. H. Davis the year after Gilbert died.

GINTZBURTER, M.
Amateur active c. 1895; member of Vancouver Camera Club.

GODREY, W.
Amateur active c. 1897; member of Vancouver Camera Club.

GOOD, H. L.
Active in Cache Creek, 1898. Amateur who served as telegraph operator and express agent at Cache Creek.

GOODIE
 Amateur active in Esquimalt, 1873.

GOODMURPHY, HERBERT FULLER
Born 1879(?); died 1962. Active in Vancouver, 1899-1917. Worked for A. E. Savard, 1899-1900, 225 Carrall Street; operated his own studios in Vancouver and North Vancouver, 1901-17.

GORE, THOMAS SINCLAIR
Born in Gore's Landing, Ontario, 1851; died in Victoria, 1937. Active in Victoria, 1886. A surveyor by profession, he photographed the arrival of the first CPR train at Port Moody, July 4, 1886, and was mentioned as an amateur photographer in the *Colonist*, February 1886.

GOULD, W. J.
An itinerant active in Revelstoke, 1894; Vernon, 1897; Golden, 1899. He maintained headquarters in Winnipeg, 1893; Medicine Hat, 1894; Regina, 1896; Golden, 1899.

GRAY, ANDREW
Amateur active 1886.

GREAT EASTERN PHOTOGRAPHIC & ADVERTISING COMPANY
Itinerant studio active in Vancouver, Victoria and Nanaimo, 1888. Operated by T. J. Fletcher in Nanaimo and R. H. Gardiner in Victoria.

GREEN BROTHERS
Studio in Victoria, 1870-72, on Fort Street, south side near Government Street managed by George R. and Rowland E. Green. The business was purchased from Frederick Dally, 1870. One brother accompanied Governor Anthony Musgrave aboard the HMS *Sparrowhawk* to Knights Inlet and the Stikine River. The equipment and negatives were sold when the brothers reneged on their payment, August 1872; probably acquired by Richard and Hannah Maynard.

GREEN, GEORGE R.
Active in Victoria, 1870-72, partner-manager with brother Rowland E. of the Green Brothers studio.

GREEN, L. D.
Employed by Peterson's Photographic in Victoria at 112 Government Street, 1885.

GREEN, ROWLAND EDWARD
Active in Victoria, 1870-72, partner-manager with brother George R. in the Green Brothers studio.

GUEST, JOHN JAMES
Active in New Westminster, 1890, working for S. J. Thompson, Columbia Street, Hamley Block.

GUNTERMAN, MATTIE
Born in La Crosse, Wisconsin, 1872; died in Beaton, 1945. Moved to Seattle, c. 1890; married Bill Gunterman, December 19, 1891. The couple moved to Beaton (Thompson's Landing), walking the entire distance. Along the way Mattie took photographs which survived when her home was destroyed by fire.

HACKING, FREDERICK LOUIS
Active in Vancouver, 1899-1900+. Photo printer with the Wadds Brothers, 1899, 68 Cordova Street; by 1900, was running his own studio at 445 Granville Street in the Fairfield Block.

HAINES, J. C.
Amateur active in the Kootenay region, 1887.

HALL & LOWE
Active in Victoria, 1885-92, at Government Street over London House, 1885-87(?); 63 Government Street, 1889-92; operated by Skene Lowe. The studio was active in Vancouver, 1887-92; at 416 Cordova Street, 1887-91; 518 Cordova Street, 1892; operated by J. D. Hall. The partnership was dissolved, May 1892. Hall & Lowe were primarily portrait photographers, but also engaged in landscape work.

HALL, JAMES DEAKIN
Born in Londonderry, Ireland, 1854; died in Victoria, 1936. Hall immigrated with his parents to Ontario, Canada, 1867. Prior to moving to British Columbia, he worked for R. Walker & Sons, Toronto; with Notman & Fraser, c. 1869; in Winnipeg, 1881, partner with William Johnston as Johnston & Hall; partner with Skene Lowe, 1883, in Hall & Lowe. Moved studio to Victoria, operating 1885-86. After working as itinerant in Medicine Hat, 1886, he opened the Vancouver Photographic Company in Vancouver, 1887-1892. The Hall & Lowe partnership was dissolved, May 1892, and Hall sold the Vancouver studio to David Wadds. Hall became sheriff of Vancouver, continuing until 1917.

HALL, WILLIAM
Active in Trail, 1898-99, Bowery Alley; Grand Forks, 1900.

HALLIDAY, WILLIAM MAY
Born in Drayton, Wellington County, Ontario, 1866; died in Victoria, 1957. Active in Victoria, 1893(?)-1900+. Amateur photographer; Indian Agent for the Kwakewlth Agency, 1906-32. His autobiography, *Potlatch and Totem*, was published, 1935.

HAMILTON, LAUCHLAN ALEXANDER
Born 1852; died in Ontario, 1941. Active in Vancouver, 1885-86. The CPR deputy land commissioner and surveyor, he was also a watercolour artist and amateur photographer.

HAMMOND, HENRY
Active in the Kootenays, 1890s-1910s; believed to have worked logging and mining camps with his brother Thomas as itinerants.

HAMMOND, JOHN
Born in Montreal, Quebec; died in Sackville, New Brunswick. Active in British Columbia, 1871, an assistant to Benjamin Baltzly on the Geological Survey of Canada expedition. He became a landscape artist who secured commissions from CPR President Van Horne. Hammond began work with the Notman studio in Montreal, August 1870.

HAMMOND, THOMAS
Active in the Kootenays, 1890s-1910s, working with his brother Henry as an itinerant in logging and mining camps.

HASTINGS, OREGON COLUMBUS
Born in Illinois, 1846; died in Victoria, 1912. Active in Victoria, 1874-99. Primarily a portrait photographer, although he visited Metlakatla with I. W. Powell on an inspection tour, August 1879. He was the manager of Spencer's studio, 1874; partner with S. A. Spencer as Spencer & Hastings, 1882; bought out Spencer the following year. He sold the studio, located on Fort Street, 1889. Commissioned to take photographs at Ft. Rupert for ethnologist Franz Boas, 1894.

HASTINGS STUDIO
Active in Victoria at 56 Fort Street, 1892-95, run by O. C. Hastings; by 1895, was managed by John Savannah.

HATHERLY, JAMES THOMAS
Born in England, 1865; died in Vancouver, 1948. Active in Kualt, 1897-99.

HAYNES
Active in Trail, 1897, a partner in Hendee & Haynes.

HECKLEY, ALBERT
Active in New Westminster, 1891, at the Caledonia Hotel.

HECKLEY, JOSEPH WOODWARD
Active in New Westminster, 1891-95, at 437 Columbia Street, 1891; 417 Columbia Street, Room 3, 1895. Partner and assistant to Albert Mountain, 1891, Mountain & Heckley; photographed on his own, 1892-95. On August 31, he photographed the steamer *Surrey* and her crew for reproduction in the *Dominion Illustrated*.

HECKMAN, JOSEPH WILLIAM
Born 1854 (?); died in Montreal, Quebec, 1937. An amateur, active in British Columbia and Victoria, 1885. A civil engineer employed by the CPR he photographed along the railway line and took a portrait of the British Columbia senators and "commoners" on a stopover in Victoria, June 1885.

HEGG, ERIC A.
Born in Sweden, 1867 or 1868; died in San Diego, California, 1948. E. A. Hegg has become the photographer associated most with the Klondike gold rush, although he traveled to Hawaii, 1895, taking many photographs. He was active throughout British Columbia, 1898-99, during the gold rush; Atlin, Bennett, Discovery (Pine City), and Yukon Territory, publishing souvenir albums, 1900 and 1902. Formed a brief partnership with P. E. Larss as Hegg & Larss, 1898. At the spike ceremony for the White Pass and Yukon Railroad at Lake Bennett, July 6, 1899, Hegg's camera caught three other photographers at work, including amateur E. S. Busby. See Washington.

HENDEE & HAYNES
Studio in Trail, 1896-97; partnership of Edwin Hendee and Haynes.

HENDEE, EDWIN
Active in Trail, 1896-97; partner in Hendee & Haynes. See Oregon.

HENDEE PHOTO COMPANY
Studio in Trail, 1897, operated by Edwin Hendee.

HENDERSON, ALEXANDER
Born in Scotland, 1831; died in Montreal, Quebec, 1913. Active in Vancouver, 1892, headquartered at the Oriental Hotel. An artistic landscape photographer from Montreal, he was commissioned by the CPR to photograph its engineering accomplishments and acted as their official photographer, 1892-late 1890s.

HENDERSON, HAROLD MORTON
Active in Vancouver, 1897-99. An amateur, he photographed the CPR station, October 1897, and the departure of law enforcement members for the Klondike, fall 1897.

HENNESSY, F.
Active in Vancouver, 1897, 2 Cordova Street East, working for John White.

HENRY, THOMAS E. B.
Active in Port Hammond, 1890.

HERSCKFELD, WALTER
Born in England, 1855(?) Listed in Victoria, 1878.

HILL, HENRY FYFE
Born in Ontario, 1864; died in Van Nuys, California, 1948. Worked for photographer James F. Ryder, Cleveland, Ohio, 1885-87. Active in Vancouver, 1899-1902; worked for R. H. Trueman until c. 1901-02. After living in Hawaii for five years, he moved back to Vancouver, 1907, working for John White, then returned to Honolulu. He was a staff photographer for the *Honolulu Star-Bulletin*, 1917-24. He operated his own studio, 1925-39; then retired to Southern California.

HINTON, J. H.
Active in Vancouver, 1899, 610 Granville Street, employed by S. J. Thompson.

HIRSCHFELD, ALFRED CYRIL
Born in London, England, 1866; died in San Francisco, California, 1926. Active in Alaska and Klondike towns, 1898; in Atlin, 1899. Hirschfeld's photo studio was destroyed in the fire of August, 1900.

HOAG & SON, JAMES
Active in Kaslo, 1899, on Front Street; in Nelson on Victoria Street, corner of Ward Street, operating the Dominion Photo Company, 1900.

HOAG, E. (MISS)
Active in Nelson, 1899, working for her father or brother, James Hoag of the Dominion Photo Company.

HOAG, JOHN MORLEY
Active in Nelson, 1899; and in Kaslo, 1900, managing the Dominion Photo Company.

HOGAN, JAMES J. (MRS.)
Active in Rossland, 1897-98.

HOGG, JAMES
Active in Vancouver, 1889-90; 77 Cordova Street, 1889; 75 Cordova Street, 1890. In Nelson, 1898-1900, on Victoria Street, corner of Ward; in Vancouver, 1902, working as a photographer for the Dominion Studio; in McMinnville, Oregon, 1891-92. See Oregon.

HOLLIDAY, CHARLES WILLIAM
Born in London, England, 1870; died in Victoria, 1955. Active in Vernon, 1891-99; Armstrong, c. 1899; retired to Victoria, 1937. Holliday was also an amateur painter of the Okanagan landscape.

HOLLYER, CHRISTOPHER WILLIAM
Active in Victoria, 1898.

HOMAN, CHARLES A.
Photographed British Columbia while traveling to Alaska, 1883. Topographical assistant to First Lieutenant Frederick Schwatka, U.S. Army, during Alaska reconnaissance.

HOOD, JOHN
Born in London, Ontario, 1864; died in Vancouver, 1956. Active in Vancouver, 1891-95, employed by the Bailey Brothers as a gilder-frame maker and photographer. Listed at 160 Cordova Street, 1891-94; 138 Cordova Street, 1895+.

HOOD, WILLIAM
Born 1846. Active in Vancouver, 1893-1902. An apprentice with the Bailey Brothers, 1893; photographer, 1894-95; clerk at the Bailey Brothers, 1899; printer for A. E. Savard, 1900-02. See California.

HORETZKY, CHARLES GEORGE
Born in Edinburgh, Scotland, 1838; died in Toronto, Ontario, 1900. He worked as a CPR survey photographer in British Columbia and wrote a book about his 1872 survey work.

HOWARD, J.
Active in Steveston, 1895-1900.

HOWELL, BERTRAM ARCHER
Born on the Isle of Wight, 1877; died in Victoria, 1972. Active in Victoria, 1889(?)-1900+. Amateur photographer, supposed to have been the first electrician in Victoria. Brother of Kathleen Howell, printer for J. Savannah.

HOWELL, KATHLEEN GERTRUDE (LENA)
Born 1873(?); died in Victoria, 1964. Active in Victoria, 1891-95; worked for J. Savannah and was listed as Lena Howell and K. Howell in the directories.

HOWISON, J. W.
Active in New Westminster, 1897-1900; worked for S. J. Thompson as a photographer, apprentice, and assistant photographer, 620 Columbia Street.

HOYT
Active in Victoria, 1874-(?) He was reported to have purchased Noah Shakespeare's gallery with John Uren, on Government Street, west side near View Street.

HUNT, WILLIAM
Born in England, 1865(?); died in Vancouver, 1949. An amateur active in Vancouver, 1898, in the Kitsilano district.

IMANTY, D. G.
Active in New Westminster(?), 1898; awarded a prize for best collection of amateur photos at the New Westminster Provincial Fair.

IMPERIAL ART STUDIO
Active in Victoria, 1892-1900+, operated by E. J. Eyres, at 76 Yates Street.

IMPERIAL PHOTO STUDIO
Active in Vancouver, 1896-1900+, established by A. E. Savard, at 225 Carrall Street.

INCHBOLD & FLEMING
Studio in Victoria, 1887; partnership of Stanley Inchbold, artist, and Edgar Fleming, photographer.

ITTER BROTHERS & McBETH
Studio in Rossland, 1897, managed by J. E. and W. H. Itter and McBeth, perhaps R. A. McBeth, at 23 East Columbia Avenue.

ITTER, JULIAN E.
Active in Rossland, 1897, partner in Itter Brothers & McBeth.

ITTER, WILLIAM HENRY
Active in Rossland, 1897, partner in Itter Brothers & McBeth; also working at a news depot in the post office lobby and as a clerk with McNeil, 1899.

JACKSON, JOHN
Active in Victoria, 1894, 56 Pandora Avenue.

JACOBSON, O. B.
Active in Nelson, 1900, on Stanley Street, corner of Silica.

JENKIN, WILLIAM P.
Active in Silverton, and in Summerside, Prince Edward Island, before 1900.

JOHNSON, ANDREW
Active in Nelson, 1897, on Victoria Street, near Stanley.

JOHNSON, C. (MRS.)
Active in Nelson, 1897.

JOHNSTON, NELLIE (MISS)
Active in Victoria, 1891-1900, working for Skene Lowe as artist and clerk, 61 ½ Government Street.

JOHNSTURP, EMIL
Active in Greenwood, 1899.

JONES & COMPANY
Studios in Victoria, Vancouver, Esquimalt, 1891-1900. This firm was preceded by Jones Brothers; the Vancouver branch was managed by T. M. Jones.

JONES BROTHERS
Active in Victoria, 1889-91, 104 Douglas Street, 1889; 60 Yates Street, 1890-91. Established by J. W. and T. M. Jones, 1888, the name was changed to Jones & Company, 1891, after the Esquimalt branch studio was destroyed by fire. The directories, however, do not show an Esquimalt branch until 1897.

JONES, JOHN WALLACE
Born in Ireland, 1854; died in Victoria, 1938. Active in Victoria and Esquimalt, 1889-1900, one of the brothers in the Jones Brothers studio and Jones & Company. Originally came to Canada, 1866, working in photography at Winnipeg. He may have followed the troops west to Ft. Qu'Appelle during the Riel rebellion, 1885.

JONES, ROBERT
Born in Ireland, 1860(?); died in Victoria, 1935. Active in Victoria, 1890; Jones Brothers studio, 60 Yates Street.

JONES, THOMAS McNABB
Active in Victoria, Esquimalt, and Vancouver, Jones Brothers studio. Studio in Winnipeg, 1883, and formed the Jones Brothers company by 1886. T. M. Jones managed the Vancouver branch of Jones & Company but was also listed in the Victoria directories.

JUDKINS, DAVID ROBY
Born in Maine, 1836; died in Santa Maria, California, 1909. Active in New Westminster and other locations in British Columbia, 1882, operating out of Seattle, through Puget Sound on a barge which was towed to each location. Known as Judkins' Floating Sunbeam Gallery. He operated the Pullman Photographic Gallery in Skagway, 1899. See Alaska, California, Oregon and Washington.

KEEN, JOHN HENRY
Born 1851 or 1852; died in England, 1950. Active in Masset, 1893, an amateur photographer who was an Anglican missionary to this Haida community in the Queen Charlotte Islands. He arrived at Masset from Moose Fort, 1890; remained until 1898; stationed at Metlakatla, 1900.

KELLY, MILLARD F.
Active in Union, 1895-97. See Washington.

KERR, BYRON N.
Amateur active in Vancouver, 1898.

KING, JOHN HOWARD HAVELOCK
Born in Ontario, 1873; died in Vancouver, 1963. Active in Vancouver, 1899-1900+, at 610 Granville Street, employed as a picture framer by S. J. Thompson. The List of Voters shows him as a photographer. He later ran his own studio, the King Photo Studio until 1905, then worked in New Westminster and Nanaimo as a photographer. He took portraits of Indians in all parts of Canada.

KIPLING, THOMAS
Active in Victoria, 1892-93.

KLOTZ, OTTO JULIUS
Born in Ontario, 1852; died in Ontario, 1923. An amateur photographer active in Selkirk and Rocky Mountains; an engineer with the Topographical Surveys Branch, Dominion Department of the Interior, 1879-1908. He surveyed the CPR through the mountains as a basis for delimiting the 10-mile wide Railway Belt of land granted by British Columbia to the Dominion; first to determine the heights of principal peaks along the railway and named many of them. Klotz also worked on the Alaska boundary survey, 1893-94. He was director of the Dominion Observatory, Ottawa, beginning in 1917.

LA ROCHE, FRANK
Born in Pennsylvania, 1853; died in Sedro Woolley, 1934. Landscape photographer who published souvenir album, 1898, one of the earliest of the Klondike gold rush. See California, Alaska and Washington.

LANG, WILLIAM RUSSELL
Active in Kamloops, 1893-98, on Victoria Street (over Slavin's store). He purchased Mina Gale's studio, 1893, operating as the Royal Studio.

LANGEVIN, EDWARD A.
Active in Salmon Arm, 1890; possibly an amateur.

LANGLOIS, ALBERT
Active in Vancouver, 1900, possibly an amateur from Windsor, Ontario.

LARKIN, W.
Active in Vancouver, 1899, working for John White at 14 Cordova Street West. Name may be Wellington Larkin.

LARSS & PIERCE
Studio in Nanaimo, 1892-96; partnership of P. E. Larss and W. C. Pierce, operating as Elite Photo Studio.

LARSS, PER EDWARD
Born in Sweden, 1863; died in California, 1941. His real name was Larson; worked as photographer in Minnesota, 1883-89; in Denver, 1890, worked as a mechanic for the Denver City Railway Company; traveled in Washington, Oregon, and California; in Vancouver Island, 1892, partner with W. C. Pierce; in Denver, 1896-98; in New Whatcom (Bellingham) Washington, 1898, working for Adams & Pierce and for a brother of E. A. Hegg. Larss then journeyed to Alaska, worked with both E. A. Hegg and J. E. N. Duclos; formed a partnership with Hegg, 1898 (Hegg & Larss), and with Duclos (Larss & Duclos), 1899. Larss was also active in mining and prospecting. He was married, 1904, the year he left Alaska; he and his Swedish wife moved to Nevada in the next year where Larss continued as a photographer and ran a stationery shop. He retired from photography, 1908, and moved to Oregon where he ran a hotel. In 1920, he settled in San Pedro, California.

LASSONDE, PAUL H.
Active in New Westminster, 1890-91.

LAURSEN, VIGO
Amateur active in Vancouver, 1900.

LE MUNYON, C. E.
Active in West Kootenays, Nakusp, 1894. Official photographer of the Great Northern Railway, with headquarters at Spokane, he took what were probably the last photographs of the sternwheeler *Columbia* before she was destroyed by fire, early August 1894. He visited the West Kootenays to photograph scenery along the Nakusp and Slocan Railway line.

LECKIE-EWING, R.
Active c. 1900; photographs published in *BC Mining Record*, March 1900.

LEE WAH
Active in Kamloops, late 1890s-early 1900s. His portraits of Chinese living in Kamloops are preserved in the Kamloops Museum-Archives.

LEESON, BENJAMIN W.
Born in England, 1866; died in Vancouver, 1948. Emigrated to Vancouver, 1886; an amateur active in the Cariboo District and Winter Harbour (Quatsino Sound), 1887 or 1889-1900+; his early negatives were destroyed by fire. Moved to Quatsino Sound, 1894, operating a store with his father (J. L. Leeson & Son). Noted for his portraits of brooding Indian figures and the flat-headed Kwakiutl women.

LEHMAN, BERTIE
Active in Ashcroft(?), 1893; an amateur awarded honourable mention for a collection of photographs at the Ashcroft fall fair.

LEMON, F. L.
Active in Revelstoke, 1897-99, on Douglas Street.

LEMPRIERE, ARTHUR REID
Active in New Westminster, 1859; the Superintendent of Lands & Works, Quartermaster General, also in charge of the photographic department of the Columbia Detachment, Royal Engineers, Colony of British Columbia.

LOWE, SKENE
Born in England, 1856; died in Essondale, 1920. Active in Victoria, 1885-1918(?) A partner with J. D. Hall in Hall & Lowe, he was operating the Victoria branch of their Winnipeg operation by June 1885. The partnership was dissolved, May 1892, when Hall became sheriff of Vancouver, although Lowe continued to use the name Hall & Lowe until at least the turn of the century; he was in business for several years after 1900 under his own name.

MACDONALD, EMMA
Born in Ontario, 1859(?); died in Seattle, Washington. Active in Victoria, 1880-81(?) A daughter of Hannah and Richard Maynard, married to James F. MacDonald. An assistant to her mother or father, she drowned in Seattle before the mid-90s and her portrait appears in a few of her mother's bizarre multiple exposure tableaux.

MACMUNN, CHARLES
Born in England, 1840(?); died in Victoria, 1903. Active in Victoria and British Columbia, 1883-1903, a photographer who traveled along the CPR line. Macmunn's work is among the best of that genre. The T. N. Hibben & Company bookstore sold his work as early as 1883 which it described as "Macmunn's Views of Canadian Pacific Railway, Victoria and Surroundings." His name has been variously spelled as McMunn, MacMunn, and McMann.

MAGUFFIN, JOHN
Active in Victoria, 1890; probably working for Charles Macmunn.

MALCOLM, KENNETH
Active in Vancouver, 1892-93, working for the Bailey Brothers as an assistant.

MAYNARD, ALBERT HATHERLY
Born in Ontario, 1857; died in Victoria, 1934. Active in Victoria, 1899-1900+. Son of Richard and Hannah Maynard, he was a shoemaker and photographer like his father, and took over both his father's stores.

MAYNARD, HANNAH HATHERLY
Born in England, 1834; died in Victoria, 1918. Married 1852 to

Richard Maynard, she emigrated to the Colony of Vancouver Island with her family, 1862; probably opened Mrs. R. Maynard's Photographic Gallery, 1862. Primarily a portrait photographer; she retired, 1912, boasting of having photographed just about everyone who passed through Victoria. She and Richard made a few trips together (San Francisco, 1875, Vancouver Island pleasure cruise, 1879, Banff, 1887 or 1889, Queen Charlotte Islands, 1888). Both practiced landscape photography; although it is not always clear who took which photographs. Hannah also experimented with novelty techniques; photosculpture, multiple exposure tricks, and composite imagery, mid-1890s.

MAYNARD, RICHARD
Born in England, 1832; died in Victoria, 1907. Married in 1852 to Hannah Hatherly, he mined gold in the Fraser River, 1858-59; Stikine Territory, 1862, where he reputedly made a fortune. He settled in Victoria as a boot and shoe maker and photographer; active in photography, 1864-93. He made many trips, photographing landscapes; Barkerville, 1868; accompanying Indian Affairs Superintendent I. W. Powell, 1873 on an inspection tour along the east coast of Vancouver Island and the northwest coast of the mainland; around Vancouver Island with Powell, 1874; Queen Charlotte Islands with Captain Newton H. Chittenden, 1884, and again in 1888 with Hannah. Maynard sailed to the Pribilof Islands in the Bering Sea to photograph the seal rookeries, 1892; and to Alaska for photographic purposes, 1879, 1882, and 1887.

McBETH, ROBERT ANDREW
Active in Rossland, 1897, at 23 East Columbia Avenue. He may be the McBeth of Itter Brothers & McBeth, as he is the only McBeth listed in Rossland.

McCLEERY, FITZGERALD
Amateur who won a prize for his work at the Richmond Fair, 1900.

McCLURE
Active in Vancouver, 1889. He or his partner Crowell of Crowell & McClure visited Vancouver and were reported to be photographing buildings and streets for a publication about the Pacific Northwest coast of the U.S. and Canada.

McCULLAGH, JAMES BENJAMIN
Born in Ireland, 1854; died in Prince Rupert, 1921. Active in Aiyansh by 1900; he was an amateur photographer, a missionary who arrived in 1883.

McDERMAID, ALBERT
Active in New Westminster, 1890

McDOUGALL, JAMES
Born in Scotland, 1843; died in Victoria, 1915. Active in Masset, c. 1890; a Hudson's Bay Company agent and amateur photographer.

McGREGOR, J. H.
His photographs were published in *BC Mining Record*, October 1899.

McKAY, H. D.
Active in Vancouver, 1898-99, at 2 Cordova Street East, in J. M. White's old studio.

McLAREN
Active in Vancouver, 1890, at 2 Powell Street, employed by the Stanley Brothers.

McLEAN, JAMES B.
Active in Cumberland, 1898. McLean was listed as an agent for the Esquimalt & Nanaimo Railway in 1898, possibly an amateur photographer.

McMUNN, T.
His photographs were published in *BC Mining Record*, February 1899.

MEDLOCK, E. S. (MISS)
Active in Vancouver, 1897-98, at 45 Cordova Street. She worked for the Wadds Brothers and married David Wadds on March 26, 1898, in Rossland.

MERRIFIELD, GEORGE
Active in Nanaimo, 1893-95, working for J. Sampson's Diamond City Photo Gallery. Name also spelled Merryfield, Merrfield.

MERRILL, JOSEPH
Active in Victoria, 1893-95, working for J. Savannah at 56 Fort Street.

MERRILL, MABLE (MISS)
Active in Victoria, 1897, working for G. Preston at 56 Fort Street.

MILLAR, GEORGE EDWARD
Active in Rossland, 1897-99, at 26 ½ East Columbia Avenue, partner in Carpenter & Millar; in Greenwood, 1899-1900, on Copper Street with his own studio. Name also spelled C. Milliar, or Miller. See George E. Miller in New Mexico.

MILLER
Active in Victoria, 1874, Government Street, west side near View; a retoucher from San Francisco working for S. A. Spencer in the Theatre Photographic Gallery. He replaced R. A. Desmond who had gone to work for Noah Shakespeare.

MILLER, J. A.
Active in Victoria, 1861, on a visit. The President of "The World's Panorama Company."

MILLER, N. B.
Active in Alert Bay, c. 1888-89; possibly an amateur.

MILLER, REV.
Amateur visiting Nanaimo, 1861.

MILLER, T.
Advertised a copying service for photographs and tintypes in Nanaimo, 1882.

MILLS, THOMAS
Active in British Columbia, 1890-91 and 1893, on extensive tours attached to a British farmers delegation. On the first trip he gathered over 1,000 negatives; on his second trip, 1893, he was assisted by a man named Morde.

MILNE, A.
Active in Vancouver, 1893(?) on a visit. May have also photographed or lived in New Zealand.

MILROSS & WREN
The partnership of W. T. Milross and J. Wren. The first studio in Vancouver on Cordova Street, next door to McKendry's Boot Store, it was destroyed by fire June 13, 1886. No photographs by Milross & Wren are known to have survived.

MILROSS, WILLIAM THOMAS
Active in Vancouver, 1886, a partner in Milross & Wren. Name also spelled Melrose.

MINTO, LADY MARY CAROLINE
Born in England, 1858 or 1859; died in England, 1940. The daughter of General Charles Grey and sister of the 4th Earl of Grey, she married the 4th Earl of Minto (1845-1914) in 1883. While he was Governor-General of Canada (1898- 1904), they took the train to the Klondike. Several of her photographs illustrate the published version of Graham's journal, *Across Canada to the Klondyke*.

MOORE
Active in Bella Bella, 1885.

MOORE, THOMAS HENRY
Active in Vancouver, 1895-96, at 360 Tenth East Avenue; 1896-97, at 424 Tenth Avenue East.

MORDE
Active in British Columbia, 1893, working for Thomas Mills on his second tour of the Canadian Northwest and British Columbia; they also operated as partners (Mills & Morde) in Bangor, North Wales.

MORRIS, CURTIS DEXTER
Born in Nova Scotia, 1868(?); died in Vancouver, 1950. Active in Vancouver, 1893, at 59 Cordova Street, a photographer with T. B. Straiton. Moved to the Selkirk Mountains.

MORTIMER, GEORGE
Active in Rossland, 1897-98, on Lincoln Street, near Second Avenue.

MOUNTAIN & HECKLEY
Studio in New Westminster, 1891, at 437 Columbia Street; the partnership of Albert Mountain and J. W. Heckley.

MOUNTAIN, ALBERT
Active in New Westminster, 1889(?)-91. A partner in Uren & Mountain, 1890, Columbia Street, near Church, 1890; and Mountain & Heckley, 1891, 437 Columbia Street. He was listed in error in 1891 as J. W. Mountain.

MUIRHEAD BROTHERS
Active in Sidney, Bennett(?), Atlin, and Whitehorse, 1896, 1900+. The partnership of C. H. and L. P. Muirhead. Examples of their photography can be found in *The Mining Record* (1900).

MUIRHEAD, CHARLES H.
Born in Scotland, 1872; died in Wenatchee, Washington, 1857. Active in Sidney, Bennett(?), and Atlin, 1896; 1900. A partner in the Muirhead Brothers.

MUIRHEAD, LEWIS POTTER, JR.
Born in Scotland, 1876; died in England, after 1957. Active in Sidney, Bennett(?), Atlin, and Whitehorse, 1896, 1900; partner with C. H. Muirhead as Muirhead Brothers. See Washington.

MURCHIE, ARCHIBALD
Active in New Westminster, 1890-95; located at 1411 Sixth Avenue, 1893; on Murchie Road, 1895.

MUYBRIDGE, EADWEARD JAMES
Born in England, 1830; died in England, 1904. Muybridge was an accomplished landscape photographer by the time he was appointed to accompany General William Halleck to take views of military ports and harbours of Alaska, including Nanaimo and Vancouver Island, 1868. Views from this trip were sold as 8 x 10 in. prints and stereograph cards. See California entry.

NEELANDS BROTHERS
Active in Nelson, 1891-97; on West Baker Street, 1891-95; at 21 West Baker Street, 1897. Studio was established by James F. and H. G. Neelands; Samuel was associated with the firm, 1897. The brothers were primarily landscape photographers, but probably took portraits as well.

NEELANDS, HAMILTON GEORGE
Born 1859(?); died in Seattle, Washington, 1935. Active in Vancouver, 1889-91 in Bailey & Neelands; at 227 Hastings West Street, 1889-90; 176 Cordova Street, 1890. He moved to Nelson, establishing the Neelands Brothers, 1891-97, partners with his brother James

F. and Samuel. He later served as mayor of Nelson and also owned mining property in the Nelson area.

NEELANDS, JAMES F.
Active in Nelson, 1891-97; partner in the Neelands Brothers studio.

NEELANDS, SAMUEL
Active in Nelson, 1897; partner in the Neelands Brothers studio.

NEILL, GEORGE W.
Active in Victoria, 1891-92(?), at 60 Yates Street, working as photographer and taking charge of the fininshing department of Jones & Company. He worked previously for many years as head of the same department in the Gagen & Fraser photographic firm in Toronto.

NELKIN, J.
Active in Victoria, 1895, an artist with the Berlin Portrait Company at 32 Government Street.

NEWCOMBE, CHARLES FREDERICK
Born in England, 1851; died in Victoria, 1924. Active in Victoria, 1897-1900+. An anthropologist and amateur photographer, he collected native artifacts for G. M. Dawson and Franz Boas.

NEWMAN, ALMERON
Active in British Columbia, 1897; an itinerant partner of N. J. Porter. See New Mexico.

NICKSON, RALPH
Active in Vancouver, 1897, an apprentice with the Edwards Brothers at 534 Cordova Street.

NORMAN, HENRY
Active in Vancouver, 1888-1901, as a photo-journalist for the *Pall Mall Gazette*; took views of the city from the top of the CPR Building.

NOTMAN, CHARLES F.
A brother of William McFarlane and George W., he passed through British Columbia and stopped in Vancouver, assisting William, 1889, and possibly 1897.

NOTMAN, GEORGE W.
A brother of William McFarlane and Charles, he accompanied and assisted William on the first and second trips to British Columbia and Vancouver, 1884, 1887.

NOTMAN, WILLIAM McFARLANE
Born in Montreal, 1857; died in Montreal, 1913. A son of famed Montreal photographer William Notman (1826-91), he visited British Columbia and Vancouver several times before and after the turn of the century; 1884, 1887, 1889, 1897. He was accompanied and assisted by one or both of his brothers, Charles and George W. Notman.
    Hall, Dodds and Triggs, *The World of William Notman*, David R. Godine, Boston, Massachusetts, 1993.

OBREN, JOHN
Active in Victoria, 1874. Name may also be O'Brien.

OGILVIE, WILLIAM
A Dominion Land Surveyor equipped with a camera as early as 1885; primarily active along the "Railway Belt."

OKAMURA, PAUL L. (TSUNENOJO)
Active in New Westminster, before 1900. He was listed as an artist prior to 1901, so it is probable he was photographing as an amateur in conjunction with his art work before 1900. He was listed in the 1895 directory as a professor of drawing at St. Louis College, New Westminster.

PALMER, EMILY (MISS)
Active in Vancouver, 1892-93, working for John White at 2 Cordova Street East.

PATTERSON, M.
Active in New Westminster, 1894.

PETERS, JAMES
Born in New Brunswick, 1853; died in Victoria, 1927. Active in Northwest Territories and Victoria, 1888-97. Considered Canada's first military photographer because of his work during the 1885 Northwest Rebellion while commander of the 'A' Battery of the Regiment of Canadian Artillery, Captain Peters was transferred to Exquimalt in 1887 as commander of 'C' Battery. He photographed the 'C' Battery camp on the Skeena River during a policing action, 1888.

PETERSON & CROWELL
Partnership of L. Peterson and G. W. Crowell, active in Victoria, 1885, at 112 Government Street. The gallery was known as the Elite Photo Gallery.

PETERSON, LOUIS
Active in Victoria, 1885; partner in Peterson & Crowell. See Washington. First name sometimes spelled Lewis.

PIERCE, WESLEY CUNNINGHAM
Active in Nanaimo, 1895-97; partner in Larss & Pierce and Adams & Pierce, on Church Street. See California.

PIERIE, W.
Active in Vancouver, 1897, at 603 Cambie Street. Also spelled Peierie, or W. C. Pierce(?).

PIKE, WARBURTON MAYER
Born in England, 1861; died in England, 1915. An amateur photographer, Pike was an explorer who made a canoe voyage from Ft. Wrangell, Alaska, to the Pelly Lakes and down the Yukon River to the Bering Sea, 1892-93. Photographs from his voyage were included in his account (1896) of this trip as engravings.

PILLSBURY, A. C.
Active in Discovery (Pine City), 1898-99. An itinerant, he worked the Alaska and Yukon Territory gold camps during the Klondike gold rush. He may have been assisted by a V. Cleveland. See California.

PIPER, CHARLES JAMES
Active in Victoria, 1893, working for the Queen Art Photo Studio, at 59 ½ Government Street.

PIPER, CHARLES THOMAS WOOD
Active in Victoria, 1893, proprietor of the Queen Art Photo Studio, 59 ½ Government Street.

PLATT, THOMAS C. (MRS.)
Amateur active in Vancouver, 1891.

POPULAR PHOTO PARLOUR
Studio in Vancouver, 1896, operated by C. W. Bart at 55 Cordova Street (Sullivan Block).

PORTER, NATHANIEL JOSEPH
Born 1873(?); died in Vancouver, 1953. Active in British Columbia and Vancouver, 1897(?)-99, as an itinerant with Almeron Newman. Most of the photographs were lost in a fire in Moose Jaw, Saskatchewan, in 1917.

POWER, WILLIAM
Active in Victoria, 1893, working for the Queen Art Photo Studio at 59 ½ Government Street.

PREST & COMPANY
Studio in Cranbrook, 1899-1900, operated by W. A. Prest.

PREST, WILLIAM ARCHIE
Active in Cranbrook, 1899-1900, operating Prest & Company; and in Fort Steele, 1900.

PRESTON, GEORGE
Active in Victoria, 1897-1900; located at 56 ½ Fort Street, 1897; at 56 Fort Street, 1897-1900. His studio was previously occupied by Spencer & Hastings and O. C. Hastings; J. Savannah was also located at this address.

PRICE, BARRINGTON
Born in England; died in England. Built the Keremeos Grist Mill, c. 1876-77. Possible amateur, c. 1876-1903.

PYMAN, HENRY
Active in Somenos, 1898.

QUEEN ART PHOTO STUDIO
Gallery in Victoria, 1893, 1895, at 59 ½ Government Street; operated by C. T. W. Piper, 1893; Jones & Company, 1895.

RAPPERTIE, ARTHUR S.
Born in Pennsylvania, 1854(?); died in Florida, 1923. Active Victoria, 1880(?)-1900, working for Hannah Maynard (Mrs. R. Maynard).

RATTENBURY, FRANCIS MAWSON
Born in England, 1867; died in England, 1935. Famous architect of Victoria, British Columbia. Amateur active in Bennett and Lake Bennett, British Columbia, and the Yukon, 1898, 1902-05.

REFORD, ROBERT W.
Born in Montreal, 1867; died in Montreal, 1951. Active in British Columbia, 1889-91. An amateur photographer in Victoria. He visited several towns along the coast, including the Queen Charlotte Islands (Masset), Port Simpson, Port Essington, and Metlakatla.

REID & BROWNE
Studio in Kamloops, 1889; partnership of J. D. Reid and J. L. Browne.

REID, JAMES D.
Active in Kamloops, 1889; listed as working for J. L. Browne and as a partnership.

REVELSTOKE PHOTO COMPANY
Studio in Revelstoke, 1898, on Douglas Street.

REYNARD, MARMADUKE CHARLES
Born 1872; died in Victoria (?) 1926. His father was the Rev. James Reynard (1829-75) who designed and built St. Saviour Anglican Church at Barkerville. An amateur; his photo, "The Harvest Field," was published in *Western Recreation*.

RICE & COMPANY, F. D.
Active in Greenwood, 1899; operated by F. D. Rice and A. M. Rice.

RICE, ARTHUR M.
Active in Greenwood, 1899, working for F. D. Rice & Company.

RICE, FRANK DWIGHT
Born in Ontario, 1881; died in Kelowna, 1967. Active in Greenwood, 1899, operating F. D. Rice & Company.

RICHARDSON, JAMES
Born in Scotland, 1810; died in Quebec, 1883. Active in Nanaimo, 1875. A Geological Survey of Canada officer who photographed coal mining activities around Nanaimo and possibly parts of the Queen Charlotte Island and the mainland. Probably the first to use photography in Canada to record geological features.

RISEM, A.
Active in Vancouver, 1899, working at the Excelsior Studio with O. Risem, 418 Hastings West Street.

RISEM, OLE
Active in Vancouver, 1899, working at the Excelsior Studio with A. Risem.

ROBERTSON, LORENZO E.
Active in Glenora, 1898.

ROBERTSON, WILLIAM FRANCIS
Born in New York, 1837. Active in Victoria, 1863-64; partner in Vaughan & Robertson, located in the Victoria Theatre Photographic Gallery. See Washington.

ROBINSON, GEORGE
Born in England, 1825; died in England, 1895. At Vancouver Island, 1854, employed by Hudson's Bay company to begin coal mining operations. Opened his studio in 1864, moving to the Victoria Theatre Photographic Gallery, 1865, probably purchased from J. W. Vaughan. During part of 1864 the first studio was closed while Robinson was exploring around Pachena Bay for coal. He also left the gallery in June 1865 for the Queen Charlotte Islands where he was to manage the Queen Charlotte Coal Mining Company and "take views of the surrounding country." By 1867 Noah Shakespeare was overseeing the portrait work for Robinson who was reported to be "devoting his attention exclusively to outdoor photography." Robinson sold the Theatre Photographic Gallery in May 1869 to J. A. Craigg.

ROCHE, RICHARD
Born in England, 1831; died in Isle of Wight, 1888. An amateur photographer and Lieutenant on H.M.S. *Satellite*, he was stationed at Esquimalt and took photos there, in Victoria and on San Juan Island. Some photographs previously credited to F. G. Claudet are now believed to be Roche's work.

ROCKY MOUNTAIN PORTRAIT COMPANY
Active in Vancouver, March 15, 1894; an itinerant company.

RODIER, GEORGE
Active in Victoria, 1898-99, partner in Blake & Rodier at 52 Government Street.

ROSS, ALEX J.
Active in British Columbia, 1885-86. May have photographed the

driving of the last spike at Craigellachie on November 7, 1885; left Winnipeg in mid-September 1886 for a two-month tour along the CPR and into British Columbia.

ROSS, HELEN (MISS)
Active in New Westminster, 1897-1900; worked for S. J. Thompson in 1897; E. F. Easthope, 1900.

ROTHWELL, E. L.
Active in Somenos, 1895.

ROYAL ENGINEERS
Active in British Columbia, Esquimalt and Victoria, 1893-98. The first Sappers were taught photography in 1856 by Charles Thurston Thompson at South Kensington Museum. A survey team of Royal Engineers arrived at Esquimalt in July 1858 to establish the 49th parallel and among their numbers was one photographer who deserted in the spring of 1859 to the U.S. Two Sappers trained in photography arrived as replacements in October 1859 and photographed in and around Victoria. Charles Wilson, in the field near Chilliwack, mentions taking photographs in October 1859. Most of the photographs taken in 1860-61 were made in the Ft. Vancouver, Cascades and Dalles area of Washington and Oregon. A. R. Lempriere was in charge of the photographic department of the Royal Engineers stationed in the Colony of British Columbia (a different detachment from the survey team). Joseph Davis and Henry Bruce were two others Sappers who practiced photography.

ROYAL STUDIO
Gallery in Kamloops, 1893-98, operated by W. R. Lang on Victoria Street (over Slavin's store).

SALSBURY, FREDERICK THURSTON
Born in Quebec, 1879(?); died in Kelowna, 1953. An amateur photographer active in Vancouver, 1897. He was secretary of the (Vancouver) Camera Club in 1897.

SAMPSON, JOHN WALLACE
Born in England, 1852. Active in Nanaimo, 1886-95; purchased the photographic business of E. L. Boyden, 1886, which he ran for six years. By 1892 he was calling his business the Diamond City Photo Gallery.

SAVANNAH & COMPANY
Studio in Victoria, 1889-1892(?); established by J. Savannah, successors to O. C. Hastings at 56 Fort Street.

SAVANNAH, BENJAMIN
Active in Victoria, 1897-1900, working for John Savannah.

SAVANNAH, JOHN
Born in San Francisco, California, 1868; died in Victoria, 1925. Active in Victoria, 1889-1900+. His studio, Savannah's, was among the most fashionable in Victoria. Primarily a portrait photographer, his work increased in importance after 1900.

SAVARD, ALPHONSE
Born in Quebec, 1864; died in Vancouver, 1934. Active in Vancouver, 1896-1916. Savard trained under Mr. A. R. Ray of Quebec City and established the Imperial Photo Studio in Vancouver, February 1896.

SELWOOD, ARCHIBALD
Born in England, 1881; died in Vancouver, 1973. Active in Vancouver, 1897, c. 1902+; possibly a photographer at R. H. Trueman(?). He left photography, 1898-1901, returning to it after the turn of the century when he worked for Charles M. Scott.

SELWYN, ALFRED RICHARD CECIL
Active in Quesnel, Fort St. James, and Fort St. John, 1875; he was the director of the Geological Survey of Canada, 1869-95.

SHAKESPEARE, NOAH
Born in England, 1839; died in Victoria, 1921. Active in Victoria, 1865-78. He managed G. R. Fardon's studio, 1865-66; then managed Gentile's gallery. He is believed to have leased this gallery to Uren & Hoyt in May 1874 and to have cancelled the lease in October. Employed by G. Robinson in the Victoria Theatre Photographic Gallery, 1867; took it over from S. A. Spencer, 1875. He is presumed to have sold the business to J. Uren in June 1878. Member of Parliament and Victoria's postmaster and mayor.

SHAND, M. E. (MISS)
She was employed by R. H. Trueman & Company in Vancouver, 1898-99.

SHIELDS, GEORGE OLIVER
Possibly an American amateur; mentioned in *Cruising in the Cascades*, 1889.

SINCLAIR, DANIEL WYCLIFFE
Active in Sandon, 1898-1900.

SMITH, CHARLES HENRY
Born in England; died in Victoria, 1947. Active in Vancouver and Victoria, 1899-1900+. He arrived in Canada in either 1889 or 1897, settling first on the Prairies, then participating in the Klondike gold rush. He worked in Vancouver for S. J. Thompson, then moved to Victoria where he operated C. H. Smith & Company, an art and photo supply store.

SMITH, HARLAN INGERSOLL
Born in Michigan, 1872; died in Ontario, 1940. Active in Port Essington, 1897-1900+. An ethnographer, Smith was engaged in work on the Jesup North Pacific Expedition sponsored by the American Museum of Natural History, 1897-1902. He also used a motion picture camera in his work in the1920s and 30s. He was archaeologist of the National Museum of Canada, 1911.

SMITH JAMES A.
Active in Vancouver, 1897, at 224 Thirteenth Avenue West; primarily a portrait photographer.

SMITH, M. (MISS)
Active in Vancouver, 1899, working for the Edwards Brothers at 534 Cordova Street.

SMITH, W. B.
Active in Kaslo, 1898-1900, at A Avenue.

SMYTH, H. S. ST. G.
Active in Windermere, 1897.

SMYTHE, SIDNEY ALFRED
Displayed photos of Calgary in Vancouver, October 1896. Active in as an itinerant in Vancouver, Manitoba, Calgary, Alta, Vernon, and Atlin, 1896(?)-1900. See Western Canada.

SNELL, I. B.
He attempted to operate out of a portable studio in Vancouver, June 1898, but city council refused permission. Active in Rossland, 1898-99, at 121 Columbia Avenue, East Miller Block.

SPENCER & HASTINGS
Portrait studio in Victoria, 1882-89, run by S. A. Spencer & O. C. Hastings. Hastings bought out Spencer about 1883 and the latter moved to Alert Bay. Hastings sold his photographic gallery in January 1889; the location was probably that taken over by J. Savannah at 56 Fort Street.

SPENCER, MARY (MISS)
Active in Kamloops, 1899-1906+. Her most important series of photos are of the capture and trial of train robber Bill Miner, 1906. She moved to West Summerland in 1909 and continued photography there. The photographer in the film about Bill Miner, *The Grey Fox*, is modeled on Mary Spencer.

SPENCER, STEPHEN ALLEN
Born in Connecticut, 1829(?); died in Victoria, August 15, 1911. Active in Victoria, 1858(?)-1883. One of the pioneers of 1858 who came to the Colony of Vancouver Island from San Francisco when miners poured in for the Fraser River gold rush. With Robert Burnaby, he visited the Queen Charlottes, 1863, to photograph the mines and the surrounding country; although no photos are known. His

whereabouts, 1863-70 are unknown; he was in Barkerville, 1871. Active in Victoria, 1872, when he purchased the Victoria Theatre Photographic Gallery from J. A. Craigg. He moved to Fort Street, 1875, headquarters for Spencer & Hastings, leasing the Theatre Photographic Gallery to Shakespeare. Hastings probably bought out Spencer, c. 1883. Married to Anne Hunt, a Kwakiutl. Made stereoviews of Northwest Coast Indians.

SPINKS, W. H.
Active in Eagle Pass Landing, 1886.

STAMP PHOTO COMPANY
Itinerants active in Vancouver, 1900.

STANFIELD, ARTHUR EDWIN
Born in Iowa, 1871; died in the Stikine River, 1899. Active in Cassiar District, 1897-99. He is believed to have accompanied Andrew Jackson Stone, U.S. explorer, on an expedition into Cassiar District from Wrangell, Alaska. He drowned in a canoeing accident on the Stikine River. See California.

STANLEY BROTHERS
Established in Vancouver, 1889-93; located at 2 Powell Street (Chamberlain Block), corner of Carrall, 1889-90; 8 Powell Street, 1890-93. Active in Nelson, c. 1893-95; operated by E. H., George and Gilbert M. Stanley.

STANLEY, EDWARD HALL
Active in Vancouver, 1889-93; Nelson, 1893-95; partner in the Stanley Brothers studio. See Stanley Brothers.

STANLEY, GEORGE
Active in Vancouver, 1889-93; Nelson, 1893-95; partner in the Stanley Brothers studio. See Stanley Brothers.

STANLEY, GILBERT M.
Active in Vancouver, 1889-91, Stanley Brothers studio. See Stanley Brothers for locations of studios.

STANLEY, LADY ALICE
Born 1862; died in England(?), 1967. An amateur active in Vancouver and Victoria, 1889. Also known as Alice Maud Olivia Montagu.

STARK, ERNIE
Amateur active in Vancouver, 1897.

STARK, W. F.
Amateur active in Vancouver, 1897.

STEELE & COMPANY
Active in Fernie and Trail, 1896-1900+.

STEWART, (MISS)
Active in Victoria, 1893, working for J. Savannah at 56 Fort Street.

STODDARD, SENECA RAY
Born in New York, 1844; died 1917. Visited British Columbia, 1892. Active in New York State.

STONE, ANDREW JACKSON
Born 1859; died 1918. An amateur, he was active in the Stikine River and Cassiar Districts, before 1900(?). An explorer who worked out of Wrangell, Alaska, it is believed he employed A. E. Stanfield as a photographer. References in Stone's publications indicate he might also have taken his own photos or assumed credit for those taken by Stanfield.

STORMER, JOHN BENTON
Born in Illinois, 1858. Active in Midway, 1897-98. See California.

STRAITON, THOMAS BELL
Born in Ontario, 1869; died in Florida, 1955. Active in Vancouver, 1892-94; located at 59 Cordova Street, 1892-93; 68 Cordova Street (New Sullivan Block), 1893-94. Primarily a portrait photographer, he also did landscape work. The community of Straiton atop Sumas Mountain was named after him.

STRAUBE, E.
Active in Vancouver, 1888, working for C. S. Bailey & Company at 113 Carrall Street.

SUNBEAM PHOTO STUDIO
Active in New Westminster, 1891-93, at 435 or 437 Columbia Street (Wintemute Block), 1891-92; Columbia Street, over James Ellard & Company, opposite London House, 1892-93. Operated by J. L. Browne.

SWANZY, HENRY
Active in Selkirk Mountains, 1884, 1888. An amateur photographer from England, he was a traveling companion of his cousin, Reverend William Spotswood Green. They have been credited with undertaking the first mountaineering expedition in Canada, 1888.

TANNER, GORDON
Active in Nanaimo, 1895, at 86 Prideaux.

TARVER, JAMES
An amateur active in Nanaimo, 1864.

TASHIRO, JACKSON
Active in Port Essington, 1897-1900.

TASHIRO, R. Z.
Active in Claxton, 1892-95; in Port Simpson by 1900.

TAYLOR, ISABEL C.
Amateur active in Vancouver, 1900-05. Also listed as Mrs. Archibald Duncan.

TAYLOR, L.
Active in Columbia, 1900.

TEGART, WILLIAM M.
Born 1862; died 1921. Itinerant active in Vancouver, Sault Ste. Marie, Ontario, Regina, Prince Albert and Lumsden, Saskatchewan, 1890(?)-1900+. Located at 59 Cordova Street while in Vancouver, 1890(?)-91.

THOM, ADAM B.
Active in Rocky Mountains, Vancouver, Glacier and Selkirk Mountains, 1886-89. Partnership with Fred V. Bingham, 1884-86, operating as Bingham & Thom with headquarters in Winnipeg. Thom traveled widely and visited Vancouver, 1887.

THOMAS, EDWARD C. H.
Active in Kamloops, 1898-1901. He arrived in 1898, taking over W. R. Lang's studio; published an important series of photos depicting a Passion Play performance by Kamloops Indians, 1901.

THOMPSON & BOVILL
Studio in New Westminster, 1885(?)-89, on Columbia Street, Hamley Block; partnership of S. J. Thompson and one or both of the Bovill brothers.

THOMPSON, JOHN E.
Active in Vancouver, 1888-90, at 76 Cordova Street. His first studio was in a tent.

THOMPSON, STEPHEN JOSEPH
Born in Ontario, May 27, 1864; died in Vancouver, August 7, 1929.

Active in New Westminster, 1885-89, partner with one or both Bovill brothers in Thompson & Bovill, on Columbia Street, Hamley Block. Operated his own studio at 620 Columbia Street, 1889-98; studio was destroyed by fire, 1898. He established a branch studio in Vancouver, December 1897. He was a portrait and landscape artist, photographing extensively along the CPR throughout the 1890s. Thompson visited the Chicago World's Fair, 1893; was commissioned to obtain views of farms around Edmonton, 1895. In 1898 he accompanied an official expedition to northern British Columbia and Wrangell led by the Deputy Minister of Marine and Fisheries, Louis Coste.

TIMMS, PHILIP THOMAS
Born 1874; died in Vancouver, 1973. Active in Vancouver, 1899-1900+. Timms moved to Vancouver from Toronto at age 24, 1898, and started in business as a picture framer for S. J. Thompson. He achieved fame after the turn of the century as a photographer of street scenes in Vancouver. Listed as a photographer in the 1899 directories.

TOPLEY, HORATIO NELSON
Visited British Columbia from Ottawa to document the Alaska Boundary Survey, 1894.

TREMAYNE, H. A.
Active in Port Simpson, 1900. He is of no apparent relation to Dr. Henry Ernest Tremayne (b. 1873), a physician who moved to British Columbia from Ontario, 1906.

TRUEMAN & CAPLE
Studio in Vancouver, 1890-93; 302 Cordova Street; partnership of R. H. Trueman and N. Caple. Their catalogue, published c. 1891, listed views numbered 500-985 in three sizes: 8 x 10, 5 x 8, and 4 ½ x 6 ½ (cabinet portrait size).

TRUEMAN & COMPANY, R. H.
Studios operated in Vancouver, Revelstoke, Sandon, Kaslo and Grand Forks, 1894-1910. R. H. Trueman & Company in Vancouver was first listed in 1899. Trueman frequently manned the Revelstoke and Sandon branches himself. The Sandon branch was established by 1899, and Trueman was present in May 1900 when the city burned down.

TRUEMAN, RICHARD HENRY
Born in Ontario, 1856; died in Vancouver, 1911. Active in Vancouver, Revelstoke, Sandon, Kaslo and Grand Forks, 1890-1910. He began as a tinsmith in Brampton, Ontario, and by 1886 had purchased a photo studio calling it the Popular Photograph Parlor. He sold the studio, 1888, and moved to Brandon, Manitoba. Trueman returned to Ontario, 1890, forming a partnership with Norman Caple. Trueman & Caple traveled the CPR line for about a year and then set up headquarters in Vancouver. After the partnership was dissolved, Trueman remained in Vancouver but is not listed in the directories of 1895-97, as he was traveling through the prairies and appears to have spent most of the time in Medicine Hat, 1894-99. He continued to travel extensively, and up until two months before his death was managing his Revelstoke branch studio. Trueman was a superb landscape photographer and one of the few West Coast photographers to print his negatives on platinum paper.

U.S.P. COMPANY
Itinerant firm based in Montreal; visited Donald, 1893. Their effort to photograph was thwarted by forest fire smoke.

UREN & HOYT
Active in Victoria, 1874; partnership of J. B. Uren and Hoyt, on Government Street.

UREN & MOUNTAIN
Active in New Westminster, c. 1889(?); partnership between J. B. Uren and A. Mountain.

UREN, JOHN BATREL
Born in England, c. 1842; died in Renton, Washington, 1919. Active in Victoria, Barkerville, Nanaimo, Wellington, New Westminster, Vancouver(?) and Chilliwack, 1874-1900+. He purchased or leased Shakespeare's photographic gallery next door to the Theatre Photographic Gallery, April 1874, and appears to have abandoned the studio in October. Active in Barkerville, 1875; Nanaimo, 1877; Victoria, 1878, purchasing the Victoria Theatre Photographic Gallery from Shakespeare. Active in New Westminster, 1879, in a studio at the corner of the streets leading to the Drill Shed, a few doors from Columbia Street. He invented a reversible camera back for producing multiple images in one sitting, 1880. He purchased a saloon in New Westminster, 1881, but was back at photography, 1882, on Front Street next to Mrs. Eckstein's. By 1885 he had moved to Columbia Street. He moved to Nanaimo by 1890, and was listed as a photographer in Wellington in the mid to late 1890s. By 1898, he was active in Chilliwack; then briefly in Ashcroft; back to Chilliwack, 1899, remaining there until 1900. John Uren was a prolific photographer who took many portraits and landscape views. Name also spelled Urin and Wren.

VANCOUVER PHOTO COMPANY
Active in Vancouver, 1887-92. Established by J. D. Hall as the Vancouver branch of Hall & Lowe, this studio was sold to David Wadds. Hall was active in sports circles, and a great number of group portraits of various sports teams were taken in his studio. Hall also engaged in outdoor work.

VAUGHAN & FULTON
Partnership of J. W. Vaughan and C. Fulton in Victoria, 1862, on Government Street, west side near View Street; established the Victoria Theatre Photographic Gallery.

VAUGHAN & ROBERTSON
Active in Victoria, 1863-64, on Government Street, west side near View Street. Partnership of J. W. Vaughan and W. F. Robertson affiliated with the Victoria Theatre Gallery. Vaughan operated as Vaughan's Photographic Gallery after the partnership ended.

VAUGHAN, JOHN WILLIAM
Active in Victoria, 1862-65. Vaughan founded the Victoria Theatre Photographic Gallery with his partner, C. Fulton. The following August he formed a partnership with W. F. Robertson. After their partnership was dissolved, Vaughan used the name Vaughan's Photographic Gallery. He sold the business, 1865, and announced he was leaving for Honduras. He may have gone instead to Honolulu, as a carte-de-visite portrait in the Bishop Museum bears the imprint "J. W. Vaughan."

VAUGHAN'S PHOTOGRAPHIC GALLERY
Active in Victoria, 1864, operated by J. W. Vaughan after his partnership with W. F. Robertson ended; the gallery was in the Victoria Theatre.

VAUX FAMILY
Active in Rocky Mountains and Selkirk Mountains, 1887-1900+. Beginning in mid-July 1887 with a brief stop at the newly-opened Glacier Hotel, this talented family of scholars and photographers returned for more studies of the mountains in 1894, 1897, 1898, 1899, 1900+. Outstanding examples of their photographs can be found in *Cavell's Legacy in Ice*, 1983.

VICTORIA THEATRE PHOTOGRAPHIC GALLERY
Established by J. W. Vaughan and C. Fulton in Victoria, 1862, the business was leased or purchased from Vaughan in January 1865, by G. Robinson. Robinson sold it to J. A. Graigg, May 1869; S. A. Spencer bought the business from Craigg, 1872, and Spencer refitted the gallery. N. Shakespeare leased the gallery from Spencer, 1875; J. B.

Uren purchased it from Shakespeare, 1878. By 1879, Uren was operating his own studio in New Westminster.

VIEUSSEUX, CHARLES EDWARD
An amateur active in Victoria, 1870s.

VIPOND, ARTHUR
Born in England, 1832; died in Victoria, 1889. Active in Victoria, 1858-60s. Trained by Charles Thurston Thompson who also taught photography to the Royal Engineers.

VOGEE, ANTON
Born in Norway, 1866(?); died in Vancouver, 1950. He maintained branch studios at Atlin, Bennett and Pine City (Discovery). The studio at Pine City was managed by A. A. Garrison. He was also active in Dawson, Skagway and Whitehorse, 1898-1902.

VULLINGHS, ADRIAN JOHN
Born in Holland, 1868; died in Victoria, 1940. An amateur active in Victoria, 1893-1909. In addition to landscapes, he photographed Indians of the Saanich peninsula.

WADDS BROTHERS
Studio in Vancouver, 1892-98, operated by David and G. T. Wadds. Located at 518 Cordova Street, 1892-96; 45 Cordova Street on Sullivan Block, 1896-97; 68 Cordova Street on Sullivan Block, Room 5, 1898. Branch studio in Nelson, 1897-1900, operated by David on Victoria Street, corner of Stanley. Branch studio in Brooklyn, 1898.

WADDS, DAVID
Born in Ireland, 1800s; died in Trail, 193(?). Active in Vancouver and Nelson, 1892-1900+. Emigrating to Toronto in 1882, he and his brother G. T. Wadds studied photography under H. E. Simpson, the city's leading photographer. He moved to Vancouver, May 1892, purchased the Vancouver Photo Company from J. D. Hall, and was joined by his brother operating as Wadds Brothers. He opened a branch studio in Nelson, 1897. David operated studios after the turn of the century at Crawford Bay and Fairview, British Columbia.

WADDS, GEORGE THOMAS
Born in Ireland, 1864 or 1873; died in Vancouver(?). Active in Vancouver, 1892-1900+. He emigrated with his brother David to Toronto, 1882, and studied photography under H. E. Simpson. He worked as a photo-printer for Simpson Brothers, 1889; as a retoucher for H. E. Simpson, 1890; as a photographer, 1892. George joined David in Vancouver in the Wadds Brothers studio. When David opened the branch studio in Nelson, 1897, George continued to operate under the Wadds Brothers name until 1912 when the studio was destroyed by fire. He reopened under the name George T. Wadds Studio.

WARD, H.
Active in Victoria, 1889, at 15 Churching; possibly an itinerant.

WATKINS, CARLETON EMMONS
Born in New York, 1829; died in Napa, California, 1916. Watkins' brief visit to Victoria, 1882, was part of a tour of the Pacific Northwest. He made some panoramas of the city. See California.

WATSON, CHARLES H.
Active in Kamloops, 1890.

WATTS, JOSEPH
Active in Kincolith, 1897-1900.

WEBB, WILLIAM SEWARD
Born in New York, 1851; died in New York, 1926. An amateur active in British Columbia, 1889.

WELSH & COMPANY
Established by H. M. Welsh in New Westminster, 1895-99, at 437 Columbia Street.

WELSH, HOWARD MILTON
Active in Vancouver, 1891, with J. L. Browne. Active in New Westminster, 1892-1900, as Welsh & Company at 435 and 437 Columbia Street.

WELSH, K. (MISS)
Active in New Westminster, 1897, a retoucher for Welsh & Company at 437 Columbia Street.

WEST, MINNIE
Active in Victoria, 1897, at 140 Fort Street.

WHITE, J.
Active in Victoria, 1890; probably the same person as Vancouver photographer J. M. White.

WHITE, JOHN M.
Active in Vancouver, 1889-1900+. Employed with J. Fraser Bryce in Toronto; arrived in Vancouver, 1889, and established his tent studio for tintype portraits. Moved to a building on Carrall Street; relocated to the new Graveley-Spinks Block, 1891. Primarily a portrait photographer, he also did outdoor work. His wife, Mattie, informed Major J. S. Matthews, City Archivist, in June 1939, that her husband had been in the New Westminster Asylum for the insane for 22 years and that she had operated the studio herself for fifteen years.

WHITE'S STUDIO
Established by J. M. White in Vancouver, 1897, at 2 Cordova Street, this studio was operated by his wife Mattie, c. 1924-39+.

WILCOX, WALTER DWIGHT

WILLIAMS, JOHN TOMATOA CHAWNER
Born in England, 1858; died in Vancouver(?), 1943. An amateur active in Vancouver, 1888-99. Williams was listed as president of the Camera Club in the directories of 1897-99.

WILLIAMS, ROBERT TAYLOR
Born in New York, 1849; died in Victoria, 1934. Active in Victoria, 186(?), at the Victoria Theatre Photographic Gallery on Government Street, west side near View Street.

WILSON, A. E.
Active in Yale, 1887, on Front Street.

WILSON, A. RUSSELL
Amateur active in Vancouver, 1900.

WILSON, C. K.
Active in Nanaimo before April 1882, when businesses were warned that he had skipped town without paying his debts.

WILSON, CHARLES WILLIAM
Born in England, 1836; died in England, 1905. Active around Chilliwack, 1859, a lieutenant in the Royal Engineers and secretary to the British Boundary Commission, 1858-62.

WINTEMUTE, GEORGE
Born 1872; died 19(?) Amatuer active in New Westminster, 1892; his collection of photos was displayed at the New Westminster Exhibition.

WISEMAN, SIR WILLIAM
Born in England, 1845; died in England, 1893. Active in Cowichan Lake, late 1880s; amateur stationed at Esquimalt as commander of HMS *Caroline*.

WITHROW, DAVID
Born 1800s; died 1905. Active in New Westminster, 1868-70; operated a branch studio in Moodyville, 1869. Withrow took portraits in the carte-de-visite format as well as landscape views.

WOOD, JESSIE (MISS)
Active in New Westminster, 1892, a clerk also possibly involved in photography at S. J. Thompson's British Columbia Photo & Fine Art Studio, 441 Columbia Street.

WOODSIDE, HENRY JOSEPH
Born in Arkwright, Ontario, 1858; died in Ottawa, Ontario, 1929. Active in Teslin Trail, 1898. An amateur, he was a militia major and correpondent for several U.S. and Canadian newspapers traveling with the Yukon Field Force along the Teslin Trail through British Columbia to Dawson City.

WORGAN, ALFRED DASHWOOD
Active in Vernon by 1891 or earlier, continuing until 1896 when his studio shed and house burned. He moved to Greenwood, 1897, and continued business there for at least one year.

WORLD'S PANORAMA COMPANY
Active in Victoria and the Northwest Coast, 1861.

WREN, J.
Worked in San Francisco prior to 1886, when he was active in Vancouver; partner in Milross & Wren on Cordova Street, next door to McKendry's Boot Store.

ZIMMERMAN, A. K.
Active in Vancouver, 1899-1900.

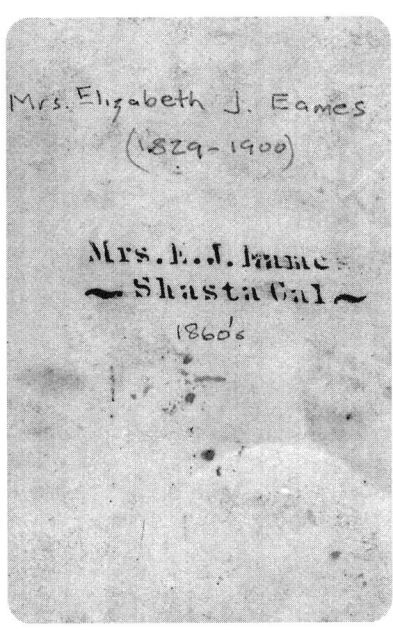

Mrs. Elizabeth J. Eames
(1829-1900)

Mrs. E. J. Eames
~ Shasta Cal ~
1860's

This section was edited by Peter Palmquist, but since the edit, extensive additions have been made. Much of the information contained in this list was derived from compilations published by Peter Palmquist, which are noted in the bibliography and should be referenced for more in-depth study.

A & A LIGHTNING VIEWING COMPANY
Publisher of stereoviews in Los Angeles at 137 South Main Street, 1870s-1920s.

ABBOTT, THEO. (MISS)
Born in California, 1880. Active in Oakland, c. 1899-1900.

ABELL
Studio in Grass Valley on Church Street, c. 1875.

ABELL & PRIEST
Operated in San Francisco, 1889-94, Bancroft's History Building, 723 Market Street; also traveling photographers.

ABELL & WELSH
Traveling photographers, c. 1876; in Sawyer's Bar, 1873-95.

ABELL, FRANK GEORGE
Born in Illinois, 1844. Active in San Francisco, 1862-74; operator with William Shew. Worked in Siskiyou County, 1869-87.

ABELL'S ART GALLERY
Active in Grass Valley, c. 1875, Mill Street near Main.

ABELL'S ART-STUDIO CAR
Traveling photography studio in California, c. 1875.

ACME PHOTOGRAPH STUDIOS
Operated by Mrs. Sarah Fletcher in San Francisco at 914 Market Street, 1881-83.

ADAMS, E. W.
Active in Pacific Grove, c. 1893.

ADAMS, FREDERICK V.
Active in Los Angeles, 1891-96, photographer with F. G. Schumacher; in San Francisco, 1898; with Boye & Habenicht; manager of the Adams Studio, 850 Market, San Francisco, 1900.

ADAMS, LAURA MAY
Active in San Francisco 1899-1902, in her studio in the Flood Building, corner of Powell and Market Streets. Continued work in Berkeley after her marriage to Sidney Armer, 1902-30s.

ADAMS, S. M.
Stereo photographer from Elgin, Illinois; active in San Francisco, 1870s-88.

ADDIS & KOCH
Active in San Francisco, 1865, 425 Montgomery Street; partnership of Robert W. Addis and John Koch.

ADDIS, ALFRED SHEA
Active in Los Angeles, 1875-78; 3 Beaudry Terrace, 1875; Bunker Hill Avenue, between Second and Third, 1878. Purchased Sunbeam Gallery, 1876.

ADDIS, ROBERT W.
Partner in Addis & Koch in San Francisco, 1865, at 425 Montgomery Street.

ADDISON, A. S.
Active in Los Angeles, 1874, studio on Main Street.

AGNER, CHARLES
Active in San Francisco, 1898, 3 Taylor Street; partner in Litchtig & Agner.

AH-SING, FONG
Gallery employee in San Francisco at 429 Montgomery Street, c. 1871.

AHASHI, KAROU
Studio photographer in San Francisco, c. 1910.

AHLMAN, H.
Active in Pasadena, 1900, 46 South Fair Oaks Avenue.

AICHBERG, CHRISTIAN
Active in San Francisco and Santa Cruz, c. 1880; operating the Philadelphia Gallery; 1884-86, in Santa Cruz, Ely Block, Pacific Avenue; and 103 Pacific Avenue, 1887-92.

ALAMEDA PHOTOGRAPH COMPANY
Presumably in Alameda, c. 1895.

ALBRECHT, OLIVER
Born in Mannheim, Germany, January 29, 1876; died in San Francisco, 1944. Professional photographer who did series on the 1906 earthquake, Chinatown and other San Francisco scenes. Also a landscape painter and married to artist Gertrude Partington . Also known as Oliver Albright.

ALDRICH, CLARENCE ULYSSES
Active in Red Bluff, 1910.

ALGER, JAMES
Active in San Francisco, 1871, 311 Montgomery Street; view photographer in James Alger & Company.

ALISKY, CHARLES
Active in San Francisco, 1897-1902, at 914 Market Street.

ALKIRE, A. S.
Active in Riverside, 1883-92.

ALLEN
Partner in Gove & Allen in Sacramento, 1877.

ALLEN & COMPANY
Partnership of Laura T. Allen and Nathaniel Weston in San Francisco, 1887-88, 6 Ellis Street and 1227 Market Street, corner of Stockton and Ellis.

ALLEN & HAY
Partnership of Mrs. Laura T. Allen, Mrs. Mary C. Hay, and her son, George Hay. Active in San Francisco at 342 Kearny Street, 1884-86.

ALLEN, BENNETT G.
Died c. 1882. Active in San Francisco, 1874-82; 523 Kearny Street, 1874-76; 342 Kearny Street, 1877-82. Partner in Wing & Allen.

ALLEN, IDA
Active in Del Norte County, c. 1897; Humboldt County, 1897.

ALLEN, LAURA T.
Active in San Francisco, c. 1874-88, as photographer and manager of Wing & Allen portrait gallery. Her husband, B. G. Allen, was a partner of Simon Wing at 342 Kearny Street. Studio located at 523

Kearny, 1874-76. After the death of her husband, c. 1882, she was a partner in Allen & Hay with Mrs. Mary C. Hay, 1884-86. Partner with Nathaniel Weston, 1887-88, operating as Allen & Company, at 1227 Market Street. She operated Allen's Ferrotype Parlors, 5 Stockton Street, 1887. Also listed as Mrs. Bennett G. Allen.

ALLHANDS, A. J.
Active in Healdsburg, 1878-80.

ALMOND, KATE
Active in Sacramento, c. 1873-80.

ALTA STUDIOS
Studio operated by W. B. Cook in Willows, 1885-95.

ALTPETER & ANDERSON
Active in Redding, 1886-88.

ALTPETER, LOUIS P.
Proprietor of the Redding Photograph Gallery, Market near the Post Office, Redding, 1886-92.

ALVERSON, FRANK
Active in Yreka, 1876.

ALWORTH & PIERCE PHOTOS
Studio in Red Bluff, 1864.

ALWORTH, N. B.
Active in Chico, c. 1864-66.

AMENIYA, R.
Active in San Francisco, c. 1910.

AMERICAN ART STUDIO
Gallery in Pleasanton, c. 1890; in Danville, c. 1895.

AMERICAN VIEW COMPANY
Publisher in Pasadena; issued views of Avalon Bay, San Pedro Bay, Mt. Lowe, southern California; photographer unknown.

AMSDEN
Active in Grass Valley, c. 1896-98.

AMSDEN & DUTKEWICH
Traveling photographers in Trinity, 1894; in the Weaverville area, c. 1895.

AMSDEN, WILLIAM OSCAR
Active in Redding, 1899-1900.

ANAYA, CHARLES
Gallery at 709 Valencia (it is possible that Valencia was a typographical error) Street, San Francisco, 1869-70; at 733 Vallejo Street, San Francisco, 1888-90. Anaya was often called Carlos Anaya.

ANDERSON
Active in Redding, 1886.

ANDERSON & POLLOCK
Active in San Francisco, 1904.

ANDERSON, BARBARA
Active in Suisun, c. 1870.

ANDERSON, E. M.
Gallery at 634 Washington, San Francisco, 1869-70.

ANDERSON, ELIZA
Ambrotypist active in Santa Rosa, 1858-59.

ANDERSON, HUGH
Born in Scotland, c. 1828. Operated in Eureka, Humboldt County, 1858-65; sold studio to Flanders & Tuttle who operated the Eureka Gallery. Anderson reoccupied studio, 1866; rented to Tuttle & Johnson, 1868; to E. Kraft, 1868; to Johnson & Tuttle, 1869-70; to A. P. Flaglor, 1871-72. Anderson operated the Sunbeam Gallery at 649 Clay Street, San Francisco, 1869; in Petaluma at 649 Main Street, c. 1875. Photographer with William Shew, San Francisco, 1876; Mission Gallery at 506 Valencia, c. 1879-85; at 726 San Jose Avenue, 1892-93.

ANDREWS & LANGE
Partnership of Thomas P. Andrews and Oscar V. Lange, active in San Francisco at 109 Montgomery Street, 1893-98.

ANDREWS, E. B.
Traveling photographer in northern California, c. 1880s.

ANDREWS, THOMAS P.
Partner in Andrews & Lange, 109 Montgomery Street, San Francisco, 1893-98.

ANGELUS STUDIO
Active in Los Angeles, 1906.

ANN TING GOCK & COMPANY
Portrait studio in San Francisco at 842 Clay Street, 1895.

ANONYMOUS
Itinerant photographer in Georgetown who was called to the Round Tent, a gambling saloon, to photograph a dead miner. He accidentally caused a fire which quickly spread. The corpse was saved, but most of the business section of town was burned in the fire, July 14, 1852. Georgetown was soon rebuilt on a new site.

ANSLEY, B. S.
Active in San Francisco, 1900-01.

ANTRIM & POWERS
Studio in Red Bluff, 1859. Partnership of B. Jay Antrim and N. B. Powers.

ANTRIM, B. JAY
Born 1818. Operated Excelsior's Daguerreotype Gallery in San Francisco before 1855; daguerreotypist in Honolulu, 1855-56. Active in Red Bluff, 1859; partner in Antrim & Powers.

APPLEGATE, J. W.
Rubber stamp imprint on a carte-de-visite, c. 1885, advertising Tintype Gallery. Only location noted is "Cal." Probably an itinerant photographer.

APPLETON & COMPANY, D. E.
Stereo photographer active in San Francisco.

ARAI
Partner in Komai & Arai at 319 and 331 6th Street, Oakland, 1909.

ARCHER, JOHN W.
Proprietor with C. H. Wescott of the Los Angeles Electric Copying House, "Solar and Bromide prints for the Trade," 314 Buena Vista, opposite the courthouse, east of Temple, Los Angeles, 1896.

ARLINGTON & REED
Partnership in Los Angeles, 1898; possibly J. C. Reed.

ARMER, LAURA ADAMS
Born in San Francisco, 1874; died 1963. Studied painting with Arthur Mathews, 1893. Active in San Francisco as Laura Adams, in the Flood Building, corner of Powell and Market Streets, 1899-1902. Continued photography in Berkeley, 1902-30s, after her marriage to Sidney Armer. Photographed the Hopi and Navaho in Arizona, 1920; produced the first Native American motion picture, *The Mountain Chant*, 1928; with her husband, she illustrated childrens' books, including *Waterless Mountain*, 1931.

ARMSTRONG, CYRUS M.
Active in Los Angeles, 1891-96; in Santa Ana as partner in Hardesty & Armstrong, 1891-94.

ARNEST, JOHN M.
Born in Missouri, 1843. Photographer with Walter H. Cook, San Francisco, 1869-70; continued in photography until 1880 or later.

ARNOLD
Studio at 1526 Park Street, Alameda, c. 1898-99.

ARNOLD, AMELIA
Active in San Francisco, 1896, at Burnett & Slatterly, 448 ½ Valencia Street.

ARNOLD, RICHARD J.
Born 1856; died 1929. Active in Monterey, Santa Barbara and San Luis Obispo, 1880-1929.

ARNOLD, WILLIAM P.
Born in Rhode Island, 1859. Active in San Francisco, 1880.

ARNOLD, WILLIAM T.
Active in Paso Robles, c. 1895.

ARRIOLA, EDWARD F.
Born in Mexico, 1850. Photographer with G. D. Morse, San Francisco, 1869-70; with William Shew, 1898-1900 or later. Operated North Beach Photo Studio, corner of Montgomery and Filbert Streets. Name sometimes spelled Ariola.

ARROWSMITH PHOTO STUDIO
Active in Oakland, 1905-14.

ARROWSMITH, W. H.
Traveling photographer in northern California, 1905-10.

ASBECK, AUGUST
Active in San Francisco at 1140 Market Street, 1893-96.

ASHER, JULIUS
Born in Bavaria, 1847. Photographer with Bayley & Winter, San Francisco, 1869-70. Moved to Sacramento and opened the Opposition Gallery by 1877; at 236 and 244 J Street, c. 1878; gallery at 810 J Street, 1883-90. Asher produced a range of quality images including portraits and views.

ASHLEY, BLANCHE
Gallery in Fort Bragg, c. 1887-88.

ATWATER & GARRISON
Stereo photographers active in San Francisco, operating as National Photo View & Copying Company at 820 California Avenue.

ATWELL, ELIZABETH
Born in Ohio, May 1872. Active in Los Angeles, 1899-1900. Also known as Atwill.

ATWOOD, B. L.
Active in San Leandro on Hayward Avenue, c. 1888.

AUFRECHT, GUSTAV
Photographer with I. W. Taber & Company in San Francisco, 1876.

AUGER, LINA
Accomplished amateur stereographer active in San Francisco.

AUSTIN & COMPANY
Operated the Sun Pearl Gallery in Stockton at 183 Main Street, 1883.

AUSTIN, CLYDE B.
Active in San Francisco, 1903-05.

AUSTIN, JAY
Partner with Charles Ironmonger on Catalina Island, 1900.

AVERY, J. W.
Active in Colusa, 1892.

AYERS, ELIZABETH N.
Operated portrait gallery in Eureka at 515 2nd Street, 1892-1906, formerly owned by J. W. Tollman.

AYRES, MILTON A.
Traveling photographer, 1914.

BABCOCK, CHARLES F.
Partner in Hutchinson & Babcock, 28 Third Street, San Francisco, 1883-84.

BACHMAN, JOHN
Studio in San Francisco at 48 Third, 1863; sold to A.W. Garrett, late 1863.

BACON BROTHERS
Partnership of J. E. and Frank W. Bacon in San Jose, 1884-88, Masonic Hall Building, 58 South First Street. Listed in Napa City, 1885-86, operated by Frank W. and J. Ed. Bacon.

BACON, EDWARD
Associated with Bacon Brothers, J. E. & F. W. Bacon, San Jose, 1884-88. Possibly the same as J. Ed. Bacon.

BACON, FRANK W.
Partner in Bacon Brothers, located at Masonic Hall Building, 58 South First Street in San Jose, 1884-87. Operated Bacon Brothers in Napa City, 1885-86.

BACON, J. ED.
Active in Salinas City, c. 1888-93. Partner in Bacon Brothers, 58 South First Street, San Jose, 1884; with Bacon Brothers, Napa City, 1885-86; photographer with W. W. Wright, San Jose, 1887.

BAGLEY, NEWTON
Photographer at the Walter H. Cook Gallery in San Francisco, 1869-70.

BAGNASCO, PETER
Born in France, 1830. Active in San Francisco, 1880. Possibly same as Policarpo Bagnasco.

BAGNASCO, POLICARPO
Chief photographer for Carleton Watkins, c. 1872-c. 1882; for I. W. Taber in San Francisco, c. 1882-c. 1892.

BAILEY
Active in Bakersfield, dates unknown.

BAILEY & CRAMER
Operated the Boston Heliographic Studio at 1713 Seventh Street, West Oakland, 1878-79.

BAILEY & PICKETT
"Heliographic Artists" at 523 Kearney Street, San Francisco, 1875; Mrs. J. Bailey and John M. Pickett.

BAILEY, A. P.
Operated the Tower Gallery at 244 J Street, Sacramento, 1864; possibly a partner in Briggs & Bailey at 111 J Street, 1864-65. Located at 189 J Street, Sacramento, 1874. Operated the Pacific Coast Photographic Art Gallery at 189 J Street, over Bale's Toy Store, c. 1870; billed as a "Heliographic Artist," c. 1875. Photographer with Joseph W. King, San Francisco, 1876; active in Tulare, 1886. Also spelled Bayley.

BAILEY BROTHERS
Operating in Santa Cruz, 1865.

BAILEY, C. H.
Gallery at 515 Seventh Street, Oakland, 1883-86. Manager of the Photographic Publishing Company, same address, 1888.

BAILEY, E. P. (MISS)
Active in Los Angeles, 1903.

BAILEY, J. (MRS.)
Photographer located at 523 Kearny Street, San Francisco, 1873-77. Partner in Bailey & Pickett with John M. Pickett, 1875.

BAILEY, MORRIS
Daguerreian artist; partner with James Heath, operating as Heath & Bailey in gallery at southeast corner of Clay and Kearny, San Francisco, 1859.

BAIRD
Active in Shasta County, c. 1880.

BAKER & CATHCART
View photographers active in San Francisco, 1886-87, 1073 ½ Market Street; 1037 Market Street, 1888. Partnership of Walter T. Baker and Walter Cathcart.

BAKER & CUSHMAN
Partnership of W. T. Baker and William H. Cushman, 8 Sixth Street, San Francisco, 1888.

BAKER, CHARLES LEVERETT
Active in Chico, 1870-92.

BAKER, CHARLES S.
Born in Ohio, 1842. Active in Oroville, 1880.

BAKER, EDWARD W.
Active in Placerville, c. 1875-76; Red Bluff, 1878. Also known as C. W. Baker.

BAKER, ELLIS WILLIAM
Active in Tehama, 1878-1910; in Red Bluff on Oak Street, 1880; San Jose, 1884; Placerville, 1884-86; Sutter Creek and Placerville, 1886; Bakersfield, 1887; Angel's Camp, 1895; Placerville, 1901, shared space with B. F. Strong; Angels Camp. 1902.

BAKER, F. N.
Active in Dunsmuir, 1907.

BAKER, G. W.
Traveling photographer, 1877-80.

BAKER, ISAAC WALLACE
Born in Beverly, Massachusetts, 1810; died in Sumatra, date unknown. Settled in California, 1853. Learned the daguerreian art from Perez M. Batchelder who employed him as a traveling photographer. Worked in Murphy's Camp, Vallecita and Sonora, recording mining scenes.

BAKER, JAMES H.
Bought out the Napa City parlor of L. H. Stockley, April 1887. Moved to a new gallery, 1889, partner with George P. Clark.

BAKER, JESSE H.
Pasadena stereo publisher.

BAKER, JOHN WILLIAM
Active in Plumas County, 1890; gallery at 18 Third Street, San Francisco, 1895; 1144 Market Street, 1896-98; active through 1904 or later.

BAKER, MINEOLA
Active in Exeter Township, Tulare County, c. 1900.

BAKER, S. F.
Active in Red Bluff, 1857-58; Shasta, 1857-60.

BAKER, WALTER T.
View photographer, partner in Baker & Cathcart, 1073 ½ Market Street, San Francisco, 1886-87; operating at 1037 Market Street, 1888. Also partner in Baker & Cushman, 1888, at 8 Sixth Street.

BALDWIN & BETANCUE
Operated in the Drennan Building, San Francisco, c. 1865. Possibly Joseph P. Betancue

BALDWIN & CLEMENTS
Partnership operating in Oroville; possibly Charles C. Clements.

BALDWIN, JOHN E. D.
Born in Pennsylvania, 1842. In California by 1874. Active in Santa Cruz, next to Dr. J. J. Dryer's Dental Rooms, through 1880. Opened gallery in Stockton at 183 Main Street; sold it to M. Monaco, 1883. Moved to Sacramento, operating gallery at 421 J Street at least through 1888. Also operated as a traveling photographer, 1884-88.

BALDWIN PHOTO COMPANY
Studio in Pasadena, 1895-1900, at 261 North Fair Oaks Avenue.

BALFREY
Active in Sawyer's Bar, 1900.

BALL, GEORGE
Stereographer and publisher active in Alameda at 1603 Oak Street.

BALLOW, ROY F.
Active in Manton, 1915.

BALOUN, EDMUND
Active in San Francisco, 1898-1901.

BANBROCK, WILLIAM E.
Born in Bath, California. Moved to Nevada where he worked in a Silver City hotel at age eleven. Worked for Peterson & Snyder in Carson City at age seventeen, and learned photography. Moved to Placer County, 1883, and went into business as a traveling photographer. Took mining views, locating first at Iowa Hill, then in Forest Hill,

c. 1895. He followed a fixed route through Placer and Nevada Counties. Later had a permanent studio in Auburn, specializing in view photography. Photographed Lake Tahoe, Donner Lake, the Winter Carnival at Truckee and the High Sierras.

BARBOUR (MRS.)
Photographer in Oroville, 1900-12.

BARNES, JOHN
Born in Maine, 1817. Active in San Francisco, 1880.

BARNETT, ED. Z.
Active in Modesto, 1888.

BARNEY, LEWIS N.
Born in New York, 1834. Active in Quincy, 1870-76. Photographic printer with R. A. Marden, San Francisco, 1876.

BARNEY, MARY S.
Born in Illinois, 1860. Active in Colfax, 1880.

BARNKISEL, H.
Active in Oleta, 1880.

BARTLEY & FELL'S
Partnership of F. H. Bartley and A. W. Fell, stereo photographers active in Salinas City, 1883-87.

BARTLEY, F. H.
Active in Salinas City, 1883-87. Partner in Bartley & Fells.

BASS, THOMAS
Active in Shasta, 1854, at the Eagle Hotel; Studio over Ross & McLean's store, Union (Arcata); in Brett's Building, Eureka, 1856.

BATCHELDER, B. P. (MRS.)
Operated portrait gallery at 345 ½ El Dorado Street, Stockton, after the death of her husband, Benjamin Pierce Batchelder, 1891.

BATCHELDER, BENJAMIN PIERCE
Born 1826; died 1850. Operated a daguerreian wagon in the Gold Country with his brother, Perez Mann Batchelder. Operated the Photographic Art Palace at 183 El Dorado Street, Stockton, 1874-91.

BATCHELDER, PEREZ MANN
Born in Boston, Massachusetts, 1818; died in Boston, Massachusetts, 1867. Active in Boston, c. 1844-50; in California by 1851; operated a daguerreian wagon on Washington Street, Sonora, 1852, which he sold to Rulofson & Cameron in 1853. While operating studios in Australia, he kept an ownership interest in several traveling daguerreotype wagons in the Gold Country which were operated by his brother, Benjamin Pierce Batchelder, and Isaac Wallace Baker, and others. Communities served include Stockton, Vallecita, Murphys Camp and Mokelumne Hill. Another brother working as a photographer was Nathaniel Batchelder. Returned to Boston, 1860, and operated with James Wallace Black the firm of Black & Batchelder, 173 Washington Street.

BATEMAN & COMPANY, GUY L.
Active in Red Bluff, 1891.

BAUMGARDT PUBLISHING COMPANY
Stereograph company in Los Angeles.

BAWDEN, J.
Stereographer in Sutter Creek.

BAXTER & BLANK
Active at 832 Market Street, San Francisco, 1880.

BAYLEY & CRAMER
Active in Plumas County, 1862-68; operated the Fine Art Gallery, next to Maquire's Opera House, San Francisco, c. 1864. Charles L. Cramer.

BAYLEY & CUINTER
Stereographer in San Francisco, 1860s-80s.

BAYLEY & O'HARA
Partnership of M. Bayley and J. D. O'Hara, operating at 622 Kearny Street, San Francisco, c. 1865.

BAYLEY, MERRILL F.
Born in Vermont, 1844. Gallery at 622 Kearny, northeast corner of Kearny and Commercial, San Francisco, 1863-64; with J. D. O'Hara at 622 Kearny Street, c. 1865-68, operating as Bayley & O'Hara; working alone at 34 Third Street, 1874. Also spelled Bailey.

BAYLEY, N. J.
Partner with W. F. Bayley, 526 Montgomery Street, San Francisco, 1874.

BAYLEY, W. F.
Partner with N. J. Bayley, 526 Montgomery Street, San Francisco, 1874; at 1102 Stockton, 1875.

BAYLEY, WILBUR FISK
Photographic artist in San Francisco, 1865; partner with Robert Winter, 618-620 Washington, 1869-70; continued active, 1876-77. Possibly associated with William F. Bayley, below.

BAYLEY, WILLIAM F.
Partner with Charles L. Cramer, 618 Washington, San Francisco, 1865-68 or later. Operated as Bayley & Cramer in West Oakland, 1877. Also spelled Bailey.

BAYLEY'S PHOTOGRAPH GALLERY
Studio in San Francisco, c. 1865, at 622 Kearney.

BAYLIS, G. E. (MRS.)
Active in Lower Lake, 1884-85.

BEAL, CHARLES H.
Gallery at 125 ½ South Spring Street in Los Angeles, 1893-99.

BEALS & WATERS
Gallery at 113 J Street, Sacramento, 1868; H. S. Beals.

BEALS, HENRY SHERMAN
Born in New York, 1822 (1880 census), or born in Connecticut, 1824 (1870 census). Established gallery at 113 J Street, Sacramento, 1867-68; partner in Beals & Waters, 1868; branch gallery at 303 Gold Hill, Nevada, 1867. Sacramento gallery located at 111 J Street, Sacramento, 1870; moved to the upstairs at 415 J Street, c. 1883; remained active in Sacramento at least through 1888. He may be the daguerreotypist Henry S. Beals of New York City, 1854-55, and may be related to the New York City daguerreotypist, A. J. Beals of 1854-55, who had a gallery in Virginia City, Nevada, c. 1878-80.

BEAR PHOTO COMPANY
Traveling photographers, 1918.

BEARD, E. W. (MRS.)
Active in San Rafael, 1888.

BEARDEN, A. J.
Born in South Carolina, 1831. In California by 1868. Active in Forest City, 1875; Grass Valley, 1880.

BEARDEN'S PHOTOGRAPHIC GALLERY
Studio at 66 Broad Street, Nevada City, c. 1875 or earlier.

BEATTY
Operated gallery on Church Street in Grass Valley, c. 1896-1900.

BEATTY & MASON
Active in Marysville, 1895.

BEATTY, CORA (MRS.)
Active in San Francisco, 1898-1901.

BECK, A. H.
Operated the Ambrotype Gallery in Mokelumne Hill on Main Street, next to Singer Hall, late 1850s-65.

BECK, ANNA
Active in Santa Cruz, 1893.

BECKETT, CHARLES W.
Photographer with F. G. Schumacher, Los Angeles, 1896.

BECKWITH, CHARLES D.
Active in Crescent City, 1858; Yreka, 1860-61.

BEEMAN, HENRY
Born in Prussia, 1851. Active in Visalia, 1870.

BEHRENDTS, RICHARD
Publisher of stereoviews in San Francisco; used Reilly negatives.

BEHRMAN, MARTIN
Amateur who made copies of early daguerreotype panoramas of San Francisco, c. 1910.

BELCHER, ROBERT
Stereographer, possibly an amateur, active in San Francisco.

BELL, GEORGE
Partner in Dickinson & Bell, traveling artists. See partnership listing.

BELL, JOHN
Amateur stereographer active in San Jose.

BELL, LEANDER
Active in Downey, 1883; Santa Ana, 1884.

BELL, WILLIAM A.
Born in Maine, 1841. Active in Hollister, 1877-81 or later; in Santa Cruz, 1882; produced stereoviews of these areas.

BELLE-OUDRY, EMMA
Born in Pennsylvania. Partner with son, Edward Henry Belle-Oudry operating gallery in Oakland, 1898-1911, in the Abrahamson Building.

BELLE-OUDRY, EDWARD HENRY
Partner with his mother, Emma, in the Abrahamson Building, Oakland, 1898-1911.

BENEDICT
Partner in Tuttle & Benedict, San Francisco, 1873; W. N. Tuttle.

BENNETT, R. (MRS.)
Active in Washington (Plumas County), 1890-93.

BENNETT. A. G.
Active in Napa City, 1892.

BENSON, Z.
Active in Arbuckle, 1885-95.

BEPP, KIROKU
Commercial photographer in San Francisco located at 426 Kearny Street, 1900-41; also listed at 1511 Fillmore Street, 1910.

BEQUETTE, BESSIE L.
Born in California, April 1883. Active in Visalia, c. 1900.

BERGEN, EDGAR
Professional ventriloquist, avid stereo photographer, active in Los Angeles; wrote "What Makes Good Stereo " published in *Realist* manual.

BERGERON, JAY PIERRE
Active in Chico, 1898-1902.

BERLIN PORTRAIT COMPANY
Studio in Los Angeles at 232 North Main, 1893.

BERTELSEN, BEATRICE
Born in California, April 1879. Active in San Francisco, 1899-1900.

BERTRAND, JOSEPH T.
Operated the Plaza Gallery in Los Angeles at 413 North Main Street, 1888-89; associated with W. F. Stein, 1890; known as Bertrand & Company, 205 ½ South Main, 1892-95. View and portrait photographer.

BEST, C.
Associated with H. C. Best in a gallery in the Ribbler Building, St. Helena, 1889.

BEST, H. C.
Partner with C. Best, gallery located in the Ribbler Building, St. Helena, 1889.

BEST, JENNIE C.
Amateur stereo photographer, active in Los Angeles; probably related to John and Robert Best.

BEST, JOHN P.
Active in Los Angeles, 1893-1904. Studio at 115 ½ North Main, 1893-94; partner with Robert Best in Best & Company, 505 ½ South Spring, Los Angeles, 1895-98; 536 South Broadway, 1904.

BEST, RAYMOND
Made stereoviews of the Best family and their inlaws; amateur active in Los Angeles, c. 1895.

BEST, ROBERT
Active in Los Angeles, 1895-1904. Located at 505 ½ South Spring, Los Angeles, 1895-96, partner with John Best in Best & Company. Studio at 536 South Broadway, 1904.

BETANCUE, JOSEPH PERCY
Studio at 402 Kearny Street, San Francisco, 1880; in Oakland, c. 1880-86; studio at 1209 Broadway, Oakland, by 1888. Possibly a partner in Baldwin & Betancue, San Francisco, c. 1865; possibly a partner with Button, proprietors of the Flying Studio in Astoria, Oregon, 1870s.

BETTERSLY, G. S.
Gallery on Commercial Street in Auburn, 1875.

BEUTHEL, W.
Amateur stereo photographer in Fresno, 1925.

BIANCHI
Partner in Vitalini & Bianchi, 233 Montgomery Street, San Francisco, 1892-99.

BICKFORD, E. L.
Amateur stereo photographer in Napa, 1913.

BICKNELL, GEORGE A.
Photojournalist in Santa Barbara and the West, c. 1890-1910. Birth surname was Yee.

BIERSTADT, CHARLES
Stereoview photographer from New Bedford, Massachusetts, who photographed Yosemite and other northern California scenes in the 1860s, many of which images were published under the imprint of the Bierstadt Brothers. Brother of the famous Hudson River School painter Albert Bierstadt who painted monumental western landscapes, many in California.

BIJOU STUDIO
Gallery in Los Angeles, 1896, 221 ½ South Spring, operated by Chester W. Burdick. Also known as Stanton Studio.

BILLINGTON, JOHN R.
Active in San Francisco, 1896-1904.

BILLINGTON, WILLIAM C.
View photographer operating the Sutro Heights Gallery in San Francisco, 1895-1900s; partner with Thomson, 1895, operating as Thomson & Billington. Perhaps related to John R. Billington

BING, JOSEPH W.
Active in Woodland, c. 1870.

BIRD & COOK
Operated studios in Placerville, Willows and Auburn, 1892-93; William Blodgett Cook and J. W. Bird.

BIRD & EILERMAN
Active in Willows, c. 1895; J. W. Bird.

BIRD, J. W.
Active in Placerville, 1891. Partner in Bird & Cook, Placerville, Willows and Auburn, 1892-93; Bird & Eilerman, Willows, c. 1895. Listed in Sacramento, 1895.

BISBEE, J. A.
Active in San Francisco, 1885-95.

BISBEE, J. A.
Gallery at 21 West First Street, Los Angeles, 1886-89; operated as Nye & Bisbee, 1886-87.

BISBEE, MARY L.
Active in Berkeley 1892-1904, at 2151 Center Street.

BLACK, FLORENCE L.
Born in California, January 1860. Retoucher in Los Angeles, 1897; photographer in San Francisco, c. 1900.

BLAIR, HOSEA
Active San Francisco, 1895-1900 or later; partner with Frances L. Matson at 6 Turk Street, 1895, operating as Matson & Blair.

BLAISDELL, SAMUEL STILLMAN
Born in Virginia, c. 1840. Active in Chico, 1870; "Heliographic Artist" on Mill Street in Grass Valley, 1871-72; Oakland, c. 1876-80.

BLAKESLY, H. H.
Partner of E. R. Healy in the Elite Studio, St. Helena, c. 1890-93. Manager of A. K. Varney studio, Placerville, 1899.

BLANCHARD & KONOLD
Active in Los Angeles, 1902, at 513 North Main and 213 ½ North Spring; James B. Blanchard.

BLANCHARD, GILBERT E.
Photographer at J. B. Blanchard's studio, Los Angeles, 1895-96.

BLANCHARD, JAMES B.
Active in Los Angeles, 1890-1902. Operated as J. B. Blanchard & Company, 569 North Main, 1890; 513 North Main, 1892-96, 1898, 1902; also listed at 715 North Main Street, 1895; also at 515 North Main Street, 1896. At 452 South Spring and 513 North Main, 1897; partner in Blanchard & Konold, 513 North Main and 213 ½ North Spring, 1902. Operated as Plaza Gallery or Galeria de la Plaza, 1896.

BLANK
Partner in Baxter & Blank, 832 Market Street, San Francisco, 1880.

BLAUERT, BERTHOLD
Studio at 339 ½ Hayes Street, San Francisco, 1898-1900 or later.

BLEDSOE, J. W.
Active in Traver, 1886-88 or later.

BLIX, AUGUST
Born in Sweden, c. 1823. Active in Los Angeles, 1878-84 or later. Worked at Wolfenstein's on Hayes Street, 1878; for Payne, Staunton & Company's Elite Gallery, 1881-84.

BLOME, J. H.
Studio at 72 South Second Street, San Jose, c. 1892. Gallery at the corner of H and Seventh, San Diego, 1888-90.

BLOOMBERG, ROBERT
Amateur stereo photographer, active in Forest Knolls.

BLOOME, J. H.
Active in San Diego, 1880-88. Possibly the same as J. H. Blome.

BLOSSER, J. A.
Traveling photographer, 1910.

BLUM, ROBERT F.
Born in Humboldt County, February 27, 1857; died in San Francisco, September 8, 1880. Apprenticed to A. P. Flaglor and took over his studio in Ferndale, c. 1874; also active in Eureka and Rohnerville. Employed at galleries in Sacramento and at Taber's studio in San Francisco, 1877-80.

BLUMANN, SIGISMUND
Born in New York, 1872; died in 1956. Photographed San Francisco earthquake, 1906.

BOBSON
Operated as Keefer & Bobson in Downieville, 1852.

BOELTE, MAX
Active in Los Angeles, 1896.

BOISVERT
Active in Willows, 1914-30.

BOLTON & STRONG
Photo lithographers in San Francisco, 1892-94.

BON TON (BOYETTE)
Studio located at 452 South Spring Street, Los Angeles, c. 1895.

BON-TON PHOTO COMPANY
Traveling photographers, 1894.

BONINE, ELIAS A.
Born Lancaster, Pennsylvania, 1843. Arrived in California, 1876. "Tent Photographer" active in southern California and based in Pasadena, c. 1880s.

BONNELL, R. A.
Stereo photographer active in Hobart Mills; possibly an amateur.

BONNINGTON, JOSIE
Colorist for James H. Crockwell in Bishop's Creek, c. 1887.

BOOTHE, LILLIE M. (MRS.)
Partner with Mrs. A. M. Hicks in Los Angeles, operating as Hicks and Boothe, 911 South Hill, 1899.

BORDWELL
Active in Riverside.

BOSTON PHOTOGRAPH COMPANY
Studio in Etna, c. 1894.

BOSTON PHOTOGRAPHIC GALLERY
Operated by B. F. Howland in Marysville, 1877-78.

BOSTON RAILROAD PHOTO CAR
Traveling photographers, 1894-95; Pacific Coast address was Sacramento, California, c. 1895.

BOSWORTH, ALBERT H.
Born 1869; died in Fall River Mills, 1951. Stereo photographer active in Fall River Mills, 1890-1910.

BOSWORTH, FRANCIS EUGENE
Gallery at 867 Fifth Street, San Diego, 1888; in Ft. Jones, 1890-93; Etna Mills, 1893.

BOSWORTH, ROSALYS JOSEPHINE (MRS.)
Photographer in Fall River Mills, 1904-51.

BOUQUET, GEORGE F.
Talented amateur who made stereoviews of San Francisco earthquake and fire, 1906.

BOWEN, C. DENION
Operated the Eureka Gallery in San Jose, c. 1880-89, at 58 South First Street.

BOWEN, C. DENION (MRS.)
Active in San Jose, 1880-89, co-owner of Eureka Gallery with husband C. Denion Bowen, 58 South First Street. Also listed as Mrs. C. E. and Mrs. J. C.

BOWEN, JULIE
Active in San Jose at 214 South Third Street, 1889. Also known as Mrs. John C. Bowen.

BOWERS, J.
Active in White Oak, 1863.

BOWLIN, NELLIE
Retoucher for C. J. Coules in Los Angeles, 1900-02; photographer at the portrait gallery of Mitchell & Frizell, 1903.

BOWMAN, E. L.
Active Santa Ana at 105 and 111 East Fourth Street, 1895-98.

BOYD, THOMAS HENRY
Active in San Francisco; photographer with George Daniels Morse, 1874; partner with I. W. Taber, 22 Montgomery Street, 1876-78 or later. Also operated as a traveling photographer, 1872-78.

BOYDSTON, D. S.
Active in Volcano, 1867-80; photographer and dentist.

BOYE, OTTO H.
Active in San Francisco, 1896-1900+; partner in Boye & Habenicht with George Habenicht, 1026 Market Street.

BOYER, M. V.
Active in San Francisco at 703 Stockton Street, 1896.

BOYER, W. P.
Active in Lassen, 1914.

BOYNTON, MAGGIE
Born in Maine, January 1872. Active in Palo Alto with J. C. Franklin, 1899-1900.

BOYSEN & STRUCKMANN
Active in Bodie, c. 1880.

BOYSEN, IWER
Established a gallery in Colusa prior to the fire of 1883 when he sustained damages valued at $1,500. Continued active in Colusa through 1903. Also operated in Nevada City. Also spelled Iver.

BRADLEY & RULOFSON
Major studio and successor of Vance's Gallery, the studio of Robert Vance and Leander Weed. Partnership of Henry W. Bradley and William Henry Rulofson, San Francisco, 1863-89. Located at 429 Montgomery Street, 1863-83; 14 Dupont Street, c. 1883-89. Also operated as traveling photographers. See Henry W. Bradley.

BRADLEY, A. S.
Active in Martinez, c. 1890.

BRADLEY, ALFRED OWEN
Active in Chico, 1882; operating the El Dorado Gallery in Georgetown, 1884; Napa City, 1884, with S. R. Dickey.

BRADLEY, HENRY W.
Born in Wilmington, North Carolina, 1813; died in Alameda, March 30, 1900. Learned daguerreotyping in New Orleans. Arrived in California, 1850. Began operating a daguerreian supply business in San Francisco at 271 Montgomery Street, then at 197 Clay Street where he also operated the National Daguerreian Gallery; branch studio at 67-68 J Street, Sacramento. San Francisco gallery moved to 622 Clay Street, 1861-63. Formed a partnership with W. H. Rulofson, purchasing Vance's old gallery from C. L. Weed, at 429 Montgomery Street, 1863. Rulofson ran the gallery, developing a highly successful business. After Rulofson's death, the firm continued as Bradley & Rulofson, but went bankrupt, 1877. Captain John H. Dall had succeeded Rulofson and was chief among Bradley's creditors.

BRANIN, R. C.
Active in Dutch Flat, 1875, 1880; operated New Art Gallery, next door to Good Templar's Hall, Visalia, 1878. Also spelled Brannan.

BRANT, EUGENE
"Heliographic Artist" in Santa Barbara, 1880.

BRATT, HENRY
Died 1915. Stereo photographer from Akron, New York. Opened gallery in San Francisco, 1886; lost everything in earthquake and fire, 1906. May be the same as James Henry Bratt of Lorillard & Bratt.

BRAYTON, JAMES G.
Born in Massachusetts, 1822. Photographic artist in Napa City, 1867, on Main Street; on Second Street, 1878-88. Alexander Fox was living in his household, 1870. Produced stereoviews and portraits. Name may also be John Gray Brayton.

BRAZELTON & MILBURN
Partnership operating in Sisson, 1890; Frank Karl Milburn.

BREMLER, ADOLPH
Active in San Francisco, 1900-01.

BRESLOW, HUGH JOSEPH
Active in Etna, 1894.

BREWER, HELEN L.
Born in Washington, D.C., October 1867. Active in Santa Monica, 1899-1900.

BREWSTER, JOHN CALVIN
Active in San Buenaventura and Avalon, 1878-80. Address on Oak Street, "A few doors South of Post Office." Active in Ventura, 1898-1900. Possibly in Ventura and Santa Paula, c. 1890. See Nevada.

BRIAN, HENRY
Partner of Harry Kies, operating as Kies & Brian in Placerville, 1887, successors to E. W. Baker.

BRICKEY, E. M.
Active in Anaheim, 1896-1909. Also spelled Bricker or Brickley.

BRIGANDI, PHILIP
Stereo photographer in Los Angeles at 1626 North Hobart Boulevard.

BRIGGS & BAILEY
111 J Street, Sacramento, 1864-65; William Briggs and possibly A. P. Bailey.

BRIGGS, E. T.
Active in Wilmington, 1883-84.

BRIGGS, THOMAS
Active in Lompoc, 1888.

BRIGGS, WILLIAM
Gallery at 111 J Street, Sacramento, 1863-65; partner in Briggs & Bailey, 1864-65, possibly with A. P. Bailey

BRIGMAN, ANNIE WARDROPE
Born in Hawaii, December 3, 1869. Fine art photographer in Oakland, 1894-1930. Married Martin Brigman, c. 1894, and separated in 1910. Her photographs were widely published and featured with her articles in *Camera Work*, 1909, and *Camera Craft*, 1905, among many others. Her work appeared in numerous gallery shows and exhibits including Corcoran Gallery, Washington, D.C., Carnegie Institute, Pittsburg, and in Hamburg, Germany. Also known as Miss Annie W. Nott, Mrs. Martin Brigman, Mrs. Annie W. Brigman.
   Anne Brigman, *Songs of a Pagan*, The Caxton Printers, Ltd., 1949
   Therese Thau Heyman, *Anne Brigman: Pictorial Photographer/Pagan/Member of the Photo-Secession*, Oakland Museum, Oakland, California, 1974.

BRINCE, H.
Active in Susanville, c. 1877-80. Brince's rural studio was used to pho-

tograph emigrants traveling the Lassen Trail.

BRINCKMAN
Produced enamelled cards in California, c. 1868.

BRIND, DAISY
Born in Utah, July 1879. Active in San Francisco, c. 1900-01, possibly associated with Brind & Brind, 984 Sutter Street.

BRINKERHOFF, AENEAS EVELYN
Active in Chico, 1874-76. Also known as E. A. Brinkerhoff.

BRITT, EMIL
Son of Peter Britt. Apprenticed to Bradley and Rulofson, 1882. See Oregon.

BRITT, PETER
Traveling from Jacksonville, Oregon, photographed Mount Shasta and other northern California scenes, 1860-70s. See Oregon.

BROCK, JOHN ALLAN.
With Brock & Company, 431 ½ South Spring, Los Angeles, 1896. Listed as photographer, 1899. See British Columbia.

BRODECK & COMPANY
Studio in San Francisco, 640 Market Street, 1876; Henry H. Brodeck.

BRODECK & SCHRODER
Partnership of Henry H. Brodeck and E. Schroder on Santa Clara Street, San Jose, 1871.

BRODECK, HENRY H.
Born in England, 1848. Photographer at Bayley & Winter, San Francisco, 1869-70. Partner in Brodeck & Schroder, Santa Clara Street, San Jose, 1871. Associated with Brodeck & Company at 640 Market Street, San Francisco, 1876. Moved to Walla Walla, Washington, c. 1880.

BRODTBECK, MATILDA A.
Born in Illinois, May 1852. Active in Los Angeles, c. 1899-1900.

BROOKLYN GALLERY
Studio of Charles H. Walker of Brooklyn, Contra Costa County, c. 1880.

BROOKS, HENRY WILLIAM
Active in Chico, dates unknown.

BROOKS, THOMAS G.
Active in Shasta, 1874-75; partner with Dr. W. P. Cool.

BROOKS, THOMAS G. & DR. W. P. COOL
Partnership operating in Shasta, 1874-75.

BROWN & EDWARDS
Active in Modesto, c. 1878-80, corner of I and Front, opposite the Ross House; William Brown and J. E. Edwards.

BROWN & OTTO
Operated the Third Street Gallery at 28 Third Street, San Francisco, 1871-72.

BROWN, ARTHUR T.
Active in San Francisco, 1898-1900, 606 Kearny Street, operating Brown's Photograph Gallery with Thomas A. and Miss Mary or May Brown.

BROWN, DR. D. P.
Active in Marysville, 1851.

BROWN, ELIZABETH
Photographer in Yuba City, 1909-10.

BROWN, IGNACIO
Born in California, 1851. Active in Bath, 1870, and probably associated with photographer James Jacobs, as they resided in the same house.

BROWN, J. M.
Active in Oakland, 1878-83; operated the Pacific Photograph Gallery, Market Street Station, 1883.

BROWN, JEANNA
Active in Coronado, c. 1900.

BROWN, JOSEPH H.
Associated with W. McClellan & Son in Los Angeles, 1896.

BROWN, MARY F. (MISS)
Active in San Francisco, 1898-1904; photographer at Brown's Photograph Gallery, 606 Kearny Street, accociated with Thomas A. and Arthur T. Brown. Also known as May Brown.

BROWN, SADIE O.
Clerk for Hector W. Vaughan, San Francisco, 1876. Partner with Max Karras in Karras & Brown, proprietors of Vaughan's Gallery, 18 Third Street, San Francisco, 1880-88 or later.

BROWN, THOMAS A.
Active in San Francisco, 1873-95 or later, at 606 Kearny Street; associated with Arthur T. Brown and Miss Mary Brown.

BROWN, WILLIAM
Born in Indiana, 1838 (1880 census shows Indiana as birthplace and County History states Iowa.); died September 16, 1893. Lived in Missouri before crossing the plains in a prairie schooner drawn by oxen. Arrived in California, 1859, and worked in Stanislaus County as stockman. Took up photography, becoming pioneer photographer of Modesto; opened gallery on Front Street, 1871. Partner with J. E. Edwards, 1878-80, operating as Brown & Edwards.

BROWNELL
Active in Ventura, 1898.

BROWNELL
Partner in Tuttle & Brownell, corner of Main and Centre Streets, Eureka, c. 1865; Kidd's Block on Main Street, c. 1869.

BROWNLEE, FRANCES C.
Active in San Francisco 1892-1911, with husband Jesse Clark Brownlee at 1229 Market Street. Gallery was later moved to 334 Church Street. Also known as Mrs. F. C. Brownlee, Mrs. J. C. Brownlee.

BROWNLEE, JESSE CLARK
Active in San Francisco 1892-1911, with wife Frances C., at 1229 Market Street. Gallery was later moved to 334 Church Street.

BRUCE, FRANK D.
Active Los Angeles, San Gabriel Township, 1880.

BRUGUIERE, FRANCIS JOSEPH
Born in San Francisco, October 16, 1879; died in London, England, 1945. Studied photography in New York. Became a member of the Photo-Secession before returning to San Francisco where he operated a portrait studio, 1906-19; produced beautiful hand tinted silver prints; moved to New York, 1919; then to London, 1928; member of the German Secession Group

BRUNDAGE, M. J.
Born in Canada, 1853. Photographer with J. R. Hodson in Santa Cruz, 1880.

BRUNNER, LOUISE E.
Active in San Francisco, c. 1895-1910.

BRUSH, J. A.
Operated at the corner of Woodward and Larned Streets, Los Angeles, 1870.

BRUSH, W. L.
Studio at 418 Downey Avenue, East Los Angeles, 1895.

BRYAN, DELZIE
Photographer in Marysville, 1915.

BRYAN, JOHN M.
Possibly a partner in May & Bryan, San Francisco, 1857; daguerreian saloon at 114 Kearny Street, 1859; 611 Clay Street, 1862-67.

BRYAN, W. B.
Stereo photographer active in Pasadena.

BRYANT & JOHNSTON
Active Sacramento, c. 1862. May be Bryan.

BRYANT, CHARLES C.
Active in Crescent City, 1857.

BRYANT, EMMA D.
Active in San Francisco, 1894.

BRYANT, MARTHA
Born in Indiana, January 1842. Active in Los Angeles, c. 1900.

BUCK, C. A.
Born in Michigan. Daguerreian artist active in Columbia on State Street near Broadway, 1854-56 or later; advertised mountain scenery, mining scenes, houses and portraits.

BUDDEN, GEORGE W. H.
Active in Weaverville, 1868-83.

BUEHMAN, HENRY
Born in Bremen, Germany, May 14, 1851; died December 20, 1912. Active in San Francisco, 1868; studio in Visalia, 1869. Traveling photographer in western states, early 1870s. Settled in New Mexico by 1874.

BUND, FONG
Active in Sacramento, c. 1900.

BURDICK, CHESTER W.
Active in Los Angeles, 1888-96. Partner in Stanton & Burdick, 1888-90, at 119-129 North Main; Burdick & Company at 221 ½ South Spring, 1892-93; Burdick & Swisher (or Swisher & Burdick), same address, 1894, 1896; listed alone, 1895, 1897-1906. Partner in Stanton Studio, also listed as Bijou Studio, 221 ½ South Spring, 1896.

BURGE, J. C.
Operated studio in Lakeport on Main Street, 1875-80; possibly a partner Everett & Burge, College City, 1881.

BURGER, JAMES S.
Active in Red Bluff, 1876.

BURGESS & CANN
Dell Cann and possibly Charles F. Burgess in Yreka, c. 1889.

BURGESS, ANDREW
Operator with James Wise in San Francisco, 1865.

BURGESS, CHARLES F.
Photographic copyist, 727 Clay Street, San Francisco, 1865; in San Diego on Sixth Street, 1882-83; gallery on Fifth Street, Colusa, 1878-89; also in Yreka, 1878-89; possibly a partner in Burgess & Cann, c. 1889. Gallery at 911 Broadway, Oakland, 1886.

BURGESS, GEORGE H.
Retoucher and engraver in San Francisco, 1865.

BURGESS PHOTO STUDIO
Operated in Red Bluff, 1862-66.

BURKHARDT, MAX
Gallery in San Francisco at 545 Washington, 1876-87; produced oil paintings and photographic views.

BURNETT & ERCANBRACK
Active in Watsonville, 1870; Castroville, 1874; operated the Pajora Art Gallery, 1875.

BURNETT & SCHACH
San Francisco at 337 Hayes, 1887-89 or later; Franklin W. Burnett.

BURNETT & SLATTERY
Active in San Francisco at northwest corner of Sixteenth and Valencia or 448 ½ Valencia, 1885-96. Partnership of Franklin W. Burnett and the Slattery brothers.

BURNETT, FRANKLIN W.
Born in California, 1860. Active San Francisco, 1880-1904 or later; partner in Burnett & Slattery, 1885-96; a second parlor at 337 Hayes in partnership with Schach, 1887-89 or later.

BURNETT, GEORGE S.
Photographer with J. Mendelssohn in San Francisco, 1900-01. Also spelled Mendelsohn.

BURNETT'S ART GALLERY
Operating in Santa Cruz, 1862.

BURNHAM, MERCEDES
Active in San Francisco, 1900.

BURNS, EMILY E.
Active in Oakland, 1898.

BURRIS, MATHEW
Active in Ukiah City, 1865.

BURT, L. S. (MRS.)
Owner of gallery in Fresno, c. 1891-92; possibly the wife of photographer T. W. Burt.

BUSH, E. E.
Active in Modoc County.

BUSH, HENRY
Born in Germany, 1830, or born in New Hampshire, 1832 (1860 census). Took up the daguerreian art, c. 1856. Studio at 219 Washington, San Francisco, 1859; operated Pacific Art Gallery, Sheil's Block, 9 Post Street, 1865-70; at the junction of Market and Kearny, 1871; 659 Clay Street, 1878-82.

BUSH, JAMES LAFAYETTE
Active in Alturas and Etna, 1888-1903.

BUSHNELL, FREDERICK H.
Born in Cincinnati, Ohio, 1861. Arrived in California in 1889. Active in San Francisco at 1510 Market, 898-1900+; at Bushnell Photo Company, 1904-16 or later. Branch galleries in Oakland, San Jose and Sacramento. Outstanding portrait studio.

BUSHNELL, G. R.
Accomplished amateur stereo photographer active in Santa Cruz.

BUSHNELL PHOTO
Located on 6th Street, Los Angeles, 1904-86 or later.

BUSHNELL PHOTO COMPANY
Operated by Frederick H. Bushnell in San Francisco, at 1510 Market, 1898-1900+.

BUTLER
Active in Salinas.

BUTLER & DORSEZ
Partnership of G. R. Butler and Fernando H. Dorsez, 715 Market Street, San Francisco, 1886.

BUTLER, CHARLES A.
Partner in Dames & Butler, 715 Market Street, San Francisco, 1883-85.

BUTLER, COOK
Active in San Rafael, 1880-82.

BUTLER, EDWARD P.
Active in Petaluma, c. 1862-63. Traveling photographer, c. 1864. Active in San Francisco, c. 1865; Santa Cruz, 1867-77 or later; in Virginia City, Nevada, partner with G. Waterhouse, 1883; in Reno, 1886.

BUTLER, G. R.
Partner in Butler & Dorsez, 715 Market Street, San Francisco, 1886.

BUTLER, T. A.
Partner in Dames & Butler, 715 Market Street, San Francisco, 1884-85.

BUTTERFIELD, S. H.
Active in Downey and Los Angeles, 1874-90s. Taught at Gallatin School, 1874, and at a Los Angeles high school, 1879-80. Proprietor of Excelsior Gallery, 221 North Main, Downey Block, Los Angeles; at 315 North Spring Street, Studio Temple Block, junction of Main and Spring, 1890s.

BUTTON & HIGGINS
Partnership of C. G. Button and , operating the Eureka Gallery in rooms formerly occupied by J. H. Heering at 342 First Street, San Jose, 1874.

BUTTON & HOGAN'S PHOTOGRAPHIC ART GALLERY
Operating at the corner of Third and D Streets, Marysville, 1875.

BUTTON, CHARLES GILBERT
Born in New York. Active in San Jose, 1870-74 or later; partner in Button & Higgins, 1874. Photographic printer with G. D. Morse in San Francisco, 1876. Also operated as a traveling photographer, 1876. Perhaps the Button of Betancue & Button's Flying Studio, Astoria, Oregon, c. 1878.

BYRAM, W. B.
Active in Lamada Park and Pasadena; specialized in stereo views and cartes-de-viste.

BYRD, DAVID
Born in Missouri, 1840. Partner in Peake & Byrd Brothers, Visalia, 1867-72 or later.

BYRD, WILLIAM
Born in Missouri, 1835. Partner in Peake & Byrd Brothers, Visalia, 1867-70 or later. Produced stereoviews of Yosemite.

BYRNS, THOMAS
Born in Ireland, 1846. Active in Nevada County, District 58, 1880.

CABONI, EFISIO
Gallery at 309 Montgomery Street, San Francisco, 1890-95.

CADY, GEORGE B.
Photographer with Alexander Edouart, San Francisco, 1869-76. Also spelled Cade.

CADY, H. C.
Born in Tennessee, 1849. Photographer in Michigan, c. 1870; San Francisco, 1880.

CAHN, (MISS)
Active in San Francisco, c. 1894. Possibly Miss Rosalie or Henrietta Cahn.

CALIFORNIA ART COMPANY
Gallery in San Jose operated by J. A. Harliss and J. O. Valpey, c. 1890.

CALIFORNIA ART COMPANY
Operated in Red Bluff, 1886.

CALIFORNIA ART PHOTO COMPANY
San Francisco firm; produced stereoviews of Oakland, San Francisco, Los Angeles and surrounding areas. Also listed as California Foto Art and California Art Foto Company.

CALIFORNIA GALLERY
Studio in San Francisco at 402 Kearny Street, corner of Pine and Kearny, operated by C. L. Cramer, 1869-1905.

CALIFORNIA PHOTO TENT
A traveling studio operated by B. L. Wilson, c. 1880.

CALIFORNIA PHOTOGRAPHIC GALLERY
Located at 402 Kearney Street, San Francisco, T. C. Lancey and J. B. Starkweather, operators, c. 1870.

CALVERY, THOMAS
Born in England, 1853. Photographic printer with Bradley & Rulofson, San Francisco, 1876. Associated with T. H. Jones in San Francisco, 1880s. Also spelled Calverley or Calverly.

CAMERON, J. D.
Daguerreian artist in partnership with W. H. Rulofson in Sonora, c. 1849. Sold his interest in the gallery to Rulofson, January 18, 1857.

CAMMERT, EDMUND R.
Photographer with Faber Photo Company, Los Angeles, 1896.

CAMPBELL, A. D.
Born in Canada, 1856. Active in San Francisco, 1880.

CAMPBELL, CHARLES ALEXANDER
Born in California, c. 1858. Listed as a photographer in Eureka, 1879.

CAMPBELL, JAMES
Born in Canada, 1853. Active in San Francisco, 1880. Probably a brother of A. D. Campbell.

CAMPBELL, S. S.
Active in Sisson, 1915.

CAMPS & OLTMAN
Active in Dunsmuir, 1898; John Oltman and possibly Frank L. Camps.

CAMPS, FRANK L.
Traveling photographer, 1898-1910.

CANN, DELL
Active in Yreka, 1889; partner in Burgess & Cann, c. 1899.

CANNON, ERON
Born in Utah, 1857, son of Marsena Cannon. Active in San Francisco, 1880.

CANNON, MARSENA
First photographer of Utah, 1850. Studio in Oakland at 1127 Broadway Street, 1870. See Utah.

CANNON, WILLIAM C.
Active in Etna Mills, 1874-75.

CANTWELL, HERBERT C.
Studio at 40 Eddy Street, San Francisco, 1893-98.

CARDER, S. M. (MRS.)
Active in Ukiah on State Street, c. 1882.

CARDOZO, ABIGAIL E.
Born in Grizzly Bluff, California, July 25, 1864; died in Ferndale, 1937. Owned the Crippen Photograph Gallery in Ferndale, 1897-1905; also called the Post Office Gallery. Also listed as Mrs. Abbie Cardozo, Mrs. O. L. Chapman, Mrs. A. E. Cardozo.

CAREY, ELODIA
Active at the Hoopa Indian Reservation, Humboldt County, c. 1900.

CARLOCK, EUGENE F.
Photographer with S. Cohen, Los Angeles, 1896.

CARLSON, CHARLES H.
Portrait and landscape artist, Mare Island, 1890.

CARPENTER, AURIELUS O.
Born in Townshend, Vermont, November 28, 1836. Participated in the survey of Topeka, Kansas, 1855. In Lawrence, Kansas, set the first type of the first newspaper in the territory. Wounded in the battle of Black Jack, 1856. Married Helen McGowan and moved to Nevada, 1857, mining at Selby Flat. Moved to Potter Valley, Mendocino County, November 1859, and helped found the *Mendocino Herald*. Appointed U.S. Assistant Assessor of the Revenue Department, 1865. Moved to Ukiah, operating Home Gallery, 1869-80 or later. Elected the first Marshall of Ukiah, 1877. He bought the *Ukiah City Press*, 1879; served as Superintendant of Highways and Road Construction, on the Board of Education, as Deputy County Assessor, and Deputy County Recorder. Co-authored a history of Mendocino County, 1914.

CARPENTER, GRACE
Born near Ukiah, California, February 1865, daughter of photographer Helen McCowen Carpenter and newspaperman-photographer Aurelius Ormando Carpenter. Active in Ukiah, c. 1880-1900. Married to William T. Davis, 1884, and Dr. John Hudson, 1890-1900.

Documented Indian culture with photographs and paintings exhibited at the Grace Hudson Museum, Ukiah.

CARPENTER, HELEN McCOWEN
Operated the family-owned Home Gallery in Ukiah, c. 1870-1900. Taught school in Potter Valley for ten years and was active member of Mendocino County Board of Education, Order of Eastern Star, Rebekahs, and the Presbyterian Church Society. Wife of A. O. Carpenter.

CARPENTER, LEE
Active in Los Angeles at 403 North Main, 1886-87; in San Francisco at 10 Sixth Street.

CARR, RICHARD
Born in Beckley, England, 1818; died 1888. Migrated to New York, 1836. Traveled to Canada, down to the Gulf Coast, up the Mississippi to Memphis, then overland to Chicago. Learned the daguerreian art in a Plumbe studio. He worked in New Orleans, Mexico, Yucatan, Belize, Nicaragua, Panama, Ecuador and Peru. He arrived in San Francisco and advertised as daguerreotypist, January 25, 1849; may have been the first photographer in California. He moved back to England later, and finally to Victoria, British Columbia.

CARRUTHERS, KATHERINE
Active in San Jose with husband W. J. Carruthers, c. 1899-1902.

CARRUTHERS, WILLIAM JOHN
Active in San Jose, c. 1899-1902.

CARSON, ADA M.
Photographer for C. J. Coules in Los Angeles, c. 1902.

CARTER, L.
Active briefly in Santa Rosa at the Third Street Gallery, 1884.

CARVALHO, SOLOMON NUNES
Born in Charleston, South Carolina, 1815; died in New York City, 1899. Portrait and landscape painter and daguerreian artist. Left Baltimore, 1853, and joined the Fremont exploring party at Westport, Missouri, travelling through the Rockies to Salt Lake City, then went to California by stage. Active in Los Angeles, 1854; San Francisco, 1854-55; returned to New York City, c. 1856. Published *Incidents of Travel and Adventure*, New York, 1859.
    Solomon Nunes Carvalho: Painter, Photographer and Prophet in Nineteenth Century America, Jewish Historical Society of Maryland, 1989 (various authors, exhibition catalogue).
    Nelson B. Wadsworth, *Through Camera Eyes*, Brigham Young University Press, Salt Lake City, 1975.

CARVER, E. M. (MRS.)
Active in Anaheim, 1898.

CARY, C. A.
Born in New York, 1850. Active in Oakland, 1878-89 or later. Studio at 1116 Broadway, 1883; corner of Seventh and Market, 1888.

CASARA, JACOB
Active in San Francisco, 1876.

CATHCART, WALTER
Partner in Baker & Cathcart, 1073 ½ Market, San Francisco, 1886. Baker was the photographer, Cathcart the manager; operated studio of his own at 1330 Turk Street, 1898.

CELAIRE, LOUIS
Jeweler and apprentice of photographer Alphonse J. Liebert in Nevada City, 1858; later became engaged in a bitter competition with his former mentor. Sold his studio to Thomas M. Wood, 1859.

CHADBOURNE, FORREST S.
Partner with George B. Rieman, 26 Montgomery Street, San Francisco, 1882.

CHADWICK, REDMOND A.
Active in Los Angeles, 1890-1905. Partner in Howland & Chadwick, selling photographic supplies, 1890-96; at 109 South Main, 1890; 211 Main Street, 1892-99. Studio at 211 South Broadway, 1900-01; 213 South Broadway, 1905.

CHALFANT, A.
Active in Mendocino, 1867.

CHALMERS & WOLFE
Studio in San Francisco at 611 Clay Street, 1865-67; Samuel A. Wolfe and James C. Chalmers.

CHALMERS, JAMES C.
Born in Scotland, 1840. Partner of S. A. Wolfe, 611 Clay Street, San Francisco, 1865-67. Photographer with Nahl Brothers, San Francisco, 1869-70.

CHAMBERLAIN
Active in Stirling City.

CHAN, ISABELLE MAY (MRS.)
Partner with husband Leo Chan in the May Studio, San Francisco, c. 1920-76.

CHAN, K. S.
Active in San Francisco, 1920s.

CHAN, LEO
Active in San Francisco, 1920-76; proprietor with wife Isabelle in the May Studio located on Sacramento Street.

CHANDLER, JESSE W.
Born in Maine, 1837. Partner in Wing & Chandler, San Jose, 1877. Operated Chandler & Company at 367 First Street, 1878-83 or later; associated with Frances Soule, 1880.

CHASE, A. W.
Supplied photographs and art to Stephen Powers for his book, *Tribes of California*, although it's not clear whether Chase, a surveyor with the Coast Survey, took the photographs.

CHASE, J. W.
Active in Point Arena, 1878.

CHASE, LORENZO G.
A Boston photographer, 1844-51; traveled to California seeking gold, 1851. Partner with Charles Hamilton, 1852; returned to Boston, late 1852.

CHAU, KA
Operated daguerreotype gallery on Sacramento Street in San Francisco, 1854.

CHENHALL, JOHN
Active in Plymouth, c. 1880.

CHERRY, EDGAR
Born in Michigan, September 14, 1845; died in Yountville, January 2, 1930. Resided in Santa Rose before starting a stationery store in San Francisco, 1882. Operated as Edgar Cherry & Company with partner Charles G. Noyes, located at 433 California Street, San Francisco. Cherry published *Redwood and Lumbering in California*, a "book-album" containing twenty-four tipped in albumen print views of log-ging scenes in the forests of Humboldt County, 1884. Photographer in Santa Rose, c. 1885; 126 Bartlett, San Francisco, c. 1885-88.

> Peter E. Palmquist, *Redwood & Lumbering in California Forests, A Reconsruction of the Original EdgarCherry Edition*, Book Club of California, San Francisco, 1983.

CHESEBRO, EDWARD C.
Active in Calistoga, 1888-90; in San Francisco, 1900-01. Also spelled Chesbro.

CHEW, AH
Photographer at studio in San Francisco, 429 Montgomery Street, c. 1871.

CHICAGO ART GALLERY
Operated by Charles Klindt at 657 Fifth Street, San Diego, c. 1895.

CHICO ART GALLERY
Operated by Woods & Son in Chico, 1884-94.

CHIN, LIN
Active in San Francisco, c. 1910.

CHIO, MING HIN
Born in San Yah, 1838. Active in San Francisco, 1880. Also spelled Ming Him Chio.

CHUNG, SIM
Born in San Yah, 1859. Active in San Francisco, 1880.

CHURCHMAN
Active in Chico, 1890-1912.

CHURCHMAN BROTHERS
Studio at 518 Broadway, Chico, 1901-05.

CHURCHMAN, J. W.
Active in Chico, 1904-05.

CHURCHMAN, S. E.
Active in Chico, 1901-10; with Churchman Brothers.

CITY MART
Gallery at the junction of Market and Kearney Streets, San Francisco, 1867.

CITY PHOTO GALLERY
Operating in Placerville, c. 1900, owned by George C. Jones and later by B. F. Strong.

CLANCY, ANDREW
Active in San Francisco, 1898-1900.

CLARK & JOHNSTON
Partnership of Peter G. Clark and James W. Johnston, 659 Clay Street, San Francisco, 1861.

CLARK, A. G.
Born in Nova Scotia, 1832. Daguerreian artist in San Francisco, 1860.

CLARK, E. L.
Active in Watsonville, 1890-98.

CLARK, GEORGE P.
Associated with J. H. Baker in Napa City, 1889.

CLARK, J. C.
Active in San Bernardino and San Diego, 1898.

CLARK, W. L.
Active in Santa Barbara.

CLARK PHOTOS
Operating in Placerville, 1895.

CLARK'S PHOTO COMPANY
Studio in Berkeley, c. 1890s-1905; taken over by J. T. Pollock.

CLAUSEN, C. H.
Studio at the corner of Market and 7th Streets, Oakland, c. 1892.

CLAWSON, C.
Stereo photographer active in Los Angeles.

CLAYBROOK, J.
Born in France, c. 1844. Active in Santa Monica, 1880.

CLAYTON, JAMES A.
Born in England, October 20, 1831. Came to America, 1839; settled in Wisconsin, 1840; came to California gold mines, 1850; clerked in his brother Charles' Santa Clara store. Went back to the mines, then to Australia still in search of gold; returned to Stockton and Santa Clara, 1851. Took up photography, operated gallery in San Jose on Santa Clara Street, 1856-70. Elected to the Common Council of San Jose, 1866.

CLEAVER, MYRA R.
Active in Santa Ana, c. 1900.

CLEMENTS & HOGAN
Partnership in Oroville, 1878; Charles C. Clements and John Hobart Hogan.

CLEMENTS & SPRAGUE
Active in Chico, 1892-93; Lucien A. Sprague and Charles C. Clements.

CLEMENTS, CHARLES C.
Partner in Collins & Clements, Oroville, 1874-90; also partner in Clements & Hogan, 1878; partner in Clements & Sprague, Chico, 1892-93.

CLENCH, F. B.
Active in Lakeport, 1885.

CLENDENON, LOUIS K.
Photographer with J. B. Blanchard, Los Angeles, 1896. Listed at 313 ½ South Spring, 1902; at 213 North Spring, 1903-05.

CLIFFORD, CHARLES A.
Studio on The Esplanade, Chico, 1894-1912.

CLIFFORD, GRANVILLE
Gallery at 198 Main Street, Stockton, c. 1870; J. P. Betancue, operator.

CLINCH, WILLIS A.
Operated the Eureka Gallery on Mill Street, Grass Valley, 1885-93.

CLOUGH, JOHN S.
Gallery at 8 Sixth Street, San Francisco, 1881-84. Also spelled Clow.

CLUNE, THOMAS
Partner with F. H. Rogers and J. F. Fitzpatrick, operating as F. H. Roger & Company, 15 First Street, Los Angeles, 1884.

CLUTE, FAYETTE J.
Born September 15, 1865; died January 28, 1921. Extremely active amateur stereo photographer in San Francisco; editor of *Camera Craft*.

COBB, DAVID
Born at Prince Edward Island of English parents, 1841. Operated Cobb's Celebrated Photographic Gallery on Mill Street near Neal Street, Grass Valley, 1867; worked for Alexander Edouart in San Francisco, 1867; for George D. Morse, 1868-69; partner in Edouart & Cobb, 504 Kearny Street, 1869-82; also operated at 1818 Post Street. Moved to 1144 Market Street and opened the Dore Gallery, 1882-c. 1900; sold out to J. G. Hucks, c. 1900.

COBURN, ROBERTA
Active in Pasadena, Los Angeles County, 1899-1900.

COFFIN
Partner in Harmon & Coffin, active in Snelling, 1867.

COFFIN & JACOBS
Partnership of I. T. Coffin and J. M. Jacobs, stereo photographers active in Dutch Flat before 1867.

COFFIN, ISAAC T.
Active in Dutch Flat; partner in Coffin & Jacobs, 1867; partner in Halsey & Coffin, 1874.

COHEN, E. A.
Born 1859; died 1939. View photographer and postcard publisher based in Alameda, 1898-1939.

COHEN, SAMUEL
Proprietor of the Garden City Photo Company, 606 East Fifth, Los Angeles, 1896.

COLE, GEORGE C.
Photographer with Silas Selleck, San Francisco, 1867-70.

COLEMAN, GEORGE
Born in New York, c. 1845. Daguerreian in Los Angeles, 1870.

COLLETTE, J. E.
Active in Los Angeles at 452 South Spring, 1895.

COLLIER, CHARLES T.
Active in Riverside, 1886-88; gallery at the corner of Eighth and Main, 1888. Operated the Collier Photo Engraving Company, 536 South Broadway, Los Angeles, 1896.

COLLINS & CLEMENTS
Operating in Oroville, 1874-90; Charles C. Clements and possibly Parker Thompson Collins.

COLLINS, META CHRISTINA
Active in Fort Bragg, 1888-90. Published four photographs as illustrations in *Overland Monthly*, October 1893. Also listed as Mrs. William Hanen after her marriage, 1890.

COLLINS, PARKER THOMPSON
Active in Chico, 1874-96.

COLLINS, WALTER
Proprietor of the Oceanside Picture Gallery, Santa Monica, 1899; at 639 East 21st, 1902.

COLLOM, WILLIAM N.
Studio at 69 Flood Building, San Francisco, 1895-99 or later. Specialized in views of residences, buildings, livestock, farms, orchards, landscapes and portraits.

COLUMBIA ART GALLERY
Located at 556 12th Street, East Oakland; in Salinas, c. 1895.

COLUMBIA PHOTOGRAPHIC TENT
Traveling photographers, 1893.

COMFORT, BELLE A.
Proprietor of the Canova Photographic Studio in Alameda at 240 ½ Santa Clara Avenue, 1897; 2427 Central Avenue, 1900-01.

COMINGS, E. S.
Active in Los Angeles at 217 ½ South Spring, 1898-99; 316 South Broadway, 1900-01.

COMSTOCK (MRS.)
Colorist and copyist in Rohnerville, 1878.

CONAWAY & HUMMEL
Gallery in Santa Ana, c. 1888.

CONAWAY, B. F.
Active in Santa Ana, 1880-90; San Bernardino, 1895-98. Partner with Clark at 5th and E, also at 567 3rd, operating as Conway & Clark, 1898. Also spelled Conaway and Conway.

CONE, F. E.
Operated in San Leandro and Hayward, c. 1899.

CONE, MAY C.
Born in New York, September 1864. Active in San Leandro, 1899; Hayward, 1900.

CONKLIN & COMPANY
Firm located in Los Angeles; published stereoviews of southern California.

CONLAN, EDWARD
Photographer with Joseph T. Silva, San Francisco, 1869-72.

CONNELL
Associated with Reed & Connell, 214 Downey Avenue, Los Angeles, 1892.

CONWAY & CLARK
Partnership in San Bernardino, 1898; B. F. Conway.

COOK & STORMER
Partnership in Willows, 1890-93; John Benton Stormer and W. B. Cook.

COOK, FRANCIS AUGUSTUS
Active in San Bernadino, 1874. Possibly a partner in Tandy & Cook, Tuscarora, Nevada, 1880. Operated at 728 Montgomery in San Francisco and partner of E. P. Butler in Reno, Nevada, 1883; traveling photographer, 1886.

COOK, I. N.
Active in Santa Barbara, 1886-89.

COOK, J. M.
Active in Quincy, 1885-1900.

COOK, JOHN E.
Traveling photographer, 1900-05.

COOK, JOHN J.
Born in New York, 1838; died prior to 1915. Settled in California, 1863. View photographer and proprietor of Watkins' Yosemite Gallery, 26 Montgomery Street, San Francisco, 1880-83. Active in Yosemite Valley and San Francisco, 1883- 1905; possibly the proprietor of the Yo Semite Valley Hotel (formerly Black's). Vice President of I. W. Taber & Company, 121 Post Street, San Francisco, by 1898.

COOK, LINCOLN HAWKINS
Active in Chico, c. 1893-96.

COOK, WALTER H.
Gallery at 28 Third Street, San Francisco, 1869-70. Successor to James Dorr.

COOK, WILLIAM BLODGETT
Active in Willows, 1866-89; Alta Studios, Willows, 1885-95; partner in Cook & Stormer, 1890-93; partner in Bird & Cook, operating in Willows, Placerville and Auburn, 1892-93; operated gallery in Colusa, Washington Block, 1895-97.

COOL, DR. W. P.
Partner with Thomas G. Brooks in Shasta, 1874-75.

COOMBS, FREDERICK
Active in St. Louis, Missouri, 1846; in Chicago, 1849. Daguerreian parlor in San Francisco, corner of Sacramento and Montgomery, c. 1850. Well known eccentric who wore patriotic costumes.

COONLEY, H. E.
Active in San Diego, 1888-96.

COOPER, CAROLINE
Active in San Jose, 1898-1900.

COOVER, D. RADNOR
Photographer with Theodore C. Marceau, San Francisco, 1898. Operated Vaughan's Imperial Photographic Studio in partnership with Rasmussen at 724 ½ Market Street, San Francisco, 1899-1900. Probably the secretary of the Photographer's Association of America, 1890.

CORL, P. S.
Active in Riverside, 1895.

CORNELIUS
Traveling photographer.

CORNELL, VIOLA G.
Active in Los Angeles, c. 1899-1900.

COSMOPOLITAN ART & PHOTOGRAPHIC GALLERY
Studio in San Francisco at 523 Kearny Street, operated by Halsey and John Calvin Scripture, 1868; with Harry De Groot, 1869-70.

COSMOPOLITAN PHOTOGRAPHIC ART GALLERY
Operated by Silas Selleck in San Francisco at 415 Montgomery, 1865-75.

COTA, JOHN
Photographer with Alexander Edouart, San Francisco, 1869-70.

COTTAGE GALLERY
Operated in Colusa at the corner of Market and Fifth. Studio was

bought by N. W. Clements, October 1895, and moved to another lot to be used as a residence.

COTTAGE GALLERY
Active in Los Angeles, 1875.

COTTON, ROSE
Amateur stereo photographer active in Santa Ana.

COTTON, WALTER S.
Amateur stereo photographer in Santa Ana; husband of Rose Cotton.

COULES & DANDO
Partnership of Charles J. Coules and F. C. Dando at 236 South Main, Los Angeles, 1895-1903; second studio at 313 ½ South Spring, 1897-1903, operated by Dando.

COULES, CHARLES J.
Active in Los Angeles at 236 South Main, 1893-1905; partner in Coules & Dando, 1895-1903; second studio at 313 ½ South Spring, 1897-1903. Coules Palace Studios at 236 South Main and 351 South Broadway, Los Angeles, 1901-05; at 535 South Broadway, date unknown.

COWAN, JOHN J.
Photographer with Louis Thors, San Francisco, 1898. Active San Francisco, 1900-01.

COX & FULLER
Gallery at 565 Stevenson Street, San Francisco, 1885.

COX, J.
Studio on Central Avenue at the foot of Webster, opposite Neptune Gardens, Alameda, 1888.

COX, P. S.
Active in Escondido, 1898.

COYLE
Active in Stockton and Oakdale, c. 1890.

CRAIG & MOSHER
Partnership of A. W. Craig and J. W. Mosher, San Francisco, 1877-93.

CRAIG, A. W.
Partner in Craig & Mosher, San Francisco, 1877-93. Studio at 638 Market Street, 1877-80; 22 Kearny Street, c. 1880-88.

CRAIG, VICTOR
Born in Wisconsin (?), 1855. Active in Oakland, 1880-88.

CRAMER, CHARLES L.
Born in Canada, 1835. Active in San Francisco, 1865-1905. Partner with William F. Bayley at 618 Washington, 1865-68. Operated the California Photographic Gallery at 402 Kearny Street, corner of Pine and Kearny, 1869-1905. Also a partner in Bailey & Cramer, West Oakland, 1877-79.

CRAMER, FRANK E.
Son of Charles L. Cramer and listed as photographer in San Francisco, 1896-1901.

CRAMER, MELINDA E.
Co-owner of gallery with husband, Charles L. Cramer in San Francisco, c. 1896-1900. Also listed as Mrs. C. L. Cramer.

CRANDALL
Active in Pasadena, 1888-1910. Official photographer on expedition with A. C. Vroman, Horatio Rust and Mrs. Thaddeus Lowe to the Southwest, 1895. Shared studio with William Henry Hill across from Vroman's bookstore, 1893-1903. Purchased Hill's share, 1905-10. Studio at 59 Street Colorado, 1893-94; 55-57 Colorado, 1895; 61 Colorado, 1897-1903. Partner in Crandall & Dewey with George N. Dewey, Pasadena.

CRANDALL & DEWEY
Partnership in Pasadena; George N. Dewey.

CRANE, J. L.
Active in Sacramento, 1863.

CRAWFORD, CHARLES FOX
Active in Buckeye, 1900.

CRAWFORD, ELLISON LASSELL
Active in Coloma, c. 1863; Greenwood, c. 1863; Georgetown, 1874-79 or later. Also editor of the *Georgetown Gem*, 1874. Operated the Universal Picture Gallery, advertised "Cheaper than the Cheapest! and views of mining claims and buildings."

CREIGHTON, JOHN M.
Active in Winters, 1886.

CRIPPEN, ABIGAIL
Active in Yosemite Valley, c. 1880.

CRISSMAN, J.
Active in Santa Ana, 1886-90s. Studio on Fourth Street, 1886. Located in Utah, 1869; in Bozeman, Montana, 1871. Accompanied Hayden's expedition through Yellowstone with William Henry Jackson, 1871.

CRITES, CARRIE
Active in Dry Creek, c. 1900. Also listed as Mrs. John W. Crites.

CROCKWELL, JAMES H.
Studio in Bishop's Creek, c. 1887. Produced a souvenir book of Marysville and Yuba City with the Albertype Company in 1895. See Utah and Nevada.

CROFOOT, DANIEL O.
Born in 1833. Photographic printer at Selleck's Gallery, San Francisco, 1865-66. Also listed as David.

CROMWELL
Active in Los Angeles, 1885-90; partner in Cromwell & Westervelt at 603 East First, 1890. Also listed as Crowell.

CROMWELL, O.
Active in Millville, 1879-80; Kennett, c. 1900.

CROMWELL, OSCAR
Active in Red Bluff, 1877-1916. Advertised in Placerville, 1881.

CROUSE, J. L.
Active in Sacramento, 1863-64.

CROMWELL & WESTERVELT
Operated the Great Eastern Photographic & Advertising Company, Los Angeles, 1890. Also spelled Crowell.

CROWELL, ARTHUR B.
Born in New York, 1858. Partner in Crowell Brothers Art Palace, San Jose, 1880-82. Married Nancy Martin, sister of Louisa who married his brother, George. Probably active El Paso, Texas, 1885-88.

CROWELL BROTHERS
George and Arthur B. Crowell operated Crowell Brothers' Art Palace, San Jose, 1880-81. Opened a studio at 739 Market Street, San Francisco, 1881.

CROWELL, GEORGE WRIGHT
Born in New York, 1856. Active San Jose, 1880-82. Married Louisa, daughter of Calvin Martin.

CRUTCHFIELD, B. F.
Partner with brother, Clarence E., in Los Angeles, 1894-99. Located at 214 Downey, 1894-95; Crutchfield Brothers at 840 East 5th, 1899.

CRUTCHFIELD, CLARENCE E.
Proprietor of the Good Gallery, 214 Downey Avenue, East Los Angeles, 1896-1900. Partner with brother, B. F. Crutchfield.

CUINTER
Partner in Bayley & Cuinter, stereographers in San Francisco, 1860s-80s.

CULVER, C.
Active in Carlsbad, 1898.

CUNNINGHAM, A. W.
Advertised as a "Portrait and View Photographer," at the Morro Street Gallery, San Luis Obispo, 1890-93.

CUNNINGHAM, J. S.
Active in Woodland, 1864.

CUNNINGHAM, JOHN
Active in Shingletown, 1880.

CUNNINGHAM, JESSIE
Partner with William H. Shattuck, Main and Placer Streets, Georgetown, 1852-59.

CUNNINGHAM, JOHN V.
May have been in Shasta, California, c. 1880. See Texas.

CURRIE, LORENZO DOW
Active in Chinese Camp, 1878-84.

CURRIER & WINTER
"Picture Dealers " at 211 Kearney Street, San Francisco, 1865.

CURTIS, C. C.
Member of the Kaweah Colony, a socialist community in Tulare County; active in Traver, 1886-88; also Hanford, Esperanza and Porterville. He recorded the dismantling of the giant Sequoia, "General Noble, " which was cut down and reconstructed at the World's Columbian Exposition in Chicago, 1993; in San Jose, c. 1896.

CURTIS, EDWARD S.
Born 1868; died in Los Angeles, 1952. Noted Indian photographer working out of Seattle, Washington, before World War I. Published *North American Indian*, 1935, in twenty volumes and portfolios; worked in Hollywood, 1940s-50s. See Washington.

CUSHMAN
Partner in Baker & Cushman, 8 Sixth Street, San Francisco, 1888.

CUSHMAN, WILLIAM H.
Active in San Francisco, 1893-98.

CUTBIRTH
Active in Sacramento at 1308 Sixth Street, c. 1896.

DAGUERRE ATELIER PHOTOGRAPHIQUE
Studio in San Francisco, 1895.

DAILEY, R.
Active in Downey, 1887-88. Possibly a partner in Fortune & Dailey, 1884.

DAILY, JOHN WILLIAM
Active in Shingletown, 1884-86.

DALL, J. H.
Operated Bradley & Rulofson studio with W. H. Rulofson, 429 Montgomery Street, San Francisco, 1880; also sold photographic materials at 618-20 Clay Street the same year. Located at Bradley & Rulofson, 14 Grant Avenue, San Francisco, 1888.

DAMES & BUTLER
Studio operated by William W. Dames and Charles A. Butler in San Francisco 715 Market Street, 1883-85.

DAMES & HAYES
Gallery at 715 Market Street, San Francisco, 1877-85; William W. Dames and Henry C. Hayes.

DAMES & KEIL
Partnership of William W. Dames and Edward A. Keil in San Francisco at 715 Market Street, 1886.

DAMES & WILLIAMS
Studio in San Francisco at 24, 26 and 28 Montgomery Street, opposite Lick House, 1871.

DAMES, DELIA C.
Co-owner of photograph galleries with husband W. W. Dames, in San Francisco, c. 1871-86; Oakland, c. 1886-1904. See William W. Dames for partnerships.

DAMES, WILLIAM W.
Born in Canada, 1842, of English parents. In California by 1867. Photographer with Alexander Edouart, San Francisco, 1869-70; partner in Dames & Williams, 26 Montgomery Street, 1871; photographer with Hector W. Vaughan, San Francisco, 1876; partner in partner in Dames & Hayes, 715 Market Street, 1877-85; Dames & Butler, same address, 1883-85; partner in Dames & Keil, same address, 1886. Operated a studio at 911 Broadway, Oakland, 1886-88.

DAMMOND, R. P.
Active in Escondido, 1898.

DAMON, MARSHALL
Born in California, 1862, son of George D. Damon, a ship carpenter. Active in San Francisco, 1880.

DAMRON, V. C.
Studio at 141 D Street, San Bernardino, 1888-93.

DANDO, FARNHAM C.
Active in Los Angeles; partner in Coules & Dando, 1895-1903. Listed at 313½ South Spring Street, 1893-1910 or later.

DARBYSHIRE
Partner in Fay & Darbyshire, Redwood City, c. 1877.

DARLINGTON, CHARLES A.
Active in Redding, 1893.

DARRAGH & GODFREY
Studio in Shasta, 1858-59. Partnership of Dr. J. C. Darragh and Professor Godfrey. Also listed as Dr. Darrah & Professor Godfrey.

DARRAGH, DR. J. C.
Active in Shasta, 1857-60; partner in Darragh & Godfrey, 1858-59.

DASSONVILLE, WILLIAM E.
Born 1879; died 1957. Studio in San Francisco, 1901. Pictorial photographer exhibiting at the San Francisco Salon shows, 1901-03. Illustrated book of poetry by George Sterling, *Yosemite: An Ode*, 1916. Published pictorial images in *Camera Craft* and other periodicals.

Retired from studio work in the 1920s and manufactured photographic paper.

DATESMAN, PETER
Active in Redding, 1893-99; operated as Progressive Art Company, 1897-99.

DAUGHERTY, CHARLES J.
Operated studio in Pasadena at 265 Street Colorado, 1897-1900; in Long Beach, 1900.

DAUGHERTY, MARY A.
Active with husband C. J. Daughtery, in Pasadena, c. 1897-1900; Long Beach, c. 1900.

DAVIDSON
Active in Woodland.

DAVIDSON, C. M.
Active in Los Angeles at 151 South Main, 1884-85; operated the San Francisco Gallery with partner, L. S. Davidson in Santa Ana.

DAVIDSON, E. M.
Active in Cloverdale, 1886. Located at 122 Main Street in Visalia by 1888.

DAVIDSON, EVA J. (MRS.)
Photographer in Cedarville, 1910.

DAVIDSON, H. & R.
Partnership in Siskiyou County, 1905.

DAVIDSON, L. S.
Studio at corner of Third and Main Streets, Los Angeles, 1884-86. Partner with C. M. Davidson operating the San Francisco Gallery in Santa Ana.

DAVIDSON, NORVALLE RICE
Born in Iowa, c. 1838. Known as N. R., he had a studio on Powell Street, Healdsburg, 1874; in Eureka by 1876. Studio at 219 Fourth Street, Santa Rosa, 1886-88. Traveling photographer.

DAVIS
Stereo photographer active in Grass Valley.

DAVIS BROTHERS
Stereo photographers active in San Francisco.

DAVIS, FLORENCE N. (MRS.)
Active in Chico, 1899-1921. Also known as Mrs. W. A. Davis.

DAVIS PHOTO
Studio in Chico, 1885-1907.

DAVIS PHOTOGRAPHY STUDIO
Operating in Red Bluff, 1907.

DAVIS, WALTER ALFRED
Naturalized Englishman, active in San Francisco, c. 1890-98; at 235 and 238 Broadway, Chico, 1904-10.

DAVIS, WALTER AUSTIN
Listed in Santa Rosa, 1890.

DE BUHR, JOSEPH
With Fairbanks, De Buhr & Goltra, view photographers, 14 Allen Block and 223 North Spring, Los Angeles, 1896.

DE GROOT & KELLOG
Partnership of Harry DeGroot and Andrew J. Kellog; in Sacramento, 1888-80; in Salinas, date unknown.

DE GROOT, HARRY
Born in New York, 1848. In California by 1854. Operated the Cosmopolitan Photograph Gallery, 525 Kearny Street, San Francisco, 1869-70. Worked as an assayer, 1876. Studio in Sisson, 1880; partner in De Groot & Kellog, Main Street, Sacramento, 1880-88; De Groot & Kellogg, Salinas, date unknown. Also spelled De Groat.

DE GROOT, HENRY, JR.
Active in Berryvale, 1887-88.

DE VERGILIO, SAMUEL
Stereo photographer active in Escondido.

DEADY, W. G.
Active in Lodi, c. 1892.

DEALEY BROTHERS
Partnership of Charles A. and George L. Dealey, 1899-1901.

DEALEY, CHARLES ALLEN
Active in San Francisco, c. 1894-1901.

DEAN & GRAY
Partnership of J. K. Dean and H. P. Gray in Selma, c. 1885. Also spelled Gay.

DEAN, GEORGE E.
Active in Anderson Valley, c. 1864; gallery on Main Street, Visalia, c. 1874.

DEAN, J. K.
Partner in Dean & Gay in Selma, c. 1885. Listed in Mariposa, 1886; in Fresno County, 1888.

DEAN, JAMES
San Francisco photographer, 1898.

DEAN, ORIE SNYDER
Active in Chico, 1897-98.

DEEK, VICTOR
Born in California, 1849. Active in San Francisco, 1870.

DELAVAN, W.
Stereo photographer active in San Francisco, c. 1868.

DELL, IRWIN
Active in Redding, 1889.

DENNIN, A. M.
Active in Sacramento, 1865-68. Also be spelled Dennien.

DENNINIGER, A. G.
Gallery in the Letitia Building, 68 South Street, San Jose, c. 1897-98.

DENNY & COE
Partnership in Grass Valley, 1865; Oliver Denny.

DENNY, OLIVER
Active in Santa Cruz, c. 1864; partner in Denny & Coe, Grass Valley, 1865; in Marysville, 1870, at D Street opposite Wells, Fargo & Company. Listed in Portland, Oregon as O. Dennie. Produced stereoviews.

DERBY, CHARLES
Operated a studio at 34 Third Street, San Francisco, 1881-82.

DERBYSHIRE, D. K.
Studio at 11 Third Street, San Francisco, 1863-64.

DESMOND, ROBERT AUXLEY BRITTAIN
Born in Louisiana, c. 1820s. Active in San Francisco, 1863-73; Colusa, 1878; Oroville, 1879; Chico and Etna, 1880; Silveyville, 1882. Traveling photographer, 1874-80. Middle name also spelled Ansley or Ainsly. See British Columbia.

DEVERAUX & LEWMAN
Active in Oakland, 512 Fifteenth, 1888; M. M. Deveraux and E. R. Lewman.

DEVERAUX, M. M.
Partner in Deveraux & Lewman, 512 Fifteenth, Oakland, 1888.

DEWEY BROTHERS
George N. and James H. Dewey, 147 South Main Street, Los Angeles, 1896.

DEWEY, GEORGE N.
Studio at 41 South Main Street, Los Angeles, 1888. Located at 147 South Main Street, Los Angeles, 1891-92, specializing in portraits and views; associated with J. H. Dewey, operating as Dewey Brothers Photographic Supplies, 1886. Partner in Crandall & Dewey, Pasadena.

DEWEY, JAMES H.
Brother of G. N. Dewey, and partner in Dewey Brothers, Kurtz Block, 147 South Main Street, Los Angeles, 1896. Dealers in photographic supplies. Partner in Hirolanc & Dewey, Los Angeles, 1910.

DEWITT & HARTEZ
Roadside studio in Sonoma, c. 1910.

DEYER, W. M.
Active in Crescent City, 1854.

DICKINSON & BELL
Partnership of John Reed Dickinson and George Bell, according to Palmquist. Traveling artists who colored photographs. Located in San Francisco, 1881; worked for Ira Perry and George Kelly in Mendocino, 1882; visited Ukiah, 1883; traveled around Humbodt County visiting many small communities, 1883-86.

DICKINSON, JOHN REED
Partner in Dickinson & Bell. See partnership listing.

DICKMAN, WILLIAM
Active in Sacramento, c. 1863-65; in San Francisco at 121 Montgomery Street, 1865. Partner in Nahl Brothers & Dickman at the same address, 1867.

DICKSON, H. A.
Active in Dicksonville, Solano County, c. 1870.

DIJEAU, ALEXANDER
Born in California, 1860, Operated gallery with various partners at 34 Third Street, San Francisco; with Weitz, 1885-86; with Wells, 1887; with Weitz, 1888; with Severin, 1895-98. Still active, c. 1901.

DILLMAN, JOSEPH
Born in Indiana, April 1851. Active in Downey, 1900.

DIMICK, FREDERICK ELLSWORTH
Active in Little Shasta, 1896.

DINGMAN, HARRY A.
Active in Los Angeles at 328   South Spring Street, 1912.

DISNEY, M.
Gallery at Lemoore, 1880.

DITEAU & SEVERIN
Operated the St. Louis Art Studio at 34 Third Street, San Francisco, 1895-99; Frank A. Severin.

DITMAS, HENRY
Proprietor of the Imperial Photographic Gallery, corner Tenth and Clay Streets, Oakland, c. 1885, B. F. Howland, operator.

DOBERER, HENRY W.
San Francisco photographic printer, 1865.

DODGE, O.
Active in Cottonwood, 1864.

DOLLARHIDE, E. F.
Photographer with George D. Morse, San Francisco, 1876.

DONALDSON, R. H.
Active in Garvanza, northeast of Los Angeles, 1895-98.

DONNELS, T.
Born in Louisiana. Daguerreotypist in Jamestown, 1856.

DONOVAN, KATIE
Active in San Francisco at 7 Mason Street, 1880.

DORAN
Active in Tulare, c. 1896.

DORE GALLERY
Operated by David Cobb in San Francisco, 1144 Market Street, c. 1885-1900.

DORNIN, GEORGE D.
Born in New York City, December 30, 1830; died in California, 1907. Left by ship for the gold rush as a teenager, and after varied experiences in San Francisco, migrated to Nevada City where he carried on several businesses including daguerreotype studios in Grass Valley and North San Juan.
    George D. Dornin, *Thirty Years Ago: Gold Rush Memories of a Daguerreotype Artist*, Carl Mautz Publishing, 1995.

DORR & MAXWELL
Third Street Gallery, 28 Third Street, San Francisco, 1870; James Dorr.

DORR, JAMES
Gallery at 28 Third Street, San Francisco, 1868-71.

DORROTHY, HARRY SEWELL
Active in Red Bluff, 1880-95.

DORSEZ, FERNANDO H.
Born in Ohio, 1860, of French parents. Active San Francisco, 1880. Partner in Butler & Dorsez, 715 Market Street, San Francisco, 1888. Active in Oakland, 1888-1901. Also spelled Dorsay and Dorsaz.

DOUGALL, W.
Active in Escondido, 1895.

DOUNING & EVANS
Active in Susanville, c. 1900.

DOVE
Partner in Dove & Moeller, 147 South Main, Los Angeles, 1898-99.

DOWE
Traveling artist in California, working alone and as partner with Rifenburg, part of the time out of Fresno, date unknown.

DOWE & MURPHY
Active 1894, base uncertain.

DOWE & PICKETT
Active in San Luis Obispo, 1884-86; partnership of O. S. Dowe and J. M. Pickett.

DOWE, ARTHUR W.
Partner in MacDonald & Dowe, 1025 Market Street, San Francisco, 1881-82; his own gallery, same address, 1882. Partner with J. M. Pickett, 1883-84, at 997 and 999 Market Street, operating as Oriental Photographic Parlors. Possibly the A. W. Dowe, proprietor of the Tivoli Exchange and Theatre, 28 First Street, San Jose, 1884. Artist at 105 Saint Ann's Building, San Francisco, 1885. Possibly connected with Arthur B. Crowell in a photogrph gallery in El Paso, Texas, 1885-88 (Refer to Rudisill). Possibly the A. W. Dowe, portrait artist at 13 West Second Street, Los Angeles, 1888.

DOWE BROTHERS
Traveling photographers, 1880-1900.

DOWE, DUANE W.
Photographer with Arthur W. Dowe, San Francisco, 1882-84. Worked as a traveling photographer, 1899; also listed in Chico, 1875-1910.

DOWE, LEWIS
Born in New Hampshire, 1838. Portrait and view photographer in Petaluma, 1877-80. Gallery in San Francisco, c. 1883; at 6 Eddy Street, c. 1886; 105 Saint Ann's Building, 1887; 410 Kearny Street, 1888-92. Also operated as a traveling photographer, 1872-90. By 1904, he was repairing musical instrument at the old 6 Eddy Street address. Possibly related to Arthur W. Dowe.

DOWE, OSCAR S.
Active in California, 1884-1919; San Luis Obispo, 1884-86; Bakersfield, c. 1888; San Francisco, 1889; Eureka, 1889-90; in Ferndale at "The Oriental Gallery, Blue Tent, lot next to the American Hotel," 1890. Operated as a traveling photographer, 1890-95. Visited Placerville, 1895; Ft. Bragg, 1919. See Idaho, Nevada, Oregon.

DOWNEY
Operated in Pleasanton, c. 1890, and probably also a traveling photographer. Listed on Front Street, Tulare, c. 1893.

DOWNEY & SON, W. M.
Firm operating in Downieville, 1864.

DOWNING & EVANS
Active in Susanville, c. 1900.

DOWNING & SMITH
Traveling photographers, 1898.

DOWNING BROTHERS
Active in Susanville and Yreka, 1880-1904.

DOWNING, D. OWEN
Active in Yreka, 1897-1904.

DOWNING, EUGENE
Active in Yreka and Ft. Jones, 1897-1904.

DOWNING, J. H.
Gallery on Center Street, Healdsburg, 1874; possibly a partner in Downing, Rea & Rauscher, Santa Rosa, 1875-78.

DOWNING, REA AND RAUSCHER
Operated the Third Street Gallery in Santa Rosa, 1875-78; H. Rauscher, T. L. Rea and possibly J. H. Downing.

DOYLE, SAMUEL
Clerk with C. E. Watkins, San Francisco, 1876.

DRENKHAHN (MRS.)
Active in Oroville, 1857. Also spelled Drenkahn.

DRESSEL
Partner in Kuchel & Dressel, San Francisco, 1858.

DREW, ADDIE
Active in Riverside, c. 1899-1902.

DUBEN, C.
Daguerreotypist at the corner of Montgomery and Clay Streets, San Francisco, 1852.

DUHEM, CONSTANT L.
Born in France, 1840. Brother of Victor Duhem; partner in Duhem Brothers, Denver, Colorado, 1869-77. With C. Duhem & Company, 739 Market Street, San Francisco, by 1880.

DUHEM, HAROLD
Photographer with V. Duhem & Sons, San Francisco, 1900; worked for the Nelson Studio, at 1019 Market Street, 1904. Probably a son of Victor Duhem.

DUHEM, JULIA (MRS.)
Born in Illinois, 1858. Ran the gallery at 1633 Polk Street, San Francisco, 1883. Wife of Victor H. Duhem.

DUHEM, VICTOR H.
Born in France, 1844. Brother of Constant Duhem and his partner in Duhem Brothers, Denver, Colorado, 1869-77. Partner with Constant in Duhem & Company, 1633 Polk Street, San Francisco, 1881-94; at 64 Third Street, prior to 1895; operated as Victor Duhem & Sons, 94 Third Street, c. 1900.

DUHEM, VICTOR L.
Born in Colorado, 1877, son of Victor H. and Julia Duhem. Lecturer on the cineograph, 1898. Photographer with V. Duhem & Sons, San Francisco, 1900-04.

DUHEM, VICTOR M.
Photographer at 64 Third Street, San Francisco, 1895; manager of the Nelson Studio at 1019 Market, 1904.

DUNHAM & BLUETT
Studio in Oakland at 1157 Broadway between 13th and 14th, 1876.

DUNHAM & COOK
Operated Palace Gallery in Oakland, c. 1870.

DUNHAM & KELSEY
Active in Susanville, 1886; O. W. Dunham and C. C. Kelsey.

DUNHAM & LATHROP
Located at 1157 Broadway, between 13th and 14th, Oakland, 1874; Allen Murray Dunham.

DUNHAM, ALLEN MURRY
Born 1834. Photographic printer with William Shew, San Francisco, 1865-70; photographic parlor in Oakland, 1872; partner with Lathrop at 1159 Broadway while he worked for George D. Morse in San Francisco, 1874; at Oakland studio, 1877; parlor in Hayward, 1880; operated Vallejo Gallery in Vallejo and New Photo Parlors at 11th and Clay Streets, 1880. Also a traveling photographer, 1850-90.

DUNHAM, EPHRAIM G.
Born 1839. Photographer for William Shew, 1865. Probably a brother of A. M. Dunham.

DUNHAM, ORLEY WYATT
Active in Greenville, c. 1880. Partner in Dunham & Kelsey in Reno, Nevada, 1886. Studio in Susanville, 1886.

DUNLAP, KNIGHT (MRS.)
Active in Diamond Springs, 1894.

DUNN, COURTNEY E.
Born in Pennsylvania, 1861. Active in San Francisco, 1880.

DUNSMUIR STUDIO
Operated by E. Paul in Dunsmuir, 1909.

DURGAN, FRANK
Active in Mayfield, c. 1867; with J. A. Todd in Sacramento, 1870.

DUROSE
Partner with A. P. Flaglor, operating as Flaglor & Durose, stereo photographers in San Francisco, 1860s-80s.

DUSY, FRANK
Born in Melbourne, lower Canada, 1836. He ran away to New Hampshire at age eleven; later went to Boston and then by steamer to the Isthmus, crossing in 24 days; arrived in San Francisco, 1858. Mined in Tuolumne County; worked on the U.S. Detective Force in Fresno County, 1864. Photographer in Millerton, 1865-70 or later (the town was abandoned, 1874). Dusy had a farm of 1,900 acres and became a well-known sheep man. He had a summer place called Dinkey about sixty miles into the Sierra Nevada from Fresno; explored the Sierras extensively, taking scenic and landscape views.

DUTCHER, EDWIN M.
Photographic printer with C. E. Watkins, 429 Montgomery Street, San Francisco, 1869-70.

DUTCHER, MOSES
Born in Massachusetts, 1850. Listed as a "Deugerien" in the Stockton census, 1870.

DUTCHER, SARAH (MISS)
Born in Australia, 1847, of English parents. Photographic retoucher, San Francisco, 1876; operated as a photograph agent by 1880.

DUTKEWICH
Traveling photographer, 1895.

DUTTON, S.
Born 1823. Active in San Francisco, 1860.

DYER & LUDERS
Partnership of William D. Dyer and Edward T. Luders at 612 Clay Street, a few doors west of Montgomery, San Francisco, 1865.

DYER, WILLIAM DENNY
Born in New Jersey, 1832. Had a daguerreian parlor at 166 Clay Street, San Francisco; partner in Dyer & Luders, 1865.

EAGLE CLIFT STUDIO
Operating in Mott, 1890.

EAGLE GALLERY
Operated by J. H. Heering, Healdsburg, 1859.

EAMES, CHARLES
Active in Shasta, 1865.

EAMES, ELIZABETH J. (MRS.)
Born 1829; died 1900. Photographer in Shasta City, 1865-69.

EAST OAKLAND GALLERY
Operated at 556 Twelfth Street, East Oakland "Come Rain or Shine," 1886-88, F. M. Harkness, photographer.

EASTBURN, FRANK P.
Active in Callahan, c. 1896.

EASTMAN, E. A. (MRS.)
Active in Stockton, operating a gallery at the corner of American and Main Streets, 1884-85.

EASTMAN, EMILY R. (MRS.)
Photographic painter, 109 Third Street, San Francisco, 1869-70; retoucher for William Shew and others, 1871-76; retoucher and artist at 235 Kearny, 1877; 23 Kearny, 1878; 11 Kearny, 1888.

EASTMAN, FRANK P.
Active in Weaverville, 1896-97.

EASTMAN, JERVIE H.
Active in Sisson, 1901-10; operated as a traveling photographer, 1909.

EASTMAN VIEW COMPANY
Operated by Jervie H. Eastman, traveling photographer, 1909.

EATON, NORA E.
Active in Placerville, 1892-93. Bought the studio of Bird & Cook.

EATON
Partner in Schwichtenberg & Eaton, Bartlett Building, Pomona, c. 1895.

ECLIPSE PHOTO CAR
Traveling car active in Santa Barbara producing stereoviews.

EDDY, LINDLEY
Portrait and stereo photographer in San Diego at 418 Logan Avenue.

EDGAR, FRANCES
Active in Berkeley, c. 1899-1901.

EDOUART & COBB
Active in San Francisco, 504 Kearny Street, corner of California, c. 1869-81; Alexander Edouart and David Cobb. Also operated as traveling photographers, 1880.

EDOUART, ALEXANDER
Born in England, 1825. Portrait painter and daguerreian artist; operated photographic gallery at 634 Washington, San Francisco, 1862; at 504 Kearny Street, corner of California, 1867; with David Cobb operating as Edouart & Cobb, c. 1869-c. 1881. Operated gallery at 6 Turk Street, 1883-88; Edouart & Son located at 121 or 217 ½ South Spring, 1890-92.

EDRIS, P. J.
Active in Ft. Jones, 1866.

EDWARDS, HELEN (MRS.)
Photographer with J. E. Edwards, Merced, 1884-90; in Santa Barbara, c. 1900.

EDWARDS, J. E.
Partner with William Brown in Brown & Edwards, Modesto, 1878-80; gallery on K Street between Front and Main, Merced, 1883-88 or later; in Santa Barbara, 1890-98; Ventura, 1898.

EGGAN, H. P.
Active in Los Angeles at 123 South Main, 1895.

EHMANN, CHARLES E.
Active in San Francisco, 1880-1900 or longer. Gallery at 115 Fourth Street, 1880-86; 116 Twelfth Street, 1887; 111 Fourth Street, 1889-1900.

EHRMANN, CHARLES S.
Photographic printer with G. D. Morse, San Francisco, 1883.

EICHENBERGER, EMIL
Gallery at 503 Montgomery Street, San Francisco, 1894-95.

EICHENBERGER, L.
Gallery at 510 Seventh Street, Oakland, 1888.

EICHLER, OSCAR
Active in Orland, 1893-94; Suisun, 1896.

EILERMAN
Active in Willows, 1900; partner in Bird & Eilerman, c. 1895.

ELDRIDGE, IRVING
Active in Sawyer's Bar, 1890s.

ELDRIDGE, JONATHAN EDGAR
Gallery on I Street, Crescent City, 1867-84.

ELIOTT'S PHOTOGRAPH GALLERY
Studio at Third and Main Streets, Woodland, c. 1880; advertised views, india ink, watercolors and oil portraits; specialized in children.

ELITE
Operated by T. E. Stanton at 119 and 129 North Main Street, Temple Block, Los Angeles, c. 1885.

ELITE
Studio in J. B. Scott's New Building, Salinas City, c. 1890.

ELITE
Studio of Jones & Lotz, 838 Market Street, San Francisco, c. 1880.

ELITE GALLERY
Also known as Elite Studio, partnership of H. H. Blakesly and E. R. Healy in St. Helena, c. 1890.

ELITE GALLERY
Studio in Los Angeles on the Temple Block at Spring and Main, Los Angeles, 1881-83; 119-129 North Main, 1883-84. E. W. Pierce, proprietor, 1886-87. Also called Elite Photograph Gallery, and Payne, Stanton & Company.

ELITE GALLERY
Studio of Henry Kemp Van Ee, located on Tenth, between H and I Streets, Modesto, c. 1885.

ELITE PHOTO STUDIO
Traveling gallery based at 107 Grove Street, San Francisco, c. 1891.

ELITE PHOTOGRAPH GALLERY
Operated by J. P. Lowe, Tulare Street, near K, Auburn, 1883.

ELITE PHOTOGRAPHIC GALLERY
Studio in San Francisco; 1880-1900+ at 838 Market Street; also known as Jones, Robinson & Company and Elite Photographic Studio. Operated by Thomas H. Jones with partners G. M. Robinson and W. H. Rulofson, 1880; by Robinson, 1881-83; by Paul Lotz, 1885-89 or later.

ELITE PHOTOGRAPHIC GALLERY
Active in Marysville, corner Third and D Streets over Joe Lask's Store; operated by LaRosh & Tieman, c. 1880; owned by Philip W. Griffiths, 1880-88.

ELITE STUDIO
Operated by Mrs. E. H. Turner in San Diego, 1895-98.

ELITE STUDIO
Active in Red Bluff, c. 1895.

ELITE STUDIO
Partnership of Strunz & Woodworth, Lodi, c. 1895.

ELITE STUDIO
Partnership of H. H. Blakesly and E. R. Healy in St. Helena, c. 1890. Also known as Elite Gallery.

ELITE STUDIO
Operated by George F. Owings in Etna, 1902.

ELLICK, GEORGE H.
Photographic printer, San Francisco, 1869-70.

ELLIOT, ORMAN
Active Woodland, 1880; in Stockton, 1882-91 or later, operating the Elite at 305 Main Street; in Marysville, 1888, gallery located on Fourth Street, between B and C Streets. Active in Chico, 1890.

ELLIOTT, EFFIE
Active in San Francisco, 1900.

ELLIS & SON
Active in Los Angeles, 1881-84; located at 55 Main Street, 235 Main Street, and 114-116 New High Street. Partnership of Lemuel and L. S. Ellis.

ELLIS, L. S.
Partner in Ellis & Son, Los Angeles, 1881-84.

ELLIS, LEMUEL
Daguerreotypist in Boston, 1854. Listed as Ellis & Son, 1881-86.

ELWELL, F. F.
Traveling photographer, 1855.

EMANUEL, E. V.
Photographic artist, 997-999 Market Street, San Francisco, 1883.

EMIG
Partner in Schoene & Emig, Santa Clara, c. 1875.

EMMONS, CLARA
Active in Los Angeles, c. 1899-1900.

ENGLE
Active in Redwood City, c. 1900.

ENSIGN, W. H.
Active in Chico, 1900. See Oregon.

EPPLER, ARTHUR O.
Operated Luline Studio, 1319 ½ Larkin Street, San Francisco, 1895; at 1314 Larkin, 1898.

ERCANBRACK
Partner in Burnett & Ercanbrack, Castroville, 1874. Operated Pajora Art Gallery, c. 1875.

ERICSON, AUGUSTUS WILLIAM
Born in Orebro, Sweden, April 26, 1848; died in Arcata, August 15, 1927. Came to America, 1866; to Trinidad, California, 1869. Worked at lumbering until 1876; settled at Arcata, working as telegrapher and opening a stationery store. Active in photography, 1885-1925; scenic photographer, partner with his brother, Richard; recorded local views, Indians, railroads and logging camps.
    Peter Palmquist and Lincoln Kilian, *The Photographers of the Humboldt Bay Region*, Vol. 7., Peter E. Palmquist, 1989.
    Peter E. Palmquist, *Fine California Views: the Photographs of A.W. Ericson.*, Interface California Corporation, 1975.

ERWIN, JAMES W.
Amateur stereo photographer, active in San Francisco.

ESBECK, AUGUST
Studio at 1140 Market Street, San Francisco, 1898.

ESTERLE, ALBERT MARK
Gallery on the northeast corner of J and Third Street, Sacramento, 1865-74.

ETNA ART PARLORS
Operated by C. A. Miller in Etna, 1906-08.

ETNA GALLERY
Operating in Etna, 1894.

EUREKA ART & PHOTOGRAPHIC STUDIO
Operated in San Francisco, c. 1880.

EUREKA GALLERY
Operated in Grass Valley by W. A. Clinch, c. 1880, and Kendell & Clinch, c. 1885.

EUREKA GALLERY
Operated by C. Denion Bowen in San Jose at 58 South First Street, c. 1880.

EUREKA GALLERY
Operated by Button & Higgins from rooms formerly occupied by J. H. Heering at 342 First Street, San Jose, 1874.

EVANS
Partner in Downing & Evans, Susanville, c. 1900.

EVANS & VAN ETTEN
Operated gallery at 1065 Washington Street, Oakland, c. 1893.

EVANS, FRANK E.
Active in Los Angeles at 168 East First, 1888; 31 Post Office Block, 1890.

EVANS, J. G.
Active in Los Angeles at 305 North Main, 1883-87; also claimed to be a resident of New York's Boyle Heights.

EVANS, Z. W.
Active in Los Angeles at 3020 South Grand Avenue, 1893.

EVELYN & HOGARTH
Active in Chico, 1875.

EVERETT
Partner in Picket & Everett, College City, c. 1877; in Colusa on Market Street, 1878.

EVERETT & BURGE
Partnership in College City, 1881; A. J. Everett and possibly J. C. Burge.

EVERETT, ANDREW JACKSON
Partner in Pickett & Everett, 1870s-78; produced stereoviews from Amador City, 1870s; built a photograph gallery on Market Street, Colusa, opposite the Sun building, February 1877; in College City, c. 1877-78. Also listed as Everett & Pickett. Partner in Everett & Burge, College City, 1881.

EVERITT, E. F.
Active in Redlands, c. 1900. See Oregon.

EWING, CHARLES G.
Studio at 111 Montgomery Street, San Francisco, 1871-73.

EXCELSIOR ART GALLERY
Operated by M. Monaco in Stockton, 183 Main Street, 1883-89 or later.

EXCELSIOR FINE ART GALLERY
Partnership of James Riley Mains and C. A. Marston, active in San Francisco at 523 Kearny Street, 1868-74.

EXCELSIOR GALLERY
Studio in Los Angeles, 207 North Main Street, 1888; also at 221 North Main, 6 Downey Block; operated by William Lawrence; also known as Lawrence & Son.

EXCELSIOR PHOTO GALLERY
Operated by Henry S. Simmons in Los Angeles at 352 South Broadway, 1896.

EXCELSIOR PHOTOGRAPHIC PARLORS
Operated by E. K. Peacock in Colton on Commercial Street, 1884.

EXCELSIOR STUDIO
Gallery in San Francisco; originally located at 500 Valencia Street; moved to 409 Stanyan Street, c. 1890.

EYRE, WILLIAM
Photographer with Kingsley, San Francisco, 1869-70. Gallery at 659 Clay Street, San Francisco, 1874-77.

FABER PHOTO COMPANY
Operated by F. W. Hennessy and A. F. Welton in Los Angeles at 217 South Spring, 1896.

FAGERSTEEN, GUSTAVUS
Photographer in San Francisco at 315 Montgomery Street before 1875; portrait painter and photographer in San Jose, 1875, at 355 and 361; in Merced, 1877; issued stereoviews in association with S. C. Walker in Stockton and Yosemite, 1870s; gallery near Barnard's Hotel, Yosemite Valley, 1883; gallery in Madera, 1886; in Fresno at 225 Mariposa Street, 1888.

FAIRBANKS, DE BUHR & GOLTRA
Active in Los Angeles, 1896, 14 Allen Block and 223 North Spring; William W. Fairbanks, Edward B. Goltra and Joseph De Buhr.

FAIRBANKS, WILLIAM W.
Active in Elk; in Point Arena, c. 1888. With Fairbanks, De Buhr & Goltra, view photographers, 14 Allen Block and 223 North Spring, Los Angeles, 1896.

FAIRCHILD, E. N.
Stereo photographer active in San Francisco area, 1900-10s.

FAIST, CHARLES G.
Operated from the corner of Market and Fourth Streets, San Francisco, c. 1878. Partner in Lanier & Faist, 31 Third Street, 1885. His own gallery at 3 Fourth Street, 1886-88 or later.

FARDEN, GEORGE ROBINSON
Born in Birmingham, England, 1806; died in Canada, 1886. Came to America, 1849, first to New York and to San Francisco by 1856. Daguerreian saloon located at 203 Clay Street, San Francisco, 1859. Landscape and view photographer; an album of his San Francisco photographs on paper was published, 1856-57, the first album of photographs of an American city ever published. Some of the images in Farden's album may have been taken by James M. Ford or Carleton E. Watkins. Farden moved his studio to Ft. Victoria, Vancouver Island, 1858; his photographs of that island were published in the *Illustrated London News*, January 10, 1863. Retired from photography in Canada, 1870.

> *San Francisco in the 1850s: Photographic Views* by G. R. Fardon. Facimile of Fardon's book, *San Francisco Album*. Inroduction by Robert A. Sobieszek. George Eastman House and Dover Publications, 1977.
>
> Peter E. Palmquist, "Carleton E. Watkins, A Biography," Chapter 4, *The Daguerreian Annual*, Eureka, California, 1991.

FARRELL, WILLIAM. M.
Active in San Francisco, 1896-1901.

FARRERE, MANUEL
Worked for Joseph Silva, San Francisco, 1865.

FAVORITE, IRENE R.
Born in Pennsylvania 1839. Active in Los Angeles and Downey, 1880s; in Garberville, Rohnerville, Trinidad, c. 1881- 82. Also listed as Irena. See Oregon and Texas.

FAY & DARBYSHIRE
Operated in Redwood City, c. 1877.

FAY & JEROME
Operated at 32 Kearny Street, San Francisco, 1867.

FEDERSPIEL, ANNA S.
Active in San Francisco, 1897-1903.

FELL, A. W.
Partner in Nobel & Fell, Main Street, Petaluma, 1874; gallery in Lompoc, 1878; gallery opposite Williams Hotel, Gilroy, 1892; in Watsonville on Main Street, c. 1881-1906+. Partner in Bartley & Fells, Salinas City, 1883-87.

FELLOWS
Stereo photographer active in Mirror Lake.

FENN, S. T.
Active in Yreka, 1861-62; licensed in Ft. Jones, 1863.

FENNESSEY, GLADYS
Photographer in Chico, 1909-10.

FERNDALE GALLERY
Active in Pasadena, 1882, operated by George Weingarth at his ranch in Walnut and Orange Grove.

FERRAND, CHARLES
Born in France, 1824. Operated gallery at 48 Pine Street, Nevada City, 1863-80.

FERRAR
Partner in Kraft & Ferrar, 659 Clay Street, San Francisco, 1877.

FESSENDEN
Partner in May & Fessenden, San Francisco, 1855.

FESSENDON, CHARLES. P.
Active in San Diego, 1869-80.

FETROW, WILLIAM PARKER
Partner in Freese & Fetrow, Eureka, 1888.

FETZER, AUGUST W.
Active in Trinity County, 1897-1900.

FIELDING, JOHN
Born in New York, 1856. Active in Oakland, 1875-81.

FIELDS, J. G.
Traveling photographer, 1897.

FIGG, ADELE
Active in San Francisco, 1898.

FINCH, O. R.
Active in Cottonwood, 1900-05.

FINDLEY, MARGARET
Active in Colton, c. 1888-90. Also known as Maggie.

FINK, J. F.
Active in Chico, 1914.

FISCHER, M.
Operated El Paso de Robles Gallery, c. 1890.

FISKE, C. C.
Traveling photographer, 1908.

FISKE, GEORGE
Born in Amherst, New Hampshire, 1835; died in Merced, 1918. Fiske was employed as a clerk in his half-brother's bank, next door to Vance's Gallery where Charles Leander Weed worked and produced the first images of Yosemite Valley. Fiske worked for Carleton E. Watkins, 1864; photographer for T. Housewworth & Company, 1869-73. In 1874, Fiske returned to work for Watkins, Houseworth's rival, and stayed with him until Watkins' bankruptcy. Fiske had helped in Watkins' Yosemite Art Gallery for years, and may have visited Yosemite with Muybridge, 1872, 1879. He became Yosemite's first year-round photographer, with a studio opposite the church in Yosemite Valley. Fiske was close friends with Galen Clark, Yosemite's first "Guardian," and spent many years photographing the Yosemite, its residents and visitors.

> Paul Hickman and Terence Pitts, *George Fiske, Yosemite Photographer*, Northland Press, 1980.

FISKE, JAMES
Born in Massachusetts, 1820. Active in San Francisco, 1870.

FITCH, ANITA
Active in San Francisco, c. 1899-1900.

FITCH, HERBERT R.
Born in Andover, Connecticut, 1868; died in San Diego, c. 1952. After attending M.I.T., he moved to San Diego because of his health, 1895; operated a studio and photographed maritime subjects, 1897-1952.

FITZGERALD, INEZ G.
Born in Michigan, August 1852. Active in San Francisco, 1889-92; Gilroy, 1892-1908; Redding, 1910. See Oregon.

FITZGERALD, MYRA
Active in Oakland, 1899-1900.

FITZPATRICK, JOHN F.
Partner in F. H. Rogers & Company, 15 First Street, Los Angeles, 1884.

FLACH, G. A.
Stereo photographer active in Alameda.

FLAGLOR & DUROSE
Partnership of A. P. Flaglor and Durose, stereo photographers in San Francisco, 1860s-80s.

FLAGLOR & GREGOR
Active in Eureka, Humboldt County, 1874; Alexander Gregor.

FLAGLOR, AMASA P.
Born in New Brunswick, Canada, December 24, 1848; died in Decoto, Alameda County, March 2, 1918. Arrived in San Francisco, 1862; worked for William Shew, 1862-68; photographer with Bradley & Rulofson, San Francisco, 1869-70; Flaglor & Parker, Cosmopolitan Gallery, 523 Kearny Street and Flaglor & Durose, c. 1870; photographer with Oscar Foss, 606 Kearny Street, 1870-71. Opened the Eureka Photograph Gallery in Eureka, 1871-80; branch galleries in Arcata, 1876; Rohnerville, 1878. Traveled to Jacksonville, Oregon, 1878, where he was befriended by Peter Britt; due to poor business, he returned to Eureka. Operated a gallery in San Francisco, southeast corner of Market and Ninth, 1885- 88.

FLANDERS & GODFREY'S ART PHOTOGRAPHIC PARLOR
Operated in Los Angeles, c. 1873.

FLANDERS & TUTTLE
Partnership of Dudley P. Flanders and William N. Tuttle, active in Arcata, Eureka and Rohnerville, 1865-66.

FLANDERS & VANCE
Active in Grass Valley on Church Street, opposite Hamilton Hall, late 1860s; produced "Flander's Patent Enameled Cards" on Mill Street, 1868.

FLANDERS, DUDLEY P.
Born in Massachusetts, c. 1840. Partner in Flanders & Tuttle, 1865-66; bought out Tuttle, 1866, and operated as Eureka Photographic Gallery. Active in San Francisco, 1865-67; Grass Valley, 1867-72; with Edgar Henry Vance as Flanders & Vance, late 1860s; Truckee, 1868; 205 Third Street, Los Angeles, 1873; with Godfrey in Flanders & Godfrey's Art Photographic Parlor, Downey's Block, 727 Main Street, 1873. See Arizona.

FLECKENSTEIN, LOUIS
Born in Faribault, Minnesota, 1866; died in Long Beach, California, 1943. Pictorialist photographer in Los Angeles, 1907.

FLEISCHMANN, ELIZABETH
Died 1905. Active in San Francisco, 1896-1905. A pioneer in the field of X-ray photography, she opened the first laboratory in California at 611 Sutter Street; worked with Army physicians during the Philippine War, and the Surgeon-General of the Army rated her work as the best known. She married Israel J. Ascheim, 1900; she died from the results of exposure to radiation. Also listed as Mrs. E. Fleischmann-Ascheim.
    Peter E. Palmquist, *Pioneer X-Ray Photographer*, Judah L. Magnes Museum, Berkeley, California, 1990.

FLETCHER, HENRY
Active in San Francisco, 1869-70; retoucher, 1883.

FLETCHER, SARAH S. (MRS.)
Proprietor of the Acme Photograph Studios in San Francisco, 914 Market Street, 1881-83.

FLETCHER, WILLIAM H.
View photographer from Vermont; moved to Los Angeles, 1885.

FLIGGLE, J. E.
Active in Vallejo, 1864; Suisun, 1865.

FLORENCE PHOTOGRAPH GALLERY
Operated by A. Provo Kluit in San Francisco, 28 Third Street, 1875.

FLOWER, W. B.
Active in San Bernardino, 1895; 448 Stowell Block, Los Angeles, 1899.

FLY, CAMILLUS S.
Active in San Francisco until 1879; moved to Tombstone, Arizona, where he worked until his death. Photographed Geronimo and participants in the Apache campaigns and some participants of the gunfight at O.K. Corral. See Arizona.

FLYING PHOTOGRAPHER
The traveling photographer, George Henry Ramsdell, 1890.

FLYING STUDIO
Studio operated by Edweard J. Muybridge and Silas Selleck in San Francisco, c. 1864. Also known as Helios-the Flying Studio.

FONG, C. W.
Active in Oakland at 511 8th Street, 1904.

FONG, EDWARD
Active in San Francisco at 743 Grant Aveenue, c. 1920s.

FONG GET
Operated studio at 914 Stockton Street in San Francisco, c. 1900.

FORBES, ANDREW ALEXANDER
Born in Ottowa Township, Wisconsin, April 21, 1862; died in southern California, 1921. Traveling photographer in Kansas, Colorado, New Mexico, Arizona, Texas and Oklahoma, 1880s-90s. Active in Gutherie and Oklahoma City, Oklahoma, c. 1889. Known today for his scenes of cowboy life. Arrived in California, 1898; operated out of Santa Ana, 1898-1902; studio in Bishop, 1902-16.
    Owenulph, "No Trade for Heroes," *The America West*, 1968.
    Bosak, Jon, "Andrew A. Forbes — Photographs of the Owens Valley Paiute," *Journal of California Anthropology*, Banning, California, Summer 1975.

FORD, H. C.
Active in Santa Barbara, 1878.

FORD, JAMES M.
Brother of Frank Ford, photographer in Ravenna, Ohio. Arrived in California, 1849; operated in Sacramento as Wheeler & Ford, 1852; gallery in Sacramento City and on Clay Street, San Francisco, 1854; sold out to H. A. Kendrick, 1854; gallery in San Jose, 1855; also in San Francisco, operating as Ford's Daguerrian Gallery, 1855. He

claimed he was first to make ambrotypes in California. Carleton Watkins served as a Ford operator before opening his own studio. Ford competed with Robert Vance for pre-eminence in San Francisco's gold rush era photography market. He left for Ohio, c. 1858, and his studio was operated by S. P. Howes. Ford returned in 1861 and shared a studio with Watkins.

FORTIN, J.
Active in San Diego before 1890.

FORTUNE, E. W.
Active in Los Angeles, 1888-93; 151 South Spring, 1888-90; 523 Downey Avenue, 1888-89; 239 ½ South Spring Street, 1890-93.

FORZELL, C.
Active in Lompoc, c. 1895.

FOSS & HALSEY
Gallery in San Francisco at 606 Kearny, 1868-74.

FOSS & HICKOX
Partnership of Oscar Foss and A. A. Hickox, stereo photographers operating in San Francisco, 1860s-70s.

FOSS, OSCAR
Born 1830. Associated with Bayley Brothers, c. 1864. Gallery in San Francisco at 841 Mission and at 606 Kearny Street, in association with A. J. Perkins by 1865; continued alone, 1865-74. Sold photographic and ambrotype material with partner Alonzo T. Ruthrauff at 606 Kearny, 1867-69; at 410 Kearny Street, c. 1874-81 or later.

FOSTER
Active in Fresno, c. 1900.

FOSTER, J. L.
Active in San Diego, 1898.

FOWZER
Partner in Fowzer & Samuels in Colusa; produced photo of lynching victim Hong Di, July 11, 1887.

FOWZER & HAYES
Partnership of Jacob Fowzer and Henry C. Hayes in San Francisco at 115 Fourth Street, 1883.

FOWZER & SAMUELS
Studio active in Colusa, 1887.

FOWZER, GEORGE J.
Operated in San Francisco, c. 1900.

FOWZER, JACOB
Partner with Henry C. Hayes, 115 Fourth Street, San Francisco, c. 1883-95; continued business alone at 1228 Market Street, 1895; 1148 Market Street, 1898-1900+.

FOX, ALEXANDER
Born in England, 1823. Established Alexander Fox & Company at 606 Kearny in San Francisco by 1867; moved to 649 Clay Street, c. 1869. Associated with James Brayton in Napa City, 1870. Partner with Charles W. Symons in Salt Lake City, 1874-82.

FRANKLIN & DARLINGTON
Partnership operating in Redding, 1893.

FRANKLIN & HOWELL
Operating in Yreka, c. 1891; Redding, 1891-93.

FRANKLIN & WHITE
Operating in Redding, c. 1890.

FRANKLIN, J. C.
Active in Palo Alto, c. 1900.

FRANKLIN, JOHN C.
Operated in Redding, c. 1890-93; also a traveling photographer, 1889-93.

FRANKLIN, LENA
Born in Oregon, July 1864. Partner with Charles Johnson in San Francisco, c. 1898-1903; gallery at 31 Third Street 1898; 55 Third, 1899-1900.

FRANKLIN, MAURICE A.
Sold drugs and medicines and operated the Premium Photographic Gallery over his drug store in San Bernardino, 1864-67.

FRAUENHOLZ, ELEANOR
Active in San Francisco, 1897-99.

FRAZER, D. H. (MISS)
Active in San Diego, 1889-90.

FREEMAN, EDMUND R.
Born in Greeley, Colorado, 1879; died 1939. Husband of Emma B. Freeman; married in Denver, Colorado, November 26, 1902. After the couple moved to Eureka, Edmund had learned photography by 1910, opened the Freeman Art Company and purchased the studio of J. A. Meiser. Edmund traveled and documented the countryside. He made lantern slides of the building of the Panama Canal and the route of the new Northwestern Pacific Railroad, and presented lectures. He also took motion pictures of the joining of the rails celebration at Cain Rock, Humboldt County, 1914, and was an official photographer at the 1915 Panama-Pacific International Exposition. See Emma B. Freeman.

FREEMAN, EMMA B.
Born in Nebraska, 1880; died in San Francisco, March 26, 1928. Emma Belle Richart married Edmund R. Freeman in Denver, Colorado, November 26, 1902. They moved to San Francisco, 1904, and opened an art shop. Emma enrolled in the art school of Giuseppe Cadenasso and learned to draw and paint. The 1906 earthquake destroyed the art shop and the couple moved to Eureka, opening another art shop. At the Freeman Art Company they sold framed photographs by the Pillsbury Picture Company, among many other things. Emma operated the store and continued her art training under Charles Harmon. She also learned photography and specialized in artistic portraits and landscape, including a series of hand colored images of local Indians. The Freemans divorced in 1915, and Emma continued to operate the Freeman Art Company. She published illustrated articles about native culture and art in the *Overland Monthly*, *Pacific Outdoors*, and *Camera Craft*. Emma offered approximately two hundred images of Native Americans, known as the northern California Series, had a major display at the 1915 Panama-Pacific International Exposition, and won national recognition. After a period of great success, however, she became over-extended and her business failed.

Peter E. Palmquist, *With Nature's Children: Emma B. Freeman [1880-1928] - Camera and Brush*, Interface California Corporation, 1976.

FREEMAN, EVA P.
Active in Chico on Barber Street and Salem, 1909-10.

FREESE & FETROW
Operated in Eureka, c. 1888-90.

FRENCH, IRA G.
Operated in San Francisco, 1852-62.

FRENCH, JAMES A.
Born in New Hampshire, 1830. Active in San Francisco, 1870.

FRENCH, JULIA A. (MRS.)
Studio on the northeast corner of Kearny and Washington, San Francisco, 1869-71.

FRICK, R. N.
Active in Los Angeles, 1880s.

FRIEND, A. O.
Active in Folsom, 1867.

FRIEND, HERVE
Studio in Los Angeles at 314 West First Street, 1895; also located at 513 North Main and 205 ½ South Main, unknown dates.

FROST, EDWARD SANDS
Born in Lyman, Maine, 1843. Moved to Pasadena, 1877; began photographic work with son, George Henry Frost, c. 1882. Operated as E. S. Frost & Son, located on north side of Colorado Boulevard, east of Fair Oaks Avenue, 1882-87. Also listed as E. B. Frost & Son.

FROST, GEORGE HENRY
Born in Beddeford, Maine, 1868. Moved with family to Pasadena and worked with his father, Edward Sands Frost, in E. S. Frost & Son, 1882-87.

FRY & JENKINS
Active in Chico on 2nd Street, 1875-95.

FRYE BROTHERS
Operated by Hiram H. Frye in Grass Valley, 1877.

FRYE, HIRAM HAMILTON
Born in Michigan, 1842. Studio in Davisville, c. 1872; in Vallejo at 136 ½ Georgia Street, by 1874; partner in Frye Brothers, 6½ Mill Street, Grass Valley, 1877; in Chico, 1874-1900, on 2nd Street. An H. H. Frye & Company appears in Woodland, Washington, around 1875.

FRYETT, FRANK C.
Photographer in Silver City, New Mexico, 1882; active in Los Angeles at 742 South Fort, 1886-87; in Redlands and San Francisco, c. 1894.

FUHRMAN, R. H.
Active San Diego, 1895-98. Also spelled Furman.

FUJII, M.
Active in San Francisco, c. 1910.

FULLARD, WILLIAM
Born in California, 1854. Active in San Francisco, 1880-88.

FULLER & WILLIAMS
Gallery at 1150 Market Street, San Francisco, c. 1887.

FULLER, A. W.
Photographer with William H. Fuller, 1150 Market Street, San Francisco, 1886.

FULLER, C. (MRS.)
Active in San Diego, c. 1886. Her photographs were published in *Sketch of San Diego*, 1886, by Charles Turrill.

FULLER, WILLIAM H.
Gallery at 1150 Market Street, San Francisco, 1885-87. Edward A. Williams became a partner, 1887-88.

FULLERTON PHOTO COMPANY
Partnership of Samuel J. Fullerton and Edward A. Williams, active in San Francisco, 1887-88. Located at 1150 Market Street, 1887; 1140 Market Street, 1888.

FULLERTON, SAMUEL J.
Operated at 1398 Market Street, San Francisco, c. 1898; partner with Edward A. Williams in the Fullerton Photo Company.

GADION, D.
Partner in Strong & Gadion in Placerville, 1899-1900, located behind Wonderly's Blacksmith Shop, formerly operated by T. A. Ley.

GAGE, EDWARD F.
Born in Massachusetts. Photographer with George D. Morse, San Francisco, 1869-70.

GAGE, HERMAN KIMBALL
Born in Massachusetts, 1834. Active in Aurora, Nevada, at Pine Street, c. 1863. Parlor at the corner of Church and Bridge in Truckee, Nevada County, 1874-86.

GAGE, M. D. (MRS.)
Gallery at 205 Third Street, San Francisco, 1871-72. Possibly related to portrait photographer H. K. Gage.

GAGNE, ED.
Operated the North Beach Gallery at 706 Filbert Street, San Francisco, c. 1890.

GAINES
Operated the People's Gallery, 627 J Street, Sacramento, 1880.

GAINES, A. F.
Active in Redding, 1889.

GAINES, FLANE HENRY H.
Gallery on North Main Street, Red Bluff, c. 1884-90.

GALERIA DE LA PLAZA
Operated by J. B. Blanchard, 513 North Main Street, Los Angeles, c. 1895. Also known as the Plaza Gallery.

GALLAHER, STELLA
Amateur active around Lotus and Coloma, 1887.

GANTER & GANTER
Born in Wisconsin; Nell Stephanie Ganter died, c. 1947; Bertha "Berd" Theresa Ganter died 1970. They settled in San Francisco as young girls, studied photography, then moved to Napa City and operated a gallery 1898-1946. Also listed as Ganter sisters.

GANTER SISTERS
See Ganter & Ganter.

GARARD, A.
Licensed in San Juan, 1865.

GARDEN CITY PHOTO COMPANY
Operated by James T. and A. M. Pollock in Los Angeles at 606 East Fifth Street, 1896-1902; proprietor, Samuel Cohen, 1896.

GARDET, ALFRED
Photographer for the architect, Victor Hoffman; active in San Jose, 1871.

GARDINER, ROSWELL H.
Born in Maine, 1853 or 1856. Operated the Great Eastern Photographic and Advertising Company in Downey, c. 1885-98; Whittier, 1900; Fresno, 1900. See British Columbia. Also spelled Gardener.

GARDNER, GEORGE D.
Stereo photographer active in San Francisco.

GARDNER, WINNIFRED
Born in New York, April 1873. Active in Redlands, c. 1899-1900.

GARNIERE, EMMA
Partner with Mrs. L. M. Hellen in portrait gallery, Hellen & Garniere, Oakland, 1900.

GARRETT, A. W.
Operating at 48 Third Street, San Francisco, 1862-63. Sold out to John Bachman, 1863.

GARRETT, EDWIN
Stereo photographer operating studio in Ferndale, c. 1905-20.

GARRISON
Partner in Atwater & Garrison, stereographers in San Francisco, operating as National Photo View & Copying Company at 820 California Avenue.

GARTHORNE, CHARLES A.
Photographer with Joseph T. Silva, San Francisco, 1869-70; with D. B. Taylor & Company, 1876. Also spelled Gauthorne.

GASTON, ANDREW A.
Active in San Jose, c. 1871-73.

GATES, FRANKLIN QUIRK
Active in Anderson, 1893-1908.

GATES, PETER C.
Amateur active in Pasadena and the Camera Club. Photographed with A. C. Vroman in the Southwest.

GEE, GEORGE E.
Active in San Francisco, 1893.

GELDERT, E. L.
Active in Riverside, 1900.

GELVIN, D. N.
Active in Los Angeles at 214 Downey Avenue, 1893.

GENTHE, ARNOLD
Born in Berlin, Germany, 1869; died in Connecticut, 1942. He received a doctorate at the University of Jena and studied at the Sorbonne, Paris; moved to San Francisco and opened a portrait studio, 1897. He won a *Camera Craft* gold medal, 1901; renowned for his portrait work. He established his reputation as an art photographer when he published his images of the Chinese in San Francisco's Chinatown in the book, *In Old Chinatown*, 1913. He moved to New York, 1911, continuing his portrait work, often of celebrities, and became known for his dance images of Isadora Duncan and Pavlova. He published a book of images depicting New Orleans and his autobiography, *As I Remember*, 1936.
    Richard H. Dillon, *The Hatchet Men: The Story of the Tong Wars in San Francisco's Chinatown*, Coward-McCann, Inc., New York, 1962.
    Arnold Genthe, *As I Remember*, Reynal & Hitchcock, New York, 1936.
    Will Irwin, *Old Chinatown: A Book of Pictures* by Arnold Genthe, Mitchell Kennerley, New York, 1908.

GENTILE, CHARLES
Studio on Fort Street, British Columbia, 1864. Landscape photographer; took views of the Leech River during the gold rush, 1864; accompanied Governor Seymour to the Upper Country of Canada, 1865. Established a studio at 400 Kearny Street, San Francisco, 1867; Santa Barbara, 1869. The Gentile of Chicago in later years. See British Columbia and Arizona.

GENTRY, C.
Active in Etiwanda, 1898.

GENUIT, J. H.
Operated the Pacific Coast Gallery in Stockton with H. Eshbach, printer, 1877.

GERHARD, AUGUST L.
Operated California Photo Engraving Company in San Francisco, c. 1904.

GESENKIRCHEN, JOSEPHINE
Born in California, 1863, of Russian parents. Active in San Francisco, 1880.

GET, FONG, SR.
Active in San Francisco at 960 Grant Street, c. 1910-20s.

GIBBS & WHEELER PHOTO COMPANY
Operated in French Gulch, 1890.

GIBSON, JAMES L.
Studio at 811 Market Street, San Francisco, 1880.

GILBERT, GEORGE H.
Died in Placerville, June 17, 1884. Operated daguerreotype rooms in the Baker Hotel, Placerville, 1855-56; Georgetown, 1859-60; at White & Company Building, Placerville, 1861; upstairs at the northeast corner of Main and Coloma Streets, 1862; opposite Cary House, 1864; corner of Plaza and Main Streets, 1874-84.

GILBERT, J. Z.
Stereo photographer active in southern California, c. 1909; possibly a partner of F. C. Winter.

GILFILLIAN, A. W.
Active in Ferndale, 1893-96.

GILHOUSEN BROTHERS
Partnership in Colusa, 1898.

GILL, FRANK
Studio at the corner of Third and E Street, San Bernardino, 1886-92.

GILL, R. BAYLEY
Partner in Stiffler & Gill, view photographers, 120 ½ South Spring, Los Angeles, 1896.

GILLES, D.
Licensed in Grass Valley, 1863. Also spelled Gillis.

GILLETT
Active in Colusa, 1910.

GILLETTE, CHARLES
Gallery at 1144 Market Street, San Francisco, 1885.

GILLIAM, E. W.
Active in Sisson and Williams, c. 1890.

GITCHELL, CORWIN
Operated in San Francisco, c. 1900-02.

GITO MOTO, FRANK
Active in Alameda County, c. 1910.

GIVEN
Partner in Vale & Given, operating a photographic car in southern California, listed in San Bernardino, c. 1880s.

GIVENS, JAMES D.
Operated in San Francisco, c. 1900-10.

GLAISER, THOMAS
Born in Cumberland Company, England, June 12, 1824. Ship builder who came to America, 1849; clerked in a Chicago drugstore; learned the daguerreotype art in New York City, 1854; photographer in Australia until 1869. Settled near Sonoma, California; may never have practiced photography professionally in California, since he shortly went into the grape-growing business and became the leading viticulturist of Sonoma Valley.

GOCK & COMPANY, ANN TING
Portrait studio in San Francisco at 842 Clay Street, 1895.

GOCK, HEN YEN
Active in Oakland at 329 ½ 9th Street and 918 Webster Street, 1907-09.

GODEUS, JOHN DAVID
Born in Holland, c. 1832; died in San Francisco, March 14, 1895. Settled in San Francisco, c. 1866, opening gallery at 444 ½ Third Street; sometimes called South Park Photograph Gallery; moved his People's Art Gallery to 34 Third Street, 1874-81 or later; at 10 Sixth Street, 1895. Mrs. M. C. Godeus continued the business until 1900. Also known as Johannes David Godeus.

GODEUS, MARY ANNA CLIFTON
Born in Britts Landing, Tennessee, April 1849. Married to portrait photographer J. D. Godeus and partner in the business. She continued the business after his death, 1895-1900, operating with her daughter, Mary Clara (Levy).

GODEUS, MARY CLARA
See Mary Clara Levy.

GODFREY, H. J.
Photographer in Live Oak, c. 1895.

GODFREY, PROFESSOR
Partner with Dr. Darragh, operating in Shasta as Darragh & Godfrey, 1858-59.

GODFREY, WILLIAM M.
Opened the Sunbeam Gallery in Los Angeles at 55 North Main Street, 1854. Partner with D. P. Flanders, establishing Flanders and Godfrey's Art and Photographic Parlor in the Downey Block, Main Street, 1873. He sold out to Valentin Wolfenstein, 1870s.

GOETZ, H.
Active in Nevada City, 1880.

GOLDEN STATE PHOTOGRAPHIC GALLERY
Operated by Alfred A. Hart in Sacramento, c. 1860s. Produced stereoviews and photographs of the Central Pacific Railroad. Located at 65 J Street corner of Third, Sacramento, 1869.

GOLSH, A. C.
Operated the Plaza Photograph Gallery, Tintype Gallery and the Imperial Gallery of southern California, opposite the Pico House, 411 Main Street, in Los Angeles, c. 1885.

GOLTRA, EDWARD B.
With Fairbanks, De Buhr & Goltra, view photographers, 14 Allen Block and 223 North Spring, Los Angeles, 1896.

GOOD GALLERY
Studio in East Los Angeles at 214 Downey Avenue, 1896-1900, operated by brothers, C. E. and B. F. Crutchfield.

GOODENOUGH & COMPANY
Operated a daguerreian saloon at 201 Clay Street, San Francisco, 1859.

GOODMAN, C.
Active in Coulterville, 1867.

GOODWIN, LOUISE S.
Active in Pasadena, 1886-88.

GOODYEAR, CHARLES EUGENE
Active in Weaverville, 1900.

GORDON, PETE
Took views for the Central Pacific Railroad book on Tahoe, 1887.

GORR, FRANCES E. (MRS.)
Active in San Jose, 1890-92.

GOULD
Born in Massachusetts, 1828. Daguerreian in San Francisco, 1860.

GOULD, GILBERT E.
Gallery at 1708 Fillmore, San Francisco, 1895.

GOULD, J. W.
Active in Castroville, 1878.

GOVE & ALLEN
Operated by O. M. Gove at 187 J Street, Sacramento, c. 1876-78.

GOVE, O. M.
Photographer from Boston, Massachusetts. Studio at 187 J Street in Sacramento, c. 1875-78; partner in Gove & Allen, 1876-78.

GRAFF, MAMIE (MISS)
Active San Franciso, 1898.

GRAFTON, ELIZA C.
Active in Woodland, c. 1899-1900.

GRAHAM, CLARA (MISS)
Photographer in Tehama County, 1899-1900.

GRAHAM, EMMA
Born in Washington, D.C., December 1867. Active in Woodland, 1893-94; San Francisco, c. 1899-1900. Probably the wife of photographer L. A. Graham.

GRAHAM, L. A.
Active in Red Bluff and Woodland, c. 1893-94.

GRAHAM, W. M.
Partner in Graham & Morrill, Los Angeles, 1897-98. Studio at 119 South Spring Street, 1897; 125 ½ Spring Street, 1898. Sole proprietor at 119 South Spring Street, operating as the Graham Photo Company, 1899-1905.

GRAND ART PHOTOGRAPH GALLERY
Studio at the corner of Third and Jessie Street, San Francisco, c. 1880.

GRANT
Partner in Treat & Grant, traveling photographers in Mendocino City, 1877.

GRANT, MARTIN HOWE
Born in New Brunswick, Canada, 1831; died February 12, 1889. Arrived in California, c. 1876; traveling photographer with A. R. Treat in Mendocino County, 1877; photographer for A. P. Flagler in Arcata, 1876; his own gallery, 1878; established in Eureka by 1876; Arcata, c. 1880. Gallery at Third Street between E and F streets, 1881-86 or later. Continued in Eureka until 1889. Perhaps a partner in Mains & Grant, producers of California stereoviews, 1876.

GRASETT, E. H.
Active in Los Angeles, 1886-88. Listed as Grasett & Boys, Room 14, Roeder Block, 1886-87; 23 South Spring, 1888.

GRAVES, SEWELL F.
Active in Howland Flat, Sierra County, 1868.

GRAY, H.
Partner of J. K. Dean, operating as Dean & Gray in Selma, 1885; in Mariposa, 1886. Gallery in Fresno County, 1888. Also spelled Gay.

GRAYBIEL, EDWIN
Gallery on Santa Clara Avenue, opposite the Post Office in Alameda, 1886, 1888. May also have been in Hayward.

GREAT EASTERN PHOTOGRAPHIC & ADVERTISING COMPANY
Operated by Cromell & Westervelt, Los Angeles, 1890. Also spelled Crowell.

GREEN
Studio at 439 San Pablo Avenue, Oakland, c. 1900.

GREEN, A. S.
Active in Dunsmuir, 1914-15.

GREEN, ARTHUR H.
Active in Vina, 1891-93; Castle Crag, c. 1895.

GREEN, C. C.
Active in Marysville, 1914-17.

GREEN, FLORIDE (MISS)
Born in Mobile, Alabama, 1863. Active in San Francisco, c. 1892-1912. Exhibited in the first San Francisco Photographic Salon, 1901; reviewed by *Camera Craft*. Also listed as Florine.

GREENALL, CHARLES
Born in England, August 1858. Arrived in U. S., 1881. Photographer in Catalina Island, 1900.

GREGOR, ALEXANDER
Born in Brackley Point, New Brunswick, Canada, April 16, 1843; died in Eureka, October 14, 1891. Arrived in California, 1863. Partner of A. P. Flaglor for a short time, 1874.

GREGORY, A. O.
Active at 502 and 504 J Street in Sacramento, 1886-90.

GREGORY, W. G.
Partner with W. I. Williams in the manufacture of the San Francisco Dry Plates. Their offices were at 914 Market Street, San Francisco, 1887.

GRIFFITH, BENJAMIN A.
Active in Half Moon Bay, San Mateo County, 1880-82.

GRIFFITHS & SAMSON
Stereo photographers active in Marysville.

GRIFFITHS, H. S.
Active in San Diego, 1898.

GRIFFITHS, PHILLIP WILLIAM
Born in California, 1857, of Welsh parents. Griffiths had a gallery on Montgomery Street in Oroville by 1878. Active in Chico, 1878. Opened the Elite Gallery in Marysville on the southwest corner of D and Third Street, 1880-88 or later. Also listed as Griffith.

GRIME, CICERO
Operated the I.C.U. Photograph Car. He was later active in Arizona, operating the California Art Gallery.

GROSS, G. E.
Active in Santa Inez, 1898.

GROVE
Active in Santa Cruz, c. 1896-98.

GROVE & MERRILL
Partnership of traveling photographers, 1874-78.

GROVE & STINSON
Operated a gallery on the east side of Harbison Avenue, Quincy, c. 1875.

GROVE, E. K.
Marysville photographer, 1870-78; operating on the corner of Third and D Streets, 1870.

GROVER, FORREST E.
Active in Los Angeles, 1895-1905. Studio at southwest corner of Bellevue Avenue and Upper Main, 1895; 619 Upper Main Street, 1896; 619 San Fernando, 1897-1903; 314 Bellevue Avenue, 1904-05.

GRUBER, F.
Active in San Francisco. Produced "Zoographican" series of stereoviews, a rotating tableau of history.

GRUSS, FRANCIS X.
Photographer with C. L. Cramer, San Francisco, 1869-70.

GUERIN, JOHN M.
Operated in San Francisco, c. 1904. Also spelled Guerrin.

HAAS, IDA (MISS)
Active in Oakland, c. 1900-01. Employed by Hellen & Garniere, 565 12th Street, 1900; by Mrs. E. Swaney, 439 San Pablo Avenue, 1901.

HABENICHT, GEORGE
Active in Boye & Habenicht, 1026 Market Street, San Francisco, 1896-1900+.

HABENICHT, RUDOLPH
Operated in San Francisco, c. 1904.

HAELSIG
Partner in Plummer & Haelsig, traveling stereo photographers operating in the Mojave Desert area; may also have worked in Arizona.

HAGANS, EDWARD
Active in San Jose, 1871.

HAGLAN, ALBERT
Born in New Brunswick, 1848. Active in San Francisco, c. 1870.

HAINES, CHARLES M.
Active in McCloud.

HALE, HERBERT A.
Active in San Diego, 1888-89; Downey, c. 1890.

HALEY, GEORGE W.
Operated in San Francisco, c. 1904.

HALL, ADA A.
Born in Canada, 1861. Active in Oakland, c. 1880; sister of Lillie E. Hall.

HALL, CHARLES A. B.
Operated Cottage Photograph Gallery at Fourth and Spurgeon, Santa Ana, 1881-84.

HALL, E. W.
Active in Grass Valley, 1867.

HALL, G. B.
Active in Pasadena, 1895-1903. Studio at 176 East Colorado, 1895; 24 North Marengo Avenue, 1897-1903.

HALL, LILLIE E.
Born in Canada, 1860. Active in Oakland, c. 1880; sister of Ada A. Hall.

HALSEY
Partner in Foss & Halsey, 606 Kearny, San Francisco, 1868-74.

HALSEY & COFFIN
Studio in Dutch Flat operated by Henry H. Halsey and Isaac T. Coffin, landscape photographers, 1874.

HALSEY & SCRIPTURE
Proprietors of the Cosmopolitan Art & Photograph Gallery, 523 Kearny Street, San Francisco, 1868; John Calvin Scripture.

HALSEY, HENRY H.
Born in New York, 1840. Partner in Halsey & Coffin, Dutch Flat, 1874; Grass Valley and Dutch Flat, 1874-80 or later.

HALSEY, HIRAM H.
Born in New York, 1839. Active in Dutch Flat, 1870. Possibly the same as Henry H. Halsey. Had a son, Henry B. Halsey, born c. 1868 in California.

HALSEY, I. S.
Photographer, surgeon and dentist in Volcano, 1867; operating in Vallejo on Georgia Street, c. 1868.

HAMILTON
Active in Yreka, 1859.

HAMILTON & JACKSON
Studio operated by Charles A. Hamilton & Jackson in San Francisco on Eddy Street, 1877-80.

HAMILTON & KELLOG
Partnership of Charles F. Hamilton and Andrew J. Kellog at 513 Montgomery Street, San Francisco, 1865-70+.

HAMILTON & SHEW
Partnership of Charles F. Hamilton and Jacob Shew at 163 Clay Street, San Francisco, 1854. Produced stereoviews.

HAMILTON & TIDBALL
Gallery at 513 Montgomery Street, San Francisco, c. 1864.

HAMILTON, CHARLES A.
Born in Ohio, 1853. Photographic painter, San Francisco, 1880. A partner in Hamilton & Lovering, 1861; Hamilton & Jackson, Eddy Street, 1877-80.

HAMILTON, CHARLES F.
Born in Ireland, 1823. Established Hamilton & Company Daguerreian Parlor, 111 Montgomery Street, San Francisco, by 1859. Partner with Jacob Shew, 1863; associated with Andrew Kellog in studio at 513 Montgomery Street, 1865-70 or later.

HAMILTON'S GALLERY
Operated by Wise & Prindle, 417 Montgomery Street, 1867.

HAMMERSMITH, JOHN E.
Gallery at 415 Kearney Street, San Francisco, 1862.

HAMMERTON, CHARLES HENRY
Born in Downey, California, June 1, 1866. Active in Downey, 1889-95. Studio on Crawford Street opposite pavillion, 1891. Associated with partners Cromwell and Westervelt in the Great Eastern Photographic and Advertising Company.

HAMMOR
Partner in Judkins & Hammor, Downieville, 1867. Also spelled Hamor or Hamon.

HANAWAY, DANIEL
Photographer with W. W. Wright, San Jose, 1871.

HANDLEY, J. C.
Active in Sacramento and traveling, 1901.

HANSCOM, ADELAIDE MARQUAND
Born in Empire City, Oregon, 1876; died in California, 1932. Studied at Mark Hopkins Institute of Art in San Francisco. Fine art photographer active in San Francisco and Berkeley, c. 1900-20; she took over the portrait studio of Laura Adams, 1902. Her work was published by *Sunset Magazine*, 1903 and 1906, *Camera Craft*, 1903, 1906, *Photographs of the Year*, 1904, and others. She illustrated *The Rubaiyat of Omar Khayyam*, 1905, *Sonnets from the Portuguese*, 1916. After the 1906 earthquake destroyed her studio, she moved to Seattle, Washington, and opened a new studio. Later she moved with her children to Danville, California, set up a small darkroom, and began work on illustrations for nursery rhymes; the work was never finished due to the onset of mental illness.

HANSCOM, MOSES
Active in Marysville, 1852-59.

HANSEN, CARL
Active in San Francisco, 1879-80; Bakersfield, c. 1884.

HANSEN, CHARLES
Born in Germany, 1854. Active in San Franciso by 1880; studio on Mariposa Street, next to the Grand Central Hotel; in Fresno City, 1884.

HANSEN, FLORA
Active in San Francisco, 1894.

HANSEN, JACOB
Operated the Yreka Photograph Gallery in Yreka, 1869-95.

HANSON
Active in Susanville, c. 1880. Possibly the same Hanson who pho-

tographed mining scenes in the Feather River area in large format, c. 1870.

HANSON, J. A.
Active in Anderson House, 1880; proprietor of the Oakland Picture Tent, "Pictures taken and finished in ten minutes," c. 1880.

HANSON, JOHN
Photo-printer with Miss F. L. Matson, San Francisco, 1898.

HANSON, V. C.
Active in Lakeview, Oregon, c. 1890; also in Alturas and Ft. Bidwell, northern California.

HARADA, T.
Active in San Francisco, 1919-c. 1930; located at 1633, 1712 and 1720 Fillmore Streets.

HARDESTY & ARMSTRONG
Partnership of Cyrus M. Armstrong and Frank Hardesty, stereo photographers active in Santa Ana, 1891-94.

HARDESTY, FRANK
Born in Missouri, c. 1854. Active in Orange, c. 1885; in Los Angeles at 734 South Main, 1890; partner in Hardesty & Armstrong, Santa Ana, 1891-94; in Willowbrook, 1900; Downey, 1911-20. Sold his studio at 907 North Crawford Street, 1930.

HARDY, EDNA
Active in Pomona, c. 1893. Probably the daughter of Mr. and Mrs. J. Hardy.

HARDY, JOHN
Active in Pomona, c. 1886-92, operating studio in partnership with his wife.

HARDY, JOHN (MRS.)
Partner in gallery with her husband. Active in Pomona , c. 1886-93. Probably the wife of photographer Jonathan or John Hardy, active in Pomona, 1886-92.

HARDY, W. H.
Active in Scott River, 1890.

HARE, ALICE A.
Active in San Jose, c. 1895-1912. Her photographs illustrated articles in *Sunset Magazine* and *Camera Work*, 1902-03.

HARKER, A.
Artist and photographer, 66 South First Street, San Jose, 1887-88 or later.

HARKER, W. T.
Active in Relief Hill, Nevada County, 1895.

HARKNESS, F. M.
Turk Street Gallery, 6 Turk Street, San Francisco, date uncertain. Operated the Sacramento Gallery in partnership with Leftwich, 421 J Street, Sacramento, c. 1880. Gallery at 556 East Twelfth Street, East Oakland, 1886-88.

HARLAN, D. M.
Licensed in Santa Clara, 1865.

HARLBOG, CHARLES
Active in Los Angeles, 1899-1905. Studio at 228 Downey Avenue, 1899; 1828 Downey Avenue, 1902-05.

HARLISS, J. A.
Operator with J. O. Valpey at the California Art Company, 1890.

HARLOW, MINNIE
Worked for John O. Tucker in his studio, 72 South 2nd Street in San Jose, 1899-1900.

HARMON & COFFIN
Active in Snelling, c. 1867.

HARMON, RAWSON ALFRED
Licensed in Visalia, 1864.

HARNISH
Active in Albany, c. 1895.

HARRINGTON, WILLIAM M.
Purchased Rulofson's old gallery in Sonora from his uncle, Thomas W. Wells, operating it until 1942.

HARRIS, MARY ELIZABETH COOLEY
Born in Eugene, Oregon, October 20, 1855. Active in Santa Barbara, c. 1890. Traveling photographer in Oregon, 1892; worked for portrait photographer Theodore C. Marceau at 826 Market Street, San Francisco, 1893.

HARRIS, W.
Stereo photographer arriving in California, 1867, with J. D. Whitney, California State Geological Survey.

HARRISON, W. H.
Manager of the Pioneer Photograph Gallery owned by J. P. Spooner at 198 Main Street, Stockton, 1888-90.

HART, ALFRED A.
Born in Norwich, Connecticut, 1816; died in Alameda, California, March 3, 1908. Landscape photographer and painter operating out of Sacramento, 1860s. He produced an impressive series of stereoviews along the route of the Central Pacific Railroad and attended and photographed the celebration of the joining of the rails at Promontory, Utah, 1869. His Golden State Photographic Gallery was located at 65 J Street, corner of Third, Sacramento, 1869. Hart's CPRR negatives were licensed to Frank Durgan and Eli S. Dennison who reproduced them under their own imprint. Apparently J. H. Heering of San Jose also published some of Hart's views. Carleton Watkins purchased the Hart negatives and reproduced them under his own imprint. The negatives were destoyed in the San Francisco earthquake, 1906.

> Mead B. Kibbey, *The Railroad Photographs of Alfred A. Hart, Artist*, California State Library Foundation, 1995.
>
> Kraus, George, *High Road to Promontory: Building the Central Pacific Across the High Sierra*, American West Publishing Company, Palo Alto, California, 1969.

HARTEZ
Partner in Dewitt & Hartez, operating a roadside studio in Sonoma, c. 1910.

HARTSOOK, FRED
Born in Marion, Indiana, October 26, 1876. His father, John Hartsook, was a photographer for forty-four years; his grandfather was a daguerreotype artist and the first to open a studio in Virginia; two uncles were also successful photographers. He worked in his father's studio, Grant County, Indiana, until he moved to California, 1898; opened a studio in Santa Ana, then in Santa Barbara, closing them when he established a studio on Mercantile Place and South Broadway in Los Angeles; he eventually had twenty studios in California. He was also a rancher, with thousands of acres in Kern County; also owned forty-one acres in Los Angeles near Lankershim, Vineland and San Fernando Boulevard.

HARVEY, SAMUEL
Active in San Francisco, c. 1898.

HASKELL, W. J.
Active in Redlands, 1898.

HASKINS, CARRIE L. (MISS)
Operated a gallery in Berkeley, 1891-1900; moved to Honolulu and remained active, c. 1901-03+.

HASSELMAN
Partner in Parker & Hasselman in Los Angeles, Downey Block.

HASTINGS, J. H.
Born in Massachusetts, 1812. A daguerreian artist in Stockton, 1870.

HATFIELD, J. S.
Active in Anaheim, 1895.

HATHAWAY
Stereo photographer active in Sebastopol.

HATTA, YATSUTARO
Active in Sacramento at 600 M Street, 1916.

HATTON, CHARLES E.
Active in Healdsburg, 1883.

HAUSER, EDWIN
Operated in San Francisco, c. 1904.

HAUSSLER, FREDERICK O.
Studio at 911 Broadway, Oakland. Presumably the same as Professor Haussler who operated a studio at 68 South First Street, in the Letitia Building, San Jose, c. 1885. Operated a studio at 731 Market Street, San Francisco, 1898-1900s.

HAWES, A. L.
Studio at 272 First Street, San Jose, 1874.

HAWES, CHARLES W.
San Jose photographer working for Bacon Brothers, 1884.

HAWTHORN, CHARLES
Born in Louisiana, 1848. Active San Francisco, 1870.

HAY, EMILY P. B.
Active in San Francisco, c. 1890s.

HAY, GEORGE
Born in Maine, 1847. Son of Mary Hay. Operated gallery in San Francisco, 1880; photographer at Wing & Allen, 342 Kearny Street, 1883; partner with Mrs. Laura T. Allen in Allen & Hay, same location, 1884-86.

HAY, MARGARET A. (MISS)
Partner in M. C. & M. A. Hay Studio, 342 Kearny Street, San Francisco, 1888.

HAY, MARY C. (MRS.)
Born in Ireland, 1821. Mother of George Hay and partner in Allen & Hay at 342 Kearny Street, San Francisco, 1886. Partner with Miss Margaret Hay in portrait gallery, Hay & Company at the same address, 1887-88. Partnership changed to Hay & Hay (Mary C. Hay and Robert F. Hay), 1889, and was later taken over by her son, Robert F. Hay.

HAY, ROBERT F.
Studio at 821 Market Street, San Francisco, 1887-88.

HAYASHI, ICHI (MRS.)
Active in Sacramento in studio at 1114 4th Street with her husband, c. 1908-09. Also listed as Mrs. U. Hayashi.

HAYASHI, SHIGERU
Active in San Francisco, c. 1910.

HAYASHI, T.
Active in Sacramento in studio at 1114 4th Street , c. 1910-24.

HAYASHI, UTARO
Active in Sacramento with wife, Mrs. Ichi Hayashi, at 1114 4th Street, 1905-07; 1324 4th Street, 1913.

HAYES & FOWZER
Partnership of Henry C. Hayes and Jacob Fowzer, San Francisco, 1883, at 115 Fourth Street.

HAYES, HENRY C.
Born in New York, 1842. Partner in Dames & Hayes, 715 Market Street, San Francisco, 1877-85; partner in Hayes & Fowzer, 115 Fourth Street, 1883.

HAYNES, THOMAS
Born in California, 1863, of Irish parents. Active in Santa Rosa, c. 1880.

HAYS
Partner in Tresslar & Hays, 213 ½ North Spring, Los Angeles, 1893-94.

HAYS, E. S.
Stereo photographer active in Santa Barbara.

HAYWARD & MUZZALL
Partnership of E. J. Hayward and H. W. Muzzall, Santa Barbara, 1874-83, on State Street, opposite the Occidental Hotel.

HAYWARD, E. J.
Born in Canada, 1838. Active in Santa Barbara, 1868-83. Partner in Hayward & Muzzall, State Street, opposite the Occidental Hotel, 1874-83; produced stereoviews, landscapes and portraits.

HAYWOOD, J. D.
Operated Haywood & Company with W. M. Deyer, Crescent City, 1854.

HAYWOOD, S. J.
Gallery on 612 Clay Street, San Francisco, 1865. Also spelled Heywood.

HAZELHURST, EMMA V.
Born in California, 1877. Active in San Francisco, 1894-1900.

HAZELTINE & SON, L. S.
Traveling photographers, 1914.

HAZELTINE, GEORGE IRVING
Arrived in California with his brother, M. M. Hazeltine, 1853. They opened a daguerreotype saloon in San Francisco; he sold out to his brother, c. 1855, and went to Coloma where he married, gold mined and took daguerreotypes. Located in Luna House, 1857-59; Red Bluff and Trinity County, 1859; Red Bluff, 1861. Operated a studio in Canyon City, Oregon, c. 1860-94. See Oregon.

HAZELTINE, MARTIN MASON
Born in Vermont, July 31, 1827; died in Baker City, Oregon, February 16, 1903. Active in Vermont, New York, Chicago and St. Charles, Illinois, before arriving in San Francisco in December, 1853. Worked as a miner; by 1857 in partnership with his brother, George Irving Hazeltine,

doing business as Hazeltine Brothers, Daguerreotypists, 1853-55. Operated on Mormon Island, c. 1863; in Sacramento, c. 1864; in U Bet, c. 1865; in Nevada, c. 1865. Operated out of Stockton, 1868-78, issuing stereoviews alone and in association with J. J. Reilly; in Mendocino City, 1874, 1882-84; Yosemite Valley, 1876-78; Sierra and Plumas Counties, 1879. Active in the Sierra Butte Mine and Yosemite Valley (date uncertain); one large format view of Brownsville, California, verified with a date of 1874. Operated later out of Baker, Oregon. Hazeltine was a highly respected traveling photographer, c. 1893, whose stereoviews depict many scenes in California, Oregon and Idaho. Some work in Alaska and Washington indicated. See Oregon, Idaho and Traveling.

HAZLETT, J. W.
Licensed in Sacramento, 1865.

HEAD, T. D.
Painter and photographer in Stockton, c. 1885; Modesto, c. 1888.

HEALY, ADDIE G.
Born in California, July 1860. Active in Oakland, 1881-82, 1885-90; San Francisco, c. 1884-85, at 73 Street, Ann Building; St. Helena, 1890-95; Petaluma, 1896-1905+, at 816 ½ and 816 Main Street. Partner with husband Edwin Ruthven Healy.

HEALY, EDWIN RUTHVEN
Partner of H. H. Blakesly in the Elite Studio, also listed as Elite Gallery, in St. Helena, c. 1890-93.

HEATH & BAILEY
Partnership of James Heath and Morris Bailey, San Francisco, 1859, corner of Clay and Kearny.

HEATH, JAMES
Partner in Heath & Bailey, corner of Clay and Kearny, San Francisco, 1859. At the same time had a parlor in Marysville. Perhaps the daguerreotypist partner of John Kelsey, Rochester, New York, 1853.

HECKER, ALICE
Photographer in Oroville, 1899-1914.

HEDGE, FREDERICK A.
Born in Missouri, 1859. Active San Francisco, 1880.

HEDUM & BISHOP
Active in Jamestown, c. 1895.

HEERING, JOHN H.
Born in Prussia, 1816. Daguerreotypist in Healdsburg, operating the Eagle Gallery, 1859; San Jose, 1860. First Premium Photograph Studio, on First Street, San Jose, 1867-71. Published some of A. A. Hart's Central Pacific stereoviews.

HEIDRICK, A. C.
Born 1887; died 1955. Active in Monterey, 1907-45. Made views around Monterey Peninsula.

HEINNINGER, C. P.
Established Heinninger & Company at 411 ½ California Street, San Francisco, by 1887; at 22 Sansome Street, 1893; 533 Market Street, 1898.

HELIO-ART STUDIO
Operated by W. N. Tuttle.

HELIOS
Studio operated by Eadweard J. Muybridge and Silas Selleck in San Francisco, c. 1864. Also known as Helios - the Flying Studio.

HELLEN, LOTTIE M. (MRS.)
Born in Oregon, December 1873. Active in Redding, c. 1898-1900; Oakland, c. 1900-01. Partner with Miss E. Garniere in Hellen & Garniere at 565 12th Street, 1900; partner with Mrs. Emma Warren in Hellen & Warren.

HELLER, LOUIS HERMAN
Born in Herre Darmstat, Germany, August 11, 1839; died in San Francisco, June 28, 1928. Emigrated to the U.S., c. 1855; came to California, early 1860s. Active in Yreka, 1864-69. Moved to Ft. Jones, operating a gallery and photographing the Modoc War, 1872-1900, in competition with Eadweard Muybridge. Sold the Modoc War negatives to C. E. Watkins, who re-issued them under the Watkins imprint. Heller also issued a few untitled stereoviews of local scenes and citizens on cabinet-sized yellow mounts. He made at least one trip to Oregon; photographed in Ashland, 1884.

> Peter E. Palmquist, "Photographing the Modoc Indian War: Louis Heller versus Eadweard Muybridge." *History of Photography*, Volume 2, Number 3, July 1978.
>
> Peter E. Palmquist, "Jewish Photographer of the Modoc Indian War.," *Western States Jewish History*, Volume XXII, No. 4, July 1990.

HEMINGWAY & HOLMES
Stereo photographers active in Salinas and Santa Cruz.

HEMMINGER, C. B.
Active in Chico, 1910-20, at 320 Broadway.

HENDEE, DENNY H.
Born in Vermont, 1828. He learned the daguerreian art in New York, c. 1846, and became a traveling photographer in the eastern states. Came to California during gold rush, mined for a time, then opened a parlor in Sonora, late 1849. He made images of mining camps and landscapes, working out of the Stockton and Sonora areas. Established a daguerreotype and ambrotype gallery on Huntoon Street, Oroville, with his brother Edwin B; married Miss Vineyard and moved to Oregon, 1853. An itinerant photographer for several years; established a permanent gallery in Portland by 1856.

HENDEE, EDWIN B.
Born in New York, 1839. Accompanied his brother, D. H. Hendee, to California, 1849, and opened a daguerreotype parlor in Sonora with him. In Marysville, 1851; Shasta, 1855-56; Weaverville, 1856-57; gallery on Huntoon Street, Oroville, with brother Denny H. Hendee; Downieville, 1860. Operated a gallery at the "North side of Montgomery Street, 3 Doors West of Myers, Up Stairs," Oroville, c. 1865, advertising "Pictures of all kinds taken - from life size down."

HENDERSON, LINCOLN
Born in California, 1862, son of a blacksmith. Active San Francisco, 1880-81.

HENDRICKS, HORACE GATES
Licensed in Quincy, 1863; Susanville, 1864.

HENFIELD, JOHN
Active in Mountain View, c. 1862. Galleries in San Jose and Gilroy, 1867. Worked for Bradley & Rulofson, 1869-70.

HENNESSY, FRED W.
Partner of A. F. Welton in the Faber Photo Company, 217 South Spring, Los Angeles, 1896.

HENRY, WILLIAM ALEXANDER
Licensed in Presidio, 1865; Woodland, 1866.

HENSHAW, HENRY WEATHERBEE
Active in Chico, 1890-94.

HERRICK, W. A.
Active in Siskiyou County, 1880.

HEWITT, FREDERICK HORACE
Active in Oroville, 1881-85; also in Chico, 1883.

HEYWOOD, S. J.
Gallery on 612 Clay Street, San Francisco, 1865. Also spelled Haywood.

HICKOX, A. A.
Partner in Foss & Hickox in San Francisco, 1870s.

HICKOX, L. P.
Active in Santa Ana, 1895-1903.

HICKS, ADA M.
Active in Los Angeles 1899-1902, partner in the firm of Hicks & Boothe with Mrs. Lillie M. Boothe at 911 South Hill Street.

HICKS, JOHN ROSS
Born in New York, 1832. Active in Columbia, c. 1864-66. Studio at 143 Fourth Street, San Francisco, 1869. Active in San Francisco, 1880.

HICOK (MRS.)
Photographer in Colusa, 1912.

HIGA, Y
Active in San Diego, c. 1923.

HIGGINBOTHAM, JOHN BAPTISTE
Born in New York, 1820. Licensed in Shasta, 1865; active in Red Bluff, 1864-70. Also spelled Higinbotham.

HIGGINS
Partner in Button & Higgins operating the Eureka Gallery at 342 First Street, San Jose, 1874.

HIGGINS & HOWLAND
Studio in Fresno, 1901; E. R. Higgins and Clarence A. Howland.

HIGGINS & JOHNSON
Partnership of Thomas J. Higgins and George Howard Johnson. Gallery at 659 Clay Street, San Francisco, 1865.

HIGGINS, E. R.
Studio at 117 J Street, Sacramento, 1867; Hanford, 1878; in Merced by 1880; Madera, 1886. Also in Fresno, 1886, with studio on 138 Mariposa Street. Active in the Fresno area, 1900s; partner in Higgins & Howland, 1901.

HIGGINS, IDA M.
Born in California, June 1881. Active in San Jose, c. 1899-1902. Worked at the studio of John O. Tucker, 72 South 2nd Street, 1900-01; for William J. Carruthers at 26 South 1st Street, 1902.

HIGGINS PHOTOGRAPHIC GALLERY
Operating on Main Street, Odd Fellows Hall, Stockton, 1865.

HIGGINS, THOMAS J.
Active in Sacramento, c. 1860; at 659 Clay Street, San Francisco, 1863-65.

HILER, M.
Active in Woodland, c. 1878.

HILL & DEJOINER
Studio operated in San Jose.

HILL & WATKINS
Active San Jose, 1890-91.

HILL & YARD
Stereo photographers active in San Jose.

HILL, ANDREW PUTNAM
Artist and photographer in San Jose, 1878-1901.

HILL, F. M.
Stereo photographer active in El Monte.

HILL, FLORENCE W.
Born in California, 1859. Active in San Jose, c. 1899-1900. Wife of Andrew Putnam Hill.

HILL, JAMES
Active in Newcastle, c. 1867.

HILL, L. P.
Partner in Lussier & Hill, San Jose, 1878.

HILL, R.
Active in Lower Lake, 1880.

HILL, WILLIAM HENRY
Born in Asbury Park, New Jersey, 1845; died 1925. Moved to Pasadena, mid 1880s; operated studio, 1893-1910. Official photographer for Thaddeus Lowe, 1891-95, photographing the construction of Mount Lowe Railroad. Shared studio with Charles J. Crandall and sold studio to him, c. 1905-10.

HILLS & JACKSON
Partnership of Rufus Hills and Joseph Jackson, licensed in Brandy, 1863.

HILLS, RUFUS
Born in 1824. Active in San Francisco, 1866-67; associated with E. M. Sammis at 14 Second Street, 1867.

HIN, WAI CHEU
Active in San Francisco, 1892-94, at 800 Stockton Street.

HING, AH
Born in China, 1839. Active in San Francisco, c. 1870.

HINTHORNE, B. H.
Traveling photographer, also active in Ashland, 1917.

HIROLANC & DEWEY
Partnership in Los Angeles, 1910; James H. Dewey.

HIRSCH, KAHN, & COMPANY
Stereo photographers active in San Francisco, operating as "Manufacturing Opticians" at 333 Kearny Street.

HO, WAR TONG
Active in San Francisco, c. 1870.

HODGKINS, G. W.
Active in Taylorville, c. 1867.

HODSON, JOHN R.
Born in Illinois, 1851, of English parents. Active in Sacramento, 1875; on Pacific Avenue in Santa Cruz, 1880; in San Francisco at 406 Geary, 1896-98, operating the Sun Pearl Studio. His wife was Angela Mason Hodson.

HOEBEL & LUTHER
Operated the South Park Photographic Gallery at 444 ½ Third Street, San Francisco, 1872-73; Henry Luther.

HOFFMAN, JOHN D.
See Idaho.

HOFFSTETTER, G.
Born in France, 1825. Active in San Rafael, c. 1870.

HOGAN, JOHN HOBART
Born in Massachusetts, 1856. Partner in Clements & Hogan, Oroville, 1878; listed alone, 1880-1910; operated the New Photographic Art Gallery, next to Bell's Wholesale Grocery Store on Montgomery Street. Operated from Kusel's Building, c. 1880, then Kusel's New Building, and finally Sovereign's Building opposite the Odd Fellow's Hall. Also active in Chico, 1877-1920.

HOGARTH
Active in Chico, partner in Evelyn & Hogarth, 1875.

HOLHM, HANSEN
Born in Prussia, 1839. Active in San Francisco, c. 1870.

HOLLAND, JAMES
Born in Ohio, 1846. Active in San Francisco, c. 1880.

HOLLER, JOSEPH
Operated gallery in San Francisco, 1888-1900+, at 8 Sixth Street.

HOLM, SOREN H.
Studio at 143 Fourth Street, San Francisco, c. 1871-73.

HOLMES
Partner in Hemingway & Holmes, stereo photographers in Salinas and Santa Cruz. Probably R. R. Holmes.

HOLMES, MARY
Born in Indiana, 1825. Active in Sacramento with H. S. Beals, 1870.

HOLMES, MATHEW (DR.)
Won the prize for the best ambrotype and melaineotype at the Agricultural Fair in Placerville, 1860.

HOLMES, R. H.
Traveling photographer, 1894.

HOLMES, R. R.
Active in San Luis Obispo, c. 1877-83, as "Heliographic Artist."

HOME GALLERY
Studio in Ukiah, 1869-95, operated by A. O. Carpenter.

HOME STUDIO
Operated by Mrs. Frances E. Gorr at St. Mary Street, San Jose, c. 1890-92.

HONN, BESSIE
Active in Redding, c. 1900-04.

HOOD, WILLIAM
Active in San Francisco, 1915. See British Columbia.

HOOPES, H. E.
Amateur active in Pasadena and the California Camera Club; made photography trips with A. C. Vroman to photograph Southwest Indians and their ceremonies.

HOOVER, HATTIE
Active in Gilroy, 1890-91.

HOPKINS, HELEN R. (MISS)
Gallery at 18 Third Street, San Francisco, 1898; also in Oakland.

HOPKINS, JESSIE (MISS)
Born in California, 1881. Active in San Francisco, c. 1899-1900.

HOPPERSTAD, CARRIE
Active in Stockton, 1876-77.

HORD, J. R.
Opened a studio in San Francisco, 1862; San Jose, 1864; in San Francisco by 1865, at 143 Fourth Street.

HORN, JOHN PATRICK
Active in Yreka, 1890-1905.

HOSSACK, HUGH MOULE ALEXANDER
Active in Yreka and Oak Bar, 1894-96.

HOUGH, ELIZABETH
Born in Missouri, October 1847. Active in San Leandro, c. 1899-1900+.

HOUGH, REVEREND J. W.
Active in Brooklyn; made stereoviews of Monterey coast and religious sites; editor of *Christian Union*. Also listed as J. W. H.

HOUGHTALING, ABRAHAM J.
Born in New York, 1830. He was in California by 1861. Photographer for William Shew, San Francisco, 1865-70 or later.

HOUSEWORTH, THOMAS
Born in New York City, June 21, 1828; died April 13, 1915. Partner in Lawrence and Houseworth, opticians and publishers of stereo and landscape views, 317 Montgomery Street, San Francisco, 1864-67. Formed Thomas Houseworth & Company, c. 1867, located at 9 and 12 Montgomery Street, 1874-86; 1903 Mission Street, 1888. Leading retailer and publisher of photographs in the city, often employing or purchasing the negatives of other photographers and selling prints under the Houseworth imprint. In 1865 the firm submitted a group of San Francisco photographs for copyright, thereby prompting other local photographers to copyright their own work after c. 1867. His son, Harrison, was born in 1863; Frederick in 1866.
    Peter E. Palmquist, *Lawrence & Houseworth, Thomas Houseworth & Company: A Unique View of the West 1860-86*, National Stereoscopic Society, 1980.

HOUSTON, H. H.
Active in Mott, c. 1890.

HOVEY, GUY CARLETON
Active in Ontario, San Bernardino County, 1898-1900.

HOWARD, JAMES SOLOMAN
Born in Iowa, c. 1860. Active in Pomona, 1892-1903.

HOWE, ITHAMAR
Traveling photographer, 1878.

HOWE, JOHN MILTON
Studio at 6 Eddy Street, San Francisco, 1886; Anne's Building, 68 Eddy Street, San Francisco, 1887-1902.

HOWELL, EDGAR WADE
Active in Yreka, 1891-1900.

HOWES, SAMUEL P.
Ambrotypist in San Francisco, c. 1858; operator for Vance; took over Ford's studio when Ford left San Francisco, 1858.

HOWLAND
Active in Fresno with Higgins & Howland, c. 1900.

HOWLAND & CHADWICK
Partnership in Los Angeles, operated by Frederick T. Howland and Redmond A. Chadwick, 1890-96, selling photographic supplies. Located at 109 South Main, 1890; 211 Main Street, 1892-96.

HOWLAND & DEWEY
Operated in Los Angeles, c. 1912.

HOWLAND & FAGERSTEEN
Studio known as the Art and Photograph Gallery, 315 Montgomery Street, San Francisco, 1873.

HOWLAND & PETERS
Partnership of B. F. Howland and John Henry Peters in San Francisco, c. 1869-77; studio at 25 and 27 Third Street.

HOWLAND & VASCONCELLES
Studio in San Francisco, at 25 and 27 Third Street, 1865, operated by B. F. Howland and Vasconcelles.

HOWLAND, BENJAMIN FRANKLIN
Born in New Bedford, Massachusetts, March 1, 1828; died in Oakland, California, August 6, 1900. Retired as sea captain, 1851, and went to the gold fields of California. Returned to New Bedford, 1854. Went to Jacksonville, Oregon, 1856, opened a store with a partner and ran a pack train of fifty mules between Jacksonville and Crescent City, California. Later he quartz-mined in California. Moved east and opened a photographic gallery in Syracuse, New York, c. early 1860s. Sold out to Bonta & Curtis, moved to San Francisco, and opened Howland & Vasconcelles at 25 and 27 Third Street, 1865. Partner with J. H. Peterson (later Peters) in the New York Gallery, c. 1869-77. Howland opened a gallery at 359 First Street, San Jose, 1877. In 1879 he sold his interest in the New York Gallery to Daniel Sewell. Operated the Boston Photograph Gallery in Marysville, c. 1880; also operated and managed the Aldine Studio at 811 Market Street in San Francisco. Worked for Bradley & Rulofson, San Francisco, 1882-84. Established a gallery in Napa City, 1886; Oroville, 1886. By 1888, opened a gallery on the southwest corner of Tenth and Clay, Oakland.

HOWLAND, CLARENCE A.
Photographer at B. F. Howland and J. H. Peters' New York Gallery, San Francisco, 1871-78. Manager of the Imperial Photo Gallery, 1882, 724 ½ Market Street, run by Mrs. Hector W. Vaughan; became proprietor, 1890s. The gallery was sold c. 1900 to D. Radnor Coover and J. Charles Rasmussen, continuing into the 20th century. Possibly active as Higgins & Howland in Fresno, c. 1900.

HOWLAND, FREDERICK T.
Partner in Howland & Chadwick, 211 South Main Street, Los Angeles, 1896, dealing in photographic supplies. In business for himself 1903, 213 South Main Street, dealing in photographic supplies, views and Kodaks. By 1906 associated with William Ford in Howland & Company, 510 South Broadway. The company became Howland & Dewey by 1910, photographic suppliers, composed of F. T. Howland, William Ford, J. H. Dewey, and H. S. Wallace.

HOWLAND, H. A.
Operated Howland's New Gallery at 25 Third Street, San Francisco, c. 1875; 811 Market Street, 1878.

HOWLAND, JAMES F. S.
Clerk at Howland & Company, Los Angeles, 1903; operated his own gallery by 1906 at 310 South Broadway, Los Angeles.

HOWLAND, M. F. R.
Active in San Francisco, c. 1875-78. Possibly a daughter of B. F. Howland.

HOWLAND, R. P.
Gallery at 811 Market Street, San Francisco, 1878.

HOYT, HIRAM
Active in Red Bluff, 1873-75; studio on 3rd Street, over Farmer's Store, Santa Rosa, Sonoma County, 1875.

HUBBELL (MISS)
Active in San Jose, c. 1890s. Partner in gallery with Miss Lily E. White.

HUBBELL, VIOLA T.
Worked for J. H. McGee in Los Angeles, 1899, at the Plaza Gallery, 513 North Main Street.

HUBLEY, GRACE
Fine art photographer active in Colfax, c. 1900-06; in Sacramento, c. 1906-16. Her work was published in *Camera Craft*, 1902, and she had numerous exhibits; portrait studio in the Stoll Building, c. 1906.

HUCKS, GEORGE A.
Born in California, 1876. Son of J. G. Hucks. Photo printer with J. G. Hucks, Dore Photo Studio, San Francisco, 1898.

HUCKS, J. GEORGE
Born in England, 1850. In California by 1876. Studio at 811 Market Street, San Francisco, by 1880; moved to 914 Market Street, 1880; bought out John H. Peters' half interest in the New York Gallery, 25 Third Street, becoming a partner of Daniel Sewell, c. 1881-87; Hucks bought out Sewell, 1887; moved to 1144 Market by 1890; at 1228 Market, 1898. Proprietor of the Dore Photo Studio at 1380 Market, by 1900, taking it over from David Cobb. Hucks continued in business into the 20th century.

HUDDLESTON, LOLA L.
Born 1861. Active in Los Angeles 1900-03+. Probably the wife of photographer Foster G. Huddleston. Employed by Theodore C. Marceau, 227 South Spring Street, 1899-1903.

HUDSON
Active in Redding, 1898.

HUDSON (MISS)
Photographer and gallery owner in Oroville, 1857.

HUGHES, CHARLES
Active in Red Bluff, 1890-1900.

HUMMEL
Partner in Conaway & Hummel, Santa Ana, 1880s.

HUNT, CHARLES E.
Active in San Francisco, 1865. Worked for Bradley & Rulofson, 1869-70.

HURLBURT, I. (MRS.)
Photographer in Orland, 1884-85.

HUSTON, H. H.
Active in Mott, 1890.

HUTCHISON, DAVID
Gallery with Charles F. Babcock at 28 Third Street, San Francisco, 1883-84; continued at the same address alone, 1885-88. Also operated the Eureka Gallery.

HUTTIE, AGNES
Active in San Francisco, 1894-95.

HYDE, JETTORA WATKINS
Born in California, 1851. Photographer and gallery owner in San Jose, 1892-1900. Studio at 79 West Santa Clara Street, 1895-97; operated as Hyde & Company, 1898.

HYDE, WILLIAM
Active in Chico, c. 1870.

HYDEY, J. JOSE
Possibly Jethora Hyde, San Jose.

HYNES & COMPANY
Partnership of W. J. Hynes and Shingoro Mashino in San Francisco, 1896-1905, located at 426 Kearny.

HYNES & OKUBO
Studio at 24 Antonio, San Francisco, 1895.

HYNES, WILLIAM J.
Established W. J. Hynes & Company at 426 Kearny, San Francisco, c. 1898.

I.C.U. PHOTOGRAPH CAR
Operated in California by itinerant photographer, Cicero Grime. He was later active in Arizona, operating the California Art Gallery.

IDEAL STUDIO
Gallery at 573 Third Street, San Bernardino, c. 1895.

IGUCHI, C. S.
Partner with J. Z. Mayaki in Sacramento, 1915-16, at 1221 4th Street.

IIDA, K.
Active in San Francisco, c. 1923.

IMAI ART STUDIO.
Gallery at 1950 Bush Street and Polk Street, 1922, in San Francisco.

IMAI, TSUNEKISHI
Active in San Francisco, 1898-1910. Also listed as Tsuenkichi Imai.

IMATO, MORISEKE
Active in San Jose, c. 1910, where he owned a gallery.

IMPERIAL GALLERY
Operated in Oakland.

IMPERIAL PHOTOGRAPHIC GALLERY
Studio in San Francisco, 724 ½ Market Street, 1877-1900. Begun by Hector W. Vaughan, operating 1877-80; operated by Mrs. Emma Vaughan, c. 1880; Clarence A. Howland, c. 1890s; by J. C. Rasmussen and D. Radnor Coover, c. 1900.

IMPERIAL PHOTOGRAPHIC PARLOR
Studio in San Bernardino, 1884-88, operated by M. A. and H. B. Wesner and located on D Street between Third and Fourth, 1884; at 217 Third Street, 1888. Also known as Wesner Brothers.

INGERSOLL, WILLIAM B.
Born in Massachusetts, 1834. Came to California by 1861; photographer in San Francisco, 1865; gallery in Oakland on Sixth Street, c. 1867; studio at 1069 Broadway, Oakland, 1872-86. Perhaps the W. B. Ingersoll who published stereoviews from New York City, early 1860s.

INGLESTON, R. H.
Active in Weed, 1915.

INONG, CHIN FONG
Active in San Francisco, 1909.

INTERNATIONAL GALLERY
Studio in San Francisco, c. 1869-80+, operated by Joseph T. Silva. Located at 64 Third Street, corner of Mission, San Francisco, c. 1869-78; at 28 Third Street, 1880.

INTERNATIONAL VIEW COMPANY
Chicago company publishing stereoviews of Big Trees and San Francisco.

IRONMONGER, CHARLES
Born in Ohio, August 1869. Partner with Jay W. Austin on Catalina Island, 1900.

IRVIN, GEORGE C.
Active at 305 Main Street, Stockton and in Dixon, 1886; San Leandro, 1892-93.

ISAACS
Partner in Weintraub & Issacs, 28 Third Street, San Francisco, 1881.

ISHIGURO, C. J.
Active in San Francisco, 1902-08, at 1509, 1609, and 1930 Fillmore Street, where he owned a gallery. Also known as C. I. Ishiguro.

JACKMAN, ARTHUR
Active in Oroville, 1910.

JACKSON, B. D.
Active in Glendale, at 710 East Elk Avenue; produced stereoviews of Mariposa Big Trees.

JACKSON, JOHN
Licensed in San Francisco, 1863.

JACKSON, JOSEPH
Born in New Brunswick, 1841. Active in Howland Flat, 1867; La Porte, 1870.

JACOBS, BENJAMIN F.
Photographic printer with William Shew, San Francisco, 1865.

JACOBS, JAMES MONROE
Born in Ohio, 1832. Ran away from home, 1850s, and crossed the plains to California; mined and later photographed in Placer County. Photographer in Bath, 1870, probably associated with Ignacio Brown. Main studio in Auburn, c. 1887 or later, taking views and portraits, and making an annual circuit to the mining camps in Colfax, Michigan Bluff, Forest Hill, Dutch Flat, Yankee Jim's and Iowa Hill. Perhaps the first permanent photographer in the gold country; produced stereoviews.

JACOBSEN, C.
Studio at 103 Pacific Avenue, Santa Cruz, 1888.

JAMES, GEORGE WHARTON
Born in Gainsborough, England, September 27, 1858; died 1923. Author, lecturer and photographer. Made his home in Pasadena and was active in California and western states, 1880s-1900+. Part of the Arroyo community; known for his studies of California Indians.

JAMES, WILLIAM E.
Born in Wales, 1830. Active in San Francisco, 1880; Santa Cruz, 1887.

JARVIS, BENJAMIN
Born in England, 1835. Opened photo studio in Marshalltown, Iowa, c. 1865; moved to Pasadena, 1886. With his son, Luciene, he bought the E. S. Frost studio, operating 1887-90s. Studio located at 33 West Colorado Street, 1900; 49 East Colorado Street, 1893.

JARVIS, LUCIENE EMERSON
Born in Marshalltown, Iowa, son of Benjamin Jarvis. Moved to Pasadena, 1886, and worked in the E. S. Frost studio. Partner with his father, 1887-90s. Also spelled Lucien.

JAYCOX, D. L.
Studio on San Pablo, between Fifteenth and Sixteenth, Oakland, 1878.

JEFFERS, WELLS & KIPPS
Studio in San Francisco, 1880-82; William H. Jeffers.

JEFFERS, WILLIAM H.
Partner in Jeffers, Wells & Kipps, "Artists & Photographers," 1436 Market Street, San Francisco, 1880-82. In business for himself, 1886, at 1202 Mission Street.

JELLUM, H. LEE
Active in Yreka, 1900-16.

JENKINS, J. C.
Active in Chico, 1881, at Main and 3rd streets.

JENKS, NELLIE F. (MISS)
Photographer in Sutter County, 1880-1900.

JEROME
Partner in Fay & Jerome, 32 Kearny Street, San Francisco, 1867.

JETZLER, CARL LUCAS
Active in Carters and Yosemite, c. 1900; Dunsmuir, 1902-08. Also spelled Jezler.

JOHNS, WILLIAM F.
Active in Johnsville, 1890.

JOHNSON
Partner in Knight & Johnson, 811 Market Street, San Francisco, 1881.

JOHNSON & SULLIVAN
Operated the Portable Photograph Gallery, 1870.

JOHNSON, A. M.
Partner with Solomon N. Carvalho, August 31 to September 21, 1854, in Los Angeles. Johnson moved to San Francisco and Carvalho to New York City.

JOHNSON, A. P.
Gallery at 645 and 649 Clay Street, San Francisco, 1862-68.

JOHNSON, B. R.
Premium Gallery on Main Street, Phoenix Block, Petaluma, 1867.

JOHNSON BROTHERS
Edward E. and Josiah Johnson, stereo photographers active in Sacramento, 1870s.

JOHNSON, C. E.
Stereo photographer active in Los Angeles, 1890s.

JOHNSON, CHARLES M.
Born in Ohio, 1846. Came to California, 1870s; active in Oakland, 1880; in San Francisco, 1883; gallery at 31 Third Street, San Francisco, 1898; at 10 ½ Sixth Street, 1904.

JOHNSON, CHARLES WALLACE JACOB
Born in Maryland, August 3, 1833; died in Salinas, January 17, 1903. Arrived in California, 1857; worked the gold fields and performed as a traveling musician in the gold camps. Probably operated a gallery in San Francisco before leaving for Eureka, 1868; rented Anderson's Eureka Photography Gallery with William N. Tuttle, 1869-70. Johnson moved back to San Francisco, 1870, and bought the Cosmopolitan Photograph Gallery at 523 Kearny Street with Tuttle. By 1874 he was operating a portable gallery in partnership with Al Sullivan; working solo based in Watsonville, 1875-80. He purchased A. W. Fell's gallery in Monterey, 1880, and the opening of the Hotel Del Monte provided him with ample business through the 1890s. Johnson was a major producer of photographs, well-known for his stereoviews and boudoir card views of scenes of the Monterey Peninsula.
     Peter E. Palmquist with Lincoln Kilian, *The Photographers of the Humboldt Bay Region* 1865-1870, Volume 2, Peter E. Palmquist, Arcata, California, 1986.

JOHNSON, CLINTON
Photographer in Los Angeles; produced stereoviews of San Francisco earthquake, 1906.

JOHNSON, EDWARD E.
Stereo photographer active in Sacramento.

JOHNSON, GEORGE
Born in New York, 1840, of Scotch parents. Active in San Francisco, c. 1880.

JOHNSON, GEORGE HOWARD
Born in New York, 1823. One of the great daguerrian artists of the gold rush era; active in San Francisco, 1860, at 645 and 649 Clay Street; in Great Salt Lake City, late 1860s.

JOHNSON, J. B.
Gallery on Monterey Street, Gilroy, 1874-79; Los Gatos, 1886; San Jose, 1887-88 or later, at 58 South First Street.

JOHNSON, LYNETTE (MRS.)
Photographer in Willows, 1910.

JOHNSON PHOTO COMPANY
2109 East First Street, Los Angeles, 1891.

JOHNSON, RICHARD T.
Active in San Francisco, c. 1883.

JOHNSON, TOM
Traveling photographer, 1895.

JOHNSON, WILLIS
Licensed in Woodland, 1865.

JOHNSTON, JAMES W.
Born in Louisiana, 1810. Came to California by 1854; operated a daguerreian parlor at 56 Montgomery Street, San Francisco, 1865-66.

JOHNSTON, LOUISA
Born in England, 1859. Active in San Francisco, c. 1880.

JONES & LOTZ
Operated the Elite at 838 Market Street, San Francisco, 1880-96.

JONES, A. J.
Active in Fresno and Tulare City, c. 1883.

JONES, CHARLES
Traveling photographer with his wife, Dorothy, 1900.

JONES, DOROTHY
Photographer in Red bluff, 1900; also traveling. Also known as Mrs. Charles Jones.

JONES, GEORGE C.
Operated the City Photo Gallery in Placerville, c. 1900.

JONES, I. G.
Studio located on south side of Jersey Bridge, Downieville, 1870-80. Also listed as I. F.

JONES, J. W.
Active in Fresno, 1880.

JONES, J. WESLEY
Daguerreian artist who led group of artists and daguerreians eastward from San Francisco, c. 1850-51, William Shew, Jacob Shew, and S. L. Shaw among them, across the plains, daguerreotyping cities and landscapes. From the 1500 daguerreotypes taken, a panorama painting was made and exhibited as the "Pantascope of California" in New York as late as 1854. These historical daguerreotypes are now lost.

JONES, N. W.
Photographic painter, 6 Eddy Street, San Francisco, 1880.

JONES, ROBINSON & COMPANY
Partnership of Thomas H. Jones and G. M. Robinson in San Francisco, c. 1880s.

JONES, RODNEY C.
Studio on Ocean Terrace, San Francisco, 1895-1904; associated with Luther W. Kennett, 1898.

JONES, RULOFSON & COMPANY
Studio located at 838 Market Street, San Francisco, c. 1888.

JONES, THOMAS H.
Born in Wales, 1851. Operated the Elite Gallery, 838 Market Street, San Francisco, 1880-89. Studio also known as Jones, Robinson & Company, with partners G. M. Robinson and W. H. Rulofson, 1880; Robinson, 1881-83; Paul Lotz, 1885-89 or later; and Thomas Calverly, date uncertain. The Elite Gallery continued into the 20th century.

JOSLIN, A. J. T.
Active in Yreka, 1909.

JOSLIN, J.
Stereo photographer active in Chico.

JOSSELYN, LEWIS
Born 1883; died 1964. Active in Carmel, 1914-40.

JUDD, ALINDA M.
Born in New York, January 1863. Active in Los Angeles, c. 1893-1903+. Partner with husband at 26 Downey Building, 1903.

JUDD, C. W.
Partner in Parker & Judd, 1880s, in San Diego. Active in Los Angeles, 1899, at 113 Second.

JUDKINS & HAMMOR
Partnership of Judkins and A. B. Hammor, stereo photographers active in Downieville, 1866-68. Also spelled Hamor, Hamon.

JUDKINS, DAVID ROBY
Died in Santa Maria, 1909. Moved from Seattle to San Francisco, 1903, opening a gallery at 853 Market Street; opened the Santa Maria Photograph Gallery at 200 West Main Street, Santa Maria, in partnership with E. D. Shull, 1906. The studio was destroyed by fire, 1908, and Judkins' glass negatives were lost; the studio was rebuilt and operated by Judkins as the Judkins Gallery until his death. Thereafter, the gallery was operated by Judkins' daughter Hazle and her husband, Miles Franklin Weaver, for a short time before the studio was moved to Brea. See Washington.

KAHN, GEORGE H.
Studio at 201 Kearny Street, San Francisco, 1898. Photographed in Placerville, 1898.

KAMAGUCHI, SHIGIRA
Active in San Francisco, c. 1910.

KARRAS & BROWN
Max Karras and Sadie O. Brown in San Francisco, 1880-88.

KARRAS, MAX
Active in San Francisco, 1869-88. Enameler with H. W. Vaughan at 18 Third Street, 1869; partner with Sadie O. Brown, forming Karras & Brown, proprietors of Vaughan's Photograph Gallery, 18 Third Street, 1880-88.

KATTENHORN, OTTO
Active in Gazelle, 1900.

KAY, WALLACE
Born in Fall River, Massachusetts, 1829; died 1908. Moved to California during gold rush; operated parlor in Jackson, 1860s-1908. He was a musician and leader of the Ione Cornet Band and the Georgetown Band, owned a successful variety store and erected an office building in Jackson. Employed L. C. Swain as an operator, c. 1895.

KEANWAY, DANIEL
Born in Indiana, 1851. Photographer with Wilbur Wright, San Jose, 1870.

KEEFER & BOBSON
Partnership in Downieville, 1852; possibly Henry Keefer.

KEEFER, HENRY
Active in Marysville, 1857.

KEIL, EDWARD A.
Born in California, 1862. Operated a gallery in San Francisco, 34 Third Street, 1880; partner in Dames & Keil, 715 Market Street, 1886. Also spelled Kiel.

KEITH
Partner in Vaughan & Keith, 14 Grant, San Francisco, 1899-1904.

KEITH, WILLIAM
Born 1839; died 1911. One of California's most famous painters, known for his landscapes. Located in San Francisco, working throughout the western states. His photography is less well known.

KELLOG
Partner in De Groot & Kellog, Main Street, Sacramento, 1880-88; Salinas, date uncertain. Also spelled Kellogg.

KELLOG, ANDREW J.
Partner with Charles F. Hamilton in Hamilton & Kellog, 513 Montgomery Street, San Francisco, 1865.

KELLOG, G. P.
Active in Petaluma, 1856-62.

KELLY & McDONOUGH
Cabinet card, c. 1890, with an imprinted firm name and "Helena, Montana" on the bottom of the card, but the city and state are crossed out and "Benecia, Cal" is written above. The back of the cabinet card advertises the "San Francisco Gallery" at Galen's Block, Main Street, Helena, Montana.

KELLY & RUNNELS
31 Third Street, San Francisco, 1880.

KELLY & SOBIESKI
Studio in Los Angeles, 1886-87, on Twenty-First Street; G. Kelly and F. C. Sobieski.

KELLY, FREDERICK
Photographer with E. M. Anderson, San Francisco, 1869-70.

KELLY, G.
Partner in Kelly & Sobieski, Twenty-First Street, Los Angeles, 1886-87.

KELLY, GEORGE
Partner with Ira Perry, Mendocino, c. 1885.

KELSEY, C. C.
Partner in Dunham & Kelsey, Susanville, 1886; listed alone in North Bloomfield, c. 1890.

KELTON, CHARLES H.
Active in Watsonville, 1867.

KEMP & COLEMAN
Operated on Main Street, Bodie, 1880-82.

KEMP & KLUIT
Traveling photographers using People's Art Gallery in San Francisco as a base, 1870-75.

KEMP & VANCE
Partnership of R. H. Vance and William Kemp, stereo photographers active in Modesto.

KEMP, HENRY
One imprint proclaims Great Celebrated Centennial Flying Photograph Gallery, c. 1876. Active in Chico, 1878; Bodie, 1880; Modesto, 1884, at the corner of Tenth and I Street. Perhaps the same or related to J. C. Kemp, as both studios used an unusual script exactly the same on the reverse of buff colored cartes-de-visite mounts, c. 1876, the centennial year.

KEMP, J. C.
Operated the Celebrated Great Flying Photograph Gallery, c. 1875; the Celebrated Flying Photograph Gallery at 27 North C Street, Virginia City, Nevada; the Great Flying Gallery at 211 J Street, Sacramento; and Flying Photograph Gallery. See Henry Kemp above.

KEMP VAN EE, HENRY
Active in Santa Rosa, 1878; Modesto, c. 1885, at Tenth between H and I Streets.

KEMP, WILLIAM
Artist in the Elite Gallery, Modesto, 1884.

KENDALL & CLINCH
Operated the Eureka Gallery on Mill Street in Grass Valley, c. 1885.

KENDALL, R. A.
Gallery at 33 Mill Street, Grass Valley, 1874; possibly a partner in Kendall & Clinch, c. 1885; in Modesto by 1886.

KENDRICK, H. A.
Purchased James M. Ford's San Francisco gallery, 1854; leased it back to Ford, 1855.

KENNEDY, AMELIA G.
Active in San Francisco, 1895.

KENNETT & JONES
Gallery in San Francisco, 1898, on B near Ocean Boulevard, and at 301 49th Street; Luther W. Kennett and Rodney C. Jones.

KENNETT, LUTHER W.
Studio at 607 and 612 Stanyan, San Francisco, 1895; partner in Kennett & Jones with studios at B near Ocean Boulevard, and at 301 49th Street, 1898; in Los Angeles, 1902.

KERLIN, THEODORE J.
Born in Ohio, 1861. Active in Sacramento, 1880; at 318 and 320 J Street, 1886.

KERWIN, ROSE
Active in San Francisco, 1895-1900.

KIEFER & SAMMIS
Active in Visalia, c. 1867.

KIES & BRIAN
Active in Placerville operating Baker's old stand before 1887; Henry Brian and Harry Kies.

KIES, HARRY
Working in Sacramento, 1886; opened gallery with Henry Brian in Placerville, 1887, replacing E. W. Baker.

KILDARE & COMPANY, E. L.
Operated in Kern County, c. 1875.

KILDARE & THWAITES
Advertised "Art and Photographic Rooms, E. J. Kildare, Artist - Late of Bradley & Rulofson," and "Joseph Thwaites, Photographer - Late of G. D. Morse," San Francisco, c. 1875. Operated in Visalia, c. 1880, corner of Main and Church Streets, over Baker's Drug Store.

KILDARE, E. J.
Active in San Francisco, c. 1875; Red Bluff, 1876.

KILDARE, E. S.
Active in Oakland, 1872.

KINCAID, J. T.
Active in Chico, c. 1910.

KING BROTHERS
Active in Santa Paula, 1895-98.

KING, J. L.
Gallery on the southeast corner of Clay and Kearny, San Francisco, 1869-70.

KING, JOSEPH W.
Operated in Woodland and San Francisco, 1874-80.

KINGSLEY, JOHN L.
Operator with William Shew, San Francisco, 1865; gallery at 659 Clay Street, c. 1869-71, associated with Eyre.

KINGSLEY, JOHN L. (MRS.)
Active in San Francisco, 1870-71; operated the Clay Street gallery after her husband's death.

KINT, C.
Stereo photographer active in San Diego. Probably Charles Klindt.

KIPPS, ALFRED K.
Portrait and landscape painter in San Francisco, studio at 618 Washington Street, 1865; at 415 Montgomery Street, 1869-70. Operating the Palace gallery in Oakland by 1872, southwest corner of Broadway and Ninth, Wilcox Block. Possibly a partner in Jeffers, Wells & Kipps, 1436 Market Street, San Francisco, 1880.

KLAIN, NATHAN M.
Landscape and view photographer, San Francisco, 1865-87; studio at 564 Ninoma, 1865-77; thereafter at 921 McAllister.

KLECKNER, WARREN
Partner in Scholl & Kleckner, Los Angeles, 1896.

KLEINHAMER, IDA M. (MISS)
Photographer in Yreka, 1905-30.

KLENCH, FLORA
Active in Stockton 1878, working with John Pitcher Spooner.

KLINDT, CHARLES
Operated the Chicago Art Gallery at 657 Fifth Street, San Diego, c. 1895. Probably also known as C. Kint.

KLINE, CHARLES W.
Traveling photographer, 1897.

KLOSTERMANN, CORRINO CAESARINA
Born in Central Point, Iowa, October 1849; died 1909. Crossed the plains with her parents, c. 1865, and moved to Humboldt County, c. 1866. Married Frederick Klostermann, 1869. Active in Eureka, c. 1893-98, with studio in her home at 1822 Albee Street. Married Homer H. Lambert, 1894, and became partner in Shaw & Lambert with her husband's sister Sophronia Caroline Shaw, gallery at 601 F Street. The studio was engaged in commercial photography and some prints were published in the *Overland Monthly*, 1896.

KLUIT, A. PROVO
Operated the Florence Gallery at 28 Third Street, San Francisco, 1875.

KNAPP, CHARLES H.
Active in Bloomfield, 1878-80.

KNIGHT & JOHNSON
Gallery at 811 Market Street, San Francisco, 1881; George H. Knight.

KNIGHT & PALMER
Active in Chico, c. 1890-92, at 307 Main Street.

KNIGHT, GEORGE H.
Born in England, 1851. Portrait painter in San Francisco, 1880; photographer in San Francisco, 1881-1900+. Partner with Johnson at 811 Market Street, listed as Knight & Johnson, 1881; at 19 Sixth Street,

1886; 721 Sutter Street, 1895; practiced commercial photography and photo printing at 568 Sutter Street, 1904. Active in Chico, 1906-07.

KNOWLES, JOSEPH E.
Sold photographs, pictures, newspapers, magazines and cutlery at 621 Kearny Street, San Francisco, 1869-70.

KOCH, JOHN
Partner in Addis & Koch, 425 Montgomery Street, San Francisco, 1865.

KOCHENRATH, CHARLES
Photographer with Joseph T. Silva, San Francisco, 1865.

KOHLER, E. F.
Active in Pasadena, 1895-1903.

KOHRN, W.
Stereo photographer active in San Francisco, at 1 Franklin Street.

KOMAI & ARAI
Partnership at 319 and 331 6th Street, Oakland, 1909.

KONOLD
Partner in Blanchard & Konold, Los Angeles, 1902, at 513 North Main and 213 ½ North Spring.

KONRAD, LEWIS
Active in St. Helena, 1886-88.

KORNMANN, E.
Worked for California Art Foto Company, producing stereoviews of Oakland, San Francisco, Los Angeles and surrounding areas.

KRAFT & FERRAR
659 Clay Street, San Francisco, 1877.

KRAFT & WORTHINGTON
Edward Kraft and William Thomas Worthington, operating in San Francisco at 5 Stockton Street,1890.

KRAFT, EDWARD
From New York City. Established the Third Street Gallery, Santa Rosa, 1868; Downing, Rea & Rauscher succeeded him. Visited Eureka, 1868, renting Anderson's daguerreian gallery. Operated in San Francisco as Kraft & Farrar at 659 Clay Street, 1877; alone at 706 Filbert Street; partner in Kraft & Worthington at 5 Stockton Street, 1890. Listed at 64 Third Street, 1892; 1303 Polk, 1895. See Oregon.

KRAUS, G. E.
Active in Los Angeles, 1895, at 133 ½ Spring Street.

KRAUS, H. D.
Active in Los Angeles, 1892-94, at 426 Downey Avenue.

KRUSE, LOUIS
Active in San Francisco, 1865.

KUCHEL & DRESSEL
Operated in San Francisco, c. 1858.

KUSEL, EDWARD ABRAHAM
Born in Mecklenburg Schwerin, Germany, 1824. Came to New York, 1849, and walked most of the way to Chicago. Went to St. Louis, joined an ox team, 1852, and rode a mule to Sacramento. Moved to Marysville, then to Oroville, 1856, and took up photography. Built general merchandise store and established his photographic parlor in the rear. The store became known as the Kusel Building. Practiced

photography at least until 1878; also operated in Chico, 1868-89. Published stereoviews and large format landscape images; published books on the local school system, and was active in his community.

KUSEL, LOUIS E.
Operating in Oroville, c. 1885.

KUYKENDALL, F.
Active in Santa Rosa, 1878.

LA ROCHE, FRANK
Active in Colusa, 1880. Opened a gallery in partnership with B. F. Sooy in Ogden, Utah, 1883. Landscape and view photographer, working in the western states. Worked out of Seattle, Washington, 1890s, and was one of the early photographers of Alaskan Indians. Also spelled La Roch and La Rosh. See Alaska, British Columbia and Washington.

LA ROSH & ATIEMAN
Operated the Elite Photographic Studio at the corner of Third and D Streets, over Joe Lask's Store, 1880, Marysville.

LAI YONG
Portrait painter and photograph gallery, located at 743 Washington Street, corner of Dupont, San Francisco, 1869-81.

LAMB, C. Y.
Active in Cuffey's Cove, 1878.

LAMBERT, EICHENBERGER BROTHERS
Operated in San Francisco, c. 1890.

LAMSON, JOSEPH H.
Active in Los Angeles, 1889-92. Partner in Steckel & Lamson, 120 ½ South Spring Street, 1889-90; operated his own studio, J. H. Lamson Company, 1892, at 313 ½ Spring Street; also known as Lamson Studio.

LANCEY, T. C.
Owned the California Photographic Gallery with J. B. Starkweather, operator of the gallery at 402 Kearney Street, San Francisco, 1870.

LANEY
Active in Redlands, 1898.

LANEY, GRACE E.
Born in Pennsylvania, November 1872. Active in Redlands, 1897-1900, in gallery she purchased from J. H. Young.

LANGE & NEWTH
Partnership of Oscar V. Lange and Ernest W. Newth, stereo photographers in San Francisco at 620 Clay Street, before 1870s.

LANGE, OSCAR V.
Born in New Jersey, 1855, of German parents. San Francisco photographer specializing in architectural, landscape and mining; also a landscape painter. Produced stereoviews in association with Ernest W. Newth, c. 1868-78. Gallery at 1023 ½ Market Street, 1883, business manager, J. W. Farnell; at 1025 Market Street, 1885-86; 26 Montgomery Street, 1887; in business with T. P. Andrews as Andrews & Lange at 109 Montgomery Street, by 1895. Published an article on William Shew in *Camera Craft*, Volume 5, Number 3, July 1902.

LANGERNOR, ELLA
Born in Tennessee, May 1877. Active in Sacramento, c. 1899-1900.

LANGEVIN, EDWARD A.
Active in Milton, late 1880s; in Enderby, British Columbia, 1890; in Salmon Arm, 1891; San Francisco, 1902.

LANGFORD, OLIVE
Born in Iowa, January 1868. Partner with Corry Bushnell in Fresno gallery, c. 1899-1900.

LANIER, CHARLES
Gallery at 31 Third Street, San Francisco, 1885-95. Associated with Charles G. Faist, 1885; operated a second gallery at 715 Market, 1887-95. Was awarded a medal at the Mechanic's Fair, 1885.

LANKIN, GEORGE W.
Active in Chico, 1880.

LARE, CHARLES A.
Active in Etna, 1895-96.

LARISON, C. A.
Active in Yreka, 1890-1900.

LARSON, SELMA
Active in Ferndale, 1899, in the Brien Building, Ocean Avenue.

LARUE, E. C.
Stereo photographer, possibly an amateur, active in Pasadena.

LASLEY, MARGARET ROSE
Born in California, April 1874. Active in Blue Lake and Ferndale, c. 1894-98, partner with husband, C. C. Lasley. Operated the Elite Gallery, formerly operated by Adam W. Gilfillian, 1896.

LATHROP
Partner in Dunham & Lathrop, 1159 Broadway, Oakland, 1874.

LAUGHLING, SADIE
Active in San Diego, 1888-90, at 740 5th Street.

LAUSKIN, MARIE
Born in Italy, November 1870. Immigrated to the United States with her parents, 1889. Active in San Francsico, c. 1899-1900.

LAWHUN & ZWERNER
Partnership in San Francisco at 1303 Polk Street, 1899; Miss Marion Lawhun and Anna Zwerner.

LAWHUN, MARION (MISS)
Active in San Francisco, 1899, partner in Lawhun & Zwerner.

LAWHUN, SAMUEL
San Francisco, 1898.

LAWLESS, E. J.
Active in Sisson, 1911.

LAWN STUDIO
Operating in Sacramento, c. 1895.

LAWRENCE & HOUSEWORTH
Partnership of optician George S. Lawrence and photographer Thomas Houseworth, 1864-67; produced many of the best of the early stereoviews of California and the earliest mammoth plate views of Yosemite Valley by C. L. Weed. See Thomas Houseworth.
   Peter E. Palmquist, *Lawrence & Houseworth, Thomas Houseworth & Company: A Unique View of the West 1860-86*, National Stereoscopic Society, 1980.

LAWRENCE & SON
Excelsior Gallery, 207 North Main Street, Los Angeles, 1888; also at 221 North Main, 6 Downey Block, date uncertain. Operated by William Lawrence. Also known as Lawrence & Sons.

LAWRENCE, GEORGE E.
Studio at 133 ½ Spring, Los Angeles, 1894-98; 321 ½ South Spring, 1904, and 203 Mercantile Place, 1905. Probably the son of William Lawrence.

LAWRENCE, GEORGE S.
An optician; after an unsuccessful try at mining in Calaveras County, joined with one of his mining partners, Thomas Houseworth, to found the firm of Lawrence & Houseworth, opticians and photographers.

LAWRENCE, H. F.
Picture agent and photographer, Church Street near Fifth, Gilroy, 1884-88 or later.

LAWRENCE, WILLIAM
Partner in William Lawrence & Son, Los Angeles, 1884-89. Studio located at 6 Downey Block, 1884-88; 207 North Main, 1888-89; 221 North Main, Downey Block; 317 North Main, 1890.

LAWRENCE, WILLIAM H.
Gallery at 427 Montgomery Street, San Francisco, 1881-87.

LAWSON, BENJAMIN W.
Studio at 147 South Main Street, Los Angeles, 1894-96; 228 Mercantile Place, 1905.

LAWTON, LENA W.
Photographer at 29 Kearny Street, San Francisco, 1877.

LE FORGE, F. M.
Active in Shasta County, 1880.

LE PLONGEON, AUGUSTUS
Daguerreian active in San Francisco, 1856.

LEARNED
Active in Oak Bar and Oakdale, 1890.

LEAVENWORTH, JOHN RANDOLPH
Born in Connecticut, 1836. San Francisco photographer, 1865-88. Worked for Thomas Houseworth, 1869-70; partner in Leavenworth, Stone & Company, 1228 Market Street, 1887; listed alone at same address, 1888.

LEAVENWORTH, STONE & COMPANY
Gallery in San Francisco, 1887, at 1228 Market Street operated by John Randolph Leavenworth.

LEAVITT, DIANA S.
Active in Oakland, 1883-84, at 911 Broadway. Possibly the wife of F. L. Leavitt.

LEAVITT, F. L.
Operated the Oakland Photograph Gallery in Oakland, 911 Broadway, 1883-84.

LEBO
Partner in Rhein & Lebo, 114 South Spring, Los Angeles, 1892.

LEE, LE ROY
Active in Sisson, 1911.

LEE, W. THOMAS
Photographic printer with George D. Morse, San Francisco, 1869-70; partner with W. N. Tuttle, Temple Block, Los Angeles, 1874; studio in Virginia City, Nevada, 1877.

LEE, WILLARD MALCOMB
"Artist" in Chico, c. 1865-66; studio on the 100 Block, Main Street.

LEFTWICH, JOHN WARWICK
Born in Virginia, 1845. Studio at 421 J Street, Sacramento, 1880-84; listed in Plumas County, 1881-95.

LEFTWICH, MARY F.
Born in Virginia, 1852. Operated the studio of her husband, J. W. Leftwich, Sacramento, 1885-86.

LEHR, O.
Stereo photographer; worked with H. Schoene in San Francisco, 1871.

LEMOS, W.
Studio at 47 Wilson Block, Los Angeles, 1893.

LENTZ, WILLIAM H.
Born in Maryland, 1847. "Late of Johnson's," located at Main Street, Petaluma, c. 1867; San Francisco, 1870.

LENZ, J. M.
Gallery at 657 Fifth Street, San Diego, 1888-98.

LESHER, CHARLES
Studio at 314 West Second, Pomona, 1898.

LEVI, I. G.
Studio at 245 Third Street, San Francisco, 1871.

LEVY, LEAH A.
Born in California, January 1881. Active in San Francisco, c. 1900.

LEVY, MARY CLARA
Born in San Francisco, California, December 1866. Daughter of photographers John David Godeus and Mary Anna Clifton Godeus. Active in San Francisco, 1890-1901. Worked as a photographer for her father at 10 Sixth Street, 1892, and after his death, operated the studio with her mother.

LEWIN, OTTO
Stereo photographer; worked with H. Schoene in San Francisco, 1871.

LEWIS, E. B.
Active on Monterey Street, San Luis Obispo, c. 1895.

LEWIS, MARY S.
Active in Santa Clara, 1899-1900.

LEWIS, W. S.
Stereo photographer active in Hollywood and Los Angeles; offered hand-colored views of desert flora, Mono and Kern Counties, national parks.

LEWMAN, E. R.
Partner in Deveraux & Lewman, 512 Fifteenth Street, Oakland, 1888.

LEY, MARY M.
Active in Woodland, c. 1890-94. Wife and partner of Thomas Allen Ley in gallery on Main Street.

LEY, THOMAS ALLEN
Operated the Palace Gallery on Main Street near Third, Woodland, 1883-89 or longer. Partner with his wife, Mary M. Ley. Perhaps the Thomas A. Ley of Dayton, Washington Territory, uncertain date. Operating in Auburn, c. 1896; Placerville, opposite the Democrat Office, 1898-99.

LICHTIG & AGNER
Studio in San Francisco, 1898, operated by Bernard Lichtig and Charles Agner at 3 Taylor Street.

LICHTIG, BERNARD
Partner in Lichtig & Agner, 3 Taylor Street, San Francisco, 1898.

LIEBERT, ALPHONSE J.
Born in France, c. 1827; died in Paris, France, 1914. An officer in the French navy, he resigned to pursue a career in photography, 1848. Daguerreian studio in Nevada City, 1857; published paper prints in Nevada City, 1857; published a book with tipped in prints, *La Photographie en Amerique*, 1864; his studio burned, 1858; active on Broad Street, opposite the Hotel de Paris 1859; raffled daguerreian jewelry; sold his studio, 1862. He returned to France, 1863, continuing his career as a tintypist, published several books and invented an electric light system for studios. Trained Louis Celarie but later engaged in bitter competition with him in Nevada City.
> Peter E. Palmquist, "Raffle Wars: A Chronology of Alphonse J. Liebert in California and France," *The Daguerreian Annual*, The Daguerreian Society, 1992.

LILJEGREEN, A.
Active in Weaverville, 1885-1910; traveling photographer, 1890s; in Happy Camp by 1900.

LILLIBRIDGE, CLARK
Born in New York, 1820. Probably in Illinois, 1865, when his son, Clark, was born. Active in Auburn, 1880.

LINGFELTER, J. M.
Stereo photographer active in Los Angeles, c. 1893, at 426 Downey Avenue.

LINK, WILLIAM
Active in Weed, 1913.

LIPPINCOTT ART PHOTO COMPANY
Los Angeles, 1900-01.

LISK, J. H.
Active in San Jose, 1877; Salinas, 1878.

LIVE YANKEE GALLERY
Operating in Shasta, 1875-76.

LLOYD, HAROLD
Famous movie comedian, 1920s-30s, and stereo photographer; made thousands of views of motion picture stars.

LLOYD, W. S.
Active in San Andreas, 1867.

LOBBELL, S. A.
Active in Lemoore, 1880.

LOCHMAN, R. E.
Active in Chico, 1881, at Salem and 5th Street.

LOCKE, ALICE E.
Born in Georgia, December 1846. Active in San Francisco, c. 1899-1901.

LOCKE, I. S.
Daguerreian artist in Stockton on Main Street, 1863; his studio on wheels was burned in the Stockton fire of September 4, 1865.

LOCKWOOD, J. R.
Studio located on Whipp Block, Pomona, c. 1895; 169 South Main, 1896-97.

LOFLAND, DAVID R.
Proprietor of the Oriental Photographic Gallery, Watsonville, 1884-87; in San Lucas, 1888.

LOGAN, A.
Active in Verdugo, 1898.

LOGAN, CHARLES W.
Active in Modoc County, 1885-1905.

LONERGAN
Associated with Clarence A. Howland in the Imperial Photographic Gallery, 724 ½ Market Street, San Francisco, 1895.

LONG, A. W.
Partner in Pierce and Long, Los Angeles, 1888, at 523 Downey Avenue; listed under his own name at 418 Downey Avenue, 1890.

LONG, C. B. (MRS.)
Gallery operator active in Azusa, c. 1892-94. Possibly the same as Cora W. Long.

LONG, C. B., & L. R. SCOTT
Partnership operating in Susanville, 1880.

LONG, CORA W.
Active in Los Angeles, 1891.

LONG, SACK
Active in Cherokee, 1864-65.

LOOMIS, ARTHUR W.
Active in Redding, 1898-1914.

LOOMIS, BENJAMIN FRANKLIN
Active in Redding, 1900-30.

LORENZ, HELEN W.
Active in Los Angeles, 1894. Probably the wife of John A. Lorenz.

LORENZ, JOHN A.
Active in Los Angeles, 1892-97. Listed at 317 North Main, 1892, 1897; 6 Downey Block, 1893-95; studio in his home, Downey Block, 307 North Main Street 1895-96.

LORILLARD & BRATT
Partnership operating portrait and view gallery on 4th Street, 1898-1900; Eva Lorillard and James Henry Bratt.

LORILLARD, EVA
Born in Oregon, February 1860. Active in San Rafael, 1898-1900. Purchased an interest in the McMillan Gallery, 1898; partner with James Henry Bratt, operating the Lorillard & Bratt portrait and view gallery on 4th Street, 1898-1900.

LORYEA & MACAULEY
Gallery in San Jose, 1883-86; Milton and Archibold Loryea and John M. Macaulay.

LORYEA, ARCHIBALD
Associated with his brother, Milton Loryea, in the Souvenir Photographic Studio, 26 South First Street, San Jose, 1884-89 or later. John W. Macaulay was a partner in the company, 1883-86.

LORYEA, MILTON
Born in California, 1860. Photographer in San Francisco by 1880. Opened the Souvenir Photographic Studio in San Jose, partner with John W. Macaulay on 315 Santa Clara Street, by 1883; also operated as Loryea & Macaulay. Located at 26 South First Street, c. 1886, when Macaulay left the firm; Loryea, with his brother Archibold, formed Loryea Brothers Souvenir Photographic Studio, continuing through 1889 or later.

LOS ANGELES ELECTRIC COPYING HOUSE
Studio in Los Angeles, 1896, at 314 Buena Vista, operated by C. H. Wescott and J. W. Archer.

LOTZ, PAUL
Born in Tennessee, 1858, of German parents. Photographer in San Francisco, 1880; partner in Jones & Lotz Elite Gallery, 838 Market Street, 1885-89; in business alone in the same address, 1898.

LOUCKS, R. N.
Stereo photographer, Pomona; also operated a book and stationery shop.

LOUIS, A.
Licensed in San Francisco, 1864.

LOVEJOY & WILLIAMS
Studio in San Francisco, c. 1874-76, at 128 Kearny; William E. Lovejoy.

LOVEJOY, HARVEY P.
Born in New York State, 1833. Lived in Indiana, Michigan and Kentucky before practicing photography in San Francisco, c. 1880.

LOVEJOY, WILLIAM E.
Born in New Hampshire, 1836. An artist in Alexander Edouart's gallery, San Francisco, 1865; associated with Williams at 128 Kearny, 1874; in business for himself at 22 Kearny, 1876; photographer with the Pacific View Company, 1883. He was a bartender for William A. Scollay, 1885, but practiced photography in San Francisco, 1887-98 or later.

LOVELACE, ESTHER
Photographer in Colusa County, 1903.

LOVEWELL
Tintypist in Los Angeles, c. 1870.

LOVEWELL, GEORGE, H.
Born in Iowa, 1854. Active in Red Bluff, 1878; Chico, 1878-80; studio in Auburn, 1880.

LOVEWELL, S. J.
Active in Stockton, 1877.

LOWE, J. P.
Active in El Dorado, c. 1866; Auburn, c. 1867; proprietor of the Elite Photograph Gallery on Tulare Street near K, 1883. Also a winch maker and agent for New Home and New Wilson Sewing Machines.

LUDERS, EDWARD T.
Partner in Dyer & Luders, 612 Clay Street, San Francisco, 1865.

LUMMIS, CHARLES FLETCHER
Born in Lynn, Massachusetts, 1859; died 1928. After attending Harvard University, Lummis walked from Ohio to Los Angeles, 1884-85. Worked as an editor for the *Los Angeles Times*, learning photography, 1885-88. Lived at Isleta Pueblo, New Mexico, 1888-92, and published an account of his cross-country walk, *A Tramp Across America.* Settling in Pasadena, Lummis became a leader of the emerging artists' community and engaged in numerous activities involving writing and photography in southern California and New Mexico. He published many postcards and was the prime mover in establishing the Southwest Museum in Pasadena, 1913.

Charles F. Lummis - The Centennial Exhibition Commemorating His Tramp Across the Continent, Morieta, Daniela P. (Editor), Southwest Museum, 1985.
Patrick T. Houlihan and Betsy E. Houlihan, *Lummis in the Pueblos*, Northland Press, 1986.
Mary A. Sabers, *Charles F. Lummis: A Bibliography*, University of Arizona Library, Tucson, 1977.

LUSSIER, L. O.
San Jose photographer, 1878, associated with L. P. Hill.

LUTHER, HENRY
Born in Prussia, 1824. Studio in 444 ½ Third Street, San Francisco, 1872-86 or longer. Partner in Hoebel & Luther, 1872-73. Also known as Hans Luther.

LYDSTON, ARTHUR F.
Born in Massachusetts, 1844. Active in San Jose, 1880. Musician and photographer; gallery at 66 South First Street, San Jose, 1884-87.

LYNN, ANNIE E.
Born in Missouri, January 1871. Active in Los Angeles, 1891-1900.

LYON, CORNELIA
Active in Stockton, 1881-88. Portrait photographer with B. P Batchelder.

MACAULAY, JOHN W.
Studio at 367 First Street, San Jose, 1874-1877. Partner in Loryea & Macaulay's Souvenir Photographic Studio, 315 Santa Clara Street, San Jose, 1883; with the same company at 26 South First Street, 1884-1886. Addressed "Three doors from Central Market, No stairs to climb." In 1887 became a salesman with T. W. Hobson & Company, clothiers and tailors, San Jose.

MACDONALD & DOWE
Operated at 1025 Market Street, San Francisco, 1881-82; also offered portrait painting.

MACDONALD, A. J.
Stereo photographer in Springfield, Ohio, 1860s; partner with Lewis Dow in San Francisco, 1881-92.

MACDONALD, JOHN C.
Proprietor of gallery at 1504 Market Street, San Francisco, 1900-02.

MACDONALD, NELLIE
Active in San Francisco, 1900-02. Wife of John C. MacDonald, proprietor of gallery at 1504 Market Street, where Nellie presumably worked.

MACHINO, SHINGORO
Partner with William J. Hynes in Hynes & Company gallery, San Francisco, 1896-1905.

MACKENZIE, G. J.
Operated MacKenzie's Art Studio, 125 ½ Spring, Los Angeles, 1893. Listed under his own name, 1894 at the Spring Street address; as G. J. MacKenzie & Company at 92 Potomac Block, 1895.

MAINS & CLEMENTS
Operating on Huntoon Street in Oroville, c. 1875.

MAINS & M. H. GRANT
Operating in San Francisco, c. 1875.

MAINS & SHIPPY
Stereo photographers active in Sucker Flat, 1870s; photographed aftermath of robberty at the Blue Point Mining Company, mining scenes; James Riley Mains.

MAINS & VON HASSLEN
Produced enameled cards, c. 1868; carte-de-visite in author's collection with Mains & Von Hasslen imprint is copied from a Mumler "spirit photograph," c. 1875. Partnership of stereo photographers active in Camptonville; J. R. Mains.

MAINS, JAMES RILEY
Born in Maine, 1833. Photographer with Jacob Shew, San Francisco, 1865; partner with Charles A. Marston, c. 1867, establishing the Excelsior Fine Art Gallery of Photography, 523 Kearny Street. Published a number of California stereoviews with Grant (probably Martin H. Grant), 1868-78; opened a gallery in La Porte, 1874.

MALLORY, F. L. (MRS.)
Photographer in Shasta Springs, 1900.

MANSFIELD, C.
Born in Austria, 1854. Active in Oakland, c. 1880.

MANSIR, HENRY C.
Born in Massachusetts, 1840. Active in San Francisco, 1880.

MARCEAU, THEODORE C.
Active in Plumas County, 1892. Bought out George Daniels Morse and established himself at 826 Market Street, San Francisco, 1895. Had galleries in Cincinnati, Indianapolis and Los Angeles. Active in Los Angeles, 1898-1906, at 227 South Spring.

MARCHAND, A. P.
Studio at 380 South First Street, San Jose, 1887.

MARDEN, ROBERT A.
Studio called Marden's National Art Gallery located at 28 Third Street, San Francisco, 1876-79.

MARIE, LOUIS ARMAND
Active in Weaverville, 1871-75.

MARNELL, DAVID
Active in Etna, 1898-1900.

MARSTON & MAINS
Gallery in San Francisco, c. 1867-69, at 523 Kearny Street; C. A. Marston and J. R. Mains.

MARSTON, CHARLES A.
Born in Boston, Massachusetts. Partner with Jacob Shew in San Francisco at 315 Montgomery Street, 1865-67; partner with J. Riley Mains, operating as Excelsior Fine Art Gallery at 523 Kearny Street, near Sacramento Street, 1867; in business alone at 806 Kearny Street, 1869; opened a second gallery at 652 Washington, 1871; operated gallery in Carson City, Nevada, 1872-c. 1886. Directories show that while he had his gallery in Carson City, 1886, he was Deputy Collector of U.S. Internal Revenue in San Francisco, 1885-86.

MARTIN
Active in Sisson, 1895.

MARTIN & TUTTLE
Active in Los Angeles, c. 1867.

MARTIN & VALENTINE
Operating at 650 Washington, San Francisco, 1864.

MARTIN & WEILE
Partnership operating in Sisson, 1890-1900.

MARTIN, J. A.
Licensed in Silveyville, 1864.

MASON
Partner in Beatty & Mason, Marysville, 1895.

MARX, GERTRUDE (MISS)
Photographer in Etna, 1905.

MATTHEWS, GEORGE
Active in Chico.

MATTHEWS, GEORGE L. & ROSA
Partnership in Cedarville, 1900.

MATTHEWS, ROSA (MRS.)
Active in Dunsmuir, c. 1887-90; in Cedarville, c. 1900. Wife of photographer George L. Matthews, with whom she owned a traveling photography wagon.

MATHIASON, P. B.
Active in Los Angeles, 1898-1904. Listed at 6th Floor, Byrne Building, 1898, and at 239 ½ South Spring, 1902-04.

MATLACK, IDA
Born in Missouri, May 1863. Photographer and retoucher in Riverside, 1893-1920; employed by S. P. Tresslar, Rubidoux Building, 1893-94; by H. E. Scott, 773 Main Street, 1911.

MATSON & BLAIR
Partnership of Frances (Fanny) L. Matson and Hosea Blair at 6 Turk Street, San Francisco, 1894-95.

MATSON, FRANCES L. (MISS)
Active in San Francisco, 1894-1914. Partner in portrait studio at 6 Turk Street with Frank L. Blair, 1894-95; sole proprietor, 1896-1900; located at 410 Kearny Street, 1900-04; Emmet Place, 1909; Stockton Street, 1913-14. Also listed as Fanny.

MATTISON, ROBERT
Licensed in Santa Cruz, 1862-63.

MAUDE, FREDERICK H.
Partner in Maude & Company, landscape photographers and producers of stereoviews, 21 West First Street, Los Angeles, 1896-1900+; photographed southern California Indians. Studio also located at 101 ½ South Broadway, 1897-98; 8 Hammond Block, 1899; 110 West Second, 1902; 1718 Brooklyn Avenue, 1905. Maude worked with George Wharton James, perhaps as a partner. Some confusion reported over attributions with E. E. Hall and Ben Wittick.

MAURER, OSCAR
Born in New York, 1871; died in Berkeley, 1965. Brother of Currier & Ives artist, Alfred Maurer. Began career in 1886 in San Francisco, shared studio with Arnold Genthe until the studio was destroyed in the 1906 earthquake; studio on Le Roy Avenue, Berkeley, 1907.

MAXWELL
Partner in Dorr & Maxwell, 28 Third Street, San Francisco, 1870.

MAXWELL BROTHERS
Gallery on West Street, Healdsburg, 1867. Possibly C. T. and J. D.

Maxwell of Maxwell Brothers, Spokane Falls, Washington, 1886.

MAY
Advertised as "The Photographer " in Wheatland, c. 1895. Probably George W. May.

MAY & BRYAN
Active in San Francisco, 1857. Possibly John M. Bryan and Professor H. J. May.

MAY & FESSENDON
San Francisco, 1855.

MAY & NYE
Active in Stockton, c. 1875.

MAY, C. W.
Active in Dutch Flat, 1878.

MAY, GEORGE W.
Born in Pennsylvania, 1843. Active Healdsburg and Oroville, c. 1880; in Lebanon, Oregon, 1886; Porterville, California, c. 1890; San Francisco, 1895.

MAY, PROFESSOR H. J.
Possibly involved in partnerships of May & Fessenden, 1855; May & Bryan, San Francisco, 1857; May & Nye, Stockton. Stereo photographer in San Jacinto; San Francisco, 1859-61; licensed at 606 Kearney Street, 1861; in Riverside County, c. 1880s.

MAY STUDIO
Operated by Isabelle May Chan and Leo Chan on Sacramento Street, San Francisco, c. 1920-76.

McALPIN, ARTHUR BANCROFT
Studio in San Francisco at 427 Montgomery Street, 1879. See Oregon.

McCARTHY, MICHAEL H.
Active in Scott River, 1890-1905.

McCAUSTLAND, EDITH M.
Born in Wisconsin, October 1869. Active in San Jose, c. 1899-1900. Employed by photographer Mrs. J. W. Hyde, 79 West Santa Clara Street, 1900. Sister of Ellen McCaustland.

McCAUSTLAND, ELLEN
Born in Wisconsin, April 1876. Active in San Jose, c. 1899-1900. Sister of Edith M. McCaustland.

McCLELLAN, WILLIAM C.
With McClellan & Son, wholesale portraits and frames, 2 Temperance Temple, northwest corner of Temple and North Broadway, Los Angeles, 1896. Also listed as William S.

McCONNELL
Partner in Pierce & McConnell, 515 or 517 North Main, Los Angeles, 1893-94.

McCORMICK, J.
Active in Grizzly Flat, 1886.

McCRARY, SYLVESTER
Gallery at 4 Odd Fellows Building, Marysville, 1865-67. Also listed as McCray.

McCREARY, ROLLAND
Licensed in Downieville, 1865.

McCULLOUGH
Studio at 21 North El Dorado Street, Stockton, c. 1900.

McCURRY
Traveling photographer; also in Sacramento, 1914.

McCUTCHAN, J. M.
Licensed in Nevada [City], 1863.

McDONALD, A. J.
Born in St. Andrews, Canada, 1840. Served in the Civil War, Company K, 18th New York Infantry, Newton's Brigade, First Division, 6th Army Corps. After his service, he went to Buffalo, New York, where he learned photography; active in Pennsylvania, Ohio, West Virginia and New Orleans, arriving in San Francisco, California, 1887. Published California views. Father of George A. McDonald.

McDONALD, GEORGE A.
Son of A. J. McDonald. In business with his father, San Francisco, 1892. Gallery at 2103 Webster, 1895-98 or later.

McELROY, H. S.
Licensed in San Francisco, 1861.

McEVOY, JOHN JAMES
Active in Redding and Keswick, 1897-1900.

McFARLIN & WOODS
Operating in Placerville on Main Street, 1868.

McFARLIN, S. L.
Active in Placerville over Harris' Variety Store, at the corner of Main and Plaza, 1865-69.

McGARRY, EARL A.
Traveling photographer, 1890-1907.

McGEE, J. H.
Active in Los Angeles, 1899-1901, at 513 North Main.

McGINLEY & SCHUBERT'S FLYING PHOTOGRAPH GALLERY
Operating in California, late 1860s.

McGINLEY, THEODORE B. G.
Probably the partner in McGinley & Schubert's Flying Photograph Gallery operating in California, late 1860s. Gallery on Fifth Street, Hollister, 1874; gallery in Fresno City on Mariposa Street, 1884.

McGINN, ANNA (MISS)
Active in San Francisco, 1863-68. Gallery at 234 Kearny Street, 1863; at 2 O'Farrell Street, corner of Market, 1865-68.

McINTOSH, WILLIAM
Active in Livermore, 1877.

McINTYRE, S. S.
Mentioned in Humphrey's Journal, 1851, having lost his establishment in a fire and five half-plate daguerreotypes of San Francisco and six of the same size of the gold diggings. Probably the same as S. C. McIntyre.

McINTYRE, STERLING C.
Daguerreotypist in Tallahassee, Florida, 1844-45, 1848-49; in New York at 663 Broadway, 1850-51; San Francisco, California, 1851; Nevada City, 1851-55; also practiced dentistry, 1851; operated out of Kilbourn's Daguerrean Room, 1853. A panorama of San Francisco which he made out of five daguerreotypes was displayed at the

Crystal palace Exhibition in London; also made daguerreotypes of the gold fields. Probably the same as S. S. McIntyre.

McKEAN & RECHT
125 Pacific, Santa Cruz, 1888.

McKENNELT, MARY E.
Born in England, June 1851. Immigrated to the U.S., 1855. Active in Los Angeles, c. 1899-1900.

McKINNON, M. A.
Active in Shasta, 1862-63.

McMILLAN
Active in Ferndale, c. 1885.

McMILLAN
Active in Merced, c. 1895.

McMILLAN, A.
Active in Mammoth City, 1880.

McMILLAN BROTHERS
Partnership of Charles, George and John McMillan, operating in San Francisco at 8 Sixth Street, 1883-87.

McMILLAN, CHARLES
Born in Kingston, Canada, 1853. Went to Chicago and took up photography at age sixteen. Opened a gallery which survived the fire, and operated it until he left for California, 1881. Partner in McMillan Brothers with his brother, John, 8 Sixth Street, San Francisco, 1883-87 ; brother George joined partnership, 1886; photographed the entire state, building up an extensive collection of views. Opened McMillan Brothers in Santa Maria, 1888; in Vallejo, c. 1891-1912 or later, first in a tent, then a gallery. See Oregon.

McMILLAN, GEORGE
Partner in McMillan Brothers with Charles and John, 8 Sixth Street, San Francisco, 1886.

McMILLAN, JOHN
Partner in McMillan Brothers, 8 Sixth Street, San Francisco, 1883-86. Perhaps went to Oregon and ran McMillan Brothers in Marshfield (Coos Bay), Oregon, 1886. Studio in Santa Maria, California, 1892-98. See Oregon.

McMILLEN, F. H.
Gallery at the Evans Block, Riverside, c. 1880; at the corner of Main and 8th Streets, c. 1895.

McMILLEN, ZEPHONIA
Partner in gallery with her husband, F. H. McMillen, in Riverside, 1892-95.

McMILLER, MAUDE W. (MISS)
Photographer in Marysville, 1907-10.

McMULLEN, C. A.
Publisher of stereoviews in Oakland.

McNICOLL, E.
Licensed in San Francisco, 1863.

McNICOLL, JOHN
Gallery in San Francisco; on Mission, 1882-88; active 1903.

McWAIN, O. G.
Active in Los Angeles, 1900-01, at 601 Byrne Building.

MEACHAM, MARK
Active in Redding, 1894.

MEAD, A. H.
Licensed in Woodland, 1863.

MEDINA, F.
Active in Merced, c. 1895.

MEEK, MARIE (MISS)
Photographer in Marysville, 1900.

MEISER, JESSE A.
Studio in Eureka, 1908. Sold out to Edmund and Emma B. Freeman.

MEISTER, CECELIA
Active in Chico, 1920-21.

MELVIN
Active in Redlands, 1898.

MENDELSSOHN, G. (MRS.)
Artist with Morse Photograph Company, 1898, San Francisco.

MENDELSSOHN, JOSEPH
Photographer in San Francisco, 1897-1901; with C. E. Ehmann, 1898. Also spelled Mendelsohn.

MENDENHALL, H.
Traveling photographer; gallery at 227 Fifth Street, San Diego, 1888-89.

MERRIAM, EDSON WINFIELD
Active in Chico.

MERRIAM, ESRA DALY
Born in 1838. Studio at 618 Washington, San Francisco, 1866.

MERRICK, ANNA F.
Born in Kansas, March 1868. Active in Auburn, c. 1899-1900.

MERRILL, STEWART
Active in Yreka, 1876-78; gallery at 659 Clay Street, San Francisco, 1886-98.

MERSEREAU, FREDERICK E.
Gallery at 2239 Mission Street, San Francisco, 1894-98. See Oregon.

METCALF & HUTCHINSON
Gallery at 650 Washington Street, San Francisco, 1863-66.

MEYER, CHARLES A.
Active in Hayfork and Harrison Gulch, 1895.

MEYER, JACOB EMERY
Active in Junction City, 1869.

MEYER, P. J.
Active in Knob, 1890.

MEYERS, FREDERICK
Active in San Francisco, c. 1880.

MEYERS, FREDERICK, JR.
Active in Harrison Gulch, 1895; San Francisco, c. 1898.

MIDDLEMISS, B.
Active in Redding, 1897-98.

MILBURN, FRANK KARL
Active in Sisson, 1890s; partner in Brazelton & Milburn, 1890.

MILHOLLAND, T.
Active in Valle Vista, San Jacinto Township, 1898.

MILLER & CHASE
Gallery located at 335 F Street, Eureka, c. 1895.

MILLER, CAROLINE
Born in Nevada, March 1869. Active in San Francisco, 1899-1900.

MILLER, CHARLES ALDRICH
Operated the Etna Art Parlors in Etna, 1896-1908; also active in Hamburgh, 1906-08.

MILLER, CHARLES RICHARD
Active in Sisson and McCloud, 1905-18.

MILLER, GEORGE W.
Active in Humboldt County, 1890.

MILLER, HIRAM
Worked with Bradley & Rulofson in San Francisco, 1871; active in Woodland, 1883.

MILLER, JOE F.
Active in Corning, 1916.

MILLER, R.
Active in Sisson, 1903.

MILLER, SARAH ELOISE
Born in California, August 1888. Active in Santa Rosa, c. 1899-1900.

MILLS, C. H.
Stereo photographer in Humboldt County; possibly an amateur.

MILLS, WILLIAM ALLISON BLAIR
Active in Yreka, 1877.

MILNE, CHARLES
Active in Scott Bar, 1912-14.

MILTZ & OVERTON
Partnership of Theodore G. Miltz and N. R. Overton, operating in Nevada City and Grass Valley, c. 1883.

MILTZ & SWART
Partnership of Theodore G. Miltz and John H. Swart operating in San Francisco, c. 1875; Santa Rosa, 1877-81.

MILTZ, THEODORE G.
Born in New York, 1848. Bought out Gustavus Fagersteen and operated the St. Louis Art and Photographic Gallery with J. Swart and R. Schad, 315 Montgomery Street, San Francisco, c. 1875. Partner of John H. Swart in the San Francisco Gallery, 180 Fourth Street, Santa Rosa, 1877-81. Partner with N. R. Overton in Nevada County, 1883, operating galleries in Nevada City and Grass Valley. Also spelled Mitz.

MINOR, ROBERT
Born in Massachusetts, 1828. Daguerreian artist active in Stockton before 1870.

MITCHELL& FRIZELL
Gallery in Los Angeles, c. 1900.

MITCHELL, MAYBELLE G.
Active in San Jose, employed by W. J. Carruthers at 26 South First Street, 1899-1900.

MITH, G. B. (MRS.)
Photographer in Red Bluff, 1914.

MOELLER, JOHN R.
Born in Germany, c. 1858. Studio at 319 West Fourth Street, Santa Ana, c. 1895; partner in Dove & Moeller, 147 South Main, 1898-99.

MOJONIER, A. LOUIS
Born in Highland, Illinois, October, 28, 1869. Operated studio in Los Angeles, California, 1896-1913. Located at 127 West First Street, 1896; 217 ½ South Spring, 1897; 205 ½ South Main, 1899; 326 ½ South Broadway, 1900-04; 1023 South Figueroa, 1905; 644 South Alvarado Street, 1913.

MONACO, JOHN B.
Born in Verscio, Italy, December 12, 1856; died in San Francisco, December 12, 1938. A trained artist who worked as a colorist for his brother, Louis, in Eureka, Nevada, 1875, and later as an operator. Studio in San Francisco at 1228 Market Street, 1888-94; 702 Market, near the Palace Hotel, 1894-97; at North Beach, the location of "Little Italy," 205 Columbus Avenue (then Montgomery Avenue), 1902. He lost his studio in the earthquake and fire, 1906, and rebuilt a temporary studio on Broadway; studio at 234 Columbus Avenue, 1920-37. J. B. was a portrait artist and also photographed the city of San Francisco and life around North Beach. His name was originally Giovanni Battista Monaco.
    Dillon, Richard, *North Beach: The Italian Heart of San Francisco, Photographs by J. B. Monaco, (*1856-1938), Presidio Press, Novato, California, 1985.

MONACO, LIBERTA
Widow of Louis Monaco; after his death, she ran the studio in San Francisco, 1898-1900.

MONACO, LOUIS
Died in San Francisco, 1897. Operated the City Photograph Gallery, Eureka, Nevada, 1875-87; in San Francisco, 1888-97. See J. B. Monaco.

MONACO, LOUIS P.
Probably a son of Louis and Liberta Monaco; photographer in the Louis Monaco studio, San Francisco, 1898-99 or later.

MONACO, MARINO
Born in Canton Tecino, Switzerland, 1854. Came to America, 1869, and lived at Gold Hill, Virginia City and Eureka, Nevada, until c. 1875. Worked in Batchelder's gallery, Stockton, California, 1876. Opened the Pioneer Photograph Gallery at 198 Main Street, 1878; bought out J. D. Baldwin at 183 Main Street, operating as Excelsior Art Gallery, 1883-89 or later. Won four first premiums for his artistic photographs. Brother of Louis and J. B. Monaco.

MONAHAN, WILLIAM
Operated the City Mart Photographic Gallery in San Francisco, 1869, at the junction of Market and Kearny Streets; also in real estate business with Timothy P. Riordan in Monahan & Company.

MONMONIER, WILLIAM B.
Born in Maryland, 1820. In California by 1858. In business with his son, William D. Monmonier, at 205 Third Street, San Francisco, 1869.

MONMONIER, WILLIAM D.
Born in Rhode Island, 1855, son of William B. Monmonier. Active in Monmonier & Son, 205 Third Street, San Francisco, 1869.

MONOTTI, GIUSEPPE
Active in San Francisco, c. 1898.

MONROE, E. B.
Partner in D. B. Taylor & Company, 415 Montgomery Street, San Francisco, 1876; partner in Monroe & Potter, same address, 1878.

MONSEN, FREDERICK
Born in Bergen, Norway, 1865; died 1929. Son of a Norwegian photographer; arrived in Utah Territory, 1868; worked as a photo journalist with W. H. Jackson; with General Crook in the Apache campaign; worked on the Brown-Stanton Survey; photographed Death Valley, 1893; active in Yosemite, 1896; visited the Southwest with A. C. Vroman; established a San Francisco Studio which operated until the 1906 earthquake. Later lived in Pasadena and lectured in the East.

MOODY, H. W.
Active in Los Angeles at 238 ½ South Spring, 1890.

MOOERS, J. L.
Studio at 217 ½ South Spring, 1900-01.

MOON
Active in Red Bluff, 1920-22.

MOON, CARL
Born in Ohio, 1879; died 1948. Photographer for Santa Fe Railroad, known primarily for his photographic work among the Indians of New Mexico, Arizona and Oklahoma. Active in Pasadena, California, 1914-48. Author of *Indians of the Southwest,* 1936, which included fifty atlas-folio photographic prints; also painted Indian subjects. His wife, Grace Purdie, produced extensive western illustrations for children's books and magazines. Also spelled Karl. See New Mexico.

MOORE
Active in Nevada City, c. 1895.

MOORE & SKELTON
Operated in Arbuckle, c. 1880.

MOORE, A. R.
Active in Gilroy, 1882-86.

MOORE, G. E.
Active in Lakeport, 1887-93.

MOORE, GEORGE
Active in Oakland, 1877; possibly in Seattle, Washington, 1878.

MORDOFF, NELLE L. (MRS.)
Active in Chico, 1918-40.

MOREHEAD, JAMES FRANKLIN
Traveling photographer, 1898-1920.

MORELAND, A. W.
Gallery at 997 Market Street, San Francisco, 1885.

MORGAN, SAMUEL M.
Born in Virginia, 1847. Photographer with Bradley & Rulofson, San Francisco, 1869.

MORRILL
Partner in Graham & Morrill, Los Angeles, 1897-98. Studio at 125 ½ South Spring, 1897; at 119 South Spring, 1898.

MORRIS, ELLA M. (MRS.)
Born in Massachusetts, 1852, daughter of C. H. Butterfield. Gallery at 166 Pacific Avenue, Santa Cruz, 1883-87. Her husband, S. I. Morris, joined her in the studio, 1886-87.

MORRIS, SAMUEL I.
Born in Illinois, 1850. Upholsterer in Santa Cruz, 1878-80. Later had a shop dealing in furniture and picture frames. Joined his wife, Ella M., in the Morris Photographic Gallery, 1886-87.

MORRISON, E. G.
Operated "In tent, On the Beach, Near Santa Monica Bath House," c. 1885, Santa Monica.

MORSE, GEORGE DANIELS
Born in New York, 1835. Operator for William Shew in San Francisco, 1865; operated his Palace of Art at 315 Montgomery Street, c. 1867-81; located in the Phelan Building, 826 Market Street, 1881-95. Sold out to Theodore C. Marceau, c. 1895, but continued to practice photography at 916 Market Street. Also operated as a traveling photographer, 1859-89.

MORSE, JAMES, JR.
Gallery in Guadalupe, 1878.

MORTON, DAISY A.
Born in California, January 1882. Active in San Francisco, c. 1900.

MOSHER
Gallery at 146 Lake Street, San Francisco, 1868.

MOSHER, J. W.
Partner with A. W. Craig, operating as Craig & Mosher in San Francisco, 1877-93; at 638 Market Street, 1877-80; 22 Kearny Street, c. 1880-88.

MOULIN, GABRIEL
Partner with R. J. Walters, San Francisco, 1898.

MUDGE, A. C.
Active c. 1900.

MUELLER, C. R.
Studio at 412 West Eighth, Los Angeles, 1900-01.

MUELLER, META C. (MISS)
Listed in Los Angeles, 1897, at 802 Downey Avenue.

MUNDY, WILLIAM B.
Operated in Lakeport, 1880; also in Chico, dates unknown.

MUNROE & POTTER
Successors to D. B. Taylor & Company, operating the Temple of Art at 415 Montgomery Street, San Francisco, 1880.

MUNROE, E. B.
Born in Ohio, 1838. In California by 1874; active in Oakland, 1880. Sometimes listed as E. R. Munroe.

MURPHY
Partner in Dowe & Murphy, 1894, base uncertain.

MURRAY & COMPANY, E. E.
Company originally from Chicago; produced stereoviews in Stockton, c. 1880s.

MUYBRIDGE, EADWEARD J.
Born in Kingston-upon-Thames, England, 1830; died in Kingston-upon-Thames, 1904. Immigrated to New York, 1851; worked as a book merchant and met daguerreotypist Silas T. Selleck. Moved to San Fran-

cisco, 1855, established a bookstore at 113 Montgomery Street, and became involved in Bohemian and literary circles. Injured in a stagecoach accident in Texas, 1858; traveled between New York and England, 1858-64. Associated in photography with Silas Selleck in San Francisco, operating as Helios–the Flying Studio; also affiliated with the Nahl Brothers. He is primarily known for the series of stereoviews and larger format views published by Bradley & Rulofson. Muybridge's mammoth plate views of Yosemite Valley rivaled those of Watkins and Weed, as did his travel images taken on excursions to Alaska, Central America, and the Modoc War in northern California, 1873. He produced a spectacular panorama of San Francisco and began the famous motion studies of running horses under the auspices of Leland Stanford. At the University of Pennsylvania he continued the photographic studies of people and animals in motion that were later published. He is considerd by many as the father of the motion picture for his invention of the zoopraxiscope.

> Robert Bartlett Haas, *Muybridge, Man in Motion*, University of California Press, 1976.
> Mary V. Jessup Hood and Robert Bartlett Haas, "Eadweard Muybridge's Yosemite Valley Photographs, 1867-72," *California Historical Quarterly*, March 1963.
> *Edward Muybridge: The Stanford Years*, 1872-82, Stanford University Catalogue for an exhibition of Muybridge images, 1972.
> Weston Naef, *The Rise of Landscape Photography in the American West, 1860-85: Era of Exploration*, The Metropolitan Museum of Art, 1977.
> Kevin MacDonnell, *Eadweard Muybridge: The Man Who Invented the Moving Picture*, Little, Brown & Company, Boston, Toronto, 1972.
> Peter E. Palmquist, "Photographing the Modoc Indian War: Lewis Heller versus Eadweard Muybridge," *History of Photography*, July 1978.

MUZZALL, H. W.
Born in Indiana, 1844. Partner in the firm of Hayward & Muzzall, producing stereoviews, portraits and landscapes, Santa Barbara, 1874-83.

MYERS & LOOMIS
Traveling photographers.

MYSTIC STUDIO
Operated by G. W. Yount in Weaverville, 1896.

NAHL & WENDEROTH
Partnership of Charles Christian Nahl and Frederick A. Wenderoth, operating a daguerreian parlor at 79 Broadway, San Francisco, 1854.

NAHL BROTHERS & DICKMAN
Traveling photographers, 1862-68. Studio in San Francisco, 1867-71; partnership of Charles Christian Nahl, Hugo Wilhelm Nahl and William Dickman. Also known as the Art & Photographic Gallery.

NAHL, CHARLES CHRISTIAN
Born in Germany, 1819; died 1878. Came to California, 1850. Artist and photographer; operated a daguerreian parlor in San Francisco with A. Wenderoth and his half-brother, Hugo Wilhelm Arthur Nahl, at 79 Broadway, operating as Nahl Brothers, 1854-57. Operated as the Art & Photographic Gallery of Nahl Brothers & Dickman at 121 Montgomery Street, 1857-71. Famous artist who captured the spirit of early California in large, genre depictions in oil on canvas.

NAHL, HUGO WILHELM ARTHUR
Half-brother of Charles Christian Nahl and his partner in a daguerreian parlor and photography studio in San Francisco, 1850s-70s.

NAST
Studio in Alameda at Park and Santa Clara, c. 1890; also in San Francisco.

NATIONAL PHOTO VIEW & COPYING COMPANY
Operated by Atwater & Garrison in San Francisco, 820 California Avenue.

NEAL (MISS)
Retoucher and coloring artist at the gallery of George W. Valleau, Fifth Street, Colusa, 1875; located over Spittler's drugstore.

NELCKE, THERESA
Wife of photographer Felix Nelcke, active in San Francisco, 1897-99.

NELSON & BAILEY
Partnership of stereo photographers active in Bakersfield, 1880s; C. A. Nelson.

NELSON, A. A. (MRS.)
Active in Woodland, 1893.

NELSON, CHRISTOPHER A.
Active in San Francisco, 1886, at 444 ½ Third Street; in Bakersfield, 1880s-90s.

NELSON, ETTA B.
Born in California, September 1878. Active in Oakland, c. 1899-1900.

NELSON STUDIO
Gallery in San Francisco, 1904, operated by Harold and Victor M. Duhem at 1019 Market Street.

NESEMANN, ENNO
Operated Woods Gallery in the Odd Fellows Building, Marysville, 1883-1900.

NESS, JOSEPH
Born in Massachusetts, 1850. Active in Chico, 1880.

NEW ERA PORTRAIT COMPANY
506 South Broadway, Los Angeles, 1897.

NEW YORK GALLERY
Studio in San Francisco, 1869-87; operated at various times by B. F. Howland and J. H. Peters, Daniel Sewell and J. G. Hucks, 1880-87; located at 25 and 27 Third Street, 1869-79.

NEWARK GALLERY
L. Richardson, proprietor, at 31 Third Street, San Francisco, 1880.

NEWCOMB, T. J.
Active in Pomona at 383 Second, 1895-97; in Santa Ana at 312 Bush, 1905.

NEWDICK, ALFRED P.
Active in Los Angeles, 1890-96. Studio at 354 South Spring, 1890; 452 South Spring, 1892-93; 17 Summers Block, 114 South Spring Street, Los Angeles, 1894-96.

NEWTH, ERNEST W.
Born in New York, 1854. San Francisco photographer, c. 1868-78; produced stereoviews alone and in association with Oscar V. Lange. Gallery located at 620 Clay Street, 1880-81.

NEWTON, W. L.
Active in Santa Barbara, 1895-98.

NICHEL, H. T.
Active in Grafton, c. 1900.

NICHOLS, A. E.
Partner in Nichols, Norton & Company, Los Angeles, 1875; also known as A. E. Nichols & Company.

NICHOLS, L. M. (MISS)
Active in Santa Clara, 1890-91.

NICHOLS, NORTON & COMPANY
Operated by A. E. Nichols in Los Angeles, 1870s.

NICHOLS, SHELDON K.
Daguerreotypist in Hartford, Connecticut, and San Francisco. Exhibited his work in New York City, 1853-54.

NIESON, CARRIE (MISS)
Born in California, April 1881. Active in Marysville, c. 1900. Also listed as Cordie.

NOBLE & FELL
Studio on Main Street, Petaluma, 1874.

NOBLE, SKELTON STANFORD
Born in Missouri, c. 1833. Licensed with the 2nd Division, 1863. Traveling and studio photographer; in Gold Run, 1867; Eureka, c. 1867-70; Truckee, 1868-72; North San Juan, 1872-74; with Noble & Fell, Petaluma, 1874; Sierra City, 1875- 76; Nevada City, c. 1875; operating the Sunbeam Gallery on Main Street in Petaluma, c. 1876; Cambria, 1880.

NOE, CHARLES B.
Born in New York, 1849. Active in San Francisco, 1870; Grass Valley, c. 1875; Redding, 1886.

NOE, MIGUEL, JR.
Studio in 1102 Stockton Street, San Francisco, 1876-77; Napa City, 1884.

NORCROSS & HIGINBOTHAM
Partnership in Weaverville, 1864.

NORCROSS, OLIVER H. P.
Born in Maine, July 1824; died in Weaverville, April 1871. He sailed from the East seeking gold, 1849. First advertised a daguerreotype studio in Weaverville, 1854, where he served as Justice of the Peace and practiced law. Employed Raenhart as an operator, 1856; in Union (Arcata), 1857. Moved his studio to Wellendorff's Drug Store, 219 Main Street, Weaverville, 1863. Joined with J. B. Higinbotham in Junction City, 1864, operating a traveling gallery; in Weaverville, 1867; Red Bluff, 1868; Weaverville, 1868-69; Shasta City, 1870.

NORRIS, J. E.
Active in Dunsmuir, 1908.

NORTH BEACH GALLERY
Operated by Ed. Gagne at 706 Filbert Street, San Francisco, c. 1890.

NORTON
Associated with Nichols, producing stereoviews in Los Angeles, 1870s.

NORTON, E.
Partner in Williams & Norton, 914 Market Street, San Francisco, 1885-87.

NORTON, T. G.
Issued stereoviews from Pasadena, 1870s; partner in Nichols, Norton & Company, Los Angeles, 1875.

NOTT, ELIZABETH W.
Fine art photographer in Oakland, c. 1900-03; photographs published in Camera Craft, 1902; one was exhibited in the San Francisco Salon, 1903. Sister of art photographer, Annie W. Brigman.

NOWLIN & COMPANY
Listed at 21 West First Street, Widney Block, Los Angeles, 1886-87.

NOY, FONG
Active in San Francisco, c. 1871, employed by Bradley & Rulofson at their studio, 429 Montgomery Street.

NURSE & SLYLES
Licensed in Benicia, 1862.

NUSBAUM, ABRAHAM B. O.
Active in Red Bluff, 1867-69.

NYE
Partner in Nye & Bisbee, 21 West First, Los Angeles, 1886-87; partner in May & Nye, operating in Stockton, dates unknown.

O. K. STUDIO
Gallery in Pasadena producing stereoviews.

O'CONNOR, EMMA OLIVE
Born in Rough and Ready, California, February 1858, the daughter of William and Tacy Harris. Active in Blocksburg, Hydesville and Fortuna, Humboldt County, c. 1893-1900.

OAKLAND PHOTOGRAPHIC GALLERY
Operated by A. P. Bailey in Oakland, 1883-88, at 515 Seventh Street; Pacific Photographic Publishing Company at the same address.

OAKLAND PICTURE TENT
J. A. Hanson, proprietor; "Pictures taken and finished in ten minutes," c. 1880.

OCEANSIDE PICTURE GALLERY
Studio in Santa Monica, 1899-1902, operated by Walter Collins; at 639 East 21st, 1902.

OFFAC
San Francisco.

OGELVIE, B.
Active in Angels, 1890.

OHIO VIEWING COMPANY
Located on East First, Los Angeles, 1895.

OLIPHANT, O. F.
Active in Anderson, 1894.

OLSEN, H.
Studio at 650 and 652 Washington Streets, opposite Hall of Records, San Francisco, 1865-68.

OLTMAN, JOHN
Partner in Camps & Oltman, Dunsmuir, 1898l; listed alone in Sisson, 1898-99. Possibly John D. or E.

ONG, VINCENT B.
Studio at 112 North Alameda, Los Angeles, 1894-1903.

OPPOSITION GALLERY
Gallery in Sacramento, 1877-90, operated by Julius Asher; produced quality portraits and views. Located at 236 and 244 J Street, c. 1878; 810 ½ J Street, 1883-90.

OPPOSITION PHOTOGRAPH GALLERY
Located at 638 Market Street, San Francisco, 1875.

OPPOSITION PHOTOGRAPHIC GALLERY
Operating in Plumas County, 1874.

OREGON & CALIFORNIA RAILROAD
Traveling photographers, 1890.

ORIENTAL PHOTOGRAPHIC GALLERY
Studio in Watsonville, 1884-87, operated by D. R. Lofland.

ORIENTAL PHOTOGRAPHIC PARLORS
Gallery in San Francisco, 1883-84, operated by A. W. Dowe and J. M. Pickett at 997 and 999 Market Street.

ORMSBY, ELON D.
Born in Michigan, 1845. Produced stereoviews in Stockton, operating the Photographic Art Palace with Reilly at 183 El Dorado Street, 1870s; in Oakland, 1878-88.

ORR, L. P.
Active in Bishop, 1890.

ORR, L. P. (MRS.)
Active in Bishop with her husband or son, 1890.

OSBON, C.
Active in Fresno, 1890s-1906 or later; produced stereoviews of San Francisco earthquake and fire.

OSBORN, DR. WILLIAM B.
Born in New York. Came to California in Colonel Stevenson's regiment, 1847; opened the first drugstore in Los Angeles, 1850; appointed Postmaster, 1853; frequently acted as Deputy Sheriff. An amateur photographer who made the first daguerreotypes in Los Angeles in association with Moses Searles, August 1851. Spoke Spanish and also signed his name Guillero B. Osbourn; name also spelled Osborne.

OSBORNE, ALBERT W.
Born in Massachusetts, c. 1835. May be A. W. Osborne, daguerreotypist of Richmond, Virginia. Located in Virginia City, Nevada, c. 1865; Woodland, 1870; operating New York Gallery on F between Second and Third Streets, Eureka, 1872; Merced, 1873; Eureka, 1875; Honolulu, Hawaii, c. 1875.

OTTO, RICHARD
Photographer with Walter H. Cook, San Francisco, 1869-70; partner in Brown & Otto, 1871; at 10 Sixth Street, 1888.

OVERTON, N. R.
Partner in Miltz & Overton, Grass Valley and Nevada City, 1883.

OWEN, DAN
Stereo photographer active in Redlands.

OWEN, E. S.
Active in Forbestown, 1864-65.

OWEN, M. B. (MRS.)
Active in Chico, 1903.

OWINGS, GEORGE F.
Operated the Elite Studio in Etna, 1902-04.

O'HARA, J. D.
Partner with Merrill F. Bailey at 622 Kearny Street, c. 1865-68, operating as Bayley & O'Hara.

PACIFIC ART GALLERY
Traveling photographers, 1882.

PACIFIC ART GALLERY
Studio in San Francisco operated by D. H. Woods, 1864-66; at Sheil's Block, 9 Post Street, operated by Henry Bush, c. 1865-70.

PACIFIC COAST GALLERY
Active in Stockton, 1877, operated by J. H. Genuit with H. Eshbach, printer.

PACIFIC COAST PHOTOGRAPHIC ART GALLERY
Studio in Sacramento, c. 1870-75, at 189 J Street, over Bale's Toy Store; operated by A. P. Bailey.

PACIFIC GALLERY
Located at Market Street Station, Oakland, 1880.

PACIFIC PHOTO GALLERY
Studio in Santa Monica, 1888-1908 or later, operated by H. F. Rile.

PACIFIC PHOTOGRAPH GALLERY
Active in Oakland, 1883, operated by J. M. Brown at the Market Street Station.

PACIFIC STEREOSCOPIC PHOTO COMPANY
Publishers of stereoviews, Compton, 1890s.

PACIFIC VIEW COMPANY
San Francisco studio; employed photographer W. E. Lovejoy, 1883.

PAGE, WILLIAM D.
Active in Yreka City, c. 1863-64.

PAJORA ART GALLERY
Operated by Burnett & Ercanbrack, Jr., in Pajora, c. 1875.

PALACE ART GALLERY
Studio in Woodland, 1883-89 or later, operated by T. A. and Mary M. Ley on Main Street, near Third.

PALACE STUDIO
Active in Los Angeles, 1901-02, at 236 South Main and 351 South Broadway, operated by C. J. Coules.

PALMER
Photographer in Los Angeles.

PALMER, JOHN D.
Active in Dunsmuir, 1890; Chico and Shingle Springs, 1893.

PAPE, DAISY L.
Born in Arcata, California, June 1878. Active in Eureka, c. 1904-10, employed by Joshua Vansant, Jr., 310 F Street.

PARDOW, GEORGE, JR.
Photographic printer with Addis & Koch, San Francisco, 1865.

PARK, FRANK L.
Operated as Frank L. Park & Company in Los Angeles, 1898-1903. Studio at 211 West First, Los Angeles, 1898; 609 East Sixth, 1899-1901; 37 South Raymond Avenue, Pasadena, 1900; 120 ½ South Spring, Los Angeles, 1902-03.

PARKA, FRANK
Born in New York, 1834. Active San Francisco, 1870.

PARKER & PARKER
Gallery on F and Sixth Street, San Diego, 1874.

PARKER & SON
Landscape and portrait photographer on Fifth Street, between F and G, San Diego, 1870.

PARKER, EMMA
Born in Massachusetts April 1872. Active in San Diego, c. 1900.

PARKER, FRANCIS
Studio at 523 Kearny Street, San Francisco, 1871; in Los Angeles at 740 5th Street, Downey Block, partner in Parker & Hasselman, 1878-80; also operated as Tuttle & Parker. Studio in San Diego, 1880s, operating as Parker, Parker & Company, Parker and Judd, and Parker & Son, West Side Fifth Street between F and G, 1885.

PARKER, J. C.
Gallery in 738 Fifth Street, San Diego, 1886; landscape and portrait artist, 740 Fifth, 1888.

PARKS, MYRA A.
Active in San Jose, 1893-94.

PARSONS, D. H.
Active in Columbia, 1860s.

PARTAIN, JOE
Active in Lemoore, c. 1900.

PARTRIDGE, A. C.
Born in Vermont, 1821. Active in West Virginia, 1855-64; Massachusetts, 1869. Active in San Francisco, 1880. Father of the Partridge brothers, Edward J., William H. and Sam C., all successful in photography business.

PARTRIDGE, EDWARD J.
See Oregon.

PARTRIDGE, SAM C.
Died in Berkeley, 1900. Son of A. C. Partidge of Wheeling, West Virginia, a daguerreotypist and photo supply store owner; brother of William H. and Edward J. Partidge. Operated a photo supply store, at times the largest such supply house on the coast. Began on Market Street, 1880s, moved to 520 Commercial Street, later to 226 Bush Street, San Francisco.

PARTRIDGE, WILLIAM H.
See Oregon.

PASSMORE, LEE
Died in San Diego, 1959. View photographer in San Diego, 1908-59; specialized in maritime subjects. Later turned to nature photography and became known for original research on the trapdoor spider and carpenter bees. Official photographer for the San Diego Museum of Natural History until his death.

PATTERSON, FRANK
Travelled through out northwest California c. 1915, from Ashland, Oregon; produced an extensive line of stereoviews and postcards. See Oregon.

PAUL, E.
Operated the Dunsmuir Studio in Dunsmuir, 1909.

PAXTON, A. B.
Active in Santa Clara, c. 1867. Possibly Andrew B. Paxton of Oregon.

PAYNE
Active in Monrovia, c. 1890.

PAYNE
Active in Shasta, 1869.

PAYNE & BAGLEY
Gallery at 205 Third Street, 1868.

PAYNE, DANIEL R.
Born in Illinois, 1847. In California by 1871. Active in Los Angeles, 1880 or earlier. Partner in Payne, Stanton & Company's Elite Gallery, Temple Block, 119 and 129 Main Street, Los Angeles, 1881-86.

PAYNE, HENRY T.
Los Angeles photographer, gallery, 65 Main Street, Los Angeles, 1874; on the Downey Block, 1875. Partner in Payne, Stanton & Company's Elite Gallery, Temple Block, 119 Main Street, junction of Spring, 1881-86; branch parlor in Room 6, Downey Block, 1883-84 or later. Produced views of Santa Monica and other Los Angeles suburbs. Exhibited nearly 1000 of his wet plate stereoviews of southern California in Philadelphia, 1876.

PAYNE, STANTON & COMPANY
Partnership of Daniel R. Payne, Henry T. Payne and and T. E. Stanton, operating in Los Angeles, 1881-86.

PEABODY, HENRY G.
Born in St. Louis, Missouri, April 27, 1855; died in Glendora, California, March 27, 1951. Photographer for the Boston & Maine Railroad and Detroit Publishing Company, with studios in Boston, 1886-1900; branch in Chicago associated with Alexander Hesler; moved to Pasadena, California, 1900. Published stereoviews of Arizona, California and Mexico and other subjects. See Arizona.

PEACOCK, E. K.
Proprietor of the Excelsior Photographic Parlors, Commercial Street, Colton, 1884. Probably the same as E. R.

PEACOCK, E. R.
Active in Cloverdale, 1886. Probably the same as E. K.

PEAKE & BYRD BROTHERS
Active in Visalia, c. 1867-72.

PEARCE, FRANK
Photographer with A. F. Bayley's Gallery, Sacramento, 1870.

PEERS, ALEX
Born in England, 1836. Daguerreian active in San Jose, 1860.

PEISER, THEODORE EMANUEL
Born in California, 1853. Active in San Francisco, 1880; Colusa, 1885-90.

PELLEGRIN, ALFRED L.
Born in Ohio, c. 1863. Active in Santa Ana, 1880; Anaheim, 1881-89, gallery on Center Street.

PENCE, J. S. (MRS.)
Active in Colton, 1895. Also known as Mrs. J. L. Pence.

PENELON, HENRI
A French artist, fresco painter and photographer; in Los Angeles by 1853. Worked on the renovation of the old Plaza, 1861, later took up photography; parlor on Main Street, 1867-70s.

PEOPLE'S ART GALLERY
Studio of J. D. Godeus, operating at 34 Third Street, San Francisco, 1874-81 or later.

PERA & COMPANY
Active in San Francisco, c. 1900.

PERCIVAL, O. C.
Produced stereoviews of Nevada City, 1880s.

PERCIVAL, RICHARD
Studio located on Main Street, Petaluma, 1865-75.

PERKINS & FOSS
Partnership of Alfred J. Perkins and Oscar Foss, operating a studio at 606 Kearny Street, San Francisco, 1865.

PERKINS, ALBERT
Born in Germany, 1845. Active in Oakland, 1880.

PERKINS, ALFRED J.
Born in California, 1867, son of Alfred Judkins Perkins, and brother of Florence and Ivy Perkins, also photogaphers. Active in San Francisco.

PERKINS, ALFRED JUDKINS
Born in Illinois, 1839. Partner in Perkins & Foss, 606 Kearny Street, San Francisco, 1865; photographer with Bradley & Rulofson, 1869; gallery at 12 Kearny Street, 1877; 337 Haynes, 1880-83; 1217 Polk, 1885; 26 Montgomery Street, 1887. Reportedly produced stereoviews of Vallejo, 1880s. Photo printer in San Francisco, 1898.

PERKINS, ALFRED JUDSON
Active in San Francisco and traveling, 1889.

PERKINS, FLORENCE
Born in California, May 1869. Active in San Francisco, c. 1899-1900. Daughter of photographer Alfred J. Perkins and Jennie E. Perkins. Her brother, Alfred J. Perkins, and sister, Miss Ivy M. Perkins, were also photographers.

PERKINS, IVY M.
Born in California, April 1880, the daughter of Alfred Judkins Perkins. Active in San Francisco, c. 1899-1900. Sister of Alfred J. and Florence Perkins.

PERKINS, MARY
Born in Wisconsin, 1848. Active in Ferndale, c. 1880.

PERKINS, WILLIAM A.
Studio on Sacramento Street between Oak and Pine, Lodi, 1886-88.

PERROTT, C. E.
Active in Eureka, 1893.

PERRY & KELLY
Partnership of Ira Perry and George Kelly, c. 1882.

PERRY & RUMSDELL
Partnership of J. C. Perry and G. Rumsdell, operating in Oakland, 1880.

PERRY, IRA C.
Active in Mendocino, operating the Imperial Photo Gallery, 1886; also active in Elk and Fort Bragg. Partner in Perry & Kelly with George Kelly, c. 1882.

PERRY, J. C.
Partner in Perry & Ramsdell, Oakland, 1880. Sometimes listed as J. E. Perry.

PERSHBAKER, DOLLY
Born in Oregon, September 1868. Active in Oakland, c. 1899-1900.

PETERS, CLARA (MISS)
Photographer with Peter's Photograph Gallery, 914 Market Street, San Francisco, 1896-98.

PETERS, JOHN HENRY
Born in Germany, 1832. Known as John H. Peterson until c. 1876. Arrived in New York, 1851; sailed on the ship *Rockland*, arriving in California in October. Mined in Tuolumne County, then took up photography. Active in Sonora, 1863-65. Photographer with B. F. Howland, San Francisco, 1865-69; partner in Howland & Peterson's New York Gallery, 25 and 27 Third Street, 1869-79. Daniel Sewell bought out the Howland interest, c. 1880; Peters sold his interest to J. G. Hucks, 1885. Bought out W. I. Williams' gallery in 914 Market Street, calling it Peters' Photograph Gallery, also known as J. H. Peters & Company. Operated in Plumas County, 1890. Possibly died before 1898, when Clara Peters was the only Peters listed as working in the gallery.

PETERSON, ANDREW W.
Died 1893. Active in Minneapolis, 1883. Opened a studio in Templeton, San Luis Obispo County, c. 1888, and bought a farm in Willow Creek.

PETERSON, FRED
Active in Stockton, 1900-01.

PETERSON, LETA
Born in Germany, April 1873. Immigrated to the United States, 1882. Active in San Francisco, c. 1899-1900.

PETERSON, SARAH B.
Active in Stockton, 1900-02. Wife of photographer Fred Peterson with studio at 407 East Market Street.

PHARES, ALICE O. (MRS.)
Photographer in Oroville, 1890-10. Middle name may be Ophelia.

PHARES, MORRIS E.
Active in Oroville, 1884-1915.

PHILBROOK, JAMES MILTON
Born in Maine. Apprenticed to R. H. Vance, San Francisco, 1860; engaged in photography at least through 1866.

PHILIPPI, R. G.
Active in Redlands, 1889-96, specializing in panoramic outside views. Also listed as R. J.

PHILLIPS, J. B.
Studio at 316 Boyd, Los Angeles, 1897.

PHILPOTT, ALICE
Born in Australia, 1884. Immigrated with her family to the United States, 1887. Active in San Francisco, c. 1899-1900.

PHOTOCHROME COMPANY
Branch at 640 Howard Street, San Francisco, c. 1876; represented by H. M. Barnes and later, C. H. Turner. The company provided "Silver Type Pictures" which were copies of images on iron, presumably tintypes, and finished in India ink or painted.

PHOTOGRAPHIC PARLORS
Gallery at Downey Block, 65 Main Street, Los Angeles, 1880.

PHOTOGRAPHIC PUBLISHING COMPANY
Business operated in Oakland, 1888, by C. H. Bailey, at the same address as his gallery, 515 Seventh Street.

PIATT, C. E.
Active in Grass Valley, c. 1880; Healdsburg, 1886.

PICKETT & EVERETT
Produced stereoviews from Amador City, 1870s; built a photograph gallery on Market Street, Colusa, opposite the Sun Building, February 1877. Listed in College City, 1877-78. A. J. Everett and J. M. Pickett. Also listed as Everett & Pickett.

PICKETT, JOHN M.
Active in Colusa, 1874-86. Also partner in Bailey & Pickett with Mrs. J. Bailey, 523 Kearny Street, San Francisco, 1875; studio at 22 Kearny Street, San Francisco, 1877. Partner in Dowe & Pickett's Oriental Photographic Parlors, 997 and 999 Market Street, with another studio at 337 Hayes Street, 1883. Active in Hollister and Willows, 1886.

PIERCE
Partner in Swaney & Pierce, Main Street, Los Gatos, 1888.

PIERCE & BLANCHARD
Partnership of James P. Blanchard and Charles C. Pierce, stereo photographers operating the Plaza Gallery in Los Angeles, 1890s-1900s.

PIERCE, CHARLES C.
Active in Los Angeles, 1886-1905. Studio at 513 North Main Street, 1896; also listed as 515 or 517; 313 South Spring Street, 1889-1905. Partner in Pierce & McConnell, 515 or 517 North Main, 1893-94. Acquired the Indian negatives of George Wharton James.

PIERCE, E. W.
Operated the Elite Gallery, Los Angeles, 1886-87. Possibly a partner in Pierce & Lohn, 523 Downey Avenue, 1888.

PIERCE, G. A.
Active in San Jose, 1900. Possibly B. A. Pierce.

PIERCE, W.
Active in Red Bluff, 1864-66.

PIERCE, WESLEY CUNNINGHAM
Active in Los Gatos, 1889-92.

PIERCE, WILLIAM
Born in Ohio, 1854. Clerk in photographic studio, San Francisco, 1870.

PIGGOTT & SHAW
Stereo photographers active at the Third Street Gallery, 434 ½ Third Street, Santa Rosa, 1888; J. K. Piggott.

PIGGOTT, JAMES K.
Born in Bodega, California, 1861; son of Dr. J. K. Piggott who pioneered in Placer County, 1844. He bought out Rauscher's interest in the Third Street Gallery, Santa Rosa, 1884, becoming a partner with Rea; Shepherd then bought out Rea and later Piggott bought out Shepherd. Piggott sold a one-half interest in the gallery to Shaw, 1885; Piggott sold his interest to Shaw, 1888, opening the Souvenir Photograph Studio. Third Street Gallery was opposite the Court House, 1886; Piggott & Shaw were at 434 ½ Third Street, 1888; Souvenir Photograph Studio was on the southwest corner of Fourth and B Streets, 1888-(?). Produced scenic stereoviews, landscapes and portraits.

PILLINER DAGUERREAN GALLERY
Operated by W. H. Pilliner in Red Bluff, 1858-61.

PILLINER, WILLIAM H.
Born in England, 1828. Active in Red Bluff, 1858-68; at 14 Second Street, San Francisco, 1865; in Grass Valley, 1870; Carson City, Nevada, 1878.

PILLSBURY, ARTHUR CLARENCE
Born in Medford, Massachusetts, October 9, 1870; died in Oakland, March 5, 1946. Located in Palo Alto, 1897. He claimed he invented the circuit camera for panorama work and marketed panoramas, orotones and large format views as the Pillsbury Picture Company. Went to the Klondike gold rush, 1898, and stayed two years as a photographer, then moved to Seattle. Moved to Los Angeles and exhibited at the Los Angeles Salon; 1902 San Francisco Salon; staff photographer for the *San Francisco Examiner*, 1903-06; photographed the aftermath of the 1906 San Francisco earthquake and fire. Operated studio in Yosemite, 1907-27; sold to the Curry Company after it burned, 1927; photographed San Francisco from a hot air balloon, 1909, narrowly avoiding disaster after it came loose and went up to an estimated 5,000 feet and drifted more than 30 miles before landing. Took up motion picture work, 1920, and also involved in botany. By 1928, Pillsbury called himself a "Photographer/Botanist and Naturalist/Lecturer;" he authored several books.

PIMENTAL, J. M.
Operated Pimentel's Cosmopolitan Gallery in San Rafael, c. 1868; studio in San Francisco, 1883. Also spelled Pimentel.

PINDELL, S.
Licensed in Napa, 1862.

PIONEER PHOTOGRAPH GALLERY
Studio operated in Stockton, c. 1870s-90s; by M. Monaco, 1878; later by J. P. Spooner; W. H. Harrison, manager, 1888-90.

PISER, THOMAS E.
Active in Colusa, 1893-94.

PITCHFORD, EMILY
Born in Gold Hill, Nevada, 1878; died in 1954. Attended Mark Hopkins Institute of Art in San Francisco; bronze medal at Alaska-Yukon Pacific Exposition in Seattle; shared studio with Laura Adams Armer; published often in *Camera Craft*.

PLAZA PHOTO GALLERY
Studio in Los Angeles, operated by J. T. Bertrand, 1888-89; Bertrand and W. F. Stein, 1890; J. B. Blanchard, 1896. Located at various times at 413 and 513 North Main.

PLEASANTS, JOSEPH B.
Active in Shasta, 1854-55; Eureka, 1857-58. Also listed as Joseph P.

PLUMMER & HAELSIG
Traveling stereo photographers operating in the Mojave Desert area; may also have worked in Arizona. Sample view shows Plummer & Haelsig's traveling wagon; C. A. Plummer.

PLUMMER, HARRY W.
Rubber stamp overprint of Bird & Cook imprint on a cabinet card, c. 1880. Located in Placerville, 1898.

PLUMMER, M. V. (MRS.)
Active in San Francisco, 1900, at 46 O'Farrell Street. Possibly the same as Margaret V. Plummer.

PLUMMER, MARGARET V.
Born in Iowa, September 1851. Active on Catalina Island, 1900. Married to a druggist, Elijah J. Plummer. Possibly the same as Mrs. M. V. Plummer.

POKORNEY, LUDWIG L.
Operator for Hartsook prior to 1914. See Oregon.

POLLOCK, A. M.
Associated with the Garden City Photo Company, 606 East Fifth Street, Los Angeles, 1896-1902; partner with James T. Pollock.

POLLOCK, JAMES T.
Associated with the Garden City Photo Company, 606 East Fifth Street, Los Angeles, 1896-1902; partner with A. M. Pollock. Took over Clark's Photo Company in Berkeley after 1900.

POLLOCK, JAMES T.
Traveling photographer, 1899.

POMEROY, EDGAR
Active in San Jose at 342 First Street, 1871.

POND, CHARLES L.
Stereo photographer from Buffalo, New York; visited California, 1870, and was noted for the Yosemite and gold country views published in his "American Scenery" series.

PORTER, D. A.
Photographic artist, Main Street, Santa Rosa, 1864-66.

POST, A. B.
Studio in Pasadena, 1898, at 176 East Colorado.

POTTER
Partner in Stiffler & Potter, 10 Hammond Block, Los Angeles, 1897.

POTTER, G. W.
From Montana; arrived in Placerville, 1902, and purchased the City Photo Gallery from B. F. Strong. Operated until at least 1907.

POTTER, H. N.
Partner in D. B. Taylor & Company, 415 Montgomery Street, San Francisco, 1876-77; also known as the Photographic Temple of Art. Partner in Monroe & Potter, same address, 1878.

POTTER, J. W. A.
Active in Ontario, 1898.

POWERS
Partner in Lawson & Powers, 147 South Main, Los Angeles, 1895; partner in Konold & Powers, 513 North Main, 1903-05.

POWERS, JOSEPHINE C.
Born in California, August 1874. Active in San Jose, 1893-1910. Photographer in Paul Haussler's studio, 68 South First Street, 1893-99; at 42 South First Street, 1900-06. Operated her own studio, 1910.

POWERS, N. B.
Active in Red Bluff, 1859. Partner with B. Jay Antrim in Antrim & Powers.

PRATHER, E.
Active in Diamente, Riverside County, 1895.

PRATSCH, CHARLES R.
Active in Oregon and traveling in California, 1889.

PRATT
Active in Dunsmuir, 1914.

PRATT & GREEN
Partnership in Dunsmuir, 1914.

PRAY, FRED H.
Partner in Rieman & Pray, 26 Montgomery Street, San Francisco, 1885-87.

PRENTICE & HART
Active in San Francisco and traveling.

PRENTICE, HELEN M.
Born in Oregon, May 1872. Active in San Francisco 1900.

PRETZ, J. C.
Studio in Los Angeles, 1900-05, at 340 ½ South Broadway.

PREZEAU & TOUGAS
Billed as "Home Photographers," 158 Fifth Street, San Francisco, c. 1900.

PRICE & VOELKER
Partnership of Andrew Price and J. A. Voelker, c. 1888, at 1069 Broadway, Oakland.

PRICE, ANDREW
Born in Ireland, 1843, son of Patrick Price. Traveling and studio photographer active in California, 1870s-80s. Gallery in Napa City on Second Street, 1878; Dixon, c. 1880; listed in Healdsburg, 1880-86; also in St. Helena, c. 1885; parlor in Colusa, 1885; one week in Georgetown, 1886; partner with Voelker, establishing a gallery at 1069 Broadway, Oakland, 1888. Also advertised branch galleries in Geyser Springs, Cloverdale and Windsor. Specialized in landscapes and stereoviews.

PRICE, ANDREW
Active in Colusa, 1878-90.

PRICE, THOMAS
Born in Canada. Active in San Francisco, 1870.

PRIEST, CHARLES F.
Partner in Abell & Priest, traveling photographers based in San Francisco, 1889-94; active in Chico, 1893. Operated gallery alone at 723 Market Street, 1895; at 2518 Mission Street, 1898.

PRINCE, H.
Active in Taylorsville, 1878. Possibly Herman Brince of Susanville.

PRINCE, J. K.
Active in Oroville, 1918.

PRINDLE, BENJAMIN A.
Born in New York, 1844. Photographic printer in San Francisco with James Wise, 1865; in San Francisco, 1880.

PROGRESSIVE ART COMPANY
Operated by Peter Datesman in Redding, 1897-99.

PURSER, SPENCER
Born in England, c. 1821; died in Leavenworth, Kansas, August 20, 1890. Photographer in Baltimore, Maryland, 1860. Private in the 23rd Pennsylvania during the Civil War. Sign painter in Eureka, 1875; first librarian in Eureka, 1878; unclear if he took photographs while in California.

PUTNAM & VALENTINE
Partnership of J. R. Putnam and W. S. Valentine, stereo photographers active in Los Angeles, c. 1898-1912.

PUTNAM, ARION
With J. R. & A. Putnam, commercial photographers, 79 Temple Block, junction of North Spring and Main, Los Angeles, 1895-1902.

PUTNAM, JOHN R.
With J. R. & A. Putnam, Los Angeles, 1895-1902, at 79 Temple Block. Partner in Putnam & Valentine, c. 1898-1912.

QUIGLEY PHOTO
Active in Siskiyou, 1895.

QUIRK & BOWDEN
Active in Sutter Creek, 1875.

QUIRK & HALSEY
Operated gallery in Grass Valley and Nevada City, c. 1885.

QUIRK, JAMES
Born in New York, 1853. Probably in California by 1855. Active in Grass Valley, 1880-84.

RADER, R. F.
Operated a gallery in Centerville, c. 1880.

RAENHART
Active in Weaverville, 1856.

RAMSDALE, GEORGE
Born in Massachusetts, 1846. Active in Bodega, 1880.

RAMSDELL, GEORGE HENRY
Associated with Perry & Ramsdell, Oakland, 1880. Traveling as the "Flying Photographer," 1890; in Fort Jones, 1889-95.

RANDALL, STEPHEN
Stereo photographer associated with Francis A. Parker in San Diego, 1880.

RANKIN, GEORGE W.
Active in Nevada City, c. 1880; Placerville, 1881; traveling, 1890; College City, 1893-94.

RASMUSSEN, J. CHARLES
With D. Radnor Coover purchased the Imperial Photographic Studio in San Francisco, c. 1899, at 724 H Market Street; manager of the studio, 1900; at 744 Market Street, 1904.

RASMUSSEN, N. F.
President of Coover & Rasmussen, operating as Imperial Photographic Studio, 724 ½ Market Street, San Francisco, 1900.

RATH, FRANK
Born in California, 1861. Active in Sonora, 1880.

RAUSCHER, H.
Associated with Downing and T. L. Rea in the Third Street Gallery, Santa Rosa, 1878-84. Sold out to J. K. Piggott, c. 1884; moved to Fresno and established a parlor on J Street, 1886.

RAUTHRAUFF, A. T.
Stereo photographer active in San Francisco.

RAY, AFFLECT ARCHIE
Active in Red Bluff, 1910.

RAYMOND
Stereo photographer active in Pasadena.

REA, THOMAS L.
Born in Pennsylvania, 1847. Partner with Rauscher and Downing, operating the Third Street Gallery, Santa Rosa, 1878-84. Later a partner with Piggott at the same address before selling his interest to Shepherd.

REA, W. J.
Operated a gallery in San Luis Obispo, c. 1880; in Santa Barbara at the corner of State and Haley, 1886-88 or later. Also spelled Rhea.

READ, G. W.
Studio at the corner of Main and Walnut Streets, Red Bluff, 1858-59.

READMAN, J. B.
Active in Riverside, c. 1885-95.

RECHT
Partner in McKean & Recht, 125 Pacific Avenue, Santa Cruz, 1888.

REDDING PHOTOGRAPH GALLERY
Studio in Redding on Market near the post office, operated by Louis Altpeter, 1886-92.

REDEKER
Active in Chico, 1913-16.

REDINGTON, DANIEL C.
Established the St. Louis Art and Photographic Studio, 34 Third Street, and another studio at 743 Howard, San Francisco, by 1883, when he also had an office at 237 Kearny Street. Perhaps the Redington who had the St. Louis Art Studio in Portland, Oregon, c. 1885.

REED & CONNELL
Operated studio at 214 Downey Avenue, East Los Angeles, c. 1890.

REED, CHARLES
Active in Gridley, 1880.

REED, GEORGE W.
Amateur stereo photographer from Berkeley; may have been the husband of Ida Reed who later owned *Camera Magazine*.

REED, J. C.
Partner in Reed & Connell, 214 Downey Avenue, Los Angeles, 1892. Possibly a partner in Arlington & Reed, 1898.

REED, J. H. S.
Operated a gallery in Santa Barbara, c. 1878.

REED, JOHN Q.
Born in Massachusetts, 1842. Active in Stockton, 1870; gallery on Main Street, Petaluma, c. 1874-88; Santa Barbara, 1870-88.

REED, N. H.
Active in Santa Barbara, c. 1890-1900, opposite Clock Building.

REED, P. FISKE
Operated a gallery in Santa Barbara, c. 1878.

REED, V.
Active in Selma, 1895.

REED, WILLIAM
Gallery at 306 Turk Street, San Francisco, 1895.

REED, WILLIAM L.
Born in Canada, 1824. Gallery in Sacramento, 1864, at 70 J Street; at 117 J Street, c. 1870-80.

REES, M. A.
Active in Santa Barbara, c. 1875.

REESE, MARTIN A.
Gallery at 125 Pacific Avenue, Santa Cruz, 1884-89.

REICHLING, OSCAR H.
Active in Chico, 1893-1910.

REIFF & MEYERS
Active in Fort Jones, 1869.

REIFF & PAYNE
Partnership in Shasta, 1869.

REIFF, JACOB BENJAMIN
Active in Fort Jones, c. 1869.

REILLY & HAZELTINE
Partnership of John J. Reilly and Martin Mason Hazeltine, stereo photographers in San Francisco, 1870s-80s.

REILLY & ORMSBY
Partnership of J. J. Reilly and Elon Delamore Ormsby, stereo photographers in Stockton and San Francisco, 1870s-80s.

REILLY & SPOONER
Association of J. J. Reilly and John Pitcher Spooner, stereo photographers in Stockton and San Francisco, 1870s-80s.

REILLY, JOHN JAMES
Born in Scotland, 1834; died in San Francisco, 1893. Produced stereoviews of Niagara Falls, New York, c. 1866-70. In Stockton by 1870; may have formed a working agreement with J. Pitcher Spooner. Photographed Yosemite and tourists, 1870-75; became a friend and companion of John Muir. Located in San Francisco at 729 California Street, c. 1875; produced stereoviews in association with M. M. Hazeltine, E. D. Ormsby, and John Pitcher Spooner. Proprietor of Wood's Gallery in the Odd Fellows Building, Marysville, 1879-86. (Amos Woods moved to Oakland, c. 1880.) Reilly abandoned his wife and business, the latter to Enno Nesemann, and moved to San Francisco, 1886, where he associated with Oscar Foss. He worked in Eureka, 1893, but committed suicide later that year in San Francisco. Reilly won awards during his life and produced a respectable body of stereoviews of Niagara, Yosemite, railroads, and portraits and western images.
  Peter E. Palmquist, *J. J. Reilly: A Stereoscopic Odyssey* 1838-94, Community Memorial Museum, Yuba City, California, 1989.

REINHART & DORROTHY
Active in Red Bluff, c. 1890.

REINHART, JOHN D.
Active in Red Bluff, c. 1893-99; Chico, 1905.

REMBRANDT GALLERY
Studio located at 337 Hayes Street, San Francisco, c. 1880.

REMBRANDT STUDIO
Gallery at 1156 I Street in Fresno, c. 1895.

RENDALL & GODFREY
Operating in Los Angeles, c. 1867.

RENDALL, STEPHEN ARNOLD
Born in England. Came to Los Angeles, 1860s. Raised Angora goats and photographed Los Angeles. In 1867, Rendall produced a large panorama of Los Angeles, made in sections; later a partner with Francis Parker. An imprint has been verified from Santa Rosa, c. 1875, where he had property and visited frequently.

REYNOLDS, J. A.
Studio in Los Angeles, 1898-1901, at 213 ½ North Spring; at 331 ½ South Spring, 1902-05.

RHEIN, C. G.
Partner in Rhein and Lebo, 114 South Spring, Los Angeles, 1892; sole proprietor, 1893-1901. Studio located at 1327 West 12, 1900-01. Also listed as G. C. Rhein.

RICE, J. M.
Active in Columbia, 1880; also in Orland and Colusa County.

RICHARDSON, LEONARD
Born in Maine, 1847. Operated Neward Gallery in San Francisco, 1880-98. Located at 31 Third Street, 1883; 1227 Market Street, 1895.

RICKETSON, MARJORIE A.
Born in Minnesota. July 1878. Active in Los Angeles, 1898-1900.

RIDDERHOF, N. L.
Photographer and publisher of stereoviews, Los Angeles, 1870s.

RIEDER, M.
Publisher of half-tone lithoviews of southern California, Los Angeles, 1900-15.

RIEGLE, HENRY
Partner in Riegle & Wells, 428 Third Street, San Francisco, 1874-77; 836 Market Street, 1878; 234 Post Street, 1878.

RIEMAN & COMPANY
Studio in San Francisco, c. 1882; partnership of George B. Rieman and Forrest S. Chadbourne, at 26 Montgomery Street.

RIEMAN & PRAY
Partnership of George B. Rieman and Fred H. Pray in San Francisco, c. 1886.

RIEMAN & TUTTLE
Active in San Francisco, c. 1880-82, operated by George B. Rieman and Tuttle at 26 Montgomery Street.

RIEMAN, GEORGE B.
Worked as an agent for Bradley & Rulofson, San Francisco, 1876; as clerk, 1877. Partner in Rieman & Tuttle at 26 Montgomery Street, 1880-82; partner with Forrest S. Chadbourne in Rieman & Company, c. 1882-86; partner with Fred H. Pray, 1886. Later Rieman worked as superintendent for I. W. Taber.

RIFENBURG & DOWE
Partnership of A. G. Rifenburg and Dowe, traveling photographers operating a portable building in Fresno, c. 1880; at 925 I Street, 1885.

RIFENBURG, A. G.
Traveling photographer with Dowe, covering various California towns from a base in Fresno at least part of the time, c. 1880s. Opened the Imperial Photograph Studio, Main Street, Salinas City, c. 1886; studio in San Jose at 241 South First Street, 1895-97.

RIGBY, S. H.
Studio in Los Angeles, 1894, at 205 ½ South Main.

RIGDON, ALICE M.
Born in California, February 1870. Active in San Jose, c. 1899-1900.

RIGGS & TAYLOR
Studio at 916 Broadway, Oakland, c. 1889-90.

RIGGS, AUSTIN R.
Studio at 514 Kearny Street, San Francisco, 1895-96.

RILE, HARRY FRANZ
Born in Philadelphia, December 1, 1860. Learned photography in Philadelphia, c. 1878; worked in Chicago, Kansas City, Portland and San Francisco, 1878-87; operated Pacific Photo Gallery in Santa Monica on North Beach, 1888-1908 or later.

ROBERTS
Active in Chico, 1892-93. Possibly H. F. Roberts.

ROBERTSON, J. DONALD
Galleries in San Francisco at 119 Third Street and 32 Kearny Street, 1865; 109 Third Street, 1867.

ROBINSON, E.
Active in Stirling City, 1905.

ROBINSON, G. M.
Associated with Jones, Robinson & Company, 838 Market Street, San Francisco, 1880-93.

ROBINSON, IDA
Born in California, November 1866. Active in Orosi Township, Tulare County, c. 1899-1900.

ROBINSON, R. E.
Gallery in Centerville, 1880.

ROBISON, FRANCES WOOLSEY
Lady photographer in Vina, 1920-30; sister-in-law of Hana Robison.

ROBISON, HANA
Active in Berkeley, c. 1896-1901, associated with portrait photographer, George Wilcox. In San Francisco, c. 1901-05, partner in Wilcox & Robison. Also spelled Robeson.

ROBLES, C.
Active in Davisville, c. 1867.

ROCKWELL, BESSIE
Active in San Francisco, c. 1899-1900; employed by Stanford Photo Studio, 1900.

RODGERS, R.
Studio located opposite Cary House, Placerville, 1865. May be same person as R. Rogers.

RODRIGO & WOLFENSTEIN
Active in Los Angeles, 1868.

ROGERS, A. H.
Gallery at 433 Third Street, San Bernardino, 1885; in Redlands operating the New Excelsior on Cajon Street, between Vine and Olive Streets, 1895; in Santa Barbara, 1898.

ROGERS, DR.
Operated the Gilroy Photo Gallery, over Bigg's & Clifton's Drug Store in Gilroy, c. 1875.

ROGERS, F. H.
Active in Dixon, c. 1875; in Los Angeles, 1884, partner in F. H. Rogers & Company with J. F. Fitzpatrick and Thomas Clune, 15 First Street. Produced stereoviews, 1880s-90s.

ROGERS, LUCY (MRS.)
Born in Illinois, March 1868. Active in Los Angeles, 1900-03+.

ROGERS, R.
Active in Placerville with McFarlin, 1868; in Suisun, Solano County, 1870, then returned to Placerville same year. May be same person as R. Rodgers.

ROGERS, WILLIAM
Active in Mud Springs, 1864.

ROLLINS, IDA
Active in Oakland, 1888-89.

ROOS
Partner in Snow & Roos, stereo photographers operating in San Francisco at the depot of Goupil & Company.

ROOT, JANE L.
Active in San Francisco, 1895.

ROSE, GEORGE L.
Studio in Pasadena specializing in children's portraits, 33 West Colorado Street, 1895. Photographed the Southwest during several journeys with George Wharton James.

ROSS & ORMSBY
Active in Petaluma, c. 1868.

ROSS, GEORGE
Born in Edinburgh, Scotland, February 2, 1832. Immigrated to U.S.; lived in Louisiana; went to San Francisco after working as a miner at Sigar Bar on the Yuba River. In business as painter in San Francisco; worked in Benicia for the Pacific Mail Steamship Company; settled in Petaluma, 1855. Operated photographic parlor, 1863-88; also gave dance lessons in Petaluma area until 1877. Studio at 36 Main Street, "opposite American Hotel; Snow's Cheap Cash Store; and Allen's Paint Store." Ross also had a studio in Placerville, 1863+.

ROSS, WILLIAM
Photographer with J. A. Todd's gallery in Sacramento, 1870. Probably W. H. Ross, listed as "Negro," 1870.

ROTH, HERMINA
Born in Hungary, November 1872. Immigrated to U.S., 1887. Active in San Francisco, c. 1899-1900.

ROTHERY, GARRITY (MRS.)
Photographer in Chicago, 1886-93; in Los Angeles after 1893.

ROTHROCK, G. H.
Stereo photographer operating gallery in Bakersfield before 1875; itinerant and gallery owner in Arizona after 1875.

ROUSE, CHARLES
Employed as a retoucher in San Francisco, 1871, 1874.

ROUSSEL & PALMER
Traveling photographer, 1891; operated "The Flash," 307 Main Street, Chico, c. 1891-93.

ROUSSEL, GEORGE ONEZIME
Active in Sisson, 1891-92.

RUDOLPH, JULIA F. (MRS.)
Daguerreian from Utica, New York where she owned and operated a gallery, 1852-55, as Mrs. Julia A. Raymond. Took over G. O. Kilbourn's gallery in Nevada City, April 1856, but it burned on July 19th, along with much of the business district. Opened gallery at 10 Commercial Street in September, operating under her maiden name, Julia A. Swift; married James Ferdinand Rudolph, a druggist, in December. Her gallery was located in the Democrat Building, Broad Street, near the post office, June 1857; at 21 Commercial Street over Dr. Rudolph's Drug Store, August 1857. She operated two galleries, dividing her time between them because of her husband's allergies; in Sacramento, 1860-90 and Nevada City, 1856-90. Sacramento galleries on K Street near 4th, 1865; 91 K Street, 1866; 627 J Street 1884-90. She may have bought out P. T. Collins in Nevada City, c. 1880.

RUE, LEWIS M.
Gallery in Grass Valley, 1864-66; in Woodland on Main Street, 1874.

RULE & EDWARDS
Studio on Main Street in Mokelumne Hill, c. 1868.

RULE, EUGENE L.
Licensed in St. Helena, 1863-64.

RULOFSON, WILLIAM HENRY
Born in Hampton, New Brunswick, September 27, 1826; died in San Francisco, November 1, 1878, by falling from the roof of his gallery, perhaps intentionally. Learned the daguerreotype art from a relative, James C. Melick, then embarked on extensive travels through France and England, 1846-49; first studio in New Brunswick, 1847; St. John's, New Foundland, 1848, corner of King and York Streets; left for California, late 1848, photographing en route. Arrived in San Francisco, June 13, 1849; fitted out portable gallery and daguerreotyped mining areas while looking for gold. Briefly offered daguereotyping services in Stockton, July 1849. Partner with J. D. Cameron in gallery in Sonora, c. 1849; brought his family to Sonora, 1850; bought Batchelder's "Old Stand" on Main Street, June 17, 1852, setting up his portable daguerreian gallery. He and Cameron moved to the corner of Dodge and Washington in October 1855; he bought out Cameron, continuing operation, 1857-63; leased gallery to Daniel Sewell, 1863; sold it to him, 1865. Partner with Henry W. Bradley in San Francisco, 1863-78; purchased the old Vance/Weed gallery at 429 Montgomey Street, operating as Bradley & Rulofson. Bradley ran his old business at 618-620 Clay Street, dealing in photographic materials; Rulofson operated their gallery, known for high quality work and high prices. An association with Eadweard Muybridge in the early 1870s led to many awards for excellence in view photography. Apparently involved in Jones, Rulofson & Company, 1888. The company employed many young photographers who later established successful studios of their own. Rulofson was a member and the first photographer of the Bohemian Club; also operated as a traveling photographer, 1865-78.

> Robert Bartlett Haas, "William Herman Rulofson, Pioneer Daguerreotypist and Photographic Educator," *California Historical Society Quarterly*, December 1955, and March 1956.
> Peter E. Palmquist, "William Herman Rulofson: The P. T. Barnum of American Photography," *The Daguerreian Annual*, 1993, The Daguerreian Society, Eureka, California.

RUNNELS, BENJAMIN F.
Born in Maine, 1846. Photographer in San Francisco, 1870; associated with Runnels & Kelly at 31 Third Street, 1880-82; partner in Runnels & Stateler at 957 Market Street, 1883-88.

RUSSELL, GEORGE H.
Active in Plano, 1880-81.

RUSSELL, KATHERINE L.
Born in Ireland, June 1868. Active in Los Angeles, c. 1903.

RUSSELL'S STUDIO
Studio located on Alvarado Street, Monterey, c. 1890.

RUTH, J.
Daguerreian, ambrotypist and photographer at the St. Charles Hotel, Shasta City, 1855-59; D Street, opposite the Ham House, Marysville, 1856.

RYAN, J. M.
Active in San Francisco, 1865.

SACKRIDER, DELZIE BROWN
Photographer in Marysville, 1915-36.

SACKRIDER, HENRY
Died in San Francisco, September 27, 1944. Active in Marysville, California, 1914-36. See Oregon.

SACRAMENTO GALLERY
Studio operated by Leftwich & Harkness, 421 J Street, Sacramento, 1875.

SAFFORD, O. D.
Licensed in Mainville and Petrolia, 1865.

SAGE, W. W.
Active in Long Beach prior to 1900.

SAKATA, Z.
Stereo photographer in San Francisco, 1915 or earlier; captions in Japanese.

SAKURAI, S.
Printer in San Francisco, c. 1900.

SALB, A. (MRS.)
Photographer in Redding, 1910-11.

SALMON, WILLIAM
Operated Salmon's Daguerrean Gallery located on Main Street, two doors down from the Philadelphia Hotel, 1854-55.

SAMMIS & HILLS
Partnership at 14 Second Street in San Francisco, 1867; Edward M. Sammis.

SAMMIS, EDWARD M.
Studio on Fourth Street near Main, Olympia, Washington, 1860-61; in Seattle, 1861-66; partner in Sammis & Hills, 14 Second Street, San Francisco, 1867.

SAMSON
Partner in Griffiths & Samson, stereo photographers active in Marysville.

SAMSON, EVA (MISS)
Active in Red Bluff, 1892-99, at the corner of Main and Oak streets.

SAMUELS
Partner in Fowzer & Samuels as indicated by cabinet card imprint on photo of lynching victim, Hong Di, July 11, 1887, Colusa.

SAMUELS & FORZANI
Studio in San Francisco, 1898, 309 Montgomery Street; Michael A. Samuels and Forzani.

SAMUELS, MICHAEL A.
Partner in Williams & Samuels, corner of Tenth and Clay, Oakland, 1883-87; partner in Samuels and Forzani, 309 Montomery Street, 1898; in business for himself, same address, 1900.

SAN FRANCISCO ART & PHOTOGRAPH GALLERY
Operated by John Swart and T. Miltz on Second Street, next to the Revere House, Napa, 1870.

SAN FRANCISCO GALLERY
Studio in Santa Rosa at 180 Fourth Street, operated by T. Miltz and John Swart, 1877-80.

SAN FRANCISCO GALLERY
Partnership of C. M. and L. S. Davidson, Santa Ana, c. 1880s.

SANDERS
Licensed in Oroville, 1863.

SANDERS & STINSON
Located at the corner of Third and D Streets, Marysville, 1867.

SANDERS, STEPHEN P.
Born in Nova Scotia, 1835. Active in Marysville, c. 1860; operated gallery in San Francisco, 1865; San Jose, 1874-80 or later, at 282 First Street. Also a traveling photographer.

SANDO, ANTONIO
Worked with Joseph Silva in San Francisco, c. 1865.

SANTA CLARA GALLERY
Studio owned by H. Schoene & Emig in Santa Clara, c. 1875.

SANTA MARIA PHOTOGRAPHY GALLERY
Gallery operated by E. D. Shull and D. R. Judkins in Santa Maria, 1906-08; destroyed by fire, 1908.

SARVER, M.
Publisher of "Centennial Series of Mammoth Grape Views," Santa Barbara, c. 1875. Some photographs by W. N. Tuttle.

SAUNDERS
Active in Ukiah, c. 1885-1900.

SAUNDERS, FRED
Born in England, 1845. Active in San Francsico, 1870.

SAUNDERS, VIOLET
Born in Texas, April 1870. Active in Los Angeles, c. 1899-1900.

SAVAGE, C. R.
Traveled through California on a number of occasions, 1860s-70s. See Utah.

SAWYER, F. W.
Active in Hornbrook, 1890.

SAYERS, B. (MRS.)
Born in Minnesota, August 1861. Active in Sacramento, 1900.

SCHACH
Partner in Burnet & Schach, 337 Hayes, San Francisco, 1887-89.

SCHAD, R.
Partners in St. Louis Art and Photographic Gallery with T. Miltz and J. Swart at 315 Montgomery Street, San Francisco, 1875; bought out Gustavus Fagersteen.

SCHAFER, HENRY A.
Active in Red Bluff, 1900-60.

SCHAFFER, C. E.
Active in Benecia, c. 1895; Oakland, c. 1897-1910.

SCHATTMAN, A. L.
Long Beach, 1898.

SCHENCH, GEORGE
Studio in Los Angeles, 1890, at 23 South Spring Street.

SCHEUCH
Studio located on south east corner of 11th and Broadway, Everts Block, Oakland, c. 1887, 1895-97.

SCHILLER, RUDOLPH
Active in San Diego, 1868-74.

SCHMIDT, VIOLA
Photographer in Marysville, 1918.

SCHNEIDER, MAX
Studio located at Montgomery Avenue and Green Street, San Francisco, c. 1885.

SCHOENE & EMIG
Partnership with Herman Schoene. Operated Santa Clara Gallery in Santa Clara, c. 1875.

SCHOENE, HERMAN
Born in Prussia, 1841. In New York by 1870. Active in Santa Clara, 1877; gallery in Santa Cruz, 1878; San Francisco, 1880-1900+. Located at the corner of Montgomery and Filbert, 1880; northeast corner of Montgomery and Gaven, 1881; 504 Kearny, 1885-88; 64 Third Street, 1888; 14 Third Street, 1895; 18 Third Street, 1898. Many examples of fine studio work in cabinet card format exist from Shoene's studio.

SCHOLL & KLECKNER
Studio operated by Ameilian Scholl and Warren Kleckner, top floor Byre Building in Los Angeles, 1896.

SCHOLL, AMEILIAN
Partner in Scholl & Kleckner, Los Angeles, 1896; listed alone, 1897; operated Scholl Gallery at 317 West Third, 1898; located at 253 South Broadway, 1900-01. Also spelled Amelian, Armilian and Aemillian.

SCHRAMM, MATHIEU
Born in Prussia, 1847. Gallery at 28 Third Street, San Francisco, 1875; in Oakland, 1880, operating the Pacific Gallery at Market Street Station; in San Diego, 1886; Santa Rosa (?); Nevada City, c. 1890.

SCHROEDER, E.
Partner in Brodeck & Schroeder, San Jose, 1871; in business alone at 342 First Street, 1874; operating the New Photographic Studio on Santa Clara Street near Market, over Spring & Company store, 1875.

SCHROEPELL, GUST.
Carte-de-visite imprint includes an engraving of a business named the "Alhambra," but it is not clear if the Alhambra is a photo gallery or another business altogether, San Diego, c. 1865.

SCHUBERT
Partner in McGinley & Shubert's Flying Photograph Gallery, operating in California, mid-1860s.

SCHUBERT, E.
Gallery at 6 Ellis Street, San Francisco, 1888.

SCHUBERT, GUSTAVE H.
Active in Nelson Point, c. 1885; Quincy, c. 1900; La Porte and Port Wine. Worked throughout Plumas County, 1890-1907.

SCHUFFLER, CHARLES J.
Active in Yreka and Ft. Jones, 1905-17.

SCHULZE, HORTENSE
Active in San Francisco, c. 1897-1903, operating gallery at 116 Stockton Street; partner with W. H. Schulze in Schulze & Schulze, 1903. Specialized in photographing Chinese children. Illustrated the article by Mary Davison, "The Babies of Chinatown," *Overland Monthly*, 1899. Exhibited twelve prints at the Second San Francisco Photographic Salon, 1902, reviewed in *Camera Craft*.

SCHULZE, W. H.
Partner with Hortense Schulze in San Francisco, 1903, at 116 Stockton Street; known as Schulze & Schulze.

SCHUMACHER, FRANK G.
Born in Los Angeles, April 21, 1861. Parlor at 9 North Spring Street, opposite the post office, Los Angeles, 1884; at 107 North Spring Street, 1896; continued active into the 20th century.

SCHUMACHER, LEO
Born in Prussia, 1828; died in Weston, Oregon, 1878. Arrived in the U.S., 1850; worked in the family lithography business in Philadelphia and learned photography, 1852. He was active in Union (Arcata), 1859; Sawyer's Bar, 1860; Weaverville, 1861; on Main Street in Weaverville, 1863; on Miner Street, Yreka, 1863; San Francisco, 1863. Moved to Austin, Nevada, 1863; to Weston, Oregon, 1878. See Nevada, Oregon and Washington.

SCHUMAN & BRUNER
Active in California, c. 1890.

SCHUMAN, CARL
Cabinet card imprint, c. 1890, gives only California as a location. Probably a traveling photographer.

SCHWEITZER, J. B.
Active in Redding, 1896-1902.

SCHWEITZER, O. (MRS.)
Gallery in Wilmington, 1895. Also known as Mrs. F. M. Schweitzer.

SCHWICHTENBERG & EATON
Studio located in the Bartlett Building; also the Avis Building next to the Post Office, Pomona, c. 1895. Also spelled Schvichtenberg.

SCHWICHTENBERG, H. E.
Active in Pomona, 1895-98, at 158 West Second; partner in Schwichtenberg & Eaton, Bartlett Building, c. 1895. Possibly the same Schwichtenberg who worked in Albina Oregon, 1890.

SCOTT (MRS.)
Photographer in Dunsmuir, 1915.

SCOTT, C.
Licensed in Mariposa, 1864.

SCOTT, J. W.
Active in Chico on Broadway, 1868.

SCOTT, L. R.
Partner with C. B. Long, Susanville, 1880.

SCOTT, W. R.
With Hamilton & Kellogg, San Francisco, 1865.

SCOTT, WINFIELD
Operating Palace Gallery at 481 Seventh Street, corner of Market and 7th Streets, Oakland, c. 1895.

SCRIPTURE & STILLMAN
Active in Auburn, c. 1865.

SCRIPTURE, JOHN CALVIN
Partner in Halsey & Scripture's Cosmopolitan Art & Photograph Gallery, 523 Kearny, San Francisco, 1868. In San Andreas, Angel's Camp and Mokelumne Hill, 1877; also active in Big Trees; in Dunsmuir, 1898-1903. Also listed as I. C. Scripture.

SEARLES, MOSES
Pioneer house and sign painter in Los Angeles. He began making daguerreotypes in association with Dr. Osburn, August 1851, perhaps the first in Los Angeles.

SEARS, B. W.
Photographic painter in San Francisco, 1869.

SEARS, CARRIE
A Los Angeles photographer, c. 1883-84.

SEARS, CHARLES
Born in Massacusetts, 1850. Active San Francisco, 1870. Probably a brother of John Sears.

SEARS, CHARLES L.
Born in Connecticut, 1849. Partner in Wells & Sears, Sonora, 1880; in San Bernardino, 1886, parlor at 141 D Street; at 182 Third Street, 1888.

SEARS, JOHN
Born in Massachusetts, 1852. Active in San Francisco, 1870.

SECOR, H. H. (MRS.)
Photographer in Dunsmuir, 1915-19.

SEGERBERG, BERN
Gallery at 119 Powell, San Francisco, 1895.

SEIDENECK, GEORGE J.
Born 1885; died 1972. Active in Carmel, 1920-40.

SEIFERT
Active in Redding, 1898.

SEIFERT & HUDSON
Partnership operating in Redding, 1900.

SELDNER, MORRIS
Gallery at 415 J Street, Sacramento, 1886.

SELLECK & FISHER
Located at 415 Montgomery Street, next to Wells, Fargo & Company, San Francisco, 1872-73.

SELLECK, SILAS
Operated gallery in New York City where he met the young Eadweard

Muybridge. Opened a daguerreian saloon at 163 Clay Street, San Francisco, 1859; operated his Cosmopolitan Photographic Art Gallery at 415 Montgomery, 1865-75. Selleck sold his negatives to D. B. Taylor & Company, c. 1876. Muybridge worked in Selleck's studio in San Francisco.

SERDINKO
Partner in Strelow, Sedinko & Company, 147 South Spring Street, Los Angeles, 1888.

SERON, HENRY M.
Active in Marysville, 1914-19.

SEVERIN, FRANK A.
Partner in Dijaeu & Severin, 34 Third Street, San Francisco, 1895-99.

SEWELL, DANIEL
Born in Staleybridge, Lancashire, England, June 12, 1836. Came to America with his parents, 1847, and settled in Wappinger's Falls, New York. Learned carpentry and joinery trades; worked in Poughkeepsie. Arrived in San Francisco, 1859, settling in Sonora and working as a builder and contractor until c. 1863. Member of Sonora Hose Company, 1861-76, serving four times as Chief Engineer; elected Trustee of the City of Sonora several times; served three times as City Clerk. After learning the art of daguerreotyping, he rented Rulofson's gallery when Rulofson moved to San Francisco, 1863, and purchased it, 1865. Sewell sold his gallery to Thomas W. Wells, 1879; moved to San Francisco and purchased the Howland interest in the New York Gallery, 25 Third Street, becoming a partner of J. H. Peters. He and Peters were probably acquainted c. 1863-65, when Peters was active in Sonora. They continued together in the New York Gallery, producing landscapes and portraits until 1885, when J. G. Hucks bought out Peters. Sewell also sold out to Hucks, c. 1886, and opened a gallery at 1025 Market Street, San Francisco, remaining active there at least through 1905.

SEWELL, EDITH
Active in Sacramento, 1902.

SHAFF, MARTIN V.
Studio at 239 ½ Spring, Los Angeles, 1895-99; 239 Spring, 1900-01.

SHAFFER, DAVID N.
Photographer with Payne, Stanton & Company, Los Angeles, 1881.

SHAGUE, H. L.
Active in Pomona, 1886.

SHANNON & BIRD
Licensed in Rough and Ready and Orleans Bar, 1865.

SHANNON, JULIA (MRS.)
A midwife and the first female photographer in California. Daguerreotype parlor at the corner of Clay and Dupont, San Francisco, 1850-52.

SHARP, WILLIAM
Active in Jackson, 1874.

SHASTA COUNTY VIEW COMPANY
Operating in Redding, 1886.

SHATTUCK, WILLIAM H.
Daguerreian gallery on Main Street, Georgetown, 1854; associated with Jessie Cunningham.

SHAUG, H. L.
Active in Pomona, 1883-86. Also spelled Shague.

SHAW & LAMBERT
Billed as "Practical Photographers," Eureka, c. 1895.

SHAW, H. W.
Active in Riverside, c. 1885.

SHAW, SETH LOUIS
Born in Vermont, March 22, 1816; died in Ferndale, California, November 22, 1872. Arrived in California after crossing the continent in a wagon train, 1850, to seek his fortune in the gold fields. He joined William and Jacob Shew (at least part of the way) on J. Wesley Jones' expedition to St. Louis, daguerreotyping scenes and cities; the result was a panorama painting entitled "Pantascope of California," which was exhibited in New York. He became a partner with George H. Johnson in the Eureka Daguerrean Rooms, 197 Montgomery Street, San Francisco, 1852. Moved to Ferndale, 1854, where he farmed, made wine, served as Justice of the Peace, won an award for portrait painting, and served as coroner, but is not known to have taken any photographs.

SHAW, SOPHRONIA CAROLINE
Born in Iowa, July 6, 1847. Active in Eureka, 1893-1910. Possibly a partner in the firm of Shaw & Lambert with Homer H. Lambert and his wife, Corrino, Sophronia's sister at 601 F Street, 1895-99.

SHAW, WILLIAM
Born in Canada, 1842. Grew up in Michigan; moved to Santa Rosa, 1875; worked as an iron molder and miller before taking up photography. Shaw bought a half-interest in Kraft's old Third Street Gallery, 1885, from J. K. Piggott; bought out Piggott, 1888; produced portraits, landscapes and stereoviews.

SHELDON, JOHN KIRK
Born in New York, 1843. Bricklayer in San Francisco, 1865; became a photographer, 1866; owned gallery at the corner of Kearny and Pine, 1867.

SHEPHERD
Shepherd bought Rea's interest in Rea & Piggott's Third Street Gallery, Santa Rosa, c. 1884-85; sold his interest to Piggott soon after.

SHEPPARD, EDWARD
Born in Australia, 1848. Active in San Francisco, 1870.

SHEPPARD, GEORGE
Licensed for Tomales Bay, c. 1864.

SHEPPARD, L. T.
Gallery in Point Arena, 1880-84; in San Jose at 241 South First Street, c. 1885; gallery in Petaluma at 59 ½ Main Street, 1888.

SHERIFF, THOMAS B.
Active in Sacramento City, c. 1860; replaced T. J. Higgins at #70, corner of 3rd and J. Sacramento; partner in Sheriff Brothers, 659 Clay Street, San Francisco, 1867; operator with James Welch at the same time.

SHERRIFF, JOHN A.
Born in Canada, 1833. Partner in Sheriff Brothers, 659 Clay Street, San Francisco, 1867; continued active in San Francisco until c. 1878. Gallery in San Diego at the corner of Fifth and E Street, 1878; branch gallery in Oceanside, 1886; continued active in San Diego area at least through 1898; view and portrait photographer.

SHERRIFF'S GALLERY
Studio at 70 J Street, Sacramento; W. Reed, operator, c. 1862.

SHERWOOD, LOU
Active in Pasadena, 1900.

SHEW & BRADFORD
Studio at 914 Market Street, San Francisco, c. 1890.

SHEW, JACOB
Born 1826. A pupil of Samuel F. B. Morse; active as daguerreian artist in Baltimore, 1841; associated with Plumbe's Gallery. Accompanied J. Welsey Jones' party securing Pacific coast and western views, 1849-50. Active in San Francisco, c. 1854-78; partner with Charles F. Hamilton, 1863; gallery with C. A. Marston at 315 Montgomery Street, 1865; in business alone at same address, c. 1865-78. Brother of Myron, William and Trueman Shew. Sacramento imprint noted on a daguerreotype mat, c. 1854.

SHEW, MYRON
Born 1824. A pupil of Samuel F. B. Morse, active as daguerreian artist in Philadelphia, 1841-51; associated with Plumbe's Gallery; dealer in photographic materials, 116 Chestnut Street. Moved to San Francisco by 1865; worked for his brother, William, at least through 1872. Examiner of Invoices at the Custom House, 1874; active in photography on his own at 523 Kearny Street, 1887, producing views of residences and other buildings. Brother of Jacob, Trueman, and William Shew.

SHEW, WILLIAM
Born in Providence, Fulton County, New York, 1820; died 1903. Learned the daguerreotype art from Samuel F. B. Morse; active in Boston, 1841, superintendent of J. Plumbe's Gallery; manufactured daguerreotype cases. Came to California during the gold rush, daguerreotyped the Pacific coast and western views in J. W. Jones' group preparing material for the "Pantascope," c. 1849-50. He left New York, 1851, traveling via the Isthmus, arriving in San Francisco on the ship, *Tennessee*, March 4th. His cameras and equipment were shipped via the Isthmus, and while awaiting their arrival, he tried his hand at mining. He set up a portable daguerreian saloon on the Plaza, on Kearny Street, between Clay and Washinton, then moved to a vacant lot on Washington Street. Later his saloon was located at the corner of Clay and Dupont; his daguerreian gallery was at 113 Montgomery Street, 1859; 421 and 423 Montgomery, 1865; 121 Kearny Street, c. 1871; 115 Kearny Street (sometimes referred to as the Shew Building), 1874-80; 523 Kearny Street, 1881-1900+. Numerous photographers were trained by and worked for William Shew before setting up galleries of their own. Aside from his early daguerreotypes, Shew was widely known as a portrait artist. In the 1850s, Shew actively participated in politics; the first Free-Soil Convention was held at his rooms on the Plaza, October 8, 1852; he served on the Board of Education at one time.

    Wendy Cunkle Calmenson, "Likenesses Taken in the Most Approved Style: William Shew, Pioneer Daguerreotypist," *California Historical Quarterly*, Spring, 1977.

SHIMANOTO, F.
Active in Los Angeles, 1903, at 128 North Main Street.

SHIPPY
Partner in Mains & Shippy, stereo photographers in Sucker Flat, 1870s; photographed aftermath of robbery at the Blue Point Mining Company and mining scenes.

SHORT, H. N.
Active in San Bernardino, 1874.

SHOWERS, ANDREW
Gallery in 402 Kearny Street, San Francisco, 1879-80.

SHUBERT, JAMES T.
Active in Red Bluff, 1875-84.

SHULL, E. D.
Operating the Santa Maria Photography Gallery in partnership with D. R. Judkins at 200 West Main Street, Santa Maria, 1906.

SIBLEY, A. L.
Stereo photographer in Oakland, c. 1906; produced views of San Francisco earthquake damage.

SILVA, FRANK
Photographer with J. T. Silva, San Francisco, 1869.

SILVA, JOSEPH T.
Born in Portugal, 1830. Daguerreian saloon on the southwest corner of Clay and Kearny, San Francisco, 1859; at 402 Kearny, 1865; 649 and 703 Clay Street, 1867; International Gallery at 64 Third Street, c. 1869-78; 28 Third Street, 1880.

SILVEIRA, A. S.
Stereo photographer active in Sacramento, c. 1890.

SILVER
Active in Merced, c. 1895.

SILVER, EMMA B.
Born in California, December 1874. Active in San Francisco, c. 1900.

SILVER IMAGE
Studio in Orland, 1914.

SILVER, O. B.
Licensed in Dutch Flat, 1865.

SILVESTER
Stereo photographer employed by Lawrence & Houseworth in San Francisco, c. 1860s.

SIMAS & JOHNSTON
Partenrship of Emanuel Simas and R. T. Johnston, Placerville, 1895; Carson City, Nevada, 1896.

SIMAS, EMANUEL
Active in Placerville, taking over Baker's old stand from Kies & Brian, 1887-90; San Francisco, 1890, in partnership as Swain & Simas; returned to Placerville, 1895, in partnership with R. T. Johnston as Simas & Johnston; sold out to A. K. Varney, 1897; Taylor Mine in Garden Valley, 1897; partnership of Waston & Simas, Sutter Creek, 1897; Jackson, c. 1900.

SIMMONS, HENRY S.
Proprietor of the Excelsior Photo Gallery, 352 South Broadway, Los Angeles, 1896; partner in Simmons & Van Craigh, 133 ½ South Spring, 1900-01.

SIMS, JOHN
Active in San Francisco, 1865.

SING SUNG & COMPANY
Active in San Francisco, 1882-83, at 743 Washington Street; also known as Yong, Lai & Brother.

SISKIYOU PORTRAIT STUDIO
Operated in Fort Jones, 1898.

SKELTON
Partner in Moore & Skelton, Arbuckle, 1880.

SKINNER, C. E.
Partner with his wife in San Francisco, 1899, gallery at 724 ½ Market Street. Operated in Chico, 1895-97.

SKINNER, C. E. (MRS.)
Partner with her husband in their gallery at 724 ½ Market Street, San Francisco, 1899.

SLADKY, ANTHONY
Born in Austria, 1853, son of Joseph Sladky. Active in San Francisco, 1880.

SLATTERY, MICHAEL F.
Born in Massachusetts, 1860, of Irish parents. Brother of Thomas Slattery. Active in San Francisco, 1880; printer with Jones, Robinson & Company, 1883.

SLATTERY, THOMAS
Born in Massachusetts, 1862, son of Denis and Johanna Slattery and brother of Michael Slattery. Active in San Francisco, 1880. Partner in Burnett & Slattery, corner of Sixteenth and Valencia, San Francisco, 1885-96 or later.

SLEVIN, LEWIS S.
Born 1879; died 1945. Active in Carmel, 1905- 35.

SLIGHT, CHARLES
Active in Los Angeles, 1883.

SLINGSBY, T. H.
Active in Crescent City before 1860.

SLOAN
In Placerville, 1898.

SLOAN, S. S.
Active in Cottonwood and Corning, 1897.

SLOCUM, J. E.
Active in San Diego, 1880s. Photographed Laguna Pueblo in New Mexico.

SLUMMER, MARGARET V.
Born in Iowa, September 1851. Active in Los Angeles, c. 1899-1900. Probably Margaret V. Plummer.

SMALL, J. E.
Active in San Bernardino, 1877-78.

SMALLFIELD, CARRIE
Active in Stockton, 1881-88, working for J. P. Spooner at 173 Main Street.

SMART, ADELAIDE (MISS)
Born in California, December 1863. Active in Dutch Flat, c. 1899-1900. Sister of photographer Emma D. Smart.

SMART, EMMA D. (MISS)
Born in California, April 1867. Active in Dutch Flat, c. 1899-1900. Sister of photographer Adelaide Smart.

SMITH
Traveling photographer, 1898.

SMITH & PERKINS
Operated the Solano Art Gallery in Vallejo, c. 1875, at 164 Georgia Street; A. J. Perkins, operator, James G. Smith, proprietor.

SMITH & TUCKER
Active in Los Angeles, 1878.

SMITH, ALFRED L.
Gallery at 244 J Street, Sacramento City, c. 1875; at 234 J Street, Sacramento, c. 1880; also in Hollister, 1880; Bishop Creek, 1883.

SMITH, C. A.
Active in Sacramento and traveling, 1887.

SMITH, C. J.
Born in New York, 1828. Active in San Francisco, 1860.

SMITH, CAROLINE
Born in Ohio, March 1871, daughter of Birnhardt and Sally R. Hergburn. Active in San Francisco, c. 1899-1900.

SMITH, CHARLES
Active in Iowa, 1858; San Francisco, 1880.

SMITH, CHARLES EDMOND
Active in Chico, 1887.

SMITH, CLARA SHELDON
Born in California, July 1862. Active in Marysville, c. 1896-1935. Owned and operated the Ramona Art Studio, specializing in portraits and outdoor photography; contracted with the Marysville City Council to take photographs of prisoners, 1900-08. Studio located at 226 ½ D Street, c. 1900. Sold her studio to C. C. Green of Red Bluff, 1908, retaining half the room to operate a "Kodak business."

SMITH, EMMA GILLIS.
Born in Iowa, 1848. Widowed by 1876 when she was a photographer in San Francisco; in Nevada, c. 1868-72.

SMITH, FLORENCE E.
Born in English Canada, March 1882. Her parents immigrated to U.S. with their family, 1885. Active in San Jose, c. 1899-1900.

SMITH, GEORGE H.
Licensed in San Leandro, 1862; North Almaden, 1863.

SMITH, HARRY
Born in San Francisco, 1883; died in San Francisco, 1973. A talented amateur who recorded life in San Francisco, the 1906 earthquake, fire and aftermath.
    Stephen White, *Harry Smith: Magic Moments*, Stephen White Editions, Los Angeles, 1981.

SMITH, HENRY
Born in California, 1855. Active in San Francisco, 1880.

SMITH, J.
Active in Oakland, 1877.

SMITH, J. F.
Licensed in Forest Hill, 1864.

SMITH, JAMES GIRARD
Born in Cheltenham, England, January 27, 1836. Immigrated to U.S., 1857; lived in Rochester and Leavenworth, Kansas; worked as cattle drover to Salt Lake City. Walked from Salt Lake City to Sacramento, arriving November 1858. Farmed along the Feather River and mined in Nevada City, 1860. Mastered photography and operated his Solano Art Gallery, 164 Georgia Street in Vallejo, 1864-89; produced portraits and views. Partner with A. J. Perkins, c. 1875, Smith & Perkins gallery at same address; Perkins, operator and Smith, proprietor.

SMITH, JASON
Photograph and tintype Gallery at 1716 Seventh Street, West Oakland, 1886-89 or later.

SMITH, MINNIE (MISS)
Retoucher in San Jose, 1887.

SMITH, W. J.
Studio at the corner of Sixteenth and Clay, Oakland, 1893-1910.

SMITH, W. S.
San Francisco photographer producing stereoviews, 1860s.

SMITH'S CALIFORNIA PHOTO CAR
Operating in California, c. 1885.

SMYTH, THOMAS P.
Licensed in Ukiah, 1863; Point Arena, 1864.

SMYTHE, ARTHUR L.
With Taber Photo Company, 1898.

SMYTHE, W. H.
Active in San Francisco, 1898. Possibly related to Arthur L. Smythe.

SNEAD, FRANCES
Born in New York, 1858. Married Carlton E. Watkins and worked in his gallery in San Francisco.

SNOW & ROOS
Stereo photographers in San Francisco at the depot of Goupil & Company.

SOBIESKI, F. C.
Partner in Kelly & Sobieski, 21 First Street, Los Angeles, 1886-87.

SOHON, G.
Licensed in San Francisco, 1863-64.

SOLANO ART GALLERY
Gallery in Vallejo, 1870-89 or later, at 164 Georgia Street; James G. Smith, proprietor.

SONG, W. F.
Active in San Francisco, c. 1900, at 800 Washington Street.

SONNICHSEN, CHARLES
Stereo photographer in San Diego.

SOO, AH
Active in San Francisco, 1870.

SOOY & COMPANY
Portrait studio in Oakland, 1900, at 1065 Washington Street.

SOPER, EMMA K.
Born in Pennsylvania, January 1868. Widowed by 1900 when she was listed as a photographer in Los Angeles.

SORENSON
Active in Oroville.

SOULE, FRANCES
Born in Maine, 1835. Photographer associated with Jesse McChandler, San Jose, 1880-81.

SOURISSEAU, T.
Stereo photographer in San Jose.

SOUTH PARK PHOTOGRAPH GALLERY
Studio at 444 ½ Third Street, San Francisco, John D. Godeus,

proprietor, 1868.

SOUTHARD, DR. W. F.
Amateur stereo photographer, active in San Francisco, 1913; produced view of Bohemian Grove.

SOUTHERN PACIFIC RAILROAD COMPANY
Traveling photographers, 1887-1900.

SOUTHWORTH, ALBERT SANDS
Famous Boston daguerreotypist and partner of Josiah J. Hawes; Southworth made the trip to California, 1849, but returned without riches, 1850.

SOUVENIR PHOTOGRAPH STUDIO
Gallery in Santa Rosa, c. 1888, operated by J. K. Piggott on the southwest corner of Fourth and B Streets.

SOUVENIR PHOTOGRAPHIC STUDIO
Studio in San Jose, 1883-86. Partnership of Milton Loryea and J. W. Macaulay, located at 315 Santa Clara Street, 1883; 26 South First Street, 1884-86.

SPANG, AMELIA
Born in Ohio, 1838. Active in San Francisco, 1870.

SPATZ (MRS.)
Active in Shasta City, 1865-66. Possibly Miss Agnes Miers who married J. H. Spatz, 1855.

SPAULDING & A. CHALFANT
Obtained a tax license to operate in Ukiah, 1864.

SPAULDING, G. W.
Born in New York, 1832. In California, 1855; active in Bloomfield, 1867; operated the first gallery in Point Arena, 1869-70.

SPEAR, CLARA
Active in San Francisco, 1892.

SPERRY, MYRA E. (MISS)
Born in Ohio, January 1862. Active in Salem, Oregon, c. 1889-96; in Los Angeles, California, c. 1899-1900.

SPESERT, MARY
Photographer active in Fortuna and Hydesville, c. 1915; issued stereo postcards.

SPLANE, CHARLES U.
Born in Pittsburg, October 31, 1849. Moved to California, 1896; active in Los Angeles into the 20th century.

SPOONER, JOHN PITCHER
Born in Massachusetts, 1845. Photographer with Bradley & Rulofson, San Francisco, 1865-70. Opened the Pioneer Photograph Gallery, 171 Main Street, Stockton, c. 1870, later moving to San Joaquin Street; produced stereoviews in association with J. J. Reilly, 1870s; continued in Stockton at least through 1894. Spooner was a major producer of stereoviews of Yosemite and other northern California scenes.

SPOONER, SUSAN M. B. (MISS)
Daughter of J. P. Spooner; worked for him in Stockton, 1896-99.

SPRAGUE, LUCIEN A.
Active in Chico, c. 1890-1910; partner in Clements & Sprague, 1892-93; successor to W. A. Clinch, Grass Valley, 1895.

SPRAGUE, T. A.
Licensed in Lincoln, 1865.

SPROUL & SANDERS
Licensed in Suisun, 1865.

ST. LOUIS ART & PHOTOGRAPHIC GALLERY
Partnership of T. Miltz, J. Swart and R. Schad; bought out the studio of Gustavus Fagersteen, located at 315 Montgomery Street, San Francisco, c. 1875.

ST. LOUIS ART & PHOTOGRAPHIC GALLERY
Operated by D. C. Redington in San Francisco, c. 1883, at 34 Third Street.

STAFFORD, M.
Born in England, 1830. In California by 1856. Active in Napa City, 1870.

STANFIELD, ARTHUR EDWIN
Active in Pasadena, 1892.

STANGENWALD, HUGO
Daguerreotypist in Marysville before 1853. See Hawaii.

STANLEY, EDITH (MISS)
Born in California, September 1888. Active in San Francisco, c. 1899-1900.

STANSBURY, DR. OSCAR
Active in Chico, 1883.

STANTON & BURDICK
Studio in Los Angeles, 1888-90, at 119-129 North Main Street; Thomas E. Stanton and Chester W. Burdick.

STANTON, THOMAS E.
Born in Iowa, 1854. Active in Los Angeles by 1880; partner in Payne, Stanton & Company's Elite Gallery, 119-129 North Main Street, 1881-87; partner with Burdick, same address, 1888-90; possibly operating as Stanton Studio, 221 ½ South Spring, 1896.

STAPLES, H. A.
Active in Chico, 1910-78.

STARKWEATHER, HERBERT J.
Born in New York, 1853. Son of Joseph B. Starkweather. Photographic printer with George D. Morse, San Francisco, 1876; with David Cobb, 1883. Also listed as Herbert I.

STARKWEATHER, JOSEPH B.
Born in New York. Gallery at 248 Third Street, San Francisco, 1869-72; partner with T. C. Lancey, 1870; active in San Francisco at least through 1899. Father of Herbert J. Starkweather.

STARR & JOHNSON
Partnership in San Francisco, 1854; George Howard Johnson. Made rare stereo daguerreotypes.

STATELER, JOHN
Partner in Runnels & Stateler, 957 Market Street, San Francisco, 1883-89 or later.

STEARNS, S. S.
Photographer in San Francisco, c. 1906; issued rare views of aftermath of San Francisco earthquake.

STECKEL, GEORGE
Born in Allentown, Pennsylvania, December 20, 1864. Worked in a photographic parlor in Philadelphia, 1877-78; operated his own parlor in Allentown, c. 1878-82; in real estate business in Kansas City, c. 1882-88. Partner in photographic studio in Los Angeles with Lamson, opposite the Hollenbeck Hotel, 1888-90; opened his own gallery, 1890. Located at 220 South Spring Street, 1896; 336 ½ South Broadway, 1905-20s. Second vice president of the National Photographic Association of America, 1897; first vice president, 1898. Won a bronze medal at the association's convention in Buffalo, 1890; the first award of merit at the convention in Boston, 1898; two gold medals for portraits and the Committee of Awards medal at the Chicago meeting, 1893. Won all five medals at the Mechanics Institute in San Francisco, 1893, and a silver medal in the 1900 Paris Exposition.

STEELE, J. F.
Gallery on North J Street near Fresno Street, Fresno, 1887-88.

STEIN, WILLIAM F.
Studio at 205 ½ South Main, Los Angeles, 1896-99; associated with J. T. Bertrand at the Plaza Gallery, 413 North Main, date uncertain.

STEINERT, D. A.
Studio at 229 South Main, Los Angeles, 1892.

STELLMAN, LOUIS
Born in Baltimore, 1877; died in San Francisco, 1961. Gifted amateur photographer, journalist, poet and friend of Arnold Genthe; Stellman chronicled the life of Chinatown after Genthe's departure to New York, 1911, and illustrated *The Vanished Ruin Era*, 1910, a book about the 1906 earthquake and fire, and *That Was a Dream Worth Building*, 1916, a chronicle of the Panama Pacific Exhibition, 1916.
    Richard Dillon, *Images of Chinatown: Louis J. Stellman's Chinatown Photographs*, The Book Club of California, 1976.

STENDER, H.
Born in Germany, December 1838. Immigrated to U.S., 1875. Portrait painter in studio at 126 Kearny Street, San Francisco, 1881; photographic studio at 504 Kearny Street, 1883-98. Partner in "Stender-Ware New Method of Photography," Downey Block and 102 Bryson Block, Los Angeles, 1898; in Stender & Ware, 326 ½ Broadway, 1899. First name possibly Herman.

STEPHENS, A. J.
Studio in Pomona at 383 West Second, 1898.

STEREOSCOPIUM COMPANY
Firm in San Diego; produced stereoscopic still lifes.

STEVENS, B. F.
Traveling photographer in the Sierra Nevada Mother Lode region, particularly around Sonora, 1870s. He advertised "photographs, gems, copying and enlarging." Studio in Riceville, 1879.

STEWART, GEORGE
Traveling photographer in El Dorado County, 1887-91. Also sold insurance.

STEWART, JOHN J.
Active in Watsonville, 1887.

STEWART, W. J.
Born in Maine, 1837. Active in Stockton, 1870.

STIFFLER & GILL
Partnership of F. M. Stiffler and R. B. Gill, 120 ½ South Spring, Los Angeles, 1896.

STIFFLER & POTTER
Partnership at 10 Hammond Block, 1897; Frank M. Stiffler.

STIFFLER, FRANK M.
Partner in Stiffler & Gill, view photographers, 120 ½ South Spring, Los Angeles, 1896; partner in Stiffler & Potter, 1897, at 10 Hammond Block; in business alone, same address, 1898.

STIFFLER, GEORGE L.
Photographer with Stiffler & Gill, Los Angeles, 1896.

STILLMAN, W. B.
Active in Auburn, 1867.

STINSON, A. E.
Active in Red Bluff, 1915, when he signed a hand-tinted silver print of the eruption of Mount Lassen.

STINSON, LEWIS JACKSON
Born in Tennessee, 1833. Gallery at the corner of Third and D Street, Marysville, 1862-75; studios in Susanville, Lassen County, and Quincy, Plumas County, 1880.

STINSON, MABEL E.
Photographer in Mott and Red Bluff, 1909-20. Also known as Mrs. Robert E. Stinson.

STINSON, ROBERT E.
Traveling photographer, 1908-20.

STOCKLEY, A.
Active in Napa City, c. 1886.

STOCKLEY, L. H.
Active in Napa City, c. 1886; sold out to James H. Baker, 1887.

STOCKTON ART GALLERY
Located at 305 Main Street, Stockton, c. 1880.

STODDARD, F. C.
Born in New York, 1853. Active in San Francisco, 1880; studio in Navarro, 1888.

STONE
Partner in the firm Leavenworth, Stone & Company, 1228 Market Street, San Francisco, 1887.

STORKE, C. A.
Active in Santa Barbara, 1883.

STORMER & NELSON
Partnership in Colusa, 1893.

STORMER, JOHN BENTON
Active in Colusa, 1890-93; also a partner in Cook & Stormer, Willows, 1890-93.

STRADER
Partner in Tilton & Strader, 318 ½ Temple, Los Angeles, 1895.

STRATFORD
Active in Dunsmuir, 1915.

STREBECK, W. M.
Operated Strebeck & Company, 216 ½ O'Farrell, San Francisco, 1886-89.

STREETER, G. A.
Active in Gilroy, 1893-95.

STREI, DORA (MISS)
Born in California, March 1878. Active in San Francisco, 1899-1900.

STRELOW, SERDINKO & COMPANY
147 South Spring Street, Los Angeles, 1888-89.

STRIGHT, CHARLES
Photographer at the Elite Gallery, Los Angeles, 1883; also known as Payne, Stanton & Company.

STRINGFIELD, ALFRED MOORE
Born in Bloomington, Illinois, July 10, 1849; died in Santa Barbara, September 16, 1886. In Ferndale on Church Street between Ocean and Brown, 1877; gallery at the Clock Building, Santa Barbara, 1880-88. The studio was operated by Mrs. Mina Stringfield after Alfred's death.

STRINGFIELD, MINA (MRS.)
Wife of Alfred Moore Stringfield. Operated Santa Barbara studio after the death of her husband, 1886.

STRONG & GADION
Gallery in Placerville, behind Wonderly's Blacksmith Shop, formerly operated by T. A. Ley, 1899. Partnership of D. Gadion and B. F. Strong.

STRONG, B. F.
Partner with D. Gadion, Placerville, 1899. Purchased the City Photo Gallery from George C. Jones, Placerville, 1901; shared his studio with E. W. Baker, 1901; sold out to G. W. Potter, 1902. Shared space in Angels Camp with Baker, 1902; traveled to Grizzly Flat, 1904.

STRONG, C. C.
Licensed in Watsonville, 1863.

STRONG, CHARLES
Born in Michigan, 1837. Active in San Francisco, 1870.

STRONG, J. D.
Active in Oakland, 1877-81.

STRONG, MARK HOPKINS
Born in Oakland, March 10, 1862; died in Napa, January 13, 1945. Brother of Nathan B. Strong and worked in his studio, 1884. Sold his studio to Edward Boan and Charles R. Ashley, 1924. Studio at the corner of Main and Third, Napa City, 1888.

STRONG, NATHAN B.
Born in Oakland, California, 1860. Purchased A. P. Flaglor's Eureka Gallery on Second Street in Eureka, 1880; moved to Vance's Block, 1881; sent Charles E. Carter to solicit copying and coloring work, 1883; Palmquist speculates that Strong was involved in producing the photographs which illustrated Edgar Cherry's book, *Redwood and Lumbering in California Forests*, 1884; moved to the Cooper Building, 1887; sold studio to Wunderlich Brothers and moved to Chicago, Illinois, 1888; moved to San Francisco, 1889, operating as a photo-processor; later moved to Weaverville, then to Redding, and back to San Francisco where he operated in partnership of Bolton & Strong, photo-lithography, 1892-94; photo-engraver, Oakland, 1908-09. Produced high quality boudoir card scenes of redwood logging. Strong also was an artist and produced good quality sketches and displayed art in his studio.

STRONG, WALLACE KEALOLA
Born in Honolulu, Hawaii, October 18, 1856; died in Eureka, July 21, 1928. Court reporter for Humboldt County, 1876. Brother of Nathan B. and Mark Hopkins Strong. Began studio work when he

took over W. B Toll's gallery in Ferndale, 1881. His professional career did not last long, although he continued as an amateur for many years.

STRUCKMANN
Partnership in Bodie, c. 1880.

STRUNZ & WOODWARD
Operated the Elite Studio in Lodi, c. 1895.

STUART, WILLIAM McCORSIN
Fine Art Gallery at 198 Main Street and later on El Dorado Street, Stockton, c. 1868.

STUBBS & PHILLIPS
Billled as an "Art Studio" in Hollister, c. 1885.

STURTEVANT, A.
Studio in Los Angeles, 1897-98, at 125 East 23rd.

SUCK, KAI
Active in San Francisco, c. 1868, at 929 Dupont Street.

SULLIVAN & JENKINS
Operated on 2nd Street in Chico, c. 1880-90.

SULLIVAN, P. J.
Grand Art Gallery at 28 and 33 Third Street, San Francisco, 1874-77. Listed as a real estate agent at 31 Third Street, 1878.

SULLIVAN, TIMOTHY ALFRED
Active in Chico, 1879, on 2nd Street.

SULLIVAN, WILLIAM L.
Active in Eureka, 1882.

SUMMERHAYS, WILLIAM
Gallery at 612 Clay Street, San Francisco, 1872-85 or later.

SUNBEAM GALLERY
Active in Los Angeles at 55 North Main Street, operated by William M. Godfrey; purchased by A. S. Addis, 1876.

SUNBEAM GALLERY
Studio at 31 Third Street, San Francisco, c. 1880.

SUTTERLY & DART
Traveling photographers in California, c. 1885.

SUTTERLY BROTHERS
Partnership of C. and J. K. Sutterley, traveling photographers; in Nevada, c. 1860, 1864-65; in Utah, c. 1863; in Quincy, California, 1865; partner with J. Junk in Boise and Idaho City, 1865-66; Salt Lake City, 1866-67; Nevada, 1868; California, 1871-75; Nevada, c. 1873-74, 1881. Also involved in partnerships of Sutterly & Dart in California, Pilliner & Sutterley in Nevada, and Sutterley & Rendall. Studio in Napa City, 1871.

SUTTERLY, CHARLES
Licensed in San Francisco, 1863.

SUTTERLY, CLEMENT
Photographer in Chicago, Illinois, 1859-62. Partner with J. K. Sutterly in the firm of Sutterly Brothers on B Street, corner of Taylor in Virginia City, Nevada, 1867. Traveling photographer in California. With Sutterly Brothers parlor located in Napa City, 1871; Placerville, 1884; corner of Jackson and Buena Vista Streets, Ione, 1886. Imprint

has also been noted for Ukiah. See Idaho.

SUTTERLY, J. K.
Born in New Jersey. Daguerreotypist in Chicago, c. 1856-60. Active with his brother, Clement, in Nevada, 1867; in Napa City, California, 1871; in San Jose, 1870s. See Idaho.

SUTTON
Active in Shasta, 1876.

SUTTON & CROMWELL
Partnership in Shasta, 1875-76.

SUTTON, CORA (MISS)
Photographer in Dunsmuir, 1902.

SWAIN
Traveling photographer, 1876.

SWAIN & SIMAS
Partnership of Emanuel Simas and Swain in San Francisco, 1891.

SWAIN & WELSH
Traveling photographers, 1876.

SWAIN, ALICE (MISS)
Active in San Diego, 1889-90.

SWAIN, LEWIS C.
Operator for W. Kay in Jackson, c. 1895; parlor in San Francisco at the corner of San Jose and Plymouth Avenue, 1898.

SWANEY & PIERCE
Gallery at Main Street, Los Gatos, 1888.

SWANEY, EMMA I.
Born in Placerville, California, c. 1857. Active in Oakland, 1900-03.

SWART, JOHN S.
Born in Iowa, 1835. Partner with Miltz & Swart's San Francisco Gallery, 180 Fourth Street, Santa Rosa, 1877-80; in Petaluma by June 1880; studio on Broad Street in Nevada City, 1886, operated by F. V. Yeager. See St. Louis Art and Photographic Gallery.

SWASEY & BEARDSLEY
Partnership of Benjamin Swasey and J. S. Beardsley, licensed to operate in California, 1864.

SWASEY & BUTTON
Partnership operating in Shasta, 1876.

SWASEY & KLINE
Traveling photographers, 1897.

SWASEY & SON
Active in Shasta, 1877.

SWASEY, ALICE
Photographer in Redding, 1895-98.

SWASEY, BENJAMIN
Born in New Hampshire, 1822. Gallery at 205 Third Street, San Francisco 1865-67; worked for Oscar Foss, 1867-69; for George D. Morse, 1874-77; in Redding, 1876-91; gallery in Shasta, 1880-86 or later.

SWASEY, FRANK MARSHALL
Active in Shasta County, 1877.

SWASEY, FRED P.
Gallery at 26 Montgomery Street, San Francisco, 1888-96; also traveling, 1897-99.

SWENSON, NOREN F.
Born in Iowa, December 1860. Active on Catalina Island, 1900.

SWISHER, A. W.
Partner in Burdick & Swisher at 221 and 221 ½ South Spring, Los Angeles, 1894-96.

SYLAR, J. L.
Active in Kelseyville, c. 1895.

TABER, ISAIAH WEST
Born in New Bedford, Massachusetts, August 17, 1830; died February 22, 1912. At sea on a whaler, c. 1845-49; left for California on the ship *Friendship*. Mined at Chinese Camp, Mississippi Bar on the American River, at Beals Bar and at Secret Ravine near Ruckland, 1851-52; ranched in area that later became the Parker Whitney Ranch. Returned to New Bedford, 1854; took up dentistry and photography. He soon dropped dentistry and made photography his vocation, opening a studio in Syracuse, New York with his brother, Freeman Augustus Taber, at 6 Franklin Building, East Genessee Street, early 1860s; partner with B. F. Howland. Returned to San Francisco and worked for Bradley & Rulofson, 1864-73; worked for George Daniels Morse. Opened I. W. Taber & Company in association with Thomas H. Boyd at 26 Montgomery Street, c. 1875. In business alone, c. 1877-1906. Studio at 8 Montgomery Street, 1880; later at 121 Post Street. He produced a variety of large format images of scenes in Chinatown, San Francisco, Los Angeles, Alaska, Oregon, Yosemite Valley, and portraits of prominent people and stereoviews. G. B. Rieman supervised the business at 8 Montgomery Street, and J. J. Cook was vice president of the company after it moved to Post Street. Married Mary F. R. Howland, sister of his old friend and colleague, B. F. Howland, on April 9, 1857, and had two daughters. His second wife was Anne Slocum, married September 29, 1871, in San Francisco. Awarded photographic concession at the Midwinter Fair, 1893-94. Photographed the grand pageant during the Queen Victoria Jubilee in London, 1897; went to Marlborough House and photographed King Edward VII.

TABOR, I. W. & T. H. BOYD
Isaiah West Tabor and Boyd, traveling photographers, 1875-93.

TABOR, R. L.
Stereo photographer; issued west coast scenery views.

TALLMAN
Active in Sisson, c. 1895.

TANDY, H. C.
Active in Lemoore, c. 1885; Hanford, c. 1890-93.

TAPE, MARY (MRS.)
Active in San Francisco, c. 1890.

TATE, M. J. (MRS.)
Studio in Lakeport, 1886-88.

TAYLOR
Active in Marysville, 1912.

TAYLOR, D. B.
Born in Massachusetts, 1843. Took up photography, c. 1859; formed D. B. Taylor & Company's Photographic Temple of Art, c. 1876, 415 Montgomery Street, San Francisco, when he bought out Silas Selleck; associated with H. N. Potter and E. B. Monroe.

TAYLOR, FREDERICK ALLEN
Active in Red Bluff, 1872-80.

TAYLOR, J.
Stereo photographer in San Francisco.

TAYLOR, JOSEPH
Traveling photographer in Placerville, 1903.

TENT GALLERY
Operated in Dunsmuir, 1908.

THE PALM
Billed as a "Ground Floor Gallery" located at 565 12th Street, Oakland, c. 1890.

THIRD STREET FOTOGRAF GALLERY
Studio at 28 Third Street, San Francisco, 1885.

THIRD STREET GALLERY
Located in Santa Rosa, owned and operated at various times by Kraft, Downing, Rea, Rauscher, Piggott, and Shaw.

THOMAS, G. N.
Operated the Yolo Photographic Art Gallery in Woodland, 1880-82.

THOMAS, JOHN
Active in Orland, 1910-14.

THOMAS MANUFACTURING COMPANY
San Francisco firm; issued stereo views of San Francisco fire, photographer unknown.

THOMBERGER, MARTIN
Born in Vermont, 1820. Active in San Jose Township, 1870.

THOMPSON, CORNELIUS
Born in Missouri, 1851. Active in Chico, 1880-81.

THOMPSON, D.
Active in Chico.

THOMPSON, DR. RANSOM
Physician and photographer in Chico, c. 1875, on Main Street; in Cloverdale, 1892-93. Possibly Cornelius Ransom.

THOMPSON, E. M. (MISS)
Active in San Jose, 1875-78, at the studio of W. W. Wright, 284 Santa Clara Street.

THOMPSON, HARRY
Active in Chico, 1861-67. Primarily a portrait photographer, he also produced stereoviews at his studio, Main at 4th Street. Listed in Etna, 1870.

THOMPSON, P. J.
Active in Modoc County, 1900-24.

THOMSON & BILLINGTON
Gallery at Sutro Heights, San Francisco, 1895.

THORNBROUGH
Active in Auburn, c. 1894.

THORS, GERTRUDE M. (MRS.)
Born in California, 1867. Second wife of photographer Louis Thors, married 1891, and active in San Francisco, c. 1891-1910. Part owner of the Thors Gallery at 14 Grant Street, San Francisco, c. 1891-98. Gallery located in the Phelan Building, 1899-1900. Operated a

branch gallery in Palo Alto, 1895-98. Also listed as Mrs. Louis Thors.

THORS, KATHERINE
Born in Ohio, 1853. First wife of Louis Thors. Worked in gallery at various locations on Larkin Street, 1879-90. By 1891, she had either died or was divorced from Louis.

THORS, LOUIS
Born in Holland, 1845. Educated in France where he served in the Merchant Marine. Came to California from the East Indies, 1876; set up his photographic studio in San Francisco by 1880. Gallery at 1023 and 1025 Larkin Street, 1880-89 or later; operated Thors Photographic Company, 14 Grant Street, 1895-1900+. He used the "Nadar process," which gave a soft tone to photographic portraits through an application of photogravure, and won the Bronze Medal in the 1889 Paris Exposition.

THRASHER, A. F.
Licensed in Solano County, 1862.

THUNEN, WILLIAM
Stereo photographer active in Cherokee, 1899; in Weed and Oroville, c. 1906.

THWAITES, JOSEPH
Born in New York, 1838. Active in San Francisco, 1869-70 or later. Studio in Portland, Oregon, by 1883. Also spelled Twaite.

TIDBALL, ALEXANDER SCOTT
Born in Virginia, c. 1828. Photographer, retoucher and artist; partner in Vaughan & Tidball, 513 Montgomery Street, San Francisco, 1867; photographic artist, 429 Montgomery, 1869-70; retoucher, 409 California Street, 1874; 204 Montgomery Street, 1875-76; 26 Montgomery Street, 1881; artist at 11 Kearny Street, 1883.

TIDD, A. M. (MISS)
Active in Yreka, 1864.

TIEMAN, CHARLES H.
Active in Marysville, 1880-81.

TODD, JOHN A.
Born in England, 1828. Operating at 81 J Street, Sacramento by 1865; at J Street between Third and Fourth, 1867; gallery at 84 J Street, 1870; at 318 and 320 J Street, c. 1879. Operating in San Francisco, 1887, at 2126 Fillmore Street. Friend of Charles R. Savage, prominent photographer of Salt Lake City.

TOLL, WILLIAM B.
Born in Wisconsin, c. 1848. Located at 282 Santa Clara Street, San Jose, c. 1874; "Art and Portrait Gallery" in Santa Rosa, c. 1874; Rohnerville, 1878; Ferndale, 1879-82.

TOLLMAN & OLTMAN
Traveling photographers, 1897.

TOLLMAN & PRATSCH
Traveling photographers, 1889.

TOLLMAN, JOHN W.
Traveling photographer active in Shasta County, 1889, 1897; Mendocino County, 1894; Humboldt County, 1895-96; Trinity County, 1897; Siskiyou County, 1897-98. Also listed as John W. Tollman & Wife.

TOLLMAN, JOHN W. (MRS.)
Traveling photographer with husband, John W. Tollman, active in northern counties, 1889-98; Eureka, 1897-98; Washington and Oregon, 1899-1909.

TOMKIN, HERBERT
Gallery at 1227 Market Street, San Francisco, 1897-1900+.

TONGE
Partner in Wax & Tonge, operating the Universal Art Studio in Redding, 1898.

TOWNE, B. C.
Active in Portland, Oregon, and traveling in California, 1890.

TOWNE, WILLIAM H.
Born in New Hampshire, 1835. Worked for Alexander Edouart, 634 Washington, San Francisco, 1865. Active in Oakland and San Francisco area, 1880. Moved to Oregon and operated the San Francisco Gallery on the southwest corner of First and Morrison, Portland, 1883. Became an associate of Joseph Buchtel in Portland.

TOWNSEND, SMITH PLATT
Licensed in Marion, 1863; Ford Valley, 1863; Taylorsville, 1864.

TOY, CHIN K.
Active in San Francisco, c. 1900, at 842 Clay Street.

TRAIN, EDGAR HENRY
Licensed in Scott Bar, 1863-64.

TREAT & GRANT
Operated in Mendocino City, 1877.

TREAT, A. R.
Stereo photographer; partner with Martin Howe Grant in Mendocino, 1877.

TREAT, ARCHIBALD
Prominent amateur from Sausalito, c. 1900; attorney in San Francisco.

TRESSIDER, JOHN
Photographer with W. W. Wright, San Jose, 1887.

TRESSLAR, ELKANAH P.
Active in Los Angeles, 1892-1912. Studio at 213 ½ North Spring, 1892-97; 522 South Hill, 1898-1901; 512 South Hill, 1902; 500 ½ South Broadway, 1904-05. Partner in Tresslar & Hays at Spring Street address, 1893-94.

TRESSLAR, MABLE H.
Active in Los Angeles, 1898-1901. Presumed daughter of Elkanah P. Tresslar.

TRESSLAR, S. P.
Partner with E. P. Tresslar, Los Angeles, 1892; Riverside, 1895-c. 1900.

TRUPP, WILLIAM
Stereo photographer; worked with H. Schoene in San Francisco, 1871.

TUCKER
Partner in Smith & Tucker, Los Angeles, 1878.

TUCKER
Studio at 72 South Second Street, San Jose, 1893-98.

TUCKER, CLARENCE W.
Active in Randsburg, 1897-98; Covina, c. 1900-30s.

TUCKER, JOHN O.
Active in San Jose, 1890-1917.

TUCKER, JOHN O. (MRS.)
Active in Santa Clara, 1890+; in San Jose with husband, John, in the partnership of Judkins & Tucker, c. 1890-1917. Located at 72 South Second Street, 1899-1901; 58 South Second Street, 1903; in the Porter Building, 1904-17.

TURK STREET GALLERY
Studio in San Francisco, 6 Turk Street, operated by F. M. Harkness.

TURNBULL, RALPH R.
Photographer with C. Beal, Los Angeles, 1896.

TURNER, A. M.
Active in Riverside, 1883.

TURNER, DAVID H.
Born in Pennsylvania, c. 1839. Active in Los Angeles, 1870.

TURNER, E. H. (MRS.)
Proprietor of the Elite Studio, San Diego, 1895-98.

TURNER, E. K.
Gallery in San Diego, 1888, 806 Fifth Street.

TURNER, GEORGE A.
View photographer, 26 Mongomery Street, San Francisco, 1897-99.

TURNER, HARRY
Worked for Silas Selleck, San Francisco, 1865.

TURNER, R. H.
Active in Etna, 1905.

TURNEY & COMPANY, J. H.
Stereo photographer active in Oakland, c. 1906; issued views of the aftermath of the San Francisco earthquake.

TURRILL, CHARLES BEEBE
Born 1854; died 1927. Photographer in San Francisco and traveling, c. 1886-1900; befriended Carleton E. Watkins in his later years, helped him when he was blind and had suffered catastrophic loss in the 1906 earthquake; became Watkins' first biographer. Published the photographs of Mrs. C. Fuller in Sketch of San Diego, 1886.

TUTT, GEORGE B.
Photographer with Jacob Shew, San Francisco, 1869.

TUTTLE & BENEDICT
Active in San Francisco, 1873; W. N. Tuttle.

TUTTLE & BROWNELL
Located at the corner of Main and Centre Streets in Eureka, advertising enameled cards and sun pearls, c. 1865; at Kidd's Block on Main Street, c. 1869.

TUTTLE & COMPANY'S PHOTOGRAPHIC PARLORS
Operating in Stockton, 1868.

TUTTLE & FITZGERALD
Billed as "Heliographic Artists," 1875, in Santa Barbara.

TUTTLE & JOHNSON
Billed as "Heliographic Artists" on Mill Street, Grass Valley, 1875.

TUTTLE & LEHE
Operating in Stockton, 1868. Lehe is probably a mispelling of Lee.

TUTTLE & PARKER
Operated the Helio Art Studio on the Temple Block in Los Angeles, 1885.

TUTTLE & PAYNE
Operated in Los Angeles.

TUTTLE & SULLIVAN'S ROTUNDA ART GALLERY
Operating c. 1880, location unknown.

TUTTLE, T. G.
Parlor in Sutter Creek, date uncertain.

TUTTLE, WILLIAM NUTTING
Born in Massachusetts, 1844; died in Australia, 1895. With Flanders & Tuttle in Eureka, 1865-66; Tuttle & Brownell, 1867; Tuttle & Lehe, Stockton, 1868; rented Anderson's Eureka Photography Gallery in Eureka with C. W. J. Johnson, 1869-70; bought the Cosmopolitan Photograph Gallery at 523 Kearny Street with Johnson, 1870; Grass Valley, 1870; Chico, 1872; with Tuttle & Benedict in San Francisco, 1873; Tuttle & Lee, Temple Block, Los Angeles, 1874; Tuttle & Fitzgerald, Santa Barbara, 1873-75; Tuttle & Lee, Viginia City, Nevada, 1876. Tuttle & Company's Helio Art Studio, Temple Block, Los Angeles, was also listed as Tuttle & Payne and had a branch gallery at Second Street, Chico, 1878-79. Associated with George B. Rieman, 26 Montgomery Street, San Francisco, 1880, in the Rotunda Art Gallery. May have been a partner in Tuttle & Parker, Los Angeles, 1880s. Possibly owned Tuttle & Company in Australia and New Zealand, 1881-92. Produced stereoviews.

TWAITES, W.
Born in England, 1832. Active in San Francisco, 1860.

TWIST, JULIA S.
Active in California, c. 1861. Maiden name probably Peck.

TYLER, O. E.
Active in Los Angeles, 1883-84, at 18 South Main.

UBARTO, CESARE
Active in San Francisco, c. 1898-1900+.

UCHIGAMA, H. U.
Gallery at 141 Powell Street, San Francisco, 1901.

UNDERHILL
Partner in White & Underhill, 643 Washington, San Francisco, 1867.

UNIVERSAL ART COMPANY
Operated by William Wax in Redding, 1898.

UPTON, CHARLES E.
Possibly an amateur working around Placerville, 1895-1900.

VALE & GIVEN
Partnership of traveling photographers, W. A. Vale and Given, c. 1875; operated a railroad car out of San Bernardino.

VALE, W. A.
Born in Indiana, July 15, 1847. Studio in San Bernardino, 1874-81, on 3rd Street. Operated a photo car called the "Southern California," using P. O. Box 55 in San Bernardino as his address, 1870s; partner with Given, c. 1875, in the Vale & Given Photographic Car.

VALENTINE
Active in Lewiston, c. 1900.

VALENTINE & DARLINGTON
Traveling photographers, 1893.

VALENTINE, W. S.
Active in Redding, 1909-29.

VALLEAU, GEORGE W.
Gallery on Fifth Street, over Spittler's drugstore in Colusa, c. 1868-88 or longer.

VALPEY, J. O.
Worked with J. A. Harliss at the California Art Company, c. 1890.

VAN BURKLEO, LEROY
Advertised as a "Practical Photographer," operating a gallery at 425 3rd Street in Eureka, c. 1893-1908.

VAN BUSKIRK, C.
Studio at 124 South Main, Los Angeles, 1899.

VAN COURT, JAMES E.
Bookkeeper for William Shew in San Francisco, 1865; operator for Shew, 1869-70. Operated a gallery in Belmont, 1884; in Redwood City on Main and Schoolhouse, 1886-88 or later.

VAN CRAIGH
Partner in Simmons & Van Craigh, 133 ½ South Spring, Los Angeles, 1900-01.

VAN DER ZWEIP, JAMES
Born in Holland, 1840. Probably in New Jersey, 1875. Gallery at 64 Third Street, San Francisco, 1880-87. Also spelled Vandersweep.

VAN DIVEER, WILLIAM J.
Active in San Francisco, 1864; Windsor, 1865; Salinas City, 1877; Suisun, 1878; Woodland, 1880; Salinas City, 1883.

VAN DUYN, J. J.
Daguerreian artist from New York City; opened galleries in Sonora and Columbia, 1852.

VAN EATON, C. D. (MRS.)
Active in San Jose, 1894.

VAN EE, H. KEMP
Operated a gallery in the Glenn Building, Santa Rosa, 1888.

VAN ROSSEN, M. E. (MRS.)
Born in English Canada, March 1867. Immigrated to U.S., 1895. Active as photographer and gallery proprietor in Pasadena, 1900.

VAN WINKLE, EDNA B.
Born in Illinois, August 1874. Active in Fresno, 1900.

VAN WINKLE, EMMA (MISS)
Born in Maine, c. 1856. Displayed tinted photographs of flowers at the Humboldt County Fair, 1878. Trained at the Art School of San Francisco, 1888-90. Resident of Ferndale.

VANCE, E. H.
Partner in Flanders & Vance on Church Street opposite Hamilton Hall, Grass Valley, c. 1868.

VANCE, ROBERT H.
Born in Maine, 1825; died in New York, 1876. Active in California, 1851-62. Vance operated galleries in Sacramento, Marysville and San Francisco. His whole-plate daguerreotypes of miners, mines and west coast towns were exhibited in New York City, 1851, but were lost after being left in the custody of the Fitzgibbon studio in St. Louis. Vance operated a gallery on the corner of Montgomery and Sacramento, in San Francisco, 1856-61, which he sold to Charles L. Weed; Weed sold the gallery to Bradley & Rulofson, 1864. Sometimes called the Brady of the West, Vance's studio work was consistently superior.
  Edith M. Coulter and Jeanne Van Nostrand, *A Camera In the Gold Rush*, The Book Club of California, 1946.

VANCE, T. WILLIAM
Active in San Francisco, 1883. Probably William H. Vance.

VANCE, WILLIAM H.
Born in Maine, 1826. Daguerreian parlor at the corner of Clay and Montgomery, San Francisco, 1859; active in San Francisco, 1880. He was Robert Vance's brother. Probably the same as T. William Vance.

VANSANT, JOSHUA, JR.
Studio located at Rick's Building on F Street in Eureka, 1885-1908.

VANSANT, WILLIAM PRESCOTT
Active in Eureka, 1891-96.

VARELA, A. C.
View photographer with a studio in Los Angeles, 1878, perhaps working from his residence at 221 Olive Street.

VARNEY, A. K.
Studio located at 521 J Street, Sacramento, c. 1900. Purchased studio from Johnston & Simas in Placerville, 1897; Johnson & Simas may have operated both of Varney's studios for him for a time.

VASCONCELLES, JOSEPH J.
Partner in Howland & Vasconcelles, 25 and 27 Third Street, San Francisco, 1865-66. Later went into the hardware business. Also spelled Vasoncelles, Vasconcelles.

VAUGHAN
Active in Chico, 1868-86, at 18 Third Street.

VAUGHAN & KEITH
Studio in San Francisco, 1899; H. M. Vaughan.

VAUGHAN, EMMA (MRS.)
Born in England, 1846. Wife of Hector W. Vaughan and proprietor of the Imperial Photograph Gallery, 724 ½ Market Street, San Francisco, 1879-87.

VAUGHAN, HECTOR M.
Born in California, 1863, son of Hector W. Vaughan. Photographer with Mrs. Emma Vaughan's Imperial Photograph Gallery, 724 ½ Market Street, San Francisco, 1883-85; proprietor of the same gallery with his brother, R. K. Vaughan, 1885-88 or later; photographer in that gallery under C. A. Howland, 1898; partner in Vaughan & Keith, 14 Grant Avenue, 1899-1904 or later.

VAUGHAN, HECTOR W.
Born in Ireland, 1830. In California by 1863. Partner in Vaughan's Gallery with Scott Tidball, 1867-68, at 513 Montgomery Street, San Francisco; won the Silver Medal at the Mechanics Fair, 1868; at 18 Third Street, c. 1869; operated a second studio, the Imperial Photograph Gallery, at 724 ½ Market Street, 1877-c. 1880. Mrs. Vaughan began running the Imperial and Max Karras became proprietor of Vaughan's Gallery, c. 1880; Clarence A. Howland managed the Imperial for Mrs. Vaughan until her sons took over; Howland became proprietor, 1890s. The Imperial was sold to Rasmussen & Coover, c. 1900.

VAUGHAN, HIRAM G.
Born in California, May 20, 1870, son of Hector W. Vaughan. Partner in Vaughan & Keith, San Francisco, 1899-1904.

VAUGHAN, JOHN W.
Born in England, 1835. Perhaps the J. W. Vaughan, portrait painter, with a studio at 6 O'Farrell, San Francisco, 1871. Possibly related to Hector W. Vaughan; photographer at Hector W. Vaughan's studio, 724 ½ Market, c. 1880. In June 1880, an inmate of the insane asylum in Stockton.

VAUGHAN, RUFUS K.
Born in California, 1865, son of Hector W. Vaughan. Photographer with Mrs. Emma Vaughan at the Imperial Photographic Gallery, 724 ½ Market Street, San Francisco, 1883; proprietor of that gallery with his brother, H. M. Vaughan, 1885-89.

VAUGHAN'S FIRST PREMIUM PHOTOGRAPH GALLERY
Operated in San Francisco at various times by H. W. Vaughan, Max Karras, and Sadie O. Brown.

VERSER, JOHN H.
Born in California, 1862, son of Henry and Tillie Verser. Active in San Jose, 1880.

VINCENT, J.
Active in Anaheim, 1878.

VITALINI & BIANCHI
Partnership of E. C. Vitalini and Bianchi, active in San Francisco, 1892-99.

VITALINI, E. C.
Partner in Vitalini & Bianchi, 233 Montomery Street, San Francisco, 1892-99.

VOELKER, J. A.
In partnership with Andrew Price, operating as Price & Voelker, 1069 Broadway, Oakland, 1888.

VON FALKOWSKY, OVAN
Operated a gallery on Third, east of Main Street, Chico, 1888. Also spelled Falowsky.

VON HASSLEN
Partner in Mains & Von Hasslen, stereo photographers active in Camptonville. Also spelled Hasselin or Hasseln.

VROMAN, ADAM CLARK
Born in LaSalle, Illinois, April 15, 1856; died in Altadena, July 24, 1916. Moved to Pasadena, 1892, due to his wife's tuberculosis; she died, 1894. Vroman opened the first of his bookstores several months later. He took his first trip through the Southwest, 1895, and took numerous photographs. Vroman was representative of the talented amateurs of the late 19th century who had the resources to pursue the art of photography. Fortunately, Vroman befriended native peoples in the regions he visited, and produced a fine archive of their images during their radical aculturation. Member of the Camera Club with H. E. Hoopes and Peter C. Gates; associated with Charles Lummis and W. R. Harned; partner in Glasscock & Vroman, 60 East Colorado, Pasadena, 1895, 1897.

> Beaumont Newhall, Introduction; *Photographer of the Southwest: Adam Clark Vroman*, 1856-1916, Ruth I. Mahood, Editor, The Ward Ritchie Press, 1961.
> William Webb and Robert A. Weinstein, *Dwellers at the Source: Southwestern Indian Photographs of A.C. Vroman*, 1895-1904, Grossman Publishers, 1973.

WAGNER, AVA (MRS.)
Born in Michigan, March 1867. Active in Los Angeles, c. 1899-1901.

WAI CHEN HIN
Active in San Francisco at 800 Stockton Street, c. 1885.

WAITE, CHARLES B.
View photographer active in Los Angeles, 1894-97. Studio at 211 West First Street, 1894, 1896-97; 217-18 Kaweah Block, 254 South Broadway, 1896.

WAITE, MEDEA L. (MRS.)
Born in Ohio, November 1857. Active in Los Gatos, 1899-1901, gallery on Main Street.

WALBRIDGE, CYRUS EDMUND
Active in Chico, 1865-76.

WALDRON, MAY M. (MISS)
Born in California, January 1877. Employed by P. W. Griffiths in the Elite Photograph Gallery in Marysville, 1899; purchased Griffiths gallery, operating 1900-04.

WALKER
Active in Redding, c. 1900.

WALKER & FAGERSTEEN
Association of Sela Clarence Walker and Gustavus Fagersteen, stereo photographers active in Stockton and Yosemite, 1877-88; made views of Yosemite and Mammoth Trees. Both men had been assistant photographers for J. J. Reilly; many of their cards are Hazeltine mounts and images overprinted "Successors to M. M. Hazeltine, Photographed by Walker & Fagersteen."

WALKER & HEMENWAY
Active in Winters, c. 1900.

WALKER, C. M.
Active in Elk, c. 1890.

WALKER, CHARLES H.
Born in Missouri, 1845. Studio at 556 Twelfth Street in Brooklyn, c. 1880. Gallery in Oakland, 1883, at 556 Central Avenue, corner of Eleventh.

WALKER, JOHN A.
Active in San Francisco, 1898.

WALKER, S. C.
Associated with Fagersteen in Stockton and Yosemite, 1870s. Operating from 535 East Main Street, Stockton, c. 1895.

WALKER, SAMUEL
Born in England, 1838. Son of Samuel Walker, San Francisco portrait painter and landscape artist. Photographer with George D. Morse, San Francisco, 1869.

WALLACE, J. A.
Active in Weaverville, 1892-93.

WALLACE, J. M.
Active in Chico, c. 1875.

WALTERS, N.
Operated for H. S. Beals in Sacramento at 115 J Street, c. 1867; partner in Walters & Company, 70 J Street, 1870.

WALTERS, S. R.
Born in Canada, 1842. Active in Sacramento, 1870.

WALTON, EMMA F.
Born in California, 1857. Enameler of pictures, San Francisco, 1880; sister of James W. Walton.

WALTON, JAMES W.
Born in California, 1862. Active in San Francisco, c. 1880.

WARE
Partner in Stender-Ware New Method of Photography, Downey Block and 102 Bryson Block, Los Angeles, 1898; partner in Stender & Ware, 326 ½ Broadway, 1899.

WARE
Operated a daguerreian saloon in the Gault House, Center and Market Streets, Stockton, 1850.

WARNER
Stereo photographer active in San Bernardino.

WARREN & SON, W. E.
Stereo photographers in San Jose; produced views of Mendocino County.

WARREN, EMMA A. (MRS.)
Active in Oakland, 1900-01; partner in portrait gallery of Hellen & Warren with Lottie M. Hellen, 565 12th Street.

WASTON & SIMAS
Partnership of Emanuel Simas and Waston in Sutter Creek, 1897.

WATERHOUSE, GEORGE
Photographer with C. L. Cramer, San Francisco, 1869. Perhaps a partner with E. P. Butler, Virginia City, Nevada, 1883.

WATERS
Active around Shasta, 1894 and 1900, as evidenced by silver prints of the mountains and surrounding areas. A rubber stamp imprint on the reverse of the prints contains the name K. S. Denison, Oakland Pier, presumably the retailer of the Waters' prints. The author has also verified a 20 x 24 inch print of a downtown San Francisco office building c. 1910 signed Waters.

WATERS
Partner in Beals & Waters, Sacramento, 1868.

WATERS, RAPER JAMES
Studio in Virginia City, Nevada, 1886; Gold Hill. Gallery at 110 Sutter, San Francisco, and traveling, 1895-1900; at 717 Market Street, 1915-16.

WATKINS, CARLTON E.
Born in Oneonta, New York, November 11, 1829; died in California, 1916. He migrated to California during the gold rush, 1851. Worked and learned photography in James Ford's gallery in San Jose. Watkins began photographing Yosemite, 1861; produced glass stereoviews of Yosemite and Mendocino, early 60s; he became famous and known as a master of the medium when he produced his mammoth plate (17 by 20 inch) views. Located in San Francisco at 425 Montgomery, 1865; 22 and 26 Montgomery, c. 1874; 425 and 427 Montgomery, 1880-88; 1249 Market Street, 1898. Watkins traveled to Oregon, 1867, making exceptional views of the Portland area and the Columbia River gorge. During a financial panic in the mid-1870s, Watkins lost control of his gallery and many of his negatives; they passed to Isaiah Taber, who published them under his own imprint, a common practice, as evidenced by Watkins' own use of the negatives of A. A. Hart. By 1906, Watkins was blind and his studio and negatives were lost in the earthquake and fire. He was committed to the California State Hospital, 1910, and died there.

The Early Pacific Coast Photographs of Carleton E. Watkins, Water Resources Center Archives, Archives Series Report No. 8, University of California, 1960.

Peter E. Palmquist with Lincoln Kilian, The Photographers of the Humboldt Bay Region, Volume 5, Edgar Cherry & Company, Peter E. Palmquist, Arcata, 1987.

Peter Palmquist, Carleton E. Watkins, Photographer of the American West, University of New Mexico Press for the Amon Carter Museum, 1983.

Carleton E. Watkins, Photographs of the Columbia River and Oregon, James Alinder, Editor, with essays by David Featherstone and Russ Anderson, The Friends of Photography in association with the Weston Gallery, 1979.

Carleton E. Watkins, Photographs 1861-74, essay by Peter Palmquist, Fraenkel Gallery in association with Bedford Arts, 1989.

Richard Steven Street, A Kern County Diary, The Forgotten Photographs of Carleton E. Watkins, 1881-88, Kern County Museum, 1983.

WATROUS, STEPHEN W.
Born in Massachusetts, 1845. Photographic printer with Jacob Shew, San Francisco, 1876. Active in Visalia, 1880-88 or later; gallery was in the Holt Block where he also sold and bought musical instruments, 1888.

WATSON, A. R.
Active in Santa Rosa, c. 1860.

WAX & TONGE
Partnership of William Wax in the Universal Art Studio, Redding, 1898.

WAX, WILLIAM
Active in Diamond Springs, 1893; operated the El Dorado Gallery, c. 1890, Redding; partner in Wax & Tonge, Universal Art Studio, 1898; in El Dorado, 1899; Big Canon Mine, 1899.

WEATHERWAX, LULU (MISS)
Best view award at Placerville Agricultural Show, 1899.

WEAVER, DAVIDSON ROBY
Son of Hazle Judkins Weaver and Miles Franklin Weaver; active in Santa Cruz; later operated Weaver's Camera Shop in Santa Maria.

WEAVER, HAZLE JUDKINS
Daughter of D. R. Judkins; moved from Seattle to San Francisco, then to Santa Maria with her father. She helped in the darkroom and operated the Santa Maria studio with her husband, Miles Franklin Weaver, after her father's death, 1909. Moved the studio to Brea, 1909.

WEAVER, HENRY E.
Active in Visalia, c. 1867.

WEAVER, MILES FRANKLIN
Son-in-law of D. R. Judkins. Operated the Judkins Gallery in Santa Maria after Judkins' death, 1909, then moved the studio to Brea. Became famous for panoramas of Los Angeles. Father of photographer Davidson Roby Weaver.

WEBB, GEORGE
Studio at 400 Pacific Avenue, Santa Cruz, 1889-1907.

WEBSTER, B.
Active in Bakersfield, c. 1885.

WEBSTER, F. A.
Studio at 1069 Broadway, corner of 12th Street, Oakland, 1889-1934.

WEED, CHARLES LEANDER
Born in New York, July 17, 1824; died in Oakland, August 31, 1903. Came to California from Wisconsin and opened a gallery in Sacramento. Worked for R. H. Vance at Third and J Street, 1858; also worked for Vance in San Francisco, 1858. A landscape photographer, he made the first photographs of Yosemite, 1859. Weed bought Vance's gallery in San Francisco, 1861; sold it to Bradley & Rulofson, 1863, then moved to Yosemite. Weed made the first mammoth plate views in Yosemite, 1864; photographs published in Hutchings' *Calfiornia* magazine; traveled later to Hawaii where he made mammoth plates of the volcanoes. See Hawaii.

WEED, ELIZABETH (MISS)
Active in San Francisco, 1896.

WEGENER, VIRGINIA E. (MISS)
Born in California, January 1882. Active in San Francisco, c. 1899-1900.

WEIDNER, CHARLES
View photographer with a studio at 121 Post Street, San Francisco, 1898; at 787 Market Street, 1915-16.

WEILE
Active in Sisson, 1895.

WEINGARTH, GEORGE
Born in Shelbyville, Indiana. Photographer in Shelbyville; arrived in Pasadena, 1879; operated the Ferndale Gallery at his ranch in Walnut and Orange Grove, 1882.

WEINTRAUB & ISAACS
Active at 28 Third Street in San Francisco, c. 1881.

WEITZ & DIJEAU
Operated the St. Louis Art Studio at 34 Third Street, San Francisco, 1885-86, 1888.

WEITZ, HUGO
Partner in Weitz & Dijeau, operating the St. Louis Art Studio at 34 Third Street, San Francisco, 1885-86, 1888; also operated in Chico, 1885-90, possibly on Salem Street; operated Weitz & Company, 512 Jessie, San Francisco, 1898.

WELCH & STEPHENS
James Henry Welch and W. B. Stephens licensed in Grass Valley, 1865.

WELCH, JAMES
Operator with Thomas J. Higgins, San Francisco, 1865; gallery at 659 Clay Street, 1867.

WELDING, JOE
Active in Oroville, 1888.

WELLER, D.
Active in Los Angeles, 1894, at 232 North Main; an attorney and notary, c. 1896.

WELLS
Partner in Jeffers, Wells & Kipps, "Artists and Photographers," at 1436 Market Street, San Francisco, 1880-82.

WELLS & DIJEAU
34 Third Street, San Francisco, 1887.

WELLS & LADY
Operated the California Art Gallery in Alturas, c. 1868.

WELLS & SEARS
Partnership of Thomas Wells and Charles Sears, stereo photographers active in Sonora, 1880.

WELLS, FRANK
Partner in Reigle & Wells, 428 Third Street, San Francisco, 1876; at 836 Market, 1877.

WELLS, GEORGE N.
Active in Redding, 1890.

WELLS, THOMAS W.
Born in California, 1858. Purchased Daniel Sewell's gallery in Sonora, 1879; partner with Charles L. Sears, 1880; Wells sold out to his nephew, William M. Harrington.

WELSH
Partner in Abell & Welsh, traveling photographers c. 1876; listed in Sawyer's Bar, 1873-95. Possibly Delos or John Oliver Welsh.

WELSH & CROMWELL
Active in Shasta, 1884.

WELSH, DELOS
Licensed in Los Angeles, 1862; Sonora, 1864; Suisun, 1864-65.

WELSH, JOHN OLIVER
Active in Red Bluff, 1863-85; Willows, c. 1880; Redding, 1886.

WELTON, ARTHUR F.
Partner of F. W. Hennessy in the Faber Photo Company, 217 ½ South Spring Street, Los Angeles, 1896.

WENDEROTH, FREDERICK A.
Daguerreian artist in partnership with Charles Nahl, 79 Broadway, San Francisco, 1854.

WENDT, HENRY
Active in Fort Jones, 1908-10.

WENZLER, MARTHA (MISS)
Born in Germany May 1884. Her family immigrated to the U.S., 1886. Active in San Francisco, c. 1899-1900.

WERNER, FRED
Operator for A. K. Varney studio, Placerville, 1899.

WESCOTT, C. H.
Proprietor with J. W. Archer of the Los Angeles Electric Copying House, 314 Buena Vista, Los Angeles, 1896.

WESNER, H. B.
Partner in Wesner Brothers Imperial Photographic Parlor with M. A. Wesner, D Street between Third and Fourth, San Bernardino, 1884. His wife was a milliner. Studio was at 217 Third Street, 1888; also at 441 Third Street, date uncertain.

WESNER, MICHAEL A.
Operated Wesner Brothers Photo Car out of San Bernardino, c. 1880; partner in Wesner Brother's Imperial Photographic Parlor, D Street between Third and Fourth, San Bernardino, 1884. Studio in Los Angeles at 129 West First, 1892; 120 North Spring Street, 1896-1907 or later.

WESTALL, E. (MISS)
Photographer in Susanville, 1905.

WESTERN PHOTO COMPANY
Publisher of stereoviews in Oakland; issued views of San Francisco earthquake and fire, April 18, 1906.

WESTERVELT, JAMES D.
Born in Michigan City, Indiana, August 21, 1844; began working there as photographer, 1857. Studio at 18 South Main Street, Los Angeles, 1884-89; partner in Cromwell & Westervelt, 603 East First, 1890; listed alone at 124 South Main, 1892-94; 218 South Broadway, 1895-96; 340 ½ South Broadway, 1897. Partner in Cromwell, Westervelt & Hammerton, The Great Eastern Photographic and Advertising Company, dates uncertain.

WESTON, EDWARD
Born in Highland Park, Illinois, March 24, 1886; died in Carmel, January 1, 1958. One of the world's great photographers, Weston arrived in California in 1906, taking portraits door-to-door. Studio in Tropico (now Glendale), 1911; founding member of Los Angeles Camera Pictorialists, 1914; member of the London Salon, 1917; travels in Mexico, 1923-26; studio with Johann Hagemeyer in San Francisco, 1925; studio in Carmel with photographer son, Brett, 1928; founded Group f/64, 1932; studio in Santa Monica with Brett, 1935; moved to Wildcat Hill, Carmel, 1938; published *California and the West*, 1940, and *50th Anniversary Portfolio*, 1952.

WESTON, HENRY
Active in Red Bluff, 1883-1900; studio on North Main Street, 1888; also in Anderson, 1886-1900.

WESTON, NATHANIEL
Photographic artist at 14 Second Street, San Francisco, 1865; photographic enameler, 1869; studio on First Avenue between Fourteenth and Fifteenth, 1878; partner with Laura T. Allen in Allen & Company, 1227 Market Street, 1887-88.

WESTWOOD, F. H.
Active in Gridley, 1890.

WESTWOOD, FRED
Active in Bangor, 1875.

WHEELER, FRANK
Produced "Improved Genuine Enameled Cards," probably in San Francisco, 1868.

WHIGHAM, RICHARD P.
Studio at 22 Kearny Street, San Francisco, 1896-1900; 739 Market Street and 1515 Fillmore, 1912-13; 739 Market Street and 2780 Mission "at 24," c. 1923+; operated as Whigham Studios, 1914.

WHISLER, H. D.
Active in San Diego, 1898.

WHITE
Active in Redding, 1890.

WHITE (MISS)
Active in San Jose, c. 1890s, partner in portrait gallery, "Misses White & Hubbell." Possibly Miss Lily E. White who was later active in Portland, Oregon.

WHITE & UNDERHILL
Studio in San Francisco, 1867-68, at 643 Washington; operated by George R. White.

WHITE, ELIZABETH (MISS)
Born in Missouri, May 1879. Active in Los Angeles, c. 1899-1900.

WHITE, G. WILLIAM (MRS.)
Active in Pasadena, 1886.

WHITE, GEORGE R.
Born in Maine, 1832. Operator with Addis & Koch, San Francisco, 1865; partner in White & Underhill, 643 Washington, 1867-68; photographed with Howland & Peters (or Peterson), 1869. Active in San Jose at 359 First Street, 1878-85.

WHITE, P. C.
Studio at 222 High, Los Angeles, 1883-84.

WHITE, PHILANDER CRAWFORD
Born in Pennsylvania, c. 1830. Registed as photographer in Eureka, 1884.

WHITE, RUFUS D.
Born in Ohio, 1835. Photographer with H. S. Beals, Sacramento, 1870.

WHITE, WILLIAM G.
Active in Pasadena, 1886.

WHITEFIELD, FRANK
Active in Red Bluff, 1910.

WHITNEY, MAY (MISS)
Active in Santa Barbara, c. 1900.

WHITTEN, C. H.
Active in Nevada City, c. 1900.

WIDDER, FREDERICK O.
Active c. 1895; partner in Blauert & Widder, San Francisco, 1904.

WIGGINS, ADA M. (MRS.)
Born in Vermont, May 1864. Active in Los Angeles, c. 1899-1900.

WIGHTMAN, M. (MRS.)
Active in Colton, c. 1890.

WIKER
Active in Lakeport, c. 1895.

WILBUR, PARKER B.
Advertised "Wilbur's Enameled Cards" in Colusa and Marysville, 1862-70; located at the Odd Fellows Building in Marysville, c. 1866. Also listed as P. R.

WILDMAN, C. E.
Mining engineer who took views of the Consumnes Mine area, El Dorado County, 1899.

WILKINSON, WILLIAM RYAN
Active in Horsetown, 1869-71.

WILLIAMS
Partner in Dames & Williams, 26 Montgomery Street, San Francisco, 1871.

WILLIAMS
Partner in Lovejoy & Williams, 128 Kearny, San Francisco, 1874.

WILLIAMS & NORTON
Studio located at 914 Market Street, San Francisco, c. 1885.

WILLIAMS & SAMUELS
Operated the Palace of Art on the corner of Tenth and Clay, Oakland, 1883.

WILLIAMS, B. S.
"Ground Floor Gallery," Healdsburg, c. 1890.

WILLIAMS, EDWARD A.
Partner in Fuller & Williams at 1150 Market Street, San Francisco, 1887; 1140 Market Street, 1887; 1140 Market Street, 1888.

WILLIAMS, H. E.
Active in Cassel, 1900; Shasta Springs, 1921-33. Initials may be H. N.

WILLIAMS, JOHN CALVIN
Photographer with Bayley & Winters, San Francisco, 1869; studio at 644 Market, 1877. Operated the Yolo Photographic Art Gallery, Woodland, 1885-94.

WILLIAMS, JOHN F.
Active in Dunsmuir, 1904.

WILLIAMS, MYRTLE (MISS)
Born in Missouri, July 1882. Active in San Diego, c. 1899-1900.

WILLIAMS, NELSON
Born in Canada, 1850. Active in Oakland, 1880.

WILLIAMS, S.
Traveling photographer, 1910.

WILLIAMS, S. N.
Born in Ohio, 1845. Active in Oakland, 1880; perhaps in Nevada, 1868.

WILLIAMS, SYLVESTER M.
Photographic printer with Bradley & Rulofson, 1865-70; photographic enameler at 319 Kearny Street, 1883.

WILLIAMS, W. I.
Partner in Williams & Norton, Baldwin Hotel Block, 914 Market, San Francisco, 1885-86; partner with W. G. Gregory in W. I. Williams & Company, 1887-88; sold out to J. H. Peters prior to 1895; active San Francisco, 1898; view photographer.

WILLIS
Active in Yreka, 1859.

WILLIS & HAMILTON
Studio in Yreka, 1859.

WILLOUGHBY, J. R.
Gallery at 638 Market Street, San Francisco, 1874.

WILSON, B. L.
Traveling photographer operating the California Photo Tent, c. 1880.

WILSON, GEORGE S.
Studio at 342 Kearny Street, San Francisco, 1895-98.

WILSON, MARY LEE (MRS.)
Born 1862; married to Ezra Morton Wilson, editor of the Adin newspaper, *Argus,* July 1889. Operated a photographic studio upstairs in her home in Adin, c. 1895-1905; continued active as photographer, c. 1917.

WILSON, W.
Born in England, 1826. In California by 1857. Daguerreian artist in Sacramento, 1860.

WILTON, THOMAS H.
Marine view photographer at 513 Folsom, San Francisco, 1887; worked as marine photographer with Elite Photo Studios, 1898.

WINBERG, JOHN ALBERT
Born in South Carolina, 1848. Photographic printer, San Francisco, 1869; operating in Chico, 1870; San Francisco, 1874-78; gallery at 650 Kearny Street, 1874-76; 652 Washington Street, 1877-78. Active in Sacramento, c. 1880. Also spelled Winburg and Wineberg.

WING & ALLEN
Partnership of Simon Wing and Bennett G. Allen, active in San Francisco, 1874-80. The company was run by George Hay and Mrs. B . G. Allen, 1883, and was called Allen & Hay by 1885.

WING & CHANDLER
Partnership of Jesse W. Chandler and John A. Wing, San Jose, 1877.

WING, JOHN A.
Partner in Wing & Chandler, San Jose, 1877.

WING, SIMON
Partner in Wing & Allen, 1874-80, San Francisco; gallery at 523 Kearny, 1874; at 342 Kearny, 1877.

WINGROVE, BESSIE (MRS.)
Active in Monson, c. 1894 or later, where she also served as Wells Fargo agent.

WINSLOW, MARY (MISS)
Born, c. 1870. Traveling photographer active in San Francisco, Yosemite, southern California and other locations, 1892-95+.

WINTEMUTE, J. S.
Active in Montague, Siskiyou County, 1895-1900.

WINTER, F. C.
Stereo photographer active in southern California, c. 1909; possibly partner of J. Z. Gilbert.

WINTER, ROBERT
Born in England, 1821. Photographic artist in San Francisco, 1866, at 605 Sacramento Street; partner with Wilbur F. Bayley, 618-620 Washington, 1869-70; listed as artist, 1871.

WISE & PRINDLE
Partnership of James Wise and Benjamin Augustus Prindle at 417 Montgomery Street, San Francisco, 1863-65.

WISE, C. T.
Active in Pitville, 1884.

WISE, JAMES
Photographic art gallery, 417 Montgomery Street, San Francisco, 1865-68; landscape painter at 645 Market Street, 1869-71.

WISKOTSCHILL, I. N.
Studio at 811 Market Street, San Francisco, 1879; B. F. Howland, operator.

WISMER, CHRISTIAN
Gallery at the corner of Encinal and Willow Street, Alameda, 1885; Santa Rosa, 1886, at 520 Fourth Street.

WITHINGTON, ELIZA W. (MRS.)
Born in New York, c. 1825, and married to George Withington. Came overland, 1852; excerpts of her diaries, owned by Huntington Library, were published in *Ho for California! Women's Overland Diaries,* 1980. Operated the Ambrotype Gallery in Ione City on Main Street, 1857-76. Descriptions and praise of her work was printed in the *Philadelphia Photographer,* 1874.

WITT & YOUNG
Active in Yreka, 1854.

WITZEL, A. W.
Born in Deadwood, South Dakota. Began photography work, c. 1896. Active in Los Angeles at 543 South Main, 1905; three studios, c. 1925, at 536 South Broadway, 6324 Hollywood Boulevard, and 1011 West Seventh Street.

WOHLEB, A. (MRS.)
Active in Oakland, 1896-97. Henry Wohleb may have been her son.

WOHLEB, HENRY
Operated the East Oakland Gallery, 556 12th Street, East Oakland, 1892-97.

WOLFE & KILDARE
Active in Sacramento, c. 1880, operating Capital Photographic Rooms at the southwest corner of J and 5th Streets.

WOLFE, H. F.
Studio at 166 Pacific Avenue, Santa Cruz, 1888.

WOLFE, JOSEPH M.
Photographer with Walter H. Cook, San Francisco, 1869.

WOLFE, SAMUEL A.
Born in Pennsylvania, 1845. Photographer with J. M. Ryan, San Francisco, 1865; partner in Chalmers & Wolfe, 611 Clay Street, 1867; photographer with Oscar Foss, 1869. Moved to Sacramento and bought out J. A. Todd at 84 J Street, 1875; 428 ½ J Street, 1880-88. Also spelled Wolf.

WOLFENSTEIN, VALENTIN
Born in Sweden; died in Los Angeles. Wolfenstein served in the Union Army during the Civil War; went to New Mexico afterward, and learned photography in Las Vegas. Opened a studio at Fort Sumner, 1868. Worked for Bradley & Rulofson in San Francisco, date uncertain; listed as a portfolio maker, 1869. Opened gallery in Los Angeles, top floor of the Temple Block; bought William Godfrey's Sunbeam Gallery, operating it until 1879. Photographed the Navaho and Apache. He returned to San Francisco and operated a gallery at 1144 Market Street, 1880. Wolfenstein traveled to Guatamala, Mexico, and back to Stockholm, opening galleries in each place.

WOOD & MICHEL
Active in Placerville, 1859, opposite the Cary House. Advertised a mammoth camera and took photographs of Hank Monk and Horace Greely.

WOOD, ALLY M. (MISS)
Active in San Jose, 1889.

WOOD, E. H.
Licensed in Marysville, 1864; Birchville, 1865.

WOOD, ROMANZO E.
Traveling landscape stereo photographer active in Marysville, Tahoe and vicinity, Santa Cruz, 1875-1905.

WOOD, T. W.
Active in Lower Lake, c. 1886.

WOOD, THOMAS M.
Purchased studio of Louis Celaire in Nevada City, 1859. See traveling.

WOODARD, E. A.
Stereo photographer in Fair Oaks; issued mining scenes.

WOODBURY (MRS.)
Active in San Buenaventura, c. 1886.

WOOD'S ART & PHOTOGRAPH GALLERY
WOOD'S ART GALLERY
WOOD'S GALLERY
WOOD'S PHOTOGRAPH GALLERY
WOOD'S PHOTOGRAPHIC ART GALLERY
Gallery operated under various names in Marysville in the Odd Fellows Building, northeast corner of D and Third, 1874-86. Owned by Amos Woods, 1874-79; by J. J. Reilly, 1879-86.

WOODS & THOMPSON
Licensed at 28 Third Street, San Francisco, 1865.

WOODS, AMOS
Operated a gallery in the Odd Fellows Building, northeast corner of D and Third, Marysville, 1870-79; sold out to J. J. Reilly, 1879, although Reilly continued to use the name Wood's Gallery until 1886. He moved to Oakland, operating a gallery at 451 Sixteenth Street, 1880-86.

WOODS, DAVID HOLMES
Born in Ohio. Daguerreian artist in La Grange, California, 1856; artist and photographer with a studio in Chico, date uncertain; operated Pacific Art Gallery, 1864-66; studio in San Francisco at 28 Third Street, 1866-68; artist at 645 Market Street, 1869. Moved to Sacramento, c. 1870. Active in Chico at 8th and Broadway, 1884-90.

WOODS, EDWARD L.
Active 1880-89.

WOODS, GEORGE REYNOLDS
Active in Chico, 1884-85.

WOODS, R. E.
Photographer and proprietor of the *Tahoe Tattler*, Tahoe City, 1883.

WOODWARD
Partner with Strunz in Elite Studio, Lodi, c. 1895.

WOODWARD, R. B.
Stereo photographer active in San Francisco.

WOODY, H. C.
Studio in Los Angeles, 1888, on west side of Alameda near Walters.

WORDEN, WILLARD E.
Born in Philiadelphia, Pennsylvania, November 20, 1968; died in Palo Alto, September 6, 1946. Began photography as a soldier in the Spanish-American War. Opened his first studio at the Cliff House, San Francisco, 1902; later on Stockton Street. Major art photographer who was awarded first prize in the photography competition at the 1915 Panama-Pacific International Exposition. Known for his pictorial images of the Golden Gate, full-rigged sailing ships, Chinatown, the 1906 earthquake aftermath, architectural and sculptural subjects, and many others.

WORTHINGTON, W. D.
Active in Chico on Main Street, 1877-78.

WORTHINGTON, WILLIAM THOMAS
Born in Indiana, 1844. Studio in Red Bluff, 1870-88; in Chico, 1880. Perhaps the W. T. Worthington of New Tacoma, Washington, 1883. Partner in Kraft & Worthington, San Francisco, 5 Stockton Street, 1890; 500 Valencia, 1895-96; 2025 San Jose Avenue, 1909.

WRIGHT, DANIEL F.
Operator with James T. Wise, San Francisco, 1865; photographer with William Shew, 1869.

WRIGHT, E. C.
Active in Santa Ana, 1898-1903; at 319 or 329 West Fourth Street, 1903.

WRIGHT, N. J. (MRS.)
Active in Coronado, 1893-95.

WRIGHT, PETER
Daguerreotype studio in his rooms behind the Benicia Iron Works, Benicia, 1855-57.

WRIGHT, WILBUR W.
Born in New York, 1840-42. Active in San Jose, c. 1870-88. Located at 284 Santa Clara Street, 1871; 289 First Street, 1883; 24 West Santa Clara, 1884; 34 West Santa Clara Street, 1886; corner of First and Santa Clara over the First National Bank, 1887; 24 West Santa Clara, 1888.

WULZEN, ALBERT H.
Born in Hanover, Germany, November 21, 1844; died in Berkeley, July 10, 1917. Arrived in San Francisco, 1856; became a citizen, 1868; employed by Dames & Williams, 1871; by Carleton E. Watkins, 1871-73; operated as a photographer, 1874-76; in Oakland, 1877-79, when he produced a seven-panel panorama of Oakland; traveling photographer operating the Pacific Art Gallery out of Weaverville, 1882; Oakland, 1886-1911; Berkeley, 1911. See Oregon.

WULZEN, OTTO
Photo printer with G. D. Morse, San Francisco, 1898.

WUNDERLICH
Billed as an "Instantaneous Photographer," operating a gallery at the corner of 4th and F Streets, Eureka, c. 1890.

WUNDERLICH BROTHERS
Bought the studio of Nathan B. Strong in the Cooper Building, Eureka, 1888.

WUTH, GUSTAV
Photo printer with Peters' Photo Gallery, San Francisco, 1898.

WYLIE, E.
Studio in Los Angeles, at 442 ½ South Spring, 1898; 341 South Spring, 1899.

WYLLIE, E. A. S.
Studio at the corner of L and Tulare in Tulare, 1886-89.

WYMAN, F. O.
Gallery at 2008 Mission, San Francisco, 1895.

YAMAGUCHI, TETSO
Colorist in San Francisco, c. 1900.

YAN LEE
Active in San Francisco, c. 1893.

YANDELL, ELIZABETH (MRS.)
Born in California, June 1864. Active in Inyo County, 1900.

YARD
Partner in Hill & Yard, stereo photographers in San Jose.

YATES, ELIZABETH B. (MISS)
Born in California, August 1871. Active in San Francisco, c. 1899-1900.

YEE, WY
Active in Los Angeles, c. 1890-1910.

YOLO PHOTOGRAPHIC ART GALLERY
Studio in Woodland; J. C. Williams, operator, G. N. Thomas, proprietor, 1875.

YONG, LAI
Born in China, 1840. Portrait painter and photographer, San Francisco. Gallery at 659 Clay Street, 1867; 743 Washington, 1871-75. Also known as Yong, Lai & Brother.

YONG, LAI & BROTHER
Active in San Francisco, 1882-83, at 743 Washington Street. Also known as Sing, Sung & Company.

YOSEMITE ART GALLERY
San Francisco. See C. E. Watkins.

YOUNG (MISS)
Traveling photographers operating as William S. Young & Daughter, active in Fresno County, c. 1874.

YOUNG & DAUGHTER, WILLIAM S.
Traveling photographers in Fresno County, c. 1874.

YOUNG, ANNIE C.
Born in Iowa, 1847. Photographic colorist, San Francisco, 1880. Wife of printer Jacob Young.

YOUNG, CONRAD
Active in Colusa, 1880; studio in Sacramento, 1890, at 415 J Street.

YOUNG, J. H.
Active in Redlands, 1896; Riverside, 1898.

YOUNG, JACOB
Printer in San Francisco, 1880s.

YOUNG, WILLIAM A.
Photographer with D. B. Taylor & Company, San Francisco, 1877.

YOUNG, WILLIAM J.
Active in Susanville, 1862-63; sold out to Townsend, 1863. Justice of the Peace in Susanville, 1864, resigned in June 1865.

YOUNG, WILLIAM S.
Traveling photographer operating as William S. Young & Daughter, active in Fresno County, c. 1874.

YOUNT, G. W.
Operated the Mystic Studio in Weaverville, 1896.

YREKA PHOTOGRAPH GALLERY
Studio in Yreka, 1880-93, operated by Jacob Hansen.

ZINK, HARRY FRANKLIN
Active in Chico, 1918-25.

ZINK, JOSEPH FRANZ
Active in Chico, 1912-28.

ZUBER, WILLIAM L.
Traveling daguerreotypist. Located in Mokelumne Hill, 1858; San
Andreas, 1859. Licensed in Drytown, 1864.

ZWARG
Active in Marysville, 1920.

ZWERNER
Active in San Francisco, 1899, partner in Lawhun & Zwerner with
Miss Marion Lawhun at 1303 Polk Street.

ZUBER, WILLIAM L.
Traveling daguerreotypist. Located in Mokelumne Hill, 1858; San
Andreas, 1859. Licensed in Drytown, 1864.

DENVER
PHOTOGRAPHIC ROOM,
CORNER F & LARIMER STS.,
DENVER, C. T.

This section owes much of its information to the pioneer work of Opal Harber, as it appeared
in Colorado on Glass: Colorado's First Half Century as Seen by the Camera *by Terry*
Wm. Mangan, Sundance Limited, Silverton, Colorado, 1975. The list was augmented
in several instances by Robert Lewis.

ABBOTT, C. L.
Active in Alamosa, 1880. Partner in Warnky & Abbott.

ABEL, DOLA (MRS.)
Operated studio at 135 Broadway in Denver, 1901.

ABRAHAM & ISAACS
Represented themselves as photographers in Denver, 1868, but bilked their customers. Also known as J. H. Abrahams & Company.

ACHLEITNER, OTTO
Active in Denver, 1897.

ACME GALLERY
Studio at 1232 Larimer Street in Denver.

ADAMS BROTHERS & COMPANY
Partnership operating in Goldfield, 1900-01.

ADAMS, E.
Active in Silverton, 1892.

ADAMS, F. S.
Active at 4th and Santa Fe in Pueblo, 1897.

ALEXANDER
Partner in Mulhall & Alexander, stereo photographers in Denver.

ALLEN, C. F.
Active in Denver, 1860s.

ALLEN, EDWIN S.
Active in Denver with W. G. Chamberlain, 1875-76.

ALLEN, INCREASE
Active in Colorado Springs, 1896.

ALLYN, MARK
Active in Central City with Henry Faul, 1861; partner in Rankin, Paris & Allyn in Denver, 1861.

ALTER, C. F.
Active in Denver, 1865-66.

ANDERSON & COMPANY, CHARLES W.
Studio in Denver with E. N. Clements, 1889, 1893-94. Located at 1705 Champa, 1893; 906 15th, 1894. Studio in Leadville, 1895-97. Located at 219 Harrison, 1895; 406 ½ Harrison, 1896-97.

ANDERSON & LEON
Gallery at 705 Champa, Denver, 1893; T. J. Leon. Also listed as Leon & Anderson.

ANDERSON, E. W.
Active in Boulder, 1898.

ANDERSON, J. AUGUST
Gallery at 428 16th, Denver, 1899.

APPEL, GUSTAVE R.
Active in Central City, 1887-89. Studio in Denver, 1892-1901; located at 1529 Larimer, 1892-96; Iron Building, 1897- 99; 1623 Curtis, 1900-01.

ARMANNTROUT, M. J.
Active in Golden, 1897-98, 1900. Also spelled Armentrout.

ARMINGTON, W. R.
Active in Brighton, 1897-1900.

ARMSTRONG, A. (MISS)
Worked with Mrs. S. Harkullas in Trinidad, 1876.

ARRINGTON, ED.
Active in Brush, 1900.

ATKINS, MASSARD & COMPANY
Active in Black Hawk, 1865.

AUGUSTINE, G. W.
Active in Aspen, 886.

AUGUSTINE, WILLIAM R.
Photographer in Aspen, 1885, 1887; also a grocer.

AULLS & CANNON
Parthership of H. L. Aulls and O. R. Cannon in Oro City.

AULTMAN, O. E.
Partner with J. F. Cook in Trinidad, 1891-1900, operating as Cook & Aultman. Also listed as A. E. Aultman.

AVERY, J. C.
Active in Lamar, 1888.

AVERY, JULIAN M.
Gallery in Denver at 1740 Larimer, 1893; 2862 Larimer, 1894.

BABBITT & HOWARD
Partnership of J. P. Babbitt and Howard operating in Buena Vista, 1881-82.

BABBITT, J. P.
Partner in Babbit & Howard operating in Buena Vista, 1881-82; listed alone, 1883.

BAKER, ELLIS W.
Gallery at 6 and 7 McClellan(d) Block, Denver, 1888-90.

BAKER, F. E.
Active in Greeley, 1894, 1896-1901.

BAKER, G. G.
Gallery at 800 14th, Denver, 1890.

BAKER, JOSIAH C.
Operated in Denver, 1882.

BALDWIN, GEORGE
Studio in the Iron Building, Denver, 1893.

BALDWIN, S. S.
Studio at 115 South 4th, Cripple Creek, 1900-01.

BALLOUGH, MONTE GEORGE
Active in Rico, c. 1895-1903.

BALSTER, F. S.
Active in Durango, 1893.

BANGLEY, C. W.
Active in Ft. Collins, 1882

BARBER, JOHN F.
Studio at 1515 California, Denver, 1897.

BARKER & GATCH
Partnership active in Colorado Springs, 1875.

BARKER & MELLEN
Stereo photographers in Gunnison, c. 1880s; probably George E. Mellen.

BARKER, A. W.
Active in Colorado Springs, 1873.

BARLEY & VILA
Partnership of Harie C. Barley and Joseph Vila operating at 16th northwest corner of Platte, Denver, 1890.

BARNEY, B. F.
Studio at 219-200 Symes Block, Denver, 1901.

BARNHART
Partner in Brubaker & Barnhart, operating in Black Hawk, 1885.

BARNHOUSE & WHEELER
Partnership of T. E. Barnhouse and Wheeler, operating in Lake City, 1877-79.

BARNHOUSE, T. E.
Active in Lake City, 1876-85; partner in Barnhouse & Wheeler, 1877-79. Operated in Grand Junction, 1885 when he was also a watchmaker; photographer, 1890-93.

BARRETT (MRS.)
Listed in Del Norte, 1878-79.

BARRY, DAVID F.
See Dakota.

BARTHELMESS, CHRISTIAN
See New Mexico.

BASS
Partner in Hosier & Bass, active in Boulder, 1889; in Manitou Springs, 1890; proprietors of Iron Springs Pavillion, Manitou Springs, 1892.

BASS, LAWRENCE P.
Active in Boulder, 1890-92, 1896-97.

BASTIAN, THOMAS H.
Active in Denver, 1882

BASTON, J. A.
Active in Durango, 1885-92.

BATES & MUHR
Studio at Larimer and 16th, Denver, 1883.

BATES & NYE
Partnership of William L. Bates and Willis A. Nye, operating in Denver on Larimer, corner of 15th, 1880; also listed at 141 West 2nd.

BATES & WEBB
Studio at Tabor Block, Denver, 1884-85.

BATES, WILLIAM L.
Partner in Bates & Nye, Denver, at 40, 41 and 52 Tabor Block, 1880; partner in Bates & Muhr, 1883, at Larimer and 16th; partner in Bates & Webb in the Tabor Building, 1884-85.

BEAMAN, E. O.
See Arizona.

BEATTY, FRANK
Operated with C. H. Wells, Denver, 1890.

BEAUCHAMP, LEVI
Active at Mountain City, 1860.

BECKNER, U. S.
Worked with W. H. Lawrence & Company in Denver, 1890.

BEEBE, CHRISTOPHER K.
Worked with J. E. Beebe in Denver, 1887-90.

BEEBE, JOHN E.
Active in Denver at 438 or 1716 Arapahoe, 1885-87; 1716 Arapahoe, 1888-92.

BEECHER
Active at Dawson City, 1896.

BEEHIVE PHOTOGRAPHIC STUDIO
Gallery in Denver producing stereoviews.

BELL, WILLIAM A.
Photographer with the Kansas Pacific Railroad, 1867.

BELLMAN, W. A.
Studio at 112 South Tejon, Colorado Springs, 1901.

BELLSMITH, H. S.
Studio at 1113 16th or 16th and Arapahoe in Denver, 1891-98.

BENECKE, ROBERT
Photographer with the Kansas Pacific Railroad, 1873.

BENELL, MARY
Active in Mosca, 1895-96.

BENFORD & COMPANY
Studio operated by Thomas Benford on Lawrence, southeast corner of 15th, Denver, 1883.

BENNET, AMOS S.
Active in Craig, 1893-96.

BENNETT, A. E.
Active in Leadville; located at 15 Emmett Block, 1889; 502 Harrison, 1900; operating Bennett's Studio, 1900; at 502 Harrison, 1901.

BENNETT, LESTER J.
With W. H. Jackson in Denver, 1882.

BENNETT, WILLIAM
Active at Denver, 1889.

BENSON, O. B.
Active in Fremont, 1891-92. See British Columbia.

BIERSTADT, ALBERT
Artist with Captain Lander's Expedition. Bierstadt was the premier Hudson River School painter working in the Western United States. Brother of Charles Bierstadt, stereo photographer from Boston who photographed Yosemite and other Northern California scenes in the 1860s.

BIGGART, ROBERT
With H. W. Watson, 1884.

BILLMAN, WILLIAM A.
Studio at 116 West Huerfano in Colorado Springs, 1896; Grand Junction, 1898; at 112 South Tejon, Colorado Springs, 1899-1901. Also spelled Billinan.

BINGHAM, ROBERT R.
Active in Denver, 1889; with H. Rothberger, 1890.

BINGLER, CHARLES
Active in Denver, 1877.

BINGLEY, DR. C. W.
Active in Golden, 1878-80.

BISHOP BROTHERS
Partnership operating in Delta, 1896-98.

BLACK, BELLE (MRS.)
Active in West Las Animas, 1885.

BLACK, C. H.
Active in Denver, 1887.

BLACK SISTERS
Partnership in Boulder, 1896-98.

BLACKLIDGE, CASSIUS F.
Active in Denver with H. W. Watson, 1883; Crested Butte, c. 1885.

BLAKE, F. P.
Active in Canon City, 1891.

BLANCHARD & SON
Studio operated by T. E. Blanchard and his son in Rifle, 1900-01.

BLUE, MONTE
Active in Rico, 1901.

BLUSH, EDWARD K.
Active in Denver with Albert E. Lickman & Company, 1023 17th Street.

BOHM, C. (MRS.)
Studio at 284 15th Street in Denver, 1886.

BOHM, CHARLES
Active in Denver; operating alone, 1870-72; partner with Charles M. Perry, 1872-75; studio at 284 15th Street.

BOHM, GEORGE
Active in Denver, 1877.

BOSTON & ZIEGLER
Partnership of Canon City, 1880.

BOSTON, J. A.
Partner in Boston & Ziegler in Canon City, 1880; Silverton and Durango, c. 1885; Durango, 1888-90; operating the Boston Studio in Denver at 906 17th Street, 1891; the Boston Photo Gallery in Durango, 1892-99; in Crested Butte, 1901.

BOTTOMLEY, J. B. (MISS)
Active in Pueblo at 239 North Union, 1895; in Lamar, 1899-1901.

BOTTOMLEY, T. F.
Studio at 239 North Union in Pueblo, 1893-94.

BOYCE & FABLING
Studio at 25-1617 Lawrence in Denver, 1899.

BOYCE, H. N.
Active in Aspen Junction, 1894.

BOYTON, ORVILLE R.
Gallery located at Harrison, corner of 4th, Leadville, 1894.

BRADLEY
Active in Denver, 1862.

BRADLEY
Partner in Kellum & Bradley, Pueblo, 1882.

BRADLEY, H. C.
Active in Ft. Collins, 1900-01.

BRANDT, EUGENE
Operated studio in Colorado Springs, c. 1875-76; sold out to L. K. Oldroyd, 1876.

BREWER
Partner in McEwen & Brewer, Denver, 1861.

BRICKER
Active in Denver, 1860. Also spelled Brecker.

BRIDGE, M. L.
Active in Colorado Springs, 1874.

BRISBOIS, ALFRED
Studio at 501-503 Harrison, Leadville, 1881-92. Also listed as M. L.

BRITTON, GEORGE FRANCIS
Active in Colorado Springs, 1897-98; located at 112 South Tejon, 1898.

BRITTON, WALTER R.
Active in Denver, 1894.

BROHM, A. C.
Studio at 1605 Market, Denver, 1892.

BROOKS & DRAKE
Active in Creede, 1893-94.

BROOKS, PERCY E.
Studio in Denver; located at 808 17th, 1895; 926 16th, 23 Tritch Block, 1896-97; 16th and Stout, Barth Block, 1898- 1900; 809 16th, 1901.

BROOKS, T. B.
Stereo photographer in Trinidad.

BROWN, HARMAN
Produced stereoviews in Leadville.

BROWN, WILLIAM H.
Active in Denver, 1886.

BRUBAKER & BARNHARDT
Partnership operating in Black Hawk, 1885.

BRUMFIELD, M.
Active in Gunnison, 1881-82; Ouray, 1892-96; Silverton, 1897, 1899-1900; Ouray and Silverton, 1898.

BUCKWALTER, C. E.
Partner with H. H. Buckwalter in Buckwalter Photographic Company, Denver, 1898-1900.

BUCKWALTER, HARRY H.
Active in Denver, 1897, at 713 Lincoln; partner with C. E. Buckwalter in Buckwalter Photographic Company, Denver, 1898-1900; listed alone at 713 Lincoln, 1901.

BUELL, J. E. (MRS.)
Active in Denver, 1900-01.

BUELL, OLIVER B.
Active in Denver, 1879. See British Columbia.

BUNKER, THOMAS.
Active in Walsenburg, 1896-98.

BUNN & SECKNER
Active in Ft. Collins, 1891.

BURK, EDWARD
Active in Denver, 1899.

BURLISS, WILLIAM
Active in Osler, 1901.

BURNHAM & CUTLER
Partnership of D. D. Burnham and M. L. Cutler operating in Aspen, 1889-90.

BURNHAM, D. D.
Active in Canon City, 1878; Leadville, 1879; Aspen, 1887-88; partner with M. L. Cutler in Burnham & Cutler, Aspen, 1889-90.

BURNS & COMPANY
Active in Boulder, 1893.

BUTTREE
Partner in Fore & Buttree, operating in Cripple Creek, 1900, at 406 East Bennett.

BYLES, C. W.
Active in Boulder, 1893-94.

CABLE, RUFUS E.
Possibly took the first photographs along Cherry Creek when Denver was still part of Kansas Territory, 1858. He opened an ambrotype gallery in the Denver Herald Building, 1860. Active in West Denver, 1860; left with Oliver Case, September 1860, setting up business in Colorado City. Also listed as Cables.

CALHOUN
Partner in Hosier & Calhoun, Denver, 1868, 1877-80, at 372 Larimer.

CAMPBELL, CHARLES
Active in Denver, 1881.

CANNON, O. C.
Active in Cortez, 1888.

CANNON, OTHNIEL R.
Active in Denver; studio at 100 Opera House Block, 1885; 16 Timerman Block, 1886. Partner in Aulls & Cannon, Oro City, with H. L. Aulls.

CANNON, W. A.
Active in Denver, 1880.

CARIBOU, COLORADO
Photographic gallery, 1871.

CARLSON, PETER
Active in Leadville; studio at 423 Harrison, 1897; 501 Harrison with Frank W. Grove, 1900; 425 Harrison, 1901.

CARLZEN, S. M.
Central City, after 1880.

CARMEN, THEODORE THOMAS
Studio at 1232 Larimer, Denver, 1895-97.

CARPENTER & TAYLOR
Active in Telluride, 1890-91, 1893.

CARPENTER, D. W.
Active in La Junta, 1890-93, 1895-98. Also listed as E. W.

CARPENTER, W. J.
Active in Silverton, 1889.

CARR, J. E.
Active in Rocky Ford, 1896.

CARVALHO, SOLOMON NUNES
Traveling with Fremont in Colorado, 1853. See California.

CASE, OLIVER
Left West Denver in 1860 with Rufus E. Cable, setting up business in Colorado City.

CASEMAN, FREDERICK
Active in Denver in 1890 with W. H. Jackson.

CASEY
Partner in Gilbert & Casey, Leadville, 1893.

CASTOR, W. H.
Studio in Denver, 1901, at 30-33, 1131-15th, McClelland Block.

CASWELL, A. E.
Active in Cripple Creek; at 255 Bennett, 1899-1900; 201 Lode, 1901.

CATTON, CHARLES
Active in Colorado Springs, 1874. Also spelled Cotton.

CECIL & HUNTER
Partnership of William W. Cecil and Hunter, operating at 1635 Stout, Denver, 1896.

CECIL, WILLIAM W.
Active in Leadville, 1892, at 425 Harrison; partner in Cecil & Hunter in Denver, 1896; studio at 1635 Stout, 1899; 1528 Champa, 1900-01.

CENTRAL PHOTO C0MPANY
Studio in Pueblo, 1894, at 407 Santa Fe.

CENTRAL PHOTO PARLORS
Studio at Fifteenth and Lawrence Streets, Denver, c. 1895.

CHADBAND, FRED J.
Active in Denver, 1882, with Benford & Company.

CHAIN & HARDY
Agents for W. H. Jackson & Company.

CHAMBERLAIN, WALTER A.
Son of William G. Chamberlain who learned photography in his father's studio. Worked for W. H. Jackson for a short time, 1881, then moved to Boulder.

CHAMBERLAIN, WILLIAM G.
Born in Newburyport, Massachusetts, November 9, 1815. Learned to make daguerreotypes in Peru. Visited California gold regions, 1850s; moved to Chicago, 1855. Active in Denver, 1861-89. Located at 1400 block of Larimer, 1862; assisted by Frank M. Danielson, 1864; at Larimer northwest corner of 15th, 1864-77; operating as Chamberlain & Son, 1881; sold his studio to Francis D. Storm, 1881. Operated with W. H. Jackson, 1887-88; part-time with W. H. Jackson, 1889. Prolific producer of stereoviews of mining districts and other scenes.

CHAPMAN, J. G.
Active in Walsenburg, 1894-95.

CHASE
Studio in Pueblo, 1899, at 304 North Main.

CHASE & LEWIS
Dana B. Chase and Lewis, stereo photographers active in Ouray, c. 1873-97.

CHASE & SWANSON
Partnership operating in Denver, 1887, at 1469 Larimer.

CHASE & WOLCOTT
Dana B. Chase and Wolcott, stereo photographers active in Trinidad, c. 1873-95.

CHASE, B. B. (MRS.)
Studio at 916 16th, Denver, 1898-1901. Probably the wife of Dana B. Chase.

CHASE, DANA B.
Operated the Erie Photograph Company with Henry O. Morris, traveling photographers active in Pueblo, Canon City, Fairplay, Lake City and Saguache, 1873-76; in Garland and Alma, 1878-79; partner in Wheeler & Chase in Del Norte, 1878-79; Canon City and Trinidad, 1879; Trinidad, 1880-85, 1887-89; Denver, 1890-91, at 15th southwest corner of Lawrence; Colorado Springs, 1892; Denver, 1893-95, at 910 16th; 910 13th, 1896; 916 16th, 1897.

CHASE, E. S.
Active in Silverton, 1892.

CHASE, H. L.
Active in Holyoke, 1901.

CHASE, JOHN A.
Active in Las Animas, 1876; Pueblo, 1878-79.

CHASE, MORTON E.
Active in Denver, 1888, at Larimer northwest corner of 15th; Greeley, 1890-93; operated Chase & Company in Louisville, 1893; Ouray, 1901.

CHASE'S PHOTO GALLERY
Owned by D. B. Chase in Trinidad, 1888, at 101 ½ East Main; J. F. Cook, operator and manager.

CHESTER, BENJAMIN
Active in Denver, 1889.

CHEW & JANDUS
Partnership of N. I. Chew and William Jandus, 372 Larimer, Denver, 1877.

CHEW, N. I.
Partner in Hawkins & Chew, Denver, 1876; partner in Chew & Jandus, 1877, at 372 Larimer.

CHILDERS, B. L.
Stereo photographer active in Boulder, 1884-85.

CHILDS, ALFRED R.
Partner in Parks & Childs, Leadville, 1881, at 103 East 5th.

CHRISTENSEN, D. E.
Active in Sanford, 1898-99.

CHRISTOPHER & COMPANY, E.
Active in Denver, 1882; Pueblo, 1883.

CHRISTY & SON
Active in Colorado Springs, 1892-93.

CHURCHILL, W. D.
Active in Breckenridge, 1882-88. Produced stereoviews.

CLARK & ERDLEN
Active in Salida and Buena Vista, 1889.

CLARK, C. H.
Active in Gunnison 1884; Salida, 1886-88.

CLARK, CHARLES B.
Active in Denver, 1876; with Charles Bohm, 1876-81.

CLARK, D. G.
Active in Boulder 1896-1900. Also listed as D. E. and D. G. Clark.

CLARK, FRANK E.
Active in Denver, 1888, with Alex Lozo.

CLARK, JOHN F.
Active in Denver, 1888.

CLARK, ROBERT A. (MRS.)
Active in Black Hawk, 1870-71.

CLARKE, EDWIN R.
Active in Pueblo, 1876-82, 1878-79; partner with F. A. Nims in Clark & Nims, Colorado Springs, 1883-84. Also spelled Clark; Colorado Springs also listed as Colorado City.

CLEGG, H. B.
Active in Victor, 1895-99; partner with H. M. Phillips, 1897, operating as Clegg & Phillips; studio at 102 South 4th, 1899. Also spelled Cleggett and Glegg.

CLEMENTS & ROSS
Partnership of E. N. Clements and J. L. Ross, at 1617 Champa, Denver, 1892.

CLEMENTS & VAN HORN
Partnership of E. N. Clements and J. W. Van Horn, operating in Leadville, 1881-82, studio at 103 East 4th.

CLEMENTS, EDWARD N.
Studio in Leadville, 1880-87; partner with G. Wakely, operating as Wakely & Clements, 1880, studio at 103 East 4th; partner with J. W. Van Horn, operating as Clements & Van Horn, 1881-82, studio at 103 East 4th; partner with W. Hutchinson, 1883, operating as Hutchinson & Clements, 103 and 105 East 4th; Harrison southeast corner of 4th, 1883- 84; 105 East 4th, 1885; 613 Harrison, 1886-87. Active in Denver, 1888-1901; studio at 1617 Champa, 1888-1900; partner with J. L. Ross, operating as Clements & Ross, 1892; at 1624 Curtis, 1901.

CLEVELAND, E. L.
Active in Canon City, 1900-01.

CLINTON, J. L.
Successor to F. A. Nims. Studio at 18 South Tejon Street, Colorado Springs, 1888-94, 1896; partner in Rudy & Clinton, 1889. Published boudoir views of scenes in New Mexico and Colorado for the the Colorado Midland Railway, Pike's Peak Route.

CLOUGH, H. R.
Active in Pueblo, 1883.

COLBY
Active in Denver and Pike's Peak Region, 1860.

COLLIER, JOSEPH M.
Born in Aberdeenshire, Scotland, July 15, 1836; died in Denver, 1910. Arrived in Central City in 1871 where he operated a studio until 1878; partner in Collier & McLean, 1874-75; in Denver, 1878-1901; studio at 415 Larimer, 1878-86; 1643 Larimer, 1887-1901. Photographed the Ute.

COLLIER, ROBERT
Active in Denver, 1883-84; with J. Collier, 1883.

COLLINGS, C. H.
Stereo photographer active in Georgetown.

COLLINS & GREGG
Active in Boulder, 1878.

COLLINS, M.
Stereo photographer in Boulder City.

COLLINS, RICHARD B.
Active in Boulder, 1876-77; Central City, 1878; Leadville, 1880, at 54 Harrison; Durango, 1882; Denver, 1883.

COLLINS, WALTER
Studio at 802 Harrison, Leadville, 1892.

COLORADO ARTOTYPE COMPANY
Operated by H. M. Williamson, also known as Williamson & Company in Denver, 439 16th, opposite Courthouse, 1886; 333 16th, 1888; 329 16th, 1889.

COLORADO SPRINGS COMPANY
Stereoview publishing company in Colorado Springs.

COLORADO STEREOGRAPH COMPANY
Operated in Boulder, c. 1907; George H. Hall, photographer.

COLORADO VIEW COMPANY
Partnership of Ed Tangen and George H. Hall, stereo photographers active in Boulder.

COLPAS, THOMAS J.
Active in Denver with H. M. Williamson, 1889.

COMSTOCK, H. L.
Operated the H. L. Comstock & Company studio in Denver, 1892, 1894; studio at 906 15th, 1892; partner in Voice & Comstock, 1893; H. L. Comstock & Company, 1894; studio at 2100 Larimer, 1893-94.

CONCANNON, THOMAS M.
Studio at 18th, southeast corner of Blake, Denver, 1884-85.

CONLEY & COMPANY
Studio at 325 Santa Fe, Pueblo, 1895-96.

CONVERSE, H. C.
Studio at 11 Evans Block, Denver, 1901.

COOK & AULTMAN
Partnership of J. F. Cook and O. F. Aultman operating in Trinidad, 1890.

COOK, J. F.
Operator and manager of Chase's Photo Gallery, Trinidad, 1888, at 101 ½ East Main; partner with O. F. Aultman, operating as Cook & Aultman, 1890.

COOKER, A.
Active in Silver Cliff, 1901.

COOPER, H. D.
Studio at 25 South Weber Street, Colorado Springs, 1898.

CORNISH, J. J.
Active in Del Norte, 1880-88; Chromo, 1890-98. Also listed as J. I. Cornish.

CORRTNEY, O. W.
Active in Telluride, 1897.

CORY & GOHNER
Partnership of A. S. Cory and Gohner, Durango, 1890.

CORY, A. S.
Active in Durango, 1889-90; partner in Cory & Gohner, 1890.

COWARD, F.
Studio at 115 West 4th, Pueblo, 1893.

CRAM, ELLA
Active in Golden, 1899.

CRONYN, W. W.
Active in Pueblo, 1889-91; studio at 523 Santa Fe, 1889; 6th and Santa Fe, 1890-91.

CROOKHAM, GEORGE
Partner with Charles Bohm in Denver, 1876.

CROOKS
Active in Gunnison.

CROOKS & MILLER
Active in Monte Vista, 1895-1901. Also listed as Cooks & Miller.

CROSS, WALTER
Active in Denver with Horace E. Hunt, 1890.

CUNNINGHAM & COMPANY
Studio of Alexander M. Cunningham in Colorado Springs, 1884-85.

CUNNINGHAM, ALEXANDER M.
Active in Colorado Springs operating the Cunningham & Company studio, 1884-85.

CURRAN, THOMAS J.
Partner with H. M. Williamson in Denver, operating as Williamson & Curran at 16th and Tremont, 329 16th, opposite the Courthouse, Denver, 1890.

CURRIER, FRANK
Studio in Omaha, Nebraska. Produced stereviews of Colorado scenes.

CURTISS, FRANK F.
Active in Pitkin, 1881.

CUTLER, M. L.
Active in Aspen, 1889-90, partner with D. D. Burnham, operating as Burnham & Cutler.

DAGGETT, FRANCES (MRS.)
Active in Fulford, 1900-01.

DALES, G. S.
Active in Denver, 1873.

DALGLEISH, GEORGE
Active in Georgetown, 1890-1901; partner in Dalgleish Brothers, 1890.

DANIELSON, FRANK M.
Active in Denver with W. G. Chamberlain, 1864; Central City, 1864-68; in Denver with George M. Silsbee, 1870; with Charles Stimson, 1868-72; studio at 377 Larimer, 1874. Also spelled Donaldson and Donelson.

DARE, D. D.
Photographer from Cheyenne, Wyoming, who produced stereoviews.

DAVID, V. E.
Active in Pueblo, 1872.

DAVIS, C. L.
Active in Lansing, 1889.

DAVIS, O. T.
Active in Walsenburg, 1893; La Veta, 1898.

DAVIS, ROBERT M.
Studio at 1107 16th, Denver, 1887.

DAYTON, M.
Active in Brush, 1899-1900.

DEAN, FRANK E.
Active in Gunnison, 1883-89; Crested Butte, Gunnison and Lake City, 1890-94; Gunnison and Lake City, 1895; Crested Butte, Gunnison and Lake City, 1896-1900; Grand Junction, 1901. Also listed as F. F. Dean.

DELAVAN, W.
Active in Denver, November 1868; Central City, 1868-69. Also spelled Delevan. A deaf mute artist, Delavan proposed to paint a panorama of all the major towns along the route of the Union Pacific Railroad. May have taken the photograph of the hanging execution of Sanford Dougan, 1868.

DEMAREE, CHRISTOPHER
Active in Denver, 1884.

DEMAREE, W. HARVEY
Studio at 1126 15th, Denver, 1895.

DEMAREE, WILLIAM H.
Active in Denver 1882-97; with M. E. Chase, 1888; with F. E. Post, 1889. Also spelled Demare.

DENNIS & FEW
Partnership of A. W. Dennis and William E. Few, operating in Canon City, 1884-85. Also spelled Dennes.

DENNIS, A. W.
Active in Canon City, 1881-84; partner with W. E. Few, operating as Dennis & Few, 1884-85; in Colorado Springs, 1888-1901. Also spelled Dennes.

DENVER PHOTO COMPANY
Located at 203 Times Building, Denver, 1898.

DENVER PHOTOGRAPHIC STUDIO
Operated by A. French in Denver, 1889, at 910 16th; managed by L. C. Graves.

DESMOND, D. C.
Active in Antonito, 1892; Trinidad, 1894-1900. Also listed as DesMond.

DIAMOND, DANIEL
Studio in Craig, 1897-99.

DICKERMAN, ALLEN
Studio in Holden Block Number 2, Pueblo, 1892.

DICKERSON, A. C.
Stereo photographer active in Idaho Springs and Silver Plume.

DODGE, FRANK
Active in Denver with W. H. Watson, 1884; with Stephan, George & Company, 1888.

DOER, GEORGE E.
Studio at 72 Railroad Building, Denver, 1890.

DRAKE
Partner in Brooks & Drake operating in Creede, 1893-94; partner in Hoer & Drake, 1895.

DRENKEL, D. R.
Active at Aspen, 1890-91, 1893-95, 1899; studio at 209 Monarch Street, c. 1895.

DRUMFIELD
Active at Silverton, 1896.

DUDLEY, M.
Active at Grand Junction, 1893.

DUHEM BROTHERS
Partnership of Constant and Victor M. Duhem, active in Denver, 1869-72; studio at 448 Larimer, 1872-79. Produced a great volume of stereoviews of Colorado scenes. The studio ended in bankruptcy, 1874.

DUHEM, CONSTANT
One of the Duhem brothers and married to Maggie Hoak, an assistant in the Duhem Brothers studio.

DUHEM, VICTOR M.
One of the Duhem brothers.

DUNTON, OSCAR E.
Active in Leadville, 1892, 1901; studio at 223 East 6th, 1892; 802 Harrison, 1901.

DYER, JOHN W.
Active in Denver; with Wells & King, 1888; at 1113 16th, 1890; 2413 16th, 1892; 730 15th, 1893.

EASTMAN, C. H.
Active in Gunnison, 1901.

EASTMAN, G. L.
Active in Georgetown, 1880; with the Jackson Party, 1881.

EASTMAN'S PHOTOGRAPH & FERROTYPE GALLERY
Active in Denver, 1880s.

EATON, W. H.
Active in Colorado Springs, 1891.

EDGEWORTH, REUBAN M.
Active in Denver, 1880-81; with H. W. Watson, 1880.

EDWARDS, THOMAS
Active in Erie, 1888-89.

EGGLESTON BROTHERS
Partnership of E. M. and Wellington K. Eggleston active in Boulder, 1865; Georgetown, 1870-71.

EICHLER
Active in Denver, 1885.

ELITE PHOTO STUDIO
Located at 425 South Tejon, Colorado Springs, 1901.

ELITE PHOTOGRAPHIC GALLERY
Operated by D. J. Ryan or Ryan & Company, proprietors of the studio at 16th and Curtis and Cass and Graham Block, Denver, 1893-95.

ELITE STUDIO
Gallery in Leadville, 1895-98; located on the Union Block, 1897-98.

ELLINGSON, JOHN O.
Active in Telluride, 1898; Denver, 1900-01, at 1740 Larimer.

ELLINGTON, GEORGE
2100 Larimer, Denver, 1894. Also spelled Ellingston.

ELLIOT, J. A.
Active in Pueblo, 1883-84.

ELLIOTT, R. F.
Active in Georgetown, 1873-76, 1878-81; Silver Plume, 1882; Georgetown, 1883-88. Name also spelled Elliot. See Reiff & Elliot.

ELLIS, A. B.
Active in Trinidad, 1893.

ELLIS, CARLETON F.
Active in Denver 1884-87; with J. E. Beebe, 1885. Also spelled Charleton.

ELY & HILDRETH
Partnership of W. S. Ely and Hildreth, active in Longmont, 1898-1901; also listed as Hildreth & Ely.

ELY, W. S.
Active in Georgetown, 1897-1901. Partner in Hildreth & Ely or Ely & Hildreth operating in Longmont, 1898-1901.

ELZE, EDWARD
Active in Silver Cliff, 1897.

EMERY, CHARLES E.
Operated the New Photograph Rooms, 1880; in Silver Cliff, 1882, 1884-85; Canon City, 1886-91; Colorado Springs, 1893-1901, at 18 South Tejon.

ENDLESS
Active in Salida, 1895.

ENDSLEY & COMPANY, DAVE
219 and 318 Harrison, operating as Leadville Photo & View Company, 1899.

ENSMINGER, CLARA
Active in Hyde, 1888; Yuma, 1891.

ENSMINGER, MARCELLA
Active in Yuma, 1893.

ERDLEN, C. W.
Active in Buena Vista, 1885-87; Salida and Buena Vista, 1889; Salida, 1890; Saguache and Salida, 1891; Buena Vista, Moffat, Monarch, Saguache, St. Elmo, Salida and Villa Grove, 1892; Salida, 1893, 1896-98. Also spelled Erdler.

ERICKSON, C. A.
Active in Ridgway, 1891; Montrose, 1892; Montrose and Ridgway, 1893; Delta and Telluride, 1894; Rico and Telluride, 1895; Telluride, 1896; Florence, 1897-1900.

ERIE PHOTOGRAPH COMPANY
Operated by traveling photographers Dana B. Chase & Henry O. Morris, 1873-76, in Canon City, Fairplay, Lake City, and Saguache.

EUREKA GALLERY
Located at 2200 Larimer, Denver, 1893.

EVANS, ALBERT L.
Active in Denver with D. Lamon, 1887.

FABLING
Partner in Boyce & Fabling, Denver, 1899; studio at 25 1617 Lawrence.

FARMER, ALBERT
Active in Denver, 1890.

FARR, H. L.
Studio at 525 Santa Fe, Pueblo, 1892.

FAUL & ALLYN
Partnership of H. Faul and Mark Allyn, Central City, 1861.

FAUL & SAINT
Partnership of H. Faul and T. G. Saint, Central City, 1862.

FAUL & WALDO
Partnership of H. Faul and Waldo, Central City, 1861.

FAUL, HENRY
Studio in Central City, 1861-64. Partner in Faul & Waldo and Faul & Allyn, 1861; partner in Faul & Saint, 1862; partner with J. Glendinen, 1862, operating as Glendinen & Faul; in Denver, August-October 1864. In Central City at the Astor House, 1863; near the corner of Blake and Cherry Creek, across from the Elephant Corral, 1864. Faul is purported to have taken the first photograph of a hanging in Colorado, the execution of William S. Van Horn, October 1864.

FEN, W. E.
Active in Montrose, 1888.

FERRIS, D. (MISS)
Active in Golden City, 1860.

FEW, WILLIAM E.
Partner with A. W. Dennis in Canon City, 1884-85; operating alone, 1886.

FINN, CHARLES E.
Studio at 300 Larimer, Denver, 1881.

FISHER, M.
Studio at 2nd and Bennett, Cripple Creek, 1896; 32 North Tejon, Colorado Springs, 1901. Also listed as M. A. Fisher.

FISK, HAROLD
Active in Loveland, 1896.

FLACH, GUSTAVE A.
Studio at 1617 Champa, Denver, 1887.

FLEISCHER, A. H.
Active in Denver, 1875.

FOOS, W. W.
Active in Burlington, 1871. Also spelled Foose.

FOOTE, THOMAS R.
Active in Denver, 1888.

FORE & BUTTREE
Studio at 406 East Bennett, Cripple Creek, 1900.

FOREMAN & EHRLICK
Active in Boulder, 1900.

FOREMAN, WALTER H.
Active in Denver, 1886-95; studio at 377 Larimer, 1886; 1529 or 1537 Larimer, 1887-95; in Boulder, 1899.

FORSDAHL, M.
Active in Colorado Springs, 1890; Greeley, 1899-1900.

FOX, H.
Active in Denver, 1870.

FRANCIS & GRIFFIN
Data unknown.

FRASER, W. C.
Active in Denver, 1892-98; studio at 2108 Larimer, 1892-93; 2052 or 2055 Larimer, 1894-95; 2058 Larimer, 1896; 2052 or 1527 Larimer, 1897; 1827 Larimer, 1898. Also listed as W. A. Fraser.

FREEDMAN & COMPANY, T.
Active in Denver, 1890.

FREEMAN, ALFRED
Active in Colorado Springs, 1892-1901. Studio at 117 East 4th, Pueblo, 1892; 32 North Tejon, 1895-1901.

FREEMAN, J. B.
Active in Pitkin, 1884; White Pine, 1885-86.

FREEMAN, W. E.
Active in Denver, 1890.

FRENCH, ARTHUR
Operated the Denver Photographic Studio in Denver, 1889, at 910 16th; managed by L. C. Graves.

FRICKE & COMPANY
Active in Canon City, 1892-1901. Also spelled Frick, Fricks, Frickle.

FROST, ADDIE (MRS.)
Active in Hooper, 1897.

FROST BROTHERS
Active in Idaho Springs, 1896-98.

FROST, S. F.
With Captain Lander's Party.

FULLILORE, H.
Active in Las Animas, 1898.

FURMAN, R. H.
Studio at 325 Santa Fe, Pueblo, 1893.

GALBRAITH & COMPANY, HARVEY
Stereo photographers at Manitou; successors to H. W. Stormer. Also spelled Galbreaith.

GALBRAITH, H. (MRS.)
Stereo photographer in Manitou, 1878-85; bought Thurlow's studio, 1878. Possibly the wife of H. Galbraith. Also spelled Galbreaith, Galbreath.

GALBRAITH, HARVEY & LYLES
Stereo photographers operating in Manitou, c. 1885.

GARBANATI, HENRY
Active in Central City, 1864-66.

GARRISON BROTHERS
Active in Rifle, 1901.

GATCH
Partner in Barker & Gatch, Colorado Springs, 1875.

GAYLORD, C. W.
Active in Leadville, 1899.

GEM PHOTO COMPANY
Located at 115 East Pikes Peak Avenue, Colorado Springs, 1901.

GHORMLEY
Partner in Spracklen & Ghormley, Trinidad, 1880.

GILBERT & CASEY
Active in Leadville, 1893.

GILBERT, JOHN E.
Active in Ouray, 1883; Silverton, 1885.

GILL, DELANCY
Listed in Trinidad directory, 1888.

GILLE, CHARLES
Active in Denver, 1875. Also spelled Gillei.

GILLEN, WILLIAM J.
Active in Denver, 1885-92. Studio at 300 Larimer, 1885; 326 Larimer, 1886; 1510 Champa, 1887; 1332 Larimer, 1888; with W. H. Foreman, 1889; on Ashland, northwest corner of Gallup Avenue and Highlands, 1890-91; Golden Avenue southwest corner of Morrison Road and Colfax, 1892. Studio in Cripple Creek, 1893-97; at North 4th or 116 1st, 1895-97. Name also spelled Gillian.

GILLINGHAM, CHARLES L.
Active in Colorado Springs, 1882-90, 1901; at 324 Huerfano, 1901. Also spelled Gilligan.

GILPIN, JOSEPH A.
With W. H. Jackson in Denver, 1887.

GLENDINEN & FAUL
Partnership of J. Y. Glendinen and H. Faul, Central City, 1862. Also spelled Glendiner.

GLENDINEN, JOHN Y.
Visited the gold regions 1859-60; partner with Henry Faul, Central City, 1862; listed alone, 1863-64. Name also spelled Glendenen, Glendenin, Glendinin, Glendiner.

GLENN
Partner in Harlan & Glenn, Colorado Springs, 1893. Also listed as Glem.

GLEW, EUGENE E.
Partner in Harlan & Glew, Colorado Springs, 1892. Studio at 27 South Weber, Colorado Springs, 1900-01.

GLOBE PHOTO COMPANY
Located at 906 15th, Denver, 1895-96.

GOEHNER & COMPANY
Located in Denver.

GOEHNER, GUSTAVE A.
Active in Denver; with Charles Bohm, Denver, 1876-78; operating alone, 1880.

GOEHNER, GUSTAVE A. (MRS.)
Active in Denver, 1876.

GOEHNER, H.
Active in Denver, 1876.

GOERKE & SON, PAUL
Active in Colorado Springs, 1900; Manitou, 1901.

GOFF, O. S.
See Dakota.

GOHNER
Partner with A. S. Cory, operating as Cory & Gohner in Durango, 1890.

GOINS, JAMES
Studio at 348 Larimer, Denver, 1881.

GOLDSBERRY & COMPANY
Active in Manitou Springs, 1897.

GONNER & HURD
Active in Durango, 1892.

GONNER, FRANK
Active in Durango, 1891-1901.

GOODMAN & BROTHERS
Active in South Pueblo, 1880.

GOODMAN, CHARLES H.
Active in Pueblo, 1882; Pitkin, 1883; Montrose, 1887-88; Silverton, 1900; Bluff, Utah, 1901. Also listed as J. H. Goodman.

GORE
Partner in Grove & Gore, active in Pueblo, 1864-73.

GORMER, FRANK
Active in Durango, 1899.

GOSHA & COMPANY, C. E.
Active in La Junta, 1894; Pueblo, 1897-98, at 304 North Main.

GRABILL, JOHN C. H.
See Dakota.

GRAHAM, JAMES B.
Active in Denver, 1875.

GRAHAM, S. B.
Active in Colorado Springs, 1892-93.

GRANGER, D.
Active in Loveland, 1892.

GRAVES, LEMUEL C.
Manager of the Photographic Studio, 910 16th, Denver, 1889; operating with A. French.

GREEN, JOHN I.
Studio in Denver, 1885-1901. Located at Blake southeast corner of 18th, 1885-86; 18th and Holladay, 1889; 1800 Market, 1890-1901.

GREEN, ROBERT H.
With F. D. Storm, Denver, 1885.

GREGG, B. FRANK
Partner in Collins & Gregg, Boulder, 1878; partner in Harlan & Gregg, Colorado Springs, 1891.

GREGG, THADDEUS
With J. E. Beebe, Denver, 1886; listed alone, 1890.

GREGORY
Partner in Neel Brothers & Gregory, Trinidad, 1889.

GRIFFIN
Partner in Francis & Griffin.

GRIGG, SAMUEL A. D. F.
Active in Denver, 1882-90; with W. H. Jackson, 1882; with F. D. Storm, 1889.

GROSS
Partner in Kerwin & Gross, Aspen, 1901.
GROSS, NICHOLAS
Active in Denver, 1898.

GROVE & GORE
Partnership in Pueblo, 1864-73; Frank W. Grove
.
GROVE & HELME
Studio at 41 Union Block, Leadville, 1887.

GROVE & LUKE
Studio at Union Block 425 Harrison, Leadville, 1888.

GROVE, CHARLES ELMORE
Studio at 1625 Welton, Denver, 1899-1901.

GROVE, FRANK W.
Active in Pueblo, 1864-73, partner in Grove & Gore; also in Las Ani-

mas, 1873. Listed alone in Colorado Springs, 1874; studio in Leadville, 1887-96. Partner in Grove & Helme, 1887, at 41 Union Block. Partner in Grove & Luke, 1888; located at Union Block or 425 Harrison, 1888-91; 523 Harrison, 1893-96. Studio in New Castle, 1897. Gallery in Leadville, 1898-1901; at Harrison and 7th, 1898; 5th and Harrison, 1899-1901.

GROVE, S.
Listed as partner in Smith & Grove in Pueblo, 1864-73.

GROVES, R. W.
Stereo photographer active in Pueblo.

GURNSEY & BRANDT
Partnership of Byron H. Gurnsey and Eugene Brandt, stereo photographers in Colorado Springs, 1875.

GURNSEY, B. H. (MRS.)
Active in Colorado Springs, 1881-82. Possibly the wife of Ben Gurnsey, continuing the photography business after his death.

GURNSEY, BYRON "BEN" H.
Active in Pueblo, 1872-75; with Eugene Brandt 1875; in Colorado Springs, 1872-80.

GYRA, RUDOLPH
Studio at 313 Larimer, Denver, 1884.

HAFFNER, FRANK J.
With J. E. Beebe, 1890; Iron Building, 17th southeast corner of Arapahoe, Denver, 1892.

HALL, C.
Active in Elizabeth, 1895.

HALL, GEORGE H.
Stereo photographer in Boulder, c. 1907; manager of Colorado Stereograph Company.

HAMILRON & KENDRICK
Studio at 906-910 17th Street, Denver.

HANNA
Active in Las Animas, 1877.

HANNA, A. J.
Active in Cortez, 1895.

HANNA, O. R.
Active in Mancos, 1887, 1895.

HANSMANS
Partner in Williams & Hansmans, Alamosa, 1884-85.

HARDING, C. C.
Active in Telluride, 1889-1900.

HARGROVES, J. J.
Partner with Mrs. Strong, operating as Strong & Hargroves, Ft. Collins, 1880; also active in Buena Vista.

HARKULLAS, S. (MRS.)
Partner with Miss A. Armstrong, Trinidad, 1876; operating alone, 1878-81. Also listed A. Herkules.

HARLAN & GLENN
Partnership in Colorado Springs, 1893; Also listed as Glem.

HARLAN & GLEW
Partnership in Colorado Springs, 1892; Eugene E. Glew.

HARLAN & GREGG
Active in Colorado Springs, 1891; Frank B. Gregg.

HARLAN, ANDREW JAMES
Active in Fremont, 1891-92; in Victor and Barry, 1896-98.

HARPER
Partner with George E. Mellen, operating as Mellen & Harper in Gunnison, 1881.

HARRIS, HENRY
Active in Denver, 1891.

HARRISON, C. H.
Active in Golden, 1875.

HARTMAN & HUBBARD
Partnership of William F. Hartman and E. W. Hubbard at 1625 Welton, Denver, 1898.

HARVEY
Stereo photographer; partner in Galbreaith, Harvey & Lyles and Galbreaith, Harvey & Company, in Manitou, c. 1885.

HARVEY DRY PLATE COMPANY
Active in Manitou, 1884.

HASSELL
Partner in Smith-Hassel Company, studio at 1644 Broadway, Denver, 1899-1901.

HASSELL, GILBERT
With W. H. Jackson, Denver, 1890.

HASTINGS, C.
Studio at 25 South Weber, Colorado Springs, 1897.

HATHAWAY, FRANK H.
Partner in Townsend & Hathaway, 6 McClelland Block, 15th and Lawrence, Denver, 1894-96.

HAVIS, J. M.
Active in Colorado Springs, 1898-1900.

HAWES, M. A.
Active in Las Animas, 1897-97, 1901.

HAWKINS, B. A.
Active in Denver, 1873-82; partner with N. I. Chew, 1876, operating as Hawkins & Chew; located at 377 Larimer, 1877.

HAYNES, F. J.
See Dakota.

HAYTER, C. H.
Active in La Junta, 1897-1900.

HEAD, EDWARD J.
Active in Denver, 1884.

HEADLEY & MORGAN
Partnership of E. B. Headley and Morgan, Colorado Springs, 1886.

HEADLEY, E. B.
Stereo photographer in Colorado Springs; partner with Morgan, 1886.

HEIN BROTHERS
Active in Canon City, 1900-01.

HELME, WILLIAM
Partner with F. W. Grove, operating as Grove & Helme, 41 Union Block, Leadville, 1887.

HEMENWAY
Active in Colorado Springs, 1873.

HENTIG, ARTHUR S.
Studio at 48 Jackson Building, Denver, 1890.

HERSOM, C. E.
Active in Manitou Springs, 1892-93.

HETHERINGTON, G. H.
Active in Rocky Ford, 1899.

HICKS, A. W.
Studio at 45 King Block, Denver, 1899-1900.

HIESTAND, J. G.
Active in Colorado Springs; operated Ute Iron Springs Photo Gallery in Ute Pass before 1891.

HILDRETH & ELY
Partnership of W. S. Ely and Hildreth in Longmont, 1898-1901; also listed as Ely & Hildreth.

HILLERS, JOHN L.
See Arizona.

HILTON, E. F.
Active in Alamosa, 1890-91; Bachelor and Creede, 1893; Creede, 1894.

HINCKE, CHARLES
Active in Parker, 1890-97.

HINE, T.
Stereo photographer in Manitou Springs intermittently with Chicago, Illinois, 1864-78. Made stereoviews of Colorado published by Copelin & Son, Chicago.

HISTELHAUBER, JOSEPH
Studio at 318 Harrison, Leadville, 1899.

HOAK, MAGGIE
Colorist in Duhem Brothers gallery; became the wife of Constant Duhem.

HOER & DRAKE, J. A.
Active in Creede, 1895.

HOLT, ALEX
Active in Aspen, 1893.

HOOK, W. E.
Operated the Hook View Company at Manitou Springs, 1880-90; Colorado Springs, 1891-97; studio at 509 North Tejon, 1896-97.

HOPKINS & REED
Active in Coal Creek, 1897.

HOPKINS, BENJAMIN "BENNIE" SANDERSON
Born in St. Catherines, Ontario, Canada; died in Denver, March 26, 1915. Arrived in Colorado in 1881, and began working for Rose & Company in 1885. Partner with J. K. Rose, 1886-96; known as Rose

& Hopkins, 1896-1901. Studio located at 16th Street, corner of Laramie, c. 1890; 40, 41, and 52 Tabor Block, 1896-98.

HOPKINS, S. D.
Active in Florence, 1897-99.

HOPKINS, T. E.
Active in Colorado Springs, 1880-82.

HOPKINS, THADDEUS E.
Active in Colorado Springs, 1878-81.

HOPPING, CHARLIE H.
Active in Central City, 1860-63.

HOSE, ORVILLE L.
Active in Crested Butte, 1882-84, at the Mazzula coal mine; also located at the Railroad Station.

HOSFORD, C. H. (MRS.)
Studio at 506 Harrison, Leadville, 1895.

HOSIER & BASS
Active in Boulder, 1889; Manitou Springs, 1890-92; proprietors of Iron Springs Pavillion, 1892.

HOSIER & CALHOUN
Studio at 372 Larimer, Denver, 1868, 1877-80.

HOSIER, F. H.
Active in Denver, 1883; Boulder, 1884-87. Also listed as I. H. Hosier.

HOUGHTON, A. S.
Active in Durango, 1899-1900.

HOVER BROTHERS
Active in Saguache, 1891.

HOWARD
Partner in J. P. Babbitt & Howard, Buena Vista, 1881-82.

HOWARD, E. A.
Active in Canon City, 1892.

HOWARD, M. B.
Studio at 115 West 4th, Pueblo, 1891-1901.

HOWE
Partner with N. H. Talbot in Evans, 1880.

HOWES, M. A.
Active in Las Animas, 1896.

HUBBARD, E. W.
Partner in Hartman & Hubbard, at 1625 Welton, Denver, 1898.

HUBBELL, J. ALBERT
Studio at Times Building or 1547 Lawrence, Denver, 1899-1901.

HUBBELL, ROYAL
Active in Canon City, 1896-1901.

HUDSON, JOSEPH L.
Studio at 372 Larimer, Denver, 1883.

HULL, ARUNDEL C.
See Nebraska.

HUNT, HORACE E.
Active in Denver, 1887-88; with W. H. Foreman, 1226 14th, 1888.

HUNTER
Partner in Cecil & Hunter, operating at 1635 Stout, Denver, 1896.

HUNTER, ELIJAH C.
Studio at 33-1617 Lawrence, Denver, 1898-1901.

HURD
Partner with Frank Gonner, operating as Gonner & Hurd, Durango, 1892.

HUTCHINSON & CLEMENTS
Partnership of William Hutchinson and Edward N. Clements, at 103 and 105 East 4th, Leadville, 1883.

HUTTON, J. D.
Missouri River Reynolds Expedition, 1860.

IMES, LEWIS
With Hiestand in Manitou Springs, 1890.

INES, LEWIS
Studio at 1 Alkire Block, Denver.

IRISH, ELWOOD W.
Studio at 523-525 Charles Building, 15th corner of Curtis, Denver, 1891-92.

IRON SPRINGS PAVILLION
Operated by Hosier & Bass in Manitou Springs, 1892.

ISAACS, CHARLES
Partner in Abraham & Isaacs; represented themselves as photographers in Denver, 1868, but bilked their customers. Also known as J. H. Abrahams & Company.

IVES, LIEUTENANT
Colorado River, 1857.

JACKMAN, BRYON D.
Active in Denver, 1890.

JACKSON, D. LINCOLN
16th and Arapahoe or 1113 16th, Denver, 1900-01.

JACKSON, FREDERICK D.
Active in Denver 1880-90; with A. E. Rinehart, 1881; with W. H. Jackson, 1885, 1887-89.

JACKSON, WILLIAM HENRY
Active in Colorado, 1879-97. See Nebraska.

JACKSON-SMITH PHOTO COMPANY
Located in Denver, 1898-99.

JACOBS, A. L.
Studio in 309 South Tejon, Colorado Springs, 1898; 61 Good Block, Denver, 1900.

JAMERSON & TOWNSEND
Studio in 1617 Lawrence, Denver, 1899.

JAMES & MAULL
Active in Colorado, 1874.

JAMES & SON
Studio at Steele Block, Denver, 1883-84.

JAMES & STURTEVANT
Active in Boulder, 1891. Also mispelled Strutevant.

JAMES, C. (JOHN) (WILLIAM H.)
Studio at Room 9, Steele Block, Denver, 1883.

JAMES, C. C.
Active in La Junta, 1901.

JANDUS, WILLIAM
Partner with N. I. Chew, operating as Chew & Jandus, 372 Larimer, Denver, 1877.

JENNINGS & RUSSELL
Studio at 326 Larimer, Denver, 1884.

JENNINGS, CHARLES H.
Active in Denver, 1884-88; with J. E. Beebe, 1885; with W. H . Russell, 1888.

JENSON, A. M.
Studio at 304 Main, Pueblo, 1900-01.

JERREL & MOTZ
Active in Canon City, 1876.

JOHNSON & WOODRING
Active in Crawford, 1887.

JOHNSON, A. D.
Studio at 1740 Larimer, Denver, 1898.

JOHNSON, A. P.
Active in Denver, 1899.

JOHNSON, ADOLPH R.
Active in Denver, 1887.

JOHNSON, C. H. (MRS.)
Active in Del Norte, 1896. Listed as Mrs. C. H. Jones, 1893-1901.

JOHNSON, CHARLES
Active in Denver, 1886-90.

JOHNSON, I. M.
Operated the Rocky Mountain Gallery of Art, Greeley, 1870-74. Also listed as J. M. or M. Johnson.

JOHNSON, JOHN P.
With H. Watson, Denver, 1882.

JONES & LEHMAN
Active in Denver, 1897-99; studio at 1615 Arapahoe, 1897; 1113 16th, 1898-99.

JONES, A. H.
Active in Grand Junction, 1894-95.

JONES, C. H. (MRS.)
Active in Del Norte, 1893-1901. Listed as Mrs. C. H. Johnson, 1896.

JONES, J. WESLEY
See California.

JONES, THOMAS
Active in Denver, 1889.

JORDON, C.
Located at 16 1132 15th, Denver, 1901.

JUDKINS, DAVID R.
With C. C. Wright, Denver, 1885.

JUDSON, FRED D.
With W. H. Jackson, Denver, 1890.

KALLISCHER, MAX
Active in Denver, 1893-94; at 16th and Curtis, 1893; Cass and Graham Block, 1894.

KAUFFMAN, M. E.
Active in Leadville, 1896; Louisville, 1898.

KAY, WILLIAM
Active in Georgetown, 1893.

KEARNEY, L. A.
Active in Aspen, 1901.

KELLEY, JAMES H. "HORSETHIEF"
Born in Eaton, Maine, 1850; died in Aspen, 1928. Itinerant photographer working around Aspen at the turn-of-the- century. Traded photographs for food for himself and his horse.
    Janet Landry and Joan Lane, "Horsethief" Kelley and his Camera, Estate of A. Bertha Masterson, Aspen, Colorado, 1972.

KELLIHER' S PHOTOGRAPH GALLERY
Active in Georgetown, 1870.

KELLUM & BRADLEY
Active in Pueblo, 1882.

KENNADY, M. A.
Monte Vista, 1887-94. Also known as Bert Kennedy.

KENNETT, R.
Active in Denver, 1890-91; at 1023 17th, 1890; 19-21 Times Block, 1891.

KEPLER, V. M. (MRS.)
Active in Central City, 1895-99.

KERR
Partner in Opie & Kerr, Aspen, 1891.

KERWIN & GROSS
Active in Aspen, 1901.

KILGORE, WILL A.
Active in Longmont, 1892-93.

KING, JOHN H.
Active in Denver, 1882.

KING, WILLIAM S.
Partner in Wells & King, 1136 15th, Evans Block, Denver, 1887-93.

KIRBY, J. MARTIN
Stereo photographer active in Boulder.

KIRKLAND BROTHERS
Partnership of Charles D., George W. and P. G. Kirkland, with stu-

dio at 377 Larimer, Denver, 1874-75.

KIRKLAND, CHARLES D.
Born in Ohio, 1851; died in Denver, August 20, 1926. Worked for William Chamberlain in Denver c. 1868, together with brother George W. Kirkland. Partner with George W. and P. G. Kirkland, operating as Kirkland Brothers in Denver at 377 Larimer, 1874-75. Moved to Cheyenne, Wyoming, where he augmented his photography with the manufacture of lithium printing-out paper under the label Kirkland Lithium Paper Company. He moved the company to Denver in 1894 and sold it to the George Eastman Company of Rochester, New York, a few years later. Opened a studio at 1617 Champa, Denver, 1901, and sold it in 1926.

KIRKLAND, GEORGE W.
Partner with Charles D. and P. G. Kirkland, operating as Kirkland Brothers, studio at 377 Larimer, Denver, 1874-75. With R. F. Elliot, Georgetown, 1876.

KIRKLAND, P. G.
Partner with Charles D. and George W. Kirkland, operating as Kirkland Brothers, studio at 377 Larimer, Denver, 1874- 75.

KLINE, JOSEPH L.
Denver printer for Charles Bohm, 1878; with J. M. Goins, 1881.

KNEELAND, IRA D.
Studio at 2200 Larimer, Denver, 1893.

KNIGHT, FRED L.
Active in Akron, 1897-99, 1901.

KNIGHT, H. C.
Active in Lake City, 1897-98.

KNOERZER
Active in Denver.

KOESTER, EMIL
With Charles Bohm, Denver, 1881.

KOONZ & SON
Active in Greeley, 1886.

KRUEGER, CARL E.
Studio at 24-26 East Bijou, Colorado Springs, 1901.

KUHN & WHEELER
Active in Del Norte.

KUHN, S. M.
Active in Colorado Springs, 1873-74; Del Norte, 1875. Also listed as S. N. Kuhn.

KULL, A. F.
Listed at 907 17th, Denver, 1898.

KURTZ
Partner in Slack & Kurtz, operating in Boston and Springfield, 1889. Also listed as Kurts.

KUYKENDALL & WHITNEY
Active in Ouray, 1884-85.

KUYKENDALL, FRANK
Active in Silver Cliff, 1881-82; Maysville, 1882-83.

KUYKENDALL'S NEW GALLERY
Located at southwest corner of Ohio and Emery. Also spelled Kuy Kendall.

L'IMPEROALE PHOTOGRAPH GALLERY
Located at 10-13 Iron Building or 17th, corner of Arapahoe, Denver, 1893.

LAMON, DAVID
Active in Denver; at 1740 Larimer, 1887; 1634 Larimer, 1891-92.

LAND, LEWIS G
Active in Bellevue, c.1880.

LANG, MARY L.
Active in Langdon, 1911-12.

LARIMER (MRS. & MRS.)
Listed in the Trinidad directory, 1888.

LARIMER, WILLIAM J.
Active in Denver, 1865, on Larimer Street; in Julesberg, 1867.

LARKINS, E. W.
Active in Colorado City, 1890-92.

LAW, FREDERICK
Active in Boulder, 1881-84.

LAWRENCE & COMPANY, W. H.
Active in Denver, 1890-92; studio at 1108-1114 16th, 1892.

LAWRENCE, A. J.
Located at 16th and Lawrence, Denver, 1873-74.

LAWRENCE, C. S.
Studio at 219 Harrison, Leadville, 1901.

LAYCOCK, F. M.
Active in Hygiene (also spelled Higiene and Hygene), 1887-92; partner in F. M. Laycock & Son, 1891-92; also in Delta, 1891-92.

LAYCOCK, HENRY E.
Active in Berthoud, 1893; Hygiene, 1894-95, 1897.

LEACH, J. A.
Active in Akron, 1888.

LEADVILLE PHOTO & VIEW COMPANY
Located at 219 and 318 Harrison, Leadville, 1899, operated by Dave Endsley & Company.

LEHMAN
Partner in Jones & Lehman in Denver, 1897-99; studio at 1615 Arapahoe, 1897; 1113 16th, 1898-99. Partner in Schedlin & Lehman, 412 Bennett, Cripple Creek, 1900-01. Also spelled Schedin.

LENARD
Partner in Lockhart & Lenard, Longmont, 1873.

LEON & ANDERSON
Located at 1705 Champa, Denver, 1893. Also listed as Anderson & Leon; also spelled Lion.

LEON, T. J.
Located at 910 16th, Denver, 1892; partner in Anderson & Leon at 705 Champa, 1893.

LETELLIER, THOMAS R.
Active in Pueblo, 1886-93; studio at 19 Union, south side, 1886; 19 ½ Union, 1887; 122-126 South Union, 1888-93.

LETTLE, E.
Active in Wetmore, 1884-85.

LEVY, H. M.
Located at Santa Fe and 16th, Pueblo, 1899-1901. Initials also reversed, M. H.

LEWIS, C. C.
Active in Lawson, 1890.

LEWIS, EMMA C. (MISS)
Active in Denver, 1880. Employed by B. E. Hawkins.

LICKMAN, ALBERT E.
Located at 1023 17th or 17th and Arapahoe, Denver, 1890.

LIEBHOLDT, GUSTAVE
Active in Denver, 1887-89; with G. A. Flach, 1887.

LINGUIST, N.
Active in Julesberg, 1898.

LINQUIST, B. A.
Active in Central City, 1886.

LITTLE, EMMET
Active in Rosita, 1881; Silver Cliff, 1887-88; Siloam, 1893.

LOAR, WILLIAM H.
Active in Denver, 1876.

LOCKHART & LENARD
Active in Longmont, 1873.

LOGAN, FENAMORE J.
With H. W. Watson, Denver, 1883.

LONGSHORE & WARD
Active in Leadville, 1882.

LORENZEN, HENRY
Active in Central City, 1867.

LOTUS PHOTO STUDIO
15 Evans Block, Denver, 1901.

LOVEJOY, E.
Active in Henry (formerly Lariat), 1886.

LOWE, MINNIE (MRS.)
Active in Westcliff, 1899-1900.

LOWELL, N. T.
Active in White Pine, 1887-89, where he also operated a drugstore.

LOWELL, W. J.
Active in Del Norte, 1885, 1888-90. Initials also reversed, J. W.

LOZO, ALEX
Studio at 910 16th, Denver, 1890-91.

LUKE & WHEELER
Located at 427 Harrison or Harrison opposite Clarendon Hotel, Leadville, 1879-81.

LUKE, J. W.
Partner in Russell & Luke, Colorado Springs, 1874-76. Also listed as Russell & Lake.

LUKE, WELLINGTON O.
Active in Leadville, 1882-92. Studio at 41 Union Block Harrison and 4th, 328 Harrison, 1882-86; 103 East 5th, 1888- 89; 422 Harrison, 1890; Hall's Corner, 1891; 523 Harrison, 1892. Studio in New Castle, 1893. Also listed as W. A. Luke.

LUNDQUIST, N.
Active in Julesberg, 1887-89.

LUPEIN, EDWARD REAL
Active in Denver, 1894-99; studio at 1624 Curtis, 1898.

MACKIE, J. M.
Active in Brush, 1901.

MACOMBER, ALONZO
Active in Denver, 1885.

MACURDY, J. C.
Stereo photographer in Leadville, at 9 Morgan Street, c. 1880s.

MADDEN, T. H.
Active in Ft. Morgan, 1901.

MAFFIT, L. H.
Active in Colorado Springs, 1875.

MAHER, NELLIE (MISS)
Active in Denver, 1890.

MARCHINGTON, C.
Active in Idaho Springs, 1901.

MARSH, A.
Active in Georgetown, 1886.

MARSH, B. T.
Active in Greeley, 1875-90. Also listed as B. F.

MARSH, C. M.
Active in Greeley, 1891-1901; operated as Marsh & Son, 1901.

MARSHALL, EDWARD S.
Studio at 1367 Larimer, Denver, 1888-91.

MARTIN & MILLS, M. E.
Partnership operating at Gold Hill and Wall Street, 1896.

MARTIN & PEERS
Active in Central City, 1879-80.

MARTIN, A. P.
Active in Victor, 1900.

MARTIN, ALEXANDER
Born in Scotland; died in Denver, 1929. Active in Boulder, 1874-78; Central City and Denver, 1879; Georgetown, 1884, 1888. Operating in Denver, 1888-1901; studio at 1634 Larimer, 1888-90; Clear Creek Avenue, southeast corner of Coyote, 1893; 1740 Larimer, 1894-97; 53 Tabor Block, 1898; 2500 19th, 1899-1900; 1629 Platte, 1901.

MARTINDALE, C. S. (MRS.)
Active in Aspen, 1892.

MASONHEIMER, JOHN
Active in Denver, 1889-90; with W. H. Jackson, 1889.

MASSARD
Partner in Atkins, Massard & Company, Black Hawk, 1865.

MASTER, G. H. (MRS.)
Active in Ft. Collins, 1874.

MASTERS & TAYLOR
Located at 372 Larimer, Denver, 1874.

MASTERS, O. E.
Studio at 201 West Bennett, Cripple Creek, 1900.

MASTERS, WILLIAM H.
Studio at 372 Larimer, Denver, 1873-75.

MATTESON, SUMNER W.
Born in Decorah, September 15, 1867; died 1920. Active in Denver, 1897. Traveled by bicycle around the U. S., particularly the Southwest, taking photographs of Indians and giving illustrated lectures.

MAULL
Partner in James & Maul, operating in Colorado, 1874.

MAYES, N. M.
Active in Pueblo, 1885-86, at 122 ½ Union; in Denver, 1886, at 15th and Larimer; 6 McClelland Block, 1887; in Pueblo, 1888-91, at 407 and 413 ½ Santa Fe.

MAYNE, W. J.
Active in Denver, 1875.

McBETH, CHARLES S.
Active in Denver, 1876.

McCLINTOCK, J. A. (MRS.)
Active in Julesburg, 1899-1901.

McCLURE, LEWIS
Active in Denver, 1887-99; with W. H. Jackson, 1895; on his own, 1899. Also spelled Louis.

McCORMICK, JAMES A.
Active in Denver, 1890.

McDONALD & COMPANY, GEORGE W.
Active in Denver, 1890-1901. Studio at 12th and Larimer or 1206 Larimer, 1890-95; 1740 Larimer, 1896; 1537 Larimer, 1897; 1031 17th or Iron Building, 1899-1901.

McDONALD, J.
Active in Denver, 1874.

McDONALD, ROBERT
Active in Denver, 1863-68; partner in William & McDonald, 1867-68.

McEWEN & BREWER
Active in Denver, 1861.

McGILLYCUDDY, V. T.
Active in Black Hills, 1857.

McGRAW, E. E.
Active in Boulder, 1889-90.

McGREGOR, A. Q.
Active in Boulder, 1878.

McKEE, A. F. (MRS.)
Active in Montrose, 1899-1901. Also listed as A. S. Montrose

McKEE, THOMAS M.
Born in Scary Creek, West Virginia, March 17, 1854. Raised in Nashville, Tennessee, McKee studied painting and traveled the South pursuing his art. He studied photography in St. Louis, Missouri. He opened a gallery in Montrose, Colorado, 1887, and later in Ouray and Old Dallas. He made views along the line of the Rio Grande Southern, made some of the first x-ray photographs, and used the first motion picture camera, a Kinetescope, in Colorado, 1895. He made many photos of Ute Indians and the ruins at Mesa Verde.

McKINNEY, ALBERT S.
Active in Black Hawk and Central City, 1866-68, 1874; Georgetown, 1868-69; Central City, 1870; partner in Reed & McKinney, Denver, 1871-72, and in Central City and Georgetown, 1873; operating alone in Georgetown, 1875. Also spelled McKinny, McKenney.

McKIRAHAN, ANDREW
Active in Denver, 1882, with W. H. Jackson.

McKIRRAHN & WHITTER
Partnership of C. A. McKirrahn and Whitter, studio in Georgetown, 1883; Leadville, 1888-89, at 506 Harrison. Also spelled McKirhan. Produced stereoviews.

McLEAN, LACHLAN
Active in Denver, 1874; Central City, 1875-77; Georgetown, 1878-81; Golden, 1884; Idaho Springs, 1885-86, 1890, 1892-1901.

MEALEY & PHILLIPS
Active in Pueblo, 1879-81.

MEALEY & SAVIGNY
Pueblo, 1884.

MEALEY, MARTIN W.
Active in Pueblo, operating A. W. Martin & Company, 1880-89. Studio at 4th and Santa Fe, 1880-84; 115 West 4th, 1886-89.

MEALY & SON
Studio located in the Holden Block on South Union, Pueblo, 1893.

MEILE & STURTEVANT
Active in Boulder, 1893-94.

MEILE, LOUIS
Active in Boulder, 1888, 1897-99; Denver, 1889-92; partner in Voice & Meile, 1890-92, at 21st and Larimer. Also spelled Meille or Miele.

MELLEN & HARPER
Partnership of George E. Mellen and Harper, Gunnison, 1881.

MELLEN & COMPANY, GEORGE E.
Active in Gunnison, 1881-83; Colorado Springs, 1888; in Denver with W. H. Jackson, 1889; in Manitou Springs with J. G. Hiestand, 1890; also in Denver, 1890.

MEYERS, L.
Studio at 2615 Larimer, Denver, 1899.

MEYERS, ROSCOE H.
Active in Denver with George Stephan, 1887.

MICHAELIS, H.
Active in Denver, 1889.

MICHEL, J.
Active in Denver, 1888.

MICKEL, D. E. (MISS)
Active in Denver, 1860.

MICKEY, D. E.
Active in Del Norte, 1896-98.

MILLER
Partner in Crooks & Miller, Monte Vista, 1895-1901. Also listed as Cooks & Miller.

MILLER & NUTT
Partnership of Thomas C. Miller and James W. Nutt in Alma; portrait, landscape and stereo photographers.

MILLER, HARRY
Billed as the "Tramp Photographer," 1890s.

MILLER, R. B. (MR. & MRS.)
Active in Trinidad, 1893, 1895-97.

MILLER, T. C.
Active in Alma, 1881, 1883-84, 1886.

MILLON, G.
Active in Gunnison, 1884.

MILLS, CHARLES H.
Active in Denver, 1889-90; operating Mills Engraving Company, 1889. Studio in Pueblo, 1893, at 407 Santa Fe.

MILLS, M. E.
Partner in Martin & M. E. Mills, Gold Hill and Wall Street, 1896.

MILNER
Partner in Shaffner & Milner, stereo photographers in Pueblo.

MINER'S PHOTOGRAPHING COMPANY
Active in Victor, 1897.

MINTON & TRASK
Partnership of Ray S. Minton and Trask, studio at 343 Gallup Avenue, Highlands, Denver, 1894.

MITCHELL, A. M.
Active in Canon City, 1889.

MITCHELL, A. W.
Active in Denver, 1889-98; studio at 505 Times Block, Denver, 1889; 78 Barth Block, 1890; 329 16th, 1897-98.

MITCHELL, LILLIE L. (MRS.)
Studio at 710 Santa Fe Avenue, Denver, 1900.

MONROE-THOMPSON PHOTOGRAPH COMPANY
Located at 808 16th, Denver, 1901.

MOORE, G. L.
Active in Boulder, 1891.

MOORE, G. W.
Active in Ouray, 1892-93.

MOORE, H. C.
Active in Telluride, 1889, 1899-1900; in Rico, 1891-93.

MOORE, HARRY G.
Partner in Royer & Moore with W. C. Royer, at 1645 Curtis, Denver, 1893.

MORGAN, D. P.
Partner in Headley & Morgan with E. B. Headley in Colorado Springs, 1886. Active in Longmont, 1890; Cripple Creek, 1894-97, located at 113 2nd, 1894-96; 10 Wilbur Block, 1897.

MORGAN, SAMUEL
Active in Denver, 1900.

MORRIS, HENRY O.
Operated the Erie Photograph Company with Dana B. Chase, traveling photographers active in Pueblo, Canon City, Fairplay, Lake City and Saguache, 1873-76.

MORRISON, E. G.
Active in Canon City, 1880-83.

MORRISON, ROBERT
Active on Rose Street, Georgetown, 1891-92.

MORTIMER, FRANK L.
Active in Leadville, 1882, at 223 Harrison; also in Denver, 1882, with W. H. Jackson.

MOTENDALE, C. S. (MRS.)
Active in Aspen, 1892.

MUHR
Partner in Bates & Muhr in Denver, 1883, located at Larimer and 16th.

MUHR, ADOLPH
Studio at 48 King Block, Denver, 1893.

MULHALL & ALEXANDER
Partnership in Denver producing stereoviews.

MURPHY, A. C.
Active in Evergreen, 1891-99.

NAST & COMPANY, CHARLES A.
Died in Denver, 1931. Nast arrived in Denver from Cincinnati, Ohio, in 1875. Initially, he worked as a reporter for the Denver Tribune and covered the Black Hills Gold Rush where he fought in the Sioux with Captain Jack Crawford and Wild Bill Hickock. Active in Denver, 1880-1901. Located at 372 Larimer, 1880-81; with H. Watson, 1882; with Charles Weitfle, 1883; with C. C. Wright, 1884; with A. E. Rinehart, 1885-90; at 1624 Curtis, 1891-93; on Harman, 1893-96; 1624 Curtis or 16th and Curtis, 1897-1901.

NAST & MARTIN
Partnership of Alexander Martin and Charles A. Nast in Denver at 372 Laramie Street; also active in Central City. Portrait, landscape and stereo photographers.

NAST BROTHERS
Studio at 372 Larimer, Denver, 1882.

NAST, JOHN E.
Active in Denver, 1881-84; with H. W. Watson, 1884. Partner in Needles & Nast, 229 ½ Union, Holden Block, Pueblo, 1888.

NEAL, A.
Active in Morrison.

NEEDLES & COMPANY, JOHN T.
Active in Leadville, 1881-84. Studio at 116 East 4th, 1881; 116 East 4th or 600-613 Harrison Avenue, 1881-84. Operated in Pueblo, 1887-91; studio at 229 ½ Union, 1887; 14 Holden Block, 1888-91.

NEEDLES & NAST
Located at 229 ½ Union, Holden Block, Pueblo, 1888.

NEEDLES, JOHN T.
Partner in Stone & Needles, Holden Block, or 39 ½ Union, South Pueblo, 1884-86, 1888.

NEEL BROTHERS
Located at Trinidad, 1888-92; also operated as Neel Brothers & Gregory, 1889.

NEEL BROTHERS & GREGORY
Active in Trinidad, 1889; also known as Neel Brothers.

NEEL, J. W.
Active at Erie, 1888.

NELLES, W. A.
Partner with R. M. Pollard, operating as Pollard & Nelles in Denver, 1889.

NELSON, AARON
Active in Central City, 1890, 1892-93.

NELSON, L. E.
Located at 1017 Pearl, Boulder, 1900-01.

NELSON, O. A.
Studio at 19 Harrison, Leadville, 1897-98.

NEVILLE, DAVID S.
Studio at 111 South Tejon, Colorado Springs, 1900-01.

NEVINS, GEORGE O.
Stereo photographer in Colorado Springs.

NEW PHOTOGRAPH ROOMS
Operated by Charles E. Emery, 1880.

NEW YORK PHOTOGRAPH GALLERY
Perhaps a trade name for Abraham & Isaacs, who reputedly cheated their customers.

NEWBY & COMPANY, L. C.
Active in Aspen, 1892-95; Victor, 1899, west of Hotel Victor.

NEWBY & WILSON
Located at 125 South 3rd, Victor, 1900.

NEWBY, M. W. (MRS.)
Active in Denver with B. E. Hawkins, 1881.

NEWTON, HOWELL DEWITT
Active in Salida, 1890-1901; also practiced dentristry, 1893.

NICHOLS, GEORGE B.
Active in Colorado City, 1888.

NILSON, CARL
Active in Denver, 1881.

NIMS & COMPANY
Operated by F. A. Nims and E. R. Clarke in Colorado Springs, 1886.

NIMS, F. A.
Active in Colorado Springs, 1882; partner with E. R. Clark in Clarke & Nims, 1883-84; partner in Nims & Company, 1886. Sold out to J. L. Clinton.

NOBLE, OLIVER D.
Active in Denver, 1887; with A. E. Rinehart, 1888; with C. H. Wells, 1890.

NOCKIN, EDWARD
Partner in Oiler & Nockin, 1617 Champa, Denver, 1898. Operated as Nockin Photo Company, 1899-1901.

NOFTS, ROBERT W.
Goldfield, 1896.

NONPAREIL PORTRAIT & PUBLISHING COMPANY
Active in Colorado Springs, 1898, at 24-26 East Bijou Street; Denver, 1899, at 1625 Weston; 1615 Arapahoe, 1899.

NORTHWESTERN PORTRAIT COMPANY
Located at 10 Tabor Block, Denver, 1899.

NOTT, VICTOR E.
Active in Denver with E. S. Marshall, 1890.

NUTT, JAMES W.
Active in Denver with E. S. Marshall, 1885; also in Alma, 1885, partner in Miller & Nutt, stereo photographers.

NYE, WILLIS A.
Partner in Bates & Nye, 141 West 2nd, Leadville, 1880.

O' KEEFE & STOCKDORF
Partnership of C. F. O' Keefe and Stockdorf at 5th and Harrison, Leadville, 1894-97.

O' KEEFE, C. FRANK
Studio at 425 Harrison, Leadville, 1892-93.

O' KEEFE, M. T.
Studio at 503 Harrison, Leadville, 1885.

O' NEAL, L.
Active in Grand Junction, 1892.

OGDEN & COMPANY, JOHN T.
Active in Denver, 1889-90; studio at 14 Braisie Block, 1889-90; 523 and 525 Charles Building; 15th, corner of Curtis, 1890.

OGDEN & IRISH
Studio at 525 Charles Block, Denver, 1891.

OILER & NOCKIN
Studio at 1617 Champa, Denver, 1898.

OILER PHOTO COMPANY, N. R.
Active in Denver, 1899-1900.

OILER' S PHOTOGRAPH GALLERY
Studio in Denver, operated by Frank E. Oiler at Riche Block, 16th and Curtis, 1896-97; 1615 Arapahoe, 1899.

OLDROYD, L. K.
Active in Colorado Springs, 1873-82; bought Eugene Brandt' s business, 1876. Produced stereoviews.

OPIE & KERR
Active in Aspen, 1891.

ORR, J. E.
Active in Rocky Ford, 1895-1901. Also spelled Ore and Orris.

OWEN, GEORGE
Active in Wray, 1895-99.

PAGE CAMERA COMPANY
Active in Denver, 1895.

PAINTER, ORRIN C.
Denver with W. H. Jackson, 1886.

PALACE ART STUDIO
Located at 1113 16th, Denver, 1901.

PALMER, CHARLES H.
Active in Denver, 1890.

PARIS
Partner in Rankin, Paris & Allyn, Denver, 1861.

PARK, H. S.
Denver, 1889.

PARKS & CHILDS
Partnership of Alfred R. Childs and Parks, Leadville, 1881, at 103 East 5th.

PARKS & VAN HORN
Partnership of John W. Van Horn and Parks, operating in Leadville, 1882, at 424 Harrison.

PARKS, ARTHUR L.
Active in Denver with H. Rothberg, 1889; operating alone, 1890.

PASAMORE, WILLIAM G.
Studio at 623 Colorado, Colorado City, 1896-1901.

PASCOE, ELMER E.
Active in Denver, 1888-92; at 16th southeast corner of Court Place, 1889; partner in Stephan & Pascoe, 1226 Larimer, 1890; 1232 Larimer, 1892. Also in Creede, 1891-92.

PAYNE & STOCKDORF
Partnership of D. R. Payne and Fred Stockdorf; studio at 613 Harrison, Leadville, 1887-89.

PEERS, O. L.
Partner in Martin & Peers, Central City, 1879-80.

PEIRSON & COMPANY
Gallery operated by H. F. Peirson in Denver, 1894-1900. Located at 1609 Arapahoe, 1894; 1615 Arapahoe, 1895-96; Opera House Block, 1897-99; 1617 Lawrence, 1900. Name also listed as Howard F. or Howard T.

PENDIKE STUDIO
Partnership of William Pennington and L. C. Updike, active in Durango, Colorado, c. 1908-13. Travelled extensively, photographing in the Four Corners area including New Mexico.

PERRY & BOHM
Partnership of Charles M. Perry and Charles Bohm in Denver, 1872-75.

PERRY, O. H.
Studio at 2028 14th, Boulder, 1901.

PETERS, GEORGE
Located at 3rd and Carr, Cripple Creek, 1901.

PETERS, OTTIS
Active in Denver, 1881.

PETERSON, FOUNTAIN L.
Active in Ft. Collins, 1866.

PETERSON, JOHN F.
Active in Leadville, 1879-80; at Main Street near Harrison; 119 East 3rd, 1880. In Denver, 1883, at 326 Larimer.

PHILLIPS
Partner in Mealey & Phillips, Pueblo, 1879-81.

PHILLIPS & SCHEDIN
Located at 412 Bennett, Cripple Creek, 1899.

PHILLIPS & SMITH
Active in Grand Junction, 1899.

PHILLIPS, E. F.
Active in Sterling, 1893-95. Also E. T. Phillips.

PHILLIPS, H. M.
Partner with H. B. Clegg, operating as Clegg & Phillips in Victor, 1897.

PHILLIPS, L. R.
Active in Saguache, 1888; Pueblo, 1897, at 239 North Union.

PHILLIPS, RUSSELL T.
Active in Denver with J. Collier, 1881.

PHOTO NOVELTY COMPANY
Located at 1624 Curtis, Denver, 1899.

POLEY & COMPANY, HORACE S.
Operated as Sooy & Poley, 112 North Tejon, Colorado Springs, 1889-91; as Horace S. Poley & Company, 1892-1901, at 713-715 North Tejon.

POLLARD & NELLES
Partnership of R. M. Pollard and W. A. Nelles, Denver, 1889.

POLLEN, C. A.
Stereo photographer in Colorado Springs.

PORTER, C. Y.
Active in Cockrell, 1890-91.

PORTER, GEORGE
Active in Mt. Sneffels.

PORTER, J. H.
Active in Georgetown with Eggleston Brothers, 1871.

POST, FREDERICK E.
Active in Denver, 1889-1901; studio at 1459 Larimer, 1889-91; 1759 Larimer, 1892; 1206 15th, 1893-1901.

POTTER, C. T.
Active in Cockrell, 1889.

POWELL, CLEMENT
Photographer with the Powell Surveys.

POWELL, W. A.
Active in Ouray, 1897.

POWER, EUSTACE B.
Active in Denver, 1892.

POWERS, W. C.
Active in Holyoke, 1891-1900.

PRICE, N. B.
Active in Chromo, 1900-01.

PRUDEN
Partner in Sturtevant & Pruden, Boulder, 1889.

PURCELL, C. E.
Stereo photographer in Berthoud; specialized in landscapes.

QUACKENBUSH, RICHARD M.
Located at Larimer northwest corner of 27th, Denver, 1885.

RANDALL, A. FRANK
Active in Denver, 1890, at 4, 5, 10 and 16 Curtis.

RANKIN & COMPANY
Active in Central City, 1861.

RANKIN, PARIS & ALLYN
Active in Denver, 1861.

RAPIN, A.
Active in Silver Plume, 1892.

RAY, F. L.
Active in Salida, 1899-1901.

READ & REED
Active in Delta, 1901.

REALL, JOHN A.
Active in Denver, 1894-98; at 2330 Larimer, 1897-98.

REAVES, H. D. P.
Active in Ouray, 1889.

REED & McKENNEY
Partnership of Albert S. McKenney and William H. Reed. Active in Denver, 1870-72; Central City and Georgetown, 1873; their studio was destroyed by fire, c. 1874.

REED AND KELLUM
Active in Colorado Springs, 1879.

REED, MELVILLE
Active in Leadville, 1884-85; at 103 East 5th, 1884; Harrison and East 5th, 1885.

REED, S. E.
Studio at 425 South Tejon, Colorado Springs, 1897-98.

REED, WILLIAM H.
Active in Central City, 1869-70. Partner with Albert S. McKenney, operating as Reed & McKenney, 1870-74; in Denver, 1870-72; Central City and Georgetown, 1873; their studio was destroyed by fire, c. 1874.

REES & COMPANY, C. E.
Active in Aspen, 1894-95; Creede, 1899-1901.

REEVE, H. D. P.
Active in Pueblo, 1888, at 115 West 4th; in Ouray, 1890.

REICHENEKER, W. C.
Active in Golden, 1872; Denver, 1873. Also spelled Reichenecker.

REIFF & ELLIOT
Possibly working in Georgetown.

REIMAN, LEROY
Active in Eads, 1890-91.

REISTLE, FRANK
Active in Denver and Steamboat Springs, 1889; Denver, 1901, at 1420-1422 Lawrence.

REITZE, GEORGE
Active in Denver with W. H. Jackson, 1888.

RICH, V. E.
Active in Walden, 1896-97. Also spelled Riche.

RICHARD, CHARLES
Active in Pueblo, 1870; Canon City, 1871.

RICHARD, E. S.
Active in Rocky Ford, 1893-94.

RICHARDSON, MARY (MRS.)
Active in Durango, 1900-01.

RICHMOND, E. O.
Active in Durango, 1899.

RIDDLE, J. R.
Active in Loveland, 1881-90s.

RIENHART, E. W.
Active in Florence, 1901.

RINEHART & W. H. JACKSON
Partnership of Alfred E. Rinehart and William Henry Jackson, operating in Denver, 1880-81.

RINEHART, ALFRED EVANS
Active in Denver, 1876-97. Associated with G. W. Kirkland, 1876; with Charles Bohm, 1875-80; partner with W. H. Jackson, operating as Rinehart & W. H. Jackson, 1880-81; at 413 Larimer, 1881-86; 1637 Larimer, with William H. Rinehart, 1887; 1630 Arapahoe, 1888, 1898-1901; Londoner Block, 1889; 1830 Arapahoe, 1890-94; 827 16th, 1895- 97.

RINEHART, FRANK A.
Born 1862; died in Illinois. With Charles Bohm, 1879-81. Son of Alfred E. Rinehart. Worked at his father' s studio at 413 Larimer, 1881-86; Studio in Omaha, Nebraska, at 1520 Douglas Street, 1886-90, 1893-1901; 1524 Douglas Street, 1891-92. Official photographer for the Trans Mississippi and International Exposition at Omaha, 1898, where he photographed many of the most famous Indians of the day. Rinehart and his assistant and successor, George Marsden, made exquisite prints from the negatives of the Indians, many on platinum paper, and some were bound into albums.
    Royal Sutton, *The Face of Courage: The Rinehart Collection of Indian Photographs*, Fort Collins, Colorado, The Old Army Press, 1972.

RINEHART, WILLIAM H.
With A. E. Rinehart, Denver, 1883.

ROBERTS, O. U.
Located at 710 Santa Fe, Denver, 1900.

ROBINSON & SHIPLER
Partnership of James William Shipler and Robinson, stereo photographers active in Denver, c. 1870s.

ROBINSON, ROLAND A.
Studio at 372 Larimer, Denver, 1874; partner in Shipler & Robinson, 1875.

ROCKY MOUNTAIN GALLERY OF ART
Operated by I. M. Johnson, Greeley, 1870-74.

ROCKY MOUNTAIN VIEW COMPANY
Operated by George E. Mellen in Colorado Springs, Gunnison and Denver; Manitou Springs, 1882-90.

RODSTROM, E.
Active in Craig, 1900.

ROGERS, ORLANDO
Active in Independence, 1897-99.

ROGERS, THOMAS J.
Active in Denver, 1888.

ROLOSON
Partner in Whitney & Roloson, Ouray, 1889.

ROOD, EDGAR H.
Studio in Denver, 1884-90; located at 9 Steele Block, 1884-85; 291 16th, 1886; 1113 16th or 16th and Arapahoe, 1887- 90.

ROSE & COMPANY
Partnership of John K. Rose and Benjamin S. Hopkins in Denver, 1886-96; known as Rose & Hopkins, 1896-1901. Studio located at 16th Street, corner of Laramie, c. 1890; at 40, 41 and 52 Tabor Block, 1896-98.

ROSE & HOPKINS
Partnership of B. S. Hopkins and J. K. Rose, landscape photographers, Tabor Block, Denver, 1896-1901. Photographed many Indians in their studio. Formerly Rose & Company, 1886-96.

ROSE, CHARLES E.
Active in Denver, 1884, 1888, 1895-1901; studio at 1232 Larimer, 1893; with George W. McDonald, 1884; 1206 Larimer, 1896-97; 1740 Larimer, 1898-99.

ROSE, JOHN K.
Born in Ayr, Ontario, Canada, November 15, 1849. Arrived in Colorado in 1881, and worked at the Bohm Photography Studio in Denver. Worked for the W. L. Bates Photography Studio, Denver, 1882-84. Rose worked in Chicago, Illinois, in 1885, but returned to Denver and purchased the Bates Studio the same year, renaming it Rose & Company. Partner with B. S. Hopkins, operating in Denver as Rose & Company, 1886-96; as Rose & Hopkins, 1896-1901. Studio located at 16th Street, corner of Laramie, c. 1890, and at 40, 41 and 52 Tabor Block, 1896-98.

ROSS, H. E.
Active in Salida, 1882.

ROSS, J. LEASKE
Partner with E. N. Clements in Clements & Ross, at 1617 Champa, Denver, 1892.

ROSS, JOHN
Active in Aspen, 1889.

ROTHBERGER, HENRY
Active in Denver, 1882-1901; with H. W. Watson, 1882; on 18th, northwest corner of Larimer, 1883; 910 16th, 1888; 1539 Arapahoe, 1889-1901.

ROUFF, HENRY
Active in Denver, 1888.

ROWLEY, M. V.
Active in Denver, 1888.

ROYER & MOORE
Partnership of W. C. Royer and Moore, located at 1645 Curtis, Denver, 1893.

RUDASILL, H. M.
Studio at 25 South Weber, Colorado Springs, 1898.

RUDY & CLINTON
Partnership of J. L. Clinton and Rudy, Colorado Springs, 1889; possibly W. Ira Rudy.

RUDY, W. IRA
Studio at 18 South Tejon, Colorado Springs, 1892.

RUNKLE, MAUD (MISS)
Active in Denver with H. Rothberger, 1889.

RUSSELL & LUKE
Active in Colorado Springs, 1874-76. Also listed as Russell & Lake.

RUSSELL BROTHERS
Partnership of Frederick C. and Warren H. Russell in Denver, 1885-89; studio at 281 Larimer, 1886.

RUSSELL, WARREN H.
Partner in Jennings & Russell, 326 Larimer, Denver, 1884; operating alone, 1885; at 1354 Lawrence, 1887.

RYAN, D. J.
Active in Denver, 1893-1900; studio at Cass and Graham Block, 16th and Curtis, 1893-99; known as Elite Photographic Gallery, 1893-95; also at 913 16th, 1899. Partner in Van Tassell & Ryan, 931 16th, 1900. Also known as Ryan & Company.

SABINE, JAMES E.
Active in Gold fields, 1859.

SAINT, T. G.
Active in Central City, 1862-67; with Henry Faul, August 1862; with Henry Garbanati, 1864. Also in Denver with W. G. Chamberlain, 1867.

SAMELSON & COMPANY
Gallery owned by A. J. Samelson, 428 16th, Denver, 1899-1901.

SANBORN, G. B.
Located at 529 East 5th, Leadville.

SAVAGE AND OTTINGER
See Utah.

SAVAGE, CHARLES ROSCOE
See Utah.

SAVAGE, N. W., JR.
Studio at 229 South Union, Pueblo, 1891.

SAVIGNY
Partner in Mealey & Savigny, Pueblo, 1884.

SCARBROUGH, CHARLES W.
Studio at 219 Harrison, Leadville, 1900.

SCHAFFER
Studio at 244 15th, Denver, 1878.

SCHAWALTER, FRED
Active in Denver with W. H. Forman, 1887.

SCHEDIN
Active in Cripple Creek; partner in Phillips & Schedin, 412 Bennett, 1899; Schedin & Lehman, 1900-1901.

SCHEDIN & LEHMAN
Studio at 412 Bennett, Cripple Creek, 1900-01.

SCHERT & TAYLOR
Partnership in Denver producing stereoviews.

SCHNEIDER, R.
Active in Parrott City, 1877.

SCHUMACHER, C. E.
Active in Denver with H. Rothberger, 1888-89.

SCOTT
304 North Main, Pueblo, 1900.

SCOVILL, HOMER W.
Active in Denver, 1884.

SEAVY, F. D.
Active in Del Norte, 1876.

SECKNER, S. H.
Active in Fort Collins, 1891-1901; partner in Bunn & Seckner, 1891. Also spelled Sackner.

SEGERBERG, BERN
Active in Denver, 1890-91; at 1213 19th, 1891.

SEITZ, PERRY
Operated with H. W. Watson, 1884; Denver, 1885-86, at 556 Larimer; 2100 Larimer, 1890.

SEYMOUR, JAMES
Active in Aspen, 1888; Colorado Springs, 1890.

SHAFFNER & MILNER
Stereo photographers in Pueblo.

SHAFFNER, C. H.
Active in Georgetown, 1882.

SHAVER, J. C.
Active in Georgetown, 1900.

SHAW, J. W.
Active in Pueblo; at 115 West 4th, 1892; Santa Fe corner of 6th, 1893-95. In Cripple Creek, 1894.

SHELDON PHOTO COMPANY
Active in Hotchkiss, 1901.

SHERHOLTZ
Active in Denver, 1880.

SHIPLER & COMPANY
Studio in Denver operated by J. W. Shipler, 1878-80; at 448 Larimer, 1880.

SHIPLER & ROBINSON
Studio at 372 Larimer, Denver, 1875.

SHIPLER & SHEW
Active in Denver, 1875.

SHIPLER & WILLIAMSON
Studio at 377 Larimer, Denver, 1877.

SHIPLER, JAMES WILLIAM
Gallery in McKeesport, Pennsylvania, c. 1870-89. Active in Denver, 1872, 1875, 1877-80; partner in Shipler & Robinson and Shipler & Shew, 1875; partner in Shipler & Williamson, 1877. Operated as Shipler & Company, 1878-80. See Montana and Utah.

SHIRLEY, GEORGE A.
Studio at 2052 Larimer, Denver, 1897.

SILSBEE, GEORGE M.
Operated in Denver with Frank M. Danielson, 1870.

SIMMONS, COURT J.
Studio at Emerald Avenue, corner of 6th and Highland, Denver, 1886-87.

SIMPSON, W. P.
Studio at 133 or 331 Symes, Denver, 1899; 205 North Main, Pueblo, 1900-01.

SINCLAIR, WARREN A.
Studio at 24 South 11th Street, Denver, 1900.

SKINNER, C. E.
Active in Salida 1893, 1901.

SKOLAS, JULIA (MISS)
Studio at 222 South Tejon, Colorado Springs, 1899-1901.

SLACK & KURTZ
Active in Boston and Springfield, 1889. Also listed as Slack & Kurts.

SMALLWOOD & BALL
Partnership of William Smallwood and George Ball, 275 8th, Denver, 1876.

SMITH & GROVE
Partnership of Stephen S. Smith and S. Grove, Pueblo, 1864-73.

SMITH & REED
Active in Pueblo, 1868.

SMITH, JAMES
Studio in Denver, at 11439 18th, 1887-88; 18th Street, corner of Holladay, 1889.

SMITH, STEPHEN S.
Partner in Smith & Grove, active in Pueblo, 1864-73.

SMITH-HASSELL COMPANY
Located in Denver, 1899-1901, 437 17th; studio at 1644 Broadway. Photographed Ute Indians in the field and studio.

SNIDER
Produced stereoviews in Rainbow Falls.

SODERBERG, PONT
Artist in Kokomo, 1885.

SOLONS, ANTON
Artist in Coal Creek, 1888-89.

SONNBERGER
Artist in Georgetown, 1867.

SOOY & POLEY
Located at 112 North Tejon, Colorado Springs, 1889-91.

SOOY, BENJAMIN F.
With C. Weitfle, 1884. Artist in Boulder, 1888, 1892. Also spelled
Sovy.

SOPER, ROY W.
2323 West 30th Avenue, Denver, 1900.

SOURS & COMPANY, CHARLES W.
Studio in Denver; at 1705 Champa, 1889-91; partner with R. S.
Sours, 1890-92; 906 15th, 1895-96. Operating with R. S. Sours in
Leadville, at 219 Harrison, 1899-1900. Also known as Robert S.
Sours & Company, c. 1890-92.

SOURS & COMPANY, ROBERT S.
Partner with C. W. Sours in Denver at 1705 Champa, 1890-92; listed
alone, 1895, at 2100 Larimer. Studio in Cripple Creek, 1897; with C.
W. Sours in Leadville, 1898-99, at 217 or 219 Harrison.

SOURS BROTHERS
C. W. and R. S. Sours, 407 Santa Fe, Pueblo, 1897.

SPRACKLEN & GHORMLEY
Active in Trinidad, 1880.

STANLEY, J. M.
U.S. Government photographer, 1853.

STATES, H. L.
Active in Delta, 1894-95; New Castle, 1898-1900.

STEELE, WILLIAM C.
Active in Denver, 1886-90; with H. W. Watson, 1886; with Wells &
King, 1887.

STEIN, R.
Studio in Denver; at 2617 Larimer, 1897; 2207 Larimer, 1898.

STEPHAN & COMPANY, GEORGE
Operated studio in Denver, 1884-89; at 300 Larimer, 1885-86; 1226
and 1232 Larimer, 1887-89.

STEPHAN & COMPANY
Located at 1232 Larimer, Denver, 1891.

STEPHAN & PASCOE
Partnership of Elmer E. Pascoe and George Stephan in Denver; located
at 1226 Larimer, 1890; 1232 Larimer, 1892.

STEPHAN, GEORGE
Active in Denver; operated as George Stephan & Company, 1884-89;
partner in Stephan & Pascoe, 1890, 1892. Listed as Stephan & Company,
1891.

STEPHENS, A. J.
Active in Paonia, 1890, 1892-96; Montrose, 1891. Also spelled
Stevens.

STEVENS, F. P.
Located at 24 East Bijou, Colorado Springs, 1899-1901.

STEVENS FOTOGRAFERIE
Located at 24-26 East Bijou, Colorado Springs, 1900.

STEVENS, ISAAC N.
Active in Denver, 1873-74. Also spelled Stephens.

STEVENS, LEWIS G.
Active in Denver, 1887-88.

STEWART, WILLIAM
Active in Denver, 1884.

STIFFLER & SON
Active in Longmont, 1887-88.

STIFFLER, GEORGE W.
Active in Golden, 1881; South Pueblo, 1883; Longmont, 1884,
1890-92.

STILES, H. L.
Active in Colorado Springs; at 117 Pikes Peak, 1899; 116 Pikes Peak,
1900; 115 East Pikes Peak, 1901.

STIMSON, CHARLES
Active in Denver with Frank M. Danielson, 1868-72. Also spelled
Donaldson and Donelson.

STIVERS, JOHN O.
Active in Colorado Springs, 1889.

STOCKDORF, FREDERICK T.
Studio in Leadville; partner with D. R. Payne operating as Payne &
Stockdorf, 1887-89, at 613 Harrison; partner with C. F. O' Keefe
operating as O' Keefe & Stockdorf at 5th and Harrison, 1894-97; listed
alone at 501 Harrison, 1897.

STOLL, GEORGE
Active in Leadville, 1883-84; at Chestnut southeast corner of Harrison,
1883.

STOLL, LOTTIE N. (MRS.)
Studio in 105 East Chestnut, Leadville, 1884-85

STONE & COMPANY
Stereo photographer; studio in Georgetown.

STONE & NEEDLES
Studio in Holden Block, or 39 ½ Union, South Pueblo, 1884-86,
1888.

STONEMAN, J. S.
Active in Coal Creek, 1898.

STORM BROTHERS
Active in Arvada, 1881.

STORM, FRANCIS D.
Stereo photographer employed in William G. Chamberlain' s studio
in Denver. He purchased it, 1881, and continued operating until
1901. Studio at 359 Larimer northwest corner of 15th, 361 Larimer,
1883; Lawrence southeast corner of 15th, 1884; on the Cass and

Graham Block, Iron Building, 906 15th, 1887-1901. Also known as Frank D. Storms.

STORMER & COMPANY
Partnership of W. H. and H. W. Stormer at Manitou Springs, 1882, 1884.

STORMER, H. W.
Stereo photographer in Manitou, 1880s. Succeeded by Galbraith.

STOTT, GEORGE
Active in Leadville, 1884.

STREETER, J. E.
Active in Boulder, 1880-82.

STRINGFELLOW, F. W.
Active in Anaconda, c.1898.

STRONG & HARGROVES
Partnership of J. J. Hargroves and Mrs. Strong, Ft. Collins, 1880.

STUDEBAKER
Studio on the Oriel Block, Colorado Springs, 1900.

STUEHRK, JULIUS
Amateur stereo photographer active in Colorado; views mounted by Julius Wendt.

STURTEVANT & PRUDEN
Active in Boulder, 1889; Joseph Bevier Sturtevant.

STURTEVANT, JOSEPH BEVIER
Active in Boulder, 1887-1901; partner in Sturtevant & Pruden, 1889; partner in James & Sturtevant, 1891; partner in Meile & Sturtevant, 1893-94; studio at 1761 12th, 1900-01.

SULLIVAN, MARY (MISS)
With Hosier & Calhoun, Denver, 1879.

SWAN BROTHERS
Active in Gunnison City, 1882; Crested Butte, 1886-87. Also listed as Brothers.

SWAN, JUSTUS C.
Studio in Denver at 1206 Larimer, 1897-99; 18th and California, 1900; 1962 California, 1901.

SWANSON, AARON
Active in Denver; partner with D. B. Chase, operating as Chase & Swanson, 1887, at 1469 Larimer; operating alone, 1888, at 1740 Larimer.

SWANSON, JOHN
Active in Denver, 1888; Central City, 1891-92.

TALBERT, Z. E.
Studio at 14 Mack Block, Denver, 1898.

TALBOT & HOWE
Active in Evans, 1880.

TALBOT & NELSON
Stereo photographers in Alma.

TALBOT, CHALMERS W.
Active in Canon City, 1874-77.

TALBOT, NATHANIEL H.
Active in Evans, 1873-76, 1880-81, 1886-90; partner in Talbot &

Howe, 1880. Studio in Loveland, 1893-1901; operated Talbot's Photograph Gallery, 1894. Also listed as A. H. Talbot.

TAYLOR
Partner in Carpenter & Taylor, Telluride, 1890-91, 1893.

TAYLOR, G. L.
With W. H. Masters, at 372 Larimer, Denver, 1874.

TAYLOR, LEVE (MISS)
Active in Denver, 1889-90; with E. S. Marshall, 1889.

TEITZEL, LOUIS
Active in Idaho Springs, 1899-1900.

TERINGTON, J. P.
With Charles Bohm in Denver, 1877.

THAYER, S. N.
Active in Leadville, 1895-96.

THEILKUHL, GUSTAV
Studio at 25 South Weber, Colorado Springs, 1900.

THOMAS, A. M.
Active in Central City, 1900-01.

THOMASON, SOPHIE (MRS.)
Active in Trinidad, 1881-86. Listed as Mrs. S. Thompson, 1881-84.

THOMPSON
Operated the Monroe-Thompson Photograph Company, 808 16th, Denver, 1901.

THOMPSON, ALVAH B.
Studio at 77 Barth Block, 16th corner of Stout, Denver, 1895.

THOMPSON, H. LAWRENCE
Active in Boulder, 1869-74.

THOMPSON, T. A.
Studio at 2200 Larimer, Denver, 1892-93.

THOMPSON, Z.
Active in Eldora, 1899.

THROWBECK, SAMUEL J. O.
Active in Denver; located at Cass and Graham Block, 1892; 827 16th, 1897-1901. Also spelled Thorbeck, Throbeck.

THURLOW, JAMES
Born in England, 1831; died in Manitou, 1878. Arrived in America, c. 1874; came to Manitou, 1878, and opened portrait and landscape studio, also producing stereoviews. After his death, his negatives were bought by Weitfle, and his studio sold to Mrs. Galbraith.

TITTLER, L. L.
Active in Hotchkiss, 1897.

TOWNER, C. S. (MRS.)
Active in Buena Vista, 1898-1901.

TOWNER, HENRY C.
Studio at 322 Blake, Denver, 1878.

TOWNSEND
Partner in Jamerson & Townsend, 1617 Lawrence, Denver, 1899.

TOWNSEND & HATHAWAY
Studio at 6 McClelland Block, 15th and Lawrence, Denver 1892-93.

TRACHT, WILLIAM W.
Studio at 999 Ruxton Avenue, Manitou Springs, 1898-1901.

TRAEUMER, GEORGE
Studio at 58 Skinner Block, Denver, 1892-93.

TRASK, ROBERT T.
Partner in Minton & Trask with Ray S. Minton; studio at 343 Gallup Avenue, Highlands, Denver, 1894.

TRAVIS, W. R.
Active in Delta, 1899-1901.

TRENDEL, JOHN A.
Studio at 1420 Larimer, Denver 1891-92.

TROUTMAN
Active in Boulder, 1871.

TURNER, J. E.
Studio at 14th and Pearl, Boulder, 1901.

TWEED, A. M. (MISS)
Studio at 322 North Nevada Avenue, Colorado Springs, 1896.

UDELL, A. A.
Active in Denver, 1885.

UTE IRON SPRINGS PHOTO GALLERY
Studio operated by J. G. Hiestand in Ute Pass, before 1891.

VAN ALSTINE, E. W.
With A. S. McKenney, Denver , 1873.

VAN DERMAN, MAX
With C. James, Denver, 1883.

VAN HOFE, GEORGE D.
Studio at 326 Larimer, Denver, 1882.

VAN HORN, JOHN W.
Partner with E. N. Clements, operating as Clements & Van Horn, Leadville, 1881-82; studio at 103 East 5th. Partner in Parks & Van Horn, 1882, at 424 Harrison; listed alone, 1883.

VAN TASSELL & RYAN
Studio at 931 16th, Denver, 1900.

VAN TASSELL, WALTER S.
Studio at 931 16th, Denver, 1901. Also known as Frank M. Van Tassell.

VARNEY, HIRAM
Active in Denver; with Bates & Nye, 1880; listed alone, 1887-89; with Beebe, 1890.

VELARDE, BARTHOLOMEW
Studio listed at "F(15th) & Holladay (Market)," Denver 1872-76.

VILA, JOSEPH
Partner with Harie C. Barley, operating as Barley & Vila at 16th northwest corner of Platte, Denver, 1890.

VOICE & COMPANY
Studio operated by Ulysses A. Voice in Denver; with Stephan & Pascoe, 1890; located at 21st and Larimer, 1891.

VOICE & COMSTOCK
Ulysses A. Voice and H. L. Comstock; operated studio at 2100 Larimer, Denver, 1893.

VOICE & MEILE
Studio at 21st and Larimer, Denver, 1890-92.

VOICE, ULYSSES A.
Active in Denver; operated as Voice & Company, 1890, with Stephan & Pascoe, 1890; partner in Voice & Meile, 1890-92; partner in Voice & Comstock, 1893.

VOORHEES, C. M. (MISS)
Active in Alamosa, 1897.

WAGNER
Partner in Wildhack & Wagner, Meeker, 1888.

WAGNER, F. S.
Studio at 233 South Union, Pueblo, 1899-1901.

WAKELEY, GEORGE D.
From Chicago, Illinois, he arrived in Denver as an actor. By 1859, Wakeley was advertising ambrotypes. He closed his studio, 1863, but returned to photograph the aftermath of the Cherry Creek flood, 1864. He left for New York in 1864, and returned to Leadville, 1879-80. Partner with E. N. Clements, 1880, operating as Wakely & Clements.

WAKELY & CLEMENTS
Partnership of E. N. Clements and G. D. Wakeley, 103 East 4th, Leadville, 1880.

WALDO
Partner in Faul & Waldo with Henry Faul, Central City, 1861.

WALKER, J. W.
Active in Golden, 1887, 1892-97.

WALKER, WILLIAM H.
Studio in Denver, 1887-97, at 710 Santa Fe; in Idaho Springs, 1891.

WALLIHAN, ALLEN GRANT
Active in Craig, 1893-94; Lake City, 1894; Lay, 1895; Craig and Lay, 1896.

WARD
Partner in Longshore & Ward, Leadville, 1882.

WARNKY & ABBOTT
Partnership of F. C. Warnky and C. L. Abbott, Garland, 1878; in Alamosa, 1879.

WARNKY, F. C.
Active in Fairplay, 1876. Partner in Warnky & Abbott in Garland, 1878; Alamosa, 1879.

WARRINGTON BROTHERS
Active in Montrose, 1901.

WATERS, F. E.
Active in Burlington, 1890-91; Denver, 1892, at 1645 Curtis.

WATSON, HENRY W.
Studio in Denver at 274 16th, 1880; 300 Larimer, 1881-85; in Longmont, 1882-83; Golden, 1883; Denver, 446 Larimer, 1886; with George Stephan & Company, 1899; 1232 Larimer, 1895.

WATSON, O. T.
Active in Golden, 1881.

WEBB, J. T.
Partner in Bates & Webb in Denver, 1885, Tabor Block.

WEBB, JOHN
With Charles Bohm, Denver, 1881.

WEBSTER BROTHERS
Active in Greeley, 1888-89.

WEBSTER, H. D.
Studio at 3rd and Carr, Cripple Creek, 1899-1900.

WEITFLE, CHARLES
Active in Central City, 1878-85; Denver, 1883-84, 377 Larimer.

WEITFLE, PAUL
Active in Denver, 1884; operated studio with Charles Weitfle; also listed with C. C. Wright.

WELCH
Active in Denver, 1859.

WELLS & KING
Studio at 1136 15th, Evans Block, Denver, 1887-93.

WELLS, CHARLES H.
Active in Denver, 1886, 1890; at 1136 15th, 1894-95.

WESTERMAN, OTTO
Active in Breckenridge, 1889-1901.

WESTLAKE, W. J.
Active in Lakeside, 1884-85.

WHEELER & CHASE
Active in Del Norte, 1878-79.

WHEELER & COMPANY
Studio operated by Danforth N. Wheeler in Colorado Springs, 1885; Grand Junction, 1891-1901.

WHEELER, C. L.
Active in Colorado Springs, 1884.

WHEELER, DANFORTH N.
Partner with T. E. Barnhouse in Lake City, operating as Barnhouse & Wheeler, 1877-79. Partner in Luke & Wheeler, operating in Leadville, 427 Harrison or Harrison opposite Clarendon Hotel, 1879-81. Operated the Wheeler & Company studio in Colorado Springs, 1885; Grand Junction, 1891-1901; also a partner in Kuhn & Wheeler, in Del Norte.

WHEELER, UNA (MISS)
Active in Ouray, c.1899.

WHITCOMBE & COMPANY
Active in Ft. Collins, 1888.

WHITE, A. D.
Active in South Pueblo, 1882.

WHITE, CHARLES W.
Studio at 1131 15th, McClelland Block, 15th corner of Lawrence, Denver, 1900.

WHITE, MARTIN
Active in Denver, 1882.

WHITE, P. C.
Active in Denver, 1886.

WHITE, S. G.
Active in Ouray, 1891.

WHITE, WILLIAM A.
Active in Rosita, 1880; in Wet Mountain Valley, Rosita, Querida, Florence, Canon City, 1880-81; Denver, 1882-84, at 571 Larimer.

WHITNEY & ROLOSON
Partnership of W. H. Whitney and Roloson, active in Ouray, 1889.

WHITNEY, W. H.
Active in Ouray, 1887-89; partner in Whitney & Roloson, 1889; in Denver, 1890.

WHITTER, JACOB
Partner with C. A. McKirrahn operating McKirrahan & Whitter studio in Georgetown, 1883; in Leadville, 1888-89, at 506 Harrison. In Denver, 1892-99; studio at 31 Corbett, 1892-97; North-South Corbett between Stanton Avenue and 22nd, 1898-99. Produced stereoviews.

WILDER, EDWIN A.
Active in Rico, 1881-82; Durango, 1884-85, 1887-89.

WILDHACK & WAGNER
Active in Meeker, 1888.

WILDHACK, H. A.
Partner in Wildhack & Wagner in Meeker, 1888; operating alone, 1889-96.

WILHEM
Photographer from Madison Avenue, New York, active in Cripple Creek, 219 Meyers.

WILKINS, E. I. & G. T.
Active in Ft. Collins, 1884-85.

WILKINS, G. T.
Studio located on College Avenue, Ft. Collins, 1881-82; 1886-99.

WILLETT, C. G.
Active in Colorado Springs, 1890.

WILLIAMS & BROTHERS
Stereo photographers in Denver.

WILLIAMS & HANSMANS
Active in Alamosa, 1884-85.

WILLIAMS & McDONALD
Robert McDonald and partner, active in Denver, 1867-68.

WILLIAMS, H. G.
Active in Walsenburg, 1900.

WILLIAMS, W. L.
Active in Alamosa, 1887-89, 1893; Antonito, 1891; Pueblo, 1895-97, at 231 Union; 2 Holden Block, 1898.

WILLIAMSON & COMPANY
Studio operated by Harry M. Williamson in Denver; also known as the Colorado Artotype Company. Located at 439 16th, opposite

Courthouse, 1886; 333 16th, 1888; 329 16th, 1889.

WILLIAMSON & CURRAN
Partnership of H. M. Williamson and Thomas J. Curran, active at 16th and Tremont, 329 16th, opposite Courthouse, Denver, 1890.

WILLIAMSON, M. A.
Partner in Shipler & Williamson, 377 Larimer, Denver, 1877.

WILSON
Partner in Newby & Wilson, 125 South 3rd, Victor, 1900.

WILSON, J. G.
Active in Cripple Creek, 1893.

WING'S PHOTOGRAPH GALLERY
Located at 506 Harrison, Leadville, 1889-90.

WISPA
Partner in Yelton & Wispa, stereo photographers in Cripple Creek.

WITHER, ADA (MRS.)
Active in Steamboat Springs, 1894.

WITTER, JACOB
Active in Denver, 1882.

WOLCOTT
Partner in Chase & Wolcott, stereo photographers in Trinidad, c. 1873-95.

WOLF, J. L.
Active in Alamosa, 1895-96.

WOOD, G. M.
Active in Georgetown, before 1900.

WOODBURY, C.
Active in Central City, 1867.

WRIGHT, CHARLES C. (MRS.)
Studio at 910 16th, Denver, 1887.

WRIGHT, CHARLES C.
Active in Central City, 1885; Denver, 1883-87; studio at 359 Larimer, northwest corner of Larimer and 15th, 1883-86; 910 16th, 1887.

WRIGHT, G. WALLACE
Active in Greeley, 1881.

WRIGHT, WILLIAM J.
Active in Denver, 1890; Ft. Collins, 1891.

YALE, D. B.
Active in Boulder, 1888-89.

YELTON & WISPA
Stereo photographers active in Cripple Creek.

YELTON, E. A.
Active in Cripple Creek, 1899-1900; at 357 Bennett, 1899; 127 West Eaton, 1900.

ZAHNER, JACOB
Active in Denver, 1888.

ZEOVY (MRS.)
Active in Del Norte, 1875.

ZEREGA, CLARENCE
Active in Breckenridge, 1883-84.

ZIEGLER
Partner with J. A. Boston in Canon City, 1880, operating as Boston & Ziegler.

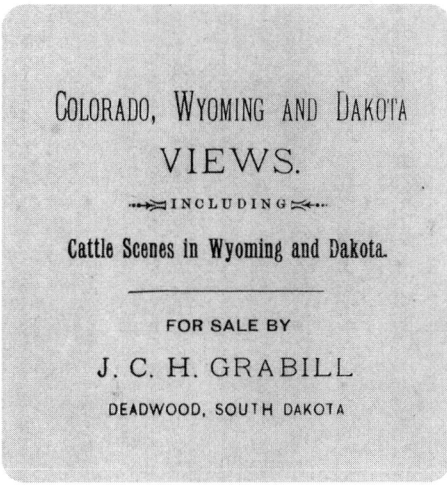

COLORADO, WYOMING AND DAKOTA
VIEWS.
⋯⋯⋙ INCLUDING ⋘⋯⋯
Cattle Scenes in Wyoming and Dakota.
_____
FOR SALE BY
J. C. H. GRABILL
DEADWOOD, SOUTH DAKOTA

Unless otherwise noted, the photographer's imprint designated "Dakota" alone without distinguishing between North Dakota, South Dakota or Dakota Territory.

ALLISON, W. C.
Stereo photographer in Custer.

AMERICAN VIEW COMPANY
Issued stereoviews; may have been associated with C. B. Manville.

ANDERSON
Associated with the Viking View Company, Dakota Territory.

ANDERSON, JOHN A.
Active on the Rosebud Reservation, South Dakota, 1889-1930s.

ANDERSON, P. G.
Stereo photographer in Redfield.

ARNOLD
Active in Watertown, South Dakota, 1885.

BAILEY, DIX & MEAD
Active in Ft. Randall, Dakota Territory, 1882; known for their portraits of Plains Indians. Josiah J. Mead was one of the partners.

BALL
Partner in Ball & Rindahl, Grafton, North Dakota, 1890; partner in Ball, Dix & Mead, Ft. Randall, Dakota Territory.

BALL & RINDAHL
Active in Grafton, North Dakota, 1890.

BALL, DIX & MEAD
Partnership operating in Ft. Randall, Dakota Territory, producing

stereoviews; Josiah J. Mead was one of the partners.

BARRY, DAVID F.
Born in Honeoye Falls, New York, March 6, 1854; died in Superior, Wisconsin, March 6, 1934. Barry learned photography from O. S. Goff when Goff was an itinerant photographer operating from Portage, Wisconsin; he managed Goff's studio in Bismark while Goff toured and photographed the Plains' forts. Goff and Barry worked together for years and developed a major archive of Indian photographs. Barry traveled to many of the forts in the area with a portable photography wagon, capturing cavalry and Indians in portraits and genre settings. Barry moved his studio to West Superior, Wisconsin, 1890, and to New York City, 1897. He returned to Superior, Wisconsin, 1898.

> Thomas M. Heski, *The Little Shadow Catcher: D. F. Barry*, Superior Publishing Company, 1978.

BARTON, M. B.
Studio in Alexandria on North Main Street, c. 1875.

BEAN, L. V.
Active in Sioux Falls, Dakota Territory, 1885.

BELGIUM STUDIO
Operating in New Rockford, N. D., c. 1900.

BENJAMIN
Partner in Staley & Benjamin, operating in Watertown, Dakota Territory, 1875. Listed alone in Watertown, Clark, Lake Preston and Elton, Dakota Territory, 1890.

BENTLEY, A. A.
Active in Fargo, 1895.

BERG, J.
Active in Grand Forks, North Dakota.

BERG, JACOB
Partner with A. S. Bratlee in Bratlee & Berg, stereo photographers in Devils Lake, 1880s.

BETHANE
Stereo photographer; partner with C. Moore in Pembina, 1880. Also listed as Bethune.

BLACK HILLS ART GALLERY
Operated by Silas Melander in Deadwood Gulch, 1876.

BLACK HILLS VIEW COMPANY
Located on Sherman Street in Deadwood, Dakota Territory. Josiah J. Mead probably was associated with the company.

BLACKBURN
Active in Grand Forks, Dakota Territory, 1885.

BLANCHARD
Stereo photographer active in Dakota Territory, 1870s-80s; partner in Rodocker & Blanchard in Deadwood.

BLUNT PHOTOGRAPHIC STUDIO
Operated by W. A. Ryan in Blunt, 1880.

BOUTON, C. L.
Active in Sioux Falls, Dakota Territory, 1885-95.

BOWMAN, O. E.
Stereo photographer in Montrose.

BOYDEN
Partner in Pollock & Boyden, stereo photographers in Deadwood, Dakota Territory, corner of Lee and Sherman Streets, 1880-82.

BRANDMO & POORE
Partnership active in Britton, c. 1885.

BRATLEE & BERG
Partnership of A. S. Bratlee and J. Berg, stereo photographers in Devils Lake, 1880s.

BRATLEE, A. S.
Stereo photographer; partner with J. Berg in Devils Lake, 1800s.

BROOKS
Partner in Hamel & Brooks, active in Yankton, 1880.

BROWN
Active in Wahpeton, North Dakota, c. 1895.

BROWN, C. B.
Active in Minot, c. 1895.

BROWN, E. J.
Stereo photographer in Sioux Falls.

BURLEY
Active in Rolla, North Dakota, c. 1900.

BURR, H. C.
Active in Yankton, Dakota Territory, 1870-88.

BUTLER, H.
Active in Vermillion, 1870-75. Also spelled Butler.

BUTTERFIELD & RALSTON
Partnership in Sioux Falls, Dakota Territory; produced scenic views.

CARLI, C. H.
Produced views in Groton, Dakota Territory.

CARROLL, JOHN W.
Stereo photographer active in Sanborn, c. 1912.

CASWELL & DUFFIN
Studio in Grand Forks, Dakota Territory, 1880.

CASWELL, W.
Active in Grand Forks, Dakota Territory, 1875; partner in Caswell & Duffin, 1880.

CITY GALLERY
Operated by Sampson & McMillen in Huron, Dakota Territory, 1885-87.

CLOW, WILL F.
Active in Lisbon, North Dakota, 1895.

COULES & McBRIDE
Partnership producing stereoviews in Deadwood, Dakota Territory.

CRAIG, J. T.
Active in Scotland, 1885.

CROSS, WILLIAM R.
Photographed Plains Indians and life around Deadwood and other mining areas in the Black Hills. See Nebraska.

CURRIER & PARKINSON
Partnership active in Jamestown, North Dakota and Mayville, 1890.

CURRIER, FRANK
Active with the Standing Rock Agency. See Nebraska.

DAVIDSON
Partner in Hamilton & Davidson, active with the Pine Ridge Agency, Dakota Territory, 1875.

DE GRAFF, W. H.
Active in Bismark, North Dakota, 1890.

DELONG, W. W.
Stereo photographer from Iowa; active in Yankton, Dakota Territory.

DESMET
Active in Coolidge, c. 1890.

DIX
Partner in Bailey, Dix & Mead and Ball, Dix & Mead, stereo photographers operating in Ft. Randall, Dakota Territory.

DUFFIN
Partner in Caswell & Duffin, active in Grand Forks, Dakota Territory, 1880.

DUGANNE
Partner in Pollock & Duganne, stereo photographers in Deadwood, Dakota Territory.

DUNN & EASTON
Partnership of O. W. Easton and Dunn, stereo photographers active in Sioux Falls, Dakota Territory.

EASTON, O. W.
Partner in Dunn & Easton, stereo photographers in Sioux Falls, Dakota Territory.

EINKOPF, PAUL
Active in Tripp, South Dakota, 1890.

ELITE PHOTO
Studio in Watertown, 1900.

ELITE STUDIO
Gallery in Lead, South Dakota, 1890.

EMMONS, W. W.
Active in Miller, 1885.

FALLMAN
Active in Eureka, South Dakota, 1890.

FISHER & COMPANY
Partnership active in Valley City, North Dakota, 1895, 1900.

FLATEN, G. E.
Billed as the successor to F. Jay Haynes in Fargo, c. 1885.

FOSTER, E. H.
Active in Jamestown, Dakota Territory, 1885.

FOX & WILTSE
Active in Mitchell, 1885.

FOX, G. W.
Active in Sioux Falls, Dakota Territory, 1895.

FRITZ & MALNIGHT
Studio in Valley City, Dakota Territory, 1885.

FROVARP, C. R.
Stereo photographer in Grafton, Dakota Territory.

FRYKLUND, OSCAR
Active in Bismark, North Dakota, c. 1900.

GAYLORD, E. E.
Active in Brookings, 1880.

GIBBON, A.
Active in Parkston, South Dakota, c. 1895.

GIBBON, W. C.
Active in Scotland, 1885-1900.

GILBERT & MILLER
Stereo photographers active in Mandan, Dakota Territory, 1870s.

GLAVIND
Partner in King & Glavind, active in Pierre, 1900.

GLENUM
Stereo photographer in Devils Lake, Dakota Territory. Also spelled Glerum.

GOFF, ORLANDO SCOTT
Born in East Haddam, Connecticut, September 10, 1843; died in Idaho, 1917. Served in the Union Army, 10th Connecticut Infantry. Learned photography in Lyons, New York, and worked as an itinerant around Portage, Wisconsin. Moved to Yankton, 1871, and established its first gallery. He hired Stanley J. Morrow, 1871. Studio in Bismark, 1873; moved his studio to Ft. Abraham Lincoln later that year, where he photographed Custer and his circle. Moved back to Bismark, 1877. Goff embarked on a photographic tour of the Plains' forts, 1878, and left his studio in the charge of David F. Barry, his former protege' at Portage. Took the first photograph of Chief Joseph, 1877, and Sitting Bull, 1881, after their respective surrenders. Operated studio at Fort Custer, Montana Territory, late 1870s, and opened studios in Havre and Ft. Assiniboine, Montana, 1896. Goff retired, 1900, while in Montana and later served in the state legislature.

GRABILL, JOHN C. H.
Active in Deadwood, Strugis Pine Ridge, Rockerville and Lead City, South Dakota, 1875-91. Photographed the aftermath of the slaughter at Wounded Knee; sold views of Colorado, Wyoming and Dakota.

GRAHAM, FRED S.
Active in Ellendale, 1870.

HAIT, W. C.
Active in Wahpeton, North Dakota, 1885.

HALLIFAX, B. E.
Active in Jamestown, North Dakota, 1890.

HALSTED & KEHM
Partnership active in Sioux Falls, South Dakota, 1890.

HAMEL
Active in Yankton, 1880.

HAMEL & BROOKS
Active in Yankton, 1880.

HAMILTON & DAVIDSON
Active with the Pine Ridge Agency, Dakota Territory, 1875.

HAMILTON & ROCKAFELLOW
Stereo photographers in Deadwood, Dakota Territory; James H. Hamilton.

HAMILTON, C. L.
Active in Ft. Randall, Dakota Territory, 1865.

HAMLIN, J. R.
Active in Casselton, Dakota Territory, 1875.

HANSEN, H. T.
Active in Fargo, North Dakota, 1895.

HART, J. A.
Stereo photographer in Bismark, Dakota Territory.

HASKIN'S
Active in Aberdeen, Dakota Territory, 1885.

HATTER, GEORGE L.
Active in Huron.

HAYNES, F. JAY
See Minnesota.

HAYNES, FRED E.
Active in Fargo, Dakota Territory, 1880; brother and co-worker with the renowned F. Jay Haynes.

HERUM, J.
Active at Devil's Lake, N.D., c. 1900.

HIKELL, SUPH
Photographer located over Sogen's store in Beresford, South Dakota, c. 1895.

HILL
Partner in Lewis & Hill, active in Huron, South Dakota, 1890; in Madison, South Dakota, 1895.

HILSTAD
Partner in Lassensen & Hilstad, stereo photographers in Sioux Falls, Dakota Territory.

HINGTGEN
Active in Wahpeton, North Dakota, c. 1890-1900.

HOFFMAN BROTHERS
Active in Bangor, c. 1895.

HOIT, W. C.
Active in Wahpeton, North Dakota, c. 1885.

HORNING, A.
Active in Mellette, 1885.

HORSWILL, A. J.
Active in Aberdeen, 1900.

JANOUSEK, L.
Active in Yankton, 1890.

JENSEN
Active in Sioux Falls, South Dakota, 1898.

JOHNSON, C. W.
Stereo photographer active in Mitchell, Dakota Territory; partner with H. F. Quiggle in Rapid City, 1900-10s, operating as Quiggle & Johnson at 204 West 2nd Street.

JOHNSON, JOHN
Active in Centrero, Centreville and Beresford, South Dakota, c. 1890.

JUDD, C. L.
Active in Jamestown, 1882-95.

JUDKINS, L. D.
Stereo photographer in Bismarck, Dakota Territory.

KEHM
Partner in Halsted & Kehm, active in Sioux Falls, South Dakota, 1890.

KEITHLEY, J. T.
Active in Faulkton, South Dakota

KELLY
Active in Pierre, Dakota Territory, 1880.

KELLY & ODELL
Partnership of R. L. Kelly and M. B. Odell, stereo photographers in Deadwood, Dakota Territory, c. 1880.

KELLY, R. L.
Stereo photographer; partner with M. B. Odell in Deadwood, Dakota Territory, c. 1880; worked alone in Pierre, 1880s.

KIDDER
Active in Parker, South Dakota.

KING & GLAVIND
Active in Pierre, 1900.

KINGTGEN
Active in Wahpeton, North Dakota, 1890.

KLENZE, H. G.
Successor to D. F. Barry in Bismark and Standing Rock, Dakota Territory; also in Fort Assiniboine, Montana Territory, c. 1890.

KRAUSE, CHRIST
Active in Huhn, North Dakota, 1895.

LASSENSEN & HILSTAD
Stereo photographers active in Sioux Falls, Dakota Territory.

LASSESEN, P. E.
Active in Sioux Falls, 1885.

LAWSON
Partner in Steinhouer & Lawson, active in Groton, Dakota Territory, 1885.

LEE, C. J.
Active in Fargo, North Dakota.

LEE, F. J.
Partner in Moe & Lee with O. J. Moe, active in Milbank, South Dakota, 1890.

LEELAND ART & MANUFACTURING COMPANY
Active in Mitchell, 1900.

LEGRUD
Active in Canton, S. Dak, c. 1895.

LEWIS & HILL
Active in Huron, South Dakota, 1890; in Madison, South Dakota, 1895.

LEWIS, A. J. (MR. & MRS.)
Stereo photographers in Sioux Falls, Dakota Territory.

LEWIS, A. T.
Active in Madison, South Dakota, 1885-90.

LIEN, C. K.
Active in Mayville, Dakota Territory, 1880.

LOCK
Partner in Rounds, Lock & McBride, operating in Lead City, South Dakota, before 1885.

LOCKE & PETERSON
Active in Deadwood, South Dakota, 1890.

LOCKE BROTHERS
Active in Canton and Sioux Falls, 1880.

LOCKE, H. R.
Partner in Locke & Peterson, active in Deadwood, 1890.

LOGAN
Active in Fargo, Dakota Territory, 1885.

LOGAN, S. H.
Gallery in Fargo, North Dakota; branch studio in Lisbon and
Casselton, 1885.

LOOCK
Studio in Lawrence, c. 1860s.

MACY, I. M.
Operated Templeman's Gallery in Miller, Dakota Territory.

MALNIGHT
Partner in Fritz & Malnight, active in Valley City, Dakota Territory,
1885.

MANVILLE, C. B.
May have been associated with the American View Company, issuing stereoviews.

MARKEL, M. G.
Active in Rolla, North Dakota, c. 1895.

MATSON BROTHERS
Active in Kimball, 1890.

MAYBERRY, T. S.
Active in Miller, South Dakota, 1890.

McBRIDE
Partner in Coules & McBride, producing stereoviews in Deadwood,
Dakota Territory. Partner in Rounds, Lock & McBride, operating in
Lead City, South Dakota, before 1885.

McCULLOCH
Partner in Varney & McCulloch, stereo photographers in Sioux Falls,
Dakota Territory.

McGREGOR, J. G.
Active in Armour, c. 1890.

McINTIRE, J. J. (MRS.)
Active in Spencer, South Dakota.

McMILLEN
Partner in Sampson & McMillen, operating the City Gallery in
Huron, Dakota Territory, 1885-87.

McMILLEN, F. H.
Active in Sioux Falls, South Dakota, 1885.

McNAMARA, J. J.
Produced stereoviews in Rapid City, Dakota Territory.

MEAD, JOSIAH J.
Partner in Bailey, Dix & Mead and Ball, Dix & Mead, operating in Ft.
Randall, Dakota Territory; produced stereoviews. Probably associated
with Black Hills View Company on Sherman Street in Deadwood,
Dakota Territory.

MEDDAUGH
Active in Lead, 1890.

MELANDER, SILAS
Operated the Black Hills Art Gallery in Deadwood Gulch, 1876.

MEYER, F.
Stereo photographer in Alcester, Dakota Territory.

MILLER
Partner in Gilbert & Miller, stereo photographers active in Mandan,
Dakota Territory, 1870s.

MILLER & VAN BUSKIRK
Partnership in Aberdeen, Dakota Territory; produced stereoviews.

MILLER, F. Q.
Stereo photographer in Groton, Dakota Territory.

MILLER, J. F.
Active in Aberdeen, South Dakota, 1895. Published a portrait of Sitting Bull and his family.

MILLER, R. H.
Made stereoviews in Sioux Falls, Dakota Territory.

MOE & LEE
Partnership of O. J. Moe and F. J. Lee, active in Milbank, South
Dakota, 1890.

MOE, O. J.
Operating in Brookings, 1880; partner in Moe & Lee operating in
Milbank, South Dakota, 1890; listed alone in Milbank as O. J. Moe
& Company, c. 1895.

MOORE & BETHANE
Stereo photographers in Pembina, Dakota Territory, 1880. Also listed as Bethune.

MOORE, C.
Stereo photographer active in Pembina, Dakota Territory; partner
with Bethane, 1880.

MORROW, STANLEY J.
Born in Richland County, Ohio, May 3, 1843; died in Dallas, Texas,
December 10, 1921. Raised in Wisconsin; fought as a member of the 7th
Wisconsin Volunteer Infantry, later part of the Iron Brigade. Learned
photography from Brady's operators, and returned to Columbia County,
Wisconsin. Opened a gallery in Yankton, Dakota Territory, on Fuller's
Block, 1869. Took many trips up the Missouri River to record life at the
forts, and made numerous Indian portraits. Morrow made frequent
trips into Montana to photograph Indians, and eventually took over
Goff's studio in Bismark, 1878. Accompanied Captain Sanderson for
Custer reburial at the Custer battlefield, and became Fort Custer photographer, 1879. Sold his studio at Fort Keogh to L. A. Huffman, 1879,
along with the negatives of the reburial which Huffman reproduced
under his own imprint. Morrow made a famous series of stereoviews of
the Black Hills region and another of Crook's Army in the field, Operating mainly out of Deadwood, 1876. The Crook negatives were sold
to B. P. Batchelder of Stockton, California. Morrow closed his gallery in
Yankton, 1883, and he moved to Florida, 1888.
    Wesley R. Hurt and William E. Lass, *Frontier Photographer: Stanley J. Mor-
    row's Dakota Years*, University of South Dakota and University of Nebras-
    ka Press, 1956.
    Paul L. Hedren, *With Crook in the Black Hills: Stanley J. Morrow's 1876
    Photographic Legacy*, Pruett Publishing Company, 1985.

MUNSON
Active in Sioux Falls; in Madison, South Dakota, 1900.

NEWCOMBE, C. H.
Active in Watertown, Dakota Territory, and Huron, South Dakota,
1885.

NORCOTT, C. K.
Active in Flandreau, South Dakota.

NORTHWESTERN VIEW COMPANY
Produced stereoviews in Chamberlain, Dakota Territory.

NYE, B. A.
Operated Nye's Fine Art Gallery in Milbank, 1885.

NYE, C. O.
Stereo photographer operating a Parlor Car in Rapid City and Aberdeen, Dakota Territory.

ODELL, M. B.
Stereo photographer active in Deadwood, Dakota Territory; partner in Kelly & Odell, c. 1880.

OPPENHEIMER, BEN
Stereo photographer in Vermillion and Viewville, Dakota Territory. Advertised as a mute.

ORR, FRANK A.
Studio at South Mill Street, Lead City, South Dakota, c. 1890.

OSTBOG, P.
Active in Park River, North Dakota, c. 1895.

PARKINSON
Partner in Currier & Parkinson, active in Jamestown, North Dakota and Mayville, 1890.

PERRY, H. B.
Studio in Chamberlain, 1888. Photographed at the Lower Brule Agency.

PETERSON
Active in Clark, c. 1885. Partner in Locke & Peterson, active in Deadwood, South Dakota, 1890.

PETERSON, I. B.
Active in Bryant, South Dakota, 1885.

PIERCE & POTTER
Studio in Leeds, N. D., c. 1895.

PIKE, J. W.
Stereo photographer in Hot Springs, Dakota Territory, c. 1895.

PIONEER GALLERY
Operated by J. N. Templeman in Miller, Dakota Territory.

PITMAN, GENERAL JOHN T.
Active in Bismark and Ft. Abraham Lincoln, 1880.

PIXLEY, S. E.
Active in Church's [Church's Ferry?], Dakota Territory, 1885.

POLLOCK & BOYDEN
Portrait and stereo photographers in Deadwood, Dakota Territory; located at the corner of Lee and Sherman Streets, 1880-82.

POLLOCK & DUGANNE
Active in Deadwood, 1885.

POLLOCK, A.
Stereo photographer active in Deadwood, Dakota Territory, 1870s-80s; partner in Pollock & Boyden, 1880-82; partner in Pollock & Duganne, 1885.

POORE
Partner in Brandmo & Poore, active in Britton, c. 1885.

POWELL, J. F.
Operated Powell's Studio in Wahpeton, 1890.

PYWELL, WILLIAM R.
Active in Bismark and on Stanley's Northern Pacific Railroad Survey, 1873-74.

QUIGGLE & JOHNSON
Partnership of C. W. Johnson and H. F. Quiggle, stereo photographers in Rapid City at 204 West 2nd Street, 1900-10s.

QUIGGLE, H. F.
Active in Doland, 1887; partner in Quiggle & Johnson, operating in Rapid City, 1900-10s.

RALSTON
Partner in Butterfield & Ralston in Sioux Falls, stereo photographers in Dakota Territory.

RAU, CARL
Active on the Sisseton Reservation, 1897.

REIMAN, JOHN
Active in Kulin, North Dakota, 1895.

RILEY, E.
Stereo photographer active in Cross Roads, Dakota Territory.

RINDAHL
Partner in Ball & Rindahl, active in Grafton, North Dakota, 1890.

ROBINSON
Active in Hurley, S. Dakota.

ROBINSON, F. N
Stereo photographer in Howard, Dakota Territory, 1884.

ROCKAFELLOW
Stereo photographer; partner with James H. Hamilton in Deadwood, Dakota Territory.

RODOCKER & BLANCHARD
Stereo photographers in Deadwood, Dakota Territory.

ROOT, D. O.
Active in Woonsocket, South Dakota, 1890.

ROUNDS, A. A.
Partner in Rounds, Lock & McBride in Lead City, South Dakota, before 1885; operated alone after 1885.

ROUNDS, LOCK & McBRIDE
Partnership operating in Lead City, South Dakota, before 1885.

RUH, O. L.
Active in Flandau, Dakota Territory, 1880.

RYAN, W. A.
Operated Blunt Photographic Studio in Blunt, 1880; listed as Ryan's Photographic studio, 1886.

SALTER & TAYLOR
Active in Langdon, c. 1895.

SAMPSON & McMILLEN
Partnership operating the City Gallery in Huron, Dakota Territory, 1885-87.

SANDERS, A. M.
Active in Valley City, North Dakota, 1895.

SASSE, JOSEPH
Active in Deadwood, South Dakota, 1895.

SCOTT, GEORGE W.
Active in Ft. Yates, c. 1880s. Photographed the Lakota.

SERDINKO, J.
Stereo photographer in Fargo, Dakota Territory.

SETHEN, I. J.
Active in Minnewaukon, N. D., c. 1895.

SHORTREAD
Stereo photographer in Gaddes, Dakota Territory.

SKRIVSETH, J. L.
Photographer in Hillsboro, North Dakota, 1890.

SPARKS, W. A.
Active in Tripp, South Dakota, 1895.

STALEY
Partner in Staley & Benjamin, operating in Watertown, Dakota Territory, 1875; listed alone on Brizee Block, Watertown, South Dakota, 1900.

STALEY & BENJAMIN
Active in Watertown, Dakota Territory, 1875.

STAR GALLERY
Studio in Sioux Falls, Dakota Territory, 1895.

STEINHAUER, H.
Operated gallery in Groton with branches in Webster, Bristol and Bradley, 1890.

STEINHOUER & LAWSON
Active in Groton, Dakota Territory, 1885. Possibly the same person as Steinhauer.

STILLWELL, L. W.
Active in Deadwood. May have photographed Indians, but published copies by others, particularly D. F. Barry and George E. Spencer.

STOBIE, C. S.
Photographed the Lakota, working out of Chicago.

STONE, A. C.
Active in Grand Forks, Dakota Territory, 1888; in Clark, South Dakota, c. 1890.

STRAUSS, B. F.
Active in Bismark, c. 1900.

SWEM, THOMAS M.
Active in Fargo, North Dakota, 1908(?). See Oregon.

TAYLOR
Partner in Salter & Taylor, active in Langdon, c. 1895.

TEMPLEMAN, J. N.
Stereo photographer operating the Pioneer Gallery in Miller, Dakota Territory; also owned Templeman's Gallery, operated by I. M. Macy. Photographed the Lakota.

VAN BUSKIRK
Partner in Miller & Van Buskirk, stereo photographers in Dakota Territory.

VARNEY & McCULLOCH
Partnership in Sioux Falls, Dakota Territory, producing stereoviews. Studio located at 220 Eighth St., c. 1890, successor to L. V. Bean.

VIKING VIEW COMPANY
Produced stereoviews in Sioux Falls, Dakota Territory; associated with Anderson.

WAGNER, JAMES
Active with the Rosebud Agency, 1890.

WELCH, C. E.
Active in Mandan, North Dakota, 1885.

WHITTLESLEY
Stereo photographer in Tower City, Dakota Territory.

WILTSE
Partner in Fox & Wiltse, active in Mitchell, 1885.

WIMBERLY'S STUDIO
Active in Ft. Mead, 1890.

Special thanks to Bruce Erickson and Lynn Davis for their substantial contributions to this list.

AH HEE
First Chinese photographer to reach prominence; studio at 76-78 Nuuanu Avenue.

ALOHA GALLERY
Operated by T. P. Severin before 1893; joined by Alexander Bolster, 1893.

AMAYA, K.
From Yokahama, Japan; operated studios in Honolulu and Lihue, Kauai, 1894-97.

ANDREWS, C. B.
Active in 1898.

ANTRIM, B. JAY
Born 1818. Operated Excelsior's Daguerreotype Gallery in San Francisco before 1855; daguerreotypist in Honolulu, 1855-56.

BAKER, RAY JEROME
Prolific photographer and film maker, originally from California. He traveled, illustrated lectures, researched and preserved earlier photographer's history; printed and published numerous books with photographs. Best known of Hawaiian photographers.

BENSON, WILLIAM
Arrived from New South Wales on the ship Harmony, 1850; located over the Advertiser, June 28, 1856; sold his gallery to W. F. Howland, 1857.

BERTRAM, G.
A priest from Dayton, Ohio; photographed Honolulu fire of 1900; returned to mainland, 1905.

BEW, Y. M.
Listed in Hawaii, 1880.

BINDT, FRANZ R.
Bought Froebe's business and operated an ambrotype and daguerreotype gallery, August 1859-61; sold out to E. Durand, 1861.

BOLSTER, ALEXANDER
Worked with J. J. Williams until 1891; joined T. P. Severin at the Aloha Gallery, 1893.

BONNEY, FREDERICK
An English amateur who worked with dry plates to record Hawaiian volcanoes, c. 1881. Bonney was apparently in Hawaii for only one month during a stopover while en route from Australia to England. May have also used the name Frank.

BRADLEY & RULOFSON
Famous San Francisco firm visiting the islands, 1875; photographed royalty and notables.

BRIGHAM, WILLIAM T.
Brigham was a much traveled scientist and amateur photographer during the 1860s, arriving on the *Symiote* from San Francisco, May 5, 1864. Professor at Oahu College; the first curator of the Bishop Museum in Honolulu, 1894.

BRIGMAN, ANNIE W.
Granddaughter of Lorrin Andrews. Went to mainland and became a famous Pictorialist photographer, part of Stieglitz' inner circle; returned to Hawaii, 1928.

BROCKWAY, WILLIAM F.
Daguerreotypist from San Francisco who arrived on the ship *Flying Dart*, 1855.

BRODIE, DR. JOHN
Formerly the House Surgeon at London Hospital, Brodie operated a photography business around Hotel and Fort Street, 1879-95.

BURGESS, CHARLES
Born 1835; died 1870. An English painter and jeweler; Honolulu agent for George & Charles Burgess, operating a photography studio, 1865-67. He taught John Meek and Horrace Crabbe photography and sold his studio to them, 1867.

BURGESS, GEORGE H.
Lithographer active in Honolulu, 1858-66.

CHALLENGER EXPEDITION
British oceanographic expedition around the world, 1875.

CHASE, HENRY L.
Born in California, 1832; died in Maui, June 1, 1901. Took over the gallery of J. W. King in Honolulu, operating as Cosmopolitan Photographic Gallery, 1862-74. He moved to Keene, New Hampshire, for two years; returned to Honolulu, 1876-85, operating the Cosmopolitan Photographic Gallery on Fort Street; his gallery burned down, 1877. Moved studio to Waikuku, Maui, 1886-1901. Chase purchased and published negatives of San Francisco photographer C. L. Weed.

CHILD, L. C.
Skilled amateur active in the Big Island, 1907.

CHING CHOW
Active in 1898.

COSMOPOLITAN PHOTOGRAPHIC GALLERY
Operated by H. L. Chase in Honolulu, 1862-74; on Fort Street, 1876-85.

CRABBE, HORACE
Born in Hawaii, 1837; died 1903. Learned photography from Charles Burgess; bought Burgess' studio, operating it with his brother-in-law, John Meek, Jr., until 1868, when he became Surveyor and Guard of the Port of Honolulu.

DAVEY, FRANK
Born in London, February 27, 1860; died in California. Son of William Turner Davey. Worked for Waleri, Sarony, and Tabor on the mainland; arrived in Hawaii, 1880. Photographed many famous people; his studio and negatives went to Perkins.

DE MELLO, JOHN, SR.
Portuguese photographer in Kohala, Hawaii, 1892-99. De Mello operated his studio from his plantation home.

DEVHILL, W. E. H.
Died 1905. Amateur photographer and operator of a hotel at Hanolei, Kauai, offering a darkroom for other amateurs at his hotel.

DICKSON, MENZIES
Born 1840; died 1891. Moved to Hawaii from Ohio, and took over Chase' s Studio, 1867; sold out to his manager, J. J. Williams, c. 1882.

DURAND, E. D.
Bought studio from Franz R. Bindt, 1861; it was taken over by Joseph W. King, 1862.

FROEBE, THEODORE W.
Bought Stangenwald' s business, operating as Honolulu Ambrotype and Daguerreotype Gallery, 1858-59; sailed on the ship Yankee to San Francisco, May 30, 1859.

FURNEUX, CHARLES
Died in Hilo, 1913. He was a well-known artist who came from Boston, 1878; worked for Montano, 1885.

GARTLEY, ALONZO
Skilled amateur noted for platinum prints of panoramas. Some of his negatives and prints were published by R. Perkins for Hawaii promotions, c. 1890.

GONSALVES, JOAQUIN AUGUSTO
Born in Portugal, 1855; died 1931. Immigrated to Hawaii, 1879, after working in a newspaper office in Madiera, Canary Islands. Gonsalves worked for A. A. Montano, apprenticed with J. J. Williams, then opened his own studio in Honolulu. Principal competitor of J. J. Williams.

GOODFELLOW, STEPHEN
Born in Clearfield County, Pennsylvania. Daguerreotypist from San Francisco, California; arrived in Hawaii with Stangenwald, 1853; left for Australia on the *Lauritta*, May 7, 1853.

GURREY, ALFRED R.
Operated Gurrey' s Art Shop in Honolulu, c. 1890s-1918; married Caroline Haskins, 1903. He eventually turned from photography to painting.

GURREY, CAROLINE HASKINS
Worked for J. J. Williams, 1898-1902; later operated her own studio; married Alfred R. Gurrey, 1903. Her beautiful Pictorialist style is compared to Annie Brigman; photos are highly sought.

HAWAIIAN CAMERA CLUB
Organized in 1889 by fifty amateur enthusiasts, the club offered lectures and programs under the leadership of president Christian J. Hedemann. Political upheaval in the early 1890s caused the demise of the club, 1894.

HEDEMANN, CHRISTIAN JACOB
Born in Denmark, 1852; died 1932. Moved to Hana, Maui, 1878, and to Honolulu, 1884, working for the Honolulu Iron Works. Prominent amateur photographer who presided as president of the Hawaiian Camera Club.
  Lynn Ann Davis, with Nelson Foster, *A Photographer in the Kingdom: Christian J. Hedemann' s Early Images of Hawai' i*, Bishop Museum Press, 1988.

HENSHAW, H. W.
U.S. Government biologist based in Hilo; made scenic platinum prints sold through Honolulu Photo Supply.

HITCHCOCK, EDWARD N.
Born in Hawaii; died at age 31. Amateur photographer active on the Big Island, 1890-1901; produced hundreds of glass plates.

HITCHCOCK, HARVEY REXFORD
Born 1835; died 1891. Amateur photographer who used a cdv camera, c. 1874, to capture landscapes around the islands.

HONOLULU AMBROTYPE ROOMS
Studio operated by W. F. Howland, 1857; by J. W. King, 1858-70.

HONOLULU PHOTO SUPPLY
Marketed scenic platinum prints made by H. W. Henshaw, C. 1902.

HOWLAND, W. F.
Operated Honolulu Ambrotype Rooms in Benson's old place, 1857-61. Sold out to King and left for San Francisco, 1861.

JAGGER, THOMAS AUGUSTUS
Volcanologist and amateur photographer who used his photos as scientific records, c. 1912.

KELSEY, THOMAS
Skilled amateur phtotographer; recording Hawaiian ethnography.

KING, JOSEPH W.
Bought Howland's studio, operating as King's Ambrotype Rooms, 1858-62; moved to Stangenwald's studio, 1862; later moved to Bindt's studio, then Durnad's. He had unaccounted absences, 1863-68. He was arrested and fined for making obscene photographs of hula dancers, then was banished from Honolulu, 1870

LEBLEUX, FERDINAND
French daguerreotypist in Honolulu, 1847, arriving from Lima, Peru.

McCANDLESS
Listed in Hilo, Hawaii, 1898.

MEEK, JOHN KANIPOOKALANI, JR.
Born in Hawaii, 1848; died 1879. Son of Chiefess Kepookalani. Taught by Charles Burgess; operated studio with brother-in-law Horace Crabbe, 1867; had his own gallery, 1868-77.

METCALF, THEOPHILUS
Born in America, c.1818; died 1866. Engineer who attempted to create the first daguerreotypes in Hawaii, 1845. No images by him have been identified to date.

MITCHELL, ALFRED A. A.
Born in New York. Amateur photographer who visited Hawaii, 1886 and 1892.

MONTANO, ANDREAS AVELINO
Worked initially for Dickson, c. 1870. Operated a successful Honolulu gallery and made many island views and royal portraits; trained Charles Furneaux. He continued in photography until his eyes failed, 1883.

MUNION, LEE
Operated Honolulu Photo Supply Company, 1900.

NAGAYAMA, T.
Listed in Hilo, Hawaii, 1898.

ON CHAR
Worked with Perkins, 1904-07, producing over 90,000 negatives, primarily of Chinese community. Continued active until 1954.

OSBORNE, ALBERT W.
Arrived from San Francisco, 1870; produced 3000 cdvs in three months.

OSHIMA, T.
Listed in Honokaa, Hawaii, 1898.

PERKINS, ROSCOE
Arrived from San Francisco with Arthur W. Rice, 1901; in business together until Rice left, c. 1908. Perkins acquired F. Davey's studio and negatives, c. 1904; he left for California, c. 1927.

RAMOS, MARIA J.
Printer for Gonsalves' studio, 1888; operated her own studio by 1890.

RHODES, F. C.
Active in 1898.

ROCK, JOSEPH
A botanist and amateur photographer, illustrated books, c. 1908; published many tree photographs.

SCOTT, WILLIAM P.
Originally from Ohio; Scott arrived in Hawaii, February 1850, and left for Manila two months later.

SEMITA
Active in Hilo, Hawaii, 1898.

SESSER, WILLIAM F.
His advertisements appeared in 1891; he spent six weeks in Volcano and Honolulu.

SEVERIN, THEODORE P.
Owned one of the largest galleries in Honolulu, employing six men, 1885-86; photographed the Royal Family. Partner with J. J. Williams, 1886.; worked with Henry Poor on the Hawaii Expedition to Samoa, 1887. Later was the proprietor of Aloha Gallery, working with Alexander Bolster, c. 1893.

SILVA, JOSE
Operated a studio in California after the Gold Rush; worked in the Hilo area, c. 1889. Also listed as Joseph.

SRIRAI
Active in Hilo, 1898.

STANGENWALD, HUGO
Born 1829; died 1899. Daguerreotypist from Marysville, California, who operated a studio in Hilo, 1853-58. Partner with Stephen Goodfellow for three months, 1853; Goodfellow went on to Australia; Stangenwald returned to the mainland and practiced medicine after 1858.

STOLPE, HERMAN
Photographer with the Vanadis Expedition, 1883-85; stopped in Hawaii, 1884.

STRONG, JOSEPH D., JR.
Artist who also photographed with Henry Poor on Hawaii Expedition to Samoa, 1887.

SUMIDA
Active in Hilo, 1898.

SUWA, T. R.
Listed in Honakaa, Hawaii, 1898.

TAI SING LOO
Active in Gurrey Art Shop, 1909-18; as Navy photographer in Pearl Harbor, 1918-49.

TIEMAN, C. H.
Active in Hawaii, 1898.

TOBITA, U.
Active in Lahaina, Maui, 1898.

TRANSIT OF VENUS EXPEDITION
American, British, French and German parties in the Pacific, 1874, each accompanied by photographers.

VALENTINE, JOHN
From San Francisco, Valentine visited Kauai and sold negatives to Crabbe and Meek before returning to San Francisco.

VANADIS EXPEDITION
Swedish expedition stopping in Hawaii, July 1884.

VANIMAN, MELVILLE
"Trapeze photographer" who took panorama views of Honolulu Harbor which were widely distributed, c. 1901.

WALKER, FREDERICK G. EYTON
Expedition photographer to northwest island chain, 1892. Visited Nihoa, Laysan and Midway. Operated studio in Honolulu, 1892-1900.

WEED, CHARLES LEANDER
Born 1824; died 1903. Pioneer California photographer who worked for Robert Vance and rivaled Carleton Watkins in creating mammoth plate views of Yosemite Valley. Weed worked in Honolulu for nine months, operating the Weed Brother's Gallery with J. A. or F. M. Weed, 1865. He made the arduous climb to the Haleakala Crater where he was the first to photograph this scenic wonder, the result being a series of mammoth plate images. Weed left for Hong Kong, 1865; his negatives went to Henry Chase. See California.

WILLIAMS, JAMES A.
Son of James J.; continued his father's business.

WILLIAMS, JAMES J.
Born 1853; died 1926. Partner with Dickson, 1879-82; purchased the studio, 1882, and ran a very successful business offering a wide array of styles of portraits and various popular scenes. Four generations of his decendants continued the business.

YAT SING
Took over the studio of Joseph W. King, c. 1870.

ZABLAN
Listed in Hilo, Hawaii, 1898.

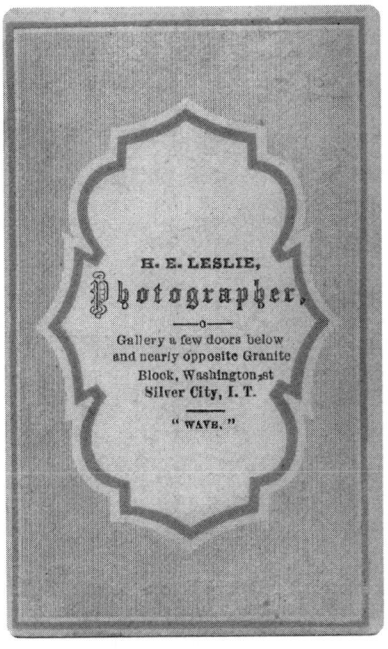

Special thanks to Bruce Hooper for his substantial contribution to this section. For more detailed reference to the photographers of this State, see Arthur A. Hart's Camera Eye on Idaho: Pioneer Photography 1863–1913, *Caxton Printers, Caldwell, Idaho, 1990.*

ALLEN, JAMES A.
Active in Hailey, 1909-11.

ALLEN, W. T.
Active in Boise at the corner of Fifth and Main Streets, c. 1892-93; also listed on Odd Fellows Block, 1893.

ALLISON
Active in Coeur d'Alene, 1885.

ALLISON, J. L.
Active in Missoula, Montana Territory, c. 1875; Murray, Idaho Territory, c. 1885; Chloride, Santa Fe and Kingston, New Mexico, 1886-92.

ALLSWORTH, SAMUEL
Born in England, March 1858. Arrived in U.S., 1874; active in Preston, 1900.

AMOS, LEAH
Born in Louisiana, 1878. Active in Twin Falls, 1908-13; partner in Helm & Amos, 1908; partner in Amos & Flower, 1910; continued alone until 1913.

ANDERSON, C. J.
Born in Sweden, November 1863. Arrived in U.S., 1870. Active in Blackfoot, 1900.

ANDERSON, J. STANLEY
Born in Utah, 1866. Brother of George Edward and Adam Anderson, photographers in Utah. Active in Rexburg, 1904- 17; branch gallery in Rigby, and later in Preston; partner in Anderson & Widerberg,

1906. The Rexburg studio was taken over by Anderson's son, Stanley L. Anderson.

ANDERSON, MARY E.
Born in Utah, 1871. Active in Rexburg, 1910-12.

ANDERSON, STANLEY L.
Son of J. Stanley Anderson and nephew of George Edward Anderson, Springville, Utah. Operated his father's studio in Rexburg after studying photography at Rick's Academy and the American School of Art.

ANDREAS, P. M. (MRS.)
Active in St. Anthony, 1903-04.

ARMSTRONG, CHARLES B.
Active in Idaho Falls, 1911-13.

ART STUDIO
Operated by A. P. and Henry Fair on Main Street in Lewiston, 1899; taught painting and photography and sold artists' materials, cameras, and views of Lewiston.

BAILEY, F. S.
Active in St. Johns, Oneida County, 1889-91.

BAKER, E. W.
Active in Nampa, 1901-03.

BAKER, J. H.
Active in Lewiston, 1889.

BARKER, GEORGE V.
Active in Grangeville, 1906-13.

BARNARD, PAUL
Born in Iowa, April 1876. Active in Wallace, 1900.

BARNARD, THOMAS NATHAN
Born in Waukon, Iowa, 1861; died in Los Angeles, California, February 1916. Active in Waukon, Iowa, c. 1861-80; printer and assistant to Laton Alton Huffman in Miles City, Montana Territory, c. 1881-83. Active in Coeur d'Alene region, Idaho Territory, c. 1886-87; photo studio in Murray, c. 1887; Wardner, c. 1887-89; Wallace, c. 1889-1913.

BARNES, JAMES
Active in Victor, 1903-04.

BARTER, E. E.
Active in Silver City, c. 1867; Custer City, c. 1880; Idaho City, c. 1887.

BARTLETT, ORVILLE O.
Active in Coeur d'Alene, 1901-02.

BATES, JAMES E.
Born in Iowa, 1886. Active in Payette, 1908-10.

BEAL, G. I.
Specialized in lantern slide exhibitions in Idaho City, c. 1883.

BEARD, JAMES
Born in Nebraska, 1887. Active in Arco, 1910.

BEATON, ALEXANDER
Active in Mountain Home, 1906.

BELL, LILLIAN
Photographer for the Camas Prairie Railroad, 1908.

BELLUS & STAMPER
Partnership in Boise, 1896; possibly Frank M. Stamper.

BENNETT & MESSEREAU
Partnership of James H. Bennett and William L. Messereau operating in Gold Hill, Nevada, 1871-75; in Boise, Idaho Territory, 1884-85. Also spelled Mersereau.

BENNETT, JAMES H.
Born in England, 1849; died January 17, 1885. Active in Virginia City, Nevada, c. 1884. Partner with Messereau in Boise, Idaho Territory, on Main Street opposite City Hall, c. 1884-85.

BENSON, LABAN
Born in Nebraska, July 1871. Active in Teton, 1900.

BEVINS, L. A.
Active in Ashton, 1909-11.

BILLINGTON, C.
Active in Caldwell, 1893.

BISBEE, CLARENCE E.
Born in Nebraska, 1876; died 1954. Active in Twin Falls, 1906-13; Jerome, 1910.

BISHIP, T. A. (MRS.)
Active in Bonners Ferry, 1908.

BISHOP, ALLEN K.

Born in Illinois, August 1867. Partner with C. C. Hedum in Hedum & Bishop, operating in California, c. 1895. Active in Silver City, Idaho, 1896-1900; operated Hedum & Bishop's Photographic Studio and Art Store, c. 1896-98; also in Delamar, 1895. Illustrated the August 23, 1895 issue of Idaho Avalanche; toured Meadow and Rock Creeks, the Junipers, Big Springs, Bruneau, Big Flat and Duck Valley Reservations, southern Idaho and northern Nevada, 1895; conducted stereopticon show in Silver City, 1896. Also known as Bishop & Hedum.

BIXBY, NAHUM E.
Born in Iowa, 1858. Active in Wallace, 1910.

BLACK STUDIO
Active in Pocatello, 1903.

BLACKWELDER, E.
Photographer with the United States Geological Survey, 1911.

BODE, OSCAR W.
Born in Minnesota, 1887. Active in Buhl, 1909-10.

BOMAR & BUTLER
Partnership of A. C. Bomar and Professor Gilbert Butler in Idaho City, corner of Montgomery and Wall Streets, 1880; in Bonanza, 1881.

BOMAR & CURRIE
Partnership of A. C. Bomar and Thomas Currie, stereo photographers in Idaho City, 1876-79.

BOMAR & KINGSLEY
Partnership of A. C. Bomar and C. R. Kingsley, stereo photographers in Idaho City, 1877.

BOMAR, ALBERT C.
Born in Illinois, 1849. Active in Boise, 1871; Corine, Utah, Boise and Silver City, Idaho Territory and Winnemucca, Nevada, 1875; Idaho City, Idaho Territory, c. 1876-80. Partner with Thomas Currie, 1876-79, operating as Bomar & Currie. Partner with Professor Gilbert Butler, 1880, operating as Bomar & Butler; continued partnership with Butler in Bonanza, 1881. Married Florence Dodge, December 1883, in Bonanza. Active in Bonanza City, 1886-92. Worked at Volunteer Signal Station at Bonanza for daily meteorological observations, April 1890. Active in Challis, 1894-1900; Idaho Falls, 1910.

BONHORE, EUGENE J.
Born in California, 1855; Active in Lewiston, 1880, 1890-92.

BORGLUM, PAUL M.
Active in Pocatello, 1904-06.

BOWEN, C. F.
Photographer with the United States Geological Survey, 1911-13.

BRAMWELL, CLAUDIUS E.
Born in England, July 1863. Arrived in U.S., 1869. Active in Rexburg, 1900.

BROCKMAN, JOHN A.
Born in Missouri, June 1880. Active in Harrison, 1900; Kellogg, 1912-13.

BROWN, CARL B.
Born in Switzerland, August 1845. Arrived in U.S., 1879. Active in Payette, 1896, 1900.

BROWN, WILLIAM
Born in Ohio, 1872. Active in Coeur d'Alene, 1910. Possibly the same as the previous Brown.

BROWN, WILLIAM
Born in Iowa, 1877. Active in Coeur d'Alene, 1910.

BRUCE, HORACE
Active in King Hill, 1910.

BRYANT, H. C.
Active in Pocatello, 1889-90.

BUNDY, OLIVER C.
Born in Saratoga or Cattaraugas County, New York, August 21, 1827; died in Virginia City, Montana, December 1891. Worked as a miner and photographer in California, 1852-63; in Boise, Idaho Territory, 1863-66; Idaho City, 1863; photographed on railroad car expeditions, 1872-76; in Montana Territory, 1876-91.

BUNNELL, ROSA M.
Born in Missouri, December 1877. Active in Grangeville, 1900, 1909-13.

BUNNELL, WALTER E.
Born in California, May 1875. Active in Grangeville, 1900-02, 1910.

BURNS & RAYMOND
Active in Coeur d'Alene, 1910-11.

BURNS BROTHERS
Partnership of Bruce and Ida Burns operating in Lewiston, 1905.

BURNS, BRUCE
Born in Idaho, June 1880. Active in Moscow, Idaho, c. 1900-03; Lewiston, 1903-13; partner in Burns Brothers, 1905. Photographed the flood at Kendrick, 1900.

BURNS, IDA A.
Active in Lewiston, 1905-13; partner in Burns Brothers, 1905.

BURNS, JAMES GROVER
Active in Caldwell, Idaho, 1912; Boise, Idaho, 1913.

BURNS, ROBERT
Active in Kendrick and Lewiston, 1903.

BURROUGHS, E. R.
Active in Pocatello, 1898.

BURTON, GEORGE
Active in Murray, 1910.

BUTLER, PROFESSOR GILBERT
Born in Plymouth, England, May 13, 1847; died near Hailey, Idaho Territory, June 19, 1884. Graduated from the South Kensington Art School, winning a Queens Scholarship. Artistic painter in the studio of his uncle, Sir John Gilbert, K.C.B., a noted artist. Came to the United States, 1869. Founded the Healdsburg Institute in California, 1873. Taught school in Owyhee, Boise and Alturas Counties, Idaho Territory. Photographer in Idaho City, 1879-83; partner with A. C. Bomar at corner of Montgomery and Wall Streets (on the site of the old St. Charles Hotel), 1880; in Bonanza with A. C. Bomar, 1881; in Bellevue and Hailey, 1883-84. Gallery on Main Street, 1883; on the corner of First Avenue and Bullion Street, 1884.

CALKINS, F. C.
Photographer with the United States Geological Survey, 1903, 1910-12.

CALVIN, WILLIAM T.
Born in Iowa, 1859. Active in Council, 1910.

CANOVA
Active in Boise, 1906.

CANOVA GALLERY
Located at New Sonna Block, Boise, Idaho, 1895.

CAREY, DELIA (MRS.)
Active in Idaho Falls, 1896.

CAREY, EDGAR E.
Born in Maine, September 1873. Active in Idaho Falls, 1900-02.

CAREY, IMOGENE
Born in Utah, November 1876. Active in Idaho Falls, 1900.

CARTER, W. JAMES
Active in Boise, 1908.

CARYL, FLOYD E.
Active in Coeur d'Alene, 1911-13.

CASTLEMAN, PHILIP F.
Active in Silver City, 1866.

CHANDLER, GERALD A.
Active in Post Falls, 1912-13.

CHAPMAN, C. C.
Active in Idaho City, Idaho. Tent on the lot south of the Murphy brick building, c. 1896.

CHENEY, B. F.
Worked for OSL Railroad, c. 1880s.

CHENEY, WILLIE TUTTLE
Born 1869; died 1949. Active in Spencer, 1890s.

CHINN, GEORGE W.
Born in Missouri, October 1963. Active in Caldwell, 1900.

COCHRAN & WARNOCK
Active in Idaho Falls, 1906.

COCHRAN, M. C.
Born in Indiana, 1875. Active in Pocatello, 1910.

COLBORN, JENNIE (MRS.)
Active in Aberdeen, 1914-15.

COMSTOCK, EDITH
Born in Idaho, 1888. Active in Lewiston, 1910.

CONNOR, MORRIS
Active in Silver District and Idaho City, 1887-88. Produced twelve albums for sale, displaying one at the Idaho World office, 1888. Active in Rockwell City, Iowa, c. 1895.

CONTINENT STEREOSCOPIC COMPANY
New York City publisher of stereographs; published stereographs of Idaho Territory, c. 1870-80s.

COOK, FRANCIS AUGUSTUS
Born in New York, c. 1832. Active in Arizona Territory, 1864-72; California, 1879-80; Nevada, 1880; California, 1881- 82; Nevada, 1883-88. Studio in Silver City, Idaho Territory, at the end of the foot bridge on Courthouse Street, 1885, 1889-90. Studio on Main Street, Boise, next door to Masonic Hall, 1887. In Iowa, late 1880s. See Arizona.

COULTER, G. H.
Partner in Wood & Coulter, Idaho City, 1873-74, on Commercial Street opposite the Court House.

CRAIG, F. M.
Active in St. Anthony, Idaho, c. 1895.

CRAIG, FRANK
Active in Twin Falls, 1906.

CRAMER, W. A.
Active in St. Maries, 1911-12.

CRANE, S. W.
Active in Harrison, 1903-06.

CROMWELL, W. J.
Active in Idaho City, partner with E. H. Train on Main Street between Wall and Commercial Streets, c. 1864; Pioneer City, c. 1866.

CROSBY, MARGARET
Born in Michigan, 1875. Active in Twin Falls, 1910.

CUMMINGS BROTHERS
Active in Lewiston, 1891-92.

CUMMINGS, EVERETT G.
Born in Iowa, August 1861. Active in Lewiston, 1900-02.

CUMMINS, THOMAS
Active in Boise, 1912-13; Nampa, 1916.

CURRIE, THOMAS
Partner with A. C. Bomar, 1876-79. Located in Placerville, 1876; Pioneerville, 1876-77; Idaho City, 1877-79; Centerville, 1879-96.

CURRY, ISAAC B.
Born in Pittsburgh, Pennsylvania, c. 1840; died in Boise, Idaho Territory, March 7, 1884. Union Soldier during the Civil War. Operator for John Junk in Idaho City and Boise, 1864-67; in Boise, 1869-84.

CURTIS, ASAHEL
Visited Idaho, 1911. See Washington.

CUTTER, C. P.
Active in Idaho Falls, 1911-12.

CUTTER, JOSEPH H.
Active in Pocatello, 1895; Blackfoot, 1906-12.

DAHLQUIST, W. A.
Active in Oakley, 1908-11, partner in Dahlquist Brothers.

DAVIS BROTHERS
Daguerrian artists from Portsmouth, New Hampshire, 1860-1901; L. G. B., Charles, Marion T. visited the Snake River region, c. 1870 or c. 1880.

DAVIS, CHARLES
Partner in Davis Brothers from New Hampshire; visited the Snake River region, Idaho Territory, c. 1870 or c. 1880.

DAVIS, H. A.
Stereo photographer active in Moscow; may have worked with F. M. Spencer of Mansfield.

DAVIS, JOHN
Born in Kansas, 1882. Active in Pocatello, 1910.

DAVIS, LEWIS G. BREWSTER
Partner in Davis Brothers from New Hampshire; visited the Snake River region, Idaho Territory, c. 1870 or c. 1880.

DAVIS, MARION T.
Partner in Davis Brothers from New Hampshire; visited the Snake River region, Idaho Territory, c. 1870 or c. 1880.

DAY, ERNEST
Active in St. Maries, 1911-12.

DEARINGER
Partner in Sethen & Dearinger, Mountain Home, 1908.

DENNIS, AUGUSTUS
Born in Main, 1857. Active in Hagerman, 1910.

DENNISTON, DEWITT C.
Active in St. Maries, 1912-13.

DIAMOND BROTHERS
Active in Pocatello, 1893.

DICKERSON, A. E.
Active in Coshocton, Ohio, c. 1870. Visited Colorado, Idaho and Utah, c. 1890.

DODGE, HORACE D.
Born in Idaho, 1885. Active in Idaho Falls, 1907-08, as partner in Lundburg & Dodge; listed alone, 1910.

DOOMES, C. H.
Active in Troy, 1910.

DOWE, OSCAR S.
Active in DeLamar, c. 1893. Also operated as itinerant in California, Oregon and Nevada up to 1893. See California, Oregon and Nevada.

DREWERY, HARRY
Born in England, 1871. Arrived in U.S., 1892. Active in Soda Springs, 1908-13.

DUNLAP, J. F.
Active in Sagle, Bonner County, 1906-13.

DURAY, JOHN H.
Operated the Bonanza Art Gallery in Salmon City before May 1880; in Challis, May-July 1880; Bonanza, c. 1880s, in the frame building of C. C. Carlisle on Main Street opposite Clasbey & Hogle's Saloon; Salmon City, 1887-90.

DURRANT, WALTER H.
Active in Driggs, 1911-13.

EASTMAN, GILMAN L.
Born in Maine, October 1848. Active in Boise, 1900.

EDGERTON, R. L.
Born in Iowa, 1874. Active in Emmett, 1910.

EGGAN, HALVOR P.
Born in Norway, 1856. Arrived in U.S. 1876. Active in Moscow, 1905-13.

EGGAN, JAMES P.
Born in Norway, 1873. Arrived in U.S. 1880. Active in Moscow, 1910.

EKEBERG & THORILD
Partnership of Minnie Ekeberg and Annie Thorild, active in Wallace, 1901-04.

EKEBERG, MINNIE
Partner in Ekeberg & Thorild operating in Wallace, 1901-04.

ELECTRIC GALLERY
Operated by Arthur M. Whelchel, Emmett, 1905.

ELITE STUDIO
Active in Nampa, 1908, operated by Fred C. Keller

ELITE STUDIO
Active in Twin Falls, 1910, operated by W. S. Rensimer.

EMERY, WILLIAM G.
Active in Moscow, 1890s. Published the first history of Moscow. See Oregon and Washington.

ENGLISH, HARRY P.
Born in Canada, February 1879. Arrived in U.S., 1900. Active in Mullan, 1900, 1912-13.

ERICHSON & HANSON
Partnership of John A. Hanson and Henry Erichson. Mounted a panoramic exhibition at Champion Hall, Silver City, September 1882. Active in Jordan Valley, Oregon, September 1882. Operated as Erichson & Hanson in Moscow, Idaho, 1885, 1891-92; Also known as Hanson & Erickson.

ERICHSON, HENRY
Born in Germany, 1856. Arrived in U.S., 1871. Partner in Erichson & Hanson, 1882-85, 1891-92. Active in Oregon, 1882; Moscow, Idaho, 1884-1908; operated alone, c. 1890. Also spelled Erickson.

ERICSSON, CHARLES T.
Born in Sweden, 1874. Arrived in U.S., 1891. Active in Blackfoot, 1910, 1913.

EXCELSIOR PHOTOGRAPHIC PARLORS
Operated by J. M. Moriarity in Hailey, May 1884, on the 2nd floor over the Oldham Building, two doors south of T. R. Jones' Bank, west side of Main Street, between Bullion and Croy Streets.

FAIKE, HARRY M.
Born in Minnesota, 1883. Active in St. Anthony, 1910.

FAIR & HENRY, A. P.
Operated the Art Studio on Main Street in Lewiston, two blocks east of the courthouse. Taught painting and photography classes, sold artists' materials, etchings, cameras; landscape and interior photographers.

FAIR & THOMPSON
Partnership active in Lewiston, 1904; Henry Fair.

FAIR, HENRY
Born in New Jersey, August 1856. Active in Lewiston, 1899-1900, 1904-08; partner in A. P. & Henry Fair, 1899, operating the Art Studio on Main Street; partner in Fair & Thompson, 1904.

FAULKNER, CHARLES
Born in Ohio, 1870. Active in Coeur d'Alene, 1910.

FEHSE
Partner in Finn & Fehse, operating in Wallace, 1908.

FENTON & MASON
Active in Boise, 1910-11.

FINK, HENRY
Born in Iowa, 1867. Active in Nez Perce, 1906-13; partner in Fink Brothers, 1910.

FINK, JOHN
Active in Nez Perce, 1910, with Henry Fink, operating as Fink Brothers.

FINN & FEHSE
Partnership in Wallace, 1908.

FOOR, GEORGE W.
Active in Portland, Oregon, 1888-90; Boise, Idaho, 1889-90; Weiser, 1890; Placerville and Idaho City, c. 1890-95.

FORTIN, JOSEPH
Active in Lewiston, 1902-05.

FOWLER, WILLIAM B.
Born in Tennessee, May 1863. Active in Payette, 1890s; Salmon, 1900-13.

FRENCH, THEODORE D.
Born in Michigan, 1874. Active in New Plymouth, 1906-13.

FROST, GEORGE A.
Active in Lewiston, 1874.

FURCHT, DELIA E.
Born in Michigan, 1855. Active in Gooding, 1910.

GAETZ, ELLA
Active in Atlanta, 1890s, 1900.

GALE, H. S.
Photographer with the United States Geological Survey, 1909-13.

GALLIGER, MARTIN
Born in New York, 1858. Active in Wallace, 1910.

GARVEY, W. E. (MRS.)
Active in Pocatello, 1913-14.

GAY, E. JANE
Amateur photographer accompanying Bureau of Indian Affairs Anthropologist, Alice Cunningham Fletcher, to Idaho Territory, 1889; unofficial photographer for the Dawes Commission, 1889-93; photographed the Nez Perce at their reservation in Lapwai, Idaho.

GIBBONS, GERTRUDE (MRS.)
Born in Kansas, 1877. Active in Grangeville, 1909-11.

GILBERT & VINCENT
Partnership active in Idaho Falls, 1911-12.

GILBERT, F. G.
Active in Rathdrum, 1910.

GILBERT, FRANK M.
Partner in Gilbert & Vincent, Idaho Falls, 1911-12.

GILBERT, G. K.
Photographer with the United States Geological Survey, 1899.

GIMBLE, MARY RENICK
Born 1866; died 1942. Active in Coeur d'Alene, c. 1890-1912.

GLANVILLE, GEORGE W.
Born in Iowa, 1867. Active in Blackfoot, 1903-13.

GOMOND, JOSEPH W.
Born in Canada, December 1866. Arrived in the U.S., 1870. Operated Gomond's Photograph Gallery in Lewiston, upstairs opposite the Raymond House, 1899-05; in Wallace, 1908-13. Also spelled Gomand.

GOODHUE, IRA D.
Active in Cottonwood, 1912-13.

GORDON PORTRAIT COMPANY
Active in Soda Springs, 1910.

GRAHAM, LAVINIA J.
Born in Iowa, 1870. Active in Emmett, 1910.

GRAVES, TIMOTHY L.
Active in Boise, 1889-93.

GREGORY, C. A.
Active in Stanley, c. 1900.

GRIFFIN, H. J. (MRS.)
Partner in Tonkin & Griffin, Boise, 1896.

HAGEN, E. B.
Active in Coeur d'Alene, 1910-11.

HALES, STEPHEN
Active in Rexburg, 1903-04.

HALL, JOHN W.
Boise, 1906-07.

HALL, PETER J.
Born in Idaho, 1885. Active in Genessee, 1910-13.

HALL, WILLIAM N.
Active in Coeur d'Alene, 1887-90.

HAMILTON, JAMES W. M.
Active in Madison, Wisconsin, 1879-80. Listed in Boise, c. 1883, at the engineering office of James M. Hamilton and J. A. Richardson, selling cameras and darkroom supplies and offering instructions on taking stereoscopic pictures.

HAMLEY, EMILY
Active in Kendrick, 1903-04.

HANCOCK, EDWARD S.
Born in Canada, 1852. Active in Cottonwood, 1903-13; also in Grangeville, 1908.

HANSEN, AXEL
Active in Pocatello, 1906-07.

HANSON
Operated The Elite in Grangeville and Stuart, c. 1895.

HANSON & ERICHSON
Partnership active 1882-85. Mounted a panoramic exhibition at Champion Hall, Silver City, September 1882. Also in Jordan Valley, Oregon, September 1882. In Moscow, Idaho, operating as Erichson & Hanson, 1885. Also spelled Erickson.

HANSON, CHARLES W.
Born in Minnesota, April 1867. Active in Genessee, 1900-08.

HANSON, FREDERICK
Born in Utah, 1875. Active in Preston, 1910.

HANSON, JOHN A.
Born in Denmark, September 1854. Arrived in U.S., 1872. Partner in Hanson & Erichson, 1882-1885; in Oregon, 1882; Moscow, Idaho, 1885, 1891-92; Grangeville, 1892-1910; partner in Hanson & Parker, 1910.

HARGEN & SKATRUD
Partnership in Coeur d'Alene, 1910-11.

HARGEN, ELIAS B.
Born in Norway, 1870. Arrived in U.S., 1900. Partner in Hargen & Skatrud, Coeur d'Alene, 1910-11.

HARNES, F. E.
Itinerant in Idaho Territory, Montana, Wyoming, Oregon and Utah, 1886-87. Partner with Thomas J. White, headquartered at Eagle Rock, Idaho Territory and Dillon, Montana. Active in Eagle Rock, c. January 1887, in "White's New Photograph Gallery."

HART & SON, W. H.
Partnership of Elmer W. Hart and his father, William H. Hart, operating in Ilo, 1908-13; Vollmer, 1913.

HART, ELMER W.
Born in Colorado, 1887. Son of William H. Hart. Active in Ilo, 1908-13; Vollmer, 1913; Ilo and Vollmer were later named Craigmont; partner in W. H. Hart & Son. See Oregon.

HART, HARRY L.
Cottonwood, 1912-13, partner in Lenox & Hart.

HART, WILLIAM H.
Born in Iowa, 1861. Active in Ilo, 1908-13; Vollmer, 1913; Ilo and Vollmer were later named Craigmont; partner in W. H. Hart & Son.

HARVEY, C. EDWIN
Partner in Whyte & Harvey, Boise, 1901-13, with William Whyte.

HASFURTHER, JOSEPH M.
Active in Genesee, 1891-92.

HASSING, F. H.
Blackfoot, 1914.

HASTIE, GEORGE, D.
Died in Silver City, March 13, 1866. Active in Silver City, 1865-66.

HAYES & STENMARK
Partnership in Wardner, 1910-11.

HAYES, C. W.
Photographer with the United States Geological Survey, 1903.

HAYNES, FRANK JAY
See Minnesota.

HAZELTINE, LELAND S.
Active in Montana, 1880; Idaho City and Boise Basin, 1884. Active in Montana, c. 1894-97, 1900. Also listed as L. F. Hazeltine.

HAZELTINE, MARTIN MASON
Active in Boise, Idaho Territory, at 9th near Grove Street, December, 1883-October or November, 1884. During 1886, itinerant in Idaho Territory in Idaho City, west side of Main street, opposite Temperance Hall, July, 1886-August, 1886; Banner, July-August, 1886; Center-

ville, August, 1886; Garden Valley, Fall, 1886; Emmett, Fall, 1886. See California, Oregon and Traveling.

HEDUM & BISHOP
Partnership of C. C. Hedum and A. K. Bishop active in California, c. 1895. Active in Silver City, Idaho, as Hedum & Bishop's Photographic Studio and Art Store, c. 1895. Illustrated the August, 23, 1895 issue of the Idaho Avalanche. Photographic tour through southern Idaho and northern Nevada by A. K. Bishop, mid October-late November 1895. Stereopticon show advertised by A. K. Bishop at the Courthouse, Silver City, Idaho, late July 1896. Active in Delamar, c. 1895; branch gallery, 1896-98.

HEDUM, CHARLES C.
Born in Norway, August 1875. Arrived in U.S., 1888. Partner in Hedum & Bishop, c. 1895-98; in Delamar and Silver City; toured Meadow and Rock Creeks, the Junipers, Big Springs, Bruneau, Big Flat and Duck Valley Reservations; also in southern Idaho.

HELM & AMOS
Partnership of Milton H. Helm and Leah Amos, active in Twin Falls, 1908.

HELM, DANIEL
Born in Kansas, June 1870. Active in Troy, 1900.

HELM, MILTON H.
Born in Indiana, 1883. Partner in Helm & Amos, operating in Twin Falls, 1908; listed alone in Mountain Home, 1910- 13.

HELSOM, EDWIN
Born in England, March 1868. Arrived in U.S., 1879. Active in Lewiston, 1900.

HENLEY, G. A.
Active in Pocatello, 1906.

HEROY, W. B.
Photographer with the United States Geological Survey, 1912.

HEWITT, D. F.
Photographer with the United States Geological Survey, 1913.

HILDRETH, CARL F.
Active in Caldwell, 1906-10.

HILL, ROY F.
Born in Missouri, 1884. Active in Gooding, 1910-13.

HIMES, RICHARD B.
Born in Ohio, 1871. Active in Kendrick, 1906; Sandpoint, 1909-13.

HINTHORNE, B. H.
Active in Blackfoot, 1912-13.

HOFFMAN, JOHN D.
Photographer on Major R. S. Williamson's expedition in California and Idaho, 1865.

HOFMANN, HENRY
Active in Taho, Idaho County, 1913-14.

HOGAN
Active in Grangeville, c. 1905.

HOLLAND, JAMES S.
Born in Utah, 1882. Active in Rigby, 1910.

HOMER, JOHN A.
Born in Utah, February 1878. Active in St. Anthony, 1900.

HOWELL, L. R.
Active in Preston, 1906.

HOWER, ATLIN B.
Active in Montana, 1888-92; Pocatello, Idaho, 1892. See Oregon.

HUDSON, ARTHUR
Active in Genessee, 1905-08.

HUNTINGTON, C. L.
Active in Boise, 1909.

HURSH, F. D.
Active in Franklin, 1910-11.

HURT, F. E.
Active in Boise, 1912-13.

HUTCHINS, CHARLES
Active in Sandpoint, 1903-13.

HUTTEBALLE, H. C.
Stereo photographer in Idaho Falls.

HUTTSTAND, FRED
Born in North Dakota, 1889. Active in Wallace, 1910.

INTERNATIONAL VIEW COMPANY
Operated by C. L. Wasson in Dacatur, Illinois, c. 1899-c. 1910. Located in Idaho, c. 1902.

JACKSON, WILLIAM HENRY
Photographed and stereographed Idaho Territory on the Hayden Survey, 1871 and 1872; revisited Idaho, 1892, with painter, Thomas Moran. Photographs of the Snake River and Shoshone falls appeared in J. M. Goodwin's article, "The Snake River Country: A Wild Part of Idaho," Overland Monthly, January 1898. See Nebraska.

JACOBSON, PHILIP
Born in Michigan, 1884. Partner in Nadeau & Jacobson, active in Sandpoint, 1909-13.

JELLUM, HERBERT LEE
Born in Norway, 1869. Arrived in U.S., 1885. Active in Nampa, 1900, 1909-13.

JENKS, JOEL ALONZO
Born in Utah, 1873. Active in Monpelier, 1903-06; Paris, 1910-13.

JOHNSON & SON
Ansgar E. and his father, Jons P. Johnson, active in Boise, 1911-13.

JOHNSON, ANSGAR E.
Born in Minnesota, September 1893; died 1981. Active in Boise, 1911-13, operating as Johnson & Son with his father, Jons P.

JOHNSON, E. G.
Active in Monitor, Kootenai County (later Black Rock), 1908.

JOHNSON, JONS P.
Born in Sweden, March 1863; died 1941. Partner with his son, Ansgar E., operating as Johnson & Son in Boise, 1911- 13.

JOHNSON, T. R. (MRS.)
Active in Emmett, 1906.

JONES, AMOS KENDALL
See Oregon.

JONES BROTHERS
Itinerants in Idaho Territory and Oregon, c. 1880-c. 1891; Boise, Idaho City and Placerville, Idaho Territory, 1880; Silver City, photographic tent on Washington Street, 1881. W. L. and W. R. Jones, and possibly others. See Traveling and Oregon.

JONES, CHARLES M.
See Oregon.

JONES, L. I.
Active in Wallace, 1906.

JONES, ROBERT A.
Active in Preston, 1908-13.

JONES, WILLIAM H.
Active in Rathdrum, 1908.

JOSLIN, J. B.
Active in Potlatch, 1911.

JOY, EMIL W.
Born in Oregon, 1890. Active in Montpelier, 1910; Grace, 1913.

JUNK, JOHN
Born in Bakersfield, California. Photographer in Idaho City, 1864-70, rebuilt studio on Main Street three times after fires. Partner with Isaac B. Curry and also in Sutterly Brothers & Junk, 1865-66; partner with Curry, operating as Junk & Curry, 1867-68. In Silver City, 1866-68, partner with Hiram E. Leslie, studio over Wells, Fargo & Company's Office, operating as Junk & Leslie. Also known as Junk & Company, 1865-70. John Funk died at Stein's Mountain, Idaho Territory, January 18, 1882 (posssibly John Junk).

KELLER, FRED C.
Operated the Elite Studio in Nampa, 1908-13.

KEMBLE, CHARLES M
Active in Spink, Boise County, 1912-13.

KENDRICK
Active in Latah County, c. 1875.

KINGSLEY, CHARLES R.
Born in Portland, Oregon, 1857 (or 1859 according to Hart); died 1940. Active in Idaho City, 1876-81; Boise, 1881-90; partner with Bomar, 1877; studio at the corner of Montgomery and Wall Streets, 1884-87; Kingsley's New Art Gallery, east side of 7th Street, two doors north of Idaho Street, 1881-89; at corner of 7th and Idaho Streets, 1890-91. Also in Placerville and Silver City, 1883, 1888. Also known as Charles R. Kingsley, Jr., and Charles S. Kingsley.

KIRBY, O. A.
Active in Post Falls, 1908.

KNAPPEN, C. G.
Active in Boise, 1889.

KOCH, GEORGE W.
Active in Rathdrum, 1901-06, operating as George W. Koch & Company.

KOCH, JOHN L.
Active in Rathdrum, 1901-04.

LADLEY, GEORGE
Born in Minnesota, 1878. Active in Bonners Ferry, 1908-13.

LAMBRECHT'S STUDIO
Active in Blackfoot, 1914.

LANE, THOMAS
Born in New York, September 1872. Active in Pocatello, 1900.

LANEY, FRANCIS BAKER
Active on the Nez Perce Reservation, 1890s(?)

LANGMAID, GEORGE W.
Born in Idaho, September 1878. Active in Boise, 1900, 1905.

LARSON, OLAF P.
Born 1879, Nordfjordeid, Norway; died in San Francisco, 1971. Gallery in Moscow, 1890s; farmed in Squirrel, c. 1900- 10s, and continued taking stereographs.

LAVERING, E. C.
Active in Caldwell, 1903-06; Twin Falls, 1907.

LAW & MILLER
Partnership of John Law and George W. Miller operating in Idaho City, 1864; Boise, 1864-65, as the New Photograph Gallery, corner of Idaho and Eighth Streets.

LAW, D. J.
Active in Soda Springs, Idaho, c. 1890.

LAW, JOHN
Partner in Law & Miller, Idaho City, 1864; Boise, 1864-65.

LAWRENCE & COMPANY, GEORGE R.
Chicago company active in Arco, 1909.

LEE, ALICE I.
Active in American Falls, 1912-13.

LEE, ANTON
Active in Deary, 1910-13.

LEE, H. V.
Active in Boise, 1909.

LEEK, NORMAN
Active in Nampa, 1901.

LEIGHTON, M. O.
Photographer with the United States Geological Survey before 1913.

LENOX & HART
Partnership of Harry H. Lenox and Harry L. Hart, operating in Cottonwood, 1912-13.

LENOX, HARRY H.
Partner in Lenox & Hart, Cottonwood, 1912-13.

LEONARD
Active in Boise, 1898; possibly Joe Leonard.

LEONARD, JOE
Born in Idaho, 1881. Active in Boise, 1910-11.

LESLIE, HIRAM E.
Born in Amherst, Ohio, July 30, 1835; died May 31, 1882. Active in Silver City, 1865-74. Partner with John Junk, over Wells, Fargo &

Company's office on Washington Street, 1867; operated alone at same location, 1867-69; Leslie's Photographic Rooms, a few doors below and nearly opposite Granite Block, Washington Street, 1869-70; studio at the lower end of Washington Street, 1871-73. Partner with H. C. Tandy, Nevada, 1874; with J. C. Potter, Winnemucca, Nevada, 1875. Operated gallery again in Silver City, 1877-81. Gallery was located one door north of the Idaho Avalanche Office, 1880-81. Active in Boise, 1870-71, opposite Masonic Hall, upstairs on Main Street.

LESTER, D. CURTIS
Born in Pennsylvania, 1852. Active in Lewiston, 1880.

LEWEIS, FRED
Active in Rexburg, 1914.

LEY, ALFRED M.
Active in Boise, 1908; Parma, 1910; Caldwell, 1912-13.

LIEUALLEN
Partner in Smith & Lieuallen, active in Coeur d'Alene, 1903-04.

LINDGREN, WALDEMAR
Photographer with the United States Geological Survey, 1896-98.

LOGAN, W. H.
Operated Logan's Art Gallery in Boise, Idaho Street adjoining Dr. Arnold's Dental Office, in Dr. Arnold's lot, between 8th and 9th Streets, July 20-November 9, 1875.

LORTON, JOSEPH S.
Born in Missouri, March 1873. Active in Salubria, 1900.

LUBKEN, WALTER J.
Born in New York City (Hart lists Idaho as birthplace), July 24, 1883; died in Boise, 1960. Official Photographer for the U.S. Reclamation Service, 1903-10; assistant to John M. Miller, 1905-08. Active in Arizona, 1904-10; Boise, Idaho, 1910, 1912-13. Also photographed water projects in New Mexico, Colorado, Nevada, Oregon, Nebraska, Montana, California, and Utah. Name also spelled Lubkin.

LUDLOW, CHARLES
Born in New Jersey, 1877. Active in St. Anthony, 1910-13.

LUNDBURG & DODGE
Partnership active in Idaho Falls, 1907-08.

LUPTON, C. T.
Photographer with the United States Geological Survey, 1913.

LYON, T. E.
Active in Victor, 1901-02.

MAALAND, KNUT
Born in Norway, 1886. Arrived in U.S., 1906. Active in Wallace, 1910.

MACKEY, G. W.
Itinerant in Oregon, Washington and Idaho, c. 1890-c. 1891. Active in Halsey, Oregon, 1890; Portland, Oregon c. July 1891. Pitched his "Travelling Gallery" tent in Caldwell, Idaho, July 20-August 3, 1891.

MAGDEN, ETTA M.
Born in Michigan, 1896. Active in Mountain Home, 1910.

MALLORY, MARTYN E.
Born 1880; died 1936. Active in Hailey, c. 1900-13.

MANSFIELD, G. R.
Photographer with the United States Geological Survey, 1909-13.

MARCKEL, W. E.
Active in Pocatello, Idaho, c. 1894-95. Also spelled Markell.

MARSH, DANIEL
Active in Colfax, Washington Territory, c. 1885; Weiser, Idaho, c. 1890, 1903-06; visited and stereographed Yellowstone National Park.

MARSHAL, MILTON A.
Active in Blackfoot, 1901-02; Weippe, 1903-06.

MARTIN, M. B.
Active in Albion, c. 1900; Gooding, c. 1909.

MARTY, FRED
Active in Buhl, 1912-13.

MASON
Partner in Fenton & Mason, active in Boise, 1910-11.

MASON, MORTON G.
Partner in Mason & Thomas, operating in Boise, 1909-13.

MASON, PETER
Born in Denmark, February 1863. Arrived in U.S., 1877. Active in Coeur d'Alene, 1900.

MAXWELL BROTHERS
Partnership of W. W., C. T., and J. D. Maxwell operating galleries in Washington, 1875-1900, also known as Maxwell Photograph Company. Opened a branch gallery in Lewiston, Idaho, in a tent located on east Main Street, a few doors east of G.A.R. Hall, June-December 24, 1899. See Washington.

MAXWELL, C. T.
See Maxwell Brothers.

MAXWELL, CHARLES N.
Active in Moscow, 1900.

MAXWELL, J. D.
See Maxwell Brothers.

MAXWELL, W. W.
See Maxwell Brothers.

McCAFEE, W. C.
Active in Darius; listed in Davis, c. 1890.

McCANDLESS, DAVID C.
Operated the Rex Gallery in Boise, 1901-13.

McCARTNEY, HERMAN G.
Born in Missouri, June 1877. Active in Harrison, 1900.

McCLAIN, J. D.
Active in Logan, Ohio, c. 1880; Garnett, Kansas, c. 1890. Listed in Boise, Idaho on Main Street, between 10th and 11th Streets, August-September 1891.

McCLAIN, WILLIAM W.
Listed in Boise City, 1891-92. Also spelled McLain.

McEVOY, JOHN JAMES
Partner with C. L. Glendenen in Eagle Rock and Rexburg, c. 1889; listed alone in Idaho Falls, April-May 1892; Photographed the Black-

foot in Eagle Rock, c. 1889; Idaho Falls, Pocatello and Montpelier, 1891-93. Active in Trinity County, California, April 1897-1900.

McINTYRE, H. A.
Born in Ohio, 1843. Active in Rocky Bar, 1870.

McKENZIE
Partner in States & McKenzie, active in Council, 1908.

McMEEKIN, JOSEPH P.
Born in Ireland, April 1859. Arrived in U.S., 1872. Active in Pocatello, 1903.

McMILLAN, J. S.
Active in Portland, Oregon, c. 1870. Photograph enlarger in Boise Basin and Idaho City, Idaho Territory, c. June 1877. May be the John McMillan active in San Francisco, California, 1883-86; may also be with the McMillan Brothers, Charles, John and George, in San Francisco and Santa Maria, California, 1883-87. McMillan Brothers also active in Marshfield, Oregon, 1886. Name also spelled McMilleon.

MELCHER, JOHN R.
Born in Ohio, 1863. Active in Peck, 1910.

MERRIFIELD, EDWARD G.
Active in Shoshone, 1908-13.

MESSEREAU, WILLIAM L.
Partner with J. H. Bennett operating as Bennett & Messereau in Gold Hill, Nevada, 1871-75; Boise, Idaho Territory, 1884-85, on Main Street opposite City Hall. Also spelled Mersereau.

MIDDLETON, DELIA
Born in Maine, September 1854. Active in St. Anthony, 1900.

MILL-APS, W. F.
Active in Hailey, 1889-90. May be misspelling of Millsap.

MILLER, C. A.
Partner in Miller & Pyfer, Pocatello, 1901-02.

MILLER, GEORGE W.
Partner in Law & Miller, operating the New Photograph Gallery at the corner of Idaho and Eighth Streets in Boise, 1864-65. Listed alone in Boise and Idaho City, c. 1878-c. 1879.

MILLS, RICHARD I.
Born in Utah, March 1871. Active in Oakley, 1900-06; Burley, 1908.

MOBLEY, PROFESSOR ROBERT
Gave lantern slide shows in Boise, 1883-84; operated his photographic tent in the vacant lot behind the Overland Hotel, 1884-86.

MONTGOMERY, J. H.
Active in Oregon, 1860-77; Washington Territory, 1873; Boise, Idaho Territory, 1877; Caldwell, 1893. See Oregon.

MOORE, FRANCIS
Born in England, 1827; died in the U.S., April 1898. Arrived in U.S., 1848. Active in Boise, c. 1875, 1878-82. Partner with A. C. Bomar on 7th Street, between Main and Idaho Streets opposite Dr. Dansman's office, 1878-79; gallery directly opposite the Ladies Store in the Central Hotel, 1879-80. Studio was destroyed by fire, March 15, 1880; located in new gallery on 7th Street, 1880-88. Active in Caldwell, 1888-98; studio at Kimball Street, 1890-93. Operated in the Snake River area and Silver City on Washington Street, 1889; in Weiser 1890; Nampa, 1891. Also listed as Frank. See Oregon.

MORIARITY, J. M.
Active in Austin, Nevada, c. April 1884; Hailey, Idaho Territory, May 1884. Operated Excelsior Photographic Parlors on the 2nd floor over the Oldham Building, two doors south of T. R. Jones' Bank, west side of Main Street, between Bullion and Croy Streets. Active in Wardner, 1906.

MORRIS, CHARLES A.
Born in California, 1867. Active in Lewiston, 1910.

MOSS & RICKETTS
Active in Silver City, c. 1900.

MUDGE, THE MISSES
Active in Blackfoot, c. cabinet card era. Photographed Shoshoni.

MURRAY, J. W.
Active in Placerville, c. 1905.

MYERS, CHARLES E.
Active in Malad, 1912-13.

MYERS, HORACE C.
Possibly active in Ohio, c. July 1889. Operated Myers' Studio in Boise, Idaho Territory, at E. M. Reed's Old Stand on Main Street, owned by his brother, John C. Myers until late July 1890; also sold etchings, lithographs, books, bibles, easels, souvenirs and novelties. Studio name changed to Myers' Picture and Photographic Gallery, then to Myers' Photograph Gallery, c. July 1890-July 1895. Operated a photographic tent in Idaho City in the lot above the Idaho World office, August 1 - 6, 1890; also active in DeLamar and Silver City, c. July 1891; Idaho City, 1894-95. Active in the eastern United States, c. August 1893. Studio in Boise, 1889-1911; partner in Myers & Rice, 1912-13.

MYERS, JOHN C.
Brother of Horace C. Myers. Worked in some of the best galleries of the eastern United States before 1888; operator for Charles R. Kingsley in Boise and Placerville, c. 1888; operated the J. C. Myers Photo Art Temple (tent) in Boise, behind Overland Hotel, August-late November 1888. Purchased Frank Struckmann's gallery opposite the Post Office, late 1888; operated Myers' Art Temple, 1888-89; relocated to E. M. Reed's Old Stand, Main Street, c. April 1889-c. July 1890. Operator for Horace C. Myers, c. 1893-c. 1894. Itinerant in Idaho, 1894, active in Placerville and Idaho City; photographed Chinese who desired to register in the Basin, February-March 1894; in Silver City operating a photograph tent, c. July 1894; in Delamar and Silver City, c. July-November 1894. Myers and George Wheel were arrested near Caldwell, Idaho, for making silver dollars out of block tin, and sent before the U.S. Commissioner in Boise, December 1894.

NADEAU & JACOBSEN
Partnership active in Sandpoint, 1909-13.

NELSON, B. S.
Active in Anderson, Idaho, c. 1900-05.

NELSON, J. H.
Active in Mackay, 1906.

NELSON, NELS
Active in Troy, 1905-08.

NEWCOMB
Active in Silver City, c. 1890.

NEWELL, MABELLE
Active in Meridian, 1909-13.

NOCK, G. R.
Active in Hailey, 1906.

NORTON, S.
Active in Silver City, Idaho Territory as photographer and millwright,
April-June 1871.

NUTT BROTHERS
Active in Bonners Ferry, 1906.

O'CONNOR, MAURICE
Operated the "Photographic Studio of Idaho City, Photo Tent" on
Main Street, July-November 1891, August 1892, August 1893. Specialized in the photographing of mines, tunnels, dark interiors,
machinery, by the new lightning flash, and also photographed objects
in motion. He photographed the planet Mars using a flexible glass
negative, producing a four inch circular image, August 1892. Active in
Idaho until c. 1896.

O'HAVER, HELEN
Active in Idaho Falls, 1906.

O'SULLIVAN, TIMOTHY H.
Born 1840; died 1882. Photographed Idaho Territory while on the King
and Wheeler Surveys, 1868, 1874. King Survey stereographs published,
1873, 1876-80; Wheeler Survey stereographs published 1874-76.

ODDEN, CRIST
Active in Troy, 1905-08.

OLIVER & WORMER
Traveling stereopticon exhibition in the Western United States; in
Idaho City, Centerville, Pioneer City and Placerville in Idaho Terri-
tory; also in Washington, Oregon, and California. While in Idaho
City, the exhibition was located at the Jenny Lind Theatre, c. Octo-
ber 1866; William Oliver, agent, M. Wormer, proprietor.

OLSON, HALVAR
Born in Norway, 1850. Arrived in U.S., 1873. Active in Coeur d'A-
lene, 1908-13.

OLSON, JOHN E.
Born in Iowa, 1875. Son of Halvar Olson. Active in Coeur d'Alene,
1910-13.

ORVIS, SPENCER
Born in Canada, August 1875. Active in Caldwell, 1900.

OYLEAR, M. M.
Active in Leland, 1906-08.

PALMER, FRANK
Born in Missouri, December 1864. Active in Rathdrum, 1900.

PARK, RALPH F.
Active in Emmett, 1912-13.

PARKER
Partner in Hanson & Parker, Grangeville, 1910.

PARSONS, CHARLES J.
Active in Homedale, 1910.

PARTAIN, JOSEPH
Active in Lewiston, 1908.

PICKETT, EDWARD
Born in Minnesota, May 1870. Active in Stuart (Kooskia), 1900.

PILLINER, FREDERICK J.
Worked with William H. Pilliner, operating studios in California, Idaho
and Montana. Photographed in Ketchum, Idaho, 1889-90; Silver City
at the "Old Cook Stand," c. December 1889-June 1890; Wood River
Country, winter, 1890; DeLamar, c. 1891; Silver City, 1891-92.

PILLINER, WILLIAM H.
Born in England, April 1828 (Hart lists birthdate as 1826). Arrived in
U.S., 1835. Studios in California, Nevada, Montana, c. 1800s. Active
in Malad, Idaho, 1880; Salmon, 1887; Silver City, gallery above Sam
Heidelberger's General Merchandise Store, September-October, 1891.
Took a series of mountain views around Silver City and DeLamar,
September 1891, 1892; Mountain Home, 1910.

PITTENGER, WILLIAM
Born in Kansas, 1872. Active in Heyburn, 1910.

POTTER, J. C.
Active in Elyria, Ohio; partner in J. C. Potter & Son with W. E. Potter, c. 1870. Active in Winnemucca, Nevada as J. C. Potter, c. July
1875; Silver City, Idaho Territory, 1875, partner in Leslie & Potter
with Hiram E. Leslie.

PRATER, WILLIAM J.
Born in Wales, 1882. Arrived in U.S. 1899. Active in Pocatello, 1907-
13. Partner in Prater & Williams, 1910.

PRESCOTT, JOHN J.
Born in Massachusetts, 1857. Active in Weiser, 1903-04; Caldwell,
1906-13.

PRICE, D.
Active in Reubens, 1912-13.

PYFER
Partner in Miller & Pyfer with C. A. Miller, operating in Pocatello,
1901-02.

RALSTON, JOHN E.
Born in Indiana, September 1866. Active in Boise, 1900.

RANSOM, J. G.
Active in Pine, 1909-10.

RANSOME, F. L.
Photographer with the United States Geological Survey, 1901, 1904.

RAYMOND
Active in Coeur d'Alene; listed alone, 1908; partner in Burns & Raymond, 1910-11.

READ, BENJAMIN F.
Active in Pocatello, 1905. See Oregon.

REDPATH, CHARLES
Active in Sandpoint, 1906.

REELS, G. W.
Active in Payette, 1906.

REICHARDT, J.
Active in Twin Falls, 1906.

REIMANN, NATHAN
Born in South Dakota, 1888. Active in American Falls, 1910-11.

REMBRANDT STUDIO
Active in Nampa, 1908.

RENSIMER, WILLIAM S.
Born in Missouri, 1874. Active in Twin Falls, 1910-13.

REX GALLERY
Operated by David C. McCandless in Boise, 1908.

RHODES, J. W.
Active in Weiser, 1891-92.

RICE, C. PERRY
Partner in Myers & Rice, Boise, 1912-13.

RICHARDS, R. W.
Photographer with the United States Geological Survey, 1908, 1911.

RICKETTS
Partner in Moss & Ricketts, active in Silver City, c. 1900.

RIGGS, J. W.
Active in Lewiston, 1880-87, 1891.

RINEHART, ELLIS W.
Born in Oregon , 1871. Active in Montpelier, 1901-13.

ROBINSON, EDITH
Active in Burley, 1912-13.

ROEDER, V. C.
Active in Pocatello, 1898-99.

ROSE, JOSEPHINE (MRS.)
Active in Orofino, 1906.

ROSENGRANT, DAN L.
Born in Kansas, June 1876. Active in Stuart (Kooskia), 1900.

ROSS, DANIEL W.
Born in Ohio, 1868. Active in Coeur d'Alene, 1908-11.

ROUGH, CHARLES
Born in Pennsylvania, 1885. Photographer for the OSL Railroad, in Pocatello, 1910.

ROYCE, L. M.
Active in Sandpoint, 1908.

RUNDLE, WILLIAM
Lewiston, 1912.

RUSH, CHARLES
Born in Virginia, 1879. Active in Coeur d'Alene, 1910.

RUSSELL, I. C.
Photographer with the United States Geological Survey, 1901.

SAMMIS, EDWARD M.
Born in New York c. 1839. Active in Washington Territory, 1860-66. Operated studio in Lewiston, Washington Territory (town became part of Idaho Territory, 1863) on D Street, August 1862. Active in California, 1867-71. See Washington and California.

SANDER, LOUIS
Photographer from Chicago; active in Utah, c. 1890. Operator for Charles R. Kingsley in Kingsley's Photograph Gallery, "Old Stand," corner of 7th and Idaho Streets, Boise, Idaho, 1890.

SARGENT, FRANCIS H.
Born in Nebraska, 1874. Active in Sandpoint, 1908-10.

SAVAGE, CHARLES ROSCOE
See Utah.

SAVIDGE, CHARLES
Born in Minnesota, 1889. Active in Emmett, 1910.

SAWLEY, MILDRED
Active in Monitor, Kootenai County, 1906-08.

SCHULTZ, A. R.
Photographer with the United States Geological Survey, 1910-11.

SETHEN, I. J.
Partner in Sethen & Dearinger, Mountain Home, 1908.

SHEPARD, W. N. P.
Active in Paris, 1889-92.

SHERMAN, CLIFTON G.
Active in Weiser, 1912-13.

SIGLER, R. HAROLD
Active in Boise, 1911-13.

SIMMONS, ALLEN A.
Born in Illinois, June 1869. Active in Nampa, 1895.

SKATRUD
Partner in Hargen & Skatrud, operating in Coeur d'Alene, 1910-11.

SMITH & LIEUALLEN
Partnership in Coeur d'Alene, 1903-04.

SMITH, ED.
Active in Lewiston, 1891; Boise, 1900.

SMITH, HANNIBAL H.
Born in North Carolina, 1879. Active in Oakley, 1909-13.

SMITH, IDA B.
Active in Jerome, 1909-11.

SMITH, MATTIE G.
Active in Rupert, 1912-13.

SMITH, RAY S.
Born in Iowa, February 1871. Active in Idaho Falls, 1900-04.

SMITH, THOMPSON J.
Active in Heyburn, 1910-13.

SMITH, W. E.
Active in Kooskia, 1906.

SMITH, WILLIAM B.
Active in Bellevue, 1889-90.

SNODGRASS, LUCIEN B.
Operated the Snodgrass Picture Shop in Caldwell, 1910-13.

SNODGRASS, MARGARET
Daughter of L. B. Snodgrass; active in the Snodgrass Picture Shop in Caldwell, 1910-38.

SNODGRASS, MARY
Daughter of L. B. Snodgrass; active in the Snodgrass Picture Shop in Caldwell, 1910-38.

SNODGRASS PICTURE SHOP
Operated by Lucien B. Snodgrass in Caldwell, 1910-13; by Margaret and Mary Snodgrass, 1910-38.

SOOY, B. F.
Active in Caldwell and Boise, 1893.

SOULE, W. A.
Active in Stanley, c. 1910.

SOURS, CHARLES W.
Studios in Colorado, 1889-91, 1895-96. Studios in Boise, Idaho, located at 8th Street between Idaho and Bannock, May-August 1893. Partner in William Whyte & Charles W. Sours, operating at 8th and Bannock Streets, August 1893. Operated in Colorado, 1899-1900.

SOURS, R. S.
Active in Pocatello, 1893.

SOUTHERLAND SISTERS
Active in Coeur d'Alene, 1906.

SPENCER, F. M
Active in Mansfield, producing stereoviews; may have worked with H. A. Davis of Moscow.

STAMPER, CALVIN F.
Born in Iowa, January 1866. Active in Boise, 1898-13.

STAMPER, FRANK M.
Active in Oswego, Kansas, November 1883. Active in Hailey, Idaho Territory, c. 1883; operated Stamper's Art Gallery in Boise, c. 1895-96. Possibly a partner in Bellus & Stamper, 1896.

STAMPER, J. L.
Active in Boise, 1901-06.

STANDOW, L. C.
Active in Burke, Idaho.

STANDOW, RICHARD
Born in Germany, 1883. Arrived in U.S., 1897. Active in Mullan, 1910-13.

STANTON, T. W.
Photographer with the United States Geological Survey, 1906-16.

STATES & McKENZIE
Partnership in Council, 1908.

STATES, H. L.
Active in Cambridge, 1910-11.

STEEN, JOHN H.
Active in Boise, 1909-10.

STENMARK
Active in Wardner, 1910-11; partner in Hayes & Stenmark, 1911.

STERNER, JOHN J.
Born in Pennsylvania, 1870. Active in Moscow, 1905-13.

STERRETT, D. B.
Photographer with the United States Geological Survey, 1910.

STEVENS, GEORGE A.
Born in Iowa, 1871. Active in Emmett and Notus, 1909-10.

STEVENSON, JOHN A.
Born in Canada, September 1870. Active in Pocatello, 1900.

STEWART, MABEL A.
Active in Boise, 1908.

STOCKBRIDGE, NELLIE JANE
Born in Pana, Illinois, March 19, 1868; died in Wallace, Idaho, May 1965. Retoucher in Pana, Illinois; trained as a photographer in Chicago, c. 1890-98. Active in Wallace, Idaho, 1898-1965. Assistant and retoucher at Barnard's New Studio, 1898. Took complete charge of the studio, c. 1900, because of Barnard's involvement in politics, other business pursuits and his deteriorating health due to tuberculosis. She bought one quarter interest in studio, 1907, and moved to the Barnard Building on Cedar Street between 6th and 7th Streets; continued active until 1965. Began taking mug shots for the Police Department, 1910.

STRAFFIN, FRED D.
Born in Massachusetts, 1873. Active in St. Maries, 1910.

STRANG, AMELIA (MRS.)
Operated "Daguerrian Rooms" in Lewiston, on C Street between 4th and 5th, October 19, 1864.

STRUCKMAN, FRANK
Born in Minnesota, July 1857. Operated portrait gallery in California, 1879, c. 1882; in Oregon, late 1880s. Active in Boise, Idaho Territory, operating Struckman's Art Gallery, opposite the Post Office, February-November 1888; sold out to John C. Myers, December 1888; worked in Idaho City, c. 1888; itinerant in Idaho, 1894. Operated in Silver City, 1894, photographing Chinese for the Geary Act of 1892, located in the Dewey Building recently vacated by A. Byrd. Listed in DeLamar, photographing Chinese, March 1894; Glenns Ferry, 1900, 1910. Name also spelled Struckmann. See Traveling.

SUTTERLEY BROTHERS & JUNK
Partnership of C. and J. K. Sutterly and John Junk, active in Boise and Idaho City, 1865-66.

SUTTERLEY, CLEMENT
Partner with J. K. Sutterly in Boise, 1865; rented John Law's Gallery, operating Sutterley & Brothers Photographic Rooms, corner of 8th and Idaho Streets, July-October 1865; sold out to W. J. Young, October 1865. Active in Idaho City, operating Sutterley Brothers & Junk with partner John Junk, on the east side of Main Street, second door above post office, 1865-66. See California.

SUTTERLEY, JAMES KIMBALL
Partner with Clement Sutterly and John Junk in Idaho City, 1865-66, operating as Sutterley Brothers & Junk on the east side of Main Street, second door above Post Office. See California.

SUTTERLY BROTHERS
See California.

TACHA, ERNEST
Active in Shoshone, 1901-022; Twin Falls, 1906.

TANDY, H. C.
Active in Nevada, c. 1868, c. 1876. Partner with Hiram E. Leslie in Silver City, Idaho Territory, September 1874-July 1875; independently, 1875-c. 1876, opposite the War Eagle Hotel. Listed in Boise, October 1875-October 1876. Active in Idaho City, 1876; partner with A. C. Bomar on Main Street, Idaho City, c. March; with Bomar as operator on Main Street, opposite the Good Templar Hall, March-October 1876. Active in Nevada, 1878-81; California, 1893.

TATE, CHARLES
Operated the Union Pacific Photograph Car, photographing Indian Braves in Shoshone, May 1883; in Hailey, May-June 1883, including a Stereopticon Exhibition at the Schoolhouse, showing over 100 views of California and Nevada; in Wood River, June-October 1883; Bullion, August 1883. Tate photographed Main Street, Hailey and the Mineral Springs in the vicinity, June 1883, and copied Hailey's town plat, c. 1884. Photographed George Pierson, murderer of Johnny-Behind-the-Rocks, in his photograph car.

THAYER, OLIVER P.
Born in Massachusetts, 1875. Active in Idaho Falls, 1910-13.

THOMA, CLARA M.
Active in Gooding, 1910-13.

THOMAS, CHARLES O.
Partner in Mason & Thomas, Boise, 1910-13.

THOMPSON
Partner in Fair & Thompson, active in Lewiston, 1904.

THOMPSON, CHARLES
Active in Post Falls, 1891-92.

THOMPSON, W. C.
Active in Hailey, 1905; Gooding and Shoshone, 1909.

THORILD, ANNIE
Partner with Minnie Ekeberg, operating as Ekeberg & Thorild in Wallace, 1901-04.

THRASHER, A. F.
Died mid-1870s. Operator for William J. Young in his new rooms in Kline's Building opposite Bilicke & Logan's Store, Boise, c. 1866. Active in Deer Lodge, Montana, c. 1867-70; itinerant photographer, 1870, in Idaho Territory and Montana; Montana, 1870-72. Probably traveled through Idaho Territory en route to the Union Pacific Railroad, early 1872; active in the eastern United States after 1872.

TOLLMAN, JOHN W.
Active in Boise, 1908. See Oregon.

TONKIN & GRIFFIN
Partnership in Boise, 1896; Mrs. H. J. Griffin and George E. Tonkin.

TONKIN, GEORGE E.
Active in Boise, 1899-1904; partner in Tonkin & Griffin, operating in Meridian, 1906-07; Boise, 1909-10.

TOPPING, ADA (MRS.)
Retoucher in Boise, 1910.

TOPPING, H. H.
Born in Michigan, 1875. Active in Boise, 1910.

TRAIN & CROMWELL
Partnership of E. H. Train and W. J. Cromwell, stereo photographers in Idaho City, 1864-65.

TRAIN, EDGAR HORACE
Partner in Train & Cromwell, stereo photographers in Idaho City, 1864-65. See Montana.

TRAPHAGEN, V. C.
Active in Hope, 1910.

TUCKER, HERMAN A.
Active in Wardner, 1908-13. See Oregon.

UNION PACIFIC PHOTOGRAPH CAR
Operated by Charles Tate, photographing Indian Braves in Shoshone, May 1883; in Hailey, May-June 1883; in Bullion, August 1883.

UNTERNAHRER, ANTON
Active in Boise, Idaho, c. 1895-1908. Also spelled Antone.

VADER, L. M.
Active in Kendrick, 1908.

VAN GRAVEN, PAUL
Partner in Van Graven & Son, in Nampa, 1903-08.

VAN GRAVEN, PHIL
Active in Weiser, 1908-13.

VAN SLYKE, LIZZIE (MRS.)
Active in Boise, 1905-07.

VAN WINKEL, ISAAC L.
Active in Culdesac, 1905-06.

VAUGHN, JOHN W.
Born in Iowa, April 1867. Active in Kendrick, 1900-02.

VEATCH, A. C.
Photographer with the United States Geological Survey, 1910.

VERNON, WILLIAM N.
Born in Ohio, August 1868. Active in Boise, 1900-02.

VINCENT
Partner in Gilbert & Vincent, Idaho Falls, 1911-12.

VOIGHT, LEO O.
Active in Montpelier, 1891-92.

WALCOTT, C. D.
Photographer with the United States Geological Survey, 1898, c. 1913.

WALTER, EYER FISHER
Born in Pennsylvania, 1878. Active in St. Anthony, 1908, 1910; Idaho Falls, 1911-13.

WARD, MARY T. (MRS.)
Active in Hailey, 1902-13.

WARNER, ISAAC V.
Born in Pennsylvania, 1868. Active in Malad, 1906-10.

WARNOCK
Partner in Cochran & Warnock, active in Idaho Falls, 1906.

WASSON, C. L.
Operated the International View Company in Decatur, Illinois, c. 1899-c. 1910. Located in Idaho, c. 1902, when he published some stereographs of Idaho.

WATKINS, CARLETON EMMONS
Stereographed Idaho Territory during a special railroad journey through Oregon, Idaho and Yellowstone, winter, 1884- 85. See California.

WATSON, O. W.
Itinerant photographer from Spokane, Washington, in Post Falls and Idaho Falls, Idaho, c. 1900.

WEBSTER, JOHN W.
Born in Ohio, 1858. Active in Lewiston, 1908-13.

WEENINK, HENRY D.
Born in Wisconsin to first generation immigrant Dutch parents, 7-1862. Active (?) in Wisconsin until 1889. Active in Dillon, Montana, 1889, c. 1891, 1894-95, 1900-03. Photographed in Blackfoot, Idaho Territory, May, 1890; photo tent in Eagle Rock, Idaho Territory, c. May-June 1890. In Idaho Falls, (formerly Eagle Rock), Idaho Territory; operated a large photo tent on the lot south of Alma Marker's store, c. June, 1891. Itinerant in Idaho Territory, 1890-91. Last name also spelled Weernich, Weeninks, and his first name sometimes shown as Harry.

WEIDER, J. H. (MRS.)
Born in Oregon, 1867. Active in Payette, 1906-13; Nampa, 1910.

WEIGEL
Active in Idaho City, c. 1900.

WELCH, F. W.
Active in Spirit Lake, 1912-13.

WELLS, L. B.
Photograph copier for the Universal Copying Company, San Francisco, California, c. 1880; possibly an operator or agent. Active in Boise, Idaho Territory, at the Central Hotel, c. December 1880, c. January 1882; in Baker City, Oregon, January 1882. Wells took orders and delivered copies and enlargements to patrons.

WENDEL, JAMES F.
Active in Ashton, 1914-15.

WHELCHEL, ARTHUR M.
Born in Kansas, August 1879. Active in Emmett, 1902-13; partner in Whelchel Brothers, 1912-13; branch gallery in Boise, 1909-10.

WHELCHEL, WALTER C.
Partner in Whelchel Brothers, active in Boise, 1909-10; Emmett, 1912-13.

WHITE, THOMAS J.
Itinerant in Idaho Territory, Montana, Wyoming, Oregon and Utah, 1886-87; in Oregon, 1885-93. Partner with F. E. Harnes, 1886-87, headquartered at Eagle Rock, Idaho Territory and Dillon, Montana. White operated a tent opposite a depot, 1886; a studio on Main Street, rear of C. Bunting's Store, c. October 1886; operated "White's New Photograph Gallery" with F. E. Harnes, c. January 1887. Traveling in Montana, January-March 1887; Pocatello, Idaho Territory, c. April 1887; Blackfoot, c. May 1887; in Montana, June 1887, c. 1895.

WHITNEY, EDWARD B.
Born in Oregon, February 1862. Active in Boise, 1900-13.

WHITNEY, J.
Active in Albion, 1903-04.

WHITNEY, JOHN M.
Born in Oregon, 1875. Active in Idaho Falls, 1906-13.

WHYTE & HARVEY
Partnership in Boise, 1901-13; William Whyte and Edwin C. Harvey.

WHYTE, WILLIAM
Itinerant in Idaho, 1891-93; operating a tent in Boise, corner of 7th and Idaho Streets, c. 1891-93. Partner with Charles W. Sours in Boise at 8th and Bannock Streets, August 1893; independently at same address, c. 1893-April 1894. Studio at 802 Idaho Street, opposite

Boise National Bank, c. April 1894; partner in Whyte & Harvey, 1901-13; also listed as partner in Whyte & Sons. Also spelled White.

WIDERBERG, LAFAYETTE
Born in Utah, 1881. Active in Rexburg; partner in Anderson & Widerberg, 1906; listed alone, 1910.

WILCOX & WILCOX
Itinerant photographers working in Caldwell, June-July 1888; Shoshone, c. July 1888. Also known as Wilcox & Wilson.

WILCOX & WILSON
Partnership of George Wilcox and B. L. or John W. Wilson, itinerant photographers in Caldwell and Shoshone, 1888. Also known as Wilcox & Wilcox.

WILCOX, GEORGE
Traveling photographer, c. 1860; in Albany and Eugene, Oregon, c. 1880. Partner with B. L. or John W. Wilson, itinerant photographers in Idaho Territory, 1888; known as Wilcox & Wilcox and Wilcox & Wilson.

WILKINSON, H. W.
Active in Potlatch, 1905-06.

WILLIAMS, HERBERT J.
Born in Idaho, 1888. Partner in Prater & Williams, operating in Pocatello, 1910.

WILLIS, B.
Photographer with the United States Geological Survey, c. 1898, c. 1901.

WILSON, B. L.
Possibly a partner of George Wilcox, itinerant photographers operating as Wilcox & Wilson, 1888. Wilcox's partner may have been John W. Wilson.

WILSON, CHARLES E.
Born in Maine, 1876. Active in Gooding, 1910.

WILSON, HENRY
Meadows Valley, c. 1900.

WILSON, JOHN W.
Born in Ohio, October 1872. Possibly partner with George Wilcox, itinerant photographers in Idaho Territory, 1888, operating as Wilcox & Wilson. Active in Montana, 1897, 1900-03. Wilcox's partner may have been B. L. Wilson.

WILVERT, S. A.
Active in Pocatello, 1905.

WOMACH, WALTER
Born in Idaho, 1883. Active in Emmett, 1910.

WOOD & COULTER
Partnership of S. W. Wood and G. H. Coulter, operating in Idaho City, 1873-74, on Commercial Street opposite the Court House.

WOOD, FRANK
Photographer in Lagrande, Idaho, c. 1893.

WOOD, S. W.
Partner with G. H. Coulter in Idaho City, on Commercial Street, opposite the Court House, c. 1873-74.

WOOD, THOMAS M.
Active in California, 1858-61; itinerant in Oregon and Idaho Territory, 1863-64; Lewiston, 1863; studio in Oregon, 1865-66; itinerant in Idaho Territory, 1868-69; studio in Silver City, at 777 Jordan Street, December 1868-July 1869. Active in Winnemucca, Nevada, c. 1876. Studio in Walla Walla, Washington, 1866. See Traveling.

WOODARD, A. B.
Photographer from Portland, Oregon, visiting Idaho, 1866, with an operator named Hurd; took views of Lewiston, Idaho City, South Boise, the New York and Idaho Gold and Silver Mining Company, Nez Perce Indians, and other scenes. See Oregon and Washington

WRENSTED, BENEDICTE
Born in Hjorring, Denmark, February 10, 1859; died in Los Angeles, California, January 19, 1949. Arrived in Pocatello, 1895; purchased studio of A. B. Howe, November 1895. She had a thriving trade in potraits and views of town activities; also known for numerous portraits of Fort Hall Reservation Indians, particularly the Northern Shoshone, Lemhi Shoshone and Bannock tribes. She sold her business, 1912, and moved to California.
    An Idaho Photographer In Focus, Joanna Cohan Scherer, ed., Idaho State University Press, Pocatello, Idaho, 1993.

WRENSTED, ELLA
Born December 27, 1892; died in California, June 6, 1986. Travelled by train at age twelve, taking post-mortem photographs. By 1909, she was an assistant to her aunt, Benedicte Wrensted, at her studio in Pocatella. She may have been the photographer of many outdoor images produced under the Wrensted imprint. She left for California with her aunt, 1912, later working for Mrs. Garvey in Pocatella and Caspar, Wyoming. After marrying Harry J. Boone, she operated a studio in Bellflower, California for many years.

YOUNG, I. L.
Twin Falls, 1905.

YOUNG, WILLIAM E.
An itinerant in Idaho; active in Nampa at the Capitol Hotel, c. 1895; Boise, c. December 1895; in Payette, c. 1896, at Overland Hotel; in Boise, March 1896.

YOUNG, WILLIAM J.
Photographer in California, c. 1862-63. Bought out Sutterley Brothers in Boise, 1865; located on Main Street, a few doors above Crawford & Slocum's, October 1865-June 1866; at Kline's Building opposite Bilicke & Logan's Store, June-December 1866. Sold out to John Junk of Idaho City, December 1866.

(See Oklahoma)

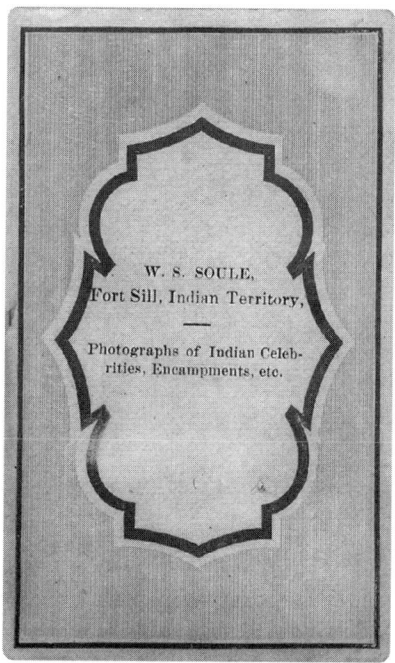

W. S. SOULE,
Fort Sill, Indian Territory,
—
Photographs of Indian Celeb-
rities, Encampments, etc.

Special thanks to David A. Reeh for his editing and substantial contribution to this section.

BALDWIN
Active in Durant.

BEAN & BEAN
Partnership active in Pauls Valley. Also spelled Beane & Bean.

BENECKE, ROBERT
Major St. Louis photographer who took stereoviews in the Indian Territory for the M K & T Railroad, c. 1873.

BENSON, W. C.
Active in Teral, c. 1897.

BEUGLER, J. B.
Active in Iron Bridge, c. 1906.

BLISS, W. P.
Photographed the Indians of the Southwest with George Ben Wittick at Ft. Sill, 1878-79. See Traveling.

BRASEL, J.
Active in Muskegee, c. 1870-80.

CALLAHAN, T. M.
Active in Uinita.

CLINKSCALES
Active in Caddo.

COLE, S. S.
Active in Ardmore.

CONNOR
Active in Purcell.

COSANA & MOSSER
Partnership active in Ft. Reno.

COTTEN
Active in Ryan, c. 1895.

COVEY, J. W.
Active in Poteau.

CRESCENT PHOTO PUBLISHING COMPANY
Operated in Uinita.

CROCKETT
Active in South McAlister.

DOWNING
Active in Ardmore.

DRUM, OSCAR
Active in Nowata, Indian Territory, and Pawhuska, Oklahoma Territory, c. 1885-1910; produced stereoviews, city panoramas and portraits.

FOWLER
Active in Uinita.

GANNAWAY
Active in South McAlister.

GATEWOOD
Active in Durant.

GILLIAM & TRIMBLE
Partnership active in Cornish.

HALLBERG'S ART STUDIO
Operated in South McAlister, c. 1895.

HAMLY
Active in Pauls Valley.

HARTUNG
Operated a studio in Cardmore, late 1880s.

HUFF
Active in Cherokee.

HUGHES
Active in Tulsa, c. 1895.

IRWIN & MANKINS
Partnership active in Chickasha and Duncan.

JENKINS
Active in Ardmore.

JONAS
Active in Nowata.

KELLY
Active in Duncan.

LEE
Active in Wynnewood.

LEEPER'S ART STUDIO
Active in Ravia.

MACURAY'S STUDIO
Active in Coalgate.

MANKINS
Partner in Irwin & Mankins, active in Chickasha and Duncan.

MARTIN & TROUTMAN
Partners from Paris, Illinois; took stereoviews in the Indian Territory, c. 1872.

MAYNARD
Active in Wetward.

McAFEE, W. C.
Active in Daris, c. 1895.

McCARTY
From Baxter Springs, Kansas; took stereoviews in the Indian Territory, c. 1873-74.

McCLANNAHAN
Active in Sapulda.

MOSSER
Partner in Cosana & Mosser, active in Ft. Reno.

NORVELLE
Active in Chickasha.

ORSBORN
Active in Tahlequah.

ROBERTSON & COMPANY
Active in Muskogee; photographed Creek Indians, early 1890s. Listed as Robertson, c. 1899.

ROGERS
Active in North Pond Creek.

SAUNDERS
Active in Davis.

SHEPARD
Active in Uinita.

SNYDER
Active in Marietta, c. 1861.

SOULE, WILLIAM S.
Born August 28, 1836. Brother of Boston photographer and publisher, John P. Soule. Served as a photographer in the Union Army, with a studio in Chambersburg, Pennsylvania by 1865. Moved to Ft. Leavenworth and Ft. Dodge, Kansas, 1867; located at Ft. Sill and Camp Supply, Indian Territory, where he photographed soldiers and Indians, late 1868.

Russell E. Belous & Robert E. Weinstein, *Will Soule: Indian Photographer at Ft. Sill, Oklahoma, 1869-74*, Ward Ritchie Press, 1973.

STANDARD PHOTO COMPANY
Operated in Hartshorne.

STANDIFORD, J. F.
Active in the 1890s; billed as "The Only Licensed U.S. Photographer in the Indian Territory." Headquartered at Muskogee, Creek Nation, he made regular visits with his portable gallery to Tahlequah, Vinita, Eufaula, Wagoner and other major points in the Territory. He advertised as a "Travelling Photographer in the Indian Territory with Resident Headquarters at Parsons, Kansas," claiming he had the most "complete photographic tent and outfit in existence," and McAlester was added to the list of towns to visit.

TAYLOR, A. D.
Active in Norman, c. 1889.

TAYLOR, J. A.
Active in Purdy.

TRIMBLE
Partner in Gilliam & Trimble, active in Cornish.

TROUTMAN
Photographer from Paris, Illinois, partner in Martin & Troutman, Indian Territory, c. 1872.

WEBB
Active in Ardmore.

WINGO
Active in Checotah, c. 1885; also active in Wagoner, Muscogee and Eaeala.

WINKLER, CHRISTIAN
Active in Ft. Sill.

ZILAR, L. B.
Active in Miami.

—FROM—
E. C. WALKER,
Dealer in Freethought Books, &c.,
Box 881   CEDAR RAPIDS, IOWA.

ACKER, G. C.
Active in Bedford, 1895-96.

ADAMS, ASA W.
Partner in Adams & Shear in Decorah, 1860s, with S. R. Shear; studio on Water Street, 1870.

ADAMS & LARSON
Active in Waterloo, 1895-96.

ADAMS & SHEAR
Partnership of Asa W. Adams and S. R. Shear, stereo photographers in Decorah, 1860s.

ADAMS, E. (MRS.)
Active in Davis City, 1895-96.

ADAMS, G. H.
Active in Griswold, 1895-96.

ADAMS, O. E.
Active in Sac City, 1895-96.

ADAMS, O. R.
Studio in Union, c. 1880, on Center Street.

ADAMS, W. G.
Stereo photographer in Waterloo; partner in Adams & Larson, 1895-96.

ADDIS, ALFRED SHEA
Stereo photographer operating gallery with Porter in Dubuque, 1879.

AGNEW, J. E.
Active in Creston, 1895-96.

ALLEN
Partner in Chatfield & Allen, active in Keokuk, 1885; produced stereoviews.

ALLEN, A. H.
Active in Davenport, 1895-96.

ALLEN, C. F.
Active in Fairbank, 1895-96.

ANDERSON, C. M.
Successor to Florence's Art Gallery in Sioux City, 1881-94. Studio at 400B Pearl Street, 1880-81; 416 Pearl Street, 1883; 607 4 Street, 1884-94.

ANDERSON, H. A.
Active in Forest City, 1895-96.

ANDERSON, PETER
Active in Shelby, 1895-96.

ANDERSON, W. C.
Active in Des Moines, 1895-96.

ANSCHUTZ
Partner in Hassall & Anschutz, active in Keokuk, 1895-96.

APFEL, HENRY
Active in Shell Rock, 1895-96.

APLIN & WILLIAMSON
Active in Eagle Grove, 1890.

APLIN, H. N.
Active in Eagle Grove, 1890-96. Partner in Aplin & Williamson, 1890.

ARAAH, PROFESSOR A.
Stereo photographer in Oxford Junction.

ARGANBRIGHT, CHARLES
Active in Hedrick, 1895-96.

ARMSTRONG, C. M.
Stereo photographer in Leon.

ARMSTRONG, J. A.
Active in St. Charles, 1895-96.

ARMSTRONG, S.
Stereo photographer in Washington.

ARNOLD, E. F.
Active in Ottumwa, 1895-96.

ASHTON, GEORGE
Studio at 18 Main Street, Council Bluffs, 1893-94.

ASKREN
Traveling photographer; partner in Askren & Baldwin; permanent address at East Des Moines, 1892.

ASKREN & BALDWIN
Traveling photographers; permanent address at East Des Moines, 1892.

ATHERTON, A. C.
Active in Charles City, 1895-96.

ATKINSON, C. A.
Stereo photographer in Davenport.

ATKINSON, S. P. (MRS.)
Active in Cambridge, 1895-96.

ATWOOD & MARSHALL
Active in Winterset, 1875.

AYERS, PERRY
Active in Ames, 1895-96.

AYERS, W. G. (MR. & MRS.)
Active in Estherville.

AYRES, E.
Active in Webster City, 1895-96.

BABCOCK, CHARLES
Active in Shenandoah, 1895-96.

BABCOCK, W. D.
Studio in Grinnell, c. 1870; produced stereoviews.

BACON, F. C.
Active in Beaconsfield, 1895-96.

BACON, GEORGE
Stereo photographer in Chariton.

BAIRD & TWIFORD
Studio at southeast corner of Fourth and Jefferson Streets, Burlington, 1865.

BAKER, J. G.
Stereo photographer in Columbus Junction.

BAKER, W.
Stereo photographer in Marshalltown.

BALDWIN
Traveling photographer; partner in Askren & Baldwin; permanent address at East Des Moines, 1892.

BALDWIN & DAUGHERTY
Partnership in East Des Moines producing stereoviews.

BALDWIN, C. F.
Studio at 415 4 Street, Sioux City, 1896-97.

BALDWIN, C. M.
Stereo photographer in Des Moines.

BALDWIN, H. O.
Active in Williams, 1895-96.

BANCROFT, C. D.
Active in New Hampton, 1895-96.

BARKE
Stereo photographer operating the Excelsior Gallery in Council Bluffs.

BARKHUFF, JOHN
Active in Swedesburg, 1895-96.

BARKS
Stereo photographer in Missouri Valley and Council Bluffs. Possibly the same as Barke.

BARLOW, HENRY
Active in Des Moines, 1895-96.

BARNARD
Partner in Huffman & Barnard, stereo photographers in Waukon, 1880, 1895-96.

BARNES & KENNEDY
Stereo photographers in Newton.

BARNETT, L. M. G.
Stereo photographer in Des Moines and Davenport.

BARTON, M. B.
Active in Le Mars, 1895-96.

BATES, G. A.
Active in Newton, 1895-96.

BATES, O. B.
Active in Hampton, 1895-96.

BAUMAN, G. C.
Active in Burlington, 1895-96.

BAUMWART, B. M.
Active in West Union, 1895-96.

BEACH, A. W.
Active c. 1895-96.

BEAMER, F. H.
Studio at 415 4 Street, Sioux City, 1900-01.

BEATTY & SHANAFELT
Studio at northwest corner of square in Sigourney, c. 1875.

BEATTY, J. S.
Active in Carroll, 1895-96.

BEATTY, WILLIAM
Active in Sigourney, c. 1875; partner in Beatty & Shanafelt at northwest corner of square.

BEEDY, F. N.
Active in Postville, 1895-96.

BELL & COURTRIGHT
Active in Fort Madison, 1895-96.

BELL, I. A.
Active in Donnellson, 1895-96.

BELLINGER, J. A.
Active in Union, 1895-96.

BELVEAL, E. S.
Stereo photographer in Ottumwa.

BERGER, T. N.
Photographer and retoucher in Elgin, c. 1870; also worked as a piano tuner, music teacher, dealer in pianos and organs, and agent for Inman & Allan Ocean Liners.

BERGER, T. N. (MRS.)
Active in Elgin 1875; in Eldora, 1895-96.

BERNARD, A. L.
Stereo photographer in Avoca.

BERTRAND, E. E.
Stereo photographer in Cresco.

BEST & COMPANY
Studio at the north side of the square in Chariton, c. 1885; successors to Bridge & Wright.

BEVERAGE & JESSUP
Stereo photographers in Marshalltown, 1895-96; M. C. Beverage.

BEVERAGE, MAURICE C.
Active in Marshalltown, c. 1880; partner in Beverage & Jessup, 1895-96.

BILBROUGH, J. E.
Studio at southwest corner of Main and Eighth Streets, Dubuque, 1865-80, 1895-96. Also spelled Billbrough.

BILLINGS, C. F.
Active in Kensett, 1895-96.

BINGHAM, F. V.
Stereo photographer in Clermont; views published by J. P. Calvin.

BITTENDENDER, L. C.
Active in Knoxville, 1875, 1895-96. Also spelled Bittenbenders.

BLACKHALL, J.
Studio in Clinton, c. 1860. Produced stereoviews.

BLAIR & TAYLOR
Partnership active in Keokuk, c. 1864.

BLAIR, L. G.
Produced stereoviews in Ida Grove.

BLAIR, R. H.
Active in Keokuk, c. 1864-65; partner in Blair & Taylor, c. 1864.

BLAIR, W. E.
Active in Rock Rapids, 1895-96.

BOECKH, EDWARDS, JR.
Active in Lansing, 1895-96.

BOHANAN, W. F.
Active in Corning, 1895-96.

BOND
Partner in Willeford & Bond, active in Ft. Madison, 1895-96.

BOOTH
Partner in Davidson & Booth; studio at 712 4 Street, Sioux City, 1888-89.

BOOTH, J. O.
Studio at 522 7 Street West, Sioux City, 1892-93; in Harlan, 1895-96.

BORLAUG, W. A.
Stereo photographer in Colmar and Decorah. Also spelled Borloug, Borlong.

BORLONG, J. E.
Active in Decorah, 1895-96.

BOSISTO, A. (MRS.)
Active in Cumberland, 1895-96.

BOWEN, W. N.
Active in Montezuma, 1895-96.

BOWERS, J. W.
Active in Mapleton, 1895-96.

BOYD
Operated the Eagle Studio in Des Moines, 1885.

BRADLEY, W. A.
Active in Albia, 1885, 1895-96.

BRANCH, E. B.
Active in West Union, 1895-96.

BRANDT BROTHERS
Operated the Brandt Brothers Art Studio in Avoca and Walnut, 1890; in Davenport and Avoca, 1895-96.

BRASCH, H. K.
Stereo photographer in Waterloo.

BRENEMAN, C. D.
Active in Marion, 1895-96.

BREWER, W. H.
Stereo photographer in Shenandoah.

BRIDGE & WRIGHT
Partnership active in Chariton, before 1885; studio at the north side of the square. Sold out to Best & Company, c. 1885.

BRIGGS & COMPANY
Studio in Ottumwa.

BRIGGS, J. B.
Stereo photographer in Mitchell. Also listed as J. P. Briggs.

BRIGHAM, L. E.
Active in Ogden, 1895-96.

BRINCE, H.
Active in Pella, 1865-70.

BRINKLEY
Partner in Keyser & Brinkley, active in Belle Plaine, 1895.

BROLINE, CLARA V.
Active in Gowrie.

BROOKS
Partner in Johnston & Brooks on North Main Street, Mt. Pleasant, c. 1875.

BROOKS, H. F. L.
Active in Hartley, 1895-96.

BROWN & SILVER
Active in Rock Valley, 1895-96.

BROWN & WAIT
H. R. Brown and partner, operating studio at 413 4 Street, Sioux City, 1890-92.

BROWN, C. A.
Studio at 813 Main Street, Lemars, 1898.

BROWN, C. F.
Active in Burlington, 1895-96.

BROWN, EDGAR
Active in Webster City, 1895-96.

BROWN, F. E.
Studio at 605 Pearl Street, Sioux City, 1891-92.

BROWN, H. P.
Operated the Premium Gallery four doors east of Bremer House, Waverly, c. 1868.

BROWN, H. R.
Studio at 413 4 Street, Sioux City, 1889-90; partner in Brown & Wait, 1890-92.

BROWN, J. R.
Active in Le Mars, 1890.

BROWN, T. A.
Active in Marshalltown, 1895-96.

BROWNING, J. G.
Active in Clarinda, 1895-96.

BRYAN & HARVEY
Operated studio in Burlington, c. 1880, at the corner of Fourth and Jefferson Streets.

BRYAN, L. T.
Active in Burlington, 1875.

BRYAN, S. T.
Active in Burlington, 1895-96.

BULL
Partner in Veatch & Bull, active in Cedar Falls, 1895-96.

BURCHELL, W. W.
Active in Sutherland, 1895-96.

BURLINGAME, D. W.
Active in Algona, c. 1875.

BURNETT, LOU (MISS)
Active in Humeston, 1895-96.

BURNSIDE
Partner in Weingartle & Burnside, active in Cedar Rapids, 1895-96.

BUSER & SON
Active in Cedar Rapids, 1895-96.

BUSER, HENRY R.
Stereo photographer operating the Star Gallery in Cedar Rapids.

BUSER, J. S.
Active in Mount Vernon, 1895-96.

BUSH, C. T.
Active in Dubuque, 1895-96.

BUTLER STUDIO
Gallery in Ft. Dodge.

BUTTERS, WILLIAM
Active in Dubuque, 1895-96.

BYERLY, ORISON
Active in Parkersburg, 1895-96.

BYRNES, J. C.
Active in Livermore, 1895-96.

CALIFORNIA GALLERY
Operated by J. S. Sayre at northwest corner of Walnut and East 5th Streets, Des Moines, 1870s-80s.

CALKINS, J. T.
Photographer and colorist, Iowa City, c. 1862.

CALVIN, J. P.
Published stereoviews in Clermont, taken by F. V. Bingham.

CAMMACK
Partner in Stubbs & Cammack, stereo photographers in Marshall-town.

CAMPBELL, MARTHA
Active in Eagle Grove, 1895-96.

CAPITAL GALLERY
Operated by L. H. Freeborn in Des Moines, c. 1875, on 5th Street.

CARD, B. F.
Stereo photographer in Leon.

CARPENTER, J. B.
Active in Panora, 1895-96.

CARTWRIGHT
Active in Forest City, 1885.

CARTWRIGHT, C. A.
Active in Marengo, 1895-96.

CARY, GEORGE
Active in Ossian, 1895-96.

CHAPMAN, A.
Stereo photographer in Adel.

CHASE & EGBERT
Stereo photographers W. P. Egbert and Chase operating in Davenport, c. 1860s-80s.

CHASE, C. W.
Active in Guttenberg, 1895-96.

CHATTERTON & SON
Partnership operating studio in Cherokee and Marcus, 1890.

CHATFIELD & ALLEN
Active in Keokuk, 1885; produced stereoviews.

CHATTERTON, F. C.
Active in Marcus, 1895-96.

CHATTERTON, H. D.
Stereo photographer in Centreville, c. 1875; also active in Villisca.

CHILD, ARTHUR
Active in Grinnell, 1895-96.

CITY GALLERY
Operated by G. W. Stiffler in Des Moines, 1875.

CITY PHOTOGRAPH GALLERY
Studio in Marshalltown, 1867.

CLARK, F. W.
Active in Irvington, 1895-96.

CLARK, L.
Stereo photographer in Webster City.

CLAUSEN, A. J.
Stereo photographer in St. Ansgar.

CLAUSEN, C. M.
Active in St. Ansgar.

CLAUSEN, ELFRED
Studio in Sioux City, 1888-90, at 603 Pearl Street.

CLEMENS, F. E.
Active in Griswold, 1895-96.

CLIFFORD & SON
Active in Muscatine, 1895-96.

CLIFFORD, L.
Stereo photographer in Newton.

CLINTON
Partner in Reed & Clinton, active in Warrenburg, 1880.

CLOUGH, J. F.
Stereo photographer in Audubon. Also listed as Cloughly.

CLUTTERD & DAFT
Stereo photographers in Newton.

COFFIN, W. J.
Active in Ida Grove, 1895-96.

COLE, D. S.
Active in Ft. Madison and Washington, 1895-96.

COLLINS, C. H.
Stereo photographer in Wyoming.

COLLINS, J. H.
Active in Pomeroy, 1895-96.

COMAN
Stereo photographer in Storm Lake.

COMING, E. S.
Active in Cedar Rapids, 1895-96.

CONKLIN, H. P.
Active in Des Moines, 1895-96.

CONLEY, NINNIAN H.
Active in Primghar, 1895-96.

CONNERS
Active in Clarinda.

CONNOR
Active in Rockwell City, 1895.

COOK
Partner in Cornell & Cook, stereo photographers in West Union.

COOK, I. N.
Stereo photographer in Davenport, operating Cook's Gallery.

COOK, J. C.
Photographer and publisher of stereoviews in Webster City.

COOK, L. H.
Active in Ogden, 1895-96.

COOK, N. G.
Ferrotypist and stereo photographer in Onawa, 1895-96.

COON & MARTIN
Studio at the corner of Beach and Main Streets, Belle Plaine, c. 1895.

COON, S. H.
Stereo photographer in Malcom.

COOVER BROTHERS
Operated the Elite Gallery in Iowa City, 1895-96.

COPE BROTHERS
Stereo photographers in Lyons.

CORNELL & COOK
Stereo photographers in West Union.

CORNELL, ERASTUS A.
Active in Marshalltown, 1895-96.

CORNING
Partner in Samson & Corning, operating in Osage, 1885; continued active, 1886.

CORWIN
Active in Guthrie Center, c. 1895.

CORWIN, F. H.
Active in Waverly, 1895-96.

COTTAGE GALLERY
Operated by Santee & Temple in Clinton, 1880.

COTTER, JOHN
Active in Sterling, 1895-96.

COTTRELL
Photographer in Dunlap.

COUP, J. B.
Active in Bedford, 1895-96.

COURTRIGHT
Partner in Bell & Courtright, active in Fort Madison, 1895-96.

COUVENS, J. W.
Stereo photographer in Waverly.

COWAN'S STUDIO
Operating in Council Bluffs, c. 1880, at 534 Broadway.

COWIN, JOHN
Active in Norway, 1895-96.

COYLE
Gallery on North Cedar Street in Monticello, c. 1880; billed as "General Photographer."

COYLE, F. A.
Active in Cedar Rapids, 1895-96.

COZIER'S GALLERY
Tintype gallery in Albia, c. 1860.

CREES, J. H.
Active in Grand River, 1895-96.

CRESCENT GALLERY
Studio at 413 4 Street, Sioux City, 1892-93.

CROSBY
Active in Nashua, 1885.

CROSS, D. H.
Active in Des Moines.

CUNDILL, WILL
Active in Maquoketa, c. 1880, 1895-96.

CURTISS, E. H.
Operator for the Union Photograph Gallery, P. O. Box 255, Waterloo, c. 1862.

CUTLER, SCHUYLER
Active in Mount Pleasant, 1895-96.

CUTLER, VIOLA E.
Active in Creston.

CUTTER
Partner in Root & Cutter, active in Dubuque.

CUTTER, E.
Active in Dubuque, 1863.

DABB, J. V.
Operated the New Art Gallery in Le Mars, 1885, on the Union Block.

DABB, R. I.
Active in Le Mars, 1890, 1895-98; studio at 714 Main Street, 1898.

DAFT
Partner in Clutterd & Daft, stereo photographers in Newton.

DAGGER, O. P.
Active in Paulina, 1895-96.

DAHMS, GUSTAV
Active in Davenport, 1895-96.

DAMMAND, R. P.
Active in Harland, 1895-96.

DANIELS, M. T.
Active in Monterey, 1895-96.

DARRAH, HUGH
Active in Malvern, 1895-96.

DATESMAN, P.
Stereo photographer in Eldora.

DAUGHERTY
Partner in Baldwin & Daugherty, stereo photographers in East Des Moines.

DAVIDSON
Traveling photographer in Des Moines, with Peelstrom as operator.

DAVIDSON & BOOTH
Studio at 712 4 Street, Sioux City, 1888-89.

DAVIS, J. F.
Active in Sumner, 1895-96.

DAVIS, W. H.
Active in Denison, 1895-96.

DAWSON, F. E.
Active in Albia, 1895-96.

DAYTON STUDIO
Gallery in Dayton, c. 1895.

DE LANO, FRANK H.
Active in Russell, 1895-96.

DELONG, W. W.
Stereo photographer in Sioux City; brother of photographer C. A. Delong.

DEMPSIE, G. M.
Active in Elkader, c. 1875; produced stereoviews.

DENNIS, E. G.
Stereo photographer in Waverly.

DINGMAN, W. H.
Active in Des Moines, 1895-96.

DINSMORE, F. H.
Active in Anita, 1895-96.

DITTS
Stereo photographer in Eagle Grove.

DOAN, J. W.
Active in Vinton, 1870.

DOLEN, J. O.
Active in Lake Mills, 1895-96.

DOOLITTLE, A. P.
Stereo photographer in Columbus Junction; studio on Front Street, c. 1875.

DOTY, ELIAS
Active in Cedar Rapids, 1895-96.

DOUGHERTY, H.
Stereo photographer in Waterloo.

DOUGLAS, G. A.
Active in Manson, 1895-96; in Lemars, 1898, at 903 6 Street.

DOUGLAS, J. A.
Active in Osage, 1895-96.

DOUGLAS, L. A.
Active in Manchester, 1895-96.

DOUGLASS
Partner in Hickox & Douglass, stereo photographers in Waverly.

DUNCAN, W. A.
Studio at northwest corner of square, north of City Hall, first floor, in Oskaloosa, c. 1875, 1895-96.

DUNHAM
Traveling photographer based in Liscomb, c. 1890.

DUNHAM, F.
Active in Whitten, 1895-96.

DUNLAP, J. H.
Active in Brooklyn, 1875.

DUNLAP, T. A.
Active in Bloomfield, 1895-96.

DWIGHT, F. E.
Studio at 407 4 Street, Sioux City, 1890-96.

DWIGHT, JOSEPH F.
Active in Remsen, 1895-96.

DYALL, H. C.
Active in Clarinda, 1895-96.

DYALL, T. W.
Active in New London, 1895-96.

EAGLE STUDIO
Operated by Boyd in Des Moines, 1885.

EARL, J. P.
Active in Reinbeck, 1895-96.

EATON'S GALLERY
Tintype gallery in Centreville, c. 1860.

EBERHARDT, C. E.
Active in Davenport, 1895-96.

EBERHART, H. C.
Traveling photographer based in Tama City and Springville; produced stereoviews.

EBERHART, M. H.
Stereo photographer in Mt. Vernon.

ECKERMAN, A. L.
Active in Centerville, 1895-96.

EDDY, F. E. (MRS.)
Active in Wesley, 1895-96.

EDSON, P. L.
Active in Clarence, c. 1880.

EDWARDS, ADA
Active in New Sharon, 1895-96.

EGBERT, W. P.
Photograph and ambrotype artist in Davenport, c. 1860; partner in Chase & Egbert, operating in Davenport, c. 1860s- 80s; in Atlantic, 1895-96.

EGNES, JOHN
Stereo photographer in Story City.

ELDER, G. W.
Active in Forest City, 1895-96.

ELITE GALLERY
Operated by Coover Brothers in Iowa City, 1895-96.

ELITE STUDIO
Gallery in Des Moines.

ELLINWOOD, W. P.
Active in Leon, 1895-96.

ELLIOT BROTHERS
Partnership operating studio in Marshalltown, 1875.

ELLIOT, W. H.
Active in Marshalltown.

ELLIOTT & HUNT
Partnership active in Marshalltown, c. 1870.

ELLIOTT, H. I. (MRS.)
Active in Marion, 1895-96.

ELLIOTT, W. H.
Partner in Jones & Elliott, stereo photographers in Davenport; worked alone in Marshalltown, 1870s.

ELLISON, E. O.
Active in Traer, 1895-96.

ELVING
Stereo photographer in Albert City.

EMERSON, J. H.
Stereo photographer in Keokuk.

EMERY, J. F.
Stereo photographer in Northwood.

EMPORIUM OF ART
Operated by A. K. Lucas in Council Bluffs, c. 1864, at 337 Broadway.

ENSMINGER & FULK
Active in Independence, c. 1864.

ENSMINGER BROTHERS
Active in Independence, 1895-96.

ERB, JOHN
Active in Parkensburg, 1885.

ESKILDSEN, J. P.
Operated in Lawler, 1895-96.

ESMAY, JOHN
Active in Sabula, 1885, 1895-96.

EVANS, F. E.
Active in Muscatine, 1875.

EVANS, J. G.
Stereo photographer in Muscatine.

EVANS, OLIVER
Active in Rock Rapids, 1895-96.

EVERETT, JAMES E.
Stereo photographer in Des Moines, c. 1882.

EVERETT, R. S.
Active in Jewell, 1895-96.

EVERSON, EDWARD
Active in Winterset, 1895-96.

EXCELSIOR GALLERY
Operated by Barke in Council Bluffs; produced stereoviews.

FAHR, G. E.
Active in Keosauqua, 1895-96.

FAHR, G. R.
Active in Bonaparte, 1895-96.

FAIRBANKS, J. A.
Active in Center Point, 1895-96.

FARR
Partner in Taylor & Farr, active in Nashua, 1895-96.

FARR, H. R.
Portrait, landscape and stereo photographer in Dubuque, c. 1870s-90s.

FARRINGTON, THEO.
Stereo photographer in McGregor.

FAVORITE
Stereo photographer in What Cheer.

FELKEY, DANIEL
Active in Armstrong, 1895-96.

FELLOWS, E. G.
Active in Vinton, opposite the Post Office, c.1885, 1895-96.

FERALD & WAHL
Active in Wellman, 1895-96.

FERGUSON, W. F.
Active in Clinton, 1895-96.

FIELDS, WILLIAM
Active in Lyons, 1895-96.

FIELDS, WILLIAM B.
Stereo photographer in Burlington.

FINE ART GALLERY
Operated by Arthur Nott in Maquoketa, c. 1880, on Main Street.

FINE ART GALLERY
Operated by J. R Tewksbury in Farmington and Ft. Madison. Also known as Gem City Photograph Rooms, Fine Art Rooms and New Photograph Rooms, all at Front Street, between Ferry Landing and Railroad Depot, c. 1885.

FINE ART GALLERY
Operated by Hover & Brother in Ottumwa, c. 1870, at Market Street, Post Office Block.

FINE ART ROOMS
Operated by J. R Tewksbury in Farmington and Ft. Madison. Also known as Gem City Photograph Rooms, New Photograph Rooms and Fine Art Gallery, all at Front Street, between Ferry Landing and Railroad Depot, c. 1885.

FINK, U.
Active in Garrison, 1885.

FINNEY
Active in Washington, 1880.

FISHER
Partner in Hastings, White & Fisher, operating gallery at 324 Brady Street, Davenport, 1885.

FISHER, C. WILL
Active in Harlan, c. 1880.

FISHER, G. C.
Stereo photographer in Vinton.

FISHER, GEORGE
Active in Clarksville, c. 1875.

FISK, H. S.
Active in Spirit Lake, 1895-96.

FLANDERS, C. M.
Active in Glenwood, 1895-96; also in Corydon.

FLEISHMAN, ESAU
Studio at 603 Pearl Street, Sioux City, 1887-88.

FLEMING, JENNIE (MISS)
Active in Council Bluffs, 1870.

FLOE
Partner in Legreed & Floe, active in Sioux Rapids, 1895-96.

FLORENCE, A. M. (MRS.)
Studio at 214 4 Street, Sioux City, 1889-90.

FLORENCE, CHARLES W.
Studios in Sioux City at 53 Pearl Street, 1875-76; 66 Pearl Street, 1876-77; 212 4 Street, 1886-89.

FLORENCE, DAVID
Studio at 216 4 Street, Sioux City, 1883.

FLORENCE'S ART GALLERY
Operated in Sioux City before 1881; succeeded by C. M. Anderson.

FORD, EDWIN A.
Active at the corner of Reeve and Third Streets in Hampton, c. 1880; in Grundy Center, 1895-96.

FORMAN, F. R.
Active in Lineville, 1895-96.

FOSNOT & HUNTER
Partnership of L. C. Fosnot and Hunter, stereo photographers in Keosauqua.

FOSNOT, L. C.
Stereo photographer; partner in Fosnot & Hunter active in Keosauqua.

FOUCHEK, S. A.
Active in Bridgewater, 1895-96.

FOX, G. A.
Active in Kingsley, 1895-96.

FRANTZ, A. L.
Active in Ackley, c. 1895.

FREDERICKSON, G. A.
Active in Dayton, 1895-96.

FREDLUND
Partner in Ralph & Fredlund, active in Carroll, 1895-96.

FREEBORN, L. H.
Studio in Des Moines on Court Avenue, c. 1862; operated the Capital Gallery on 5th Street, c. 1875; also active 1895- 96.

FREUND
Partner in Prendergast & Freund, billed as "P & F" in Jefferson, c. 1880.

FREY, E. S.
Active in Odebolt, 1895-96.

FRITZ, J. H.
Traveling stereo photographer in Gutenburg and Waverly.

FRITZ, RALPH
Active in Clinton, 1895-96.

FRITZ, T.
Active in Gutenberg, 1865.

FROST, CHARLES
Active in Grundy Center, 1895-96.

FRUSH, MABEL
Active in New Hampton, 1895-96.

FRY
Stereo photographer in Villisca.

FRY, W. D.
Operator for Park's Ground Floor Gallery in Clarinda, c. 1880.

FULK
Partner in Ensminger & Fulk, active in Independence, c. 1864.

GALLERY OF ART
Operated by Warner & Pierce in Hopkinton, c. 1880.

GAMBLE
Partner in Hampton & Gamble, stereo photographers in Whittier.

GAMER, LOUIS
Active in Council Bluffs, 1895-96; in Omaha, Nebraska, 1898.

GARDNER, E. S.
Active in Des Moines, 1895-96.

GARNER'S ART GALLERY
Studio in Waverly, 1880.

GARDNER, R. G.
Stereo photographer in Maquoketa.

GARRISON BROTHERS
Stereo photographers in Ft. Dodge.

GARRISON, C. F.
Active in Laurens, Marathon, and Rolfe, 1895-96.

GARRISON, F. A.
Active in Ft. Dodge, 1890, 1895-96.

GAUL, J. D.
Active in Nashua, c. 1880.

GEIST, D. H.
Active in Montezuma, 1895-96.

GEM CITY PHOTOGRAPH ROOMS
Operated by J. R Tewksbury in Farmington and Ft. Madison. Also known as New Photograph Rooms, Fine Art Rooms and Fine Art Gallery, all at Front Street, between Ferry Landing and Railroad Depot, c. 1885.

GENELLI
Active in Sioux City, 1890.

GENELLI PHOTOGRAPH GALLERY
Operated by M. W. Starks in Sioux City; located at 416 Pearl Street, 1884-85; 607 4 Street, 1886-87, 1896-97. Also listed as Gennelli Photograph Studio.

GERRITSON, HENRY
Active in Maurice, 1895-96.

GESMAN & HEINY
Active in Knoxville, 1895-96.

GILCHRIST, G. K.
Studios in Cedar Falls and Fairfield; produced stereoviews. Also spelled Gilchrest.

GILLEN, BYRON
Active in Lamont, 1895-96.

GILLETT, BERT
Active in Sigourney, 1895-96.

GILSON, WILSON
Active in Blanchard, 1895-96.

GLAU, E. F.
Active in Charter Oak, 1895-96.

GOESER, ANTONY
Active in Neola, 1895-96.

GOLDSBERRY & BRIGGS
Active in Ottumwa, 1895-96.

GOLDSBERRY, B. E.
Stereo photographer in Bedford.

GOODALL, H. S.
Active in New Hampton, 1895-96.

GOODENOUGH, OTIS
Active in Farmington and Mount Sterling, 1895-96.

GOODNOW & SON, A. H.
Active in Mediapolis, 1895-96.

GORANSON, FRANK
Active in Madrid, 1895-96.

GOSLING
Partner in Pierson & Gosling, active in Carson, 1895-96.

GOSTING, GEORGE G.
Active in Manchester, corner of Main and Franklin Streets, c. 1868-75; in Akron and Le Mars, 1895-96.

GOULD
Studio in Hamburg, at 250 Maine Street, over Gould's Furniture Store, c. 1875.

GRAACK, N. P.
Gallery at southeast corner of Main and Second Streets, Davenport, c. 1875. Produced stereoviews.

GRAVENSLUND & JACKSON
Active in Muscatine, 1895-96.

GRAVES, E. A.
Active in Osceola, 1895-96.

GREEN & POST
Partnership operating gallery in Ottumwa, c. 1880.

GREEN & SMITH
Stereo photographers in Ottumwa.

GREEN, L. H.
Active in Brighton, c. 1880.

GREENE, FRANK L.
Active in Blanchard, 1895-96.

GREENLEE
Partner in Miles & Greenlee, active in Belle Plaine.

GREGG, G. C.
Active in Eldon, 1895-96.

GRIFFITH, HENRY
Active in Preston, 1895-96.

GRIFFITH, V. A.
Active in Primghar, 1895-96.

GRONEMAN
Active in Ft. Dodge, 1880.

GROSSHEIM, ALEXANDER
Active in Muscatine, 1895-96.

GROSSHEIM, OSCAR
Active in Muscatine, 1895-96.

GROSVENOR & HARGER
Stereo photographers in Dubuque.

GROUND FLOOR GALLERY
Operated in Clarinda, 1880, 1895-96, opposite the Page Company Bank. O. F. Park, proprietor; W. D. Fry, operator.

GURNSEY & ILLINGWORTH
Partnership of W. H. Illingworth and Byron H. Gurnsey, stereo photographers in Sioux City. Studio at Third Street, one door west of the Post Office, c. 1860.

GURNSEY, B. H.
Partner in Gurnsey & Illingworth active in Sioux City, c. 1860. Listed alone in studio at 400 Pearl Street, 1871-72.

HAGEN, H. W.
Active in Monticello, 1895-96.

HAL, D. W. C.
Active in Elkader, 1895-96.

HALL, J. P.
Active in Monroe, 1895-96.

HALL, J. R.
Operator of the Premium Art Gallery in Monroe, c. 1862.

HALL, MIDA
Active in Woodbine, 1895-96.

HALLOPETER, C. S.
Active in Red Oak, 1895-96.

HALVORSEN, J. R.
Stereo photographer in St. Ansgar.

HAMILTON & HOYT
Studio at 714 Street, Sioux City, 1875-76.

HAMILTON & KODYLEK
Studio at 200B Pearl, Sioux City, 1871-72.

HAMILTON, I. B.
Active in Shenandoah, 1895-96.

HAMILTON, J. H.
Studio in Sioux City; at Pearl Street, between 2nd and 3rd, c. 1866; 407 4 Street, 1876-90.

HAMMON, JOHN
Active in Lakeport, 1895-96.

HAMMOND, HARRY
Active in Vail, 1895-96.

HAMPTON & GAMBLE
Stereo photographers in Whittier.

HAMRICH, WESLEY
Active in Brighton, 1895-96.

HANES, S. A. (MRS.)
Active in Maynard, 1895-96.

HANSEN, NEIL
Active in Ida Grove, 1895-96.

HARGER
Partner in Grosvenor & Harger, active in Dubuque.

HARLACHER & MELENDY
Partnership of C. B. Melendy and G. H. Harlacher operating in Cedar Falls, c. 1875.

HARLACHER, G. H.
Active in Cedar Falls, c. 1867-75; partner in Harlacher & Melendy, c. 1875.

HARMON, H. S.
Studio at 3 Street, Studio in Sioux City, 1871-81.

HARNER
"Quick'rn a Wink" photographer in Boone, c. 1880.

HARPER, C. C.
Active in Audubon, 1895-96.

HARPER, D. W.
Active in Dubuque, 1880.

HARPER, O. L.
Active in Bancroft, 1895-96.

HARRINGTON, HARRY
Active in York Center, 1895-96.

HARRINGTON, WALTER
Active in Williamsburg, 1895-96.

HARRIS, PROFESSOR C. H.
Active in De Witt, 1875.

HART, T.
"Favorite Photographer" at What Cheer.

HARVEY
Partner in Bryan & Harvey, operating in Burlington, c. 1880. Studio at the corner of Fourth and Jefferson Streets.

HARVEY, H. P. (MRS.)
Active in Maquoketa, 1875.

HARVEY, L. L.
Active in Greene, 1895-96.

HARWOOD & MOONEY
Studio in Charles City, 1875; produced stereoviews.

HASSALL
Active in Keokuk, 1898.

HASSALL & ANSCHUTZ
Active in Keokuk, 1895-96.

HASTINGS, H. A.
Active in Iowa Falls, 1895-96.

HASTINGS, WHITE & FISHER
Partnership operating gallery at 324 Brady Street, Davenport, 1885.

HAUGH, G. C.
Active in Davenport, 1895-96.

HAWKES, M. E.
Active in West Union, c. 1885, 1895-96.

HAWKINS, B. K.
Active in Fonda, 1895-96.

HAWKINS, L. D.
Active in Lake City, 1895-96.

HEALD, D. M.
Active in Washta, 1895-96.

HECKART, W. P.
Active in Richland, 1895-96.

HEIM, J. G.
Active in Sibley, 1895-96.

HENEKS, WILLIAM C.
Active in Cedar Rapids and Linn Grove, 1895-96.

HENRY, LEVI
Active in Bonaparte, c. 1875.

HESLER, ALEXANDER
Portrait, stereoview and landscape photographer in Dubuque, 1850-51. Moved to Chicago and established a leading photography studio, 1855-94.

HICKOX & COMPANY
Stereo photographer in Waterloo, 1870s.

HICKOX & DOUGLASS
Stereo photographers in Waverly.

HIESTER
Active in Chariton, c. 1880.

HILDRETH, YOUNG & COMPANY
Studio in Clinton, 1880.

HILL
Partner in Monfort & Hill, operating New Art Gallery at Sweny's New Block, 27 and 29 Third Street, Burlington, c. 1875, 1895-96.

HILLBRAND, CLARA O.
Active in Gowrie, 1885.

HILLMAN, C. C.
Active in Oelwein, 1895-96.

HINSHAW
Partner in Walthall & Hinshaw, active in Oskaloosa, 1895-96.

HIRD, J. P.
Active in West Bend, 1895-96.

HOFF
Operating in Denison and Manning, c. 1875.

HOIT, W. C.
Studio in Sioux City at 1109 4 Street, 1891-94; in the Massachusetts Building, 1894-98; also listed in Tama, 1895-96.

HOLBROOK
Stereo photographer in Charles City; partner with Slocum in Nora Springs, 1870s.

HOLBROOK & SLOCUM
Stereo photographers in Nora Springs, 1870s.

HOLE, J. O.
Active in Muscatine, 1895-96.

HOLLAND, DANIEL
Active in Clinton, 1895-96.

HOLLINGSWORTH, G. P.
Active in Lehigh, 1895-96.

HOLMES, B. A.
Stereo photographer and optician in Hampton.

HOOT
Active in Waterloo, c. 1890, partner in Hoot & Read.

HOOT & READ
Stereo photographers in Waterloo, c. 1890.

HORTON & COMPANY
Portrait and stereo photographers, in Des Moines at 210 6th Street West.

HOUGHTON & POWELL
Stereo photographers in Lansing.

HOUGHTON, A. A.
Active in Lansing, c. 1885.

HOUSE, H. L.
Active in Rockford, c. 1890.

HOVER
Operated the Fine Art Gallery in Ottumwa, at Market Street, Post Office Block, c. 1870. Active in West Union, c. 1875, operating the Gallery of Art located in Sturgis Block.

HOVER & BROTHER
Operated the Photographic and Fine Art Gallery in Mt. Pleasant, c.

1866. Operated the State Premium Art Gallery, on Market Street in Ottumwa, c. 1875.

HOVER & WYER
Stereo photographers in Decorah.

HOYT, B. F.
Partner in Hamilton & Hoyt, at 714 Street, Sioux City, 1875-76; worked alone in Manchester.

HUDSON, J. L.
Active in Tipton; in Eldora, c. 1864.

HUEBINGER BROTHERS
Partnership operating gallery in Davenport.

HUFFMAN & BARNARD
Studio in Waukon, 1880, 1895-96.

HUFFMAN, C. M. (MRS.)
Active in Waukon.

HUFFMAN, P. C.
Studio opposite Lathrop House in Frankville, c. 1865.

HUGHES BROTHERS
Active in Blanchard, 1870.

HUGHES, H. W.
Active in Adair, 1895-96.

HUNT
Partner in Elliott & Hunt, active in Marshalltown, c. 1870.

HUNT, C. H.
Active in Strawberry Point, 1885.

HUNTER
Partner in Fosnot & Hunter, stereo photographers in Keosauqua.

HUNTER, J. M.
Active in Eldora, 1895-96.

HURD
Gallery in Maquoketa, c. 1880.

HURD'S ART GALLERY
Operating in Clarence, c. 1895.

HUSTON, C. W.
Active in Ottumwa, 1895-96.

HUTCHINGS, S. H.
Stereo photographer in Hamburg.

HUTCHINS, H. E.
Studio at 66 Pearl Street, Sioux City, 1875-76.

HYDER, E. C. H.
Active in Winterset, 1875, 1895-96.

IDEAL PORTRAIT COMPANY
Active in Des Moines, 1895-96.

IDSO
Partner in Peterson & Idso; possibly agents producing stereoviews in Story City.

IKENBERRY, I. U.
Active in Newton, 1895-96.

ILLIAS, J. A.
Active in Storm Lake, 1895-96.

ILLINGWORTH, W. H.
Partner in Gurnsey & Illingworth, stereo photographers in Sioux City at Third Street, one door west of the Post Office, c. 1860.

INGALLS, F. O.
Active in Nevada, 1895-96.

INKABALL, JOHN
Studio at 301 Broadway Street West, Council Bluffs, 1893-94.

IOWA VIEW COMPANY
Publisher of stereoviews in Iowa City, corner of Clinton and Washington Streets, 1878.

JACKSON
Partner in Gravenslund & Jackson, active in Muscatine, 1895-96.

JACOBS, W. H.
Active in Oelwein, 1895-96.

JACOBY, F. C.
Active in West Liberty, 1895-96.

JACOBY, J. F.
Active in Columbus Junction, 1895-96. Operated the Daisy Car with a home address in Iowa City, c. 1885. See Traveling.

JAMES
Studio at 126 Clinton Street, ground floor, Iowa City, c. 1895. Presumably the son of David James.

JAMES & COMPANY
Gallery operated by David E. James, daguerreotypist, ambrotypist and stereo photographer in Iowa City, 1850s. Also known as James & Son. Listed as "Photographers and Stationers" eight doors south of the Post Office, c. 1875.

JAMES & PRATT
Stereo photographers in Des Moines, 1870s.

JAMES & SON
Partnership operating studio in Iowa City, 1875.

JAMES, DAVID E.
Stereo photographer operating as James & Company in Iowa City, 1850s.

JAMES, N. W. (MRS.)
Active in Iowa City, 1895-96.

JAMES, TOM
Active in Des Moines, 1895-96.

JARVIS, B.
Partner in Manville & Jarvis, stereo photographers in Marshalltown; worked alone, 1870s-80s.

JESSUP
Partner in Beverage & Jessup, stereo photographers in Marshalltown.

JEWETT, E. C. (MRS.)
Active in Cresco, c. 1875.

JOHNSON & COMPANY, G. W.
Studio at 143 Broadway Street West, Council Bluffs, 1895-98.

JOHNSON & MONTGOMERY
Studio at 513 4 Street, Sioux City, 1899-1900.

JOHNSON, C. O.
Active in Sioux City, 1892-99, 513 4 Street.

JOHNSON, E. W.
Active in Graettinger, 1895-96.

JOHNSON, F. O.
Studio at 513 4 Street, Sioux City, 1900-02.

JOHNSON, G. F.
Active in Webster City, 1895-96.

JOHNSON, G. G.
Studio at the corner of Main and 5th Streets, Dubuque, 1865.

JOHNSON, G. W.
Studio at 347 Middle Broadway, Council Bluffs, c. 1870; 143 Broadway Street West, 1893-98; operated as G. W. Johnson & Company, 1895-98.

JOHNSON, J. E.
Studio at 705 4 Street, Sioux City, 1887-92; in Boone, 1895-96.

JOHNSON, P.
Stereo photographer in Rockford.

JOHNSTON & BROOKS
Studio on North Main Street, Mt. Pleasant, c. 1875.

JOHNSTON, E. (MRS.)
Active in Waucoma, c. 1880.

JONES & ELLIOTT
Partnership of C. E. Jones and W. H. Elliott, stereo photographers in Davenport.

JONES, C. E.
Partner in Jones & Elliott, stereo photographers in Davenport.

JONES, J. G. F.
Issued "Western Stereoscopic Views" in Muscatine.

JONES' PHOTOGRAPH GALLERY
Studio at the corner of 3rd and Brady Streets, Davenport, c. 1867.

JORDAN & MACY
Studio on Main Street, opposite Carter House, Cedar Falls, c. 1880. Produced stereoviews.

JORDAN, H. A.
Stereo photographer in Cedar Falls, Waterloo and Vinton, 1870s-80s; possibly a partner in Jordan & Macy, active in Cedar Falls.

JOSEPH & SON, C. A.
Active in Farley, 1895-96.

KADGHIN, H. H.
Active in Cedar Rapids, 1895-96.

KAHN'S STUDIO
Gallery in Waverly, 1882.

KAMBER, F. J.
Active in Alton, 1895-96.

KAVANAUGH, J. J.
Active in Dubuque, 1895-96.

KEABLE'S ART STUDIO
Gallery in Pella, 1885.

KEITH BROTHERS
Active in Alta and Schaller, 1895-96.

KELLETT & WIFE, F. A.
Active in Laporte City.

KENNEDY
Partner in Barnes & Kennedy, stereo photographers in Newton.

KESTEN & COMPANY, WILLIAM
Active in Tama City, c. 1885.

KEYES, WILLIAM M.
Active in Elkader, 1865-66. Also spelled Keys.

KEYSER & BRINKLEY
Photographers in Belle Plaine, 1895.

KIDDOO, E. E.
Active in Afton, 1895-96.

KILBORN & RIFENBURG
Partnership of A. G. Rifenburg and W. F. Kilborn, stereo photographers in Cedar Rapids.

KILBORN, W. F.
Associated with A. G. Rifenburg at 1 and 3 South Commercial Street, Cedar Rapids, c. 1865-75.

KILBOURNE, J. F.
Stereo photographer in Tipton.

KING, J.
Active in Festina, 1895-96.

KING, J. P.
Active in Waterloo, c. 1885-90.

KING, M. L.
Active in Laporte City, 1895-96.

KIPPENBROCK, O. C.
Active in Muddy, 1895-96.

KIRBY & COMPANY, L.
Gallery in Marshalltown, 1868.

KIRBY, F.
Studio at the first door west of J. H. Smith's Brick Block in Eldora, c. 1875.

KIRK, H. P.
Studio on the east side of Commercial Street in Mason City, c. 1880, 1895-96, 1900.

KITCHEN, JOSEPH
Active in Ft. Dodge, 1895-96.

KNIGHT
Partner in Schrack & Knight, active in West Union, 1875.

KNOWLTON, G. E.
Active in Albia, 1895-96.

KODYLEK
Partner in Hamilton & Kodylek, stereo photographers in Sioux City at 200B Pearl, 1871-72.

KRACAW'S FINE ART GALLERY
Operated by A. Krawkaw in Washington, c. 1868.

KRAMER, I. N.
Active in Des Moines, 1895-96.

KRAMER, I. W.
Active in Des Moines, 1885.

KRAWKAW, A.
Active in Washington, c. 1868-75. Operated Kracaw's Fine Art Gallery. Also spelled Kracaw.

LA TIER, J. D.
Active in Waterloo, 1895-96. Also listed as Latier.

LANE, I. M. C.
Active in Boone, 1895-96.

LAIR
Partner in Sharp & Lair, active in Centerville, 1870.

LANCASTER
Stereo photographer in Cedar Falls.

LANE, M. L. (MRS.)
Active in Columbus Junction, 1895-96.

LARSON
Partner in Adams & Larson, with W. G. Adams, active in Waterloo, 1895-96.

LAWRENCE & O'CONNOR
Studio in Lyons, c. 1880.

LE FEVRE, W. L.
Active in Monroe, 1895-96.

LEACH, F. M.
Active in Ft. Dodge.

LEGREED & FLOE
Active in Sioux Rapids, 1895-96.

LEISENRING BROTHERS
Partnership of J. and K. Leisenring operating studio opposite the Brazelton House, Mt. Pleasant, 1870, 1895-96.

LEISENRING, J.
Partner with K. Leisenring, operating as Leisenring Brothers in Mount Pleasant, 1870, 1895-96. Active in Ft. Dodge, operating the New Photograph and Fine Art Gallery located at the corner of Market Street and the public square, Ft. Dodge, 1875; town also listed as "Ford Dodge."

LEISENRING, K.
Active in Mount Pleasant, 1870, 1895-96.

LENZ BROTHERS
Active in Dubuque, 1895-96.

LENZ, J. M.
Active in Davenport.

LEUPTON, O. L.
Active in Burlington, 1895-96. Also spelled Lupton.

LEWIS, J. F.
Active in Riverton, 1895-96.

LEWIS STUDIO
Gallery in East Des Moines producing stereoviews.

LIBBY, E. P.
Active in Manchester, c. 1867; operated as New Photograph Parlors, corner of 6th and Main Streets, Keokuk, c. 1875. Produced stereoviews.

LIND, J. A.
Active in Des Moines, 1895-96.

LINN, W. G.
Studio at 310 Iowa Savings Bank Building, Sioux City, 1897-98.

LITTLE, ERNEST I.
Stereo photographer in Oskaloosa.

LITTLE, H. N.
Stereo photographer in Oskaloosa.

LITTLEFIELD
Stereo photographer in Iowa.

LITTS
Active in Eagle Grove, 1890.

LOGUE & SANDERS
Active in Fertile, 1895-96.

LOHRER, O. F.
Stereo photographer in Dubuque, at 576 Main Street.

LONG, C. B.
Active in Britt, 1895-96.

LONG, J. D.
Active in Sanborn, 1895-96.

LOOFBOUROW
Studio at the corner of Main and Platte Streets, Maquoketa, c. 1880.

LOVELL, J. S.
Active in Council Bluffs, 1895-96.

LOVEWELL
Active in Dubuque, 1865.

LUCAS, A. K.
Operated the Emporium of Art at 337 Broadway, Council Bluffs, c. 1864.

LUNDERMEYER, J. F.
Active in Burt, c. 1895.

LUDWIG
Active in Keystone, c. 1890.

LUSCOMBE, JAMES
Active in Iowa City, 1895-96.

LYDEN, C. E.
Active in Manning, 1895-96.

LYNN, JOHN
Active in Leigh, 1890-91; in Friend, Nebraska, 1893; in Ida Grove and Woodbine, Iowa, 1895-96.

LYONS, G. H.
Active in Lohrville and Rockwell City, 1895-96.

MACARTHUR, M. H.
Stereo photographer in Hopkinton.

MACEY, O. W.
Active in Belle Plaine, c. 1890; in Cedar Rapids, 1895-96. Also listed as Macy.

MACKENZIE, A. H.
Studio at corner of 17th and Clay Streets, Dubuque, 1895-96.

MACY
Active in Vinton, 1880.

MACY
Partner in Jordan & Macy on Main Street, opposite Carter House, Cedar Falls, c. 1880. Produced stereoviews.

MAGNUSSEN, G. A.
Active in Dubuque, 1895-96.

MALMBERG, J. O.
Active in Milton and Atlantic, 1895-96.

MANGOLD BROTHERS
Active in Des Moines, 1895-96.

MANNING GALLERY
Tintype studio in Salem, c. 1860.

MANVILLE & JARVIS
Partnership of W. A. Manville and B. Jarvis, stereo photographers in Marshalltown.

MANVILLE, W. A.
Partner in Manville & Jarvis, stereo photographers in Marshalltown; worked alone, 1870s.

MARBLE SISTERS
Active in Vinton, 1895-96.

MARSHALL
Partner in Atwood & Marshall, active in Winterset, 1875.

MARTIN
Partner in Coon & Martin; studio in Belle Plaine, c. 1895, at the corner of Beach and Main Streets.

MARTIN, J. PAUL
Studio at the corner of Eighth and Keeler Streets, Boone, c. 1880, 1895-96.

MASON, C. W. (MRS.)
Active in Creston, 1895-96.

MATHER, H. S.
Active in Clear Lake, 1895-96.

MAXWELL, M. B.
Active in Bedford and Mt. Ayr, 1895-96.

McADAM BROTHERS
Partnership operating in Mt. Pleasant, 1870.

McADAMS, JAMES
Active in Ottumwa, 1895-96.

McCLANAHAN, J. A.
Active in Mt. Ayr, 1895-96.

McCORD, A.
Active in North McGregor, 1895-96.

McCOY, J. R.
Active in State Center, 1880.

McELHOSE, E. H.
Active in Sheldon, 1895-96.

McGREGOR, J. G.
Active in Malvern, c. 1880.

McINTYRE
Active in Ames, 1885.

McKAY, ARTHUR L.
Stereo photographer in Decorah, 1872; also active in Cresco.

McMAHON'S PHOTO & GEM GALLERY
Also known as McMahon's Star Gallery in Mt. Pleasant, 1875, at north side of square.

McMANUS, C. C.
Stereo photographer in Nevada.

McMULLEN, C. F.
Active in Adel, 1895-96.

MEDLAR, F. W.
Active in Spencer, 1895-96.

MELENDY, C. B.
Stereo photographer in Cedar Falls, c. 1875, as partner in Harlacher & Melendy.

MERRIAM, S. A.
Active in Sigourney, 1895-96.

MESKIMEN, A. W.
Studio at 413 4 Street, Sioux City, 1899-1900.

MIKLEBUST
Active in Eagle Grove, 1900.

MILES & GREENLEE
Stereo photographers in Belle Plaine.

MILES, WILLIAM
Active in Oskaloosa, c. 1864.

MILL, BERT P.
Stereo photographer in Correctionville.

MILLARD'S GALLERY
Active in Boonsboro, c. 1862.

MILLER
Partner in Turner & Miller, active in Wyoming, c. 1875.

MILLER & COMPANY
Gallery at the corner of 3rd and Brady Streets, Davenport, 1880.

MILLER, F. E.
Active in Clarksville, 1895-96.

MILLER, J. W.
Active in Anamosa, c. 1880; in Sioux City at 911 and 1109 4 Street, 1894-99. Also listed as Millern.

MILLER, PETER
Active in Kimballton, 1895-96.

MILLER, W. E.
Active in Tipton, 1895-96.

MILLER, WILLIAM
Active in Burlington.

MILLS, C. B.
Operated the Premium Photographic Studio in Clear Lake and Manchester, 1875.

MILLS, N. A.
Operator at Johnson's Premium Photograph Gallery, Dubuque, c. 1865

MONFORT & HILL
Operated the New Art Gallery at Sweny's New Block, 27 and 29 Third Street, Burlington, c. 1875, 1895-96.

MONROE, W. H.
Active in Fayette, 1895-96.

MONTGOMERY
Partner in Johnson & Montgomery, at 513 4 Street, Sioux City, 1899-1900.

MOONEY
Partner in Harwood & Mooney, operating in Charles City, 1875; produced stereoviews.

MOORE, J. S.
Active in Toledo, 1867, 1895-96.

MOORE, S. E. L.
Studio on Main Street, near the Post Office in Albia, 1885.

MORAN, EDGAR
Active in Red Oak, 1895-96.

MORGAN, G. W.
Stereo photographer in Lansing.

MORHISER, W. H.
Active in Dubuque, 1895-96.

MORLAN & NICHOLS
Stereo photographers in Clinton.

MORRET'S BLUE FRONT PICTURE ROOMS
Tintype gallery in Centreville, c. 1860.

MORRISON, MARTIN
Stereo photographer in Story City and Ames, late 1880s.

MORSE'S SUNBEAM PHOTOGRAPH GALLERY
Studio in Fairfield, 1875.

MORTON, L.
Active in Pella, 1865.

MOSHER, S. V.
Studio in Robinson's Building on Commercial Street, Waterloo, c. 1875

MOTT, M. M.
Active in Anamosa, 1895-96, 1900.

MOURER, J. F.
Studio at 127 Front Street, between Pine and Cedar, Ft. Madison, c. 1862.

MUDGE, KATE RAYMOND
Active in Randalia, c. 1891.

MUELLER, J.
Stereo photographer in Council Bluffs.

MUMA, CHARLES
Active in Kingsley, 1895-96.

MUSGROVE, A. E.
Active in Farmington, 1895-96.

MYERS, J. B.
Active in Fairfield, 1895-96.

MYNSTER, W. R. C.
Active in Council Bluffs, 1895-96.

NEAL, E. E.
Active in Keota, 1895-96.

NEEDHAM, J. H.
Active in Humeston, c. 1880.

NEFF
Partner in Scarff & Neff, stereo photographers in Pella.

NEFF, CHARLIE
Operated the Star Gallery in Dewitt, on the west side of Jefferson Street, over McMurrey's, c. 1864. Another studio for Chas. Neff over Crosby & Eastman's Furniture Store, Clarence, c. 1860.

NEIL, G. R.
Active in Denison, 1895-86.

NEIL, T. J.
Active in Moulton, 1895-96.

NELSON, N. A.
Stereo photographer in Dike.

NEW YORK ART GALLERY
Operated by Ormsby in Davenport.

NEWBURY, C. S.
Stereo photograher in Davenport.

NEWCOMB, J. L.
Active in Laporte City, 1895-96.

NEWTON, J. J.
Stereo photographer in Council Bluffs.

NEWVILLE, C. H. (MRS.)
Active in Maxwell, 1895-96.

NICHOLS
Partner in Morlan & Nichols, stereo photographers in Clinton.

NICKOLS, A. W.
Active in Corning, 1895-96.

NICKOLS, C. O.
Active in Villisca, 1895-96.

NICOULIN, J. F.
Active in Algona, 1895-96.

NIXON ART STUDIO
Photographic parlor in Dayton.

NOLAN, ADAM
Active in Hubbard, 1895-96.

NORTHRUP, CHARLES
Active in Monticello, 1895-96.

NORTON, A. C.
Jeweler and photographer in Monona, c. 1880. Produced stereoviews.

NOTT, ARTHUR
Operated the Fine Art Gallery on Main Street, four doors south of Pleasant Street, Maquoketa, c. 1880. Produced stereoviews.

NOYES, D. P.
Studio at the southwest corner of Main and Eighth Streets, Dubuque, c. 1864.

NUNNAMAKER, H.
Jeweler and photographer, Ottumwa, c. 1864.

O'CONNOR
Partner in Lawrence & O'Connor, active in Lyons, c. 1880.

O'HARA, H. A.
Active in Keokuk, 1895-96.

OBERHOLTZER, J. W.
Stereo photographer in Webster City.

OGGEL, J. H.
Active in Orange City, 1895-96.

OLMSTEAD, P. A.
Operated Olmstead's Photograph and Gem Gallery in Davenport, c. 1870, on Brady Street, between 3rd and 4th Streets; produced stereoviews. A carte-de-visite with an oval window for a tintype has been verified with the Olmsted [sic] imprint on the reverse and a Black & Case imprint on the bottom left front and Boston on the bottom right front.

OLSON, J. C.
Active in Lake Mills, 1895-96.

ORMSBY
Operated the New York Art Gallery in Davenport.

N. S.
Studio in Sioux City at 923 4 Street, Sioux City, 1894-1901. Also listed at 413 4 Street.

ORR
Partner in Thomas & Orr, stereo photographers in Columbus Junction.

ORVIS, J. R.
Active in Fayette, 1880.

OTTO, W. H.
Active in Davenport, 1895-96.

OWEN, R. A.
Active in Manilla, 1895-96.

OWEN, WILLIAM H.
Active in Lyons, 1865, operating the Union Gallery.

OWENS, M. W.
Active in Washington, 1880.

OYLES, G. G.
Active in Ossian, 1895-96.

PAGE & COMPANY, A. L.
Gallery in Lenox, 1895-96.

PAGE, H.
Active in Fairfield, 1865.

PALMER
Stereo photographer in Lansing.

PALMER, S. D.
Operated a book, stationery and photography shop in Marshalltown; made stereoviews of local scenery.

PANRY, C. W.
Active in Guthrie Center, 1895-96.

PARAMORE, J. H.
Active in Hawarden, 1895-96.

PARDOE, H. W.
Active in New Sharon, 1880; in Newton, 1895-96.

PARK, O. F.
Active in Clarinda, 1880, 1895-96; proprietor of the Ground Floor Gallery opposite the Page Company Bank; W. D. Fry, operator.

PARKER
Partner in Shear & Parker, active in New Hampton, 1875.

PARKER, A. T.
Active in Perry, 1895-96.

PATCH, F. H.
Studio at 413 4 Street, Sioux City, 1892-94.

PATTERSON, J. C.
Active in Bode, 1895-96.

PATTY, M. F. (MISS)
Active in Adel, 1895-96.

PEARSON, O. E.
Active in Des Moines, 1895-96.

PEASLEY & VAN GORDER
Active in Keokuk, 1895-96.

PEAVEY, L.
Studio over French's Jewelry Store, McGregor, c. 1865. Produced stereoviews.

PEELSTROM & WALLINE
Traveling photographers, active in Des Moines.

PEELSTROM, CARL
Active in Maxwell, 1895-96.

PEIRCE & COMPANY
Active in Des Moines, 1865.

PETERSON
Partner in Jensen & Peterson, active in Cedar Falls, 1895-96.

PETERSON
Partner in Schaub & Peterson, operating Photographer's Palace on the Savery Block, Walnut Street, c. 1880, Des Moines. Possibly operated as Peterson's Fine Art Studio.

PETERSON & IDSO
May have been agents; handled Martin Morrison stereoviews in Story City.

PETERSON, A. L.
Active in Algona, 1895-96.

PETERSON, J. F.
Studio at 317 Broadway Street West, Council Bluffs, 1898.

PETERSON, J. W.
Active in Reinbeck, 1895-96.

PETERSON'S FINE ART STUDIO
Gallery at 413 Walnut Street, Des Moines, 1880; possibly operated by Schaub & Peterson.

PFLAMM, JOHN
Active in Colfax, 1895-96.

PHELPS
Active in Ottumwa, 1875.

PHELPS, EDWARD
Active in Knoxville, 1895-96.

PHELPS, J. P.
Photographer in Muscatine, c. 1885.

PHILLIPS, JOHN
Stereo photographer in Ft. Madison; in Lake City, 1880-90.

PHILLIPS, L. H.
Active in Independence, 1895-96.

PHILLIPS, M. F.
Active in Hamburg, 1895-96.

PHOTOGRAPHER'S PALACE
Operated by Schaub & Peterson on the Savery Block, Walnut Street, c. 1880, Des Moines.

PHOTOGRAPHIC & FINE ART GALLERY
Operated by Hover & Brother in Mt. Pleasant, c. 1866.

PIERCE
Partner in Warner & Pierce, active in Hopkinton, c. 1880.

PIERCE, HARRY C.
Active in Colfax, 1895-96.

PIERCE, N. E.
Active in Waverly, 1895-96.

PIERSON & GOSLING
Active in Carson, 1895-96.

PINCKNEY, J. W.
Stereo photographer in Sioux City.

POOK, C.
Active in College Springs, 1895-96.

PORTER
Operated gallery in Dubuque, 1879, with Alfred S. Addis.

PORTER & SON, R.
Active in Birmingham, 1895-96.

POST, A. B.
Stereo photographer in Ottumwa; partner in Green & Post, c. 1880.

POWELL
Partner in Houghton & Powell, stereo photographers in Lansing.

PRATT
Partner in James & Pratt, stereo photographers in Des Moines, 1870s.

PREMIUM ART GALLERY
Operated by J. R. Hall in Monroe, c. 1862.

PREMIUM PHOTOGRAPHIC STUDIO
Operated by C. B. Mills in Clear Lake and Manchester, 1875.

PRENDERGAST & FREUND
Billed as P & F in Jefferson, c. 1880.

PROCTOR, JEFFERSON
Active in Corning, 1895-96.

RALPH & FREDLUND
Active in Carroll, 1895-96.

READ
Stereo photographer; partner in Smith & Read, operating in Osceola; partner in Hoot & Read, active in Waterloo, 1890.

REED & CLINTON
Partnership operating in Warrenburg, 1880.

REED & SON GALLERY
Active in Emmetsburg, 1895-96.

REED BROTHERS
Active in Missouri Valley, 1895-96.

REED, J. H.
Stereo photographer in Clinton.

REEDER, J. D.
Active in Pleasantville, 1895-96.

REEVES BROTHERS
Active in Bloomfield, 1895-96.

REINECKE, WILLIAM I.
Active in Wapello, 1895-96.

RELF, J. T.
Operated studio at the north side of Water Street, Decorah, 1880.

RENAAS, ALBERT
Active in Decorah, 1895-96.

RENVER & SEARFF'S
Partnership operating studio in Pella, 1875.

REUVENS, J. H.
Active in Pella, 1895-96.

REYNOLDS & COMPANY
Stereo photographer in Harlan.

REYNOLDS, A. C.
Stereo photographer in Griswold.

REYNOLDS, A. E. (MRS.)
Active in Lake View, 1895-96.

REYNOLDS, ALLIE
Active in Lancaster, 1895-96.

REYNOLDS, B. J.
Active in Decorah, 1895-96, studio on the Bear Block.

REYNOLDS, FRANK M.
Stereo photographer in Des Moines.

REYNOLDS, H. J.
Active in Jefferson, 1895-96.

REYNOLDS, H. M.
Stereo photographer in Alden.

REYNOLDS, J. A.
Active in Nevada, 1895-96.

REYNOLDS, J. H.
Active in Burlington, 1895-96, at 211 1/4 & 321 ½ Jefferson Street; also in Creston.

RICE, H. B.
Stereo photographer in Lovilia.

RICH & SHERMAN
Active in Nashua, c. 1875.

RICH, J. E.
Studio on the corner of Main and Clark, Charles City, 1865-80; in Osage, 1895-96.

RICHARDSON, F. F.
Active in Martinsburg, 1895-96.

RICHTER, W. C.
Active in Sioux City, 1891-92, on 4 Street.

RICKEY, J. N.
Active in Indianola, 1895-96.

RIFENBURG, A. G.
Partner with W. F. Kilborn, operating studio as Kilborn & Rifenburg at 1 and 3 South Commercial Street, Cedar Rapids, c. 1875. Awarded first premium at the Iowa State Fair.

RILEY & SHERRADEN
Studio at 43 Main Street South, Council Bluffs, 1893-96.

RILEY, C. A.
Studio at 404 Broadway Street West, Council Bluffs, 1898.

RITCHER, W. C.
Studio in Sioux City at 313 Pierce Street, 1889-91; 901 4 Street, 1892-96.

ROBERTS, D. B.
Active in Morning Sun, 1885; in Sheldon, 1895-96.

ROBINSON BROTHERS
Active in Osceola, 1895-96.

ROBLIN, FRANK E.
Stereo photographer in Spirit Lake.

ROHNER, J. A.
Active in Carroll, 1895-96.

ROOD, W. I.
Active in Spencer and Emmettsburg, c. 1880; in Spencer, 1895-96.

ROOT & CUTTER
Partnership of Samuel Root and Cutter, stereo photographers in Dubuque.

ROOT, SAMUEL
Operated Root's Gallery in Dubuque at 166 Main, c. 1865; the corner of Main and 8th Streets, Sanford Block, 1880.

ROSE, CLARENCE
Active in Charlton, 1895-96.

ROSSITER, J. E.
Active in Wyoming, 1895-96.

ROTH, E. H.
Stereo photographer in Strawberry Point.

ROWE, G. W.
Active in Strawberry Point, 1895-96.

RUGG, ELLIOTT S.
Studio at 625 4 Street, Sioux City, 1899-1901. Also listed as E. I.

RUSSELL, F. E. (MRS.)
Active in Cresco, c. 1895.

SAMSON & CORNING
Gallery in Osage, 1885.

SAMSON, W. H.
Stereo photographer in Osage; partner in Samson & Corning, 1885.

SANDERS
Partner in Logue & Sanders, active in Fertile, 1895-96.

SANDOURD, GOULD
Active in Garden Grove, 1895-96.

SANTEE & TEMPLE
Operated the Cottage Gallery in Clinton, 1880.

SATTERLEE, L. D.
Active in Ireton, 1895-96.

SAUL, P. F.
Active in Humboldt, 1895-96.

SAVAGE, CHARLES R.
Famous Utah photographer who operated a tent gallery in Council Bluffs while awaiting the departure of his wagon train to Salt Lake City, 1860. See Utah.

SAYRE, J. S.
Operated California Gallery at northwest corner of Walnut and East 5th Streets, Des Moines, 1870s-80s. Landscape and stereo photographer. Also listed as Sayres.

SCARFF & NEFF
Stereo photographers in Pella.

SCHAEFFER SISTERS
Active in Clarion, 1895-96.

SCHAUB & PETERSON
Partnership operating Photographer's Palace on the Savery Block, Walnut Street, c. 1880, Des Moines.

SCHAUB, OTTO
Active in Des Moines, 1875; possibly a partner in Schaub & Peterson, c. 1880.

SCHERRADEN, C. H.
Studio at 43-45 Main Street South, Council Bluffs, 1898.

SCHMIDT, HENRY
Studio at 406 Broadway Street West, Council Bluffs, 1895-98. Also listed as Harry.

SCHMITT
Partner in Scott & Scmitt, stereo photographers in Osage and Waterloo.

SCHMITZ, MATHIAS, SR.
Active in Mt. Pleasant, 1895-96.

SCHNECKENBERGER, O.
Active in Burlington.

SCHNEIDER, A. H.
Active in Garner, 1895-96.

SCHOEFER SISTERS
Photographic parlor in Clarion.

SCHOOLEY, L. A. (MRS.)
Active in Indianola, c. 1885, 1895-96.

SCHOONOVER, L. W. (MR. & MRS.)
Stereo photographers in Vinton.

SCHRACK & KNIGHT
Gallery in West Union, 1875.

SCHUELER, JOHN
Active in Davenport, 1895-96.

SCHULTZ BROTHERS
Active in Moulton, c. 1890.

SCHULTZ, HOWMAN R.
Active in Moulton, 1895-96.

SCHWARTZ, A.
Active in Stuart, c. 1880. Town is sometimes misspelled Stewart.

SCOTT & SCHMITT
Stereo photographers in Osage and Waterloo.

SEARFF
Partner in Renver & Searff's, active in Pella, 1875.

SEARLES, W. W.
Active in Lime Spring, 1895-96.

SEELEY, E. C.
Active in Sutherland, 1895-96.

SELLERS
Operated Photographic Gallery at 78 Main Street, Keokuk, c. 1865.

SEYMOUR, H. A.
Studio in Sioux City at 601 Pierce Street, 1893-95; 923 4 Street, 1896-97; 407 4 Street, 1897-1901.

SEYMOUR, N. S.
Studio at 407 4 Street, Sioux City, 1898-99.

SHAFFER & SON, S. W.
Active in Coggon, 1895-96.

SHAFFER, S. W.
Active in Central City, 1895-96.

SHANAFELT
Stereo photographer in Sigourney, c. 1875; partner in Beatty & Shanafelt.

SHANNON, T. E.
Active in Malvern, 1895-96.

SHARP & LAIR
Gallery in Centerville, 1870.

SHEAR & PARKER
Partnership operating studio in New Hampton, 1875.

SHEAR, S. R.
Stereo photographer in Ossian; partner with Asa W. Adams in Decorah, 1860s, operating as Adams & Shear.

SHEPARD, F.
Stereo photographer in Iowa Falls.

SHERIDAN, C. H.
Stereo photographer in Council Bluffs.

SHERMAN
Partner in Rich & Sherman, active in Nashua, c. 1875.

SHERRADEN
Partner in Riley & Sherraden, active at 43 Main Street South, Council Bluffs, 1893-96; possibly C. H. Sherraden.

SHERRADEN, C. H.
Stereo photographer in Council Bluffs, 1870s. Also spelled Sheridan.

SHOMBER, A. JUDSON
Active in State Center, 1895-96.

SIEFKEN, GEORGE
Active in Middletown, 1895-96.

SILVER
Partner in Brown & Silver, active in Rock Valley, 1895-96.

SIMMONS & LATIER
Stereo photographers in Waterloo.

SIMMONS, F. D.
Active in West Liberty, c. 1880.

SIMMONS, V. L.
Active in Waterloo, 1895-96.

SIOUX CITY PORTRAIT & ENGRAVING COMPANY
Studio at 33 Evans Block, Sioux City, 1891-92.

SLOCUM, ORVILLE W.
Stereo photographer in Clear Lake; partner with Holbrook in Nora Springs, 1870s, operating as Holbrook & Slocum.

SMALE, W. B.
Active in Des Moines, 1895-96.

SMALLEY, J. W.
Active in Van Horn, 1895-96.

SMITH
Partner in Green & Smith, stereo photographers in Ottumwa.

SMITH & READ
Stereo photographers in Osceola.

SMITH, C.
Studio at 511 4 Street, Sioux City, 1898.

SMITH, C. J.
Active in Fairfield, 1895-96.

SMITH, CHARLES
Active in Clarence, 1895-96.

SMITH, DWIGHT
Stereo photographer in Hopkinton.

SMITH, E. A.
Studio at 321 ½ Jefferson Street, Burlington, c. 1880.

SMITH, H. A.
Active in Osceola, 1895-96.

SMITH, W. H. H.
Active in Oskaloosa, 1895-96.

SMITH, WILLIAM ALEXANDER
Active in Kanesville, Iowa, 1852. See Utah.

SMRCEK, JOSEPH O.
Active in Traer, 1895-96.

SNOW
Active at Ft. Dodge, 1890.

SNOW, C. A.
Active in Lime Spring, 1895-96.

SOLBERG, O. T.
Active in Ceresco, 1895-96.

SORENSON, CLAUS
Active in Cedar Falls, c. 1880, 1895-96.

SPAULDING BROTHERS
Active in Onawa, 1895-96.

SPECHT, J. F.
Active in Marengo, 1895-96.

SPERRY
Active in Iowa City, c. 1885. Used the slogan, "Make Hay While the Sun Shines," Artisitc Photography.

SPOONER, MAUDE
Active in Onslow, 1895-96.

SPURR, E. W.
Active in Decorah, 1895-96.

STACY, CARRIE
Active in Woodward, 1895-96.

STALLINGS, W. F.
Active in Des Moines, 1895-96.

STAMPER, I. M.
Active in Pella, 1865.

STAR GALLERY
Operated by Henry R. Buser in Cedar Rapids; produced stereoviews.

STAR GALLERY
Operated by Charlie Neff in Dewitt, c. 1864, west side of Jefferson Street, over McMurrey's.

STARKS, FRED R.
Partner in Baldwin & Starks, active in Sioux City; 415 4 Street, 1897-98; listed alone at 413 4 Street, 1898-99.

STARKS, L. C.
Active in Jessup, 1895-1900.

STARKS, M. W.
Operated Genelli Photograph Gallery, 607 4 Street, Sioux City, 1887-1901.

STATE PREMIUM ART GALLERY
Operated by Hover & Brother on Market Street in Ottumwa, c. 1875.

STAUNTON, E. A.
Stereo photographer in Davenport.

STEELE, R. R.
Active in Waukon, 1895-96.

STEELHEAD, A.
Active in Smithland, 1900.

STEWART, FRANK
Active in Scranton City, 1895-96.

STICH, H. H.
Active in Sidney, 1895-96.

STIFFLER, G. W.
Operated the City Gallery in Des Moines, 1875.

STONESTREET, M.
Active in Victor, 1895-96.

STOOPS, L. M.
Active in Perry, 1895-96.

STOOPS, WILLIAM
Active in Bloomfield, 1875.

STRAININGER & McKEE
Operating the Star Gallery in Tipton, c. 1880.

STREUSER, M. J.
Active in Bellevue, 1895-96.

STROINSTEN, J. M.
Active in Corydon, 1895-96.

STRONSTEN, SOPHIA
Active in Allerton, 1895-96.

STRUSSER, J. J.
Active in Cascade, 1895-96.

STUBBS & CAMMACK
Studio in Marshalltown; produced stereoviews.

SUNIB, A. J.
Active in Silver City, 1895-96.

SUNNES, NELS
Active in Belmond, 1895-96.

SUSONG
Stereo photographer in Des Moines.

SWAN, B. P.
Active in Lynnville, 1895-96.

SWARTZ, ADAM
Active in Stuart, 1895-96.

SWEET, W. H.
Studio at 712 4 Street, Sioux City, 1887-88.

SWEM, E. L.
Active in Cedar Rapids, 1895-96.

TALMEDGE
Active in Mason City, 1900.

TANGEMAN, B. G.
Active in Garnaville, 1895-96.

TAYLOR
Partner in Blair & Taylor, active in Keokuk, c. 1864.

TAYLOR & FARR
Active in Nashua, 1895-96.

TAYLOR, C. N.
Studio at 401 Pearl Street, Sioux City, 1891-94.

TAYLOR, G. P.
Active in Sibley, 1895-96.

TAYLOR, W. P.
Studio at Perkins Block in Ames, c. 1890, 1895-96.

TEMPLE
Partner in Santee & Temple, operating the Cottage Gallery in Clinton, 1880. Possibly Gilbert Temple.

TEMPLE, GILBERT
Active in Clinton, 1895-96. Possibly a partner in Santee & Temple, 1880, operating the Cottage Gallery.

TEWKSBURY, E. C. (MRS.)
Active in Ft. Madison, 1895-96.

TEWKSBURY, J. R.
Stereo photographer in Farmington and Ft. Madison. Studio names included New Photograph Rooms, Gem City Photograph Rooms, Fine Art Rooms and Fine Art Gallery, all at Front Street, between Ferry Landing and Railroad Depot, c. 1885.

TEWKSBURY, R. W.
Stereo photographer in Farmington. Also spelled Tewkesbury.

THAYER, G. D.
Active in Grand Junction, c. 1885, 1895-96.

THOMAS & ORR
Stereo photographers in Columbus Junction; possibly J. W. Thomas.

THOMAS, G. W.
Active in Columbus Junction, c. 1875; in Ottumwa, 1895-96.

THOMAS, J. W.
Stereo photographer in Lansing, 1870; possibly a partner in Thomas & Orr, operating in Columbus Junction.

THOMPSON, C. C.
Active in Rockford and Nora Springs, 1895-96.

THOMPSON, HARRY
Active in Waukon, 1895-96.

THORNBRUE, G. H.
Active in Anita, 1895-96.

TIERNEY, H.
Stereo photographer in Clinton.

TILLOTSON, F. B.
Active in Hawarden, c. 1880.

TIMPE, AUGUST
Operated Studio in Davenport, c. 1865, at the northwest corner of Main and 2nd Streets, above Kuhnen's Tobacco Store and next to Demokrat Office. Advertised "Deutsch Photography." Active in Wheatland, 1895-96.

TOLMAN, T. W.
Active in Glenwood, 1880; in Nebraska City, 1884-85, 1888-93; in Macedonia, 1895-96.

TORP, A. N.
Active in Story City, 1895-96.

TOSDAL, H. H.
Active in Estherville, 1895-96.

TOWNSEND, I. L.
Stereo photographer in Iowa Falls and West Branch; issued same views as J. N. Townsend.

TOWNSEND, J. N.
Stereo photographer in Iowa Falls; issued same views as I. L. Townsend.

TOWNSEND, L. M.
Stereo photographer in West Liberty.

TOWNSEND, T. W.
Studio at the corner of Clinton and Washington Streets, Iowa City, 1875.

TRITZ, M. J.
Active in Waterloo, 1895-96.

TROTH, W. H.
Studio at the corner of Reeve and Third in Hampton, c. 1880. Produced stereoviews.

TURK, B. W.
Active in Morning Sun, 1895-96.

TURNER & MILLER
Studio located on Main Street, Wyoming, c. 1875.

TWIFORD
Partner in Baird & Twiford, operating in Burlington, 1865. Studio at southeast corner of Fourth and Jefferson Streets.

TWINING, H. N.
Stereo photographer in Burlington.

UNION GALLERY
Operated by William H. Owen in Lyons, 1865.

UNION PHOTOGRAPH GALLERY
Operated by E. H. Curtiss, P. O. Box 255, Waterloo, c. 1862.

UPSON, D. D.
Active in Mason City, 1895-96.

VAN DEN BERG, J. F.
Active in Orange City, 1895-96.

VAN DYKE, E. M.
Active in Baxter, 1895-96.

VAN GORDER
Partner in Peasley & Van Gorder, active in Keokuk, 1895-96.

VAN GRIEKEN'S GALLERY
Studio at 82 Main Street, Keokuk, c. 1870.

VANDERMEULEN, G. A.
Active in Pella, 1860-75.

VEATCH & BULL
Partnership active in Cedar Falls, 1895-96.

VOSBURGH, M. H.
Active in Charles City, 1885-98, operating Vosburgh's Gallery.

WAIT
Partner in Brown & Wait, stereo photographers in Sioux City, 1890-92. Studio at 413 4 Street.

WAITLEY, E. B.
Active in Dunlap, 1895-96.

WALDRON & WILSON
Stereo photographers in Marion.

WALES, C. A.
Active in Centerville, 1891, 1895-96.

WALES, T. L.
Active in Keokuk, 1895-96.

WALKER, CHARLES L.
Active in Cedar Rapids, Box 881, "Dealer in Freethought Books," c. 1875; in Grinnell, c. 1880. Produced stereoviews.

WALLACE, W. C.
Active in Marshalltown, 1895-96.

WALLINE
Partner in Peelstrom & Walline, traveling photographers active in Des Moines.

WALLINE, A. L.
Stereo photographer in Gowrie.

WALLINE, A. S.
Active in Gowrie, 1895-96.

WALTER & WEIDMAN
Active in Manchester, c. 1880.

WALTER, H. L.
Studio on Main Street opposite the Post Office, Manchester, c. 1875. Produced stereoviews.

WALTERMIRE, C. W.
Studio at 201 4 Street West, Sioux City, 1898-99.

WALTERMIRE, P. C.
Photographer in Nebraska, 1882-89. Studio in Sioux City, 1891-1901; 603 Pearl Street, 1891-92; Riverside Park, 1893-94; 201 4 Street, 1894-1901.

WALTHALL & HINSHAW
Partnership active in Oskaloosa, 1895-96.

WARD
Active in Winterset, c. 1890.

WARD, H. T.
Active in Logan, 1895-96.

WARNER & PIERCE
Operated the Gallery of Art in Hopkinton, c. 1880.

WARNER, P. H.
Stereo photographer in Hopkinton. Possibly a partner in Warner & Pierce, operating the Gallery of Art, c. 1880.

WARREN, D. W.
Active in Hull, 1895-96.

WARREN, M. B.
Active in Correctionville, 1895-96.

WARRINGTON, A. W.
Eureka Picture Gallery, northeast corner of the public square, Oskaloosa, c. 1866; continued active, 1882. Produced stereoviews.

WASHBURN, W. W.
Active in Cresco, c. 1885.

WATSON, GUY
Active in Dakotah, 1895-96.

WATTERS, S. E.
Active in Eldora, 1895-96.

WEATHERLY, C. L & J. A.
Stereo photographers in Iowa City.

WEBB, J. F.
Active in Coon Rapids, 1895-96.

WEBSTER, F. W.
Active in Des Moines, 1895-96.

WEIDER
Active in Burlington.

WEIDMAN
Partner in Walter & Weidman, active in Manchester, c. 1880.

WEIGEL, MARY
Active in Dyersville, 1895-96.

WEINERT, J. L.
Active in Sheldon, 1895-96.

WEINGARTLE & BURNSIDE
Active in Cedar Rapids, 1895-96.

WELCH, O. D.
Active in Glenwood, 1895-96.

WERTS, P. D.
Active in Iowa City, 1895-96.

WEST, H. E.
Active in Oakland, 1895-96.

WESTON, E. D.
Active in Prairie City, 1895-96.

WETHERBY
Operated a "Gallery of Photographs & Paintings" on Clinton Street in Iowa City, c. 1860-70. Awarded first premium at the State Fair.

WETHERBY & COMPANY
Active in Rock Valley, 1895-96.

WHEELER, R. S.
Active in What Cheer, c. 1880, 1895-96.

WHEELER, S. F.
Active in Toledo, 1895-96.

WHITCOMB, D. W.
Active in Kellogg, 1895-96.

WHITE
Partner in Hastings, White & Fisher, operating gallery at 324 Brady Street, Davenport, 1885. Listed alone, 1895.

WHITE, A. P.
Active in West Union, c. 1860-70.

WIGGINS, S. T.
Active in Cedar Rapids, 1890, 1895-96.

WIGMAN
Active in Tama, c. 1895.

WILCOXON, WILLIAM A.
Active in Bonaparte, 1895-96.

WILKER, T. J.
Active in Ft. Dodge, 1895-96.

WILKINS, G. T.
Active in Clinton, 1880.

WILKINS, IRA
Active in Charles City, 1865. Studio on Main Street, opposite Charles City Bank, c. 1875.

WILLARD
Active at Lake City, c. 1890.

WILLCUTT, C. F.
Active in Exira, 1895-96.

WILLEFORD & BOND
Ft. Madison, 1895-96.

WILLIAMS
Active in Manson, 1875.

WILLIAMS, L. F.
Active in Moville, 1895-96.

WILLIAMSON
Partner in Aplin & Williamson, active in Eagle Grove, 1890.

WILSON
Partner in Waldron & Wilson, active in Marion.

WILSON, FRED
Stereo photographer in Gravity.

WILSON, J. C.
Active in Cherokee, 1875-90, 1895-96.

WILSON, J. W.
Active in Cherokee and Le Mars, c. 1880. Produced stereoviews.

WINGATE "THE LEVY"
Active in Mt. Pleasant, 1895.

WINN, J. M.
Active in Ottumwa, 1895-96.

WINSLOW, L. B.
Stereo photographer in Osage.

WISE, S. H.
Active in Wilton Junction, 1895-96.

WOLFGANG, L. M. (MISS)
Worked at the Reed & Son Gallery, Emmetsburg, 1895-96.

WOLLETT, A. E.
Active in Ottumwa.

WOOD, C. S.
Studio at 623 Pearl Street, Sioux City, 1886-87.

WOODBRIDGE'S PHOTO ART GALLERY
Active in Nashua, 1885.

WOODWARD, W. H.
Active in Winterset, 1895-96.

WOOLLETT, A. E.
Active in Ottumwa, 1895-96.

WRIGHT, G. WALLACE
Studio on the northwest corner of the square, Chariton, c. 1875; partner in Bridge & Wright before 1885. Sold out to Best & Company, c. 1885.

WYER
Partner in Hover & Wyer, stereo photographers in Decorah.

YEOMANS, O. L.
Active in Gladbrook, 1895-96.

YOUNG
Partner in Hildreth, Young & Company, stereo photographers in Clinton, 1880.

YOUNG, E. S.
Active in Leon, 1885.

YOUNG, WILLIAM
"Photographic Artist" in De Witt, c. 1864.

ZAHM, C. W.
Studio at 511 4 Street, Sioux City, 1895-99.

ZARLEY, C. W.
Active in Indianola, 1895-96.

Much of the information contained in this list is based on research by the staff of the Kansas Historical Society.

ACKER, G. G.
Stereo photographer active in Olathe.

ADAMS & SKEELS
Operated over the country store, Lawrence, c.1862; J. O. Adams.

ADAMS & THOMSON'S
Listed at 135 Massachusetts Street, Lawrence; specialized in Indian photographs.

ADAMS, A. W.
Studio at 1114 North Quincy Street, Topeka, 1899-1900.

ADAMS, J. O.
Partner in Adams & Skeels in Lawrence, c. 1862; operated the Photograph & Fine Art Gallery, c. 1863; operated the Sunbeam Gallery, c. 1865.

ADDIS & NOEL
Partnership of A. S. Addis and Noel, 48 Delaware Street; stereo photographers in Leavenworth. Also listed as Noe.

ADDIS, ALFRED SHEA
Partner with John T. Needles in Leavenworth, 1859-64; Needles & Addis studio at 56 Main, 1859-60; partner in Stevenson & Addis, 1860-62. Partner in Addis & Noel, operating at 48 Delaware, c. 1862-64. Addis left his negatives of Cheyenne and Arapaho with Stevenson when he left the partnership, 1862.

AHLSTROM, CHARLES
Active in Lawrence, 1883.

ALBRECHT, HUGO
Active in Topeka, 1885-86.

ALDEN, D. R.
Operated the Photographic Villa in Topeka, 1882-86, at 287 Topeka Avenue. Probably the same as D. R. Aldin.

ALDIN, D. R.
Active in Topeka, 1882-83, 207 Topeka Avenue. Probably the same as D. R. Alden.

ALDINE PHOTO-VILLA
Studio in Topeka, 1880; probably D. R. Aldin.

ALDRIDGE, GEORGE
Studio in Topeka, 1887-1902, 1013 North Kansas Avenue.

ALLEN, FRANK
Active in Leavenworth, 1882-83.

ALLEN, J. H.
Active in Russell, c. 1890.

ALLEN, THOMAS
Active in Topeka, 1899-1900, at 529 Topeka Avenue.

ALMA ART GALLERY
Active in Alma, 1885.

AMES, N. F.
Portrait, landscape and stereo photographer in Emporia at 170

Commercial Street; listed at Sixth Avenue, c. 1868.

ANDERSON, P.
Active in Topeka, 1887-88, at 314 West 7th.

ANDERSON, THOMAS
Photographer with Joseph Haag in Leavenworth, 1882.

ARLAUD, ADOLPH A.
Active in Leavenworth, 1894-95, at 801 South 5th; southeast corner of 5th and Olive, 1895-1900.

ARMANTROUT, M. I.
Active in Anthony, 1895.

ATCHERSON, C. E.
Listed at 317 Commercial, 1872-73, Atchison. Possibly an assistant of R. Stevenson.

ATCHISON PORTRAIT COMPANY
Studio in Atchison, 1899-1900.

ATHERTON, H. M.
Studios in Topeka, 1885-88, at 174 and 200 Kansas Avenue, North Topeka.

ATKINS
Active in Kinsley, c. 1890.

ATKINSON
Active in Lawrence, 1911.

ATKINSON, CHARLES W.
Photographer with Bauer in Leavenworth, 1893-94.

AVERY, C. D.
Operated the Ground Floor Studio in Concordia, c. 1900.

AVERY, J. C.
Active in Sedan, c. 1895.

BABBERGER, WILLIAM
Studio at 317-319 Commercial, Atchison, 1891, 1899-1900.

BABBITT, J. P.
Gallery at 40 and 42 Delaware, Leavenworth, 1865-67.

BAECHLE, OSCAR H.
Artist and portrait painter in Leavenworth, 1876-97; photographer at 825 Kickapoo, 1880-81.

BAILEY
Partner in Kent & Bailey, active in Yates Center, c. 1885.

BAILEY, M. W.
Active in Hutchinson, 1908-09.

BAIRD, J. A.
Advertising as the "Portrait and Landscape Photographer, Lightning Process, 16 Years Experience," operating in Dighton, c. 1875.

BALBERGER
Studio in the Ingalls Building, Atchison, c. 1890.

BALDWIN & OSTERGREN
Studio at 88 Douglas Avenue, Wichita, c. 1885.

BALDWIN & SON
Studio in Wichita, c. 1880.

BALDWIN, F. C.
Active in Westmoreland.

BALDWIN, NEREUS
Active in Wichita, 1876.

BALDWIN'S ART GALLERY
Located east of Eagle Block, Wichita, c. 1870.

BANKS, E. J.
Active in Wichita, 1916.

BARBER, W. B.
Active in Topeka, 1899-1900.

BARKER
Active in Ottawa, 1885-95.

BARKER & GREGG
Partnership of Henry J. Barker and Alexander Gregg in Leavenworth, 1855-60; studio at South Delaware, between Main and 2nd.

BARNARD & JOHNSON
Operating at East Spring Avenue, Conway Springs, c. 1885.

BARR, JOHN M.
Artist at northeast corner of Oak and 7th, Leavenworth, 1859-60.

BAUER & SON, S.
Active in Leavenworth, 1885-87; Sebastian Bauer with son, P. H. Bauer in S. Bauer & Son. Also spelled Baur.

BAUER, MARY (MISS)
Photographer in Leavenworth with S. Bauer & Son, 1886-87; with P. H. Bauer, 1888.

BAUER, P. H.
Photographer in Leavenworth, 1878-1900; with S. Bauer, 1878-79; listed separately at 421 Delaware, 1879-80, 1882; with his father, Sebastian & P. H. Bauer, 1883; located at 420 Delaware upstairs, 1884-89; studio at northwest corner of Shawnee and Fifth Streets, 502 Shawnee, Leavenworth, 1890-1900.

BAUER, SEBASTIAN
Active in Leavenworth, 1866-87; at 99 Shawnee, 1866-67; 409 Shawnee, 1874-76; 421 Delaware, 1877-83; 420 Delaware, 1884; continued at that location with son, P. H. Bauer in S. Bauer & Son, 1885-87.

BAUM'S ART STUDIO
Active in Hanover.

BAUMAN, PHEOBE (MRS.)
Active in Leavenworth, 1897-1900, at 111 and 113 South 4th.

BEACHLE, CHARLES F.
Active in Leavenworth, 1874-76. Possibly Baechle.

BEAN, R. T.
Active in Washington, 1897.

BEARDSLEY, GEORGE O.
Active in Topeka, 1899-1900.

BECHTLE, JOHN
Active in Topeka, 1896-97.

BECK & DILLON
H. Beck and H. Dillon, active in Winfield, 1879.

BECK, H.
Partner in Beck & Dillon, Winfield, 1879.

BEECHER, LULU
Artist in Ft. Scott, 1889-90.

BEIGHTLE
Active in Valley Falls.

BEISNER, H. F.
Active in Louisville.

BELL, DR. WILLIAM A.
Photographed on Union Pacific route, 1867.

BELL, FRANK
Active in Atchison, 1891.

BELL, ROBERT
Active in Topeka, 1899-1900.

BENDER, H. A.
Active in Independence, 1890.

BENECKE, ROBERT
Photographer on Union Pacific route, 1864. See Missouri.

BENEY, WILLIAM G. F.
Listed at 56 Delaware in Leavenworth, 1860-61.

BENNETT, HARRY O.
Partner of H. W. Rose in Leavenworth, 1884, operating as Rose & Bennett, 218 South 5th Street.

BENTON PORTRAIT COMPANY
Studio in Topeka, 1896-97, 21 Office Block.

BERGLOF, H. M. (MRS.)
Active in Concordia, 1895.

BERNSTEIN, AARON
Active in Leavenworth, 1899-1900.

BEST, H. E.
Active in Topeka, 1887-88.

BEST, THOMAS B.
Active in Leavenworth, 1861-62, at 56 Delaware.

BETTERLY, J. G.
Stereo photographer in Kansas City, advertised as the "Roving Photographer."

BILL, E. C.
Active in Topeka, 1896-97, at 1913 West 10th Avenue.

BIRD, D. R.
Active in Ft. Scott, 1879.

BIRDSALL, GEORGE B.
Active in Leavenworth, 1884-92; with E. E. Henry, 1884-85; listed separately, 1886-87; studio at 412 Delaware, 1889-92.

BISCHOFF BROTHERS
Active in Minneapolis, c. 1885.

BITTMAN & RICHEY
Partnership in Wamego.

BLACK, CHARLES H.
Active in Leavenworth, 1897-98.

BLISS, W. P.
Studio at Sixth Avenue, Topeka, c. 1868. See New Mexico and Traveling.

BOLES & DA LEE
Active in Lawrence, 1860; A. G. Da Lee.

BOLMAR, LYDIA M.
Active in Topeka, 1899-1900.

BONEBRAKE, M. P.
Active in Topeka, 1882-83.

BONSALL, ISAAC H.
Active in Leavenworth, 1859-60, at 24 fi33 Delaware; in Kansas City and later Arkansas City, c. 1875. Also listed as J. H.

BORDEAUX & SINCLAIR
Operated the B & S Photo Company in Wichita, c. 1890.

BOSS, EDITH S.
Active in Leavenworth, 1895-99.

BOURE
Active in Delphos, 1880.

BOURQUIN, JULES A.
Active in Horton.

BOVINE, E. A.
Active in Ft. Scott, 1871-72.

BOWER & JOHNSON
M. B. Bower and W. S. Johnson, stereo photographers in Kansas City, c. 1870s-80s.

BRADBEER, ANDREW D.
Photographer with G. B. Birdsall in Leavenworth, 1888.

BRADEN, CHARLES
Active in Elsmore, c. 1904.

BRADLEY, H. E.
Stereo photographer in Kirwin.

BRIGGS, ZENO & LUTA
Active in Atchison, 1899-1900, operating the Z. T. Briggs & Company studio and photographer's supply shop.

BRONNER
Active in Dodge City, 1890.

BROWN, A.
Stereo photographer in Independence.

BROWN, E. C.
Active in Ellsworth.

BROWN, J. C.
Stereo photographer in Holton.

BROWN, JOHN E.
Active in Lawrence.

BROWN, WILLIAM A.
Photographer for Topeka & Southwestern Railroad in Leavenworth, 1882.

BRUMFIELD
Photographer and portrait artist, Dodge City, c. 1890.

BRUNDIGE, H. T.
Stereo photographer in Cherryvale.

BRUNER, C. A.
View photographer in Topeka, 1896-97.

BUCK
Active in Paola.

BUCKLEY, SAMUEL W.
Photographer with Stevenson in Leavenworth, 1862-63.

BUELL, H. H.
Studio at 11 5th Street East, Topeka, 1882-83.

BUFFHAM, A. T.
Listed at 115 Scott Avenue, Ft. Scott, 1898.

BULL, JOHNNIE
Active in Manhattan, 1885.

BUMBARGER
Partner in Spicer & Bumbarger, Topeka, 1914.

BUNKER, MARY
Active in Topeka, 1896-97, 1899-1900.

BURGOYNE, GEORGE
Gallery operated in Manhattan, c. 1870. Succeeded by Dewey who advertised that the studio was established in 1859.

BURLINGTON, FORD H.
Stereo photographer in Kansas City.

BURT, GEORGE
Active in Leavenworth, 1884, upstairs at 311 Delaware.

BUSH, J. E.
Operated the Floral Art Gallery in Burlingame, c. 1885.

BUTLER, R. S.
Gallery listed at 107 North 7th, Atchison, 1887. Also listed as B. S. Butler.

C & S STUDIO
Active in Lawrence.

CAMPBELL, M. L.
Active in Topeka, 1899-1900, at 111 West 6th Avenue; operated the M. L. Campbell Portrait Company, 722 Kansas Avenue, 1902.

CAPITAL GALLERY
Studio in Topeka, 1882-83, operated by I. J. Martell at 71 Kansas Avenue.

CARD, B. F.
Operating at 173 Commercial Street, Emporia, c. 1868. Billed as a landscape and portrait photographer in Humboldt, c. 1875.

CARDEN & DOWNS
Partnership of C. H. Carden and E. J. Downs, in Ft. Scott, 1885.

CARDEN, C. H.
Active in Ft. Scott, 1885, with E. J. Downs, operating as Carden & Downs.

CAREY, HENRY
Active in Leavenworth, 1874-75.

CARVALHO, S. N.
See California.

CARY, C. I.
Active in Leavenworth with S. Bauer, 1874.

CASE, E. M.
Active in Topeka, 1899-1900.

CASSELLA & HAAG
Partnership of John Cassella and Joseph Haag at 102 South 5th, Leavenworth, 1899-1900.

CASSELLA & HUNT
Partnership of John Cassella and J. Howard Hunt at 105 North 5th, Leavenworth, 1898-99.

CASSELLA, JOHN
Active in Leavenworth, 1898-99, at 105 North 5th with partner J. Howard Hunt; at 102 South 5th, 1899-1900, with partner Joseph Haag.

CATTON, C. W.
Active in Coffeeville, 1875.

CAUDLE, ART B.
Active at 132 fi3 West 6th Street, Concordia, c. 1885. Manager of the Elite Studio, c. 1890.

CHALLIS, M. (MISS)
Listed as an artist in Atchison, 1885.

CHAMBERLAIN, MARY L.
Active at 125 West 7th Street, Topeka, 1902.

CHANDLEE, MARIETTA
Active in Leavenworth, 1895-1900; studio at 427 Cherokee, 1899-1900.

CHANNEL, ELIAS
Active in Topeka, 1896-97.

CHAPMAN, C. G.
Active at 527 Kansas Avenue, Topeka, 1896-97.

CHARLES, A. (MISS)
Photo retoucher in Ft. Scott, 1885.

CHASE, JOHN A.
Operated studio in Atchison, 1870-73; on Commercial between 4th and 5th, upstairs, 1870-71; 412 and 414 Commercial, Atchison, 1872-73.

CHIDISTER, B. F.
Active in Leavenworth at 814 South 5th, 1880-81; 518 South 5th, 1882.

CHURCH, ALENA
Studio at 622 West 8th Avenue, Topeka, 1896-97.

CHURCHILL, D. J.
From Joplin, Missouri. Portrait artist on the 2nd floor of the McElroy Block, Ft. Scott, 1885.

CIRRK'S PHOTO COMPANY
Active in Anthony, 1912.

CITY FINE ART GALLERY
Operated by Parker & Company in Ft. Scott, 1871-72, at 3 Wall Street; J. T. Parker, proprietor.

CLARK
Partner in Corwin & Clark, active in Ottawa, c. 1890.

CLARK, C. F.
Listed at 317 Commercial, Atchison, 1887.

CLARK'S PHOTO COMPANY
Active in Anthony, 1910.

CLAYMAN, BIRDY (MISS)
Active in Leavenworth, 1888.

CLUTE, EDWARD E.
Active in Leavenworth, 1884.

COBB & LOCKE
Stereo photographers in Kirwin, c. 1870s-80s; Phillipsburg, c. 1895.

COBB, C. S.
Active in Kirwin.

COLE, ELLA J. (MRS.)
Active in Leavenworth, 1865-66, at 56 Delaware; 214 Delaware, 1874-75.

COLLINS, CORA C. (MISS)
Active in Leavenworth, 1891-97.

COLLINS, G. B. & J. L.
Studio at 63 Delaware Street, Leavenworth, c. 1868.

COLOMBIN, MICHAEL
Active in Leavenworth, 1874-77. Located at northeast corner of 5th and Cherokee, 1874; 228 Shawnee, 1877.

COLVER, JOHN P.
Active in Leavenworth, 1863-64.

COLVILLE, JOSEPH P.
Active in Topeka, 1896-97, 1899-1902; partner with C. J. Rolfe at 632 Kansas Avenue, operating the Rolfe & Colville Studio, 1902.

CONCANNON, J. H. & T. M.
Studio over Rowland, Elliot & Company grocery store in Masonic Block on Wall Street, Ft. Scott, c. 1868.

CONCANNON, J. H.
Operated the Temple of Fine Art, at 5 Wall Street, Ft. Scott, 1869-70; partner with his brother, T. M., in Ft. Scott, c. 1868.

CONCANNON, TOM M.
Partner with his brother, J. H., in Ft. Scott, c. 1868. Studios in Cainey and Baxter Springs; traveled the Indian Territory photographing Osage Indians.

CONKLIN & KLECKNER
Partnership of M. A. Kleckner and S. L. Conklin in Atchison, 1881.

CONKLIN & STEVENSON
Stereo photographers in Atchison, c. 1870s-80s; Richard Stevenson and probably S. L. Conklin.

CONKLIN, S. L.
Partner in Naughton & Conklin, Atchison, 1880, at 507 Commercial; partner with M. A. Kleckner, 1881; listed alone at 509 Commercial, Atchison, 1885. Probably also a partner in Conklin & Stevenson, c. 1870s-80s.

CONNELY, S. E.
Listed on Howard Avenue, Atchison, 1899-1900.

COOK, ANDREW I.
Active in Garnett, 1879-84.

COOK, D. L.
Active in Ft. Scott, 1891-92, 1896; at 209 Market, 1891-92; Main and Wall Streets, 1896.

COOLIDGE & COMPANY, WILLIAM H.
Listed at the Dental & Photographic Depot, southwest corner of 4th and Delaware, Leavenworth, 1863-64.

CORNISH, GEORGE B.
Partner with W. S. Prettyman, operating as Prettyman & Cornish, Arkansas City, 1889; listed alone, 1906-09.

CORWIN & CLARK
Active in Ottawa, c. 1890.

CORWIN, E. M.
Partner in Corwin & Clark, Ottawa, c. 1890.

COSAND & MOSER
Stereo photographers in Caldwell.

COTTAGE GALLERY
Studio operated by A. C. Nichols in Leavenworth, 1866-82; corner of 7th and Broadway, 1866-67; 193 Delaware, 1870-71; 308 Pottawatomie, 1880-82.

COTTAGE STUDIO
Active in La Crosse, 1903.

COTTRELL, D. H.
Operating at the corner of Main and State Streets, Seneca, c. 1885.

COULTER, C. K.
Active in Topeka, 1887-88, at 119 West 5th.

COURTNEY, S. L.
Active in Topeka, 1896-97, 1899-1900, 1902, at 905 North Kansas Avenue.

COWLEY, L. L.
Active in Ottawa.

CRAMER'S ART ROOMS
Active in Cherryvale.

CREESE, M. P.
Active in Mankato, c. 1885; in Topeka at 629 Kansas Avenue, 1896-97.

CREW & MORGAN
Active in Leavenworth, c. 1875.

CRISTOPH, J.
Active in Ellinwood.

CROCKETT, I. B. (MISS)
From Missouri. Listed as art student in Ft. Scott, 1888.

CROFT & CUSICK
Stereo photographers in Arkansas City.

CROFT, THOMAS
Active in Arkansas City; partner in Croft & Cusick.

CRONICE, ELLEN
Active in Leavenworth, 1894-95.

CRONIN, E. J. (MISS)
Active in Leavenworth, 1888, corner of 5th and Marion Avenue.

CROOK, C. J.
Photographer with S. Bauer & Son in Leavenworth, 1887.

CULP, MARETTA
Active in Topeka, 1902.

CULVER, WILLIAM
Active in Topeka.

CUNNINGHAM, C. C.
Operating in LeRoy, c. 1890.

CURTIS, EMMA M.
Active at 627 Kansas Avenue, Topeka, 1887-88. Also spelled Curtiss.

CUSICK
Partner in Croft & Cusick, stereo photographers in Arkansas City.

D'OLE, S.
Listed in Ft. Scott, 1891-92.

D'OLE, T. W.
Active in Ft. Scott, 1891-92.

DA LEE, A. G.
Active in Lawrence, 1858-79; partner in Boles & Da Lee, 1860; with Elmer Willis operating Willis-Da Lee's Art Gallery, 1858-79.

DABBS, J. V.
Studio in Ft. Scott, 1888-98; at 203 and 205 Market Street, operating as Dabbs Photo Gallery, 1888; 207 Market, 1891- 92; 18 fi East Wall, 1898.

DAUGHTERY, S.
Active in Ft. Scott, at the corner of Wall and Main, 1871-72; partner with J. T. Parker, operating as Parker & Daughtery, c. 1875.

DAVENPORT, C. F.
Active in Wellington, 1885.

DAWSON
Stereo photographer in Beloit; partner in Dobler & Dawson.

DAYLIGHT STUDIO
Active in Topeka, 1885.

DELAHAY, MARY E.
Active in Leavenworth, 1893-94.

DENTAL & PHOTOGRAPHIC DEPOT
Operated by William H. Coolidge & Company in Leavenworth, 1863-64, southwest corner of 4th anad Delaware.

DENTON, B. F.
Active in Newton.

DEWEY, GEORGE F.
Successor to George Burgoyne in Manhattan. Studio on Poyntz Avenue, c. 1890. Partner in Dewey & Dewey, c. 1895.

DEWEY'S
Active in Mound City.

DICKEY, M. P.
Active in Leoti.

DICKS, A. E.
Stereo photographer in Larned.

DILLON, H.
Partner in Beck & Dillon, Winfield, 1879.

DITTUS, ALMA
Active in Topeka, 1896-97.

DOBLER
Active in Beloit; partner in Dobler Brothers, c. 1882-88; partner in Dobler & Dawson; listed alone, 1895.

DOBLER BROTHERS
Partnership in Beloit, c. 1882-88.

DOBLER & DAWSON
Stereo photographers in Beloit.

DOOMES, C. H.
Kansas photographer, c. 1890.

DOUTHITT, ADA
Active in Topeka, 1887-88.

DOUTHITT, LAURA
Active in Topeka, 1887-88.

DOUTHITT, LOUISE
Active in Topeka, 1887-88.

DOWNING, GEORGE
Active in Topeka, 1875-1902. Studio located at 197 Kansas Avenue, 1877-86; 617 Kansas Avenue, 1887-1902. Located in the Union Hall Building, over Barnum & Co's dry goods store," c. 1870. Produced stereoviews.

DOWNS, EDSON J.
Active in Ft. Scott, 1885-90. Partner with E. J. Downs, 1885, operating as Carden & Downs; listed alone at 122 East Wall Street, 1888-90.

DRESSER
Active in Winfield, 1890.

DRESSER, GEORGE H.
Active in Independence.

DRUM, O.
Stereo photographer in Longhorn.

DUDLEY, GEORGE
Active in Topeka, 1882-83, with Hunter & Son.

DUNN, IVO M.
Active in Leavenworth, 1897-98.

DUNN, THOMAS C.
Active in Leavenworth, 1897-98.

DURLAND & COMPANY
Studio at the corner of Massachusetts and Henry Streets, Lawrence, c. 1865.

DUTLER, D. S.
From Sedalia, Missouri; in Atchison, 1885, at 805 Commercial.

DUZENBERRY, HURON
Active in Lynden, 1872-74.

DYER
Active in Lyle, 1882.

EDINGTON
Active in Marysville.

EGGERS STUDIO
Active in Augusta and Douglas, 1913.

EGGLESTON, MATTIE S. (MISS)
Listed as artist in Atchison, 1885.

ELITE GALLERY
Operated in Wellington by Snell & Sargent, stereo photographers.

ELITE STUDIO
Gallery in Concordia, c. 1890, managed by Art B. Caudle.

ELWOOD, W. C.
Active in Troy, 1899.

EMENS, R. B.
Active in Topeka at 908 North Kansas Avenue, 1902.

EMERY, A. G.
Operated studio over the Post Office in Junction City, c. 1880.

ENSLOW
Active in Highland.

EVANS, J. G.
Active in Muscaline.

EWING, E. B.
Active in Topeka, 1902; art instructor at Bethany College.

FAIRCHILD, C. E.
Active in Topeka, 1899-1900.

FARRELL, EDITH (MISS)
Active in Leavenworth, 1887, 1894-95, 1898-1900.

FARROW, WILLIAM F.
View photographer in Topeka at 811 Kansas Avenue, 1894-1902.

FEATHER
Active in Minneapolis; partner in Soule & Feather, 1885; partner in Feather & McCloughlin, 1890.

FEATHER & McCLOUGHLIN
Active in Minneapolis, 1890.

FENTON, JAMES
Artist with Inter-State Portrait Company, Atchison, 1899-1900.

FENTON, JAMES. H.
Active in Leavenworth, 1899-1900, artist with J. H. Smith.

FERGUSON, J. HENRY
Active in Leavenworth, 1874-88. Located at 112 South 5th, 1874-77; 420 Delaware, 1879-83; 414 Delaware, 3rd storey, 1884-86; 416 Delaware, 1888.

FISHBACK, LEE
Active in Florence.

FISHBACK, M. L.
Active in Ft. Scott, 1888.

FLAGG, B. A.
Active in Junction City.

FLORAL ART GALLERY
Operated by J. E. Bush in Burlingame, c. 1885.

FLOYD, F. G.
Stereo photographer in Paola.

FORD, CHARLES E.
Active in Leavenworth, 1891-95; with Birdsall, 1891-92; at 412 Delaware, 1893-95.

FORD, HARRY
Active in Lynden, 1884.

FORD'S VIEWS
Active in Burlington.

FORDICE, W. H.
Stereo photographer in Council Grove.

FORNEY
Stereo photographer in Abilene.

FORRELL, C.
Active in McPherson, 1885.

FOSTER, R. M.
Stereo photographer in Cawker City, 1886.

FOWLER
Active in Seneca.

FOX, LAURETTA
Artist in Topeka, 1896-97, 1899-1900, 1902; at 500 Lane Street, 1896-97.

FRANCIS, HELEN
Artist in Topeka, 1902.

FRASER, WILLIAM A.
Ambrotypist at northeast corner of Commercial and 5th, Atchison, 1859-60.

FREDERICK, D. A.
Active in Ashland.

FREEMAN, D. G.
Studio at 606 Kansas Avenue, North Topeka, 1883-84.

FRENCH, F.
Stereo photographer and publisher in Lawrence, c. 1895.

FRENCH'S STEREOSCOPIC VIEWS
Active in Lawrence, 1875-90.

FRICHOT, BRUTUS
Active in Leavenworth, 1885-1900; with J. T. Mason, 1885-88; with
J. S. Sauerman, 1890-95 at 505 Shawnee; listed alone at same address,
1895-1900.

GALBRAITH STUDIO
Active in Chanute.

GARDNER, ALEXANDER
Famous Civil War and Washington D.C. photographer working in
Lawrence, Leavenworth, Elsworth and Hays, 1867.

GARDNER PHOTOGRAPH GALLERY
Active at 174 Kansas Avenue, Topeka, 1877.

GARNETT
Active in McLain, 1890.

GARRITE, T. J.
Active in Leavenworth, 1870-71.

GARY, EMMA R. (MISS)
Active in Leavenworth, 1888-89.

GEBHART, J. D.
Active in Olathe.

GEM PHOTOGRAPHY GALLERY
Operated by Richard Stapleton at 318 East 4th, Topeka, 1887-88.

GHENT, MILAN H.
Active in Topeka, 1899-902.

GIBBONEY, HOWARD E.
Photographer with J. H. Leonard in Topeka, 1896-97.

GIBBS, D., JR.
Active in Dunlap, c. 1882.

GIFFORD, BENJAMIN A.
Partner in Tresslar & Gifford, stereo photographers in Ft. Scott. See
Oregon.

GILMORE, JOHN S.
Active in Fredonia, 1912.

GLASS, C. G.
Active in Coffeyville, c. 1870.

GLENDENING
Active in Little River, c. 1880.

GLOBE STUDIO
Gallery in Leavenworth, 1896-98; operated by P. H. Bauer at 412
Delaware, 1896-97; 102 South 5th, 1897-98, F. W. Swan, manager.

GOFF, EDMOND
Active in Topeka, 1902.

GOODHOLM, F.
Active in Lindsborg.

GOODNIGHT'S STUDIO
Active in Lawrence.

GOODRICH, P. (MISS)
Active in Topeka, 1883-84. Also listed as Miss B. Goodrich.

GRAHAM, ELLA (MISS)
Active in Beloit, 1889, 1898.

GRAHAM, H. M.
Agent for D. J. Churchill, a portrait artist in Ft. Scott, 1885.

GRAHM, J. WILLIAM
Photographer in Leavenworth with P. H. Bauer, 1896-97.

GRANT, C. M.
Active in Topeka, 1902.

GRAY BROTHERS PARLOR GALLERY
Active in Elsworth.

GRAY, GRACE (MISS)
Artist in Ft. Scott, 1885.

GREENWOOD, W. H.
Active in Beloit.

GREGG, ALEXANDER
Partner in Barker & Gregg, operating in Leavenworth on South
Delaware, between Main and 2nd, 1855-60; listed alone, 1860-61.

GREGORY, WILLIAM
Active in Leavenworth, 1859-60.

GRIFFITH, PROFESSOR W. A.
Active in Lawrence.

GRIGGS, A. D.
Active in Topeka, 1883-88, 1896-1902. Partner with Elijah W. Griggs, operating as Griggs Brothers, 1885-88.

GRIGGS BROTHERS
Partnership of A. D. and Elijah W. Griggs in Topeka, 1885-88; at
111 5th Street East, 1885-86; 226 Kansas Avenue, 1887-88.

GRIGGS, ELIJAH W.
Active in Topeka, 1883-88, 1896-1902. Partner with A. D. Griggs,
operating as Griggs Brothers, 1885-88.

GRIGGS, W. S.
Gallery at 122 6th Avenue, Topeka, 1882-83.

GRONDAL, B. G.
Aristotypist active in Lindsborg, 1890.

GUTZKOW, EDWARD
Active in Leavenworth, 1860-61.

HAAG, JOSEPH
Active in Leavenworth, 1870-99. Partner in Ploetz & Haag, 1870-71,
at 99 Shawnee; studio at 404 Delaware Street, 1876-80; 404 and 406
Delaware Street, 1882-97. Retoucher at Bauer's Studio, 1897-98;
partner with John Cassella at 102 South 5th, 1899-1900, operating as
Cassella & Haag. Also listed as Hague.

HAAG, JULIA
Active in Leavenworth, 1896-97; possibly Joseph Haag's daughter.

HAAS, EMMA
Active in Leavenworth, 1895-97.

HADDAN
Active in Coffeyville.

HAGAN, JOSEPH C.
Listed at 409 Commercial, Atchison, 1899-1900.

HAGAN, WILLIAM
Listed at 409 Commercial, Atchison, 1880.

HAGUE, JOSEPH
See Joseph Haag.

HAHN, JULIUS A.
Active in Ft. Scott at 101 South Main, 1898.

HALL
Active in Havens, c. 1890.

HALL, W. R.
Active in Smith Center, 1885.

HALL, WILLIAM E.
Active in Leavenworth, 1891-92, 1895-96.

HALLADAY
Active in Great Bend and La Crosse, c. 1885.

HAMILTON
Active in Junction City, 1910.

HAMILTON, A. C.
Active in Lawrence, 1886.

HANEY, J. W.
Active in Miltonvale, 1900-01.

HANSBROOK, W. A.
Active in Leavenworth, 1865-66.

HANSBROUGH
Active in Abilene, 1890.

HAPGOOD, C. (MISS)
Active in Ft. Scott, 1893.

HARDEN, HOMER T.
Active in Wichita, 1908.

HARDING, FREDERICK
Studio at 112 Woodlawn Avenue, Topeka, 1899-1900.

HARLOW, MABEL
Retoucher in Leavenworth, 1894-95.

HARP
Photographer with Mason in Leavenworth, 1885.

HARRIS, LILLIE
Active in Leavenworth, 1899-1900, at 422 South 5th.

HARVEY
Operated the Harvey Studio in Council Grove.

HATHAWAY, HARRY
Artist in Ft. Scott, 1871-72.

HATHEWAY, NATHANIEL
Active in Leavenworth, 1870-71, at 5th between Delaware and Shawnee.

HAYNES, HANNIE
Active in Topeka, 1887-88.

HAYS, GEORGE
Photo printer with Elkanah Tresslar in Ft. Scott, 1885.

HAYS, J.
Active in Ft. Scott, 1891-92.

HAYS, L. (MISS)
Active in Ft. Scott, 1888.

HAYWOOD, M. C.
Active in Topeka, 1882-84, at 195 and 273 Kansas Avenue.

HECKMAN, DANIEL G.
Active in Topeka, 1899-1900.

HEINE, HANNAH (MRS.)
Listed at 501 South Main in Ft. Scott, 1893.

HENRY, E. E.
Operated in western Canada before 1870. Active in Leavenworth, 1870-99. Gallery at 82 Delaware Street, 1870-71; 322 Delaware Street, 1874-94; 420 Delaware, 1897-99. Partner of Harrison Putney, operating as Putney & Henry, 1870-71, 1894-97. Published stereoviews as early as 1870.

HENRY, R. H.
Photographer with E. E. Henry at 322 Delaware Street, 1882-83.

HICKOX, R. A.
Active in Emporia.

HIGGINS, W. C.
Active in Salina with C. E. Libbey.

HILL, JOSEPH C.
Listed at 409 Commercial, Atchison, 1899-1900.

HINMAN, E. B.
Active in Pittsburg.

HIXON STUDIO
Active in Lawrence.

HOAGLAND, N.
Active in Wyandotte.

HOFFMAN, L.
Active in Leavenworth, 1874.

HOFFMASTER, HARRY
Active in Topeka, 1896-97.

HOGE, E. G. (MISS)
Photographer and retoucher with Elkanah Tresslar in Ft. Scott, 1885, 1888.

HOLCOMB, O.
Stereo photographer in Salina, 1890; partner in Hopkins & Holcomb, c. 1880s.

HOLMES & SON
Active in Hiawatha, c. 1885.

HONEY, J. W.
Active in Miltonvale.

HOOBS, I. N.
Studio at Capital House, Topeka, 1884-83.

HOOK, WILLIAM M.
Active in Leavenworth, 1859-61.

HOOP, S. W.
Active in Manhattan.

HOOPER
Active in Washington, c. 1895.

HOOVER, D. F.
Active in Topeka, 1887-88.

HOPKINS & HOLCOMB
Stereo photographers in Salina, c. 1880s.

HOPKINS, FRANCIS M.
Active in Ft. Scott at 113 East Wall, 1898.

HOPKINS, GEORGE B.
Artist at 16 Office Block in Topeka, 1887-88.

HOPKINS, S. D.
Active in Junction City, 1890.

HOPPE, E. L.
Active in Holton, c. 1885.

HORACEK, WILLIAM
Active in Topeka at 708 Kansas Avenue, 1902.

HORKMANS, D. M.
Active in Lawrence, 1903-04.

HORRUP, C. A.
Active in Leavenworth at 608 Pottawatomie, 1883; with J. T. Mason, 1884.

HOUSE, E.
Artist in Topeka, 1899-1900.

HOVER, J. W.
Assistant to Hunter in Ft. Scott at the corner of 1st and Main, 1891-92.

HOWARD
Active in Paola, 1875; in Clay Center, c. 1880.

HOWARD, C. H.
Agent of American Portrait Company, Leavenworth, 1891-92.

HOWARD, GEORGE
Active in Leavenworth at 913 and 914 Pottawatomie, 1886-98.

HOWARD, N. W.
Stereo photographer in Eureka.

HUEY'S ART GALLERY
Active in Independence, 1870.

HUNT, J. HOWARD
Active in Leavenworth, 1898-99; partner with John Cassella, operating as Cassella & Hunt at 105 North 5th.

HUNTER
Active in Dodge City and Wellington, 1880.

HUNTER & SON
Topeka, 1882-83.

HUNTER, J. W.
Photographer at Hunter's Photograph Gallery in Ft. Scott at the corner of 1st and Main, 1891-92.

HURRLE & BROTHER, EDWARD D.
Active in Leavenworth at southwest corner of 5th and Delaware, 1882; 511 Delaware, 1883.

HURRLE, ALFONSO
Active in Leavenworth, 1883, with brother E. D., 511 Delaware.

HURRLE, FREDRICK G.
Active in Leavenworth, 1883, at 511 Delaware, operating as Edward D. Hurrle & Brother.

HUTCHINGS, V.
Active in Smith Center, 1880.

HUTCHINS, S. H
Active in Burlington.

HUTCHINSON, C. C.
Active in Newton.

IFLAND
Stereo photographer active in Sedan; partner in Ross & Ifland.

INGRAM, E. A. (MRS.)
Active in Leavenworth, 1889-92, at 106 South 4th.

INTER-STATE PORTRAIT COMPANY
Studio in Atchison, 1899-1900, at 715 Commercial; M. M. Mishler, manager.

IRELAND, W. R.
Partner in Oaks & Ireland, stereo photographers in Holton, c. 1880s. Produced stereoviews.

ISAACS, G. G.
Active in Mound Ridge, 1890.

ISERMAN, HELEN
Active in Topeka, 1896-97.

JAMESON, ARTHUR E.
Active in Leavenworth, 1891-96.

JAYCOX, P. L.
Active in Mitchell County.

JENKINS, CHARLES
Active in Topeka, 1882-83.

JENKINS, JOHN E.
Active in Topeka, 1887-88.

JENNINGS, JOSEPH
Active in Scandia, 1898.

JEPSON
Active in Stockton, 1910-12.

JIPSON, F. B. (MISS)
Active in Ft. Scott, 1898.

JOHNSON
Partner in Barnard & Johnson, Conway Springs, c. 1885.

JOHNSON, SAMUEL
Active in Leavenworth, 1897-98.

JOHNSON, SELMA
Art teacher in Topeka, 1896-97.

JONES, NATIE M.
Operated art studio at 833 North Kansas, Topeka, 1902.

KALIN, JOHN
Active in Scandia.

KANSAS CITY PHOTOGRAPH ROOMS
Studio in Kansas City at Third Street, east of Main; J. G. Wertz, proprietor.

KASSABAUM, CHARLES H.
Portrait artist at 409 Hill Block, Ft. Scott, 1888; 418 Commercial, 1900.

KEITH, MARY I.
Artist in Atchison, 1891.

KELLAM BOOK & STATIONARY COMPANY
Active in Topeka, 1899-1900, selling artists materials at 711 Kansas Avenue.

KELLNER, ANTHONY
Active in Leavenworth, 1897-98, at 68 Delaware.

KELLY, PETER
Picture agent in Topeka, 1902.

KEMPER, MORRIS
Active in Topeka, 1899-1900.

KENDERDINE, FRANCON C.
Artist in Topeka, 1896-1900, at 727 Topeka Avenue.

KENNEDY & COMPANY, M. A.
Gallery at 125 Mass Street, Lawrence, c. 1868.

KENNEDY, L. G.
Active in Kansas City.

KENT & BAILEY
Active in Yates Center, c. 1885.

KENT, I. N.
Active in Humboldt, c. 1895.

KEYSTONE VIEW COMPANY
Active in Scammon.

KIERNAN, ANNIE S.
Active in Topeka, 1896-97, 1902.

KIMBALL, HOWARD A.
Active in Leavenworth, 1865-67, at 63 Delaware. Operated as Kimball & Company, 1867.

KIMBALL, R. H.
Studio at 63 Delaware Street, Leavenworth, c. 1865.

KING, J. R.
Active in Clyde, c. 1885.

KINNEY & TOOLEY
Active in Concordia.

KINNEY, JOHN
Active in Leavenworth, 1891-92.

KIRKHAM, JOHN W.
Active in Leavenworth, 1874-79, 1882-85, 1893-94. Operated at 412 Delaware, 1874-76; 112 South 5th, 1878-79.

KIRMEYER, JOSEPH
Photographer with H. S. Stevenson in Leavenworth, 1894-98. Listed separately, 1898-1900.

KISSEL, S. W.
Manager of Noble's Gallery in Leavenworth, 1875, at 328 Delaware.

KLECKNER & SNYDER
Partnership of M. A. Kleckner and George H. Snyder, at 703 Commercial, Atchison, 1899-1900.

KLECKNER, M. A.
Photographer from Bethlehem, Pennsylvania. Photographer in Atchison, 1881-91; partner in Conklin & Kleckner, 1881; at 409 Commercial, 1885-91; partner with G. H. Snyder, operating as Kleckner & Snyder, 1899-1900; also in Osborne City, 1885-91.

KLEIN
Active in Topeka; partner in Weber & Klein.

KNIGHT, CAPTAIN J. LEE
Operated the Riverside Gallery at 174 Kansas Avenue, Topeka, 1867-75.

KNIGHT, GEORGE M.
Active in Topeka, 1899-1900, at 900 West 6th Avenue.

KNIGHT, O. LEE
Operated the Riverside Gallery in Topeka, 1865.

KOENTZ, C. E.
Active in Onaga; Olsburg, c. 1900.

KOMO PHOTO COMPANY
Active in Lawrence.

KRAPF, RUTH
Active in Topeka, 1899-1900.

KRIGER, ALLIE (MISS)
Art student in Ft. Scott, 1891-92.

KUHNS, O. D.
Photographer with McLeod's Gallery in Atchison, 1891.

LAIRD, E. L.
Active in Mulberry, 1890.

LAMON, W. H.
Studio at 125 Massachusetts Street, corner of Massachusetts and Henry, Lawrence, 1865-86.

LAMY, ALNIE
Portrait painter in Topeka, 1896-97.

LANDON, O. B.
Active in Garnett, c. 1861.

LARE, CHARLES A.
Stereo photographer in Beloit and Downs.

LARKIN, EMMA (MISS)
Active in Ft. Scott, 1879, at the corner of Wall and Scott Avenues.

LAURENT, C. M.
Artist in Topeka, 1899-1900, 1902.

LAWRENCE, ALFRED
Active in Lawrence, 1906-11; operated the Lawrence Studio after 1911.

LEAN & COMPANY, E. L. (MRS.)
Gallery in Ft. Scott, 1875, 1879, 1885, at 101 Scott Avenue, 2nd floor.

LEAN & COMPANY, J.
Active in Ft. Scott, 1885, above southeast corner of Wall and Scott Avenues.

LEE & COMPANY, J. B.
Active in Anthony, 1904.

LEE, FREDERICK
Active in Topeka, 1885-86.

LEE, T. H.
Active in Seneca.

LEEK, NELLIE M.
Active in Leavenworth, 1898-99.

LEMLEY, GEORGE W.
Artist in Topeka, 1899-1900.

LEONARD & MARTIN
Partnership of J. H. Leonard and H. T. Martin in Topeka, 1877-86; at 187 Kansas Avenue, 1877; 613 Kansas Avenue, 1882-86.

LEONARD, ELLA
Active in Topeka, 1887-88, at 615 Kansas Avenue.

LEONARD, I.
Active in Topeka, 1890.

LEONARD, J. H.
Active in Topeka, 1877, 1882-88, 1896-97, 1902. Partner of H. T. Martin, 1877, 1882-86, with studios at 187 and 613 Kansas Avenue; listed as sole owner, 1887-88, 1896-97, 1902.

LEONHARD, FRANK O.
Druggist, apothecary and photographer in Severance, c. 1885.

LEROY, ROBERT
Active in Leavenworth, 1891-92, at 427 Delaware.

LESEUR, J. H.
Active in Leoti, 1885.

LEVI, H. (MRS.)
Active in Abilene, 1875.

LEVI, LAURA
Artist in Topeka, 1899-1900.

LEWIS, E. HARRIE
Artist from New York, active in Atchison at 118 South 4th, 1885, 1887.

LEWIS, EDWARD
Listed at 420 South Crawford, Ft. Scott, 1889-90.

LIBBEY, C. E.
Active in Salina with W. C. Higgins.

LINGFELTER
Active in Wabaunsee, 1891.

LINNEY
Stereo photographer in Miltonville and Concordia.

LOCKE
Partner in Cobb & Locke, stereo photographers in Kirwin, c. 1870s-80s.

LOCKE, BENJAMIN
Photographer with P. H. Bauer in Leavenworth, 1893-96.

LOCKE, GEORGE A.
Active in Stockton, c. 1885.

LOFFINCK, R. E.
Active in Manhattan.

LOGAN, E. L.
Active in Pratt, 1885.

LONG, WILLIAM
Active in Hoxie, 1908-28.

LONGACRE, J. K.
Listed at 215 North Jones, Ft. Scott, 1879.

LOOMAS
Active in Lawrence.

LOOMIS
Active in Blue Rapids, 1908.

LOOMIS, D. A.
Active in Fredonia, 1881.

LOTUS STUDIO
Active in Morrill.

LUCAS, WILLIAM H.
Active in Topeka, 1902.

LUKE, WELLINGTON O.
Stereo photographer active in Colorado, Arizona and Abilene, Kansas, 1879-93.

LUTES, FRANK C.
Active in Topeka, 1896-97; at 511 Kansas Avenue, 1902.

LUTES, JOHN W.
Active in Topeka, 1887-88, 1896-97, 1899-1900. Studio at 805 Kansas Avenue, 1899-1900.

MALL, A. G.
Active in Clay Center, 1908.

MANGRUM, C. W.
Stereo photographer active in Paola.

MARBLE, L. W.
Published stereoviews in Larned, c. 1880s.

MARSHALL, JAMES P.
Active in Leavenworth, 1863-66. Located at Southwest 3rd between Delaware and Shawnee, 1863-64; with Richard Stevenson, 1865-66, operating as Stevenson & Marshall.

MARSHALL, NATHAN T.
Active in Leavenworth, 1894-95.

MARTELL, I. J.
Active in Topeka, 1882-83, operating Capital Gallery at 71 Kansas Avenue.

MARTIN, H. T.
Active in Topeka, 1885-88, at 721 Kansas Avenue.

MARTIN, W. H.
Active in Ottawa, 1895-98, 1909.

MARTINDALE, M. H. (MRS.)
Artist in Topeka, 1885-86, at 715 Harrison Street.

MASON, JOHN T.
Active in Leavenworth, 1874-87. With E. E. Henry, 1874, 1877; at 412 Delaware, 1879-87.

MASTERS, CHARLES H.
Apprenticed with W. H. Masters in Princeton, Illinois, 1866-69; operated studio, 1869-95. Traveled to Atchison to make stereoviews.

MASTERS, W. H.
Art Gallery in Pleasanton, Linn County, c. 1885.

MASTERS, WILLIAM H.
Born in Kentucky, 1823. Ambrotypist in Princeton, Illinois, c. 1850s-60s. Operated gallery in Ft. Scott, 1869.

MATHEWS, SHIRLEY
Active in Topeka, 1899-1900.

MATROT, SIMON
Artist in Topeka, 1896-97, at 312 Kansas Avenue.

MAYNER, G.
Active in Ft. Scott, 1871-72.

McCARTY
Photographer from Baxter Springs, Kansas, who took stereoviews in the Indian Territory, c. 1873-74.

McCARTY, A. W.
Active in Parker.

McCLAIN
Active in Garnett and Osawatomie, c. 1890.

McCLELLAN, WILLIAM
Active in Atchison, 1880.

McCLOUGHLIN
Partner in Feather & McCloughlin, active in Minneapolis, 1890.

McCULLOUGH, W. H.
Active in Ft. Scott, 1893.

McDONALD
Partner in Vancil & McDonald, active in Dodge City, 1885.

McDONALD, L. E.
Active in Minneapolis, 1880.

McFARLAND
See W. S. Prettyman.

McGLANE, F. E.
Stereo photographer in Ellsworth.

McKEE, C. F.
Active in Topeka, 1887-88, at 400 Madison.

McKIRAHAN, CHARLES A.
Active in Leavenworth, 1887, at 505 Shawnee.

McLEOD & COMBS
Active in Kansas City, 1875-80.

McLEOD, D.
Photographer in Atchison, 1887, 1891; operated as McLeod's Gallery, 1891; studio at 519 Commercial Street; later at 509 Commercial Street.

McMASTER, L.
Operating at North Main Street, Winfield, c. 1885.

McNULTY, H. B.
Active in Topeka, 1887-88.

MEDLAM, J. L.
Active in Norwich, 1895.

MEIER
Portrait and view photographer in Alma, c. 1885.

MERRILL, R. S.
Active in Leavenworth, 1870-71, at 48 Delaware.

MERWIN, FRED
Art student in 1896-97.

MESSENGER, MILTON M.
Active in Ft. Scott, 1898.

METTNER, F. F.
Operated the Riverside Studio in Lawrence, 1883-96.

MEYER, WESLEY
Stereo photographer in Macksville.

MILLER
See W. S. Prettyman.

MILLER, DEWITT
Artist in Topeka, 1887-88.

MILLER, E. W.
Active in Overbrook, c. 1875.

MILLER, FLOYD
Artist in Topeka, 1899-1900.

MINNICH, IRA
Active in Wichita, 1907.

MINTURN, JOHN
Photographer with Concannon in Ft. Scott, 1869-70.

MISHLER, M. M.
Manager of the Inter-State Portrait Company, Atchison, 1899-1900; located at 715 Commercial.

MITCHELL, CARRIE M. (MISS)
Retoucher in Ft. Scott, 1898.

MITCHELL, D. S.
Active in Lawrence, 1875.

MODEL STUDIO
Operated in Minneapolis.

MOHLER & COMPANY
Partnership of James W. Mohler and J. C. Rector, operating in Topeka, 1882-83, at 111 5th Street East.

MOHLER, J. W.
Studio at 111 5th Street East, Topeka, 1882-83; partner with J. C. Rector, operating as Mohler & Company.

MONTEITN, W. W.
Active in Topeka, 1887-88.

MOORE, WILLIAM
Active in Leavenworth, 1891-92.

MORGAN
Partner in Crew & Morgan, active in Leavenworth, c. 1875.

MORRIS, J. L.
Active in Lawrence, 1904.

MORROW, FRANK
Active in Leavenworth, 1896-1910.

MORSE, D. D.
Traveling photographer living in Leavenworth, 1883.

MOSER
Partner in Cosand & Moser, stereo photographers in Caldwell.

MULIT, H. S.
Operated Mulit's Art Gallery in Concordia, 1882-85. Also listed as N. S. Mulit.

MUNN, J. M.
Studio in Atchison at Commercial between 3rd and 4th, 317 Commercial, 1872-73; partner in Ragan & Munn, 1880, same address.

MUNTFERING, HERMAN
Active in Topeka, 1885-88.

MURRAY
Active in Cunningham, 1913.

NAUGHTON & CONKLIN
Listed at 507 Commercial, Atchison, 1880.

NEEDLES & ADDIS
Partnership of John T. Needles and Alfred S. Addis in Leavenworth, 1859-64; studio at 56 Main, 1859-60; 48 Delaware, 1862-64.

NEEDLES, JOHN T.
Active in Leavenworth, 1855-64; with partner Alfred S. Addis, 1859-64; studio of Needles & Addis at 56 Main, 1859- 60; 48 Delaware, 1862-64.

NEISWANGER, CHARLES G.
Active in Osborne, 1909.

NEREUS, BALDWIN
Active in Wichita, 1875-c.1885.

NEW YORK PHOTOGRAPH GALLERY
Studio in Leavenworth, 1862-66, operated by A. C. Nichols; at 62 Delaware, 1862-64; South Delaware between 7th and Broadway, 1865-66.

NEWBERG, P. A.
Photographer with Bauer & Son in Leavenworth, 1885.

NEWBY, S.
Active in Morehead.

NEWCOMB, M. W.
Active in Marysville.

NICHOLAS, JAMES A.
Active in Topeka, 1885-88.

NICHOLS, A. C.
Active in Leavenworth, 1862-67, 1870-71, 1875, 1880-84. New York Photograph Gallery at 62 Delaware, 1862-64; South Delaware between 7th and Broadway, 1865-66; Cottage Gallery, corner of 7th and Broadway, 1866-67; 193 Delaware, 1870-71; 308 Pottawatomie, 1880-82. Photographer with J. T. Mason, 1882-84.

NICHOLS, C. D.
Active in Lawrence, 1901.

NICHOLS, H. C.
Active in Leavenworth, 1800s.

NOBLE & COMPANY, JAY
Active in Leavenworth, 1870-71, at 88 Delaware, J. Noble, proprietor.

NOBLE, C. B.
Active at Noble's Gallery, 328 Delaware, Leavenworth.

NOBLE, C. B. (MRS.)
Active in Leavenworth, 1863-64, at 328 Delaware.

NOBLE'S GALLERY
Active in Leavenworth, 1874-79 at 328 Delaware, S. W. Kissel, manager. Alexander St. Clair, manager, 1875-77. Studio known as Noble's Photography & Chromotype Gallery, 1877.

NOBLE'S PHOTOGRAPHY & CHROMOTYPE GALLERY
Studio in Leavenworth, 1877, formerly Noble's Gallery, at 328 Delaware.

NOE
Stereo photographer in Leavenworth; partner in Addis & Noe. Also listed as Noel, Noell.

NOEL, C.
Photographer with Addis in Leavenworth, 1863-64. Also listed as Noell.

NOLTE, JOSEPH
Active in Seneca and Hanover, 1914-16.

NORTHCRAFT & COMPANY, C. E.
Operated in Abilene, c. 1900s.

O'NEIL, WILLIAM N.
Picture agent in Topeka, 1883-84.

O'NEILL, JAMES R.
Active in Leavenworth, 1863-64.

OAKS & IRELAND
Stereo photographers in Holton, c. 1880s; W. R. Ireland.

OAKS, W. M.
Partner in Oaks & Ireland, stereo photographers in Holton, c. 1880s.
Also active in Oakley.

OFFIELD, HARRY
Active in Topeka, 1902.

OHLSON, CHARLES G.
Active in Leavenworth, 1876-92; at 117 and 117 fi Delaware, 1878-80; northeast corner of 3rd and Shawnee, 1880-81; Room 4, 1st National Bank Building, 1884; 314 Delaware, 1886-87; 314 Shawnee, 1888-90; 228 Shawnee, 1891-92.

OLIVER, PROFESSOR J. K.
Operated the Sunflower Portrait Gallery at 1024 South Scott Avenue, Ft. Scott, 1888. Listed as artist, 1893.

ONG, LEE W.
Studio on Douglas Avenue, Wichita, c. 1875.

ORR, S. C.
Active in Manhattan.

ORTMAN, MARY T.
Active in Leavenworth, 1899-1900, at 1114 South 4th.

OSTERGREN
Partner of Baldwin in Wichita, c. 1885, at 88 Douglas Avenue.

OSTLUND
Active in Leonardville, c. 1890.

PADGETT, LIZZIE
Active in Topeka, 1896-97.

PAGE, HARRY
Located at 222 East 2nd and 207 Kansas, Topeka, 1896-1900.

PAGE, L. S.
Active in Emporia, 1887.

PAINE & WILLIAMS, A. B.
Wholesale photographic supplies at 523 South Main, Ft. Scott, 1891-93.

PARAMORE, H. B.
Active in Ottawa, 1895-98.

PARKER & COMPANY
Listed as City Fine Art Gallery, J. T. Parker, proprietor, at 3 Wall Street, Ft. Scott, 1871-72.

PARKER & DAUGHERTY
Palace of Fine Art at 1 North Main, corner of Wall and Main Streets, Fort Scott, c. 1875.

PARKER & TOMLINSON
Partners John F. Parker and James Tomlinson at corner of Jones and Scott Avenue, Ft. Scott, 1865-66.

PARKER, DELL
Active in Topeka, 1899-1900.

PARKER, JOHN T.
Listed at 1 North Main, corner of Main and Wall, Ft. Scott, 1869-70, Parker's Palace of Art Photographs. Operated as the City Fine Art Gallery, 1871-72, at 3 Wall Street; 109 Market, 1875. Also listed as Parker's Photography Gallery.

PEACOCK, ELLA
Active in Topeka, 1887-88, at 517 West 8th; partner with sister, Nina, operating as the Peacock Sisters, 1897-98.

PEACOCK, NINA
Active in Topeka, 1896-97, at 517 West 8th; partner with sister, Ella, 1897-98, operating as the Peacock Sisters.

PECK, J. R.
Active in Leavenworth, 1876.

PECK, MAYTIE (MISS)
Photo printer with Tresslar in Ft. Scott, 1888.

PENNELL & ZELLNER
Partnership of E. D. Zellner and J. J. Pennell; studio in Junction City, 1891. Also listed as Zellner & Pennell.

PENNELL, JOSEPH JUDD
Active in Junction City, 1880s-1905. Partner in Ramsour & Pennell, 1889; in Pennell & Zellner, 1891. Also listed as Zellner & Pennell.

PERKINS, W. M. C.
Active in Leavenworth, 1866-67, at 47 3rd Street.

PERSIAN PORTRAIT COMPANY
Gallery in Topeka, 1899-1900, operated by partners G. and E. N. Requa.

PETEFISH & POTTER
Active in Scott City and Dighton, 1897.

PETERSON BROTHERS
Active in Topeka, 1899-1900, at 511 Kansas Avenue.

PICKARD, HOWARD S.
Active in Topeka, 1896-97.

PIERSON, JOHN
Active in Topeka, 1899-1900.

PLAISTED, JESSIE C.
Active in Topeka, 1899-1900.

PLOETZ & HAAG
Active in Leavenworth, 1870-71, at 99 Shawnee; J. Haag.

POLAND, J. W.
Star Gallery, at "G. H. Falls, Kansas," c. 1868.

POMEROY, CHARLES T.
Stereo photographer active in Rochester, New York, 1880-84; in Leavenworth, Kansas, 1885-86.

PONIZZARDI, L. C.
Active in Topeka, 1887-88.

POTTER
Partner in Petefish & Potter, Scott City and Dighton, 1897.

POWELL
Partner in Young & Powell, active in Emporia.

POWELL, M. (MISS)
Photo printer with Elkanah Tresslar, Ft. Scott, 1885.

POWELL, NETTIE M. (MISS)
Photo retoucher in Ft. Scott, 1898.

PRESCOTT, ROSE MABLE
Active in Topeka, 1902.

PRETTYMAN & CORNISH
Partnership of W. S. Prettyman and G. B. Cornish, Arkansas City, 1889.

PRETTYMAN & McFARLAND
See W. S. Prettyman.

PRETTYMAN & MILLER
See W. S. Prettyman.

PRETTYMAN, W. S.
Born in Princess Anne County, Maryland, November 12, 1858; died in Los Angeles, California, 1932. He arrived in Emporia, 1879, and soon apprenticed to Civil War photographer, I. H. Bonsall, in Arkansas City. Prettyman opened his own gallery and took the portrait of Bob Dalton, Deputy U. S. Marshal in the Osage Agency. He took portraits of Indians who came to him from the Indian Territory, and who attended the local Indian school. Beginning in 1883, Prettyman made trips through the Indian Territory to photograph Indians in their villages. He photographed the Oklahoma "Boomers" as they invaded the territory in wave after wave. Backmarks indicate partnerships of Prettyman & McFarland, Prettyman & Miller, and Prettyman & Cornish. Partner with George B. Cornish in Arkansas City, 1889.
  Robert E. Cunningham, *Indian Territory: A Frontier Photographic Record by W. S. Prettyman*, University of Oklahoma Press, 1957.

PROCTOR, J. H.
Active in Girard, 1880.

PROCTOR, JESSIE
Studio at 707 Western Avenue, Topeka, 1896-1900.

PURCELL
Partner in Young & Purcell, photographers and ambrotypists at the corner of Commercial and 6th Avenue, Emporia, c. 1865.

PURCELL, I. D.
Listed as artist, 728 Barbee, Ft. Scott, 1893.

PURSLEY, J. J.
Active in Wetmore.

PUTNEY & HENRY
Partnership of Harrison Putney and E. E. Henry in Leavenworth; at 82 Delaware, 1870-71, 1894-97.

PUTNEY, HARRISON
Active in Leavenworth, 1870-1900. Partner in Putney & Henry, 1870-71, 1894-97.

RAGAN & MUNN
Partnership of William O. Ragan and J. M. Munn, listed at 317 Commercial, Atchison, 1880.

RAGAN & SHANNON
Stereo photographers in Kansas City.

RAMEY & COMPANY, R. A.
Listed at 104 Market, Ft. Scott, 1879.

RAMSOUR & PENNELL
Studio in Junction City, 1889; J. J. Pennell.

RAMSOUR, L. A.
Active in Manhattan.

RANDALL, FRED
Active in Leavenworth, 1865-66.

RANKIN
Active in Leavenworth, 1855.

RECTOR, J. C.
Partner with J. W. Mohler in Topeka, 1882-83, operating as Mohler & Company at 111 5th Street East.

REED, C. E.
Active in Norton, 1909.

REES, MAGGIE J.
Active in Leavenworth, 1891-95.

REES, N. B.
Active in Lincoln Center.

REID & STONE ART STUDIO
Active in Topeka, 1902, in the Crawford Block. Possibly George Stone.

REID, HAL
Active in Liberal.

REQUA, GEORGE & E. N.
Partners active in Topeka, 1899-1900, operating Persian Portrait Company.

REYNOLDS, A. C.
Active in Topeka, 1899-1903, at 629 Kansas Avenue. Operated the Reynolds Art Gallery at the same address, 1902.

RHODES, WILLIAM
Active in Topeka, 1883-84.

RICHEY
Stereo photographer in Wamego; partner in Bittman & Richey.

RIDDLE, J. R.
Gallery at 237 Kansas Avenue, Topeka, 1872-86.

RITCHIE BROTHERS
Active in Kingman, c. 1890.

RITTER, CHARLES
Listed at 5th and Andrick, Ft. Scott, 1889-90.

RITTER, HENRY
Active in Topeka, 1885-88.

RIVERSIDE GALLERY
Active in Topeka, 1865, operated by O. Lee Knight.

RIVERSIDE STUDIO
Operated by F. F. Mettner in Lawrence, 1883-96.

ROBERTS, GEORGE M.
Active in Topeka, 1899-1900, at 805 Kansas Avenue.

ROBINSON
Active in Kansas City.

ROBINSON, P. H.
Active in Leavenworth, 1866-67, at 107 Shawnee.

RODOCKER, D.
Born in Ohio, October 1840. Active in Winfield, c. 1885. Photographed Comanche and Apache.

ROGERS, W. S.
Active in Wichita, 1890.

ROLFE & COLVILLE STUDIO
Operated by Joseph P. Colville and C. J. Rolfe, partners in the studio located at 632 Kansas Avenue, Topeka, 1902.

ROLFE, C. J.
Active in Topeka, 1902, at 632 Kansas Avenue with partner Joseph P. Colville, operating the Rolfe & Colville Studio.

ROSE & BENNETT
Active in Leavenworth, 1884, at 218 South 5th Street; H. W. Rose and Harry O. Bennett, partners.

ROSE & SON
Active in Chetopa, 1800s.

ROSE, H. W.
Active in Leavenworth, 1884, at 218 South 5th Street; partner with Harry O. Bennett.

ROSS & IFLAND
Active in Sedan.

RUDD & RUNYAN
Active in Marion, 1890.

RUDIGER & COMPANY, J.
Active in Topeka, 1885-86, at 177 Kansas Avenue.

RUDOLPH, H. W.
Listed at 409 Commercial, Atchison, 1899-1900.

RUNYAN
Partner in Rudd & Runyan, active in Marion, 1890.

RUSSELL, W. F.
Active in Kingsley and North Topeka, 1885.

SANGER, I. S. (MRS.)
Photographer with Mrs. E. L. Lean & Company, Ft. Scott, at 101 Scott Avenue, 1875. Listed as Mrs. J. Sanger, 1888, and Jane Sanger, 1889-90. Operating at the corner of Wall and Scott, 1888-92.

SANKEY, R. A. (MRS.)
Active at 100 West Central Avenue, Arkansas City, c. 1895.

SARGENT
Partner in Snell & Sargent, stereo photographers in Wellington operating the Elite Gallery.

SAURMAN, J. S.
Active in Leavenworth, 1885-95. Located at South Shawnee between 5th and 6th, 1885-88; 505 Shawnee, 1889-95. B. Frichot, manager, 1893-94. Also spelled Sauerman.

SCANLON
Stereo photographer active in Wyandott.

SCHATTNER, F.
Active in Leavenworth, 1865-67. Located at 80 Shawnee, 1865-66; with J. P. Babbitt, 1866-67.

SCHMIDT, MAGGIE (MISS)
Listed as an artist, Atchison, 1887.

SCIBIRD, H. W.
Listed at 313 Commercial, Atchison, 1887.

SCOTT
Active in Independence, 1900.

SCOTT, S. B. (MRS.)
"Artist, (?) Kansas," is penciled on the reverse of a tintype of a couple from Mount Pleasant, Iowa.

SELBY, BELLE (MISS)
Listed as artist, 3rd floor Union Block, Ft. Scott, 1888.

SELLON, OSCAR
Active in Cheney.

SHAFER, JOHN
Active in Topeka, 1896-97, at 316 Kansas Avenue.

SHAMBEAU STUDIO
Operated in Hiawatha.

SHANE & SON
Operated by J. B. Shane in Lawrence.

SHANE, J. B.
Active in Lawrence; possibly June Belle Shane.

SHANE, JUNE, BELLE
Active in Lawrence.

SHANNON
Partner in Ragan & Shannon, stereo photographers in Kansas City.

SHARP, W. A.
From Chicago, active in Atchison, 1885.

SHELLABARGER, G. G.
Active in Valley, c. 1875.

SHELLY
Active in Lawrence, 1903.

SHEPARD
Active in Great Bend, c. 1895.

SHEPERD, FRANK L.
Active in Topeka, 1896-97, at 112 West 7th Street.

SHEPHARD, W. B.
Listed as employee of Dabbs Photo Gallery, Ft. Scott, 1888.

SHOOT, C.
Photographer with Concannon, Ft. Scott, 1869-70.

SHORT & STONE
Active in Leavenworth, 1863-64, at Delaware between 2nd and 3rd. Partnership of H. N. Short and D. W. Stone.

SHORT, HARVEY N.
Photographer with Addis in Leavenworth, 1862-63. Partner of D. W. Stone at Delaware between 2nd and 3rd, 1863-64.

SHORT, JAMES H.
Photographer with Addis in Leavenworth, 1862-63.

SHROUT
Active in Wichita, 1919.

SIMPSON, T. S.
Active in Leavenworth, 1884, 1889.

SINCLAIR
Partner in Bordeax & Sinclair in Wichita, 1890, operating the B & S Photo Company.

SIPPEL, WILLIAM
Active in Marysville, 1880-89.

SIPPLE'S ART STUDIO
Operating at the southwest corner of Central and Johnson Avenues, Parsons, c. 1880. Photographed the Osage.

SKEELS
Partner in Adams & Skeels in Lawrence, c. 1862, over the country store.

SMITH
Active in Ottawa.

SMITH, E. FRANCIS (MISS)
Active in Topeka, 1885-86, in Office Block.

SMITH, FRANK
Active in Lyona. Also listed as Will Smith.

SMITH, JAMES H.
Active in Leavenworth, 1899-1900, at 319 Delaware.

SMITH, M. (MISS)
Active in Topeka, 1885-86, with studio at 79 10th Avenue.

SMITH, R. G.
Photographer with J. S. Sauerman in Leavenworth, 1885-86.

SNELL & SARGENT
Stereo photographers in Wellington, operating the Elite Gallery.

SNELL, E. B.
Partner in Snell & Sargent, stereo photographers in Wellington. Operated the Elite Gallery. Photographed the Cheyenne.

SNOOK
Worked at Riverside Portrait Studio in Lawrence, c. 1880s.

SNYDER
Active in Osage City, c. 1890.

SNYDER
Active in Harper, 1911.

SNYDER, CHARLES J.
Active in Topeka, 1882-1902. Studio at 174 Kansas Avenue, 1882-84; 214 Kansas, 1885-86; 632 Kansas, 1887-97; 722 Kansas, 1899-1902.

SNYDER, ROBERT
Active in Topeka, 1887-88, at 528 Kansas Avenue.

SOULE
Active in Glasco, c. 1900.

SOULE & FEATHER
Active in Minneapolis, 1885.

SOULE, WILLIAM S.
See Indian Territory.

SOUTH WESTERN PUBLISHING COMPANY
Listed at 201 Scott Avenue, Ft. Scott, 1891-92, W. K. Larkin, manager.

SPALLER, HENRY T.
Active in Leavenworth, 1888.

SPAULDING, JOHN
Photographer with P. H. Bauer in Leavenworth, 1890.

SPICER & BUMBARGER
Active in Topeka, 1914.

SPITZEY, EDWIN
Photographer with Henry in Leavenworth, 1883; with J. T. Mason, 1884-85. Also spelled Spitze.

SQUIRES, CON. F.
Photographer with P. H. Bauer in Leavenworth, 1893-1900, at 907 North Broadway, also operating as Squires Photo in Lawrence. Also listed as Connie.

ST. CLAIR, ALEXANDER
Operated of Noble's Gallery in Leavenworth at 328 Delaware, 1875; manager, 1877-80.

ST. CLAIR, FRED E.
Assistant photographer for Alexander St. Clair, 1879-80; photographer with J. T. Mason, 1886.

STAMPER, FRANK M.
See Idaho.

STANDIFORD, J. F.
Active in Parsons, Kansas, c. 1890. See Indian Territory and Traveling.

STAPLETON, RICHARD
Operating Gem Photography Gallery at 318 East 4th, Topeka, 1887-88.

STAUGHT, BELLE
Listed at Parker's Photography Gallery or Parker's Palace of Art Photographs, Ft. Scott, 1869-70.

STAYNER, JOHN V.
Billed as the "Practical Photographer" at 205 Market, Ft. Scott.

STEELE STUDIO, M.
Active in Dodge City.

STEINHOSS, JOHN
Active in Topeka, 1887-88.

STEVENSON & ADDIS
A. S. Addis and Richard Stevenson, active in Leavenworth, 1860-61, at 40 Delaware.

STEVENSON & MARSHALL
James P. Marshall and Richard Stevenson, operating at 40 Delaware Street, Leavenworth, 1860s.

STEVENSON, HORACE S.
Active in Leavenworth, 1886-1900; studio at 102 South 5th, 1888-96; 412 Delaware, 1897-1900.

STEVENSON, R.
From Pennsylvania; studio in Atchison, 1872-85; at 325 Commercial, 1872-73, 1880; 317 Commercial, 1885.

STEVENSON, RICHARD
Active in Leavenworth, 1859-95. Alfred S. Addis joined Stephenson 1860, operating as Stephenson & Addis; Addis left in 1862, leaving his negatives of Cheyenne and Arapaho with Stephenson. Partner in Stevenson & Marshall, 1860s; at 40 Delaware, 1859-64; 48 Delaware, 1865-71; 102 South 5th, 1887-90. Also listed at 210 Delaware Street (old No. 48), c. 1885-95. Also listed as Richardson Stevenson and Richard Stephenson.

STONE, D. W.
Partner in Short & Stone, active in Leavenworth, 1863-64, at Delaware between 2nd and 3rd.

STONE, ELMER B.
Listed at 207 Market, Ft. Scott, 1898.

STONE, GEORGE
Active in Topeka, 1885-1902. Located in Office Block, 1885-86; 501 Jackson Street, 1886-87; 501 Jackson Street, 1899-1902.

STONER, HOPEWELL M.
Active in Topeka, 1899-1900.

STONER, S. B.
Artist in Lancaster, 1899-1900.

STOWE
Successor to the Trader Studio, Emporia, c. 1890.

STOWE, H. D.
Operated at 212 Fourth Street, Louisville.

STRAIN
Active in Garnett.

STRATHMANN, F. B.
Active in Axtell, 1908.

STRATHMANN, F. J.
Active in Seneca, 1914.

STREETER, G. A.
Active in Junction City, 1900-01.

STREETER, SOLOMON
Active in Solomon and Gypsum.

STRICKROTT, JOHN F.
View photographer in Topeka, 1898-1902; at 531 Kansas Avenue,

1899-1900; 515 Kansas, 1902. Also listed as John T.

STROUD
Active in Hutchinson, c. 1895.

STUDIO GRAND
Operated in Concordia.

STUDIO JACKSON
Operated in Lawrence.

SULLIVAN, PATRICK
Active in Topeka, 1887-88.

SUMMERS, GEORGE
Listed as a photographer at O. D. Kuhn's studio, Atchison, 1891.

SUN PUBLISHING COMPANY
Operated in Glasco, c. 1908.

SUNDERLAND, J. C.
Active in Girard, c. 1880.

SUNFLOWER PORTRAIT GALLERY
Operated by Professor J. K. Oliver in Ft. Scott at 1024 South Scott Avenue, 1888.

SWAN, FRED W.
Manager of Globe Studio in Leavenworth at 102 South 5th, 1897-98.

SWEARINGEN, BELLE
Active in Topeka, 1896-1902.

TEACHOUT, A. W.
Listed as an artist, 400 Commercial, Atchison, 1899-1900.

TEEPLE, CHARLES B.
Active in Humboldt, c. 1870.

TEITZEL, LOUIS
Active in Junction City, 1903-17. Produced stereoviews.

TEMPLE OF FINE ART
Studio in Ft. Scott, operated by H. H. Concannon, 1869-70, at 5 Wall Street.

THOMPSON
Partner in Adams & Thomson's, operating in Lawrence at 135 Massachusetts Street.

THOMPSON, D. A. L.
Active in Topeka, 1883-84.

THOMPSON, ISABELLA M.
Active in Topeka, 1896-97.

THOMPSON STUDIO
Operated in Lawrence.

TICE, ARTHUR L.
Listed as an artist, Atchison, 1899-1900.

TIDERMAN, B. C.
Active in Leavenworth, 1894-95, at 427 Delaware.

TOOLEY
Partner in Kinney & Tooley, stereo photographers in Concordia.

TOWNSEND, L. L.
Active in Topeka, 1882-83.

TRADER, F. A.
Operated the Trader Studio in Emporia, 1885, at 518 Commercial Street.

TREAT, A. R.
Listed at 725 Commercial, Atchison, 1887.

TRESSLAR & GIFFORD
Stereo photographers in Ft. Scott; Benjamin A. Gifford.

TRESSLAR, ELKANAH P.
Active in Ft. Scott, 1873-90. Partner in Tresslar Brothers, c. 1880-85, at 108 Market Street; listed alone on 2nd floor of 104 Market Street, 1885; corner of Main and 1st Streets, 1888; 101 South Main, 1889-90.

TRESSLAR, HERBERT
Photo printer with S. P. Tresslar, Ft. Scott, 1885.

TRESSLAR, S. P.
Active in Ft. Scott, 1873-85, at 108 and 110 Market Street, 2nd floor; partner with brother, E. P. Tresslar in Tresslar Brothers.

TRIGG
Active in Abilene.

TRIULZI, CHRISTOPHER
Active in Leavenworth, 1898-99, at National Hotel.

TROTT, A. P.
Active on Washington Street, Junction City, c. 1865.

TRUBY, F. M., JR.
Apprentice photographer in Leavenworth, 1888; photographer with Birdsall, 1889-90.

TRUMBULL, W. L.
Active in Topeka, 1896-97, at 720 Kansas Avenue.

TUCKER, E. S.
Active in Lawrence.

TURNER, E. WINSLOW
Active in Topeka, 1885-86, at 238 Kansas Avenue.

TURNWELL, MARY J. (MISS)
Listed as artist in Ft. Scott, 1888.

TUTTLE, INEZ
Active in Topeka, 1899-1900.

ULLOM, ELLA (MISS)
Listed as artist, Ft. Scott, 1891-92.

UNDERWOOD & UNDERWOOD
Active in Ottawa, 1903.

URELL PHOTO
Active in Towanda, c. 1919.

VANCIL & McDONALD
Active in Dodge City, 1885.

VOGENITZ, L. V.
Active in Topeka, 1899-1900, at 623 Kansas Avenue.

VOGENRT'S ART PHOTOS
Active in Wichita, 1895.

VOLT & MARTELL
Partnership of J. G. Volt and I. J. Martell in Topeka, operating Capital Gallery loctated at 71 Kansas Avenue, 1882-83.

VOLT, J. G.
Active in Topeka, 1882-83, with partner, I. J. Martell operating Capital Gallery.

WADE, MADISON W.
Active in Leavenworth, 1897-98.

WAITE, S. H.
Active in Emporia; partner in Willett & Waite, c. 1880; studio at West Sixth Avenue, c. 1890. Also listed as A. H.

WAITE, V. H.
Active in Topeka.

WAKELY, GEORGE
Daguerrean artist in Leavenworth, 1859-60, at South Seneca, between 4th and 5th. See Colorado.

WALBRIDGE, LOUIE C.
Active in Russell County, c. 1892-1910.

WALKER
Stereo photographer in Kansas City.

WALLACE, JEAN
Active in Topeka, 1899-1900.

WALSH, ANNA M.
Active in Topeka, 1902.

WAMSLEY, WILLIAM
Active in Topeka, 1883-84.

WAREHAM, C. H.
Active in Ft. Scott at 205 and 209 Market Street, 1888-92. Produced stereoviews. Also known as Warcham.

WARNER, J.
Active in Topeka, 1882-83, at 273 Kansas Avenue.

WARNER, JOSEPH
Active in Leavenworth, 1875, with Crew & Morgan.

WASSON, R. M.
Active in Topeka, 1896-97, at 832 Kansas Avenue.

WEAVER, J. L.
From Glen Falls, New York; studio in Topeka, 1882-83; in Atchison at 509 Commercial, 1885.

WEAVER, WILLIAM S.
Active in Leavenworth, 1899-1900.

WEBER
Active Topeka with Klein, operating as Weber & Klein.

WEBER & KLEIN
Partnership in Topeka.

WEEKS, J. H.
Active in Lawrence, 1880.

WEEKS, R. E.
Active in Lawrence, 1886.

WEHE, LYDIA E.
Active in Topeka, 1896-1902, at 707 Kansas Avenue.

WEIBLING, HARMON G.
Active in Leavenworth, 1859-60.

WELCH, JESSIE (MISS)
Artist in Ft. Scott, 1891-92.

WELCH, RUTH K.
Active in Topeka, 1899-1900.

WENDELL, DELLA
Photograph retoucher in Topeka, 1883-84.

WERTZ, J. G.
Active in Chanute. Proprietor of Kansas City Photograph Rooms at Third Street, east of Main, Kansas City.

WESTERN VIEW COMPANY
Active in Lawrence.

WHEELER, C. M.
Active in Junction City, 1890.

WHEELER, FRED
Active in Burlingame, c. 1885.

WHITAKER, GEORGE C.
Studio in Leavenworth, 1874-88; at 220 Delaware, 1876-81; 118 4th Avenue, 1882; 327 Delaware, 1883; 104 Delaware, 1884; 317 Delaware, 1888.

WHITAKER, W.
Active in Leavenworth, 1876.

WHITE, MINNIE E.
Active in Topeka, 1896-97.

WHITE, W. A.
Active in Wilson, c. 1885.

WHITESIDE, HULDAH
Active in Topeka, 1887-88.

WHITESIDE, JOSEPH K.
Active in Topeka, 1883-84.

WILCOX, HIRAM P.
Active in Topeka, 1896-97, at 314 West 3rd.

WILDER, MARTHA
Active in Topeka, 1899-1900.

WILLETT & WAITE
Studio at Sixth Avenue, Emporia, c. 1880.

WILLETT, CLARENCE G.
Active in Topeka, 1895-1900.

WILLIAMS, C. R. (MRS.)
Active in Belleville.

WILLIAMS, FRANK
Active in Barnesville, 1885.

WILLIAMS, TILLIE J.
Retoucher with Bauer's Studio in Leavenworth, 1898-99.

WILLIS, ELMER
Partner with A. G. DaLee in Lawrence, c. 1858-79, in Willis-DaLee's Art Gallery; proprietor of Willis Studio, c. 1800s.

WILLIS STUDIO
Operated by Elmer Willis in Lawrence, c. 1800s.

WILLIS-DALEE'S ART GALLERY
Operated in Lawrence by A. G. DaLee and Elmer Willis, c. 1858-79.

WILSON, E. B.
Active in Topeka, 1887-88.

WILSON, FRED H.
Active in Topeka, 1902.

WILSON, WILLIAM H.
Active in Topeka, 1899-1900.

WIMBERLY, J. H.
Photographer in Muscotah, 1899-1900.

WINCHESTER, H. A. (MISS)
Active in Leavenworth, 1889-92; studios at 106 South 4th, 1889; 609 Shawnee, 1890-92.

WINNE, MAGGIE
Active in Topeka, 1887-88.

WITTICK, GEORGE B.
Active in Pawnee Rock.

WITWER, MARIE
Active in Topeka, 1902, at 812 Kansas Avenue.

WOLF, H. L.
Active in Garden City.

WOODMAN, SHELDON J.
Active in Topeka, 1882-97.

WOOLSEY & GITHENS
Active in Randall, c. 1875.

WORRALL, HENRY
Studio in Topeka, 1882-97; at 231 Polk, 1882-83, 1885-86; 259 Kansas Avenue, 1883-84; 715 Polk and Delineator, 1887-88; 807 Kansas Avenue, 1896-97.

WORTMAN, JESSIE
Active in Topeka, 1902.

WRIGHT, BELAH
Active in Lynden, 1870s.

WRIGHT VIEW COMPANY
Active in Hartford.

WYATT, C. B.
Active in Colony, 1900.

YALE, FRANK T.
Active in Topeka, 1896-1900.

YOEMAN, EMERSON
Active in Topeka, 1899-1900.

YORDY, CHRIST
Active in Ft. Scott, 1891-92.

YOUNG & POWELL
Active in Emporia.

YOUNG & PURCELL
Billed as photographers and ambrotypists at the corner of Commercial
and 6th Avenue, Emporia, c. 1865.

YOUNG, O. F.
Active in Burlingame.

ZELLNER & PENNELL
Studio in Junction City, 1891, operated by partners E. D. Zellner
and J. J. Pennell. Also listed as Pennell & Zellner.

ZELLNER, E. D.
Post photographer at Ft. Riley with a studio at Junction City, c. 1890.
Partner with Pennell, 1891.

Mrs. JAS. McPHEE,

Photo Artist,

Cor Second St. and Nicollet Avenue,

MINNEAPOLIS, MINN.

Born on the Island of Greenland

Much of the information in this section is based on research done by Tracey Baker of the Minnesota Historical Society.

ANDERSON & PETERSON
Active in Granite Falls, c. 1890.

ANDERSEN, N. B.
Active in Redwood Falls, c. 1885-90.

ANDERSON, E.
Stereo photographer active in Minneapolis, c. 1902.

ANDERSON, H. A.
Studio at 428 Nicollet Avenue, Minneapolis, c. 1890.

ANDERSON, OLE
Active in Montevideo, 1880.

ANGELL & WEEKS
Active in Litchfield, 1875-95.

ANGELL, C. L.
Art gallery on Marshall Avenue, Litchfield, c. 1868; stereo photographer, 1875-95; partner with Weeks.

ART STUDIO
Active in Cloquet, 1885.

AUSTIN, J.
Active in Fergus Falls, 1870-80.

AYERS, ELLIS
Active in Dodge Center, 1875-85.

BACON
Wigwam of Art, Litchfield, c. 1885.

BAGNE
Partner in Manderfeld & Bagne, Waseca, c. 1875.

BAINES, W. L.
Studio at Simpson's Block, Center Street, Winona, c. 1880.

BANCROFT
Active in St. Peter, c. 1895.

BANGS, D.
Active in Sleepy Eye, c. 1890.

BANKS BROS.
Active in West Duluth, c. 1890.

BARNES, J. H.
Stereo photographer in Chatfield.

BARNES, W. L.
Active in Winona, 1875.

BARTRAM
Partner in Huntington & Bartram, Minneapolis, 1870-80.

BARTRAM & TAYLOR
Stereo photographers in Minneapolis, 1870s-80s.

BATCHELDER
Partner in Fearon & Batchelder, Minneapolis, 1870-80.

BEACH, E. A.
Photograph artist, Hastings, c. 1863.

BEAL & BURT
Partnership of Charles H. Beal and I. K. E. Burt in Minneapolis,
1885-87.

BEAL, ALONZO H.
Born in Saco, York County, Maine, July 10, 1833. Active in Minneapolis, 1860. Burned out twice, his last studio was located on Washington Avenue, 1874. Beal's Art Gallery was described as a "bower of
art" with rare plants and flowers, song birds, and could accommo-
date up to two thousand people. Credited with introducing the first
scenic cartes-de-visite to Minnesota by publishing small views of the
Falls of St. Anthony, c. 1860. His sons, Charles and Eugene, ran the
gallery for a short period after Beal retired, 1885.

BEAL BROTHERS
Partnership of Charles H. Beal and Eugene C. Beal in Minneapolis,
1890.

BEAL, CHARLES H.
Born in Boston, Massachusetts, 1859, son of Alonzo Beal. Employed
in Minneapolis by family firm as photo retoucher, 1877-85. Became
the senior partner in Beal & Burt with I. K. E. Burt, 1885-87. Worked
again for his father, 1887-89, and with his brother, Eugene C., as
Beal Brothers, 1890. Photographer with A. B. Rugg, 1891-92. Moved
to Los Angeles, 1892.

BEAL, EUGENE C.
Born in Maine, 1856; died in Pasadena, California, June 21, 1896.
Son of Alonzo Beal; worked for his father as office manager and in
other capacities. Partner with his brother, Charles H., in Beal Brothers, 1890. Photographer for A. B. Rugg, 1891-93. Moved to Pasadena, California, 1894.

BEAL'S ART GALLERY
Studio operated by Alonzo Beal in Minneapolis, 1874-85, and thereafter by his sons, Charles and Eugene. Located at 18 South 4th Street,
c. 1880.

BELL, N. D.
Studio in Minneapolis, c. 1900.

BELL, N. D. (MRS.)
Retoucher in husband's studio in Minneapolis, c. 1900.

BENJAMIN
Active in Pipestone, 1890.

BENNETT
Partner in Washburn & Bennett, Red Wing, 1860-70.

BERG, GUSTAF
Scandinavifka Photograph Gallery, Main Street, Red Wing, c. 1875.

BERGERSON
Active in Lake Park, 1875.

BERGERSON, W. O.
Active in Albert Lea, 1870.

BILL, GEORGE
Partner with W. H. Illingworth in Illingworth & Bill, St. Paul, 1860-70.

BINGHAM, F. U.
Active in Northfield, 1870-90; partner in Sumner & Bingham,
Rochester and Northfield, 1870-80; also in Bedford, 1880. Initials also
given as F. V.

BIRD, L. & COX, S. P.
Stereo photographers in Minneapolis.

BISHOP & SONS, B.
Active in Watertown, c. 1860.

BISHOP BROTHERS
Gallery on the Syndicate Block, Minneapolis, c. 1890.

BLAND & COMPANY, J. L.
Active in Anoka, 1880.

BOWRON & COX
Partnership involving George Bowron in Minneapolis.

BOWRON, GEORGE
Ambrotypist in the Woodman Building, Minneapolis, 1858-59. Associated with Bowron & Cox.

BOYD, CARRIE V.
Ambrotypist in St. Anthony, c. 1860; won first prize for her work.

BRANDMO, A.
Active in Candy, 1880-85; also active in Montevideo.

BREWER, KENNEYARD
Active in Redwood Falls, c. 1895.

BRIGGS, E. M. (MRS.)
Active in Minneapolis, 1890.

BROCKHAM, WILLIAM
Portrait, stereo, and landscape photographer, c. 1879.

BROWN
Partner in Eldrige & Brown, Mankato, 1885.

BROWN & RILEY
Stereo photographers in Winona; possibly W. H. Brown.

BROWN, W. H.
Active in Red Wing, 1870.

BROWN, WILLIAM
Studio at 41 Washington Avenue South, Minneapolis, 1875-80.

BROWNELL, J.
Active in St. Paul, 1875-90.

BRUSH, JAMES A.
Studio at 223 Nicollet Avenue in Minneapolis, c. 1875; 609 Nicollet
Avenue, 1885-90.

BURCH, C. E. (MRS.)
Amateur active in St. Paul, winner of a first prize in salon competition.

BURFIELD, THOMAS
Active in Waconia.

BURNAM, D. D.
Active in Spring Valley, 1875.

BURNHAM, A. F.
Studio on Barron House Block, Main Street, Faribault, 1870-80.

BURRITT & PEASE
Active in St. Paul, 1870-80.

BURRITT, E. H.
Stereo photographer in St. Paul, 1870s-80s.

BURT, I. K. C.
Partner in Beal & Burt, Minneapolis, 1880-90. Also listed as I. K. E. Burt.

BUTLER, W. E.
Active in Minneapolis, 1870-80; West Superior, c. 1895.

CALESON'S GALLERY
Studio at 305 Washington Avenue South, c. 1880.

CANNING & RUST
Stereo photographers in Hastings.

CANNING, M. A. (MRS.)
Active in Hastings, c. 1860s.

CARLI, CHRISTOPHER, JR.
Stereo photographer active in Stillwater, 1870s. May be the same as C. J. Carli of Groton, Dakota Territory, 1880s.

CARLSON, A.
Active in Wheaton, c. 1890-1900.

CARLZEN, S. M.
Stereo photographer active in Wilmar.

CARPENTER & COMPANY, C. E.
Successors to M. Watkins, St. Paul, c. 1863.

CARVER, E. M.
Stereo photographer in Tracy.

CASWELL & DAVY
Active in Duluth, 1870-80.

CASWELL, H. C. (MRS.)
Active in Garden City, c. 1860s.

CHASE
Active in Minnehaha Falls (now part of Minneapolis), 1875-90.

CHASE, C. B.
Stereo photographer active in Minnehaha Falls and Minneapolis, 1875-90; partner with M. Nowack in Minneapolis, 1880s.

CHESLEY, G. W.
Active in Owatonna, 1870-80. Stereo photographer. Also listed as C. W.

CHRISTMAN, E. J.
Active in Waterville, c. 1870.

CLARK, M. L. (MRS.)
Active in Kenyon, c. 1880.

CLAUSSON, O. A.
Stereo photographer active in Great Falls.

COFFIN, J. H.
Active in St. Peter, 1870-80.

COLBURN, R. W.
Active in Jordan.

CONGER
Active in Brainerd, 1880.

COOK & JONES
Photographers active in Winona, c. 1860.

COOK, J. C.
Active in Rochester, 1880-90. Stereo photographer who made views of 1883 cyclone. Also recorded as J. A.

COOLEDGE & HASKINS
Partnership in Zumbrota, 1870-80.

COOLEDGE, H. W.
Active in Zumbrota, 1877-78.

COOPERATIVE VIEW COMPANY
Produced views in St. Paul.

COX, SAMUEL P.
Stereo photographer in Minneapolis, 1880s; partner in L. Bird & S. P. Cox.

CRANDALL & FLETCHER
Stereo photographer active in Duluth.

CRANDALL, H. S.
Active in Cloquet, c. 1890.

CRESSEY, R. M.
Partner in McLeish & Cressey, St. Paul, 1870-80.

CROWELL, E. S.
Active in Rochester, 1870-80.

CURTISS, E. A.
Stereo photographer in Minneapolis.

DANIELS, CRAIG F.
Produced stereoscopes and stereoviews in Red Wing, operating as Red Wing View Company.

DAVENPORT, JAMES
St. Paul entrepreneur who sold stereoviews by Huntington & Bartram and Whitney & Zimmerman.

DAVIS, WILLIAM
Active in Mankato, 1885.

DAVY
Partner in Caswell & Davy, active in Duluth, 1870-80.

DE GUIRE, L. J.
Active in Winona, 1895.

DE LONG, C. A.
Operated the Sunbeam Gallery on Central Avenue in Minneapolis East, c. 1875; also had a studio in St. Anthony, 1870-80 (annexed to Minneapolis, 1872).

DELLING
Stereo photographer; partner in Palmer & Delling, active in St. James and Medelia.

DENISON
Partner in Hardy, Denison & Robertson, stereo photographers in Fergus Falls.

DENISON & POTTER
Studio at the corner of Main and Third Streets, Faribault, c. 1867.

DICKERSON, A. E.
Stereo photographer from Coshocton, Ohio; made views of Colorado, Idaho and Utah, c. 1890s; later associated with Cooperative View Company in St. Paul, Minnesota.

DICKINSON'S BAZAR
Dealer in stereoviews in Minneapolis at 321 Nicollet Avenue; marketed Nowack views with his imprint.

DILLEY, S. B.
Active in Lake City, c. 1885.

DRESSEL, G. A.
Active in Le Sueur.

EASTON, JAMES H.
Operating Easton's Photo Gallery in Rochester, 1863-c.1889.

EASTON, LUCY JANE BOLTON (DR.)
Operating Easton's Photo Gallery in Rochester, 1863-c.1889. Spiritualist who performed clairvoyant healings and augmented her magnetic powers with herbal remedies.

EBERT, E. F.
Stereo photographer active in Mankato.

ECKEL, F. C.
Active in Le Sueur, 1900.

EDWARDS, C. G.
Operated the Edwards' Gallery in Rushford, 1870.

EDWARDS' GALLERY
Studio operated by C. G. Edwards, active in Rushford, 1870.

EGGAN, HALVOR P.
Active in Minneapolis, 251 Cedar Avenue, 1887-88.

EGGAN, OLE
Active in Minneapolis, 251 Cedar Avenue, 1890.

EGGAN, S. P.
Active in Minneapolis, 251-253 Cedar Avenue, 1896-1915.

EGGAN, STEPHEN
Active in Minneapolis, 251 Cedar Avenue, 1900.

EGGAR
Active in Minneapolis, 1880.

ELDRIDGE & BROWN
Active in Mankato, 1885.

ELDRIDGE & PRICE
Stereo photographers in Mankato.

ELLICKSON, ANDREW L.
Active in Lanesboro, c. 1875.

ELLIOT & POWERS
Studio at 46, west side of Bridge Street, Minneapolis, c. 1866.

ELLIOT, RUFUS
Daguerreotypist located in the Goodwin & Fuller Building, later the Burt & Hoad Building, Minneapolis, 1856-65.

ELLIS (MRS.)
Opened a gallery in Pipestone with Mrs. R. L. Rynolds, 1889.

ELMER & TENNEY
Operating at 18 Center Street, Winona, 1870-90. Produced stereoviews.

ELWELL, TALMADGE
Born in Candor, New York, July 18, 1828. First daguerreotypist to open studio in St. Anthony Falls, Minnesota Territory; in Minneapolis, 1852. His flamboyant advertisements are the best of the era. His studio and gallery included a 225-square-foot skylight, which allowed him to make shorter exposures to catch squirmy children and to photograph at "all hours of the day." Operated in Granite City (Morrison County), 1857-62, when the Dakota Conflict made him feel unsafe. Lived in Little Falls, St. Cloud, and Cottage Grove, Minneapolis; founded the Elwell Manufacturing Company which made spring beds, 1873.
    James Taylor Dunn, "The Diary of Tallmadge Elwell: Pioneer Daguerreotypist, 1852," *The Daguerreian Annual 1992*, The Daguerreian Society, Eureka, California, 1992.

EMERSON, H. N.
Stereo photographer in Minneapolis.

ERICKS & WHITSTRUCK
Star Gallery at 301 Washington Avenue South, Minneapolis, c. 1880.

ERICKS, ANDERSON & CO'S
Studio at 111 E. Seventh Street, corner of Jackson, Saint Paul, c. 1880.

ERICKSON & COMPANY
Active in Minneapolis, 1890.

ERICKSON, C. T.
Active in Minneapolis; at 65 Eastman Avenue, 1897; at 716 Northwestern Building, 1898.

ERICKSON, J. A.
Active in Minneapolis, 529 Washington Avenue South, 1891-94.

ERICKSON, JOHN
Active in Minneapolis, 313 Washington Avenue South, 1906-10.

ERICKSON, JULIUS
Active in Minneapolis, 315 Cedar Avenue, 1891-92.

ERICKSON, VICTOR
Active in Minneapolis, 1433 Franklin Avenue East, 1912-15.

ESSERY & BROWN
Partnership of Ida M. Essery and Joseph H. Brown, operating in St. Paul, 1888-90, at 211 East Seventh Street.

ESSERY, IDA M. (MRS.)
Active in St. Paul, 1886-92, at 211 East Seventh Street. Wife of Robert W. Essery who died in 1886. Partner in Essery & Brown with Joseph H. Brown, 1888-90; listed alone, 1890-92; operated Essery Photograph Gallery, 1891, as Mrs. I. M. Johnson. Sold out to J. C. Varney, 1891.

ESSERY, ROBERT W.
Born in Canada; died in St. Paul, 1886. Photographer in St. Paul, 1873-86; at 135 or 137 East Seventh, 1873-81; at 211 East Seventh, 1882-88. Also spelled Ossery.

EVERITT, E. F.
Active in Mankato, 1870-80.

EXCELSIOR PHOTOGRAPHY GALLERY
Studio operated by Newton J. Trenham, Main Street, Alexandria, 1880-86.

FAIRBANKS
Active in Austin, c. 1900.

FALKENSHIELD, ANDREW
Operated out of Joel E. Whitney's studio in St. Paul, c. 1850-60s. Had his own studio at 136 3rd Street, c. 1866.

FARR, H. R.
Active in Minneapolis, 1875-90. Farr's wife advertised hairdressing services on his cartes-de-visite mounts, free with photos.

FEARON & BATCHELDER
Partnership of R. N. Fearon and Batchelder, Minneapolis, 1870-80. Also spelled Bacheller.

FEARON, R. N.
Active in Minneapolis, 1865-80. Partner in Fearon & Batchelder.

FENTON, R. N.
Stereo photographer in Minneapolis.

FLATEN & SKRIVSETH
Partnership in Moorhead, 1870s-80s, producing stereoviews; made rare views of Manitoba, 1875. Known as Norsk Atelier.

FLATEN, O. E.
Partner in Flaten & Skrivseth, Moorhead, 1870s-80s.

FLETCHER
Partner in Crandall & Fletcher, stereo photographers in Duluth.

FLOE, IVER I.
Active in Blue Earth City.

FLOWER
Partner in Flower & Hawkins, St. Paul, 1870-75.

FLOWER & HAWKINS
Active in St. Paul, 1870-75.

FLOYD & POWER
Partnership of G. W. Floyd and Power, Minneapolis, 1870s-80s, studio on Nicollet Avenue, corner of 5th Street.

FLOYD, G. W.
Partner in Floyd & Power, Minneapolis, 1870-80. Had his own studio at 11 and 13 Hale Block, Minneapolis, c. 1880- 90.

FOUCH, JOHN H.
Fouch maintained studios in Excelsior, Jordan, New Prague and Montgomery, Minnesota, 1880s. See Montana.

FULLER, J. A.
Stereo photographer in Albert Lea; listed in Madison, Wisconsin, operating Fuller's Temple of Art and Stereoscopic Gallery, 1860-65.

GALLERY OF ART
Operated by M. L. Smith in Long Prairie, 1875.

GAUSMEL, P. A.
Active in Kenyon, 1885.

GAYLORD & THOMPSON
Partnership in Duluth, 1870-80.

GAYLORD, EDWIN
Stereo photographer in Belvidere.

GAYLORD, P. B.
Studio at 93 East Superior Street, Duluth, 1870-80.

GAYLORD, ZIMMERMAN & SARGENT
Partnership of stereo photographers in St. Croix.

GOODWIN, OLIVE
Operated a daguerreotype and ambrotype studio in Minneapolis, 1859-60; gallery on Bridge Square was in competition with John Monell, C. C. Nelson, and Charles Robinson. Traded pictures for "good grain." She developed a disease of the throat, "partly occasioned by the use of cyanide of potassium in finishing of Daguerrian work," and after suffering intense pain, committed suicide, September 1860.

GROSSFIELD, G. G.
Active in Lanesboro, c. 1875.

HAGER
Partner in More & Hager, active in Blue Earth City, 1875-90.

HARDY & DENISON
Partnership operating a studio opposite Bell's Hotel, Fergus Falls, c. 1875.

HARDY, DENISON & ROBERTSON
Studio on Court Street, Fergus Falls, c. 1880.

HARDY, JOHN
Active in Fergus Falls, 1870-80; partner in Hardy & Denison, c. 1875; partner in Hardy, Denison & Robertson, c. 1880.

HARREY, G.
Active in Minneapolis, 1860-70.

HARVEY, EDWIN
Active in Minneapolis, 1860-70.

HASKINS
Partner in Cooledge & Haskins, active in Zumbrota, 1870-80.

HASKINS, GEORGE
Active in Osakis.

HASKINS, NYE
Active in Sauk Centre.

HASSAN, NELSON
Active in Glencoe, 1895.

HAWKINS
Partner in Flower & Hawkins, St. Paul, 1870-75.

HAWS, S. C.
Studio located on the ground floor of 134 West 7th Street, St. Paul, c. 1890.

HAYNES, F. E.
Active in St. Paul, 1890-1900; purchased photography business from William H. Jacoby, early 1890s.

HAYNES, F. JAY
Born in Saline, Michigan, October 28, 1853; died in St. Paul, March

10, 1921. Learned photography from S. C. Graham in Beaver Dam, Wisconsin, 1873. Worked for William H. Lockwood of Ripon, Wisconsin, 1875. He piloted the excursion boat *Camera* at Green Lake Resort for Lockwood. In 1876, Haynes opened his studio in Moorhead and contracted with the Northern Pacific Railroad to produce views for their promotional purposes. He developed one of the finest inventories of stereoview images of the Dakota country, in part due to a commission to photograph for the Black Hills Stage Company. In 1879 he opened a larger studio in Fargo, North Dakota. James Paris was a key contributor to Haynes' studio and remained with him until 1905. In 1881, Haynes added the Canadian Pacific Railway to his patrons and traveled through western Canada taking views. He traveled to Yellowstone, 1882, capturing a great number of views. Haynes traveled through Oregon and Washington for the Northern Pacific, and in 1883, he became the official photographer for President Chester A. Arthur's excursion to Yellowstone. He obtained a license to operate a photographic concession in Yellowstone at Mammoth Hot Springs, 1883, opening the Log Cabin Studio which served Yellowstone for many years. He operated a railroad car gallery dubbed Haynes Palace Studio, 1885-1905. In 1889, Haynes moved his studio from Fargo to St. Paul. In 1891, he traveled through Alaska for the Puget Sound and Alaska Steam Ship line. Haynes was one of the most prolific of the West's early photographers, and one of the finest.

Freeman Tilden, *Following the Frontier with F. Jay Haynes: Pioneer Photographer of the Old West*, Alfred A. Knopf, 1964.

Montana Historical Society, *F. Jay Haynes, Photographer*, Montana Historical Society Press, 1981.

HEIGHSTEDT, A. W.
Active in Minneapolis, 1895.

HEINEN, HENRY
Active in Norwood.

HELLING, JAMES
"Travelling Photographer & Artist," active in Minneapolis.

HENNEPIN STUDIO
Active in Minneapolis, c. 1893-1908.

HICKOX & COMPANY
Stereo photographers in St. Paul.

HILDAHL, G. S.
Active in Austin, 1880-90.

HILL
Studio over Murphy & Ryan's Shoe Store, Anoka, c. 1876.

HILL & KELLEY
Partnership involving Joseph Hill, the ambrotypist.

HILL, E. A.
Active in St. Cloud, c. 1890.

HILL, J.
Studio on Washington Avenue between St. Germain and Lake Streets, St. Cloud, 1860-70.

HILL, JOSEPH
Daguerreotypist and ambrotypist located in Minneapolis and St. Paul, 1857-63, in association as Hill & Kelley; also listed in St. Anthony, c. 1860; in Anoka, c. 1880.

HILLMAN, W. J.
Active in Cannon Falls, 1880-90.

HINDE
Partner in Maddison & Hinde, active in Huntington and St. Ires.

HINSHAW, GRANT
Amateur stereo photographer, member of the United Stereoscopic Society, 1913, in St. Paul.

HIRSCH BROTHERS
Stereo photographers in Wheaton.

HOARD & TENNEY
Studio at 40 East Second Street, c. 1870; on Center Street between Second and Third, Winona, 1875-80. Produced stereoviews.

HOLAND
Partner in Overland & Holand, active in Fergus Falls, 1875-90.

HOOKER, A. E.
Active in St. Paul, 1885, at 105 East Third Street.

HOWITT, C. (MISS)
Active in Chatfield, c. 1860s.

HUDSON, C. H.
Active in St. Paul, 1870-75.

HUGHES, ELIZABETH D.
Amateur active in St. Paul, c. 1899. Winner of a prize for interiors.

HUFFMAN, L. A.
See Montana.

HUNTINGTON & BARTRAM
Partnership active in Minneapolis; possibly related to the Huntington & Company listed in St. Paul, 1870s-80s.

HUNTINGTON & COMPANY
Publisher of stereoviews in St. Paul, 1870s-80s; published some of Illingworth's views. Possibly in partnership with Bartram in Minneapolis, 1870s, also with Bartram and Taylor in Minneapolis, 1870s-80s.

HUNTINGTON & COMPANY, CHARLES J.
Studio at 53 East Third Street, St. Paul, 1870-80. Also known as Huntington & Company.

HUNTINGTON & WINNE
Photo studio in St. Paul destroyed by fire, 1874.

ILLINGWORTH & BILL
Partnership of W. H. Illingworth and George Bill, active in St. Paul, 1860-70.

ILLINGWORTH & McLEISH
Partnership of W. H. Illingworth and McLeish, active in St. Paul, 1870-80.

ILLINGWORTH, WILLIAM HENRY
Born in Leeds, England, September 20, 1842; died in St. Paul, March 16, 1893. Stereographer active in St. Paul, 1863-c. 1880. Studio moved to Red Wing, 1865; returned to St. Paul, 1866. Joined Powell expedition with assistant, George Bill, selling negatives to Chicago photographer, John Carbutt, who then sold stereoviews with his own imprint and no credit to Illingworth. Went to England, March 1874, mainly to claim a legacy but also to photograph the birthplaces and former homes of a number of St. Paul citizens and to sell Minnesota views. Accompanied General Custer on an expedition to the Black Hills, July-August 1874, contracting with Huntington & Winne of St.

Paul to publish approximately 60-70 stereoviews of the dramatic terrain and the wagon train. Soon after he was charged with embezzling and misappropriating government funds, because he had not supplied the expedition's chief engineer with six sets of stereoviews as promised. It is possible that he was prevented from doing so by a fire that destroyed the photo gallery of Huntington and Winne, although the Black Hills negatives were not in their possession at that time. The charges were dropped within days. He advertised sole ownership of the carbon process, 1878; his career began failing, 1880s; he succumbed to alcoholism and committed suicide.

INGALLS, FRANK M.
Active in Le Sueur and Jordan, 1880.

INGERSOLL, TRUMAN W.
Born in St. Paul, February 19, 1862; died, June 1922. Active with a thriving business in landscape and commercial work in St. Paul, 1880-1900. His studio was located on the site of the present (1922) public library. Famous for his photographs of Theodore Roosevelt, 1870s. He sold the very first Kodak (made by his friend, Mr. Eastman), early 1880s. Moved to Buffalo, c. 1911.

INGERSOLL VIEW COMPANY
Active in St. Paul, 1890-1900.

JABE
Active in Winona, c. 1870.

JACOBY & SON
Partnership of W. H. and his son, C. L. Jacoby, Minneapolis, mid-1880s-90s; sold to F. E. Haynes, early 1890s.

JACOBY, CHARLES L.
Son of W. H. Jacoby. Began working in the family business, 1878; became partner, mid-1880s, when the firm's title was W. H. Jacoby & Son; assumed control, 1887, when his father retired.

JACOBY, HIRAM J.
Born in Ohio, 1838; died in Minnesota, 1909. Active in Minneapolis with his brother, William H., in Bridge Square, 1867; in St. Peter, 1868-88.

JACOBY, WILLIAM H.
Born in Massillion, Ohio, May 24, 1841; died in Los Angeles, February 1, 1906. Operated Jacoby's Champion Art Gallery, 46 Nicollet Street, corner of Third, c. 1870; Jacoby's Photographic Art Palace in Minneapolis with his brother, Hiram, 1867-87, at Bridge Square; published stereoviews, specializing in Minneapolis, St. Paul, and Lake Minnetonka; known for very fine portraiture. Produced "imitation porcelain pictures" printed on paper to look like porcelain; also invented the "Combination Printing Frame." After the famous robbery in Northfield, September 7, 1876, he published the robbers' portraits as cartes-de-visite; competed strongly with Alonzo H. Beal. Took his son, Charles L., as partner, mid-1880s, when firm's title was W. H. Jacoby & Son; retired, 1887, turning the studio over to Charles; sold the photography business to F. E. Haynes, early 1890s.

JACOBY'S ART GALLERY
Located in St. Peter, J. H. Coffin, operator, c. 1880.

JACOBY'S PHOTOGRAPHIC ART PALACE
Operated by William H. Jacoby in St. Paul, 1867-87.

JARVIS, WILLIAM H.
Dentist and daguerrean in St. Paul, 1850 on Fifth Street. Reputedly one of two photographers active in Minnesota in 1850; the other was Sarah Judd.

JENSEN BROTHERS
Active in Albert Lea and Alden, 1895-1900.

JOHNSON, CHARLES F.
Active in Duluth, 1865-80.

JOHNSON, J. E.
Active in Morgan, c. 1895.

JOHNSON, JOSIE
Active in Fertile, c. 1890s.

JOHNSON, O. F.
Active in Hastings, c. 1862.

JONES, F. V.
Active in Cloquet, 1885.

JUDD, SARAH
Born in Connecticut; moved with her family to Marine, Illinois, and then to Sillwater, Wisconsin Territory, later eastern Minnesota. Daguerreotypist in Stillwater, 1848-50; possibly the first photographer in Minnesota (then Wisconsin Territory); married Ariel Eldridge, 1849, perhaps leaving photography for family life. No known examples of her work survive.

KEENE, GEORGE E.
Studio at 803 and 805 South Front Street, Mankato, c. 1890.

KELLEY, JAMES H.
Photographer in St. Anthony, c. 1860.

KELLOGG, J. D.
Active in Red Wing, 1870-90.

KRECH, M. (MRS.)
Active in St. Paul, c. 1860s.

KRUGER, PAULINE
Studio in Minneapolis, c. 1899. Known also as a musician, painter, designer and book illustrator; she designed a badge to commemorate President McKinley's 1899 visit.

KUHN, JOHN M.
Stereo photographer in Stillwater, 1882-1904.

LAKE, MALONA
Stereo photographer in Park Rapids; also known as Mrs. E. C. Lake.

LARSON, ANTON
Active in Minneapolis, 1875-90.

LASBY, DR. WILLIAM F.
Amateur stereo photographer in Minneapolis, member of the United Stereoscopic Society, 1913.

LEE BROTHERS
Partnership active in Minneapolis, c. 1912; joined by Frank Sweet, 1912.

LHOTHKA, FRED
Active in Winstead, c. 1900.

LIDEN, L. N.
Active in Duluth.

LOOMIS, FRANK E.
Active in Stillwater, 1870-80. Stereo photographer.

LYNN, E. A.
Active in Winona, 1890.

MADDISON & HINDE
Partnership active in Huntington and St. Ires.

MADSEN, S. C.
Active in Sleepy Eye and New Ulm, 1880.

MANDERFELD & BAGNE
Studio in Waseca, c. 1875.

MANDERFELD, H.
Fine Art Gallery, Waseca, c. 1875.

MANN, GERTRUDE E.
Operated a studio in the Handicraft Guild Building, Minneapolis, c. 1908. Initially an amateur who exhibited in England and Italy.

MARTIN, JAMES E.
Active in St. Paul, 1860-70.

MARTIN'S ART GALLERY
Active in St. Paul, 1885.

MATSON, S. C.
Stereo photographer in Sleepy Eye.

MAXIM, A. L.
Amateur stereo photographer in Minneapolis; member of United Stereoscopic Society, 1913.

MAYO, E. D.
Amateur stereo photographer in Minneapolis; member of United Stereoscopic Society, 1913.

McFARLAN, JOHN R.
Daguerreotypist in St. Anthony, c. 1860.

McLEISH & CRESSEY
Partnership active in St. Paul, 1870-80.

McLEISH & PASEL
Active in St. Paul, 1875-80.

McLEISH & PEASE
Partnership of William McLeish and F. O. Pease, stereo photographers in St. Paul, c. 1870s.

McLEISH, WILLIAM
Partner in McLeish & Pease, active in St. Paul, c. 1870s.

McPHEE, CATHERINE
Stereo photographer in Minneapolis; owned a gallery on the corner of Nicollet Avenue and 2nd Street. Also known as Mrs. James McPhee.

MELANDER
Partner in Naumann & Melander, active in Duluth, 1880-90.

MERRILL, RANDALL & COMPANY
Partnership in St. Paul, 1870-80; the company was also an outlet for books, guides, chromos, tourist supplies. They offered 1,000 views of the west, and "Merrill's Collection of Minnesota Views," containing 300+ Minnesota views. Also listed as D. D. Merrill, Randall & Company.

MESSER, ASA
Active in Red Wing, 1875-80.

MILLER & CRESSEY
Details unknown; views rare, some of Carver's Cave.

MINNE HA HA GALLERY
Operated by Michael Nowack.

MITCHELL, GERTRUDE F.
Amateur active in Minneapolis, known for her portraits of both adults and children in their homes, c. 1900.

MONELL, JOHN
Studio in Saint Anthony, 1854-60, on Main Street, overlooking the Falls of Saint Anthony; specialized in ambrotypes and daguerreotypes of the Falls.

MOOERS & PLUMMER
Partnership active in Minneapolis, 1870-80.

MORE & HAGER
Active in Blue Earth City, 1875-90.

MORE, A. R., JR.
Active in Blue Earth City, 1870-80.

MORGENEIER, ROBERT
Active in Winona, c. 1875.

MORROW, S. J.
See Dakota.

MYHRE
Active in Sacred Heart, c. 1885.

NAUMANN & MELANDER
Active in Duluth, 1880-90.

NEAL & SIMMONS
Stereo photographers in Little Falls.

NELSON, C. C.
Daguerreotypist in Minneapolis, c. 1860.

NELSON, F. A.
Active in Little Falls, 1890.

NELSON'S PHOTOGRAPHIC STUDIO
Active in Anoka, 1895.

NESBITT, A. F.
Stereo photographer in Minneapolis.

NEWT, A. F.
Active in Minneapolis, 1890.

NOWACK & CHASE
Partnership of M. Nowack and C. B. Chase, stereo photographers in Minneapolis, c. 1870s-90s. Published their own views and many pirated views from the rest of the U.S.

NOWACK, MICHAEL
Minne Ha Ha Gallery at 117 Washington Avenue North, Minneapolis, 1870-90.

NYE
Active in Duluth, 1875-90.

OERTER
Active in Chaska.

OLESON, ANNA G.
Photographer active in Minneapolis at 228 and 307 Washington Avenue South, 1882-90; wife of photographer John H. Oleson; continued work after his death, c. 1888.

OLESON, JOHN H.
Died in Minneapolis, 1888. Successful photographer active in Minneapolis, 1871-87. Began at W. H. Jacoby's gallery, 1871-72; established his own studio at 305 Washington Avenue South, 1874-75; moved to 307 Washington Avenue South, 1876-79. Erected new building at 226-228 Washington Avenue South, 1881, continuing until his death, c. 1888. His wife, Anna G., also a photographer, ran the business until c. 1890. The studio at 307 remained a tintype gallery operated by the Oleson's.

OLSON, EMMA
Studio in St. Paul, c. 1879, at 844 Payne Avenue; Perham, c. 1889.

OLSON, H. L.
Active in Granite Falls, 1870-80.

OPSAHL
Active in Minneapolis, 1890-1900.

OSWALD BROTHERS
Active in Minneapolis.

OSWALD, CHARLES
Active in Minneapolis.

OVERLAND & HOLAND
Partnership active in Fergus Falls, 1875-90.

OVERLAND, A. P.
Active in Fergus Falls.

PALMER & DELLING
Partnership active in St. James and Medelia; stereo photographers.

PALMER, A. A.
Active in Minneapolis and Minnehaha Falls, 1870-80. Photographed Chippewa.

PALMER, FRED
Studio at the corner of 2nd and Elm Streets, Waseca, c. 1875.

PALMER, J. W.
Stereo photographer, partner in Palmer & Delling, active in St. James and Medelia; also worked alone in St. James.

PARK & LAWRENCE
Active in Rochester, c. 1862. Produced stereoviews.

PARK, A. O.
Billed as "photographer and artist in ink, caryon [sic] and water colors," c. 1880. Name crossed out and "J. M. Wood" inserted. Bunched with Minnesota cartes-de-visite, so assumed to be Minnesota photographers, but no place included in the imprint.

PARK, A. V.
Partner in Park Brothers, Rochester, 1870-75. Successor to Park Brothers, located at 2 Bank Block, c. 1875.

PARK BROTHERS
Active in Rochester, 1870-75.

PASEL
Partner in McLeish & Pasel active in St. Paul, 1875-80.

PASEL, O. C.
Stereo photographer; partner with William McLeish in St. Paul, 1875-80.

PEARCY, L.
Active in Faribault, 1880-90.

PEASE
Partner in Burritt & Pease active in St. Paul, 1870-80.

PEASE, F. O.
Stereo photographer active in Lincoln, 1878; Clinton, 1882.

PEAVEY, L.
Active in Faribault, c. 1885.

PECK, C. S.
Photographer and publisher of stereoviews in Zumbroata; produced series depicting "Wanderings Among the Wonders and Beauties of Minnesota," 1880-90. Also known as C. J.

PEOPLE'S PHOTO GALLERY
Studio at 93 East Seventh Street, St. Paul, owned by Weatherby; purchased by Harry L. Shepherd, 1887. By 1888, was named People's Portrait Company; moved gallery over New England Shoe Store on Seventh, between Robert and Jackson; became Shepherd Photographic Company at 418-420 Wabasha Street, 1892.

PEPPER & SON, A. H.
Partnership of A. H. Pepper and T. M. Pepper, father and son active in St. Paul, 1875-90.

PEPPER, A. H.
Partner in Pepper & Son, active in St. Paul, 1875-90.

PEPPER, T. M.
Partner in Pepper & Son, active in St. Paul, 1880-90.

PERKINS, O.R.
Artistic photographer, Red Wing, c. 1880.

PHILLIPS
Active in Red Wing, 1890.

PHILLIPS, J. & A.
Active in Lake City, 1875-90. First name possibly John.

PHILLIPS, JOHN
Active in Lake City, 1880-90.

PHILLIPS, W. W.
Stereo photographer in White Bear Lake.

PINGREY, R. H.
Stereo photographer in Taylors Falls.

PLUMMER
Partner in Mooers & Plummer, active in Minneapolis, 1870-80.

POWER
Partner in Floyd & Power, Minneapolis, 1870s-80s, located on Nicollet Avenue, corner of 5th Street.

PRESCOTT, J. J.
Active in Melrose, c. 1898-99.

PRICE
Partner in Eldridge & Price, stereo photographers in Mankato.

PRINDLE, M. M.
Amateur active in Duluth, c. 1899. Won a prize for interiors.

PROCTOR, J. H.
Rooms over First National Bank, Hastings, c. 1864. Made stereoviews of Turkey River Railroad.

PROUD, JOHN
Stereo photographer in Rochester; studio on Daniel's Block, Broadway, c. 1870; rare, single view known of Minnehaha Falls.

RANDALL
Partner in Merrill, Randall & Company, stereo photographers and dealers in books and tourist supplies in St. Paul, 1870-80.

RANSOM, R. W.
Stereo photographer active in St. Paul, offering Minnesota, "American and European Views."

RED WING VIEW COMPANY
Operated by Craig F. Daniels in Red Wing.

REITZ, J. A.
Active in Chaska, c. 1894-95.

RENTFROW, W. E.
Active in Minneapolis, c. 1865.

REYNOLDS & KEENE
Studio in Redwood Falls, c. 1895.

REYNOLDS, R. L. (MRS.)
Opened a gallery in Pipestone, 1889 with Mrs. Ellis; operating alone as the Lincoln Photograph Gallery by 1898, publishing stereoviews of the falls and quarries.

RIBBLES, G. H.
Active in St. Peter, 1894-95.

RICH
Active in Sauk City, c. 1885.

RICH, J. E.
Studio at 129 Washington Avenue South, Minneapolis, 1875-90.

RILEY
Partner in Brown & Riley, stereo photographers in Winona.

RINGE
Partner in Thrane & Ringe, stereo photographers in Minneapolis, 1880s-1900.

ROBERTS & SUMMER
Operated the Champion Gallery in Northfield, c. 1873.

ROBERTS, Z.
Partner in Roberts & Summer's Champion Gallery, Northfield, c. 1873.

ROBINSON, CHARLES
Active in Minneapolis, 1859-62.

ROE, GEORGE
Photographer in Alexandria before 1876.

RUGG, A. B.
Studio at 41 Washington Avenue, Minneapolis, 1870-1915.

RUH, O. L.
Active in Northfield, c. 1880.

RUST
Partner in Canning & Rust, stereo photographers in Hastings.

RYERSON, R. D.
Active in Detroit City (now Detroit Lakes), 1875-90.

RYERSON, R. D. (MRS.)
Active in Detroit City (now Detroit Lakes), c. 1898.

SARGEANT
Purchased the studio of Amanda Wahlstrom, 1906.

SARGENT, S. C.
Stereo photographer active in Taylors Falls; made views of the railroad, Dalles of the St. Croix and loggers.

SCANDINAVIFKA PHOTOGRAPH GALLERY
Operated by Gustaf Berg in Red Wing, c. 1875.

SCHLATTMAN BROTHERS
Active in St. Paul, 1875-80.

SEITER, E. E.
Active in New Ulm, 1875-90.

SHEPARD
Active in Minneapolis, 1895.

SHEPHERD PHOTOGRAPHIC COMPANY
Studio operated by Harry R. Shepherd in St. Paul, 1887-c. 1905.

SHEPHERD, R. HARRY
Born in Virginia, January 1854. Bought the People's Photo Gallery on East Seventh Street, St. Paul, from Weatherby, 1887, and renamed it the People's Portrait Company, 1888; half-owner of Annex Gallery, located opposite People's, mid-1889; full owner, October 1889. Opened Shepherd Photographic Company, 1891, over New England Shoe Store, on Seventh Street between Robert and Jackson; the earliest black proprietor of a photographic studio in the state. Owned three galleries by 1890; Made tintypes, photos on ivory, watch dials and silk handkerchiefs; won gold medal at State Fair, 1891, embossing it on the front of his cabinet portraits thereafter. Appointed official photographer for the Afro-American exhibit at the Paris Exposition, 1900. Shepherd claimed to make $18-20,000 per year at his studio. No studio records survive to confirm this, but hundreds of examples of his work remain to illustrate his popularity. May have moved to Chicago, May 1905.

SIDDALL, H. E.
Active in Minneapolis, 1880-85.

SIMMONS
Partner in Neal & Simmons, stereo photographers in Little Falls.

SINCLAIR, JAMES
Active in Stillwater, 1870-80.

SIVERTS, PETER
Active in Canby, 1880.

SKRIVSETH, J. L.
Partner in Flaten & Skrivseth, stereo photographers in Moorhead, 1870s-80s. Studio on the corner of Main and 2nd Streets, Faribault, c. 1880.

SLEYSTER, A. L.
Operating the Sleyster Studio of Fine Art, c. 1898.

SLEYSTER, BESSIE E.
Operating the Sleyster Studio of Fine Art, c. 1898.

SMITH, M. L.
Operated the Gallery of Art in Long Prairie, 1875.

SMITH, R. I.
Active in Austin, 1865-79.

SNOW, H. H.
Active in Zambrota, 1895.

SNYDER BROTHERS
Partnership operating at 727-729 Hennepin Avenue, Minneapolis, c. 1905.

SPRAGUE, E. J. (MRS.)
Active in St. Paul, c. 1860s.

STADON, J. E.
Active in Minneapolis, 1875-80.

STAFFORD & COMPANY
Studio owned by O. F. Stafford, active in Minneapolis, 1900.

STAFFORD, O. F.
Operated the studio of Stafford & Company, in Minneapolis, 1900.

STAR GALLERY
Active in St. Cloud, 1885.

STEBBINS, A. L.
Stereo photographer active in St. Charles.

STEELE, R. E.
Active in St. Paul, 1895-1910.

STEVENS, J. A.
Active in Spring Valley, 1880-90.

STIFF, CHARLES W.
Active in St. Paul, 1870-80.

STOHLMANN, GUSTAV
Active in New Ulm, 1870-80.

STRIDBORG, J. A.
Studio on the corner of Main Street and Commercial Avenue, Stillwater, c. 1880.

SUMNER & BINGHAM
Active in Rochester and Northfield, 1870-80.

SUMNER, IRA E.
Active in Northfield, 1870-90.

SUNBEAM GALLERY
Operated by C. A. De Long in Minneapolis East, on Central Avenue, c. 1875.

SUNDERLAND, W. F.
Stereo photographer in Grand Forks.

SWAIN, ALLEN
Operated Swain's Gallery in St. Paul, 1866-93.

SWAIN, L. A. (MRS.)
Active in St. Paul, 1863.

SWAIN'S GALLERY
Studio operated by Allen Swain, 130 Third Street, St. Paul, 1866-93.

SWEET, FRANK
Born in Minnesota, 1868 or 1870. Active in Minneapolis, 1897-1912+. Partner with his brother, Louis Sweet, 1897-1912, in Sweet Studio; joined a rival portrait studio, Lee Brothers, c. 1912.

SWEET, LOUIS
Born in Minnesota, 1868 or 1870. Operated the Sweet Studio in Minneapolis, 1897-1930; partner with his brother, Frank Sweet, 1897-1912.

SWEET STUDIO
Stylish studio in Minneapolis in the Syndicate Arcade on Nicollet Avenue; operated by Louis and Frank Sweet, 1897-1912; Louis continued alone until 1930. Specialized in landscape and portrait photography, printing 8 x 10 inch landscapes and encased large portraits in elegant folders. Their negatives included 19th century images after they purchased the William Jacoby archive.

SWEM, THOMAS M.
Active in St. Paul, 1885. See Oregon.

TAYLOR, F. A.
Active in St. Paul, 1870-80.

TAYLOR, S. M.
Born in Wisconsin. Portrait and landscape artist, 134 West Seventh Street, St. Paul, 1883-88; galley known as Taylor's Seven Corners Gallery.

TAYLOR'S GALLERY
Located at 148 Third Street, St. Paul, c. 1880.

TAYLOR'S SEVEN CORNERS GALLERY
Studio operated by S. M. Taylor in St. Paul, corner of Exchange and West Seventh Streets (134 West Seventh), 1883.

TENNEY, CHARLES A.
Born in New Hampshire, 1847; died in Ohio, October 1917. Learned photography in Chicago, 1869; came to Winona and established studio on Second Street, near Center, 1871. Studio moved to 115 Center Street, 1874. Partner in Hoard & Tenney, 1875-80. Although a portrait photographer, he also specialized in scenic and stereoviews of Winona. By 1883, he had sold over 25,000 prints of his snow views of winter, 1880-81. Moved to Creston, Ohio, 1893. Also spelled Tenny.

THIEL & COMPANY, CHARLES
Partnership active in Duluth, 1883-84.

THOMAS, J. E.
Active in Fergus Falls, 1880.

THOMAS, WILLIAM W.
Active in Owatonna, 1870-85.

THRANE & RINGE
Partnership in Minneapolis, 1880s-1900.

THRANE ART COMPANY
Photographers and publishers of stereoviews; made rare stereoviews of Norway with titles in Norwegian for immigrants in the upper midwest, c. 1906.

THRANE, P. E.
Stereo photographer active in Minneapolis; partner in Thrane & Ringe, 1880s-1900; owned and operated Thrane Art Company, c, 1906.

THUNE
Active in Ada, c. 1890.

THURMOND, R.
Stereo photographer in Minneapolis.

TOYBERG, L. J.
Studio at Simpson's Brick Block, Sinona, c. 1862.

TRENHAM, NEWTON J.
Came from Canada via New York; operated studio in Alexandria, 1875-c. 1896. Within six months he drove out his only competition, George Roe. Opened new gallery on Main Street, 1880, the Excelsior Photography Gallery. Specialized in landscape stereoviews around Alexandria and Glenwood; photographed extensively in Otter Tail County. Reportedly worked for Zimmerman, January 1887; also had a studio in Fergus Falls, 1895. Moved to Florida, c. 1896, and helped settle a new town, Fulford (now North Miami Beach).

TUTTLE, MOSES C.
Daguerreotypist in St. Paul, c. 1860; won first premium for his work. Advertised daguerreotypes and ambrotypes of Indian chiefs. Studio at Whitney's Gallery on the corner of 3rd and Cedar; later at 3rd, between Wabashaw and St. Peter Streets, 1858.

UPTON & MARTIN
Partnership of Benjamin Franklin Upton and James E. Martin.

UPTON, BENJAMIN FRANKLIN
Born in Dixmont, Penobscot County, Maine, August 3, 1818. Daguerreotypist in Maine, c. 1844-51. Began work in St. Anthony, 1856; in Big Lake, Sherburne County, c. 1857-65, spending summers at Lake Minnetonka; in St. Anthony, c. 1865-75. Operated from a wagon every day except Sunday. Notable for his portraits of the Dakota Indians imprisoned at Ft. Snelling after the 1862 conflict, published as cartes-de-visite and stereoviews. Also photographed the Ojibwa in the field. Moved to Florida, c. 1875, continuing photography.

VANCE, GEORGE
Stereo photographer in Winona, 1874-81+. Began photographic career in S. T. Wiggin's Winona studio, 1874; later worked for the studio of Hoard & Tenney (later became Elmer & Tenney). Took "Minnesota Snow View Series of 1881," published by Elmer & Tenney.

VANDERWARKER & NALLY
Stereo photographers in Minneapolis.

VARNEY, J. C.
Purchased the Essery Photograph Gallery in St. Paul, 1891.

VIKING VIEW COMPANY
Active in Minneapolis. Produced stereoviews of Scandinavia, Russo-Japanese War, Minnesota towns; titles in Norwegian.

WAHLSTROM, AMANDA
Active in Wadena, c. 1896-1906. Sold studio to Mr. Sargeant and returned to Sweden.

WARGE
Active in Hawley, 1885.

WARNER, F. S. (MRS.)
Active in Dawson, 1886.

WASHBURN & BENNETT
Partnership active in Red Wing, 1860-70.

WATKINS, MARGARET
Active in St. Paul, c. 1860. Succeeded by C. E. Carpenter.

WEBB, D. W.
Active in Minneapolis, 1870-80.

WEDMAR
Active in Pine Island, 1900.

WEEKS
Partner in Angell & Weeks, active in Litchfield, 1875-95.

WESTBERG, L. E.
Active in Duluth.

WHEELER, L. G. (MRS.)
Active in Kasson, c. 1860s.

WHITCOMB (MRS.)
Active in Brownton, 1875.

WHITNEY & ZIMMERMAN
Joel E. Whitney hired Charles A. Zimmerman as his assistant, 1858, until Zimmerman left to become a soldier in the Civil War, 1862-65. He returned to Whitney's studio after the war, became a partner, 1870; purchased the business, 1871.

WHITNEY, JOEL EMMONS
Born in Phillips, Maine, May 18, 1822; died in St. Paul, January 20, 1886. Daguerreotypist active in St. Paul, 1850-71; Whitney's Gallery located above Elfelt's store on Third and Cedar Streets, 1851; studied under Alexander Hesler of Chicago and Galena, Illinois, 1852. On August 15, 1852, they took a hike which became legendary, resulting in 80 views; the view of Minnehaha Falls was Henry Wadsworth Longfellow's inspiration for *The Song of Hiawatha*. One of the first Minnesota photographers to adopt the new collodion negative and albumen paper print process, 1855; introduced cartes-de-visite to St. Paul, 1861, specializing in portraits of Indians (capitalizing on the great public interest during the age of treaty delegations and news reports of friendly and hostile encounters). Opened the Art Depot in the Lambert Building at Third and Cedar, 1866. Partner with C. A. Zimmerman, 1870; sold out to Zimmerman, 1871, due to ill health; moved to Georgia and Tennessee; returned to St. Paul, 1880.

WIGGINS & BARNES
Studio on the corner of Second and Lafayette Streets, Winona, c. 1864.

WIGGINS, S. T.
Studio on Post Office Avenue, Winona, 1865-70.

WILLIAMS, S. M.
Active in Minneapolis, 1870-75.

WILSE, ANDERS BEERS
See Washington.

WILTSE, G. G.
Stereo photographer in Red Wing.

WOOD, J. W.
Active in Lake City, 1880-90.

WOODBURY, I. DORA
Active in Rochester, 1865.

WOODS, J. M.
Active in Anoka, c. 1880.

WRIGHT
Issued local stereoviews in Kenyon.

YATES, LILIAN
One of the Yates sisters operating in Waseca. Opened her first gallery in 1888; in Worthington, over the newspaper office, 1901-1911.

YATES, MARGARET
One of the Yates sisters operating in Waseca, c. 1889; briefly in Waterville.

YATES SISTERS
Lilian and Margaret Yates, operating as partners in Waseca, c. 1890.

ZIMMERMAN
Partner in Gaylord, Zimmerman & Sargent, stereo photographers in St. Croix.

ZIMMERMAN BROTHERS
Partnership of Edward O. and Charles A. Zimmerman, active in St. Paul, 1873-c. 1900; published *The Northwestern Amateur*, a photography journal, 1898-1900; eventually became Eastman Kodak Company of St. Paul.

ZIMMERMAN, CHARLES A.
Born in Strasbourg, Alsace, France, 1844. Came to America with his parents, 1848; moved to St. Paul, 1856. By age 14, he built a simple camera and was astute enough to bring it to the best photographer in town. Whitney was impressed and hired him as his assistant until Zimmerman left to become a Civil War soldier, 1862-65. He returned to the studio after the war and became a partner by 1870; he purchased the studio, 1871. John Wesley Powell asked him to be his expeditionary photographer down the Colorado River, 1871. He declined with "regrets but would be away from family too long" and "have just obtained a gallery which I have to run myself." Gold embossed images of his national gold medals appear on some of his cabinet-sized portrait mounts. In 1872, he opened a four-story gallery at 9 West Third Street on St. Paul's Bridge Square, offering diverse goods: cameras, chemicals, lenses, stereoscopes, and photography supplies, while maintaining his portrait studios, art galleries, a tintype gallery, and a landscape department "from which are daily turned out over 1000 views." He took some of the era's finest landscape photos of Minnesota, specializing in stereoviews of the Twin Cities area. Also traveled to Odanah, Wisconsin, and to Lake Pepin as well. On November 28, 1869, he almost lost his life to his art. "Wishing to obtain winter views of a place Longfellow has immortalized in his classic verse, Mr. Zimmerman passed under the falls." A large icicle, weighing between two and three hundred pounds, fell and knocked him senseless, but he was found and rescued one hour later.

ZIMMERMAN, EDWARD O.
Partner with brother, Charles A., in the Zimmerman Brothers, St. Paul, 1873-c. 1900.

ZINN, W. S.
Stereo photographer in Minneapolis.

ZWEIFEL, JOSHUA
Active in Duluth, 1895.

ZWEIFEL, TOBIAS
Active in Duluth, 1895.

ADAMS, R. F.
Successor to McConnell. Studio at 215 North Fourth Street, old No. 62, on the west side between Pine and Olive, St. Louis, 1865-80.

AINSWORTH
Stereo photographer in Pleasant Hill; also made cartes-de-visite and cabinet cards.

ALVORD, E. D.
Active at Palmyra, c. 1864.

ANDREWS, J. A.
Operator for Greene in St. Louis, c. 1880.

BABBITT & SHANNON
Stereo photographers in Kansas City, c. 1870s.

BARCAFER
Stereo photographer active in Springfield.

BARNUM & RIDGEWAY
St. Louis "Travelling Photographers, Views taken in any part of state or area, homes and businesses a specialty."

BARTELS, K. L.
Amateur stereo photographer, active in St. Louis.

BARTRAM, ROBERT
Stereo photographer in Independence.

BEARDEN, W. L.
Stereo photographer active in Princeton.

BECK & FRANK
Medical partnership of Joseph C. Beck, M.D., and Ira Frank, M.D., in St. Louis; wrote 131-page booklet and made 300 stereoviews of plastic surgery techniques. "A Stereoscopic Atlas of Plastic Surgery of the Face, Head, and Neck." Photos are from surgery being done on cadavers. The set was sold cased in green cloth/cardboard box, published by C. V. Mosby Company, St. Louis.

BEENCK, P.H.
Tintype studio at 2409 Broadway, near Sturgeon Market, St. Louis, c. 1864.

BELLE STUDIO
Active in St. Louis.

BENECKE, ROBERT
Major studio in St. Louis; southeast corner of Fourth and Market Streets, c. 1875. Produced stereoviews of the Indian Territory.

BENEDICT, R.
Stereo photographer in St. Louis; member of American Stereoscopic Exchange Club, 1867-69.

BENTON
Active in Waverly, c. 1880.

BEOHL & KOENIG
Partnership active in St. Louis.

BEST, STEPHEN R.
St. Louis social worker by profession; made stereoviews of sculptures.

BIGELOW & PARCELL
Operated the Photo and Art Company, Frederick Avenue, St. Joseph, c. 1890. Awarded the Medal of Honor at the Paris Academy of Science and Invention, 1891.

BOOTH, R. J.
Active in Columbia, c. 1867.

BOOTH STUDIO
Gallery at Rich Hill, c. 1900.

BOWER & JOHNSON
Partnership active in Kansas City, producing stereoviews, 1870s; possibly M. B. Bower and W. S. Johnson.

BOWER, BOWER & JOHNSON
Partnership of M. B. Bower and W. S. Johnson, stereo photographers in Kansas City, 1880s.

BOWER BROTHERS
Partnership of M. B. Bower and others, active in West Kansas City, 1870s.

BOWER, M. B.
Stereo photographer in Kansas City, 1870s-80s.

BOYETT
Stereo photographer in St. Louis.

BRIGGS, C. W.
Active in Maryville, 1860.

BRINCE, HERMAN
Stereo photographer formerly in the Susanville region of California, active in St. Louis.

BROWN & SONS, N.
Studio at 41 North Fourth Street, St. Louis, c. 1868.

BROWN, NICHOLAS
Daguerreotypist in St. Louis, 1857-66; 41 or 43 North Fourth Street; changed to ambrotypes by 1860, later working in New Mexico and Mexico with sons William Henry and John O. Brown.

BROWN, WILLIAM
Studio at 70 North Fourth Street, St. Louis, c. 1862.

BROWN, WILLIAMS & COMPANY
Studio at 41 North Fourth Street, St. Louis, c. 1868.

BRYANT, G. W.
Stereo photographer in Plattsburg.

BUCK, F. A.
Active in Hopkins, c. 1880.

BURDGE, R. R.
Active in Appleton City. Produced stereoviews.

BURNHAM'S GALLERY
Active in Hannibal, c. 1870.

BURNS, W. K.
Stereo photographer in St. Louis.

BUSHNELL, E. P.
Stereo photographer active in Springfield, Ohio, and Jefferson City, c. 1870.

CALOHAN, C. W.
Stereo photographer; partner with his brother, George, Eureka Springs, Arkansas, 1880s; in Hannibal, Missouri before 1879.

CASSILLY, C. W.
Operated a studio at 723 Franklin Avenue, St. Louis, c. 1885.

CASTOR BROTHERS
Active in Carthage, c. 1885.

CHOATE, W. W.
Stereo photographer in Holden.

CITY ART GALLERY
Studio in Lexington.

CONSAUL BROTHERS
Active in Lamar, c. 1880, operating the New Gallery at Northeast Main Street.

COOPER, B. S.
Active in Arrow Rock, Saline County, c. 1875; also active in Waverly, producing stereoviews. Active in California, Missouri, c. 1885.

COREY, A. S.
Active in Clinton, 1867.

CORNELIUS, S. C.
Stereo photographer; operated the Sun Gallery on the square in Columbia.

COTTON, J. G.
Traveling stereo photographer based in St. Louis.

COTTRELL, D. E.
Operated the Picture Gallery at Cameron, c. 1862.

CRAMER, G.
Active in Carondelet, c. 1864; 1001 South Fifth Street, corner of Chouteau, St. Louis, c. 1880.

CRAMER, GROSS & COMPANY
Studio at 1200 and 1264 South Fifth Street, below French Market, St. Louis, c. 1875.

CREAGER, R. C.
Stereo photographer in Kansas City, 1909.

CREEL, W. R.
Amateur stereo photographer in Carrolton.

CROCKER & COMPANY
Produced stereoviews in St. Louis.

CROSBY, GEORGE L.
Active in Hannibal, c. 1864-75. Produced stereoviews.

CROWTHER BROTHERS
See New York Gallery.

DAVIESS
Active at Lee's Summit, c. 1885.

DAVIS
Operating the Cottage Gallery at Sixth and Charles Streets, St. Joseph, c. 1890. Possibly the same as O. A. Davis.

DAVIS, JAMES M.
Publisher of stereoviews and "General Agent" in St. Louis. Agent and distributor for Kilburn's views, starting c. 1890. May also have been photographer.

DAVIS, O. A.
Stereo photographer in St. Joseph.

DE HART
Active in Butler, c. 1890.

DEANE BROTHERS
Partnership of stereo photographers active in Kansas City.

DEERING, AMOS
Stereo photographer in Rolla.

DETWILER, O. W.
Active in Canton, c. 1880. Produced stereoviews.

DOPP, J. C.
Photograph and ambrotype artist, southwest corner of 4th and Poplar Streets; 97 Washington Avenue, St. Louis, c. 1864.

DOWNING, J. C.
Active in Warrensburg, 1870.

DUNCAN, W. A.
Stereo photographer active in Pierce City.

DUNLAP, W.
Active in Chillicothe, c. 1868. Produced stereoviews.

DUNN
Partner in Parsons & Dunn, stereo photographers in St. Louis.

DURANT, G. S.
Stereo photographer, active in Maryville, 1883.

DUVALL, J. H.
Operated the Art Gallery at 77 ½ Main Street, Lexington, 1870.

EAMES & ELLIOTT
Stereo photographers in St. Louis.

EDETTE DEUTSCHE BUCHHANDLUNG
German book store in St. Louis at 710 Franklin Avenue; sold views with their sticker or rubber-stamped with their imprint. Photographers unknown.

EASTERLY, THOMAS
Born in Guilford, Vermont, 1809; died in St. Louis, 1882. Daguerreotypist initially in Liberty; in St. Louis, 1847-82. Operated John E. Ostrander's gallery, 1848. Listed at times with Martin and Philomena Easterly. Photographed the Sauk and Fox Indians. Easterly was a brilliant artist who continued to daguerreotype scenes around St. Louis, long after the process had lost favor around the world.
    Dolores A. Kilgo, *Likeness and Landscape: Thomas M. Easterly and the Art of the Daguerreotype*, Missouri Historical Society Press, 1994.

ELITE STUDIO
Active in Trenton, 1890.

ELLIOTT
Partner in Eames & Elliott, stereo photographers in St. Louis.

EULASS, T. H.
Traveling photographer based in Joplin; produced stereoviews.

FAIRLEIGH, A. E.
Stereo photographer in Mexico, Missouri, c. 1885.

FARADAY, G. C.
"Travelling Photographer & Artist," active in Missouri.

FARRINGTON, GEORGE
Active in St. Louis, 1870.

FAULHABER, G. L.
Stereo photographer active in Sedalia.

FELLOWS & CRANDELL
Active in Glasgow, c. 1864.

FELLOWS, HOMER
Active in Carrollton, c. 1868.

FERGUSON
Operated the Cottage Gallery in Springfield, c. 1880; advertised solar printing for the trade.

FIDDLER, JAMES
"Artistic Photographer" in Joplin; produced stereoviews.

FIELDS, J. P.
Stereo photographer in Harrisonville.

FINDLAY, W. W.
Stereo photographer active in Kansas City.

FITZGIBBON, JOHN H.
Born in London, England, c. 1816; died 1882. Daguerreotype artist who opened studio in St. Louis, 1846. Gallery at northeast corner of 4th and Market Streets, St. Louis, 1848-52. Purchased the now missing Vance collection of outdoor Pacific Coast daguerreotypes from Jeremiah Gurney, 1853. Studios at 1 Fourth, 1854-59; 65 North 4th, 1860. Moved to Vicksburg, Mississippi, 1861; returned to St. Louis, 1866; established his studio at 116 North 4th, 1867-76. Published the *St. Louis Photographer*, 1877, and helped his wife, Mrs. J. H. Fitzgibbon, who operated a studio at 415 Franklin Street, 1878-79. See Fitzgibbon & Bourges in Texas.

FORNEY, S. P.
Active in Albany, 1890.

FOSTER, CHARLES E.
Parlor Gallery, Nevada, c. 1875.

FOX, A. J.
Studio at Fourth and Olive Streets, c. 1868; Ground Floor Gallery and Frame Store at 205 North Fifth Street, St. Louis, c. 1875.

FRANK
Partner in Beck & Frank, medical doctors who made stereoviews of plastic surgery techniques. See Beck & Frank.

FRAZER & SIMPSON
Active in St. Louis, c. 1880.

FRAZER (MRS.)
Stereo photographer active in St. Genevieve.

FRENCH'S STEREOSCOPIC VIEWS
Active in Kansas City.

FRIDEN, E. H.
Stereo photographer in Poplar Bluff.

FRITTS, C.
Active in Liberal, c. 1890.

FULTS
Partner in Rundle & Fults in Gallatin, 1880.

FURLONG & COMPANY
See New York Gallery.

GALWORTHY, M. M.
Operated Galworthy's Gallery in St. Louis; stereo photographer.

GARDNER, J. C.
Operating as the "Artist" at the Star Gallery in Brookfield, c. 1870.

GARDNER, R. G.
Active in Kansas City, 1885.

GAUSE, J. L.
First National Photograph Gallery, at the junction of Main and Delaware Streets, Kansas City, c. 1868.

GENELLI
Active in St. Louis.

GENELLI STUDIO
Gallery at 923 Olive Street, operated by the Hulbert Brothers, in St. Louis, 1885.

GIFFORD, BENJAMIN
Apprentice of William Latour in Sedalia; eventually became one of Oregon's outstanding landscape photographers, working out of The Dalles.

GILHOUSEN, W. H.
Artist active in Kahoka, c. 1875.

GLENDENNY, N.
Stereo photographer in Kansas City.

GODFREY, P.
Active in Fulton, c. 1875. Produced stereoviews.

GOEBEL, R.
Portrait and landscape photographer in St. Charles, c. 1856; produced "Stereoscopic Views of St. Charles & Vicinity," c. 1880.

GOODWIN, JAMES H.
Studio northwest of the Court House Square, Lineus, c. 1867.

GRAHAM, E. D.
Stereo photographer active in Mexico, Missouri. Operated Graham's City Gallery, c. 1863; Graham's Art Gallery, 1870.

GRAHAM, J. W.
Active in Trenton, 1890.

GRAHAM'S ART GALLERY
Operating at the southeast corner of the Public Square, Mexico, 1870.

GRAHAM'S CITY GALLERY
Studio at the southeast corner of the Square, Mexico, c. 1863.

GRANT, W. WALLACE
Studio at 215 North Fifth Street, St. Louis, c. 1880.

GREENE
Studio at 606 Olive Street, St. Louis, c. 1880. J. A. Andrews, operator.

GRILEY, T. R.
Stereo photographer in Wilcox.

GROSS
Partner in Cramer, Gross & Company, and Kramer & Gross, stereo photographers in St. Louis.

GUERIN, FRITZ W.
Studio at 906 North Sixth Street, St. Louis, c. 1880. Bought out by George A. McMillan.

GUILD, F. D.
Active in Lebanon, 1890.

GUIN & LANE
Studio at 35 and 37 Franklin Avenue, between 4th and 5th, St. Louis, c. 1864.

GULICK, THEO.
Traveling photographer based in Joplin; "Any Size Photo Made Anywhere."

HALL, GEORGE P.
Studio at 63 and 65 North Fourth Street, St. Louis, c. 1863.

HALLWIG & COMPANY
Studio at the northeast corner of Olive and 7th Streets, St. Louis, c. 1885.

HALLWIG, G. O.
Stereo photographer active in St. Louis.

HAMMER, L. F.
Stereo photographer in St. Louis.

HAMMERSLY, CHARLES V.
Stereo photographer from Aberdeen, Mississippi; studio at 520 Franklin Avenue, St. Louis, c. 1875.

HANSARD, J. W.
Active in Verona, c. 1880; also in Fayetteville, Arkansas; took railroad views.

HARDESTY & BROWN
Traveling landscape and portrait photographers based in St. Louis; made stereoviews of towns in Texas and Missouri, c. 1880s. Possibly Frank Hardesty.

HARDESTY & DEAN
Partnership of traveling photographers based in St. Louis; active in Texas and Missouri, c. 1880s; Frank Hardesty.

HARNWOOD
Stereo photographer active in Joplin.

HART, R.
Stereo photographer in Independence.

HARVEY, GEORGE H.
Active in Cameron, c. 1862.

HAYS, R. H.
Active in Kansas City.

HEAD, J. G.
Active in Mexico, 1890.

HEALD & STIFF
Successors to Troxell & Brother, west corner of Fourth and Locust Streets, c. 1865. Produced stereoviews.

HEMINGWAY'S ART GALLERY
Studio in Cameron, c. 1885.

HENRY, LEVI
Active in Trenton, 1890.

HESTON, W.
Stereo photographer in Carthage; made views of Indians at Quawpaw Mission and Oklahoma Modocs. Also known as Wat Heston.

HICKS, J. T.
Stereo photographer active in Liberty.

HOELKE & BENECKE
Partnership of H. Hoelke and Robert Beneke; studio at the northeast corner of 4th and Market Streets, St. Louis, c. 1862-80. Produced stereoviews.

HOLBRON, H.
Active in St. Louis, c. 1880s.

HOLSTEAD, J. D.
Photo artist, Atlanta, c. 1880.

HUFF SISTERS
Active in Stockton.

HUGHES, T. HARRY
Born in 1841. Active in Alabama, c. 1857. Successor to W. L. Troxel, southwest corner of Fourth and Locust, St. Louis, c. 1867; partner with Josephus Lakin. Also known as Henry Hughes.

HULBERT & BROTHERS
Active in St. Louis; proprietors of Genelli Studio, 1885.

HURR, J. F.
Photographer in Odessa, c. 1888; produced stereoviews, cartes-de-visite and cabinet cards.

HUTCHINGS
Active in St. Louis.

JACKSON, C.
Operated the Old Reliable Gallery, 105 North Main Street, Hannibal. Published his own stereoviews, and some credited to C. W. Calohan.

JAMES, T., JR.
Studio at 421 and 423 Franklin Avenue, near the corner of Fifth Street, St. Louis, c. 1870.

JEWETT
Active in Macon, c. 1870.

JOHNSON, W. S.
Portrait and landscape photographer in Springfield; partner in Bower, Bower & Johnson in Kansas City, 1870s-80s. Produced stereoviews.

JUDD, W. S.
Stereo photographer active in Carthage.

JULIAN, DR. J. J.
Amateur stereo photographer in Kansas City.

KAUT, JOHN
"Stereo and Art Photographer," 1105 Buchanan Street, St. Louis.

KENDIG & SON, C.
Active in Burlington Junction, 1885.

KENDIG, C.
Active in Burlington Junction, 1880.

KETCHUM, W. G.
Stereo photographer in LaGrange.

KINNAIRD, W. W.
Active in Potosi, c. 1870.

KIRKPATRICK
Active in Kansas City.

KLOTTER & SCHERER
Partnership active in Lexington, 1875. "Photograph Art Gallery" at 906 and 908 North 6th Street, St. Louis, c. 1880.

KOENIG
Partner in Boehl & Koenig, stereo photographers in St. Louis and Corondolet.

KRAMER & GROSS
Partnership active in St. Louis; produced stereoviews; probably Herman Gross.

LATOUR, IRA HINSDALE
Born in Sedalia, 1878; died in California, 1931. Son of William Latour; learned photography from his father. Operated a gallery in Joplin; married Ruth Arnold after meeting her during a portrait sitting. Represented the Aristo company in San Francisco, California, c. 1900; was a founding member of the Photographer's Association of California, 1903.

LATOUR, LIONEL L.
Son of William Latour; worked for him in Sedalia.

LATOUR, WILLIAM
Born in Eslingen, Germany, October 4, 1845; died in Columbus, Ohio, October 23, 1914. Began taking daguerreotypes, 1852, and may have been the youngest daguerreotype operator. At one time an actor with Edwin Booth. Photographer in Sedalia, 1866-84. Sons Lionel L. Latour and Ira Hinsdale Latour were also photographers. Had studios in Ohio and Kansas. Opened the first studio at the corner of Fourth and Ohio Streets after the Civil War; at 62 or 162 Main Street, 1875-84. Also at Newkirk Road, north side of Main Street, second door west of Ohio Street. Operated Latour's Photographic Gallery & Studio of Portrait Painting. One studio was near Scott Joplin's studio. Benjamin Gifford was an apprentice of Latour's and eventually became one of Oregon's outstanding landscape photographers, working out of The Dalles.

LATOUR'S PHOTOGRAPHIC GALLERY & STUDIO OF PORTRAIT PAINTING
Operated by William Latour in Sedalia, 1875-84. Located at 62 Main Street, opposite Smith's Hall, and at 162 Main Street.

LEFTWICH BROTHERS
Stereo photographers active in Carrollton.

LEONARD, P. F.
Studio at 60 Rollins Street, over Jewett's Singer Machine office, Macon, c. 1885.

LETTON'S ART STUDIO
Operating in Hannibal, c. 1885.

LINENSCHMIDT, H. E.
Active in Wellsville, c. 1885. Produced stereoviews.

LITTLE & SPRAGUE
Active in Pleasant Hill, c. 1875.

LOZO, ALEX
Studio at the corner of Fourth and Edmond Streets, Saint Joseph, c. 1885.

MACURDY, J. C.
Studio on Morgan Street, Boonville, c. 1880. Produced stereoviews.

MAITLAND
Active in Lexington.

MANSFIELD'S CITY GALLERY
Studio opposite the entrance to the Planter's House, St. Louis, c. 1868. Advertised "Facilite," two skylights and multiplying cameras.

MARKS, ELLSWORTH
Active in Clinton.

MARSTON, JAMES
New York Gallery, Chillicothe, c. 1870

MARTIN, C. L.
Gallery in Kansas City, c. 1863; Holden, c. 1885.

MARTIN CITY GALLERY
Operating in Carthage, c. 1895.

MARTLAND, T. C.
Active in Fulton, c. 1885, operating the Art Photography Gallery on Main Street.

MARTYR, C. J. J.
Operated a gallery at 591 and 593 Pine Street, Norborne, c. 1875.

McAHRON, C. O.
Studio one door north of Hall's Opera House, Golden City, c. 1880.

McCONNELL, G. H.
Studio at 62 North Fourth Street, St. Louis, c. 1860.

McFARLAND
Stereo photographer in Tarkio.

McGILLICUDY, V. T. M.
Photographer for Jenney's Black Hills expedition, based in St. Louis.

McLAUGHLIN, T. C.
Stereo photographer in Breckenridge.

McLELLAN
Stereo photographer in Joplin.

McMILLAN, GEORGE A.
Successor to Fitz W. Guerin, studio at 906 North Sixth Street, St. Louis, c. 1880.

MELCHERY, F. W.
Stereo photographer active in Ft. Joseph.

MERINE, WILLIAMS & THOMSON
Photographers and portrait painters, 612 Main Street, Kansas City, c. 1880. Carte-de-visite indicates Merine was cancelled out of partnership.

MERRITT, T. J.
Successor to T. L. Rivers, southeast corner of Fourth and Olive Streets, St. Louis, c. 1860.

MILLER & DANNENBERG
Studio at 25 South Fourth Street, St. Louis, c. 1862.

MITCHELL, T. L.
Stereo photographer active in St. Louis.

MITCHELL, WALTER
Studio at the corner of Second and Francis Streets, c. 1862.

MITCHELL'S GROUND FLOOR GALLERY
Located at the corner of Fifth and Edmond Streets, St. Joseph, c. 1880.

MOBERLY, L.
Studio at the northeast Public Square, Chillicothe, c. 1867.

MORRIS, J. H.
Active in Kirksville, c. 1870.

MOULTON, D. S.
Stereo photographer active in St. Louis.

MUNSON, J.
Stereo photographer in Joplin.

NEEDHAM
Active in Grant City, c. 1880.

NEW YORK ART COMPANY
Active in St. Joseph, 1890.

NEW YORK GALLERY
Studio at the north side of Market Square, St. Joseph, c. 1868. Owned by Furlong & Company, and succeeded by Crowther Brothers.

NICHOLS & BROTHER'S
Gallery at 60 North Fourth Street, St. Louis, c. 1864.

OSTELLO, J. K.
Stereo photographer in Carthage.

OUTLEY, J. J.
Began as a daguerreotypist, 1851; made rare stereo daguerreotypes and paper views; studio in St. Louis; partner in J. J. Outley & Bell. Palace of Art, 39 Fourth Street, opposite the Planter's House, St. Louis, c. 1862.

PARCELL
Active in Kirksville, c. 1880.

PARKINSON, L. D.
Stereo photographer in Kansas City, c. 1906.

PARSONS
Active in St. Louis.

PARSONS & DUNN
Stereo photographers active in St. Louis.

PAYNE, A. B.
Born in Iowa, 1867; died in Missouri, 1953. Chief staff photographer for Keystone View Company, 1897-1908; A. B. and O. E. Payne ran the St. Louis branch with other family members, 1899-1908. Operated studio in Branson and Webster Groves, c. 1908.

PECKHAM, G. E.
Stereo photographer in Trenton.

PERKINS, W. C.
Active in Washington, Pacific, St. Claire and Cuba, 1875.

PETERS
Active in Higginsville, c. 1885.

PHILLIPS
Stereo photographer active in Joplin.

PHILLIPS, J. H.
Studio at the corner of Third and Washington Streets, St. Louis, c. 1864.

PINE STREET GALLERY
Studio in Warrensburg, 1860.

PLOETZ, J.
Stereo photographer active in Kansas City.

POWERS
Active in Perryville, c. 1975.

PRICE & SOURS
Partnership in St. Joseph producing stereoviews.

PRICE, D. A.
Artistic photographer at the corner of 5th and Felix Street, St. Joseph, c. 1880.

PRITCHARD
Active in Louisana, c. 1875.

QUIN & LANE
Studio at 35 and 37 Franklin Avenue, Saint Louis, c. 1864.

RAGAN & WINANS
Operating at 514 Main Street, between 5th and 6th, Kansas City, 1862.

RAGAN'S PHOTOGRAPH ROOMS
Operating in Kansas City, c. 1885.

REA, W. J.
Grand Central Gallery, corner of Fourth and Edmond Streets, St. Joseph, c. 1880.

REUTCH & LADY, W. W.
Active in Warrensburg, 1870.

REYNOLDS, B. F.
Studio at the corner of Eleventh and Salisbury Streets, St. Louis, c. 1880.

RICE, T. J.
Stereo photographer active in Rockport.

RIDINGS, GEORGE T.
Active in Monroe City, c. 1880

RINO, AUGUST
"Photograph Art Gallery" at the northwest corner of 8th and Franklin Avenue, St. Louis, c. 1875. Produced stereoviews as A. Rino.

RIPPEL
Partner in Uhlman & Rippel, stereo photographers operating in St. Joseph.

RIVERS, T. L.
Studio at Southeast 4th and Olive Streets, St. Louis, c. 1862.

ROBERTSON, N. A.
Active in Trenton, c. 1870.

RODGERS, W. J.
Amateur stereo photographer, active in St. Louis; member of Stereoscopic Society, 1925.

ROGERS, CHARLES THOMAS
See Arizona.

ROSCH
Active in St. Louis.

ROSS, J. B.
Active in Linneus, c. 1868.

ROSS, P. F.
Active in Tipton, 1885.

ROSWALL, FRED. A.
Active in Macon, c. 1885.

ROTH
Partner in Setzer & Roth, active in St. Louis.

RUGG, D. B.
Studio on the west side of Pine Street, Rolla, c. 1875.

RUNDLE & FULTS
Active in Gallatin, 1880.

SAUNDERS' CITY ART GALLERY
Studio at 97 5 Main Street, opposite Courthouse, Lexington, 1870.

SAURMAN
Active in St. Joseph.

SCHLATER, P.
Stereo photographer active in Kansas City.

SCHNEIDT & DIPPEL
Partnership operating the Belle Studio in St. Louis.

SCHOLTEN, J. A.
Studio at 301 and 303 North 5th Street, corner of Olive, 1863; 82 North 4th Street, c. 1864; 273 South Fourth Street, corner of Convent, c. 1864; 920 and 922 Olive Street, corner of 10th Street, re-opened in 1879; corner of Fifth and Olive Streets, 1885, St. Louis.

SCHOO & CROUCH
Successor to J. A. Scholten, 273 South Fourth Street, corner of Convent, c. 1864, St. Louis.

SCHWARTZ & SON
Active in Kansas City.

SCOTFORD, J. H.
Stereo photographer in Kansas City.

SEIBERT, J. A.
Studio at 9 South Fifth Street, between Market and Walnut, St. Louis, c. 1875.

SETZER & ROTH
Active in St. Louis.

SHAFF
Active in Cameron, c. 1885.

SHANNON
Partner in Babbit & Shannon, stereo photographers active in Kansas City, 1870s-90s; also may have been partner with Ragan, c. 1870s.

SITTLER
Operated gallery in Springfield, producing stereoviews, c. 1880.

SHOCKLEY, J. R.
Studio on the west side of Main Street, Hannibal, c. 1862.

SIPPLE & THOMASON
Active in Mexico, 1890.

SMITH
Active in Trenton, 1890.

SOURS, R.
Active in St. Joseph, 1885.

SPEAKE
Active in St. Joseph.

STAFFORD, CHARLES
Active in Palmyra, c. 1875.

STARK, HENRY
Photographer from St. Louis, Missouri; traveled through Texas making photographs, 1895-96. A handmade book of his photographs was reprinted as *Views in Texas*.

STIFF
Partner in Heald & Stiff, stereo photographers active in St. Louis, c. 1865.

STONE, J. G.
Studio at 311 Felix Street, St. Joseph, c. 1885.

STOUT
Gallery in Unionville, c. 1875.

STOWE, E. G.
Stereo photographer in Fayette.

STRAUSS
Studio at 1245 Franklin Avenue, St. Louis, 1893.

SWAN & TAYLOR
Partnership active in Lamar; stereo photographers.

SWAN, CARTER G.
Active in Nevada.

SWEM, T. M.
Stereo photographer active in Macon.

TAINTER, G. W.
Stereo photographer in Linn.

TAYLOR
Partner in Swan & Taylor, stereo photographers in Lamar.

TAYLOR, A. E.
Active in Clinton, c. 1880.

TAYLOR, L.
Studio at the northeast corner of square, Carthage, c. 1870.

THOMAS, FRANK
Partner in Williams & Thomas, stereo photographers in Kansas City, 1875; possibly Frank Thomas. Active in Columbia.

THOMASON
Partner in Sipple & Thomason, active in Mexico, 1890.

THOMPSON
Operating at West Cherry Street in Nevada, c. 1890.

THOMPSON & COMPANY, D. P.
Photographers active in Kansas City, 1878-83; also issued views by M. B. Bower.

THOMPSON ARTS
Studio in Newhope, c. 1862.

THOMSON, D. P.
Active in Kansas City, 1895. Possibly Thompson.

THORNE, WILLIAM E.
Stereo photographer in Kansas City.

TILFORD, WILLIAM H.
Stereo photographer active in St. Louis.

TOBIAS
Active in Carondelet, c. 1870.

TOBIAS & COMPANY
Studios at 1264 and 1266 South Fifth Street, and 2 North Fourth Street, St. Louis, c. 1880.

TOMKINS, E. P.
Active in Holden, 1885. Also known as Tompkins.

TOMLINSON BROTHERS
Partnership active in Hannibal; stereo photographers.

TROXELL & BROTHER
Active in St. Louis, 1864.

TROXELL, W. L.
Gallery on the southwest corner of Fourth and Locust Streets, St. Louis, c. 1860.

TULL, GEORGE W.
Active in Kirksville, c. 1880.

TUSSEY, J. C.
Active in Clinton, north side square, c. 1880.

UHLMAN & RIPPEL
Stereo photographers in St. Joseph; R. Uhlman.

UHLMAN, RUDOLPH
Studio at 51 Edmond Street, St. Joseph, c. 1867; 225 Edmond Street, St. Joseph, c. 1885. Partner in Uhlman & Rippel. Perhaps also spelled Uhlmain.

URIE, A. T.
Studio at northeast corner of 4th and Market Streets, St. Louis, c. 1868.

VAN BUSKIRK, H.
Active in Savannah.

WADELL, A. J. V.
Active in Warrensburg, 1865-85.

WALKER ART COMPANY
Active in Joplin.

WARNKY, F. C.
Active in Independence.

WELLS
Studio on Vine Street, c. 1875.

WHEN
Located at 1631 Franklin Avenue, St. Louis, c. 1890. Awarded 1st Premium award at St. Louis County Fair, 1888. Imprint is overprinted on mount of H. Holborn.

WICKISER, S. H.
Active in North Springfield.

WILKINSON, J. W.
Stereo photographer active in Ironton.

WILLIAMS & CORNWELL
Studio at 60 North 4th Street, St. Louis, c. 1862.

WILLIAMS & THOMPSON
Studio in Kansas City, 1875. Also spelled Thomson.

WILLIAMS, F. L.
Studio at 104 Main Street, Sedalia, c. 1880.

WINTER, F.
Stereo photographer active in Kansas City.

WISE, E. W.
Rooms over Buchanan & Blair's on Main Street, Hannibal, c. 1868. Operator and retoucher at Wise's Art Gallery at North Main Street, Cape Girardeau, c. 1885.

WOLFROM & EMERY
Studio at 215 North Fifth Street, St. Louis, c. 1880.

WOOD, A. W.
Studio at the corner of Fourth and Market Streets, St. Louis, c. 1868-70.

WRIGHT & COMPANY, C. H.
Studio at 215 North Fifth Street, St. Louis, 1875.

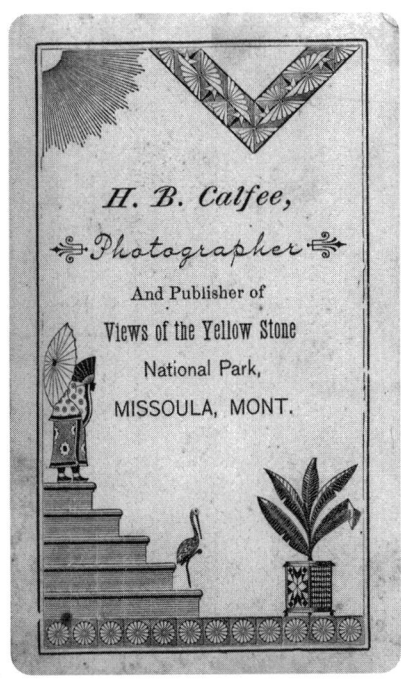

ALLISON, J. L.
Active in Missoula, 1875.

AYRES
Partner in Beal & Ayres, stereo photographers in Big Timber.

BALL & SON, J. P.
Operated a gallery on Broadway opposite the U. S Assay Office in Helena, c. 1885. Later the firm operated two studios in Helena, one on Main Street, near 6th Avenue and the other on Helena Avenue, opposite Turner Hall; advertised their studios were located at the "Sign of Red Ball." Is this the Ball who is famous as the black daguerreotypist in Cincinnati, Ohio?

BARKER, G.V.
Active in Glendive.

BARRY, D. F.
One of America's most prolific and finest photographers of Native Americans, operating from Fort Custer, summer 1883. See Dakota.

BARTHELMESS, CHRISTIAN
Born in Klingenberg, Germany, 1854; died in Fort Keogh, April 10, 1906; came to the U.S., 1870s. Served in U.S. Army as bandsman/photographer at Ft. Apache, Arizona Territory, 1876-81. Photographer at Fort Wingate and Fort Bayard, New Mexico, 1881-87; operated as Barthlemess & Schofield at Fort Wingate. Later he moved to Fort Lewis, Colorado; moved to Fort Keogh, Montana and photographed the formation of Casey's scouts, 1888. Photographed the Northern Plains Indians (Cheyenne, Crow), and the Southwest

Indians (Apache, Hopi, Navaho, Zuni).
Maurice Frink with Christian Barthlemess, *Photographer on an Army Mule*, University of Oklahoma Press, 1965. Reprinted later.

BEAL & AYRES
Stereo photographers active in Big Timber.

BECKWITH & BOMEN
Partnership active in Helena, 1890.

BECKWITH, R. H.
Active in Helena, 1885; partner with Bomen, 1890.

BELVEAL, E. S.
Stereo photographer in Butte.

BENJAMIN, J. A.
Active in Livingston & Billings, 1885-1900.

BENNETT, J. J.
Stereo photographer active in Bozeman.

BERKIN, JOHN
Active in Boulder, 1890.

BOMEN
Partner in Beckwith & Bomen, Helena, 1890.

BRACY
Partner in Deland & Bracy, Great Falls, 1867.

BRENNAN, L. L. (MRS.)
Operated the Elite Studio, Butte, 1890.

BRENNAN, T. J.
Active in Butte.

BREWSTER & COMPANY, J. C.
Licensed in Helena, 1867.

BROADWAY GALLERY
Active in Helena.

BROWN, HENRY W.
Operated the Rocky Mountain Art Gallery in Glendale, 1879.

BUNDY & TRAIN
Gallery on Cutler Street near the head of Main Street, Helena, 1875.

BUNDY, O. C.
Operating in Montana, c. 1875-80.

CALFEE & CATLIN
Stereo photographers in Bozeman, c. 1880s; Henry Bird Calfee.

CALFEE, HENRY BIRD
Came to Montana, 1870; active in Bozeman. Produced early panoramic stereoview photos of Yellowstone, 1871, 1877, 1878, 1879. Conducted Yellowstone lectures with W. W. Wylie, 1881-82, and his photographs were published in Wylie's guidebook, *Yellowstone National Park,* or the *Great American Wonderland,* 1882. Active in Missoula, 1885. See Wyoming.

CAMERON, EVELYN JEPHSON
Born near Streatham, England, August 26, 1868; died in Fallon, December 26, 1928. Members of the English upper class, she and her husband and settled near Terry, a town between Miles City and Glendive, 1889. Cameron learned photography, 1894, and captured western life, landscapes and fauna of the plains of eastern Montana. With ranching unprofitable, Cameron began selling her services as a photographer in Terry, 1899, and later Fallon. She illustrated several magazine articles for *Country Life.*
    Donna M. Lucey, *Photographing Montana 1894-1928: The Life and Work of Evelyn Cameron,* Alfred A. Knopf, 1991.

CARPENTER, W. J.
Active in Philipsburg, 1890.

CARROLL, J. S.
Licensed in Bannack, 1865.

CARTER, A. C.
Partner in Pickett & Carter, Virginia City, 1865; Operated the Montana Picture Gallery on Jackson Street, and advertised views of Virginia City, Great Salt Lake City, mountain scenery, mills, buildings and celebrities, 1866-68.

CASWELL, WILLIAM M.
Born in Vermont, 1843. Partner in Caswell & Davy, Duluth, 1870s. Listed in Billings, 1880. Photographed Ojibwa Indians.

CATLIN
Partner in Calfee & Catlin in Bozeman, c. 1880s.

CITY PHOTOGRAPH GALLERY
Operating in Helena.

COMFORT, E. W.
Operated the Imperial Gallery, Butte, 1895.

CRISSMAN, J.
Active in Bozeman; photographed Yellowstone National Park. Chief photographer for Barlow/Heap expedition of army engineers, summer, 1871 (coincided with Hayden expedition). Knew Jackson prior to that time; made his darkroom available to Jackson in Utah; Jackson loaned him a camera in Yellowtone, 1871. Also may have been in Ogden, Utah.

DELAND & BRACY
Active in Great Falls, 1867.

DOUGLAS, M.
Stereo photographer active in Helena.

DUSSEAU, A. J.
Studio over the Post Office, Butte City, Montana Territory, c. 1880; at the corner of Main and Granite Streets, opposite Centennial Hotel, Butte, 1880-1900.

DUTRO & REED
Partnership of Daniel Dutro and Roland Reed in Havre, 1880s-97.

DUTRO, DANIEL
Born in Missouri, c. 1850; died in Montana, 1918. Served as a drummer boy in the Union Army, and later was a vigilante opposing Quantrill's Raiders in Missouri. He took up photography and painting at Fort Benton, Montana, and later at Havre; Roland Reed served as his apprentice and later partner, 1880s-97.
    Ralph W. Andrews, *Picture Gallery Pioneers,* Superior Publishing, 1964.

ECKERT, M. A.
Studio in Helena, c. 1880.

ECKERT, M. A. (MRS.)
Stereo photographer operating studios in Virginia City and Helena.

EITNER
Partner in Walender & Eitner, Philipsburg and Granite, c. 1885.

ELITE STUDIO
Active in Great Falls, 1895.

ELLIOTT
Partner in Harves & Elliott, Anaconda, 1875. Studio on the Gans and Klein Block, Main Street, Butte City, Montana Territory, 1900.

FINN, C. E.
Active in Livingston, 1890.

FORSYTH, N. A.
Active in Butte, c. 1890-1910. Known for his friendship with cowboy painter Charles Russell, Forsyth issued a broad range of fine stereoviews and postcards depicting buffalo, Blackfeet Indians, mining and Montana towns.

FOUCH, JOHN H.
Studio at Contonment Tongue River (later Fort Keogh), 1877; photographed Chief Joseph after his surrender and imprisonment there. First to photograph the Custer battlefield at Little Big Horn and Curley, Custer's Crow scout. Issued a stereoview series of Yellowstone country, now rare. His studio was taken over by S. J. Morrow, 1878, then by L. A. Huffman. Fouch maintained studios in Minnesota before and after his stay at Fort Keogh.
    James S. Brust, M.D., "John H. Fouch, First Post Photographer at Fort Keogh," *Montana, the Magazine of Western History,* Spring 1994.

GEM STUDIO
Active in Butte, 1890.

GENELLI
Active in Great Falls, 1890.

GOFF, ORLANDO SCOTT
Studio at Ft. Custer where he took the famous portrait of Chief Joseph after Joseph's surrender, 1877. The portrait was also printed by and credited to both Haynes and Barry. See Dakota.

GRAHAM
Active in Great Falls, 1890.

HAMILTON, S. C. R.
Operated studio in Bozeman, c. 1890-95.

HARVES & ELLIOTT
Active in Anaconda, 1875.

HAUPT
Operated the New York Photographic Gallery opposite Grand Opera House on Broadway, Butte City, 1890; Lewis Jones, Manager.

HAWES, W. S.
Active in Anaconda, Granite and Philipsburg, 1895.

HAYNES, F. JAY
See Minnesota.

HAZELTINE, LELAND S.
Post photographer in Fort Assinaboine, 1880; at 433 South Arizona, Butte City, 1900.

HONGELL, A.
Active in Red Lodge, 1895.

HOUGH
Active in Livingstone, 1887.

HOWER, ATLIN B.
Partner in Rice & Hower, Deer Lodge, 1890; active in Philipsburg, 1895. Advertised "Cut Rate Cabinets" on the face of his photo mounts. See Idaho and Oregon.

HUFFMAN, LATON A.
Born in Iowa, 1854; died in Billings, 1931. An understudy of F. Jay Haynes; replaced S. J. Morrow as post photographer at Fort Keogh, 1878, two years after Little Big Horn. He opened a studio at Miles City, 1880, and photographed the Indians, cowboys, buffalo herds and northern plains life. Huffman moved to Chicago, 1890; returned to open studios in Billings and Miles City, 1896. He closed his last studio,1905, but continued to publish from his negatives. Formats include cabinet cards, stereoviews, postcards, and prints in albumen, platinum, silver and collotype.
>   Mark H. Brown and W. R. Felton, *Before Barbed Wire: L. A. Huffman, Photographer on Horseback*, Bramwell House, 1956.
>   Mark H. Brown and W. R. Felton, *The Frontier Years*, Bramwell House, 1955.

HUNTER
Active in Butte, 1895.

INGLIS
Active in Kalispell, c. 1895.

JACKSON
Studio at 61 West Park, Butte, 1900.

JONES, D. L.
Operated the Elite, Missoula, 1885.

JONES, LEWIS
Manager of the New York Photographic Gallery, Butte City, 1890.

KAHN, LEO
Active in Livingstone, 1880.

KELLER'S STUDIO
Active in Helena, 1895.

KELLY & McDONOUGH
Studio billed as the San Francisco Gallery on Galen's Block, Main Street, Helena, c. 1890.

KINSEY, DARIUS
Made stereoviews of Yellowstone, 1904. See Washington.

LAURENS
Active in Billings, c. 1900.

LAURENS, A.
Operated Par Street Gallery in Livingstone, 1890.

LAWSON
Active in White Sulphur Springs and Billings, c. 1890.

LE MUNYON, C. E.
Operated a gallery at 13 Park Drive, Great Falls, c. 1890. Photographer for the Great Northern Railway; advertised views of scenes in Montana, Washington and Idaho.

LORD, HERBERT W.
Made rare stereoviews, some of Canadian lynx in the forest. Active in Darby; probably an amateur.

LOWRY, HOWARD J.
Studio in rooms 28-29, 35-36, Pittsburg Block, Helena, c. 1885.

MACKEY, M. C.
Licensed in Nevada City, 1865.

MADISON, M.
Active in Butte, 1900.

MARSH, D.
Photographed and published stereoviews, some of Yellowstone National Park. Active in Bozeman.

McDONOUGH
Partner in Kelly & McDonough, operating the San Francisco Gallery on Galen's Block, Main Street, Helena, c. 1890.

McINTYRE
Active in Red Lodge, 1890.

MILLER, FRED
Born in Chicago, 1868; died in Hardin, 1936. Miller learned photography in Bloomfield, Iowa, and operated studios in Nebraska and Iowa. In 1898, he became assistant clerk at the Crow Reservation, photographing residents and entertaining artists Joseph Sharpe, Edgar Paxson and Frederic Remington. Adopted into Crow Nation.
>   Nancy Fields O'Connor, *Fred E. Miller, Photographer of The Crows*, University of Montana Press, 1985.

MONTANA VIEW COMPANY
Produced "Views in and near Helena."

MORRIS, CHARLES E.
Active in Chinook.

MORROW, STANLEY J.
Morrow made frequent trips into Montana to photograph Native Americans, and eventually took over Goff's studio, 1878. See Dakota.

NESBITT
Partner in Rutter & Nesbitt in Glendale, c. 1870s.

OSBON
Produced stereoviews of the construction of the railway's Mullen Tunnel, c. 1870s.

PANSY STUDIO
Operated in Kalispell, c. 1895.

PAR STREET GALLERY
Operated by A. Laurens in Livingstone, 1890.

PETZOLDT, W. A.
Minister and photographer in Montana, 1890-1910.

PICKETT & CARTER
Licensed in Virginia City, 1865.

PICKETT, J. M.
Licensed in Virginia City, 1868.

PILLINER
Active in Dillon.

POTTER, G. W.
Active in Livingstone 1900.

REED, ROLAND
Born in Fox River Valley, Wisconsin, 1864; died 1934. Apprenticed to Daniel Dutro at his studio in Havre, where he began a long career photographing Native Americans. Reed published many photographs in association with the Great Northern Railroad. He opened a studio at Bemidji, Minnesota, 1890, and also operated studios in Fort Benton, Montana, and Ortonville, Minnesota. Reed photographed the Alaska Gold Rush, 1897. In 1907, with aspirations similar to Edward S. Curtis, Reed launched a study of Indian peoples but did not achieve the scale or pictorial accomplishment of Curtis.

RICE & HOWER
Active in Deer Lodge, 1890.

RICE & KOEHLER
Active in Great Falls, 1889.

RUSSELL & VAUGHN
Licensed in Virginia City, 1864; C. Vaughn and George Russell.

RUSSELL, GEORGE
Partner in Russell & Vaughn, Virginia City, 1864; licensed in Virginia City, 1865.

RUTTER & NESBITT
Stereo photographers in Glendale, c. 1870s; Thomas H. Rutter.

RUTTER, THOMAS H.
Portrait and landscape photographer, center of Main and Broadway, Butte City, 1885-90.

SCHLECHTEN BROTHERS
Stereo photographers in Bozeman, c. early 1890s. Made views of soldiers of the late Indian Wars, dressed in cavalry uniforms.

SHIPLER, JAMES WILLIAM
Active in Great Falls, 1889. See Utah and Colorado.

SKAGE, C.
Studio in the Johnson Building, 323 West Superior Street, Duluth, c. 1895.

SUN PEARL GALLERY
Active in Deer Lodge City, 1870.

SUNBEAM GALLERY & STUDIO
Studio on the Galen Block, Main Street, Helena, 1890. Awarded two first premium prizes at the 1885 Territorial Fair.

TAYLOR, H. W.
Active in Helena, 1895.

THE ELITE
Studio of D. E. Jones, Missoula, 1885.

THRASHER, A. F.
Active in southwestern Montana, c. 1867-68. Operated the Sun Pearl Gallery in Deer Lodge, Montana, 1868-69; worked as "Daguerrian Artist" in Bannock, c. 1870; itinerant photographer, spring-October 1870; in Idaho Territory and Montana, summer 1870; in Deer Lodge, Montana, October 1870-January 1872; partner with William Hyde, c. March 1871; operated Montana Stereopticon, spring-July 1871. See Idaho and Traveling.

TRACIE, E. H.
Licensed at Deer Loop, 1867.

TRAIN, EDGAR H.
Born in Stockholm, St. Lawrence County, New York, January 1, 1831; died in Helena, Montana, June 10, 1899. Miner and photographer in California, 1852-63. Partner with W. J. Cromwell, operating as Train & Cromwell in Idaho City, Idaho, on Main between Wall and Commercial Streets, c. 1864-65; worked independently in Idaho City c. 1866. Active in Grizzly Gulch, Montana, 1866. He opened the first photo gallery in Helena with A. C. Bundy, c. 1867; toured Montana and Northwest, 1866-c. 1876. He eventually turned to other pursuits and purchased the Utah Assay Office, 1889.

TRIMBLE, R.
Licensed in Helena City, 1865.

VAUGHN
Operated the Palace in Great Falls, 1895.

VAUGHN, C.
Partner in Russell & Vaughn, Virginia City, 1864; licensed in Helena City, 1865.

WALANDER & BURKHART
Operated the Broadway Gallery in Butte, opposite the Grand Opera House, c. 1880.

WALENDER & EITNER
Active in Philipsburg and Granite, c. 1885.

WEENINK, HENRY D.
Active in Dillon, Montana, 1889-1903.

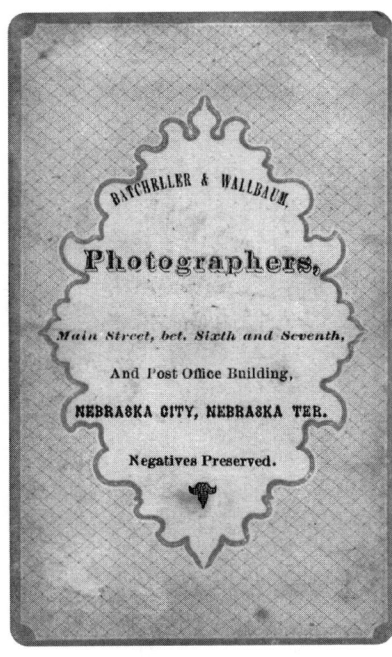

Much of the information contained in this section is based on research conducted by John Carter and the staff of the Nebraska Historical Society.

ABBOTT, WARREN D.
Studio in Peru, 1882-85; Brownsville, 1884-85; Auburn, 1886-87; Peru, 1888-93.

ACME VIEW COMPANY
Active in Lincoln and Omaha, c. 1870s, operated by J. M. Calhoun.

ADMIRE, C. A.
Studio in Cowles, 1886-87.

ADRIEN, J.
Gallery in Henderson, 1890-91.

AGNEW, E. W.
Studio in Sterling, 1884-85.

AHLMANN, W. C.
Studio in Norfolk, 1884-85.

ALBEE, E. S.
Active in Plainview, 1886-87.

ALEXANDER, A. D.
Active in Syracuse, 1884-85.

ALEXANDER, C. G.
Active in Scotia, 1886-87.

ALLEN
Partner in Hughes & Allen, active in Humboldt, 1894-95.

ALLEN, A. W.
Active in Omaha, 1884-85, at 903 24 Street North; 996 24 Street North, 1896; 1206 24 Street North, 1897-1900. Possibly Arthur W. Allen.

ALLEN, ARTHUR W.
Active in Ewing, 1888-89.

ALTINE
Partner in Shepard & Altine, active in Lincoln, 1899.

ALVORD
Partner in Hughes & Alvord, operating in Omaha, 1888-89, at 992 24 Street North.

AMERICAN VIEWING COMPANY
Studio in Omaha, 1891, operated by Morledge.

AMERMON, ADA (MRS.)
Active in Weeping Water, 1884-85.

AMES, W. P.
Active in Fairmont, 1894-95.

ANDERSON, A. E.
Active in Beatrice, 1900-01, at 418 Court.

ANDERSON, A. T.
Active in Kearney, 1888-95; studio at 1808 Central Avenue.

ANDERSON BROTHERS
Studio in Plainview, 1884-85.

ANDERSON, C.
Active in Valentine, 1886-87.

ANDERSON, C. J.
Active in Stromsburg, 1884-85, 1890-93.

ANDERSON, E. C.
Active in Gothenburg, 1893; Hildreth, 1894-95.

ANDERSON, J. H.
Active in Valpariaso, 1884-85.

ANDERSON, JOHN A.
Active in Ft. Niobrara and Valentine, 1885-93.

ANDERSON, N. J.
Active in Wahoo, 1880-93.

ANDERSON PHOTOGRAPHIC COMPANY
Produced stereoviews in Miller.

ANDERSON, W. F.
Active in Loup City and Arcadia, 1893.

ANDRESEN, J. M.
Active in Wilber, 1884-85; 1893.

ANDREWS, GEORGE
Active in Brownsville, 1888-89.

ANDREWS, HOWARD L.
Active in Lincoln, 1884-1900, at 1034 O Street.

ANGELL, JAMES
Active in David City, 1888-89.

ARMSTEAD & SON
Active in Wahoo and North Bend, 1884-85; South Bend, 1886-88; North Bend, 1888-95. Also listed as G. W. Armstead & Son, and G. W. Armstrong & Son, 1888-89.

ASHER, J. W.
Active in Wakefield, 1886-87.

ASHLEY, A. O.
Active in Weeping Water, 1886-87.

AUSTIN, D.
Active in Ewing, 1890-91.

AUSTIN, DANIEL
Active in O'Neil, 1893.

AYERS
Partner in Smith & Ayers, active in Odell, 1886-87.

BACKUS, E.
Active in Shelby, 1886-87.

BACON
Partner in Lowell & Bacon, active in Wymore, 1886-87.

BAILLIE, W. L.
Active in Seward, 1893; Beatrice, 1894-95.

BAILOR, J. M.
Active in Culbertson, 1886-93; studio on Taylor Avenue, 1886. Also listed as G. M.

BAKER, C. O.
Active in Sidney, 1893.

BALDRY, A. S.
Active in Sidney, 1886-87.

BANGS, HENRY
Operated Bangs Studio in Broken Bow, 1893-95. Also known as Harry.

BANKS
Partner in Erskine & Banks, active in Lincoln, 1888-89.

BANNING, GARNETT (MRS.)
Active in Rising City, 1888-89.

BARBE, C. L.
Active in Talmage, 1886-87.

BARBER, ANDY
Active in Indianola, 1886-87, on Fourth Avenue. Produced stereoviews.

BARLING, M. (MRS.)
Active in Gordon, 1886-87.

BARRETT & HART
Active in Sidney, 1886-87.

BARRETT, A. E.
Active in Plattsmouth, 1884-85.

BATCHELLER & WALLBAUM
Partnership operating in Nebraska City, Nebraska Territory, 1862.

BATES (MISS)
Partner in Bates & Hawley, Harvard, 1879-80.

BATES & HAWLEY
Harvard, 1879-80. Also listed as Misses Bates & Hawley.

BAUMAN
Partner in Fitzsimmons & Bauman, active in Crawford, 1893.

BAUMANN, G. J.
Studio in Grand Island, 1898, at 117 3 Street West.

BAUMANN, H.
Active in Rushville, 1888-89.

BEARD & BROTHER, T. J.
Omaha, 1886-87.

BECKMAN & KNAPP
Partnership in Hastings, 1890-91.

BEDELL, S. W.
Active in Alma, 1888-91.

BEEHIVE GALLERY
Operated in Omaha. Managed by Daniel S. Mitchell, 1879-84, at 211 and 213 16 Street North. Operated by Howard E. Gray in Omaha, 1886-89, at 213 16 Street North. Also listed as Bee Hive Studio.

BELL, L. C.
Active in Madison, 1884-85.

BELL, T. C.
Active in Madison, 1893; in Fremont, 1898, at 145 6 Street East.

BENNETT & LIEBENDORFER
Partnership in Pawnee City, 1893.

BENNETT & SMITH
Partnership active in Pawnee City, 1884-85.

BENNETT, C. E.
Active in Pawnee City, 1890-91.

BENSON, LEROY
Active in Rushville, 1893.

BENSON, NELS
Active in Omaha, 1900, at 508 10 Street South.

BENTLEY, F. M.
Active in Pender, 1884-85.

BENTLEY, F. N.
Active in Coleridge, c. 1895.

BENTON, H. M.
Active in Milford, 1890-91.

BERNHARDT, JACOB
Active in Chadron, 1888-89.

BIDDLE, JOHN
Active in Silver Creek, 1886-87.

BIERSTADT, ALBERT
Active in Ft. Laramie, 1859, and with the Simpson Expedition.
Famous Hudson River School painter renowned for his monumental
western landscapes.

BILES, C. W.
Active in Fairfield, 1888-91.

BINGHAM, FRED D.
Studio at 1612 Farnam, Omaha, 1893. Also listed as F. V.

BISHOFF, C. S.
Active in Wymore, 1886-87.

BISHOP BROTHERS
Partnership in Riverton and Republican City, 1884-85; Alma and
Bloomington, 1894-95.

BISHOP, C. D.
Active in Elwood, 1886-87; Plum Creek, 1888-89; Elwood, 1893.

BISHOP, F. L.
Active in Sutton, 1884-85.

BLACK, ANDREW
Active in Oakdale, 1879-80.

BLACKWOOD, L. D.
Studio in Omaha, 1897, at 1446 13 Street South.

BLACO, ALBERT
Active in Fairbury, 1890-95

BLAIR, L. G.
Active in South Omaha, 1888-89; Ainsworth, 1890-91.

BLAKER, A. M. (MRS.)
Active in Tekamah, 1879-80.

BLAKESLY, H. H.
Active in North Platte, c. 1880. Produced stereoviews.

BLANCHARD, F. A.
Active in Omaha, 1893, at 311 16 Street North.

BLATTER, J. A.
Studio in Nebraska, 1870, at 300 Main.

BLOOM, F. O.
Active in Valentine, 1893.

BON TON ART GALLERY
Operated by partners Trager & Kuhn in Chadron, 1889-91.

BON TON STUDIO
Operating in Wahoo, c. 1890.

BOOTH, ALBERT
Active in Schuyler, 1893; Howell, 1894-95.

BOSTON RAIL ROAD PHOTO CAR
Stationed in Kearney.

BOUER, J. H.
Active in Wahoo, 1886-87.

BOVEE, W. L.
Active in Gibbon, 1886-87.

BOWEN, J. B.
Active in Ravenna, 1884-85.

BOWMAN
Active in Omaha, c. 1870.

BOWMAN, C. M.
Studio in Omaha, 1888-93, at 205 16 Street North.

BOWMAN, HUGHES & COMPANY
Operated in Omaha, 1889-93, 205 16 Street North; C. M. Bowman.

BRADBROOK, F.
Active in Red Cloud, 1888-93.

BRADLEY, W. A.
Traveling photographer located at 1108 Farnam Street, Omaha, c.
1890. See Traveling.

BRANDT, C. M.
Active in Steele City, 1882-83.

BREECE, E. E.
Active in Indianola, 1884-85.

BRENTON, H.
Active in Bennet, 1890-91.

BRIGGS, J. W.
Active in Friend, 1886-91.

BRINCKMAN BROTHERS
Partnership in Madison, 1886-87. Also spelled Brinckmann.

BRINCKMAN, P.
Active in Madison, 1886-91; partner in Brinckman Brothers, 1886-
87. Also spelled Brinkmann.

BRINER, L.
Active in Callaway, 1893.

BRISTOL, T. C.
Active in Hebron, 1879-80.

BRITTINGHAM, J. G.
Active in Lincoln, 1900, at 1222 O Street.

BROACH & HAMMEL
Partnership in North Platte, 1888-89.

BROACH, W. H.
Active in North Platte, 1884-93; partner in Broach & Hammell, 1888-89.

BROCKWAY, CHARLES T.
Studio in Lincoln, 1884-85; 1890-94. Located at 1026 O Street, 1891-92; Studio La Grande, Ground Floor, 124 12 Street South, 1893-94.

BROKAW, C. W.
Active in Blue Springs, 1884-85; Albion, 1886-87.

BROKAW, E. A.
Active in Albion, 1888-89.

BROWN & CHURCHILL
Partnership active in Hastings and St. Paul, 1882-83.

BROWN, G. W.
Active in Fairfield, 1886-87.

BROWN, H. F.
Active in Tekamah, 1888-91; Falls City, 1890-95; Gothenburg, 1894-95. Also listed as F. H.

BROWN, OSCAR
Active in Nemaha City, 1884-85.

BRUCKERT, G. G.
Active in Nelson, 1884-85.

BRUNO, L.
Active in Tekamah, 1884-85. Probably the same as L. Burno.

BRYNER, ISAAC
Active in Callaway, 1890-91.

BUCKRIDGE, J. J.
Active in Pierce, 1886-87.

BULKLEY, J. A.
Active in Red Cloud, 1888-89, 1893.

BUNN, BUDD
Active in Overton, 1886-87.

BURNHAM
Active in Nelson, 1875-85.

BURNO, L.
Active in Tekamah, 1882-83. Probably the same as L. Bruno.

BURRIDGE, CHARLES
Active in Falls City, 1893.

BURROWS, H. G.
Active in Weeping Water, 1893.

BUSSE, ROBERT
Active in Chadron, 1888-89.

BUTCHER, SOLMON D.
Active in Jefferson, 1884-85. Traveled through western Nebraska, specifically Custer County, during the late 19th century. Butcher created an extensive record of life on the Great Plains; photographed at Pine Ridge Agency, Dakota Territory, during Wounded Knee Massacre, 1891.

John E. Carter, *Solomon D. Butcher: Photographing the American Dream*, University of Nebraska Press, 1985; reprinted in 1995.

BUTLER, H.
Stereo photographer in Vermillion, at Main and Ravine Streets.

CAESAR & COMPANY, CHARLES
Gallery at 1521 Douglas Street, Omaha, 1887.

CALDWELL, W. T.
Active in Alliance, 1894-95.

CALHOUN, J. M.
Operated the Acme View Company in Lincoln and Omaha, c. 1870s.

CAMP, C. D.
Active in Geneva, 1882-85, 1888-95; listed as C. D. Camp & Company, 1882-83.

CAMP, G. A.
Active in Platte Center, 1888-89.

CAMPBELL, A. R.
Active in Beatrice; partner in Moody & Campbell, 1884-85; listed alone, 1886-89; located at 405 Court, 1886-88.

CAMPBELL, W. H.
Stereo photographer active in Clarks.

CANNELL, M. J.
Active in Omaha, 1886, at 1109 Farnam Street.

CAR, H. S. (MRS.)
Active in Wymore, 1890-91.

CARBUTT, JOHN
Prolific Chicago photographer who served as official photographer with Union Pacific Railroad survey, 1866, and produced stereoviews of scenes along the route.

CARLSON, T. A.
Active in Holdredge, 1894-96.

CARLSON, THOMAS
Active in Bertrand; partner in Pattison & Carlson, 1888-89; listed alone, 1893.

CARMAN, S. O.
Active in Chester, 1884-85; Beaver City, 1888-89.

CARMAN, S. P.
Active in Belvidere, 1879-80.

CARMON
Operated the Sunbeam Gallery in Hastings, c. 1895.

CARNAHAM, G. E.
Active in Fairbury, 1880, 1886-87; gallery at north side of Park, c. 1880.

CARPENTER, S. O.
Active in Axtell, 1894-95.

CARR, H. S. (MRS.)
Active in Wymore, 1888-89.

CARRUTH, F.
Active in Plattsmouth, 1879-85.

CARSON, C.
Active in Gothenburg, 1886-87.

CARTER, WILLIS
Active in Peru, 1886-87.

CARY, C. L.
Stereo photographer in Plattsmouth.

CASE, F. R.
Studio in Beatrice, 1882-93. Located at 400B Court Street, 1886-87; 122 4 Street South, 1888.

CASE, S. G.
Active in Syracuse, 1886-87.

CASTEEL, MILTON
Active in Ravenna, 1893.

CATHEY, WILLIAM M.
Active in Hastings, 1884-87.

CATTERLIN, D. W.
Active in Peru, 1890-91.

CENTRAL PHOTOGRAPH GALLERY
Located in Omaha, c. 1875-90. Also listed as Central Photograph Company.

CENTRAL PORTRAIT STUDIO
Active in Nebraska City, 1870-85.

CHAMBERS, ARTHUR
Active in Seward, 1886-87.

CHAPMAN & ROLOSON
Studio in Hamilton, 1879-80.

CHAPMAN, A.
Stereo photographer active in Omaha.

CHAPMAN, J. P.
Active in Aurora, 1884-87; partner in Leon & Chapman, 1886-87.

CHASE, F. R.
Stereo photographer; partner in Young & Chase with V. H. Young in Lincoln.

CHENOWETH, D. W.
Active in Kearney, 1884-89.

CHICAGO PHOTO AND VIEW COMPANY
Operated in Lincoln, 1892, 1034 O Street. Listed as Chicago Gallery, 1893.

CHOICEN
Active in Omaha, c. 1890.

CHOICENER, J. F.
Active in Omaha, 1890-91.

CHRISTENSEN, H. P.
Active in St. Paul, 1884-85; Grand Island, 1894-95.

CHRISTIANSEN
Partner in Moore & Christiansen, active in Sydney, 1886-87.

CHURCHILL & COMPANY
Studio in Fremont, 1894-95.

CHURCHILL, GEORGE O.
Studio in Hastings, 1880-95; partner in Brown & Churchill, 1882-83; located at 720 ½ 2 Street, 1893.

CITY PICTURE ROOMS
Operated by A. M. Smith in Nebraska City, c. 1866.

CLARK & HEYDE
Active in Omaha, 1870-80.

CLARK, A. M.
Active in Omaha, 1886-87.

CLARK, C. C.
Active in Seward, 1886-87.

CLARK, C. E.
Active in Osceola and Shelby, 1884-85; Holdrege, 1888-93; Stromsburg, c. 1900.

CLARK, D. G.
Active in York, 1882-85; partner with L. F. Kennedy, operating as Kennedy & Clark in York, 1882-83. Also listed as Mr. & Mrs. D. G. Clark.

CLARK, D. G. (MRS.)
Active in York, c. 1885, listed as Mr. & Mrs. D. G. Clark.

CLARK, WILLIAM F.
Active in Omaha, 1886-87.

CLARK'S FINE ART STUDIO
Active in Lincoln, c. 1880.

CLAYTON & PROVINS
Operating in Ord, 1886-87.

CLEMENTS, E. G.
Studio in Lincoln, 1879-1900; located at 129 11 Street South, 1891-1900; branch studio in Wahoo, 1888-93.

CLINE, D. A.
Active in Nebraska City, 1870; Lincoln, 1879-80.

CLINKENBEARD, W. H.
Active in Lincoln, 1893; Auburn, 1894-95.

CODY, J. H.
Active in St. Edward, 1884-85; Genoa, 1894-95.

COLGROVE, J. H. (MRS.)
Active in Madison, 1884-85.

COLLINGS, H. A.
Studio in Lincoln, 1891, at 1029 O Street.

CONKLIN & SAVITZKY
Located in Omaha at the Granite Block, 1893; and 213 16 Street North, 1896.

CONKLING, O. C.
Studio in Omaha, 1892, at 1406 Farnam.

COOK, A. A.
Active in Shelby, 1886-87.

COOPER & DENISON
Studio in Beatrice, 1879-80.

CORBETT, ALVIN H.
Active in O'Neill, 1884-85, 1888-93.

CORWIN, C. W.
Active in Guide Rock, 1884-85.

COSMOPOLITAN VIEW COMPANY
Studio at 141 12 Street South, Lincoln, 1893.

COTTAGE PHOTO STUDIO
Active in Omaha, c. 1890.

COTTON
Partner in Lear & Cotton, operating in Omaha, c. 1890.

COUPER, G. R.
Active in Blue Springs, 1888-91.

COWAN, H.
Studio at 2121 Cuming, Omaha, 1892-93. Also listed as Cowing.

COWLES
Partner in Gulwits & Cowles, active in Sutton, 1879-80.

COWLES, A.
Active in Peru, 1879-80.

COX, H. D.
Active in Plum Creek, 1886-87.

COYLE, J. H.
Active in Lanham, 1890-91.

CRABTREE, ISAAC
Active in Stella, 1890-91.

CRAIG, EULIUS B.
Active in Greenwood, 1894-95.

CRANDELL, N. H.
Active in Gordon, 1894-95.

CRAVEN, C. M.
Active in Wayne, 1884-85.

CREAGER, JOHN P.
Active in Wisner, 1888-89.

CROLEY, W. A.
Active in Stuart, 1884-85.

CRONIN, DAN
Active in Sutton, 1886-87.

CROOKHAM, M. E.
Active in Osceola, 1882-83; Sutton, 1884-85; Republican City, 1888-89. Also spelled Crookhem.

CROSS, W. R.
Born in Vermont, c. 1843. Studio in Omaha at Caldwell Block, 1868; southwest corner of Dodge and 15th Street, 1870; in Niobrara, c. 1875-85; also in Norfolk; Meade, 1885-88. Active in Hot Springs, South Dakota. Photographed Plains Indians and life around Deadwood and other Black Hills mining areas. John A. Anderson apprenticed with Cross and bought his Nebraska studio, 1889.

CROW, FRANK W.
Studio in Nebraska City, 1898, at 810 Central Avenue.

CULVER, L. W.
Active in Fairbury, 1879-80.

CURD, J. C.
Studio in Omaha, 1887-89, at 1402 13 Street South.

CURRAN, A. B.
Active in O'Neill, 1886-87.

CURRIER & JARVIS
Partnership of Frank F. Currier and Jarvis, active in Omaha.

CURRIER, FRANK F.
Possibly associated with Julius Meyer, dealer in Indian artifacts in Omaha. Studios in Omaha at 232 Douglas St., 1872-73; 235 Douglas Street, 1874-76; 559 and 561 15th, corner of Dodge, 1878; 113 North 15th, 1879; 1316 Farnam, 1880; 1212 Farnam, 1883-85; 1720 St. Mary's Avenue, 1886. Photographed Plains Indians and published stereoviews. Also listed as F. E.

CURRY, D. W.
Studio in Nebraska City, 1884-85, 1888-93; at 720 Central, 1891-92.

CURTIS, W. F.
Active in Wood River, 1886-87; Nebraska City, 1890-91.

CURTIUS, K. E.
Active in Plainview, 1893.

CUTLER, W. E.
Active in Plattsmouth, 1888-89.

CUTTER, PLATTSMOUTH DAVIES
Active in Omaha, c. 1895.

DAHL & HALVORSEN
Partnership operating in Minden, 1884-85.

DARING, O. H.
Active in Grafton, 1879-80.

DATSMAN, P.
Active in Blue Springs, 1886-87.

DAVIDSON, T. M.
Active in Talmage, 1888-91.

DAVIES
Partner in Waldron & Davies, operating in Omaha, 1884-85.

DAVIES, JOHN
Studio in Omaha, 1896-98, at 113 16 Street South.

DAVIS
Partner in Marcellus & Davis, active in Weeping Water, 1888-89.

DAVIS
Partner in Ferrier & Davis, active in Fullerton, 1890-91.

DAVIS & GARRETT
Partnership in Franklin, 1893.

DAVIS, C. H.
Active in Franklin, 1888-91, 1894-95.

DAVIS, W. L.
Active in Craig, 1893.

DAY, E. M.
Active in North Platte, 1875-90; Ogallala, 1886-87.

DAY, E. M. (MRS.)
Active in North Platte, 1882-83; Ogallala, 1888-91.

DAY, M. A.
Active in North Platte, 1882-83.

DAY, S. C.
Active in Leigh, 1884-85.

DAY, T. J.
Active in Burwell, 1894-95.

DEEDS & ANDERSON
Partnership in Gothenburg, 1890-91.

DELANOY, J. A.
Active in Aurora, 1882-83; Ainsworth, 1884-87.

DEMMER, JOHN
Active in Creighton, 1880-95; Plainview, 1888-89. Also spelled Denner.

DENISON
Partner in Cooper & Denison, active in Beatrice, 1879-80.

DEPUY, I.
Active in Springfield, 1886-87.

DEVENDORF, J. C.
Located in Wahoo, 1886-87.

DICKINSON, W. F.
Operating in Red Cloud, 1884-85.

DIVIGHT, F. E.
Active in Fremont, dates unknown. Possibly a misspelling of F. E. Dwight.

DODGE, C. O.
Active in Niobrara, 1890-93.

DOLLARSHIDE
Partner in Pallett & Dollarshide, operating in Broken Bow, 1890-91.

DOLLINDS, J. S.
Active in Alexandria, 1879-80.

DON, HARRY H.
Active in Omaha, 1886-87.

DONAVAN, M. F.
Active in St. Paul, 1886-87.

DOUGHERTY
Partner in Macy & Dougherty, Norfolk, 1888-93.

DRAPER, EDGAR
Active in Central City, c. 1900.

DUHLING
Active in Fairfield, c. 1875-90; partner in Stayner & Duhling with John V. Stayner.

DUIS, B. R.
Active in Salem, 1890-91.

DUNCAN, MINNIE
Active in Wakefield, 1884-85.

DUNLAP, W. L.
Active in Tecumseh, 1879-83.

DWIGHT, D. W.
Active in Fremont, 1888-89.

DWIGHT, F. E.
Studio in South Sioux City, 1890-91; Fremont, 1898, at 625 Main Street North.

DYE, D. S.
Active in Chapman, 1890-91.

EADER, G. A.
Active in Pawnee City, 1886-87.

EASON BROTHERS
Stereo photographers in Chadron; possibly E. L. Eason.

EASON, E.
Active in Chadron, 1894-95.

EAST, THOMAS
Active in North Loup, 1884-93.

EASTMAN L. (MRS.)
Active in Rushville, 1888-89.

EASTON, W. J.
Active in Republican City, 1890-91.

EATON, E. L.. Operated as Eaton's Gallery of Art, Omaha, 1860-92, 1320 Farnam Street, 1886-92.

EBERSPACHER, FRED
Studio at 912 24 Street North, Omaha, 1897.

ECKER, J. T.
Active in Albion, 1882-85.

ECLIPSE STUDIO
Operating in Lincoln; 1222 O Street, 1892; 1216 O Street, 1893.

EDMONDS
Partner in Fisher & Edmonds, active in Pierce, 1886-87.

EDOFF, C. J.
Active in Mead, 1884-85; Ashland, 1893-95.

EIMERS, W.
Stereo photographer in Humphrey.

ELITE GALLERY
Operated in Lincoln.

ELITE STUDIO
Active in Omaha, 1884-85, 1893.

ELITE STUDIO
Operated by T. W. Townsend in Lincoln, 1898, 226 11 Street South.

ELLINGSON, M. A.
Active in Cambridge, 1894-95.

ELLIOTT, C. W.
Active in Omaha, 1886-87.

ELLIOTT, N.
Active in Omaha, 1886-87.

ELLIS, HOWARD
Operated in Pawnee, 1879-85.

ELLWANGER, H. S.
Operated in Rushville, 1884-85, 1893; Omaha, 1900, at 218 ½ 16 Street North.

ELROD, T. E.
Active in Pawnee City, 1886-87.

ELSFELDER, H. E.
Active in Pawnee City, 1886-87.

ELWOOD, SYLVANUS
Active in Anselmo, 1893.

EMERSON, E. O.
Studio in 1034 O Street, Lincoln City, 1891.

EMORY, H. S.
Operated in Omaha, 1884-85, 1893-1900. Located at 612 16 Street North, 1893-96; 213 16 Street North, 1897-1900.

ENGDALE, C. E.
Active in Oakland, 1884-85.

ENGLISH, HERMAN H.
Operated in Fremont, 1884-85. In Omaha, 1888-93; at 1402 13 Street South, southwest corner of 13th and Williams Streets, 1889-93.

ERSKINE & BANKS
Active in Lincoln, 1888-89.

ESMOER, L. P.
Studio at 1406 Farnam, Omaha, 1896.

EVANS, ELIAS
Active in Silver Creek, 1884-85.

EVERS, B. J.
Active in Omaha, 1886-87.

EWING
Partner in Pryse & Ewing, active in Hastings, c. 1875; Red Cloud, c. 1880.

EXCELSIOR PORTRAIT COMPANY
Studio in Omaha, 1893.

FABER, C. J.
Active in Auburn, 1893.

FABER, H. (MRS.)
Active in Blair, 1894-95.

FACKLER, G. R.
Active in Springfield, 1893.

FAULKNER, M.
Active in Seward, 1886-87.

FAXON, CHARLES
Active in Blue Springs, 1882-83.

FEARN, W. B.
Active in Haigler, 1893.

FERGUSON
Partner in Taylor & Ferguson, operating in Liberty, 1884-85.

FERGUSON, J. H.
Active in Talmage, 1884-85, 1890-93.

FERRIER & DAVIS
Active in Fullerton, 1890-91.

FIGLEY, J. M.
Active in Superior, 1884-85.

FIKE, GEORGE W.
Operated in Wilber, 1882-89; Tobias, 1884-85; Dewitt, 1888-89; Alexandria, Ohiowa, Tobias and Swanton, 1893.

FISHER & EDMONDS
Active in Pierce, 1886-87.

FISHER, C.
Active in Emerson, 1893.

FISHER, H. M.
Active in Gresham, 1894-95.

FISHER, J. J.
Active in Central City, 1870-80.

FISK, J. W.
Active in Syracuse, 1886-87.

FITCH, WILLIAM
Active in Miller, 1893.

FITZSIMMONS & BAUMAN
Active in Crawford, 1893.

FLEISHMAN & MALMQUIST
Studio at 1210 13 Street South, Omaha, 1891.

FLEMING, A. J.
Active in Exeter, 1882-83.

FLINT
Partner in Lewis & Flint, active in Western, 1890-91.

FLORENCE, C. W.
Active in Norfolk, 1882-85.

FLOWER, W. A.
Active in Weeping Water, 1884-85.

FLOWERDAY, G. R.
Studio at 501 2 Street, Hastings, 1898.

FORBES, JOHN
Active in Tecumseh, 1888-89.

FOSTER, H. W.
Active in Syracuse, c. 1885.

FOSTER, J. C.
Active in Pawnee City, 1884-85, 1888-89.

FRANKLIN & LESCHINSKY
Partnership in Harvard, 1880-90.

FRANKLYN, F. J.
Active in Fairbury, 1882-83.

FRARY, EMERY
Active in Pender, 1886-87.

FRAZIER, J. FRANK
Operated in Omaha; 1010 Jones, 1889; 1516 Capitol Avenue, 1893.

FRITZ & GOOD
Active in West Point, 1893; Fremont, 1894-95.

FRITZ, W. P.
Active in Scribner, 1884-85, 1890-93; listed in Fremont, 1898, at 331 Main Street North.

FROM & COMPANY
Active in Newman Grove, 1884-85, 1893.

FYOCK, D. E.
Operated in South Omaha, 1884-85; Omaha, at 218 ½ 16 Street North, 1896-97.

GAMER, LOUIS
Omaha, 1884-85, 1893; Council Bluffs, Iowa, 1895-96; Omaha, at 702 16 Street South, 1896-1900.

GARMON, C. M.
Studio at 505 2 Street, West Hastings, 1893.

GARRETT
Partner in Davis & Garrett, operating in Franklin, 1893.

GARRISON, W. E.
Active in Syracuse, 1884-85.

GIESE, FREDERICK
Active in Falls City, 1870-85.

GILBERT
Partner in Kilborn & Gilbert, active in Lincoln, 1894, at 1029 O Street.

GIVENS, W. D.
Active in Seward, 1882-93. Also listed as W. S.

GODKIN, W. R.
Active in Ainsworth, Long Pine and Ft. Niobrara area, 1884-85; Long Pine, 1886-87.

GOLDSMITH, M. A. (MRS.)
Active in Bingham, 1894-95.

GOOD
Partner in Fritz & Good, active in West Point, 1893; Fremont, 1894-95.

GOODRICH & LEWIS
Verdon, 1886-87.

GOSS, ALBERT
Active in North Auburn, 1884-91.

GOTTULA, L.
Active in Tecumseh, 1886-87.

GRABILL, J. C. H.
See Dakota.

GRAHAM, WALTER T.
Active in Gering, 1894-95.

GRAND CENTRAL GALLERY
Operated by Herman Heyn in Omaha, c. 1886-88, at 217 16 Street North.

GRANT, U. S.
Active in Lincoln, 1890-91.

GRAY, HOWARD E.
Active in Omaha, 1884-93; listed at 213 16 Street North, 1891-93. Operated the Bee Hive Studio, 1886-89, 213 16 Street North. Also listed as Beehive Gallery.

GREAT WESTERN PHOTO PUBLISHING COMPANY
Operating in Omaha, 1870-80.

GREENE, A. W.
Active in Sidney, 1888-89.

GREGORY, B. F.
Active in Fullerton, 1886-87.

GREGSTON, W. H.
Active in St. Paul, 1886-87.

GRIER, A.
Active in Brock, 1884-85.

GRIFFIN, C.
Active in Fremont, c. 1865.

GRIFFIN, WILLIAM
Active in Hebron, 1884-95.

GRIFFITH, J. W.
Active in David City, 1882-83.

GROVER & PATTON
Active in Bennet, 1884-85; F. A. Grover.

GROVER, F. A.
Active in Bennet, 1882-87; partner in Grover & Patton, 1884-85.

GULICK, E. L.
Active in Merna, 1893.

GULWITS & COWLES
Active in Sutton, 1879-80.

HAHN, A.
Active in Albion, 1890-93.

HAINES, O. P.
Active in Chadron, 1886-87.

HALL & COMPANY
Active in Lawrence, 1888-91.

HALL, C. I.
Active in McCook, 1884-85.

HALL, C. J.
Active in Ponca, 1879-80.

HALL, H. G.
Active in Schuyler, c. 1880, 1884-85; opposite Odd Fellows Block, in Broken Bow, c. 1890-95.

HALLIDAY, JOHN
Active in Seward, 1886-87.

HALLORAN, J. J.
Active in O'Neill, 1886-87.

HALVORSEN
Partner in Dahl & Halvorsen, active in Minden, 1884-85.

HAMANN, WILLIAM
Active in Stanton, 1886-87.

HAMEL, E. H.
Active in Lexington, 1890-93.

HAMILTON & TAYLOR
Active in Lyons, 1890-91.

HAMILTON, GRANT C.
Active in Ponca, 1884-85, 1888-91.

HAMILTON, J.
Studio in Omaha City, Nebraska Territory, early 1860s, upstairs in first building north of Post Office.

HAMMEL
Partner in Broach & Hammel, operating in North Platte, 1888-89.

HAMMOND, S. G.
Active in Hardy, 1884-85; Tobias, 1890-91.

HAMMOND, W. A.
Active in Randolph, 1884-85, 1893.

HANSEN, C.
Studio at 2113 Cuming, Omaha, 1897.

HANSON, H. P.
Photographer and ferrotyper, Omaha, 1879-80.

HARE, G. B.
Active in Syracuse, 1879-83.

HARMON, CHARLES
Active in Omaha, 1886-87.

HARMON, J.
Active in Arapahoe, 1890-91.

HARPER, P. PEARSON
Active in York, 1886-87.

HARRINGTON, J. H.
Active in Oakdale and O'Neill, 1884-85; Dubois, c. 1885.

HARRIS
Partner in Love & Harris, active in Danbury, 1894-95.

HARRIS, CHARLES H.
Active in Blair, 1875-91. Also listed as C. C.

HARRIS, H. (MRS.)
Active in Blair, 1893.

HARRIS, H. G.
Active in Arapahoe, 1890-91.

HART
Partner in Barrett & Hart, operating in Sydney, 1886-87.

HART, G. T.
Active in Blair, 1893.

HARTFORD, E. P
Active in Schuyler, 1882-83.

HARTSON, D.
Active in Omaha, 1886-87.

HARVEY, S. D.
Active in Shelton, 1888-89.

HAS, E. W.
Active in Schuyler, 1884-85.

HASSEBROCK, WILLIAM
Studio at 119 16 Street North, Omaha, 1900.

HATCH, H. M.
Active in Kearney, 1882-85.

HAWLEY (MISS)
Partner in Bates & Hawley, Harvard, 1879-80.

HAYDEN, A. F.
Active in Lincoln, c. 1888.

HAYDEN, J. A.
Operated in Lincoln, 1884-1900; 1214 O Street, 1892-96; 1029 O Street, 1897-1900.

HEBARD & SONS, E. A.
Studio at 1808 Cherry Street, Lincoln, 1892.

HEBARD, C. E.
Active in Table Rock, 1890-91; Lincoln, 300 11 Street South, 1891; 1343 O Street, 1900.

HEBARD, F. L.
Operated in Lincoln, 1884-85; 218 12 Street South, 1894.

HECKER, A. E.
Active in Hooper, 1894-95.

HEFFNER, H. C.
Active in Guide Rock, 1886-89.

HELMERICK, PHILIP
Active in Stanton, c. 1885; Stratton, 1888-89; Stanton, 1890-93.

HENDERSON, C. G.
Operated in York, 1884-85; St. Paul, 1888-91.

HENINGER, W. J.
Active in Elkhorn, 1894-95.

HENRY, J. W.
Active in Cedar Rapids, 1886-87.

HEWITT, H. A.
Active in Stromsburg, 1886-87.

HEYDE
Active in Omaha, 1870-85; partner in Clark & Heyde, 1870-80.

HEYN & COMPANY, S.
Omaha, 1893.

HEYN, G. (MRS.)
Operated in Omaha, 1884-85, 1893.

HEYN, GEORGE
"Heyn, The Photographer" active in Omaha, 1870-99. Studio on Granite Block, 1886; 313B 15 Street South, 1887; 315 15 Street South, 1888; 300B 15 Street South, 1889; 1312 Farnam, 1891; 300B 15 Street South, 1891; 315-317 15 Street South, 1892.

HEYN, HERMAN
Active in Omaha, 1884-93; operated the Grand Central Gallery, 217 16 Street North, 1886-88; 1406 Farnam, 1891-93.

HEYN PHOTO SUPPLY
One of the Heyns' many photo business interests in Omaha, 1893.

HEYN, S.
Omaha, 1890-91.

HEYN STUDIO
Omaha, 1898, 317 15 Street South.

HICKS, E. J.
Active in Table Rock, 1884-85; Falls City, c. 1885-89; Salem, 1893.

HILDRETH, G. K.
Active in Tekamah, 1886-87.

HILL, J. A.
Active in Steele City, 1890-91.

HILL, LEO
Studio at 206 13 Street North in Omaha, 1900.

HILL, M. V.
Active in Rising City, 1886-87.

HINE
Helped photograph the Union Pacific Railroad route, 1866.

HINES, W. B.
Operated in Kenesaw, 1884-85; Hastings, 1894-98; at 200B Lincoln Avenue, 1898.

HINMAN, L.
Active in Beatrice, 1882-83.

HOBART, C. M.
Active in Omaha, 1900, 1515 ½ Farnam.

HOBBS, I. C.
With Cooper & Denison in Beatrice, 1879-80.

HOBBS, I. N.
Stereo photographer from Washington; active in Crete, at 226 South 26th, c. 1890.

HODGES ART STUDIO COMPANY
Studio at 1222 O Street in Lincoln, 1898.

HOFFMASTER, H.
Active in Fremont, 1888-89.

HOFFMEISTER, EMIL
Operated in Fremont, 1882-95; 255 5 Street East, 1891-92.

HOLST, PETE
Active in Papillion, 1886-87.

HONEY, D. A.
Active in Inman, 1888-89.

HOOVER, W. M.
Active in Tecumseh, 1893; Falls City, 1894-95.

HORNER
Partner in Mason & Horner, active in Falls City, 1884-85.

HOUGH & SON
Studio at 110 5 Street South in Beatrice, 1888.

HOUGH, E. H.

HOUGHTAYLEN, S. A. (MRS.)
Active in Stella, 1884-85, 1893.

HOVER & SHAW
Partnership in Tecumseh, 1890-91.

HOVER, WILLIAM M.
Active in Beatrice, 1879-80; Seward, 1884-85; Beatrice, 1886-89; Tecumseh, 1888-89.

HOWARD, F. L.
Operated in Nebraska City, 1879-80.

HOWARD, J. B.
Active in Nelson, 1888-91.

HOYER, F. M.
Active in Norfolk, 1884-85, 1893; Osceola, 1890-93.

HUBBARD, W. H.
Active in Waverly, 1886-87.

HUGHES
Partner in Bowman, Hughes & Company with C. M. Bowman,

Omaha, 1890-93, 205 16 Street North; C. M. Bowman.

HUGHES & ALLEN
Partnership in Humboldt, 1894-95.

HUGHES & ALVORD
Partnership in Omaha, 1888-89, 992 24 Street North.

HUGHES & COMPANY
Operated by B. E. Hughes, Omaha, 1890-92, 991 24 Street North.
Also known as B. E. Hughes & Company.

HUGHES & POE
Partnership in North Auburn, 1884-85.

HUGHES & SANDBERG
Partnership in Omaha, 1884-85, 1893-1900, 205 16 Street North.

HUGHES, ARTHUR A.
Active in Humboldt, c. 1884-93.

HUGHES, B. E.
Active in Omaha, 1887-88, 1509 Douglas Street.

HULL, ARUNDEL C.
Born in Fort Wayne, Indiana, April 14, 1846. Learned photography in
St. Paul, Minnesota, 1862. Opened his first gallery at age 17 in St. Cloud,
Minnesota. Moved to Omaha, 1866, and worked for E. L. Eaton. He
spent the summers traveling and photographing scenes in Colorado,
Wyoming and Utah. By 1868, Hull worked in the Jackson Brothers
Studio. Traveled with William Henry Jackson and did a significant
amount of the photographic work on the Union Pacific Railroad con-
tract, 1869. Studio in Fremont, 1870; sold to Fritz & Good, 1895.
   Miller, Nina Hull, *Shutters West*, Sage Books, Denver, 1962.

HUNT & RYLEY
Operated in Omaha, 1886-87.

HURD BROTHERS
Active in Wahoo and Utica, 1890-91.

HUSTON, J. A.
Active in Fairbury, 1884-85; Auburn, 1890-93; Weeping Water,
1890-91.

HUTCHINGS & MATSEN
Operated in Omaha, 1900, 1406 Farnam. Also listed as Hutchings
& Matzen.

JACKSON BROTHERS
Active in Omaha, 1865-70.

JACKSON, WILLIAM HENRY
Born in Keesville, New York, April 4, 1843; died in New York City,
June 30, 1942. Perhaps the most prolific of 19th century Western photographers, and certainly one of the most famous. He learned photography in the studio of C. C. Schoonmaker of Troy, New York, 1857,
and worked with Frank Mowry in Rutland, Vermont, 1860. Jackson
served in the Union Army during the Civil War; worked as a retoucher in Mowry's studio, and later in F. Styles' studio in Vermont. In 1866,
Jackson went west, sketching scenes along the way. He worked for
Hamilton in Omaha, 1867, and later bought his studio; also associated with E. L. Eaton's studio and opened the Jackson Brothers studio
with his brother Edward the same year. Jackson's assistants included
John Jarvis, later of Washington D.C., Arundel Hull and Ira T. Johnson. In 1869, he traveled by railroad to Cheyenne with Hull. He
became the official Hayden Survey photographer, 1870, which led to
his famous photographs of the area that became Yellowstone National

Park. He sold his Omaha studio to Parker & Johnson and moved to
Washington D.C. to work on survey publications, 1871. In 1879, he
opened a studio in Denver with Frank Smart as an assistant, and was in
partnership with Alfred E. Rinehart by 1881. He also began to work
for the Denver & Rio Grande Railroad, photographing extensively
along the line, 1881; he made a wide variety of images in Mexico. His
son Fred worked in his Denver studio, and he entered a partnership
with Chain & Hardy, booksellers c, 1884, producing many "view
books" related to Colorado and the Rocky Mountain region. Jackson's
assistant was Louis Charles McClure at the time. His studios were
located at 413 or 414 Larimer, 1880-86; 1609-1615 Arapahoe, 1887-
93; 433 Colfax, 1894-97. He incorporated W. H. Jackson Photography & Publishing Company, 1892 and traveled throughout the world
as the photographer for the World Transportation Commission, 1894-
99. In 1897, Jackson moved to Detroit and became a principal in the
Detroit Publishing Company; the company published his photographs
as postcards and prints, utilizing a color process that produced images
called photochroms. With the bankruptcy of the Detroit Publishing
Company, 1924, Jackson moved to Washington, D.C. where he
worked on paintings and his memoirs, and in 1929, he moved to New
York City. Jackson became the research secretary for the Oregon Trail
Memorial Association and produced many sketches under their auspices; some were reproduced in a number of histories published by
the association. In 1936, Jackson painted murals for the Works
Progress Administration. His autobiography, *Time Exposure,* was published, 1940. He died at age 99.
   Books by and about Jackson are legion, and the best reference to further
reading is *William Henry Jackson, An Annotated Bibliography (1862 to
1995)* by Thomas H. Harrell, Ph.D., Carl Mautz Publishing, 1995.

JACOBS, W. E.
Published stereoviews in Bancroft; made views of the lynching of Loris
Higgins, c. 1907.

JACOBS, W. L.
Active in Oakland, 1884-85, 1898-93.

JACOBSEN, J.
Active in Hooper, 1886-87.

JAMES & COMPANY
Partnership in Omaha, 1889, 217 16 Street North.

JANOUSEK, L.
Operated in Niobrara, 1886-87.

JARVIS
Partner in Currier & Jarvis, active in Omaha.

JEFFERY, H. M.
Active in Aurora, 1890-95. Also listed as Jeffreys, Jefrey.

JEFFRYES, F. H.
Active in Diller, 1894-95.

JENKINS & SON
Active in Schuyler, 1886-87.

JENNINGS, T. J.
Active in Oxford, 1886-87.

JEWELL, FLORA
Active in Harvard, 1894-95.

JEWELL, GEORGE
Operated in Palmyra, 1886-87.

JOHNS, C. C.
Active in Lincoln, 1888-89.

JOHNSON, C. J.

JOHNSON, F.
Active in Raymond, 1890-91.

JOHNSON, GEORGE E.
Active in Nebraska, c. 1865.

JOHNSON, IRA T.
Worked in W. H. Jackson's studio in Omaha in 1868, purchased the Jackson studio with Charles Johnson, operating as Parker & Johnson.

JOHNSON, J. C.
Active in Hay Springs, 1893.

JOHNSON, R.
Active in Blue Springs, 1882-83.

JOHNSTON
Partner in Leon & Johnston, operating in Omaha, 1888-89.

JONES & COMPANY, L.
Active in Ponca, 1886-87.

JONES & SON
Active in Tobias, 1886-87.

JONES, GEORGE
Active in Palmyra, 1886-87.

JONES, H. P.
Active in Ewing, 1894-95.

JORDAN, C.
Active in Omaha, 1886-87.

JORGENSEN, HANS
Active in Dannebrog, c. 1890; listed in Danbury, 1894-95.

KAY, WILLIAM
Active in Wakefield, 1884-85.

KEENE, F. N.
Active in David City, 1894-95.

KEEP, W. C.
Active in Elm Creek, 1894-95.

KEITGES, JOHN
Studio at 1518 Douglas, Omaha, 1889.

KEITH & COMPANY
Studio at 938 P Street, Lincoln, 1896.

KEITH, T. D.
Active in Lyons, 1882-83.

KELLEY & COMPANY
Active in Lincoln, 1884-89. Also listed as H. W. Kelley & Company.

KELLEY, I. P.
Active in Broken Bow, 1886-87.

KELLY & TAYLOR
Active in St. Edward, 1886-87.

KELSO
Partner in Page & Kelso, operating in Omaha, 1865-70.

KENEMEDY, J. F.
Listed at 132 12 Street South, Lincoln, 1898. Misspelling of I. F. Kennedy.

KENNEDY & CLARK
D. G. Clark and I. F. Kennedy, active in York, 1882-83.

KENNEDY, I. F.
Active in York, 1884-85; partner in Kennedy & Clark, 1882-83; listed alone, 1888-89; in Lincoln, 1892-96; studio at 1029 O Street, 1892-96; 132 12 Street South, 1898-1900. Also listed as J. F. Kenemedy, 1898.

KENNEDY NOBLE STUDIO
Operating in Lincoln, c. 1890.

KERIM
Active in South Omaha, c. 1890.

KIBBE
Active in Hartington, 1890-94.

KILBORN & GILBERT
Partnership in Lincoln, 1894, 1029 O Street.

KILBORN, W. D.
Active in Lincoln, 1884-85; at 1029 O Street, 1895; partner in Kilborn & Gilbert, 1894.

KILBORN, W. F.
Active in Grand Island, 1888-93.

KING, W. W.
Active in Beemer, 1894-95.

KINKEAD BROTHERS
Active in Plattsmouth, 1886-87.

KLEINHANS, C. F.
Studio at 116 4 Street South, Beatrice, 1896.

KNAPP
Partner in Beckman & Knapp, active in Hastings, 1890-91.

KNOWLTON & COMPANY
Studio at 1026 O Street, Lincoln, 1895-1900.

KNOWLTON, CHARLES
Studio at 311 16 Street North, Omaha, 1892.

KOON, W. J.
Active in Plattsmouth, 1890-93.

KOON, WILLIAM
Active in Imperial, 1890-95.

KORTRIGHT, GEORGE W.
Active in Wayne, 1880-91. Operated as Kortright & Company in Wayne, 1893-98; in Wakefield, 1890-91.

KOSTERS, HENRY A.
Active in Omaha, 1886-87.

KOUPAL, J.
Active in West Point, 1893.

KREITZ & SONS, W. A.
Active in Plum Creek, 1886-87.

KUBETZKI, C.
Active in Roca, 1886-87.

KUHN
Partner in Trager & Kuhn, operating the Bon Ton Art Gallery in Chadron, 1889-91; operated galleries in Crawford and Pine Ridge, 1890-01.

KURTZ, A.
Active in Stanton, 1893.

KURZ
Active in Wisner, dates unknown.

LA BLATT, H. D.
Active in Grand Island, 1890-91.

LANCASTER, HABNEMANN
Operated in Omaha, 1884-85, 1896-1900. Located at 1518 Dodge, 1896-98; 1312 Farnam, 1900. Also spelled Hahneman, Hahnemann.

LANE, V. B.
Active in Rising City, 1884-85, 1890-93. Also listed as V. R.

LANGER, ANTON
Studio in West Point, 1880-1900.

LASMOTH, J. M.
Active in Alma, 1884-85.

LATHAM, N. G. (MRS.)
Active in Benkelman, 1894-95.

LAWRENCE, WILLIAM
Active in Neligh, 1879-83.

LAWSON, B.
Active in Red Cloud, 1882-83.

LEACH, ED. A.
Active in Hastings, 1884-85; McCook, 1885-91.

LEAR & COTTON
Active in Omaha, c. 1890.

LEE, W. L.
Operated in York, 1884-85, 1890-93; Benedict, 1894-95; York, Central City and Aurora, 1895.

LEGISLATIVE GALLERY
Studio at 129 11 Street South, Lincoln, 1900.

LEHMAN, H.
Active in Omaha, 1886-87.

LEHMER, C. I. (MRS.)
Active in Syracuse, 1884-85, 1888-93.

LEON & CHAPMAN
Partnership in Aurora, 1886-87.

LEON & JOHNSTON
Active in Omaha, 1888-89. Possibly D. L. Leon.

LEON, D. L.
Active in Curtis, 1888-89. Possibly a partner in Leon & Johnston, 1888-89.

LEON, JOHN J.
Studio at 1509 Douglas, Omaha, 1889.

LEONARD, CARL
Active in Louisville, 1884-85.

LEONARD, V. V.
Active in Plattsmouth, 1879-93; Nebraska City, 1898, 509 Main Street.

LESCHINSKY, JULIUS
Partner in Franklin & Leschinsky, active in Harvard, 1880-90; operating alone in Grand Island, 1890-98; at 109 3 Street East, 1898. Also spelled Lechinsky, Leschinisky, Lescininsky.

LESCHINSKY, MAX
Active in Grand Island, 1888-89; Loup City, 1893. Also spelled Loschinsky, Lesehinsky.

LEWIS
Partner in Goodrich & Lewis, active in Verdon, 1886-87.

LEWIS & FLINT
Partnership in Western, 1890-91.

LEWIS, A. L.
Active in Salem, 1886-87.

LEWIS, HARRY
Active in College View, 1894-95.

LIEBENDORFER
Partner in Bennett & Liebendorfer, operating in Pawnee City, 1893.

LINBERG, O.
Active in Wakefield, 1886-87.

LIND, V. L.
Active in Ord, 1884-85; partner in Westberg & Lind, 1893.

LINSTROM & STAYNER
Active in Edgar, 1893; John V. Stayner.

LLOYD, J. A.
Active in York, 1890-91.

LOAR, W. R.
Operated in Wymore, 1882-83; Nelson, 1884-85; Superior, 1888-91; Guide Rock, 1890-91.

LOCKE, GILBERT
Active in Tekamah, 1886-87.

LOCKE, J. T.
Active in Ulysses, 1888-89.

LOUCKS, W. H.
Active in Arapahoe, 1890-91.

LOUTZENHISER, F.
Active in Plainview, 1886-87.

LOVE & HARRIS
Active in Danbury, 1894-95.

LOVEALL, Z.
Active in Hay Springs, 1894-95.

LOWELL & BACON
Active in Wymore, 1886-87.

LUCE & MORGAN
Active in Shelton, 1893.

LUCE, ALICE
Operated the Bon Ton Gallery in Chadron, 1889; sold out to Trager & Kuhn.

LUCE, H. L.
Active in Shelton, 1884-85; Gibbon, 1894-95.

LUCE, SAMUEL
Active in Union, 1884-85.

LUNDY, H. R.
Active in Columbus, 1884-87; Silver Creek, 1888-89.

LUSK, G. E.
Active in Omaha, 1893.

LUTHOLD, CHARLES C.
Studio at 1402 Davenport Street, Omaha, 1887.

LYMAN, M. E.
Active in Champion, 1894-95.

LYNN, JOHN
Operated in Leigh, 1890-91; Friend, 1893; Ida Grove, 1895-96.

MACDONALD, C.
Active in Stratton, 1886-87.

MACDONALD, D. J.
Operated in Carleton, 1879-80, 1888-89.

MACKEY, T. M.
Active in Superior, 1884-85, 1893.

MACKPRANG, J. H.
Stereo photographer in Cedar Bluffs.

MACY & DOUGHERTY
Partnership in Norfolk, 1888-93; I. M. Macy. Also spelled Doughty.

MACY, I. M.
Active in Norfolk, 1888-93, partner in Macy & Dougherty. Also listed as J. M.

MADDEN, T. H.
Active in Ashland, 1886-87.

MADISON, J. H.
Active in Nebraska City, 1879-80.

MADSEN, ANDREW
Active in Omaha, 1890, 325 25 Street North; South Omaha, 1893-94.

MAGARRELL, W. W.
Studio at 1611 24 Street North, Omaha, 1898.

MAHAN & MEEK
Partnership in Pawnee City, 1884-85, 1893.

MAHAN & WALLACE
Active in Pawnee City, 1890-91.

MAHAN, W. H.
Active in Osceola, 1886-87; Pawnee City, 1888-89.

MAHONEY, C. C.
Active in Central City, 1879-80.

MALICK, W. H.
Active in Plattsmouth, 1886-87.

MALMQUIST, HANS O.
Operated in Omaha, 1882-96; 3100 Walnut, 1887; 2121 31 Street South, 1888-92; 1440 13 Street South, 1896.

MARBLE, L. W.
Located on Main Avenue in McCook, 1884-86.

MARCELLUS & DAVIS
Partnership active in Weeping Water, 1888-89.

MARCELLUS, P. W.
Active in Fairbury, 1886-87; Imperial, 1893; Lincoln, 1894-97; 2221 O Street, 1894; 1543 O Street, 1895; 1222 O Street, 1897.

MARKS & COMPANY, D.
Active in Aurora, 1894-95.

MARSH, A. (MRS.)
Active in Clay Center, 1893.

MARSH, FRED W.
Operated in Omaha, 1888-89, 1896-1900; 2615 Decatur. Also listed as Fohn W.

MARTIN, H. A.
Studio at 113 16 Street South, Omaha, 1900.

MARTIN, W. H.
Active in Schuyler, 1884-85, 1888-91.

MASON & HORNER
Partnership active in Falls City, 1884-85.

MASON (MRS.) & MYERS
Active in Falls City, 1879-80.

MASON, P. G. (MRS.)
Active in Falls City, 1879-83; partner in Mason & Myers, 1879-80.

MATHENY, A. D.
Active in Long Pine, 1884-85.

MATHEWSON, T. C.
Active in Hastings, 1884-85; North Platte, 1886-87.

MATHISON, I. L.
Active in Tekamah, 1884-85, 1893.

MATSEN, JAMES
Active in Omaha, 1896-98; 912 24 Street North, 96; 1406 Farnam, 1897-98, operating as Matsen & Company; partner in Hutchings & Matsen, 1900, same location. Also spelled Matzen.

MAYER
Partner in Peirson & Mayer, active in Broken Bow, 1888-89.

McALLISTER, J. S.
Active in Columbus, 1882-83, 1886-87; Genoa, 1884-85.

McBRIDE, C. C.
Active in Crawford, 1894-95.

McCLANE, F. E.
Active in Benkelman, 1886.

McCOY
Active in O'Neill, c. 1885.

McCRYSTAL, A. M.
Active in Cozad, 1894-95.

McCULLOUGH, S. H.
Operating in Central City, 1884-85; Schuyler, 1880-91.

McELHINEY, H. H.
Active in Nebraska City, 1881-93, 173 Main; 1891-92, 705 Central.
Also spelled McElhinney.

McELWAIN, M.
Active in Plattsmouth, 1886-87.

McFARLAND, WILLIAM
Active in Leigh, 1888-89.

McGOWAN, JOSEPH H.
Stereo photographer active in Omaha at the southwest corner of 12th
and Harney; also partner with Mitchell, 1870-75, operating as
Mitchell, McGowan & Company. Photographed Plains Indians.

McINNES
Produced "Stereoviews of the North West" in Omaha; photographed
the Sioux Indians.

McKAY, WILLIAM H.
Active in Omaha, 1882-87, 1897; 2400 Commercial, 1887; 5125
24 Street North, 1897.

McKINNEY, P.
Active in Waho, 1886-87.

McMAHILL, JAMES A.
Studio at 418 Court, Beatrice, 1894-98.

MECKELS, E.
Active in Hooper, 1886-87.

MEDDAUGH, J. S.
Studio in Rushville, 1890-91. Made photographs of the Lakota Indians' Ghost Dance at Pine Ridge. Also listed as J. E.

MEEK
Partner in Mahan & Meek, operating in Pawnee City, 1884-85, 1893.

MELOY
Active in Omaha, dates unknown.

MENTGEN, F.
Active in Blue Hill, 1894-95.

MERGELL & ROSENZWEIG
Active in Omaha, 1886-87.

MERRIAM
Active in Weeping Water, c. 1890.

MERRILL, M. R.
Active in St. Paul, 1884-85.

MESSERVEY, O. E.
Active in Odell, 1886-87.

MEYER, JULIUS
Omaha photographer who was also an "Indian Trader and Dealer in
Indian, Chinese and Japanese Curiosities," and issued rare views of
Union Pacific and Central Pacific Railroad. Unknown whether views
are original or pirated; at least some are original, since they show him
posed with Indians.

MIELENG & NENOW
Active in Stanton, 1884-85.

MIELENZ
Active in Stanton, c. 1885; Columbus, 1898, at 1221 Olive Street.

MILLER, C. C.
Active in Loup City, 1886-87.

MILLER, G. A.
Active in Cozad, 1893.

MILLER, G. H.
Studio at 1318 29 Avenue South, Omaha, 1897-98.

MILLER, JAMES
Active in Doniphan, 1893-95.

MINER, NETTIE M.
Operated in Omaha, 1900, 918 24 Street North.

MITCHELL, DANIEL S.
Born c. 1837; died in Maine. Partner with Joseph H. McGowan in
Omaha, 1878-83; manager of Bee Hive Gallery, 211 and 213 North
16th, 1879-84; also listed as Beehive Gallery or Studio; propietor of
Pioneer Photographic House, 1883. In Norfolk, 1885; sold to I. M.
Macy and C. E. Doughty, 1886. Photographed the Plains tribes.

MITCHELL, McGOWAN & COMPANY
Studio at southwest corner of 12th and Harney, Omaha, 1870-75.

MOELLER, J. R.
Active in Grand Island, 1884-91.

MONTGOMERY & TARKINGTON
Active in Minden, 1884-85.

MOODY & CAMPBELL
Active in Beatrice, 1884-85; A. R. Campbell.

MOORE & CHRISTIANSEN
Active in Sidney, 1886-87; G. H. Moore.

MOORE, G. H.
Active in Sidney; partner in Moore & Christiansen, 1886-87; listed
alone, 1890-91.

MOOREHEAD, T. P.
Active in Dubois, 1899-91.

MORGAN
Partner in Luce & Morgan, operating in Shelton, 1893.

MORLEDGE, CLARENCE GRANT
Operated the American Viewing Company in Omaha, 1891, active at
Pine Ridge Agency, Dakota Territory, during Wounded Knee Massacre the same year. Many of his images were issued by Trager, but bear
the intitials, "C. G. M.," in the negatives, and are numbered 1000-
1600. Convicted of grand larceny in Missourri, 1900.

MORRIS, J.
Active in Oxford, 1888-91.

MORTON, W. H.
Active in Pierce, 1886-87.

MULVANE, O. H.
Active in Raymond, 1893.

MURPHY, M.
Active in Grand Island, 1870-89.

MURPHY, T.
Active in Superior, 1886-87.

NANKIVEL, W. M.
Active in Bloomington, 1884-85.

NAU
Partner in Wegmann & Nau, operating in Blue Hill, 1893.

NAU, H.
Active in Lawrence, 1893.

NEIBURG, A.
Active in West Point, 1886-87.

NEIHART, A. W.
Active in Nebraska City, 1884-87; operated as Neihart & Company in
Fairmont and Nebraska City, 1886-87; Elmwood, 1888-95; operated as A. W. Neihart & Company, 1893-95; Weeping Water, dates
unknown. Also listed as A. L.

NEIHART, M. W.
Studio at 910 Central Avenue, Nebraska City, 1898.

NELIGH, V.
Active in West Point, 1886-87.

NELSON, JAMES
Active in Cedar Rapids, 1893; Fullerton, 1894-95.

NELSON, JOHN
Stereo photographer active in Ericson, c. 1902-17.

NELSON, O. R.
Studio at 222 13 Street South, Omaha, 1886.

NELSON, T. K.
Active in Upland, 1884-85.

NENOW
Partner in Mieleng & Nenow, active in Stanton, 1884-85.

NEWCOMB, J. F.
Active in Syracuse, 1886-87.

NEWCOMB, T. J.
Active in Humboldt, 1879-80; Fairbury, 1888-89.

NICHOLAS, J. K.
Active in Louisville, 1884-87.

NICHOLS, E. P.
Active in Hastings, 1886-87.

NICHOLS, G. C.
Active in Plattsmouth, 1879-80.

NIELSEN, L.
Active in Auburn, 1898.

NIELSON & COMPANY
Located at 617 Pacific, Omaha, 1888.

NOBLE, H. E.
Active in Lincoln, 1882-91.

NOBLE, JOHN
Active in Palmyra, 1886-87.

NOBLE, P. W.
Active in Lincoln, 1888-91.

NOLESTEIN, W. R.
Active in Columbus, 1890-93.

NORTH, I. E.
Studio at 307 14 Street North, Omaha, 1887.

NORTH, J. E.
Studio at 1010 Jones, Omaha, 1888.

NORTH OMAHA PHOTOGRAPH GALLERY
Located at 2121 Cuming, near 22nd Street, Omaha, c. 1885.

NORTH PHOTOGRAPHIC GALLERY
Operating in Omaha, 1870-80.

NORTHWEST PHOTOGRAPHIC COMPANY
Company formed by George Trager and Joe Ford in Chadron, 1891,
to make prints of Trager and Moreledge's Wounded Knee Massacre
images.

NORTON & ROWLEY
Studio at 418 Court Street, Beatrice, 1886-87.

NOTESTEIN, W. R.
Active in Fullerton, 1888-89; Columbus, 1894-95.

NUTE, C. N.
Active in Hastings, 1888-95; 914 2 Street West, 1893.

O'DONOGHUE, J. B.
Active in Wahoo, 1884-85.

OBERHOLTZER, J. W.
Operated in Fairmont, 1888-91. Also spelled Oberholdzer.

OLDROYD, L. K.
Active in Columbus and Falls City, 1875-90.

OLDS, C.
Active in Steele City, 1886-87.

OLSEN, RICHARD
Active in Omaha, 1888-89.

OLSEN, THORSTEIN
Active in Newman Grove, 1888-91. Also spelled Olson.

OMAHA PHOTOGRAPHING COMPANY
Operating at 311 16 Street North, Omaha, 1889-91.

OPP, JACOB
Active in Avoca, 1893.

OSTERMAN, CHARLES
Active in Cedar Bluffs, 1894-95.

OWEN, C. A.
Active in Red Cloud, 1886-87.

OWEN, LEONARD M.
Omaha Photographer and publisher of colored card views and Realist slides of Nebraska, Missouri, Arizona, Colorado and Utah.

PAGE & KELSO
Active in Omaha, 1865-70.

PALLETT & DOLLARSHIDE
Active in Broken Bow, 1890-91.

PALMGREN, H.
Active in Stromsburg, 1884-85.

PARKER & JOHNSON
Partnership of Charles Parker and Ira T. Johnson; purchased Jackson's Omaha studio. Studio at the corner of 15th and Douglas Streets, Omaha, 1871.

PARKER, CHARLES
Partner of Ira T. Johnson in Parker & Johnson.

PARKER, E. O.
Active in Plainview, 1886-87.

PARKINSON, H.
Active in Tecumseh, 1884-85.

PARMLEY, E.
Active in Jackson, 1893.

PARRISH, C.
Active in Table Rock, 1886-87.

PARSONS
Active in Ainsworth, c. 1895.

PARSONS
Partner in Rice & Parsons, active in Omaha, 1886-87.

PARTCH, R. N.
Active in Davenport, 1886-87.

PASSMORE, W. G.
Active in Alliance, 1890-91.

PATTERSON, JAMES
Active in Bloomfield, 1894-95.

PATTERSON, JOSEPH
Albion, 1890-95.

PATTERSON, R.
Active in Albion, 1890-91.

PATTISON & CARLSON
Active in Bertrand, 1888-89.

PATTISON, J. A.
Active in Minden, 1884-85, 1893. Partner in Pickels & Pattison, 1890-91. Also spelled Patteson.

PATTON
Partner in Grover & Patton, active in Bennet, 1884-85.

PAWWMORE, W. G.
Active in Alliance, 1893.

PAYNE
Active in Hastings, c. 1900.

PAYNE, J. L.
Active in Stuart, 1886-87.

PEALE, F. R.
Active in Ogallala, 1886-87.

PEARSON, G. Q.
Active in Cozad, 1890-91; Eustis, 1893. Also listed as S. Q.

PEIRCE, H. A.
Active in Harrisburg, 1893.

PEIRSON & MAYER
Active in Broken Bow, 1888-89.

PEIRSON, H. F.
Partner in Speake & Peirson, active in Lincoln, 1892; listed alone, 1893.

PERCY, W. H.
Active in Wilber, 1886-87.

PERKINS, W. M. C.
Active in Brownville, 1860-70.

PERRY, O. H.
Active in Dewitt, 1884-87; Wymore, 1884-94.

PERSON, A. J.
Active in Weeping Water, 1884-85.

PETERSEN, PETER CARL
Active in Omaha, 1890-93; 996 24 Street North, 1890-93; also listed at 1612 Farnam, 1891. Also spelled Peterson.

PETERSON, C. E.
Listed in South Omaha, 1884-85, and Omaha, 1890-91. Possibly Peter Carl Peterson or Petersen.

PETERSON, E. W.
Active in Wymore, 1886-87.

PETERSON, W. S.
Active in Humboldt, 1882-85.

PHELPS, A. M.
Active in Lyons, 1884-85.

PHILIPS, CHARLES W.
Operated in Nebraska City, 1879-93; 179 Main, 1881; 711 Central, 1891-92.

PICKELS & PATTISON
Partnership of J. A. Pattison and J. W. Pickels, active in Minden, 1890-91. Also spelled Patteson.

PICKELS, J.
Active in Table Rock, 1879-80.

PICKELS, J. W.
Active in Stella and South Auburn, 1884-85; Minden, 1888-91; partner in Pickels & Pattison, 1890-91. Listed in South Auburn, 1898.

PIETZ, HENRY
Studio at 1406 Farnam, Omaha, 1888-89. Also spelled Pletz.

PIKE, J. W.
Active in Orleans, 1888-89; Grand Island, 1893.

PIONEER PHOTOGRAPHIC HOUSE
Operated by Daniel S. Mitchell in Omaha, 1883.

POE
Partner in Hughes & Poe, active in North Auburn, 1884-85. Possibly P. E. Poe.

POE & WOODS
Studio at 132 12 Street South, Lincoln, 1895-96; P. E. Poe.

POE, P. E.
Active in Cortland, 1890-91; Valparaiso, 1893. Active in Lincoln, 1895-96, partner in Poe & Woods, 132 12 Street South.

POWE, T. H.
Operated in Omaha, 1884-85, 1896-97; at 1400 13 Street South, 1896-97.

POWELL, W. A.
Active in David City, 1894-95.

POWERS, D. R.
Stereo photographer active in Nebraska.

PRATT
Partner in Sanford & Pratt, active in Ainsworth, 1893-95.

PRESTON, H. C.
Active in Columbus, 1870-80; Seward, 1882-89; Scotia, 1884-85; Greeley Center, 1893.

PREWITT, W. L.
Operated in Lincoln, 1884-85, 1894-1900; 1026 O Street, 1894; 218 12 Street South, 1895; 1216 O Street, 1896-99; 1214 O Street, 1900.

PREY
Partner in Smith & Prey, active in Lincoln, 1898-99, at 1214 O Street.

PRIMIK, FRANK I.
Active in Wilber, 1890-91.

PROCTOR BROTHERS
Active in Omaha, 1884-85. Possibly Edward L. and J. H. Proctor.

PROCTOR, EDWARD L.
Active in Omaha, 1891-1900; 1509 Douglas, 1891; 616 16 Street South, 1896-1900.

PROCTOR, J. H.
Active in Omaha, 1892-1900; 512 16 Street South, 1892; 320 16 Street North, 1896-98; 420 16 Street North, 1898-1900.

PROVINS
Partner in Clayton & Provins, operating in Ord, 1886-87.

PRYSE & EWING
Partnership in Hastings, c. 1875; Red Cloud, c. 1880.

PURSLEY, J. J.
Active in Hubbell, 1888-89; Ashland, 1894-95.

PUTNAM & SNYDER
Partnership in Scribner, 1886-87.

RAGAN, G. C.
Located at 2 Street, Hastings, 1898.

RAGAN, H. D.
Active in York, 1890-91; Exeter, 1893.

RECHER
Partner in Stinson & Recher, operating in Blair, 1890-91.

REED, CHARLES
Active in Palmyra, 1886-87.

REED, VIRGIL
Active in Dewitt, 1890-91.

REEDER, O. B.
Active in Fairbury, 1894-95; Beatrice, 1900-01, at 201 6 Street North.

REEF, W. E.
Active in Neligh, 1890-91.

REEVES, THOMAS
Active in Stockville, 1884-85.

REGAN, H. D.
Active in Exeter, 1890-91.

REHARD, J. W.
Active in Lexington, 1884-85.

REIGEL, O.
Active in Wahoo, 1879-80.

REIS, F. L.
Active in North Platte, 1879-80.

REITZ, ED (MRS.)
Operated in Imperial, 1890-91.

RELF, W. E.
Active in Neligh, 1884-93.

REYNOLDS, F. M.
Active in Dacatur, 1888-89; David City, 1890-95.

REYNOLDS SISTERS
Partnership in Beatrice, 1894-95.

RICE
Partner in Tyson & Rice, active in Nebraska City, 1900-01, at 711 Central Avenue.

RICE & PARSONS
Active in Omaha, 1886-87.

RICE, H. B.
Active in Dewitt, 1893; Western, 1884-85.

RICHARDS, M. W.
Operated in Lincoln, 1884-85.

RICHTER & COMPANY, W. C.
Partnership operating in Page, 1884-85.

RIFENBERG, GEORGE
Active in Loomis, 1893.

RILE, J. L.
Active in Nebraska City, c. 1870.

RILEY, A. L.
Active in Clay Center, 1890-91.

RILEY, A. L. (MRS.)
Active in Sutton, 1882-83.

RIMER, H. E.
Active in Schuyler, 1888-91.

RINEHART, FRANK A.
Active in Omaha, 1886-1900s. 1520 Douglas Street, 1886-89, 1893-1900; 1524 Douglas, 1891-92.

RIPSOM & COMPANY
Active in Fairmont, 1893.

ROBBERTS, J. F.
Studio at 704 16 Street North, Omaha, 1888-89.

ROBINSON, G. L.
Mascot, 1884-85.

ROBINSON, J. W.
Active in Franklin, 1893-95.

RODSTROM, GUSTAF
Active in Holdredge, 1894-95.

ROGERS & COMPANY
Studio at 628 16 Street South, Omaha, 1892-93.

ROGERS, J. D.
Gallery at 628 16 Street South, operating as Rogers & Company, Omaha, 1893.

ROGERS, ORLANDO
Active in Wallace, 1884-85, 1893.

ROGGEN, A.
Active in Milford, 1893.

ROLOSON
Partner in Chapman & Roloson, operating in Hamilton, 1879-80.

ROONEY, E.
Active in O'Connor, 1888-89.

ROSE, J.
Active in Wood River, 1884-85.

ROSENZWEIG
Partner in Mergell & Rosenzweig, operating in Omaha, 1886-87.

ROSS, A. J.
Active in Chadron, 1886-87.

ROSS BROTHERS
Active in Rushville, 1886-87.

ROSS, EDWARD
Active in Lynch, 1884-85.

ROSS, H. R.
Active in Burnett 1888-89; Battle Creek, 1888-91. Also listed as H. R.

ROWEL, WILLIAM
Active in Sterling, 1886-87.

ROWLETT, E.
Active in Ulysses, 1882-83; Madison, 1884-85. Also spelled Rowlette.

ROWLETT, J. W.
Active in Norfolk, 1884-85.

ROWLEY
Partner in Norton & Rowley, operating in Beatrice, 1886-87.

ROWLEY BROTHERS
Active in Kearney, 1886-87.

ROWLEY, E. A.
Operated the Palace Studio in Omaha, c. 1890.

RUSHVILLE ART GALLERY & COPYING COMPANY
Studio in Rushville, c. 1880.

RUSSEL, A. J.
Active in Omaha, c. 1868.

RYAN & COMPANY, T. W.
Active in Wymore, 1884-85.

RYLEY
Partner in Hunt & Ryley, active in Omaha, 1886-87.

SANDBERG
Partner in Hughes & Sandberg, active in Omaha, 1884-85, 1893-1900; located at 16 Street North.

SANDY, WILLIAM
Active in Elwood, 1894-95.

SANFORD & PRATT
Partnership in Ainsworth, 1893-95.

SAVAGE, H. F.
Active in Stratton, 1886-87.

SAVITZKY
Partner in Conklin & Savitzky, active in Omaha; located in the Granite Block, 1893; 213 16 Street North, 1896.

SAXTON, W.
Active in Neligh, 1884-87.

SCHLANGE, F.
Active in Greeley Center, 1890-91.

SCHMIDT, F. W.
Active in Fairbury, 1893-95.

SCHNABE, HERMAN
Studio at 2121 Cuming, Omaha, 1882-89. Also listed as Schwabe.

SCHNACK, PETER
Active in Franklin, 1890-91.

SCHOEMBOHN, WILLIAM
Active in Elkhorn, 1888-91.

SCHWABE, HERMAN
Studio at 2121 Cuming Street, Omaha, 1882-89. Also listed as Schnabe, 1888.

SCOTT
Partner in Smith & Scott, active in York, 1888-89.

SCOTT & STEWART
Active in York, c. 1890.

SCOTT, M. F.
Active in Campbell, 1894-95.

SEELEY, S.
Active in Bellwood, 1894-95.

SELLARS, M. J.
Active in Hubbell, 1886-87.

SELLARS, M. J. (MRS.)
Active in Hubbell, 1884-85.

SEVERSON, O.
Active in Ord, 1886-87.

SHAMPANG, B. A.
Active in Central City, 1894-95.

SHAVER, J. C.
Studio at 4134 Hamilton, Omaha, 1897.

SHAW, A. G.
Active in Ft. Niabrara, 1885.

SHAW, C. M.
Active in Tecumseh, 1884-85; partner in Hover & Shaw, 1890-91.

SHEPARD & ALTINE
Studio at 1238 O Street, Lincoln, 1899.

SHEPARD, WILLIAM E.
Active in Nebraska City, 1884-85; Friend, c. 1890; Nebraska City, 1891-92, partner in Trimble & Shepard, 106 9 Street North; listed alone, 1893. Active in Lincoln, 1900, 1238 O Street. Also spelled Sheppard.

SHEUEY, M.
Active in Burchard, 1888-89.

SHIREY, C. R.
Active in Crete, 1879-80; Friend, 1884-85.

SHUCK, JOSEPH
Active in Columbus, 1890-95.

SHULTZ, W. B.
Active in Stromsburg, 1888-89.

SILVIS, J. B.
Operated the Pacific Railroad Photograph Car, headquartered in

Omaha, 1860-80. See Traveling and Utah.

SIMPSON, A.
Active in Grafton, 1894-95.

SKINNER, C. E.
Active in Beatrice, 1882-83.

SMART, F.
Active in McCook, c. 1894.

SMART, J. H.
Active in McCook, 1890-93.

SMITH
Partner in Bennett & Smith, active in Pawnee City, 1884-85.

SMITH & AYERS
Active in Odell, 1886-87.

SMITH & PREY
Studio at 1214 O Street, Lincoln, 1898-99.

SMITH & SCOTT
Active in York, 1888-89.

SMITH & ZIMMERMAN
Active in Rulo, 1884-85.

SMITH, ANDREW
Active in Fairmont, 1879-80; Crete, 1882-95.

SMITH, C. O.
Active in Arapahoe, 1894-95.

SMITH, D. C.
Operated in Blair, 1879-80; Omaha, 1884-93. 322 16 Street South, 1892.

SMITH, D. M.
Active in Nebraska City, 1870, 179 Main.

SMITH, DR. A. M.
Operated the City Picture Rooms in Nebraska City, c. 1866.

SMITH, FRANK
Active in Falls City, 1890-91.

SMITH, LUKE
Active in Geneva, 1888-89.

SMITH, R. G.
Active in Norfolk, 1884-85.

SNIDER, W. H.
Active in Aurora, 1888-93.

SNYDER
Partner in Putnam & Snyder, active in Scribner, 1886-87.

SODERBERG, PONT
Active in Sulton, c. 1880; Harvard, 1882-85; Sutton, 1884-91; Geneva, 1886-87. Also spelled Soderbert, Soderburgh, Sodreberg.

SPAKES, J. G.
Active in Broken Bow, 1888-89.

SPEAKE & PEIRSON
Partnership of H. F. Peirson and J. Grant Speake, operating in Lincoln at 124 12 Street South, 1892.

SPEAKE, J. GRANT
Lincoln, 1891-93; 124 12 Street South, 1891; partner in Speake & Peirson, 1892; at 1026 O Street, 1893.

SPENCER, E. G. M.
Active in Greenwood, 1884-85.

SPOONER, A. E. (MRS.)
Studio at 882 27 Street North, Lincoln, 1900.

STAMM, A. N.
Active in Omaha, 1888-89.

STAMPER, E. J.
Active in Tecumseh, 1882-85.

STAR PHOTO COMPANY
Active in McCook, c. 1890.

STAYNER & DUHLING
Partnership in Edgar and Fairfield, 1875-90.

STAYNER, JOHN V.
Active in Edgar, 1875-93; partner in Stayner & Duhling, 1875; partner in Linstrom & Stayner, 1893.

STEADMAN, F. M.
Active in Clarks, 1888-89; Fremont, 1890-93; studio at 643 Broad Street North, 1891-92; partner with G. Trager in Trager & Steadman, 1893.

STEARNS, O. A.
Active in Columbus, 1879-87. Also listed as O. H.

STEEL, GEORGE
Active in Gandy, 1893.

STEELE, FRANK B.
Active in Blue Hill, 1886-91. Also listed as F. P.

STEELE, G.
Active in Thedford, 1890-91.

STEELE, I. H.
Active in Herman, 1893.

STEIDBORG, J. A.
Active in Kearney, 1882-83.

STERN, O. E.
Active in Columbus, 1888-89.

STEVENS, W. T.
Active in Seward, 1884-85.

STEWART
Partner in Scott & Stewart, active in York, c. 1890.

STEWART, N. D. (MRS.)
Active in Lincoln, 1879-80.

STIFFLER, M. T.
Active in Minden, 1888-89.

STINSON & RECHER
Partnership in Blair, 1890-91.

STOCK, H. W.
Active in Genoa, 1894-95.

STONE, J.
Active in Omaha, 1884-85.

STONECYPER, E. A.
Active in Gothenburg, c. 1885.

STOUT, B. D.
Active in Lincoln, 1882-83.

STOVER, A. C.
Active in Lincoln, 1884-85.

STRASBURG, HENRY
Active in Omaha, 1870-83.

STRAUSS, A. C.
Studio at 1209 Olive Street, Columbus, 1898.

STRIDBORG, J. A.
Active in Kearney, 1884-85.

STROMSTON, J. M.
Active in Orleans, 1884-85.

STULE, F. P.
Active in Blue Hill, 1884-85.

STURDEVANT, J. B.
Active in Wahoo, 1879-83; Valentine, 1884-85; Atkinson, 1884-95.

STUTSMAN, W. G.
Active in Central City, 1884-95.

SUNBEAM GALLERY
Operated by Carmon in Hastings, c. 1895.

SUNBEAM STUDIO
Located on the east side of the Square, Broken Bow, c. 1890.

SUNDY, H. R.
Active in Columbus, 1882-83.

SWANSON, CHARLES
Active in Mead, 1886-89.

SWEET, C. A.
Studio at 114 6 Street East, Fremont, 1898.

SWINNERTON, VICTOR N.
Amateur stereo photographer in Omaha, c. 1913; took hundreds of area views; some were pirated and sold commercially.

SYKES, F. R.
Active in Brownville, 1870-75.

TALBOT, W. E.
Active in Fairbury, c. 1880-91.

TALBOTT BROTHERS
Active in Fairbury, 1893.

TANNAR, M. E. (MRS.)
Active in Brownsville, 1882-83.

TARKINGTON
Partner in Montgomery & Tarkington, active in Minden, 1884-85.

TAYLOR
Partner in Kelly & Taylor, active in St. Edward, 1886-87.

TAYLOR & FERGUSON
Active in Liberty, 1884-85.

TAYLOR, B. F.
Active in Beatrice, 1880-98. Operating from 405 Court Street, 1880; 201 6 Street North, 1896; 600B Ella Street, 1898.

TAYLOR, W. F.
Active in Lyons, 1884-93; partner in Hamilton & Taylor, 1890-91.

TAYLOR, W. H.
Active in Ogallala, 1886-87.

TEILBORG, C. C.
Active in Wausa, 1884-85.

TENNANT, EARLE
Active in Red Cloud, 1884-85.

THOMAS, W. L.
Active in Plattsmouth, 1860-70.

THOMPSON
Partner in Tillotson & Thompson, operating in Norfold, 1890-91.

THORNE, WAYNE
Active in Roseland, 1884-85.

TILLOTSON & THOMPSON
Active in Norfolk, 1890-91.

TITUS, T. J.
Studio at 938 P Street, Lincoln, 1899-1900.

TOLLMAN, JOHN W.
Active in Omaha, 1886-87, 702 16 Street North. Operated Tollman & Company, 1886. See Oregon and Washington.

TOLMAN, T. W.
Active in Nebraska City, 1884-93; Macedonia, 1895-96.

TOMPSETT, WILLIAM
Active in Sidney, 1886-87.

TORELL, S. P.
Active in Oakland, 1886-87.

TOWNSEND, A. C.
Studio at 226 11 Street South, Lincoln, 1899-1900.

TOWNSEND BROTHERS
Active in Hastings, 1886-87.

TOWNSEND, C. O.
Active in Bassett, 1888-89.

TOWNSEND, I. L.
Active in Hastings, 1888-91.

TOWNSEND, J. A.
Studio at 224 Lincoln Avenue North in Hastings, 1893-95.

TOWNSEND, J. W.
Active in Hastings and Lincoln, 1880-90.

TOWNSEND, T. W.
Active in Lincoln, 1884-85, 1891-98. Studio at 226 11 Street South, 1891-98; known as Elite Studio, 1898. Also listed as F. W.

TRABER, P. J.
Active in South Omaha, 1884-85.

TRAGER & KUHN
Partners operating the Bon Ton Art Gallery in Chadron, 1889-91; operated galleries in Crawford and Pine Ridge, 1890-91.

TRAGER & STEADMAN
Fremont, 1893; partnership of George Trager and F. M. Steadman.

TRAGER, ERNEST
Nephew of George Trager; partner in studio in Crawford, 1890.

TRAGER, GEORGE
Born in Gefell, Germany, 1861; died in New York, 1948. Arrived in America, 1876. Studied photography in Whitewater, Wisconsin. Opened studio in Mazomanie with Frederick Kuhn, 1888. Trager and Kuhn migrated to Chadron, Nebraska, and purchased Bon Ton Art Gallery from Miss A. Luce, 1889. Opened studio in Crawford, then at the Pine Ridge Agency, 1890; photographed the Ghost Dance; first to photograph the aftermath of the Wounded Knee massacre; formed the Northwestern Photographic Company to market the Wounded Knee images. Sold Chadron studio and moved to Yellowstone National Park, 1892. Formed partnership of Trager & Steadman in Fremont, 1893. Also known as Gus.

TRAULSEN BROTHERS
Active in Dodge, 1893-95.

TRAULSEN, PETER
Active in Hooper, 1894-95.

TRILOFF, WILLIAM
Active in Table Rock, 1886-87.

TRIMBLE & SHEPARD
Active in Nebraska City, 1891-92, 106 9 Street North. Also spelled Sheppard.

TRIMBLE, J. M.
Active in Blair, 1886-87.

TRIMBLE, R. W.
Active in Nebraska City, 1884-1901; partner in Trimble & Shepard with William E. Shepard, 1891-82. Studio at 9 Street North, 1898; 810 Central Avenue, 1900-01.

TRIPP, H.
Active in Arlington, 1894-95.

TRIVELPIECE, R. P.
Active in Gibbon, c. 1885.

TURNER, A. B.
Active in Creighton, 1882-83.

TURNER, A. V.
Active in Creighton, 1886-87. Possibly A. B. Turner.

TURNER, S.
Active in Creighton, 1884-85.

TWO JOHNS
Operating in Lincoln, c. 1885.

TYSON & RICE
Located at 711 Central Avenue, Nebraska City, 1900-01.

VALE & COMPANY
Operating from 996 24 Street North, Omaha, 1891.

VAN ALSTINE, C. W.
Studio at 2111 Central Avenue, Kearney, 1890-95. Also spelled Vanal-
stine.

VAN LIEW, A. J.
Active in Ulysses, 1884-85; Aurora, 1886-87; Ulysses, 1890-93. Also
spelled Vanliew.

VAN LIEW, GEORGE
Active in Western, 1886-87. Also spelled Vanliew.

VANDEWALL & COMPANY, W. B.
Studio at 612 16 Street North, Omaha, 1897-98.

VANDEWALL & VIELE
Active in Blair, 1894-95.

VANDIKE BROTHERS
Operated in Arcadia, 1890-91.

VIELE
Partner in Vandewall & Viele, active in Blair, 1894-95.

WAGNER, JAMES
Studio in Valentine, 1890. Photographed at the Rosebud Agency. Possibly the same as James Wagoner.

WAGONER, JAMES
Active in Ft. Niobrara area, c. 1885.

WAIT
Active in Stratton, 1886-87.

WAKELY, GEORGE D.
Active in Omaha; issued views of Rocky Mountains, Garden of the
Gods, and a "Smithsonian Series," c. 1865-67. Listed in Denver,
1859-64; Leadville, 1879.

WALDRON
Active in Omaha, c. 1895.

WALDRON & DAVIES
Partnership in Omaha, 1884-85.

WALDTER, LOUIS
Active in Wymore, 1886-87.

WALKER, N. P.
Active in Shelton, 1886-87.

WALLACE
Partner in Mahan & Wallace, active in Pawnee City, 1890-91.

WALLACE, C. W.
Active in Burchard, 1894-95.

WALLACE, E. E.
Active in McCook, 1893.

WALLBAUM, C. C.
Partner in Batcheller & Wallbaum, operating in Nebraska City, 1862.
Studio above the Post Office Building, c. 1863-70; later at 500 Main.

WALLINGFORD, J. L.
Active in Cortland, 1894-95.

WALTER BROTHERS
Active in Wayne, 1886-87.

WALTER, C. P.
Studio at 1551 Hill Avenue, Lincoln, 1892-98.

WALTERMIRE, P. C.
Active in Ashland, 1879-85; Lincoln, 1886-89, listed as Waltermire's
Fine Art Studio; Sioux City, Iowa, 1895-98. Also spelled Wallermire.

WALTERS, F. E.
Active in Hastings, 1880-83. Also listed as Waters.

WALTERS, J. F.
Active in Riverton, 1882-83.

WALTMIRE, N. J.
Active in Ashland, 1886-87. Possibly a misspelling of Waltermire.

WARD, M. T.
Active in Orleans, 1879-80.

WATSON, D. D.
Active in Grant, 1888-93.

WEBER, C. C.
Active in Red Cloud, 1879-80.

WEBSTER, A. F.
Active in Beaver City, 1894-95.

WEBSTER STEREOSCOPE COMPANY
Active in Gothenburg.

WEGMANN & NAU
Active in Blue Hill, 1893.

WEGMANN, J. H.
Active in Red Cloud, 1884-85.

WEIKERT, A. N.
Active in Indianola, 1888-89; Imperial, 1890-91. Also listed as A.
M.

WELCH
Active in North Platte, 1875-88.

WELCH, C. A.
Active in Crab Orchard, 1894-95.

WELCH, E. (MRS.)
Active in North Platte, 1893.

WELD, F. A.
Active in Stanton, 1886-87.

WELDIN & SON
Partnership in Kearney, 1884-85.

WELLS, N. G. (MRS.)
Active in Superior, 1882-83.

WELLS, THOMAS
Active in Western, 1886-87.

WESCOTT, D. K.
Studio at 2018 34 Street North, Omaha, 1896.

WEST END STUDIO
Gallery on Rottman Boulevard, Nebraska City, 1900-01.

WESTBERG & LIND
Active in Ord, 1893.

WESTBERG, H. G.
Active in Dannebrog, 1888-89; Ord, 1890-91, partner in Westberg & Lind.

WESTBERG, W. G.
Active in Arcadia, 1894-95.

WHEAT, O. H.
Active in Lincoln, 1882-83.

WHEELER, C. A.
Active in Loup City, 1890-91.

WHEELER, F.
Active in Tecumseh, 1884-85.

WHEELER, W. D.
Active in Sterling, 1888-89.

WHITE, A. J.
Active Nebraska City, c. 1870-75; 153 Main, 1870.

WHITMORE, L.
Active in Unadilla, 1886-87.

WHITNEY, A. C.
Active in Dorchester, 1894-95.

WHITTEMORE, F. H.
Active in Ashland, 1888-91.

WHYMAN, ROBERT
Active in Adams, 1894-95.

WICKHORST, E. A.
Active in Hooper, 1888-93. Also spelled Wiekhorst.

WIKER, T. J.
Active in Cortland, 1886-87.

WILD, L. (MRS.)
Active in Dewitt, 1879-80.

WILDER, E. A.
Active in North Platte, c. 1878.

WILLIAMS, B. S.
Active in Belvidere, 1888-89.

WILLIAMS BROTHERS
Active in Culbertson, 1894-95.

WILLIAMS, G. S.
Active in Indianola, 1894-95.

WILLIAMS, W. C.
Studio at 228 Main, Nebraska City, 1879-81.

WILSON, B. A.
Active in Plum Creek, 1884-85.

WILSON, B. L.
Active in Liberty, 1890-91.

WINDHEIM, P.
Active in Omaha, 1886-87.

WINSLOW, R. A. (MRS.)
Active in Oakdale, 1884-85.

WOLCOTT, H. B.
Active in St. Paul, 1886-87.

WOOD, E.
Active in Brownville, 1884-85.

WOODS
Partner in Poe & Woods, active in Lincoln, 1895-96; studio at 132 12 Street South.

WOODS, J. H.
Active in Kearney, 1888-89; Beatrice, 1893-1901; 509 Court, 1896-1901.

WOODWORTH, H. S.
Active in Chapman, 1886-89.

WORDEN, W. E.
Active in Hay Springs, 1890-91.

WYATT, M. J.
Active in Holdrege, 1888-93. Also listed as N. J.

WYATT, M. J. (MRS.)
Minden and Wilcox, 1884-85; Holdrege, 1886-87.

WYATT, W. A.
Active in Rushville, 1886-87.

YOHO, B. W.
Studio at 418 Court, Beatrice, 1888.

YOUNG & CHASE
Partnership of F. R. Chase and V. H. Young in Lincoln, c. 1875.

YOUNG, A. J.
Active in Harvard, 1890-93

YOUNG, V. H.
Partner in Young & Chase with F. R. Chase in Lincoln; also worked alone.

ZENITH STUDIO
Gallery at 938 P Street, Lincoln, 1897.

ZIMMERMAN
Partner in Smith & Zimmerman, active in Rulo, 1884-85.

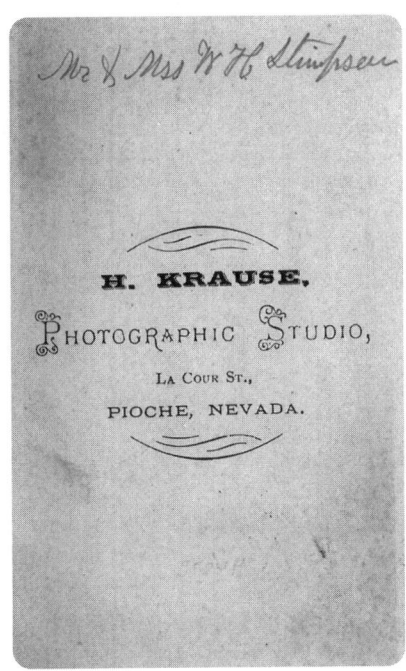

ASHBY, E. (MRS.)
Active in Wadsworth, c. 1900; photographed the Piute.

BAKER, E. W.
Active in Virginia City, c. 1900.

BANBROCK, WILLIAM E.
Active in Carson City, 1881-83.

BEALE, T. L.
Proprietor of the New York Gallery, Virginia City, c. 1886.

BEALS & WATERHOUSE
Partnership active in Virginia City, 1878; A. J. Beals and G. Water-house.

BEALS, A. J.
Active in Virginia City, 1878-80; partner with G. Waterhouse, 1878, operating as Beals & Waterhouse.

BEALS, H. S.
Active in Gold Hill, 1867.

BENNETE, J. J.
Active in Pioche.

BREWSTER, JOHN CALVIN
Born in Ohio, 1841. Photographer in California, 1862-64. Operated R. H. Vance's gallery in Virginia City by 1864. Opened a studio for the Sutterly Brothers in Ruby City, Idaho, and in Salt Lake City, Utah.

Operated a tent studio in nearby Douglas, Utah. A carte-de-visite with Brewster's 140 South C Street address in Virginia, c. 1866, has Hurd's Gallery rubber stamp imprint on the front. See California.

BUDDEN, G. W. H.
Active in Reno, 1878.

BUTLER, E. P.
Active in Reno and Virginia City, 1883-95; Reno Art Gallery.

CADE, H. C.
Active in Carson City

CANN
Active in Virginia City, 1895.

CARSON & NOE
Active in Carson City, 1874.

CITY PHOTOGRAPH GALLERY
Operated by Louis Monaco in Eureka, 1878-87.

CLINCH, WILLIS A.
California photographer located in Grass Valley, Nevada, c. 1870s.

COOK & BUTLER.
Partnership of F. A. Cook and E. P. Butler, active in Reno, 1883.

COOK & SCHNEIDER
Active in Reno, c. 1880s.

COOK, F. A.
Partner with E. P. Butler, operating as Cook & Butler in Reno, 1883; also active in Winnemucca.

CROCKWELL, JAMES H.
Studio in Virginia City, Nevada, at 29½ C Street, 1888; employed Al Smith, 1888-89. Closed his gallery after his daughter was killed in a studio fire, 1889. Published a book of photographs of Nevada mining towns and activity, *Souvenir of the Comstock*. Partner with Marston, c. 1891. Crockwell traveled extensively in Nevada and Utah photographing mining camps and other scenes, printing many images in boudoir card format. See California, Traveling and Utah.

CROCKWELL, MILLIE BASSETT
Wife of James H. Crockwell who, out of necessity, re-opened his gallery without his knowledge in1889-90, while he traveled to Los Angeles to promote ideas for souvenir books.

DEADY, WILLIAM G.
Active in Belmont, 1883.

DOWE, OSCAR S.
Active in Lovelock, Nevada, 1891, 1901, 1904; in Silver City, operating the " Big tent below the Catholic Church." See California, Idaho, Oregon.

DUNHAM & KELSEY
Partnership in Reno, 1886; O. W. Dunham.

DUNHAM & LATHROP
Active in Reno, 1880.

ESSELBRUEGGE, FRED
Active in Eureka, c. 1900.

EVANS
Active in Reno, 1870.

FAIRBANKS, G. R.
Active in Wadsworth, c. 1900; photographed the Piute.

GAGE, H. K.
Active in Aurora at Pine Street, c. 1863.

GAGE, M. D.(MRS.)
Active in Elko, c. 1870.

GROVE, ELBRIDGE K.
Active in Reno, 1883.

HART, A. A.
See California.

HAZELTINE, MARTIN MASON
An important western photographer active in Reno, 1878. See California, Idaho, Oregon and Traveling.

HEPBURN
Stereo photographer in Gold Hill; issued rare views of Idaho, mines and towns.

HURD, E.
Active in Virginia City, 1875. An enameled card, with Hurd's Gallery imprinted at the bottom of a portrait of a soldier, implies an earlier date. A carte-de-visite with J. C. Brewster's 140 South C Street address in Virginia, has Hurd's Gallery rubber stamp imprint on the front, c. 1866. Also listed at 82 South C Street, Virginia.

JOHNSON, GEORGE H.
Operated Pioneer Gallery in Landin County, 1860.

JOHNSTON & COMPANY.
Partnership active in Virginia City, 1875.

KRAUSE, H.
Studio in Austin, 1867; in Pioche, c. 1875, on LaCour Street.

LARSON
Active in Gold Hill.

LEE, W. THOMAS
Active in Virginia City, 1877.

LESLIE, HIRAM E.
See Idaho.

LUDLOW, E. C.
Active in Carson City, 1865.

LUDLOW, F. G.
Active in Carson City, 1867.

MARSTON, CHARLES A.
Active in Carson City, 1875-86.

MIDDLEMISS, B.
Active in Carson City, c. 1900.

MONACO, LOUIS
Operated the City Photograph Gallery in Eureka, 1878-87.

MORIARITY, J. M.
See Idaho.

MUSHET & SLATER
Landscape and view photographers working around Virginia City, c. 1880. Partnership of J. MacFarlane Mushet and H. Slater.

MUSHET, J. MacFARLANE
Active in Virginia, c. 1880.

NOE & LEE
Active in Virginia City, 1878-80.

NOE, JOHN S.
Studio at 82 South C Street, Virginia City, 1886.

O'SULLIVAN, TIMOTHY H.
Famous Civil War photographer who worked for Matthew Brady. The official photographer for the King Survey, 1867, who took some of the most striking photographs of frontier Nevada. See Arizona.

OSBORNE, ALBERT W.
Active in Virginia City, c. 1865. See California.

PETERSON & COMPANY
Active in Virginia City, 1878.

PETERSON & SNYDER
Partnership active in Carson City, 1881.

PETERSON, C. E.
Active in Carson City, 1880-86.

PICKETT, J. M.
Studio on the corner of Main and Dunn Streets, Hamilton, c. 1863.

PILLINER, WILLIAM H.
Born in England, 1828. Gallery at 14 Second Street, San Francisco, 1865. Active in Grass Valley, 1870. By 1878, he moved his gallery to Carson City, Nevada. Billed as the "Pioneer Artist" while operating in Tuscarora, c. 1895.

PIONEER GALLERY
Operated by George H. Johnson, 1860, in Landon County.

POTTER, J. C.
See Idaho.

RENO ART GALLERY
Studio in Reno, 1885.

RIFENBURG & DOWE
Traveling photographers, c. 1885-90; headquartered in Reno, 1890.

RIVERSIDE PHOTO GALLERY
Operated by C. E. Skinner in Reno, 1895.

SCHUMACHER, LEO J.
Active in Austin, 1866-69; Unionville, 1872-73. See California, Oregon and Washington.

SCHNEIDER, MAX
Partner of F. A. Cook in Reno, c. 1880s.

SCRIPTURE, JOHN CALVIN
Prominent photographer from California; traveled to Nevada, c. 1860s-70s, photographing mines, mills and smelters.

SIMAS & JOHNSTON
Active in Carson City, 1896. See California.

SKINNER, C. E.
Active in Reno, 1895, operating Riverside Photo Gallery.

SLATER, H.
Active in Virginia City, c. 1880.

SMITH, AL
Worked with James H. Crockwell in Virginia City, 1888-90. Later active in Tonapah.

STIMLER, H. P.
Owner of the Sunbeam Photograph Gallery on Main Street in Austin, c. 1875. L. A. Weller, Operator.

SUNBEAM GALLERY
Studio in Austin, Lander County, c. 1906.

SUNBEAM PHOTOGRAPH GALLERY
Studio of H. P. Stimler, Austin, c. 1875.

SUTTERLEY & NOE
Partnership of J. S. Noe and J. K. Sutterley, active in Virginia City, c. 1870s. Successor to Sutterly Brothers, 29 South C Street, ground floor.

SUTTERLY BROTHERS
The studio of Clement and J. K. Sutterly operating in Virginia City, 1867.

SUTTERLY, CLEMENT
Operated the Sutterly Brothers gallery with his brother, J. K. in Virginia City, 1867. See California.

SUTTERLY, J. K.
Partner with his brother, Clement, in the Sutterly Brothers gallery, Virginia City, 1867. See California.

TANDY & COOK
Active in Tuscarora, 1880.

TANDY, H. C.
Active in Idaho, 1870s, before moving to Nevada. Partner with Leslie in Winnemucca, 1878; with Cook in Tuscarora, 1880-81. See Idaho.

WATERHOUSE & BUTLER
Partnership of G. Waterhouse and E. P. Butler, active in Virginia City, 1883.

WATERHOUSE, G.
Partner of E. P. Butler, operating as Waterhouse & Butler, Virginia City, 1883.

WATERS, R. J.
Active in Virginia City, 1886; also in Gold Hill.

WATKINS, CARLETON E.
See California.

WELLER, L. A.
Operator for H. P. Stimler's Sunbeam Photograph Gallery in Austin, c. 1875; listed alone, 1878-86.

WOOD, THOMAS M.
See Idaho.

Much of the information contained in this section derives from the compilation of Richard Rudisill, Curator of the Museum of New Mexico, and published in Photographers of the New Mexico Territory 1854-1912, *Museum of New Mexico, Santa Fe, 1973.*

ABBOTT, C. L.
Active in Abiquiu, 1879, with F. C. Warnky, operating as Warnky & Abbott.

ADAMS
Active in Socorro, 1895-1905.

ADAMS, F. S.
Active in Albuquerque, 1899, 113 North Third Street; probably an operator for Mrs. Franc Luse Albright.

ADDIS, ALFRED SHEA
Active in Las Cruces, House of Christian Duper, October 1880; in Silver City, Main Street, April 1881-October 1882; in Lake Valley, October 1882.

ALBRIGHT ART PARLORS
Studios operated in Santa Fe by Mrs. Franc Luse Albright, 1880-1912. See Mrs. Franc Luse Albright.

ALBRIGHT, FRANC LUSE (MRS.)
Married to newspaperman John G. Albright, she came from Kansas to Santa Fe, 1880, opening The New Art Parlors, also known as the Albright Art Parlors. Located at the corner of the Democrat Printing Office, 1880-82; with Mrs. Woodruff at Tertio-Millenial Exposition Building, then southwest corner of Plaza, 1883. Operated the Art Parlors in Albuquerque at Gold Avenue at Front Street, 1882-87; 113 or 113 ½ North Third Street, 1887-1904; 312 West Lead Avenue, 1907-08; 121 ½ North Third Street, 1909-12. Also listed as Mrs. Emma L. Albright, Mrs. E. L., Mrs. F. L., and Mrs. J. G. Albright.

ALEXANDER & GREEN
Gallery in El Paso, 1912, at 109 El Paso, operated by Jim A. Alexander and Green.

ALEXANDER, JIM A.
Operated studios c. 1908-mid-30s; located in Alamogordo, winters; in Cloudcroft, summers; also operated seasonally in El Paso, c. 1909-30s; operated as Alexander & Green at 109 South El Paso, 1911-12.

ALISON, JOHN
Active in El Paso, 1886-87, operating Parker's Photograph Gallery at 13 El Paso Street.

ALLEN, C. P.
Active in southwestern New Mexico, c. 1889-92.

ALLISON, J. L.
Traveling photographer active in Chloride on Upper Wall Street, 1886-87; in Kingston, 1892.

AMIAN, BROTHER
Probably an amateur; faculty member of Christian Brothers' College, and Territorial geologist; active in Santa Fe, c. 1885.

ANDERSON
Active in Santa Fe, c. 1885-95.

ANDREWS & COMPANY, E.
Dr. Enos Andrews, Santa Fe dentist, jeweler, and operator of circulating library, 1861-81. Father of Edwin Steck Andrews. Partner with

McKenzie in Santa Fe, at West Side Plaza during absence of Nicholas Brown. Also listed as Dr. Enos Andrews.

ANDREWS & McKENZIE
Gallery in Santa Fe, operated by Dr. Enos Andrews, c. 1871, on the west side of Plaza.

ANDREWS, DR. ENOS
See E. Andrews & Company.

ANDREWS, EDWIN STECK
Born in Santa Fe, 1867; died 1947; son of Dr. Enos Andrews. Active c. 1895-1917.

ANSLEY, W. T.
Active in El Paso, 210 North Stanton, 1912.

ARGENBRIGHT, ALVA L. (MRS.)
Active in Silver City, on Bullard Street, near Yankie, 1905-20.

ARISTO STUDIO
Active in Tucumcari, 1908, operated by O. Steihaug.

ARMSTRONG
Partner in Nall & Armstrong, active in Fort Bayard, 1905-06.

ARTS SHOP
Studio in Silver City, on Bullard Street, 1912-32, operated by William L. Spitzley.

ASPLUND, THEODORE CARL
Born 1876; died March 20, 1960. Moved to Santa Fe, c. 1909 after graduating from Daguerre Institute (Winona School of Photography), Illinois. Active in Santa Fe Camera Club, 1910-16. Studios in Santa Fe, West Side Plaza, 1909, 1913-15; Diaz Building, 1911-12; 104 Lincoln, 1912-13.

ATENCIO, J. M.
Active in Velarde, 1903-12.

ATKISSON, W. RUSSELL
Active in Dayton, 1912-13.

ATLANTIC & PACIFIC VIEW PORTRAIT COMPANY
Gallery in Eddy (Carlsbad), December 1895-January 1896, and in Tuscon, Arizona, 1902-10. Operated by Wallace B. and Joseph C. Parker.

ATTWOOD, MYRTLE (MISS)
Active in El Paso, 205 Mesa Avenue, 1905.

AULTMAN, O. E.
Brother of Otis A. Aultman. Active in Trinidad, Colorado, 1891-1900. Made photos for railroad booklet to promote gold mine area in La Belle, Taos County, May 1896.

AULTMAN, OTIS A.
Born in Holden, Missouri, August 27, 1874; died in El Paso, March 6, 1943. Schooled in Trinidad, Colorado; learned photography from his brother, O. E. Aultman. Moved to El Paso, 1907; partner with Homer Scott. Photographed meeting of President Taft and Mexican President Diaz, 1909; Madero Revolution (Mexico), Battle of Casas Grandes (Chihuahua), and Siege of Juarez (Mexico), 1911; made photos of Orozco Revolt (Mexico), and various Apache ceremonials, 1912. Motion picture pioneer work, 1916-17, for Pancho Villa and Obregon; first to photograph after Villa's raid on Columbus, New Mexico.

AUTREY, L. M. (MRS.)
Active in Gallup, 1907-08.

BACON, MAX E.
Active in Alamogordo, 1902 and Tucumcari, April-October 1903; operator for Roliene Banner in Banner Photo Car.

BAECKER, JULIUS
Active in El Paso, 309 St. Louis, 1898-99; operator for Bushong & Feldman.

BAGNASCO, POLICARPO
Itinerant Italian artist active in Santa Fe at El Dorado House, July 13, August 16, 1872, and Tucson, 1881.

BAKER & CORNELL
Studio in Roswell, 1911-12; operated by A. D. Baker and Edward M. Cornell.

BAKER & LEACH
Stereo photographers active in Raton, 1880s; possibly Don M. Leach and Raymond Baker.

BAKER, E. W.
Active in Denver, Colorado, 1888-90; in Santa Fe, on San Francisco Street, c. August 1892. Brief partnership with Skelley in Baker, 1892.

BANNER, ROLIENE E.
Photographed for El Paso and Northeastern Railroad, c. 1902-04; Mescalero Apache Indian Reservation, c. 1902-03. Operated the Banner Photo Car in Cloudcroft and Alamagordo, 1902-03; in Las Cruces, 1908, 1912-13.

BARKER, E. S.
Active in Texico, 1907-08.

BARNES, J. E.
Active in Eddy (Carlsbad) in partnership with Frank P. Pool, operating as Pool & Barnes, 1893, and independently, 1893-96.

BARNES, WILL CROFT
See Arizona.

BARNUM, CHARLES
Active in Aurora, 1911-12.

BARRETT, JACK
Active in Solano, 1907-08.

BARTHELMESS & SCHOFIELD
Partnership of Christian Barthelmess and Schofield.

BARTHELMESS, CHRISTIAN
See Montana.

BASS, EDWIN A.
Operated gallery in Socorro, 1882-85.

BAUM, DR. HENRY MASON
Photographed Acoma Pueblo and Taos Indians, 1907, for the National Photographic Library, Washington, D.C.

BEATTY, R. R.
Active in Artesia, 1907-08.

BECKAM, L. P. (MRS.)
Active in Las Vegas, 718 Ulibarri Street, 1895-96.

BECKHAM, LOUIS P.
Active in Albuquerque, 1121 South Edith Street, 1907-10.

BELL, DR. WILLIAM
Worked with Alexander Garner, photographers with Palmer-Wright-Calhoun survey for the Eastern Division of the Union Pacific across New Mexico, Arizona and California, 1867.

BENNETT & BROWN
Studio in Santa Fe, West Side Plaza, June 1880-83; George C. Bennett and W. H. Brown. .

BENNETT & BURRALL
Partnership of George C. Bennett and Burrall, 1878, in Santa Fe on Palace Avenue, near northeast corner Plaza.

BENNETT, FRANK
Name also possibly George C. Bennett.

BENNETT, GEORGE C.
Active in Santa Fe, as Bennett & Burrall, Palace Avenue, northeast corner Plaza, 1878; northwest corner Plaza, c. February-May 1880. Active as Bennett & Brown, West Side Plaza, June 1880-83, partner with William Henry Brown. Name also possibly Frank Bennett. Major producer of stereoviews. Same images appear with imprints of G. C. Bennett, Bennett & Brown and W. Henry Brown.

BENNETT, J. M.
Active in Arrey, 1903-08.

BENZINGER, FRED
Correspondent active in Taos, 1892, photographing San Geronimo Day for the Omaha Bee and the American Press Association of New York.

BERNARD, OSCAR C.
Active in El Paso at 107 Myrtle, 1901-03; 211 Myrtle, 1904-05; 407 Myrtle, 1906-07; 609 San Antonio, 1908-12.

BIBO, EMIL
Born in Brackl, Westphalia, Prussia, February 10, 1862; died March 23, 1925. Came to U.S., 1879; operated Trading Post in Cubero; photographed the Acoma and Laguna Pueblos, c. 1898-1912.

BIDDELL, J. R.
Active in Fort Wingate and Gallup, September-October 1888. Name also listed as Biddle; may be misspelling of Riddle.

BIRT, GEORGE O.
Active in El Paso at 508 El Paso (or South El Paso), 1903-04; 602 South El Paso, 1905-10; 506 ½ or 605 ½ South El Paso, 1911; 207 ½ South Stanton, 1912.

BLACK, J. M., JR.
Active in Kirtland, San Juan County, 1911-12.

BLISS, W. P.
Active in Santa Fe, c. 1878 or 1879; sometimes with partner George Ben Wittick, operating as Wittick & Bliss. See Kansas and Traveling.

BLOCHE, ARTHUR E.
Active in Lucero, 1903-08.

BLUE, FRANK O.
Active in Clayton, 1912-13.

BLUE TENT GALLERY
Operated by George Ben Wittick in Albuquerque, 1881-82, in partnership with R. W. Russell.

BOATMAN, R. J.
Active in Carlsbad, 1905-06.

BODDY, EDWARD V.
Active in Elida as Boddy & Sons, 1907-08. Listed alone in Artesia and Elida, 1911-12; in Artesia, 1912-20; in Albuquerque at 302 ½ West Central Avenue, 1922-26.

BOLTON, THOMAS C.
Active in Santa Fe, West Side Plaza, c. May-December 1885; at El Paso at Oregon Street between San Antonio and Texas, 1886-87; at 319 and 213 El Paso Street, 1888-89.

BONITTA, MACK
Active in El Paso, northeast corner of Texas and North Stanton or 405 Myrtle, 1909-10.

BONITTA, ROSA (MRS)
Active in El Paso, 405 Myrtle Avenue, 1911-12.

BONNER
Partner in Park & Bonner, active in Santa Fe, June 1885. Advertised as representing the New York Graphic.

BOOTH
Operated studio in Las Vegas, 1868; trained Valentine Wolfenstein.

BOOTH, A. J.
Active in Roswell, 1900, operating the Chicago Viewing Company.

BOSTON ART COMPANY
Gallery in El Paso, 217 Stanton, 1900, operated by Claud E. Guivey.

BOSTON RAIL ROAD PHOTO CAR
Active in Las Vegas and Santa Fe, March 1891.

BOTTOMLEY, T. F.
Active in Raton, March 1896, operating the C. A. Harris Gallery.

BOYLE
Partner in Payne & Boyle, in Santa Fe, Exchange Hotel, 1885-86.

BRAY, EDWARD M.
Active in Socorro, December 1889.

BRENNAN, MICHAEL J.
Active in El Paso, 209 North Florence, 1904.

BROOKS, P. H.
Active in Melrose, 1907-08.

BROWN & SON, N.
Studio in Santa Fe operated by Nicholas Brown, 1866-72.

BROWN & THOMAS
Partnership operating the Stephenson Gallery in Las Cruces, 1895; listed as Thomas Brothers, 1897.

BROWN, A. T. (MRS.)
Active in West Quay County, 1911-13.

BROWN, FANNIE (MRS.)
Widow of William Henry Brown; photographer for Francis Parker in El Paso, 1889. Also listed as Fanny.

BROWN, HARRY C.
Active in El Paso, as photographer for F. J. Feldman, 1902.

BROWN, LORIN W., SR.
Born c. 1857; died December 29, 1902. Newspaper editor in Red River, Elizabethtown and Taos, c. 1885-1902; studio photographer in Taos, located between Dibble's Hotel and the Post Office, 1889-90s.

BROWN, NICHOLAS
One of the earliest New Mexico photographers, active in Santa Fe, 1866-72. Located next door to Santa Fe Hotel, August 1866, January-April 1867; Johnson Building, c. February 1868; West Side Plaza, c. September 1868-January 1871, November 1871-c. January 1872. Also listed as N. Brown, N. Brown & Son, Brown E'Hijo.

BROWN, W. CALVIN
Came to Albuquerque c. 1882; lieutenant in Territorial Militia. Travelled throughout northwestern New Mexico, c. 1882-89. Studio located at Gold Avenue, Albuquerque; studio was managed by E. Gregg, late 1880s, while Brown served as Marshall. Partner with George H. Wonfor, 1888-89; sold out to William Henry Cobb, 1889.

BROWN, WILLIAM HENRY
Born in 1844; died in El Paso, 1886. Son of Nicholas Brown; partner with father, 1866-67 in Santa Fe; in Fort Union, 1866; in Santa Fe, 1866-67; in Chihuahua, Mexico, 1867-69. Employed cameramen Genevus, John Burke and possibly his wife Fannie. Partner with George C. Bennett in Santa Fe, 1880-84, on West Side Plaza. Studio in Parral, Mexico, 1884-85; in El Paso, 1885. Published George C. Bennett's stereoviews under his own imprint.

BRYANT, A. J.
"Traveling Artist," headquartered in Alamogordo, New Mexico, 1898-1906.

BRYANT, J. W.
Traveling photographer, c. 1890-95.

BRYANT, M. A. (MRS.)
Active in Silver City, 1900 and 1905-06; studio at North Bullard Street, 1900.

BUCK, A. J.
Traveling photographer active c. 1898-1906, headquarters in Alamogordo. Active in Alamogordo and La Luz, 1899- 1900; in Alamogordo, 1901. Operated livery stable, 1905; undertaker, 1909.

BUEHMAN, HENRY
Born in Bremen, Germany, May 14, 1851; died December 20, 1912. Arrived in San Francisco, California, 1868, working for photo studio. Itinerant through Arizona, California, Nevada, New Mexico and Utah, 1871-74. Settled in Tucson, Arizona, 1874, acquiring studio of Julio Rodrigo. Also worked as surgeon-dentist and was mayor of Tucson, 1894-98. See Arizona and California.

BUQUOR, J. OSCAR
Active in El Paso, 511 El Paso or South El Paso, 1903-13.

BURGE ART PARLORS
Studio owned by J. C. Burge. After his death, Mrs. Burge sold it to Clinton D. Curtis, c. 1898. Sold to P. L. Weitfle, 1900. Located on Mills block, Little Plaza, El Paso.

BURGE, J. C.
Born c. 1839; died January 1, 1897. Active in Phoenix, Arizona and Montezuma, c. 1881; in Flagstaff, Arizona, c. 1883- 84; in Globe, 1884; in Kingston, c. 1885-91; in Deming operating a branch studio under W. A. Gilmore, 1888-89; intermittently in Hermosa, 1890; in Las Cruces, c. 1891; in El Paso at 212 Santa Fe, 1895-96.

BURK, JOHN
Partner in Stiles & Burk or Burke, active c. 1882, Santa Fe, c. May 1882; in San Pedro and Golden, c. June 1882; in Fort Stanton, c. July 1882; in Tularosa, c. July-August 1882; in Organ Mountain area, c. September 1882. Photographer for William Henry Brown, c. 1883. Also spelled Burke.

BURKHART, E. C.
Active in White Oaks, c. 1877.

BURN, W. L.
Active in El Paso, manager for F. A. Remington at 111 South El Paso, 1905.

BURNHAM
Active in Las Vegas, c. 1881-82.

BURRALL
Partner with George C. Bennett in Santa Fe, 1878, operating as Bennett & Burrall.

BURTNESS, CONNER C.
Active in Magdalena, 1912-13.

BUSHONG & FELDMAN
Studio in El Paso, 111 El Paso, 1895-1901; John C. Bushong and Frederick J. Feldman.

BUSHONG, JOHN C.
Leased studio to Feldman, 1895, to study in the East; entered four-year partnership upon returning, but sold to Feldman, 1901. Also listed as John S. Bushong.

BUTLER, J. FREDERICK
Active in Eddy (Carlsbad), c. 1896-98, partners with Frank P. Pool in Pool & Butler; active in Carlsbad, 1903-13.

BUTMAN, W. C.
Photographer active in Albuquerque, 1904, 215 West Railroad Avenue. Also known as Butman's Studio. Name often misspelled Batman.

BUTMAN, W. W.
Stereo photographer active in Albuquerque.

CABLE, R. E.
"Ambrotype Artist" in Santa Fe, 1861.

CALVAR, FRANK
Anglicized name of Francisco Calvarusso, see below.

CALVARUSSO, FRANCISCO
Active in El Paso, 1911-13, 610 South El Paso. Also known as Frank Calvar.

CARPENTER
Active c. 1905-07, photographing Indians.

CARTER
Active in Santa Fe, March 1882; sent cameraman to photograph fire ruins in Albuquerque.

CARTER, WILLIAM P.
Died December 22, 1882. Active in Albuquerque, 1882-83; studio on the corner of Lead Avenue and First Street, opposite the Armijo House.

CASTER, LEE L.
Active in Forrest, Quay County, 1911-12.

CENTENNIAL PHOTOGRAPHIC COMPANY
Philadelphia firm operating photo concession of the 1876 Centennial Exposition involving Edward L. Wilson, editor of The Philadelphia Photographer. Issued stereoviews of Santa Fe and Albuquerque, 1876-82.

CENTER, ADDISON P.
Active in Las Cruces, 1901-04.

CHAIN
Traveling operator for William Henry Jackson.

CHANDLER, DELL
Active in Gallup, 1897.

CHASE, DANA B.
Died c. 1897. Owned studio in Santa Fe, 1884-92, on West Side Plaza; operated by L. Fetter and E. B. Headley, 1884- 85.

CHASE, N. W.
Active in Las Cruces and Deming, c. 1894.

CHICAGO VIEWING COMPANY
Studio operated by A. J. Booth in Roswell, 1900.

CLAIBORNE, C. E.
Active in Clovis, 1911-12.

CLARK, MAY (MISS)
Clerk-secretary for the Bureau of American Ethnology, Washington, D.C. Accompanied Mrs. Matilda Coxe Stevenson to Zia Pueblo, 1890, photographing ceremonials and shrines.

CLEVELAND, CHARLES
Active in Red River, 1903-06.

CLEVELAND, R. D.
Amateur photographer; illustrated a trip by railroad rate agents on a chartered train from Chicago via Denver and New Mexico to Chihuahua, Mexico, 1882.

CLINTON, J. L.
See Colorado.

CLINTON, P.
Active in Las Vegas, corner of 7th and Douglas Avenues, 1907-08.

CLINTON STUDIO
Gallery in El Paso, 1898-1900, operated by Clinton D. Curtis.

COBB, EDDIE ROSS (MRS.)
Born in Leavenworth, Kansas, 1862; died 1945. Daughter of U.S. Senator Edmund G. Ross. Active in photography in Albuquerque, 1889-1942. Receptionist in Albright Art Parlors, 1889; retoucher for William H. Cobb, 1890; married him, 1891. She continued in business after his death, 1909-1942, retiring at age 80.

COBB STUDIO
Gallery operated by William Henry and Mrs. Eddie Ross Cobb.

COBB, WILLIAM HENRY
Born in New York, 1860; died March 6, 1909. Active in Albuquerque, 1889-1909. Studio at 115 West Gold Avenue, 1889-97; 210 West Gold Avenue, 1901-09. Mrs. Eddie Ross Cobb continued the business after his death, 1909.

COFFMAN, CHARLES
Active in Mills, 1911-12.

COLE, FAY-COOPER
Born in 1881. Anthropologist and archaeologist; active in Chaco Canyon, making numerous lantern slides for use in lectures.

COLLOM
Partner in Cortell & Collom, operating in Deming with Andrew Jackson Cortell.

COLPAS
Partner in White & Colpas, stereo photographers active in Raton, 1880s-1900s.

COLTMAN, REVEREND
Amateur photographer; faculty member of Presbyterian Indian School, active in Albuquerque, 1889.

CONSAUL & SWEETLAND
Active in Elizabethtown, 1896

CONTINENT STEREOSCOPIC COMPANY
Active New York, c. 1878-98, reprinting or pirating the work of New Mexico photographers Nicholas Brown, William Henry Brown, and George C. Bennett.

COOKE
Active in Nara Visa, third lot west of Hotel King, January 1908.

CORKINS
Active Santa Fe, early 1866.

CORNELL, EDWARD M.
Partner in Baker & Cornell, active in Roswell, 207 West 4th, 1912-14.

CORT
Partnership of Porter & Cort, active c. 1900.

CORTELL, ANDREW JACKSON
Born in Norwich, New York; son of John Patterson Kettle. Name changed to Kittell and then to Cortell. Active in Santa Fe, West Side Plaza, 1888, in partnership with George W. Mack operating as Mack & Cortell; in Deming, Copper Avenue, Hopkins Cottage, 1889. Also partner in Cortell & Collom. Lived in Mexico and Texas.

COUGHLEN, D. R.
Active in Raton, 1905-06.

COX BROTHERS
Active in Albuquerque, East Side Plaza (Old Town), April-June 1881; Los Lunas, c. June 1881.

CRAUSBAY, J. M.
Active in Santa Fe, leasing the Kaadt Studio, Delgado Building, West Side Plaza, c. June 1901; 112 Lincoln, 1903-04.

CRAYCRAFT, AARON B.
Born c. 1856; died August 21, 1918. Active in Santa Fe at Plaza Studio, West Side Plaza, 1904-05; Plaza, 1911-12; 112 Lincoln Avenue, 1912-13; Plaza, 1913-15; 129 Palace Avenue, 1918. Also known as Craycraft Foto, c. 1904-18.

CRISPELL, A. H. (MRS.)
Probably the widow of T. Crispell. Active in East Las Vegas, 702 Douglas Avenue, 1895-96.

CRISPELL, T.
Operating studio for James N. Furlong, Furlong & Crispell, 1885-90; located at Bridge Street, Las Vegas,1888-89; opened his studio, mid-1891 at New Plaza, Douglas Avenue. First name is probably Theron.

CROWELL & COMPANY
Arthur B. Crowell with Arthur W. Dowe leased William Henry Brown's studio in Santa Fe, 1886-87, on Oregon Street near San Antonio.

CROWELL, ARTHUR B.
Partner with Arthur W. Dowe in Crowell & Company.

CRUM'S MEXICAN CURIOSITY BAZAAR
Issued stereoviews in Santa Fe; photographer unknown.

CUNNINGHAM & COMPANY
Studio operated by Alexander M. Cunningham in Colorado Springs, Colorado, 1884-85. Made stereographs for Atcheson, Topeka & Santa Fe Railroad. May have bought out Franklin Nims, since some views are on printed cards of Nims overstamped by Cunningham.

CURRAN, THOMAS J.
Died January 15, 1919. Active in Santa Fe, 1891-99. Bought studio from Dana B. Chase, 1892; operated studio on West Side Plaza, 1892-99; sold it to P. L. Weitfle, 1899. Produced large format, artistic views of Santa Fe. Name is often misspelled Curren.

CURTIS, CLINTON D.
Active in El Paso, 1898-1900, purchasing C. Burge's studio from Mrs. Burge, July 27, 1898; sold out to P. L Weitfle, September 17, 1900. Clinton Studio and Burge Art Parlors located on Mills Block, Little Plaza, El Paso, 1900.

CURTIS, EDWARD S.
One of America's legendary photographers. Main work in New Mexico, 1903-04, 1925. See Washington.

CUYLER, BEN
Active in Santa Fe with assistant Vreeland, 1890.

DARTON, NELSON HORATIO
Born 1865; died 1948. Noted geologist active in New Mexico and southwest, c. 1900. He sometimes used the work of others, such as Ward's Studio of Alamogordo.

DAVIS, BENJAMIN F.
Partner of William M. Pennington in Pennington & Davis, active in Albuquerque at 309 West Central Avenue, 1907-08.

DAVIS, O. T.
Active in La Belle, New Mexico, May 1895-April 1896.

DAVIS, R. C.
Active in Santa Fe, Plaza, 1903-04.

DE LONG, O. V.
Active in El Paso at 21-26 Plaza Block, 1907; 4 ½ Little Plaza, 1907-08.

DEAKINS, E. D.
Active in Roosevelt, 1907-08.

DEMMON, E. F.
Partner with W. A. White in White & Demmon, active in Springer and Santa Fe, May-June 1890.

DENNIS, S. K.
Active in East Las Vegas in 1887.

DETROIT PHOTOGRAPHIC COMPANY
Represented by W. H. Jackson who visited New Mexico, 1899, photographing the Acoma and Laguna Pueblos; in Albuquerque, 1902-04, c. 1908. Jackson was a part-owner of the company and leased his images for publication.

DILLINGHAM, J. E.
Active in Watrous, 1897.

DIXON, DR. JOSEPH K.
Active photographing American Indians, 1908-13; probably actual photographer of pictures attributed to Rodman Wanamaker. Published The Vanishing Race, 1913.

DOMINGUEZ, JOSE
Active in Mesilla, 1875, at Court Street, taking over the studio of H. T. Heister.

DONATI, AUG.
Active in Tucumcari, 1912-13.

DORMAN, HENRY HOWARD
Born May 14, 1872; died October 28, 1960. Landscape photographer in Santa Fe, 1902-20.

DOUBLEDAY & PATTON
Active in Las Cruces.

DOUGLAS, O. F.
Active in Albuquerque, 1884-85.

DOWE, ARTHUR W.
Partner in Crowell & Company in El Paso with Arthur B. Crowell, 1886-87; studio at 202 El Paso Street. Listed alone, 1888.

DOWE, O. L.
Active in Las Vegas.

DOWNING, MORTIMER A.
Active in Santa Fe c. 1893; in Silver City, c. May 1, 1893; in Hillsboro, c. May 15, 1893; in Eddy (Carlsbad), c. May 29, 1893.

EASON, D.
Active in Melrose, 1907-08.

EATON, ALLAN
Active in Deming, 1884-85.

ECKMEYER, C. (MR. & MRS.)
Probably amateurs, although possibly making studies for cousin E. W. Deming, a New York painter. Active in 1894, when they photographed several pueblos, particularly Santa Clara, San Juan and Jemez.

EDGINGTON
Partner in Smith & Edgington, active in Taos, 1912-13.

EL PINON STUDIO
Active in Santa Fe, c. 1905.

ELDERKIN, HAROLD A.
Active in Las Vegas as successor to F. M. Sargent, c. 1885; Montezuma View Company with Wooster, c. August 1886. Active in Santa Fe, May-November 1886; Plaza Art Studio, Delgado Building, West Side Plaza, November 1886- December 1887; West Side Plaza, 1888. Partner in Wooster & Elderkind active in Las Vegas, August 1885-May 1886. Also worked under the name of Montezuma View Company.

ELITE PHOTO STUDIO
Active in Alamogordo, across from Courthouse and Alamogordo Hotel, 1903.

EMANUEL, E. V.
Active in Santa Fe, 1889-90, representing Victor Portrait Company.

ERICKSON, C. A.
Active in Raton, 1900-04. Studio at Saunders Avenue and 3rd Street, June 1900-01.

ESSERY, R. W.
Studio operator from St. Paul, Minnesota, who spent winter of 1885-86 in Santa Fe, presumably for his health, at St. Vincent's Sanitarium. Photographed Santa Fe.

ESTIELL, B. F.
Active in Logan, Quay County, 1910.

EVANS, DAVID E.
Active in Albuquerque, 1909.

EVANS, FRANK E.
Active in East Las Vegas, 1881-87; photographed Penitente activities, 1884. Studio at 311 Grand Avenue, 1881; 410 Grand Avenue, 1883; nearly opposite Optic Office, 1885.

EWING & HILTON
Active in Albuquerqu,e c. 1908, photographing Pueblo and Navajo Indians.

FARNSWORTH, NORMAN
Operated the studio for Harold A. Elderkin in Santa Fe, 1886, in the Delgado Building, West Side Plaza.

FARR, H. R.
Born in Vermont, 1839; died March 17, 1893. Active in Albuquerque, 1892-93, after buying the studio of M. B. Howard.

FELDMAN, FREDERICK J.
Born in San Jose, California, 1873; died 1923. Worked on trains between Tucson, Arizona and El Paso, Texas. Tintypist in Tucson, 1893; leased Bushong studio and partnership, 1897-1901; eventually bought out studio, operating there until his death.

FETHERSTON
Active in Albuquerque, 1872.

FETTER, W. L.
Operator for Dana B. Chase, West Side Plaza, Santa Fe, 1884. Active in Gallup, opposite the Plummer & Wickham Building, October 1889-February 1890.

FEWKES, DR. JESSE WALTER
Born in 1850; died in 1930. Noted anthropologist and archaeologist active in the southwest, c. 1890-1929. Worked in New Mexico, c. 1890-92, c. 1909-10, c. 1915, c. 1925-29; at Zuni Pueblo, 1890.

FISKE, HONORABLE E. A.
U.S. Attorney for New Mexico and amateur photographer, 1891.

FITES, SAMUEL
Active in Albuquerque, 117 ½ South 2nd, 1908-09.

FITZSIMMONS, THOMAS
Worked with banquet and panoramic cameras; active in Raton, 1905-14.

FLY, CAMILLUS S.
Arizona photographer; his studio possibly located in Santa Fe, on San Francisco Street, next to J. Gold's, c. June 1892. See Arizona.

FORREST, EARLE R.
Born in 1883. Amateur active in Four Corners area and on Navajo Reservation, summer 1902.

FORTIN, J.
Active in Albuquerque, c. 1890. Prints appear on W. H. Cobb's card mounts, 3rd and Silver Avenues, Albuquerque, c. 1885. Name is sometimes misspelled Forton.

FROST, C. B. F.
Active in Santa Fe at Herlow's Hotel, San Francisco Street, January 1886. Practiced "Egyptian Crystal" method of coloring images.

FROST, FRANK
Active in Roswell, 1903-04; in Hagerman, 1910-13.

FRYETT, FRANK C.
Active in Silver City, 1882, in the studio of Lucas & Fryett, with Harry W. Lucas on Main Street near Broadway.

FURLONG & CRISPELL
T. Crispell operated the studio for James N. Furlong in Las Vegas, 1885-90; located at Bridge Street, 1888-89.

FURLONG, JAMES N.
Active in Las Vegas 1875-1906. Studio at 131 ½ Bridge over Post Office, 1879-85; East Side, 1895-96; Douglas and 7th, 1903-06. Studio operated by T. Crispell, 1885-90, while Furlong was in California and Texas in the cattle business.

GAIGE, GEORGE A.
Active in Albuquerque, South Side Plaza, May-September 1863. May be the same as J. G. Gaige.

GAIGE, J. G.
Died in Camp Goodwin, Arizona, July 1869. Daguerreotypist, ambrotypist, and photographer regularly traveling the Arizona-New Mexico Territory. Active in Santa Fe, c. 1862. Photographer for New Mexico Military District, 1865. Active at Fort Sumner where the Navajo Indian Nation was in captivity, February-March 1866. Studio at Southwest Corner Plaza, opposite Perea's. Name sometimes misspelled Gage. May be the same as George A. Gaige.

GARRETT, C. E.
Active in Otto, Santa Fe County, 1911-12.

GENEVUS
Operator for William Henry Brown, Santa Fe, 1883.

GENTHE, ARNOLD
Visited New Mexico in 1894, 1897, and on two more occasions before 1912; photographed around Acoma Pueblo, See California.

GENTRY, M.
Active in Albuquerque, c. 1892. See Texas.

GERIKEN, GEORGE O.
Active in San Marcial, 1888.

GILBERT, W. L.
Active in Gallup, opposite Plummer and Wickham Building, January-September 1889.

GILLAM, W. F.
Active in Aztec, 1907-08.

GILLOT, N. H.
Active in Taos, 1900-01, in the old Government building. Also listed as N. R. Gillot.

GILMORE, W. A.
Operator for J. C. Burge; studio in Deming, Gold Avenue, opposite the bank, 1889.

GLASCOCK
Partner in Lopez & Glascock, operated by Paul C. Lopez in El Paso, 506 ½ South El Paso, 1912-13.

GLASER, ADOLPH
Active in Albuquerque, 1900.

GOLD, J.
Dealer in stereoviews and Indian and Mexican curiosities in Santa Fe, c. 1880s.

GOMEZ & VILLALOBOS
Studio in El Paso, 316 South Stanton, 1906.

GOMEZ, J. LUZ
Active in El Paso at 401 ½ South El Paso, 1907; 517 South El Paso, 1908-10; 506 South El Paso, 1911-12. Name may also be J. L. or G. L. Luz.

GOMEZ, M. F.
Active in El Paso, 610 South El Paso, 1911.

GONZALES, G.
Stereo photographer active in Las Vegas.

GOODALE, C. M.
Active in Las Vegas, Railroad Avenue, 1888-89.

GOODLOE, GUY
Active in El Paso, 212-214 South Santa Fe, 1901-07.

GOODMAN, CHARLES
Studio over the Evening Citizen office, in Albuquerque, 1893.

GOSPER, ETHEL
Active in Orton, Quay County, 1911-12.

GOTTLIEB, HARRY JOSEPH
Born in New York, 1882; died in 1936. Worked for itinerant wagon photographer at age 12 in New York and at Coney Island for lady tintypist. Opened studio in Florida, photographing Admiral Dewey. Active in El Paso and Las Cruces, c. 1907, as operator for A. N. Segal; in El Paso, operating his own studio in the Plaza Block, c. 1909-23, then relocated to Alamogordo. Active in Ruidoso, c. 1924, doing itinerant portrait work in Deming and Roswell. Commissioned by Mescalero Apache tribe to photograph old scouts, c. 1930-35.

GRAY, W. L.
Amateur active in Raton, 1899; his snapshot of Theodore Roosevelt was widely sold.

GRAY, W. M.
Active in Albuquerque, 219 Central Avenue, 1910-14, operating Gray Studio.

GREEN
Active in El Paso, 1912, at 109 El Paso; partner with Jim A. Alexander operating as Alexander & Green.

GREGG, E.
Manager for W. Calvin Brown; studio in Albuqerque, 1888-89.

GRENNAN, JOHN
Active in Artesia, 1911-14.

GRIGSBY, R. L.
Active in El Paso, 506 ½ South El Paso, 1911.

GUIVEY, CLAUD E.
Operated the Boston Art Company in El Paso, 217 Stanton, 1900.

GULLETTE, REVEREND JOHN COLUMBIA
Died July 27, 1906. Amateur active in Santa Fe, c. 1890-1900, making photographs during several trips from New Mexico to Minnesota.

GUSTAFSON, CHARLES
Active in El Paso, 21-26 Plaza Block, 1904.

GUTEKUNST, FREDERICK
Proprietor of leading firm in Philadelphia, c. 1860-95. Uncertain if he personally worked in New Mexico, but his firm was commissioned to photograph the boundary markers between Mexico and the U.S. west of the Rio Grande during the re-survey of the boundary, 1892-95.

HADDIX, ANDREW J.
Photographer for Pecos Valley & North East Railroad, in Roswell and Pecos Valley area, 1899. Studio in Roswell, 1899-1902.

HAGEDORN, C. H.
His photograph, "Pines, N. M.," was published in The Albuquerque Booster, November 15, 1908.

HAIGHT, ERNEST
Active in Raton, 1912-13.

HANCE & MAST
Los Angeles firm, operated by G. W. Hance photographing in Albuquerque, 1905.

HANCE, G. W.
Partner in Hance & Mast, active in Albuquerque, 1905.

HANDY & WALDON
Photographers with group expedition under Dr. Ladd, President of University of New Mexico in Santa Fe, 1883; worked in Red Rock Canyon and in the area of modern Bandelier Monument.

HARRIS, C. A.
Operated gallery in Raton, c. 1895-97.

HARRIS, ELMER E.
Active in Raton, c. 1893-June 1899, when he died.

HARRISON, C. H.
Active in Albuquerque (Old Town), Main Street opposite Post Office, May-June 1877.

HARROUN, PHILIP EMBURY
Born in Chicago, July 14, 1867; died October 26, 1947. Active in Santa Fe, 1888-98; in Albuquerque, 1898-1902. Photographed Indian pueblos and people, ceremonies of Santa Fe.

HARVEY, SERGEANT CHARLES
Army man in Quartermaster Service; active c. 1880s.

HAWLEY, PERCY J.
Active in Albuquerque, 1908-29. Studios at northeast corner of Silver and 2nd, c. 1908-09; at 705 West Central, 1910- 29.

HAYWOOD, M. C.
From Topeka, Kansas, a partner in Leonard & Haywood with J. H. Leonard, active in Las Vegas, 1881.

HEADLEY, E. B.
Active in Santa Fe, 1884-85; operator for Dana B. Chase.

HECOX
Active in El Paso, 1911-12. Studio at February 3 Gem Building, 1911; partner in Hoffman Brothers & Hecox, 206 ½ South, 1912.

HEISTER, HENRY T.
Made stereo views of the Rio Grande Basin, New Mexico, and of reservations in Arizona and New Mexico. Active in Santa Fe, 1871-78, and in Mesilla, 1874. Studios located at West Side Plaza, Santa Fe, c. 1871-74; Main Street, September 1874-March 1875, Mesilla; South Side Plaza, September 1876-77, Santa Fe. Name also spelled Hiester.

HENDRICK, H. G.
Ambrotypist in Mesilla, Old Plaza, October 1860; in Santa Fe, April-May 1861.

HENRY BROTHERS
Stereo photographers in Santa Fe.

HERINGA, EDWARD
Active in Aztec, 1911-12.

HESS & COMPANY
Active in Roswell, 1907-08.

HIGGINS, FREAME M.
Printer for Bushong & Feldman in El Paso, 1898-99.

HILLERS, JOHN K.
Worked many times in the New Mexico and Arizona region; pictured many of the New Mexico Pueblos during his visit, 1879. See Arizona.

HILTON
Partner in Ewing & Hilton, active in Albuquerqu,e c. 1908, photographing Pueblo and Navajo Indians.

HINMAN, O. C.
Active in Silver City, (?)-1906.

HINSHAW, THOMAS
Partner with Orson Pratt Huish operating an itinerant tent and wagon, c. 1898-99; Huish & Hinshaw.

HINSON, O. A.
Partner with T. J. Ray in studio of Ray & Hinson, active in Roswell, 1907-08.

HODGMAN, C. C.
Arrested in Pinos Altos for stealing camera, 1905; hired by W. O. Thomas of Silver City to photograph southwestern New Mexico mining towns.

HODGSON, JOHN
Active in Gallup, 1903-08.

HODSOLL & STRINGFELLOW
Partnership of F. G. Hodsoll and Stringfellow, active in White Oaks, June-August 1891.

HODSOLL, F. G.
Englishman who came to Pecos Valley region, late 1880s. Active in Roswell, c. 1889-90; also in White Oaks. Partner in Hodsoll & Stringfellow, June-August 1891; returned to England, 1897, photographing Queen Victoria's Diamond Jubilee and the Kaiser in Germany. Active in Carlesbad, 200 block of Fox Street, 1915-16. Name also spelled Hodsall, Hodsell. Sold studio to Ray Davis, 1916.

HOFFMAN & COMPANY, J.
Active in Albuquerque, September 1873.

HOFFMAN BROTHERS & HECOX
Active in El Paso, 206 ½ South El Paso, 1912.

HOOK, WILLIAM E.
Produced photographs in Santa Fe and Rocky Mountain region, 1891-92, for the Wholesale View Company.

HOPKINS, BENJAMIN S.
Operated Rose & Hopkins with John K. Rose. Listed in Denver, 1896-1901. Publication in 1901 carries ad for Denver engraving shop with picture of "Elote, Chief of Apaches," copyright 1900.

HOPKINS, PROFESSOR F. LOOSEHIMSELF
Active in Las Cruces, 1901. Possibly an amateur who may have been on the staff of New Mexico State University.

HORNER
Partner in Skinner & Horner, at the Imperial Photograph Gallery in Gallup, 1900, at Coal Avenue and Second Street; in Taos, 1901.

HORTON, J. A.
Active in Las Cruces, Lower Main Street, c. 1909-13. Name is sometimes misspelled Horten.

HOWARD, M. B.
Operated studio in Albuquerque, c. 1890-92, sold out to H. R. Farr, 1892.

HOYT, H.
Active in Cimarron, December 1877; in Albuquerque (from San Francisco), opposite Centennial Hotel, February 1878.

HUBBELL, ROYAL
Produced views for J. Gold's Curio Shop in Santa Fe, c. 1900; wholesale view photographer from Florida.

HUISH & HINSHAW
Partnership of Orson Pratt Huish and Thomas Hinshaw, itinerant tent and wagon photographers, active c. 1898-99, travelling extensively through Utah, Colorado, New Mexico and Arizona.

HUISH, ORSON PRATT
Itinerant tent and wagon photographer with Thomas Hinshaw, operating as Huish & Hinshaw, active c. 1898-99, in Utah, Colorado, New Mexico and Arizona.

HUMPHRIES PHOTO COMPANY
Active in El Paso at 22-28 Mills Building, 1905-06; 129 San Francisco, 1907-09. Also known as Humphrey's and W. R. Humphries.

HUNTZING, H. G.
Active in Raton, 22 First Street, operating the Old Adobe Gallery, October-December 1900.

HUSHER
Active in Albuquerque, c. 1902-08, as operator for W. H. Jackson; his photographs of Alvarado Hotel were attributed to Jackson.

IMPERIAL PHOTOGRAPH GALLERY
Active in Gallup, 1900, at Coal Avenue and Second Street; in Taos, 1901. Also known as Skinner & Horner.

IRVINE & McKENZIE
Santa Fe firm; distributed stereoviews by Henry T. Hiester.

JACKSON, WILLIAM HENRY

His own writings indicate that he first worked in New Mexico on a brief visit, 1877, but that his efforts completely failed because of the experimental new dry plates he was using. His first significant body of New Mexico work dates from summer 1881; his Denver studio opened, 1880. The pictures produced on this trip are not exclusively his, since he was accompanied by a long-term assistant, Mr. Chain, and others. It is a problem to determine his work out of the vast body of images produced. During the 1881 visit, Jackson presented a number of pictures to the recently reborn New Mexico Historical Society, and they became a cornerstone for the present collections of the Museum of New Mexico. Presumably in return for this gift, Jackson was voted to honorary membership, and he may have visited the area again before the turn of the century. Jackson revisited New Mexico for the Detroit Photographic Company, 1899, 1902-04, concentrating on photographing Acoma and Laguna Pueblos. The newly completed Alvarado Hotel complex in Albuquerque was photographed in detail. Although Jackson supervised the work, not all negatives were his; other names, such as Husher, appear on a number of them. See Nebraska.

JAMES, GEORGE WHARTON

Born 1858; died 1923. Traveler and anthropologist active in Southwest, c. late 1880s; photographed Indian life, particularly Hopi Snake Dance. Authored several books; stereopticon lecturer. Also listed as Wharton-James.

JEANCON, JEAN ALLARD

Born 1874. Archaeologist and photographer, c. 1911.

JERRELL, W. L.

Died February August 1884. Itinerant in New Mexico and Mexico, c. 1876-78. Active in Bernalillo, February 1876; in a tent in Albuquerque, South Side Plaza, February-March 1876; in Los Lunas, March 1876; in Las Cruces, Mesilla and El Paso, May 1876; in Taos and Santa Fe, November 1877; in Las Cruces, Adkins Store, December 1877-March 1878. Shot to death by stagecoach robbers while serving as special deputy tracking other bandits near Abilene, Texas.

JOHNSON

Partner in Pankey & Johnson, active in Tucumcari, 1907-08.

JONES, FREDERICK L.

Operated a portrait studio in El Paso, 1898-99, at 22 Bronson Block.

JONES, R. W.

Active in Portales, 1905-06.

JOSEPH, ANTHONY

Territorial Delegate to Congress in intermittent terms, 1860s-90s. Owner and manager of Ojo Caliente Hot Springs into the twentieth century. Also listed as Antonio Joseph.

KAADT & WHITLOCK

Partnership in Santa Fe, c. 1902; C. G. Kaadt. Produced view cards for Gold's Curio Store.

KAADT, CHRISTIAN G.

Born in Denmark, March 1868; died May 10, 1905. Operated the Santa Fe Art Studio in Santa Fe, 1899-1905; at Lower San Francisco Street, June-July 1899; West Side Plaza, April 1900-02; 110 Lincoln, 1903-04, 1905. Produced large collection of view cards for Gold's Curio Store, 1902, some imprinted with Kaadt & Whitlock; official photographer for the Santa Fe Central Railroad, c. 1903. Made copies of others' work for wholesale trade, particularly John K. Hillers, but published them under the Kaadt imprint.

KAADT, LUCY (MRS.)

Widow of Christian G. Kaadt, who continued operating husband's studio after his death, 1905.

KAADT STUDIO

Operated by J. M. Crausbay in Santa Fe, Delgado Building, West Side Plaza, c. June 1901.

KEENUM, CHARLES W.

Active in Columbus, 1912-13.

KELEHER, THOMAS F., JR.

Born November 19, 1882, died August 1959. Active in Albuquerque with Carl Moon, in the Moon-Keleher Studio, 313 ½ West Railroad Avenue, 1905-06.

KELLOGG, C. R. (MISS)

Operated "The Studio" in Las Cruces, Murphy Building, Main Street, July-December, 1906.

KEM, S. A.

Active in Raton, North Second Street, August-September 1898; in Albuquerque, 115 Gold Avenue, 1899, operating as Kem's Art Studio.

KEMERER, GEORGE

Instructor in Chemistry at New Mexico Technical, Socorro; active photographer, early 1900s.

KEMMERER

Partner in Showell & Kemmerer, Albuquerque, 313 ½ Central, 1907-08.

KISSEL, E. L.

Operated a "Photo Car," c. 1890s.

KNORR, JOSEPH G.

Partner with Frank L. Smith in Smith & Knorr, active in Albuquerque, 206 West Silver Avenue, 1912-13.

KNOWL, R. E.

Active in Dawson, Colfax County, 1911-12.

KOCH, M. H.

Active in White Oaks, 1903-05; in Tucumcari, c. 1905.

LA GARZA BROTHERS

Active in El Paso, 718 South Stanton, 1912-13.

LAS CRUCES ART GALLERY

Active in Las Cruces, Near Rio Grande Hotel, 1892.

LAS CRUCES PHOTOGRAPH GALLERY

Studio in Las Cruces selling ambrotypes and porcelain prints, next to the Borderer office, 1872.

LEACH, DON M.

Itinerant photographer in Texas and New Mexico, c. 1886. Active in Raton as partner with Raymond Baker in Baker & Leach; with William A. White, White & Leach; in Mineral Wells with Zant, operating as Zant & Leach.

LEE, WILLIAM A.

Active in Raton, 1912-13.

LEMMON, MARK J.

Photographer in El Paso, 1895-99. Studio at 414 El Paso, 1895-96; on the south side of East 7th, between El Paso and Utah, 1898-99.

LEONARD & HAYWOOD

Partnership of J. H. Leonard and M. C. Haywood, from Topeka, Kansas, active in Las Vegas area, July 1881.

LEONARD, J. H.
From Topeka Kansas, a partner in Leonard & Haywood with M. C. Haywood, active in Las Vegas, 1881.

LIPOVETZKY, CHARLES
Studio in El Paso, 1908-09; at 217 South Stanton, 1908; 506 or 506 ½ South El Paso, 1909. Also spelled Lipowetzky.

LOCKE, E. A.
From La Jara, Colorado; active in Taos, September 1900.

LOOMIS & COMPANY
Active in Socorro, 1886.

LOOMIS, EMERSON R.
Active in Alamogordo, 1908; in Cloudcroft, summer 1908.

LOPEZ & GLASCOCK
Operated by Paul C. Lopez in El Paso, 506 ½ South El Paso, 1912-13.

LOPEZ, PAUL C.
Operated Lopez & Glascock in El Paso, 506 ½ South El Paso, 1912-13.

LOWELL
Active in Cerrillos, 1894; visited Bland in August.

LUCAS & FRYETT
Partnership of Frank C. Fryett and Harry W. Frank, active in Silver City, 1882, on Main Street near Broadway.

LUCAS, HARRY W.
Active in Silver City, 1882-85. Located at Main Street working for Alfred S. Addis, 1882; Main Street near Broadway, 1882; with Frank C. Fryett, c. 1882-83, in the studio of Lucas & Fryett. He absconded with the Silver City Masonic Lodge treasury, December 1893, and fled to Mexico.

LUMMIS, CHARLES FLETCHER
Noted photographer, journalist and writer. Active in New Mexico c. 1884-1925, producing around 10,000 prints, and books: A Tramp Across the Continent, 1892; The Land of Poco Tiempo, 1925; Mesa, Canon and Pueblo, 1925. See California.

LUZ, J. L.
See J. Luz Gomez.

MACK & CORTELL
Partnership of George W. Mack and A. J. Cortell, active in Santa Fe, West Side Plaza, December 1887-c. April 1888.

MANKER, R. E.
Operator for Roliene E. Banner in Alamogordo, 1902-03.

MARKS, CHARLES W.
Active in Las Cruces, located in a tent on South Main Street, September-December 1890; in Mesilla, c. December 1890; in White Oaks, 1892; in Silver City, August 1896.

MARSHALL, J. W.
Active in Las Palomas Hot Springs, c. 1905-08.

MARTIN & COMPANY, GEORGE T.
Stationer and bookseller in Santa Fe in 1869 dealing in photographs, photo albums, stereoscopes and views.

MARTIN, JOHN
Ambrotypist in Santa Fe, Hovey House, 1863.

MARTINEZ, J. B.
Active in Las Vegas on Bridge Street, 1903-04.

MAST
Partner in Hance & Mast with G. W. Hance in Albuquerque, 1905.

MASTERS, WILLIAM G.
Photo printer for Bushong & Feldman, c. 1900.

MATHEWS, W. H.
Partner with G. W. Overman in Overman & Mathews, active in Deming at 105 Silver, 1912-13.

MATTESON, SUMNER W.
Active in Four Corners area as bicycling intinerant, c. 1899-1900, photographing for Field and Stream magazine; with Wetherill expeditions at Pueblo Bonito, Chaco Canyon.

MAYES
Active in Albuquerque, Hughes Block above The Citizen office, 1893-94.

McCLURE, LOUIS CHARLES
Born c. 1872; died February 26, 1957. Operator for William Henry Jackson in Denver, 1895-97; in his own studio thereafter. Photographed New Mexico Pueblo Indians, c. 1900-20.

McELWAIN, GUY W.
Photographer in El Paso, 1912-13; studio at 210 North Stanton.

McEWEN, PROFESSOR
Daguerreotypist in Santa Fe, 1858; also visited Las Vegas Hot Springs. Traveled down the Rio Grande Valley, October 1858.

McKENZIE
Partner in E. Andrews & Company in Santa Fe, c. 1871, operating as Andrews & McKenzie, West Side Plaza. Partner in Irvine & McKenzie, a firm distributing stereoviews by Henry T. Hiester.

McSCHOOLER, T. W.
Active in Raton, 1905-06, 1911-12.

MERNIN, T. G.
Active in Las Vegas, c. 1885-90; in Albuquerque after 1890. Uncertain when he was a photographer; he was also in book, stationery and music business.

MILLER
Partner in Stirrat & Miller, operated in Las Vegas, 1905-06.

MILLER, G. EDWARD
Died c. 1950. Active as photographer, c. 1900-20; itinerant throughout Otero County region. Worked in North Cloudcroft on the Stewart Lot, July 1904; in Mayhill, 1906, 1907-08, 1911-12.

MILLER, GEORGE T.
Born in Chicago, c. 1864-65; died 1909. Moved to Hillsboro, New Mexico, 1892, and operated a drug store until his death. Active as photographer, 1906-08, recording stagecoaches in the Caballo Road and Palomas Gap areas near Elephant Butte; photographs were published in land development stock sale brochure.

MILLER, H.
Assistant to Jim A. Alexander, Alamogordo, 1910.

MILLETT, E. M.
Proprietor of the Millett Studio in Albuquerque at 215 West Railroad (Central), 1907-08.

MILLETT, IDA (MRS.)
Photographer at the Millett Studio in Albuquerque at 215 West Railroad (Central), 1907-08; 215 West Central Avenue, 1909-10. Also listed as Mrs. E. M. Millett.

MISHLER & WALKER
Partnership of Calvin S. Mishler and Horace H. Walker, active in Gallup, 1905-08, 1911-13.

MISHLER, CALVIN S.
Partner in Mishler & Walker with Horace H. Walker, active in Gallup, 1905-08, 1911-13.

MONTEZUMA VIEW COMPANY
Partnership of Harold A. Elderkin and Wooster, active in Las Vegas, 1885.

MONTFORT, E.
Photographer and undertaker in Albuquerque, c. 1885-95.

MOON, CARL E.
Born in Wilmington, Ohio, 1878. Worked for various photographers in Ohio, West Virginia and Texas before arriving in Albuquerque, 1903. In 1906, Moon's art studies of southwest Indians were used as illustrations by museums and magazines. Moon moved his studio to El Tovar at the Grand Canyon, 1907, and he contributed images to the Fred Harvey Collection of Southwest Indian pictures. He was also a partner with Thomas F. Keleher, Jr. in the Moon-Keheler Studio at New Grant Block, 313 ½ West Railroad (Central), Albuquerque. Official photographer for Santa Fe Railroad, 1909s. His large format silver prints were sold through Fred Harvey outlets, and now command substantial prices in the art market. An artist trained by Thomas Moran, Moon moved to Pasadena, California, 1914, where he painted oils for the Smithsonian Institution. In 1923, Moon sold three hundred large format photographs and twelve oil paintings to Henry E. Huntington.He produced Indians of the Southwest, a four volume atlas-folio set containing one hundred photographs, 1936; however only ten copies were printed. Moon illustrated many childrens' books, a number of them written by his wife, Grace. Also listed as Karl Moon.
    Haines, Robert D. Jr., *Carl Moon; Photographer & Illustrator of the American Southwest*, Argonaut Bookshop, San Francisco, 1982.
    Tom Driebe and Dave Palmiter, *In Search of the Wild Indian: Photographs and Life Works by Carl & Grace Moon*, Maurose Publishing Co., Moscow, Pennsylvania, 1996.

MOONEY, JAMES
Born 1861; died 1921. Anthropologist for Bureau of American Ethnology, writing mainly on the Cherokee Indians. Produced text and photographs for the definitive study of The Ghost-Dance Religion and the Sioux Outbreak of 1890. Claimed to have made the only picture of Wovoka, Paiute initiator of the Ghost Dance cult.

MOON-KELEHER STUDIO
Partnership of Carl Moon and Thomas F. Keleher, Jr. Active in Albuquerque at 313 ½ West Railroad Avenue, 1905- 06.

MOORE, S. E.
Active in Portales, 1907-08, 1911-13.

MYERS, L. S.
Active in Taos, 1899-1900. Possibly a partner in Phillips & Myers; possibly in Smith & Myers, 1911-12.

NALL & ARMSTRONG
Active in Fort Bayard, 1905-06.

NAST'S GALLERY
Active in Santa Fe, San Francisco Street, opposite store of Joe Hirsch,

October 12, November 7, 1882. Presumably the firm of C. A. Nast, Denver, 1880-91.

NEFF, HARRY L.
Partner with Milton E. Porter in Porter & Neff, active in Albuquerque, 220 West Gold Avenue, 1909-10.

NEIS, CORAL MAE (MRS.)
Worked as photographer in Tucumcari, 1909-14, after the death of her husband.

NETO, J. B.
Active in Albuquerque, 1905-06; also a barber.

NEW, SYLVA
Active in Endee, Quay County, 1912-13.

NEWMAN, ALMERON
Known for his panoramic pictures, he was active throughout New Mexico, c. 1905-20s. Headquartered in Silver City, c. 1910-15; in Raton, dates uncertain. See British Columbia.

NICKLAS, W. H.
Active in Redlake, Roosevelt County, 1911-14.

NIELSEN, A. P.
Active in Santa Fe, San Francisco Street, tent next to U.S. Revenue Office, August-c. October 1886.

NIMS, FRANKLIN A.
Listed in Colorado Springs at times with partner Clark, 1882-83, and 1886. Photographer with Brown-Stanton Expedition down the Canyon of the Colorado, 1889-90. May have sold views to Cunningham, c. 1883, since some of his printed card labels are overstamped for Cunningham.
    The Photographer and the River, 1889-90 (Diary of F. A. Nims), Dwight L. Smith, ed., Stagecoach Press, Santa Fe, 1967.

NOBLE, RALPH KENDAL
Active in Albuquerque at 501 South Walter, 1908-09. Also known as The Booster Man and The Booster Press.

NOWELL, ROBERT A.
Active in Portales and Tucumcari, 1903-04.

NUSBAUM, JESSE LOGAN
Born in Greeley, Colorado, September 3, 1887. Came to Santa Fe, 1909, as the first employee of Museum of New Mexico, School of American Archaeology. Active photographer in Las Vegas and Santa Fe areas, c. 1908-15.

OLD ADOBE GALLERY
Operated by H. G. Huntzing in Raton, 22 First Street, October-December 1900.

OSTERGREN, G. A.
Active in Albuquerque, 1882.

OVERMAN & MATHEWS
Partnership of G. W. Overman and W. H. Mathews, active in Deming, 1912-13; studio at 105 Silver.

OVERMAN, G. W.
Partner with W. H. Mathews in Overman & Mathews, active in Deming at 105 Silver, 1912-13.

PADILLA, FRANCISCO
Active in Puerto de Luna, Guadalup County, 1907-08.

PAIRES, L. A.
Active in Belen, 1897.

PANKEY & JOHNSON
Partnership active in Tucumcari, 1907-08.

PARK & BONNER
Partnership of H. S. Park and Bonner, active in Santa Fe, June 1885. Advertised as representing the New York Graphic.

PARK & WICKMILLER
Partnership of H. S. Park and Wickmiller, active in Albuquerque, November-December 1882. Advertised as representing the New York Graphic.

PARK, H. S.
Partner in Park & Wickmiller, active in Albuquerque, November-December 1882; and in Park & Bonner, active in Santa Fe, June 1885. Both firms advertised that they represented the New York Graphic.

PARKER, FRANCIS F.
Listed in El Paso, 1884-1908; at 13 El Paso Street, 1886-87.

PARKER, R. M.
Active in Roswell, c. 1897. Also listed A. M. Parker.

PARKER, WALLACE B. & JOSEPH C.
Partnership operating as the Atlantic & Pacific View Portrait Company. Active in Eddy (Carlsbad), December 1895- January 1896; in Tuscon, Arizona, 1902-10.

PASEVICH, JACOB
Photographer in El Paso, 1901, in Room 25 of the Plaza Building.

PATTON
Partner in Doubleday & Patton, active in Las Cruces.

PAYNE & BOYLE
Operated by D. R. Payne in Santa Fe, Exchange Hotel, 1885-86.

PAYNE, D. R.
Operated with a partner in Payne & Boyle. Active in Santa Fe, Exchange Hotel, November 1885-June 1886.

PEARCE, WALTER
Active in Santa Fe, July 1883; advertised as representing the London Graphic.

PENDIKE STUDIO
Partnership of William Pennington and L. C. Updike, active in Durango, Colorado, c. 1908-13. Travelled extensively, photographing in the Four Corners area including New Mexico.

PENN, R. W.
Active in Red River, 1903-08.

PENNINGTON & DAVIS
Partnership of William M. Pennington and Benjamin F. Davis, active in Albuquerque at 309 West Central Avenue, 1907- 08.

PENNINGTON, WILLIAM
Born 1875; died c. 1939. Active in Four Corners area on trips with partner, L. C. Updike, 1907-32. Possibly the same as William M. Pennington.

PENNINGTON, WILLIAM M.
Active in Albuquerque at 121 ½ North Third Street, 1904; 309 West Railroad Avenue (Central), 1905-06; Partner in Pennington & Davis, 309 West Central Avenue, 1907-08; Guadalupita, 1911-12. Possibly the same as William Pennington.

PEOPLE'S STUDIO
Active in Albuquerque, 212 South Third, 1907-08.

PHELPS, WILLIAM
Active in San Marcial, c. 1885-95.

PHILLIPS & MYERS
Partnership active in Taos, c. 1898-99; possibly L. S. Myers.

PHILLIPS & SHEEK
Partnership of Ren Phillips and Sheek, active in Roswell area, 1892-93, promoting region for fair displays, including the Columbian Exposition in Chicago.

PICKETT, W. B.
Active in Raton, c. 1894.

PLAZA ART STUDIO
Firm name used in Santa Fe in late 1880s by both Harold A. Elderkin and his successors.

POLEY, HORACE SWARTLEY
Born c. 1864; died June 1949. Photographed Indians of Santa Clara, San Juan, San Ildefonso, and the Rio Grande Pueblos of New Mexico.

POLLOCK, RALPH F.
Active in Alamogordo, 1905-13; at Tenth Street, 1912-13. He spent summers in Cloudcroft while his wife ran the Alamogordo studio.

POOL & BARNES
Partnership of Frank P. Pool and J. E. Barnes, active in Eddy (Carlsbad), 1893.

POOL & BUTLER
Partnership of Frank P. Pool and J. Frederick Butler, active in Eddy (Carlsbad), c. 1896-98.

POOL, FRANK P.
Active in Eddy (Carlsbad) May-June 1893; partner with J. E. Barnes in Pool & Barnes, June-July 1893; and with J. Frederick Butler in Pool & Butler, c. 1896-98.

POORE, H. R.
Artist from Philadelphia who photographed in Santa Fe area, 1890.

PORTER & CORT
Active c. 1900.

PORTER & NEFF
Partnership of Milton E. Porter and Harry L. Neff, active in Albuquerque, 220 West Gold Avenue, 1909-10.

PORTER, MILTON E.
Photographer and Kodak finisher, active in Albuquerque, 1901-10. Located at 212 South 2nd, 1907; 220 West Gold Avenue, 1908-09; partner with Harry L. Neff in Porter & Neff, 220 West Gold Avenue, 1909-10.

POSACK, A.
Active in El Paso at 110 Stanton, 1903-04, and in Socorro, 1905-06.

POSADA, JOSE
Active in San Rafael, Valencia County, 1907-08.

POTTER, FLORENCE E. (MISS)
Active in Albuquerque, 1901, 1904-06, 115 West Gold Avenue.

POTTER, SADIE (MISS)
Photographer in studio of Dana B. Chase, Santa Fe, 1890.

PRENTICE, SERGEANT ROYAL
He sold photographs made in Cuba while serving in the Spanish-American War with Troop E of the Rough Riders, 1899; probably an amateur.

PRICE, ROBERT C.
Photographed Indian dancers and Governor Hagerman, c. 1907; studio possibly in Santa Fe.

RAGAN, GEORGE C.
Operated Ragan's Plaza Studio in Las Vegas, 1900, 1903-04, 1907-08, 1911-14. Also listed as J. C. Ragan.

RANDALL, A. FRANK
Itinerant in wide area, c. 1883-88, based in Wilcox, Arizona. Correspondent for Leslie's on Crook Expedition, 1883. Photographs of Apache Indians present problems of attribution. Musum of New Mexico has George Ben Wittick copy negatives of photos copyrighted by Randall; Arizona Historical Society has prints on Randall's card mounts which are captioned in the print in Wittick's handwriting. It has not been determined whether trade, sale, partnership or outright piracy was involved. Listed in Las Cruces at Montezuma Block, November 1885-May 1886.

RAY & HINSON
Partnership of T. J. Ray and O. A. Hinson, active in Roswell, 1905-06.

RAY, T. J.
Partner with O. A. Hinson in Ray & Hinson, active in Roswell, 1907-08.

REALL, J. A.
Active in Taos, as Simpson & Reall, May 1891. Listed in Las Vegas, northwest corner Plaza, c. October 1899. Also operated as Reall's Art Studio; also spelled Real.

REED, BYRON
Active in Albuquerque and Las Vegas, March-April 1881.

REEVES, ENOCH J.
Photographer in El Paso, 1902-03, 25 Plaza Block.

REID, E. L.
Active in Tucumcari, Third Street fronting Livery Stable, 1903-04.

REIS, T. E.
Active in Albuquerque, 1904.

REMINGTON, FREDERICK A.
Operator for Francis Parker; in El Paso, 1888-89; 1905-06; in Las Cruces, 1889.

RENNIE & STANLEY
Active in Las Cruces, 1889, first door east of corner opposite the Post Office.

RHODY, F. (MRS.)
Active in El Paso, 1907-10, at 212 West Overland.

RICHARDSON, R.
Active in Yeso, De Baca County, 1911-12.

RICHARDSON, W. S.
Stereo photographer active in New Mexico; may have been associated with H. T. Heister.

RIDDLE, J. R.
Active as itinerant with the firm of Leonard & Martin, Topeka, Kansas in 1880s, following the route of the Santa Fe Railroad, using tents. Active in Santa Fe, May 1886; in Las Cruces, at Plaza, May 1888.

RISDON, O. A.
Operated studio of Thomas & Risdon, active in Clifton, New Mexico, and Metcalfe, Arizona, 1909-12.

ROBB & COMPANY
Active in Carlsbad, 1907-08, 1911-12.

ROBERTS, W.
Active in Silver City, 1897.

ROBINSON, H. F.
Photographed Hopi, Navajo, Pueblo and Blackfoot Indians as an avocation, c. 1904-20.

ROBINSON, ROBERT O.
Active in Clovis, 1912-13.

ROBINSON, T. G.
Active in Las Cruces, 1905-06.

RODDEN STUDIO
Active in Roswell, c. 1910.

ROESSLE & (?)
Active c. 1900-05, possibly near Tucumcari.

ROHNER, J. A.
Active in Raton, 1884-85.

ROIBAL, SOLOMON
Active in Tusas, Rio Arriba County, 1911-12.

ROMERO, A.
Active in Arroyohondo, Taos County, 1911-12.

ROSE & HOPKINS
Studio operated by John K. Rose and Benjamin S. Hopkins. Listed in Denver, 1896-1901. Publication in 1901 carries ad for Denver engraving shop with picture of "Elote, Chief of Apaches," copyright 1900.

ROSE, A. A.
Active in Las Cruces, 1897.

ROSE, C. A.
Active in Las Cruces, c. April 1904.

ROSE, CHARLES A.
Active in in El Paso, 103 South Campbell, 1895-96.

ROSE, JOHN K.
Operated Rose & Hopkins with Benjamin S. Hopkins. Listed in Denver, 1896-1901.

ROSS, EDDIE (MISS)
Maiden name of Mrs. Eddie Ross Cobb; see individual listing.

RUDY, W. IRA
Active in Santa Fe, 1888-91. Worked with Jake Gold, 1888; worked along routes of Santa Fe and Colorado Midland Railroads, November 1890.

RUITZ, H.
Active in San Rafael, Valencia County, 1911-12.

RUSSELL, R. W.
Partner in Wittick & Russell with George Ben Wittick in Santa Fe and Albuquerque, 1880-84. Albuquerque studio at Gold Avenue, between First and Second Streets, 1881-84.

SABINE, JAMES E.
Clockmaker and jeweler, selling guns, magazines and stationery, c. 1851-60. Operated as daguerreotypist in Santa Fe, 1855-57; at East Side Plaza, c. November 1855. Also listed as Santiago E. Sabine in Spanish advertisements.

SALE, GEORGE E.
Active in San Jon, Quay County, operating as Sale Brothers with J. A. Sale prior to June 1910; San Jon, Endee, Bard City, Tipton and Glenrio, c. June 1910-September 1911; in Tucumcari as Sale Brothers, 1915.

SALE, J. A.
Operated studio, Sale Brothers, with George E., in San Jon, c. 1910; in Tucumcari, 1915.

SAN FRANCISCO PHOTOGRAPH GALLERY
Operating in Albuquerque, tent on corner of Railroad Avenue and Fourth Street, October 1882. Listed in San Marcial, c. October 1882.

SANTA FE ART STUDIO
Operated by Christian G. Kaadt in Santa Fe, 1899-1905.

SANTA ROSA PORTRAIT COMPANY
Studio in Santa Rosa, 1907-08.

SARGENT, F. M.
Active in East Las Vegas, c. 1885. His successor was Harold A. Elderkin.

SCHMIDT, HENRY A.
Born in Germany, 1861; died August 1944. Arrived in U.S., 1878; came to Chloride, New Mexico as member of survey team, 1882. Primarily an assayer, sometimes operating photo studio in Chloride, Lake Valley, Winston and Tyrone, c. 1890-24.

SCHOFIELD
Partner with Christian Barthelmess in Barthelmess & Schofield.

SCHUSTER, M.
Stereo photographer in Las Vegas and Hot Springs.

SCHWEMBERGER, BROTHER SIMEON
Franciscan monk who operated a photo studio in Gallup and Window Rock area, c. 1909.

SCOTT, HOMER
Partner of Otis A. Aultman, active in El Paso, 1907-13. Also listed as Scott Photo Company.

SEGAL, A. N.
Active in Las Cruces, 1906-07, on Main Street, Murphy Building, operating the Segal Photographic Company.

SELIGMAN, SIEGMUND
Born December 1830; died October 4, 1876. Earliest photographer in New Mexico known by name, he operated a daguerreotype studio in Santa Fe, 1854-56. Also spelled Sigismund, Sigismundo, Selegman.

SHAW, GEORGE M.
Died January 12, 1888. Amateur active in Socorro area, c. 1882; in

Socorro and Santa Fe, 1883; participated in Territorial fairs, and displayed new techniques.

SHEEK
Partner with Ren Phillips in Phillips & Sheek, active in Roswell area, 1892-93.

SHOWELL & KEMMERER
Active in Albuquerque, 313 ½ Central, 1907-08.

SHUFELDT, DR. R. W.
Active in Fort Wingate as U.S. Army surgeon, 1887, photographing Navajo tanning process. Photographs used in article, "The Navajo Tanner," Proceedings of United States National Museum.

SIMPSON
Operated studio, Simpson & Reall, with J. A. Reall in Taos, May 1891.

SIMPSON & REALL
Studio in Taos, 1891.

SIMPSON, WILLIAM H.
Photographed Navajo and Hopi Indians in area of Navajo Reservation, c. 1900-02.

SKELLEY, L. A.
Active in Silver City, c. 1888-92; brief partnership with E. W. Baker, 1892.

SKINNER & HORNER
Operated the Imperial Photograph Gallery in Gallup, 1900, at Coal Avenue and Second Street; in Taos, 1901.

SLOAN, JACK
Active in El Paso, 1907-10, at 506 ½ and 508 South El Paso.

SLOCUM, J. E.
Active in Laguna Pueblo, late 1880s, working for Santa Fe Railroad; his studiowas in San Diego, California.

SMITH & EDGINGTON
Active in Taos, 1912-13. Possibly the same person who was partner in Smith & Myers, or J. L. Smith.

SMITH & KNORR
Partnership of Frank L. Smith and Joseph G. Knorr, active in Albuquerque, 206 West Silver Avenue, 1912-13.

SMITH & MYERS
Active in Taos, 1911-12. Possibly the same as J. L. Smith, and also with Smith & Edginton.

SMITH, ERWIN
Resident of Bonham, Texas; made approximately 10,000 hand camera negatives of cattle ranch life in Texas, Arizona, Mexico and New Mexico in early years of twentieth century. He worked with writer George Pattulo on many famous ranches of the day, and produced illustrated articles for Saturday Evening Post, and other magazines.

SMITH, FRANK L.
Partner with Joseph G. Smith in Smith & Knorr, active in Albuquerque, 206 West Silver Avenue, 1912-13.

SMITH, J. L.
Active in Questa, 1897-98; in La Belle, Taos County, c. 1897-98. Possibly a partner in Smith & Myers, or Smith & Edgington.

SMITH, JOSEPH E.
Born in Massachusetts, September 27, 1858; died January 25, 1946. Active in Socorro, c. 1885-98 on California Street; branch studio in San Marcial.

SMITH, WILFRID H.
Active in Fort Sumner, 1907. Partner with Alb Turner operating as Turner Studio in Roswell, 1911-13; also known as Turner & Smith.

SMITH, WILLIAM A.
Ambrotypist in Santa Fe, operating with Wertz as Wertz & Smith, summer 1866. Photographic assistant with Indian Commissioner Julius K. Graves, photographing treatment of Indians during captivity at Fort Sumner.

SOLIS, ALBERTO L.
Listed in El Paso, 1907-12, at 418 South Stanton.

SPITZLEY, WILLIAM L.
Operated the Arts Shop in Silver City, Bullard Street, 1912-32.

SPONAUGLE, M. L.
Active in Clayton, 1912-13. Sometimes misspelled Shonaugle.

STANLEY
Partner in Rennie & Stanley, in Las Cruces, 1889, first door east of corner opposite the Post Office.

STARR, CLARA (MRS.)
Active in El Paso, 1907, at 212 West Overland.

STAUFFER, JOHN K.
Photographs reproduced in special edition on El Camino Real of the Santa Fe Daily New Mexican, May 30, 1905. Pallbearer at the funeral of Christian G. Kaadt.

STEELE, F. M.
Active in Santa Rosa, 1910.

STEIHAUG, O.
Active in Tucumcari at Gallegos Building, c. 1907, 1911-12; operated the Aristo Studio, 1908.

STEPHENSON GALLERY
Operated by Brown & Thomas in Las Cruces, 1895; listed as Thomas Brothers, 1897.

STEVENSON, MATILDA COXE (MRS.)
Born 1850; died 1915. Noted early ethnologist of Southwest; participated with husband in founding Bureau of Ethnology under Powell, 1879. Active in photographing the Zia and Zuni Pueblos, c. 1879-98. Sometimes was accompanied by assistant Miss May Clark.

STILES & BURK(E)
Partnership of William Stiles and John Burk or Burke, on extensive photo tour, c. 1882. Photographed in Santa Fe, c. May 1882; in San Pedro and Golden, c. June 1882; in Fort Stanton, c. July 1882; in Tularosa, c. July-August 1882; in Organ Mountain area, c. September 1882.

STIRRAT & MILLER
Studio operated by J. A. Stirrat, Las Vegas, 1905-06.

STIRRAT, J. A.
Active in Las Vegas, 1905-06. Las Vegas, Gallinas Park and the Scenic Highway by Ward, 1904, contains several Stirrat photographs. Also known as Stirrat & Miller.

STONECYPHER, E. A.
Manager of Western Stereoscope Company, Deming and Las Cruces, c. 1902.

STRINGFELLOW, E. T. & F.
Active in Eddy (Carlsbad), Canon Street opposite Hotel Hagerman, January 1891-August 1892; Fox Street opposite Bronson Block, August 1892-April 1893. May have been partner in Hodsoll & Stringfellow in White Oaks, June-August 1891.

STUART, W. F.
Active in El Paso, 1906-23.

STULTZ, H. P.
Involved in various ventures; photographed public and private buildings, c. 1885.

SUMERLIN, J. F.
Uncertain if actually photographer or painter; listed as artist for Mrs. Albright's Art Parlor in Albuquerque.

SWEETLAND
Partner in Consaul & Sweetland, active in Elizabethtown, 1896.

TACKETT BROTHERS
Active in Artesia, 1905-06.

TELLES, ANTONIO M.
Active in Alamogordo, 1904-06. New York Avenue and 11th Street, 1905; New York Avenue and 7th Street, 1906.

THOMAS & RISDON
Operated by O. A. Risdon in Silver City, c. 1900-10.

THOMAS BROTHERS
Active in Las Cruces, operating as Brown & Thomas, Stephenson Gallery, 1895; listed as Thomas Brothers, 1897.

THOMAS, CHARLES E.
Photographer for Thomas C. Bolton in El Paso, 1888.

THOMAS, P. W.
Active in Silver City, listing only "Thomas," opposite Post Office, 1900; definite listing 1903-05. Possibly a partner in Thomas & Risdon. Also listed as W. O. Thomas.

THURLOW, JAMES
Photographer with the Hayden Survey. Listed in Manitou, Colorado, 1874-79. Made stereograph of Juanita, wife of Navajo Chief Manuelito.

TOMLINSON, JAMES A.
Physician, surgeon and druggist active in the southern and eastern part of New Mexico, c. 1890s. Uncertain where or when he practiced photography.

TOOKER, JOHNATHAN L.
Listed in Las Vegas, 1905-32, operating Tooker's Plaza Studio.

TORRES & BROTHERS
Studio operated by A. C. Torres with M. Torres, 1905-08.

TORRES, A. C.
Active in Socorro with M. Torres, as Torres & Brothers, 1905-08.

TORRES, M.
Operated studio in Socorro, 1903-08; partner with his brother, A. C., 1905-08.

TOSSELL, W. P.
Active in Deming, 1905-08.

TROUTMAN, EDWARD A.
Operated studio in Cimarron, c. 1910.

TURNER & SMITH
Partnership of Alb Turner and Wilfrid H. Smith, Roswell, 117 West 4th, 1911-13. Also called Turner Studio.

TURNER, E. WINSLOW
Uncertain whether he was photographer only, or also a sketch artist. Reported as "artist in the employ of the Mexican Central railroad" taking "views and sketches" in Santa Fe, July 14, August 22, 1885.

TWO-BIT TINTYPIST
Active in Santa Fe, c. 1870s; low-priced tent itinerant. Tent in Santa Fe, near Loretto Chapel, February-April 1877.

UPDIKE, L. C.
Born in Texas, May 25, 1890. Partner with William Pennington, operating Pendike Studio in Durango, Colorado; traveled to Four Corners region, c. 1908-13.

VAN TINE, HENRY
Active in Virsylvia, Taos County, 1912-13; in Bernalillo, 1924-26.

VASQUEZ, MANUEL
Active in El Paso, 1912-13; studio at 217 ½ South El Paso.

VELARDE, B.
Leading photographer of Chihuahua, Mexico; active in Mesilla, New Mexico, April 1878.

VENEGAS, ALVINO
Active in El Paso, 1912, at 712 South El Paso.

VICTOR PORTRAIT COMPANY
Active in Santa Fe, 1889-90, operated by E. V. Emanuel.

VIERRA, CARLOS
One of the notable New Mexico painters of the Santa Fe group; did considerable photography as reference for his paintings. Probably also a member of the Santa Fe Camera Club; operated a studio in Santa Fe, West Side Park, 1907- 08. Also used the name Charles Vierra.

VILLALOBOS
Partner in Gomez & Villalobos, operating in El Paso, 316 South Stanton, 1906.

VOORHEES, FREDERICK W.
Born September 29, 1869; died March 6, 1943. Active in Albuquerque, 1897-1901, working for Mrs. Franc Luse Albright at the Art Parlors; opened his own studio, c. 1898. Located at 208 West Railroad Avenue, 1899; 215 West Railroad Avenue, 1901.

VOORHEES, RUSSELL E.
Brother of Frederick W. Voorhees and assistant to him, 1901.

VREELAND
Active in Santa Fe, assistant to Ben Cuyler.

VROMAN, ADAM CLARK
One of the major photographers of the southwest. Made several substantial trips to New Mexico, 1894-1904. See California.

WAITE, C. B.
Active near Gallup, c. 1890s, traveling from studio in Los Angeles.

WAITE PHOTO STUDIO, V. H.
Active in Las Vegas, 1903-04, at 513 ½ 6th.

WALDON
Operating as Handy & Waldon, reported as photographers with group expedition under Dr. Ladd, President of University of New Mexico in Santa Fe; worked in Red Rock Canyon and area of modern Bandelier Monument.

WALKER, HORACE H.
Partner in Mishler & Walker, with Calvin S. Mishler, active in Gallup, 1905-08, 1911-13.

WALTER, PAUL A. F.
Photographed the El Camino Real between Santa Fe and Las Vegas with John K. Stauffer, c. 1905. Photographs were reproduced in special edition of the Santa Fe Daily New Mexican, May 1905.

WALTON, WILLIAM R.
Active in Roswell, 1905-06; in Albuquerque at 313 ½ West Central Avenue, 1908-22.

WANAMAKER, RODMAN
Possibly not actually a photographer. Heir to the department store fortune, he financed a number of Indian congresses and expeditions. Pictures are published in both original prints and books with attribution to him, but they may actually be by Dr. Joseph K. Dixon.

WARD'S STUDIO
Active in Alamogordo, c. 1903-08.

WARNKY & ABBOTT
Studio operated by F. C. Warnky and C. L. Abbott, active in Abiquiu, 1879; from Alamosa, Colorado.

WARNKY, F. C.
Partner with C. L. Abbott in Warnky & Abbott, Abiquiu, 1879. Also active in Independence, Missouri.

WARREN, JOHN
Active in Mora, 1903-08, 1911-12.

WATERMAN, GEORGE E.
Listed in Las Vegas, 1912-13.

WEITFLE, P. L.
Active in Santa Fe, 1899-1900. Bought studio of Thomas J. Curran, 1899; bought out Clinton D. Curtis, successor to J. C. Burge in El Paso, 1900. Studio at West Side Plaza, Santa Fe, June-October 1899. Sometimes listed mistakenly as P. F. Weitfle.

WENDELL, FRANK R.
Active in Santa Fe and Albuquerque, 1882-89, operating the Albright Art Parlors.

WENZ, ADOLPH
Active in Ariolo, Union County, 1907-08.

WERTZ
Active in Santa Fe and Fort Union, 1866; partners with William A. Smith operating as Wertz & Smith.

WERTZ & SMITH
Partnership of William A. Smith and Wertz, ambrotypists in Santa Fe and Fort Union, 1866.

WESTERN STEREOSCOPIC COMPANY
Active in Silver City and Fort Bayard, c. 1906; may have been in Las

Cruces, 1902; possibly represented by manager, E. A. Stonecypher of Kansas or Galesburg, Nebraska.

WESTERVELT, E. J.
Railroad agent for the Santa Fe; active as photographer in Anthony and Mesilla Park, 1889-90; in Engle, c. 1895-97.

WESTMANN, ORLOFF
Studio in Elizabethtown, 1871. Photographed the Apache and Pueblo.

WHARTON-JAMES, GEORGE
Alternate spelling of George Wharton James.

WHITE & COLPAS
Partnership of William A. White and Colpas, stereo photographers active in Raton, 1880s-1900s.

WHITE & COMPANY, DR. A. D.
Active in Santa Fe, Room 13, Hotel Capital, c. October 1890.

WHITE & DEMMON
Partnership of W. A. White and E. F. Demmon, active in Springer and Santa Fe (from Raton), May-June 1890.

WHITE & LEACH
Partnership of William A. White and Don M. Leach, stereo photographers in Raton, 1880s-1900s.

WHITE, WILLIAM A.
Active Raton, c. 1885-1902. Traveled northeast quarter of New Mexico; Springer, Elizabethtown, Clayton, Folsom, Cerrillos, Las Vegas. Photographed San Geronimo Day at Taos Pueblo. Partner with E. F. Demmon in White & Demmon, in Springer and Santa Fe, May-June 1890. Partner in White & Colpas, stereo photographers active in Raton, 1880s-1900.

WHITLOCK
Partner in Kaadt & Whitlock, c. 1902.

WHOLESALE VIEW COMPANY
Operated by William E. Hook in Santa Fe, 1891-92.

WHORLEY'S STUDIO
Active in Socorro, c. 1907-08.

WICKMILLER
Partner in Park & Wickmiller, active in Albuquerque, November-December 1882. Advertised as representing the New York Graphic.

WILDER, EDWIN A.
Active in Tierra Amarilla, c. 1885-88.

WILKINSON, EDWIN H.
Active in Roswell, 1903-18. 124 North Main, 1912-13; 2nd and Main, 1913-15; 124 ½ West 2nd, 1918.

WILLIS, J. R.
Photographer and painter working around Navajo Reservation and Canyon de Chelly, c. 1903; in Gallup, c. 1920s.

WILSON, J. K.
Active in Las Cruces (from California), c. November 1890.

WIMBERLEY, E. M.
Active in Texico, 1911-12.

WING, PAUL M.
Active in Fort Bayard, 1907-08.

WITHAUP, LOUIS C.
Active in Albuquerque, Main Street, two doors south of Post Office, March-April 1870.

WITTICK & BLISS
Partnership of G. B. Wittick and W. P. Bliss, stereo photographers in Santa Fe, 1880s.

WITTICK & RUSSELL
Partnership of George Ben Wittick and R. W. Russell, operating in Santa Fe and Albuquerque, 1880-84. Albuquerque studio at Gold Avenue, between First and Second Streets, 1881-84.

WITTICK, ARCHIE
Born July 14, 1873; died September 28, 1912. Son of George Ben Wittick; assisted his father in studio at Gallup, c. late 1890s; at Fort Wingate, until father's death, 1903.

WITTICK, GEORGE BEN
Born in Huntingdon, Pennsylvania, January 1, 1845; died July 30, 1903. Active in Santa Fe, c. 1878-79, as partner with W. P. Bliss; with R. W. Russell, c. 1880. Moved studio to Albuquerque, 1881, occupying Blue Tent gallery until summer 1882. Partnership dissolved, 1884. Wittick opened studio in Gallup, until selling out to Imperial Photograph Gallery, 1900. See Arizona.
Patrick Janis Broder, *Shadows On Glass: The Indian World of Ben Wittick*, Rowman & Littlefield, 1990.

WITTICK, THOMAS
Son of G. B. Wittick; associated with his father in Gallup, before 1900, producing stereoviews.

WOLFE, FRANCIS B.
Active in El Paso, 1905, 25 Plaza Block; in Albuquerque, 115 South 2nd Street, 1907-12.

WOLFENSTEIN, VALENTINE
Born in Sweden. Active in Fort Sumner, 1868, after learning photography from Mr. Booth in Las Vegas. Photographed last part of Navajo Captivity, treaty negotiations and signing between General Sherman and Navajo leaders allowing restoration of Navajos to homeland. Moved to California, c. 1870, buying Godfrey's Sunbeam Gallery in Los Angeles, c. 1872.

WONFOR, GEORGE H.
Landscape and scenic painter from St. Louis. Came to Albuquerque in December 1888, forming partnership with W. Calvin Brown. Operated in various parts of New Mexico, 1889, and moved to Tucson, Arizona, 1890. Listed in Albuquerque (with Brown), December 1888; in East Las Vegas, 1889; in Chloride, June 1889; in Las Cruces, Wesche Building opposite Amador Hotel, December 1889-January 1890; in Tucson, Arizona, East Congress, 1890. Name is often listed with wrong initials or added E.

WOODRUFF (MRS.)
Partner of Mrs. Franc Luse Albright in Santa Fe during period of Tertio-Millennial Exposition, summer 1883, and later part of year before Santa Fe branch studio was suspended. Listed in Santa Fe, Southwest Corner Plaza, August-September 1883.

WOODWARD, GEORGE
Mentioned in diary of William A. Smith as photographic member of the Graves Party to Santa Fe and New Mexico, early 1866.

WOOSTER & ELDERKIN
Partnership of Harold A. Elderkin and Wooster, active in Las Vegas, August 1885-May 1886. Also worked as Montezuma View Company.

WORD, THOMAS
Active in Santa Fe, Mrs. Sena's Placita, March-April 1865.

WRIGHT & PARKER
Listed in El Paso, 1906, 21-25 Plaza Block. Possibly Francis Parker.

YONTZ, HARRY C.
Jeweler in Santa Fe, c. 1895-1912; practiced photography as an avocation.

ZACZYNSKI, B. (MRS.)
Wife of gunsmith and jeweler, active as photographer in Gallup, mid-1880s-c. 1906. Studio at top of hill, at head of Third Street, c. 1888.

ZANT & LEACH
Partnership of Zant and Don M. Leach, Mineral Wells.

OKLAHOMA
(See Indian Territory)

Special thanks to David A. Reeh for his substantial contribution to this section.

ADDISON, GEORGE A.
Active in Ft. Sill, Oklahoma Territory, c. 1890-95.

AMES BROTHERS
Active in Okarche, Oklahoma Territory, c. 1895-1900.

ARLINGTON & DANA
Studio in Blackwell, Oklahoma Territory, c. 1895-1900.

ARMSTRONG, MARTIN
Photographed the Land Run, 1889; from Milon, Kansas.

BLISS, W. P.
Itinerant and stereographer at Ft. Sill, 1873-75. See Traveling and New Mexico.

BODDY, E. V.
Active in Okarche, Oklahoma Territory.

BRASEL, J.
Active in Muskogee, Indian Territory, c. 1870-80; Muskogee later became Oklahoma.

BRETZ, GEORGE W.
Active in Ft. Sill, Oklahoma Territory, c. 1895.

BRASEL, L.
Stereo photographer in Muskogee.

BROOKS, W. E.
Active in Norman and Shawnee, Oklahoma Territory.

BROWN
Stereo photographer in Oklahoma, c. 1900.

BRUCE
Partner in Taylor & Bruce, operating the People's Gallery in Guthrie, Oklahoma Territory, c. 1890.

BRUNK, J. D.
Active in Pond Creek, Oklahoma Territory.

BRYAN & ELLIOTT
Active in Stroud, Oklahoma Territory.

CAMPBELL & EDWARDS
Active in Shawnee, Oklahoma Territory.

CAPITAL CITY GALLERY
Studio in Guthrie, Oklahoma Territory, c. 1893, operated by W. A. Flower.

CIMARRON GALLERY
Active in Perkins, Oklahoma Territory.

CONCANNON, T.
Stereo photographer in Osage.

COTTAGE GALLERY
Operated by the Martin Brothers in Wynnewood.

CRAFT, THOMAS F.
Active in Oklahoma, Oklahoma Territory, c. 1895.

343

CRANSON, L.
Active in Lexington, Oklahoma Territory.

DAKE
Active in Edmond, Oklahoma Territory.

DANA
Partner in Arlington & Dana, Blackwell, Oklahoma Territory, c. 1895-1900.

DAUGHERTY
Active in Guthrie.

DAVIS, CALVIN LEE
Active in Hobart, c. 1902-13; photographed the Kiowa.

DICKMAN
Active in Cleveland, Oklahoma Territory.

DRAKE
Active in Ponca City, Oklahoma Territory.

DRUM, OSCAR
Active in Nowata, Indian Territory, and Pawhuska, Oklahoma Territory, c. 1885-1910. Produced stereoviews, cityscape panoramas, and portraits.

EATON
Active in Chandler, Oklahoma Territory, c. 1895.

EDWARDS
Active in Enid, Oklahoma Territory.

EDWARDS
Partner in Campbell & Edwards, Shawnee, Oklahoma Territory.

ELLIOTT
Partner in Bryan & Elliott, Stroud, Oklahoma Territory.

ENRIGHT, B. P.
Stereo photographer active in Lahoma, 1910.

EWING, R. A.
Active in Oklahoma City.

FLOWER, W. A.
Operated Capital City Gallery in Guthrie, Oklahoma Territory, c. 1893.

FORBES, ANDREW ALEXANDER
Active in Guthrie and Oklahoma City, c. 1889. Traveling photographer in Texas and Oklahoma, 1880s-90s; known for his scenes of cowboy life. Active in Bishop, California, after 1909. See California.

FORRESTEL, ELLA J.
Active in Wagoner.

GARSIDE
Active in Newkirk, Oklahoma Territory.

GENTRY, M.
Active in Texas and Oklahoma. See New Mexico.

GREEN, G. T.
Active in Waynoka, Oklahoma Territory.

HAINLINE, SAMUEL R.
Active in Hydro.

HAMILTON
Active in Oklahoma City, Oklahoma Territory, c. 1895.

HANGROUG & SON
Active in Shawnee.

HARPER BROTHERS
Stereo photographers in Ryan, 1907.

HAYCRAFT
Active in Chandler, 1898.

HAYES, DR. J. J.
Amateur in Oklahoma City; member Stereoscopic Society, 1939.

HERINGER
Active in Shawnee.

HIXSON, J. W.
Stereo photographer active in Newkirk, 1907.

HOSNER, Y. P.
Born in Illinois, 1869. Owned the Imperial Gallery in Weatherford, Custer/Cedar Township, Sayre area, c. 1900.

HUFF
Active in Cherokee.

HUGHS
Active in Perry, Oklahoma Territory. and in Tulsa and Uinita, Indian Territory.

HUME, C. R. (MRS.)
Active in Anadarko, Oklahoma Territory.

IMPERIAL GALLERY
Owned by Y. P. Hosner in Weatherford, Custer/Cedar Township, c. 1900.

INGRAM, W. R.
"Stereoscopic and View Artist" in Deer Creek; photographed the crowd preparing for the opening of the border for the land rush.

KEM, S. A.
Active in El Reno, Oklahoma Territory.

KENT STEREOSCOPIC VIEW COMPANY
Factory and studio in Chandler, offices in Los Angeles and Detroit. Also produced good-quality lithoviews for advertising giveaways for businesses. Issued view of Quanah Parker, Comanche Chief.

KINGHAM, J. B.
Operated a studio in Oklahoma City, Oklahoma Territory, c. 1895, at 113 South Broadway.

KLEPFER, G. W.
Active in McCloud, Oklahoma Territory, operating the Klondike studio.

KLONDIKE
Active in McCloud, Oklahoma Territory; operated by G. W. Klepfer.

LAMBERT, ALEXANDER
Stereo photographer in Frederick; made views of Teddy Roosevelt visiting Frederick, 1905; possibly an amatuer.

LIVINGSTON
Active in Hobart, Oklahoma Territory.

LOSEY
Active in Oklahoma City.

MANDEL
Active in Pawnee, Oklahoma Territory.

MARTIN BROTHERS
Operated the Cottage Gallery, Wynnewood.

McBRIDE
Active in Lexington, Oklahoma Territory, c. 1895.

McMULLEN, V.
Amater stereo photographer; member Stereoscopic Society, 1939.

MILLER, D. A.
Active in Oklahoma City, c. 1889.

MILLER, E. W.
Active in Chandler, c. 1900.

MOON, CARL
See New Mexico.

OLIVANT
Active in Hennessey, Oklahoma Territory.

OLIVER, E. W.
Stereo photographer in Oklahoma City; made view of priest posing with two Indian boys.

PARKER
Active in Newkirk, Oklahoma Territory.

PARSON, GEORGE W.
Born in Arkansas, March 1845. Photographed the Osage; studio in Pawhuska, Indian Territory and Oklahoma Territory.

PEOPLE'S GALLERY
Gallery in Guthrie, Oklahoma Territory, c. 1895, operated by Taylor & Bruce.

PRETTYMAN, W. S.
He made long trips into Indian Territory after 1883, photographing various tribes, particularly the Civilized Tribes. Prettyman also photographed the Boomer camps around Arkansas City when support was growing for the Boomer invasion encroaching on Indian lands. He joined the Boomers, 1889, and migrated to Oklahoma, operating in Guthrie for many years. See Kansas.

PURNELLE, H. J.
Active in Augusta and Perry, Oklahoma Territory.

RENSIMER
Active in Augusta, Oklahoma Territory.

RICH, C. P.
Operated a gallery in Guthrie, Oklahoma Territory, 1894, located at 118 East Oklahoma Avenue.

RISING STUDIO
Active in Kingfisher, Oklahoma Territory.

ROBINSON, H. P.
Active in Ft. Sill, Oklahoma Territory, 1895; photographed Arapaho and Comanche in the field and in his studio.

ROGERS
Active in North Pond Creek.

RUSSELL
Active in Anadarko, Oklahoma Territory; photographed Kiowa.

SALMON BROTHERS
Active in Woodward, c. 1895.

SAUNDERS ART GALLERY
Active in Woodward, c. 1890.

SHIFFERT, FRED R.
Studio in El Reno, 1890-1915.

SHORE, J. T.
Active in Cushing, Oklahoma Territory.

SIMES
Active in El Reno.

SOULE, WILLIAM S.
See Indian Territory.

SPOTTS, J. B.
Active in Tryon and Fouts, Oklahoma Territory.

STALL, JOHN
Portrait photographer in Ada, 1920-46; also used panoramic view camera for photographs of large groups. Produced outdoor business and documentary views.

STEVENSON
Stereo photographer in El Reno; produced stereoview of two Indian men in eastern dress. Photographed the Cheyenne.

STILLWATER PHOTO STUDIO
Active in Stillwater, Oklahoma Territory, c. 1898.

STOTZ, C. C.
Active in El Reno, Oklahoma Territory, c. 1890.

STREETER
Active in Shawnee, Oklahoma Territory.

SWEARINGEN, H. T.
Active in Guthrie, opposite the Post Office, c. 1895.

TACKETT BROTHERS
Active in Enid, Oklahoma Territory, c. 1895.

TAYLOR & BRUCE
Operated the People's Gallery in Guthrie, Oklahoma Territory, c. 1890.

THAT MAN STONE
Active in Chickasaw, c. 1900.

THORNLEY
Partner in Wilcox & Thornley, Stillwater, Oklahoma Territory.

TURNER, J. H.
Active in McAlister.

VREELAND STUDIO
Operated the R.R. Palace Photo Car from a base in Alva.

WAGY, J. S.
Active in Oklahoma City.

WANTLAND
Operated at North Main Street, Stillwater, c. 1890.

WARD, G. R.
Active in Techumseh.

WERNER, GEORGE P.
Active in Lexington, Oklahoma Territory.

WHITE, WILLIAM A.
Active in Colorado, New Mexico and Oklahoma, c. 1870s; partner
with Colpas, 1870s-80s; with Don M. Leach, 1880s.

WILCOX & THORNLEY
Partnership active in Stillwater, Oklahoma Territory.

WILLIAMS, W.
Active in El Reno, Oklahoma Territory.

WINKLER, C.
Stereo photographer in Ft. Sill.

YOUNG, D. W.
Active in Enid, Oklahoma Territory.

Special thanks to Tom Robinson for his substantial contribution to this section. For more detailed reference to the photographers of Oregon, see Oregon Photographers: Biographical History and Directory 1852-1917, *by Thomas Robinson, Portland, Oregon, 1992.*

ABELL & PRIEST
Partnership of Frank G. Abell and Priest in San Francisco, c. 1885.

ABELL & SON, FRANK G.
Operated by Frank G. Abell in Portland at 29 Washington Street, 1884-85. Associated with Abell-Herrin Company, 1898-99.

ABELL & WELSH
Studio in Portland, 1880, operated by J. O. Welsh and Frank G. Abell.

ABELL, FRANK G.
Born c. 1844; died in Tacoma, Washington, 1910. Active in Portland, 1878-99. Studio located on 1st Street, 1878-83; operated studio with J. O. Welsh, known as Abell & Welsh, 1880; operating as Frank G. Abell & Son at 29 Washington Street, 1884-85; on the 4th Floor of Labbe Building, 1886-87; operating as Abell-Herrin Company, 1898-99. He also operated a studio in San Francisco, Abell & Priest, c. 1885; in Colfax, Washington, 1888. Associated with the Abell-Herrin Company, 1898-99. Abell published or sold stereo and large format views of landscapes of various sights from the Northwest Coast and Yosemite Valley. See California.

ABELL, GEORGE L.
Traveling photographer, 1876-77. Active in Portland, 1878-88; partner in Abell & Son in Corvallis, 1886; partner in Abell-Herrin Company, Portland, 1897-1900.

ABELL-HERRIN COMPANY
Partnership of David C. Herrin and George L. Abell, operating in Portland, 1897-1900. Frank G. Abell was associated with the studio, 1898-99.

ABRAMS, JAMES L.
Active in Sumpter, 1901.

ACADIA STUDIO
Operated by William G. and Mrs. Emma E. Cutberth in Portland, 1910-16.

ACME VIEW & ADVERTISING COMPANY
Active in Portland at 81 Fourth Street, 1890(?)-1900(?).

ADAMS & MARTIN
Studio operating in Corvallis.

ADAMS, LUELLA M.
Active in The Dalles, 1907.

ADVANCE PORTRAIT HOUSE
Operated by Charles E. Griffith in Portland at 43 H 1st Street, 1891.

AERNE & NORDSTORM
Studio in Portland at 133 H 5th, operated by Christopher Aerne, Jr. and Carl H. Nordstrom, 1902.

AERNE, CHRISTOPHER, JR.
Active in Portland 1897-14. Partner with Carl H. Nordstrom, 1902; operated studios at 133 H 5th, 1902-08; 129 H 5th, 1909-11; 352 H Washington, 1912; 345 H Washington, 1913. Also listed as Christian Aerne, Jr.

AERNE, ROBERT
Active in Portland, 1891-1903. Photographer for M. S. Eastman, 1891; operated as a photographer from his residence at 88 14th North, 1892; printer for Aune, 1893; printer for McAlpin & Lamb, 1894. Photographer at 515 East Clay, 1895; 534 East 8th, 1902-03.

AINSWORTH, MAUD
Born 1874; died 1962. Member of the Oregon Camera Club; active in Portland 1899-23. Also known as Mrs. Maud Babbitt.

AKERS, E. M.
Active in Ione, 1890s; operated as W. L. Richards & E. M. Akers, with headquarters at the Morrow Art Hall.

ALBRIGHT, M. (MISS)
Member of the Oregon Camera Club; active in Portland, 1900.

ALDRICH, FRANK C.
Active in Portland, 1910-20. Located at 128 ½ 5th, 1910; photographer for Angelus Commercial Studio, 1911-15; Vice President of Oregon Commercial Studio, 1917; a photographer again, 1920.

ALLATT
Photographer for Sherman Company in Sherman County, 1897.

ALLEN, FREDERICK C.
Active in Portland, 1910.

ALLEN, O. G.
Active in Pendleton, 1911.

ALLEN, RATA (MISS)
Photographer for Hazeltine's in Baker City, located at the right front corner of Auburn Avenue, 1899.

ALLYNA STUDIO
Gallery in Willamina.

ALVERSON, FRANK
Active in Eugene, 1875.

ALVORD, CHARLES A.
Active in Portland, 1894-17. Photographer for J. S. Potter, 1892-93; in McMinnville, 1895.

AMBROSE, THOMAS
Active in Portland at 248 ½ 1st, 1917.

AMERICAN PORTRAIT COMPANY
Active in Tillamook, c. 1900.

AMERICAN VIEW COMPANY
Studio in Sumpter at 33 North Street, 1900; in Portland, c. 1905(?).

ANALYTIS, JAMES
Active in Portland, 1913-15; partner in Genatis & Anayltis with George Genatis at 11 5th North, 1915. Names also spelled Analetis and Genatas.

ANDERSON, ALFRED
Member of the Oregon Camera Club; active in Portland, operating as A. Anderson & Company, printers and lithographers, 1894. Made views of the 1894 Portland flood.

ANDERSON, C. W.
Landscape photographer in Portland at 128 Third Street, 1880s-90s.

ANDERSON, E. H.
Operated gallery in Dallas, 1880.

ANDERSON, J. B.
Active in Eugene, 1911-17; operating the Tollman Studio after buying it from Lulu Ehrhardt, the former wife of J. W. Tollman.

ANDERSON, L. E.
Member of the Oregon Camera Club; active in Portland, 1905-13.

ANDERSON, L. M.
Member of the International Photographic Association; active in Merrill, 1908.

ANDREWS, A. (MISS)
Member of the Oregon Camera Club; active in Portland, 1900.

ANDREWS, BYRON
Active in Portland at 244 Burnside, 1917.

ANGELUS STUDIO
Active in Portland at 525 Abington Building, c. 1911-17. Also known as Angelus Commercial Photographic Company.

APPLEGATE, JAMES W.
Active in Portland, 1891-1925; located at Cordray's Theatre, 1891; 537 Albina Avenue, 1894-95; 508 Williams, 1896; 2 6th North, 1897-1911; 167 ½ 1st, 1918-25.

AREY, HERBERT L.
Born in New Hampshire, 1867; died in Portland, 1938. Railroad engineer and amateur photographer who specialized in trains, active in Portland, early 1900s.

ARLETA STUDIO
Operated by S. E. Stone and Kearney in Portland, 1910-14.

ARMATAGE (MRS.)
Member of the Oregon Camera Club; active in Portland, 1900.

ARMSTRONG & DEAN
Partnership active in Creswell, c. 1913; A. J. Armstrong and Dean.

ARMSTRONG, A. J.
Operated the Grove Studio in Cottage Grove, 1910-17. Active in Creswell, 1913, partner in Armstrong & Dean.

ARMSTRONG, J. N.
Active in Astoria, c. 1870.

ARNOLD, BENJAMIN D.
Professional photographer and member of the Oregon Camera Club; active in Astoria at 528 Commercial, 1901.

ARNOLD, HOSMER K.
Member of the Oregon Camera Club; active in Portland, c. 1900.

ARTCLIFF PHOTO STUDIO
Active in Milwaukie and Portland.

ARTCRAFT
Studio in Grants Pass.

ASH, ORMSBY M.
Member of the Oregon Camera Club; active in Portland, 1904-25.

ASHFORD, FRANCIS
Active in Portland, 1918; photographer and picture framer.

ATKESON, LAURA
Active in Salem prior to April, 1865, when her gallery was destroyed by fire.

ATKESON, WILLIAM T.
Operated a gallery in Baker City, 1870; husband of Laura, who owned gallery in Salem, 1865.

ATLANTIC PHOTO-VIEW & ADVERTISING COMPANY
Itinerant c. 1889; in Portland, c. 1892, operated by Mrs. R. H. Gardiner.

ATWOOD, H. A. (MRS.)
Active in Corvallis, 1881.

AUNE, AASTA (MISS)
Active in Portland, 1892-97, with Amante, Peter O., and Struck Aune.

AUNE, AMANTE
Active in Portland, 1892-94, with brothers Struck and Peter O. Aune, and sister, Aasta.

AUNE BROTHERS
Partnership of brothers Struck, Peter and Amante, and sister, Aasta, operating in Portland, 1891.

AUNE, PETER O.
Active in Portland, 1890-95; operated as Aune Brothers with Struck, Amante and Aasta, 1891. Studio also in Trondhjem, Norway.

AUNE, STRUCK
Active in Portland, 1890-1915; operated as Aune Brothers with Peter, Amante and Aasta, 1891. Partner in Aune-Ball, Inc., 1921-22. Known as Aune Studio, 1923-25. Studio also in Trondhjem, Norway.

AUNE-BALL, INC.
Studio in Portland, 1921-22; Struck Aune.

AVERY, D. A.
Member of the Oregon Camera Club; active in Portland, 1900.

AVERY, WILLIAM L.
Active in Portland, 1864; operating as Rendall & Avery, in the New Building, corner of 2nd and Alder Streets.

BACKER, L. J.
Active in Summerville, 1888.

BACKUS, MORGAN
Born 1869; died 1903. Active in Astoria, 1889. Photographer, editor and publisher of the Pacific Coast Photographer, monthly journal of the Oregon Camera Club.

BADGER
Active in Sodaville, 1890s(?).

BAECHLER & COMPANY, C.
Partnership of Charles Baechler, Louis and Charles Wagner, operating in Portland, 1891-92, at 776 Glisan. Also known as Baechler & Wagner Brothers.

BAECHLER & WAGNER BROTHERS
Partnership of Charles Baechler, Louis and Charles Wagner, operating in Portland, 1891-92, at 776 Glisan. Also known as C. Baechler & Company.

BAECHLER, CHARLES
Active in Portland, 1880-94. Operated as C. Baechler & Company

or Baechler & Wagner Brothers, 1889-93, with Louis Wagner, at 776 Glisan. Also known as C. Baechler & Company.

BAGLEY, H. T. (MRS.)
Member of the International Photographic Association, active in Hillsboro, 1914.

BAGNASCO, POLICARPO
Active in Portland in the fall of 1866, employed by Joseph Buchtel. An itinerant Italian photographer traveling through Arizona and New Mexico, early 1870s. See California.

BAILEY, ARLIE A., JR.
Linotypist active in Portland, 1918; member of the Oregon Camera Club.

BAILEY, J. L.
Member of the Oregon Camera Club; active in Portland, 1900.

BAIRD, WILLIS
Active in Seghers, 1913.

BAKER
Active in Dufur, 1913, operating studio as Baker & Koehler.

BAKER & KINSON
Studio in Eugene, 1917, at 982 Willamette; Carl R. Baker and partner. Also known as Kodak Shop.

BAKER & KOEHLER
Studio in Dufur, 1913.

BAKER, CARL R.
Active in Eugene, 1917, listed as Baker & Kinson and Kodak Shop, 982 Willamette.

BAKER, H. H.
Active in Wollowa County; H. H. Baker Portrait Company.

BAKER, JAMES H.
Active in Lewiston, Idaho, 1889; in Baker City, Oregon, and Napa, California, 1899; in Union, Oregon, 1903. Located at the corner of 3rd and Washington, in Baker City, 1899.

BAKER PORTRAIT COMPANY, H. H.
Studio in Wollowa County.

BAKOWSKI, B. B.
Active in LaGrande, 1910, LaGrande.

BALDWIN, JAMES R.
Born in Ohio, c. 1850. Active in Sheridan, 1880.

BALDWIN, MAUDE E.
Scenic photographer in Klamath Falls, 1899-1925.

BALL
Partner with Struck Aune, operating as Aune-Ball, Inc., Portland, 1921-22.

BALL, JAMES PRESLEY
Active in Portland.

BALL STUDIOS
Active in Corvallis from 1913 to present; established by Maurice W. Hall. Oldest continuously operating photography business in Oregon, also known as Ball Studio.

BALLWEG, PHILLIP
Member of the International Photographic Association, active in Baker, 1912.

BANKS, J. C.
Member of the International Photographic Association, active in Foster and Wren, 1913; in Sweet Home, 1915.

BARCLAY, C. EDWIN
Active in Alsea, 1907; in Corvallis, 1911-13, operating Corvallis Studio. Active in Sheridan, 1915.

BARENSTECHER (MRS.)
Member of the Oregon Camera Club; active in Portland, 1900.

BARKER, EDWARD W.
Active in Portland, 1909.

BARNARD, HUGH F.
Active in Bandon, 1901.

BARNETT, EDWARD E.
Active in Salem, 29 Liberty Street.

BARNEY & CRIST
Active in Oakland, 1872.

BARNUM & CAMPBELL
Portrait gallery in Portland, 1879-82, operated by J. T. Barnum and John Campbell at Fifth between Morrison and Yamhill.

BARNUM, JOHN T.
Active in Portland, 1879-82, operating Barnum & Campbell, Fifth near Yamhill.

BARROWS, TINA HAMBLOCK
Active in Bandon(?), 1915(?)

BARTELS, HARRY F.
Amateur active in Portland, c. 1907-15. Member of the Oregon Camera Club; agent of the Commercial Photo Company, 1915.

BARTELS, OTIS T.
Active in Carlton, 1913; in Lebanon, 1913-17; member of International Photographic Association.

BASEY, CHARLES E.
Member of Portland Society of Photographic Art and Salon Commitee, active in Portland, 1904-15.

BASSETT & WHAITE
Studio in Salem, 1911-13, operated by John E. and Frank T. Bassett and Rene Whaite at 384 State Street.

BASSETT, FRANK T.
Active in Salem, 1911-13; operated Bassett & Whaite with his brother John E., and Rene Whaite.

BASSETT, JOHN E.
Active in Salem, 1911-13; operated the studio of Bassett & Whaite with Frank T. and Rene Whaite.

BATES, PHILLIP
Active in Portland, 1894-1920, specializing in the sale of views; publisher of Pacific Northwest, 1904-15.

BAUER, CHARLES A.
Active in Portland, 1909.

BAUGHMAN, H. F.
Stereo photographer in Ashland; primarily a furniture dealer with photography sideline.

BEALL, ROBERT VINTON
Born 1878; died 1961. Active in Central Point, c. 1925.

BECKER, CHARLES F.
Active in LaGrande, 1914. Member of the International Photographic Association.

BEEBE, WALTER B.
Active in Portland, 1901-05. Member of the Oregon Camera Club.

BEEDE, CHARLES V.
Active in Portland, 1904.

BEERS & CUPP
Partnership active in Forest Grove, 1868; G. W. Beers and G. M. Cupp.

BEERS, G. W.
Active in Forest Grove, 1868, operating as Beers & Cupp with G. M. Cupp.

BELANCUE & BUTTON
Partnership of Charles G. Button and Belancue; operated the Flying Studio in Astoria, c. 1880; also listed as Blancue and Betancue.

BELL & COMPANY
Active in Astoria, 1901-03; operated by Thomas Charles Bell and Henry Wedekind.

BELL, FRANK H.
Active in St. Johns, 1909-10, operating as McDermid & Bell with Albert E. McDermid.

BELL, THOMAS CHARLES
Active in Astoria, 1901-07; in Lebanon, 1911-13; in Junction City, 1915; in Toledo, 1917. Photographer at 528 Commercial, 1905 and 583 Commercial, 1905-07; with Henry Wedekind as Bell & Company, 1901-03.

BELLAY, FRANCIS
Retoucher active in Portland, 1866, possibly employed by Hendee.

BENNETT, COLUMBUS
Active in Wolf Creek., c. 1885.

BENNETT, E. D.
Active in Hillsboro, 1897(?)-1902(?), operating as Pope & Bennett.

BENNETT, MILTON H.
Active in Kent, 1889; photographer and postmaster.

BENNETT, N. S.
Stereographer active in Medford, 1880.

BENNING, HENRY
Active in Portland, 1903, at 606 Williams Avenue.

BENSON, JOHN R.
Active in Myrtle Point, 1891.

BENZ, CHARLES A.
Member of Oregon Camera Club; active in Portland, 1917.

BERGER, HENRY, JR.
Born 1877; died 1939. Active in Portland, 1900-39, operating as Berger's Barn Studio and Berger-Putnam Studio. Operated a prestigious portrait studio, 1900-15, and won many awards in international exhibitions and salons. Clients included artists, dancers, actors, authors, musicians, sculptors and socially prominent and wealthy individuals. Studios at 108 South 10th, 1918; 329 Pittock Block, 1921; 205 Blue Moose Theater Building, 1923; 205, 408 Washington, 1924; 293 Broadway South 1927; 345 Salmon, 1930.

BERGIN, MABEL E.
Finisher active in Portland, 1910, at H. A. Hale Studio. See H. A. Hale.

BERNSTEIN, ALEXANDER, JR.
Member of the Oregon Camera Club; active in Portland, 1898-1900.

BERTHOLD, CHARLES
Active in Portland, 1909-14, operating Rose City Studios.

BETANCUE
Active in Astoria, c. 1880, operating Betancue & Button and Flying Studio. Also listed as Belancue, Blancue.

BETHKE, L. A. (MISS)
Member of the Oregon Camera Club; active in Portland, 1900.

BEYERS, J. P.
Portrait and landscape photographer in Coquille City.

BICKNELL, WILFRED
Operated the Centennial Art Studio in Portland, 1906-16, at 203 ½ 1st Street.

BIGLOW, J.
Member of the Oregon Camera Club; active in Portland, 1900.

BIRDSALL, THORNTON
Active in Portland, 1903-18. Photographer at 203 Vine with Thornton Photography; President of Pacific Photo Company, 1907-14; worked as "T. Birdsall, Commercial and Advertising Photographer" at 203 Vine, 1914-18.

BIRKIN, DAZIE R.
Photgrapher active in Portland, 1910.

BISSELL, GARDINER P.
Born in Ada, Michigan, 1880; died in Portland, 1949. Active in Portland, 1906-49.

BIXBY, C. F.
Active in Grants Pass, 1913-15.

BJORKLUND, ERIK
Active in Portland, 1910.

BLACKWELL, CLARA
Active in Sheridan pior to 1913; advertised fully equipped studio for sale in *Camera Craft*, 1913.

BLACKWOOD, EDWARD C.
Born 1879; died in Portland, 1954. Active in Portland, 1900-1950; operated the Portland Camera Exchange, early 1920s.

BLAIN, J. W. (MRS.)
Active in Portland, 1900; member of the Oregon Camera Club.

BLAIR
Active in Ashland.

BLAIR, FRANK L.
Active in Oregon City, 1891, managing Watson's Photograph Gallery; in Portland, 1891-92, photographer with J. E. Watson.

BLAKE, DR. W. E.
Active in Ashland, 1913; member of International Photographic Association.

BLAKELY, GEORGE C.
Active in Forest Grove, 1910.

BLEDSOE, JAMES W.
Born 1863. Active in Bend, 1905; in Dinuba, California, 1909.

BLOOM, ERNEST J.
Active in Hood River, 1913.

BLOSSOM, R. H.
Active in Portland, 1900; member of the Oregon Camera Club.

BOATMAN, J. W.
Active in Oregon City, 1901.

BOGARDUS, E. M.
Active in Myrtle Creek, 1911.

BOHLMAN, HERMAN T.
Born in Portland, 1872; died in Portland, 1933. Active in Portland, c. 1904-20; nationally acclaimed bird photographer.

BONAVENTURA, MICHELE
Active in Portland, 1907-21; located at 653 4th Street, 1910. Name also spelled Mikel, Michael.

BOND, ALFRED
Photo enlarger active in Portland, 1906.

BOND, N. E.
Operated the Bond Studio in Klamath Falls, 1917-18.

BOND STUDIO
Operated by N. E. Bond in Klamath Falls, 1917-18.

BONELL, FRANK
Active in Portland, 1906; in Tacoma, Washington, 1907. Member of the Photographer's Association of the Pacific Northwest.

BONGE, FREDERICK
Active in Portland, 1904, at 508 Williams Avenue.

BONNEY, ROBERT B.
Member of the International Photographic Association, active in Woodburn, 1912.

BONSER, STEPHEN D.
Born in Ohio, 1830; died in The Dalles, 1917. Active in Sauvies Island, 1888.

BOOS, J. C.
Active in Forest Grove, 1882.

BORDER, A. W.
Active in Myrtle Point, 1880.

BOSCO & MEGLER
Studio in Portland, 1875-76; operated by Carl Bosco and A. J. Megler.

BOSCO, CARL
Photographer active in Portland, 1871-76. Employed by Buchtel & Stolte, 1872-73; operated Bosco & Megler studio with Alex J. Megler, 1875-76.

BOSTON STUDIO
Operated by Gardner B. Frost in Portland, 1903-04, at 185 ½ Morrison.

BOSWELL, W. H.
Active in Newberg, 1913.

BOWLES, LINDLEY M.
Member of the International Photographic Association, active in Dallas, 1911.

BOWMAN & LEE
Partnership in Pendleton at 906 Main Street.

BOWMAN, WALTER S.
Born c. 1862; died in Pendleton, November 27, 1938. Traveling photographer, 1887-90, in eastern Oregon; major studio in Pendleton, 1890-1925; photographed Umatilla and Cayuse Indians and was among the first to record the Pendleton Round-Up rodeo. Bowman was a close friend of Major Lee Moorhouse and influenced his photographic work.

BOYCE & EASTOM
Partnership of Charles A. Boyce and Charles E. Eastom, portrait photographers in Portland, 1907, at 126 12th Street.

BOYCE, A. Y.
Active in Hillsboro, 1867.

BOYCE, CHARLES A.
Portrait photographer active in Portland, 1907, with Charles E. Eastom, operating as Boyce & Eastom at 126 12th Street.

BOYCHUK, WALTER
Born in Austria. Portrait studio in Portland, 1912-61.

BOYD, H. S.
Active in Eugene, c. 1890(?)

BOYD, HENRY J.
Partner with Frank A. Rankin in Rankin & Company, Eugene, 1891. Itinerant in Eugene, 1891; in Lebanon, 1901; in Ashland, 1903-17.

BOYD, JAMES N.
Active in Cottage Grove, 1901; in Lebanon, 1903.

BOYLE, J. R.
Portrait photographer active in Burns, 1856-1900. Also listed as J. F. Boyle.

BOYLE, KATE (MRS.)
Photographer active in Harrisburg, 1901-05.

BRADFORD, CORWIN W.
Born 1870. Active in Roseburg, 1903-11.

BRADLEY
Partner in Lantz & Bradley, active in Woodburn, 1895; Elmer G. Lantz.

BRADLEY, D. F.
Active in Wasco, c. 1900.

BRADLEY, DARWIN
Studio in Wasco, 1900(?); Portland, 1904; Oregon City, 1909.

BRADLEY, J. W.
Active in Endersley, 1895.

BRADLEY, L.
Active in Yaquina, 1888; also in Forest Grove and traveling, headquartered in Dayton, 1885.

BRADSHAW, CHARLES H.
Active in Newport, 1909-11.

BRADY, WILLIAM F.
Member of the Oregon Camera Club; active in Portland, 1909.

BRAINARD, SHERMAN H.
Member of the Oreon Camera Club; active in Portland, 1909-10.

BRANCH, JOHN W.
Active in Grants Pass, 1907-09.

BRANDBERG, JOSEPHINE (MRS.)
Photographer active in Huntington, 1903.

BRATT, JAMES HENRY
Active in San Francisco until 1893; in Astoria, 1893-95; San Rafael, California, 1899.

BREEDING, W. G.
Active in Woodville, 1891.

BRESSLER, JOHN B.
Studio in Grass Valley, 1903-13.

BRETHERTON, W. W.
Member of the Camera Club; active in Arlington; in Portland, 1885-1915.

BREWSTER, WILLIAM K.
Active in Enterprise, 1905.

BREYMAN, BERTHA M. (MISS)
Member of the Oregon Camera Club; active in Portland, 1904-05.

BRIDGE STUDIO
Operated by Joe Lum in Portland 1910-12, at 185 ½ Morrison.

BRIGGS, A. C.
Active in Creswell, 1889-91.

BRIGGS, JOHN A.
Active in Pendleton, 1884-88. Also active in Pleasant Hill and as an itinerant photographer; operated as the Portable Photographic Studio.

BRINK, J. F.
Portrait painter and enlarger active in Portland, 1865.

BRINKERHOFF, A. E.
Operated a portrait gallery in Salem on State Street, opposite Bennet House.

BRITT, EMIL
Son of Peter Britt; spent one year training at the studio of Bradley and Rulofson in San Francisco where he learned the gelatin dry-plate method of photography. He returned to his father's business, 1883, and his assistance allowed Peter Britt to practice the oil painting skills he had learned as a youth in Switzerland.

BRITT, PETER
Born in Obstalden, Switzerland, March 12, 1819; died in Jacksonville, 1905. Trained as an artist in Switzerland. Britt was one of the great early photographers of the Far West. He trained under J. H. Fitzgibbon in St. Louis, 1847, and operated a daguerreotype gallery in Highland, Illinois, 1847-52. He made the trek to Oregon, 1852, and after a brief stint in the gold fields, set up his studio in Jacksonville where he worked until 1900. Britt was one of the first to try each new process as it was announced and produced daguerreotypes, ambrotypes, melainotypes, opalotypes, tintypes, stereoviews, cdvs, cabinets, boudoirs and larger format albumen prints. His son, Emil, helped with the business in later years, as Peter Britt & Son, using bromide, carbon and other papers including postcard stock. Beginning in 1868, Britt took the first photographs of Crater Lake, and traveled through the area around Mt. Shasta, California, recording the scenery. Britt was also a musician, a horticulturalist renowned for his gardens, a breeder of exotic fish, a wine maker with his own label, an innovative orchardist, climatologist, bee keeper, and successful businessman. Britt was a favorite among the Chinese, who were largely ostracized by the community, and he produced portraits of Chinese citizens which are now among the collectable treasures of Britt memorabilia.
  Allen Clark Miller, *Photographer of a Frontier: The Photographs of Peter Britt*, Interface, Eureka, California, 1976.

BRITTEN, J.
Active in The Dalles.

BROBECKS, CHARLES
Photographer active in Portland, 1892.

BROCK
Active in Pendleton.

BRODECK, HENRY H.
Born 1836; died in Walla Walla, Washington, 1886. Active in Portland, 1877-78; in Alaska and California, 1881; in Walla Walla, Washington, 1880-c. 1891.

BRONQUIST, EDWARD
Active in Portland, 1904-15.

BROOKS & COMPANY, THOMAS
Studio in Astoria, 1881, operated by Thomas Brooks.

BROOKS, S. F.
Active in LaGrande.

BROOKS, THOMAS G.
Active in Astoria, 1881, operating as Thomas Brooks & Company.

BROUGHMAN, H. T.
Oregon stereographer who produced a few California views, c. 1900.

BROWER, C. C.
Active in Astoria, 1880s.

BROWN
Active in Eugene, operating as Winter & Brown, over A. V. Peters' store.

BROWN, ARTHUR M.
Active in Mill City and Stayton, 1891.

BROWN, F. J.
Active in Salem, at 243 Commercial Street, ground floor.

BROWN, HARRY C.
Manager of Angelus Commercial Photographic Company in Portland, 1915, 525 Abington Building. Also listed as Angelus Studio.

BROWN, I. S.
Member of the Oregon Camera Club; active in Portland, 1900.

BROWN, JAMES T.
Active in Oregon City, 1895; in Portland, 1894-25. Worked as a photo finisher for E. W. Moore, 1895, 1898 and 1899; for C. W. Short, 1896; for G. L. Eastman, 1897; also worked as a printer for E. W. Moore, 1899. He is listed as a photographer, 1894-97; as a photographer, c. 1900-25.

BROWN, JEDDY
Active in Fossil, 1891.

BROWN, NELLIE (MRS.)
Active in Vale, 1915.

BROWN, SIDDY
Active in Mitchell, 1886.

BROWNING, FLORA H. (MRS.)
Retoucher for B. C. Towne in Portland, 1888-89, at 167 ½ 1st Street. Manager of the San Francisco Gallery, 1895 at the same address; proprietor and photographer, 1896-1908, operating as Browning Photo Gallery. Active in Newburg, c. 1911.

BROWNING, GEORGE W.
Active in Portland, c. 1896-1902, photographer for the Browning Photo Gallery at 167 ½ 1st.

BROWNING PHOTO GALLERY
Operated by proprietor and photographer, Flora H. Browning in Portland, 1896-1908, at 167 ½ 1st Street. Formerly the San Francisco Gallery.

BRUNN, C. D. (MRS.)
Member of the Oregon Camera Club; active in Portland, 1900.

BRUNO STUDIO
Gallery in Salem producing stereoviews.

BRYANT, GEORGE ARCHIBALD
Born near Gaston, Oregon, 1879; died in Eugene, 1959. Active in San Francisco; in Portland, 1907; in Forest Grove, 1907-19; also known as Pacific Art Studio.

BRYSON, W. R.
Active in Eugene, 1890s(?), operating as McClanahan & Bryson with Edward J. McClanahan.

BUCHTEL & CARDWELL
Partnership of Joseph Buchtel and Byron P. Cardwell, stereo photographers in Portland, 1859-64. Cardwell sold his interest in the studio to his brother, J. R., 1864; J. R. remained a partner until the business was sold to F. Dalton, 1865.

BUCHTEL & HOLLAND
Joseph Buchtel and Holland, operating in Portland, 1857, in the Canton House, over the Crockery Store; in Oregon City, 1858.

BUCHTEL & STOLTE
Joseph Buchtel and E. H. Stolte, stereo photographers in Portland and Salem, 1873-78.

BUCHTEL, ALBERT Z.
Born July 5, 1857; died in Portland, July 11, 1880. Son of Joseph Buchtel, active in Portland, 1878-80.

BUCHTEL, FRANK S.
Active in East Portland, 1881-83.

BUCHTEL, JOSEPH
Born 1830; died in Portland, August 10, 1916. Learned daguerreotyping and worked in Urbana, Illinois, 1851-52; in Portland by 1853; puchased Wakefield's daguerreotype studio, 1853, but traveled with a portable gallery to various towns along the Columbia and Willamette Rivers. Buchtel & Holland opened for business in Portland, 1857, in the Canton House, over the Crockery Store; in Oregon City, 1858. He visited San Francisco and bought cameras from William Shew and Robert Vance, then returned to Portland. Partner with Byron Cardwell, 1859-65, operating as Buchtel & Cardwell; sold the studio to F. Dalton, 1865. He operated A. B. Woodard's gallery, 1865-66; purchased the gallery, 1866, and opened the Pioneer Gallery at the corner of Front and Morrison. Parisian photographer Policarpo Bagnasco served as operator. Buchtel opened a new studio in the Shelby Building, 1867; moved to 91 First Street, 1869. By 1873 he had formed the partnership Buchtel & Stolte with E. H. Stolte, and in 1875 the firm moved to the corner of First and Morrison. The same year Buchtel purchased the firm of Bosco & Megler located down 1st Street, overprinting their imprints with his own name. Bosco became Buchtel's operator. He apparently sold his studio to W. H. Towne, an experienced photographer from San Francisco, 1880, who printed some of Buchtel's images under his own imprint. Buchtel was one of Portland's leading citizens, serving as fire chief and Sheriff of Multnomah County, and was the city's foremost photographer for many years. He produced photographs in all of the popular formats, including stereoview.

BUCHTEL, SAMUEL
Died in California, 1901. Younger brother of Joseph Buchtel. Active in Portland, 1865-97; operator for Buchtel & Stolte, and later for Davidson; in California, 1897-1901.

BUCK, M. E.
Active in Sherwood, 1911-15.

BUCKLEY, J. W.
Member of the Oregon Camera Club; active in Portland, 1909-11.

BULLOCK, MAE C.
Active in Salem, 1913, with Wilkins A. Bullock, her husband. Formerly Mrs. M. C. Lewis.

BULLOCK, WILKINS A.
Studio in Salem, 1913, with Mae C. Bullock, his wife. Also known as Bullock Studio.

BUNNELL, W.
Active in Bandon(?).

BURKHART, D. C.
Active in Lebanon, 1907-11; in Albany, 1911.

BURNS & OHSFELDT
Partnership in Portland at 313 ½ Morrison, 1899.

BURNS BROTHERS
Partnership of M. Bruce, Robert M. and William (or Walter), operating in Pendleton, 1903-05, at 916 Main Street.

BURNS, K. (MISS)
Member of the Oregon Camera club; active in Portland, 1900.

BURNS, M. BRUCE
Operated as Burns Brothers in Pendleton, 1903-05, at 916 Main Street, with brothers Robert M. and William (or Walter).

BURNS, OWEN SPENCER
Active in Upper Albina, c. 1890, at 508 Williams and 313 ½ Morrison; in Portland, 1894-1900.

BURNS, ROBERT
Active in Kendrick and Lewiston, Idaho, 1903; in Pendleton, 1903-07; with brothers Bruce and William (or Walter) operating as Burns Brothers, 1903-05, at 916 Main Street.

BURNS, WILLIAM J.
Active in Pendleton, 1903-05, at 916 Main Street, with brothers Robert M. and M. Bruce, operating as Burns Brothers. Active in Warner, Idaho, 1907; in Coeur d'Alene, Idaho, 1910-11. Name also given as Walter.

BURRELL, J. B.
Active in Pendleton; in Ontario, 1915.

BURTON
Partner in Lloyd & Burton, active in Eugene.

BURTON, DOROTHY M.
Active in Portland, 1905-06. Clerk at E. H. Moorehouse & Company, 1905; at Rembrandt Photo & Portrait Studio, 1906.

BUSH, JAMES
Active in Myrtle Point, 1886.

BUSHBY & COMPANY
Studio in Portland, 1890, operated by Asa C. Bushby and Clarence J. Messer.

BUSHBY, ASA C.
Born in Massachusetts, 1835; died in Pierce County, Washington, January 21, 1897. Active in Portland, 1890, operating Bushby & Company with Clarence J. Messer; in Pierce County, Washington, 1897.

BUSHNELL, CORRY A.
Born c. 1866; died 1941. Active in Ellensburgh, Washington, 1891-95; in Eugene, 1896; Yakima, Washington, 1898; Seattle, 1902-14; and in Portland, 1915-25. Operated at Columbia Building, 6th Floor, 365 Washington, 1915-25.

BUSHNELL, FRANK P.
Active in Portland, 1910.

BUSHNELL-LANGFORD PHOTO COMPANY
Active in LaGrande and Union, c. 1899, operated by Miss Olive Langford.

BUTLER & FRANKS
See Franks & Butler.

BUTLER, BENJAMIN D.
Born in North Carolina, 1819; died in Bickelton, Washington, 1890. Active in The Dalles, 1852-70; partner in Franks & Butler, 1852-65, with F. D. Franks on Main Street. Also listed Butler & Franks.

BUTTERWORTH, CHARLES
Born near Cincinnati, Ohio, 1858; died in Portland, 1936. Active in Portland, 1898-1936. Worked for Aune, 1898-1900; at Krauch Studio, 1902. Operated at 345 ½ Washington, 1903-12; at 301 Globe Building, 1914-17; 207 Globe Building, 1917-22; 407 Washington, 1923-25; 315 Fliedner Building, 1927-33.

BUTTON, CHARLES GILBERT
Born 1835. Active in Astoria, c. 1878-80, operating Belancue & Button and the Flying Studio. Partner's name also spelled Blancue, Betancue.

BYBEE
Active in Willamina, 1913, operating studio of Bybee & Cannon.

BYBEE & CANNON
Studio in Willamina, 1913.

BYERS, BERNARD L.
Active in Portland and Stayton, 1903.

C. C. M. COMPANY
Active in Portland, 1900, operated by John R. Cawthon and Samuel B. Crow. It became the Crow Photo Company, 1901; and the Unique Portrait Company, 1902-09.

CALDWELL, CHESTER M.
Active in Corvallis, 1909-11.

CALDWELL, JOHN
Active in Canyonville, 1880.

CALIFORNIA GALLERY
Active in Astoria, 1880, operated by Samuel Crow.

CALIFORNIA STUDIO
Gallery in Salem producing stereoviews.

CALLAGHAN
Active in Portland, c. 1910, operating as "Mayer & Callaghan, Stereographers."

CALVERT, ALVIDA
Active in Portland, 1910, with Harry, Charles E. and Grace Calvert, operating a postcard portrait studio known as Calvert's Studio, Ten Minute Postcard Man and City Park Gallery.

CALVERT, CHARLES E.
Postcard portrait studio in Portland, 1906-15; at 796 Washington 1910-15. Operated with Alvida and Harry, 1910; with Harry and Grace, 1910-17. Active in Oregon City, at 6th North, 1916-23; at 305 Buchanan Building, 1923-25; at 607 Woodlark Building, 1927-30. Known as Calvert's Studio, Ten Minute Postcard Man, City Park Gallery.

CALVERT, GRACE E.
Operated with Alvida, Harry and Charles E. in Portland, 1910; in Oregon City, 1915-18, with Harry and Charles E. Known as Calvert's Studio, Ten Minute Postcard Man, City Park Gallery.

CALVERT, HARRY
Active in Portland, 1910-17, operating with Grace and Charles E. Calvert; also with Alvida, 1910. Known as Calvert's Studio, Ten Minute Postcard Man, City Park Gallery. See Charles E. Calvert.

CALVERT'S STUDIO
Active in Portland, 1910-15, at 796 Washington; in Oregon City, at 6th North, 1916-23; at 305 Buchanan Building, 1923-25; at 607 Woodlark Building, 1927-30. Operated by Harry, Alvida, Charles E. and Grace E. Calvert. Also known as City Park Gallery and Ten Minute Postcard Man.

CAMMACK & JOHNSON
Partnership in Portland, 1902, at 171 1st Street; Fred M. Cammack and Walter H. Johnson.

CAMMACK, FRED M.
Active in Portland, 1902, 171 1st Street, operating as Cammack & Johnson.

CAMPBELL
Featured at meeting of Oregon Camera Club in Portland, 1917, showing slides of birds.

CAMPBELL, HAMILTON
Born in West Virginia, June 12, 1812; murdered in Mexico, June 12, 1863. Traveling daguerreotypist based in Corvallis, 1854-59. Uncle of Byron P. Cardwell of Buchtel & Cardwell. Working in San Francisco, 1859.

CAMPBELL, JOHN
Active in Portland, 1879-82, operating as Barnum & Campbell with J. T. Barnum, at Fifth near Yamhill..

CAMPS, FRANK L.
Active in Olympia, Washington, 1891; Ashland, 1901-17.

CANADAY, H.
Active in Burns, 1891.

CANARIS, CATHERINE
Died, c. 1938. Active in Portland, c. 1894-1905. Operated the studio at 466 Alder, 1895-99. Photographer for William Sandeen, 1899-1900; on her own, 1901; photographer for E. W. Dill, 1905.

CANARIS, FRANK H.
Born in Reine Provene, Russia, February 4, 1854; died in Long Beach, Washington, 1937. Active in Portland, c. 1894.

CANDLIN, L. M. (MRS.)
Member of the Oregon Camera Club; active in Portland, 1900.

CANN
Active in Portland, operating as Cann Studio.

CANNON
Active in Willamina, 1913, operating as Bybee & Cannon.

CARABERIS & NICKAS
Partnership in Portland, 1917; Christ Nickas and George Caraberis, 207 Globe Building.

CARABERIS, GEORGE
Active in Portland, 1917, operating as Caraberis & Nickas.

CARDWELL & ELLSWORTH
Studio in Portland, 1867, at 89 First Street, operated by Byron P. and J. R. Cardwell and Frank Ellsworth. Also known as Ellsworth & Cardwell, and Cardwell Gallery.

CARDWELL, BYRON P.
Born 1832; died 1903. Active in Portland, 1859-65. Learned daguerreotyping from his uncle, Hamilton Campbell. Operated as Buchtel & Cardwell, 1859-65.

CARDWELL GALLERY
Studio in Portland, 1867, at 89 First Street, operated by Byron P. and J. R. Cardwell and Frank Ellsworth. Also known as Ellsworth & Cardwell, and Cardwell & Ellsworth.

CARDWELL, J. R.
Brother of Byron and R. H. Cardwell; a dentist who purchased the interest of his brother Byron in the Buchtel & Cardwell gallery, 1864, remaining a partner until the business was sold to F. Dalton, 1865. Partner in Ellsworth & Cardwell, operating studio at 89 First Street, 1866-67. Also known as Cardwell & Ellsworth and Cardwell Gallery. R. A. Desmond was Cardwell's operator. J. R. was also taxidermist, and operated a museum of stuffed animals that offered a diversion for portrait customers.

CARDWELL, R. H.
Active in Portland, 1868; in Seattle, Washington, 1876, operating a photograph gallery over the Seattle Market. Brother of Byron P. and

J. R. Cardwell; nephew of daguerreotypist Hamilton Campbell.

CAREY, ZOOK ANGUS
Studio in Portland, 1910-17; at 501 Beck Building, 1910; at 525 Beck Building, 1913-17. He changed his name from Carey A. Zook, 1914.

CARR, CLARENCE
Active in Milton, 1903.

CARRATT
Active in Arlington.

CARRUTHERS, GRACE
Active in Astoria, 1889, with Zoe Carruthers.

CARRUTHERS, ZOE
Active in Astoria, 1889, with Grace Carruthers.

CARSTONS, E.
Member of the Oregon Camera Club; active in Portland, 1900.

CARTER, HERBERT S.
Active in Salem, 1910-16, operating the Trover-Carter Studio; in Astoria, 1911, operating Carter's Portrait Studio.

CARTER'S PORTRAIT STUDIO
See Herbert S. Carter.

CASTLEMAN, PHILLIP F.
Born 1827; died 1913. Itinerant active in East Cascades, 1853-78; Portland, 1869-70; also in Eugene and Astoria, 1870. Produced "Birds-Eye View" lithographs of cities.

CATCHING, S. E.
Member of the Oregon Camera Club; active in Portland, 1900.

CATTERLIN & HICKS
Partnership of Lute J. Hicks and Frances J. Catterlin, active in Salem, 1888, at 160 State.

CATTERLIN & LUSSIER
Partnership of Frances J. Catterlin and William Lussier in Portland, 1889, at 160 State Street.

CATTERLIN, FRANCES JUDD
Active in Salem, 1886-93. Operated as Pickerill & Catterlin, 1886; at 160 State as Catterlin & Hicks with Lute J. Hicks, 1888; with William Lussier, 1889, operating as Catterlin & Lussier. Sold out to Anna Cronise in 1893.

CATTERLIN, WILLIAM H.
Possibly an itinerant, 1872. Active in Salem, c. 1873-76; operated as Catterlin & Rogers, 1874; in Portland, 1894-1911. Located at 166 5th, 1894-98; 89 ½ 4th, 1899-1904; 89 4th, 1905-10.

CAWTHON & WARREN
Partnership of James B. Cawthon and Warren in Portland, 1885.

CAWTHON, ETHEL (MISS)
Operator of Unique Portrait Company in Portland, 1902, for John R. Cawthon.

CAWTHON, J. W.
Active in Union and Enterprise.

CAWTHON, JAMES B.
Active in Portland, 1888-89; also operated as Cawthon & Warren, 1885. Name also spelled Cawthorn.

CAWTHON, JOHN R.
Active in Portland, 1888-89; 1894-1910; operated as C. C. M. Company, 1900; Crow Photo Company, 1901; Unique Portrait Company, 1902-09.

CELEBRATED PHOTOGRAPH STUDIO
Operated by Joseph Fortin in The Dalles, 1891-97; in Lewiston Idaho, 1902-05. Also active in Huntington.

CENTENNIAL ART STUDIO
Active in Portland, 1906-16 at 203 ½ 1st Street, operated by W. Bicknell.

CENTENNIAL PHOTO STUDIO
Active in Portland, 1910 at 52 North 6th Street, operated by Louis A. Kearney.

CHASE, E. T.
Member of the Oregon Camera Club; active in Portland, 1898-1900.

CHATTERTON, M. (MISS)
Member of the Oregon Camera Club; active in Portland, 1900.

CHENEY & GRIMM
Active in Mill City; also called the Star Studio.

CHENEY, EDITH C.
Operated Cheney's Art Gallery in Oregon City, 1896-1905, corner of Ninth and Main Streets.

CHENEY, ESTON S.
Active in Oregon City, 1896-1901.

CHENEY, ETHEL
Active in McMinnville, 1905-07, with Bessie Krumm operating Cheney & Krumm. Edith or Ethel may also have operated as Cheney & Grimm, Mill City.

CHENEY'S ART GALLERY
Operated by Edith C. Cheney in Oregon City, 1896-1905, corner of Ninth and Main Streets.

CHERRINGTON BROTHERS
Stereo photographers in Salem, 1895. Also listed as Cherrington & Brothers.

CHERRINGTON, THOMAS J.
Active in Salem, 1888-91. Partner with brother William M., 1891, on Commercial or Chemeketa Street, operating as Cherrington Brothers or Cherrington & Brothers. Active in Dallas, 1901-11, at 4 Wilson Building.

CHERRINGTON, WILLIAM M.
Active in Salem, 1891, with brother Thomas J. on Commercial or Chemeketa Street, operating as Cherrington Brothers or Cherrington & Brothers.

CHILDREN'S ART GALLERY COMPANY
Studio in Portland, 1894-95, at 410 East Morrison, possibly operated by William Emery.

CHINLUND, ELMER A.
Active in Portland, 1910-12. Located at 303 ½ Washington with Frantz W., operating as Chinlund Brothers, 1910; listed as photographer, 1911-12.

CHINLUND, FRANTZ WILLIAM
Active in Portland, 1910, operating at 303 ½ Washington as Chinlund Brothers with Elmer A.

CHINNERY, J. H.
Member of the International Photographic Association; active in Woodville, 1911; in Portland, 1912.

CHRISTIANI, CHARLES O.
Member of the International Photographic Association; active in Prineville, 1911.

CHRISTY STUDIO
Active in Portland and Seattle, Washington, 1901-11.

CHURCHLEY & HARGRAVE
Partnership of Arthur G. Churchley and Hargrave, based in Kelso, Washington and photographing in the Hillsboro area of Oregon, 1895.

CHURCHLEY, AMY G.
Retoucher and photographer in Portland, 1901-05, with Arthur G. Churchley at 145 ½ 3rd.

CHURCHLEY, ARTHUR G.
Born c. 1871; died in Portland, 1928. Based in Kelso, Washington, operating as Churchley & Hargrave and photographing the Hillsboro area, 1895. Active in Portland, 1900-28; located at 145 ½ 3rd, 1900-11; 616 Northwest Building and 327 ½ Washington, 1912-18; 616 Raleigh Building, 1920-28.

CLAPP & PRATT
Active in Marquam, c. 1915; O. Clapp and G. A. Pratt.

CLARK
Partner in Fritz & Clark, active in Forest Grove before 1900.

CLARK & CLARK
Studio in Roseburg, 1917, operated by James H. and Charles W. Clark. Operated as Clark Brothers, 1908-16.

CLARK & WOOD
Partnership of Frank W. Wood and John C. Clark in LaGrande, 1891.

CLARK BROTHERS
Studio in Roseburg, 1908-17, operated by James H. and Charles W. Clark. Also listed as Clark & Clark, 1917.

CLARK, CHARLES W.
Active in Roseburg, 1908-17; with brother James H. as Clark Brothers; also listed as Clark & Clark, 1917.

CLARK, F. MELVIN
Operated Clark's Studio in Eugene, 1913-15, at Seventh and Willamette Streets.

CLARK, FRED A.
Commercial photographer in Portland, 1914-16, at 310 Macley Building. Also listed at McKay Building.

CLARK, GEORGE
Active in Independence, 1888.

CLARK, JAMES H.
Active in Roseburg, 1908-17; with brother Charles W. as Clark Brothers; also listed as Clark & Clark, 1917.

CLARK, JOHN C.
Born in Illinois, 1853. Active in LaGrande, 1889-91; in Portland, 1896-97. Partner with Frank W. Wood, 1891, operating as Clark & Wood.

CLARK, L. WILSON
Active in Olympia, Washington, 1881-87; in Albany, Oregon, 1887-89.

CLARK'S STUDIO
Active in Eugene, 1913-15, at Seventh and Willamette Streets, operated by F. Melvin Clark.

CLARKE, J. F.
Member of the Oregon Camera Club: active in Portland, 1900.

CLAUSSENIUS, HERMAN
Member of the Oregon Camera Club; active in Portland, 1900.

CLAVERING, ROBERT K.
Active in Oregon City, 1896-97; in Portland, 1894-95, operating the Motor Gallery at 410 Morrison.

CLAXTON, INEZ
Retoucher active in Portland, 1904-05.

CLEAVES, J. R.
Active in Marshfield, 1878-89.

CLEMENS, RUTH (MRS.)
Active in Grants Pass, 1913.

CLEMENT, EDLAND C.
Member of the Oregon Camera Club; active in Portland, 1900.

CLEVELAND, MARSHALL
Active in Oregon City.

CLEVENGER, CHARLES L.
Active in Grants Pass, 1901-07.

CLIFFORD, C. E.
Operated studio in Albany, 1915-17.

CLUTTER
Active in Forest Grove; operating as Clutter & Company in Medford, c. 1880-81.

CLUTTER & COMPANY
Operated in Medford, c. 1880-81.

COCHRAN, M. C.
Active in Cottage Grove, 1907.

COE, ELMER A.
Active in Astoria, 1906-11, at 110 11th.

COFFEY, CHESTER M.
Born in Oregon, 1887. Active in Corvallis, 1907-09; Portland, 1909, 1927-33; in McMinnville, 1916-26. Operated Coffey's Photo Service.

COHEN, I. L.
Member of the Oregon Camera Club; active in Portland, 1898-1907. Operated the Oregon Photo Stock Company, 1903-07; Blumauer Photo Supply Company, 1909-12.

COLE, J. J.
Member of the Oregon Camera Club; active in Portland, 1900.

COLLINS, PAUL
Active in Albany, 1911.

COLLINS, RICHARD B.
Enlarger and photographer in Dallas, 1884-91; in Victoria, British Columbia, 1892.

COLUMBIA COMMERCIAL STUDIO
Operated by J. H. Gensler in Portland, 1917, at 167 4th Street.

COLUMBIA GALLERY
Operated by Seifert & Leopold in Forest Grove, 1904-05.

COLUMBIA PHOTOGRAPH GALLERY
Operated by Albert L. Jackson in Eugene or Portland, 1882. Also known as the Columbia Photo Gallery.

COLUMBIA STUDIO
Active in Oregon City, 1895(?), 29 North Third Street.

COLVIG, VOLNEY
Active in Canyonville, 1867.

COMMERCIAL PHOTO COMPANY
Located in Portland, 1915, H. F. Bartels, agent.

COMMONWEALTH PORTRAIT STUDIO
Operated by Vassar L. Northrup in Portland, 1910, at 308 Commonwealth Building.

CONE & McKERCHER
Active in Portland, 1879; a bookstore that sold photographs.

CONN
Partner in Wilcox & Conn, active in Albany, 1891.

CONN & UNDERWOOD
Partnership of Richard E. Conn and J. L. Underwood, active in Corvallis, 1891.

CONN, R. J.
Active in Oregon City, c. 1895.

CONN, RICHARD E.
Born c. 1853; died 1947. Partner with J. L. Underwood in Corvallis, 1891, operating as Conn & Underwood. Listed alone in Portland, 1892-1902. Operated at 121 ½ Russell, 1892-1900.

CONNOR, CHARLES T.
Active in Portland, 1896, operating as Frost & Connor.

CONNOR, OLIVE
Active in Holley, 1907.

COOK, H. M.
Active in Pendleton, 1909; in John Day, 1913.

COOPER, C. V.
Member of the Oregon Camera Club; active in Portland, 1900.

COOPER, CHARLES J.
Born c. 1852. Active in Camas Valley, 1880.

COOPER, HENRY L.
Partner with James J. Owings in North Bend, 1905, operating as Owings & Cooper.

COOPER, RAYMOND O.
Active in Baker City, 1907-11, operating the Elite Studio.

COOS BAY PHOTO & CRAYON COMPANY
Operated by George McMillan in Marshfield, 1886-91.

COOVERT
Operated a gallery in McMinnville prior to October 26, 1878, when it was destroyed by fire.

CORBETT, E.
Active in Portland at 508 Williams Avenue, 1893.

COREY
Traveling photographer, Hillsboro area, c. 1867; partner in Roberts & Corey.

COREY & SCOTFORD
Studio in Portland at 127 ½ Fourth Street, operated by Justin C. Corey and John H. Scotford, 1898.

COREY, JUSTIN C.
Active in Portland, operating as Corey & Scotford with John H. Scotford, 127 ½ Fourth Street, 1898.

CORPRON, O. B.
Active in Lafayette, 1901.

CORVALLIS STUDIO
Gallery in Corvallis, operated by Edwin C. Barclay, 1911-13.

COSPER & TALIFERRO
Studio in Salem, formerly occupied by W. P. Johnson & Company; operated by Romeo Cosper and Taliferro, 1878. Also spelled Taliafero.

COSPER, ROMEO
Active in Salem, 1878-89; operated as Cosper & Taliferro, 1878, at a gallery formerly occupied by W. P. Johnson & Company.

COTTEL, W. I.
Member of the Oregon Camera Club; active in Portland, 1900.

COTTON, WALTER S.
Member of the International Photographic Association; active in Portland, 1914.

COUSIN & CHURCHLEY
Stereo photographers in Salem, 1890s.

COUSIN, ALBERT B.
Active in Portland at 410 East Morrison, 1892-93.

COVER, FRANK C.
Member of the Oregon Camera Club; active in Portland, 1898-1900.

COWDEN, JOHN W.
Active in Sumpter, 1901-05.

COWGILL, H. E., JR.
Member of the Oregon Camera Club; active in Portland, 1900.

COWHERD, LUTHER
Active in Madras, 1913.

COX
Operated the Cox Studio in Hood River, 1917.

COX, ALFRED
Active in Portland at 516 Worcester Building, 1914-15.

COX, C. M.
Member of the Oregon Camera Club; active in Portland, 1898-1900.

COX, M. B. (MRS.)
Active in Salem at 418 Hubbard Building, 1917.

COX STUDIO
Operated in Hood River, 1917.

CRAMER, MARY E.
Active in Stayton, 1901.

CRANDALL & ELLIS
Partnership in Hillsboro operating Ellis Studio, 1904. Possibly Rudolph Crandall.

CRANDALL & McBRIDE
Studio in Hillsboro operated by Rudolph Crandall and McBride, 1891.

CRANDALL, A. B.
Active in Hillsboro, 1891.

CRANDALL, RUDOLPH
Active in Hillsboro operating as Crandall & McBride, 1891; possibly a partner in Crandall & Ellis, 1904.

CRANE, EPHRAIM MARTIN
Active in Roseburg, 1862; Oakland, c. 1870-72; operated as Sawyer & Crane, 1872.

CRANE, S. W.
Active in Roseburg, 1862; Oakland, 1872; brother of E. M. Crane.

CRAVEN, DAVID H.
Active in Salem, 1893; partner in Cronise & Craven, c. 1893, possibly with Thomas J. Cronise. Active in Portland, 1901-15; listed as a photographer with Pike & Markham & Company, 1915.

CRAVENS (MISS)
Active in Salem, 1893, working for Cronise & Cronise. Possibly a misspelling of Craven and related to David H. Craven, who was a partner of Cronise.

CRAWFORD & HUTCHINS
Studio in Lebanon, possibly after 1905.

CRAWFORD & LITTLER
Partnership of James G. Crawford and Littler in Albany, 1889.

CRAWFORD & PAXTON
Active in Albany, 1891; partnership of James G. Crawford and Andrew B. Paxton at 72 First Street, Briggs Building.

CRAWFORD BROTHERS
Partnership of Orville and James G. Crawford, active in Albany, 1886.

CRAWFORD, GEORGE
Active in Arlington, 1915.

CRAWFORD, JAMES G.
Born 1850. Active in Harisburg, 1877-84; in McMinnville, 1884; in Portland, 1885; in Albany 1886-1917. Partner with his brother Orville, 1886, operating as Crawford Brothers; partner with Andrew B. Paxton, 1891, operating as Crawford & Paxton at 72 First Street; partner with Littler, 1889. Also employed by I. G. Davidson.

CRAWFORD, ORVILLE
Active in Albany with brother James G., operating as Crawford Brothers, 1886.

CREGO, GIBSON S.
Active in Portland, 1912-17.

CRIST
Active in Oakland, 1872; partner in Barney & Crist. Possibly in business in Portland, 1873.

CROCKET, ETHEL M.
Retoucher in Portland, 1905-10; worked for Mrs. R. M. Hogan, 1907, 1910.

CROMWELL, OSCAR
Born 1838. Active in Salem, 1860s. Partner with S. E. Gray in Gray & Cromwell, Salem, 1870. Listed alone in Lakeview, 1880; also in Bonanza..

CRONISE & CRAVEN
Active in Salem, c. 1893; David H. Craven possibly with Thomas J. Cronise.

CRONISE, ANNA LOUISE
Active in Salem as photographer for Francis J. Catterlin, 1892; with her brother, Thomas J., operating as Cronise & Cronise, 1893; with Tom Cronise Photo Studio, 1903-07. She married Howard D. Trover, her brother's partner.

CRONISE, THOMAS J.
Born in Illinois, 1853. Active in Salem, 1882, 1893-1917. Worked as printer for A. L. Stinson, 1882; possibly a partner in Cronise & Craven with David H. Craven, c. 1893; operated as Cronise & Cronise, 1893, with his sister, Anna L., at 160 State Street; part time at Cronise Photo Studio, 1894-1902; operated as the Tom Cronise Photo Studio, 1902-1923; as Trover-Cronise with Howard D. Trover, 1909.

CROSLEY, HARRY A.
Born 1866; died 1953. Active in Independence, 1888; partner in Fritz & Crosley, Hillsboro, 1889-91; in Forest Grove, 1890-1911.

CROSS & DIMMITT
Studio in Portland operated by E. L. Dimmitt and Arthur B. Cross; located at 414-415 Merchants Trust Building, 1916- 25; at 1801 Sandy Boulevard, 1925.

CROSS, ARTHUR B.
Active in Portland, 1909-35. Photographer for Leonard J. Miller at Electric Studio, 145 6th, 1910; at 392 ½ Washington, 1912-13; at 414 Washington, 1915. Partner in Cross & Dimmitt with E. L. Dimmitt, 1916-25, at 414-415 Merchants Trust Building; at 1801 Sandy Boulevard, 1925.

CROUSE, C.
Active in Portland, 1904-05.

CROW & CROW
Active in Portland, 1901; operated by Samuel B. Crow, John W. and Miss Minnie Crow.

CROW & LUSSIER
Partnership of Samuel B. Crow and William Lussier, operating in Portland at Labbe Building, corner of 2nd and Washington, 1894.

CROW & SNYDER
Partnership in Coquille City, 1876; Samuel B. Crow and Snyder.

CROW, JOHN W.
Active in Calapooya Precinct, 1870; in Knappa, 1886-91; operating with S. B. Crow as the Crow Photo Company in Portland, 1899. Worked with S. B. and Miss Minnie Crow as Crow & Crow, 1901.

CROW, MINNIE (MISS)
Active in Portland with John W. and Samuel B. Crow, operating as Crow & Crow, 1901.

CROW PHOTO
Active in Portland, operated by John R. Cawthon, 1901.

CROW PHOTO COMPANY
Operated in Portland by S. B. Crow, 1895-1900; by J. W. Crow, 1899.

CROW PHOTOGRAPH COMPANY
Active in Astoria, operated by Samuel B. Crow, 1884-91.

CROW, SAMUEL B.
Active in Coquille with partner operating as Crow & Snyder, 1876; in North Canyonville, 1880. Active in Astoria, c. 1884-91, operating as the Crow Photograph Company; in Portland with William Lussier, operating as Crow & Lussier at the Labbe Building, corner of 2nd and Washington, 1894; as Crow Photo Company, 1895-1900; as Crow & Crow with John W. and Miss Minnie Crow, 1900-01. Active in Vancouver, Washington, operating the Elite Studio, 1903; Port Townsend, Washington, 1915-16. Also operated as CCM Company in Portland, 1900.

CROXALL
Active in Bandon.

CRYSLER, RALPH
Member of the Oregon Camera Club; active in Portland, 1900.

CUMMINGS, CHARLES C.
Active in Portland, 1889.

CUMMINGS, E. C.
Active in Athena.

CUMMINGS, OLIVER G.
Active in Portland, 1904.

CUNNINGHAM, BURTON S.
Active in Ft. Klamath, 1903.

CUPP, G. M.
Operating as Beers & Cup in Forest Grove with G. W. Beers, 1868.

CUTBERTH, EMMA E. (MRS.)
Active in Spokane with Cutberth Brothers, 1901; operating the Rembrandt Photograph & Portrait Studio in Portland with W. G. Cutberth, 1902-04; photographer at 801 Dekum Building, 1905-06.

CUTBERTH, WILLIAM G.
Active in Spokane with Cutberth Brothers, c. 1901; operating the Rembrandt Photograph & Portrait Studio in Portland with Emma E. Cutberth, 1902-04; at 801 Dekum Building, 1905-15; listed at 216 Pittock Block, 1916. Operated as Acadia Studio in Portland, 1910-16; also in Acadia.

CUTSFORTH, JARVIS E.
Active in Tillamook, 1915; Sheridan, 1917; member of the Photographers Association of the Pacific Northwest.
DAHLGREN, JOHN
Active in Tillamook, 1915; Sheridan, 1917.

DAILEY, JONAS
Active in Elgin, 1909.

DAILEY, MARY (MRS.)
Active in Hillsboro, 1881.

DAIVSON, C. K.
Active in Zena, 1895(?); possibly Dawson.

DALGLEISH, GILBERT
Member of the Oregon Camera Club; active in Portland, 1898-1900.

DALTON, FRANK
Active in Portland, 1865.

DANA
Operated as Dana Studio in Ashland, 1917.

DANNER, THEODORE D.
Active in Heppner and Lexington, 1889-91; in Pendleton, 1903-05, operating as as Danner & Lubken; in Athena, 1907; in Milton, 1911-17.

DARLING & INGERSOLL
Studio in Forest Grove, 1915-19; Belle Darling.

DARLING, BELLE
Operating as Darling & Ingersoll in Forest Grove, 1915-19.

DATESMAN, PETER P.
Active in Portland, 1904-10.

DAVENPORT, LIZZIE (MRS.)
Active in Silverton, 1884-88.

DAVIDSON, D. A.
Partner in Hanson & Davidson, Monmouth, 1911-17

DAVIDSON, EDGAR L.
Active in Oregon City, 1897; partner in Davidson & Wells with Ebenezer Wells, 1903-04.

DAVIDSON, ISAAC GRUNDY
Born 1845; died 1922. Active in Portland, 1878-88; in Tacoma, Washington, c. 1888. One of the Northwest's premier photographers, Davidson published an extensive series of scenic photographs covering many aspects of life and scenes throughout Oregon, Washington and Alaska. He operated portrait studios, a traveling gallery, and contracted with the Northern Pacific Railroad under the names of Shuster & Davidson, 1876-77, Palace Gallery and Gilman & Davidson, 1878, and Davidson Brothers, 1878-79. In 1878 he hired Andrew Wulzen who had worked for Carleton Watkins during his memorable 1867 tour of the Columbia River and the Portland area, and Wulzen produced some of the best views published by Davidson. He produced a series of boudoir-format prints of the Indian School at Forest Grove. Robinson proposes that Davidson, an accountant by profession, was never an operator in his photography business, but was a keen businessman who produced the finest photographic record of Oregon during the 1870-80s. His employees included James G. Crawford, Samuel Buchtel, O. S. Dowe, Mrs. A. L. Jackson, Albert L. Jackson, Asel E. Severance, Charles W. Short and Andrew Wulzen.

DAVIDSON, J.
Operated Davidson's Studio in Linkville, 1886.

DAVIDSON, JOHN S.
Active in Portland, 1875-94. Assistant to Oliver Dennie, 1875; partner in Shuster & Davidson, 1876-77, at the southwest corner of 1st and Yamhill; partner with his brother, I. G., operating as Davidson

Brothers, 1878-c. 1888; alone, 1890; for G. W. Davies, 1891-94. He operated Davidson's Studio in Monmouth, 1910.

DAVIDSON, LE ROY
Active in Portland, 1896-98.

DAVIES, GEORGE W.
Born 1855; died 1929. Active in Portland, 1879-1928. Printer for F. G. Abell, 1879-82; operated Davies Studio with his stepson, Clarence A. Defries, 1901-25.

DAVIS & TULL
Gallery in Lakeview, 1909; operated by Irene Tull and L. M. Davis.

DAVIS, A. LEAMAN
Operated the Sarony Studio in Portland at 342 ½ Washington, 1910-14.

DAVIS, HUGH C.
Active in Wallowa, 1903; in Flora, 1907-13.

DAVIS, L. M.
Partner in Davis & Tull with Irene Tull, operating in Lakeview, 1909.

DAVIS, MARSHALL P.
Active in Sandy, 1911-17.

DAVIS, S. P.
Active in Oregon City at 927 Madison Street, 1904, 1914, 1916.

DAVIS, W. B.
Active in Union, c. 1900.

DAVIS, W. W.
Active in Portland at 89 First Street, 1865.

DAVIS, WILLIAM
Active in Portland, 1906.

DAWSON, C. B.
Active in Zena, 1895.

DAY
Partner in Holland & Day, opposite George Abernethy & Company's brick store in Oregon City, 1858.

DAY & LYON
Partnership in Prairie City, 1905; Lewis L. Day.

DAY, LEWIS L.
Partner in Day & Lyon with Mrs. Lyon in Prairie City, 1905.

DAY, SARAH E. (MRS.)
Active in Portland at 537 Albina Avenue, 1892-93.

DE MONBRUM, DAVID
Active in Newberg, 1915.

DE WERT, MAE M. (MISS)
Member of the Oregon Camera Club; active in Portland, 1900.

DEALEY, CHARLES A.
Active in Portland, 1895-97. Viewer for W. H. Ribelin in the Elite Studio, 1895; on his own, 1896-97.

DEAN
Partner in Armstrong & Dean, Cottage Grove and Creswell, 1913.

DEAN, JAMES
Printer and photographer in Portland, 1909-25.

DEANE
Active in The Dalles, c. 1900.

DEFRESNE, JOSEPH Z.
Active in Portland, c. 1907-12.

DEFRIES, CLARENCE A.
Photographer and manager in Portland at the studio of his stepfather, G. W. Davies, 1901-25.

DEGROOT & MORRIS
Charles Morris and Henry DeGroot in Corvallis, 1884-86.

DEGROOT, HENRY
Partner in DeGroot & Morris with Charles Morris in Corvallis, 1884-86.

DEITY PHOTO STUDIO
Active in Hood River at 121 State Street, c. 1910.

DEITZ, HORACE C.
Active in Hood River, 1907-15.

DEMEYER, M. (MRS.)
Attendant at the studio of W. G. Cutberth in Portland, 1910.

DENNIE, OLIVER
Came from California, 1871; operated a studio in Portland, 1871-75; also in Tacoma and Olympia, Washington, 1873. Also listed as Denny. See California.

DENNING, P. HARRY
Active in Portland, 1892-1914; located at 606 Williams Avenue, 1892-1910.

DENNY, OLIVER
See Oliver Dennie.

DERBY, F. L.
Member of the International Photographic Association; active in La Fayette, 1908-14.

DEREMO, VICTOR H.
Operated the Penny Studio in Portland at 104 11th, 1914.

DESMOND, R. A.
Worked for Buchtel & Cardwell in Portland, 1864-66.

DEWERT
Amateur photographer in Portland, 1890; newspaper account describes photographing cave exploration.

DICKMAN, C. W.
Active in Salem, c. 1890s.

DILL, BENJAMIN
Born c. 1838; died 1906. Active in Portland at 386 East Morrison, 1904-05.

DILL, EBBIN W.
Active in Portland at 386 East Morrison with Benjamin Dill, 1905.

DIMMITT, EDWARD W.
Born in Columbia, Missourri, 1881; died in Portland, 1963. Active in Portland, 1914-30s; operated the Electric Studio, 1914-15; partner

with A. B. Cross, operating as Cross & Dimmitt at 414-415 Merchants Trust Building, 1916-25; 1801 Sandy Boulevard, 1925.

DIX STUDIO
Gallery operated by T. H. Dix in Independence, 1914-15.

DIX, T. H.
Operating the Dix Studio in Independence, 1914-15.

DODD, E. ARTHUR
Exhibited his photographs at the Mechanics Fair in Portland, 1886.

DODGE, KATE E.
Active in Portland, 1904.

DODGE, ORVIL
Active in Jacksonville, 1864; in Roseburg, 1867; in Oakland, 1871; in Myrtle Point, 1880(?).

DOHSE, H. M.
Born c. 1858. Active in Corvallis on Main Street, operating as Stryker & Dohse with Mr. & Mrs. David S. Stryker, 1869; partner with S. E. Gray in Gray & Dohse, Roseburg, 1870; listed alone in Roseburg, 1871; in Douglas County, 1880.

DOLSON, CHARLES
Died 1882(?). Partner in Hack & Dolson with Truman L. Hack, Portland, 1864-65.

DONNERBERG, FRED W.
Born c. 1887; died in Portland, 1981. Member of the Oregon Camera Club; active in Portland, 1913.

DOOMES, CHARLES
Active in Baker, 1913.

DORRIS, SUE (MISS)
Proprietor of Dorris Art Gallery in Eugene, 1891-1917.

DOUBLEDAY, R. R.
Photo postcard company in Pendleton, 1913-27.

DOUGLAS, GEORGE A.
Active in Portland, 1907-25; operating as Northwestern Photo Company with brother Roy A., 1914-25.

DOUGLAS, ROY A.
Active in Portland, 1909-25; operating as Northwestern Photo Company with brother George A., 1914-25.

DOUGLAS, WILLIAM
Active in North Bend, 1909.

DOUGLASS, JOHN H., JR.
Active in Newberg, 1907-11.

DOUGLASS, JOHN H., SR.
Active in Newberg, 1903-05.

DOWE, OSCAR S.
Retoucher in Portland with Davidson Brothers, 1879-80. See California, Idaho, Nevada.

DOWELL, ALEX
Member of the International Photographic Association; active in Mercer, 1913.

DRAKE, EMERY R.
Active in Silverton operating individually and as Drake Brothers with June D. Drake, 1901-42. Drake Brothers were known for their art photography and won several important contests.

DRAKE, JUNE D.
Active in Silverton, 1901-42, operating individually and as Drake Brothers with Emery R. Drake.

DRAPER, WILLIAM G.
Active in Portland, 1903-05.

DUFRENE
Partner in Shanahan & Dufrene, Portland, 1865.

DUFRESNE, JOSEPH Z.
Operated the Dufresne Studio in Portland, 1907-12.

DUMMERMUTH, FRANK E.
Operated as Penny Photo Company in Portland at 253 ½ Washington, 1901. Also spelled Dumermuth.

DUNCAN, FRANK
Active in Klamath Falls, 1913.

DUNHAM, R. M.
Active in Hood River, 1911.

DUNLAP, ROBERT H.
Born in Michigan. Active in Applegate, 1870.

DUNN, CARRIE E. (MRS.)
Scenic photographer in Portland at 1037 Belmont, 1909-10.

DURHAM, GEORGE C.
Member of the Oregon Camera Club; active in Portland, 1900.

DURKEE, B. S.
Born 1872; died 1920. Member of the Oregon Camera Club; active in Portland, 1909-13.

DURSTON, GLENN A.
Active in Portland, 1910.

DUVALL, CLARKE
Born 1852. Active in Hillsboro, 1872; partner with William Hall in Hall & DuVall, East Portland, 1873; listed alone, 1874-75; in The Dalles, 1875-90; Washington and Idaho, 1890. Also listed as Charles M.

DWYER, DENNIS J.
Partner in Sawyer & Dwyer with Carlton S. Sawyer, Portland, 1911; known as Rose City Art Store.

EARL, MILES W.
Active in St. Johns, 1900.

EAST SIDE PHOTO STUDIO
Operated by A. U. Payson in Portland, 1917.

EASTMAN, GILMAN L.
Born in Maine, October 1848. Active in Colfax, Dayton, Olympia, Pullman and Walla Walla, Washington. Listed in The Dalles, Oregon, 1891; Portland, 1887-97; Oregon City, 1890.

EASTMAN, J. H.
Active in Gold Hill, 1913.

EASTMAN, MELTON S.
Active in Portland and Cascade Locks, 1891; Pullman, Colfax and Moscow, Idaho, 1895; Seattle, Washington, 1903. Also spelled Milton.

EASTON, CHARLES E.
Active in Portland, 1906-07. Partner in Boyce & Eastom [sic] with Charles A. Boyce, 1907.

EATON, FRANK B.
Died 1938. Member of the Oregon Camera Club, 1887.

EATON, J. M.
Active in Dallas, 1913.

EATON, JAMES H.
Active in Portland, 1894-09. Worked for Alvord, 1894; for J. S. Potter, 1895-96. Listed at 285½ 1st Street, 1898-09. Active in Scotts Mills, 1913.

EBY, FELIX G.
Partner in Mulit & Eby, Woodburn, 1889-91.

EDDY, C. J.
Member of the Oregon Camera Club; active in Portland, 1900.

EDDY, JOHN
Member of the Oregon Camera Club; active in Portland, 1900.

EDDY, RALPH J.
Active in Portland, 1910; Oregon City, 1915.

EDGAR, WARREN B.
Active in Portland at 15 East 16th North, 1907-09.

EDWARDS, JOHN R.
Active in Ballston near Sheridan, 1891.

EDWARDS, JOSEPH H.
Active in Portland, 1897-05. Located at 351 Morrison 1897-01; operated the Pacific Picture Place at 408 3rd, 1901-05.

EGGAN, H. P.
Active in Seattle, Washington, 1891 and 1907; in Moscow, Idaho, 1901-03; in Wallowa, Oregon, 1915; Portland, 1917.

EGGMAN, JOHN I.
Active in Portland, 1910.

EHRHARDT, LULU (MRS.)
Formerly Mrs. John W. Tollman. As Mrs. Tollman, she was active in Portland, 1899; in Eugene, 1907-09. After she divorced John W. Tollman and remarried, she operated the Tollman Studio with Catherine McHardy, 1909-11; also known as Tollman & McHardy.

EIBACH, PETER
Active in Portland at 470 Taylor, 1909.

ELECTRIC STUDIO
Operated by Jones in Independence; also known as Jones' Electric Studio.

ELECTRIC STUDIO
Operated by Leonard J. Miller in Portland, 1910-15. Located at 145 6th, 1910; 392 ½ Washington, 1912-13; 414 Washington, 1915.

ELITE
Active in Tillamook, 1890.

ELITE PHOTO STUDIO
Operated by Preston M. Hart in Salem, 1899-02.

ELITE PHOTO STUDIO
Operated by Peter Hochscheid in Portland at 3 Grand Avenue, 1915.

ELITE PHOTO STUDIO
Operated by Dio D. Wilder in Portland at 245 Alder, 1917.

ELITE STUDIO
Operated by Raymond O. Cooper in Baker City, 1907-11.

ELITE STUDIO
Active in Portland at 421 Washington, 1896; operated by William H. Ribelin.

ELITE STUDIO
Operated by James J. Tyrrel and William Lussier in Portland, c. 1890s.

ELITE STUDIO
Active in Portland at 115 Morrison, 1890s.

ELITE STUDIO
Operated by Roy Van Vleet in Bend, c. 1915.

ELLERY, DANFORTH
Member of the Oregon Camera Club; active in Portland, 1898-1900.

ELLIGE, GEORGE
Active in Salem and Pendleton, 1874.

ELLIS
Partner in Crandall & Ellis, operating Ellis Studio in Hillsboro, 1904.

ELLIS, EVA F. (MRS.)
Active in Halsey, 1909.

ELLIS, HOWARD H.
Active in Portland, 1910.

ELLIS, M. D.
Active in Dallas, 1886-88.

ELLIS, PERRY
Operated the Few Studio in Hillsboro, corner of Seventh and Baseline Streets, 1899-1902(?).

ELLIS STUDIO
Operated by Crandall & Ellis in Hillsboro, 1904.

ELLISON, J. R.
Active in La Grande on C Street, 1865.

ELLSWORTH & CARDWELL
B. P. Cardwell and Frank Ellsworth in Portland at 89 First Street, 1867.

ELLSWORTH, FRANK
Partner with B. P. Cardwell, operating as Ellsworth & Cardwell at 89 First Street, Portland, 1867.

ELLSWORTH, MAGGIE V.
Active in Estacada, 1916.

EMERY, WILLIAM G.
Active in Astoria at 523 3rd, 1891. Listed in Portland, 1891-93; Studio located at 318 North East Side, 1891; 410 East Morrison, 1892; 132 ½ 3rd, 1893. In Corvallis, 1905. Also operated in Idaho and Washington.

ENGRAVES, E. G.
Active in Klamath Falls, 1913.

ENNES, T. J.
Stereo photographer in Hillsboro, c. 1900.

ENSIGN, W. H.
Born 1864. Active in Sutherlin, 1913-17. Located in Chico, California, 1900.

ENTERPRISE ART COMPANY
Operated by Herbert A. Maddock in Portland, 1910; also known as Stevens Manufacturing Company.

ERDMAN, ELIZABETH
Photographer for Sue Dorris in Eugene, 1910. Also known as Mrs. Elizabeth Romane.

ERICHSON & HANSON
Partnership of John A. Hanson and Henry Erichson, active in Jordan Valley, September, c. 1882. See Idaho.

ERICHSON, HENRY
Partner in Erichson & Hanson, Jordan Valley, c. 1882.

ERICKSON, JOHN
Active in Portland, 1913-25.

ERICSON, AUGUSTUS W.
Active in Myrtle Point, 1901.

EUGENE PHOTO COMPANY
Active in Eugene, c. 1800s.

EVANS, A. J.
Active in Myrtle Creek, 1909.

EVANS, DAVID PERRY
Active in Portland, 1903-43. Photographer for W. G. Cutberth, 1903; for Portland Finishing Company, 1904; printer for G. W. Davies, 1905-06; photographer for A. G. Churchley, 1907-08. Listed as photographer at 55 Washington Building, 1909-14; at 270 ½ Washington, operating the Rose Studio, 1915.

EVANS, OLIVER
Active in Newberg, 1915-17.

EVELAND, DAVID
Active in Portland, 1914-17. Located at 104 11th, 1914-15; at 111 Killingsworth Avenue, 1916-17.

EVERITT, ELIAS FOSTER
Born 1837. Active in Grants Pass, 1886-89; later in California.

EXCELSIOR ART GALLERY
Studio in Portland, 1880(?).

EXCELSIOR FOTO COMPANY
Operated by J. Hogg in McMinnville, 1890s; also listed as Excelsior or Escelsior Studio.

EXCELSIOR STUDIO
Active in Baker City, 1885, operated by Martin M. Hazeltine. Also known as Hazeltine's Excelsior Studio.

FAIRFIELD, HARRY
Active in Kent, 1900.

FALLGATTER, JOHN A.
Photographer and view artist in Milton, 1909.

FAVORITE, IRENA (MRS.)
Born 1839. Traveling photographer in Umatilla County with Thomas J. Favorite, 1870. See California and Texas.

FAVORITE, THOMAS J.
Born 1836. Traveling photographer with Mrs. Irena Favorite in Umatilla County, 1870.

FEIKERT, CHARLES S.
Active in Junction City.

FELBAUM
Partner in Stearns & Felbaum with May Stearns, Cove, 1917.

FELLOES, EDGAR
Born c. 1864; died in San Francisco, 1923. Amateur photographer, artist and photo engraver active in Portland, 1896- 1906. One of the founders of the Oregon Camera Club.

FERGUSON, M. F.
Active in Portland at 43 Grand Avenue, 1905.

FERGUSON, RICHARD M.
Died 1907. Active in Tacoma, 1903; in Portland at 4 Union Avenue, 1907-08.

FERO, CHARLES E. F.
Active in Eugene, 1910.

FERRIS, AMY (MISS)
Member of the Oregon Camera Club; active in Portland, 1900.

FEW STUDIO
Operated by Perry Ellis in Hillsboro, corner of Seventh and Baseline Streets, 1899.

FINLEY, CORA M.
Active in Lakeview, 1907.

FINLEY, WILLIAM LOVELL
Born 1876; died 1953. State wildlife biologist and photographer; his work was published in the books, *American Birds*, *Wild Animal Pets*, *Little Bird Blue*, and magazines such as *National Geographic, Nature, Atlantic Monthly, Life*. Active in Portland, c. 1900-c. 1945.

FISCHER, E. R. (MRS.)
Active in Tillamook operating Mrs. Fischer's Studio, 1911. Active in McMinnville, 1913.

FISHER, LUCILE
Active in Portland, 1910-11.

FISKE, BERTRAND E.
Active in Portland, 1904-05.

FITZGERALD, ALLEN
Born 1879; died 1953.

FITZGERALD, INEZ G.
Active in Gilroy, California, 1899-1907; in Grants Pass, Oregon, 1912-13.

FLAGLOR, AMASA PLUMMER
Born in New Brunswick, Canada, December 24, 1848. Arrived in U.S., 1862. Worked in San Francisco with William Shew, Bradley Rulofson and Durose; galleries and partnerships in Humboldt County. Stereo photographer in Jacksonville, Oregon, 1878. See California.

FLASHLIGHT GALLERY.
Active in Portland at 508 Williams Avenue, c. 1890s.

FLEMING, MARGARET A. (MISS)
Member of the Oregon Camera Club; active in Portland, 1900.

FLOTO STUDIO
Active at 271 ½ Morrison Street, Portland, 1910.

FLOWER, WARREN A.
Active in Athena, 1905.

FLOWERDAY
Active in The Dalles, c. 1890; Baker City, c. 1905.

FLYING STUDIO
Operated by Charles G. Button and Betancue in Astoria, 1880. Also spelled Blancue, Belancue.

FOOR, GEORGE W.
Active in Oregon before 1889; in Boise, Idaho, 1889-90. See Idaho.

FORBES, HERBERT C.
Active in Portland, 1900-05. Member of the Oregon Camera Club; operated a photo supply store.

FORBES, ROBERT LACHLAN
Active in Jacksonville, 1865; in Eugene, 1873-76.

FORD, ANNA M. (MRS.)
Partner in McCrea-Ford Company with J. P. McCrea on Commercial Street, Astoria, 1901-11.

FORD, CHARLES W.
Active in Portland, 1903-06. Located at 271 ½ Morrison, operating with John F., Richard S. and John T. Ford; also known as the Foto Studio.

FORD, F. A.
Active in McMinnville, 1867.

FORD, JOHN FLETCHER
Born c. 1862; died 1914. Active in Portland, 1900-08. Located at 185 ½ Morrison, 1900-02; 271 ½ Morrison, 1903- 08. Operated with John T., Charles W. and Richard S. Ford; also known as the Foto Studio.

FORD, JOHN T.
Active in Portland at 271 ½ Morrison, 1904. Operated with John F., Richard S., Charles W. Ford; also known as the Foto Studio.

FORD, RICHARD S.
Active in Portland, 1904-05, 1907. Located at 271 ½ Morrison. Operated with John F., Charles W. and John T. Ford; also known as the Foto Studio.

FORTIN, JOSEPH
Active in Illinois before 1885; The Dalles, Oregon, 1891-97; Lewiston Idaho, 1902-05. Operated as the Celebrated Photograph Studio. Also active in Huntington.

FOSTER
Partner in Templeton & Foster, Corvallis, 1867.

FOSTER, LAURA H.
Active in North Powder, 1910.

FOSTER, PERRY
Active in Joseph, 1915-17.

FOULKES, DAVID
Member of the Oregon Camera Club; active in Portland, 1900.

FOWLER, D. D.
Active in Portland at 107 Front Street, 1865.

FOWLER, GEORGE H.
Active in Portland, 1910-17.

FRANKS & BUTLER
Partnership of F. D. Franks and Benjamin D. Butler, stereo photographers in The Dalles on Main Street, 1852-65. Also listed as Butler & Franks.

FRANKS, F. D.
Partner in Franks & Butler with Benjamin D. Butler, operating in The Dalles on Main Street, 1852-65; also listed as Butler & Franks.

FRASER, CHARLES
Member of the Oregon Camera Club; active in Portland, 1898.

FREEMAN, S. A.
Active in Enterprise, 1901.

FRENCH, F. A. (MRS.)
Member of the Oregon Camera Club; active in Portland, 1900.

FRENCH, FRED A.
Member of the Oregon Camera Club; active in Portland, 1900.

FRENCH, H. A.
Member of the Oregon Camera Club; active in Portland, 1900.

FRITZ & CLARK
Active in Forest Grove, 1895-99; Charles Fritz.

FRITZ & CROSLEY
Partnership of Charles Fritz and Harry Crosley, Hillsboro, 1889-91.

FRITZ, CHARLES
Active in Hillsboro as Fritz & Crosley, 1889-91; in McMinnville as Fritz Superior Gallery, 1891. Active in Portland, 1892. Partner in Fritz & Clark, Forest Grove, 1895-99.

FROST & CONNER
Studio in Portland at 410 East Morrison, 1896; George B. Frost and Charles T. Connor.

FROST, GARNER B.
Active in Independence, 1886; in Portland, 1896-1906. Operated the Boston Studio at 185 ½ Morrison, 1903-04; photographer for Kiser Photographic Company, 1905. Located at 493 Market, 1906. Also listed as B. Garner.

FROST, GEORGE B.
Operating as Frost & Connor with Charles T. Connor, 410 East Morrison, Portland, 1896.

FROSTS
Active in Seaside, 1913.

FRUZENLICKER
Tintypist in Pendleton.

FRY, LESLIE H.
Active in Prineville, 1909.

FULSOM
Operated branch gallery in Arlington, 1897; main studio was in The Dalles.

FUNK, JOHN R.
Active in Portland, 1904.

GADDIS, FLOE
Member of the Photographer's Association of the Pacific Northwest; active in Portland, 1907.

GALLIEN, CHARLES L.
Active at 114 15th North, Portland, 1894-96.

GALLOWAY, MICHAEL B.
Active in Heppner, 1901-05.

GARDINER, R. B.
Itinerant active in Roseburg area, c. 1887.

GARDINER, R. H. (MRS.)
Itinerant c. 1889; in Portland, 1892; also operated as Great Eastern Photographic and Advertising Company.

GARDNER, WINFIELD S.
Active in Corvallis, 1886-13; partner in Chase & Gardner, 1905. Also listed as Walter S. Gardner, 1901.

GARLAND, THOMAS L.
Active in Portland, 1901-04.

GARNETT, A.
Active in Weston, c. 1900.

GATCH, HELEN P. (MRS.)
Born 1861; died 1942. Active in Salem, 1891-07. Also known as Helen Plummer.

GATES, B. E.
Member of the Oregon Camera Club; active in Portland, 1900.

GAVIN, A.
Member of the Oregon Camera Club; active in Portland, 1898-1902.

GEBBIE, J.
Member of the Oregon Camera Club; active in Portland, 1900.

GEHRES, FRANK J.
Born 1854. Active in The Dalles, 1879-81.

GENATAS, GEORGE
Active in Portland, 1915-17; partner in Genatas & Analytis at 11 5th Street, 1915. Also spelled Genatis & Anayltis.

GENSLER, J. H.
Active in Portland, 1910-17. Operated Columbia Commercial Studio at 167 4th Street, 1917.

GEORGE & GIBLER
Partnership active in Coquille, 1913.

GERKING
Partner in Kunselman & Gerking, Medford, 1913.

GERTH, FRANK J.
Active in Portland, 1911.

GETTY & McCOOL
Partnership of Mark Getty and Ira McCool, Lakeview, 1911.

GETTY, MARK
Partner in Getty & McCool with Ira McCool, Lakeview, 1911.

GIBBS & SCHOFIELD
James Gibbs and R. G. Schofield in Umatilla City, 1865.

GIBBS & WHEELER
Active in Medford.

GIBBS, JAMES
Partner in Gibbs & Schofield, Umatilla City, 1865.

GIBLER
Partner in George & Gibler, Coquille, 1913.

GIBSON, ALICE L.
Member of the Oregon Camera Club; active in Portland, 1900.

GIFFORD & HALE
Partnership of Benjamin A. Gifford and Herbert A. Hale, The Dalles, 1895-99.

GIFFORD & PRENTISS
Benjamin A. Gifford and Arthur M. Prentiss in Portland, 1917.

GIFFORD, BENJAMIN A.
Born 1859; died 1936. Apprenticed to William Latour in Sedalia, Missouri, 1883. Partner in Tresslar & Gifford, Fort Scott, Kansas; on his own in Chetopa, Kansas, 1883. Active in Portland, Oregon, c. 1883-95; located at 115 Morrison, 1891; 313 ½ Morrison, 1893. Partner in Gifford & Hale operating in The Dalles, 1895-99; continued alone in The Dalles, 1899-10. Listed in Portland, 1910-20; operated as Gifford's Studio, 1914, 1915-17; partner in Gifford & Prentiss, Inc., 1917. Active in Wa Ne Ka, Washington, c. 1920. Gifford was one of Oregon's finest landscape photographers, recording life along the Columbia River from his base in The Dalles.

GILBERT, GLADYS
Stereo photographer in Salem.

GILHOUSEN, WILLIAM H.
Active in The Dalles, 1879-88, sometimes operating as Gilhousen Brothers.

GILL, ESTHER A.
Printer for Aune in Portland, 1904.

GILL, JOHN
Member of the Oregon Camera Club; active in Portland, 1900-06.

GILLILAND, LEWIS T.
Member of the Oregon Camera Club; active in Portland, 1898-1900.

GILMAN & DAVIDSON
Active in Portland, 1878; Isaac G. Davidson.

GLEASON, L.
Operated a gallery over the post office in Forest Grove, 1895.

GLEN, BENJAMIN
Active in Fossil, 1903.

GLENDENNING, M. W.
Active in LaGrande, c. 1890.

GLENN, E. T.
Member of the Oregon Camera Club; active in Portland, 1900.

GLIDDEN, G. D.
Active in Joseph, 1915.

GOETHE, M. A.
Stereo photographer in Portland at 509 Columbia Street, 1890s.

GOLDSMITH, HUGO B.
Amateur in Portland, 1897-1909; active in the Camera Club; may have used Goldsmith Brothers imprint at 273 Alder Street.

GOLDSMITH, LOUIS J.
Active in Portland, 1904-25, an amateur and member of the Oregon Camera Club; may have used Goldsmith Brothers imprint.

GOLDSMITH, MILTON P.
Active in Portland, 1885-1900. Member of the Oregon Camera Club; amateur who may have used Goldsmith Brothers imprint.

GOLDSON, L.
Active in Corvallis, 1878.

GORDON, G. W.
Active in Monmouth, 1903.

GORDON, WILLIAM A.
Active in Portland with Crow Photo Company, 1895-98.

GOULTY, EARL D.
Photographer at the Council Crest Amusement Park in Portland, 1910-16.

GOURLEY, GEORGE S.
Active in Cottage Grove, 1907-09; Eugene, 1913-17. Located at 29 West 10th, 1913; at 57 10th Avenue West, 1915.

GRACHY, J. G.
Active in Agate Beach, 1913.

GRAHAM, HORTON N.
Active in Carus, 1891.

GRAHAM, SAMUEL B.
Active in East Portland, 1885-87; Corvallis, 1889.

GRAVES, CLARENCE E.
Active in Joseph, 1909; LaGrande, 1915.

GRAVES, HUBERT D.
Operated the People's Gallery in Portland, 1885; at 408 1st Street before 1887; in Roseburg at 431 Jackson, 1887-04.

GRAVES, TIMOTHY L.
Active in Boise, Idaho, 1889-93; in Oakland, Oregon, 1901; Roseburg, 1906-11.

GRAY & CROMWELL
S. E. Gray and Oscar Cromwell, Salem, 1870.

GRAY & DOHSE
S. E. Gray and H. M. Dohse, Roseburg, 1870.

GRAY, CHARLES J.
Born c. 1873; died 1923. Member of the Oregon Camera Club and Portland Society of Photographic Art Salon Committee. Active in Portland, 1905.

GRAY, S. E.
Partner in Yantis & Gray, Olympia, Washington, c. 1870. Operated in Salem, Oregon, 1867-72; listed as S. E. Gray & Company in Corvallis; partner in Gray & Cromwell, Salem, 1870; partner in Gray & Dohse, Roseburg, 1870.

GREAT EASTERN PHOTOGRAPHIC & ADVERTISING COMPANY
Itinerant company active in Portland, c. 1889, c. 1892; operated by R. H. Gardiner.

GREEN, LETHA V.
Partner with F. B. Maddock, operating as Green & Maddock in Portland at 508 Williams Avenue, 1902-03.

GREENE, T. C.
Stereographer active in Portland.

GREENLEAF, R. S. (MRS.)
Member of the Oregon Camera Club; active in Portland, 1900.

GREENWOOD, WILLIAM H.
Active in Albany, 1889; Baker City, 1891.

GREER, R. H.
Active in Forest Grove and Centerville.

GREGG, HERBERT R.
Active in Bay City, 1909-13. Located in Washington prior to 1909 and after 1916.

GREGORY, LAWRENCE A.
Active in Medford, 1911-13.

GREGORY, OWEN
Active in Portland at Towne's San Francisco Gallery, 1881.

GRIFFITHS, CHARLES E.
Active in Portland, 1889-95. Located at 17 Glisan's Block, 1889-90; operating as Advance Portrait House at 43 ½ 1st Street, 1891; at 382 Morrison, 1893; 508 Goodnough Building, 1894; 344 19th North, 1895. Also listed as Griffiths.

GRIMM, FRANK A.
Active in Mill City, operating as Cheney & Grimm with Ethel or Edith Cheney; in Mt. Angel, 1901.

GRINDSTAFF, W. H. (MRS.)
Member of the Oregon Camera Club; active in Portland, 1900.

GRINNOLD, VERN L.
Died 1920. Active in McMinnville, 1901-03. Moved to Seattle, c. 1908.

GRISWOLD, J. M. (MISS)
Member of the Oregon Camera Club; active in Portland, 1900.

GROB, JACOB
Peter Britt's apprentice and stepson; active in Jacksonville, 1886.

GROSS, L.
Active in Portland, c. 1867.

GROVE, C. ELMORE
Active in Portland, 1940-17. Located at 446 Washington, 1904-06; 362 Washington, 1907-12; 351 ½ Washington, 1913. Operated as the Residence Studio of Photographic Art or Studio of Photographic Art.

GUMP, S. & G.
Partnership active in Portland at 184 First Street, 1885.

GUNDELACH, LOIS E. (MRS.)
Member of the International Photographic Association; active in Sweet Home and Huntington, 1913.

GUNTON, WINIFRED (MRS.)
Operated a gallery in Hillsboro, 1911-17.

GURNEA, E. L
Published stereoviews of Southern Oregon, 1880s.

GUSTIN, EARL E.
Active in Pendleton, 1913; Portland, 1914-17. Operated the Sowell Studio with Etta Sowell, 1916-17.

HACHENEY, ELIZABETH M. (MISS)
Member of the Oregon Camera Club; active in Portland, 1900.

HACK & DOLSON
Partnership of Truman L. Hack and Charles Dolson in Portland, 1864-65.

HACK, TRUMAN L.
Born c. 1820; died 1874. Active in Portland, 1864-71. Partner in Hack & Dolson, 1864-65; listed as Hack & Company, 1866-71. Possibly a partner in Johnson & Hack, 1864-66.

HAGAR, D. C.
Stereo photographer in Salem.

HAINES, WALTER O.
Born in Nova Scotia, 1872; died in Portland, 1963. Member of the Portland Society of Photographic Art and Portland Salon Committee. Active in Portland, 1905.

HALE & REDMOND
Herbert A. Hale and Charles F. Redmond, 615-616 Eilers Building in Portland, 1917-18.

HALE, HERBERT A.
Born c. 1862; died 1935. Photographer for B. C. Towne in Portland, 1892-94; located at 590 Union Avenue, 1893. Partner in Gifford & Hale, The Dalles, 1895-99. Located at 145 ½ 3rd, 1895-97; 132 ½ 3rd, 1898-02; 253 Alder, 1903; 43 ½ 1st Street, 1904; 133 ½ 1st Street, 1905-15. Partner in Hale & Redmond, "Home Photographers," operating in Portland, 1916-20; located at 167 ½ 1st Street, 1916; 403 Eilers Building, 1917; 615-616 Eilers Building, 1917-18; 615 Bush & Lane Building, 1920. Also known as Hale Studio. See California.

HALE, WILLIAM S.
Operated as Stevens Manufacturing Company producing lantern slides in Portland, 1912.

HALL & DUVALL
William Hall and Clarke DuVall, East Portland, 1873.

HALL, ARIBERT F.
Active in Elgin, 1903-07.

HALL, JAMES J.
Born in Woodburn, 1871; died in Salem, 1947. Purchased studio from his employer, A. Jensen, 1905-45; operated branch studio in Canby. Published real photopostcards of Oregon scenes. Also served as Mayor of Woodburn.

HALL, LINDSLEY
Noted Egyptologist and amateur photographer, active in Portland.

HALL, LOTTIE C. (MRS.)
Active in Elgin, 1909-13.

HALL, W. MAURICE
Established Ball Studio in Corvallis, 1903. The firm is the oldest continuously operating photography business in Oregon.

HALL, WILLIAM
Partner with Clarke DuVall in Hall & DuVall, East Portland, 1873.

HALL, WILLIAM M.
Member of the Oregon Camera Club; active in Portland, 1898-1900.

HALLER, CHARLES M.
Photographer and retoucher in Portland, 1901-25.

HALLER, RUTH
Worked as a clerk at the Portland studio with her husband, 1904.

HAMACHER, EPHRIAM J.
Active in Lebanon, c. 1885. Later worked in Yakima, Washington and Alaska. Also listed as E. G. Hammacher.

HAMADA, M.
Active in Portland at 43 4th North, 1909.

HAMILL, A. S.
Active in Albany, Second Street, YMCA Block.

HAMILTON, ALBERT E.
Active in Portland, 1904.

HAMILTON, ROSE
Stereo photographer in Portland; possibly an amateur.

HAMMOND, AMELIA F. (MRS.)
Member of the Oregon Camera Club; active in Portland, 1900.

HAMMOND, HARRY E.
Active in Portland, 1890s; The Dalles, 1897. Worked in Nome, Alaska with J. A. Saaroni, operating as Saaroni & Hammond, 1901.

HANDLEY
Active in Lakeview.

HANSEN, J. JOHN
Active in Portland at 16 Healey Building, corner of Morrison and Park, c. 1907-10.

HANSON & DAVIDSON
Partnership in Monmouth, 1911-17; D. A. Davidson.

HANSON, JACOB
Active in Roseburg; Salem, 1878; partner in Vaughan & Hanson, Eugene, 1889.

HANSON, JOHN A.
Partner in Erichson & Hanson, Jordan Valley, 1882; partner in Johnson & Hanson with Rankin M. Johnson, 134 ½ East 20th, Portland, c. 1906.

HANSON, V. C.
Active in Lakeview, 1890.

HARAN, JAMES A.
Member of the Oregon Camera Club; active in Portland, 1905-09; LaGrande, 1925.

HARDEN, J. J.
Member of the Photographer's Association of the Pacific Northwest; active in Stayton, 1907.

HARDY, W. H.
Active in Lakeview and traveling, 1896.

HARLOW, MICAJAH B.
Operated the Pendleton Photo Company with J. A. McIntire at the corner of Main and Alta Streets in Pendleton before 1891. Located in Tekoa, Washington, 1907.

HARNISH, CLINTON S.
Active in Albany, 1901-11; Scio, 1901-03. Also operated as Simmons & Harnish.

HARR, ADOLPH W.
Member of the Oregon Camera Club; active in Portland, 1900.

HARRIS, BELLA (MRS.)
Active in Portland at Kern Park, 1906-07.

HARRIS, C. H.
Active in Salem, c. 1885.

HARRIS, I. B.
Active in Madras, 1915.

HARRIS, J. H.
Member of the Oregon Camera Club; active in Portland, 1900.

HARRIS, JOHN R.
Active in McMinnville, 1901-07.

HARRIS, O. M. (MRS.)
Active in Dayton, 1905.

HARRISON, HENRY D.
Active in Portland at 408 1st Street, 1888-98. Also listed as Harry.

HART, ELMER W.
Born 1887. Active in Vollmer, Idaho, 1908-13; Craigmont, Idaho, 1913; Elgin, Oregon, 1915-17.

HART, HARRY L.
Partner in Wells & Hart with H. A. Wells, Baker City, 1909. Active in Cottonwood, Idaho, 1912-13.

HART, JOHN C.
Active in Ashland and Jacksonville, 1911.

HART, PRESTON M.
Operated the Elite Studio in Salem, 1899-02. Listed in St. Johns, 1909; Oregon City, 1911-17.

HARVEY, JOE E.
Active in Roseburg.

HASBROUK, H. L.
Member of the Pendleton Camera Club, 1904-06.

HASENMAYER, OSCAR
Manager of the Angelus Commercial Photographic Studio, 525 Abington Building, Portland, 1917.

HASKIN, I. O.
Member of the International Photographic Association; active in Lebanon, 1912.

HATFIELD, EDNA
Retoucher in Portland, 1904.

HATTEN, D. A.
Active in Dallas, Wilson Block.

HAVEN, E. (MRS.)
Active in Prairie City, c. 1890s.

HAWKINS, L. B.
Member of the Oregon Camera Club; active in Portland, 1900.

HAWLEY, EDNA M.
Retoucher in Portland, 1904.

HAWLEY, J. H.
Member of the Oregon Camera Club; active in Portland, 1900.

HAY, W. H.
Member of the International Photographic Association; active in Forest Grove, 1914.

HAYDEN, EDITH
Operated the Hayden Studio in Roseburg, 1915.

HAYDON, DR. WALTON
Died 1933. Active in Marshfield.

HAYES & HAYES
Partnership of Amelia and Harry C. Hayes in Portland at 340 ½ Washington, 1904-10.

HAYES & HENDEE
Partnership of Amelia and Harry C. Hays and Otho S. Hendee in East Portland, 1889-91; located at 216 L East and 1115 4th.

HAYES & SHORT
Active in Portland, 1901, at 2 ½ Grand Avenue and 340 ½ Washington; partnership of Amelia and Harry C. Hayes and Charles W. Short.

HAYES, AMELIA
Active in Portland, 1883-1910; partner in Hayes & Hayes, Hayes & Hendee, Hayes & Short. She was the wife of Harry C. Hayes; listed as his widow, 1910, continuing to operate that year as Hayes & Hayes. See Harry C. Hayes.

HAYES, HARRY C.
Died in Portland, 1910. Active in Portland, 1883-1909. Worked for W. H. Towne; partner in Yocum & Hayes, 1886; partner with Otho S. Hendee as Hayes & Hendee at 216 L East and 1115 4th, East Portland, 1889-91. Located at 512 Williams in 1892; 2 ½ Grand Avenue, 1894-1900. Partner in Hayes & Short at the Grand Avenue address in 1901, then moved to 340 ½ Washington. Listed as Hayes & Hayes at that address, 1904-09.

HAYES, T. J.
Active in Newport, 1915.

HAZELTINE, GEORGE IRVING
Born in New York, 1836; died in Canyon City, Oregon, August 8, 1918. Active in Canyon City, 1860-91; in John Day, 2 miles North of Canyon City, 1888-92 . Brother of M. M. Hazeltine. Served as County Treasurer, Judge and Recorder in Grant County. See California.

HAZELTINE, MARTIN MASON
Pioneer photographer with studio in Baker City and extensive field work throughout the far west. See California.

HEATON, JAMES R.
Member of International Photographic Association; active in Hood River before 1911.

HECK, R. W.
Active in Burns, 1915.

HEDLUND, A.
Active in Madras on Main Street, c. 1911. Also listed as O. Hedlund.

HEINEY, ALBERT
Active in Gresham with Arthur Heiney, c. 1900.

HEINEY, ARTHUR
Active in Gresham with Albert Heiney, c. 1900.

HEINS, OTTO
Active in Tillamook, 1891-1905.

HELD, GEORGE C.
Member of the International Photographic Association; active in Portland, 1913-14.

HELD, J.
Member of the Oregon Camera Club; active in Portland, 1900.

HELLER, LOUIS
Active in Ashland, 1884. His 24-view series of the Modoc war of 1873 was published with his imprint and later by Carleton E. Watkins. See California.

HELLIWELL, CLARA L.
Photographer for H. A. Hale in Portland, 1903-04. Sister of Florence E. and Louise C.

HELLIWELL, FLORENCE EDITH
Photographer for H. A. Hale in Portland, 1904-05. Sister of Clara L. and Louise C.

HELLIWELL, LOUISE C.
Photographer for H. A. Hale in Portland, 1903-06. Sister of Clara L. and Florence E.

HEMENWAY, OSCAR E.
Active in Springfield, 1909-11; also in Eugene, 1910.

HENDEE, DENNY H.
Born 1826; died 1907. Arrived in Portland from San Francisco and took over Wakefield's studio, operating 1852-92; one of the city's first daguerreotypists. See California.

HENDEE, EDWIN L.
Active in Portland, 1881-96; in Trail, British Columbia, 1896-97.

HENDEE, OTHO S.
Active in Portland, 1884-93; partner in Hayes & Hendee, 1889-91, with Amelia and Harry C. Hayes.

HENDEE, SAMUEL L.
Active in Portland at his father's studio, 1876.

HENDRICKS, WILLIAM F.
Active in LaGrande, 1905-07; in North Powder, 1911. Member of the Photographer's Association of the Pacific Northwest.

HENLINE, ARCHIE C.
Active in Eugene, 1905; Silverton, 1907; Klamath Falls, 1915-18. Professional photographer and member of the Oregon Camera Club.

HENRICHSEN, LARS C.
Born 1839; died 1924. A prominent jeweler and amateur photographer active in Portland, 1900; member of the Oregon Camera Club.

HENRY ERICHSON
Partner in Erichson & Hanson with John A. Hanson, active in Jordan Valley, c. 1882.

HENRY, V. H.
Active in Pendleton on Main Street.

HEPBURN, MAUDE M.
Operated the Van Dyke Studio in Portland, 1912-17.

HERMAN, F. P.
Active in Portland, c. 1883.

HERRICK, M.
Active in Marmot, 1889.

HERRIN, DAVID C.
Active in Medford; in The Dalles, 1895. Listed in Portland, 1898-1901; partner in Abell-Herrin Company, 1898. Later had traveling galleries in The Dalles, Oregon and Washington. Operated with his wife, Margaret E.

HERRIN, MARGARET E. (MRS.)
Active in studios in Medford; in The Dalles, 1895; worked with her husband, David C. Herrin. Listed in Portland, 1898-1901; partner in Abell-Herrin Company, 1898. Later had traveling galleries in The Dalles, Oregon and Washington.

HERTZMAN, J. A.
Member of the Oregon Camera Club; active in Portland, 1894-1900.

HESLOP, E.
Active in Corvallis, 1881. Also spelled Heslap.

HETRICK, ALICE
Member of the Oregon Camera Club; active in Portland, 1900.

HEUSLER, FRANK
Active in LaGrande, 1867.

HEWITT, JAMES (MRS.)
Active in Portland, 1895-99; at 228 6th, 1895; operating as Hewitt's Gallery at 197 Madison, 1899; also at 183 Madison, 1899. Also listed as Mrs. Agnes Hewitt.

HICKAM, WILLIAM P.
Active in Portland, 1912-17.

HICKERSON, HAROLD J.
Active in Portland, 1911.

HICKETHIER, AUGUSTUS
Died c. 1924. Active in Drain, 1881-07; itinerant in Cottage Grove, 1883; itinerant in Roseburg, Woodville, Canyonville and Elkton, 1887.

HICKEY, MALLIE B.
Member of the Oregon Camera Club; active in Portland, 1900. Also listed as Mrs. Mollie.

HICKEY, MARGARET F.
Member of the Oregon Camera Club; active in Portland, 1900.

HICKS
Active in Burns, 1917.

HICKS, FRANK F.
Active in Bandon, 1901.

HICKS, LUCIUS J.
Partner Francis J. Catterlin as Catterlin & Hicks, active in Salem, 1888. Retoucher for J. E. Watson in Portland, 1890; photographer for B. C. Towne in Marshfield, 1891. Active in Portland, 1895-08, working for Coos Bay Photo & Crayon Company, Ballard Engraving, and as a partner in Hicks-Chatten Engraving Company. Also listed as Lute J. Hicks.

HIENS, O.
Active in Tillamook, 1901.

HILDEBRAND, G. (MISS)
Member of the Oregon Camera Club; active in Portland, 1900.

HILDEBRAND, M. (MISS)
Member of the Oregon Camera Club; active in Portland, 1900.

HILGRATH, HELEN G.
Active in Portland, 1904.

HILL, C. W.
Active in Coquille before 1912; Roseburg, 1912; again in Coquille after 1912.

HILLMAN, GEORGE W.
Picture dealer in Portland, 1872.

HILLSBORO PHOTO GALLERY
Active in Hillsboro, c. 1891.

HIMES
Active in Portland, c. 1874.

HINTHORNE & STEVENSON
Partnership in Ashland, Oregon, 1915-17; B. H. Hinthorne.

HINTHORNE, B. H.
Active in Blackfoot, Idaho, 1912-13; partner in Hinthorne & Stevenson, Ashland, Oregon, 1915-17.

HOBBS, I. N.
Born 1844; died in Forest Grove, 1900. Active in Forest Grove and McMinnville, 1896-1900.

HOBSON & PREBLE
Partnership of Samuel Hobson and Edward W. Preble in Portland at 181 ½ First Street, 1902.

HOBSON, SAMUEL
Active in Portland, 1888-16. Partner in Yocum & Hobson with Oliver C. Yocum at 4th between I and J, 1888. Photographer for C. A. Alvord, 1901; partner in Hobson & Preble, 1902. Located at 225 ½ 1st Street, 1903; photographer for H. S. P. Warren, 1905. Worked for Woodward, Clark & Company, 1907-08. Also active in Woodburn.

HOCHSCHEID, PETER
Active in Portland; at 3 Grand Avenue, 1914-16; 245 Alder, 1917.

HOEG, CHARLES H.
Active in Portland(?), 1898-1909.

HOES, J. A.
Active in St. Johns, 1912-17.

HOESTEN, WILLIAM
Active in Portland, 1889-90.

HOFFMAN & PITTMAN
Mrs. Nettie Hoffman and Miss Pittman in Forest Grove, 1907.

HOFFMAN, FRED
Active in Vale, 1913.

HOFFMAN, NETTIE (MRS.)
Active in Albany, 1896-97; Forest Grove, 1898-1906. Partner in Pope & Hoffman with Oliver M. Pope, 1901; partner in Hoffman & Pittman, 1907. Also operated as Hoffman Studio, Pacific Photo Company, Pacific Photo Gallery, and Pacific Gallery.

HOFSTEATER & PATTERSON
Partnership of Orlando M. Hofsteater and Thomas W. Patterson, active in Portland at 165 ½ 3rd, 1906.

HOFSTEATER, ORLANDO M.
Active in St. Helens, 1884; in Vancouver, Washington, 1884-99; Portland, 1900-25. Partner with Thomas W. Patterson, 1906, operating as Hofsteater & Patterson; Hofsteater Photo Studio, 1910, 1914; as Hofsteater & Company, 1888; Hofsteater Photo Gallery, 1901.

HOGAN, JAMES J.
Operated the Keystone View Company in The Dalles with his wife, Rowena M., 1895; in Portland, 1900-17. Also known as the Rembrandt Photo & Portrait Studio, c. 1900, 1907-08.

HOGAN, JOHN
Member of the Oregon Camera Club; active in Portland, 1900.

HOGAN, ROWENA M.
Operated the Keystone View Company in The Dalles with her husband, James J., 1895; in Portland, 1907-17. Operated as the Rembrandt Photo & Portrait Studio, c. 1900, 1907-08. Also listed as Mrs. J. J. Hogan.

HOGG, J.
Operated the Excelsior Studio in McMinnville, 1890s. Also spelled Escelsior.

HOLBROOK, E. (MISS)
Member of the Oregon Camera Club; active in Portland, 1900.

HOLLAND
Partner in Buchtel & Holland, located in the Canton House over the Crockery Store, Portland, 1857; also listed as Holland & Buchtel. Partner in Holland & Day, opposite George Abernethy & Company's brick store, Oregon City, 1858.

HOLLAND & DAY
Partnership in Oregon City, located opposite George Abernethy & Company's brick store, 1858.

HOLMAN, GEORGE F.
Born 1861; died 1951. Prominent attorney and amateur photographer active in Portland, 1895-1922; member of the Oregon Camera Club.

HOLMES, J. W.
Member of the Oregon Camera Club; active in Portland, 1898-1900.

HOLT, AXEL
Assistant and printer for Joseph Thwaites in Portland, 1890-91.

HOLT, JESSE W.
Member of the International Photographic Association; active in Portland, 1911-13.

HOLTZ, P.
Active in The Dalles on Second Street, 1865.

HOOD RIVER STUDIO
Operated by Miss Iris Markley in Hood River, 1913.

HOOKER, CADDIE G.
Retoucher and photographer for F. H. Browning, Portland, 1901-07.

HOOPER, R. B.
Active in Baker City.

HOPFIELD, LEONARD S.
Member of the International Photographic Association; active in McMinnville, 1909-13.

HOPKINS, F. H. (MRS.)
Member of the Oregon Camera Club; active in Portland, 1900.

HOPPER, E. A.
Active in Portland, at Mt. Tabor Villa.

HORTON, GILBERT D.
Born 1853; died 1936. Active in Pendleton on Main Street near the bridge, 1883.

HOUGHT, H. H.
Active in Harney, 1891.

HOUGHTON, ALBERT S.
Active in Portland at 72 Selling-Hirsch Building, 1910.

HOUGHTON, THOMAS A.
Itinerant active in Washington Territory, 1885; The Dalles, 1888-91; Portland, 1885-87.

HOWER, ATLIN B.
Active in Pocatello, Idaho, 1893-96; in Baker City, Oregon, 1901.

HOY, LILIAN G.
Active in Albany, 1917.

HOYT, GEORGE W.
Member of the Oregon Camera Club; active in Portland, 1898-1905.

HOYT, ROBERT W.
Active in Hillsboro, 1899-1901.

HOYT, WILLIAM R.
Active in Salem, 1884.

HUBBARD & EAST
Gallery in Portland, 1890; also known as Jennings Gallery, operated by J. Jennings.

HUBNER, GERHARDT ROBERT
Operated the Swett Studio at 719 Swetland Building in Portland, c. 1910.

HUDNALL
Active in Forest Grove, 1875.

HUDSON, CHARLES W.
Active in Forest Grove, 1880.

HUFFMAN, CHARLES
Partner with Charles Huffman, operating as McConnell & Huffman in Corvallis, 1884.

HUG, EUGENE F.
Active in Elgin, 1899-1911; partner with brother Henry H., operating as Hug & Hug, 1901. Operated as Hug Brothers, 1905; as Hug Brothers & Company with H. Towner, 1909.

HUG, HENRY H.
Active in Elgin, 1901-11; with brother Eugene F., 1901, operating as Hug & Hug. Operated as Hug Brothers, 1905; Hug Brothers & Company with H. Towner, 1909.

HUGHES
Active in Coos Bay(?).

HULIT, ALPHONSO
Active in Portland, 1904.

HULIT, LOA VALENTINE
Active in Portland, 1905-12. Also listed as Lewis V., L. W., and Louis V.

HULL, FRANK H.
Active in Medford, 1906-11.

HULSE, JOSEPH B.
Partner in Shafer & Hulse, Lakeview, 1891; alone in Elgin, 1905; LaGrande, 1907; Klamath Falls, 1909.

HUME
Partner in Templeton & Hume, Brownsville, 1867; also known as Star Gallery.

HUNT
Active in The Dalles, 1891-95.

HUNT, WILLIAM H.
Purchased Partridge's studio in Portland, corner of 5th and Yamhill, 1888. Listed at 115 Morrison, 1891.

HUNTINGTON, CLARENCE L.
Active in Portland, 1898-1903.

HUNTLEY, CLYDE G.
Operated as Huntley Brothers in Oregon City with his brother, William A., 1904-11.

HUNTLEY, WILLIAM A.
Partner in Huntley Brothers with his brother, Clyde G., Oregon City, 1904-11.

HURD
Operator with A. B. Woodard on his photographing trip to Idaho, 1866. Possibly in Independence operating as Whiteaker & Hurd, 1889.

HURLBURT, JOHN S.
Retoucher active in Portland, 1899.

HURLBURT, R. E.
Member of the International Photographic Association; active in Albany, 1912.

HURLEY & RIGGS
Partnership in Marshfield; possibly J. W. Riggs.

HUSBANDS, S.
Active in Hood River, 1886.

HUSSOCK, HERBERT
Member of the Oregon Camera Club; active in Portland, 1909.

HUSTON, MARY (MRS.)
Active in Cottage Grove, 1911-13.

HUTCHINS, C. C.
Active in White Salmon, c. 1910.

HUTCHINS, D. R.
Worked for Joseph Thwaites in Portland, 167 and 169 First Street, 1888.

HUTCHINSON, T. O. (MRS.)
Active in Myrtle Creek, 1891.

HUTCHINSON, THOMAS O.
Active in Myrtle Creek, 1891; Portland, 1901-02; Holly, 1909.

HUTCHINSON, WILLIAM A.
Active in Portland, 1902; partner with Thomas O., operating as Hutchinson & Son, 1909.

HYDE, WILLIAM
Active in Harrisburg, 1867.

HYLAND, K. U.
Active in Portland, 1894-1900. Operated at 313 ½ Morrison, 1894-95; 345 Washington, 1896-

IDEAL STUDIO
Active in Portland at 228 Sixth Street, 1890s.

IMPERIAL GALLERY
Active in Oregon City.

IMPERIAL GALLERY
Operated by Arthur B. McAlpin and Charles Lamb in Portland, 1890-93; also known as McAlpin & Lamb.

IMPERIAL GALLERY
Active in McMinnville and North Yamhill.

IMPERIAL GALLERY
Operated by Miss Bessie Krumm and Mrs. M. Emma Lewis in Portland at 800 Dekum Building, 1897-98.

INGERSOLL
Partner in Darling & Ingersoll with Belle Darling in Forest Grove, 1915-17.

INNES, L. J.
Stereo photographer active in Hillsboro.

IRVINE, ROBERT M.
Member of the Oregon Camera Club; active in Portland, 1909.

IRVINE, WILLIAM G. F.
Active in Portland at 2271 Market, 1907.

ITOW, S.
Active in Portland, 1915.

JACK, DAVE V.
Active in Long Creek, c. 1890s(?).

JACKSON, A. L. (MRS.)
Colorist for I. G. Davidson in Portland, 1884. Wife of Albert L. Jackson.

JACKSON, ALBERT L.
Active in Eugene, 1878-81; operated as Columbia Photograph Company, 1882. In Portland, 1883-87; in Tacoma, 1891- 10. Also worked for I. G. Davidson, Portland.

JACKSON, FRANK A.
Member of the Oregon Camera Club and Portland Salon Committee; active in Portland, 1897-1905.

JACOBS, A. L.
Active in Bandon, 1915.

JAMES, WILLIAM B.
Member of the Oregon Camera Club; active in Portland, 1900-10.

JARVIS
Partner in Jarvis & Potter at 586 Willamette Street, Eugene, 1910.

JENKS, E. L.
Partner in Redmond & Jenks, 615 Maegly Tichner Building, Portland, 1925.

JENNINGS GALLERY
Operated in Portland, 1890; also known as Hubbard & East.

JENNINGS, J.
Active c. 1880s-90; in Woodburn, Gervais and Hubbard; in Forest Grove, over the post office; in Portland at 318 N Street, between Fifth and Sixth. Operated as Jennings Gallery; also known as Hubbard & East in Portland, 1890.

JENNINGS, WILLIAM H.
Daguerreotypist in Portland, 1851.

JENNY, JOSEPH
Active in Mt. Angel, 1903-17.

JENSEN, ANDREW
Born 1864; died 1938. Active in Woodburn, 1905; Portland, 1904-25; McMinnville, 1911-17. Operated as Jensen's Studio, 1917.

JEWEL, IZETTA (MISS)
Member of the Oregon Camera Club; active in Portland, 1900.

JOHANNES & LUM
Partnership of John G. Johannes and Joe Lum, operating in Portland at 185 ½ Morrison, 1909.

JOHANNES, JOHN G.
Active in Portland, 1907-09; partner in Johannes & Lum at 185 ½ Morrison, 1909.

JOHNSON & HANSON
John A. Hanson and Rankin M. Johnson at 134 ½ East 20th, Portland, 1905-06.

JOHNSON, ALLIE (MRS.)
Active in Portland at 111 ½ 3rd, 1895.

JOHNSON, GLEN
Operating as Miller Photo Company in Klamath Falls, 1913-17.

JOHNSON, J. E.
Born 1861. Active in Hillsboro, 1910-17.

JOHNSON, J. W.
Partner in Johnston & Hack, Portland, 1864-66; operating as J. W. Johnson & Company, c. 1867, at 107 Front. Also spelled Johnston.

JOHNSON, JOHN F.
Active in Portland at 2 ½ Grand Avenue, 1906.

JOHNSON, L. Y.
Member of the Oregon Camera Club; active in Portland, 1907.

JOHNSON, MOLLIE
Artist for W. M. Pickel in Portland, 1904.

JOHNSON, O. R.
Member of the International Photographic Association; active in Vale, 1911.

JOHNSON, RANKIN M.
Partner with John A. Hanson in Portland, 1905-06, operating as Johnson & Hanson at 134 ½ East 20th.

JOHNSON, ROSS
Active in Burns(?).

JOHNSON, WALTER H.
Partner with Fred M. Cammack in Portland, operating as Cammack & Johnson at 171 1st Street, 1902. Also active in Woodburn.

JOHNSON, WILLIAM
Active in Newberg, 1907-11.

JOHNSON, WILLIAM C.
Active in Portland, 1907-25; photographer for E. H. Moorehouse, 1907.

JOHNSON, WILLIAM P.
Active in Salem, 1873(?)-88. Located at State Street until June 16, 1880; on Commercial, 1884; at 269 Commercial, 1886-88.

JOHNSTON & HACK
Partnership of J. W. Johnson and possibly Truman L. Hack, Portland, 1864-66. Also spelled Johnson.

JOHNSTON, J. W.
Partner in Johnston & Hack, operating in Portland, 1864-66; operating as J. W. Johnson & Company at 107 Front, 1867. Also spelled Johnson.

JOHNSTON, LILLIAN T.
Clerk at the Rembrandt Photo & Portrait Studio, 1904.

JONES
Operated as Jones' Electric Studio in Independence.

JONES, AMOS KENDALL
Died 1899. Active in Placerville, Idaho, 1880; Silver City, Idaho, 1881.

Operated as Jones Brothers, associated with Charles M. Jones in Union, Oregon, 1884-1900.

JONES, CHARLES M.
Active in Placerville, Idaho, 1880; Silver City, Idaho, 1881. In Union, Oregon, 1884-1900; operated as Jones Brothers, associated with Amos K. Jones.

JONES, E. P.
Member of the Oregon Camera Club; active in Portland, 1900.

JONES, F. D.
Member of the Oregon Camera Club; active in Portland, 1900. Also listed as F. I. or F. J.

JONES, LYNDS W.
Active in Portland, 1905-20; also operated as Woodruff & Jones.

JONES, RAY
Active in Elsie, c. 1903-07.

JONES, W. R.
Active in Eugene, c. 1865; Weston, c. 1881-87.

JONES, WILLIAM
Active in Harrisburg, c. 1867.

JONES, WILLIAM L.
Active in Silverton, c. 1889-13; Wasco, c. 1907.

JONES BROTHERS
From Idaho, active in Union, 1884-91; association of brothers Amos K. and Charles M. Jones. See Idaho and Traveling.

JORDAN, A. C.
Active in Mt. Hood, 1911.

JORGENSEN, EDWIN D.
Member of the Oregon Camera Club; active in Portland, 1900.

JORGENSEN, W. N.
Active in Burns, c. 1895.

JUDD, F. V.
Member of the Oregon Camera Club; active in Pendleton, 1899-1900.

JUDKINS, DAVID ROBY
Born 1836; died 1909. Brother of George H. Judkins; active in Sale, 1878. See Washington.

JUDKINS, EDGAR G.
Born in Maine, 1863. Son of George H. and Sophia B. Judkins; active in his parents' studio in Portland, 1889. See Washington.

JUDKINS, ELMER E.
Born in Maine, 1865; died 1922. Son of George H. and Sophia B. Judkins; active in his parents' studio in Portland, 1885-88.

JUDKINS, GEORGE HENRY
Born in Maine, 1837; died in Portland, 1887. Active in Portland, 1879-87. His wife and sons worked in the studio as photographers and carried on the business after his death. See Washington.

JUDKINS, J. S.
Active in Portland, 1880. Probably J. C. Judkins. See Washington.

JUDKINS, SOPHIA B. (MRS.)
Born in Albany, New York, 1841; died in Seattle, Washington, 1937. Wife of George H. Judkins. Active in Portland 1884-90. She continued to operate the studio with her sons after the death of her husband.

KAISER, ALFRED
Active in Salem at 277 Commercial, 1905.

KALIN, ALBERT
Member of the International Photographic Association; active in Portland, 1915.

KARTEN, STELLA M. (MISS)
Active in Portland, 1899-1925; partner with Margaret A. Paffrath, operating as Paffrath & Karten, 1902-04.

KAURIN, ODIN
Active in Springfield, 1910-13.

KEARNEY, LOUIS A.
Born 1865; died 1919. Active in Portland at 245 ½ Morrison, 1903-17. Photographer for W. E. Towne, 1903-04; for Wilfred Bicknell, 1906-12.

KEIL, EMANUEL
Active in Aurora, 1881-03.

KELLENBERGER
Active in Grants Pass.

KELLER
Operated Keller's Photo in Fossil on 1st Street.

KELLEY
Active in Pleasant Hill, c. 1895.

KELLOG, B. F.
Active in Oregon City, 1896-97.

KELLOGG, RUBY (MISS)
Member of the Oregon Camera Club; active in Portland, 1900.

KELLY, JAMES S.
Active in Prineville, 1903-05.

KELSO, THOMAS M.
Active in Clatskanie, 1911.

KENDRICKS
Stereo photographer in Ashland.

KENT, VIOLET
Operator in charge of the studio of Benjamin A. Gifford, active in The Dalles, 1898-1901.

KENYON, WILY
Active in Salem, 1854-66.

KERR, S. C.
Member of the Oregon Camera Club; active in Portland, 1898-1900.

KESTER, CHARLES M.
Active in Oregon City, 1881-88.

KEYSTONE VIEW COMPANY
Operated by Rowena M. and James J. Hogan in The Dalles, 1895; in Portland, 1900-17. Also known as the Rembrandt Photo & Portrait Studio, c. 1900, 1907-08.

KIDD, JAMES P.
Died 1934. Active in Diamond, 1891-98; Ontario, 1898-1934.

KILCOYNE, J. A. (MRS.)
Member of the International Photographic Association; active in Portland, 1911.

KIMBLE, CLARE
Active in Nehalem, 1911.

KIMBLE, E. R.
Member of the Oregon Camera Club; active in Portland, 1900.

KINCAID, J. H.
Active in Dallas, 1873.

KING, CHARLES C.
Active in Waterville, Washington, 1891; operating the Lucerne Photo Studio in Portland, 1903.

KINGSLEY, CHARLES R.
Born in Portland, 1857. Worked with A. C. Bomar in Idaho; stereo photographer in Portland.

KINSON
Operated as Baker & Kinson in Eugene at 982 Willamette, 1917.

KIRBY, ORRIN A.
Active in Myrtle Creek, 1913.

KIRK, G. W.
Active in Arlington, c. 1903.

KISER, FREDERICK H.
Partner with brother Oscar H., operating as Kiser Brothers in Warrendale, 1903-04. After Oscar's death, he moved to Portland, operating Kiser Photographic Company, 1905-21; Kiser Scenic Photo Studio or Kiser Studios Inc., 1923-25. He was a major commercial photographer, producing Oregon scenes in many formats, and also painted in oils. Official photographer for the Lewis & Clark Exposition. Employees included Miss Maie Ely, colorist; Garner B. Frost and David M. Stevens, operators.

KISER, OSCAR H.
Operated as Kiser Brothers with brother Frederick H. in Warrendale, 1903-04.

KNIGHT, J. H.
Member of the Oregon Camera Club; active in Portland, 1898.

KNIGHT, R. PERCY
Member of the Oregon Camera Club; active in Portland, 1898.

KNOTTS, RALPH
Member of the International Photographic Association; active in Albany, 1913.

KNOX, CORNELIA A. (MRS.)
Born 1864; died in Portland, 1930. Portrait photographer in Lakeview, c. 1900-c. 1925. Also known as Cornelia A. Watson.

KODAK FIEND
Street photographer in Portland, 1891.

KODAK SHOP
Operated by Baker & Kinson at 982 Willamette, Eugene, 1917.

KOEHLER, FRANK
Partner in Baker & Koehler, Dufur, 1913.

KOERNER, FREDERICK J.
Active in Portland at 388 East Morrison, 1898-99.

KRAEFT, JOHN B.
Active in Portland, 1896-1901.

KRAFT, EDWARD
From San Francisco; active in Portland at 225 ½ 1st Street, 1898-1902.

KRAUCH, CHARLES A.
Active in Portland at 345 or 345 ½ Washington, 1900-01.

KRUMM, BESSIE (MISS)
Active in Portland, 1896-1901. Partner with Mrs. Emma M. Lewis, operating as Imperial Gallery, 800 Dekum Building, 1897-98; as Lewis & Krumm, 145 ½ 3rd, 1898. Active in McMinnville, operating as Cheney & Krumm with partner Ethel Cheney, 1905-07.

KUNSELMAN
Partner in Kunselman & Gerking, Medford, 1913.

KUNZ, ETHEL L.
Finisher for H. A. Hale in Portland, 1910.

KUWAHARA, W.
Active in Portland at 43 4th North, 1910-11.

LA FOLLET, CHARLES
Active in Dallas, c. 1867.

LADD, SARAH HALL
Born 1857; died in Carmel, California, 1927. Member of the Oregon Camera Club; active in Portland, 1900-25. Produced fine platinum prints of the Columbia River Gorge. Often photographed with her friend Lily E. White, and both were members of the prestigious Photo-Secession.

LAFLER, F. E.
Active in Prineville, 1915-17.

LAGERBORG, NETTIE (MISS)
Born 1864; died 1947. Active in Portland, 1900-07; partner in Samain & Lagerborg with Charles O. Samain, 1901-02.

LAKEPORT, E. D.
Member of the International Photographic Association; active in Junction City, 1913.

LAMB & LOUIS
Partnership of Joseph Lamb and Paul M. Louis, 185 ½ Morrison, Portland, 1906-07.

LAMB, CHARLES Y.
Born in Grass Valley, California, 1855; died in Portland, 1945. Active in Portland, 1883-1903. Printer for F. G. Abell, 1883-84; retoucher for Abell, 1885-88; working with E. W. Moore, 1888; photographer with partner Arthur B. McAlpin, operating as McAlpin & Lamb, 1889-96. Located at 153 ½ 3rd, 1891. Operated as Gifford's Studio in the Chapman Block, 1915. He was an actor appearing in many amateur presentations in San Francisco and Portland. See California.

LAMB, JOSEPH
Active in Portland, 1906-07. Partner with Paul M. Louis, operating as Lamb & Louis at 185 ½ Morrison 1906; also proprietors of Leon's Studio, 115 ½ Morrison, 1906.

LAMBERT, W. S.
Active in Prineville, 1907.

LAMBERT, W. T.
Member of the Oregon Camera Club; active in Portland, 1900.

LAMMEY, A. M.
Active in Springfield, 1913.

LAMSON, ROSWELL B.
Attorney and amateur photographer, active in Portland, 1902-05. Member of the Portland Salon Committee.

LANGFORD, OLIVE (MISS)
Active in Union; in LaGrande, 1899, operating as Bushnell-Langford Photo Company.

LANTZ & BRADLEY
Partnership in Woodburn, 1895; Elmer G. Lantz.

LANTZ, ELMER G.
Active in Woodburn, 1895. Operated as Parker-Lantz Studio with partner Waldo H. Parker at 286 Commercial Street, in Eugene, 1910. Listed in Bay City, 1915; in Tillamook, 1917. Also listed as E. J. Lantz and Lantz Brothers.

LARE, CHARLES A.
Operated the Studio DeLuxe in Eugene at 29 West 10th, 1910-17.

LARSON
Operated as "The Larson" in Ashland.

LAU, J. F.
Active in Stayton, 1911-13; Albany, 1915.

LAURIE, ROBERT H. F.
Itinerant in Roseburg area, c. 1887.

LAURL
Partner in McAlpin & Laurl, Portland, c. 1880s.

LAVALLEUR, EUGENE EVERETT
Photographer for the Patton Postcard Company in Salem, 1911-13.

LAWRENCE, WILLIAM R.
Member of the International Photographic Association; active in Cloverdale, 1914.

LAYCOX, ALICE
Active in Portland at 1637 East 13th, 1903.

LAYER, AGNES
Active in Burns, 1911.

LAYTON, F. J.
Member of the International Photographic Association; active in Monfort, Wisconsin, and Coquille, Oregon, 1911.

LEAS, J. A.
Member of the Oregon Camera Club; active in Portland, 1916.

LECKENBY, A. B.
Member of the Oregon Camera Club; active in Portland, 1898-1900.

LEDER, CHARLES
Active in Jefferson, 1911.

LEDGERWOOD, EDWARD
Active in The Dalles, 1909-17.

LEE
Partner in Bowman & Lee at 906 Main Street, Pendleton.

LEEPER, GEORGE W.
Active in Philomath, 1909.

LEON
Active in Portland at 115 ½ Morrison, 1906.

LEON'S STUDIO
Active in Portland at 115 ½ Morrison, 1906; proprietors were Joseph

Lamb and Paul M. Louis; also operated as Lamb & Louis.

LEONARD, JOHN EDSON
Photographer for Aune in Portland, 1912-14.

LEONARD, JOSEPH D.
Member of the International Photographic Association; active in Portland, 1909.

LEOPOLD
Active in Forest Grove, 1904, operating as Seifert & Leopold and Columbia Gallery.

LEPPERT, E. D.
1900(?); possibly E. D. Lippert.

LEROY, ARVID L.
Born c. 1878; died in Portland, 1919. Photographer for the Rembrandt Photo & Portrait Studio in Portland, 1903; operated the Leroy Studio at 23 Lafayette Building, 313 ½ Washington, 1912-17.

LESMEISTER, CECELIA (MRS.)
Active in Central Point, 1911-15.

LESMEISTER, FREDERICK W.
Active in Medford, 1908-09.

LETZ, JAQUES
Member of the Oregon Camera Club; active in Portland, 1917-18.

LEWIS & HUTCHINSON
Partnership of C. C. Lewis and T. O. Hutchinson, stereo photographers in Monmouth, c. 1860s.

LEWIS & KRUMM
Partnership of Emma M. Lewis and Miss Bessie Krumm, operating the Imperial Gallery, 800 Dekum Building, 1897-98; at 145 ½ 3rd, 1898.

LEWIS, ABRAHAM T.
Active in Grants Pass, 1911-17.

LEWIS, CHARLES C.
Active in Monmouth, 1894-1909.

LEWIS, F. G.
Active in Portland at 289 ½ First Street.

LEWIS, G. N.
Active in Grants Pass, 1915.

LEWIS, HERBERT O.
Active in Roseburg, 1906-09; member of the Photographer's Association of the Pacific Northwest.

LEWIS, M. C. (MRS.)
Active in Salem, 1903-13. Listed at 98 Court Street, 1903-05; 338 Court Street, 1907. Operated Rex Studio, 343 Court Street, 1910. Married Wilkins A. Bullock, 1912; listed at Bullock Studio, 1913. See Mrs. M. C. Bullock.

LEWIS, M. EMMA (MRS.)
Active in Portland, 1897-98. Partner with Miss Bessie Krumm operating the Imperial Gallery, 800 Dekum Building, 1897-98; operating as Lewis & Krumm, 145 ½ 3rd, 1898.

LEWIS, O. L.
Operated gallery in Roseburg, 1902.

LEWIS, W. E.
Active in Yamhill, 1915.

LEWIS, W. H.
Active in Salem, 1866; in Portland with Buchtel & Stolte, 1875.

LING KEE
Active in Portland at 313 Alder Street, 1894. Also listed as King Kee.

LINK, WILLIAM
Active in Sumpter, 1913.

LINN, H. P.
Member of the International Photographic Association; active in Portland, 1909.

LINT, JOHN W.
Active in Bandon, 1909-11.

LINTHICUM, L. M. (MRS.)
Member of the Oregon Camera Club; active in Portland, 1900.

LIPMAN, ISAAC N.
Member of the Oregon Camera Club; active in Portland, 1898-1909.

LIPPERT, E. D.
Active in Junction City, 1917.

LITTLER
Partner in Crawford & Littler, Albany, 1889.

LIVERMORE, FRANK
Active in St. Johns, 1905.

LLEWELLYN, GUY K.
Active in Portland.

LLOYD & BURTON
Partnership in Eugene.

LLOYD, WILLIAM S.
Active in Cottage Grove, 1890s.

LOBDELL, S. A.
Active in Butteville, 1855; in Salem on State Street between Commercial and High, 1871.

LOCKLEY, FRED
Stereo photographer in Portland.

LODGE, JOHN
Active in Springfield, c. 1892.

LOGAN (MRS.)
Active in Ashland, 1891.

LOGAN, CHARLES W.
Active in Ashland, 1884-91.

LOMBARD, J. PHILIP
Member of the Oregon Camera Club; active in Portland, 1900.

LONG, J. B.
Active in Amity, 1901-13.

LONG, MARIE J.
Operating the Long Photo Company in Albany, 1898-1911.

LORAIN, LORENZO
Born in Phillipsburg, Pennsylvania, July 5, 1831; died in Ball, Maryland, March 6, 1882. Active in the Northwest, 1856-61. Served as lieutenant quartermaster at Fort Umpqua. He made large format salt prints of the area around Fort Umpqua, Portland, Oregon City, The Dalles and Klamath Lake. Lorain's prints may be the first landscape images made of the area.
    Terry Toedtemeier, "Oregon Photography: The First Fifty Years," *Oregon Historical Quarterly*, Spring 1993.

LORENZ, ALFRED C.
Active in Portland, 1911-17; operated the Multonamah Studio at 801 Dekum Building, 1916-17.

LOUCKS & MASON
Studio in Madras, 1909-13; M. L. Loucks.

LOUCKS, M. L.
Partner in Loucks & Mason, Madras, 1909-13.

LOUIS, PAUL M.
Active in Portland, 1906; partner with Joseph Lamb, operating as Lamb & Louis at 185 ½ Morrison; also proprietors of Leon's Studio.

LOUNSBERRY, GEORGE W.
Member of the Columbia Camera Club; active in Astoria, 1895.

LOVE, CHARLES
Amateur photographer active in Portland, 1904-10.

LOWELL, W. J.
Active in Ione, 1913.

LOWENFELD, RICHARD
Active in Salem at 332 State Street, 1907-13. Also spelled Loewenfeld.

LUBKEN
Partner in Danner & Lubken, Pendleton, 1903-05.

LUCERNE PHOTO STUDIO
Operated by Charles C. King in Portland, 1903.

LUETTERS, F. P.
Active in Portland, 1911-17. Employed by Kiser Photo Company, 1911-16; operated the Winter Photo Company, successor to Kiser Photo Company, at 240 East 32rd, 1917.

LUM, JOE
Active in Portland, 1909-14; partner with John G. Johannes operating as Johannes & Lum at 185 ½ Morrison, 1909; operated the Bridge Studio, 1910-12, same address.

LUSSIER, WILLIAM
Partner with Catterlin in Salem, operating as Catterlin & Lussier, 1889. Active in Portland, 1890s, operating the Elite Studio with partner James J. Tyrrell; partner with Samuel B. Crow, operating as Crow & Lussier at the Labbe Building, Washington, corner of 2nd, 1894.

LYNN, H. P.
Active in Portland at 25 ½ Yamhill, 1910.

LYON (MRS.)
Partner with Lewis L. Day in Prairie City, operating as Day & Lyon, 1905.

LYON, SARAH J. (MRS.)
Active in Central Point, 1889. May be Lyons.

MACKEY, GEORGE W.
Active in Medford, 1901-05; in Brownsville, 1911-13.

MACKEY, HENRY C.
Operated the Photo Tent in Medford, 1901-17; also known as MacKey's Studio.

MACNAB, N. C.
Active in Portland, 1914.

MACNAB, ROBERT B.
Active in Portland at 351 ½ Washington Street, 1913-17.

MACOMBER, JAMES
Member of the Columbia Camera Club; active in Astoria, 1895.

MACRUM, WILLIAM S.
Member of the Oregon Camera Club; active in Portland, 1900-05.

MADDOCK, FRANCIS B.
Active in Portland, 1893-1907. Photographer with B. F. Gifford, 1893; with B. C. Towne, 1894; partner with Mrs. Letha V. Green, operating as Green & Maddock, 1902-03.

MADDOCK, HERBERT A.
Born 1870; died 1930. Active in Portland, 1901-25. Operated the Stevens Manufacturing Company, 1910; also known as Enterprise Art Company.

MAGAZINE PHOTO COMPANY
Studio in Portland at 615 Sixth Street.

MALARKEY (MRS.)
Member of the Oregon Camera Club; active in Portland, 1900.

MANNING, FRANK M.
Born 1845; died 1904. Active in Portland, 1875-78; also known as F. M. Manning & Lady.

MANZ, SAMUEL D.
Active in Portland at 603 Northwest Building, 1915-17.

MARBLE, L. W.
Active in Ashland, 1913-15.

MARCELL, EDWARD F.
Active in Portland, 1911-25.

MARIS, H. E.
Stereo photographer active in Ashland.

MARKELL, W. H. (MRS.)
Member of the Oregon Camera Club; active in Portland, 1900.

MARKHAM, BENJAMIN C.
Active in The Dalles; in Portland, 1914-17, partner in Pike & Markham Company with Nelson G. Pike at 343 ½ Washington. Brother of Ora L.

MARKHAM, ORA L.
Active in Portland, 1904-40s. Operated the O. L. Markham & Company studio at 350 ½ Morrison, 1910; 36 Selling-Hirsch Building, 1915-16; listed as the Markham Studio at 386 ½ Washington Street, 10th and Main, 1917; 36 Selling-Hirsch Building, 1917-25; 917 Southwest Alder Street, 1935.

MARKLEY, IRIS (MISS)
Operated the Hood River Studio in Hood River, 1913-14.

MARQUAM, P.
Active in Scott's Mill, formerly Butte Creek, 1883(?).

MARSH, F. L.
Active in Forest Grove(?), 1898.

MARSH, JULIA (MRS.)
Active in East Portland, 1878.

MARTIN
Partner in Adams & Martin, Corvallis

MARTIN & WEILE
Partnership operating in Eugene, 1890-92.

MARTIN, E. F.
Active in Eugene, 1915.

MARTIN, FRANK J.
Partner with Boughton E. Sanders, operating as Sanders & Martin in McMinnville, 1884-86. Also listed as Morton, and Sanders & Morton.

MARTIN, GERTRUDE
Active in Brownsville, 1901-13. Operated the Martin Photo Company, 1901-03; changed the name to Martin Sisters, 1903-13. Operated as milliners, 1907-09, then returned to photography. Associated with her sister, Susie.

MARTIN, SUSIE
Partner with her sister Gertrude, active in Brownsville, 1901-13. Operated the Martin Photo Company 1901-03; changed the name to Martin Sisters, 1903-13. Operated as milliners, 1907-09, before returning to photography.

MARYNAM, P.
Active in Summerville, 1881.

MASON
Partner in Loucks & Mason with M. L. Loucks, Madras, 1909-13.

MASON, F. M.
Active in Marcola, 1913.

MASSEY, GERALD L.
Member of the International Photographic Association; active in Big Eddy, 1912-15.

MATHIESEN, J.
Member of the Oregon Camera Club; active in Portland, 1900.

MATHSON, MATH
Active in Astoria, c. 1890.

MATTHEWS
Active in Lakeview, 1895-96.

MAXWELL, THOMAS B.
Operated a studio in Portland, 1872.

MAY, GEORGE W.
Active in Lebanon, 1886. See California.

MAY, R. B. (MRS.)
Member of the Oregon Camera Club; active in Portland, 1900.

MAYBE, J. H. L.
Active in Cherryville, 1888-91.

MAYER & CALLAGHAN
Partnership active in Portland, 1880-1906.

MAYER, ADOLPH
Stereo photographer in Portland; partner in Mayer & Callaghan, 1880-1906; sole proprietor, 1906-10.

MAYER, W. L.
Active in Wheeler, 1915-17.

MAZZIE, VINCENT
Active in Beaverton, 1911-13.

McALPIN & LAMB
Studio in Portland operated by Charles Y. Lamb and Arthur B. McAlpin, 1889-96. Also called the Imperial Gallery, 1890-93. Located at 153 ½ 3rd, northwest corner of Morrison, 1889-92; top floor of the new Dekum Building, 1893- 96.

McALPIN & LAURL
Stereo photographers in Portland, c. 1880s.

McALPIN, ARTHUR BANCROFT
Born in Athens, Pennsylvania, 1856; died in Portland, 1947. Active in Portland, 1889-96, operating McAlpin & Lamb with partner Charles Y. Lamb; also known as Imperial Gallery, 1890-93. He was working on his own, 1897-1924; 129 7th, 1897-1911; 414 Central Building, 1911-24. See California.

McARDLE, L. D.
Member of the Oregon Camera Club; active in Portland, 1898-1900.

McARDLE, L. D. (MRS.)
Member of the Oregon Camera Club; active in Portland, 1900.

McBRIDE
Partner in Crandall & McBride, Hillsboro, 1890.

McCALEB, JOHN M.
Active in Independence, 1901-11.

McCAUSEY, G. H.
Member of the Oregon Camera Club; active in Portland, 1900.

McCLAIRE, MORT
Active in Portland 1879-84. Name also spelled Mait or Martin S.

McCLANAHAN & BRYSON
Partnership of Edward J. McClanahan and W. R. Bryson, Eugene, 1890s.

McCLANAHAN, EDWARD J.
Partner with W. R. Bryson in studio in Euguene, 1890s, operating as McClanahan & Bryson.

McCLELLAN, JOSEPH SEWARD
Active in Portland at 508 Williams Avenue, 1897.

McCLURE, FRED H.
Born 1870; died 1956. Active in Portland, 1905-11; associated with the Pacific Photo Company, 1907-11.

McCLURE, J. M. (MISS)
Member of the Oregon Camera Club; active in Portland, 1900.

McCONNELL & HUFFMAN
Partnership of John W. McConnell and Charles Huffman in Corvallis, 1884.

McCONNELL JOHN W.
Active in Corvallis with partner Charles Huffman, operating as McConnell & Huffman, 1884.

McCOOL, IRA
Active in Lakeview, 1911; partner with Mark Getty operating as Getty & McCool, offering Indian pictures.

McCRACKEN, JAMES
Died 1878. Itinerant based in Salem.

McCREA, J. P.
Active in Astoria operating the McCrea-Ford Company with partner Mrs. A. M. Ford on Commercial Street, 1901-11.

McCREA-FORD COMPANY
Operated by Mrs. A. M. Ford and J. P. McCrea in Astoria, 1901-11.

McCULLOCH, A. C. (MRS.)
Active in Oakland, 1911.

McCULLOCH, J. LYNN
Itinerant in Glendale, 1887.

McCULLOUGH, ARTHUR D.
Active in Portland, 1910-13.

McDERMID & BELL
Frank H. Bell and Albert E. McDermid, St. Johns, 1909-10.

McDERMID, ALBERT E.
Active in St. Johns, 1909-15; partner with Frank H. Bell, operating the McDermid & Bell studio, 1909-10; on his own, 1910-15.

McDONALD, RONALD P.
Active in Portland, 1899-1903.

McEITLE, GEORGE
Active in North Yamhill, 1901.

McEVOY, J. J.
Active in Portland, 1890. He was in Montpelier, Idaho, 1891; Pocatello, Blackfoot and Idaho Falls, 1893; in Redding, Keswick and Trinity County, California, 1897.

McGILL, JAMES A.
Active in Portland, 1912-17.

McGOWAN, J. D.
Active in Oregon City, 1872; photographer with O. Dennie in Portland, 1872-73; in Independence and itinerant, 1880.

McHARDY, CATHERINE
Operated the Tollman Studio with partner Mrs. Lulu Ehrhardt in Eugene, 1909-11. Also known as Tollman & McHardy. Active in Florence, 1915-17.

McINTYRE & HARLOW
Partnership of J. A. McIntyre and M. B. Harlow, Pendleton, 1880s-90s; also known as Pendleton Photo Company.

McINTYRE, J. A.
Born 1843. Active in Pendleton, 1880s-90s, operating with M. B. Harlow as McIntyre & Harlow and Pendleton Photo Company.

McKERCHER
Active in Portland, c. 1879(?).

McLENNAN, MARTHA F. (MRS.)
Active in Salem, 1899-1902, with partner Preston M. Hart, operating the Elite Studio as Hart & McLennan.

McMILLAN, CHARLES
Partner in McMillan Brothers, Marshfield, 1886-91.

McMILLAN, GEORGE
Active in Marshfield, 1886-91, operating as McMillan Brothers with Charles and John McMillan, and as Coos Bay Photo & Crayon Company. See California.

McMILLAN, JAMES W.
Active in Tillamook, 1907-09.

McMILLAN, JOHN
Partner in McMillan Brothers, Marshfield, 1886-91.

McMILLER, MAUDE
Active in Portland, 1904-06.

McMONAGLE, CLYDE V.
Active in Portland, 1906-37+.

McMORRIS, J. A.
Active in Condon, 1913.

McMULLEN
Active in Canyon City, c. 1900.

McMULLEN, ARTHUR
Active in Dayville, 1895; Wallowa, 1905.

McMULLEN, JOHN
Active in Burns, 1905-11.

McNAB
Active in Portland at 351 ½ Washington Street.

McPHERREN, CHARLES E.
Active in Falls City, 1911-13.

McWILLIS, JAMES
Active in Fossil, 1905.

MEAD, WILLIAM R.
Active in Baker City, 1911-13.

MEALEY, GEORGE
Itinerant with William Mealey in Sweet Home.

MEALEY, WILLIAM
Itinerant with George Mealey in Sweet Home.

MEEK
Partner in Weister-Meek Company, Portland, 1893.

MEGLER, ALEX J.
Died in Portland, 1900. Partner in Bosco & Megler with Carl Bosco, Portland , 1875-76.

MEINZER, F. J.
Active in Cottage Grove, c. 1895.

MEISER, J. A.
Member of the Photographer's Association of the Pacific Northwest; active in Post Orford, 1907.

MELLIS BROTHERS
Active in Portland, c. 1880(?).

MERESSE, ELISEE
Born in Northern France, 1855; died in Forest Grove, 1924. Active in Oregon City, 1897; Forest Grove, 1897-24; operated as E. Meresse & Son with his son Frank, 1903. Also active in Netarts, 1900-24.

MERESSE, FRANK
Born in France, 1882. Active in Forest Grove with his father, operating as E. Meresse & Son, 1903.

MERRIFIELD, EDWARD G.
Active in Arlington, 1903; in Condon, 1907.

MERSEREAU, FREDERICK E.
Active in Portland, 1904; San Francisco, California, 1905-06; Forest Grove, Oregon, 1907. See California.

MERTENS, HUGO H.
Born in Essen, Germany, c. 1859; died in Olympia, Washington, 1948. Active in Waterbury, Connecticut, 1881; Tacoma, Washington, 1889; Sheridan, Oregon, 1901-03; Orting, Washington, early 1900s; Centralia and Orting, Washington, c. 1908; Centralia, Washington, c. 1931.

MESARVEY & RIBELIN
Partnership of W. D. Mesarvey and W. H. Ribelin, 421 or 431 Washington, Portland, 1895.

MESARVEY & SIMMONS
Partnership in Portland, 1894; W. D. Mesarvey.

MESARVEY, WILLIAM D.
Active in Lebanon, 1891; Portland, 1892-02. Partner in Mesarvy & Simmons, 1894; partner in Mesarvey & Ribelin, 1895; operated as Mesarvey Card Company, 1900.

MESSEGEE, ACHILLES
Printer at Davies Studio in Portland, 1910.

MESSER, CLARENCE J.
Partner in Bushby & Company with Asa C. Bushby, Portland, 1890.

MESSING, EMIL F.
Member of the International Photographic Association; active in Mist, 1913.

MEYER
Partner in Shepard & Meyer, in Portland before 1895.

MEYER, M.
Member of the Oregon Camera Club; active in Portland, 1905.

MEYERS, B. K.
Itinerant c. 1870s. Also spelled Myers.

MICHAEL, RALPH
Active in Portland at 314 ½ Washington, 1900.

MIKIBBEN, JAMES H.
Active in Portland, c. 1895.

MIKKELSON, JOHANNE
Active in Junction City, 1912-13.

MILARCH, ALFRED E.
Active in Portland, 1910-15; photographer with W. H. Catterlin, 1910.

MILLARD, FRANK A.
Amateur photographer active in Portland, 1915.

MILLER, A. D.
Active in Elk City, c. 1895.

MILLER, ALVIN E.
Active in Portland, 1892-99. Photographer for McAlpin & Lamb, 1894-95.

MILLER, ARLIN D.
Member of the International Photographic Association; active in Portland, 1912.

MILLER, C.
Active in Elk City, 1890s.

MILLER, CHARLES R.
Active in Portland, 1898-02; located at 227 ½ Washington 1901-02. Studio in Klamath Falls, 1910-17; operated as Miller Photo Company and Miller Post Card Company. Associated with Glen Johnson, 1913-17.

MILLER, FRED
Partner E. E. Thum, operating as Thum & Miller in Portland at 246 Main, 1910-13.

MILLER, LEONARD J.
Operated Electric Studio in Portland, 1910-15; at 145 6th, 1910; 392 H Washington, 1912-13; 414 Washington, 1915.

MILLER, MARTIN T.
Active in Heppner, 1901.

MILLER POST CARD COMPANY
Active in Klamath Falls, 1910-17, operated by Charles R. Miller; associated with Glen Johnson, 1913-17; also known as Miller Photo Company.

MILLER, RUTH
Active in Burns(?).

MILLN, RALPH S.
Member of the Oregon Camera Club; active in Portland, 1915-17.

MINARD, THADDEUS M.
Member of the Oregon Camera Club; active in Portland, 1900.

MISER, W. L.
Active in Medford, operating as Tyler & Miser with Mae E. Tyler.

MISNER, H. E.
Member of the Oregon Camera Club; active in Portland, 1898.

MIZUNO, S.
Active in Portland, operating the Rose City Photo Studio at 66 6th, 1914-25.

MOFFITT, JOHN H.
Active in Portland, 1912-17; at Du Fresne Studio, 1912; Van Dyck Studio, 1914; Moffitt Studio, 1917.

MONGOLD, MAE (MRS.)
Active in Klamath Falls, 1911.

MONK, T. R. (MRS.)
Active in Tillamook, 1911-15; operated the Modern Studio, 1911.

MONROE, A. L.
Active in Cottage Grove, 1913-17.

MONTAG, WILLIAM J.
Active in Portland, 1910; Seaside, 1909-15.

MONTEE, FRANK A.
Operated the Montee Brothers in Salem with James W., 1889-93; at 177 Commercial, 1891; 187 Commercial, 1892-93.

MONTEE, JAMES W.
Operated the Montee Brothers with Frank A. in Salem, 1889-93; at 177 Commercial, 1891; 187 Commercial, 1892-93.

MONTGOMERY, C. E.
Active in Sunnyview.

MONTGOMERY, J. H.
Active in Salem, 1862; Portland, 1863. Took over Buchtel's Salem studio, 1863; sold it to W. H. Lewis, 1866; listed in Amity, 1866. Operator for Buchtel in Portland, 1868; in Salem, 1870-72; Walla Walla, Washington, 1873; Salem, 1876; Union, 1881; Baker City, 1884.

MOOERS, W. A.
Active in Astoria, 1880.

MOON, H. C.
Active in Woodburn, 1903-07.

MOORE, BLANCHE McNAMER (MRS.)
Active in Portland at 332 ½ Washington, 1906.

MOORE, CHARLES
Active in Pendleton, 1915.

MOORE, ELBRIDGE W.
Born in Gardiner, Maine, 1857; died in Napa, California, 1938. Moved to Portland, 1883, and worked as photographer for Abell. Partner with B. C. Towne, operating as Towne & Moore, 1884-87. He purchased Frank Abell's studio and continued in business, 1888-1915, winning many awards for both his art and photography. Also known as Moore Portrait Company.

MOORE, FRANK
Active in Baker City, 1884; Caldwell, Idaho, 1889-91.

MOORE, M. E.
Active in Medford, c. 1917.

MOORE, W. D.
Active in Kellogg, 1891; Oakland, 1907.

MOORHOUSE, LEE
Born in Marion County, Iowa, February 28, 1850; died in Pendleton, June 1, 1902. The family crossed the Plains, 1861, settling in Walla Walla, Washington. He worked as an engineer and clerk until the Bannock War, when he was appointed Lieutenant Colonel in the Militia, and serving as secretary to the Governor of Oregon for the duration. After managing a large farm for several years, Moorhouse bought and ran a general store in Pendleton. He was appointed agent at the Umatilla Reservation, 1889, where he made thousands of images of Umatilla, Cayuse and Nez Perce. Moorhouse also photographed numerous female subjects in various costumes and poses, both in the studio and outdoors. He sold photographs and published books of his photographs, and served as Mayor of Pendleton and Deputy Clerk of the Oregon Supreme Court.

    Moorhouse, Major Lee, *Souvenir Album of Noted Indian Photographs*, Lee Moorhouse, Pendleton, Oregon, 1906.

MORAN, NELLY (MISS)
Member of the Oregon Camera Club; active in Portland, 1900.

MORGAN, E. (MISS)
Member of the Oregon Camera Club; active in Portland, 1900.

MORGAN, NORRIS V.
Partner in Taylor & Morgan with Fred E. Taylor, Myrtle Point, 1907.

MORGAN, RACHEL
Employed by Benjamin Gifford in Portland, 1917.

MORGAN, WILLIAM C.
Active in Portland at 220 Marquam Building, 1910.

MORQUAM, P.
Active in Portland, c. 1883.

MORRILL, A. A.
Active in Corvallis, 1881. Also spelled Morrell.

MORRIS, A. E.
Member of the Oregon Camera Club; active in Portland, 1900.

MORRIS, CHARLES B.
Active in Corvallis, 1884-88. Operated with partner Henry DeGroot as DeGroot & Morris, 1884.

MORRIS, CORA D.
Active in Medford, 1889.

MORRIS, EDWARD D.
Active in Haines, 1905.

MORRIS, M. E. (MISS)
Member of the Oregon Camera Club; active in Portland, 1900.

MORRISON, JULIA (MRS.)
Active in Rainier, 1915.

MORRISON, R. (MRS.)
Active in Corvallis, 1889-91.

MORRISON, W. F.
Active in Empire City, 1878-80.

MORSE, C. C.
Active in Portland, 1880; owner of an art gallery and picture framing store, not a photographer.

MORTISON, O. H.
Active in Glendale, 1913.

MORTON, FRANK J.
Partner in Sanders & Morton with Boughton E. Sanders, McMinnville, c. 1884.

MOSELEY, R. C.
Active in Corvallis at 430 South Second Street, 1910.

MOSER, W. H.
Active in Portland, 1904-06.

MOSES, HENRY C.
Member of the Oregon Camera Club; active in Portland, 1917.

MOSIER, ALA O.
Member of the International Photographic Assocation; active in Canyon City, 1912.

MOTOR GALLERY
Operated by Robert K. Clavering in Portland at 410 Morrison, 1894-95.

MOUNT, LELAN
Active in Cottage Grove, c. 1870.

MOUNTJOY, SMITH
Amateur photographer active in the Eugene area, 1909-50.

MOURY, O. F. (MRS.)
Member of the International Photographic Assocation; active in Elkton, 1912.

MT. HOOD STUDIO
Active in Portland, 1914.

MULIT, HENRY S.
Partner in Mulit & Eby in Woodburn, 1889-91; listed alone in Salem, 1891-93.

MULKEY, TH.
Active in Philomath, 1891; Pleasant Hill, 1895; Eugene, 1890s.

MULLIGAN, ROBERT E.
Active in Portland, 1910-15.

MULTNOMAH STUDIO
Operated by A. C. Lorenz in Portland at 801 Dekum Building, 1917.

MURHARD, S. A. (MRS.)
Member of the Oregon Camera Club; active in Portland, 1900.

MYERS, ALBERT G.
Born in Switzerland, 1869; died in Portland, 1967. Member of the Oregon Camera Club; active in Portland, 1909-17.

MYERS, B. K.
Itinerant active c. 1870s. Also spelled Meyers.

MYERS, MARION D.
Active in Portland, 1910.

NEFF, W. E.
Active in Hood River, 1895-97.

NEICKEN, L. M. (MRS.)
Member of the Oregon Camera Club; active in Portland, 1900.

NEMYRE, LENA M.
Printer for the Unique Portrait Company in Portland, 1904.

NESS, JAMES HARRY
Active in Portland, 1912-21.

NEW YORK GALLERY
Operated by John H. Turney in Oregon City at 5th, corner of Water, 1901-04.

NEW YORK GALLERY
Operated by Robert K. Clavering in Oregon City, 1893.

NEW YORK GALLERY
Active in Portland at Fourth Street, opposite Turn Hall, operated by Joseph Thwaites.

NEWCOMB, ALTA
Photographer for the Studio De Luxe in Portland at 23 Raleigh Building, 323 ½ Washington, 1910. Associated with Marion and Ida Newcomb.

NEWCOMB, IDA
Active in Portland, 1910, photographer for the Studio De Luxe with Marion and Ida Newcomb.

NEWCOMB, MARION W.
Active in Portland, 1910-16. Operated the Studio De Luxe at 23 Raleigh Building, 323 ½ Washington, 1910-11; 604 Eilers Building, c. 1912-14. Associated with Alta and Ida Newcomb, 1910.

NEWMAN, E. (MRS.)
Member of the Oregon Camera Club; active in Portland, 1900.

NICHOLS, CLYDE B.
Active in Grants Pass, 1903.

NICKAS, CHRIST
Active in Portland, 1917, partner with George Caraberis, operating as Caraberis & Nickas, 207 Globe Building.

NICOLAI, H. T.
Member of the Oregon Camera Club; active in Portland, 1900.

NIGHSWANDER, JASPER MERLE
Amateur photographer active in Hadleyville, Lane County, c. 1905-25.

NITCHY, F. A. (MRS.)
Member of the Oregon Camera Club; active in Portland, 1898.

NOE & WIRTH
Active in Cottage Grove, c. 1895.

NORCOTT, C. K.
Active in Bandon, 1913; McMinnville, 1915.

NORDSTROM, CARL H.
Active in Portland, 1899-1902. Located at 133 ½ 5th, 1902, operating the Aerne & Nordstrom studio with partner Christopher Aerne, Jr.

NORRIS, J. E.
Active in Milton, 1885; Enterprise, 1888-89; Elgin, 1891.

NORTH PACIFIC PHOTOGRAPHIC PRINTING & ENGRAVING HOUSE
Operated by O. C. Yocum in East Portland, c. 1885.

NORTHRUP, VASSAR L.
Active in Everett, Washington, 1905; Portland, 1909-25. Operated the Commonwealth Portrait Studio at 308 Commonwealth Building, 1910; the Vassar Studio at 525 Abington Building, 1913-14.

NORTHWESTERN PHOTO COMPANY
Active in Portland, 1913-25, operated by brothers George A. and Roy A. Douglas; partners with Mrs. Anna B. Postles, 1913-14.

NYE BEACH PHOTO STUDIO
Active in Newport Beach, c. 1910.

NYLOW, J. C.
Active in Portland, c. 1890.

O'BRIEN, J. H.
Member of the Oregon Camera Club; active in Portland, 1898.

O'NEILL
Partner in Pike & O'Neill Company, stereo photographers in Salem, 1880s-90s.

OAKES, OMEGA
Operated Omega Picture Gallery in Roseburg, 1878-87; Baker City, 1889.

OHSFELDT, ANNIE C. (MRS.)
Active in Portland, 1899, with partner operating as Burns & Ohsfeldt, 313 ½ Morrison.

OLIVE, J. R.
Member of the Photographer's Association of the Pacific Northwest; active in Roseburg, 1907.

OLMSTEAD, J. R.
Member of the Photographer's Association of the Pacific Northwest; active in Sheridan, 1907.

OLSEN, E.
Active in Marshfield, 1884.

OLSON, EMIL E.
Active in Drewsey, 1907-11; Portland, 1910.

OMEGA PICTURE GALLERY
Operated by Omega Oakes in Roseburg, 1878-87; Baker City, 1889.

OREGON ART COMPANY
Active in Bend, 1912; Redmond, c. 1910-15.

OREGON CAMERA CLUB
Established in 1895, incorporated in 1902.

OREGON COMMERCIAL STUDIO
Active in Portland, 1917.

OREGON PHOTO STOCK COMPANY
Active in Portland, 1904-08.

OSBORN, J. Q.
Active in Walla Walla, c. 1881.

OVIATT, N. C.
Member of the Oregon Camera Club; active in Portland, 1900.

OWENS, J. E.
Member of the Oregon Camera Club; active in Portland, 1900.

OWINGS, JAMES J.
Operated the Owings & Cooper studio with partner Henry L. Cooper in Gold Hill, 1888; in North Bend, 1905. Active in Coquille, 1907-09. Also spelled Owens.

P. & VAN E.
Active in Grants Pass, opposite the Courthouse.

PACIFIC ART STUDIO
Operated by George A. Bryant in Portland, 1907; Forest Grove, c. 1908-17.

PACIFIC FILM COMPANY
Operated by Henry Thumann, Jr. in Portland, 1910.

PACIFIC PHOTO COMPANY
Active in Salem, 1915-17; located at 322 State, 1917.

PACIFIC PHOTO COMPANY
Active in Portland, 1900s. Thornton Birdsall was president, 1907-14.

PACIFIC PHOTO GALLERY
Active in Forest Grove, c. early 1900s, operated by Mrs. Nettie Hoffman. Also known as Pacific Photo Company.

PACIFIC PICTURE PLACE
Operated by Joseph H. Edwards in Portland at 408 3rd, 1901-05.

PADDOCK, W. A.
Active in Grants Pass, 1917.

PAFFRATH & KARTEN
Stella M. Karten and Margaret A. Paffrath, Portland, 1902-04.

PAFFRATH, MARGARET A. (MISS)
Active in Portland, 1900-05; retoucher for C. A. Krauch, 1900; worked for Hayes & Short, 1901; partner with Stella M. Karten operating as Paffrath & Karten, 1902-04.

PAGE, J. J.
Operated the Page Studio in Eugene at 644 Willamette Street, 1912-13.

PALACE GALLERY
Active in Portland, 1878, possibly late 1880s, operated by I. G. Davidson and Gilman.

PALACE STUDIO
Active in Tillamook.

PALMER, CLAUDE
Born 1899; died 1991. Active in Portland, 1916-1990, operating the Photo Art Studio.

PALMER, G. W.
Associated with W. P. Palmer in Milton, 1881.

PALMER, JOHN
Active in Gold Hill, 1915.

PALMER, JOHN BERNARD
Active in Portland at 147 1st Street, 1900-01.

PALMER, W. P.
Active in Milton with G. W. Palmer, 1881.

PARK & VAN DUYN
Partnership active in Oregon.

PARKER, ROLAND T.
Operated Parker's Studio in Baker City, 1899-1917.

PARKER, WALDO H.
Partner with Elmer G. Lantz in Eugene, operating the Parker-Lanz Studio at 286 Commercial Street, 1910. Active in Salem, 1910-17.

PARKER-LANTZ STUDIO
Operated by Waldo H. Parker and Elmer G. Lantz in Eugene at 286 Commercial Street, 1910.

PARKINS, C.
Active in Lexington, 1886.

PARRISH, A. H.
Member of the International Photographic Association; active in Sodaville, 1912.

PARRISH, LENA C.
Member of the Oregon Camera Club; active in Portland, 1906-10.

PARTRIDGE, EDWARD J.
Born in Wheeling, West Virginia, 1856; died in San Francisco, 1891. Active in Portland, 1884, 1887-89; The Dalles, 1884-85. Son of prominent daguerreotyper, Asa C. Partridge; associated with his brother, W. H. Partridge. Manager of Partridge Photo Company by 1888, when he sold the business and moved to San Francisco, where his brother Sam C. operated the largest photo supply house on the west coast. Returned to Portland, 1889, opening a photographic supply house; moved back to San Francisco, 1890. Together with brother W. H., he published a stunning series of scenic views of Alaska. The Partridge brothers produced splendid views of the Pacific Northwest in addition to their Alaska work.

PARTRIDGE, WILLIAM H.
Died 1939. Active in Boston, 1878-79. Moved to Portland, late 1883, and worked for Abell. Established studio with his brother, E. J., by 1884. Also owned Gilhousen's studio in The Dalles, 1884-86. After a photographing trip to Alaska, 1886, he married Emma Abell, and they moved back to Boston. He was active until 1914, one of Boston's most prominent photographers; he produced some of the finest views of the Pacific Northwest and Alaska.

PATTERSON, FRANK
Active in Hood River, 1911; in Ashland and Northern California thereafter. Major producer of stereoviews and postcards.
    Robert I. Wright, *A Patterson Postcard Checklist/Workbook*, Robert Wright, Ashland, Oregon.

PATTERSON, J. WARNER
Active in Portland, 1925.

PATTERSON, THOMAS W.
Partner with Orlando M. Hofsteater, operating as Hofsteater & Patterson, at 165 ½ 3rd, Portland, 1906.

PATTERSON, WILLIAM
Active in Portland, 1906.

PATTON, HAL D.
Operating the Patton Postcard Company in Salem, 1911-13.

PAXTON, ANDREW B.
Active in Albany, 1867-91. Operated as Thompson & Paxton, 1867-68; sold studio to John A. Winter, 1868. Listed as the Crawford & Paxton studio with partner James G. Crawford, 1889-91. Major studio and producer of stereoviews of Oregon scenes.

PAYNE, SAMUEL
Active in Linkville, 1878-80.

PAYSON, A. U.
Active in Portland, 1909-17; operated the East Side Photo Studio, 1917.

PEAKE, J.
Active in Astoria, c. 1865.

PEASLEY, ALBERT E.
Active in Portland, 1914-25. Photographer for W. G. Cutberth, 1914; proprietor of the Vassar Studio at 525 Abington Building, 1915. Operated as The Peasleys, 407 Morrison, 1916-25.

PEASLEY, ALDA B. (MRS.)
Married to Albert E.; active in Portland at the Vassar Studio or The Peasleys, 1915, 1925.

PEAT, J. H.
Active in Portland, 1906.

PEEBLES, J.
Member of the Oregon Camera Club; active in Portland, 1900.

PEEK, WILLIAM A.
Active in Yaquina, 1889-91. Also listed as Peck.

PEIR, S. S.
Member of the Oregon Camera Club; active in Portland, 1898.

PENDLETON PHOTO COMPANY
Active in Pendleton, c. 1880s-90s, operated by partners J. A. McIntire and M. B. Harlow; also known as McIntyre & Harlow. Sold to C. S. Wheeler, 1891.

PENNINGTON, JOSHUA
Active in Cottage Grove, 1891.

PENNOCK, C. (MRS.)
Member of the Oregon Camera Club; active in Portland, 1900.

PENNY PHOTO COMPANY
Operated by F. E. Dumermuth in Portland at 253H Washington, 1901.

PENNY STUDIO
Active in Portland at 104 11th, operated by Victor H. DeRemo, 1914.

PEOPLE'S GALLERY
Operated by Hubert D. Graves in Portland, 1885.

PERET, GUS
Active in Yoncalla, 1911-13.

PERFECTO
Active in Portland, c. 1895(?).

PERKINS, MARY (MRS.)
Active in Heppner.

PERNOT BROTHERS
Active in Corvallis, 1890.

PERRIN
Partner in Pike & Perrin, Salem, 1880s-90s.

PERRY, DR. J. C.
Member of the Oregon Camera Club; active in Portland, 1897-98.

PERRY, F. C.
Active in Redmond, 1912.

PERSHIN, F. R.
Active in Klamath Falls.

PETERSON, CAROLYN M.
Active in Portland, 1915.

PETERSON, L. DEAN
Member of the International Photographic Association; active in Eugene, 1912.

PETERSON, ROY J.
Active in Portland, 1911-25. Operated the "Peterson Daguerre [sic] Studio" at 214 Pittock Block, 1925.

PFLUGER, LILLIAN M.
Retoucher, clerk and photographer in Portland, 1904-25.

PHEBY, GEORGE E.
Active in Grants Pass, 1901.

PHILLIPS, EDGAR W.
Active in Corvallis, 1901-03.

PHILLIPS, EDWARD W.
Active in Portland, 1889.

PHOTOGRAPHIC COMPANY
Active in Portland, Russell Building, 165 4th Street, 1902.

PICKEL, ELSWORTH
Active in Athena, 1895; Independence, 1901-03.

PICKEL, LEWIS G.
Operated the Umatilla Art Gallery in Athena, 1899-03.

PICKEL, WILLIAM M.
Active in Portland at 2 ½ Grand Avenue, 1904-05.

PICKERILL & CATTERLIN
Partnership of F. Judd Catterlin and Frank A. Pickerill in Salem, 1884-86.

PICKERILL, FRANK A.
Active in Salem, 1884-86; operated as Pickerill & Catterlin with partner F. Judd Catterlin.

PIERCE, K. A.
Active in Cascade Locks.

PIKE & MARKHAM COMPANY
Nelson G. Pike and Benjamin C. Markham in Portland at 343 ½ Washington, 1914-17.

PIKE & O'NEILL COMPANY
Stereo photographers in Salem, 1880s-90s; possibly C. S. Pike.

PIKE & PERRIN
Stereo photographers in Salem, 1880s-90s; possibly C. S. Pike and G. B. Perrin.

PIKE, NELSON G.
Active in Portland, 1914-17. Operated the Pike & Markham Company with Benjamin C. Markham at 343 ½ Washington.

PITTMAN (MISS)
Active in Albany, 1896-97; Forest Grove, 1898-1907. Operated the Hoffman & Pittman studio with partner, Nettie Pittman Hoffman.

PLAGEMANN, JOHN P.
Member of the Oregon Camera Club; active in Portland, 1909-13.

PLUMMER, HELEN
Active in Salem, 1905. Also known as Helen Gatch.

PLUMMER, OAKES M.
Born in Bradford, Maine, 1869; died in Portland, 1945. Member of the Portland Society of Photographic Art Salon Committee; active in Portland, c. 1905.

POKORNEY, LUDWIG L.
Born in Czechoslovakia, 1877; died in Portland, 1925. In San Francisco prior to 1914. Active in Portland, 1914-25.

POLDEMAN, WILLIAM F.
Artist and photographer active in Portland at 19 Washington, 1865-72. Also spelled Podeman.

POLLOCK, THOMAS
Active in Yoncalla, 1872.

POPE & HOFFMAN
Partnership of Mrs. Nettie Hoffman and Oliver M. Pope, Forest Grove, 1901.

POPE, OLIVER M.
Born in Cash County, Missouri, 1858; died in Hillsboro, 1928. Active in The Dalles, 1891; partner with Mrs. Nettie Hoffman, operating as Pope & Hoffman, Forest Grove, 1901. Listed in Hillsboro, 1903-09; Portland, 1912-28. Major producer of postcards in Washington County.

POPE, SETH L.
Amateur photographer active in Portland, 1870s-1910(?).

PORTABLE PHOTOGRAPHIC STUDIO
Operated in the Pendeleton and Pleasant Hill area by itinerant John A. Briggs, c. 1880s.

PORTLAND CAMERA EXCHANGE
Operated by Edward C. Blackwood in Portland, early 1920s.

PORTLAND FINISHING COMPANY
Active in Portland, c. 1900s.

PORTLAND GALLERY
Active in Portland at 111 ½ Third and 167 4th, c. 1895(?). Also known as The Portland.

PORTLAND PORTRAIT COMPANY
Operated by Fred P. Wittenberg in Portland at 349 1st Street, c. 1904-10.

PORTLAND STUDIO
Gallery in Portland operated by Perry D. Sutphen, at 510 Macleay Building, 1910-17.

PORTLAND VIEWING COMPANY
Active in Portland at 228 Sixth Street, 1890.

POST OFFICE TIN TYPE GALLERY
Active in Portland at 166 Fifth, operated by Mrs. Mary A. Russ, 1884. Also known as Post Office Gallery.

POSTAL SHOP
Active in Portland, c. 1907.

POSTLES, ANNA B. (MRS.)
Active in Portland, 1909-17; partner in Northwestern Photo Company with R. A. Douglas, 1913-14.

POSTLES, WILLIAM F.
Photographer for Northwestern Photo Company in Portland, 1913-17.

POSTLETHWAITE, BENJAMIN P.
Active in Baker City, 1903-07. Operated with partner Benjamin F. Read as Read & Postlethwaite, 1903.

POTTER
Operated as Jarvis & Potter in Eugene at 586 Willamette Street, 1910.

POTTER, HENRY N.
Active in Portland, 1870-81; operated Little Gallery Around the Corner, 1870; with partner as Thwaites & Potter at Yamhill between 4th and 5th, 1881.

POTTER, J. J.
Active in Portland, c. 1895(?).

POTTER, JOHN S.
Active in Portland, 1893-99. Located at 225 ½ 1st Street, 1892-97; 285 1st Street, 1898-99.

POWELL, H. E.
Member of the Oregon Camera Club; active in Portland(?), 1905.

PRATT, GUY A.
Listed in Marquam, c. 1909-11; partner with O. Stayton in Marquam, operating as Clapp & Pratt, c. 1915.

PRATT, LOVE
Active in Portland after 1900.

PREBLE, EDWARD W.
Partner in Hobson & Preble with Samuel Hobson, in Portland at 181 ½ 1st Street, 1902.

PRENTISS, ARTHUR
Active in Portland, 1913-32; associated with George M. Weister, operating as Weister Company, 1913-16; operating as Gifford & Prentiss with Benjamin A. Gifford, 1917.

PRENTZEL, W. R.
Member of the International Photographic Association; active in Hillsboro, 1911.

PREUSS DRUG COMPANY
Active in Marshfield, c. 1913.

PRICE, L. R.
Active in Hoskins, 1885(?).

PRICE, WILLIAM V.
Active in McMinnville, 1886-88.

PRIDAY, E. A.
Active in Plush, 1911.

PRIER, RICHARD
Active in Oregon City, 1888-1909.

PRIEST
Partnership of Frank G. Abell and Priest in San Francisco, c. 1885.

PRINGLE, JOSEPH
Partner in Shanafelt & Pringle with William F. Shanafelt, Cottage Grove, 1903.

PRITCHARD, NORA B.
Active in Portland, 1909-13; proprietor of Aerne Studio, 1912-13.

PUTNAM
Partner with Henry Burger, Jr., operating as Burger-Putnam Studio in Portland, c. 1900-39. See Henry Burger, Jr.

PUTNAM, CLYDE A., SR.
Member of the Oregon Camera Club; active in Portland, 1910-40.

PUTZIEN, HERMAN
Active in Canyon City, 1890-1899, 1903-15.

QUACKENBUSH, E. H.
Member of the Oregon Camera Club; active in Portland, 1900.

QUANT, BLANCHE
Active in Oakland with sister Dora, operating as the Quant Sisters, 1905-09.

QUANT, DORA
Active in Oakland, operating with Blanche as the Quant Sisters 1905-09.

QUANT, SUMNER
Active in Oakland, c. 1880.

QUARTERMASS, C. W.
Active in Marshfield, 1913-17.

R. T. R. COMPANY
Studio in Pendleton, located over the post office; successors to J. A. Briggs.

RAEDER, BARBETTA E. (MRS.)
Photo retoucher in Portland, 1910.

RAGAN, G. C.
Active in Albany at 120 West Second Street, c. 1910-13.

RAHMEYER, B. F.
Active in Oregon, WWI era.

RAMSDELL, G. H.
Active in Marshfield, 1885-86. Also listed as G. F. Ramsdell.

RANDALL, LILLIAN M.
Member of the Oregon Camera Club; active in Portland, 1900-06.

RANDALL, WILLIAM G.
Active in Oregon City, 1907.

RANKIN, F. S.
Active in Wasco, 1891.

RANKIN, FRANK A.
Active in Eugene, 1880-91, operating as Rankin & Company; partner with Henry J. Boyd, 1891.

RANSFORD, ARTHUR L.
Active in Portland, 1916-17.

RASCH, FRED A.
Member of the Portland Society of the Photographic Art and Portland Salon Committee, 1904-05.

RAYMOND
Partner with Charles S. Woodruff, operating as Woodruff & Raymond, 327 ½ Washington Street in Portland, c. 1915(?).

RAYMOND, WILL
Born in Lenawee County, Michigan, October 15, 1894; died in The Dalles, June 3, 1943. Active in Moro, 1899-1935(?).

REA, JOSIE H. (MISS)
Active in Baker City, 1886.

READ & POSTLETHWAITE
Partnership of Benjamin P. Postlethwaite and Benjamin F. Read in Baker City, 1903.

READ, BENJAMIN F.
Partner Benjamin P. Postlethwaite, operating as Read & Postlethwaite in Baker City, 1903; in Pocatello, Idaho, c. 1905.

READ, T. L.
Member of the International Photographic Association; active in Wren, 1909.

REALSTON, ALBERT
Active in Portland, 1910.

REAS, HENRY J.
Active in Woodburn, c. 1900.

REDDING, THOMAS F.
Active in Portland at 247 ½ 5th, 1909.

REDER, A.
Active in LaGrande, 1908.

REDINGTON
Active in Portland, c. 1885; operated the St. Louis Art Studio.

REDMOND & JENKS
Partnership of Charles F. Redmond and E. L. Jenks at 615 Maegly Tichner Building, Portland, 1925.

REDMOND, CHARLES F.
Born 1875; died 1937. Active in Portland, 1907-37. Partner with Herbert A. Hale, operating as Hale & Redmond, "Home Photographers," 1916-20. Located at 167 ½ 1st Street, 1916; 403 Eilers Building, 1917; 615-616 Eilers Building, 1917-18; 615 Bush & Lane Building, 1920. Partner with E. L. Jenks, 1925, at 615 Maegly Tichner Building, operating the Redmond & Jenks studio.

REED, JESSIE B. (MRS.)
Member of the Oregon Camera Club; active in Portland, 1900-04.

REHFELD
Operated as Rehfeld & Company, Marshfield, 1917.

REID, DANIEL
Active in Portland at 282 ½ 2nd and 133 ½ 1st Street, 1909-10. Also spelled Read.

REID, J. J.
Active in Hubbard, 1881.

REID, JOHN V.
Member of the Oregon Camera Club; active in Portland, 1909-12.

REISE, H. J.
Member of the Photographer's Association of the Pacific Northwest; active in Woodburn, 1907.

REMBRANDT STUDIO
Operated by William G. and Emma E. Cutberth in Portland; at 801 Dekum Building, 1902-15; 216 Pittock Block, 1916.

REMBRANDT STUDIO
Active in Portland, c. 1900, 1907-08, operated by Rowena M., James J. and Mrs. J. J. Hogan.

RENDALL & AVERY
Partnership of Steve A. Rendall and William L. Avery, operating in Portland in the New Building, corner of 2nd and Alder Streets, 1864. Also listed as Avery & Rendall.

RENDALL, STEVE A.
Partner in Rendall & Avery, corner of 2nd and Alder Streets, Portland, 1864.

REX STUDIO
Operated by Mrs. M. C. Lewis in Salem at 343 Court Street, 1910.

REYNOLDS, A. C.
Active in Tillamook, 1891-03.

REYNOLDS, GEORGE O.
Active in Portland at 245 ½ Morrison, 1910-11.

REYNOLDS, H. BURT
Active in Portland at 163 West Park, 1911-14.

REYNOLDS, HENRY J.
Active in LaGrande, 1901-03; Eugene, 1905-16.

REYNOLDS, WILLIAM S.
Active in Forest Grove, 1899; Dayton, 1901-03.

RHINEHART, JOHN B.
Active in Eugene, 1886-91.

RIBELIN, WILLIAM H.
Partner in Mesarvey & Ribelin, operating the Elite Studio at 421 or 431 Washington in Portland, 1895.

RICE, H. M.
Active in Jacksonville, 1880s(?).

RICHARD, W. L.
Active in Union, 1899; operating as Richards & Akers in Ione, with headquarters in the Morrow Art Hall, 1890s.

RICHARDS, HARRY I.
Active in Portland at 1747 East 21st Street, 1909-10.

RICHARDSON, CLARENCE FORD
Member of the Oregon Camera Club; active in Portland, 1910-24.

RICHARDSON, WARREN
Active in Stayton, 1903.

RIGGS, GEORGE
Active in Mabel, 1888-89; McMinnville, 1891.

RIGGS, JAMES W.
Born in West Virginia, 1842. Active in Ashland, 1880-81; Lewiston, Idaho, 1883-87; Roseburg, 1887; Marshfield, 1889-13. Possibly a partner in Hurley & Riggs, Marshfield.

RIGGS, RALPH P.
Active in Portland, 1910.

RISLEY, N. C. W.
Active in Albany, c. 1883.

RITTER, HENRY J.
Active in Portland, 1894-1906; LaGrande, 1909-15.

ROBB
Operated the Robb Photo Studio in Independence, 1915.

ROBBINS, EVERMAN
Stereo photographer in Molalla.

ROBERTS
Traveling photographer in the Hillsboro area, c. 1867, partner in Roberts & Corey.

ROBERTS, W. E.
Born 1883; died 1930. Member of the Oregon Camera Club; active in Portland, 1909-10.

ROBERTS, W. O.
Active in Enterprise.

ROBERTSON, C. W.
Photographer in Eugene, 1912; advertised for position, wife available as retoucher and receptionist.

ROBINSON, J. W.
Active in Portland, 1872, East Side; Forest Grove, 1873; Brownsville, 1874. Also a partner in Williams & Robinson.

ROBINSON, SAMUEL W.
Born 1878; died 1907. Active in Portland at 364 Morrison, 1902.

ROE, H. S.
Member of Oregon Camera Club; active in Portland, 1898.

ROGERS
Operated the Catterlin & Rogers studio in Salem, 1874.

ROGERS, WILLIAM D.
Active in Hood River, 1901-09.

ROLLINS, J. P.
Active in Condon, 1909-11.

ROMANE, ELIZABETH
Photographer for Sue Dorris in Eugene, 1910. Also known as Elizabeth Erdman.

ROMIG, JOSEPH H.
Active in Joseph, 1901-07.

ROMINGER, G. T.
Stereo photographer from Spokane, Washington; made rare views of Portland.

ROPER, CHARLES
Operated studio with Theresa Roper in Newport, 1915-17.

ROPER, THERESA
Studio photographer in Newport, 1915-17.

ROSE CITY PHOTO STUDIO
Active in Portland, 1914-25, operated by S. Mizuno at 66 6th.

ROSE CITY STUDIO
Operated by Charles Berthold in Portland, c. 1909-14.

ROSE STUDIO
Active in Portland at 270 ½ Washington, operated by D. Perry Evans, 1915.

ROSIGER, F.
Member of the Oregon Camera Club; active in Portland, 1900.

ROSS, DAVID W.
Active in Portland, 1899-1905; member of the Oregon Camera Club.

ROSS, H. R.
Active in Eugene-Marcola area, c. 1900.

ROSS, JACK
Active in Portland at 29 Park North, 1894.

ROTNOR, GEORGE H.
Active in Portland, 1904-05; member of the Oregon Camera Club.

ROUSH, ADA A. (MISS)
Active in Goldendale, Washington, c. 1907; LaGrande, Oregon, c. 1907-17. Located at 108 Elm, 1913-17. Also listed as Miss Ada G. Roush.

ROUTLEDGE, FRED A.
Active in Portland, 1898-1905.

ROWIN, GEORGE
Active in Waldport, c. 1913.

ROYAL, OSMAN (MRS.)
Member of the Oregon Camera Club; active in Portland, 1900.

ROYAL, OSMAN, DR.
Amateur photographer active in Portland, 1900; member of Oregon Camera Club.

ROYCE, ORLEN
Active in Portland at 584 Umatilla Avenue, 1914-17.

RUMMELIN, P. (MISS)
Member of the Oregon Camera Club; active in Portland, 1900.

RUMSEY (MRS.)
Active in Portland, 1866.

RUSH, WILLIAM B.
Active in Clatskanie, 1901-07.

RUSS, E. R.
Active in Portland on First near Stark, 1880.

RUSS, MARY A. (MRS.)
Born 1842; died 1911. Active in Salem, 1878; in Portland, 1881-84; at 166 Fifth, 1884; operated Post Office Tin Type Gallery, 1885. Her husband, Dr. Hiram M. Russ, practiced dentistry at the same location.

RUSSELL
Active in Baker.

RUSSELL, JOHN
Active in Sweet Home(?).

S & Y
Active in Portland.

SAARI, ALFRED A.
Active in Astoria, 1903-17; at 212 14th, 1903-11; 632 Commercial, 1913.

SACKRIDER, HENRY
Died in San Francisco, California, September 27, 1944. Active in Forest Grove, 1910-13; in Marysville, California, 1914.

SAITO, I.
Operated Century Photo Studio in Portland, 1906-12.

SALB, ALBERT
Active in Salem, 1909.

SALEM ART COMPANY
Studio in Salem.

SALMELA, H.
Active in Astoria, 1917.

SAMAIN, CHARLES O.
Active in Portland, 1901-10; operated as Samain & Lagerborg with partner, Miss Nettie Lagergborg, 1901-02.

SAMMIS, EDWARD M.
Itinerant active before 1860s. Name also spelled Sammes. See Idaho and California.

SAN FRANCISCO GALLERY
Active in Portland, 1879-95. Operated by William H. Towne and associates, 1879-84, at First and Morrison Streets. Bertram C. Towne and Elbridge W. Moore operated the studio, 1884-87, taking over shortly after W. H. Towne's death. The studio was known as B. C. Towne Photograph Company, 1888-95. It was managed by Flora H. Browning, 1895. She became the proprietor, also working as photographer, 1896-1908, operating as Browning Photo Gallery.

SANBORN, VAIL & COMPANY
Picture framing company that imprinted their mounts.

SANDEEN, WILLIAM
Active in Portland, 1899-1901, at 386 East Morrison.

SANDERS & MORTON
Partnership of Frank J. Morton and Boughton E. Sanders in McMinnville, 1884-86. Also listed as Sanders & Martin.

SANDERS, BOUGHTON E.
Active in McMinnville, 1884-86, operating as Sanders & Morton. Also listed as Sanders & Martin.

SANDFORD, WILLIAM C.
Active in Stayton, 1881-92.

SANFORD, FREDERICK B.
Member of International Photographic Association, 1913, living in Grants Pass; moved to Dothan.

SARONY STUDIO
Operated by A. Leaman Davis in Portland at 342 ½ Washington, 1910-14.

SASMAN, F. F.
Active in Newport.

SAVAGE, JOHN
Active in North Yamhill, 1901.

SAWYER & CRANE
Studio in Oakland, 1872; S. W. Crane.

SAWYER & DWYER
Active in Portland; C. S. Sawyer and D. J. Dwyer.

SAWYER, CARLTON S.
Active in Portland, 1911-17, operating as Sawyer Scenic Photos Inc., Sawyer Photos Company, and Rose City Art Store; partner in Sawyer & Dwyer.

SAWYER, F. W.
Active in McMinnville, 1873.

SAYER, AGNES
Operated as Sayer Photo Company in Burns, 1915-17.

SCHLEGEL, EDWARD J.
Member of the Oregon Camera Club; active in Portland, 1900.

SCHNEIDER, MAXWELL
Active in Gresham, 1910-17; Damascus, 1911-13.

SCHOFIELD, R. G.
Active in Umatilla City, 1865.

SCHOLL, AEMILLAN
Active in Portland, 1910.

SCHUMAKER, LEO J.
Studio in Weston, 1877.

SCHURKENS, WILLIAM
Active in Oregon City, 1913.

SCHUSTER & DAVIDSON
Stereo photographers in Salem, c. 1876-77; I. G. Davidson.

SCHWICHTENBERG, HUGO E.
Active in Albina, 1890; Portland, 1889-91; Pomona, California, 1894.

SCOTFORD, JOHN H.
Active in Tacoma, Washington, 1891; Portland, 1892-98. Operated as Corey & Scotford with partner Justin C. Corey, 1898-99, then as Scotford & Company.

SEIFERT, EMIL
Active in Stayton, 1889; in Hoskins, 1891; in Forest Grove, 1904-07; in Kings Valley, 1915. Known as Columbia Gallery, 1904, operated by Seifert & Leopold. Also spelled Sifert.

SEIGMUND BROTHERS
Active in Mehama, 1889-91.

SELLECK, F. L.
Member of the Oregon Camera Club; active in Portland, 1900.

SELLWOOD PHOTO STUDIO
Active in Portland at 543 Umatilla Avenue, 1910.

SERVICE, WILLIAM
Active in Silverton, 1909; member of International Photographic Association.

SEUFERT, ARTHUR
Active in The Dalles with his father, Frank Seufert, 1911.

SEUFERT, FRANK A.
Active in The Dalles with Arthur Seufert, his son, 1911.

SEVERANCE, ASEL E.
Active in Portland, 1882-85; operating as Severance & Yocum, 1885.

SEWARD, C. G.
Active in Bend, 1913.

SEYMOUR, VIVUS
Active in Drain, 1913.

SHAFER & HULSE
Active in Lakeview, 1891; Joseph B. Hulse.

SHAFER, ROBERT A.
Active in Summerville, operating as Shafer Brothers with Samuel J., 1891.

SHAFER, SAMUEL J.
Operated as Shafer Brothers with Robert A. in Summerville, 1891.

SHANAFELT, EMMA E.
Active in Portland, 1911-15; wife of William F.; continued to operate the studio after her husband's death, 1913.

SHANAFELT, WILLIAM FULLER
Born in Berwick, Pennsylvania, June 6, 1860; died in Lawrence, Kansas, December 31, 1913. Active in Portland, 1891- 98; photographer for G. L. Eastman, 1892-93. Active in Arlington, 1901; Cottage Grove, 1903-05; with partner Joseph Pringle, operating as Shanafelt & Pringle, 1903. Worked alone in Portland at 508 Williams Avenue, c. 1905-13.

SHANAHAN & DUFRENE
Partnership in Portland, 1865.

SHAVER STUDIO
Active in Baker.

SHAW, DOUGLAS
Active in Portland, 1915.

SHEANE, ROBERT
Active in Forest Grove, c. 1880, 1886-88. Active in North Yamhill, 1884. See Washington.

SHEILDS, HAZEL
Active in Portland, c. 1910.

SHEPARD & MEYER
Partnership in Portland before 1895.

SHEPHERD, GEORGE S.
Born in Scotland, 1866; died in Portland, 1941. Attorney and photographer, active in Portland, 1890s-1941; member of the Oregon Camera Club.

SHEPPARD, D. A.
Active in John Day, c. 1895.

SHERMAN & BROWN
Stereo photographers in Crystal, c. 1903; F. J. Brown.

SHERMAN, WILLIAM A.
Member of the Columbia Camera Club; active in Astoria, 1897.

SHERWOOD, SAMUEL P.
Partner with Charles A. Alvord in Portland, operating as Alvord & Sherwood at 183 Madison, 1898.

SHEYTHE, E. G.
Active in Willamina, 1881.

SHOGREN, FRED A.
Died in Portland, 1958. Active in Portland, 1900-40; photographer for the Oregonian.

SHORT, CHARLES W.
Active in Portland, 1886-1901. Printer for Towne & Moore, Bert C. Towne, I. G. Davidson, and E. W. Moore, 1886- 95. Located in the Labbe building, 1896-99; with partners Amelia and Henry C. Hayes at 340 ½ Washington, operating as Hayes & Short, 1901.

SHORT, GORDON
Itinerant.

SHUMAKER, LEO
Active in Weston, 1878-80.

SHUPE, P. T.
Active in Walla Walla, Washington, 1865-66; LaGrande, Oregon, 1867. Also spelled Shrope.

SHURTE, MILES P.
Active in Arlington, 1911-17.

SHUSTER
Active in Tillamook, c. 1880s; photographed Tillamook Indians in his studio.

SHUSTER & DAVIDSON
H. S. Shuster and I. G. Davidson, southwest corner of 1st and Yamhill, Portland, 1876-77.

SHUSTER, H. J.
Active in Hillsboro, c. 1895.

SHUSTER, H. S.
Active in Portland, operating as Shuster & Davidson with I. G. Davidson, 1876-77. Active in Astoria, 1878; Salem, 1879-84; Astoria, 1888-91; Aberdeen, Washington, 1889.

SIBSON, W. S. (MRS.)
Member of the Oregon Camera Club; active in Portland, 1900.

SIEBLEY, CHARLOTTE
Active in Portland, 1910.

SIEGRIST, ADOLPH
Active in Cedar Mills, near Portland, late 1880s.

SIFERT, E. F.
Active in Kings Valley, c. 1915. Also spelled Seifert; possibly Emil.

SIGSBEE, BOYD
Active in Heppner, 1902-15. Also listed as Byron G. Sigsbee.

SILVERSTONE, JULIUS
Member of the Oregon Camera Club; active in Portland, 1900.

SIMMONS
Partner in Mesarvey & Simmons, Portland, 1894.

SIMMONS & HARNISH
Partnership active c. early 1900s; Clinton S. Harnish.

SIMMONS, ALLEN A.
Born 1869. Active in Portland, 1894, operating as Mesarvey & Simmons; Nampa, 1895; Eugene, 1905-10.

SIMON, LEO F.
Born c. 1891; died 1986. Active in Portland, 1907-76; operated the Sowell Studio, 1925.

SLAVENS, W. H.
Active in Portland, 1896.

SLEETH, DANA P.
Born 1878; died in Portland, 1936. Member of the Oregon Camera Club; reporter for *The Journal*, 1904; editor of the *Daily News*, 1910. Active 1900-11.

SLOAN, W. B.
Active in Eugene, 1880; in Pendleton with gallery over Allison's New Store, 1882.

SMALL, C. FREDERICK
Member of the International Photographic Association; active in Portland, 1911.

SMITH & WALLING
Active in Oakland, 1881; F. A. Smith.

SMITH, A. D.
Member of the Photographer's Association of the Pacific Northwest; active in Salem, 1907.

SMITH, B. F.
Member of the International Photographic Association; active in Tygh Valley, 1913.

SMITH, C. S.
Traveling photographer active in San Francisco, Marshfield and Eugene, 1880. See Washington.

SMITH, CHARLES T. G.
Member of the International Photographic Association; active in Astoria, 1909.

SMITH, CHRISTOPHER C.
Itinerant photographer active in Newberg, 1901-09; in Portland at 149 ½ 1st Street, 1910-13.

SMITH, CLAUDE R.
Active in Portland, 1910.

SMITH, E. A.
Active in Sumpter(?).

SMITH, FRANCES (MISS)
Active in Portland, 1902-03; printer for Aerne & Nordstrom, 1902.

SMITH, FRANCIS A.
Active in Roseburg, 1861-70; Portland(?), 1871; Salem, 1872-81; in Oakland, 1881, operating as Smith & Walling. See Washington.

SMITH, FRANK J.
Operated with F. C. Aldrich at Angelus Commercial Studio, Portland, c. 1915.

SMITH, G. GREENWOOD
Active in Salem at 480 North 15 Street.

SMITH, GEORGE O.
Active in Portland, 1910.

SMITH, H. M.
Active in Portland, c. 1902(?).

SMITH, HARRY G.
Amateur active in Portland, 1898-1905; member of the Oregon Camera Club.

SMITH, INA (MISS)
Active in McMinnville, 1909.

SMITH, J. S.
Active in The Dalles, 1876.

SMITH, JOHN J.
Active in Portland, 1906-07.

SMITH, LILLIAN (MRS.)
Member of the International Photographic Association; active in Toledo, 1911.

SMITH, M.
Member of the Oregon Camera Club; active in Portland, 1900.

SMITH, MATT K.
Daguerreotypist active in Portland, 1851.

SMITH, P. N. (MRS.)
Member of the Oregon Camera Club; active in Portland, 1900.

SMITH, PERCY H. (MRS.)
Stereographer active in Joseph, 1905.

SMITH, RAY
Active in North Bend, 1907. Possibly Roy Smith.

SMITH, SARAH (MRS.)
Active in LaGrande, 1903-05.

SMITH, STERLING C.
Active in Enterprise, 1903.

SMITH, W. D.
Born c. 1861; died 1924. Member of the Oregon Camera Club; active in Portland(?), 1905.

SMITH, W. L.
Active in Portland, 1915.

SMITH, WILLIAM (MRS.)
Operated the Smith Studio in Roseburg, 1907-09.

SMITH, WILLIAM B.
Active in Portland at 368 1st Street, 1894.

SNODGRASS, WILLIAM F.
Active in Astoria, 1896-1901; at 634 Commercial, 1901. Active in Oregon City, 1902-03.

SNYDER
Partner in Crow & Snyder, Coquille City, 1876; Samuel B. Crow.

SNYDER, CHARLES E.
Active in Lebanon, 1911-13; partner with Frank D. in Snyder Brothers, 1911. Listed separately in St. Johns, 1915.

SNYDER, FRANK D.
Active in Lebanon, 1911-13; partner with Charles E. in Snyder Brothers, 1911.

SOLOMON, R. B.
Active in Portland, 1912.

SORENSEN, J. H. C.
Active in Gresham, 1909-11.

SORENSON, A.
Photo operator, retoucher and finisher, advertising in *Camera Craft*, 1913, for position in Condon.

SOURS, LEVI L.
Active in Stayton, 1905.

SOWELL, FRANKLYN S.
Operated studio in Portland, 1911-15; known as The Photograph Man at 420 ½ Washington, 1914-15. The Sowell Studio continued after his death, operated by his widow, Etta, and Earl E. Gustin, 1916;

operated by Leo F. Simon, 1925.

SOWELL, JOSEPH CLYDE
Active in Portland, 1912-13, with his brother Franklyn S.

SPAUGH, CHARLES H.
Active in Laidlaw, 1911.

SPAULDING, W. R.
Member of the Oregon Camera Club; active in Portland, 1900.

SPERRY, MYRA E. (MISS)
Active in Salem at Commercial and Court, and 277 Commercial, 1889-99. The address on Commercial was re-numbered in 1907, becoming 197 North Commercial.

SPURGEON, JOHN M.
Stereo photographer in Clatskanie.

ST. LOUIS ART STUDIO
Operated by Redington in Portland, c. 1885.

STADDEN, J. H.
Active in Marshfield, 1913-17.

STAEHR, ANNA
Operating as the Staehr Sisters with Emma Staehr in Forest Grove, 1903.

STAEHR, EMMA
Active in Forest Grove, operating as the Staehr Sisters with Anna Staehr, 1903.

STAFFORD, EDGAR
Active in Portland at 435 and 440 East Burnside, 1913-17.

STALEY, R. A.
Operated the Victor Studio in Baker, 1913-14.

STANLEY, A. B.
Active in Lone Rock, 1908-13.

STANLEY, R. A.
Active in Baker, 1915.

STANSELL, LELIE W.
Active in Jacksonville, 1914.

STANTON, EUGENE M.
Active in Portland, 1910-11; operating with his brother, R. Raymond, 1910.

STANTON, L. M. (MISS)
Member of the Oregon Camera Club; active in Portland, 1900.

STANTON, R. RAYMOND
Operated with his brother, Eugene M. in Portland, 1910.

STAR GALLERY
Operated by Templeton & Hume, Brownsville, c. 1867.

STAUFF, ERNEST A.
Active in Marshfield, c. 1910.

STEARNS, MAY
Active in Cove, 1912-17; partner in Stearns & Felbaum, 1917. Also spelled Mae.

STEGNER, CLOID
Active in Portland, 1913-15.

STEPHENSON, LOWELL H.
Active in Portland, 1906-08.

STERNBERG, OSCAR
Active in Eugene, 1910.

STEVENS, DAVID M.
Active in Portland, 1905-09; employed by the Kiser Photographic Company, 1905; in his own studio at 602 Goodnough Building, 1906-09. Listed as physician, 1910.

STEVENS, LESTER P.
Active in Portland at 501 Behnke-Walker building, operating the Columbia Commercial Studio with partner J. H. Gensler, 1916-17.

STEVENS, LOUIS J. (MRS.)
Member of the Oregon Camera Club; active in Portland, 1898-1900.

STEVENS MANUFACTURING COMPANY
Produced lantern slides in Portland, 1910-12. Operated by photographer Herbert A. Maddock, c. 1910; by William S. Hale, 1912. Also known as Enterprise Art Company.

STEVENS, NELLIE P. (MRS.)
Active in Portland at 602 Goodnough Building, 1910-11.

STEVENSON
Active in Ashland, 1915-17, operating as Hinthorne & Stevenson.

STEWART, GEORGE
Active in Langlois, 1903.

STEWART, JAMES H.
Active in Newberg, 1891.

STEWART, T. L.
Active in Fossil, 1901.

STITT, GEORGE W.
Active in Portland at 2 ½ Grand Avenue, 1910.

STOLTE, E. H.
Born in Hamburg, Germany, 1841; died in Portland, 1909. Active in Portland, 1872-82. Partner with Joseph Buchtel, one of Portland's most prolific studio photographers, operating as Buchtel & Stolte at 91 First Street, 1873-75.

STONE, C. B.
Active in Dallas, 1913-15.

STONE, E .J.
Active in Lakeview, 1913.

STONE, S. E.
Active in Portland.

STRATFORD, J. L.
Active in Creswell, 1911.

STRATFORD, JOSEPH C.
Active in Marshfield, 1901.

STRAUS, EDWARD
Active in Portland at 615 6th, 1904.

STRINGER, A. R.
Active in Portland, 1887.

STROLE, M. A.
Stereo photographer in Portland, c. 1905.

STRONG, GEORGE M.
Worked for the Portland Finishing Company in Portland, 1900-10.

STRUBLE, W. B.
Member of the Oregon Camera Club; active in Portland, 1905-17.

STRUKMAN, P.
Active in Ontario, 1898.

STRYKER, C. M. (MRS.)
Active in Corvallis, 1867-73, operating with her husband, David S., and H. M. Dohse as Stryker & Dohse on Main Street.

STRYKER, DAVID S.
Active in Corvallis, 1867-73, operating with his wife, Mrs. C. M., and H. M. Dohse as Stryker & Dohse on Main Street.

STUART, GEORGE E.
Active in Oregon City, 1887; Dayton, 1888-91.

STUBBS, C. L.
Partner with Herbert A. and Grace S. Hale, operating as H. A. Hale & Company, Portland, 1901.

STUDIO DE LUXE
Active in Portland at 23 Raleigh Building and 323 ½ Washington, 1910; operated by Alta, Marion, and Ida Newcomb.

STUDIO DELUXE
Active in Eugene at 29 West 10th, operated by C. A. Lare, 1910-17.

STURGESS, O. G.
Active in Medford prior to 1912, when he began operating the Vitax Studio in Chico, California.

STURTEVANT, A.
Active in Portland at 476 Washington, 1909.

SULLIVAN, CORNELIUS R.
Active in Portland at Clay and 76th, 1910-11.

SUNSET PHOTO COMPANY
Active in Portland at Grand Avenue and East Ankeney Street, 1910. Also known as Sunset Studio.

SUPERIOR GALLERY
Operated by Charles Fritz and Clark in McMinnville, 1891. Also known as Fritz Superior Gallery.

SUTPHEN, PERRY D.
Active in Portland at 510 MacLeay Building, 1910-17.

SUTTON, CORA A.
Active in Salem at 98 Court, 1901.

SWAIN, JOHN J.
Active in Portland, 1910-15.

SWEM, THOMAS M.
Active in St. Paul, Minnesota, 1888; Fargo, North Dakota, 1908(?); in Medford on the Payne Block, opposite Elks Lodge, 1909-21.

SWETT STUDIO
Operated by G. Robert Hubner in Portland at 719 Swetland Building, c. 1910.

SWOPE, M. A. (MRS.)
Active in Astoria, 1903-17; listed at 178 10th, 1911, operating the Up to Date Photo Studio.

SYKES, HORACE
From Newport; advertised his photographic equipment for sale in *Camera Craft*, 1912.

TALBOT, CHARLES B.
Born in Illinois, 1841; died in Portland, 1900. Active in Portland, 1865-68.

TALIAFERO, B. W.
Active in Portland, 1876-78; in Salem, 1878, partner in Cosper & Taliferro; in Walla Walla, 1879. Also spelled Taliferro.

TALIAFERO, JODIE (MRS.)
Active in Sumpter, 1907-15.

TAYLOR, FRED E.
Partner in Taylor & Morgan with Norris V. Morgan, Myrtle Point, 1907.

TAYLOR, JESSE F.
Active in Portland at 285 ½ First Street, 1904, 1910. Operated in Oregon City, 1907.

TAYLOR, MAMIE (MRS.)
Operated the Taylor Studio in LaGrand, 1905-07.

TAYLOR'S PHOTO TENT
Active in Roseburg, 1902.

TELFORD, RAY
Born September 1, 1882; died December 30, 1967. Amateur photographer in Colstin, 1901-06; Klamath Falls, 1906-45.

TEMPLETON & FOSTER
Partnership in Corvallis, 1867; J. H. Templeton.

TEMPLETON & HUME
Operated the Star Gallery in Brownsville, 1867.

TEMPLETON, J. H.
Active in Brownsville and Corvallis, 1867. Listed as Templeton & Foster in Corvallis; as Templeton & Hume, Star Gallery, in Brownsville.

TEN MINUTE POSTCARD MAN
Active in Portland at 796 Washington, 1910-15; Oregon City, at 6th North, 1916-23; 305 Buchanan Building, 1923-25; 607 Woodlark Building, 1927-30. Operated by Harry, Alvida, Charles E. and Grace E. Calvert. Also known as Calvert's Studio and City Park Gallery.

TENNERY & WHEELER
Carl S. Wheeler and Newton H. Tenneray, Pendleton, 1889.

TENNERY, NEWTON H.
Partner with C. S. Wheeler as Tennery & Wheeler, Pendleton, 1889.

TERWILLEGER, GEORGE W.
Active in Rainier, 1907.

TEUSCHER, MABEL A. (MRS.)
Retoucher for A. B. McAlpin in Portland, 1910.

THAYER, ALICE M. (MISS)
Member of the Oregon Camera Club; active in Portland, 1900.

THOMAS, ALBERT L.
Active in Newport, 1909-11.

THOMPSON & PAXTON
Partnership in Albany, 1867-68; A. B. Paxton.

THOMPSON, B. R.
Active in Monkland, 1889-91.

THOMPSON BROTHERS
Active in Eugene, 1917.

THOMPSON, HARRY
Photographer and barber in Cottage Grove, 1880-90.

THOMPSON, JAMES
Active in Prairie City, 1913.

THOMPSON, L. A.
Active in Moro until 1899.

THORNE, H. J. (MRS.)
Member of the Oregon Camera Club; active in Portland, 1909.

THORNE, H. J.
Member of the Oregon Camera Club; active in Portland, 1905-12.

THORNTON, A. C.
Member of the Oregon Camera Club; active in Portland, 1900.

THORNTON, C. F.
Active in Riddle, 1914-17.

THORNTON PHOTOGRAPHY
Studio in Portland at 203 Vine, c. early 1900s.

THRALL, SAMUEL A.
Member of the Oregon Camera Club; active in Portland, 1900-05.

THUM & MILLER
E. E. Thum and F. Miller, 246 Main, Portland, 1910-13.

THUM, EDWARD E.
Operated as Thum & Miller with partner Fred Miller at 246 Main, Portland, 1910-13.

THUMANN, HENRY, JR.
Operated the Pacific Film Company in Portland, 1910.

THWAITES & POTTER
Joseph Thwaites and J. L. Potter, stereo photographers in Salem and Portland, c. 1881. Also listed as Thwaite.

THWAITES, JOSEPH
Active in Portland, 1880-1903. Operated as Thwaites & Potter at Yamhill, between 4th and 5th, 1881. Also operated as Little Gallery Around the Corner and Thwaites & Potter's Little Gallery Around the Corner. Located at 167 First, 1886- 96; 187 4th, 1898; 133 ½ 5th, 1899-01. Studio in St. Johns, 1906-07; 22 Holbrook Block, 1907.

TIMSON, WILLIAM
Member of the Columbia Camera Club; active in Astoria, 1895.

TINKLE, F. B.
Active in Albany, 1895(?), operating Tinkle Photo Company. Located in Los Angeles, 1914.

TOKYOKAN, Y. TAKAGI
Active in Portland, 1904.

TOLLMAN, JOHN W.
Active in Omaha, Nebraska, 1885(?)-87; in Portland, 1899-02; operated the Tollman Studio at 312-313 MacLeay Building and 67 Labbe building, 1899. Operated in Klamath Falls, 1907; Boise, Idaho, 1908. He and his wife, Lulu, also operated the Tollman Studio, 1907-09. After they divorced, she continued to operate the business until she sold it to J. B. Anderson, late 1911; Anderson operated as Tollman Studio until 1917. See Washington.

TOLLMAN, LULU (MRS.)
Active in Portland, 1899; Eugene, 1907-11. Operated Tollman Studio with her husband, John W., 1907-09; divorced John W., 1909. She continued operating Tollman Studio with partner Catherine McHardy, 1909-11, operating as Tollman & McHardy; remarried in 1909, becoming Mrs. Lulu Ehrhardt.

TOLLMAN STUDIO
Active in Eugene 1907-17. Operated by J. W. Tollman and his wife, Mrs. Lulu Tollman, 1907-09; by Mrs. Lulu Tollman (Ehrhardt) and Catherine McHardy, 1909-11, and by J. B. Anderson, 1911-17. See John W. Anderson.

TOLLMAN, THOMAS W.
Active in Portland at 67 Labbe Building, 1901; in Spokane, 1907.

TOWNE
Gallery in The Dalles, 1915; also known as the Towne Studio.

TOWNE & MOORE
Partners Bertram C. Towne and Elbridge W. Moore took over the Portland gallery of William H. Towne beginning shortly after his death. They continued to operate as San Francisco Gallery, 1884-87. The studio on First Street was known as B. C. Towne Photograph Company, 1888-95.

TOWNE, BERTRAM C.
Active in Portland, 1884-95. Took over the San Francisco Gallery in Portland, after William H. Towne's death; operated with partner Elbridge W. Moore, 1884-87, also listed as Towne & Moore. Studio operated as B. C. Towne Photograph Company, 1888-95, in association with Lucy A. Towne, 1895, and Ralph W. Towne, 1893-95. It became one of the premier galleries in Portland, employing many of the best photographers in the area. Published boudoir format scenes of Alaska, the Columbia River, Mount Hood and other Northwest scenes.

TOWNE, C. C.
Active in Baker, 1917, operating the Towne Studio. Also listed as Townes.

TOWNE, LUCY A.
Active in Portland, 1895; associated with Bertram C. and Ralph W., at the B. C. Towne Photograph Company. Widow of William H. Towne.

TOWNE, RALPH W.
Active in Portland, 1893-95; associated with Bertram C., Lucy A., and William H. Towne, at the B. C. Towne Photograph Company.

TOWNE, WALTER E.
Active in Portland, 1903-05.

TOWNE, WILLIAM H.
Born 1835; died in Portland, November 1, 1884. Active in San Francisco, as operator for Bradley & Rulofson and I. W. Taber. Arrived in Portland, 1879, with Frank G. Abell, who became his first operator.

Towne's studio was located upstairs on First Street, corner of Morrison, known as the San Francisco Gallery, 1879-84. He purchased Buchtel's studio on First Street, 1880, and acquired Buchtel's negatives from which he made new prints to order. Hired Owen Gregory, formerly of J. F. Ryder's Gallery, as an operator, 1881.

TOWNER, H.
Partner of Henry H. and Eugene F. Hug, operating as Hug Brothers & Company in Elgin, 1909.

TOWNSEND, W. J.
Born 1849; died in Portland, September 26, 1906. Active in Portland. 1895(?).

TOWNSLEY, ISAAC M.
Operated as Townsley Photo Company in Portland at 87 Yamhill, 1885; in Astoria at 384 Commercial, 1901.

TRACEY, F. B.
Member of the Oregon Camera Club; active in Portland, 1909.

TRASK, S. E.
Active in Cascade Locks, 1895; Corvallis, 1890.

TRINE, VICTOR R.
Member of the Oregon Camera Club; active in Portland, 1913-17.

TROVER, HOWARD D.
Active in Salem, 1893-30s. Operated in the Eldridge Block, 1901-03; in the Cronise Studio, over the New York Rackett Store, 1905; in the Trover-Cronise Studio in the Eldridge Building, 1907-09; at 442 State, 1910-11. Operated the Trover-Weigel Studio at the same address with partner George H. Weigel, 1913-17. Married photographer Anna Cronise.

TRUMBULL, BERNARD H.
Member of the Oregon Camera Club; active in Portland, 1900.

TUCKER, DR. ERNEST F.
Member of the Oregon Camera Club; active in Portland, 1898-1900.

TUCKER, G. F. (MRS.)
Member of the Oregon Camera Club; active in Portland, 1898-1900.

TUCKER, HERMAN A.
Active in Myrtle Point, 1915; Wardner, Idaho, 1908-13.

TULL, IRENE
Active in Lakeview, 1909, operating with partner L. M. Davis as Davis & Tull; photographed Indians.

TURNER, GEORGE H.
Proprietor of the Eugene Art Store in Eugene, 1910-11; listed as photographer, 1911.

TURNER, I. S.
Active in North Yamhill, c. 1870-80s.

TURNEY, JOHN H.
Operated the New York Gallery in Oregon City at 5th, corner of Water, 1901-04.

TURNEY, JOHN P.
Born c. 1851. Active in McMinnville, 1876-80.

TUTTLE, J. E.
Operated the Tuttle Studio in Eugene at Patterson and Thirteenth, 1912-15.

TWEEDY, WILLIAM
Active in Salem at 343 ½ Commercial, 1913.

TYLER & MISER
W. L. Miser and Mae E. Tyler, Medford.

TYLER, G. H.
Active in Ashland, c. 1895.

TYLER, MAE E. (MRS.)
Active in Ashland, 1889-91; in Medford, operating as Tyler & Miser.

TYRELL, JAMES J.
Member of the Oregon Camera Club; active in Portland, c. 1890, 1904-17. Operating as Lussier & Tyrrell, c. 1890; also known as Elite.

U.S. PHOTO COMPANY
Itinerant in The Dalles area, 1892.

UGLOW, J. C.
Active in Dallas on the Wilson Block, c. 1900(?).

UMATILLA ART GALLERY
Active in Athena, 1901-03, operated by Lewis G. Pickel.

UNDERWOOD, ELMER O.
Member of the International Photographic Association; active in Dufur, 1913.

UNDERWOOD, J. L.
Active in Corvallis, operating as Conn & Underwood with partner R. E. Conn, 1891. Also operated in Albany, at 2nd and Ferry.

UNIQUE PORTRAIT COMPANY
Operated by John R. Cawthon in Portland, 1902-09.

UP TO DATE PHOTO STUDIO
Operated by Mrs. M. A. Swope in Astoria, 1903-17; located at 178 10th, 1911.

VAN DUYN
Partner in Park & Van Duyn. Also listed as VanDuyn.

VAN DUYN, FANNY
Active in Tygh Valley, 1907.

VAN DYCK STUDIO
Active in Portland, 1915-17, operated by Maude M. Hepburn.

VAN SCHUYVER (MRS.)
Member of the Oregon Camera Club; active in Portland, 1900.

VAN SCHUYVER, H. (MISS)
Member of the Oregon Camera Club; active in Portland, 1900.

VAN VLEET, ROY
Active in Bend, 1915-20s, operating the Elite Studio.

VAN WINKLE, ISAAC L.
Active in Culdesac, Idaho, 1905-07; Athena, 1913; Barlow, 1915.

VASSAR STUDIO
Active in Portland at 525 Abington Building 1913-15; operated by Vassar L. Northrup, 1913-14; by Albert E. Peasley, 1915. Continued at another location, known as The Peasleys, 1915-25.

VAUGHAN & HANSON
Jacob Hanson and John W. Vaughan, operating near River Bridge in

Eugene, 1889.

VAUGHAN, JOHN
Operated the Novelty Studio at 21 Breyman Building over Stockton's store, at 180 North Commercial, Salem, 1917.

VAUGHAN, JOHN W.
Born 1867. Active in Eugene, 1892-96; operated as Vaughan & Hanson near River Bridge, 1889. Listed in Kendrick, Idaho, 1901-02.

VENNER, J. F.
Active in Brownsville, 1881.

VERGEE, F. I.
Member of the International Photographic Association; active in Enterprise, 1912, producing postcards.

VICTOR, F. F. (MRS.)
Photograph colorist active in Portland, 1877.

VICTOR STUDIO
Operated by R. A. Staley in Baker, 1913-14.

VINSON, ANNIE
Died 1957. Active in Medford, 1911, operating with Pheba Vinson as the Vinson Sisters.

VINSON, PHEBA
Born in Langell Valley, Oregon, January 30, 1877; died 1960. Active in Medford, 1911, operating with Annie as the Vinson Sisters.

VOORHIES, AMOS E.
Born in Greenville, Michigan, 1869; died October 27, 1960. Active in Grants Pass, c. 1900, operating a photographic supply store. He was a prominent newspaper publisher for the *Rouge River Courier* and *Grants Pass Courier*, 1897- 1960.

WAGNER, CHARLES
Active in Portland, 1891-92; operated as Baechler & Wagner Brothers with his brother Louis Wagner and Charles Baechler at 776 Glisan.

WAGNER, FRANK G.
Born c. 1865. Active in Forest Grove, 1892; Portland, 1909.

WAGNER, HENRY
Member of the Oregon Camera Club; active in Portland, 1900-05.

WAGNER, LOUIS
Operated as Baechler & Wagner Brothers at 776 Glisan, Portland, with his brother Charles Wagner, and Charles Baechler, 1891-92.

WAKEFIELD, LELAND HOWARD
Born c. 1825. Active in Vermont, 1849; Kenosha, Wisconsin, 1850; also operated in Boston and New York. Listed in Canton House, Portland, 1852-53, in daguerreotype rooms taken over by Hendee. Advertised a price reduction on daguerreotypes, available for two weeks in Oregon City, 1853.

WALKER, JESSE M.
Active in Coquille, 1903-05.

WALKER, JOHN
Active in Fossil, 1915-17.

WALKER, JOHN A.
Active in Marshfield, 1907-13.

WALKER, RALPH C.
Physician, surgeon and amateur photographer, active in Portland,

1900. Member of the Oregon Camera Club.

WALKER, ROL.
Active in Bandon, 1913.

WALKER, WILL H.
Member of the Oregon Camera Club; active in Portland, 1898-1922.

WALLICK, JODIE (MRS.)
Active in Sumpter, 1903-05.

WALLIN, HERMAN E.
Active in Portland at 245 ½ Morrison, 1913.

WALLING, J. D.
Active in Salem and Pass Creek, 1880; located at Commercial Street between State and Court, operating as Smith & Walling.

WALTON
Active in Roseburg, operating as Walton's Picture Gallery, 1869.

WARD, THOMAS CHESTER
Active in Roseburg, 1886; Pendleton, 1889.

WARNER, DANIEL D.
Member of the Oregon Camera Club; active in Portland, 1900.

WARNER, HENRI
Stereo photographer in Applegate.

WARREN
Active in Portland, operating as Cawthon & Warren, c. 1885.

WARREN, E. C.
Active in Portland at 171 3rd, 1889.

WARREN, HENRY STEPHEN
Active in Portland, 1892-24; located at 388 East Morrison, 1896; 285 East Morrison, 1903-05; with Manley Warren, 2 6th North, 1909-10.

WARREN, MANLY
Active in Portland at 2 6th North with Henry S. Warren, 1910.

WARRENS, WILLIAM H.
Member of the Oregon Camera Club; active in Portland, 1900.

WASSERMAN, FRANK C.
Member of the Oregon Camera Club; active in Portland, 1898-1900.

WATERHOUSE, JAMES
Active in Seaside, 1911-13.

WATKINS BROTHERS
Active in Forest Grove, 1901.

WATKINS, CARLETON E.
Landscape and view photographer active in Oregon, 1867, 1882, 1884, making trips from San Francisco. Photographed Portland, Oregon City, Oswego, Columbia River, Dalles City, Celilo, and the Upper Cascades (57 large negatives and 136 stereographs), 1867. He produced his "new series" boudoir and stereoviews, 1882. Pictures produced during the trip in 1884 may not be Watkins' work. See California.

WATKINS, EVERETT W.
Active in Portland, 1910.

WATSON
Operated as Watson & Woodruff in Portland, 1916.

WATSON, CORNELIA A.
Born 1864; died 1930. Portrait photographer active in Lakeview, 1903-05. Also known as Mrs. Cornelia A. Knox.

WATSON, JOSEPH E.
Active in Portland at 225 ½ 1st Street, 1890-92. Also active in Oregon City, 1891. Operated as Watson's Photograph Gallery.

WATTS, JOHN E.
Active in Athena, 1891.

WEBB, H. & A.
Active in Dallas, c. 1890.

WEBB, HELEN M. (MRS.)
Active in Dallas, 1889.

WEBB, SUSIE E. (MRS.)
Active in Portland at 380 East Washington, 1903-04.

WEBSTER, FRANK H.
Active in Portland, 1910.

WEBSTER, H. D.
Member of the Photographer's Association of the Pacific Northwest; active in Wilbur, 1907.

WEDEKIND, HENRY
Active in Astoria at 583 Commercial with partner Thomas C. Bell, operating as Bell & Company, 1901-03. He operated alone in Astoria, 1905-15; 514 Bond, 1905; 520 Bond, 1907-11.

WEIDER, J. H. (MRS.)
Active in Eugene, 1901-03.

WEIGAND, E. MAGGIE (MRS.)
Active in Prineville, 1903; Corvallis, 1910-15. Located at 127 Second Street North, 1910. Operated with her husband, Ernest, 1911.

WEIGAND, ERNEST
Active in Corvallis with his wife, Mrs. E. Maggie Weigand, 1911.

WEIGEL, GEORGE H.
Partner with Howard D. Trover, operating as Trover & Weigel at 442 State in Salem, 1913-17.

WEILE, E.
Partner in Martin & Weile in Eugene, 1890-92. Also active in Pendleton.

WEISTER, GEORGE M.
Born in Pennsylvania 1862; died in Portland, 1922. Active in Portland, 1888-1922; photographer, salesman and manager with Partridge Photo Company, 1888-92; operating as Weister-Meek Company, 1893; as Weister Company or Weister & Company, 1895-1922; partner with Arthur M. Prentiss, 1913-16.

WEISTER-MEEK COMPANY
Operated by George Weister in Portland, 1893.

WELCOME STUDIO
Active in The Dalles, 1917.

WELLS
Operated the Wells' Art Gallery in Woodburn, 1900.

WELLS & HART
Partnership of H. A. Wells and H. L. Hart, Baker City, 1909.

WELLS, EBENEZER N.
Partner with Edgar L. Davidson, operating as Davidson & Wells, Oregon City, 1903-04.

WELLS, GLADYS
Active in Echo, 1917.

WELLS, H. A.
Partner with H. L. Hart, operating as Wells & Hart in Baker City, 1909.

WELLS, J. W.
Stereo photographer active in Ashland.

WELSH, J. O.
Operated as Abell & Welsh in Portland with Frank G. Abell, 1880.

WENDT, HENRY
Born October 14, 1875; died March 27, 1955. Worked as itinerant in south Oregon and northern California until 1905. Studio in Beiber, California, 1905-09; in New Pine Creek, 1909-36(?).

WENINGER, FRANK
Operated the Portland Portrait Company at 349 1st Street in Portland, 1904-10.

WERTZ, F. B. (MRS.)
Member of the Oregon Camera Club; active in Portland, 1900.

WESSINGER, PAUL
Born in Esslingen, Germany, 1859; died 1926. Member of the Oregon Camera Club; active in Portland, 1900-04.

WEST
Active in North Powder.

WEST, ORVIL W.
Member of the Oregon Camera Club; active in Portland, 1900.

WESTERN PHOTO STUDIO
Active in Portland in the Behnke Walker Building, 1914.

WESTON, E. D.
Active in Medford, 1913-17.

WESTROP
Itinerant in Vancouver, Washington and in Hillsboro, Oregon, 1876.

WEYRICH'S STUDIO
Active in Hillsboro at 27 and 29 West Main Street, c. 1895.

WHAITE, RENE
Partner in Bassett & Whaite at 384 State, Salem, 1913.

WHAITE, WILLIAM
Active in Portland, 1887.

WHEELER
Partner in Gibbs & Wheeler, Medford.

WHEELER, A. F.
Partner with S. E. Gray, operating as S. E. Gray & Company Photographic Gallery on Main Street, Corvallis.

WHEELER, CARL S.
Born in Mount Vernon, Iowa, 1862. Partner with Newton H. Tennery, Jr., operating as Tennery & Wheeler in Pendleton, 1889; purchased Pendleton Photo Company from J. A. McIntire and M. B. Harlow, 1891; listed alone, 1891-1917; located over the Post Office, 1894-95;

at Main, corner of Alta, 1899. Also active in Baker City, 1899.

WHEELER, LOUIS I.
Active in Sheridan, 1907; Bandon, 1915.

WHEELER, WARREN D.
Active in Astoria at 120 Olney, 1891.

WHEELON, FRANK H.
Active in Big Eddy, 1913; Seattle, Washington, 1928. Member of the International Photographic Association, 1913.

WHELAN, WILLIAM W.
Member of the Oregon Camera Club; active in Portland, 1898-1900.

WHITE, LILY E.
Born in Oregon City, Oregon. Studied art in San Francisco and Chicago, settling in Oregon, 1886. Active in Portland, 1899-24. Located at 348 4th, 1902; 616 Beck Building, 1910-24. Produced fine platinum prints of the Columbia River Gorge. She often worked with her friend Sarah Ladd, and both were members of the prestigious Photo-Secession.

WHITE, T. BROOK
Died 1914. Member of the Oregon Camera Club; active in Portland, 1903(?).

WHITE, THOMAS J.
Active in Portland, 1885-93. Located at 134 5th, 1885; at 5th opposite the Post Office, 1887; 166 5th, 1888-90.

WHITEAKER & HURD
Partnership in Independence, 1889-91.

WHITEAKER, WILLIAM H.
Partner in Whiteaker & Hurd, Independence, 1889-91. Also active in Monmouth, 1891.

WHITNEY, G. A. (MRS.)
Active in Corvallis, 1883.

WIDMER, WILLIAM W.
Born in Tennessee, May 7, 1882; died February, 1959. Active in Portland at 655 East Stark Street, 1915.

WIGGINS, MYRA ALBERT
Born in Salem, December 15, 1869; died in Seattle, 1956. Began photographing, 1880s; student with the Art Students League in New York City, 1891-94. Active in Salem, 1890-1907, spending summers in Newport; in Toppenish, Washington, 1907-32. She won major national photography exhibitions, was an acquaintance of Alfred Steiglitz, and was named an associate of Photo-Secession; perhaps Oregon's most important woman photographer.

WILCOX & CONN
Partnership in Albany at the corner of 2nd and Ferry Streets, 1891.

WILCOX, GEORGE L.
Active in Eugene, 1888; in Albany at the corner of 2nd and Ferry Streets, operating as Wilcox & Conn, 1891.

WILCOX, ROBERT
Active in Lexington, 1909-11.

WILDER, DIO D.
Active in The Dalles, 1897-1913; Portland, 1917-25. Operated the Elite Photo Studio located at 245 Alder, 1917.

WILDER, LYDIA E.
Active in The Dalles with Dio D. Wilder, 1901.

WILKINS, CHARLES
Active in Myrtle Point, 1888; Coquille, 1891.

WILL, J. M.
Active in Portland at 185 ½ Morrison, 1905.

WILLIAMS
Partner in Windsor & Williams, North Bend, 1915.

WILLIAMS & ROBINSON
Partnership in Brownsville, 1874.

WILLIAMS & WARREN
Stereo photographer in Salem, 1890s.

WILLIAMS, J. HALSEY
Active in McMinnville, 1910-11.

WILLIS, HUGH J.
Active in Salem on State Street between Commercial and Liberty, 1878-81.

WILSON, C. D.
Member of the International Photographic Association; active in Chitwood, 1908.

WILSON, FRED C.
Active in Astoria, 1911-23, operating as Wilson's Studio.

WILSON, I. N.
Active in Marshfield, c. 1887-90(?).

WILSON, J. B.
Active in Agate Beach, 1913.

WILSON, J. M.
Active in Alba, 1889-91.

WILSON, L. (MISS)
Member of the Oregon Camera Club; active in Portland, 1900.

WILSON, M. E. (MRS.)
Active in Medford, 1913.

WILSON, NELLIE (MRS.)
Active in The Dalles, 1901.

WILSON, SHEDDEN F.
Amateur active in Marshfield, 1887-89.

WIMBERLY, IRA
Active in Drain, 1913, selling photographic apparatus, material and supplies. Also spelled Wemberly.

WINCH, SIMEON R.
Born 1888; died 1946. Member of the Oregon Camera Club; active in Portland, 1905.

WINCHESTER, FRANK E.
Born c. 1832; died 1914. Active in Empire City, 1872-80; Walla Walla, Washington,1886-99.

WINDSOR & WILLIAMS
Partnership in North Bend, 1915.

WINDSOR, G. F.
Active in North Bend, 1911-15; operated as Windsor & Williams, 1915. Also listed as G. T. Windsor.

WINQUIST, DAVID
Active in Russellville, suburb of Portland, 1896.

WINTEMUTE, J. S.
Active in Ashland, 1895.

WINTER
Active in Jefferson.

WINTER, CLARENCE L.
Son of John A. Winter. Active in Eugene, 1891-1906. Partner with Sue Dorris, operating the Winter Photo Company, 1891; operated with his wife Frances, 1902-05. Active in Portland, 1911-17; associated with the Kiser Photo Company, 1911-14. Partner with F. P. Luetters in the Winter Photo Company, successor to Kiser Photo Company, 1917. Active in Vancouver, Washington, 1920-26.

WINTER, FRANCES D.
Active in Eugene with her husband, Clarence L. Winter, 1902-95.

WINTER, JOHN A.
Major studio photographer who produced some stereoviews, active in Eugene, 1867-86; purchased the studio of A. B. Paxton in Albany, 1868; in Brownsville, 1891. Father of Clarence L. Winter. Rented his Eugene studio, 1877, to Frank Abell of the San Francisco firm, Abell & Welsh.

WINTER PHOTO COMPANY
Active in Eugene, 1890s; Portland, 1900s. Operated by Clarence L. Winter and Sue Dorris, and by Clarence L. and Frances D. Winter.

WINTLER, MARION A.
Retoucher and photographer active in Portland, 1898-1925; employed by Johannes & Lum, 1909. Active in Vancouver, Washington, 1913.

WIRH
Active in Medford; operating as Noe & Wirth [sic] in Cottage Grove, 1895.

WISNER, ANNA (MISS)
Active in Oregon City, 1902-05.

WITTENBERG, FRED P.
Operated as the Portland Portrait Company in Portland at 349 1st Street, 1904-10.

WOLFE, G. M.
Member of the International Photographic Association; active in Quiniualt and Woodburn, 1912.

WOLLY, A.
Active in Hubbard, 1880.

WOMAN'S ART COMPANY
Active in Salem in the Fennel Building on State Street, 1910.

WOOD, FRANK W.
Partner with John C. Clark, operating as Clark & Wood in LaGrande, 1891.

WOOD, T. M.
Active in The Dalles, 1863; Walla Walla, Washington, 1866.

WOODARD, ALONZO BIXBY
Born in Batavia, Michigan, July 16, 1840; died in Olympia, Washington, April 1918. Active in Portland, 1862-66; employed by Hendee, 1863; by Buchtel & Cardwell, 1864; his own gallery at 5 Morrison Street, 1864. Woodard made a photography trip to Idaho with Hurd, 1866, and sold his gallery to Buchtel, his operator since 1865, when he returned. Woodard advertised a new gallery at 107 Front Street, 1867, but may not have conducted any business there, moving to Tumwater, Washington. See Washington.

WOODARD, CLARK & COMPANY
Employed photographers Charles Berthold and Samuel Hobson, 1907-08.

WOODFIELD, FRANK W.
Born in Astoria, July 17, 1879. Active in Astoria, 1910-42.

WOODRUFF, CHARLES S.
Active in Portland and Philomath, c. 1915-19. Operated as Woodruff & Jones, Watson & Woodruff, Watson & Raymond, Woodruff's Kodak School.

WOODWARD, W. F.
Member of the Camera Club; active in Portland, 1887.

WOOLSEY, FRANK
Active in Portland, 1887.

WORSLEY, B.
Active in The Dalles, 1876; partner with J. W. Worsley, operating as B. Worsley & Brother on Washington Street, next door to Brooks & McFarland's.

WORSLEY, J. W.
Active in The Dalles, 1873-76. With B. Worsley, operating as B. Worsley & Brother or Brothers, on Washington Street, next door to Brooks & McFarland's, 1876.

WRENSHALL BROTHERS
Howard D. and William C., operating in Bandon, 1903-07; also known as Wrenshall & Wrenshall.

WRIGHT, BURKE
Operated Wright's Studio in Sheridan, 1910-13; Willamina, 1911. Also spelled Burt.

WRIGHT, H. F.
Active in Milton.

WULZEN, ALBERT H.
Active in Portland, 1878-80. Hired by I. G. Davidson in 1878, because of his work accompanying Watkins on his photographic trip in Oregon, 1867. Wulzen's views are the finest published by Davidson, and he made a spectacular, six-print (8 ½" x 11") panorama of Portland. Owner of Pacific Art Gallery, a traveling studio operating out of Weaverville, California. See California and Traveling.

YOCUM & HAYES
Partnership of Henry C. Hayes and O. C. Yocum, Portland, 1886.

YOCUM & HOBSON
O. C. Yocum and S. Hobson, 4th between I and J, Portland, 1888.

YOCUM, OLIVER COOPER
Born in Springfield, Illinois, 1842; died in Portland, March 13, 1928. Active in East Portland, 1882-94. Photographer with I. G. Davidson, 1882; printer, 1883-84. Partner with Asel E. Severance, operating as Severance & Yocum, 1885; also known as North Pacific Photographic Printing & Engraving House, 1885. Partner with Henry C. Hayes, operating as Yocum & Hayes and Yocum Photograph Gallery, 1886. Partner with Samuel Hobson, operating as Yocum & Hobson at 4th between I and J, 1888. Worked with Mrs. A. M. Yocum at

1115 4th, operating as Yocum & Yocum, 1888.

YODER, FLORA
Printer with A. B. McAlpin in Portland, 1904.

YOUNG, F. A.
Active in Shaniko, 1902.

ZINSLEY, A. H.
Member of the Oregon Camera Club; active in Portland, 1909.

ZOLLNER, FRANK
Active in East Portland, 1890; Canby, 1901-11.

ZOOK, CAREY ANGUS
Studio in Portland, 1910-17. Located at 501 Beck Building, 1910; 525 Beck Building, 1913-17. He changed his name to Zook A. Carey, 1914.

ZUMWAIT, DON J.
From Klamath Falls; advertised elaborate photographic equipment for sale in *Camera Craft*, 1914.

Much of the information contained in this section was compiled by David Haynes of the Insitute of Texan Cultures, and published in Catching Shadows: A Directory of 19th Century Texas Photographers, *Texas State Historical Association, Austin, Texas, 1993.*

AARON, SYDNEY D.
Born in Arkansas, 1867. Artist-photographer in San Saba, 1900.

ABERNATHY
Active in Fort Worth, 1853; possibly M. L. Abernathy.

ABERNATHY, M. L.
Active in Alvarado, 1869; Fort Worth, 1870.

ABRAHAM, A.
Stereo photographer active in El Paso.

ACADEMY OF ART
Operated by Sequin, Cevor & Scott in Waco, 1886-87, 1898-99. Partnership of Charles W. Sequin, Charles E. Cevor and A. E. Scott; studio located on Austin at Seventh, 1886-87.

ACME STUDIO
Operated by Oswald Randau in Galveston.

ADAMS
Partner in Caswell & Adams, Goliad County, 1871.

ADAMS & HILL
Partnership of Samuel B. Hill and Adams operating in the Palm Building, Austin, 1878.

ADAMS, EARNEST
Born in Tennessee, 1876. Active in Alvarado, 1900.

ADAMS, ELIAS L.
Born in Ohio, 1861. Active in Greenville, 1900.

ADAMS, WILLIAM H.
Born in Ohio, 1866. Active in Greenville, 1896-1900.

ADDISON, GEORGE A.
Billed as the "Practical Photography" in Taylor, 1882-83; Georgetown, 1884-85; Nocona, 1896-97; Georgetown, 1898-99. Also spelled Addision.

ADGATE, THEODORE
Active in Austin and New Braunfels, 1866; McKinney, 1868. Possibly F. Aagate or F. Adgate.

ADKINS, NELLIE S.
Born in Illinois, 1862. Active in Port Lavaca, 1900.

AIKERS, WILLIAM F.
Active in Grandview, 1896-97, 1900.

ALBERT, A.
Active in Orange, 1884-85. Possibly A. Alberts who was reported in Ashtabula, Ohio, during the Civil War.

ALBRIGHT, G. J.
Active in Winnsboro, 1896-97.

ALEXANDER & GREEN
Active in El Paso, 1912, operated by Jim A. Alexander.

ALEXANDER, E. R.
Active in Ennis, 1878-79.

ALEXANDER, J. A.
Active in Wise County, 1872; Hunt County, 1874.

ALEXANDER, JIM A.
Active in El Paso, 1909-12, operating as Alexander & Green.

ALEXANDER, PINCKNEY C.
Active in Texarkana, 1890-92, 1896-97.

ALEXANDER, WILLIAM
Active in Grayson County, 1873.

ALISON, JOHN
Operator of Parker's Photograph Gallery, El Paso, 1886-87.

ALLEN & WHITFIELD
Partnership in Houston, 1846-47. Possibly Henry R. Allen and E. P. Whitfield.

ALLEN, EDWIN K.
Born in Texas; died in New Orleans, February 1898. Photographer; details unknown; died of an overdose of laudanum.

ALLEN, FLETCHER
Active in Kosse, 1898.

ALLEN, GEORGE R.
Born in Connecticut, c. 1831. Listed as an artist in Williamson County, 1850; photographer or painter.

ALLEN, HENRY R.
Active in Houston, 1845-46; also operated as Houston Daguerreian Gallery. Possibly a partner in Allen & Whitfield.

ALLIN, R.
Born in Maryland, c. 1840. Active in Marshall, 1860. Possibly B. Allin.

ALLISON, J. L.
Active in Presidio, 1893-95.

ALRED, JAKE
Born in Kentucky, c. 1855. Active in Paris, 1880.

AMEN, M.
Born in Virginia, c. 1835. Photographer or painter active in Galveston, 1860.

ANDERSON
Partner in Hillyer & Anderson active in Williamson County, 1867; partner in Barrett & Anderson, Falls County, 1875.

ANDERSON & BENNETT
Active in Columbus, 1870-71.

ANDERSON & BICKEL
Partnership in Galveston, 1854-55; possibly Samuel Anderson and William C. Bickel.

ANDERSON & BLESSING
Partnership of Samuel Anderson and Samuel T. Blessing operating in Galveston, 1851-60. Studio located at Twenty-third between D and E, 1859-60. They operated a gallery in New Orleans at 120 Canal Street during the same period.

ANDERSON & COMPANY, C. B.
Operated by Charles B. Anderson in Dallas, 1893-98. Studio at 400 Elm, 1894; 398 Elm, 1896-97; 372 Elm, 1898.

ANDERSON BROTHERS
Charles B. and William H. Anderson; studio in Dallas, 1889-92.

ANDERSON, C. R.
Born in Washington (D.C.?), 1869. Active in Houston, 1900.

ANDERSON, CHARLES B.
Born in Kentucky, 1857. Partner in Anderson Brothers, active in Dallas, 1889-92; operated C. B. Anderson & Company, 1893-98; portrait copy dealer, 1900.

ANDERSON, EDWARD
Born in Texas, 1877. Active in Austin, 1900.

ANDERSON, JOHN
Active in Caldwell County, 1866. May be the J. S. Anderson reported in Racine, Wisconsin, during the Civil War.

ANDERSON, LOUIS
Active in Upshur County, 1871.

ANDERSON, SAMUEL
Born in Pennsylvania, 1825. He owned a studio in New Orleans, 1848-c. 1884, with partner Samuel T. Blessing, at 120 Canal Street. The partners also operated a studio in Galveston, 1851-60; located at Center and Post Office, 1851-54; Twenty-third between Avenues D and E, 1859-60. Anderson sold his interest in the Galveston studio to John P. Blessing, 1857; left for Europe at the beginning of the Civil War, returning before it ended. After the studio in New Orleans burned, c. 1884, he opened gallery in Houston, operating c. 1884-1901, or later. Studio was located at 85 Main, 1887-92; 403 ½ Main, 1892-1901.

ANDERSON, THOMAS B.
Partner in Anderson Brothers with William H., active in Dallas, 1889-92; operated Southwestern Portrait Company, photographic enlargers, 1893-94.

ANDERSON, WILLIAM H.
Partner in Anderson Brothers with Thomas B., active in Dallas, 1889-92; operated Southwestern Portrait Company, photographic enlargers, 1893-94.

ANKENMAN & BUTLER
Active in Mason, c. 1890. Possibly N. Ankenman and M. L. Butler.

ANKENMAN, NICHOLAS
Born in Canada, 1848. Immigrated to U.S., 1868. Active in Austin, 1887-98; at 200 East Sixth, corner of San Jacinto, 1889-90; 202 East Sixth, 1890-91; 818 and 903 Congress, 1892. Worked as retoucher for Samuel B. Hill, 1895-96; operated as Austin Photo Engraving Company, 1897-98. Active in Mason, 1900.

ANSLEY & TINKEL
Cary D. Ansley and Frank B. Tinkel active in Denison, 1892.

ANSLEY, CARY D.
Born in Georgia, c. 1851. Active in Denison, 1889-1900. Studio at 201 West Woodard, 1889; operated as Blue Gallery, 1889-90; at 201 North Austin, 1891-94; partner in Ansley & Tinkel, 1892; at 521 West Main, 1896-97; 523 West Main, 1899-1900; also listed in Grayson County, 1900 Census.

ANSLEY, ROBERT
Active in Denison, 1892.

ANSLEY, W. T.
Active in El Paso, 1912.

ANSLEY, WILLIAM
Born in Georgia, 1861. Active in Denison, 1900.

ANTHONY & HILL
Partnership of Milton M. Anthony and Eugene Hill in Marshall, 1892.

ANTHONY, MILTON M.
Born in Alabama, 1858. Active in Longview, 1890-1900; also a partner in Anthony & Hill in Marshall, 1892.

APEL, EDWARD
Active in Dallas, 1894-96; photographer or painter.

ARCHER & COMPANY
Operated by John R. Archer in Houston, 1884-85, at 130 Texas.

ARCHER, JOHN R.
Managed the New York Photographic Company in Houston, at 85 Main, 1884-85; also operated as Archer & Company, 1884-85, at 130 Texas.

ARD, JOHN W.
Born in Illinois, 1863. Active in Dallas, 1900.

ARKNA, ALFORD
Born in Illinois, 1874. Active in Dallas, 1900.

ARMSTRONG, MARTIN
Born in Illinois, 1855. Active in Velasco, Brazoria County, 1896-97, 1900.

ART GALLERY
Operated by John H. Flett in Galveston, 1884-85, at 221 Post Office.

ART SALOON
Studio operated by Adolphe F. Gouhenant, Dallas' first daguerreotypist, 1852.

ARTHUR, H. D.
Active in Saltillo, Hopkins County, 1896-97.

ARVIN & WRIGHT
Partnership in Lewisville, 1870.

ARVIN, JAMES A.
Born in Virginia, 1838. Active in Limestone County, 1873-76; Mexia, 1878-1900.

ASBERRY, C.
Active in Clarksville, 1847.

ASHBURY, STEVE
Active in Winnsboro, 1890-91.

ASHFORD, PENNY M.
Born in Missouri, 1882. Assistant photographer in Kendall County, 1900; daughter of Theodicia.

ASHFORD, THEODICIA
Born in Kentucky, 1864. Active in Kendall County, 1900.

ASHLEY, THOMAS
Operated Ashley's City Gallery in Houston on Main between Preston and Prairie, 1866.

ASHLEY'S CITY GALLERY
Operated by Thomas Ashley in Houston, 1866, on Main between Preston and Prairie.

ASKEW & GLENN
Partnership of Samuel R. Askey and T. H. Glenn, active in Tyler, 1872.

ASKEW, SAMUEL R.
Born in Texas, c. 1851. Active in Tyler, 1870; Smith County, 1871-72; partner in Askew & Glenn, 1872.

ATCHINSON, A. W.
Active in Grayson County, 1875.

ATKINSON, G. W.
Active in Navarro County, 1876.

ATKINSON, GEORGE W.
Born in Alabama, 1848. Active in Plano, 1890-92, 1896-97; Garland, 1898; Plano, 1900.

ATTWOOD, MYRTLE (MISS)
Active in El Paso, 1905.

AUBREY, CHARLES
Active in Walnut Springs, 1890-91.

AUERBACH, R.
Active in Abbott, 1896-97.

AULTMAN, OTIS A.
Active in El Paso, 1907-1943.

AUSTIN
Born in Illinois, c. 1858. Active in Luling, 1880.

AUSTIN, HUGH A.
Active in Alvarado, 1890-92.

AUSTIN, J. V.
Active in Dallas County, 1873.

AUSTIN, JOHN O.
Active in Bonham, 1856-57; advertised his services in Paris, Lamar County, and at McCown's store, March 1856.

AUSTIN PHOTOGRAPH COMPANY
Studio operated by Stone & Waggoner in Houston, 1866; W. D. Stone and possibly W. T. Wagner. Sold out to William James Oliphant, November 1866.

AUTREY, G. D.
Active in Hico, 1884-85.

BACKSTROM, ALEXANDER D.
Active in Moody, c. 1885; Temple on Sixth at Avenue D, 1892.

BACON & COMPANY, J. H.
Operated by James H. Bacon in Austin, 1866.

BACON, JAMES H.
Active in Baltimore, 1858-60; operated in Austin as J. H. Bacon & Company, 1866.

BADE, J.
Active in Cuero, 1882-83.

BAECKER, JULIUS
Operator for Bushong & Feldman at their St. Louis Street studio in El Paso, 1898-99.

BAILEY & HAND
F. B. Bailey and Hiram Hand in Houston on Main, 1856-57; Also operated as Bayou City Ambrotype Rooms.

BAILEY & TERRY
Possibly Frank B. Bailey and Anderson F. Terry, active in Palestine, 1884-85.

BAILEY, E. N.
Partner with Charles R. Blackburn, operating as Blackburn & Bailey in Houston, 1895-98, at 1008 ½ Prairie.

BAILEY, FRANK B.
Born in South Carolina, c. 1830. Partner in Bailey & Hand in Houston, 1856-57, also operating as Bayou City Ambrotype Rooms. Active in Navasota, 1870-72; Palestine, 1878-83; partner in Bailey & Terry, 1884-85; possibly a partner of R. E. Moore.

BAIN, J.
Active in Clarksville, 1848.

BAIR, JOHN
Listed in Lee County, 1874-76; may be John Pair or Pain. Also listed as Biar.

BAIRD, C. W.
Active in Chicago, 1887; Dallas, 1894.

BAKER (MRS.)
Active in Clarksville, 1854.

BAKER & LEACH
Partnership of Don M. Leach and possibly Raymond Baker, stereo photographers in Austin, 1860s-70s.

BAKER & RAYMOND
Photographers in Austin during the Civil War era; operated a drug store, published almanacs and sold photographic supplies, 1860s.

BAKER, LAWSON
Born in North Carolina, c. 1830. Active in Corpus Christi, 1860; reported in Massachusetts and Rhode Island, 1870s.

BAKER, RAYMOND
Active in Austin, 1860-70.

BAKER, W. A.
Born in Texas, 1873. Active in Calvert, 1900.

BAKER, W. H.
Active in Floresville, 1890-91.

BAKER, WILLIAM C.
Active in Clarksville, 1848; operator for Blackburn & Bailey in Houston, 1895-96.

BALDWIN & SNODGRASS
Partnership in Cass County, 1873.

BALL & SOUBY
Active in Jefferson, 1866. Possibly Bell & Souby or Ball/Bell & Sowby; may have been a partner in Chinn & Sowby.

BALLARD, C. B.
Active in Bee and Goliad Counties, 1876; possibly C. E. Ballard.

BANCROFT, EDDY
Born in Pennsylvania, c. 1864. Active in Sherman, 1880.

BANKS, THOMAS
Born in Texas, 1865. Active in Pearsall, 1900; listed in the census as black.

BANKSTON, ANDREW J.
Born in Texas, 1877. Active in Clay County, 1900.

BANKSTON, EMMET C.
Born in Georgia, 1879. Active in Clay County, 1900.

BANNIFER, W. H.
Active in Fayette County, 1873.

BANTA
Partner in Janes & Banta operating in Fayette County, 1871-72.

BARBE, C. G.
Born in England, 1853. Immigrated to U.S., 1870. Listed in Center, 1900.

BARDIN, G. M.
Born in Kentucky, c. 1859. Active in Dallas, 1880.

BARKER, CORNELIA
Born in Texas, 1863. Active in Brady, 1900.

BARKER, M. W.
Active in Austin, 1858-60; possibly a partner with W. B. Clark operating as Clark & Barker in Columbus, 1858.

BARKS, J. F.
Stereo photographer active in Houston after 1860.

BARNES, PETER BENJAMIN
Born in Maryland, 1852. Active in Floresville, 1896-97, 1900.

BARNUM, P. C.
Active in Dallas, 1877; photographer or painter.

BARR & WRIGHT
Partnership of David P. Barr and Charles J. Wright, active in Houston, 1870-80. May have had more than one studio, 1870-78, listed at Main and Preston, and Main and Congress.

BARR, DAVID P.
Born in Ohio, 1839. Reported in Mississippi during the Civil War, and in Illinois and Kentucky, 1870s. Active in Houston, 1870-80; partner in Barr & Wright; in San Antonio, 1881-1900. Studio at 283 West Commerce, 1881-84; 5 Acequia, 1884-85, 1887-92, 1896-97; 401 West Commerce, corner of Acequia, 1885-86; 103 Main, corner of West Commerce, 1894-96, 1897-1900.

BARRETT & ANDERSON
Active in Falls County, 1875.

BARRETT, CLARA M.
Born in Texas, 1882. Active in Huntsville, 1900.

BARRETT, JOHN H.
Active in Falls County, 1875, partner in Barrett & Anderson; in Waco, 1882-87. Studio at 53 ½ Austin, 1882; on Fifth, near Austin, 1884-85. Active in Pittsburg, 1892. Reported in Illinois, 1886, 1896. May be the same person as John H. Barrot.

BARRETT, THOMAS K.
Born in Texas, 1853. Active in Huntsville, 1900.

BARRON, RUSSELL J.
Born in New York, 1838. Active in Terrell, 1884-85, 1890-92, 1898-99; partner with William M. Shreves, operating as Shreves & Barron, 1884-85. In Longview, 1896-97; Dallas and Trenton, 1900.

BARRY, A.
Active in Crockett, Houston County and Palestine, 1869.

BARSANTEE & DUGGAN
Active in Brazoria County, 1874. May be Bassantect or Barsantee Dugen.

BARTHOLD, A.
Active in Rusk County, 1867.

BARTLETT & HOOKER
Frederick W. Bartlett and F. S. Hooker, in Galveston, 1868-69; studio at 159 East Market.

BARTLETT, FREDERICK W.
Born in Virginia, c. 1840. Active in Galveston, 1866-83. Operated as Lone Star Photographic Gallery, 1866-70; partner in Bartlett & Hooker, 1868-69. Studio at 159 East Market, 1870-74; on Twenty-second between Market and Post Office, 1875-76; at 174 Twenty-second, 1876-79; 221 and 223 Post Office, 1882-83.

BARTLETT, JESSE C.
Managed the branch studio of Harper & Company in Houston, 1899-1900.

BARTLETT, K. P. L.
Active in Galveston County, 1874.

BARTON, W. E.
Active in Wharton County, 1872. Possibly W. E. Barlow.

BASS, ALBERT A.
Active in Terrell, 1896-97.

BATES, JOHN S.
Born in Ohio, c. 1853. Active in Dallas, 1875, 1878-80; studio at 101 South Houston, 1875. Partner with Jesse C. Downing in Downing & Bates, 1878-79. Worked for A. C. Dayton Miller, 1884-85; for James R. Davis, 1886-87.

BATH, WILLIAM
Active in Pulaski County, Arkansas, 1860; Virginia, 1870s. Active in Dallas, 1877.

BATTERS, W. F.
Active in Click, Llano County, 1892, 1896-97.

BAUDRESSU & COMPANY, A.
Active in Corpus Christi, 1867.

BAUER, C.
Active in Columbus, Ohio during the Civil War; in Eagle Pass, Texas, 1870.

BAUM, GEORGE C.
Born in Mississippi, 1859. Active in Whitesboro, 1884-85, 1890-92, 1896-97, 1900.

BAXTER & COMPANY
Association of E. Frank DeZalba, John F. Russell, and Henry G. Baxter operating in Beaumont, 1892.

BAXTER, HENRY G.
Operated as Baxter & Company in Beaumont, 1892; firm included E. Frank DeZalba and John F. Russell.

BAXTER, S. D.
Active in Matagorda County, 1874.

BAXTER, WILLIAM
Born in Kentucky, 1867. Active in Harrison County, 1900.

BAY & WRIGHT
Stereo photographers in Houston, c. 1870s-90s; C. J. Wright.

BAYOU CITY AMBROTYPE ROOMS
Operated by Bailey & Hand in Houston, 1856-57.

BAYS, DAVIS HENRY
Itinerant tent photographer and Mormon missionary based in Bandera, 1879.

BEACH & MEEK
Partnership of Frank E. Beach and Walter H. Meek, operating in Houston, 1897-98, at 409 Travis.

BEACH, ALBERT L.
Active in Eagle Pass, 1892.

BEACH, FRANK E.
Active in Lampasas, 1892; Florence, 1896-97; partner in Beach & Meek, 1897-98; in Houston, 1899-1901, at 409 Travis.

BEACH, GEORGE
Born in Texas, 1875. Active in Liberty County, 1900.

BEAN
Active in Corsicana, 1860-61; possibly Charles N. Bean.

BEAN, CHARLES N.
Located in Vicksburg, Mississippi during the Civil War; active in Houston, 1866-68, Main at Preston. Possibly operated the Houston City Gallery.

BEARD, JOE R.
Born in Texas, 1869. Active in Sutton County, 1900.

BEAUMAN, GEORGE A.
Born in Texas, 1871. Active in Robert Lee, 1900.

BECKMANN, AUGUST
Born in Texas, 1853. Active in San Antonio, 1870.

BEDFORD, THOMAS J.
Born in Texas, 1863. Active in Dallas, 1889-1900. Partner with Carl P. Miller, operating as Miller & Bedford, 1900. Studio at 947 Main, 1889-91; 345 Elm, 1893-94; 504 Elm, 1894-96; 304 Elm, 1897.

BEDLMEYER, HENRY
Born in Germany, 1864. Active in Lavaca County, 1900.

BEEMAN, GEORGE
Born in Texas, 1872. Active in Sterling City, 1900.

BEHN, ADOLPHUS
Active in La Grange, 1847; possibly G. A. Behne.

BEHNE, G. A.
Born in Germany, c. 1825. Active in Columbus, 1860; possibly Adolphus Behn.

BELL
Possibly a partner in Bell & Souby; also listed as Ball & Souby, Ball/Bell & Sowby; active in Jefferson, 1866.

BELL & COMPANY, C. H.
Studio in Lockhart, 1859.

BELL, CHARLES
Born in New York, c. 1832. In Illinois, 1854. Active in Corpus Christi, 1860. Partner in Morrill & Bell in Indianola, Calhoun County, at Main and Fannin, 1860.

BELL, EUNICE
Born in Texas, 1878. Active in Stephens County, 1900.

BELLAIR
Partner in Morgan & Bellair, Wood County, 1871.

BENEKE, WALTER C. A.
Born in Wisconsin, 1880. Active in Howard County, 1900.

BENNETT
Partner in Anderson & Bennett in Columbus, 1870-71.

BENNETT & BURRALL
Partnership of George C. Bennet and Arthur Burrall in Bexar County, 1876; in San Antonio, 1877-78, located on Soledad between Commerce and Houston. They were operating in Santa Fe, New Mexico, 1878.

BENNETT & COLLINS
Partnership in Liberty, 1869.

BENNETT & GEORGE
Active in Galveston, 1869.

BENNETT, A. F.
Operated in Evans Point, Hopkins County, 1890-91. Also active in Leadville, Colorado, 1889, 1900, 1901.

BENNETT, COLONEL A. S.
Stereo photographer in San Antonio, 1940s.

BENNETT, GEORGE C.
Partner in Bennett & Burrall with Arthur Burrall in Bexar County, 1876; in San Antonio, 1877-78; Santa Fe, New Mexico, 1878; operated alone or with William Henry Brown in Santa Fe, 1878-83.

BENNETT, WALTER L.
Born in Texas, 1871. Active in Cleburne, 1898-1900.

BENTLEY, WILLIAM T.
Born in Georgia, 1851. Operated in Ohio, 1886-98, before locating in Atlanta, Texas, 1900.

BERGERON, J. P.
Active in Paris, 1898-99.

BERGSTROM, JOHN LOUIS
Active in Waco, 1890-95; studio at 502 ½ Austin, 1890-92; 503 ½, 1892-95. Photographed the Great Crush Collision, September 16, 1896; later worked for the Central Electric Company.

BERKELEY
Partner in Wright & Berkeley in Washington, 1857.

BERNARD, OSCAR C.
Active in El Paso, 1901-12.

BERNER, GEORGE H.
Born in Tennessee, 1866. Active in Austin, 1900.

BERRY, B. W.
Stereo photographer in Dallas; partner in Berry, Kelley & Chadwick, major publisher of stereoviews, c. 1906-15. Also worked alone and in other partnerships.

BERRY, KELLEY & CHADWICK
B. W. Berry, E. W. Kelley, publishers of stereoviews in Dallas; issued views by photographers E. W. Kelley and William H. Rau, c. 1906-15. Listed over 5,000 views in their catalog.

BEVERLY, ALBERT
Born in Texas, 1881. Brother of Ardell. Active in Galveston, 1900; listed in census as black.

BEVERLY, ARDELL
Born in Texas, 1877. Brother of Albert. Active in Galveston, 1900; listed in census as black.

BICHNELL, W. P.
Born in Pennsylvania, c. 1825. Active in Galveston, 1850.

BICKEL, WILLIAM C.
Partner in Meguire & Bickel in Houston, 1851; Meguire may have been a dentist. Partner in Anderson & Bickel in Galveston, 1854-55, possibly with Samuel Anderson.

BIGNEY, JAMES
Born in Nova Scotia, c. 1825. Artist in Rusk County, 1850; may have been a painter, possibly James Bigney Wheeler.

BILES, MAY
Born in Texas, 1881. Active in Pittsburg, 1900.

BILLOWS, ALFRED R.
Born in England, c. 1838. Active in Ottawa, Illinois, 1872. Photographer for James R. Davis in Dallas, 1880-81; for William McClellan, 1881-82. Continued active in Dallas, 1883-89, 1898-99. Listed at 705 Main, 1886-89.

BINGHAM, HENRY L.
Born in Ohio, c. 1835. Active in Kalamazoo, Michigan, 1867-72. Operated in Bexar County, Texas, 1874-75; in San Antonio, 1877-80. Studio on Commerce between St. Mary's and the river, 1877-78.

BIRDS
Partner in Yarbrough & Birds, Gillespie County, 1872.

BIRKLAND, CATHERINE
Partner with Mrs. Fannie B. Travis, operating as Travis & Birkland in Dallas, 1886-87, 1898-99. Studio at 505 Main, 1886-87. Partner in Al D. Burk & Company, Fort Worth, 1888-89; studio on Rusk at East First. Also known as Mrs. O. D. Birkland.

BIRT, GEORGE O.
Active in El Paso, 1903-12.

BLACK & LOWRY
Partnership of A. E. Black and John Lowry; Black was also a blacksmith, and Lowry a music teacher; active in Cannon, Grayson County, 1884-85.

BLACKBURN
Partner in Holladay & Blackburn, Gonzales County, 1872.

BLACKBURN & BAILEY
Charles R. Blackburn and E. N. Bailey active in Houston, 1895-98, at 1009 ½ Prairie.

BLACKBURN, CHARLES R.
Born in Mississippi, 1860. Worked for Charles J. Wright in Houston, 1890-95; worked alone, 1899-1901+.

BLACKBURN, DAVID E.
Partner in Snell & Blackburn in Cameron, possibly with William H. Snell, 1892; also listed alone in Brenham, 1892.

BLACKBURN, JOHN E.
Worked for Blackburn & Bailey in Houston, 1895-96.

BLACKWELL, ELLA (MRS.)
Active in Fort Worth, 1884-85, at 1108 Houston.

BLAGG, JOSEPHUS S.
Born in Texas, 1870. Active in Cuero, 1896-97; Bastrop, 1900. Possibly Josephus E. Blagg.

BLAIR, JOHN E.
Active in Fort Worth, 1884-85, at 508 Houston; in Fort Worth, 1885-87, 108 Main; in Farmersville, 1890-91; Dallas, 1891-92, at 502 Elm; in Fort Worth, 1898-99.

BLAIR, WILLIAM J.
Born in Bell County, Texas, 1856. Active in Lancaster, 1880; Gatesville, 1890-92, 1896-1900.

BLAKE & CHENAULT
Partnership in DeWitt County, 1871.

BLAKE, L. S.
Born in Georgia, c. 1843. Active in Huntsville, 1880.

BLANCHARD, ARTHUR L.
Born in New York, 1853. Active in Hillsboro, 1896-1900.

BLAYLOCK, J. W.
Active in Tyler, 1897, at East Ferguson, near I & GN Depot.

BLESSING & BROTHER
Operated in Houston, 1866-68, 1870-71. Located at Main between Congress and Preston, 1866; 92 Main, 1868; Main and Congress, 1870-71. Studio in Galveston, 1868-83; located at 178 East Post Office, 1868-69; 180 Tremont, 1870; 174 Tremont, 1871-79; 170 Twenty-third and 170 Tremont, 1882-83.

BLESSING & BROTHER, J. P.
John P. Blessing and Solomon Thomas Blessing in Houston, 1867-69; at 59 Main, 1867.

BLESSING & COMPANY
Located in Galveston, 1872, staffed by photographers Louis Eyth and Philip H. Rose.

BLESSING & COMPANY, J. B.
Listed in Houston, 1870-80. Probably J. P. Blessing.

BLESSING & PATRICK
Possibly John P. Blessing and T. G. Patrick; active in Houston during the Civil War.

BLESSING & ROSE
Partnership of Solomon Thomas Blessing and Philip H. Rose in Galveston, 1878-79, at 174 Tremont.

BLESSING, JOHN P.
Born in Pennsylvania, c. 1832. Partner in Blessing & Kuhn and Blessing & Fenge in Baltimore, Maryland, 1882-1904; in Brownsville, Maryland, 1899-1901. Partner in Blessing & Brother, Blessing & Patrick, J. P. Blessing & Brother. Active in Houston, 1870; Harris County, 1871.

BLESSING, JOHN T.
Born in Maryland, c. 1837. Active in Houston, 1870; Garland, 1892.

BLESSING, SAM C.
Active in Dallas, 1898-1900; also listed as S. T.

BLESSING, SAMUEL T.
Born in Maryland, c. 1832; died in St. Louis, Missouri, 1897. Partner in Anderson & Blessing in Louisiana, 1856-63; active in La Grange, 1856; partner with Anderson in Galveston and Houston. Worked for Smith and Tucker, a supply house, 1863-69.

BLESSING, SOLOMON THOMAS
Born in Pennsylvania, c. 1840; died in Dallas, 1928. Active in Galveston, 1870, 1898-99. Associated with Blessing & Brother, Blessing & Rose, Blessing's Photographic Gallery, and J. P. Blessing & Brother.

BLESSING'S PHOTOGRAPHIC GALLERY
Probably the same business as Blessing & Brother; it was run by Solomon Thomas Blessing in Houston, 1866-67. Listed at Main, Van Alstyne's building, 1866; at 92 Main, 1867.

BLISARD, THOMAS
Active in Houston, 1892-93, in a tent at 1006 Willow.

BLOUT, JOHN
Active in Upshur County, 1900.

BLUE GALLERY
Operated by Cary D. Ansley in Denison, 1889-90.

BLUNT, W. B.
Active in Hunt County, 1875.

BOARMAN, C.
Active in Greenville, 1870.

BODDY BROTHERS
Edward V. and William J. Boddy in Lufkin, 1896-97.

BODDY, EDWARD
Partner in Boddy Brothers active in Lufkin, 1896-97; operating alone in New Mexico, 1907-26.

BODDY, WILLIAM J.
Partner in Boddy Brothers in Lufkin, 1896-97.

BOEHM, L.
Active in Fayette County, 1883.

BOGGS, R. L.
Born in Tennessee, 1872. Active in Terrell, 1900; possibly R. L. Buggs.

BOGLE, JAMES P.
Born in Alabama, 1851. Active in Decatur, 1900.

BOLDDON, JOHN W.
Listed in Mason County, 1884; Del Rio, 1890-91. Possibly John W. Boldon.

BOLIE, FREDERICK O.
Active in San Antonio, 1892-93, located on Pinto at San Luis.

BOLIN, HALE W.
Born in Iowa, 1879. Listed in Honey Grove, 1900.

BOLIN, T. J.
Active in Grayson County, 1879; Denison, 1880. Also listed as Thomas Boten.

BOLTON & MITCHELL
T. C. Bolton and T. E. Mitchell, active in San Antonio at 134 or 134 ½ West Commerce, 1894-97.

BOLTON, F. G.
Active in Galveston County, 1874.

BOLTON, THOMAS C.
Active in McLennan County, 1872. Studio in Galveston, 1874-76; Twentieth Street at Post Office, 1874; 161 Market, 1875-76. Operated in Bryan, 1878-79; Denison, 1882-83. Studio in El Paso, 1885-89; located on Oregon between San Antonio and Texas, 1886-87; at 319 El Paso, 1888; 213 El Paso, 1889. Also in New Mexico, 1885. Partner in Crowell & Company with Arthur B. Crowell, El Paso, 1886-87. Possibly a partner in Bolton & Mitchell, San Antonio, 1894-97.

BOLTON, THOMAS C. (MRS.)
Active in El Paso, 1890-92.

BOMAR, SPENCER E.
Born in Texas, 1873. Active in Sherman, 1900.

BOND, J. M.
Active in Carthage, 1870.

BOND, J. W.
Active in Sabine County, 1873.

BONDURANT, JAMES
Born in Alabama, 1867. Listed in San Antonio, 1900.

BONITTA, MACK
Active in El Paso, 1909-10.

BONITTA, ROSA (MRS.)
Active in El Paso, 1911-12.

BONNER, J. WHITMILL
Born in Texas, 1851. Active in Quanah, 1892, 1896-97, 1900.

BONNER, WILLIAM J.
Active in Paris, 1884-85.

BOONE, JAMES H.
Itinerant in Marshall, 1852.

BOONE, WALTER H.
Born in Virginia, 1875. Listed in Clarendon, 1900.

BOREL, M. (MISS)
Studio in San Antonio, 1895, at 1307 West Commerce Street.

BOREL PORTRAIT COMPANY
San Antonio firm at 1307 West Commerce, c. 1895-1900; Miss M. Borel was involved with the company, 1895; Joseph F. Solsona may have been associate, c. 1900.

BORKLUND & MOORE
Partnership of Eric Borklund and Robert E. Moore in Dallas (Oak Cliff) on Lancaster between Ninth and Tenth, 1891-92.

BOSLEY, JAMES L.
Active in Gainesville, 1884-85.

BOSTON ART COMPANY
Active in El Paso, 1900, operated by Claud E. Guivey at 217 Stanton.

BOUD, N. E.
Born in Kansas, 1866. Listed in Denton, 1900.

BOUNDS, H. W.
Active in Mesquite, 1896-97.

BOURGES, EMILE
Born in the West Indies, c. 1811. Listed in 1850 census as a "grocer and artist" in Galveston; as a photographer located on Post Office in Mr. Brock's house, 1851. Partner in FitzGibbon & Bourges, with branches in Houston and Austin, 1851; partner in FitzGibbon, Bourges & Stanley in Galveston, and Stanley, FitzGibbon & Bourges in Houston, late 1851-52.

BOYD, CHARLES S.
Born in Pennsylvania, 1877. Listed in Bonham, 1900.

BOYD, FRANKE
Born in Pennsylvania, 1871. Active in Bonham, 1900.

BOYD, JOHN D.
Born in Mississippi, 1853. Active in Pittsburg, 1884-85, 1896-1900.

BOYD, P.
Active in Gilmer, 1866-67; Jefferson, 1869; possibly F. or T. Boyd.

BOYETT, E. W.
Active in Breckenridge, 1890-91.

BRACK & GIBSON
Asa A. Brack and B. M. Gibson operating in San Antonio at 113 North Alamo, 1897-98.

BRACK & RABA
Asa A. Brack and Ernst Raba active in San Antonio at 113 North Alamo, 1894-96.

BRACK & WATKINS
Partnership of Asa A. Brack and his brother-in-law, Willis M. Watkins, c. 1886; active in Beeville, San Antonio and El Paso. Also listed as Brach & Watkins.

BRACK, ASA A.
Born in Kentucky, 1862. Moved to Texas with his family, settling in Goliad, 1872. He was a confectioner's apprentice in Goliad, later a farmer in Karnes County. Learned photography from Frank Hardesty in San Antonio, c. 1884, working as an itinerant in south Texas. Partner with his brother-in-law, Willis M. Watkins, 1886. Brack bought out Hardesty, 1889. Partner in Brack & Raba, 1894-96; Brack & Gibson, 1897-98. Studio was located at 32 North Flores, 1890-92; 126 North Flores, 1892-93; 113 North Alamo, 1896-1900 and later.

BRACKEN, W. J.
Born in Texas, c. 1845. Active in Anderson County, 1871, 1874-75; Henderson County, 1875; Wharton County, 1880. Possibly W. G. Bracken or W. Y. Bracken.

BRACTON, P. L.
Operating in Eastland County, 1892.

BRADLEY, THOMAS
Active in Henderson County, 1874.

BRADSHAW, W. M.
Active in Hubbard, 1896-97.

BRADY, I. T.
Active in San Antonio at 229 East Houston, 1897-1900.

BRADY, J. S.
Active in Clio, Brown County, 1884-85.

BRANIM, LEOSIS
Born in Russia, 1862. Immigrated to U.S., 1883. Active in Brazoria County, 1900.

BRASHERS, MILLS
Born in Missouri, c. 1854. Listed in Little Elm, 1880.

BRAUNIG, HENRY JACOB
Born in Meyersville, DeWitt County, 1861; died 1945. Learned photography from Pius Fey in Cuero, c. 1878, and began working with him June 1878; the firm was known as Fey & Braunig, c. 1882-1909. Braunig opened a studio in Hallettsville, 1887-1909; located on the square, 1895.

BRIDGERS, WILLIAM W.
Born in North Carolina, c. 1833. Active in Austin, 1856-58, 1860-61; may have been active in Lampasas, summer 1858. Studio was located opposite Oliphant's Jewelry Store, 1858.

BRIDGES, W. W.
Active in Montgomery County, 1872. Possibly Bridger or Bridgers.

BRIGGS, JAMES B.
Born in Tennessee, 1849. Active in Coleman County, 1900.

BRIGHT, F. S. D.
Born in Kentucky, c. 1838. Active in Corsicana, 1869; Cleburne, 1870; Collin and Denton Counties, 1873. Possibly L. S. D. or T. S. D Bright.

BRINK & COMPANY, J. F.
Partnership listed in Bexar County, 1871.

BRITAIN, P. L.
Bought the studio of M. S. Lusby in Canyon, 1913 or 1917.

BRITTINGHAM & SAWYER
John G. Brittingham and Clifford E. Sawyer; gallery at 808 Main Street, Fort Worth, 1890-91.

BRITTINGHAM, JOHN G.
Active in Galveston, 1881-82, 1896-97; at 174 Twenty-third, 1881-82. Employed by Philip H. Rose in Galveston, 1882-83; in Illinois, 1884, 1886, 1891, 1900; partner in Brittingham & Sawyer, 1890-91.

BROADWAY, WILLIAM M.
Born in North Carolina, 1844. Active in Navarro County, 1873-76, 1880; Corsicana, 1878-79; Hubbard, 1890-92, 1896-97. Listed in Hill County, 1900.

BROCK, A. A.
Active in San Antonio, 1870-80.

BROCK, J. W.
Active in Cherokee County, 1871.

BRODIE, G. A.
Active in Comanche, 1898; possibly the same as J. A. Broidey.

BROMOWICZ, FRANCIS
Active in Laredo on Grant and Convent, 1890-92, 1896-97.

BROOKS, JOHN W.
Born in Texas, c. 1822. Active in Cameron, 1870.

BROOKS, M. A.
Active in Anderson County, 1871.

BROWN & CHAPMAN
Active in Wharton County, 1872.

BROWN & GALWAY
Active in Lee County, 1874.

BROWN & SON, N.
Nicholas and William Henry Brown; worked in New Mexico and Mexico, 1866-72; in Maverick County, Texas, 1873.

BROWN, ALFRED M.
Born in Missouri, 1863. Listed in Wise County, 1900.

BROWN, BAULDWIN
Born in Tennessee, 1875. Listed in Boyd, 1900.

BROWN, DAVID
Active in Mason County, 1871.

BROWN, FANNIE (MRS.)
Clerk for Francis F. Parker in El Paso, 1886-87; operator, 1889. Also known as Mrs. William Henry Brown. See New Mexico.

BROWN, HARRY C.
Active in El Paso, 1902.

BROWN, HENRY M.
Active in Galveston at 1905 Market, 1890-91.

BROWN, J.
Active in El Paso, 1898-99.

BROWN, J. C.
Operating in Bastrop County, 1874-75; also in Travis County, 1875.

BROWN, JAMES
Born in Tennessee, 1832. Active in Fort Worth, 1900.

BROWN, NICHOLAS
Partner in N. Brown & Son with William Henry Brown operating in New Mexico and Mexico, 1866-72; in Maverick County, Texas, 1873. Listed alone in Marshall, 1884-85, 1890-91, 1895, 1898-99.

BROWN, WILLIAM HENRY
Died in El Paso, 1886. Partner in N. Brown & Son with Nicholas Brown in New Mexico and Mexico, 1866-72; listed alone in El Paso, 1885. See New Mexico.

BRUCE & GRIFFIN
Thomas J. Bruce and Joseph K. Griffin, operating in Atlanta, 1882-83.

BRUCE, THOMAS J.
Born in Arkansas, 1856. Active in Linden, 1880; partner in Bruce & Griffin, Atlanta, 1882-83; in Marshall, 1892, 1896-97, 1900; Mineola, 1898-99; partner of Harry O. Corti, 1900.

BRUCE, WILLIAM M.
Born in Arkansas, c. 1845. Active in Marshall, 1866-80.

BRUNEKE, WALTER
Born in Wisconsin, 1880. Listed in Thurber, 1900.

BRUTON, JONAH
Born in Texas, 1874. Active in Clarksville, 1900.

BRYAN, ERNEST
Born in Alabama, 1868. Active in Elgin, 1900.

BRYAN, H. H.
Active in Elgin, 1896-97.

BRYANT, CHARLES N.
Born in Kentucky, c. 1857. Listed in Cooper, 1880.

BRYANT, WILLIAM
Born in Indiana, 1870. Active in Dallas, 1900.

BUCK, D. R.
Active in Canton, 1868.

BUCK, W. E.
Active in Clarksville, 1858.

BUCKINGHAM, FLOYD
Born in Texas, 1877. Listed in Dublin, 1900.

BUDY, FRANK E.
Born in Texas, 1867. Listed in census as "Proprieter Photograph," in Houston, 1900.

BUFFALO PHOTO GALLERY
Operated by E. K. Sturdevant in San Antonio, 1885-88; in Seguin, 1892; Galveston, 1893-94; San Antonio, 1898-99.

BUGGS, R. L.
Born in Texas, 1876. Active in Terrell, 1900. Possibly R. L. Boggs.

BULGER & HUBERT
Active in Kendall County, 1872.

BULLOCK, W. M.
Listed in Tyler, 1870; Hallsville and Upshur County, 1871; Rusk County, 1875. Possibly W. W. Bullock.

BUMGARNER, M. J.
Active in Fairy, Hamilton County, 1892.

BUNGHURST, GEORGE R.
Associated with Blessing & Brother in Houston, 1866.

BUNNELL, JESS R.
Born in Texas, 1874. Active in Rhome, 1900.

BUNNELL, WALTER A.
Born in Kansas, 1868. Active in Decatur, 1890-92, 1900; also listed in Eastland County, 1891; in Hillsboro, 1896-97.

BUNSE, CONRAD
Born in Prussia, c. 1829. Listed in San Antonio, 1870.

BUQUOR, J. OSCAR
Active in El Paso, 1903-13.

B

BURDSAL, CLAYTON W.
Active in Texarkana, 1896-97.

BURG, W. H.
Active in Galveston at 220 Tremont, 1868-69.

BURGE, J. C.
Born c. 1839; died 1897. Operated in Arizona, 1881-84; New Mexico, 1885-91. Active in El Paso, 1895-96; also known as Burge Art Parlor.

BURGE, ROBERT
Born in Ohio, 1838. Active in Ohio, 1874; Fort Worth, 1896-1900. Studio at 1005 Main, 1896-97. Also listed in Van Alstyne, 1900.

BURGESS & BUTLER
A. Burgess and C. W. Butler in Corpus Christi, 1860; studio at Water and William.

BURGESS, A.
Active in Peachtree, 1859; wrote to John A. Lloyd that he took nine photographs, but local residents were resistant; told of explosion of ammonia bottle and resulting injuries. Partner in Burgess & Butler, Corpus Christi, 1860.

BURGESS, BENJAMIN
Active in Dallas, 1893-94.

BURGESS, WILLIAM
Born in Missouri, 1862. Listed in Spanish Fort, Montague County, 1900.

BURK & COMPANY, AL D.
Partnership of Al D. Burk and Mrs. Catherine Birkland, operating in Fort Worth, 1888-89; studio on Rusk at East First.

BURN, W. L.
Active in El Paso, 1905.

BURNETT, C. G.
Active in Johnson County, 1872.

BURNS, WARREN
Born in Texas, c. 1850. Active in Cooper, 1880.

BURRALL, ARTHUR
Partner in Bennett & Burrall in Bexar County, 1876; in San Antonio, 1877-78; Santa Fe, New Mexico, 1878.

BURTON, C.
Active in Brazoria County, 1871.

BURTON, MATTHEW C.
Born in Kentucky, c. 1852. Active in Galveston, 1870.

BURTON, W. C.
Active in Matagorda County, 1871.

BUSH, EFFIE A.
Listed in Llano County, 1900.

BUSHONG & FELDMAN
Partnership in El Paso, 1897-1901; John C. Bushong and Frederick J. Feldman. Studio located at 111 South El Paso, 1898-1900.

BUSHONG, JOHN C.
Leased his studio in El Paso to Frederick J. Feldman, 1895, and went east to study photography. Became partner with Feldman upon his return, and operated studio 1897-1901; sold out to Feldman, 1901.

BUTLER, A. H.
Active in Fayette and Walker Counties, 1872.

BUTLER, C. W.
Partner with A. Burgess, operating as Burgess & Butler in Corpus Christi, 1860; studio at Water and William.

BUTLER, J. E. (MRS.)
Active in Eastland, 1892.

BUTLER, M. L.
Born in California, 1855. Listed in the 1900 census as a female photographer in Mason. Possibly a partner in Ankenman & Butler, 1890.

BYRD, W.
Active in Plano, 1878-79.

CADERAN, A. W.
Stereo photographer in Bonham.

CADMAN, A. N.
Active in Illinois, 1855, 1867-84. Active in Bonham, 1890-91.

CADWELL, AARON W.
Born in Illinois, 1843. Twin of Moses Caldwell. Active in Fayette County, 1870-76; operated alone, 1870-71; partner with Moses, 1872-76.

CADWELL, FRED B.
Born in Texas, 1880. Son of Moses Cadwell. Active in Fayette County, 1900.

CADWELL, M. & A. W.
Partnership of twin brothers, Moses and Aaron W. Cadwell, operating in Fayette County, 1872-76; also known as Cadwell Brothers, 1876.

CADWELL, MOSES
Born in Illinois, 1843. Twin of Aaron W. Cadwell and father of Fred B. Cadwell. Listed in Fayette County, 1870; partner with Aaron, 1872-76. Operated alone in Fayette County, 1885; Flatonia, 1890-92, 1896-99.

CALAHAN, H. C.
Born in Alabama, 1860. Listed in Polk County, 1900.

CALAWAY, C. N.
Active in Red River County, 1872. Possibly Alonzo Newell Callaway.

CALDWELL & SPAGLIAM
Partnership of Charles H. Caldwell and H. D. Spagliam in San Augustine County, 1873.

CALDWELL, CHARLES H.
Born in Alabama, c. 1842. Active in San Augustine County, 1871, 1873; also partner in Caldwell & Spagliam, 1873; in Beaumont, 1880.

CALDWELL, J. R.
Active in Jefferson, 1865-66; San Augustine County, 1871-72; possibly J. B. Caldwell.

CALDWELL, WILLIAM M.
Active in Paris, 1891-92, at 204 Bonham.

CALLAWAY & PETERSON
Alonzo Newell Callaway and possibly Conrad Peterson in Columbus, 1876.

CALLAWAY, ALONZO NEWELL
Born in Montgomery, Alabama, 1847. Came to Texas while a young man, served in the Confederate Army in Louisiana and fought in the Battle at Mansfield. Active in Waller County, 1874; Austin County, 1875; in Columbus, 1876, as partner in Callaway & Peterson; became sole proprietor in November, and sold out to John H. Chapman, spring 1877. Active in Brenham, 1878-79, 1882-83, operating the Fine Art Gallery; in San Antonio, 1885-1900. Studio at 413 or 413 East Houston, 1885-1892; 511 ½ East Houston, 1892-1900. Working in Tyler, c. 1910.

CALVAR, FRANK
Active in El Paso, 1911-13. Also listed as Francisco Calvarusso.

CALVIN, ROBERT
Born in South Carolina, 1845. Active in Denton, 1890-91; Fort Worth, 1900.

CAMMEL, R. H.
Born in Texas, 1867. Listed in McKinney, 1900.

CAMMEL, W. M.
Born in Tennessee, 1852. Active in McKinney, 1900.

CAMPBELL, JOHN P.
Active in New Jersey, 1855-60; Maryland, 1859-60. Active in Port Sullivan, Milam County, 1867-68; in Bryan, 1870.

CANDER, JOHN
See John Carter.

CANFIELD, E. H.
Born in New York, 1831. May have learned photography in Louisiana, 1860, working through Texas until 1862; continued in Wisconsin until c. 1881.

CARADINE & CUMMING
Partnership of James B. Caradine and Charles Menzies Cumming in Navarro County, 1876; billed as "Artist-Photographers" in Sherman and Corsicana at North Travis between Pecan and Houston, 1878-79. Also spelled Carradine.

CARADINE, JAMES N.
Born in Mississippi, 1845. Active in Grayson County, 1879, 1881; listed in Sherman on North Texas Street, 1880, 1882-94, 1898-1900; in Honey Grove, 1892; McKinney, 1896-97. Also listed in Hillsboro, 1900.

CARLYLE & SMITH
William Carlyle and partner in Tyler, 1867.

CARNAHAN & COMPANY
Active in Mount Pleasant, 1870.

CARPENTER
Partner in Wheddon & Carpenter, Texarkana, 1878-79.

CARPENTER, THOMAS H.
Active in Louisiana, 1865-67. Active in Sherman, 1876-79; on North Travis between Houston and Pecan, 1876-77; on Houston between Travis and Walnut, 1878-79. Listed in Grayson County, 1879-80; Sherman, 1882-91; at 106 South Crockett, 1887-88. Active in Bowie, 1892, 1896-97, 1900; Sherman, 1898-99.

CARR, ROBERT
Active in Maverick County, 1873.

CARRELL, J. F.
Active in Carlisle, Rusk County, 1892, 1896-97.

CARRICO, THOMAS
Born in Texas, c. 1877. Active in Bexar County, 1900.

CARSON & IRVIN
Miss Eddie Carson and Miss Oma Irvin, photographers in Crawford, 1896-97.

CARSONS, JOHN
Born in Louisiana, 1876. Partner with Sam W. Cooper in Port Arthur, 1900.

CARTER, HOWELL
Born in Texas, 1874 . Active in Longview, 1900.

CARTER, JOHN
Born in England, 1866. Immigrated to U.S., 1878. Active in Illinois, 1875. Listed in Luling, 1890-92, 1896-1900. Also listed as John Cander.

CARTWELL, W. A.
Listed in Johnson County, 1873-74; Tarrant County, 1876.

CARTWRIGHT, SHELLEY
Born in Texas, 1882. Listed as apprentice photographer in Glenwood, Tarrant County, 1900.

CASEY, ANDREW F.
Born in Mississippi, 1846. Active in Cisco, 1884-85, 1890-92, 1896-1900; in Eastland County, 1894-95.

CASEY, ROBERT H.
Active in Ellis County, 1876; in Fort Worth on Houston at Weatherford, 1878-79.

CASIDY, JOHN
Born in England, c. 1836. Active in Ennis, 1880. May be J. T. Cassidy.

CASLEY & HARINGTON
Partnership of Charles H. Casley and W. David Harrington in Nacogdoches, 1896-97.

CASLEY, CHARLES H.
Born in Illinois, 1867. Partner in Casley & Harington, Nacogdoches, 1896-97; listed alone, 1900.

CASSADAY, WILLIAM J., JR.
Worked for William J. Cassaday, Sr. in Waco, 1896-99; worked as printer after 1898.

CASSADAY, WILLIAM J., SR.
Active in Waco, 1890-1901. Listed at 106 ½ North Third, 1890-91; 122 ½ South Third, 1892-97; 121 ½ South Third, 1898-1901.

CASSADY & CRADER
Partnership in Eastland County, 1894.

CASSELL, OLIVER
Born in Indiana, 1845. Active in Houston, 1900.

CASSIDY, J. T.
Listed in Austin County, 1872; may be John Casidy.

CASWELL & ADAMS
Partnership in Goliad County, 1871.

CASWELL, C. B.
Active in Goliad, 1866; Gonzales, 1867; Corpus Christi, 1869.

CATER
Partner in Harper & Cater in Austin before 1860. W. W. Bridgers, successor.

CATRON, THOMAS B.
Partner in W. G. Walz & Company, dealing primarily in photographic supplies in El Paso, 1898-1900.

CAWKER, VICTOR
Born in Canada. He learned photography at age fourteen in St. Catharines, Ontario; worked in galleries in Paris and London, Ontario, then moved to Michigan. Active in Fort Worth, 1885; in Gainesville at Elm and North Dixon in the Hemming Building, 1887-88.

CAYLOR, JACOB L.
Active in Rockwall, 1867. Possibly a partner in Morphis & Caylor, Bonham, 1868; listed in Bonham, 1870, 1882-85.

CAYTON, JOHN P.
Active in Groesbeck, 1884-85, 1890-92, 1896-97.

CEVOR, CHARLES E.
Partner in Sequin, Cevor & Scott, operating the Academy of Art in Waco, 1886-87, 1898-99. Studio on Austin at Seventh, 1886-87.

CHADWICK
Stereo photographer in Dallas; partner in Berry, Kelley & Chadwick, major publisher of stereoviews, c. 1906-15. Also worked alone and in other partnerships.

CHAFFIN, J. H.
Active in Bowie, 1890-91.

CHALKLEY, HENRY G.
Active in San Antonio at 34 West Commerce, 1891-92.

CHALMERS & WILLIAMS
Partnership of Richard L. Chalmers and Jesse B. Williams, operating in Dallas at 913 Elm between Sycamore and Ervay, 1888-89.

CHALMERS, RICHARD L.
Born in South Carolina, 1867. Employed by William B. Mahon in Dallas, 1886-87; operating alone in Dallas, 1889-95. Listed at 913 Elm, 1889-91; 304 Elm, 1891, 1893-95; 345 Elm, 1891-92. Active in Bowie, 1895-96; Corsicana, 1900.

CHAMBERS, J. B.
Active in Brownwood, 1898.

CHAMBERS, JAMES
Advertised as cabinetmaker in Matagorda, 1851, stating that his building included daguerrean rooms; uncertain whether he was also a photographer.

CHAMBERS, JOHN
Born in Texas, 1870. Listed in Abilene, 1900.

CHANAY, E. C.
Born in Wisconsin, 1867. Listed in Winnsboro, 1900.

CHANAY, ELLA
Born in Texas, 1869. Listed in Winnsboro, 1900.

CHANDLER, WILLIAM M.
Born in Alabama, 1842. Active in Belton, 1892, 1898-99; Bell County, 1900.

CHAPMAN
Partner in Brown & Chapman, Wharton County, 1872; listed alone in Mason County, 1886.

CHAPMAN & WILLIAMS
Partnership in San Marcos, 1898-99.

CHAPMAN, ANDREW
Active in Houston, 1889-90, at 135 Congress.

CHAPMAN, E. V.
Listed in Austin County, 1876; may be E. N. Chapman.

CHAPMAN, FRANK
Born in England, 1852. Immigrated to U.S., 1880. Active in Sweetwater, 1884-85; Houston, 1900.

CHAPMAN, J. E. H.
Active in Hays County, 1887; Fayette County, 1894; San Antonio, 1898-99.

CHAPMAN, JOHN H.
Born in Texas, c. 1856. Successor to Alonzo Newell Callaway in Columbus, March 1877-80.

CHARLES, JAMES C.
Born in Ireland, 1864. Immigrated to U.S., 1884. Partner in Cozby & Charles, Lockhart, 1892; listed in Val Verde County, 1900.

CHATHAM, PERRY
Born in Texas, 1876. Listed in Waco, 1900.

CHENAULT
Partner in Blake & Chenault, DeWitt County, 1871.

CHERRY & WEATHERINGTON
Charles W. Cherry and John W. Weatherington in Decatur, 1884-85.

CHERRY, CHARLES W.
Active in Fort Worth on Houston between Fifth and Sixth, 1883-84; partner in Cherry & Weatherington in Decatur, 1884-85.

CHERRY, GEORGE R.
Active in Fort Worth, 1883-84.

CHESSEL, MADE
Born in France, c. 1844. Listed in San Antonio, 1870.

CHILDRESS, GUILDFORD B.
Born in Alabama, c. 1834. Active in Nacogdoches County, 1880; Timpson, 1892, 1896-97.

CHILDRESS, WILLIE
Born in Alabama, c. 1861. Painter or photographer listed in Nacogdoches County, 1880.

CHINN & SOWBY
Partnership in Jefferson, 1867. May be Souby.

CHIPMAN, ALICE L.
Born in New York, 1876. Listed in Childress County, 1900.

CHIPMAN, UVA
Born in Michigan, 1882. Active in Childress, 1900. Possibly Una Chipman.

CHISHOLM, C. P.
Born in Tennessee, 1868. Listed in Montague County, 1900.

CHRISTIAN, WILLIE
Born in Texas, 1879. Active in Galveston, 1900; listed in census as African-American.

CHRISTOPHER, J. D.
Active in Lampasas County, 1876.

CHUKINGER, WILLY
Born in Texas, 1872. Active in Fayette County, 1900.

CHURCH, CLIFTON
Born in Massachusetts, 1855. Active in Dallas at Elm and Murphy or 278 Elm, 1891-1900.

CHURCHILL
Partner in Wilson & Churchill, San Antonio, 1866.

CHURCHILL (MRS.)
Active in Indianola, 1852; her husband was a portrait painter and they were known for giving musical performances together.

CHURCHILL & WEST
John R. Churchill and John C. West in Brownwood, 1896-98.

CILIAZ, HERMAN
Active in New Braunfels, 1870. Possibly the same as Herman Celiaz or Ciliax.

CLAMPET, JO W.
Born in Tennessee, 1867. Listed in Trenton, 1900.

CLAPMAN, J.
Born in France, 1861. Immigrated to U.S., 1884. Active in Mineral Wells, 1900.

CLARK
Partner in Newton & Clark, operating in Temple, 1898-99.

CLARK & BARKER
W. B. Clark and possibly M. W. Barker, operating in Columbus, 1858.

CLARK, ELLEN E. (MRS.)
Active in Babyhead, Llano County, 1890-91.

CLARK, F. M.
Active in Rains County, 1871.

CLARK, W. B.
Partner in Clark & Barker, Columbus, 1858; operating alone in La Grange, 1859; Winchester, Fayette County, 1866.

CLARY & ROOT
John W. Clary and Melville E. Root, operating in San Antonio at 415 East Houston, 1883-84.

CLAY, G. B.
Active in Falls County, 1876.

CLEASBY, E. W.
Active in Galveston County, 1874; Brazos County, 1875; Galveston, 1875-77; also listed in Lee County, 1876. Located at Post Office between Twentieth and Twenty-second, 1875-76.

CLEFF, BERRY
Listed in Eagle Pass, 1896-97.

CLEGHORN
Partner in Smith & Cleghorn active in Kosse, 1871.

CLEGHORN, J. T.
Born in Georgia, c. 1845. Listed in Calvert, 1870.

CLEVELAND & OLIVE
William Cleveland and partner in Victoria at 207 West Forrest, 1900-01.

CLEVELAND, WILLIAM
Born in Texas, 1872. Active in Victoria, 1900; partner in Cleveland & Olive, 1900-01.

CLIFFS
Born in England, 1881. Immigrated to U.S., 1885. Listed in 1900 census as female photo finisher in Houston.

CLIFT, W.
Born in Arkansas, 1869. Listed in Grayson County, 1900.

CLIFTON, L.
Active in Kaufman, 1868, 1872.

CLINE, EMMA M.
Born in Tennessee, c. 1842. Active in Palestine, 1870; wife of Isaac Cline.

CLINE, ISAAC
Born in Virginia, c. 1824. Active in San Antonio on Commercial Row, over Stith and Burn's grocery, 1856-57. Listed in Anderson County, 1860.

CLINE, R. W.
Born in Anderson County, c. 1863. Listed in Lancaster, 1880.

CLOY & McCLURE
Godfrey B. Cloy and George McClure, active in Marlin, 1884-85.

CLOY, GODFREY B.
Partner in Cloy & McClure in Marlin, 1884-85; listed in Groesbeck, 1890-91; continued alone in Marlin, 1890-92, 1896-97.

CLOYD & MAXWELL
Active in Sherman, 1867; possibly Marcus D. L. Cloyd.

CLOYD, MARCUS D. L.
Active in Sherman, 1866-68; possibly a partner in Cloyd & Maxwell, 1867.

CLOYD, T. J.
Active in McKinney, 1867-70.

COBB, BENJAMIN
Active in Dallas, 1876-81; possibly employed by James R. Davis, 1876; worked for Davis, 1878-79.

COBB, WILLIAM F.
Born in Kentucky, 1869. Listed in Fort Worth, 1900; partner with George D. Wakely in McKinney, 1896-97, operating as Wakely & Cobb.

COCHRAN, HAL A.
Partner in Griffith & Cochran with Arthur W. Griffith, operating in Austin at 904 Congress, 1898-99.

COCKRELL, THOMAS J.
Active in Laredo, 1890-92.

COCKRUM, BEATRICE
Born in Texas, 1881. Listed in Holland, 1900.

COFFEY, ROBERT S.
Active in Galveston on Market, 1892.

COFFMAN, W. E.
Born in Texas, 1867. Active in Mason, 1898; San Saba, 1900.

COHEN, L. L.
Born in South Carolina, c. 1835. Active in Calvert, 1870.

COLE
Active in Plano, 1895.

COLLINS
Partner in Bennett & Collins, active in Liberty, 1869.

COLLINS, HENRY M.
Born in Louisiana, 1865. Listed in Sherman, 1900.

COLLINS, JOHN W.
Partner with David D. Dare, operating as Dare & Collins Art Store in San Antonio, 1883-84. Located at 42 West Commerce.

COLLINS, MARY (MRS.)
Born in Ohio, c. 1815. Active in Galveston, 1859; Port Lavaca, 1860.

COLLUM, MILAM
Born in Texas, c. 1830. Listed in Palo Pinto County, 1860.

COLUMBIA SKY-LIGHT GALLERY
Operated by Park & Holmes in Columbia, 1858-59; possibly Charles Holmes.

COMON, C. S.
Active in Blanco County, 1874.

CONGER, JAMES L.
Born in Texas, c. 1855. Active in Hood County, 1880; Dawson, 1882-83.

CONNER, HENRY T.
Active in McKinney, 1892, 1896-97; Sherman, 1900.

CONNER, WILLIAM
Born in Missouri, c. 1861. Listed in Mason County, 1880.

CONOLY, CLAY C.
Active in San Antonio located on Houston and Navarro, or 12 East Houston, 1883-85.

CONRAD, E. S.
Active in Wylie, 1892.

CONRADS, ARTHUR
Born in Texas, 1866. Active in Sequin, 1898-1900.

COOK, E. BELL (MRS.)
Listed in Dallas, 1883-84, at 823 Main.

COOK, J. T.
Active in Williamson County, 1876.

COOKE, C. FRANK
Partner in Guy & Cooke with Henry A. H. Guy in Houston, 1892-95, at 501 ½ Main.

COOKSEY, EUGENE
Born in Mississippi, 1871. Listed in Bell County, 1900.

COOLEY, FRED M.
Born in Texas, 1873. Active in Waco, 1900.

COOPER
Partner in Farr & Cooper, Sherman, 1870; possibly Tarr & Cooper. Active in Freestone County, 1871.

COOPER & GARRETT
Active in Smith County, 1872; Cherokee County, 1873. Possibly Fleming P. Cooper.

COOPER & ORTIZ
Spencer H. Cooper and Joseph A. Ortiz in Eagle Pass, 1890-91.

COOPER, A. H.
Active in Travis County, 1884.

COOPER, F. P. (MRS.)
Active in Belton, 1898-99.

COOPER, FLEMING P.
Born in Louisiana, c. 1845. Partner in Cooper & Garrett, Smith County, 1872; partnership continued in Cherokee County, 1873. Listed alone in Bell County, 1873, 1876, 1880; in Belton, 1882-85.

COOPER, PROFESSOR
Listed in Tyler, 1874.

COOPER, S. W.
Born in Louisiana, 1877. Listed in Beaumont, 1900.

COOPER, SAM W.
Born in Texas, 1876. Active in Port Arthur, 1900; partner with John Carsons.

COOPER, SPENCER H.
Listed in Travis County, 1884; in Austin, 1885-88, 1898-99. Located on Peach between Colorado and Lavaca, 1885-86; on West Thirteenth between Colorado and Lavaca, 1887-88. Partner in Cooper & Ortiz with Joseph A. Ortiz in Eagle Pass, 1890-91.

COOPER, URIAH M.
Worked in Jackson County, Arkansas, 1870. Active in Gainesville, 1892.

CORDES, ARTHUR
Active in Fayette County, 1900.

CORDES, RUDOLPH
Born in Germany, c. 1820. Active in Galveston, 1859-60; studio on Avenue H between Thirteenth and Fourteenth. Possibly the same as R. Cardus.

CORLEY, D. B.
Active in Sherman, 1880-90.

CORN, THOMAS J.
Active in Dallas, 1878-81; on Swiss between Crockett and Hawkins, 1878-79; at 1416 Elm, 1880-81. Also spelled Carn.

CORNELIUS, A. R.
Born in Texas, 1871. Listed in Rains County, 1900.

CORTI, HARRY O.
Born in Italy, 1869. Immigrated to U.S., 1880. Partner of Thomas J. Bruce in Marshall, 1900.

COTTAGE GALLERY
Operated by D. H. Swartz & Brother in Fort Worth, 1886-87, at 600 Main.

COTTAGE PHOTO PARLORS
Operated by A. J. T. Joslin in El Paso, 1892; studio on Texas at Stanton.

COUCHMAN, LEONA
Born in Illinois, 1875. Retoucher in Denison, 1900.

COURT STUDIO
Operated by Mullins & Gray in Victoria, 1896-97.

COURTNEY & THOMPSON
Partnership operating gallery in Gainesville, 1880.

COURTNEY, GEORGE
Active in Terrell, 1882-83; partner in Courtney & Thompson, 1884-85.

COUTNEY, ALEX
Born in Louisiana, c. 1855. Active in Cuero, 1880.

COVERTSON, T. N.
Active in Ellis County, 1876.

COX
Partner in Joiner & Cox, Fayette County, 1873.

COX, GEORGE H.
Born in West Virginia, 1861. Listed in Fredericksburg and Junction, 1900.

COX, MARTIN C.
Born in Texas, 1879. Listed in Deaton, Polk County, 1900.

COZBY & CHARLES
Oliver Cozby and James C. Charles, operating in Lockhart, 1892.

COZBY & KRUSE
Oliver Cozby and Carl G. Kruse, active in San Marcos, 1890-91.

COZBY, OLIVER
Listed in Hays County, 1889-90. Partner in Cozby & Kruse, operating in San Marcos, 1890-91; partner in Cozby & Charles in Lockhart, 1892.

COZZENS, KATE
Active in Dallas, 1894-95; painter or photographer.

CRADER
Partner in Cassady & Crader, Eastland County, 1894.

CRAIG & WAGNER
Partnership operating in Galveston on Tremont between Post Office and Church, 1866-67; S. T. Craig and W. T. Wagner or Waggoner. Also operated as Galveston Photographic Company.

CRAIG, S. T.
Partner in Craig & Wagner (Waggoner), Galveston, 1866-67; also Galveston Photographic Company.

CRAMER, WILLIAM M.
Born in Iowa, 1868. Listed in Galveston, 1900.

CRASBY, E. W.
Active in Waller County, 1875.

CRAWFORD & WHEELER
L. W. Crawford and Alonzo D. Wheeler, operating in Fort Worth, 1877-79. Listed at 7 ½ Houston, or Houston between First and Weatherford.

CRAWFORD, L. W.
Born in Virginia, c. 1844. Listed in Tarrant County, 1874-76; in Fort Worth, 1877-82. Partner in Crawford & Wheeler, 1877-79.

CRAWFORD, M.
Active in Tarrant County, 1871.

CREW, EMIL
Born in Ohio, 1833. Active in Hempstead, 1890-92, 1896-99; Waller County, 1900.

CROCKETT BROTHERS
Eli C. and William W. Crockett, operating in Blossom, 1890-92; Nathaniel C. and William W. Crockett, partners in Clarksville, 1896-98.

CROCKETT, WILLIAM W.
Active in Clarksville, 1892; partner in Crockett Brothers with Eli C. in Blossom, 1890-92; with Nathaniel C. in Clarksville, 1896-98.

CROSBY
Partner in Fitch & Crosby, Lavaca County, 1872.

CROSS, A. B.
Listed in Dallas County, 1894.

CROSS, J. Y.
Active in Brenham, 1866; possibly J. Y. Crop.

CROSSLEY, MARTIN V.
Listed in Eastland, 1900. Also spelled Crossly. Partner in Crossly Brothers, 1893.

CROSSLY BROTHERS
Active in Eastland County, 1893; Martin V. Crossley.

CROWDER, ROBERT B.
Born in Missouri, 1862. Listed in Waco, 1900.

CROWELL & COMPANY
Arthur B. Crowell and Thomas C. Bolton operating in El Paso, 1886-87.

CROWELL, ARTHUR B.
Crowell and Arthur Dowe leased the house and equipment of William Henry Brown in El Paso for a photo gallery, 1885-88; located on Oregon near San Antonio, 1886-87. Partner with Thomas C. Bolton operating as Crowell & Company, 1886-87.

CROWLEY, W. A.
Listed in Gonzales County, 1875. Also spelled Croley.

CULLUM, JOHN L.
Advertised as "John L. Cullum and Lady" in Corsicana, back room of McKinney's Confectionery, 1855.

CUMMING & SON
Charles Menzies and Edward R. Cumming operating in Corsicana, 1884-85, 1892, 1898-99. Also known as M. Cummings & Son, 1898-99.

CUMMING, CHARLES MENZIES
Born in Scotland, c. 1835. Partner with James B. Caradine, operating as Caradine & Cumming in Corsicana and Sherman, Navarro County, 1876-79; billed as "Artist-Photographers" at North Travis between Pecan and Houston, 1878-79. Listed as photographer in census, 1880. Partner in Cumming & Son in Corsicana, 1884-85, 1892, 1898-99. Also listed in Dallas, 1896. Also listed as Cummings.

CUMMING, EDWARD R.
Born in Georgia, 1860. Partner with his father, Charles Menzies Cumming, in Corsicana, 1884-85, 1892, 1898-99. Also active in Dallas, 1896. Listed in Kaufman, 1900.

CUMMING, JOHN A.
Active in Dallas, 1896.

CUMMINGS, S.
Active in Austin, 1850. Possibly newspapaperman, Samuel Cummings.

CUNNINGHAM, HOWARD D.
Born in Tennessee, c. 1838. Listed in Pittsburg, 1880, 1882-83, 1890-91.

CUNNINGHAM, J. L. (MRS.)
Active in Goliad, 1882-83.

CUNNINGHAM, JOHN V.
Born in Virginia, 1846. May have been in Shasta, California, c. 1880. Listed in Jack County census, 1900.

CURLEE, R. E.
Born in South Carolina, c. 1810. Active in Henderson, 1857; Tyler, 1860-61. Initials may be R. R.

CURRENT, LEVI
Active in Palo Pinto County, 1871.

CURTIS, CLINTON D.
Active in El Paso, 1898-1900. Purchased J. C. Burge's studio from his widow, July 1898; sold out to P. L. Weitfle, September 1900.

CURTIS, WILLIAM H.
Born in Iowa, 1862. Active in San Antonio, 1892-1902. Studio at 227 ½ Houston, 1892-97; 104 East Houston, 1897-1900.

CURTISS & GEORGE
Listed in Smith County, 1874; in Tyler on the north side of the public square, 1875, operating as Tyler Art Gallery.

CUSHING, W. H.
May have been in St. Augustine, Florida, 1870s-80s. Active in Travis County, 1884.

CUTE, J. T.
Active in Red River County, 1892.

DAHL, LOUIS
Born in Norway, 1867. Partner of O. Ramsey, operating in Runge, 1900.

DALE, C. S.
Active in Dallas at 602 Elm, 1875.

DALGLEISH, THOMAS
Born in Scotland, c. 1848. Active in Luling, 1880; successor to Andrew L. Washburn in Houston at 85 Main, 1884-85.

DALLAS COPYING & ENLARGING COMPANY
Operated by David G. Stokey in Dallas at 1413 Main, 1884-85.

DALLAS COPYING HOUSE
Operated by W. Wirt Williams in Dallas, 1892.

DALTON, SAMUEL
Born in Tennessee, c. 1825. Photographer or painter listed in Marlin, 1870.

DAMAND
Partner in Griffin & Damand, operating in Sherman, 1869.

DANIEL, ARTHUR
Born in Texas, 1873. Apprentice photographer in Houston, 1900.

DANIEL, JOSEPH E.
Born in Georgia, 1854. Active in Fort Worth, 1885-1900. Partner in Frederick & Daniel with James E. Frederick, on Houston between Fifth and Sixth, 1885-86. Operating alone at 608 Houston, 1886-87; 610 Houston, 1888-99; 700 Houston, 1899-1900. Also listed in Gordon and Weatherford, 1892; Glenwood, 1900.

DARDEN, GEORGE A.
Listed in Decatur, 1890-92; Alvarado, 1896-97; Paige, Bastrop County, 1898-99.

DARE & COLLINS ART STORE
Operated by David Dare and John W. Collins in San Antonio at 42 West Commerce, 1883-84. Left for Cheyenne, Wyoming, September 1884.

DAUGHERTY, C.
Active in Grayson County, 1873; Erath County, 1874.

DAVENPORT, PERRY F.
Active in Waxahachie, 1882-85, 1896-99. Partner with E. L. Reid, operating as Reid & Davenport, 1892.

DAVID, EDMUND
Born in Pennsylvania, 1882. Listed in Houston, 1900.

DAVIDSON, GEORGE W.
Born in Tennessee, c. 1852. Active in Mount Vernon, 1880.

DAVIS (MRS.)
Active in Houston, 1843.

DAVIS, ARTHUR
Born in Colorado, 1863. Listed in Houston, 1900.

DAVIS, C. A.
Active in Clarksville, 1854-55.

DAVIS, GEORGE A.
Active in Austin, 1848, over Mr. Dietrich's store.

DAVIS, J. P.
Born in Louisiana, c. 1841. Listed in Arlington, 1880.

DAVIS, J. W.
Active in Georgetown, 1870; Burleson and Tyler Counties, 1871; Burnet and Jefferson Counties, 1872; Bell County, 1874, 1876; Jefferson County, 1875.

DAVIS, JAMES A.
Born in Georgia, 1875. Active in Itasca, 1896-97; Cleburne, 1900.

DAVIS, JAMES R.
Born in Indiana, c. 1834. Worked in Illinois, 1864. Listed in Lancaster, 1868; Collin and Dallas Counties and Denton, 1871; Dallas, 1867, 1870, 1873-99. Studio in Dallas on Elm between Jefferson and Market, 1873-74; 313 Elm, 1875; 401 Elm, 1877; Main between Poydras and South Sycamore, 1878-79; at 705 Main, 1880-81; 609 Elm, 1881-85; 619 Elm, 1886-87.

DAVIS, M. C.
Active in Big Cypress, Camp County, 1892.

DAVISON, JOHN M.
Born in Tennessee, 1843. Active in Sulphur Springs, 1870, 1882-85, 1890-92, 1898-99. Listed in Dallas County, 1900.

DAWSON, EVERETT
Born in Missouri, 1872. Listed in Italy, 1900.

DAY, THOMAS P.
Born in Bolivar, Texas, 1844; died 1924. Active in Fort Worth at 5 ½ Houston, 1876-79. Also operated a jewelry store and a bicycle and sporting goods store.

DE LONG, O. V.
Active in El Paso, 1907-08.

DEAN
Partner in Hardesty & Dean, traveling photographers from St. Louis, Missouri, active in Texas, c. 1883.

DEAN, ROBERT D.
Born in Kentucky, 1857. Active in Dallas, 1891-1900. Studio listed on Main, 1891; Stone and Main, 1892; 419 Elm, 1896-97; 412 Elm, 1898; 453 Elm, 1900.

DEANE & MORGAN
Jervis C. Deane and Forrest T. Morgan operating in Waco at 503 ½ Austin, 1888-91.

DEANE, CLARENCE C.
Born in Virginia, 1854. Active in Houston, 1884-91, 1894-1900. Studio located at 306 Preston, 1884-88; 110 Prairie, 1890-91; 507 ½ Main, 1894-99. Operated in Galveston at 418 ½ Twenty-first Street, 1893-94. Also worked for Samuel Anderson, 1889-90.

DEANE, GRANVILLE M.
Born in Virginia, 1858. Brother of Jervis C. and Martin O. Deane. Active in Galveston, 1886-91, 1898-99; Dallas, 1892- 1900. Studio at Market and Twenty-first, 1886-89; 2020 Market, 1890-91; 300 Elm, 1892-97; 224 Elm, 1897-1900. Granville and Jervis were on the photographers' stand at the Great Crush Collision, September 15, 1896.

DEANE, JERVIS C.
Born in Virginia, 1860. Brother of Granville M. and Martin O. Deane. Worked as a house painter in Hannibal, Missouri; studied photography in Europe, 1885; toured the United States, then joined his brother in photography. Active in Waco, 1888-1901; partner with Forrest T. Morgan, operating as Deane & Morgan, 1888-91. Studio at 502 ½ Austin, 1888-89; 701-03 Austin, 1892-93; 414 ½ Austin, 1894-1901. He was active in Jefferson, 1890-92; in Temple, 1896-97. He lost an eye while photographing the Great Crush Collision, September 15, 1896; a metal fragment lodged in his brain, and he was in a coma for several months. He recovered by 1898, and resumed his work in photography.

DEANE, M. O. (MRS.)
Active in Fort Worth, 1898.

DEANE, MARTIN O.
Brother of Jervis C. and Granville M. Deane; may have been at the Great Crush Collision. Active in Waco, 1886-87, at 512 Austin; in Fort Worth, 1896-1900. Listed at 610 ½ Main, 1896-97; 112 ½ West Seventh, 1899-1900.

DEASON, C. C.
Born in Georgia, 1870. Operated a "Traveling Picture Gallery" in Dallas, 1900.

DEBERRY & BROTHER, A. A.
Active in Chappell Hill, Washington County, 1869.

DELFRAISSE, A. LEON
Active in San Antonio, 1891-97; operated the Little Brick Photographic Gallery, 1891-93. Listed at 10 East Houston, 1891-92; 110 East Houston, 1892-93; 102-104 East Houston, 1894-95; 102 East Houston, 1896-97.

DELFRAISSE, L. EUGENE
Listed in San Antonio at 126 North Flores, 1894-96; in Colorado County, 1897.

DELLIS, SAMUEL
Born in Texas, 1869. Listed in Armour, Limestone County, 1900.

DEMOSS, EUGENE
Born in Texas, 1874. Active in Marion County, 1900.

DENALLEY, LOUIS
Active in Centerville, 1867; Leon County, 1872, 1874. Also listed as Louis Dinnelly.

DENDY, JAMES S.
Listed in Rusk, 1892; Palestine, 1896-97.

DENISON ART GALLERY
Operated by William H. Snell in Denison, 1893-98. His brother, Thomas W., took over the operation and changed the studio name to Snell's Photo Studio, 1898; known as Snell Brothers, 1899-1900.

DEPLANQUE, LOUIS
Born in Prussia, c. 1837; died 1898. He worked the entire Texas Gulf coast, either as traveling photographer or with branch galleries. In Mexico, 1865; in Texas by the late 1860s. Active in Indianola, Calhoun County, 1869; Corpus Christi and Rufugio, 1870; Calhoun County, 1871; in Indianola operating in Dhame's Building, 1875; in Corpus Christi, 1878-97; Victoria, 1898-99. Studio in Brownsville during the Civil War; in Corpus Christi, 1870-80. Also listed as De Planque.

DERYEE & IWONSKI
William DeRyee and Carl G. von Iwonski in New Braunfels, 1859.

DERYEE, WILLIAM
Born in Bavaria, 1825; died in Corpus Christi, Texas, 1903. Active in San Antonio, 1858-59; partner in Deryee & Iwonski in New Braunfels, 1859-60. Also operated as the Gallery of Fine Arts in Austin, 1859. He published *The Texas Album* together with R. E. Moore, including nearly 100 tipped-in photographic portraits. He produced a magic lantern show and toured central Texas and the Mississippi and Ohio rivers with Hermann Lungkwitz and William Thielepape, 1859-60. DeRyee made multiple albumin prints of drawings that he called homeographs. He moved to Corpus Christi after the Civil War, operating as a druggist and involved in mining ventures.

DESHON, GEORGE
Active in Dallas, 1878-79.

DESMETH, H.
Active in Weatherford, 1869-70.

DESMOND
Partner with Paul H. Naschke in Galveston, c. 1890s.

DEVENPORT, P. F.
Active in Waxahachie, c. 1885.

DEZALBA, E. FRANK
Operated with the firm of Baxter & Company in Beaumont, 1892.

DICKENSON & TUCKER
Active in Parker County, 1876.

DICKENSON, W. C.
Active in Parker County, 1874-76.

DINGNOWITY, ANTHONY FRANCIS
Listed in San Antonio, 1869-70, 1872; at 70 Commerce, opposite Reed & Mather's, 1872. Also spelled Dignowity.

DOBBINS, JOHN A.
Born in Mississippi, 1879. Listed in Bowie County, 1900.

DOBINS, MARCELLUS
Born in Virginia, 1858. Listed in Montague County, 1900.

DODDS, JAMES S.
Partner in Millholin & Dodds, Georgetown, 1890-91.

DOEKERY, L. K.
Active in Moulton, 1867.

DOERR, HENRY A.
Born in Prussia, c. 1822; died in San Antonio, 1855. Active in San Antonio, 1866-72, 1881-85, 1898-99; Bexar County, 1874. Studio in Maverick's New Building over Gamble's Store, 1871; at 233 West Commerce, 1881-83; Avenue C and Travis, 1884-85. Also active in New Braunfels, c. late 1860s. Partner with Engle, 1865-66; with Jesse, 1866; with Winther, 1874; with Jacobson, 1876-80.

DOERR & JACOBSON
Henry A. Doerr and Samuel E. Jacobson, operating in San Antonio, 1876-80. Studio at 63 Commerce. Jacobson is also listed as Semmy E.

DOERR & JESSE
Henry A. Doerr and Maximilian T. Jesse, operating in San Antonio, 1866.

DOERR & WINTHER
Partnership of Henry A. Doerr and Nicholas Winther in San Antonio, Bexar County, 1874; operated "Photographic Rooms" on Commerce Street near Main Plaza, c. 1875. Also listed as Winther & Doerr.

DOOLITTLE, E. H.
Active in Fayette, Travis and Williamson Counties, 1871; Limestone County, 1872.

DOTSON
Partner in Watson & Dotson operating in Calvert, 1872.

DOUGLASS
Active in Texas, c. 1853, originally from St. Louis.

DOUGLASS, T. C.
Born in Tennessee, c. 1837. Listed in Lewisville, 1860; Swissville, Denton County, 1867.

DOUGLASS, WALTER
Active in Dallas, 1896.

DOWDY, JESSE L.
Born in Tennessee, c. 1848. Active in Erath County, 1873-74; San Saba County, 1875; in San Saba, 1878-79; Eastland County, 1880; Ballinger, 1892.

DOWE, ARTHUR W.
Active in El Paso, 1885-88; located at 202 El Paso, 1886-87. Associated with Arthur B. Crowell, 1885-88, when they leased the house

and equipment of William Henry Brown in El Paso for a photo gallery. Located on Oregon Street, near San Antonio, 1886-87.

DOWNING
Active in Dallas, 1885; possibly William C. Downing.

DOWNING & BATES
Jesse C. Downing and John S. Bates, operating in Dallas at 411 Main, 1878-79.

DOWNING, JESSE C.
Died in Waxahachie, 1878. Active in Dallas, 1877-79; located at 509 Main, 1877. Partner in Downing & Bates, 1878-79.

DOWNING, WILLIAM C.
Partner in Kinne & Downing, Gainesville, 1887-88; studio on California at Denton.

DRAKE, H. J.
Born in Arkansas, 1870. Listed in Matagorda County, 1900.

DRANE, EDWARD C.
Born in Sheby County, Kentucky, c. 1826. In Navarro County by 1850; making daguerreotypes by 1853 in Corsicana; one of the earliest photographers in Texas; also practicing dentistry.

DREYLING, GUSTAV
Active in Matagorda, 1858, 1860.

DRIVER, DOUG OTIS
Born in Texas, 1878. Listed in Commerce, 1900.

DRIVER, JOSEPH M.
Born in Texas, 1868. Active in Commerce, 1900.

DRYDEN, R. H.
Listed in Live Oak County, 1872.

DUBOIS, T. N.
Born in Alabama, c. 1857. Active in Blooming Grove, 1880; Corn Hill, 1896-97.

DUDLEY, E. T.
Active in Clarksville, 1860-62.

DUER, STUMP & COMPANY
Active in Collin County, 1873.

DUER, W. T.
Born in Tennessee, c. 1834. Active in Collin County, 1874-76; partner in Harman & Duer, 1875; in McKinney, 1880. Worked for James R. Davis in Dallas, 1881-82. May have been a partner in Duer, Stump & Company.

DUFF, N. FRANK
Listed in Hillsboro, 1892; Itasca, 1892, 1896-97.

DUFFIELD, JOHN D.
Born in Texas, 1863. Active in Navasota, 1896-97; Galveston, 1900.

DUGEN, BASSANTECT
Active in Brazoria County, 1874. May be Barsantee Dugen.

DUGGAN
Partner in Barsantee & Duggan; may be misspelling of Barsantee Dugen.

DULANEY, J. E.
Active in Lebanon, Collin County, 1867.

DULCHAN, WILLIAM
Born in Texas, 1870. Listed in Llano County, 1900.

DUNCAN
Partner in Morphis & Duncan, Cotton Gin, Freestone County, 1870. Listed as photographers "at large" in tax records.

DUNCAN, E.
Active in Henderson, 1869; Houston County, 1872.

DUNCAN, FRANCIS K.
Born in Missouri, 1878. Listed in Lufkin, 1900.

DUNK, D. T.
Born in England, c. 1855. Listed in Palestine, 1880.

DUNLAP, CRAIG
Born in Tennessee, 1880. Active in Dallas, 1900.

DUNLAP, W. T.
Active in Wise County, 1873.

DUNLEAVY, J. E.
Active in Dallas, 1895, at 107 North Ervay.

DUNN & PAYNE
Partnership in Williamson County, 1874.

DUNN, A. S. W.
Listed in Hempstead, 1870.

DUNN, G. W.
Listed in Brownsville, 1866; Columbus, 1867, 1869; Austin County, 1871.

DUNN, WILLIAM SR.
Active in Lockhart, 1868.

DUNNAWAY, ANDREW
Born in Tennessee, 1875. Listed in Midlothian, 1900.

DYER, JOSEPH M.
Active in Greenville, 1890-91.

EAKIN, J. S.
Active in Sherman, 1868.

EANES, FRANK
Born in Texas, c. 1853. Listed in Austin, 1870.

EANES, JOHN
Active in Mount Pleasant, 1882-85. Also listed as Eves.

EANES, PERRY
Active in Belton, 1870.

ECHOLS, M. V.
Listed in Lamar County, 1873.

ECKERSKORN, JOSEPH
Born in Germany, 1867. Immigrated to U.S., 1892. Active in San Antonio, 1894-1900; at 616 Water, 1894-96; 616 South Alamo, 1896-97.

EGGEL, FIDEL
Born in Germany, 1830. Listed in Coleman, 1890-92, 1896-97, 1900.

EICHELBERGER, HENRY C.
Born in Georgia, 1856. Active in Crockett, 1880, 1890-92, 1896-1900.

ELDERKIN, HAROLD A.
Active in New Mexico, 1885-88. Active in El Paso, 1888.

ELIFRITS, WILLIE
Born in Missouri, 1878. Listed in Dallas, 1900.

ELITE PHOTOGRAPHIC GALLERY
Operating in Plano, 1896-97.

ELKINS, GEORGE
Active in Johnson County, 1871.

ELLIOT, J. L.
Active in Sweetwater, 1896-97.

ELLIOT, MARTIN W.
Born in Kansas, 1871. Active in Ellis County, 1900.

ELLIS
Partner in Hoy & Ellis, Denton County, 1871.

ELLIS & COMPANY
Possibly M. G. Ellis operating in McKinney, 1867.

ELLIS, AMOS J.
Born in Georgia, c. 1846. Listed in Waxahachie, 1870.

ELLIS, CHARLES
Born in Michigan, c. 1858. Active in Austin, 1880.

ELLIS, CHARLES
Born in Tennessee, 1877. Listed in Granbury, 1900.

ELLIS, JAMES R.
Born in Alabama, 1856. Active in Waller County, 1880; Giddings, 1890-92, 1896-97, 1900.

ELLIS, M. G.
Active in Fort Worth, 1868; Stephenville, 1869. Possibly associated with Ellis & Company in McKinney, 1867.

ELLISON, J. E.
Active in Grayrock, Franklin County, 1869; Titus County, 1872.

ELMON, JACOB W.
Born in South Carolina, c. 1836. Listed in Williamson County, 1876, 1880. Possibly Jacob W. Elman or Elmore.

ELMORE, JOSEPH W.
Born in North Carolina, 1836. Active in Corsicana, 1900. Possibly Jacob W. Elmon.

ELROD, THOMAS B.
Born in Illinois, 1844. An attorney from Louisville, Kentucky; worked for David H. Swartz in Columbus and took over the businesss; active 1884-1900. He was also the mayor of Columbus, 1896-98.

EMANUEL, G. W.
Active in Austin, 1866.

EMBREY, MARTIN T.
Active in Sherman, 1866.

ENGLE & DOERR
Partnership in San Antonio, 1865-66; Henry A. Doerr.

ENGLE & LEONARD
Active in Wharton County, 1866.

ENGLE, EUGENE
Born in Virginia, c. 1835. Listed in Sherman, 1870.

ENGLISH, JAMES A.
Born in Georgia, c. 1838. Originally from Sycamore, Illinois; active in Jefferson and Starrville, 1870.

ENLOE, BENJAMIN
Born in Missouri, 1857. Listed in Home, 1900.

ENOS
Partner in Varkin & Enos, listed as "Photo view & crayon Artist."

EPPS, EMILY
Born in Texas, 1859. Listed in Junction, 1900.

ERNST, G. F.
Active in New Braunfels located on Sequin Street in Backer Hermann's house, 1855.

ERSLY, PERRY
Active in Hillsboro, 1890-92; possibly a partner in Esley & Garlington, 1898-99.

ERWIN & HOLLY
Partnership in Wadeville (now Kerens), 1869.

ERWIN, E. E.
Active in Sunset, Wise County, 1884-85.

ESKER, J. H.
Active in Bee and San Patricio Counties, 1871. Possibly J. H. Eshue.

ESLEY & GARLINGTON
Partnership in Hillsboro, 1898-99; possibly Perry Ersly.

ESTES
Partner in Flamister & Estes, Uvalde, 1868.

ESTES, HATTIE A.
Born in Texas, 1880. Listed in Hays County, 1900.

EUREKA GALLERY
Operated in Tyler by George C. Irons, 1896-97; Edward Wellington Mims, date unknown; by Mims & Rafferty, 1893, at 112 North Bois d'Arc.

EVANS, AMY
Born in Arkansas, 1865. Listed in Wise County, 1900.

EVANS, DANIEL W.
Active in Granbury, 1896-97.

EVANS, J. M.
Active in Mount Pleasant, 1898-99.

EVANS, J. W.
Active in Navasota, 1878-79.

EVANS, LESLIE D.
Born in Texas, 1868. Listed in Paris, 1900.

EVRY, G. N.
Listed in Lamar County, 1875.

EYTH, LOUIS
Born c. 1838; died 1889. Primarily a painter and illustrator; may have been a photographer.

FAGERSTEEN, GUSTAV
Photographer from Berlin; in California, 1870s. Active in New Braunfels, 1858. See California.

FAHRENBERG, ALBERT
Born in Prussia, c. 1828. Active in Kentucky, 1859; Mexico, 1870s. Active in San Antonio, c. 1870-74; at 48 Commerce Street, 1870; also listed on Market, 1870, 1872.

FAHRENBERG, OSCAR
Born in New York, c. 1854. Listed in San Antonio, 1870.

FAIRBANKS, CHARLES W.
Active in Waco at 107 ½ South Fifth, 1892.

FAIRCLOTH, THOMAS
Listed in Corrigan, 1890-91.

FARMER, JOHN
Born in England, c. 1862. Listed in San Antonio, 1880; possibly a painter.

FARQUHAR, JULIUS T.
Born in Texas, 1872. Active in Lampasas, 1896-97, 1900.

FARR & COOPER
Partnership in Sherman, 1870; may be misspelling of Tarr & Cooper.

FARR, HENRY R.
Born in Vermont, 1839; died 1893. Active in Tyler, 1890-91. May have sold out to Henry T. Hiester; moved to New Mexico and bought a studio, 1892, operating it until he died.

FARR, W. E.
Active in Collin County, 1871.

FARRINGTON, A. G.
Active in Lavaca County, 1871-72.

FAULK, WILL
Born in Alabama, 1872. Listed in Austin, 1900.

FAUMAN, D. H.
Active in McLennan County, 1874.

FAUNVILLE, W. R.
Active in San Augustine County, 1874-75. Also spelled Fonville.

FAVORITE, IRENE R. (MRS.)
Active in Burnet, 1884-85. See Oregon and California.

FAWKES, JOHN W.
Active in Paris, 1890-91.

FELDER
Born in Texas, 1879. Listed in Houston, 1900.

FELDER, SPURGEON S.
Born in South Carolina, 1858. Active in Huntsville, 1890-92, 1896-1900. Also listed as Fowler.

FELDMAN, FREDERICK J.
Born in California, 1870; died 1923. After photographing in Arizona, 1893, he moved to Texas. Active in El Paso, 1895-1912. Leased the studio of John C. Bushong in El Paso, 1895, when Bushong went east to study photography. Became his partner upon his return, 1897-1901; bought him out, 1901.

FENNELL, JESSIE
Born in Missouri, 1877. Listed in Clay County, 1900.

FERGUSON, JOHN
Active in Goliad, 1890-91.

FERGUSON, L. M.
Active in Titus County, 1872.

FERGUSON, M. M.
Active in Georgetown, 1882-83; Goliad, 1892, 1898-99.

FEY & BRAUNIG
Partnership of Pius Fey and Henry Jacob Braunig. They began working together as itinerants, both coming from Cuero and visiting the Fredericksburg area, 1878. Main gallery in Braunfels, 1870s-80s; Braunig established a branch in Halletsville, 1887, and built a brick studio on the square, 1895. The business in Cuero continued 1875-1909, when the partnership was dissolved.

FEY, PIUS
Born in Prussia, 1855. Immigrated to U.S., 1870. He bought photographic equipment from Max A. P. Krueger in Cuero and set up business, mid-1870s. After the partnership was dissolved, 1909, Fey continued in Cuero, retiring c. 1936. See Fey & Braunig.

FIELDS, T. W.
Born in Texas, 1863. Listed in Polk County, 1900.

FIGLEY, JOSEPH N.
Born in Ohio, 1850. Listed in La Porte, 1900.

FINCH, EDWIN
Active in Milford, 1868-70; Ellis County, 1871; Johnson County, 1875. Also worked in Waxahatchie and Alvarado, 1870-80.

FINE ART GALLERY
Active in Brenham, c. 1870, operated by A. N. Callaway.

FINLEY, T. C.
Born in Tennessee, 1867. Listed in Rockdale, 1900.

FINTOFPH, JAMES.
Born in Germany, c. 1830. Listed in Galveston as an "artist," possibly a painter or photographer.

FISCH, FLORENCE LILLY
Born in Indiana, 1862. Active in San Antonio, 1900.

FISCHER, WALTER
Born in Germany, 1871. Immigrated to U.S., 1888. Active in Falls County, 1900.

FISCHER, WILLIAM
Active in Gorman, 1896-97.

FISHBECK, FRANK
Born in Kentucky, 1877. Listed in Dallas, 1900.

FISHER, C. H.
Born in Louisiana, c. 1840. Active in Bryan and Calvert, 1870-80.

FISHER, G.
Active in Richmond, 1869; Columbus, 1870.

FISHER, J. R.
Active in Farmington, Grayson County, 1868.

FITCH & CROSBY
Partnership in Lavaca County, 1872.

FITCH & LINDSAY
Active in San Antonio, 1872.

FITCH, A.
Born in Massachusetts, c. 1850. Listed in Cuero, 1880.

FITZGERALD, JAMES
Born in New York, c. 1845. Stereo photographer in Galveston, 1870; possibly a partner in Patton & Fitzgerald.

FITZGIBBON & BOURGES
Emile Bourges and partner, daguerreians in Galveston, 1851. Known as FitzGibbon, Bourges & Stanley in Galveston, late December 1851, when John H. Stephen Stanley became a partner; the firm was called Stanley, FitzGibbon & Bourges at a branch studio in Houston, c. 1852. See Fitzgibbon in Missouri.

FLAMISTER & ESTES
Active in Uvalde, 1868; possibly James H. Flemister.

FLAMISTER & WALL
Partnership in Uvalde, 1869; possibly James H. Flemister.

FLEMING, C. C.
Active in Pleasant Valley, 1895.

FLEMISTER, JAMES H.
Active in Starville, Smith County, 1866; Medina County, 1871; also operated as Flemister & Company; possibly a partner in Flamister & Estes and Flamister & Wall, operating in Uvalde, 1868-69.

FLETCHER, LOTTIE
Born in Kansas, 1882. Listed in El Paso, 1900.

FLETT, JOHN H.
Active in Galveston, 1884-85, at 221 Post Office. Also operated as Art Gallery.

FLICK, J. H.
Born in South Carolina, c. 1853. Listed in Angelina County, 1880.

FONDA, J. B.
Born in Kentucky, c. 1839. Active in Sandy Mountain, Llano County, 1870; Blanco County, 1871.

FORBES, ANDREW ALEXANDER
Traveling photographer in Texas and Oklahoma, 1880s-90s. Known for his scenes of cowboy life. Active in Bishop, California, after 1909. See California.

FORD, OLIVER
Active in Grand Prairie, 1894.

FORDTRAN
Partner in Holmes & Fordtran, Columbia (now West Columbia), 1857.

FORELL, CARL
Active in Illinois, 1878; Houston, 1895-96, at 1618 Nance.

FORREST, JAMES
Born in Mississippi, 1880. Listed in San Antonio, 1900.

FORT WORTH ART GALLERY
Operated by Augustus R. Mignon in Fort Worth, c. 1880s-90s.

FOSTER, CHARLES E.
Born in Missouri, 1857. Active in Bonham, 1896-1900.

FOSTER, W. M.
Active in Lassater, Marion County, 1892.

FOUZER, C. L. (MRS.)
Active in Fayette County, 1893.

FOWLER, N. G.
Partner in Malloy & Fowler, Collin County, 1871. Listed alone in Tarrant County, 1875; Denton County, 1876.

FOWLER, S. T.
Active in Colin County, 1872-73; Denton County, 1876.

FOWLER, WILLIAM R.
Active in Terrell, 1896-97, on Francis Street.

FRANKLIN & COMPANY, W. S.
Firm operating in San Antonio, 1897, at 228 Losoya.

FRANKS, MARY E. (MISS)
Born in South Carolina, 1844. Active in Austin, 1898-1900, at 914 Congress. Also listed as a Kodak view developer.

FREDERICK & DANIEL
James E. Frederick and Joseph E. Daniel, operating in Fort Worth, 1885-86. Located on Houston between Fifth and Sixth.

FREEMAN, ALFRED
Born in England, c. 1846. Active in Dallas, 1870-85; on Elm at Houston, 1873-74; 101 South Houston, 1875; 505 Main, 1880-85. Active in Decatur, Sherman and McKinney, 1887-88; Sherman, 1890.

FREEMAN, ELIJAH M.
Born in Texas. Listed in Rockwall, 1900.

FREEMAN, GAMIEL C.
Active in Columbus, 1884; partner in Swartz & Freeman with David H. Swartz, studio in Columbus, 1882-83; listed alone, 1884. Partner with John Swartz operating as Swartz & Freeman in Denison, 1889-92.

FREEMAN, L. H.
Active in Bastrop County, 1874.

FRENCH, R. G.
Listed in Killeen, 1892.

FREY, EMIL
Born in Prussia, 1855. Active in Corsicana, 1875-1900. Studio at 102 North Beaton, 1894-95, 1898-99. Also spelled Fry.

FREY, WILLIAM
Tent photographer in Dallas at 421 Elm, 1894-95.

FRIEMAN, A.
Active in McKinney, 1898-99.

FRISBY, EDWIN
Born in Virginia, 1859. Listed in San Antonio, 1900.

FRITZ, WILLIAM
Born in Germany, 1859. Immigrated to U.S., 1875. Listed in Houston, 1900.

FROELICH, GUS
Born in Prussia, 1841. Immigrated to U.S., 1856. Active in Fayette County, 1872-76, 1883-87; Round Top, 1878-80, 1884-85, 1890-92, 1896-1900.

FROST, FANNIE L. (MISS)
Active in Dallas at 233 Elm, 1893-94.

FULLER, J. A.
Active in Clarksville, 1870.

FULSOM, L. A.
Listed in Paris, 1866-67, 1870. Also listed as G. A. Folsom.

GAIGE, J. G.
Died in Camp Goodwin, Arizona, 1869. Arizona photographer who regularly traveled into Texas and New Mexico before 1862, and visited El Paso, 1866; he may not have photographed in Texas.

GALBRATH, POLK
Born in Missouri, 1859. "Enlarging Photographer" listed in Houston in the census of 1900.

GALE, GEORGE F.
Born in North Carolina, c. 1850. Active in San Augustine County, 1880; in Dallas at 609 Elm, 1883-84.

GALLAHER, S. A.
Born in Virginia, c. 1831. Active in Dallas on the southeast corner of the public square, 1859-60.

GALLERY OF FINE ARTS
Operated in Austin by William DeRyee, 1859.

GALLWAY SAM
Active in Houston at 92 Main, 1870-7; also operated as Gem Picture Gallery.

GALVESTON PHOTOGRAPHIC COMPANY
Firm in Galveston, operated by S. T. Craig and W. T. Waggoner, 1866-67; by G. H. Joslyn, 1869. Located at 220 Tremont, 1869.

GALVESTON PORTRAIT COMPANY
Operated by J. E. Young in Galveston at 2214 Market, 1890-91.

GALWAY
Partner in Brown & Galway, Lee County, 1874.

GAMBLING
Partner in Morgan & Gambling, Hopkins County, 1871.

GARCIA, JOSE
Born in Mexico, 1873. Immigrated to U.S., 1884. Listed in Laredo, 1900.

GARLINGTON
Partner in Esley & Garlington, in Hillsboro, 1898-99.

GARNETT, W. T.
Listed in Panola County, 1871, 1875; also in Shelby County, 1875; Nacogdoches County, 1876.

GARRETH, W. E.
Active in Hardin, 1884-85.

GARRETT
Partner in Cooper & Garrett in Smith County, 1872; Cherokee County, 1873.

GARRETT, JAMES
Born in Mississippi, 1880. Active in San Antonio, 1900.

GARRETT, ORVILLE B.
Born in Kentucky, 1875. Listed in Tyler, 1900.

GARY & WRIGHT
Partnership in Austin, 1851.

GATES, J. M.
Born in Iowa, 1866. Active in Dickens County, 1900.

GEERS, JOHN B.
Active in Denton, 1882-83.

GEM PICTURE GALLERY
Operated by Sam Gallway in Houston at 92 Main, 1870-71.

GENTRY, M.
Active in Texas and Oklahoma. See New Mexico.

GENTRY, N. B.
Born in Kentucky, 1842. Listed in Midland, 1900.

GENTRY, WILLIAM T.
Active in Winnsboro, 1892.

GEORGE
Partner in Bennett & George, Galveston, 1869; partner in Curtiss & George listed in Smith County, 1874; in Tyler on the north side of the public square, 1875. Also operated as Tyler Art Gallery, 1875.

GEORGE, ELIAS E.
Born in Mississippi, 1848. Listed in Houston, 1870, 1900.

GEORGE, JAMES W.
Born in New York, 1871. Active in Albany, 1896-97, 1900.

GETZ, FERDINAND
Born in Germany, 1863. Immigrated to U.S., 1878. Active in Gonzales, 1896-97, 1900.

GIBBONS, WILLIAM
Active in Kaufman County, 1871.

GIBBS, WALTER F.
Active in Fort Worth, 1883-85. Listed on Houston between Seventh and Eighth, 1883-84; at 610 Houston, 1884-85.

GIBSON, B. M.
Partner in Brack & Gibson with Asa A. Brack, operating in San Antonio at 113 North Alamo, 1897-98.

GILDER, A.
Active in Sulphur Springs, 1870.

GILLETT, SAMUEL EMANUEL
Active in San Antonio at 215 West Commerce, 1885-86. Partner with Arthur C. Paris operating as A. C. Paris & Company at 10 East Houston, 1889-90. Apparently working on his own in San Antonio, 1898-99.

GILLIAM, H. H.
Active in La Grange, 1866; Belton, 1867.

GILLIAN, A. J.
Born in Tennessee, 1838. Listed in Tyler, 1900.

GIROUX, ALPHONSE
Active in Houston, 1889-90, 1892-95, 1897-98. Studio on Fannin,near San Jacinto, 1889-90; at 422 South Flores, 1892; 1113 Franklin, 1892-95; in a tent at 1210 Franklin, 1897-98.

GLASCOCK
Partner in Lopez & Glascock, El Paso, 1912-13.

GLENN & COMPANY, J. H.
Operating in Van Zandt County, 1872.

GLENN, B. H.
Born in Texas, 1865. Listed in Bellville, 1900.

GLENN, T. H.
Active in Tyler, 1870; partner in Askew & Glenn, 1872.

GLOCK, ALBERT
Born in Germany, 1837; died in Austin, Texas, 1923. Immigrated to U.S., 1852. Active in Kerrville, 1896-97, 1900. May have employed Emil Hzitray who lived with him, 1900.

GOBEN, EDGAR L.
Active in Gainesville and Sherman, 1887-88, while living with Perry F. Goben in Sherman. Listed in Henrietta, 1896-97.

GOBEN, JAMES L.
Active in Gainesville, 1887-88, 1890-92, 1896-97. Listed at 10 East California, 1887-88.

GOBEN, PERRY F.
Born in Missouri, 1836. Active in Grayson County, 1875-76, 1879-81. Listed in Sherman, 1876-79, 1882-83, 1890-1900; studio on Opera House Block, 1876-77; on Houston between Travis and Walnut, 1878-79; at 317 East Mulberry, 1891-92; 321 East Mulberry, 1893-1900. Listed in Denison at 231 West Main, 1887-88; in Gainesville, 1890, 1898-99.

GOBIN, G. L.
Active in Bonham, 1884-85; possibly G. L. Goben.

GOLDMAN, HENRY
Born in Georgia, 1838. Listed in Dallas, 1900.

GOLDTHONE, O. M.
Active in Brazoria County, 1875.

GOMEZ & VILLALOBOS
Studio in El Paso, 1906.

GOMEZ, J. LUZ
Active in El Paso, 1907-12.

GOMEZ, M. F.
Active in El Paso, 1911.

GOODLOE, GUY
Active in El Paso, 1901-07.

GOODWIN, JULIUS
Born in Texas, 1879. Listed in Dallas, 1900.

GOODWIN, T. J.
Active in Rusk County, 1871.

GORDON
Partner in Snider & Gordon, Collin County, 1873.

GOREN, L. F.
Operated Goren's Picture Gallery in Gainesville, 1890; also active in Sherman.

GORMAN, G. S.
Active in Bee County, 1876.

GORSUCH, NICHOLAS B.
Born in Maryland, c. 1913. Active in Columbus, 1858; Moulton, 1866; High Hill, Fayette County, 1869; Lavaca County, 1871; Fayette County, 1873; Williamson County, 1875; Snake Prairie, Bastrop County, 1880.

GOTTLIEB, HARRY JOSEPH
Active in El Paso, 1909-12.

GOUHENANT, ADOLPHE F.
The first daguerreotypist in Dallas; opened the Art Saloon Gallery, 1852.

GOVE, WILLIAM S.
Partner in Robbins & Gove with G. W. Robbins in Huntsville, 1853.

GRADT, L. W.
Active in Harris County, 1874.

GRAHAM, DONALD
Born in Oregon, 1882. Listed in San Antonio, 1900.

GRAHAM, W. A.
Active in Johnson County, 1871.

GRANT, J. W.
Active in Wise County, 1874, 1876-77; Jacksonville, 1890-91.

GRASLETT, DAN
Born in Texas, 1874. Listed in San Marcos, 1900.

GRAY, H. B.
Active in Lockhart, 1866.

GRAY, J. F.
Active in Speakville, 1870; may be Speaks, Lavaca County.

GRAY, JAMES L.
Born in Illinois, 1864. Active in Van Alstyne, 1892, 1896-97; Grayson County, 1900.

GRAY, MARY
Born in Tennessee, 1876. Listed in Dallas, 1900.

GRAY, THOMAS J.
Worked for W. Wirt Williams in Dallas, 1893-94; partner in Mullins & Gray with Robert W. Mullins in Victoria, 1896-97.

GRAY-BUTTON PHOTO PARLORS
Studio in Sherman at 124 North Travis Street, c. 1893.

GREEN
Partner in Alexander & Green, operating in El Paso, 1912.

GREEN STORE AMBROTYPE GALLERY
Operated by R. E. Moore and W. Wirt Williams in Houston, c. 1850s.

GREEN, W. A.
Traveling photographer based at 604 Tremont Street in Galveston, c. 1900.

</>

GREER, OMER C.
Born in Illinois, 1870. Active in Fort Worth, 1899-1905. Listed at 503 Main, 1899-1900.

GREGORY, JOHN T.
Born in Mississippi, 1875. Listed in Royce City, 1900.

GRIFFIN
Partner in Spiller & Griffin, Gairfield, 1868.

GRIFFIN & COMPANY
Operated in Belton, 1857.

GRIFFIN & DAMAND
Active in Sherman, 1869.

GRIFFIN, J. E.
Active in Upshur County, 1872.

GRIFFIN, JOSEPH K.
Partner in Bruce & Griffin with Thomas J. Bruce, Atlanta, 1882-83.

GRIFFIN, NATHAN T.
Active in Clarksville, 1867-68; Sherman, 1870.

GRIFFITH & COCHRAN
Arthur W. Griffith and Hal A. Cochran operating in Austin at 904 Congress, 1898-99.

GRIFFITH, LEMUEL H.
Partner in Pittman & Griffith with Francis M. Pittman operating in Austin at 510 East Sixth, 1887-88.

GRIGSBY, R. L.
Active in El Paso, 1911.

GRIMM, J. ADAM
Born in Illinois, c. 1853. Listed in Terrell, 1880.

GROGDON, ROBERT
Born in Texas, 1866. Active in Travis County, 1900.

GRONDEL & PRAYTOR
Partnership of B. G. Grondel and William B. Praytor in Round Rock, 1890-91.

GROSS, HENRIETTA
Born in Texas, 1863. Listed in Galveston, 1900.

GROSS, OLIVER
Born in Hungary, 1875. Active in Tyler, 1900.

GROW, W. M.
Active in Rains County, 1872. Also listed as Crow.

GRUNDY, ELLA
Born in Texas, 1873. Listed in Goldthwaite, 1900.

GRUNN, W. A.
Born in Illinois, 1871. Listed in Galveston, 1900.

GUENDCH, L. P.
Active in Brownsville, 1869.

GUESS, J. J.
Active in Eastland County, 1894-95.

GUIN, JOHN R.
Listed in Wood County, 1900.

GUIVEY, CLAUD E.
Active in El Paso operating the Boston Art Company at 217 Stanton, 1900.

GUNSTREAM, ADOLPHUS
Born in Louisiana, 1843. Active in Orange, 1896-97, 1900.

GURNEY, CORNELIUS L.
Active in Vernon, 1892.

GUSTAFSON, CHARLES
Active in El Paso, 1904.

GUTHRIE, HOPE
Active in Honey Grove, 1896-97.

GUTHRIE, RICHARD R.
Born in Kentucky, 1851. Listed in Honey Grove, 1900.

GUTIERREZ, SANTOS
Born in Mexico, 1875. Immigrated to U.S., 1876. Listed in Laredo, 1900.

GUY & COOKE
Partnership of Henry A. H. Guy and C. Frank Cooke, operating in Houston at 501 ½ Main, 1892-95.

GUY, HENRY A. H.
Born in Germany, 1861. Active in Houston, 1892-1901. Studio at 83 Main, 1892; 1720 Congress, 1897-1901. Partner in Guy & Cooke at 501 ½ Main, 1892-95.

HACKETT, R.
Active in Dallas before 1899, when the tax records noted a transfer of business to Weatherington Brothers.

HADDIX, ANDREW J.
Active in Decatur, 1896-97; Roswell, New Mexico, 1899, 1902.

HADEN, W. A.
Listed in Buena Vista, Shelby County, 1867; Eutaw, Limestone County, 1868.

HAGEMANN, OTTO
Born in Germany, 1872. Immigrated to U.S., 1887. Listed in San Antonio, 1900.

HAGEN, ERNEST
Active in Fort Worth at 808 Throckmorton, 1892.

HAGGARD, W. Y.
Active in Kaufman County, 1871, 1875; Grayson and Wise Counties, 1873.

HAGGITT
Active in Austin, 1882, at 819 Congress.

HAIR, THOMAS
Born in England, c. 1833. Listed in Galveston, 1880. May be Thomas Moir.

HALCOMB
Listed in Burnet County, 1873. May be Holcomb.

HALEY, JAMES
Born in Texas, 1847. Listed in Galveston, 1900.

HALL & MARSHALL
Partnership operating in Cass and Morris Counties, 1876.

HALL, CHARLES F.
Born in New York, c. 1836. Listed in El Paso, 1860; possibly a painter.

HALL, F. M.
Active in Burleson and Fayette Counties, 1872.

HALL, F. M.
Active in Lexington, Lee County, Texas, c. 1872. Taught photography to John Scott.

HALL, ICHABOD NELSON
Born in Canada, 1834. Immigrated to U.S., 1886. Active in Cotulla, 1880s; La Salle County, 1900.

HALL, N. N.
Active in Grapevine, 1884-85.

HALLER, CHARLES
Born in Michigan, 1870. Listed in El Paso, 1900.

HAMILTON PRODUCE COMPANY
Operating in Temple, 1898-99.

HAMILTON, THOMAS K.
Active in Laredo, 1884-85, 1898-99.

HAMMER, LAURENCE
Born in Alabama, 1876. Listed in Lampasas County, 1900.

HAMMOCH, JOHN G.
Born in Louisiana, 1859. Listed in Baylor County, 1900.

HAND, HIRAM
Partner in Bailey & Hand with F. B. Bailey, operating in Houston on Main, 1856-57; also operated as Bayou City Ambrotype Rooms. Partner with R. E. Moore, c. 1850s.

HANEY, ADA
Born in Texas, 1879. Listed in Wichita Falls, 1900.

HANKS, O. T.
Active in San Augustine County, 1875; Also listed as O. T. Hawks.

HANNA
Partner in Leach & Hanna, active in Cherokee and Llano, 1870s-80s; listed in Presidio County, 1896.

HANNA, ROBERT M.
Born in Missouri, c. 1838. Listed in Dallas, 1870.

HANNIG, IDA (MISS)
Active in Rockport, 1890-91; Victoria, 1890-91.

HANNIG, JULIUS
Active in Victoria, 1882-85, 1898-99.

HANSARD
Partner in Stone & Hansard, active in Denison, c. 1880s. possibly J. W. Hansard of Arkansas and Missouri, c. 1870s-80s.

HANSLEY, J. K.
Listed in Van Zandt County, 1872. Also listed as J. K. Heansley.

HANSON, BARRAUD
Active in Dallas, 1894-95; painter or photographer.

HANZAL, FRANZ
Born in Kentucky, c. 1830. Active in San Antonio, 1869-71; partner in Lungkwitz & Hanzal, 1866-69; partner in Iwonski & Hanzal, 1870.

HANZOLSH, SAM
Active in Medina County, 1872.

HARBIN
Active in Kaufman County, 1871.

HARBSCHEN
Active in Grayson County, 1875.

HARD, E.
Active in Goliad County, 1875. Also listed as Hood.

HARD, J.
Active in Falls County, 1874.

HARDESTY, FRANK
Active in San Antonio at 32 North Flores, 1885-90; sold out to Asa A. Brack, 1889; also active 1898-99.

HARDESTY, J.
Active in San Antonio, 1870-80.

HARDGRAVES, JAMES D.
Listed in Greenville, 1884-85; Ballinger, 1892. Also spelled Hardgrave.

HARDIN, AMBROSE
Born in Missouri. Listed in Palo Pinto, 1860.

HARGROVE, C. R. (MRS.)
Active in Marshall, 1855; employed S. P. Woolley.

HARGROVE, J. G.
Born in Missouri, 1864. Listed in Nocona, 1900; possibly James D. Hardgraves.

HARKEY, W.
Active in Waxahachie, 1867.

HARKEY, WILLIE
Born in Texas, 1879. Listed in Italy, 1900.

HARMAN & DUER
Partnership of James Harman and W. T. Duer, Collin County, 1875.

HARMAN, JAMES
Active in McKinney, 1870, 1878-79; Collin County, 1871-76; partner in Harman & Duer, 1875.

HARPER
Active in Fayette County, 1883.

HARPER & CATER
Active in Austin, 1860. Succeeded by W. W. Bridgers.

HARPER & COMPANY
Thomas J. Harper owned several studios; one in Houston managed by Jesse C. Bartlett at 507 ½ Main, 1899-1900+; another in Austin managed by Samuel L. Loughridge at 920 Congress, 1897-99. A third studio in Galveston operated at 2215 Market, 1898-1900.

HARPER, A. S.
Occasionally photographed in Austin, late 1850s; partner in Harper & Cater.

HARPER BROTHERS
Listed in Lancaster, 1893-94.

HARPER, THOMAS J.
Born in Arkansas, 1858. May have worked at various branches of the Tyler Art Gallery; active in Marshall, 1884-85; Bryan and Ennis, 1890-91; Corsicana, Tyler and Waxahachie, 1892. Operated Harper & Company with studios in Houston, Austin and Galveston, c. 1895-1900+. Also active in Marshall, 1896-97.

HARPER, WILLIAM D.
Born in Missouri, 1867. Listed in Clarendon, 1900.

HARPER, WILLIAM L.
Born in Arkansas, 1868. Listed in Ennis, 1892, 1896-97, 1900.

HARRAH, LEVELLA B.
Born in Kansas, 1877. Listed in Miami, 1900.

HARRINGTON BROTHERS
Partnership of Henry G. and William D. Harrington operating in Dallas at 283 Elm, 1892.

HARRINGTON, HENRY
Born in Kentucky, 1854. Partner in Harrington Brothers, Dallas, 1892; listed in Atlanta, 1900.

HARRINGTON, W. DAVID
Partner in Casley & Harrington with Charles H. Casley, Nacogdoches, 1896-97.

HARRIS
Born in Texas, 1878. Listed in Blanket, 1900.

HARRIS, CHARLES H.
Active in Houston at 1211 Liberty, 1895-96.

HARRIS, JOHN
Active in Hopkins County, 1872.

HARRIS, M. C.
Active in Hutchins and Simonds, 1893.

HARRIS, OTTIS
Born in Tennessee, c. 1877. Listed in Blanket, 1900.

HARRIS, R. D.
Active in Gladewater, 1892.

HARRIS, R. O.
Active in Belton, 1857; Harris County, 1871; San Jacinto County, 1872; in Houston at the Great Northern Depot, 1873; in Montgomery County, 1875.

HARRIS, R. P.
Active in Crackersnack, Liberty County, 1870.

HARRIS, WILLIAM H.
Born in Georgia, c. 1834. Listed in Henderson, 1870; Rusk County, 1871, 1875-76.

HARRISON, GEORGE C.
Active in Springtown, 1884-85; Mineola, 1890-92.

HARRISON, JAMES
Listed in Hopkins County, 1872.

HARRISON, M. C.
Active in Kaufman County, 1891; Dallas County, 1892.

HARRISON, M. CAROLINE (MRS.)
Active in McGregor, 1890-92, 1898-99.

HARRISON, WILLIAM
Born in Mississippi, 1868. Listed in San Antonio, 1900;

HARROW & COMPANY
Operating in Smith County, 1875.

HART, ALEXANDER
Listed in Medley, Montgomery County, 1892.

HART, J. W.
Born in Tennessee, c. 1843. Listed in Stephenville, 1880.

HART, JANIS
Born in Indiana, 1876. Listed in Nacogdoches, 1900.

HART, JOHN
Active in Hopkins County, 1872; Hunt County, 1873; Collin and Denton Counties, 1874.

HARTLEY, R. M.
Born in Iowa, 1870. Active in Brownwood, 1900.

HARTMAN, MICHAEL E.
Born in Kentucky, c. 1843. Active in Grayson County, 1874-75; Sulphur Springs, 1880; Bonham, 1882-85, 1898-99.

HARTMANN, LEOPOLD A.
Active in Houston, 1890-99. Studio at 50 West Preston, 1890-91; on Congress, 1892-95; at 409 Travis, 1895-96.

HARTSOCK, J. R.
Active in Indianola, Calhoun County, 1854.

HASKINS, SAMUEL
Born in Tennessee, 1856. Listed in Collin County, 1900.

HASMAN, JAMES
Active in Williamson County, 1873.

HASTAND, WILLIAM L.
Born in Missouri, 1870. Listed in Claude, 1900.

HAUGE, CORNELIUS
Born in Norway, 1870. Immigrated to U.S., 1886. Listed in McGregor, 1900.

HAUSER, JAMES K. P.
Born in Texas, c. 1851. Active in Red River County, 1880; Clarksville, 1882-85, 1890-92.

HAWE, H.
Active in Anderson County, 1875.

HAWKINS, GEORGE
Active in Lamar County, 1873.

HAWKS, J. P.
Listed in San Augustine County, 1872; Orange County, 1875.

HAY & WOOD
Possibly Hoy & Wood, active in Blanco and Burnet Counties, 1871.

HAY, CLAUDE
Born in Tennessee, 1871. Listed in De Kalb, 1900.

HAY, GEORGE H.
Born in Kentucky, 1867. Active in Rockdale, 1896-97; Williamson County, 1900.

HAYES & MURRAY
James Hayes and Henry L. Murray operating in Athens, 1892.

HAYES, JOHN W.
Born in Tennessee, 1862. Listed in Upshur County, 1900.

HAYWORTH, J. P.
Partner with Daniel P. Sink operating as Sink & Hayworth in Vernon, 1890-91.

HEANES, E. A.
Active in Tyler, 1869.

HEARN, THOMAS
Born in Texas, c. 1847. Listed in Avinger, 1880.

HECOX, F. C.
Active in El Paso, 1911.

HEFNER, CLAUDE S.
Born in North Carolina, 1868. Active in Nolan County, 1900

HEIRON & SCHLUTE
Possibly H. B. Heiron, or a misspelling of Heiman & Schlueter. Listed in Granger, 1896-97.

HEIRON, H. B.
Born in Texas, 1865. Active in Granger, 1900; possibly a partner in Heiron & Schlute.

HELDINGER, HENRY
Born in Illinois, 1876. Listed in Houston, 1900.

HELLIN & WESTRUP
Partnership operating in Dallas, 1898-99, at 304 Elm.

HEMMING, EDWARD
Active in Grayson County, 1879-80; Whitesboro, 1884-85.

HENAUSIN, W. F. E. C.
Active in Columbus and Oso, 1869.

HENDEMAN, JOHN
Listed in Wood County, 1900.

HENDERSON, H. A. E.
Active in Goliad County, 1870.

HENDERSON, J. F.
Active in DeWitt County, 1871.

HENDERSON, L. D.
Born in South Carolina, c. 1842. Listed in Grayson County and Wheatville, Morris County, 1870; Titus County, 1872.

HENDERSON, WILLIAM
Born in Kentucky, c. 1843. Listed in Refugio, 1870; possibly a painter.

HENDRICK, JAMES
Active in Honey Grove and Sherman, 1884-85.

HENDRICKS
Active in Denison, 1880-90.

HENDSON, WILLIAM
Listed in Linden, 1870.

HENRY, JOHNSON
Active in Clinton, DeWitt County, 1866-67.

HENTSCHELL, GUSTAVE
Born in Saxony, c. 1845. Active in Belle Plain, Callahan County, 1880.

HEPP, G. W.
Active in Bertram, 1892.

HERERA, G.
Active in Laredo, 1892.

HERWICK, J. T.
Born in New York, c. 1842. Listed in Denison, 1880; possibly a painter.

HEYLAND, HERMAN
Born in Germany, 1861. Listed in Fredericksburg, 1900.

HICKMAN, HERMAN
Born in Virginia, 1878. Listed in Galveston, 1900.

HICKS, M. W.
Active in Whitney, 1884-85.

HICKSON, CAREY L.
Born in Texas, 1866. Active in Lockhart, 1896-97, 1900.

HIELMAN, CHRISTIAN
Born in Norway, 1870. Immigrated to U.S., 1884. Listed in McLennan County, 1900.

HIESTER, HENRY T.
Died in Dallas, February 1895. Hiester began his career in photography in Tonica, Illinois, 1867, and worked in the Santa Fe, New Mexico area, 1871-78 or later. He may have bought out Henry R. Farr in Tyler and operated a studio there, 1889-95. During the same period, he also worked in Vernon and Lewisville. Also spelled Heister.

HIGGINS, FREAME M.
Born in Illinois, 1877. Worked as a printer for Bushong & Feldman in El Paso, 1898-99; also listed as active, 1900.

HILDEBRANDT, AUGUST
Born in Texas, 1879. Listed in Hays County, 1900.

HILL, EUGENE
Partner in Anthony & Hill, operating in Marshall, 1892.

HILL, JOHN M.
Born in Tennessee, c. 1841. Active in Tyler, 1860-61, 1866-69.

HILL, ROBERT E.
Born in Texas, 1876. Listed in Caldwell County, 1900.

HILL, SAMUEL B.
Born in Ohio, 1839 (1900 census), or c. 1843 (1880 census); died in Austin, 1917. Moved to Austin, 1877. He may have started in pho-

tography business as partner in Adams & Hill, 1878, continuing until c. 1906, when he worked in real estate. His studio was located at 817 Congress, 1879-83; 818 Congress, 1884-88; 916 Congress, 1889-94. A second address was given in 1892, at 909 Congress. He was at 915 Congress, 1895-1901.

HILL, SAMUEL T.
Printer for Samuel B. Hill in Austin, 1895-96; proprietor of Austin Photo Engraving Company, 1898-99.

HILLMAN, JOSHUA W.
Born in Georgia, c. 1849. Listed in Caldwell, 1880; Texarkana, 1884-85.

HILLYER & ANDERSON
Partnership operating in Williamson County, 1867.

HILLYER & SON, H. B.
Hamilton Biscoe and Charles Ernest Hillyer operating studios in Austin at 916 Congress, 1887-88; in Dallas at 701 Elm, 1888-89; in Taylor, 1890-91; Taylor and Belton, 1892.

HILLYER, CHARLES ERNEST
Born in Texas, 1866. Active in Austin, 1885-86; Bartlett, 1896-97; Belton, 1900. Partner with his father in H. B. Hillyer & Son in their studios in Austin at 916 Congress, 1887-88; in Dallas at 701 Elm, 1888-89; in Taylor, 1890-91; Taylor and Belton, 1892.

HILLYER, HAMILTON BISCOE
Born in Macon, Georgia, 1835; died in Bowie, 1903. Son of Reverend John Freeman Hillyer, the president of Mercer University and a daguerreotypist in Georgia, c. 1844, working in Athens, 1847. The family came to Galveston, 1848, later moving to a ranch on the San Antonio River. H. B. was listed in the 1850 census as a clerk and farmed around Goliad before making his first daguerreotypes, 1857. He bought an ambrotype kit, took instructions from Anderson & Blessing of New Orleans for $100, and made ambrotypes, 1858-61. He moved to Austin after the Civil War and organized tent studios that traveled to many towns. He was active in Austin, 1868-99, with studios located on Hickory, 1872-73, 1877-78; at 917 Congress, 1881-82; 916 Congress, 1883-86. Also active in Belton, 1890-91, 1896-97; Dallas and Bowie, 1890s.

HIMBLY, EUGENE
Active in Comal County, 1876.

HINSDALE, ALBERT
Born in Massachusetts, 1858. Listed in Fort Worth, 1900.

HINSDALE, LEWIS A.
Active in Bastrop, 1896-97.

HINSON, THOMAS A.
Born in England, 1874. Immigrated to U.S., 1879. Listed in San Marcos, 1896-97, 1900.

HITCHLER, ANTHONY H.
Born in Germany, 1852. Immigrated to U.S., 1853. Worked for Charles J. Wright in Houston, 1882-97; proprietor of the Wright Art Studio at 502 ½ Main, 1899; 501 ½ Main, 1900-01.

HOBLEIN, HOMER
Born in Texas, 1855. Listed in Rockport, 1900.

HODGE, JAMES H.
Born in Tennessee, c. 1835. Listed in Wheelock, Robertson County and Woodville, 1870.

HODGES, W. W.
Active in Lampasas County, 1876.

HODSALL, F. G.
Active in Mason County, 1887; New Mexico, 1889-1916. Possibly F. G. Hodsell, or Hodsoll.

HOFFMAN, A. L.
Active in Comal County, 1874.

HOFMAN, B. F.
Working in New Braunfels, 1853.

HOGAN, EUGENE
Born in Texas, 1874. Listed in Ladonia, 1900.

HOLCOMB
Partner in Soloman & Holcomb, operating in Georgetown, 1868.

HOLCOMB, JOHN M.
Born in Texas, c. 1844. Listed in Livingston, 1870.

HOLDERNESS
Active in Eastland County, 1895.

HOLLADAY & BLACKBURN
Partners operating in Gonzales County, 1872.

HOLLAND, THOMAS A.
Born in Texas, 1868. Active in Wharton, 1892; sold out to F. C. Winkelmann, 1894; in Brenham, 1896-1900.

HOLLINGSWORTH, B. F.
Active in New London, 1870.

HOLLY
Partner in Erwin & Holly operating in Wadeville (now Kerens), 1869.

HOLMES
Partner in Holmes & Fordtran operating in Columbia (now West Columbia), 1857; partner in Park & Holmes on Front, 1858-59. Also operated as Columbia Sky-Light Gallery. Possibly Charles Holmes.

HOLMES & FORDTRAN
Active in Columbia, 1857.

HOLT, N. N.
Possibly the same as N. N. Hall in Grapevine, 1884-85.

HOLT, ROBERT
Born in Louisiana, 1853. Listed in the 1900 census as operating a "Photographic Store" in Houston.

HOLT, W. U.
Born in Tennessee, 1856. Listed in Denton, 1900.

HOME STUDIO
Operated by Swafford & Swafford in Baird.

HOOD, J. R.
Born in Louisiana, c. 1835. Listed in Willis, 1880.

HOOKER, F. S.
Partner in Bartlett & Hooker with Frederick W. Bartlett operating in Galveston at 159 East Market, 1868-69.

HOPER, J. D.
Born in New Jersey, c. 1842. Listed in Weatherford, 1880.

HORN
Partner in Williams & Horn operating in Strawn, 1890-91.

HORN, JOHN W.
Active in Greenville, 1892.

HORTON, KING
Born in Texas, 1869. Listed in Greenville, 1900.

HOUCK, HAMILTON
Born in Maryland, c. 1842. Possibly a partner in Shalenberger & Houck, listed in Tarrant County, 1875; in Kimball, 1880; Kopperl, 1882-85, 1890-91.

HOUGH, R. S.
Active in Rusk County, 1871.

HOUSE, EMMETT
Born in Kansas, 1873. Listed in Cleburne, 1900.

HOUSGHEN, J. A.
Active in Brenham, 1872.

HOUSTON CITY GALLERY
Operated by Charles N. Bean in Houston, Main at Preston, 1866-68.

HOUSTON DAGUERREIAN GALLERY
Operated by Henry R. Allen in Houston, 1845-46.

HOUSTON, FORBES
Active in Navasota, 1869; also listed as Forbes Honston.

HOUSTON SKY-LIGHT AMBROTYPE GALLERY
Operated by R. E. Moore in Houston, 1856. Also known as Magnolia Sky-Light Gallery, 1857-58; R. E. Moore & Company, 1857-58, and Moore & Williams.

HOWARD, P. J.
Listed in Hill County, 1874.

HOWE, WILLIAM H.
Photographer and watchmaker from Washington, D.C. Active in Clarksville and Paris, 1859-60; Clarksville, 1861.

HOWEL, JOHN
Active in Hays County, 1889.

HOWELL, HERMAN
Born in Ohio, 1868. Listed in El Paso, 1900.

HOWELL, JOHN A.
Born in Tennessee, 1858. Active in Temple, 1896-97, 1900.

HOWELL, T. L.
Active in San Marcos, 1892.

HOY & ELLIS
Partnership operating in Denton County, 1871.

HOY, WOOD & COMPANY
Operating in Blanco County, 1871; possibly the same as Hay & Wood.

HOYT, E. E.
Active in Midland, 1895; Presidio County, 1899.

HOYT, ELMER
Partner in Roessle & Hoyt with Theodore Roessle operating in San Angelo, 1890-92.

HOYT, HIRAM
Active in New Mexico, 1877-78; in Washington before 1900. Active in San Antonio at 10 East Houston, 1885-86; in Orange County, 1887; continued in San Antonio, 1898-99.

HUBERT
Partner in Bulger & Hubert, Kendall County, 1872.

HUBSCHAM, LEWIS
Active in Grayson County, 1874; possibly Lewis Hubschmann who was later active in Illinois, 1882, 1884.

HUCKWATE, I.
Born in Texas, 1870. Listed in San Antonio, 1900.

HUDSON, ED
Active in Waxahachie, 1900.

HUDSON, FRANK
Born in Alabama, 1865. Active in Paris, 1896-1900.

HUDSON, WILLIAM
Born in Mississippi, 1867. Listed in Red River County, 1900.

HUFF
Partner in North & Huff operating in Denison, 1881.

HUFF, JOHN B.
Born in Virginia, 1844. Listed in Bowie County, 1900.

HUGH & McCLANE
Partnership in Collin County, 1871.

HUGHES & WALKER
Active in Williamson County, 1874.

HUGHES, HARRY E.
Listed in Henderson, 1896-97.

HUGHES, MILTON H.
Active in Gonzales, 1890-92.

HUGHES, MOSE E.
Born in England, 1868. Immigrated to U.S., 1868. Listed in Marshall, 1900.

HUGHES, WILLIAM F.
Born in North Carolina. Active in Colorado City, 1884-85, 1890-92, 1896-99; listed in Mitchell County, 1900.

HUGHSON & MOODMORTH
Partnership in Brenham, 1869; James A. Hughson.

HUGHSON, JAMES A.
Born in Illinois, c. 1831. Active in Springfield, Limestone County, 1866; Brenham, 1869-70; partner with Moodmorth, 1869; operating alone in San Marcos, 1880; Luling, 1884-85.

HULL, D. HAG
Born in Pennsylvania, c. 1863. Listed in Galveston County, 1880.

HUMPHRIES PHOTO COMPANY
Active in El Paso, 1905-09, operated by W. R. Humphries.

HUMPHRIES, W. R.
Active in El Paso operating the Humphries Photo Company, 1905-09.

HUNT, A. A.
Born in Illinois, 1828. "Artist Photographer" listed in the 1900 census, active in San Saba.

HUNT, JOHN
Born in Mississippi, c. 1841. Active in Troup, 1860; possibly a painter.

HUNTER BROTHERS
Partnership of Charles G. and Robert T. Hunter operating in Bryan, 1884-85.

HUNTER, CHARLES G.
Partner with Robert T. Hunter, operating as Hunter Brothers in Bryan, 1884-85.

HUNTER, ROBERT T.
Partner in Hunter Brothers, studio in Bryan, 1884-85; operated alone, 1898-99.

HUNZIKER, JOHN A.
Listed in Gillespie, Maverick and Uvalde Counties, 1872; Atascosa County, 1873; Starr County, 1874, 1876.

HURLEY & COMPANY
Advertised in Houston, 1859; possibly dealers of photographic supplies, and not photographers.

HURST, LEWIS
Active in Presidio County, 1897.

HUTCHENSON, RICHARD
Born in German, 1867. Immigrated to U.S., 1878. Listed in Gillespie County, 1900.

HUTCHINS, G. W.
Active in Dallas, 1894.

HUTCHINSON, THOMAS E.
Born in Tennessee, c. 1834. Active in Sequin, 1867-70, 1878-79.

HZITRAY, EMIL
Born in New York, 1882. Listed in Kerrville, 1900; lived with Albert Glock and may have worked for him.

INCE, R. E. W.
Listed in Johnson County, 1872.

INGLE, ELIZABETH
Active in Gainesville at 16 Boggs, 1887-88; continued active 1890-91. Also known as Mrs. Henry Ingle.

INGLE, H.
Active in Gonzales County, 1875; Ellis County, 1876; possibly Henry Ingle.

INGLE, HENRY
Active in Gainesville, 1882-83, 1898-99.

IRBY & PHILLIPS
Terry Irby and Henry S. Phillips operating in Vernon, 1892.

IRONS, GEORGE C.
Active in Tyler, 1896-97; also operated as Eureka Gallery.

IRVIN, OMA (MISS)
Partner in Carson & Irvin operating in Crawford, 1896-97.

IRVINE, A. H., JR.
Listed in San Antonio at 229 East Houston, 1899-1900.

ISH, JOHN W.
Active in Henrietta, 1890-91.

IVY, EPHRAM
Born in Georgia, 1874. Listed in Henrietta, 1890-91.

IWONSKI & COMPANY
Active in San Antonio, 1869.

IWONSKI & HANZAL
Carl G. Von Iwonski and Franz Hanzal operating in San Antonio, 1870.

IWONSKI, CARL G. VON
Born in Hilbersdorf, Silesia, 1830; died in Breslau, Silesia, 1912. Immigrated to U.S., 1845. Iwonski was a painter and art teacher for most of his life and photographer for at least ten years. Partner in DeRyee & Iwonski, operating in New Braunfels, 1859-60. In San Antonio he was a partner in Lungkwitz & Iwonski, 1866-69; in Iwonski, Lungkwitz & Hanzal, 1869; and Iwonski & Hanzal, 1870.

IWONSKI, LUNGKWITZ & HANZAL
Partnership in San Antonio, 1869; changed to Iwonski & Hanzal, 1870.

JACKSON & KNIGHT
William D. Jackson, Sr. and Fayette W. Knight; studio located at 27 ½ Austin Avenue, Waco, c. 1874-76.

JACKSON & SPILLER
Active in Llano, c. 1890.

JACKSON, CYRUS F.
Born in Canada, 1848. Listed in San Marcos, 1900.

JACKSON, GUS B.
Employed by William D. Jackson, Sr., in Waco, 1886-93. Listed in Waco at 107 ½ South Fifth, 1894-95; in Dallas at 321 Elm, 1896-97.

JACKSON, ISAAC
Born in Georgia, c. 1851. Listed in Bastrop County, 1880.

JACKSON, J. L.
Active in Navarro County, 1876.

JACKSON, J. N.
Active in Goliad County, 1874-75.

JACKSON, W. B.
Active in Brazos Santiago, Cameron County, 1866.

JACKSON, W. D.
Active in Belton, 1859; Cameron, 1866-70; possibly William D. Jackson.

JACKSON, WILLIAM D., JR.
Born in Texas, 1862. Operating in Waco, 1886-1901. Listed at 120 North Third, 1886-87; 109 South Fifth, 1888-91; 107 ½ South Fifth Street, 1892-99; 503 ½ Austin, 1900-01.

JACKSON, WILLIAM D., SR.
Born in North Carolina, 1838. Active in Waco, 1874-1901. Partner in Jackson & Knight with Fayette W. Knight, studio located at 27 ½ Austin, 1874-76; continued alone at that address, 1878-82; at 27 Austin, 1882-83; 423 Austin, 1884- 85; 120 North Third, 1886-87; 112 North Fifth, 1888-89; 109 South Fifth and 112 North Fifth, 1892-93; 112 North Fifth, 1894-1901.

JACOBI
Partner in Parks & Jacobi, Lee County, 1876.

JACOBS, SAMUEL E.
Operating in San Antonio at 2 East Houston, 1890-92. May be the same as Samuel E. Jacobson.

JACOBSEN, S. E.
Listed in Weimar, 1894-95; he left for New Orleans, November 1895. Possibly Samuel E. Jacobs or Semmy E. Jacobson.

JACOBSON, MARY E. (MRS.)
Active in San Antonio, 1889-93; listed at 2 East Houston, 1889-91; 113 North Alamo, 1892-93.

JACOBSON, SAMUEL E.
Partner in Doerr & Jacobson with Henry A. Doerr, operating in San Antonio at 63 Commerce, 1876-80. Active in Galveston, 1884-85, at 221-223 East Post Office. Also listed as Semmy E.; see Samuel E. Jacobs.

JAMES, J.
Born in Kentucky, c. 1870. Listed in Longview, 1900.

JAMES, J. WILLIAM
Listed in Edna, 1900.

JANES & BANTA
Partnership in Fayette County, 1871-72.

JANES & MAY
Operated in Bryan, 1869.

JANSON, FRED M.
Listed in Harrison County, 1900.

JARMAN, I. N.
Born in Tennessee, c. 1854. Listed in Palestine, 1880.

JAYNES & JOLLY
Partnership in Travis County, 1875.

JEFFERIES, H. L.
Active in Navarro County, 1875.

JENNINGS, R. P.
Active in San Jacinto County, 1871.

JERABEK, J. V.
Partner in Thomas & Jerabek with George E. Thomas operating in Caldwell, 1896-97.

JERNIGAN, MARTIN
Listed in Elysian Fields, Harrison County, 1869.

JERROLD, DOUGLAS E.
Active in Austin, 1875; possibly a painter.

JESSE, MAXIMILIAN T.
Born in Russia, c. 1843. Partner in Doerr & Jesse, San Antonio, 1866, with Henry A. Doerr. Operating alone in San Antonio, 1867-68, 1880; Fayette County, 1871; Lavaca County, 1872; Maverick County, 1873; Medina and Webb Counties, 1875; partner in Winther & Jesse with Nicholas Winther at 287 West Commerce, 1881-82; alone in Mason County, 1886.

JOE'S GALLERY
Studio located on Houston Street between 6th and 7th next to Gillespie's Office, Fort Worth, c. 1880.

JOHNS, W. C.
Born in Indiana, 1864. Listed in Beaumont, 1900.

JOHNSON & COMPANY, L. H.
Agents for National Copying Company of Georgia, working in Houston on Congress at Travis, 1875.

JOHNSON & STAMPS
Partnership in Caldwell County, 1871.

JOHNSON, EDWARD
Born in Texas, 1858. Listed in Ladonia, 1900.

JOHNSON, J. H.
Photographer working in Ohio, 1870s. Active in Kaufman County, 1872.

JOHNSON, J. H. (MRS.)
Active in Kaufman County, 1871.

JOHNSON, JOSEPH
Active in Laredo, 1869.

JOHNSON, LOUIS
Born in Texas, 1871. Listed in Wilson County, 1900.

JOHNSON, LUTHER C.
Born in Alabama, 1853. Active in Galveston County, 1880; Ganado, 1900.

JOHNSON, S. E.
Active in Union, Wilson County, 1882, 1896-97.

JOHNSON, THOMAS H.
Stereo photographer active in Dallas.

JOHNSON, W. D.
Listed in Hillsboro, 1884-85.

JOHNSTON, GEORGE
Born in Pennsylvania, c. 1848. Operated in Waco on North Fourth between Austin and Washington, 1880-81.

JOINER & COX
Partnership operating in Fayette County, 1873.

JOLLY
Partner in Jaynes & Jolly, Travis County, 1875.

JONES & LOCKHART
Active in Fannin County, 1867; possibly J. B. Lockhart.

JONES & MEACHAM
Charles Jones and George L. Meacham operating in Houston at 1009 Main, 1895-96.

JONES & MOFFITT
Partnership in Denton County, 1875; Pilot Point, 1878-79, 1884-85; possibly David J. Moffitt.

JONES & SCHEIER
Charles Jones and John H. Scheier, operating in Houston at 1007 Main, 1897-98.

JONES, BARNETT H.
Born in Texas, c. 1850. Listed in Polk County, 1880.

JONES, CHARLES
Born in Ohio, 1868. Active in Navasota, 1900; possibly a partner in Jones & Scheier and Jones & Meacham.

JONES, FRED S.
Listed in Gonzales County, 1875-76.

JONES, FREDERICK L.
Active in El Paso at 22 Bronson Block, 1898-99; possibly a painter.

JONES, J. R.
Active in Goliad County, 1870.

JONES, JAMES TALIFERO
Born in Georgia, 1843. Listed in Denton, 1874, 1890-92, 1894, 1896-97, 1900.

JONES, JESSE G.
Born in Alabama, c. 1843. Active in Black Jack Grove, 1869-70; also in White Oak, 1870; Hopkins County, 1880.

JONES, JOHN B.
Born in Tennessee, 1854. Listed in Floyd County, 1900.

JONES, MILTON
Born in Mississippi, c. 1836. Active in Meridian, 1860.

JONES, MOLLY E. (MRS.)
Active in Goldthwaite, 1896-97.

JONES, ROBERT
Active in Maryland, 1880. Active in Goldthwaite, 1890-91.

JONES, ROBERT E.
Listed in Prairie Lea, Caldwell County, 1867; possibly a partner in Sterzing & Jones in Burnet County, 1867.

JONES, ROBERT S.
Born in Texas, 1880. Listed in Denison, 1900.

JONES, T. R.
Active in Stonewall, Gillespie County, 1892.

JONES, TALIFERO
Born in Texas, 1880. Listed in Denton, 1900.

JORDAN, ELMER P.
Born in Maine, 1865. Active in Galveston, 1900.

JOSLIN, AMEN J. T.
May have operated as photographer in Illinois, 1874, 1878, 1882, 1884. Active in El Paso, 1892, on Texas at Stanton. Also listed as Jr.

JOSLYN, G. H.
Active in Austin, 1866; in Galveston operating the Galveston Photographic Company at 220 Tremont, 1869.

JOURNEAY, WILLIAM O.
Born in Texas, 1865. His father was a Mier Expedition survivor. Journeay was employed as a retoucher for Samuel B. Hill in Austin, 1887-90; continued active in Austin, 1891-1900. His studio was located at 818 Congress, 1891-97; 814 Congress, 1898-99.

KAISER, FRANK
Partner in Richard & Kaiser, Fort Worth at 108 Main, 1888-89; also operated as Southern Art Gallery.

KANE
Partner in Lewis & Kane, Washington County, 1875.

KARECHEL, WILLIAM
Active in Fayette County, 1896. Possibly William Kauechel.

KARNES
Partner in Wallace & Karnes, Fayette County, 1871, 1873.

KAVANAUGH, MALVIN P.
Active in Belton, 1884-85, 1898-99; Hillsboro, 1890-91; Abilene, 1892; Baird, 1896-97.

KEASLER, JOHN R.
Born in Alabama, 1860. Listed in Sulphur Springs, 1890-91; Ladonia, 1896-97, 1900; also in Honey Grove, 1900.

KEE, W. M.
Listed in Cherokee County, 1871; Upshur County, 1873.

KEELER, W. M.
Born in Scotland, c. 1850. Listed in Kinney County, 1880.

KEISER, FRED
Active in Fort Worth at 52 Houston, 1882.

KEISER, JESSE
Leased the studio of M. S. Lusby in Canyon, 1908.

KEITH & COMPANY, ROBERT J.
Operated in Beaumont, 1890-91.

KEITH, T. D.
Stereo photographer in Texas; specific area unknown.

KELLEY, E. W.
Stereo photographer in Dallas; partner in Berry, Kelley & Chadwick, major publisher of stereoviews, c. 1906-15. Also worked alone and in other partnerships in Illinois, Texas and Pennsylvania, 1890s-1910; partner in Kelley & Chadwick in Chicago, 1900s.

KELLEY, J. A.
Partner in Stephens & Kelly operating in Jefferson, 1869; listed alone in Jefferson, 1870.

KELLOGSOL, L. W.
Active in Travis County, 1879.

KELLY, COLUM
Listed in Dallas, 1891-92.

KELLY, JAMES A.
Born in Mississippi, c. 1834. Listed in Henderson, 1870; Johnson County, 1871.

KELLY, R. P.
Active in San Antonio, 1852-54. Located on southeast corner of Main Plaza, 1852. Partner in Peirce, Kelly & Peirce on Pecan, 1853-54.

KELTERINGHAM, C. B.
Born in Mississippi, c. 1840. Active in Hempstead, 1878-79; Matagorda County, 1880. Possibly C. B. Kiteringham.

KEMPTON, R. JOHN
Born in Arkansas, 1870. Listed in Hays County, 1900.

KENDALL, WILLIAM
May have been in Vermont and New Hampshire, 1870s. Active in

Fayette County, 1884, 1886-88, 1892. Possibly William Kendell.

KENDEL, W.
Active in Cibolo, 1890-92, 1896-97.

KENNEDY & PINKERTON
Listed in Denton County, 1876.

KENNEDY, WALTER B.
Partner in Whittaker & Kennedy with Daniel Whittaker in Weatherford, 1892. Listed alone in Cleburne, 1896-97.

KEPPINGHAM, CAPTAIN
Born in England, c. 1936. Listed in Houston, 1880.

KERR, M. T.
Born in Texas, c. 1854. Active in Erath County, 1876; Weatherford, 1880.

KERSTING, F. W.
Born in Prussia, c. 1819. Active in Galveston at 174 South Tremont, 1880-81. Possibly W. John Kersting.

KEULER, WILLIAM
Born in Germany, 1848. Immigrated to U.S., 1874. Listed in Guadalupe County, 1900.

KEURITZ, OTTO
Operated in Indianola, Calhoun County, 1870.

KEY, W. M.
Active in Smith County, 1872.

KEYS, M.
Born in Illinois, 1868. Listed in Kerrville, 1900.

KIBBE, EDWIN T.
Born in Texas, 1884. Active in Clarksville, 1900. Also listed as Kikle.

KINCADE, CHARLES
Employed as artist at Ashley's City Gallery in Houston, 1866.

KINNARD, J. A.
Active in Nacogdoches County, 1876.

KINNE & DOWNING
Partnership of Walter O. Kinne and William C. Downing operating in Gainesville, 1887-88. Studio on California at Denton.

KINNE, WALTER O.
Born in Mississippi, c. 1866. Photographic apprentice in Gainesville, 1880; operating as photographer, 1884-85, 1890-92.

KIRKHAM, JOHN
Born in England, 1832. Immigrated to U.S., 1850. Listed in Dallas, 1900.

KIRKPATRICK, A. W.
Active in Granbury, 1898-99.

KITE, JOHN
Listed in Palo Pinto County, 1873.

KITERINGHAM, C. B.
Active in Refugio County, 1871; possibly C. B. Kelteringham.

KLINE, MYRTLE
Born in Missouri, 1884. Listed in McLennan County, 1900.

KNIGHT, E. T.
Active in Grandview, 1896-97.

KNIGHT, FAYETTE W.
Partner with William D. Jackson, Sr., operating as Jackson & Knight, 27 ½ Austin Avenue, Waco, c. 1874-76. Partner in Mullens & Knight with John J. Mullens in Waco at 55 ½ Austin, 1878-79. Operated alone in Greenville, 1882-85, 1890-92, 1898-99.

KNOX, ED
Active in Fayette County, 1891.

KNUCKSON, J. P.
Active in Dallas, 1877.

KNUTSON, O. PETER
Born in England, c. 1853. Partner in Teagarden & Knutson active in Tyler, 1880. Also listed as Nutson.

KOCH, H.
Active in Austin County, 1871; Lee County, 1874.

KOCH, THEODORE H.
Active in Bellville, 1896-97.

KRUEGER & PIPER
Active in San Antonio, 1870-80; listed in Burnet County, 1874. Also listed as Kruger & Piper. Possibly Albert Piper.

KRUEGER, ERNEST
Partner in Works & Krueger, active in Fort Worth at 403 Main, 1894-95; operating alone, 1896-97. Also spelled Kruger.

KRUEGER, MAX A. P.
Born in Germany, 1851; died in Germany, 1927. An itinerant photographer operating from "the Texas coast to San Saba," 1873-75. He sold out to Pius Fey, mid-1870s.

KRUSE, CARL G.
Partner in Cozby & Kruse with Oliver Cozby operating in San Marcos, 1890-91. Possibly Charles G. Kruse.

KRUSE, CHARLES G.
Born in Germany, 1861. Immigrated to U.S., 1880. Active in Rockport, 1896-97; Dallas, 1900.

KUHN, FRANKLIN
Active in Maryland, 1856-57, 1874-80; in Georgia, 1866-71. Listed in San Antonio, 1882-84; located on the Main Plaza, 1882-83; also operated with David P. Barr as F. Kuhn & Comapny, 1882-83. Studio at 3 Acequia, 1883-84. Also listed as Frank Kuhn.

KUHN, H.
Active in Columbus, 1869. Worked in Atlanta, Georgia, c. 1870.

KUHN, VLEG
Active in San Antonio, 1890.

KUNZ & MUELLER
Partnership operating in Fayette County, 1893.

KYLE, A. A.
Listed in Hood County, 1873.

LA GARZA BROTHERS
Active in El Paso, 1912-13.

LABADIE, EDWARD
Partner in Mitchell & Labadie, Dallas, 1891-92; may have been painters.

LACKARD, GEORGE W.
Active in Lockhart, 1867.

LACKEY, A.
Listed in Grayson County, 1871-73; Williamson County, 1875.

LAINE, D. J.
Active in Waco, 1866.

LAMICH, C. H.
Born in Ohio, c. 1855. Active in San Antonio, 1880.

LAMKINS BROTHERS
Operated in New Braunfels, 1854.

LAMON, W. H.
Listed in Grayson County, 1874-75; worked in Lawrence, Kansas, c. 1879.

LANDY, M. L.
Active in Brownwood, 1884-85.

LANE, LUTHER C.
Born in Texas, 1876. Listed in Corsicana, 1900.

LANEY, JOHN W.
Born in Kentucky, c. 1830. Active in Lockhart, 1869-70; Caldwell County, 1871-72.

LANGE, N.
Born in Pennsylvania, c. 1845. Active in Austin County, 1871; Washington County, 1874; Waller County, 1875; Limestone County, 1880. Possibly M. Lang.

LANGENHEIM, WILLIAM
Born in Germany, 1870; died in Philadelphia, Pennsylvania, 1874. He operated the famous Langenheim Brothers gallery in Philadelphia with his brother, Ferdinand, 1840-46. He intended to relocate permanently to Texas, 1846, but fear of epidemics caused him to return to Philadelphia. The Langenheim Brothers sold the rights to Talbot's paperprint process for Texas to Maquire & Harrington of New Orleans, but calotypes are not known to have been made in Texas.

LARN & MILLER
Active in Fayette County, 1889.

LAROCHE, C. G.
Listed in Maverick County, 1874.

LASSITER, J. W.
Active in Rusk County, 1875.

LAWHON, JOHN P.
Active in Grayson County, 1875; in Sherman on the square between Crockett and Travis, 1876-77.
LAWRENCE, D. H.
Worked in Corpus Christi, 1866; Eagle Lake, 1867.

LAWRENCE, O. J.
Operated in Hill County, 1871, 1875; Tarrant County, 1874-76; Arlington, 1882-85, 1890-92, 1898-99.

LAWSON, W. H.
Born in Arkansas, 1856. Listed in Marble Falls, 1890-91; Travis County, 1900.

LAYTON, J. M.
Active in Lavaca County, 1871, 1876; Fayette County, 1872.

LEACH
Partner in Shauum & Leach, Presidio County, 1896.

LEACH & HANNA
Partnership operating in Presidio County, 1896.

LEACH & RANDOLPH
Listed in Gainesville, 1880s; Don M. Leach.

LEACH, DON M.
Partner in Baker & Leach, active in Austin, 18602-70s; partner in Leach & Randolph, Gainesville; in Zant & Leach, Mineral Wells, 1880s.

LEACH, JOE A.
Born in Texas, 1857. Listed in Llano County, 1900.

LEDBETTER, ABNER B.
Born in South Carolina, 1849. Active in Upshur County, 1900.

LEE, ELLEN (MISS)
Partner in Ratcliffe & Lee with Miss Jennie Ratcliffe, operating in San Antonio, 1892-93.

LEE, WILLIAM
Born in Texas, 1867. "Photographer Artist" listed in the census of 1900 in Newton County.

LEESON, HARRY O.
Employed by William H. Leeson in Houston, 1877-80.

LEESON, WILLIAM H.
Active in New Orleans, Louisiana, 1861, 1865-70. Active in Harris County, 1875; Houston, 1877-83. Studio at 113 Main, 1877-78; 111 Main, 1879-80; 89 Main, 1880-83.

LEFFLER, FRANK B.
Born in Ohio, 1851. Active in Fort Worth, 1894-1905 or later. Partner with James A. Thomason operating as Thomason & Leffler, 600 Houston, 1894-95; listed alone at that address, c. 1900.

LEGANER, E. R.
Born in Louisiana, 1879. Listed in Houston, 1900.

LEGTERTON, JOHN
Born in England, 1862. Immigrated to U.S., 1882. Active in Dallas, 1900.

LEIFS, ERNST
Active in Fayette County, 1875.

LEIMGRUBER, F.
Listed in Nacogdoches County, 1870.

LEINERY & PARKER
Partnership operating in Van Zandt County, 1872; possibly Hugh M. Parker.

LEISTER, H.
Active in Travis County, 1884.

LEMAN, CHARLES H.
Born in South Carolina, c. 1832. Worked in Houston, 1870-71, on Chartres Street at McKinney.

LEMMON, MARK J.
Active in El Paso, 1895-99. Located at 414 El Paso, 1895-96; East Seventh between El Paso and Utah, 1898-99.

LEMONE & TESTASUDZ
Partnership in Montgomery County, 1876.

LENMONS, C. F.
Born in Arkansas, 1865. Listed in Ellis County, 1900.

LENNOX
Partner in Williams & Lennox, operating in Denton, 1884-85, 1898-99; possibly I. Williams. Also spelled Lenox.

LENNY, WILLIAM J.
Active in Houston, 1894-96; partner in North & Lenny with Jerry E. North at 302 Chenevert, 1894-95.

LENOX, JOHN W.
Born in Missouri, 1850. Active in Brownwood, 1892; Stephenville, 1896-97, 1900.

LEONARD
Partner in Engle & Leonard, Wharton County, 1866.

LERNE, PALMER
Active in Goliad County, 1870.

LEROSIN, DAVID
Born in France, c. 1827. Listed in Henderson, 1860.

LEWIS & KANE
Partnership operating in Washington County, 1875.

LEWIS, EDWIN C.
Born in Vermont, c. 1842. May have operated in New York, 1870s. Active in Brazos County, 1879; Bryan, 1880, 1882-83.

LEWIS, J. F.
Born in Texas, 1877. Listed in Rockdale, 1900.

LEWIS, JOE R.
Born in Texas, 1874. Listed in Rio Grande City, 1900.

LEWIS, PAUL A.
Born in Texas, 1862. Active in Timpson, 1890-92; Houston, 1900.

LEWIS, W. F.
Active in Temple, 1898-99.

LEWISON, ABRAHAM
Born in Texas, 1871. Listed in San Antonio, 1900.

LEWISON, MARKS
Born in Texas, 1876. Worked in San Antonio, 1900.

LILIENTHAL, LOUIS
Active in New Orleans, Louisiana, 1867-70. Active in Galveston at 170 Tremont, 1884-85.

LIMS & OLIVER
Partnership operating in Victoria, 1866.

LIND, ALBERT H.
Partner with his brother H. C., operating as Lind Brothers in San Antonio at 228 Losoya, 1896-97; also operated as Lind & Company; in Galveston at 420 Twenty-second, 1898.

LIND, ALBERT H. C.
Brother of Albert H.; partners in Lind Brothers, San Antonio, 1896-97.

LIND BROTHERS
Albert H. and H. C. Lind operating in San Antonio, 1896-97, at 228 Losoya.

LIND, H. D.
Born in Wisconsin, 1868; listed in Morgan, 1900; possibly H. C. Lind of Lind Brothers.

LINDGREN, JOHN A.
Born in Sweden, 1847. Immigrated to U.S., 1870. Active in Cleburne, 1880, 1890-92, 1896-99. Also listed in Greenville, 1896-97, 1900.

LINDSAY
Partner in Fitch & Lindsay, active in San Antonio, 1872.

LINGO, HENRY P.
Born in Texas, 1880. Listed in Gatesville, 1900. Possibly Henry Liugo.

LINGOOBER, T. H.
Active in Gregg County, 1873.

LIONBERGER, JOHN M.
Born in Texas, 1867. Active in Weatherford, 1900.

LIPOVETZKY, CHARLES
Active in El Paso, 1908-10.

LITTLE BRICK PHOTOGRAPHIC GALLERY
Operated in San Antonio by A. Leon Delfraisse, 1891-93. Listed at 10 East Houston, 1891-92; 110 East Houston, 1892-93.

LLOYD, JAMES
Born in Alabama, 1859. Listed in McLennan County, 1900.

LLOYD, WALTER A.
Active in Wichita Falls, 1892, 1896-97.

LOCKHART, J.
Operated in Clarksville, 1853.

LOCKHART, J. B.
Possibly a partner in Jones & Lockhart in Fannin County, 1867; active in Honey Grove, 1868.

LOCQUER, A.
Active in Jefferson County, 1874.

LONE STAR COPYING HOUSE
Operated by D. H. Swartz & Brother, David H. and John, in Fort Worth, 1885-86; known as the Cottage Gallery, 1886-87.

LONG, ERNEST
Born in Missouri, 1878. Listed in San Antonio, 1900.

LONG, HORACE G.
Active in Elysian Fields, Harrison County, 1866.

LONG, J. C.
Listed in Grayson County, 1879.

LONG, J. G.
Born in Tennessee, 1872. Listed in Cisco, 1900.

LONG, JAMES E.
Born in Texas, 1871. Active in Mineola, 1896-97; Copperas Cove, 1900.

LONG, N.
Active in Travis County, 1885.

LOOMER, J. L.
Listed in Dallas, 1875.

LOPEZ & GLASCOCK
Partnership operated by Paul C. Lopez in El Paso, 1912-13.

LOPEZ, PAUL C.
Active in El Paso, 1912-13, partner in Lopez & Glascock.

LOTT, SARAH D.
Born in Texas, 1874. Listed in Arlington, 1900.

LOVEJOY, FRANK B.
Born in Missouri, 1865. Active in San Antonio at 516 South Alamo, 1894-96; in Marlin, 1900.

LOVELACE
Active in Stockdale, 1879.

LOWRY, JOHN
Partner in Black & Lowry active in Cannon, Grayson County, 1884-85. A. E. Black was also a blacksmith and Lowry a music teacher.

LOYD, JOHN A.
Born in Tennessee, c. 1820. Worked in Coldspring, 1840s-50s, 1860, 1869.

LOZANO, R.
Born in Mexico, 1876. Immigrated to U.S., 1893. Listed in Laredo, 1900.

LUCK, ALFRED
Born in Texas, 1875. Active in Austin, 1900.

LUCK, CHARLES P.
Born in Texas, 1875. Listed in Hallettsville, 1900.

LUCKER, A. W. & E. M.
Partnership in Waxahachie, 1867.

LUCORE & WARD
Emma J. Lucore and Gurney E. Ward operating in Fort Worth, 1888-91, at 109 East Third.

LUCORE, EMMA J.
Partner in Lucore & Ward with Gurney E. Ward operating in Fort Worth at 109 East Third, 1888-91; listed alone at West Ninth at Throckmorton, 1892-93. Also listed as Mrs. Basset J. Lucore.

LUFF, LUCIAN J.
Born in Tennessee, 1877. Listed in Howard County, 1900.

LUND, MARRO V.
Active in Starr County, 1871, 1873.

LUNDY, A. R.
Born in Missouri, 1879. Active in Temple, 1900.

LUNGKWITZ & IWONSKI
Hermann Lungkwitz and Carl G. von Iwonski operating in San Antonio, 1866-69.

LUNGKWITZ, HERMANN
Born in Prussia, 1813; died in Austin, 1891. Immigrated to U.S., 1850. A landscape painter for most of his career, he also became involved in photography. In San Antonio he was a partner in Lungkwitz & Iwonski, 1866-69; in Iwonski, Lungkwitz & Hanzal, 1869. Listed in Austin, 1870; reproduced maps photographically for the General Land Office, early 1870s.

LUSBY, M. S.
Active in Canyon, 1891-1913. Leased to Jesse Keiser, 1908; sold out to P. L. Britain, 1913 or 1917.

LUST, EARNEST
Active in Lee County, 1874; Lavaca County, 1875.

LUTHY, JACOB
Born in Switzerland, c. 1864. Listed in Gonzales, 1896-97, 1900.

LUX, JOSEPH
Born in Texas, 1861. Active in Sealy, 1898, 1900.

LYNCH, OSBORN
Born in Texas, 1875. Listed in Jewett, 1900.

LYNN, SAMUEL
Born in Ireland, c. 1835. Listed in Marshall, 1867; Sulphur Springs, 1868; Paris, 1869-99. Also listed in Lamar County, 1871-76.

MACCURDY, JAMES C.
Active in Denison at 103 West Main, 1893-94; possibly Macurdy.

MAGNOLIA SKY-LIGHT GALLERY
Operated by R. E. Moore in Houston, 1857-58; also known as Houston Sky-Light Ambrotype Gallery, 1856; and R. E. Moore & Company, 1857-58.

MAHON, WILLIAM
Listed in Dallas at 905 Elm, 1886-87; also active 1898-99.

MAHONEY, ANDREW J.
Born in Missouri, 1866. Active in Arlington, 1900.

MAIN, CHARLES
Born in California, 1867. Listed in Lockhart, 1900.

MAJOR, CHARLES A.
Born in South Carolina, 1863. Active in Port Lavaca, 1900.

MALLOY & FOWLER
Active in Collin County, 1871.

MALLOY, J. C.
Listed in Denton County, 1872; in Dallas at 540 Griffin, 1875.

MALONE, W. C.
Born in Alabama, 1880. Active in Comanche, 1900.

MANDEL, SIMON
Active in Mineral Well, 1890-91.

MANDERFELD & MERTENS
Partnership active in Paris, 1885; John L. Mertens.

MANDERFIELD, ALBERT
Born in Germany, 1852. Immigrated to U.S., 1854. Active in Gainesville, 1892, 1898, 1900.

MARABLE, MATTHEW M.
Born in Georgia, 1854. Listed in Pilot Point, 1896-97; Denton County, 1900.

MARCHAM, G. A.
Born in Michigan, 1851. Active in Bryan, 1900.

MARCLEAN, G. A.
Born in Michigan, c. 1851. Listed in Bryan, 1900.

MARECHAL ART COMPANY
Mail order firm in Dallas, Texas, operated by C. L. Marechal; made crayon or pastel enlargements from photographs.

MARESH, JOSEPH
Born in Texas, 1874. Active in Caldwell, 1900. Also spelled Moresh.

MARKER, MATTHEW
Born in Illinois, 1875. Listed in El Paso, 1900.

MARKHAM, WILLIAM
Active in Gorman, 1892.

MARKS, HARVEY R.
Born in New York, 1821; died in Austin, 1902. Daguerreotype artist in Baltimore, Maryland, 1848-53; may have been in Mobile, Alabama, 1855-58 (H. R. Marks). Active in Houston, 1866-70; located on Main between Preston and Prairie, 1866; Main at Congress, 1867-68. Operated a gallery in Austin, c. 1870-1901. Studio on Congress, 1872; on Congress between Pecan and Pine, 1872-73; 706 Congress, 1877-78, 1881-83; on Congress between Hickory and Bois d'Arc, 1879-80; 705 Congress, 1883-99; 612 Congress, 1900-01.

MARKS, WILLIAM R.
Born in Alabama, 1858. Listed in Fort Worth, 1900.

MARSCHALL, EDWARD M.
Born in the District of Columbia, c. 1851. Listed in Bowie County, 1876; Bonham, 1880; Honey Grove, 1882-85.

MARSH, ALONZO
Born in Texas, 1851. Active in Medina Coutny, 1900.

MARSH, CARY R.
Born in Tennessee, c. 1848. Active in Denison, 1880; Bells, 1882-83; Farmersville, 1884-85, 1891-92, 1896-99.

MARSHALL
Partner in Hall & Marshall, Cass and Morris Counties, 1876.

MARSHALL, S.
Active in Clarksville, 1878-79.

MARSHALL, W. H.
Born in Tennessee, 1877. Listed in Parker County, 1900.

MARTIN (MRS.)
Active in Austin on Congress Avenue, 1868. Possibly the wife of John R. Martin.

MARTIN, G. W.
Active in Orange County, 1887.

MARTIN, J. M.
Active in Hood and Tarrant Counties, 1874. Possibly listed as J. M. Matson.

MARTIN, JOHN R.
Born in Tennessee, c. 1833. Active in Austin, 1869; La Grange, 1870; listed in Fayette County, 1871. Mrs. Martin of Austin may be his wife.

MARTINETS, CHARLES
Born in Texas, 1877. Listed in Taylor, 1900.

MASTERS, WILLIAM G.
Printer for Bushong & Feldman in El Paso, 1900.

MATHEW, FRANCIS
Born in Louisiana, c. 1860. Listed in Polk County, 1880; possibly a painter.

MATTHEWS, WILLIAM H.
Partner with Andrew J. Mullenix operating as Mullenix & Matthews in Fort Worth at 1005 Main, 1899-1900.

MATTOCKS, BENJAMIN S.
Active in Houston at 507 ½ Main, 1897-98.

MAURER, JOSEPH M.
Died 1953. Worked for Justus Zahn, 1893-96; bought him out, 1902, operating the studio until 1948.

MAUVAIS, ANDRE F.
Listed in Johnson County, 1875-76; Dallas, 1878-99. Located at 915 Elm, 1878-79; 1059 Elm, 1881-82; 701 Elm, 1882-84; 1352 Elm, 1886-87.

MAXWELL
Partner in Cloyd & Maxwell, active in Sherman, 1867.

MAXWELL, CHARLES
Born in Mississippi, 1868. Active in Springtown, 1892; Reno, Parker County, 1900.

MAY
Partner in Janes & May operating in Bryan, 1869.

MAY & BROTHER
Listed in Burleson County, 1871.

MAY, A. J.
Active in Gonzales County, 1874.

MAYERS
Partner in Moore & Mayers operating in Carthage, 1884-85.

McALASTER, J. J.
Born in Georgia, 1864. Listed in Hopkins County, 1900.

McALISTER, CYRUS A.
Active in Dallas at 233 Elm, 1894-95.

McBRIDE, FLORENCE
Born in Kansas, 1875. Active in Denton, 1900.
McCALLUM, W. S.
Born in Texas, 1874. Listed in Wharton County, 1900.

McCARTY, A. B.
Active in Austin, 1867-68.

McCARTY, JEROME
Born in Texas, 1879. Listed in Comanche, 1900.

McCASKILL, J. B.
Active in Waco, 1876.

McCAUGHAN, A. J.
Active in Henderson, 1855.

McCAY & WILLIAMS
Partnership operating in Hunt County, 1871.

McCLANE
Partner in Hugh & McClane operating in Collin County, 1871.

McCLELLAN, LILLIAN
Born in Texas, 1877. Listed in Prairie Hill "Retouching Photographs," 1900.

McCLELLAN, WILLIAM
Active in Dallas, 1881-87; successor to James R. Davis at 705 Main. Alfred R. Billows, operator for Davis, continued to work for McClellan.

McCLOUD, W. E.
Born in Texas, 1862. Listed in Seguin, 1900.

McCLURE, GEORGE
Partner in Cloy & McClure with Godfrey B. Cloy, active in Marlin, 1884-85.

McCLURE, JOHN S.
May have worked in Canada, 1870s-80s. Active in San Marcos, 1884-85.

McCLURE, JUDSON C.
Born in Texas, 1877. Listed in Clarendon, 1900.

McCONNELL, H. C.
Active in Taylor, 1878-79.

McCORD
Partner in Spruitt & McCord, Wood County, 1873.

McCOWN & COMPANY
James L. McCown and Alfred Freeman operating in McKinney, 1884-85.

McCOWN, JAMES L.
Employed by Alfred Freeman in Dallas, 1881-82; operated as McCown & Company with Freeman in McKinney, 1884-85.

McCOWUN, H. H.
Active in Red River County, 1892.

McCOY, S. L. (MRS.)
Listed in Gordon, 1892.

McCRARY, H. F.
Active in Spring Hill, Navarro County, 1869.

McCULLOCH, JOHN
Born in South Carolina, c. 1840. Active in Clarksville, 1870.

McDANIEL, C. H.
Active in Dallas County, 1871.

McDANIEL, JOHN D.
Active in Marshall, 1884-85; Dallas, 1886-89, 1898-99.

McDAVID, J. P.
Born in Alabama, 1877. Listed in Athens, 1900.

MCDONALD
Partner in Thigpen & McDonald operating in Tyler, 1869-70.

McDONALD, G. H.
Active in Anderson County, 1873; may have worked in Chicago, Illinois, 1880-87 (George H. McDonald).

McDONALD, GRACE
Born in Kansas, 1875. Listed in Jack County, 1900.

McDONALD, S. J.
Active in Atlanta, 1878-79

McDONOUGH, J.
Active in Rusk County, 1874.

McELWAIN, GUY W.
Active in El Paso, 1912-13.

McFADDIN, W. (MRS.)
Active in Taylor, 1898.

McGEE, LEM
Born in Texas, 1877. Listed in Bowie County, 1900.

McGILL, SAMUEL
Born in Ireland, c. 1834. Listed in Eutaw, Limestone County, 1870.

McGONNEGAL, J. H.
Active in Belton in the Masonic Hall, 1857; also in Georgetown, 1857.

McGRAW, WILLIAM
Active in Greenville and McKinney, 1870; Kaufman County, 1871; Hunt County, 1872.

McHAIG, ARVIN
Born in New York, 1866. Listed in San Antonio, 1900.

McHAIN, BYRON W.
San Antonia publisher of views of "Picturesque Southwest, scenes on the lines of the Missouri Pacific Railway," c. 1880.

McINTIRE, ANNIE
Born in Indiana, 1859. Listed in Nacogdoches, 1900.

McINTIRE, JESSE
Active in De Kalb, 1896-97.

McINTIRE, JOHN
Born in Texas, 1883. Active in Nacogdoches, 1900.

McINTIRE, SAMUEL J.
Born in Illinois, 1877. Active in Lee County, 1900.

McINTYRE, KIRBY
Born in California, 1873. Active in Fort Worth, 1901.

McKAINE, JAMES
Born in Florida, c. 1853. Listed in Farmersville, 1870.

McKAY, GEORGE
Born in Texas, 1882. Active in Dallas, 1900.

McKEAN, JOHN T.
Active in Ennis, 1884-85.

McKEE & WALTERS
Partnership in Tarrant County, 1892.

McKEE, T. M.
Possibly Thomas Michael McKee, working in Montrose, Colorado,

1887, 1890, 1895-98. Active in Abilene, 1888, on Second Street; continued in Abilene, 1898-99.

McKEE, W. M.
Active in Wood County, 1873.

McKELVY, G. W.
Born in Indiana, 1872. Brother of L. F. McKelvy; active in Houston, 1900.

McKELVY, L. F.
Born in Indiana, 1874. Listed in Houston, 1900; brother of G. W. McKelvy.

McKEY, JAMES D.
Born in Tennessee, c. 1843. Active in Quitman, 1870; Rains County, 1871-72.

McKINLEY, F. M.
Active in McGregor, 1896-97.

McKISSLEY, FRANK M.
Born in Arkansas, 1861. Listed in Gatesville, 1900.

McMAHAN
Active in Denton County, 1871; possibly McMahau.

McMILLAN, J.
Born in Texas, 1863. Listed in Madison County, 1900. Possibly Jacob S. or John W. McMillan.

McMILLAN, JACOB S.
Active in Houston, 1894-95, at 1102 McKee.

McMILLAN, JOHN W.
Active in Giddings, 1884-85; Lexington, 1896-97.

McMILLAN, NEY
Born in Texas, c. 1854. Listed in Cleburne, 1880.

McMILLAN, W. M.
Active in Lancaster, 1894.

McQUILLAN, THOMAS R.
Born in Ireland, 1867. Listed in Hansford County, 1900.

McQUIRE, WILLIAM
Born in Illinois, c. 1810. Active in Galveston, 1850. Lived with W. P. Bichnell and may also have been his partner in Meguire & Bickel, 1851. Meguire may have been a dentist.

MEACHAM, GEORGE
Partner in Jones & Meacham with Charles Jones, operating in Houston at 1009 Main, 1895-96.

MEEK, WALTER H.
Partner in Beach & Meek with Frank E. Beach operating in Houston at 409 Travis, 1897-98.

MEGUIRE & BICKEL
William Meguire and William C. Bickel, operating in Houston, 1851. May be Bichnell and McQuire; Meguire may have been a dentist.

MEINERS, W. A.
Active in Fayette County, 1898.

MELCHER & MEYER
Partnership in Fayette County, 1895; possibly Louis Melcher.

MELCHER, LOUIS
Born 1870; died in O'Quinn, Fayette County, Texas, 1948. Active in Fayette County, 1892-97; possibly a partner in Melcher & Meyer, 1895.

MELTON, GEORGE
Born in North Carolina, 1873. Listed in Smith County, 1900.

MELVIN, THOMAS A.
Active in Longview, 1884-85.

MEMPHIS, J. M.
Active in Hill County, 1871.

MENDELL, M. D. (MRS.)
Active in Mexia, 1890-92.

MENDELL, S. C.
Born in Kentucky, late 1820s. Listed in Fairfield, 1869-70; Freestone County, 1880. Also spelled Mandell.

MENDEX, JOSIE
Active in Brownsville, 1898-99.

MERCER, E.
Active in Hill County, 1871.

MERIENNO & PARRA
Partnership operating in Bexar County, 1876.

MERIENNO, PAUL
Active in San Antonio, 1877-88, on the Main Plaza.

MERTENS, JOHN L.
Born in Germany, 1848. Immigrated to U.S., 1849. Partner in Manderfield & Mertens in Paris, 1885; listed alone in Paris, 1890-92; Wolfe City, 1896-97, 1900. Also listed as Mertins.

METCALF, W. H.
Active in San Antonio, 1880-90.

METHBIN
Partner in Perry & Methbin operating in Upshur County, 1871.

MEYER
Partner in Melcher & Meyer, 1895.

MEYER, CHARLES A.
Born in Germany, 1865. Immigrated to U.S., 1885. Listed in Giddings, 1896-97, 1900.

MEYER, FRIEDA
Born in Texas, 1878. Retoucher in Galveston, 1900.

MEYER, M. H.
Born in South Carolina, 1878. Active in Henderson, 1900.

MICAN, JOSEPH
Born in Texas, 1877. Active in Lavaca County, 1900.

MIGNON, AUGUSTUS R.
Born in France, c. 1843. Operated a studio in Fort Worth, 1870-99; also known as Fort Worth Art Gallery. Located at 24 Main, 1882-84; 208 Main, 1884-86; 701 Elm, 1886-87.

MIGNON, JOSEPH H.
Photographer for Augustus R. Mignon in Fort Worth, 1883-84; operating alone, 1885-99. Studio at 709 Houston, 1885-86.

MIGURSKI, CHARLES JOSEPH
Active in La Grange, 1898.

MILEHAM, W. W.
Active in Williamson County, 1875.

MILLER
Partner in Larn & Miller operating in Fayette County, 1889.

MILLER & BEDFORD
Carl P. Miller and Thomas J. Bedford operating in Dallas at 420 Elm, 1900.

MILLER & WALKER
William W. Miller and George H. Walker active in Cisco, Groesbeck and Marlin, 1892.

MILLER, A. C. DAYTON
Active in Dallas at 840 and 621 Elm, 1884-85; in Pecos, 1898-99.

MILLER, A. K.
Active in Lexington, 1869.

MILLER, B.
Active in Runnels County, 1888; possibly Benjamin J. Miller.

MILLER, B. J.
Active in Lancaster, 1898; possibly Benjamin J. Miller.

MILLER, BENJAMIN J.
Partner in Miller Brothers with J. N. in Abilene, located on Pine, 1888-91. Active in Sweetwater, 1892; Mexia, 1896-1900.

MILLER BROTHERS
Benjamin J. and J. N. Miller, listed in Abilene on Pine, 1888-92.

MILLER, CARL P.
Partner in Miller & Bedford, operating in Dallas, 1900, at 420 Elm.

MILLER, GEORGE K.
Born in Virginia, 1870. Itinerant photographer in Mineral Wells and with a partner in Garland, c. 1898; in Cooper, 1900. He operated a studio in San Marcos, 1906-16; also maintained studios in Temple, Harlingen, Wichita Falls and Marshall.

MILLER, GEORGE W.
Born in Texas, 1855. Listed in Henrietta, 1900.

MILLER, J. N.
Partner with his brother, William W., operating as Miller Brothers in Abilene on Pine Street, 1888-91.

MILLER, J. R.
Born in Louisiana, c. 1860. Listed in Tyler, 1880.

MILLER, JESSE M.
Born in Texas, 1880. Active in Henrietta, 1900.

MILLER, MAX
Born in Texas, 1880. Active in Orange, 1900.

MILLER, WILLIAM W.
Born in Texas, 1866. Partner in Miller & Walker with George H. Walker, operating in Cisco, Groesbeck and Marlin, 1892; on his own in Marlin, 1896-1900.

MILLHOLIN & DODDS
James M. Millholin and James S. Dodds, partners in Georgetown, 1890-91.

MILLHOLIN, JAMES M.
Born in Texas, 1857. Active in Georgetown, 1892; Hutto, 1896-97, 1900.

MILLS, FRANK C.
Active in La Grange, 1890-91.

MILLS, WILLIAM
Born in Texas, 1872. Listed in Cleburne, 1900.

MIMS & RAFFERTY
Edward Wellington Mims and Frank Ernest Rafferty, partners in Tyler at 112 North Bois d'Arc, 1893. Also operated as Eureka Gallery.

MIMS, EDWARD WELLINGTON
Born in Louisiana, 1878. Partner in Mims & Rafferty operating in Tyler, 1893; also known as Eureka Gallery. Operated alone in Tyler, 1896-1900. Moved to Denver after 1933.

MINDELL, S. D.
Active in Limestone County, 1872.

MINSHIFT, C. G.
Active in Collin County, 1874.

MINSHULL, CHARLES
Born in England, c. 1845. Listed in Van Zandt County, 1880.

MITCHELL & LABADIE
Arthur W. Mitchell and Edward E. Labadie, operating in Dallas at 336 Elm, 1891-92. They may have been painters.

MITCHELL, ROY
Born in Pennsylvania, 1867. Listed in Brenham, 1900.

MITCHELL, T. E.
Partner in Bolton & Mitchell with T. C. Bolton, active in San Antonio at 134 or 134 ½ West Commerce, 1894-97.

MITCHELL, THOMAS E.
Born in Illinois, 1866. Listed in Laredo, 1900. Possibly T. E. Bolton, partner in Bolton & Mitchell.

MOBERLY, LOUIS
Active in Washington County, 1876; McKinney, 1878-79, 1882-83.

MOEHRING, CLARA (MISS)
Daughter of Clara and Herman Moehring; photographer in Boerne, Comfort and Kerrville, c. 1900-10.

MOEHRING, CLARA (MRS.)
Active in Boerne, Comfort and Kerrville, c. 1900-10. Wife of Herman Moehring.

MOEHRING, HERMAN
Born in Germany, 1863; died 1908. Immigrated to U.S., 1878. Active in Boerne, 1896-97; Kendall County, 1900.

MOELK, CHARLES F.
Born in Ohio, c. 1854. Active in Fort Worth at 5 Houston between First and Weatherford, 1878-79. Listed in Arlington, 1880.

MOFFITT, DAVID J.
Born in Illinois, c. 1849. Partner Jones & Moffitt, Denton County, 1875; in Pilot Point, 1878-79, 1884-85; listed alone in Pilot Point, 1880, 1890-92.

MOHLER & PARKS
Partnership operating in Johnson County, 1871; possibly J. A. Mohler.

MOHLER & RUSH
Listed in Johnson County, 1874-75; possibly J. A. Mohler.

MOHLER, CONRAD
Born in Germany, 1877. Listed in Bell County, 1900.

MOHLER, J. A.
Active in Johnson County, 1871-73; San Saba County, 1876.

MOIR, THOMAS
Listed in Galveston, 1880-83, 1886-87, 1890-92, 1898-99. Located at 119 East Market, 1880-81; Market at Twenty-fifth, 1881-91; 2510 Market, 1891-92. Also listed as Hair.

MOLLENHAUER, EDWARD
Born in Texas, 1872. Active in Yorktown, 1896-97; listed in census as "Photographer and Merchant," 1900.

MONK, J. R.
Active in Overton, 1898-99.

MONROE, JAMES
Active in Travis County, 1875-76.

MONTGOMERY, JAMES F.
Born in Texas, 1874. Active in Yoakum, 1895-98, 1900.

MOODMORTH
Partner in Hughson & Moodmorth with James A. Hughson in Brenham, 1869.

MOON, LEROY
Born in Arkansas, 1871. Listed in Dallas, 1900.

MOON, ULETUS
Born in Texas, 1874. Listed in Jacksonville, 1900.

MOONEY, MARGARET
Born in Texas, 1872. "Artist and Photographer" listed in census, Cook County, 1900.

MOORE
Partner in Williams & Moore; possibly Obadiah S. Williams or W. Wirt Williams and possibly R. E. Moore. Possibly in Clarksville during the Civil War.

MOORE & MAYERS
Partnership in Carthage, 1884-85.

MOORE & PATTERSON
Leroy F. Moore and George W. Patterson, operating in Dallas at 412 Elm, 1900.

MOORE & WILLIAMS
Possibly R. E. Moore and W. Williams or W. Wirt Williams. Operated in Washington and Houston, 1856; Houston, 1857-58.

MOORE, CHARLES C.
Active in Texarkana, 1882-83.

MOORE, ELLA M.
Born in Texas, 1867. Listed in Parker County, 1900.

MOORE, EMMET B.
Born in Missouri, 1863. Listed in San Marcos, 1900.

MOORE, GEORGE L.
Active in Gainesville, 1890-91; may be the G. L. Moore working in Boulder, Colorado, 1891.

MOORE, GEORGE W.
Born in New York, 1854. Active in Denison at 210 West Main, 1893-1900.

MOORE, J. F.
Born in Tennessee, 1859. Listed in Dallas, 1900.

MOORE, J. P.
Active in Travis County, 1884.

MOORE, LEROY F.
Partner in Moore & Patterson with George W. Patterson, operating in Dallas at 412 Elm, 1900. Worked in Springfield, Illinois, 1911-13.

MOORE, R. E.
Associated with many photographers in Houston during the 1850s; W. Williams, possibly the same as W. Wirt Williams; partner with Hiram Hand and possibly Frank B. Bailey. Moore was associated with William DeRyee, publishing *The Texas Album*, with nearly 100 tipped-in photographic portraits. May also have been a partner in Williams & Moore in Clarksville. Moore operated as the Houston Sky-Light Ambrotype Gallery, 1856; Magnolia Sky-Light Gallery, 1857-58; R. E. Moore & Company, 1857-58. May have been involved with Williams in the Green Store Ambrotype Gallery. Moore's studio was located on Franklin, 1857-59.

MOORE, ROBERT
Born in Maryland, c. 1829. Active in Navasota, 1870.

MOORE, ROBERT E.
Partner in Borklund & Moore, with Eric Borklund in Oak Cliff (Dallas), on Lancaster between Ninth and Tenth, 1891-92.

MOORE, SOLON
Born in Wisconsin, 1867. Listed in Foard [sic] County, 1900.

MOREY, OLIVER L.
Born in Texas, 1879. Active in Howard County, 1900.

MORGAN & BELLAIR
Partnership in Wood County, 1871.

MORGAN & GAMBLING
Operated in Hopkins County, 1871.

MORGAN & McGRAW
Active in Greenville, 1870; possibly William McGraw.

MORGAN, FORREST T.
Partner in Deane & Morgan with Jervis C. Deane, operating in Waco at 503 ½ Austin, 1888-91.

MORGAN, GEORGE W.
Active in McKinney, 1884-85.

MORGAN, J.
Born in Ohio, 1834. Listed in Palo Pinto County, 1900.

MORPHIS & CAYLOR
Partnership operating in Bonham, 1868; possibly Jacob L. Caylor.

MORPHIS & DUNCAN
Listed as photographers "at large" in Cotton Gin, 1870.

MORPHIS, L. A.
Active in McKinney, 1867; partner in Morphis & Caylor operating in Bonham, 1868; listed alone in Henderson, 1869; partner in Morphis & Duncan operating in Cotton Gin, 1870; working alone in Hamilton County, 1876; Millsap, 1884-85. Also listed as Marthis, Marphis and Morphes.

MORRELL, J.
Active in Hempstead, 1859.

MORRILL & BELL
Possibly D. S. Morrill and Charles Bell operating in Indianola, Calhoun County at Main and Fannin, 1860.

MORRILL, D. S.
Active in Indianola, 1853-54.

MORRIS & HUDSON
Active in Ladonia, 1890.

MORRIS, BERNARD H.
Born in Texas, 1870. Listed in Galveston, 1900.

MORRIS, HENRY H.
Born in Texas, 1869; died 1956. Apprentice in the Galveston studio of Granville M. Deane, 1885. He operated his own studio, 1891-1900; located at 2024 Market, 1891-98; 2119 Post Office, 1898-1900.

MORRIS, J. W.
Partner in Patton & Morris, operating with Thomas Patton in Cameron, 1890-91.

MORRIS, JOHN
Born in Pennsylvania, c. 1852. Listed in Galveston County, 1880.

MORRIS, R. C.
Made the earliest surviving image of Houston, 1856.

MORROW, JOHN H.
Active in Weatherford, 1882-83.

MORTON & WILLS
Partnership in Coryell County, 1871; possibly J. M. Morton.

MORTON, J. M.
Active in Gatesville, 1870; Coryell County, 1871-72; possibly a partner in Morton & Wills, 1871.

MORTON, WILLIAM
Born in Texas, c. 1841. Active in Gatesville, 1870.

MOSES, ALPHONSE
Active in Dallas at 208 Commerce, 1878-79.

MOSES, ALPHONSE & EMMA
Partnership operating in Dallas, 1877.

MOSES, EUGENE
Active in Terrell, 1884-85.

MOSS, G. & A.
Possibly a misspelling of Alphonse and G. A. Moses; photographers in Dallas, 1877. The partners were working in Quincy, Illinois, 1870s.

MOSS, R. P.
Born in Texas, 1861. Listed in Nacogdoches, 1900.

MOULDER, N. G.
Active in Grayson County, 1874.

MOUZON & SON
Henry D. and Samuel C. Mouzon operating in Palestine, 1896-97.

MUELLER
Partner in Kunz & Mueller operating in Fayette County, 1893.

MUELLER, AUGUST
Born in Germany, 1849. Immigrated to U.S., 1857. Listed in Robertson County, 1900.

MUELLER, ISIDORE
Active in Nacogdoches, 1867. Possibly the I. Mueller in Council Bluffs, Iowa, 1860s-70s.

MULFORD, J. W.
Amateur stereo photographer in Dallas.

MULLENIX & MATTHEWS
Andrew J. Mullenix and William H. Matthews operating in Fort Worth at 1005 Main, 1899-1900.

MULLENIX, ANDREW J.
Born in Arkansas, 1874. Partner in Mullenix & Matthews in Fort Worth at 1005 Main, 1899-1900.

MULLENS & KNIGHT
John J. Mullens and Fayette W. Knight in Waco at 55 ½ Austin, 1878-79.

MULLENS, JOHN J.
Born in Kentucky or Tennessee, c. 1834. Active in Brenham and Columbus, 1858; Brenham, 1866; Waco, 1867-68, 1870, 1876, 1880-81. Partner in Mullens & Knight, 1878-79. Studio in Waco located at 55 ½ Austin, 1878-81. May have worked for Jackson & Knight and/or H. W. Pickett.

MULLER, LOUIS
Active in Galveston, 1870.

MULLINS & GRAY
Robert W. Mullins and Thomas J. Gray operating in Victoria, 1896-97; also known as Court Studio.

MULLINS, DAVID
Born in Missouri, c. 1852. Listed in Sherman, 1870.

MULLINS, F. T.
Active in Rusk County, 1888.

MULLINS, J. J.
Born in Tennessee, c. 1832. Active in Hill County, 1880.

MULLINS, JOHN
Born in Tennessee, 1846. Active in Hill County, 1900.

MULLINS, ROBERT W.
Active in Jewett, 1892; partner in Mullins & Gray, Victoria, 1896-97; also operated as Court Studio.

MUNROE, JAMES
Active in Harris County, 1875.

MURPHY, B.
Active in Milam County, 1869.

MURPHY, F. J.
Active in Clarksville, 1851.

MURRAY, HATTIE (MISS)
Listed in Chico, 1892, 1896-97.

MURRAY, HENRY L.
Born in Tennessee, c. 1849. Active in Carthage, 1880; partner in Shreves & Murray operating in Palestine, 1890-91; working alone in Dallas, 1893-94. Partner in Hayes & Murray with James Hayes operating in Athens, 1892.

MURRAY, JOSEPH F.
Born in Missouri, 1849. Listed in Alvord, 1892, 1900.

MUSE, THOMAS
Born in Texas, c. 1847. Active in Waco, 1880.

MYBUSH, ALLEN
Born in Texas, 1867. Active in Jefferson, 1900.

MYERS & COMPANY, J.
Operated in Sabine County, 1887.

NAGHEL & COMPANY, D. FRANK
Listed in San Antonio at 20 French Building, 1859-60.

NAGHEL & WILLIAMS
Active in San Antonio at 12 and 20 French Building, 1860.

NAGHEL, D. FRANK
Active in San Antonio, 1859-60, operating as D. Frank Naghel & Company, 1859-60; as Naghel & Williams, 1860. Studio at 12 and 20 French Building.

NASCHKE, PAUL H.
Born in Galveston, 1872; died 1932. Employed by Rose & Zahn in Galveston, 1888, later becoming manager. Continued as photographer, 1893-1900; operated his own studio, 1894-1900; located at 420 Twenty-second, 1893-94; 2215 Market, 1895-96; 1429 Church, 1896-1927. Moved to La Marque, 1927.

NATIONAL COPYING COMPANY
Georgia-based firm; its Houston agents, L. H. Johnson & Company, were located on Congress Street at Travis, 1875. James Nicholson was the agent in Bastrop, 1866-79.

NAUSCHUETZ, BRUNO
Born in Germany, 1861. Immigrated to U.S., 1887. Active in San Antonio, 1889-1900. Studio on Austin between Grand and Tenth, 1889-90; at Austin and Tenth, 1890-91; 700 Austin, 1891; 411 Austin, 1892; 221 Sharer, 1892-1900.

NEAL, B. F.
Active in Galveston, 1844; perhaps the newspaperman, Benjamin F. Neal.

NEAL, CHARLES B.
Born in Kentucky, 1869. Listed in Burnet County, 1900.

NEAMIS, R. P.
Active in Liberty County, 1870.

NEFF, CHARLES
Active in Orange, 1896-97.

NELSON, ALFRED N.
Born in Texas, 1876. Listed in Bartlett, 1900.

NELSON, J. D.
Born in Missouri, c. 1831. Listed in Rusk, 1850.

NELSON, VELMAN
Born in Texas, 1875. Active in Houston, 1900.

NESS, N. T.
Born in Georgia, c. 1854. Listed in Hytown, Grayson County, 1880.

NEW YORK PHOTOGRAPHIC COMPANY
Operated by John R. Archer in Houston at 85 Main, 1884-85.

NEWCOMB, T.
Born in Texas, 1865. "Photograph Painter" listed in census, Austin, 1900.

NEWTON & CLARK
Active in Temple, 1898-99.

NEWTON, LUTIE T.
Born in Iowa, 1883. Son of William H. Newton. Active in Houston, 1900.

NEWTON, WILLIAM H.
Born in Pennsylvania, 1854. Father of Lutie T. Newton. Active in Italy, 1898; Houston, 1900-01, at 501 ½ Main.

NICHOLS & WEDDINGTON
Active in Honey Grove.

NICHOLS, ARTHUR A.
Born in Illinois, 1873. Active in Fayette County, 1898; Austin County, 1900; also active in Industry.

NICHOLS, JACOB
Active in Van Alstyne, 1890-91.

NICHOLSON, JAMES
Agent for National Copying Company of Atlanta, Georgia, representing them in Bastrop, 1866-79; continued in photography business until 1881 or later.

NICKA, ALLEN A.
Born in Tennessee, 1877. Brother of Eliga A. Nicka. Listed in Galveston, 1900.

NICKA, ELIGA A.
Born in Tennessee, 1880. Brother of Allen A. Nicka. Worked in Galveston, 1900.

NIELSEN, CARL
Active in Round Rock, c. 1875.

NIELSON BROTHERS
Partnership operating in Dallas, 1894.

NIX, E. E.
Born in Tennessee, 1882. Listed in Galveston, 1900.

NORELIOUS, EFRON
Born in Sweden, 1862. Immigrated to U.S., 1869. Active in El Campo, 1900.

NORMAN, C. A. (MRS.)
Active in Whitt, Parker County, 1892, 1896-97.

NORRIS
Partner in Sims, Norris & Company, operating in Jefferson, 1868.

NORSWORTHY, L. F.
Active in Henderson, 1866; Rusk and Salem, Newton County, 1867; Sulphur Springs, 1868; Bright Star, Rains County, 1870; Hopkins County, 1871-75. Also listed as Noiseworthy, Northworthy, Nosworthy.

NORTH & HUFF
Partnership operating in Dension, 1881.

NORTH & LENNY
Jerry E. North and William J. Lenny working in Houston at 302 Chenevert, 1894-95.

NORTH, JERRY E.
Born in Indiana, 1853. Partner in North & Lenny, Houston, 1894-95; operating alone in Austin on San Jacinto between Fifth and Sixth, 1896-97; in Marlin, 1900.

NORTHERN, JOE T.
Active in Whitewater, c. 1895; Whitewright, 1896-97, 1900.

NORVILLE, GEORGE
Born in Tennessee, 1865. Active in Bowie, 1900.

NOWLIN & WILSON
Partnership active in Kendall County, 1875.

NUCKOLS, ALPHEUS B.
Born in Virginia, 1840. Active in Austin, 1893-1906; at 608 Neches, 1897-98; 1402 Lavaca, 1898-1900.

O'BANNON, JAMES F.
Active in Dallas at 354 Elm, 1898-99.

O'BANNON, JOSEPH T.
Born in Kentucky, 1865. Partner in Parish & O'Bannon with William H. Parish, operating in Dallas, 1888-97. See partnership entry for locations. Continued on his own, 1897-1900.

O'BRIEN, WILLIAM G.
Active in Austin on Pecan, 1858-59.

O'LEARY, JAMES
Born in England, 1863. Immigrated to U.S., 1870. Active in Dallas, 1896-1900; located at 423 Elm, 1896; 412 Elm, 1897; 365 Main, 1900.

O'LEARY, PATRICK
Active in Dallas, 1897.

O'REAR, A. J.
Active in Eastland County, 1891-95.

O'REGAN, M.
Active in Indianola, 1859.

OKERLUND, GUS A.
Active in Houston at 719 Main, 1897-98.

OLIPHANT, WILLIAM JAMES
Born in Laurenceberg, Indiana, 1845; died in Austin, 1930. His family moved to Houston, then to Austin, 1852. Oliphant joined the Confederate Army at age 15, serving in Company G, Sixth Texas Infantry, Pat Cleburne's Division. He was imprisoned and returned to Austin after his release at the end of the war. He bought out Stone & Waggoner, the photographers operating above his father's jewelry store, 1866, and operated the business, 1866-80. Considered a significant Texas artist, he had studios in Washington, D.C. with Alexander Gardner and T. H. O'Sullivan. Studio located at 119 Pecan between Congress and Brazos, 1873-80.

OLIVARES, ENRIQUE
Born in Mexico, 1875. Immigrated to U.S., 1875. Listed in Duval County, 1900.

OLIVARES, JOSE
Born in Mexico, 1849. Immigrated to U.S., 1856. Active in Duval County, 1900.

OLIVE
Partner in Cleveland & Olive with William Cleveland, operating in Victoria at 207 West Forrest, 1900-01.

OLIVER
Partner in Lims & Oliver operating in Victoria, 1866.

OLSON, E.
Active in Harrison County, 1871.

ORTIZ, JOSEPH
Partner in Cooper & Ortiz with Spencer H. Cooper in Eagle Pass, 1890-91.

OSBORN, JOSEPH M.
Born in Missouri, 1868. Listed in Wharton County, 1900.

OSBORN, O. P.
Born in Mississippi, 1845. Active in Jones County, 1900.

OSBORNE, J. Q.
Listed in Collin County, 1873; in Dallas on Sycamore between Main and Elm, 1873-74; also in Grayson County, 1874; Dallas, 1875.

OSHNER, MARY
Born in North Dakota, 1884. Listed in Port Arthur, 1900.

OSTEBEE, S.
Born in Norway, 1872. Immigrated to U.S., 1882. Listed in Beaumont, 1900.

OTT, J. E.
Born in Mississippi, c. 1846. Active in Grayson County, 1870.

OTTO, ALFRED
Born in Germany, 1871. Immigrated to U.S., 1894. Listed in Fayette County, 1900.

OVERMAN, JOSEPH
Born in Texas, 1881. Active in San Antonio, 1900.

OVERPACK, SILAS E.
Born in Michigan, 1872. Listed in Galveston, 1900.

OWEN, MAUD
Born in Texas, 1879. Active in Wise County, 1900.

PADGETT, AUGUSTUS
Active in Jacksonville, 1882-83.

PAIN, JOHN
Listed in Lee County, 1874-76; possibly Bair, Biar or Pair.

PALING, WILLIAM
Born in Illinois, c. 1865. Active in Bexar County, 1900.

PALLAIS, MARY E. (MRS.)
Active in Galveston at 221-223 East Post Office, 1881-82.

PALMER & LEWIS
Partnership operating in Denison, 1880.

PALMER, H. L.
Active in Lavaca County, 1871.

PALMER, JOSEPH R.
Born in Connecticut, 1850. Studio with Smith & Tucker at 56 Canal Street, New Orleans, Louisiana. Active in Galveston, 1845; Corpus Christi, 1846; Matamoros, Mexico, during the Mexican War. Published *The American Flag in Matamoros,* 1846; moved to Brownsville, Texas, 1848; listed as a printer, 1850.

PANNEWITZ, GUSTAV A.
Born in Germany, 1862. Immigrated to U.S., 1870. Partner in Tauch & Pannewitz in Fayette County, 1886-87; continued alone in Fayette County, 1889; Flatonia, 1890-91; Shiner, 1896-97, 1900. May also have been in Shiner, 1890. Listed as partner again with Tauch in Schulenburg, 1898-99.

PARDUR, WILLIAM E.
Born in Texas, 1875. Listed in Wichita Falls, 1900.

PARIS & COMPANY, A. C.
Partnership of Arthur C. Paris and Emanuel Gillett operating in San Antonio at 10 East Houston, 1889-90.

PARIS & ROTHWELL
Arthur C. Paris and Isaac N. Rothwell operating in San Antonio, 1891-96. Studio at 11 and 13 West Commerce, 1891-92; 107 West Commerce, 1891-96.

PARIS, ARTHUR C.
Active in San Antonio, 1890-96. Partner with Emanuel Gillett operating as A. C. Paris & Company, 1889-90; partner with Isaac N. Rothwell, 1891-96. See partnerships for locations.

PARIS, MARY
Active with the firm of A. C. Paris & Company in San Antonio at 10 East Houston, 1889-90.

PARISH & O'BANNON
William H. Parish and Joseph T. O'Bannon, operating in Dallas, 1888-97. Studio at 930 Elm, 1888-89; 948 Elm, 1889-91; 378 Elm, 1891-97. Another studio was operated at 254 Elm, 1894-97.

PARISH, JOHN W.
Born in Illinois, 1871. Active in Alvord, 1890-91; Springtown, 1896-97; Itasca, 1900.

PARISH, N. H.
Born in New York, 1861. Listed in Cisco, 1900.

PARISH, WILLIAM H.
Partner in Parish & O'Bannon, Dallas, 1888-97; listed alone in Dallas, 1898-1900.

PARK & HOLMES
Partnership in Columbia (now West Columbia), 1858-59, on Front Street; also known as Columbia Sky-Light Gallery. One of the partners was possibly Charles Holmes.

PARK, W. N. & J. T.
Active in Fayette County, 1875.

PARKER, FRANCIS F.
Born in Massachusetts, 1831. Active in El Paso, 1882-1908. Studio at 11 El Paso, 1886-87; 111 El Paso, 1888-89; at St. Louis and Mesa,

1895-96. Worked in California, c. 1908-10.

PARKER, H. S.
Born in Kentucky, 1851. Listed in Nacogdoches, 1900.

PARKER, H. T.
Born in Texas, c. 1852. Active in Hill and Johnson Counties, 1876; San Augustine County, 1880, 1887.

PARKER, HUGH M.
Born in Mississippi, c. 1844. Active in Independence, Washington County, 1867; Lampasas, 1870; possibly a partner in Leinery & Parker, Van Zandt County, 1872.

PARKER, JOHN H.
Born in Texas, c. 1846. Active in New Hampshire and Vermont, 1870s. Listed in Texas, operating in Hood County, 1875; Montague County, 1879; Tyler County, 1880.

PARKER, ROBERT R.
Born in Tennessee, 1865. Active in Dallas County, 1900.

PARKS
Partner in Mohler & Parks operating in Johnson County, 1871.

PARKS & JACOBI
Partnership in Lee County, 1876.

PARKS, CLYDE
Born in Texas, 1871. Listed in Bosque County, 1900.

PARKS, PERCY P.
Born in Mississippi, 1870. Active in Belton, 1898, 1900.

PARKS, W. M.
Billed as a "Photographist" in Texas, c. 1875.

PARR, SISSON J.
Born in Georgia, 1878. Listed in Howard County, 1900.

PARRA
Partner in Merienno & Parra operating in Bexar County, 1876.

PARRENBECK, HENRY
Born in Germany, 1856. Immigrated to U.S., 1884. Active in Meridian, 1900.

PARROTT & QUEENSBERRY
Partnership operating in Maverick County, 1875; Starr County, 1876. Also spelled Quesenberry.

PASEVICH, JACOB
Active in El Paso, 1901.

PATE, THOMAS G.
Born in Tennessee, c. 1850. Active in Kaufman, 1868; Charleston, Delta County and Ladonia, 1870; Delta County, 1871.

PATE, W. H.
Born in Georgia, 1822. Partner in W. H. & J. P. Pate operating in Tyler, 1870.

PATE, W. H. & J. P.
Operated by William H. Pate in Tyler, 1870.

PATE, WILLIAM
Active in Whitt, Parker County, 1892, 1896-97; Jack County, 1900.

PATEY, ARTHUR B.
Born in England, 1867. Immigrated to U.S., 1875. Listed in Lockhart, 1900.

PATRICK, T. G.
Active in Houston, 1866; Hempstead, 1867. Partner in Blessing & Patrick operating in Houston during the Civil War.

PATTERSON, GEORGE W.
Partner in Moore & Patterson with Leroy F. Moore, operating in Dallas at 412 Elm, 1900.

PATTERSON, JAMES N.
Active in Paris, 1896-97; Texarkana, 1899.

PATTERSON, JOHN W.
Active in Coryell County, 1871.

PATTON & FITZGERALD
Henry Patton and James Fitzgerald operating in Galveston on Post Office, 1870.

PATTON & MORRIS
Thomas Patton and J. W. Morris in Cameron, 1890-91.

PATTON, HENRY
Born in New Mexico, c. 1849. Partner in Patton & Fitzgerald operating in Galveston on Post Office, 1870.

PATTY, DOLPH P.
Born in Texas, 1882. Listed in Bastrop County, 1900.

PAXTON, R. S.
Active in Dallas County, 1875.

PAYNE
Partner in Dunn & Payne operating in Williamson County, 1874.

PAYNE, EDGAR
Born in Tennessee, 1871. Active in Waxahachie, 1900.

PEERY, HENRY F.
Active in Van Zandt County, 1872, 1874; Kaufman, 1890-92, 1896-97. May have operated as H. F. Peery & Company, misspelled Purey, in Red River County, 1875.

PEIRCE & BROTHER
John K. and Robert W. Peirce arrived in Galveston, 1853; traveled to Indianola, Port Lavaca, Petersburg, Gonzales, Prairie Lea and Lockhart before settling in Austin, c. 1855.

PEIRCE, JOHN K.
Partner with his brother, Robert W., operating as Peirce & Brother in Galveston, Indianola, Port Lavaca, Petersburg, Gonzales, Prairie Lea and Lockhart, 1853-55. Settled in Austin, c. 1855. Also operated as Peirce, Kelly & Peirce in Austin, 1853-54.

PEIRCE, KELLY & PEIRCE
John K. and Robert W. Peirce, partners with R. P. Kelly in Austin, 1853-54.

PEIRCE, ROBERT W.
Listed in Sequin, 1853-54; partner in Peirce, Kelly & Peirce operating in Austin, 1853-54; also partner in Peirce & Brother, 1853-55. See partnership listing for locations.

PENIX, JESSIE L.
Born in Arkansas, 1880. Active in Wood County, 1900.

PENIX, THOMAS
Born in Arkansas, 1874. Active in Wood County, 1900.

PENLEY
Active in Erath County, 1876.

PENNINGER, CORA
Born in Illinois, 1878. Listed in Stephenville, 1900.

PENNINGTON, WILLIAM
Active in McKinney.

PEOPLE'S GALLERY
Operated by William R. Works in Fort Worth, c. 1892.

PERKINS, G.
Active in Denison, 1878-79.

PERRY
Partner in Stirman & Perry operating in Kaufman County, 1871; V. I. Stirman.

PERRY & METHBIN
Partnership operating in Upshur County, 1871.

PERRY, H. H.
Active in Wood County, 1874.

PERRY, JAMES M.
Active in Lockhart, 1868; Dallas County, 1872; Navarro County, 1873.

PETERS, N. C. (MRS.)
Active in Whitt, Parker County, 1896-97.

PETERSON, CONRAD
Born in Germany, 1836. Immigrated to U.S., 1850. Active in Fayette County, 1872-1900. Listed in La Grange, 1870s, 1882-85, 1890-92, 1896-1900. Also spelled Petersen.

PETTIT, WILLIAM W.
Born in Alabama, 1866. Active in Killeen, 1900.

PETTY & TUCKER
Active in Hunt County, 1872.

PHELPS, WILLIAM M.
Manager for W. Wirt Williams in Dallas, 1894-95; continued working in Dallas, 1896-97.

PHILIPS
Listed in Dallas, 1877. Boarded with Alphonse Moses and may have worked for him.

PHILLIPS, ED
Active in Huntsville, 1900.

PHILLIPS, HENRY S.
Partner in Irby & Phillips with Terry Irby operating in Vernon, 1892.

PHILLIPS, J. F. G.
Active in Rusk County, 1888.

PICKARD, WILLIAM
Born in Louisiana, c. 1856. Listed in Angelina County, 1880.

PICKETT, H. W.
Active in Waco, 1876, at Sixth and Austin.

PIERCE, JOHN B.
Born in Alabama, 1846. Listed in Williamson County, 1900.

PIERROT, EUGENE
Born in France, c. 1825. Listed in Dallas, 1870; possibly a painter.

PINKERTON
Partner in Kennedy & Pinkerton operating in Denton County, 1876.

PINKERTON & SMITH
Partnership operating in Wise County, 1876; possibly A. Smith.

PIPER
Partner in Krueger & Piper, active in San Antonio, 1870-80; listed in Burnet County, 1874. Also listed as Kruger & Piper. Possibly Albert Piper.

PIPER, ALBERT
Born in Prussia, c. 1842. Listed in Clifton and San Antonio, 1870; De Witt County, 1871; Victoria County, 1872; Gonzales and Lavaca Counties, 1875; Lavaca County, 1876.

PITTMAN & GRIFFITH
Francis M. Pittman and Lemuel H. Griffith operating in Austin at 510 East Sixth, 1887-88.

PITTS & TUCKER
Partnership in Brazos County, 1872, 1874-75. Possibly J. M. Tucker.

PLUKTON & SMITH
Listed in Wise County, 1877; possibly A. Smith. May be the same as Pinkerton & Smith.

PLUNKETT, L. S.
Active in Rusk County, 1871.

POE & WRIGHT
Partnership operating in Walker County, 1872; possibly John T. Poe.

POE, JOHN T.
Active in Huntsville, 1865, 1870, 1878-79; Walker County, 1870-71, 1875-76; possibly a partner in Poe & Wright operating in Walker County, 1872.

POLING, WILLIAM
Born in Illinois, 1865. Listed in San Antonio, 1900.

PONCH, ADELIA
Born in North Carolina, 1875. Listed in Jacksonville, 1900. May be Ronch.

PONCH, M. G.
Born in North Carolina, 1833. Active in Jacksonville, 1900. May be Ronch.

POOL, J. F. P.
Active in Anson, c. 1895.

POPE, A. N.
Active in Brown County, 1876.

POSSE, CHARLES A.
Born in Georgia, 1869. Listed in Dallas, 1900.

POTASH, MOSES L.
Born in Louisiana, 1861; died in Victoria, Texas, 1918. Partner in Rice & Potash, Fayette County, 1887. Listed alone in Victoria, 1890-92, 1896-97, 1900-01. Located at 116 North Main, 1900-01.

POTTER
Partner in Sache & Potter operating in Galveston on Market Street, 1860.

POTTER, FLORENCE E.
Born in Michigan, 1879. Photograph retoucher in California, 1895-96. Active in Dallas at 298 Elm, 1897-1900.

POTTER, L. A.
Born in Kansas, 1875. Active in Paris, 1900.

POWEL, ELLIMARE
Born in Texas, 1874. Listed in Coke County, 1900.

POWELL, L. T.
Born in Kentucky, 1871. Active in Beeville, 1900; may have bought Watkins Brothers gallery.

POWER, G. T.
Active in Moffat, Bell County, 1884-85, 1890-92.

PRATHER, F. O.
Active in Anderson County, 1874.

PRATHER, THOMAS O.
Born in Georgia, 1847. Active in Clifton, 1890-92, 1896-97; Bosque County, 1900.

PRATT, GEORGE H.
Born in Illinois, 1858. Listed in Waxahachie, 1896-97; Paris, 1900.

PRAYTOR, WILLIAM B.
Partner with B. G. Grondel, operating as Grondel & Praytor in Round Rock, 1890-91. Active in Stephenville, 1892; Ladonia, 1896-97.

PREALINOUZ, C.
Active in La Grange, 1866-67.

PREDICK, J. B.
Active in Limestone County, 1873.

PRESCOTT, ARTHUR
Born in Texas, c. 1884. "Apprentice Photographer" listed in San Antonio census of 1870.

PREUSSER, GEORGE
Born in Germany, c. 1825. Active in Fort Concho, Tom Green County, 1880.

PREUSUER, FRANK
Born in Germany, 1857. Immigrated to U.S., 1883. Listed in Midland, 1900.

PREVOT, ANTHONY
Active in Dallas, 1886-87.

PRICE, C. C.
Active in Montague County, 1875.

PRICE, C. C.
Born in Texas, 1869. Active in Cass County, 1900.

PRICE, CARL E.
Born in Ohio, 1860. Listed in Corrigan, 1900.

PRICE, JAMES M.
Active in Athens, 1890-91.

PRICE, JOHN
Born in Tennessee, 1851. Listed in Jacksboro, 1900.

PRIESTLY, P.
Active in Austin, 1851, operating on Congress.

PROTHROW, SANDERS C.
Born in South Carolina, c. 1831. Listed in Troup, 1870; Cherokee and Kaufman Counties, 1871.

PUGH, JOHN W.
Born in Texas, 1874. Active in Reno, Parker County, 1900.

PULLEN & WAGNER
Partnership operating in Temple, 1898-99.

PURDY, J. M.
Active in Eastland County, 1894. Worked in Boston, Massachusetts, 1896-1905 or later.

PUREY & COMPANY, H. F.
Operated in Red River County, 1875; may be misspelling of Perry or Peery.

PUTTY, EDWARD
Partner in G. & E. Putty operating in Gainesville, 1896-97.

PUTTY, G.
Partner in G. & E. Putty operating in Gainesville, 1896-97.

PUTTY, G. & E.
Partnership in Gainesville, 1896-97.

PYWELL & STERZING
Possibly William Redish Pywell and F. A. Sterzing operating in Austin, 1867.

PYWELL, WILLIAM REDISH
Born in Baltimore, Maryland, 1843; died in Bunkie, Louisiana, 1887. Took up photography with Mathew Brady and Alexander Gardner during the Civil War. Worked for Charles N. Bean in Houston, 1867-68; photographed on the Yellowstone River expedition, 1873; in Tasmania, 1874. Active in Homer and Ruslin, Louisiana, 1880s.

QUEENSBURY
Partner in Parrott & Queensbury operating in Maverick County, 1875; in Starr County, 1876. Also spelled Quesenberry.

QUINN, C. W.
Born in Kentucky, 1855. Operated a "Dry Plate Factory" in Houston, 1900.

QUIRK, JAMES
Born in New York, 1852. Listed in Canadian, 1900.

RABA, ERNST
Born in Germany, 1874; died 1951. Immigrated to U.S., 1891. Partner in Brack & Raba with Asa A. Brack, active in San Antonio, 1894-96, at 113 North Alamo. Succeeded Joseph Eckerskorn, 1897-1900, operating at 211 South Alamo.

RABE, JOHN A. G.
Active in San Antonio, 1889-90.

RAFFERTY, FRANK ERNEST
Partner in Mims & Rafferty with Edward Wellington Mims in Tyler at 112 North Bois d'Arc, 1893. Also operated as Eureka Gallery.

RAGLAND, J. B.
Active in Upshur County, 1872.

RAGSDALE & BROTHER
Partnership operating in Burnet County, 1875.

RAGSDALE & WILSON
Active in Honey Grove, 1898-99; Robert B. Ragsdale.

RAGSDALE, McARTHUR CULLEN
Born in South Carolina, 1849; died 1944. Itinerant photographer based in Belton; worked in Brownwood, Fort McKavett, Mason and Fredericksburg, c. 1874-75. Moved to Fort Concho, 1875, then to San Angelo, operating on Chadbourne Street. Active in San Antonio, 1881. Listed in Bell, Hamilton and Williamson Counties, 1874; Llano and Williamson Counties, 1875; Fort McKavett, Menard County, 1880; San Angelo, 1884-85, 1890-92, 1896-99; in Tom Green County, 1900. He continued working as a photographer until c. 1915, then sold out; all his negatives were destroyed by the new owner.

RAGSDALE, ROBERT B.
Active in Honey Grove, 1891-92; continued in Honey Grove as partner in Ragsdale & Wilson, 1898-99.

RAINEY
Active in Matagorda County, 1871.

RAINS, CARVER W.
Born in Texas, 1865. Listed in San Antonio at 305 West Houston, 1894-96. Active in Houston at 1417 Congress, 1897-1901. Also listed in La Grange, 1900.

RAINWATER, TERREL
Born in Kentucky, 1846. Active in Sulphur Springs, 1892, 1896-97, 1900.

RAMSEY, O.
Born in Denmark, 1858. Active in Runge, 1890; partner of Louis Dahl, 1900.

RAND, C. A.
Born in Maine, c. 1828. Associated with C. H. Washburn of New Orleans; active in San Antonio, 1855; Brownsville, 1860.

RAND, L. O., JR.
Born in Texas, 1877. Listed in El Paso, 1900.

RANDALL, A. F.
Active in Weimar, 1897, 1899, on Columbus.

RANDAU, OSWALD
Born in Germany, 1848. Immigrated to U.S., 1867. Active in Galveston at 1727 Strand, 1895-97; 420 Twenty-second, 1899-1900. Also operated as Acme Studio, 1899-1900.

RANDOLPH
Partner in Leach & Randolph with Don M. Leach in Gainesville, 1880s.

RANDOLPH, JOHN P.
Born in Virginia, c. 1856. Active in Terrell, 1880.

RANKIN, CHARLES AUGUSTA
Born in Los Angeles, California, 1872; died in Waco, 1905. Brother of William Wesley Rankin. Active in Corsicana, 1900.

RANKIN, WILLIAM WESLEY
Born in Corsicana, 1880; died 1927. Brother of Charles Augusta Rankin. Listed in Corsicana, 1900.

RANNEY, R. H.
Active in New Braunfels, 1867.

RATCLIFFE & LEE
Miss Jennie Ratcliffe and Miss Ellen Lee operating in San Antonio, 1892-93.

RAU, J. P.
Born in Virginia, c. 1839. Active in Galveston, 1870; possibly a woman.

RAWLINS, W. J.
Born in Georgia, c. 1847. Worked in Wooster, Ohio, 1870s; may have been in Chicago, Illinois, 1875. Active in Gainesville, 1880.

RAWLS, WILLIAM J.
Born in Texas, 1872. Listed in Hillsboro, 1896-97, 1900.

RAY, W. R.
Active in Coryell County, 1871.

RAYBURN
Active in Dallas, 1877; possibly a painter.

RAYMOND
Partner in Baker & Raymond, photographers in Austin during the Civil War era; operated a drug store, published almanacs and sold photographic supplies, 1860s. Partner in Rearick & Raymond with L. B. Rearick operating in Grayson County, 1873.

REAMS, JOSHUA
Born in Tennessee, 1863. Listed in Cooke County, 1900.

REARICK & RAYMOND
Partnership operating in Grayson County, 1873.

REARICK, L. B.
Partner in Rearick & Raymond, Grayson County, 1873; continued in Grayson County, 1874.

REASLER, J. R.
Active in Ladonia, 1898.

RECKNAGEL, FRIEDERIKE (MRS.)
Born 1860; died 1856. Amateur photographer active in Fayette County, 1892-95.

RECTOR & ROBERTS
Partnership operating in Williamson County, 1874; D. W. Roberts.

REED
Partner in Stone & Reed, Red River County, 1873.

REED, BENJAMIN
Active in Daingerfield, 1870. May be the same as B. Reel.

REED. E. L.
Active in Abilene, 1898-99.

REEL, B.
Active in Lamar County, 1871. May be the same as Benjamin Reed.

REEVES, ENOCH J.
Active in El Paso, 1902-03.

REEVES, IRA
Born in Texas, 1874. Listed in Sabine County, 1900.

REHNER & SON, R.
Operated by Richard Rehner in Indianola, Calhoun County, 1866-70.

REHNER, RICHARD
Born in Germany, c. 1814. Operated as R. Rehner & Son in Indianola, 1866-70. Listed alone in Calhoun County, 1871; Matagorda County, 1872; Calhoun County, 1875-76; Goliad County, 1880. Also spelled Reiner, Relmer, Rheimer, Riener.

REID & DAVENPORT
E. L. Reid and Perry F. Davenport, operating in Waxahachie, 1892. Also spelled Devenport.

REID, E. L.
Born in Iowa, c. 1846. Listed in Hopkins County, 1872; Waxahachie, 1878-83.

REIFF, J. B.
Active in Hallettsville, 1866.

REMINGTON, FREDERICK A.
Operator for Francis F. Parker, El Paso, 1888-89; also active 1905-06.

REUGON, MARCOS
Active in Brazoria County, 1872-73; also listed as Keugan and Kruyon.

REYNOLDS, E. T.
Active in Kinmundy, Illinois, 1860. Listed in Pittsburg, Texas, 1869.

RHEA & SON
James W. and Robert H. Rhea, operating in Franklin, 1890-92.

RHEA, JAMES W.
Partner in Rhea & Son, Franklin, 1890-92.

RHEA, ROBERT H.
Listed in Carbondale, Illinois, 1864. Active in Franklin, Texas partner in Rhea & Son, 1890-92.

RHINE, GUSTAVE C.
Active in Fort Worth, 1880-99. Listed at 108 Main, 1885-86; 208 Main, 1886-89; Fourth at Main, 1890-91. Also known as Rhine's Studio, 1880-90.

RHODES, ALBERT S.
Active in Clarksville, 1896-97.

RHODES, C. J.
Active in Dallas, 1894, when the business license was transferred to Weatherington Brothers. Possibly Charles Rohde.

RHODY, F. (MRS.)
Active in El Paso, 1907-10.

RHOMBERG, CHARLES
Active in Austin, 1889-90, on Colorado at West Thirteenth; partner in Yancey & Rhomberg with Charles R. Yancey, 1890-91, at the same address. Printer for William O. Journeay, 1891-92; listed alone, 1893-94.

RIBBLE, V. A. (MRS.)
Active in Lampasas, 1892, 1896-97.

RICE & POTASH
Possibly Louis Rice and Moses L. Potash, operating in Fayette County, 1887.

RICE, D. E.
Photographer for Seymour & Company, Dallas, 1891-92.

RICE, LOUIS
Born in Baden, 1843. Immigrated to U.S., 1850. Listed in Aransas and Victoria Counties, 1872; Victoria County, 1873; Lavaca County, 1874; Jackson and Victoria Counties, 1875; Texana, Jackson County, 1880; Victoria, 1882-83; Fayette County, 1887, 1890, 1897-98; Sequin, 1896-97; La Grange, 1900. Also operated as Rice & Company in Fayette County. May have been a partner in Rice & Potash, Fayette County, 1887.

RICE, W. A.
Active in Palo Pinto County, 1873; Parker County, 1874-76.

RICE, WILSON A.
Active in Corsicana, 1859-60.

RICHARD & KAISER
Julius Richard and Frank Kaiser operating in Fort Worth at 108 Main, 1888-89; also known as Southern Art Gallery.

RICHARD, JULIUS
Partner with Frank Kaiser operating as Richard & Kaiser in Fort Worth, 1888-89. Also listed as Jules.

RICHARDSON
Active in Collin County, 1874.

RICHARDSON, ARTHUR
Born in Texas, 1872. Active in Corsicana, 1900.

RICHARDSON, JAMES T.
Born in Tennessee, 1865. Active in Leonard, 1900.

RICHARDSON, JOHN
Born in Texas, 1872. Listed in Harrison County, 1900.

RICHEY & TIERS
Possibly Theodore Richey and William C. Tiers operating in San Antonio, 1868.

RICHEY, THEODORE
Born in the District of Columbia, c. 1846. Active in San Antonio on Main Plaza, 1868-69; in Austin, 1870.

RICHMOND, ALBERT
Active in Galveston at 2024 Market, 1899-1900.

RIGBY, RUSSELL
Born in Mississippi, c. 1845. Active in Cameron, 1880.

RINES, ALFRED
Born in Minnesota, 1874. Listed in Uvalde, 1900.

RITTER, W. E.
Born in Tennessee, 1868. Active in Ferris, 1900.

RIVERS, J. E.
Active in Travis County, 1885.

ROBBERTS, HENRY L.
Born in Tennessee, 1874. Listed in Springtown, 1900.

ROBBINS & GOVE
G. W. Robbins and William S. Gove operating in Huntsville, 1853.

ROBBINS, G. W.
Active in Houston, 1852; partner in Robbins & Gove, Huntsville, 1853.

ROBERS, LOWERY
Born in Texas, 1876. Listed in San Antonio, 1900.

ROBERSON, JOHN A.
Active in Saint Jo, 1890-91.

ROBERTS
Partner in Sheldon & Roberts operating in Jefferson, 1868; Sargeant & Roberts operating in Dallas on Sycamore between Main and Elm, 1873-74.

ROBERTS, C. A.
Born in Texas, 1867. Listed in Potter County, 1900.

ROBERTS, D. W.
Active in Williamson County, 1874; partner in Rector & Roberts.

ROBERTS, O. B.
Active in San Antonio, 1899-1900.

ROBERTSON & COMPANY
Operating in Brenham, 1878-79.

ROBERTSON, GEORGE
Active in Austin, 1872-74.

ROBERTSON, JOHN J.
Active in McKinney, 1867.

ROBINS, WILLIAM N.
Born in Louisiana, 1859. Active in Ennis, 1900.

ROBINSON, GEORGE W.
Active in San Antonio at 305 West Houston, 1896-1900 and later.

ROBINSON, J. A.
Active in San Augustine County, 1872.

ROBINSON, W. A.
Active in Fayette County, 1893-94.

ROBINSON, WILLIAM N.
Listed in Kaufman, 1884-85; Temple, 1890-91; Navasota, c. 1890; Bryan, 1892; Corsicana, 1894-99. Located at 114 West Fifth, 1894-95; 306 North Beaton, 1898-99.

ROENHGEN, KUNO
Active in Travis County, 1879.

ROESBERG, GEORGE F.
Born in Indiana, c. 1823. Active in S. Louis, Missouri, 1859-60; New Orleans, Louisiana, 1870. Operating in Henderson, Texas, 1869; Upshur County, 1871; Houston and Walker Counties, 1872; Fayette County, 1873; Limestone County, 1874; Harris County, 1875; Austin and Bastrop Counties, 1876. Active in Austin on Pecan at Sabine, 1877-79. In Houston, 1880-88, 1898-99; studio located on Dallas at San Felipe, 1880-81; 129 Congress, 1882-87; 135 Congress, 1887-88.

ROESSLE & HOYT
Theodore Roessle and Elmer Hoyt operating in San Angelo, 1890-92.

ROESSLE, THEODORE
Partner in Roessle & Hoyte, San Angelo, 1890-92.

ROFF, REESE R.
Born in Texas, 1867. Photographic supply agent in Houston, 1900.

ROGERS, CHARLES
Born in Alabama, c. 1828. Listed in Galveston, 1870.

ROGERS, EARLY
Active in Weatherford, 1890-92.

ROGERS, I.
Active in Liberty, 1866-67.

ROGERS, LARRY
Born in Texas, 1861. Active in Harrison County, 1900; listed as black.

ROHDE, CHARLES
Born in Texas, 1870. Listed in Crosby County, 1900.

ROHDE, LILLIAN
Born in Ohio, 1876. Active in Crosby County, 1900.

ROMO, TOMAS
Born in Mexico, 1873. Listed in San Antonio, 1900.

ROOT & COMPANY, J. C.
Van Buren, Arkansas firm; planned to visit Clarksville, Paris, Bonham, Sherman and Preston, Grayson County during September and October, according to advertisement of August 25, 1855.

ROOT, MELVILLE E.
Partner in Clary & Root operating in San Antonio at 415 East Houston, 1883-84.

RORDEN, CHARLES
Active in Elm Mott, McLennan County, 1892.

ROSE & SCHMEDLING
Philip H. Rose and Marcus E. Schmedling operating a gallery in Galveston, c. 1875-c. 1899. Listed at 170 Tremont, 1886-87.

ROSE & ZAHN
Philip H. Rose and Justus Zahn operating in Galveston before 1887-88; Zahn bought out Rose, May 1888.

ROSE, CHALMERS
Active in Chicago, Illinois, 1874-76. Active in San Antonio, 1882.

ROSE, CHARLES A.
Active in El Paso, 1895-96, at 103 South Campbell.

ROSE, NOAH HAMILTON
Born in Kendall County, Texas, 1874; died in San Antonio, 1952. Rose made and distributed thousands of copies of nineteenth-century photographs of Texas and the West, but none of the original photographers are identified. His prints are typically 5 x 7, and subjects are identified with a typed label at the bottom. He was listed in Wichita Falls, 1900.

ROSE, PHILIP H.
Born c. 1846. Active in Galveston, 1870-99; he worked with Blessing & Brother, Blessing & Company, Blessing & Rose; partner in Rose & Schmedling, Galveston, c. 1875-c. 1899. Also a partner in Rose & Zahn before 1888, when he sold out to Zahn. Located at 159 and 161 East Market between 21st and 22nd, 1879-85.

ROSS, J. W.
Born in Illinois, c. 1815. Listed in the 1850 census as an "artist" in Galveston; studio located on Main, 1851. Also active in San Antonio, 1851.

ROSSER, J. A. (MRS.)
Active in Leesburg, Camp County, 1892, 1896-97.

ROTHBERG, H.
Active in Denison, 1898-99.

ROTHWELL, ISAAC N.
Born in Pennsylvania, 1851. Partner in Paris & Rothwell with Arthur C. Paris, operating in San Antonio, 1891-96. Studio was located at 11 and 13 West Commerce, 1891-92; 107 West Commerce, 1891-96. Continued alone at the same address, 1896-1900 and later.

ROWGLES, ALLEY
Active in San Patricia County, 1875.

ROWLAND, CAIN
Active in Dallas County, 1874.

ROWLAND, PEARL
Born in Texas, 1880. Listed in Navasota, 1900.

RUCK, D. R.
Active in Canton, 1868.

RUDDELL, JOHN B.
Listed in Denton, 1900.

RUDOLPH, A. E.
Active in Gainesville, 1870.

RUINS
Active in Williamson County, 1876.

RUSH
Partner in Mohler & Rush, Johnson County, 1874-75.

RUSH, C. A.
Active in Angelina and Hardin Counties, 1872. Also listed as Bush or Reesh.

RUSH, JOHN
Born in Mississippi, 1874. Listed in Mount Calm, 1900.

RUSHING, G. B. D.
Active in Shelby County, 1884.

RUSSELL, C.
Born in Kentucky, c. 1852. Active in Parker County, 1880.

RUSSELL, JOHN
Born in Virginia, c. 1838. Listed in Waco, 1870.

RUSSELL, JOHN F.
Associated with E. Frank DeZalba and Henry G. Baxter, operating in Beaumont as Baxter & Company, 1892.

RUSSELL, SAMUEL B.
Born in Virginia, c. 1835. Active in Waco, 1870; McLennan County, 1872; Waller County, 1874; Weatherford, 1880. May be Samuel R. Russell.

SACHE & POTTER
Partnership operating in Galveston on Market Street, 1860.

SAMSON, WILLIAM H.
Active in Montague County, 1880; Fort Worth on Main at Third, 1882; Cisco, 1884-85.

SAMUEL, TUTLEY
Born in Michigan, 1864. Active in Ysleta, El Paso County, 1900.

SANDERS, DR.
Active in Hamilton, 1884-85, 1890-91.

SANDERS, MARTIN L.
Born in Tennessee, 1859. Listed in Abilene, 1883; Brownwood, 1890-92; Waco, 1896-1901. Studio in Waco located at 503 ½ Austin, 1896-99; 509 ½ Austin, 1900-01.

SANDERS, S.
Active in Brownwood, c. 1895.

SANDIFER, P. M.
Born in Mississippi, 1851. Listed in Lampasas County, 1900.

SANDOVAL, FERNANDO S.
Active in San Antonio at 201 El Paso, 1896-97.

SARDONIC
Active in Waller County, 1875; possibly John Serdinko.

SARGEANT & ROBERTS
Partnership operating in Dallas on Sycamore between Main and Elm, 1873-74; J. P. Sargeant, also spelled Sargant.

SARGEANT, J. P.
Partner in Sargeant & Roberts operating in Dallas, 1873-74. Also spelled Sargant.

SARUSET, GEORGE
Born in Germany, 1868. Immigrated to U.S., 1882. Listed in El Paso, 1900.

SATTELLE, ED
Active in Dallas at the fairgrounds, 1894.

SAVAGE, CHARLES H.
Active in San Antonio, 1881-99. Studio at 247 West Commerce Street, 1881-88; 319 or 219 West Commerce, 1889-91; 207 West Commerce, 1892-93.

SAWDERS, W. B.
Active in Marlin, 1866.

SAWYER, CLIFFORD E.
Partner in Brittingham & Sawyer with John G. Brittingham in Fort Worth, 1890-91; gallery at 808 Main Street.

SCAGGS
Born in Georgia, c. 1854. Active in Goliad County, 1880.

SCHEIER, JOHN H.
Partner in Jones & Scheier operating in Houston at 1007 Main, 1897-98.

SCHELBERGER
Partner in Woodard & Schelberger, Williamson County, 1876. Possibly O. S. Shalenberger.

SCHLEY, JOHN
Active in Coryell County, 1874.

SCHLEY, W. A.
Active in Cass County, 1873.

SCHLUETER, FRANK J.
Itinerant tent photographer with his father and brother-in-law in Flatonia, 1891, making prints and postcards. He moved to Quanah and established a studio, operating c. 1892-c. 1898. Active in Galveston; moved to Houston, continuing in photography until c. 1968,

at 909 Branard and 3617 Main.

SCHLUETER, JAMES
Active in New Ulm, Austin County, 1896-97.

SCHLUETER, JOSEF
Born in Germany, 1846. Immigrated to U.S., 1884. Active in Austin County, 1900.

SCHLUTE
Partner in Heiron & Schlute, possibly a misspelling of Schlueter. Active in Granger, 1896-97.

SCHMEDLING, MARCUS R.
Partner in Rose & Schmedling with Philip H. Rose, operating a gallery in Galveston possibly as early as 1875, until c. 1899. Listed at 170 Tremont, 1886-87.

SCHMIDT, JOHN B.
Born in Bavaria, c. 1833. Listed in Victoria, 1866-70; Clinton, DeWitt County, 1870; Victoria and Houston Counties, 1871; Victoria County, 1872-73, 1875; Gonzales, 1875. Also listed as Smith.

SCHNEIDER, BERN
Active in Galveston County, 1873-81, located on Market at Twentieth.

SCHNEIDER, ERNEST
Born in Germany, 1870. Active in Brownwood, 1898, 1900.

SCHNEIDER, ROBERT C.
Born in Germany, c. 1853. Active in Galveston, 1880-82. Operated in the same gallery as Bern Schneider, on Market at Twentieth, 1881-82.

SCHNELL, L.
Active in Burnet County, 1871; Hill County, 1875.

SCHUNTZ, C. N.
Active in Harris County, 1872.

SCHURMAN, PAUL
Born in Germany, 1876. Listed in Galveston, 1900.

SCHUWIRTH, ANNA
Born in Germany, 1851. Immigrated to U.S., 1872. Wife of George Schuwirth; worked with him in Austin, 1900.

SCHUWIRTH, DORA
Born in Texas, 1879. Daughter of George and Anna; worked with them in Austin, 1900.

SCHUWIRTH, GEORGE
Born in Hesse, Germany, 1843; died 1906. Operated studio in Austin, 1875-1901. His daughter and wife worked with him, 1900. Studio on Pecan between Brazos and San Jacinto, 1877-82; 220 East Pecan, 1882-83; 219 East Pecan, 1882-85; 423 East Sixth, 1885-1901.

SCHWART & COMPANY, F. W.
Active in San Antonio, 1895.

SCHWART, FREDERICK W.
Active in Kerrville, 1892; operated as F. W. Schwarz & Company in San Antonio, 1895; in New Braunfels, 1896-97.

SCHWARTZ, DAVID
Born in Virginia, c. 1855. Listed in Cleburne, 1880.

SCHWARTZ, JOE
Active in Fort Worth, 1898.

SCHWING, SAMUEL
Born in Kentucky, c. 1839. Active in Gonzales, 1869-72. May be Schonig.

SCOTT, A. E.
Partner in Sequin, Cevor & Scott operating in Waco, 1886-87, 1898-99; also known as Academy of Art.

SCOTT, HENRY D.
Born in Ohio, 1859. Active in Dallas, 1891-1900. Photographer for Parish & O'Bannon, 1891-92; retoucher for Richard L. Chalmers, 1893-94; for Parish & O'Bannon, 1894-95. Continued in Dallas until 1900; listed at 304 Elm, 1898-1900.

SCOTT, HOMER
Active in El Paso operating the Scott Photo Company, 1907-13.

SCOTT, JOHN
Born in Savannah, Tennessee, 1846. Came to Bastrop County, 1853. He served in Company G, Second Texas Infantry, 1864 to the end of the Civil War. He moved with his family to Lexington, Lee County, 1865, farming and working as a clerk. He learned photography from itinerant F. M. Hall, 1872, and opened a gallery in La Grange; moved to Rockdale and continued in photography, 1874-1900 or later. Listed in Limestone and Victoria Counties, 1872; Dallas, Johnson and Limestone Counties, 1873; Limestone County, 1875-76; Rockdale, 1880-1900.

SCOTT PHOTO COMPANY
Active in El Paso, 1907-13, operated by Homer Scott.

SCROGGINS, F.
Active in Angelina County, 1874-75.

SCRUGGS, J. M.
Active in Melrose, Nacogdoches County, 1870.

SEARGEANT, V. P.
Listed in La Grange, 1866.

SELF, JIM
Active in Corsicana, 1860.

SELKIRK, JAMES
Partner with his cousin, James H. Selkirk, operating in Matagorda as James H. & J. Selkirk, 1846-58.

SELKIRK, JAMES H.
Born in New York, 1815. Operated a gallery in Matagorda with his cousin, James, 1846-58, as James H. & J. Selkirk.

SELKIRK, JAMES H. & J.
Partnership in Matagorda, 1846-58. Also listed as J. H. & J. Selkirk.

SELRING, JULIA P. (MRS.)
Active in San Antonio at 12 North Alamo, 1885-86; also listed 1898-99.

SELVIDGE, SOL M.
Born in Texas, 1868. Active in Reno, Parker County, 1900.

SENBEAUBER, F.
Active in Nacogdoches, 1870; name may be Serwegruber.

SENTER, WILLIAM B.
Listed in Navasota, 1890-91.

SEQUIN, CEVOR & SCOTT
Partnership of Charles W. Sequin, Charles E. Cevor and A. E. Scott, proprietors of the Academy of Art in Waco, 1886-87, 1898-99. Located on Austin at Seventh, 1886-87.

SERDINKO, JOHN
Active in New Braunfels, 1882-99. Also listed as Sardonic, Serkinko, Serdinke, Sedinko.

SERKINKO, JULIUS
Born in Bohemia, 1849. Immigrated to U.S., 1867. Active in Weimar, 1900. Possibly John Serdinko.

SERTZ, JOSEPH
Born in Austria, c. 1828. Listed in Galveston on Market, 1870-71.

SEVESON, GEORGE F.
Active in Grayson County, 1875.

SEVOM, GEORGE
Active in Grayson County, 1875.

SEYMOUR & COMPANY
Active in Dallas, 1891-92.

SHALENBERGER & HOUCK
O. S. Shalenberger and possibly H. Houck operating in Tarrant County, 1875.

SHALENBERGER, O. S.
Active in Grayson County, 1875; partner in Shalenberger & Houck, Tarrant County, 1875; listed alone in Kimball, Bosque County, 1876. May have been a partner in Woodard & Schelberger, Williamson County, 1876. Also listed as Shellenberges, Shellingberger.

SHANNON, JOHN C.
Active in Llano, 1896-97.

SHARP, W. E.
Partner in W. G. Walz & Company, and with William G. Walz and Thomas B. Catron, El Paso, 1898-1900; predominantly a photographic supply business.

SHAUUM & LEACH
Partnership in Presidio County, 1896.

SHAW & COMPANY, J. W.
Operated in Hill County, 1875.

SHAW, J. L.
Active in Mount Pleasant, 1890-92.

SHAW, J. W.
Born in Tennessee, 1852. Listed in Nocona, 1900. Possibly operated as J. W. Shaw & Company, Hill County, 1875.

SHELBY, WILLIAM
Active in Lavaca County, 1876.

SHELDON & ROBERTS
Active in Jefferson, 1868; possibly G. A. Sheldon.

SHELDON, G. A.
Active in Jefferson, 1868; possibly a partner in Sheldon & Roberts.

SHEPHERD, WILLIAM B.
Active in Mineral Wells, 1896-97.

SHERER, N. D.
Active in Waco, 1867.

SHERFF, L.
Born in Minnesota, 1873. Listed as female in the census, operating

in Parker County, 1900.

SHERMAN, SAMUEL W.
Born in Tennessee, 1861. Active in Amarillo, 1896-97, 1900.

SHERRELL & YATES
Partnership operating in Williamson County, 1874.

SHIELDS, GEORGE J.
Active in Palo Pinto County, 1872-73; Shackelford County, 1875.

SHIVE, WILLIAM
Born in Michigan, 1874. Listed in Athens, 1900.

SHORT, E. B.
Active in Caldwell, 1869.

SHORT, WILLIAM
Born in Texas, 1864. Listed in Jack County, 1900.

SHOTWELL
Active in Jefferson County, 1872.

SHREVES & BARRON
William M. Shreves and Russell J. Barron operating in Terrell, 1884-85.

SHREVES & MURRAY
William M. Shreves and Henry L. Murray in Palestine, 1880-1900.

SHREVES, WILLIAM M.
Born in Illinois, c. 1854. Listed in Terrell, 1880, 1882-83. Partner with Henry L. Murray in Palestine, 1880-1900; partner with Russell J. Barron in Terrell, 1884-85.

SHRUN, W. F.
Active in Upshur County, 1876.

SHULL, LAFAYETTE T.
Born in Kentucky, 1833. Active in Tyler, 1884-85, 1887, 1898-99; Greenville, 1892, 1896-97, 1898-99.

SHUN, N. D.
Active in Osage, Colorado County, 1869.

SIDES, M. J. (MRS.)
Listed in Alexander, Erath County, 1892, 1896-97.

SIMMONS, D. P.
Active in Bowie and Lamar Counties, 1871.

SIMMONS, J. R.
Active in Hempstead, 1866; Industry, Austin County, 1867, 1870.

SIMMONS, J. W.
Active in Lavaca County, 1871.

SIMPSON, JAMES
Born in Alabama, 1856. Listed in Taylor County, 1900.

SIMS
Partner in Sims, Norris & Company operating in Jefferson, 1868.

SIMS, G. W.
Listed in Leonard, 1890-92.

SIMS, NORRIS & COMPANY
Active in Jefferson, 1868.

SINGLETON, ANDREW
Active in Saint Jo, 1896-97.

SINK & HAYWORTH
Daniel P. Sink and J. P. Hayworth operating in Vernon, 1890-91.

SINK, DANIEL P.
Born in North Carolina, c. 1850; died 1931. Arrived in Calvert, 1878; operated a studio, 1880-99. Began working in Vernon, c. 1890; partner with J. P. Hayworth, 1891. Continued alone until c. 1919, when he sold out to R. B. Clifton and moved to California.

SKATES, W. T.
Active in Mount Enterprise, 1866; Panola County, 1867. Initials may be W. F. or W. I.

SKUMAND, HENRY
Born in Texas, 1870. Listed in Corrigan, 1900.

SKYLIGHT GALLERY
Operated by John H. Stephen Stanley in Houston, 1852-57.

SLEDGE
Born in Tennessee, 1854. Listed in the 1900 census as a traveling photographer in Whitewright.

SLIGER, JACK A.
Born in Tennessee, c. 1850. Active in Rosston, Cooke County, 1880.

SLOAN, JACK
Active in El Paso, 1907-10.

SLOAN, JOSEPH D.
Born in Texas, c. 1852. Active in Oso, Fayette County, 1869; listed in Fayette County, 1870, 1872. Also spelled Sloane.

SLOAN, WILLIAM H.
Active in Jefferson, 1865.

SLOAN, WILLIAM W.
Born in Tennessee, c. 1830. Active in Jefferson, 1866-83.

SLOCUM, WILLIAM
Born in New York, 1865. Listed in Hooks Switch, 1900.

SLONEKER, LITTLETON W.
Born in Texas, 1875. Active in Fisher County, 1900.

SMARLY, ALICE
Born in Tennessee, 1874. Listed in Henrietta, 1900.

SMARLY, GERTRUDE
Born in Tennessee, 1876. Active in Henrietta, 1900.

SMETTERS, S.
Active in Port Lavaca, 1857.

SMITH
Partner in Carlyle & Smith with William Carlyle, operating in Tyler, 1867; partner in Taylor & Smith, Grayson County, 1875; partner in Pinkerton & Smith, Wise County, 1876; partner in Pluckton & Smith, Wise County, 1877. Possibly A. Smith.

SMITH & CLEGHORN
Partnership operating in Kosse, 1871.

SMITH, A.
Active in Wise County, 1877.

SMITH, ALFRED
Active in Austin, 1848.

SMITH, BENJAMIN F.
Born in Missouri, c. 1843. Listed in Smith County, 1867; Tyler, 1869-70; Cleburne, 1880, 1884-85, 1890-92, 1896-99.

SMITH, CHARLES L.
Active in Orange, 1882-83.

SMITH, CHARLES W.
Born in North Carolina, c. 1817. Possibly a daguerreian; operating in Gabriel Mills, Williamson County, 1860.

SMITH, DELL
Active in Hopkins County, 1871.

SMITH, E. R.
Active in Moody, 1892.

SMITH, G. W.
Active in Mason County, 1888.

SMITH, GEORGE
Born in Missouri, c. 1854. Worked in Chicago, Illinois, 1870-79. Active in Denton County, 1880.

SMITH, GEORGE S.
Listed in Brownsville, 1866, 1870. Active in Alexandria, Virginia, 1888.

SMITH, H. H.
Born in Alabama, 1851. Listed in San Saba, 1900.

SMITH, J. B.
Active in Utica, New York, during the Civil War. Possibly the same person as John B. Schmidt operating in Texas, 1866-75. Schmidt was often listed as Smith. See John B. Schmidt.

SMITH, J. H.
Active in Kaufman County, 1874-75; Lampasas County, 1876.

SMITH, J. M.
Active in Grayson County, 1879.

SMITH, J. W.
Listed in Presidio County, 1896.

SMITH, JAMES
Born in Texas, 1874. Active in Eastland County, 1900.

SMITH, JOHN E.
Active in Crockett, 1870.

SMITH, JOHN W.
Active in Cass County, 1873-74.

SMITH, LEILA (MRS.)
Listed in Mineral Wells, 1892.

SMITH, M. D. & H. H.
Partnership in Henderson County, 1874.

SMITH, SAMUEL C.
Active in Chicago, Illinois, 1874. Listed in Burnet, 1890-92.

SMITH, TOBE
Active in San Jacinto County, 1887.

SMITH, WILLIAM E.
Born in Mississippi, 1868. Listed in Leon County, 1900.

SNELL & BLACKBURN
Possibly William H. Snell and David E. Blackburn operating in Cameron, 1892.

SNELL & THOMPSON
Active in Live Oak County, 1875.

SNELL, A.
Active in Goliad County, 1875; Fayette County, 1882.

SNELL BROTHERS
Thomas W. and William H. Snell, active in Denison, 1898-1900, at 316 ½ West Main. Also operated as Snell's Photo Studio.

SNELL, HENRY W.
Born in Tennessee, 1875. Listed in Denison, 1900.

SNELL, JENNIE B.
Born in Tennessee, 1872. Listed in Sherman, 1900; sister of William H. Snell.

SNELL, SIDNEY J.
Worked for Snell Brothers in Denison, 1898-99.

SNELL, THOMAS W.
Partner with William H. in Snell Brothers, operating in Denison, 1898-1900.

SNELL, WILLIAM H.
Born in Tennessee, 1855. Brother of Jennie B. and Thomas W. Snell. William opened the Denison Art Gallery at 316 West Main, c. 1893; his brother Thomas operated it as Snell's Photo Studio, 1898-99; as Snell Brothers, 1899-1900. William opened a second gallery in Sherman, 1896-1900, or later. He may have been a partner in Snell & Blackburn, operating in Cameron, 1892. He moved to Plainview, c. 1925.

SNIDER & GORDON
Partnership operating in Collin County, 1873.

SNODGRASS
Partner in Baldwin & Snodgrass operating in Cass County, 1873.

SNYDER
Active in Wolfe City, 1890.

SNYDER, WILSON
Born in Ohio, c. 1843.

SOLIS, ALBERTO L.
Active in El Paso, 1907-12.

SOLOMAN, T. D.
Active in Round Rock, 1866; possibly a partner in Solomon & Holcomb, Georgetown, 1868.

SOLOMON & HOLCOMB
Active in Georgetown, 1868; possibly T. D. Soloman.

SOLSONA, JOSEPH F.
Born in Spain, 1877. Immigrated to U.S., 1888. Listed in Fredericksburg, 1900. May have been associated with the Borel Portrait Company operating at 1307 West Commerce in San Antonio, c. 1900.

SOUBY
Active in New Orleans, Louisiana, 1870. Possibly a partner in Ball &

Souby and Chinn & Sowby. See partnership listings.

SOUTHERN ART GALLERY
Studio operated by Richard & Kaiser in Fort Worth at 108 Main, 1888-89.

SOUTHWESTERN PORTRAIT COMPANY
William H. Anderson and Thomas B. Anderson; listed as enlargers in Dallas, 1893-94.

SOWELL, A. D.
Born in Texas, 1880. Listed in Dickens County, 1900.

SOWELL, BURRELL
Born in Alabama, c. 1837. Active in Starrville, Smith County, 1870.

SPAGLIAM, H. D.
Partner in Caldwell & Spagliam with Charles H. Caldwell in San Augustine County, 1873.

SPARKMAN, WILLIAM
Born in Tennessee, 1846. Active in Hamilton, 1892, 1900.

SPEARMAN, I.
Born in Georgia, 1872 or 1875. Itinerant photographer active in Mansfield and listed in Fort Worth census, 1900.

SPILLER
Partner in Jackson & Spiller, active in Llano, c. 1890.

SPILLER & GRIFFIN
Partnership operating in Fairfield, 1868.

SPLITGERBEN, JULIUS
Active in Gillespie County, 1871-72.

SPRAIN, JOHN FREDERICK
Active in Brenham, 1884-85.

SPRINKS, W.
Born in Arkansas, 1859. Listed in Rockdale, 1900.

SPROUL, JAMES J.
Born in Missouri, 1844. Father of William C. Sproul. Active in Taylor, 1896-97, 1900.

SPROUL, WILLIAM C.
Born in Texas, 1875. Listed in Taylor, 1896-97, 1900.

SPRUITT & McCORD
Partnership operating in Wood County, 1873.

STAINTON, RENIE V.
Born in Canada, 1873. Immigrated to U.S., 1881. Listed in Houston, 1900.

STAMFER, F.
Active in Dallas, 1875; possibly a painter.

STAMPS
Partner in Johnson & Stamps, Caldwell County, 1871.

STAMPS & TRACY
Active in Grayson County, 1872.

STAMPS, P. R.
Active in Fayette County, 1871-72.

STANDROPER, T. S.
Active in Williamson County, 1871.

STANFORD, JOE B.
Born in Alabama, 1871. Active in Farmersville, 1900.

STANFORD, JOHN
Born in Alabama, 1874. Listed in Farmersville, 1900.

STANLEY, FITZGIBBON & BOURGES
Partnership of Emile Bourges and other daguerreians in Galveston, 1851. Known as FitzGibbon, Bourges & Stanley in Galveston, late December 1851, when John H. Stephen Stanley became a partner. The firm was called Stanley, FitzGibbon & Bourges at a branch studio in Houston, c. 1852.

STANLEY, JOHN H. STEPHEN
Born in England, c. 1799. Active in Houston, 1850-70. Partner in Stanley, FitzGibbon & Bourges, 1852; operated as Skylight Gallery, 1852-57. Stanley was a correspondent of the *Daguerreian Journal,* lecturing on astronomy and making meteorological observations for the Smithsonian Institution, 1851. He advertised that he was prepared to make stereo views, 1852. His gallery was listed on Main between Preston and Prairie, 1866; at 88 Main, 1867-68.

STAPLES, WILLIAM F.
Worked in Atlanta, Georgia, c. 1876. Active in Dallas, 1889-82, at 701 Main. He may have been in Nashville, Tennessee, 1890.

STAR GALLERY
Studio active in Sherman. Cabinet card imprint verified for a Burnet studio, c. 1885.

STARK, HENRY
Photographer from St. Louis, Missouri; traveled through Texas making photographs, 1895-96. A hand-made book with his photographs was reprinted as *Views in Texas.*

STARK, NARBONNE P.
Born in Kentucky, c. 1819. Active in Jefferson, 1869; Sulphur Bluff, Hopkins County, 1870; listed in Hopkins County, 1871-72, 1874; also in Montague County, 1874.

STARR, CLARA (MRS.)
Active in El Paso, 1907.

STEARNE, E. A.
Active in Woodville, 1869.

STEBBINS, A. T.
Listed in Travis County, 1875.

STEPHENS & KELLY
Partnership operating in Jefferson, 1869; possibly J. A. Kelley.

STEPHENSON, H. W.
Active in San Antonio at 132 West Commerce, 1892-93.

STEPP, GEORGE W.
Active in Liberty Hill, Williamson County, 1892.

STERNES, W. M.
Artist with J. P. Blessing & Brother in Houston, 1867-68; in Galveston at 178 Post Office, 1869.

STERZING & JONES
Possibly F. A. Sterzing and Robert E. Jones operating in Burnet County, 1867.

STERZING, F. A.
Active in Austin, 1865; possibly a partner in Sterzing & Jones, Burnet County, 1867; partner in Pywell & Sterzing operating in Austin, 1867.

STEVE, ROBERT M.
Born in Minnesota, 1872. Listed in Stephenville, 1900.

STEVENS, AMMON I.
Active in De Leon, 1884-85, 1890-91, 1896-99.

STEWART, GEORGE A.
Born in Alabama, c. 1843. Listed in Crockett, 1870.

STEWART, ISAAC A.
Born in Texas, 1865. Listed in Crockett, 1870.

STEWART, WILLIAM
Born in Indiana, 1847. Active in Morris County, 1900.

STILES, HARRY L.
Active in Rockwall, 1892; possibly the H. L. Stiles in Colorado Springs, Colorado, 1899-1901.

STIRMAN & PERRY
Partnership in Kaufman County, 1871; V. I. Stirman.

STIRMAN, V. I.
Partner in Stirman & Perry, Kaufman County, 1871.

STOKEY, DAVID G.
Active in Dallas at 1413 Main, 1884-85; also operated as Dallas Copying & Enlarging Company.

STONE & HANSARD
Partnership active in Denison, c. 1880s; possibly J. W. Hansard of Arkansas and Missouri, c. 1870s-80s.

STONE & REED
Partnership operating in Red River County, 1873.

STONE & WAGGONER
W. D. Stone and W. T. Waggoner operating in Austin, 1866. Also known as Austin Photograph Company. Sold out to William James Oliphant, November 1866.

STONE, EDWARD
Born in Tennessee, c. 1846. Listed in Clarksville, 1870.

STONE, ROBERT J.
Born in Texas, 1869. Active in Burleson County, 1890; Caldwell, 1890-91; Georgetown, 1900.

STONNE, H. C.
Born in Alabama, 1878. Listed in Terrell, 1900.

STORK, EUGENE B.
Born in Europe, c. 1836. Active in Houston, 1867-68; Bremond, 1870. Also listed as Storks.

STORY, ROBERT M.
Born in Mississippi, 1854. Active in Rusk, 1900.

STORY, W. P.
Born in Alabama, c. 1838. Active in Cleburne, 1870.

STOVALL & COMPANY
Listed in Bonham, 1866; also spelled Stoveall.

STOVALL, J. F.
Listed in Limestone County, 1874; Grayson County, 1875; Dallas and Ellis Counties, 1876.

STOVER
Active in San Antonio, 1860.

STOVER, ALEXANDER
Active in Carbondale, Young County, 1892.

STRAIN, FANNIE
Born in Texas, 1862. Active in Overton, 1900.

STRICKLAND, J.
Born in Tennessee, 1846. Listed in Mount Vernon, 1900.

STRICKLAND, MATTIE (MRS.)
Listed in Decatur, 1896-97.

STROOP, J. F.
Active in Johnson County, 1877.

STUART, W. F.
Active in El Paso, 1906-23.

STUMP
Partner in Duer, Stump & Company, Collin County, 1873.

STUPL, ANTON
Born in Bohemia, 1834. Immigrated to U.S., 1852. Listed in Austin County, 1900.

STURDEVANT, EUGENIO K.
Active in San Antonio, 1885-88, 1898-99. Studio at 19 West Houston, 1885-86; 10 East Houston, 1887-88. Operating in Seguind, 1892; in Galveston on Tremont and Avenue H, 1893-94.

SULLESBERY
Partner in Williams & Sullesbery, Williamson County, 1871.

SUMMERS, J. M. W.
Active in Bowie County, 1871.

SURBER, SYLVESTER A.
Born in Iowa, 1856. Listed in La Porte, 1900.

SUZLEM, C. C.
Born in Georgia, c. 1855. Active in Waco, 1880.

SWAFFORD & SWAFFORD
Operated the Home Studio in Baird.

SWAFFORD, ADOLPH
Born in Arkansas, 1872. Listed in Cooke County, 1900.

SWAIN, J.
Active in Dallas County, 1871.

SWAN, GEORGE B.
Born in Mississippi, 1869. Listed in Callahan County, 1900.

SWARTZ & BROTHER, D. H.
David H. and John Swartz operating in Fort Worth, 1885-87, 1898-99. Also operated as Cottage Gallery, 1886-87; as Lone Star Copying House, 1885-86. Located at 1013 Main, 1885-86; 600 Main, 1886-87.

SWARTZ & FREEMAN
Partnership of David H. Swartz and Gamiel C. Freeman in Columbus,

1882-83. Swartz sold out to Freeman, February 1884. John Swartz and Gamiel C. Freeman operated in Denison at 229 West Main, 1889-92.

SWARTZ, CHARLES
Born in Virginia, 1864. Secretary for the D. H. Swartz Life Size Portrait Company, 1894-95. Worked for John Swartz in Fort Worth, 1896-99. Listed in Fort Worth, 1900.

SWARTZ, DAVID H.
Born in Virginia, 1854. Active in Fort Worth, 1888-1900; Partner in Swartz & Freeman in Columbus, 1882-83; D. H. Swartz & Brother, 1885-99; Cottage Gallery, 1886-87; Lone Star Copying House, 1885-86. Operated D. H. Swartz Life Size Portrait Company, 1894-95; David H. Swartz, president, Charles L. Swartz, secretary, and William K. Swartz, advertising agent. Also operated in Dallas, c. 1888-89, listed as John Swartz. See partnership listings for locations.

SWARTZ, JOHN
Born in West Virginia, 1859. Operator for David H. Swartz in Dallas, 1888-89; partner in Swartz & Freeman, Dennison, 1889-92. Active in Fort Worth, 1896-1910, 1916-18. Also a partner in D. H. Swartz & Brother, 1885-87, 1898-99. See partnership listings for details.

SWARTZ, WILLIAM K.
Advertising agent for D. H. Swartz Life Size Portrait Company in Fort Worth, 1894-95.

SWOFFORD, E. O.
Born in Missouri, 1862. Listed in Baird, 1900.

SZMIDENSKY, STANISLAUS
Born in Poland, c. 1836. Active in La Grange, 1880.

TARR & COOPER
Active in Waco, 1869. Possibly Farr & Cooper.

TASHJIAN, ARMENEY
Active in Dallas, 1877.

TATE, ROBERT
Listed in Dallas, 1891-94.

TAUCH & PANNEWITZ
Possibly William Tauch and Gustave A. Pannewitz operating in Fayette County, 1886-87; in Schulenburg, 1898-99.

TAUCH, HENRY
Born in Texas, 1865. Listed in Fayette County, 1892-1900. Also listed as Hy Tauch.

TAUCH, WILLIAM
Active in Fayette County, 1883-91.

TAULMAN, JOSEPH EDWARD
Born in Texas, 1867. Active in Hubbard, 1896-97, 1900. Possibly in Clifton, mid-1890s.

TAWUK, A. I
Active in Palestine, 1870.

TAYLOR & SMITH
Partnership in Grayson County, 1875.

TAYLOR, HOWARD H.
Printer for William O. Journeay in Austin at 403 Congress, 1897-99.

TAYLOR, JAMES M.
Born in Kentucky, 1872. Listed in Whitewright, 1900.

TAYLOR, T. Y.
Active in Aurora, 1882-84; Springtown, 1890-92.

TAYLOR, WILLIAM
Born in Texas, 1882. Listed in Denton, 1900.

TEAGARDEN & KNUTSON
Partnership of Charles A. Teagarden and O. Peter Knutson operating in Tyler, 1879-83.

TEAGARDEN & WHERRY
Charles A. Teagarden and W. H. Wherry operating in Rusk, 1870.

TEAGARDEN, CHARLES A.
Born in Ohio, late, 1840s. Partner with W. H. Wherry in Rusk, 1870; in Houston and Trinity Counties, 1871; Houston County, 1873-74; Wood County, 1875; partner with Knutson in Tyler, 1879-83; continued in Tyler, 1884-99.

TEAGUE, JAMES H.
Active in Waxahachie, 1900.

TEEPLE, CHARLES B.
Active in Denison, 1876-77, on Austin between Main and Woodard.

TEMPLETON, T.
Active in Nacogdoches, 1859.

TENNEY, GEORGE M.
Active in San Antonio, 1857-58.

TERRELL, ANNA C. (MRS.)
Active in Bowie, 1890-91.

TERRY, ANDERSON F.
Partner in Bailey & Terry with Frank B. Bailey, active in Palestine, 1884-85.

TERRY, SAM
Born in Texas, 1863. Listed in Hillsboro, 1900.

TESTASUDZ
Partner in Lemone & Testasudz, Montgomery County, 1876.

TEWLER, THOMAS
Born in South Carolina, 1856. Active in Corpus Christi, 1900.

TEXAS PHOTO COPYING HOUSE
Operated by J. W. Weatherington & Company, John W. Weatherington and Charles W. Cherry in Lampasas, 1884-85.

TEXAS VIEW COMPANY
Published boxed set of 25 Texas stereoviews and parallel set of tinted lantern slides, probably photographed and produced by Keystone, c. 1936. The company address was Box 2192, Dallas.

THAIN, J. C.
Active in Presidio County, 1899.

THIELEPAPE, WILLIAM
Worked with Hermann Lungkwitz and William DeRyee producing a magic lantern show, then took it on tour through central Texas and up the Mississippi and Ohio Rivers, 1859-60.

THIGPIN & McDONALD
Partnership in Tyler, 1869-70; O. B. Thigpin.

THIGPIN, O. B.
Born in South Carolina, c. 1845. Active in Kickapoo, Anderson County, 1869; Tyler, 1870; partner with McDonald in Tyler, 1869-70; Smith County, 1871. Also operated as O. B. Thigpin & Company.

THOM, LAWRENCE
Active in Galveston, 1882-84, on Market at Twentieth.

THOMAS
Active in Columbus, 1859.

THOMAS & JERABEK
George E. Thomas and J. V. Jerabek operating in Caldwell, 1896-97.

THOMAS, CHARLES E.
Operator for Thomas C. Bolton in El Paso, 1888.

THOMAS, E. L.
Born in Texas, 1873. Listed in Sherman, 1900.

THOMAS, JOE
Born 1865. Active in Galveston and Houston, 1900; listed in census as black. Also listed as Thompson.

THOMAS, JOHN J.
Born in Ohio, 1838. Active in Ranger, 1900.

THOMAS, JOSEPH J.
Active in Dallas, 1894-95.

THOMAS, R. F.
Active in Rusk County, 1874; Nacogdoches County, 1875.

THOMAS, WILLIAM H.
Born in Holstein, c. 1840. Active in Schulenburg, 1878-80.

THOMASON & LEFFLER
James A. Thomason and B. Frank Leffler operating in Fort Worth at 600 Houston, 1894-95.

THOMPSON
Partner in Courtney & Thompson operating in Gainesville, 1880.

THOMPSON, GEORGE
Born in Kansas, 1870. Listed in Taylor, 1900.

THOMPSON, GUS S.
Born in Tennessee, 1869. Active in Dublin, 1898, 1900.

THOMPSON, J. S.
Active in Frost, 1892; Fredericksburg, 1896-97.

THOMPSON, JAMES R.
Listed in Bonham, 1892, 1896-97.

THOMPSON, L. A.
Born in Indiana, 1874. Active in El Paso, 1900.

THOMPSON, ROBERT M.
Born in Texas, 1876. Listed as "Photographer and Farmer" in Williamson County, 1900.

THOMPSON, RUTHA
Born in Kansas, 1880. Listed in Smithville, 1900.

THOMPSON, S. C.
Amateur stereo photographer active in San Antonio; member of Stereoscopic Society, 1939.

THOMPSON, W.
Born in Alabama, 1870. Active in Waco, 1900.

THOMPSON, W. W.
Born in New York, 1860. Active in Houston, 1900.

THOMPSON, WILLIAM S.
Active in Bonham, 1890-92, 1896-97.

THORNBLOD, OLAF L.
Active in Austin at 920 Congress, 1897-98.

THRESHKELD, HARRY
Born in Missouri, 1861. Listed in Marble Falls, 1900.

THRESHKELD, MATTIE
Born in Missouri, 1859. Listed in Marble Falls, 1900.

THUPPS, L. A.
Born in Texas, 1871. Active in Medina County, 1900.

THURMAN, A. M.
Born in Georgia, c. 1832. Active in Nacogdoches, 1860; Palestine, 1870.

TIDWELL, J. E.
Active in Beeville, 1866.

TIERS, WILLIAM C.
Born in Canada, c. 1833. Active in San Antonio, 1869-70; also in Belmont, Gonzales County, 1870. Possibly a partner in Richey & Tiers, San Antonio, 1868. Also listed as Teirs.

TINKEL, FRANK B.
Partner in Ansley & Tinkel with Cary D. Ansley, active in Denison, 1892.

TITSWORTH, C. G.
Listed in Fairview, Wilson County, 1890-92. Also listed as Fitsworth.

TOBLAR, LOUIS
Born in Russia, 1866. Immigrated to U.S., 1879. Active in Galveston, 1891-1900; located at 2608 Market, 1891-92; 2510 Market, 1893-94; Beach at Twenty-fourth, 1895-97.

TOBLER, S.
Active in Dallas, 1894.

TOE, LAER
Active in Galveston at 133 East Post Office, 1874.

TORDT, T.
Active in Webb County, 1874.

TOWNSEND, GEORGE F.
Active in Austin, 1893-97; located at 808 Congress, 1895-97; 904 Congress, 1897-98.

TRACY
Partner in Stamps & Tracy, Grayson County, 1872.

TRAMMELL, S. C.
Active in Dallas on Elm, 1875; possibly a painter.

TRANTLOW, WILLIAM C.
Born in Louisiana, 1879. Listed in Pearsall, 1900.

TRAVIS & BIRKLAND
Mrs. Fannie B. Travis and Mrs. Catherine B. Birkland operating in

Dallas at 505 Main, 1886-87; continued in Dallas, 1898-99.

TRAVIS, FANNIE B. (MRS.)
Partner with Mrs. Catherine B. Birkland operating as Travis & Birkland in Dallas, 1886-87, 1898-99.

TRIMBLE, W. U.
Born in Iowa, 1867. Listed in Bonham, 1900.

TRISEL, EMILE
Born in Germany, c. 1819. Listed in the 1850 census as an "artist" in Comal County; possibly a painter. Also listed as Tresel.

TROST, FRANK
Born in Pennsylvania, 1868. Listed in Port Arthur, 1900; brother of Phillip Trost.

TROST, PHILLIP
Born in Pennsylvania, 1859. Listed in Port Arthur, 1900; brother of Frank Trost.

TROUGH, EDWARD
Born in Pennsylvania, c. 1861. Active in Galveston County, 1880.

TUCKER
Partner in Petty & Tucker, Hunt County, 1872; partner in Dickenson & Tucker, Parker County, 1876.

TUCKER, A. W.
Active in Waxahachie, 1868.

TUCKER, E. M.
Listed in Mansfield, 1884-85, 1891-92.

TUCKER, E. N.
Active in Palo Pinto County, 1874; Oxford, Connecticut, 1884.

TUCKER, F.
Active in Clarksville, 1848.

TUCKER, HENRY C.
Born in Mississippi, 1864. Active in Cherokee County, 1900.

TUCKER, HUGH M.
Born in Texas, 1876. Active in Blum, 1896-97; Collin County and Weatherford, 1900.

TUCKER, J. L.
Active in Clarksville, 1857-58.

TUCKER, J. M.
Born in Tennessee, c. 1844. Active in Bryan, 1870; Burleson County, 1875.

TUCKER, W. A.
Active in Erath County, 1875.

TUCKER, WILLIAM A.
Active in Brownwood, 1892.

TUNE, THOMAS C.
Born in Tennessee, 1863. Listed in Forney, 1890-91, 1900.

TURNBULL, WALTER
Listed in Temple, 1892; Cameron, 1896-97.

TURNER & VAN HORN
Partnership operating in Brazos County, 1875; possibly Pitt S. Turner.

TURNER, J. A.
Active in Burnet and Williamson Counties, 1874.

TURNER, J. E.
Active in Morgan, 1884-85; Boulder, Colorado, 1901; Decatur, Illinois, 1912.

TURNER, L. T.
Born in Georgia, c. 1843. Active in Belton, 1870; Bell County, 1876.

TURNER, PITT S.
Active in Bryan, 1870, 1878-79; possibly a partner in Turner & Van Horn, Brazos County, 1875; listed in Brazos County, 1878-79.

TURNEY, CHRISTOPHER
Born in Tennessee, 1870. Listed in Tarrant County, 1900.

TURNEY, PETER
Born in Tennessee, 1850. Listed in Tarrant County, 1900.

TURPIN, J. F.
Active in Montague County, 1874.

TUTEN, JOHN A.
Born in Alabama, 1854. Listed in Rains County, 1900.

TYLER ART GALLERY
Operated by Curtiss & George in Tyler on the north side of public square, 1875.

UMSTEAD, N. L.
Active in Boonsville, Wise County, 1896-97.

UNDERWOOD, S. H.
Active in Lockhart, 1896-97.

UNI, G. M.
Active in Lamar County, 1875-76. Possibly Ensi or Urie.

VAN HORN
Partner in Turner & Van Horn, operating in Brazos County, 1875, possibly with Pitt S. Turner.

VAN HORN, C. E.
Active in Anderson, 1855.

VANCE, T. R.
Listed in Kaufman County, 1873.

VANDERMIER, ABRAHAM
Born in Michigan, 1858. Listed in Montgomery County, 1900.

VANDERMIER, JACOB
Born in Michigan, 1866. Listed in Montgomery County, 1900.

VANKAMAN, G. W.
Active in Hamilton County, 1876.

VANRIPER, C. T.
Active in Bell County, 1871-73.

VASQUEZ, MANUEL
Active in El Paso, 1912-13.

VASSALO, FRANCIS N.
Claimed to have studied in Italy and worked in Europe for ten years. Active in Austin on Congress at Bois d'Arc, 1849; also in Clarksville, 1849; continued in Clarksville, 1852-53.

VAUGHT, J. M.
Active in Indianola, Calhoun County, 1853.

VENEGAS, ALVINO
Active in El Paso, 1912.

VERKIN & ENOS
Partnership in Denison; Paul Verkin. Also listed as Varkin & Enos.

VERKIN, PAUL
Born in Germany, 1862. Immigrated to U.S., 1876. Active in Mexia, 1884-85. Listed in Denison as "Photo View & Crayon Artist" and partner in Verkin & Enos, 1887-92; operating in Galveston, 1900. Also listed as Varkin.

VERKIUS, PAUL
Stereo photographer in Galveston, c. 1870s.

VICKERS, J. C.
Active in Abilene, 1898.

VILLALOBOS
Partner in Gomez & Villalobos active in El Paso, 1906.

VINCENT, CHARLES L.
Active in Richmond, 1896-97.

VIVIER & FAGERSTEEN
P. Vivier and G. Fagersteen operating in San Antonio on Commerce, 1859; also in Chappel Hill, 1859. See Fagersteen in California.

VIVIER, P.
Born in France, c. 1814. Active in Belton at the Masonic Hall, 1858; partner in Vivier & Fagersteen operating in San Antonio and Chappel Hill, 1859; listed in Fayette County, 1860.

VOORHIES, EDWARD
Born in Tennessee, c. 1860. Active in Wise County, 1880.

VOORHIES, FREDERICK W.
Active in St. Louis. Listed in Galveston at 418 Twenty-first, 1895-97. Worked in Albuquerque, New Mexico, 1897. Moved to Dallas and continued in photography, 1902-14; retired in California.

VORON, F.
Active in Columbus, 1880-81; made crayon enlargements of photographs; possibly not a photographer.

WADE, MARION A.
Born in Mississippi, c. 1849. Listed in Navarro County, 1873; Johnson County, 1875; Falls County, 1876; McLennan County, 1880.

WAGGONER, W. T.
Partner in Stone & Waggoner with W. D. Stone operating in Austin, 1866. Also known as Austin Photograph Company. Sold out to William James Oliphant, November 1866. Partner with S. T. Craig in Craig & Wagner or Waggoner, operating in Galveston on Tremont between Post Office and Church, 1866-67; also operated as Galveston Photographic Company. Also listed as Wagner.

WAGNER
Partner in Pullen & Wagner operating in Temple, 1898-99.

WAKELEY & COBB
George D. Wakeley and William F. Cobb operating in McKinney, 1896-97.

WAKELEY, GEORGE D.
Active in Denver, Colorado, 1859-64; Leadville, 1879; McKinney, Texas, 1892, 1896-97; partner in Wakeley & Cobb, 1896-97.

WALCOTT, FRANK B.
Born in Wisconsin, 1861. Retoucher in Houston, 1900.

WALKER
Partner in S. R. Whitley & Walker operating in Iron Mountain, 1870; in Hughes & Walker, Williamson County, 1874.

WALKER, E. S. (MRS.)
Active in Jefferson, 1866-68.

WALKER, GEORGE H.
Active in Marlin, 1890-91; may have been in Vermont, 1880s.

WALKER, JOHN
Born in Texas, 1885. Apprentice photographer in Robertson County, 1900.

WALKER, SIDNEY
Born in Alabama, 1857. Listed in West, 1900.

WALKER, WILLIAM T.
Born in Missouri, 1854. Active in Cuero and Victoria, 1892; Brenham, 1896-97; Robertson County, 1900.

WALL
Partner in Flamister & Wall, operating in Uvalde, 1869; possibly with James H. Flemister.

WALL, CANE
Born in Texas, 1876. Listed in Harrison County, 1900.

WALLACE & KARNES
Partnership operating in Fayette County, 1871, 1873.

WALLACE, ELMER E.
Active in Gainesville, 1896-97.

WALLACE, J. L.
Active in Wise County, 1876.

WALLACE, LOUIS
Listed in Denton County, 1875.

WALLACE, MAT S.
Operated in La Grange, 1869-70.

WALLACE, R. W.
Born in England, c. 1828. Active in Brownsville, 1880, 1884-85, 1890-92, 1896-97, 1900. May be the same as R. H. Wallis.

WALLACE, RICHARD
Active in Rusk, 1867.

WALLER, WILLIAM
Active in Panola County, 1873; Rusk County, 1874-75.

WALLIS, R. H.
Born in England, 1828. Immigrated to U.S., 1852. Listed in Brownsville, 1866-67, 1869-70, 1878-79, 1898-99. May be the same as R. H. Wallace.

WALLIS, W. L.
Listed in Rusk County, 1871; possibly William L. Waller.

WALTERS
Partner in McKee & Walters operating in Tarrant County, 1892.

WALTGENBACH, CARL
Active in Brownsville, 1896-97; Corpus Christi, 1898-99.

WALTGENBACH, MARY
Born in Texas, 1870. Listed in Brownsville, 1900.

WALZ & COMPANY, W. G.
William G. Walz, Thomas B. Catron and W. E. Sharp; primarily dealers in photographic supplies.

WAMBLE, R.
Active in Walnut Springs, 1898-99.

WARD, GURNEY E.
Born in New York, 1862. Listed in Abilene, 1892, on Chestnut at South First; in Abilene, 1896-97; Lampasas County, 1900; cabinet card verified from G. E. Ward at Lampasas Springs, Ground Floor Studio, c. 1890. Partner in Lucore & Ward with Emma J. Lucore (Mrs. Basset J.), at 109 East Third in Fort Worth, 1888-91.

WARD, JACK
Born in Mississippi, 1863. Listed in Cleburne, 1900.

WARD, S. A. (MRS.)
Active in Hearne, 1890-91.

WARREN, MARY E.
First documented black woman in photography in the United States, active in Houston, 1866; listed as a photographic printer.

WASHBURN, ANDREW L.
Active in Houston, 1882-83. Thomas Dalgleish succeeded him in studio at 85 Main, c. 1884.

WASSON, SYLVESTER
Born in Tennessee, 1854. Active in Stephenville, 1890-91, 1898-99; Waco, 1898-1900. Listed at 516 Franklin, 1898-99.

WATERMAN, SOLOMON
Born in Alabama, c. 1855. Listed in Henderson County, 1880.

WATKINS, BRANHAM W.
Partner in Watkins Brothers with Willis M. in Beeville, 1886-1900. Active in Kaufman after 1900.

WATKINS BROTHERS
Branham W. and Willis M. Watkins operating in Beeville, 1886-1900. Studio was sold, 1900, possibly to L. T. Powell.

WATKINS, NORMAN R.
Born in Texas, 1877. Active in Eastland County, 1900.

WATKINS, W. W.
Listed in San Antonio, 1898.

WATKINS, WILLIS M.
Born in Georgia, 1868; died 1946. He began photography with his brother-in-law, Asa A. Brack, 1886; opened Watkins Brothers gallery a short time later, operating until c. 1900, when the studio was sold. Willis then worked in Palestine.

WATSON & DOTSON
Operating in Calvert, 1872; John W. Watson.

WATSON, JOHN W.
Born in Missouri, c. 1828. Active in Richmond, Virginia, 1855; Athens, Georgia, 1856; LaSalle, Illinois, 1860. Listed in Waco, 1867; Bryan, 1780; Brazos County, 1871; Hearne, 1872. Also partner with Dotson in Calvert, 1872. Operated in Raleigh, North Carolina, 1880s.

WATSON, JOSEPH W.
Active in Cass County, 1873.

WATTS, RUFUS
Born in Alabama, 1847. Listed in Lott, 1900.

WATTS, W. J.
Active in Washington, 1855-56.

WAUGH, J. C.
Active in Maverick County, 1873.

WAUS, DAN
Born in Arkansas, 1870. Listed in Mineral Wells, 1900.

WEAR, GEORGE R.
Born in Texas, 1863. Active in McKinney, 1890-92; Sherman, 1896-1900. Operated as Wear's Art Gallery at 117 ½ West Houston, 1899-1900.

WEATHERINGTON BROTHERS
George R. and John W. Weatherington active in Dallas, 1889-96, 1900. Studio at 705 Main, 1889-90; 237 and 321 Elm, 1891-92; 321 Elm, 1893-96; 334 Elm, 1900. Listed in Belton, 1896-97; Temple, 1896-98.

WEATHERINGTON, GEORGE R.
Active in Denton, 1888; partner in Weatherington Brothers with John W., operating in Dallas, 1889-96, 1900. See partnerships for locations. Operated in Belton, 1896-97; Temple, 1896-98.

WEATHERINGTON, JOHN W.
Born in Mississippi, 1856. Partner in Cherry & Weatherington, Decatur, 1884-85; also operating as Texas Photo Copying House and J. W. Weatherington & Company. Listed alone in Brownwood, 1890-91, 1898-99. Partner in Weatherington Brothers, Dallas, 1889-96, 1900; in Belton, 1896-97; Temple, 1896-98. See partnerships for locations.

WEB, RON
Born in Texas, 1880. Listed in Clarksville, 1900.

WEBB, B. F.
Born in Tennessee, c. 1850. Active in Jenny Lind, Arkansas, 1870. Active in Blossom, Texas, 1880.

WEBB, E. H.
Born in Texas, 1862. Listed in De Leon, 1892; Stephens County, 1900.

WEBB, RUFUS
Active in Freestone County, 1874; Leon County, 1875.

WEBB, WILLIAM E.
Born in Texas, c. 1862. Listed in Pittsburg, 1880.

WEBSTER, ALFRED
Active in Dallas, 1884-85.

WEBSTER, JOHN H.
Born in Mississippi, c. 1847. Active in Titus County, 1873; Harrison County, 1874, 1876; Marshall, 1875, 1878-80, 1882-83; Dallas, 1884-91, 1894-99. Studio at 701 Elm, 1884-85; 804 Elm, 1886-89; 802 Elm, 1889-90.

WEDDINGTON
Partner in Nichols & Weddington, Honey Grove.

WEDEMEYER, WILLIAM GEORGE
Amateur photographer in Texas, 1884-89 or longer, while based at Fort Concho. He was a Captain in the U.S. Army, also based at Fort Stockton, Austin, San Antonio; also in Arizona, Arkansas and Wisconsin.

WEDGE
Active in Galveston, 1861.

WEEMS, J. M.
Active in Columbia (now West Columbia), 1868.

WEITFLE, P. L.
Active in Santa Fe, New Mexico, 1899. Active in El Paso, 1898-1901. Bought studio from Clinton D. Curtis, September 1900; formerly the studio of J. C. Burge. See Colorado and New Mexico.

WESSON, JOHN A.
Active in Orange, 1892.

WEST & BROTHER, W. W.
Partnership in Kaufman County, 1873.

WEST, A. M.
Born in Virginia, c. 1831. Listed in Panola County, 1860.

WEST, BENJAMIN
Born in Mississippi, 1868. Active in Frost, 1900.

WEST, D. C.
Active in Aurora, 1890-91.

WEST, JOHN C.
Partner in Churchill & West with John R. Churchill in Brownwood, 1896-98.

WESTBROOK, J. B.
Active in Denton County, 1871.

WESTBROOK, SARAH M. (MRS.)
Active in Belcherville, Montague County, 1896-97.

WESTPHALL, GEORGE
Born in Illinois, 1861. "Enlarging Photographer" listed in the 1900 census in Houston.

WESTRUP
Partner in Hellin & Westrup operating in Dallas at 304 Elm, 1898-99.

WETHERSPOON, J. F.
Active in Upshur County, 1872; Waco, 1876; may have worked for H. W. Pickett or Jackson & Knight. Also listed as Weatherspoon.

WHATLEY, JAMES B.
Born in Georgia, 1853. Active in Garden Valley, Smith County, 1896-97; in Tyler, 1900.

WHEALDON, JOSHUA
Born in West Virginia, 1853. Active in Texarkana, 1878-83, 1890-91, 1896-1900. Possibly a partner in Wheddon & Carpenter, 1878-79.

WHEAT, HARRIET E.
Active in Clarksville, 1856.

WHEDDON & CARPENTER
Partnership in Texarkana, 1878-79; possibly a misspelling of Whealdon.

WHEELER, ALONZO D.
Active in Meriden, Connecticut, c. 1869. Listed in Tarrant County, 1876; Fort Worth, 1877-79, operating with L. W. Crawford as Crawford & Wheeler at 7 ½ Houston, or Houston between First and Weatherford. Operating alone, 1882, on Grove Street at Forth [sic].

WHERRY, W. H.
Partner in Teagarden & Wherry with Charles A. Teagarden, operating in Rusk, 1870. Active in Nacogdoches County, 1871; continued in Rusk, 1875-76.

WHITE
Active in Falls County, 1874.

WHITE, D. P.
Active in Duncanville, 1893-95.

WHITE, JOSEPH L.
Born in Texas, 1881. Listed in Caldwell County, 1900.

WHITE, SAM G.
Active in Belton, 1898-99.

WHITE, W. S.
Active in Belton, 1867.

WHITE, W. W.
Active in Dallas, 1892; Garland and Lancaster, 1893.

WHITFIELD
Partner in Allen & Whitfield, active in Houston, 1846-47; San Antonio, 1849; possibly E. P. Whitfield.

WHITFIELD, E. P.
Active in Austin, c. 1848.

WHITLEY & WALKER, S. R.
Partnership in Iron Mountain, Rusk County, 1870.

WHITLEY & WOOD
Possibly S. R. Whitley and David H. Wood operating in Rusk County, 1876.

WHITLEY, S. R.
Active in Rusk County, 1867; Henderson, 1869. Partner in S. R. Whitley & Walker, Iron Mountain , Rusk County, 1870; continued in Rusk County, 1875. Possibly a partner in Whitley & Wood, Rusk County, 1876. Listed in Overton, 1898-99.

WHITTAKER & KENNEDY
Daniel Whittaker and Walter B. Kennedy operating in Weatherford, 1892.

WHITTLE, J. C.
Active in Henderson County, 1871.

WIGHT, W.
Active in Kaufman County, 1873.

WILCOX, NATHAN MILES
Born in Mississippi, 1844. Active in Georgetown, 1890-92, 1896-97, 1900.

WILDER, EDWIN A.
Stereo photographer in Colorado, 1881-89; active in Tierra Amarilla, 1885-88.

WILEY, ROY
Born in Indiana, 1879. Listed in Greenville, 1900.

WILKES, J. C.
Active in Denison, operating in a tent at 412 West Main Street, 1887-88.

WILKINS, HARLEY
Born in Germany, 1861. Immigrated to U.S., 1888. Listed in Corsicana, 1900.

WILLGERD, JOHN B.
Active in Dallas at 237 Elm, 1896-97.

WILLIAM & HILLYER
W. Wirt Williams and Hamilton Biscoe Hillyer operating in Austin, 1867-68; continued working together, 1878-79, when they "formed a grand combination to make a tour of Texas."

WILLIAMS
Partner in Naghel & Williams with D. Frank Naghel, San Antonio, 1860; studio at 12 and 20 French Building. Partner in McCay & Williams operating in Hunt County, 1871; Chapman & Williams, San Marcos, 1898-99.

WILLIAMS (DR.)
Surgeon and dentist who also advertised daguerreotype services in Galveston, 1850.

WILLIAMS & HORN
Partnership in Strawn, 1890-91.

WILLIAMS & LENNOX
Partnership in Denton, 1884-85, 1898-99; possibly I. Williams.

WILLIAMS & MOORE
Possibly Obadiah S. Williams or W. Wirt Williams and possibly R. E. Moore, operating in Clarksville, 1860-10.

WILLIAMS & SULLESBERY
Partnership in Williamson County, 1871.

WILLIAMS, A. J.
Born in Missouri, c. 1854. Active in Montague County, 1879-80.

WILLIAMS, BERT
Active in Denton, 1898-1900.

WILLIAMS, CHARLES S.
Born in Texas, 1882. Listed in Denton, 1900.

WILLIAMS, DAVID
Born in Tennessee, c. 1853. Active in Linden, 1880.

WILLIAMS, DON H.
Born in Ohio, 1853. Active in Denton, 1900.

WILLIAMS, HALL
Born in Illinois, 1876. Listed in Dallas, 1900.

WILLIAMS, HENDLEY
Born in Georgia, 1860. Listed in Scurry County, 1900.

WILLIAMS, I.
Active in Denton, 1896-97; possibly a partner in Williams & Lennox, Denton, 1884-85, 1898-99.

WILLIAMS, J. J.
Active in Johnson County, 1876.

WILLIAMS, JESSE B.
Partner in Chalmers & Williams in Dallas at 913 Elm between Sycamore and Ervay, 1888-89.

WILLIAMS, JOHN
Active in Lancaster, 1898-99.

WILLIAMS, K. T.
Active in Denison at 523 West Main, 1898-99.

WILLIAMS, OBADIAH S.
Active in Clarksville, 1866; possibly a partner in Williams & Moore during the Civil War.

WILLIAMS, P. N.
May have operatored daguerreian rooms at Dr. Williams' dental office, March 22, 1865.

WILLIAMS, ROBERT S.
Active in Hallettsville, 1870; Lavaca County, 1871-72.

WILLIAMS, SAMUEL
Born in Texas, c. 1861. Listed in Bryan, 1880.

WILLIAMS, W.
Active in New Braunfels, 1855. Possibly W. Wirt Williams.

WILLIAMS, W. WIRT
Possibly a partner in Moore & Williams, Washington and Houston, 1856. Active in Houston, 1857-58; known as the Green Store Ambrotype Gallery on Main, 1858. Partner in Williams & Hillyer with Hamilton Biscoe Hillyer, Austin, 1867-68; in Houston, 1878-79, they "formed a grand combination to make a tour of Texas." He advertised that he had "twenty years' experience, and five years in the city of Houston." Listed in Dallas, 1889-98; 334 Elm Street, c. 1891. Known as the Dallas Copying House and Wirt Williams Art Studio, 1892. In Lampasas, 1898-99.

WILLIAMS, WALTER
Active in Sherman on the town square, 1893-94.

WILLIAMSON, F. G.
Active in Dallas, 1886-87.

WILLIAMSON, H.
Listed in Tyler, 1870.

WILLIAMSON, JESSE J.
Active in Mason, c. 1895; Ballinger, 1896-97.

WILLIS, D. H.
Active in Florence, 1892.

WILLIS, D. W.
Active in Llano, 1890-91.

WILLIS, M. D.
Listed in Bryan, 1900.

WILLMARTH, J. T.
Active in Del Rio, 1892.

WILLS
Partner in Morton & Wills, Coryell County, 1871.

WILLS, A.
Born in Texas, 1866. Listed in Round Rock, 1900.

WILLYERD, HENRY C.
Active in Alexander, Erath County, 1896-97.

WILLYERD, J. B.
Willyerd listed his address in Houston and owned a studio in Galveston, 1895-97, managed by Thomas J. Harper.

WILSON
Partner in Nowlin & Wilson, Kendall County, 1875; Ragsdale & Wilson, Honey Grove, 1898-99.

WILSON & CHURCHILL
Partnership in San Antonio on Main, 1866.

WILSON, B. H.
Active in Lavaca County, 1871; Gonzales County, 1872.

WILSON, D. W.
Active in San Jacinto County, 1873.

WILSON, DAVID
Active in Dallas, 1883-84.

WILSON, J. M.
Listed in Blanco County, 1871-72; also in Gillespie County, 1872.

WILSON, U. A.
Born in Georgia, 1853. Listed in Athens, 1900.

WILSON, WILLIAM
Born in Ohio, c. 1857. Active in Refugio, 1870; possibly a painter.

WILSON, WILLIAM D.
Active in Waco at 329 Austin, 1884-85.

WILSON, WILLIAM M.
Born in Texas, 1879. Listed in the 1900 census as "Apprentice Photographer" in Bryan.

WIMBERLEY, ELLERY M.
Active in Marble Falls, 1892; may have been in Texico, New Mexico, 1911-12.

WINDER, JOHN W.
Active in Uvalde, 1884-85.

WINKELMANN, FRED C.
Born in Germany, 1874; died 1959. Immigrated to U.S., 1893. Moved from New York to Galveston, then settled in Brenham. He bought the Thomas A. Holland Studio, renamed it Winkelmann Studio, operating c. 1894-1952; his son was in business at least until 1974.

WINNE & POE
Operated in Huntsville before 1860; possibly William Winne and John T. Poe.

WINNE, WILLIAM
Born in Texas, c. 1849. Possibly operating in Huntsville before 1860, as partner with John T. Poe; listed in Houston, 1870.

WINTHER & DOERR
Nicholas Winther and Henry A. Doerr operating in Bexar County, 1874.

WINTHER & JESSE
Nicholas Winther and Maximilian T. Jesse, San Antonio at 287 West Commerce, 1881-82.

WINTHER, NICHOLAS
Born in Prussia, c. 1839. Active in San Marcos, 1868; New Braunfels, 1869-70. Listed in San Antonio, Bexar County, 1874-76. He was a partner in Doerr & Winther, 1874-75, advertising "Photographic Rooms" on Commerce Street near Main Plaza, c. 1875; also listed as Winther & Doerr. Continued alone in San Antonio, 1877-86; on Commerce between Soledad and St. Mary's, 1877-78; at 7 Commerce, 1879-80. Partner in Winther & Jesse, 1881-82, at 287 West Commerce; continued alone at that address, 1882-84. Listed at 231 East Houston, 1884-86. He was active in San Antonio at least until 1899.

WISDOM, CHARLES H.
Born in Florida, 1861. Listed in Temple, 1890-91; Calvert, 1892; Dallas, 1897-1900. Studio at 318 Elm, 1897-99, 300 Elm, 1900.

WISEMAN, RUFUS FRANK
Born in South Carolina, 1874. Active in Hico, 1896-97, 1900.

WISEMAN, WILLIAM H.
Born in North Carolina, 1829. Active in Dublin, 1890-92, 1896-97; Hico, 1890-92, 1900.

WOHL, WILLIAM
Born in Texas, 1875. Listed in Weatherford, 1900.

WOLFE, FRANCIS B.
Active in El Paso, 1905.

WOMACK, J. N.
Active in Brown County, 1874.

WOMBLE, WILLIAM
Born in Texas, 1876. Active in Georgetown, 1900.

WONFOR, GEORGE H.
Landscape painter from St. Louis, Missouri; moved to Albuquerque, New Mexico, 1888, and began a photography business. Operated in Galveston at 418 Center, 1896-97; moved to Tucson, Arizona, 1890. Also listed as Wonfar.

WOOD
Partner in Hoy, Wood & Company, Blanco County, 1871; possibly the same as Hay & Wood.

WOOD, DAVID H.
Active in Rusk County, 1875, 1888; Henderson, 1882-85, 1898-99. Partner in Whitley & Wood, operating in Rusk County, 1876. May have been in California during the Civil War.

WOOD, E. H.
Active in Washington, Arkansas; in Clarksville, Texas, 1859-60.

WOODARD & SCHELBERGER
Partnership in Williamson County, 1876. Possibly O. S. Shalenberger.

WOODRUFF, SAMUEL
Born in North Carolina, c. 1849. Listed in Rosston, Cooke County, 1880; McKinney, 1882-83.

WOOLEY, R. M.
Born in Arkansas, 1869. Active in Burnet County, 1900.

WOOLLEY, S. P.
Born in Virginia, c. 1831. Employed by photographer Mrs. C. R. Hargrove in Marshall, 1855; listed in Clarksville, 1856; Bonham, 1860.

WOOTEN, W. H.
Active in Rusk County, 1874.

WORKS & KRUGER
James A. Works, William R. Works and Ernest Krueger operating in Fort Worth at 403 Main, 1894-95.

WORKS, JAMES A.
Worked for William R. Works in Fort Worth, 1892-93; partner in Works & Kruger, 1894-95; partner in W. R. & J. A. Works, 1896-97. See partnerships for locations.

WORKS, W. R. & J. A.
Partnership of William R. and James A. Works, Fort Worth at 401 Main, 1896-97.

WORKS, WILLIAM R.
Active in Fort Worth, 1892-1900. Operated as People's Gallery at Main and Fourth, c. 1892-93; partner in Works & Kruger at 403 Main, 1894-95; partner in W. R. & J. A. Works at 401 Main, 1896-87. Listed at 403 ½ Main, 1899-1900.

WORTHINGTON, JAMES
Born in Arkansas, c. 1848. Active in Pennington, Trinity County, 1870.

WREN, J. C.
Born in Texas, 1881. Listed in Temple, 1900.

WRIGHT
Partner in Gary & Wright Austin, 1851; Arvin & Wright, Lewisville, 1870; Poe & Wright in Walker County, 1872; possibly John T. Poe.

WRIGHT & BERKELEY
Partnership operating in Washington, 1857.

WRIGHT & COMPANY
Listed in Kaufman County, 1872.

WRIGHT & PARKER
Active in El Paso, 1906.

WRIGHT ART STUDIO
Operated by Anthony H. Hitchler in Houston at 502 Main, 1899.

WRIGHT, C. J.
Active in El Paso, 1875-90.

WRIGHT, CHARLES
Active in Brown County, 1873.

WRIGHT, CHARLES J.
Born in Massachusetts, c. 1842. Listed in Houston, 1870-99. Partner in Barr & Wright, 1870-80. May have had more than one studio, 1870-78; at Main and Preston, and at Main and Congress. Listed alone at 77 Congress, 1880-87; 82-84 Main, 1886-88; 84 Main, 1889-92; 502 ½ Main, 1892-98.

WRIGHT, E. N.
Active in Wheatville, Morris County, 1882-83. Also worked in Belfast, Maine, 1880s.

WRIGHT, JAMES L.
Born in Georgia, c. 1847. Active in Hamilton County, 1872; Comanche, 1880, 1884-85, 1890-92, 1896-97.

WRIGHT, W. W.
Listed in Ellis County, 1874-75.

WRIGHT, WILLARD
Active in Texarkana, 1884-85, 1898-99; Atlanta, 1892.

WRIGHT, WOODWARD
Born in Kentucky, 1851. Active in Bowie, 1896-97; Willis Point, 1900.

WYKES, JAMES W.
Active in Quincy, Illinois, 1872-75, 1911. Listed in Navasota, 1882-83; Lampasas, 1884-85, 1890-92, 1898-99.

YANCEY
Active in Beaumont, c. 1895.

YANCEY & RHOMBERG
Charles R. Yancey and Charles Rhomberg operating in Austin on Colorado at Thirteenth, 1890-91.

YANCEY, CHARLES R.
Printer for Charles Rhomberg in Austin, 1889-90; partner in Yancey & Rhomberg, 1890-91; in Palestine, 1892; Tyler, late 1890s.

YANCEY, E. W.
Active in Fort Bend, Lee, and Waller Counties, 1874. Possibly E. D. Yancy.

YANCEY, J. S.
Listed in Waco, 1898.

YARBROUGH & BIRDS
Partnership operating in Gillespie County, 1872.

YARBROUGH, WILLIAM
Active in Blanco County, 1871.

YATES
Partner in Sherrell & Yates operating in Williamson County, 1874.

YATES, B.
Active in Bandera County, 1876.

YEAROUT, J. T. & H. J.
Photographers from Memphis, Tennessee, active in Marshall, 1855.

YEATES & BROTHER
Active in Gonzales County, 1876.

YOUNG, CHARLES R.
Born in Missouri, 1859. Listed in Cameron, 1900.

YOUNG, H. W.
Active in Trenton, c. 1890.

YOUNG, J. E.
Operated as the Galveston Portrait Company in Galveston at 2214 Market, 1890-91.

YOUNG, JOE L.
Born in Texas, 1875. Listed in Boyd, 1900.

YOUNG, JOSEPH
Born in Texas, 1874. Active in Springtown, 1900.

ZAHN, JUSTUS
Born in Germany, 1847. Active in Galveston, c. 1879-1902. Partner in Rose & Zahn with Phillip H. Rose before 1888, when he sold out to Zahn. Located at 159 and 161 East Market between 21st and 22nd, 1879-85. Continued at 170 Tremont, 1888-89; 418 Tremont, 1890-1900. Sold out to Joseph M. Maurer, c. 1902. May have worked in Belleville, Illinois, 1882-84.

ZANT & LEACH
Active in Mineral Wells, 1880s; Don M. Leach.

ZIMMERMANN, REINER J.
Born in Hanover, Germany, 1831. Immigrated to U.S., 1854. Active in Fayetteville, 1869-70; listed in Fayette County, 1872-76. Also in Austin County, 1876; Schulenburg, 1880, 1890-91, 1896-97, 1900.

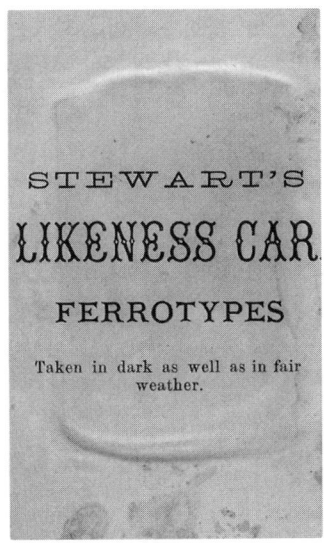

Photographers in this section worked as itinerants somewhere in North America during the pre-World War I period. It is the publisher's belief that most of them operated in the western United States or Canada, but some traveled exclusively in areas east of the Mississippi River.

ABELL, GEORGE L.
Itinerant in Oregon, 1876-77. Later operated permanent studios in Portland and Corvallis. Presumably operated Abell's Art-Studio Car.

ABELL'S ART-STUDIO CAR
Traveling photography studio in California, c. 1875.

ACTINO PHOTOGRAPH CAR
Operated by S. P. Burgert, c. 1861-69.

AIKEN, F. J.
Active c. 1860s, operating the Mammoth Traveling Saloon.

ALBRECHT, A. A.
Traveling photographer in the Northwest. See Washington and British Columbia.

ALLEN
Operated Tucker & Allen and advertised as "Champion Traveling Photographers."

ALLISON, J. L.
Active in New Mexico; Chloride, 1886-87; Santa Fe and Kingston, 1892.

AMSDEN & DUTKEWICH
Traveled in the Weaverville area of California, c. 1895.

ANDERSON, C. W.
Operated the Palace Photo Car in Oregon.

ANDERSON, GEORGE EDWARD
Headquarters located in Springville, Utah, 1877-1920.

ANDREWS, E. B.
Traveling photographer in northern California, c. 1880s.

ANONYMOUS
Itinerant photographer in Georgetown, California, who was called to the Round Tent gambling saloon to photograph a dead miner. He accidentally caused a fire which quickly spread. The corpse was saved, but most of the business section of town was burned in the fire, July 14, 1852. Georgetown was soon rebuilt on a new site.

APPLEGATE, J. W.
Rubber stamp imprint on a California carte-de-visite, c. 1885, advertising "Tintype Gallery, Cal."

ARROWSMITH, W. H.
Traveling photographer in northern California, 1905-10.

ARTZ
Partner in Fallman & Artz operating the Photo Car.

ASKREN & BALDWIN
Partnership with a permanent address at East Des Moines, Iowa, c. 1885.

ASKREN, I. M.
Partner in Askren & Baldwin, 1885.

ATKINSON, C. W.
Active in 1875.

ATKINSON'S RAILROAD GALLERY
Headquartered in Orion, Illinois.

ATLANTIC PHOTO-VIEW & ADVERTISING COMPANY
Operated in Portland, Oregon, c. 1889, by Mrs. R. H. Gardiner.

AVERY, R. S.
Operator of White's Young America Picture Gallery, billed as "The Largest Movable Establishment in America."

AUSTIN
Partner in Headley & Austin operating the Photograph Boat, c. 1875.

AX BROTHERS
Operated by H. Ax, the "Traveling Landscape & Portrait Photographer," 1885.

AX, H.
Operated as Ax Brothers, 1885.

AYLSWORTH & LOOMIS

AYLSWORTH, J. H.
Active c. 1860s.

BABBITT'S, C. W.
Operated the "Traveling Saloon" headquartered in Fitchburg, Massachusetts.

BACON, MAX E.
Active in New Mexico, 1902-13, partner with Roliene E. Banner operating the Banner Photo Car.

BAGNASCO, POLICARPO
Employed by Joseph Buchtel in Portland, Oregon, fall 1866; an itinerant Italian photographer traveling through Arizona and New Mexico, early 1870s. In Santa Fe at El Dorado House, July and August 1872; Tucson, 1881. Chief photographer for Carlton Watkins, c. 1872-c. 1882; for I. W. Taber, San Francisco, c. 1882-c. 1892.

BAKER & JOHNSTON
Active in Wyoming, c. 1870-80s.

BAKER, ISAAC WALLACE
Came from Beverly, Massachusetts, and settled in California, 1853. Learned the daguerreian art from Perez M. Batchelder and was employed by him as a traveling photographer. Worked in Murphy's Camp, Vallecita and Sonora, California, recording mining scenes.

BALDWIN
Partner in Askren & Baldwin; permanent address at East Des Moines, Iowa, c. 1885.

BALDWIN, E. A.
The "Wandering Artist," c. 1860s.

BANBROCK, WILLIAM. E.
Born in Bath, California. Moved to Nevada where he worked in a Silver City hotel at age eleven. At seventeen he was employed by Peterson & Snyder in Carson City and learned photography. Returned to Placer County, California, 1883, and worked as a traveling photographer. Took mining views while based at Iowa Hill; later headquartered in Forest Hill and photographed the mines along the divide. He had a fixed route through Placer and Nevada Counties; eventually owned a permanent studio in Auburn, specializing in view photography.

BANNER PHOTO CAR
Active in New Mexico, 1902-1913, operated by Max E. Bacon and Roliene E. Banner.

BANNER, ROLIENE E.
Active in New Mexico with Max E. Bacon operating the Banner Photo Car, 1902-13.

BARNES, WILL CROFT
Arrived in Arizona in 1880; stationed at Fort Apache as Corporal-telegrapher. Joined in forming Esperanza Cattle Ranch, 1883; entered U.S. Forest Service, 1907. Traveled the West, 1907-08.

BARNHART, J. S.
Operated the Excelsior Car, headquartered in Bellafonte, Pennsylvania, 1860s.

BARRETT BROTHERS
Operated the Photograph Boat in Wheelersburg, Scioto County, Ohio; Thomas Barrett.

BARRETT, THOMAS
Operated the Photograph Boat, headquartered in Wheelersburg, Scioto County, Ohio; also operated as Barrett Brothers.

BARRY, D. F.
See Dakota.

BATCHELDER, J. C.
Billed as the Traveling Saloon headquartered in Nashua, New Hampshire, opposite Tremont House.

BATCHELDER, PEREZ M.
Traveling daguerreian artist active in California by 1851, located on Washington Street, Sonora. His old stand was purchased by W. H. Rulofson, June 1852. He had several daguerreian wagons and trained and hired men to operate them in mining areas including Stockton, Vallecita, Murphys Camp and Mokelumne Hill, c. 1851-53.

BAYS, DAVIS HENRY
Itinerant tent photographer and Mormon missionary based in Bandera, Texas, 1879.

BEALS, G. W.
Operated a Traveling Saloon.

BENNETT
Operated as Sellon & Bennett, headquartered in Mount Hope and Colwich, Kansas, 1885.

BENNETT, GEORGE C.
Active in New Mexico, 1880-82.

BERGEN'S PORTABLE GALLERY
Active in 1870.

BETHUEL, CURTIS
Traveling photographer.

BIERSTADT, ALBERT
Active in Wyoming, 1859; traveling photographer on expedition, 1859, accompanied by assistant F. S. Frost.

BIG TENT GALLERY
Operated by J. N. Caradine in Texas, 1885.

BLANTON
Active c. 1895, location unknown.

BLATT, C. G.
Known as a "Traveling Artist," headquartered in Bernville, Pennsylvania.

BLISS PHOTOGRAPH CAR
Operated by W. P. Bliss. See Indian Territory, Kansas and New Mexico.

BLISS, W. P.
Operated the Bliss Photograph Car. See Indian Territory, Kansas and New Mexico.

BOLTON'S PHOTOGRAPH CAR
Active in Lyndon, Vermont, opposite the drug store, 1860s.

BOOEN, J. O.
See British Columbia.

BOONE, JAMES H.
Itinerant based in Marshall, Texas, 1852.

BOOTH, JAMES J.
Active in Utah, 1885. See Utah.

BORKLUND, ERIK
Operated the Photo Car, 1885.

BOSTON ART COMPANY RAILROAD PHOTO CAR
Location and dates unknown.

BOSTON RAIL ROAD PHOTO CAR
Stationed in Kearney, Nebraska.

BOSTON RAILROAD PHOTO CAR
Pacific Coast address was Sacramento, California, 1885.

BOTTORF, J. K.
Operated the Mammoth Car with C. C. Burkholder, c. 1860s; also known as Burkholder & Bottorf.

BOWMAN, WALTER S.
Born c. 1862; died in Pendleton, Oregon, 1938. Itinerant in eastern Oregon, 1887-90. Permanent studio in Pendleton, c. 1890-1917.

BOYD, HENRY J.
Itinerant in Oregon; began as a partner with Frank A. Rankin in Rankin & Company, Eugene, c. 1891; Lebanon, c. 1901; Ashland, c. 1903-17.

BOYDEN'S PHOTOGRAPH SALOON

BOYSEN & STRUCKMANN
Traveling photographers, c. 1880.

BRACK, ASA A.
Working as an itinerant in south Texas; based in San Antonio. See Texas.

BRADLEY, L.
"Traveling Artist" headquartered in Dayton, Oregon, c. 1895; Forest Grove, 1885; Yaquina, 1888.

BRADLEY, W. A.
Operated the Union Pacific Photo Car between Ogden, Utah, Butte, Montana, and Omaha, Nebraska, 1885. Headquartered at 1108 Farnam Street, Omaha, Nebraska.

BRAUNIG
Partner in Fey & Braunig operating in the Fredericksburg area, 1878; main gallery in Braunfels, 1870s-80s. See Texas.

BRAVER
Active with Hagedorn, Braver & Suden, operating the Photo Traveling Palace & Art Gallery.

BRENSINGER, FRANK
Known as the "Traveling Artist."

BRIGGS, JOHN A.
Operated the Portable Photographic Studio, c. 1884; headquarters located in Pleasant Hill, Oregon.

BRINER
Partner in Brinkley & Briner.

BRINKLEY & BRINER
Traveling photographers.

BRITAIN'S PALACE RAILROAD PHOTO CAR
Operated by P. L. Britain.

BROCK, C. F.
Traveling "Photographic Artist," c. 1860s.

BROWING'S PHOTOGRAPHIC CAR, NO. 1
Operated by D. P. Browing, c. 1860s.

BROWN, FRED M.
Operated as the Portrait & Landscape Photographic Car Gallery.

BROWN, H. J.
Itinerant photographer operating the Traveling Saloon, c. 1865.

BROWN, W. CALVIN
Arrived in Albuquerque, New Mexico, c. 1882; lieutenant in Territorial Militia. Traveled throughout northwestern New Mexico, c. 1882-89. Permanent studio on Gold Avenue in Albuquerque; studio was managed by E. Gregg while Brown served as Marshall, late 1880s. Partner with George H. Wonfor, 1888-89; sold out to William Henry Cobb, 1889.

BRYANT, A. J.
Known as a "Traveling Artist" headquartered in Alamogordo, New Mexico 1898-1906.

BRYANT, J. W.
Traveling photographer active in New Mexico, 1890-95.

BUCK, A. J.
"Traveling Artist" headquartered in Vance, Texas, and Alamogordo, New Mexico, 1898-1906. Active in Alamogordo and La Luz, 1899-1900; Alamogordo, 1901. Operated a livery stable, 1905; worked as undertaker, 1909.

BUCKEY'S TRAVELING PHOTOGRAPH & ART GALLERY
Operated by A. R. Buckey.

BUDDEN'S TRAVELING PICTURE GALLERY
Active in 1865.

BUEHMAN, HENRY
Born in Bremen, Germany, May 14, 1851; died December 20, 1912. Active in San Francisco, 1868; studio in Visalia, 1869. Traveling photographer in Arizona, California, Nevada, New Mexico and Utah, 1871-74. Settled in New Mexico by 1874.

BULLOCK'S PHOTOGRAPH ROOM
Operating c. 1860.

BURCHFIELD & BOTTORF
Operated the Mammoth Car, c. 1860.

BURGERT, S. P.
Operated the Actino Photograph Car, c. 1861-69.

BURKHOLDER & BOTTORF
J. K. Bottorf and C. C. Burkholder operated the Mammoth Car, c. 1860s.

BURKHOLDER, C. C.
Operated the Mammoth Car with J. K. Bottorf, c. 1860s; also known as Burkholder & Bottorf.

BUTCHER, SOLOMON D.
Headquartered in Custer County, Nebraska, 1900.

BUTLER, EDWARD P.
Active in Petaluma, c. 1862-63. Traveling photographer, c. 1864. Active in San Francisco, c. 1865; Santa Cruz, 1867-77 or later. Moved to Virginia City, Nevada, operating with G. Waterhouse, 1883; in Reno, 1886.

CALIFORNIA PHOTO TENT
Traveling studio in California, c. 1880, operated by B. L. Wilson.

CAMPBELL, HAMILTON
Born 1812; died 1863. Traveling photographer based in Corvallis, Oregon, 1854-59.

CARADINE'S BIG TENT GALLERY, J. N.
Active in Texas, 1885.

CARNE'S CAR, H. P.
Headquartered in Montpelier, Vermont, c. 1860s; operated by H. P. Carne.

CARPENTER, R. J.
Operated the Mammoth Car, headquartered in Richmond, Kentucky.

CASTLEMAN, PHILLIP F.
Born 1827; died 1913. Itinerant active in East Cascades, Oregon, 1853-78; Portland, 1869-70; also in Eugene and Astoria, 1870. Produced "Birds-Eye View" lithographs of cities.

CATTERLIN, WILLIAM H.
Possibly active as an itinerant in Oregon, 1872. Active in permanent studios in Salem, c. 1873-76; operated as Catterlin & Rogers, 1874; in Portland, c. 1894-1911. Located at 166 5th, 1894-98; 89 ½ 4th, 1899-1904; 89 4th, 1905-10.

CAUCH, R. & C. E.
Itinerants billed as the "Artists - Sunbeam Gallery" headquartered in Amboy, Illinois, c. 1860s. Also known as Cauch & Squire and R. Cauch & Squire.

CELEBRATED FLYING PHOTOGRAPH GALLERY
Operated by J. C. Kemp in Sacramento, California, 1875. Also called the Celebrated Great Flying Photograph Gallery, and associated with H. Kemp's Great Celebrated Centennial Flying Photograph Gallery; both studios utilized an unusual script, exactly the same, on the reverse of buff colored cartes-de-visite mounts, c. 1876.

CHAIN
Traveling photographer for W. H. Jackson in New Mexico, 1881.

CHAUDET ART COMPANY RAILWAY PHOTO CAR

CLARK, E. A.
Traveling Car, c. 1862.

CLAYTON, S. T.
Traveling artist headquartered in Chilo, Ohio, c. 1895.

COGGESHALL'S EXCELSIOR PHOTOGRAPHIC CAR

COLLINS
Partner in Morse & Collins operating as the Traveling Studio, c. 1860s.

CONE PALACE CAR

COOKE, EMMA A. (MRS.)
Operated the Traveling Photo Pavillion, 1875.

COPE
Partner in Dougherty & Cope, tintypists operating the Dougherty Mammoth Wagon, c. 1860s.

COREY
Traveling photographer in the Hillsboro area of Oregon, c. 1867, partner in Roberts & Corey.

COTTRELL'S PICTURE CAR, D. E.
Active in Oregon and Missouri. May be the same as D. R. Cottrell.

COTTRELL'S, TRAVELING PICTURE CAR, D. R.
May be the same as D. E. Cottrell.

CREE, VAN S.
Operated Cree's Car, c. 1860s.

CRESCENT TRAVELING GALLERY
Active c. 1900, probably based in Iowa.

CROCKWELL, JAMES HEZEKIAH
Traveling photographer specializing in mining views. See Nevada and Utah.

CRONYN & HIBBS
Railway photographers, c. 1890, locations unknown.

CROWNS, J. H.
"Traveling Artist" headquartered in Fox Lake, Wisconsin.

CUNNINGHAM, W. H.
Active in 1865.

CURTIS, ASAHEL
Traveled in Alaska from Seattle, Washington, 1898, employed by his brother, Edward S. Curtis.

DAISY CAR
Operated by J. F. Jacoby, home address, Iowa City, Iowa.

DANIELS, J. L.
Traveling photographer, c. 1875.

DART
Partner in Sutterly & Dart, California, c. 1885.

DAVIDSON
Traveling photographer headquartered in Des Moines, Iowa; F. R. Peelstrom, operator.

DAVIDSON, NORVALLE RICE
Traveling photographer in northern California. See California.

DAVIS, E. G.
Specialized in stereographs. Active in 1871, headquartered in Leominster, Massachusetts.

DAVIS, S. P.
Traveling photographer from E. Day's Traveling Photographic Gallery, c. 1860s.

DAWSON MAMMOTH ART GALLERY
Headquartered in New London, Wisconsin.

DAY, E.
Operating the Traveling Photograph Gallery, c. 1865.

DEAN
Partner in Hardesty & Dean, traveling photographers from St. Louis, Missouri, active in Texas, c. 1883.

DEASON, C. C.
Born in Georgia, 1870. Operated a Traveling Picture Gallery in Dallas, Texas, 1900.

DEPLANQUE, LOUIS
Worked the entire Texas Gulf coast, either as a traveling photographer or with branch galleries. In Mexico, 1865; Texas by the late 1860s. See Texas.

DIETRICT, WALLACE A.
Traveling photographer, sometimes spelled Dietricht or Dietrich.

DOUGHERTY & COPE
Operating the Mammoth Wagon out of Norristown, Pennsylvania, c. 1860.

DOUGHERTY MAMMOTH WAGON
Tintypist active c. 1860s; also operated as Dougherty & Cope.

DOUGLASS TRAVELING CAR
Active c. 1860s.

DOWE
Traveling artist in California, working alone and in partnership with Rifenburg; headquartered in Fresno at least part of the time (date uncertain).

DOWE, OSCAR S.
Itinerant in California, Oregon and Nevada, late 1880s-1919. While in California, active in San Luis Obispo, 1884- 86; Bakersfield, c. 1888; San Francisco, 1889; Eureka, 1889-90; Ferndale, 1890, at "The Oriental Gallery, Blue Tent, lot next to the American Hotel"; in Ft. Bragg, 1919. Active in Lovelock, Nevada, 1891, 1901, 1904; in Silver City, Idaho Territory, c. 1893, at the "Big tent below the Catholic Church"; in DeLamar, Idaho Territory, c. August, 1893.

DOWNEY
Operated in Pleasanton, California, c. 1890, and probably also a traveling photographer. Listed on Front Street in Tulare, c. 1893.

DRAKE, H. S.
Headquarters at 2228 Washington Street, Boston Highlands, Massachusetts, c. 1860s. "Duplicate Dozens while in town at reduced prices."

DRUM RAILROAD PHOTO CAR

DUNCAN, A. B.
Partner in Peelstrom & Duncan, with F. R. Peelstrom.

DUNHAM
Traveling photographer based in Liscomb, Iowa, c. 1890.

DUTKEWICH
Partner in Amsden & Dutkewich, traveling in the Weaverville area of California, c. 1895.

EARLE, M. R.
Specialized in stereographs. Name may be M. A. Earle.

EASTBURN, F. P.
One of the managers of Western Photograph Association with G. H. Ramsdell, 1890.

EDEL
Billed as the "Photographic Tourist," c. 1885.

EDWARDS & BROTHER, J. W.
Operated theTraveling Photograph Gallery, c. 1860s.

ELITE PHOTO STUDIO
Traveling gallery headquartered in San Francisco, California, at 107 Grove Street, 1891.

ELLENWOOD, J. G.
Operated the Mammoth Saloon, c. 1860s.

ERWIN'S PORTABLE GALLERY

EULASS, T. H.
Traveling photographer, c. 1875.

FALLMAN
Operated the Parlor Photo Car.

FALLMAN & ARTZ
Operated the Photo Car.

FAVORITE, IRENE R.
Born in Pennsylvania, 1839. Wife of photogapher Thomas J. Favorite. Traveling photographer in Umatilla County, Oregon, c. 1870. Active in Los Angeles and Downey, California, 1880s; Garberville, Rohnerville and Trinidad, c. 1881-82. Also listed as Irena. See Calfornia, Oregon and Texas.

FAZE
Known as "The Rambling Artist" advertising stereoscopic views of northern Ohio, Nelson Ledges and the Mohoning Valley; based in Newton Falls, Ohio, c. 1875.

FELDMAN, FREDERICK S.
Active in Arizona and Texas, 1893.

FEY & BRAUNIG
Partnership of Pius Fey and Henry Jacob Braunig. Began working together as itinerants in the Fredericksburg area, 1878. Main gallery in Braunfels, 1870s-80s. See Texas.

FISH'S CAR
Active c. 1860s.

FORBES, ANDREW ALEXANDER
Traveling photographer in Texas and Oklahoma, 1889-1909. Known today for his scenes of cowboy life. See California.

FRANCIS, G. D.
Operated the Palace Railway Photo Studio Car, headquartered in St. Paul, Minnesota.

FRANKLIN & SON, D.
Operator of Franklin's Traveling Photographic Tent.

FRANKLIN, E. B.
Operated the Photograph Car from Pawtucket, Rhode Island, c. 1860s.

FRASIER, F. K.
Operating a Photo Car, c. 1885.

FREEHAFER, F.
Operated the American Photographic Emporium headquartered in Brownsville (Texas?).

FRITZ, FRANK Z.
Operated his Traveling Gallery in Sippackville, Pennsylvania.

FRITZ, J.
Traveling photographer headquartered in Gutenberg, Iowa.

GAIGE, J. G.
Arizona photographer who regularly traveled into Texas and New Mexico before 1862. See Arizona.

GARDINER, R. B.
Itinerant active in Roseburg, Oregon area, c. 1887.

GARDINER, R. H. (MRS.)
Itinerant in Oregon, c. 1889; in Portland, c. 1892, operating Atlantic Photo-View & Advertising Company.

GEROULD, E. P.
Headquartered in Massachusetts and New Hampshire, c. 1860s, associated with S. A. Putnam. May be the same as P. Gerrould.

GILCHRIST, J. W.
Known as the New Photograph Gallery, headquartered at the north side of Park, Fairfield, Iowa.

GITHENS BROTHERS
Operated a Photo Car.

GOFF, O. S.
See Dakota.

GOTTLIEB, HARRY JOSEPH
Worked for itinerant wagon photographer at age 12 in New York; prominent studio photographer in New Mexico, c. 1907-25. Itinerant portrait work in Deming and Roswell, c. 1924.

GOULD, A.
Headquartered in North Bridgeton.

GREAT CELEBRATED CENTENNIAL FLYING PHOTO-GRAPH GALLERY
Operated by H. Kemp in Chico, Bodie and Modesto, California, 1875. Associated with J. C. Kemp's Celebrated Great Flying Photograph Gallery operating out of Sacramento. Both studios utilized an unusual script, exactly the same, on the reverse of buff colored cartes-de-visite mounts, c. 1876, the centennial year.

GREAT EASTERN PHOTOGRAPHIC & ADVERTISING COMPANY
Itinerant company in Portland, c. 1889, 92; operated by R. H. Gardiner, 1892.

GREEN, W. A.
Traveling photographer active in Galveston, Texas, c. 1900, based at 604 Tremont Street.

GREENE
Partner in Roshon & Greene operating the Mammoth Car headquartered at Railroad Street, Huntington, Pennsylvania, c. 1860s.

GRIME, CICERO
Operated the I.C.U. Photograph Car. He was later active in Arizona, operating the California Art Gallery.

GULASS, T. H.
Traveling photographer.

GUYER
Partner in Kirby & Guyer; operated photo cars, 1890.

HAGEDORN, BRAVER & SUDEN
Operated the Photo Traveling Palace Art Gallery.

HAGEDORN, C.
Operated the Photo Traveling Palace & Art Gallery, also known as Hagedorn, Braver & Suden.

HALL, F. M.
Itinerant out of Lexington, Lee County, Texas, c. 1872.

HALL, J.
Active c. 1860s. Possibly the same as Julius Hall.

HALL, JULIUS
Traveling photographer, c. 1860s. May be the same as J. Hall.

HARDY, W. H.
Active in Lakeview, Oregon; also worked as an itinerant in Oregon, 1896.

HARFORD, GEORGE G.
Operated the Palace Photograph Car, headquartered in Anthony, Rhode Island, 1882.

HARMON, BYRON
See Western Canada and Washington.

HARRIS & COMPANY
Active in Rock Springs and Lander, Wyoming, 1898.

HARRIS, MARY ELIZABETH COOLEY
Born in Eugene, Oregon, October 20, 1855. Active in Santa Barbara, c. 1890. After working as a traveling photographer in Oregon, 1892, she returned to San Francisco, 1893, where she worked for portrait photographer Theodore C. Marceau at 826 Market Street.

HARROD
Partner in Jorns & Harrod, operating the Palace Railway Art Car from Girard, Illinois, c. 1895.

HARZOG
Operated the Photo Boat with a partner; also known as Williams & Harzog.

HAVEN & COMPANY, C.
Traveling photographers.

HAYNES, F. JAY
See Minnesota.

HAZELTINE, MARTIN MASON
Active in the East before 1853; in California, 1853-80; Baker City, Oregon, 1880, 1884-1903; Reno, Nevada, 1878; Boise, Idaho Territory, December 1883-October or November 1884. Itinerant in Idaho Territory, 1886. See California, Idaho and Oregon.

HEADLEY & AUSTIN
Operated the Photograph Boat, c. 1875.

HEISS, W. H.
Operated the Mammoth Photograph Car, headquartered in Lancaster, Pennsylvania, c. 1860s. Also known as King & Heiss.

HENDEE, DENNY H.
Traveling photographer in the eastern states. Arrived in California during the gold rush; moved to Oregon, 1853. An itinerant photographer for several years, he established a permanent gallery in Portland by 1856. Brother of Edwin B. Hendee. See California and Oregon.

HENDERSON, E. N.
Billed as a "Traveling Artist."

HERRIN, DAVID C.
Active in studios in Medford; in The Dalles, 1895. Listed as Abell-Herrin Company in Portland, 1898. Active in Portland, 1898-01; later had traveling galleries in The Dalles, Oregon and Washington. Operated with his wife, Margaret E.

HERRIN, MARGARET E. (MRS.)
Active in Medford; The Dalles, 1895; worked with her husband, David C. Herrin. Listed as Abell-Herrin Company in Portland, 1898. Active in Portland, 1898-01; later had traveling galleries in The Dalles, Oregon and Washington.

HIBBS
Partner in Cronyn & Hibbs, railway photographers, c. 1890.

HICKETHIER, AUGUSTUS
Itinerant in Oregon; in Cottage Grove, 1883; Roseburg, Woodville and Canyonville, 1887.

HILLYER, HAMILTON BISCOE
After the Civil War he moved to Austin and organized tent studios that traveled to many towns. See Texas.

HINSHAW, THOMAS
Itinerant tent and wagon photographer in Utah, Colorado, New Mexico and Arizona, c. 1898-99, operating as Huish & Hinshaw with Orson Pratt Huish.

HODGMAN, C. C.
Traveling photographer for W. O. Thomas; headquartered in Silver City, New Mexico, 1905.

HOLMES, T.
Traveling photographer listed in Connecticut and Rhode Island.

HOUGHTON, THOMAS A.
Traveling photographer in Washington Territory, 1885; The Dalles, Oregon, 1888-91; Portland, 1885-87.

HOUSTON, FRANK K.
Listed as a "Photographic Artist" with address in Holliston, Massachusetts, c. 1860s.

HOWARD, WILLIAM L.
An itinerant active in Lonoke, Faulkner and Pulsaki Counties, Arkansas, c. 1900+.

HOWE, ITHAMAR
Traveling photographer in California, 1878.

HUESTED, R. W.
Partner in Huested & Norton, operating the "Largest Moveable Gallery in America."

HUGHES
Traveling photographer, place and dates unknown.

HUNT, ORRIS P.
Photographer operating the San Francisco Railroad Studio Car.

HUISH & HINSHAW
Active in Utah, Colorado, New Mexico, and Arizona, operated by Orson Pratt Huish and Thomas Hinshaw, c. 1898-99.

HUISH, ORSON PRATT
Active in Utah, Colorado, New Mexico and Arizona, 1898-99, operating as Huish & Hinshaw with partner Thomas Hinshaw.

HUTCHINGS BROTHERS' PHOTO CAR
Active, c. 1885. Presumably related to Hutchings Railroad Photo Car.

HUTCHINGS RAILROAD PHOTO CAR
Active in 1885.

HUTCHISON'S, J. W.
Operated the Artist Floating Gallery.

I.C.U. PHOTOGRAPH CAR
Operated in California by itinerant photographer, Cicero Grime. He was later active in Arizona, operating the California Art Gallery.

JACKSON, WILLIAM HENRY
See Nebraska.

JACOBY, J. F.
Operated the Daisy Car out of Iowa City, Iowa.

JAMES, D.
Operated the Palace Car, c. 1875. See Wisconsin.

JAYCOX, W.
Operated the Photo Car.

JERRELL, W. L.
Died February 8, 1884. Itinerant in New Mexico and Mexico, c. 1876-78. Active in Bernalillo, February 1876; operating in a tent on the South Side Plaza in Albuquerque, February-March 1876; Los Lunas, March 1876; Las Cruces, Mesilla and El Paso, May 1876; Taos and Santa Fe, November 1877; Las Cruces, Adkins Store, December 1877-March 1878. Shot to death by stagecoach robbers near Abilene, Texas, while serving as special deputy tracking other bandits.

JOHNSON & SULLIVAN'S PORTABLE GALLERY
Active in 1880.

JOHNSON, CLINTON
Operated the Palace Portrait Car, 1866.

JOHNSTON
Active in Wyoming, c. 1870-80s, partner in Baker & Johnston.

JONES BROTHERS
W. R. Jones was active in Eugene, Oregon, 1865. Jones Brothers active in Oregon, June 1880; itinerants in Idaho Territory and Oregon, c. 1880-c. 1890. Active in Boise, Idaho Territory, July 2, 1880; Idaho

City and Placerville, August 1880; Silver City, photographic tent on Washington Street, mid-June 1881. While in Oregon, active in Jordan Valley, June 28, 1881; Union, (1883-90 (Jones Brothers); Silverton, 1885-1900 (W. L. Jones); in Caldwell operating a photo tent, October 1891 (Jones Brothers). The exact number of Jones brothers is uncertain. Advertisements in Boise claim they had a multiplying camera that took 1-144 pictures in one sitting.

JORNS & HARROD
Operated the Palace Railway Art Car from Girard, Illinois, c. 1895.

JUDKINS' FLOATING SUNBEAM GALLERY
Active in Puget Sound, Washington Territory and British Columbia, Canada, 1880.

JUDKINS' TINTYPE & FERROTYPE CAR
Active c. 1860s-75.

KEIL, J. K.
Known as a "Traveling Artist" headquartered in Quakertown, Bucks County, Pennsylvania, 1865.

KEMP & KLUIT
Traveling photographers, 1870-75, based at People's Art Gallery, San Francisco, California.

KEMP, H.
Operated the Great Celebrated Centennial Flying Photograph Gallery in Chico, Bodie, and Modesto, California, 1875.

KEMP, J. C.
Based in Sacramento, California, operating a studio under the name Celebrated Flying Photograph Gallery, among others, 1875 See California.

KEYSTONE TRAVELING GALLERY
Operated by A. J. Miller.

KING & HEISS
Operated the Mammoth Photograph Wagon, headquartered in Strasburg, Lancaster County, Pennsylvania, c. 1860s; W. H. Heiss, operator.

KIRBY & GUYER
Operated Photo Cars, 1890.

KISSEL, E. L.
Operated a Photo Car in New Mexico.

KLECKNER, M. A.
Headquartered at 61 Broad Street, Bethlehem, Pennsylvania, c. 1860s.

KLUIT
Partner in Kemp & Kluit, traveling photographers based at People's Art Gallery, San Francisco, California, 1870-75.

KNECHT, GEORGE V.
Known as the "Excelsior Traveling Artist," c. 1860s, possibly associated with Josiah and R. Knecht and William Nick.

KNECHT, JOSIAH
Headquartered in Allentown, Lehigh County, Pennsylvania, operating as the "Excelsior Traveling Artist," c. 1860s. Possibly associated with George and R. Knecht and William Nick.

KNECHT, R.
Headquarters located at 138 Northampton Street, Easton, Pennsylvania, c. 1860s; possibly associated with Josiah and George Knecht and William Nick.

KOONS, W.
Traveling photographer in northwestern Kansas, c. 1895.

KRACAW
Based in Washington, Iowa, c. 1863.

KRESGE
The "Excelsior Traveling Artist" operating with Lewis P. Peter as Peter & Kresge, c. 1860s.

KRUEGER, MAX A. P.
An itinerant operating from "the Texas coast to San Saba," 1873-75. See Texas.

LAKE, JOHN E.
Traveling photographer.

LANGILL, H. H. H.
Traveling photographer, active c. 1860s.

LAURIE, ROBERT H. F.
Itinerant active in Roseburg, Oregon area, c. 1887.

LAVIGNE
Operated Mears & Lavigne Traveling Saloon, c. 1860s.

LAWRENCE, C. A.
Itinerant photographer in the Traveling Saloon, c. 1860s.

LEACH, DON M.
Traveling though Texas and New Mexico.

LEE, C. J.
Headquartered in Fargo, North Dakota, operating Lee's Photo Car.

LEE'S PHOTO CAR
Headquartered in Fargo, North Dakota, operated by C. J. Lee.

LEGERTON, JOHN S.
Traveling photographer.

LEMON, F. J.
Traveling photographer in Lander, Wyoming, 1899; representative of Slawter & Walker of Salt Lake City.

LESURE & SCOVELLS PORTABLE PICTURE PALACE.
Headquartered in Winchendon, Massachusetts.

LILJEGREEN, A.
A traveling photographer in California, 1890s-1900; operating out of Happy Camp, c. 1900.

LIVINGSTON, T.
Traveling photographer, c. 1890.

LOMBARD, JAMES
Traveling photographer.

LOOMIS
Partner in Aylsworth & Loomis.

LUFF'S CHICAGO PHOTO CAR
Active c. 1885.

MACKEY, G. W.
Itinerant in Oregon, Washington and Idaho, 1890-91. Active in Halsey, Oregon, 1890; Portland, Oregon, July 1891. Pitched his Travelling Gallery in Caldwell, Idaho, July 20-August 3, 1891.

MALLORY, D.
Operated the Photographic Car, c. 1860s.

MAMMOTH CAR
Operated by Burchfield & Bottorf, c. 1860.

MAMMOTH PHOTOGRAPHIC STUDIO
Headquartered in Mt. Pleasant, Iowa, operated by the McAdam Brothers.

MAMMOTH TRAVELING SALOON.
Operated by F. J. Aiken, c. 1860s.

MARSHALL'S TRAVELING PHOTOGRAPIC STUDIO, C. C.
Active c. 1860s.

MATTHEWS, ROSA
Active in Dunsmuir, California, c. 1887-90; Cedarville, c. 1900. Wife of photographer George L. Matthews with whom she owned a traveling photography wagon.

McADAM BROTHERS
Operated the Mammoth Photographic Studio, headquartered in Mt. Pleasant, Iowa.

McALFEE, W. C.
Successor to Boston Art Company's Railroad Photo Car, Darius, Indian Territory.

McCAFFREE, O.
Billed as a "Traveling Artist."

McCRACKEN, JAMES
Died 1878. Active before 1878, based in Salem, Oregon.

McCULLOCH, J. LYNN
An itinerant in Glendale, Oregon, 1887.

McEWEN, W. T. & J. S.
Operated the Excelsior Photograph Car or McEwen's Photograph & Art Gallery, headquartered in Lewiston, Pennsylvania, c. 1860s.

McEWENS' PHOTOGRAPH & ART GALLERY
Headquartered in Lewiston, Pennsylvania, operated by W. T. and J. S. McEwen.

McGINLEY, THEODORE B. G.
Probably a partner in McGinley & Schubert's Flying Photograph Gallery operating in California, late 1860s. Gallery located on Fifth Street in Hollister, 1874; gallery on Mariposa Street in Fresno City by 1884.

McGOWAN, J. D.
Studio photographer with O. Dennie in Portland, 1872-73 ; in Independence, c. 1880. Also operated as an itinerant.

MEALEY, GEORGE
Active in Sweet Home, itinerant with William Mealey.

MEALEY, WILLIAM
Active in Sweet Home, itinerant with George Mealey.

MEARS & LAVIGNE
Operated a Traveling Saloon, c. 1860s.

MENDENHALL, H.
Traveling photographer active in California (date uncertain). Gallery at 227 Fifth Street, San Diego, 1888-89.

MEYERS, B. K.
Itinerant in Oregon, c. 1870s. Also spelled Myers.

MILLER, A. J.
Operated the Keystone Traveling Gallery.

MILLER, G. EDWARD
Died c. 1950. Active as photographer, c. 1900-20. Headquartered in Otero County, New Mexico. Worked in North Cloudcroft on the Stewart Lot, July 1904; Mayhill, 1906, 1907-08, 1911-12.

MILLER, GEORGE K.
Itinerant photographer in Mineral Wells, Texas, and with a partner in Garland, c. 1898. See Texas.

MILLER, HARRY
Billed as a "Tramp Photographer," 1890s.

MILLER, J. W.
Traveling photographer, c. 1860s.

MILLER'S PHOTOGRAPH CAR, S. R.
Active c. 1880.

MONROE, C. R.
Traveling photographer, 1880.

MORSE & COLLINS'
Partnership operating the Traveling Studio, c. 1860s.

MORSE, D. D.
Traveling photographer living in Leavenworth, Kansas, 1883.

MOTE
Partner in Swaine & Mote's Photographic Chariot, headquartered at the corner of 5th and Main Streets, Richmond, Indiana, c. 1860s.

MUNYON, A. L.
Known as a "Traveling Artist," c. 1860s.

MYERS, JOHN C.
Operated various photo tents in Idaho.

N & N TRAVELING PHOTO
Active in 1885.

NATIONAL ART COMPANY'S RAILROAD PALACE PHOTOGRAPH STUDIO
Place and dates unknown.

NELSON, JAMES
Active in 1885.

NEW YORK TRAVELING STUDIO
Operating in New York, c. 1890.

NICK & KNECHT
Partnership of William Nick and Josiah and George V. Knecht; billed as the "Traveling Artists," c. 1860s;

NICK, WILLIAM
The "Excelsior Traveling Artist," c. 1860s.

NOBLE, SKELTON STANFORD
Operated extensively in northern California. See California.

NORTON
Operated as Huested & Norton.

OLIVER & WORMER
Traveling stereoview exhibition in the western United States; Idaho City, Centerville, Pioneer City and Placerville, Idaho Territory; Walla Walla, Washington; Oregon and California. While in Idaho City, he located in the Jenny Lind Theatre, October 1866; William Oliver, agent, M. Wormer, proprietor. The stereoptican projector used magnesium lights and projected the images onto a large canvas.

OMEGA FOTO STUDIO
Headquartered in Oroville, California, 1895.

ORMSBEE, M. H.
Operated Star Photo Car, c. 1900.

OSBORN, D. C.
Known as a "Photographic Artist," c. 1860s.

OSBORN, GEORGE B.
Operator of George B. Osborn's Ferrotype Saloon.

PACIFIC PHOTOGRAPH CAR
Headquartered in Rockford, Washington, 1895.

PACKARD, I. N.
Billed as the Traveling Saloon based in Stoughton, Massachusetts.

PALACE PHOTO CAR
Operated by C. W. Anderson.

PALACE RAILROAD PHOTOGRAPH CAR
Place and dates unknown.

PALACE RAILROAD PHOTOGRAPHIC COACH
Owned by Professor L. H. Whitson; operated by C. H. Abbott, 1880.

PALACE RAILROAD STUDIO
Active in 1895.

PALACE RAILWAY PHOTO STUDIO CAR
Headquartered in St. Paul, Minnesota.

PARKER
Partner in Shear & Parker operating the Portable Gallery; headquartered in New Hampton, Iowa, 1875.

PARSONS PALACE CAR PHOTOGRAPH COMPANY
Headquartered in St. Louis, Missouri.

PEELSTROM & DUNCAN
Operated by F. R. Peelstrom and A. B. Duncan.

PEELSTROM & WALLINE
Traveling photographers, headquartered in Des Moines, Iowa.

PEELSTROM, F. R.
Operator for Davidson in Des Moines, Iowa; also operated as Peelstrom & Duncan.

PEIRCE & BROTHER
John K. and Robert W. Peirce arrived in Galveston, Texas, 1853, traveling to Indianola, Port Lavaca, Petersburg, Gonzales, Prairie Lea and Lockhart, before settling in Austin, c. 1855. See Texas.

PENDERGAST BROTHERS ART PAVILLION
Traveling photographers in Indianapolis, Indiana.

PERKINS PHOTOGRAPH & AMBROTYPE CAR
Headquartered in Oshkosh, Wisconsin, 1860.

PERRY, CHARLES H.
Operated the Photograph Tent, 1865.

PETER & KRESGE
"Excelsior Traveling Artists," c. 1860s, operated by Lewis P. Peter.

PETER, LEWIS P.
The "Excelsior Traveling Artist," c. 1860s, partner in Peter & Kresge.

PHOTO CAR
Headquartered in Mineral Springs, Texas.

PHOTO PARLOR ON WHEELS
Headquartered in Huron, South Dakota.

PLACE, S.
Operated as a "Traveling Artist," c. 1860s.

PLECKER, A. H.
Partner in Wheeler & Plecker operating the Traveling Gallery, c. 1860s.

POLLARD, L. L.
Car near Union House, Montpelier, Vermont, c. 1860s.

PORTABLE PHOTO PARLOR
Active in 1880, as Rifenburg & Dowe.

PORTABLE PICTURE PALACE
Operating from Keene, New Hampshire.

PRETTYMAN, W. S.
See Kansas.

PRICE, ANDREW
Traveling photographer in northern California.

PURNELLE, H. J.
Operated the Railroad Photo Car, active in 1885.

PUTNAM, S. A.
Operated the Traveling Portrait & Landscape Photograph Association with E. P. Gerould.

RAGSDALE, McARTHUR CULLEN
Itinerant photographer in Texas based in Belton; worked in Brownwood, Fort McKavett, Mason, Fredericksburg, c. 1874-75. Headquartered in Cullen, Texas, 1875-81; also in San Antonio, 1881. See Texas.

RAILROAD PALACE PHOTO CAR
Operated by Vreeland.

RAILROAD PHOTO CAR
Operated by H. J. Purnelle, 1885.

RAMSDELL, GEORGE HENRY
Managed Western Photograph Association with F. P. Eastburn, 1890.

RANDALL, A. FRANK
Itinerant active in Arizona and New Mexico, 1883-88, based in Willcox, Arizona. Correspondent for *Leslie's* on Crook Expedition, 1883. See New Mexico.

RANKIN
Billed as the "Pacific Coast Photographer," 1880.

RECTOR, W. H.
Traveling photographer, c. 1860s.

RHORER'S
Operated the Mammoth Photographic Car No. 2, c. 1860s.

RICE, J. B.
Advertised "The Largest Traveling Photograph Rooms in the West," 1875.

RICE'S PHOTO CAR
Active in Minnesota, 1880; Dakota, 1890.

RICHARDSON, C. F.
Operated the Traveling Studio, headquartered in North Bridgewater, Massachusetts, c. 1860s.

RICHARDSON, L. A.
Traveling Saloon, c. 1860s.

RIDDLE, J. R.
Itinerant with the firm of Leonard & Martin, in Topeka, Kansas, 1880s; followed the route of the Santa Fe Railroad working in tents. Active in Santa Fe, New Mexico, May 1886; in Las Cruces at Plaza, May 1888.

RIDEOUT, N. R.
Operated the Picture Studio, headquartered in West Waterville, Wisconsin, c. 1860s.

RIFENBURG & DOWE
Partners operating as "Traveling Artists" in California, also known as the Portable Photo Parlor.

RIFENBURG, A. G.
Traveling photographer with Dowe, covering various California towns from a base in Fresno at least part of the time (date uncertain). Opened the Imperial Photograph Studio on Main Street in Salinas City, c. 1886. Studio at 241 South First Street, San Jose 1895-97.

ROBBINS & COMPANY, J. H.
Operated the Mammoth Traveling Daguerreian Saloon.

ROBERTS & COREY
Traveling photographer in the Hillsboro area of Oregon, c. 1867.

ROCHE, L. A.
Traveled in Alaska from Seattle, Washington, c. 1897.

ROGERS, CHARLES THOMAS
See Arizona.

ROSHON & GREENE
Operated the Mammoth Car, headquartered at Railroad Street, Huntington, Pennsylvania, c. 1860s.

ROSHON'S PHOTOGRAPHIC CAR
Probably a partner in Roshon & Greene.

SALE BROTHERS
Active in Texas and New Mexico, 1910; George E. and J. A. Sale.

SAMMIS, EDWARD M.
Itinerant in Oregon before 1860s. Also spelled Sammes.

SAN FRANCISCO RAILROAD STUDIO CAR
Orris P. Hunt, photographer.

SANDERS, STEPHEN P.
Traveling photographer in California. Made tintypes with rubber stamp imprint, "S. P. Sanders' Photograph Car."

SANTA FE KID'S RAILROAD PHOTO CAR
Active 1895.

SCHLUETER, FRANK J.
Itinerant tent photographer in Flatonia, Texas with his father and brother-in-law, 1891, making prints and postcards. See Texas.

SCHUBERT
Partner in McGinley & Schubert's Flying Photograph Gallery operating in California, late 1860s.

SCHUBERT BROTHERS
Known as the "Traveling Photo Artists" headquartered in Kiel, Wisconsin.

SCOVELLS
Operated Lesure & Scovells Portable Picture Palace, headquartered in Winchendon, Massachusetts.

SELLON & BENNETT
Traveling photographers headquartered in Mount Hope and Colwich, Kansas, 1885.

SHANE, J. B.
Operated a Railroad Photo Car.

SHEAR & PARKER
Billed as the Portable Gallery headquartered in New Hampton, Iowa, 1875.

SHORT, GORDON
Itinerant in Oregon.

SILVIS, J. B.
Operated the Pacific Railroad Photograph Car headquartered in Omaha, Nebraska, 1860-80. Official photographer for the Union Pacific Railroad.

SLEDGE
Traveling photographer in Whitewright, Texas, c. 1900. See Texas.

SMITH, C. S.
Traveling photographer active in San Francisco, California, Marshfield and Eugene, Oregon, 1880; Seattle and Port Townsend, Washington, 1881.

SMITH, CHRISTOPHER C.
Itinerant photographer active in Oregon; Newberg, 1901-09; Portland, 1910-13, at 149 ½ 1st Street. Also listed as Chris C. Smith.

SMITH, LUKE
Operated the Tent Gallery in California, c. 1880.

SMITH'S CALIFORNIA PHOTOGRAPH CAR
Active 1880.

SORENSEN, C.
Headquartered in Cedar Falls, Iowa, 1875.

SPEARMAN, I.
Itinerant based in Fort Worth, Texas; in Mansfield, 1900.

SQUIRE, E. B.
Operated Squire's Traveling Photograph Gallery offering "card ferrotypes," c. 1870.

SQUIER, L. S.
Traveling photographer. Also spelled Squire.

SQUIRE'S TRAVELING PHOTOGRAPH GALLERY
Operated by E. B. Squire, 1870. Also spelled Squier.

STACY, J. W.
Known as the "Traveling Photographic Artist" headquartered in Barre, Massachusetts, c. 1860s.

STALEY BROTHERS
Operated the Tennessee River Floating Gallery, c. 1860s.

STANDIFORD, J. F.
Active in the 1890s, and billed as "The Only Licensed U.S. Photographer in the Indian Territory." He made regular visits with his portable gallery to Tahlequah, Vinita, Eufaula, Wagoner and other important points in the Territory. Headquartered at Muskogee, Creek Nation and Parsons, Kansas, his advertisements claimed the most "complete photographic tent and outfit in existence." He also visited McAlester.

STARK, C. M.
Operated c. 1870 as C. M. Stark on Wheels. Also spelled Starck.

STARK, HENRY
Photographer from St. Louis, Missouri; traveled through Texas making photographs, 1895-96. A hand-made book of his photographs was reprinted as *Views in Texas*.

STEPHENS, A. J.
Operated the Traveling Gallery, headquartered in St. Joseph, 1880.

STERLING'S RAILROAD CAR, G. F.
"Official Photogapher" for the Michigan Central's Niagara Falls Route.

STEVENS, B. F.
Traveling photographer in the gold country of California, particularly Sonora, c. 1870s. He advertised "photographs, gems, copying and enlarging." Studio in Riceville, 1879.

STEVENSON, WILLIAM F.
Itinerant photographer, c. 1880.

STEWART, GEORGE A.
Traveling photographer in El Dorado County, 1887.

STEWART'S LIKENESS CAR
Advertised ferrotypes, c. 1870, "Taken in dark as well as in fair weather."

STONE, CHARLES E.
Billed as an "Artist" with a portable gallery, probably in the Northwest, c. 1900.

STRUCKMAN, FRANK
Operated a portrait gallery with Iwer Boysen on Main Street in Salinas, California, 1879. Active in Bodie, California, c. 1882; Portland, Oregon, late 1880s. Active in Boise, Idaho Territory, operating Struckman's Art Gallery opposite the Post Office, February-November 1888. Itinerant in Idaho, 1894. Also spelled Struckmann. See Idaho.

SUDEN
Operated as the Photo Traveling Palace & Art Gallery, also known as Hagedorn, Braver & Suden.

SULLIVAN
Partner in Johnson & Sullivan operating a portable gallery, 1880.

SUPPINGER, A. E.
See Arizona.

SUTTERLY & DART
Traveling photographers in California, c. 1885.

SUTTERLY, CLEMENT
Traveling photographer in Utah and Nevada, but mainly in California.

SWAIN, S.
Operated the Traveling Photograph & Ferrotype Saloon, c. 1860s.

SWAINE & MOTE'S PHOTOGRAPHIC CHARIOT
Headquartered at the corner of 5th and Main Streets, Richmond, Indiana, c. 1860s.

SWAN, JAMES C.
Billed as the "Practical Photographer," c. 1866.

SWEET'S ART CAR
Place and dates unknown.

SWEETSER'S PHOTOGRAPH CAR
Headquartered in East Hampton, Massachusetts, c. 1860s.

TAYLOR, JOSEPH
Traveling photographer in Placerville, California, 1903.

TEEL'S PHOTOGRAPH CAR, S. S.
Active c. 1860s.

THAYER'S MAMMOTH GALLERY, M. B.
Active c. 1860s.

THIBAULT, F. X.
Traveling photographer.

THOMAS, J. J.
Operated the Big Photograph Tent, 1865.

THOMAS' PHOTOGRAPHIC CAR
Operating c. 1865.

THRASHER, A. F.
Died mid-1870s. Operated for William J. Young in his new rooms in Kline's Building opposite Bilicke & Logan's Store, Boise, Idaho Territory, c. 1866. Active in southwestern Montana, c. 1867-68; itinerant photographer, spring-October 1870. Traveled in Idaho Territory and Montana, summer 1870; in Deer Lodge, Montana, October 1870-January 1872; partner with William Hyde, March 1871; operated Montana Stereopticon, spring-July 1871. Active in Idaho Territory, summer 1871; visited Yellowstone and toured mining camps, August-October 1871; in Virginia City, Montana, c. 1872. Probably traveled through Idaho Territory again en route to the Union Pacific Railroad, early 1872; active in the eastern United States after 1872.

TOLLMAN, JOHN W.
Traveling photographer in California; Shasta County, 1889, 1897; Mendocino County, 1894; Humboldt County 1895-96; Trinity County 1897; Siskiyou County, 1897-98.

TOLLMAN, JOHN W. (MRS.)
Traveling photographer with husband, John W. Tollman, active in northern California counties, 1889-98; in Washington and Oregon, 1899-1909.

TRAIN, EDGAR H.
Worked the Northwest and Montana in a traveling wagon, c. 1870s.

TUCKER & ALLEN
Billed as the "Champion Traveling Photographers."

TWO-BIT TINTYPIST
Low-priced tent itinerants active in Santa Fe, New Mexico, c. 1870s; located near Loretto Chapel, February-April 1877.

U.S. PHOTO COMPANY
Itinerant company active in The Dalles area, Oregon, 1892.

UNION PACIFIC PHOTO CAR
Operated by W. A. Bradley, 1885.

UNION PACIFIC RAILROAD PHOTOGRAPH CAR
Headquartered in Omaha, Nebraska, 1870-80, operated by J. B. Silvis.

UPDIKE, L. C.
Active in Texas, Colorado, Arizona and New Mexico, 1902-13. See Arizona.

VALE, W. A.
Operated the Photographic Car, headquartered in San Bernardino, California, 1875.

VANCE, M. C.
Active in 1875.

VREELAND
Operated the Palace Railroad Photo Car, c. 1890.

WALES, H. P.
Headquartered in Morrisville, New York. Located in the car near the Courthouse, c. 1860s.

WALLINE
Partner in Peelstrom & Walline headquartered in Des Moines, Iowa.

WATSON, O. W.
Active in Spokane, Washington and itinerant in Post Falls and Idaho Falls, Idaho, c. 1900.

WEENINK, HENRY D.
Itinerant in Idaho Territory, 1890-91.

WENDT, HENRY
Born October 14, 1875; died March 27, 1955. Itinerant in south Oregon and northern California until 1905. Studio in Beiber, California, 1905-09; New Pine Creek, 1909-36.

WESNER BROTHERS
Operated a Photo Car headquartered in San Bernardino, California, 1875.

WEST, W. W.
"Traveling Artist," c. 1860s.

WESTERN PHOTOGRAPH ASSOCIATION
Itinerant company managed by F. P. Eastburn and G. H. Ramsdell, 1890.

WESTROP
Itinerant in Vancouver, Washington and Hillsboro, Oregon, 1876.

WHALEN'S PORTABLE GALLERY
Active c. 1880.

WHALEY, G. V.
"Traveling Artist," 1890.

WHEELER & PLECKER
Partners known as the "Traveling Artists," c. 1860s, operated by A. H. Plecker.

WHITE, THOMAS J.
Studio photographer in Portland, Oregon, on Southwest 5th Street, 1885-93. Partner with F. E. Harnes and itinerant in Idaho Territory, Montana, Wyoming, Oregon and Utah, 1886-87; headquartered at Eagle Rock, Idaho Territory and Dillon, Montana. Traveled from Granger, Wyoming to Huntington, Oregon; and from Ogden, Utah to Butte, Montana. White operated a tent opposite the depot and a studio on Main Street, rear of C. Bunting's Store, October 1886, town unknown. Operated White's New Photograph Gallery with F. E. Harnes, January 1887. Active in Montana, January-March 1887; Pocatello, Idaho Territory, April 1887; Blackfoot, May 1887; spring Hill, Montana, June 1887; Anaconada, c. 1895.

WHITE, W. A.
Active in Colorado, New Mexico, and Oklahoma, 1882-1902.

WHITE'S YOUNG AMERICA PICTURE GALLERY
Billed as "The Largest Movable Establishment in America," operated by R. S. Avery,.

WHITSON'S PALACE RAILROAD PHOTOGRAPHIC COACH
Active 1880; owned by Professor L. H. Whitson, operated by C. H. Abbott.

WHYTE, WILLIAM
Itinerant in Idaho, 1891. Active in Boise operating a tent at the corner of 7th and Idaho Streets, c. 1891-93.

WILCOX & WILCOX
Itinerant photographers in Idaho Territory; working in Caldwell, June-July 1888; Shoshone, July 1888.

WILCOX & WILSON
Partnership of George Wilcox and B. L. or John W. Wilson, itinerants in Idaho Territory, 1888. See Wilcox & Wilcox.

WILCOX, GEORGE W.
Traveling photographer, c. 1860; Albany and Eugene, Oregon, c. 1880. Partner with B. L. or John W. Wilson, Wilcox & Wilson, itinerant photographers in Idaho Territory, 1888. Partner in Wilcox & Wilcox.

WILCOX, S., JR.
Traveling photographer, c. 1860s.

WILKIN'S PHOTOGRAPHIC CAR, IRA
Headquartered in Charles City, Iowa, c. 1860s.

WILLIAMS & HARZOG
Operated the Photo Boat.

WILLIAMS' FLOATING GALLERY
Operating out of Sistersville, West Virginia, c. 1890.

WILLISCRAFT, WILLIAM HAMILTON
See Arizona.

WILSON, B. L.
Traveling photographer in California, advertising the California Photo Tent, c. 1880.

WILSON'S RAILROAD PHOTO CAR
Dates and place unknown.

WINSLOW, MARY (MISS)
Born c. 1870. Traveling photographer in California, active in San Francisco, Yosemite, southern California and other locations 1892-95+. Featured in the *San Francisco Examiner,* March 14, 1895, in a lengthy article about her life and work.

WIXON, G. S.
Traveling photographer, 1873-80, with steamboat motif on rubber stamp imprint.

WOOD, THOMAS M.
Born in New York, c. 1822. Active in New York(?); in Grass Valley, California, rooms on Mill Street, 1858; operated the Ambrotype Gallery on Mill Street, 1859-60; Nevada City, rooms at 27 and 29 Commercial Street, September 1860-June 1861; itinerant, c. 1863. Active in Dalles City, Oregon, operating Wood's Photographic Rooms, 1863-64; T. M. Wood Studio, Main Street, 1865; Wood & Butler, Main Street, 1866. Probably toured Oregon, Washington and Idaho Territories, c. 1863-64. Itinerant in Idaho Territory, 1868-69; studio in Silver City at 777 Jordan Street, December 1868-July 1869. Active in Winnemucca, Nevada, c. 1876.

WORMER
Partner in Oliver & Wormer; see partnership listing for details.

WULZEN, ALBERT H.
Owner of Pacific Art Gallery, a traveling studio active in Ferndale, California, operating out of Weaverville, c. 1882. See California and Oregon.

YOUNG (MISS)
Traveling photographer in California working with her father and advertising as William S. Young & Daughter. Active in Fresno County, c. 1874.

YOUNG, ANNIE C.
Born in Iowa, 1847. Photographic colorist in San Francisco, California, 1880. Wife of printer, Jacob Young.

YOUNG, WILLIAM J.
Active as photographer in Susanville, Califonia; sold out to Townsend, c. 1862-63. Purchased the stock and good will of the Sutterley Brothers on Main Street in Boise, Idaho Territory, operating a few doors above Crawford & Slocum's, October 1865-June, 1866. Acquired new rooms in Kline's Building opposite Bilicke & Logan's Store, June-December 1866 (A. F. Thrasher, operator), Young's Gallery was purchased and refitted by John Junk of Idaho City, December 1866. An itinerant in Idaho identified as William Young (in Nampa, c. 1895, at Capitol Hotel; Boise, c. December 1895; Payette, c. 1896, at Overland Hotel; Boise, March 1896.) was possibly William E. Young.

YOUNG, WILLIAM S.
Traveling photographers advertising as William S. Young & Daughter, active in Fresno County, California, c. 1874.

YOUNG & DAUGHTER, WILLIAM S.
Traveling photographers in California, advertising as William S. Young & Daughter. Active in Fresno County, c. 1874. The daughter may have been Annie C. Young.

ZOLK, WILLIAM
Operated the Portable Photographic Studio.

ZUBER, WILLIAM L.
Traveling daguerreotypist. Located in Mokelumne Hill, 1858; San Andreas, 1859. Licensed in Drytown, 1864.

This section was edited by Bradley W. Richards, M. D., author of
The Savage View: Charles Savage, Pioneer Mormon Photographer,
Carl Mautz Publishing, Nevada City, California, 1995.

ACE & AEBISCHER
Stereo photographers active in Logan.

ADAMS BROTHERS
Partnership active in Ogden and Park City, 1890. Located at 71 Grand Opera House Block in Ogden, 1892.

AEBISCHER
Stereo photographer active in Logan, 1870s; partner in Ace & Aebischer.

AGRAMONTE
Stereo photographer active in Salt Lake City.

ALLEN
Partner in Lewis & Allen operating gallery in Logan, c. 1875.

ANDERSON & CRANDALL
Active in Springville and Manti, c. 1885. Partnership of George Edward Anderson and L. D. Crandall.

ANDERSON, ADAM SAIG
Apprenticed with Charles R. Savage in Salt Lake City, then with his brothers, George Edward and Jeddiah Stanley Anderson. Opened a gallery in Provo, c. 1890, and sold it to his apprentice, Thomas Christian Larson, 1910.

ANDERSON, ADDISON
Active in Provo City, 1886.

ANDERSON, GEORGE EDWARD
Born in Salt Lake City, October 20, 1860; died in Springville, May 9, 1928. Apprenticed to Charles R. Savage, 1874; opened his own studio three years later at age seventeen across the street with the help of his two brothers, Jeddiah Stanley and Adam Saig Anderson. Won first prize for tintypes at the territorial fair, 1879. Opened a studio in Springville, 1881; Manti, early 1880s; Spanish Fork and Nephi, mid-1880s; portable gallery throughout the period. Hyrum Sainsbury was employed, 1887; partner with L. D. Crandall, c. 1885. Anderson traveled extensively throughout Utah for many years. John Hafen became a partner, helping with photography and painting backdrops for portrait work. Anderson recorded the aftermath of the Scofield mine disaster, 1900. Apprentices included Effie Huntington and Joe Bagley, who set up a competing gallery across the street in Springville, 1903

Nelson B. Wadsworth, *Through Camera Eyes*, Brigham Young University Press, Salt Lake City, 1975.
Rell G. Francis, *The Utah Photographs of George Edward Anderson*, University of Nebraska Press, Lincoln and London, 1979.
Nelson B. Wadsworth, *Set in Stone, Fixed in Glass: The Great Mormon Temple and Its Photographers*, Signature Books, Salt Lake City, Utah, 1992.

ANDERSON, JEDDIAH STANLEY
Brother of George Edward and Adam S. Anderson with whom he was active in Salt Lake City, c. 1874-77.

BAGLEY, JOE
Born in Toquerville, December 17, 1874; died in Springville, 1936. Apprenticed to George Edward Anderson. He and Effie Huntington, also an apprentice, left Anderson and started a studio across the street,

operating as Bagley & Huntington, 1903-36 They were married in 1936, and Bagley died six weeks later.

BENNETT, JOHN F.
Apprenticed to Charles R. Savage in the mid-1870s; he later became a successful banker and civic leader. He created a number of lantern slides which he used to illustrate lectures.

BIERSTADT, ALBERT
Member of the Lander Expedition, 1859, as an artist and photographer. Famous Hudson River painter and brother of photographer, Charles Bierstadt, New Bedford, Massachusetts.

BOOTH, JAMES J.
Active in St. George, 1875-86; also traveled.

BREWSTER, JOHN CALVIN
Born in Ohio, 1841. Opened gallery for the Sutterlys in Salt Lake City; studio in Douglas. See Nevada.

BROWNING, DAVID
Worked in the studio of Marsena Cannon with his brother James Allen, 1855.

BROWNING, JAMES ALLEN
Worked in the studio of Marsena Cannon with his brother David, 1855.

BROWNING, JOHN W.
Replaced David Lewis in the studio " over the Book Store," 1854. S. A. Lobdale was an operator for Browning. Partner with Marsena Cannon for a short time.

BUYS, WILLIAM
Active in Heber, 1886.

CAMPBELL & COMPANY, ROBERT
Advertised in Salt Lake City, 1851.

CANNON, MARSENA
Born in Rochester, New Hampshire, August 3, 1812; died in Salt Lake City, April 1900. Cannon learned the daguerreian art from John Plumbe, Jr. in Boston where William Shew was employed. He was the first photographer in Utah, 1850, and made portraits of Mormon leaders and views of Salt Lake City buildings; partner in Chafin & Cannon, 1854; won first prize for the best ambrotype at an exhibit of the Deseret Manufacturing Association, 1859. Formed a partnership with Charles R. Savage, 1860; called by the Mormon Church to settle St. George in southern Utah, 1861. He returned to Salt Lake City, c. 1863; established a studio in Oakland, 1870.
    Nelson B. Wadsworth, *Through Camera Eyes*, Brigham Young University Press, Salt Lake City, 1975.
    Nelson B. Wadsworth, *Set in Stone, Fixed in Glass: The Great Mormon Temple and Its Photographers*, Signature Books, Salt Lake City, Utah, 1992.

CARDON & THATCHER
Active in Logan, 1883.

CARDON, THOMAS BARTHELEMY
Active in Logan, 1867-85; operated the Art Emporium; partner in Cardon & Thatcher, 1883.

CARESWELL
Partner in Smith & Careswell active in Ogden.

CARPENTER
Active in Ogden, 1895.

CARPENTER, J. W.
"Job Printer" for James J. Booth in St. George, c. 1875.

CARTER, A. C.
See Montana.

CARTER, CHARLES WILLIAM
Born in London, England, August 4, 1832; died in Midvale, January 27, 1918. Worked for Savage in Salt Lake City, 1864-67; partner with J. B. Silvis in Carter & Silvis, 1867-68, taking over the Sutterly Brothers studio. Operated as Carter's Palace Gallery & View Emporium and Carter's Mammoth Photographic Gallery on East Temple Street, 1867-96. C. W. Symons, who had shared the ship's passage with Carter from England, 1864, became an apprentice, 1869. Partner with Mikkael Faldmo, 1894; Faldmo eventually bought the business. Carter advertised his services at the Grand Pacific Hotel, 1896. In his early years, Carter produced numerous cartes-de-visite and stereoviews of Indians, emigrant trains, and other western scenes.
    Nelson B. Wadsworth, *Through Camera Eyes*, Brigham Young University Press, Salt Lake City, 1975.

CASTLETON, JAMES
Assistant to James H. Crockwell in his photographic copying and coloring business, c. 1882.

CHAFFIN & CANNON
Gallery on East Temple Street, Salt Lake City, 1854, operated by L. W. Chaffin and Marsena Cannon. Advertised that " Everything we have is new except the workmen, and they are far better than new."

CHAFFIN, L. W.
Active in Salt Lake City, 1854, operating as Chaffin & Cannon.

COMPTON, ALMA W.
Active in Ogden, 1882.

CONKLING, C. A.
Operated the Phoenix Studio in Provo City.

COVINGTON, E.
Active c. 1863.

CRANDALL, L. D.
Partner in Anderson & Crandall, Springville and Manti, c. 1885; listed alone in Springfield, 1890-1910.

CRISSMAN, J.
May have been active in Ogden. See Montana. Also spelled Cressman.

CROCKWELL, JAMES H.
Born in Woodbury, Iowa; March 21, 1855; died in Alameda, California, September 16, 1933. Worked as a colorist before learning photography from C. W. Carter in Salt Lake City, 1883. Partner with William Ottinger, son of George Ottinger, 1883-86, operating as Crockwell & Ottinger. Illustrated *Pictures and Biographies of Brigham Young and His Wives,* c. 1885. Billed as a traveling photographer specializing in mining views in Utah and Nevada with a studio at 337 G Street, Salt Lake City, c. 1886; advertised " Mining and Contract Viewing a Specialty." The son of a physician, Crockwell augmented his income with dental work while on the road. Opened gallery in Bishop's Creek, California, c. 1887. Studio in Virginia City, Nevada, at 29 ½ C Street, 1888. Produced *Souvenir of Park City, Her Mines, Mining and Pleasure Resorts,* 1891. Official Utah photographer at the Chicago World's Fair, 1893. Gallery at First West and Second South Streets, 1895. Retired from photography by 1900. See Nevada and California.

DANIELS & CONKLING
Gallery in Provo City; T. E. Daniels and C. A. Conkling.

DANIELS & HAFEN
Active in Provo City, 1883.

DANIELS, ORSON A.
Active in Provo and Payson, 1882-1900s.

DANIELS, THOMAS E., JR.
Partner in Daniels & Conkling with C. A. Conkling in Provo and Payson, 1874.

DRAPER, Z. T.
Active in Rockville, 1867-80.

DREWERY, H.
Studio at 1227 Washington Boulevard, Ogden, 1895.

ELLIS & GOODWIN
Active in Salt Lake City, 1895.

FALDMO, MIKKEL ANDREAS
Active in Salt Lake City, c. 1885-1930; partner of C. W. Carter, 1892-94, and later bought the business.

FENNEMORE, JAMES
Operator for C. R. Savage in Salt Lake City; also active in Beaver and St. George; photographer with the Powell Survey, 1872; also made stereoviews of Grand Canyon, rural scenery. See Arizona.

FOX & SYMONS
Active in Salt Lake City, 1874-83; the studio continued after Fox's death, 1883.

FOX, ALEXANDER
Died in Salt Lake City, 1882. Partner in Fox & Symons, Salt Lake City, 1874-82. His partner continued to use the name after Fox's death. Also active in California.

FROST, S. F.
Active in Lander Expedition, 1859.

GASBERY, JENS C.
Active in Brigham City, c. 1873-86. Also active in Box Elder County, 1880s; in Ogden at 276 25th Street, c. 1890. Also known as Chris Gasberg, 1895.

GOODMAN, CHARLES M.
Active in Colorado and Utah, c. 1882-1901.

GOODWIN
Partner in Ellis & Goodwin, Salt Lake City, 1895.

HAFEN, JOHN
Born c. 1856; died 1910. Apprenticed to Charles R. Savage, mid-1870s. Hafen later studied art in Paris and became a noted landscape painter.

HARDY, ALMA
Active in Ogden and Bountiful, 1862-1900s.

HEBER, H. THOMAS
Active in Ogden, c. 1890-1900.

HILL & COMPANY
Active in Provo.

HILLERS, J. K.
Active in Powell Survey, 1875.

HILLSTEAD, SARAH SYMONS
Daughter of Charles W. Symons; operated his studio while he was on a Mormon mission to England, 1889-91.

HINSHAW & JOY
T. E. Hinshaw and C. L. Joy in Salt Lake City; made stereoviews.

HINSHAW, T. E.
Partner in Hinshaw & Joy, Salt Lake City; also worked alone in Salt Lake City and Eureka.

HOFFMAN BROTHERS
Active in Ogden, 1880. Albert J. Hoffman was one of the brothers.

HOUGUARD, JOHN G.
Active in Cedar Springs, 1868.

HOWARTH
Partner in Stringham & Howarth, active in Manti and Salt Lake City, 1890.

HOYT, FANNIE (MRS.)
"Artist" at G. S. Smith's Gallery; studio at 1248 First South Street, Salt Lake City, 1880-83.

HUNTINGTON, EFFIE (MISS)
Born c. 1869; died 1949. Apprenticed to George Edward Anderson in Springville; she was deaf, and an accomplished operator. In 1903, she and another apprentice, Joe Bagley, left Anderson and started a studio across the street, operating as Huntington & Bagley until Bagley's death six weeks after their marriage, 1936. Huntington continued the business until 1939.

HUISH, ORSON PRATT
Issued rare views of local scenery in Payson.

HULL, ARUNDEL C.
See Nebraska.

HUTCHINSON
Partner in Lewis & Hutchinson operating in Ogden; possibly T. O. Hutchinson who worked alone in Oregon, 1870s-1900.

HYHAMS, ARCH
Assistant in the firm of Crockwell & Ottinger, 1883.

JENNINGS, C. P.
Active in Ogden, 1883.

JENSEN, M.
Active in Ephraim, c. 1870.

JOHNSON, CHARLES ELLIS
Born in St. Louis, Missouri, March 21, 1857; died in San Jose, February 21, 1926. A druggist and eventually a successful businessman operating the Johnson-Pratt Drug Company. Johnson backed a photography studio in partnership with Hyrum Sainsbury, c. 1884. Sainsbury & Johnson ended with Sainsbury's retirement in 1893, and Johnson became the operator of the business and advertised "Johnson Around the World." An amateur actor, he made portraits of many Salt Lake City stage personalities. Johnson traveled to Palestine and made over 2,000 images, 1903.

JONES, J. WESLEY
See California.

JOY, C. L.
Partner in Hinshaw & Joy, stereo photographers in Salt Lake City.

KEELER, E. C.
Active in Salt Lake City, 1886.

KERTZ BROTHERS
Studio at 160 25th St., Ogden, 1909.

KERTZ, JACOB
Studio in Ogden at 216 25th Street, 1862; 310 25th Street, 1909.

KING, J. B.
Photgraphed the San Francisco fire, St. Louis exposition, Niagara, southern California, Missions; views published by Pan American Publishing Company in Salt Lake City.

KNIGHT BROTHERS
Active in Salt Lake City.

LA ROCHE, FRANK & SOOY, B. F.
Active in Ogden, 1883.

LARSEN, T. C.
Active in Provo and Springfield.

LARSON, CHARLES
Active in Salt Lake City, 1866.

LARSON, THOMAS CHRISTIAN
Apprenticed to Adam Anderson; purchased his studio in Provo, 1910. The studio was later taken over by Larson's son, O. Blaine Larson.

LEWIS & ALLEN
Gallery in Logan, c. 1875.

LEWIS & HUTCHINSON
Partnership of C. C. Lewis and possibly T. O. Hutchinson, active in Ogden. Hutchinson worked alone in Oregon, 1870s-1900; Lewis in Utah and Oregon, 1880s-90s.

LEWIS, BEDLINGTON
Stereo photographer in Scofield. Made series of views of mine disaster, published by G. E. Anderson.

LEWIS, DAVID
Photographic artist operating in Logan City, c. 1883.

LOBDALE, S. A.
Operator for John W. Browning in Salt Lake City, 1854. Also spelled Lobdell.

LOWE, WILLIAM
Active in Ogden, dates unknown.

LUND, ANTHON HENRIK
Tintypist in Mt. Pleasant, c. 1868-75. Later became a merchant and a presiding elder of the Mormon Church.

MARTIN, EDWARD
Born in Preston, England; died in Salt Lake City, August 16, 1882. Migrated to Salt Lake with the first Mormon wagon train from Nauvoo, Illinois, 1846. Seved in the Mormon Battalion during the Mexican War. Studio with John Olsen, 1865. Made portraits of prominent Mormons, street scenes of Salt Lake City, and panoramic views.

MARTINEAU, JAMES H.
Active in Logan, 1863-66.

MATSON
Studio in Salt Lake City, Uintah Building, Commercial Street, 1885.

MILLS, C. C.
Active in Simpson Expedition, 1859.

MONSON, F. I.
Stereo photographer in Salt Lake City.

MORRIS & COMPANY
Gallery in Salt Lake City, 1890, at 64 West Second South Street.

NEWCOMB, R. W.
Stereo photographer active in Salt Lake City.

NEWCOMB, T. J.
Studio at 26 Wright Block, Ogden, 1892-96.

NEWCOMB, WILLIAM
Active in Salt Lake City, 1885-87.

NEWCOMBE BROTHERS
Operated a portable gallery in a covered wagon, usually located on the corner of 22nd Street and Washington Boulevard, Ogden.

OLSEN, JOHN
Danish emigrant; partner of Edward Martin. Studio in Salt Lake City, c. 1860s, at First South Temple Street. Listed in Ogden, 1867.

OTTINGER, GEORGE M.
Born in Springfield, Pennsylvania, c. 1832. Partner of Charles R. Savage, 1862-mid 1870s, operating as Savage & Ottinger. Ottinger colored photographs and painted murals or various clients, including the Salt Lake Theatre and the Mormon Church. First president of the Deseret Academy of Art.

OTTINGER, WILLIAM
Son of George M. Ottinger. Partner in Savage & Ottinger, 1862-70. Worked in Savage's studio, 1876-83; partner with James H. Crockwell in Crockwell & Ottinger, Box 2380, Salt Lake City, 1883.

PAN AMERICAN PUBLISHING COMPANY
Company in Salt Lake City issuing stereoviews; San Francisco fire, St. Louis exposition, Niagara, southern California, Missions; many photographs are by J. B. King, c. 1905.

PARKINSON, CHARLES GRAHAM
Active in Logan, 1883.

PASEVITCH, J.
Active in Ogden.

PHOENIX STUDIO
Operated by C. A. Conkling in Provo City.

PIERCY, FREDERICK C.
Active in Salt Lake City, 1851.

POND, CHARLES L.
Salt Lake City photographer; made California views of Yosemite Valley, Mammoth Trees, balloon ascension, flood, western scenes, c. 1870s.

PRATER, W. J.
Graduate of Illinois College of Photography; rented Anderson's Springville studio while he went on a Mormon mission to England, 1907.

RANCE & COMPANY, F. G.
Active in Salt Lake City and Provo, 1890.

REILLY & SPOONER
Partnership of John James Reilly and John Pitcher Spooner, California photographers who made views of Utah and Niagara Falls, 1860s-70s.

ROTHI, R. P.
Assistant to James H. Crockwell, c. 1887. See Washington.

RUSSELL, ANDREW J.
Born March 20, 1829; died in New York, 1902. Raised in Nunda, New York and worked as an artist and house painter; became a teacher at the Nunda Literary Institute, 1855. Moved to New York City, 1859, and continued his artistic training and work. Enlisted as Captain in the New York Infantry, 1862; appointed United States Military Railroad Photographer, the only official photographer of the Civil War. After the war, he became the official photographer for the Union Pacific Railroad. Russell recorded the construction of the line as it was built across the West, and created landscape images of the highest quality. At Promontory, Utah, 1869, Russell photographed the engines of the Central Pacific and the Union Pacific meeting on the tracks, an almost identical image to that captured by Charles R. Savage. Russell's photograph was the basis for a woodcut centerfold in Frank Leslie's *Illustrated Weekly*; Savage's view was used in *Harper's Weekly*. Russell was assisted by Stephen J. Sedgwick who later acquired Russell's negatives from O. C. Smith, the Union Pacific paymaster. Both Sedgwick and Smith published prints under their own names without credit to Russell, and Sedgwick made lantern slides from some negatives to illustrate lectures. After Promontory, Russell joined the Clarence King geological survey of the Bear River area as a photographer. Russell took one trip as far as Sacramento, 1869, and later was employed by Frank Leslie's *Illustrated Weekly* in New York.

Susan Williams, " The Truth Be Told: The Union Pacific Railroad Photographs of Andrew J. Russell," *View Camera*, Sacramento, California, January/February, 1886.

Barry R. Coombs, *Westward to Promontory: Building the Union Pacific Across the Plains and Mountains*, American West Publishing Company and The Oakland Museum, Palo Alto, California, 1969.

Richards, Bradley W., M.D., *The Savage View: Charles R. Savage, Pioneer Mormon Photographer*, Carl Mautz Publishing, Nevada City, California, 1995.

Weston J. Naef, *Era of Exploration: The Rise of Landscape Photography in the American West, 1860 - 1885*, Albright - Knox Art Gallery and The Metropolitan Museum of Art, New York City, 1975.

SAINSBURY & JOHNSON
Partnership active in Salt Lake City, 1890; Hyrum Sainsbury and Charles Ellis Johnson.

SAINSBURY, HYRUM
Apprentice with Charles R. Savage; employed by George E. Anderson, 1887; partner with Charles Ellis Johnson as Sainsbury & Johnson, c. 1884-93.

SAMUELSON, C.
Active in Sontaquin, 1880.

SAVAGE & OTTINGER
Partnership of Charles R. Savage and George M. Ottinger, 1862-70.

SAVAGE, CHARLES R.
Born in Southampton, England, August 16, 1832; died in Salt Lake City, February 3, 1909. After converting to the Mormon faith, Savage migrated to New York City, 1855, where he learned photography from either or both T. B. H. Stenhouse and Edward Covington. In 1860, Savage and family moved to Council Bluffs, Iowa, in preparation for crossing the plains to Utah. In a tent in Council Bluffs, he made portraits of Mormon immigrants before the departure of his wagon train. Savage was a partner of Marsena Cannon at his studio on Main Street, Salt Lake City, 1860-61; partner with George Ottinger,

an artist, operating as Savage & Ottinger, 1862-mid 1870s. Savage photographed the streets of Salt Lake City and traveled throughout Utah, capturing scenes of native and pioneer life. Ottinger turned his attention to acting, and the name of the gallery on East Temple Street changed to the Pioneer Art Gallery. In 1866, Savage traveled by Overland Stage to California; he became friends with Carleton E. Watkins before departing on a steamer to the Isthmus of Panama, then to New York City. He purchased new equipment, outfitted a traveling photo wagon, and returned to Utah across the plains, photographing scenes in Nebraska, South Dakota and Wyoming. Savage was invited to the celebration of the Joining of the Rails at Promontory, 1869, and made one of the most famous photographs in the history of western America; a woodcut of the image was a centerfold in *Harper's Weekly*. He took the first photographs of the land that later became Zion National Park in southern Utah. In 1883, the Pioneer Art Gallery burned and his negatives were lost; by the end of the year he opened the new Art Bazar in the same location. Many of his apprentices went on to successful careers, including George Edward Anderson, James Fennemore, Hyrum Sainsbury, and Walter Stringham. Savage took many trips and photographed throughout the west, especially in California and Arizona; he utilized every format developed during his career, including stereviews, mammoth plates, ambrotypes and lantern slides. His sons Ralph and George helped in the studio and eventually took over operation, 1906.

Richards, Bradley W., M.D., *The Savage View: Charles R. Savage, Pioneer Mormon Photographer*, Carl Mautz Publishing, Nevada City, California, 1995.

Richards, Bradley W., M.D., " Charles R. Savage, The Other Promontory Photographer," *Utah Historical Quarterly*, Spring, 1992.

Nelson B. Wadsworth, *Through Camera Eyes*, Brigham Young University Press, Salt Lake City, 1975.

SAVAGE, GEORGE
Son of Charles R. Savage who worked in his father's studio.

SAVAGE, RALPH
Son of Charles R. Savage who worked in his father's studio.

SEDGWICK, STEPHEN J.
Assistant to Andrew J. Russell when Russell was photographer for the Union Pacific Railroad during construction of the line across the Rocky Mountains. He later purchased Russell's negatives from O. C. Smith, paymaster for the Union Pacific, and published stereoviews with his own imprint, also making lantern slides for his lecture tours. Sedgwick became a friend of Charles R. Savage at Promontory, corresponding with him until Savage's death.

SHIPLER, HARRY
Born in Mercer, Pennsylvania, 1878; died in Salt Lake City, July 14, 1961. Son of James William Shipler, father of George William and Robert Thomas Shipler, and grandfather of William Hollis Shipler, all Utah photographers in the 20th century. See below.

SHIPLER, JAMES WILLIAM
Born in Mercer, Pennsylvania, July 20, 1849; died in Salt Lake City, 1913. Operated a gallery in McKeesport, Pennsylvania, c. 1870-87. Intermittently in Colorado in many partnerships, 1872-80; Montana, 1889; Hooper Block, Salt Lake City, 1890. His son Harry became a top news photographer by 1899, and operated the studio from 1934 into the next generation when his own sons, George William " Bill" and Robert Thomas " Bud," ran the business. George's son, William Hollis, now runs the business.

SILVIS, J. B.
Employed as the official photographer of the railroad, and partner of C. W. Carter, 1867-68. See Nebraska and Traveling.

Barry A. Swackhamer, " J. B. Silvis, The Union Pacific's Nomadic Photographer," *Journal of the West*, April, 1994

SMITH & CARESWELL
Active in Ogden.

SMITH, G. S.
Active in Salt Lake City, 1867-80.

SMITH, J.
Active in Ogden.

SMITH, O. C.
Paymaster of the Union Pacific Railroad who purchased the negatives of Andrew J. Russell and published Russell's stereoviews under his own imprint. Later sold the negatives to Stephen J. Sedgewick.

SMITH, WILLIAM
Operated a gallery in Kanesville, Iowa, 1852. Partner of daguerreotypist Marsena Cannon, 1853.

SOOY, BENTON F.
Active in Ogden, 1883-1909; partner in the company of La Roche, Frank & Sooy, 1883, later called Sooy & Laroche.

SPOONER, JOHN PITCHER
Partner in Reilly & Spooner, California photographers who made views of Utah and Niagara Falls, 1860-70s.

STEPHENS, DAVID H.
Active in Ogden, 1883.

STEPHENS, JAMES OTHA
Purchased studio from Vaughn on Washington Boulevard, between 24th and 25th Streets in Ogden; active 1867-86.

STONE, E.
Active in Ogden, 1883.

STRINGHAM & HOWARTH
Active in Manti and Salt Lake City, 1890.

STRINGHAM, JOHN
Apprentice of Charles R. Savage; active in Manti, 1880.

STURGESS, C. & TAYLOR, G. T.
Active in Salt Lake City, 1859.

SUTTERLY BROTHERS
Partnership operating a studio in Salt Lake City, 1867; J. K. and C. Sutterly. Studio taken over by C. W. Carter, 1867. See Nevada and California.

SYMONS, CHARLES W.
Born in England, c. 1845; died in Salt Lake City, July 22, 1934. Travelled aboard the same ship as C. W. Carter, 1864, making the passage to America with a Mormon group. He was Carter's apprentice, 1869-74; partner with Alexander Fox on Main Street, Salt Lake City, 1874-82, operating as Fox & Symons. After Fox died, Symons continued business under the partnership name, 1882-83. He was called to missionary duty, 1889, and his daughter, Sarah Symons Hillstead, operated the studio in his absence. Symons closed his studio December 31, 1906. Later he made mug shots of local prisoners.

T & Y
Thompson & Young, active in Provo, 1895.

TAYLER, HATTIE (MISS)
Active in Salt Lake City, 1870.

TAYLOR, GEORGE S.
Active in Provo, 1885.

TAYLOR, G. T.
Partner with C. Sturgess in Salt Lake City, 1859.

THATCHER
Partner in Cardon & Thatcher operating in Logan, 1883.

THOMAS, H. H.
Active in Ogden, Utah Territory, 1890-1910; served as superintendant of the State Industrial School. Later moved the studio to Salt Lake City.

THOMAS, HARRIS H.
Son of H. H. Thomas; worked in his father's studio in Ogden, c. 1900.

THOMPSON & YOUNG
Active in Provo, 1895; also known as T & Y.

TYE, JESSE
Active in Payson.

VAUGHAN
First photographer in Ogden, working out of a covered wagon, 1862. Sold studio to James Otha Stephens, 1867.

WARNER
Stereo photographer active in Ogden.

WHITE, A. D.
Active in Ogden, 1886.

WHITE, H. J.
Studio at 26 Wright's Block, Ogden, 1895.

WILLES, WILLIAM S.
Active in Heber City, 1885-95. Also spelled Willis.

WILSON, LAURENCE
Studio in Salt Lake City at 361 East 2nd South Street, c. 1895.

WOODMANSEE, FRANK
Assistant to James H. Crockwell, c. 1886.

WRIGHT, A. R.
First to advertise ambrotypes in Salt Lake City, 1857.

YOUNG
Partner with Thompson, operating as T & Y.

YOUNG, SAMUEL
Active in Peters and Willard, 1883-86.

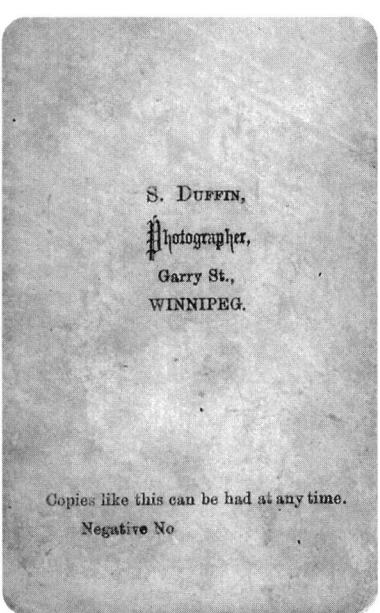

S. DUFFIN,
Photographer,
Garry St.,
WINNIPEG.

Copies like this can be had at any time.
Negative No

*Special thanks to Joan Schwartz and the staff at the National Archives of Canada
for their substantial contribution and editing to this section.*

ABBOT, JOHN
Active in Emerson, Manitoba, 1884.

ALBERTA PHOTOGRAPHIC COMPANY
Active in Calgary at Stephen Avenue, 1885.

AMERICAN ART GALLERY
Active in Winnipeg, Manitoba, c. 1885, possibly operated by G. W. Searl.

ANDERSON, GEORGE
Active in Ft. MacLeod, Alberta, 1884.

ARMSTRONG, CHARLES L.
Active in Emerson, Manitoba, 1880, 1882.

BALDWIN AND BLONDAL
Studio at 207 6th Avenue, N., Winnipeg, c. 1895.

BARBER, HARRY
Active in Winnipeg, Manitoba, 1883.

BAUSLAUGH, A.
Active in Winnipeg, Manitoba, on Hargrave Street, 1883. Possibly employed as operator for Nicholls & Parkin, 436 Main Street, 1884; 434 Main Street, 1885. Also spelled Bauslough.

BENETTO, ISRAEL
Active in Winnipeg, Manitoba, 1882-85. Partner in Bennetto & Company, Johnston & Bennett, and owner of Elite Galleries. Name also spelled Bennetto, Bennett, Berretto.

BENNETTO & COMPANY
Active in Winnipeg, 1882-85, operated by Israel Benetto at 4 McDermott Street. Second gallery at the corner of Main and Bannatyne Streets, Duffin's Block, 1883-84; 169 Ross Street, 1884-85. Also known as Elite Galleries, 1883. Photographers and photographic stock dealers, 1885. Also spelled Bennett.

BERST, J. C. F.
Active in Winnipeg, Manitoba, 98 Princess Street, Grand Union Hotel, 1885. Possibly the same as John, James, or A. J. Best.

BEST & BROTHER
Landscape photographers active in Winnipeg, Manitoba, 12 and 13 Burridge Block, corner of King and James Streets, 1883. Uncertain which of the Best brothers were involved, may have been either James or John with R. Best.

BEST, A. J.
Active in Winnipeg, Manitoba; partner in Ross, Best & Company, 1 McWilliam Street, 1885.

BEST BROTHERS
Active in Winnipeg, Manitoba, 1882, at 328 Main Street; James, William and John Best, photographers and real estate agents.

BEST, JAMES
Active in Winnipeg, Manitoba, 1882, at 328 Main Street; possibly a partner in Best & Brother, 1883; partner in Ross, Best & Company; and Best Brothers. Landscape photographer at Coffee House, Winnipeg, Manitoba, 1883. Possibly the same as J. Best, A. J. Best, J. C. F. Berst.

BEST, JOHN
Active in Winnipeg, Manitoba, 1882-84. Possibly a partner in Best & Brother, 1883; partner in Ross, Best & Company, Nixon & Best, and Best Brothers, 328 Main Street, 1882; as Nixon & Best, 229 Main Street, 1882; 7 McWilliam Street, 1884; 98 Primrose Street, Grand Hotel, 1883.

BEST, R.
Active in Winnipeg, Manitoba, 1882; 328 Main Street, partner in Best & Brother with John, A. J., or James Best.

BEST, WILLIAM
Active in Winnipeg, Manitoba, 1882, 328 Main Street; partner in Best Brothers.

BINGHAM, F. J.
Active in Emerson, Manitoba, 1882, Winnipeg Street.

BOWLES, HENRY J.
Active in Winnipeg, Manitoba. Located on Main Street N., 1876-77; 95 McDermott Street, 1880. Also spelled Bowls.

BROCK & COMPANY.
Active in Brandon, Manitoba, 1884, Rossre Avenue between 7th and 8th, operated by J. A. Brock.

BROCK, J. A.
Active in Brandon, Manitoba, 1884, operating the Brock & Company studio.

CAREY, JOSEPH
Active in Battleford, Northwest Territories, 1880, 1882; also in Prince Albert, Northwest Territories, 1882.

CARR, R. E. (MRS.)
Active in Winnipeg, Manitoba, 1884-85, at 574 ½ Main Street.

CLARKE, W.
Active in Battleford, Northwest Territories, 1880, 1882.

COLPETS, THOMAS R.
Active as photographer and postmaster in Ninette, Manitoba, 1884. Probably the same person as T. R. Colpitts of Pelican Lake. Post office of Pelican Lake is called Ninette.

COLPITTS, T. R.
See Thomas R. Colpets.

COOPER, A. D.
Active in Manitoba, 1882-83; in Portage La Prairie on Manitoba Street, 1882; in Brandon on Eighth Street, 1883.

DAVIS, W. H.
Active in London, Canada West on Dundas Street, 1865-66; in Paris, Ontario, 1873-74.

DENROCHE, W. S.
Printer for Nicholls & Parkin in Winnipeg, Manitoba, 1884, on 436 Main Street.

DIGGAN, JAMES
Active in Winnipeg, Manitoba, 1873-74.

DOHERTY, J. H.
Active in Winnipeg, Manitoba, Notre Dame Street East, 1876-77; in Portage La Prairie, Manitoba, 1880-82. Located at Manitoba Street and Portage Street, 1882.

DUFFIN & COMPANY
Studio in Winnipeg, Manitoba, operated by Simon Duffin, 1880-85. See Simon Duffin for locations. Also listed as S. Duffin & Company.

DUFFIN, SIMON
Active in Winnipeg, Manitoba, 1876-85. Located at Main Street West, 1876; Main Street South, 1876-78; 325 Main Street, 1880; 325 and/or 327 Main Street, 1882; 2 Bannatyne Street West, 1882, 1885; 474 Main Street, 1884.

DUROCHER, C. G.
Active in Winnipeg, Manitoba, 1882, at 8 Adelaide Street.

ECKERSON & COMPANY

ELITE GALLERIES
See I. Bennetto & Company.

ELLIOT

ELLIS, CHARLES
Landscape photographer in Winnipeg, Manitoba, 1882, on McDermott Street.

GARRETT, M.
Active in Winnipeg, Manitoba, 1883.

GRAHAM, THOMAS J.
Active in Neepawa, Manitoba, 1884.

GRINDLEY
Active in Calgary, Alberta, 1885, operating the Mona Gallery with Haines on Atlantic Street opposite C.P.R. Station. Also spelled Gridley.

HAINES & GRINDLEY
Partners in the Mona Gallery in Calgary, Alberta, Atlantic Street opposite the C.P.R. Station, 1885.

HALL & LOWE
Partnership of S. Lowe and J. D. Hall, active in Winnipeg, Manitoba, 499 Main Street, 1883-85; also at 82 Jemima Street, 1883-84; 13 Carey Street, 1884.

HALL, J. D.
Partner in Johnston & Hall, Winnipeg, Manitoba, 1882, at 497 Main Street; also listed at 7 Francis Street, 1882; partner with S. Lowe in Hall & Lowe at 499 Main Street, 1883-85. Also listed as J. W. Hall.

HARMON, BYRON
Born in Tacoma, Washington, February 9, 1876; died in Banff, Alberta, July 10, 1942. Studio in Tacoma, mid-1890s; became an itinerant toward the end of the century, traveling through the Southwest, East and back West through Canada. From early in the century, Harmon worked out of Banff, Alberta. By 1907 he advertised the largest collection of Canadian Rockies postcards in existence. Official photographer of the Alpine Club of Canada, Harmon's images illustrated the issues of *The Canadian Alpine Journal* for many years. His images also illustrated articles for *The National Geographic*.
    Robinson, Bart, *Great Days in the Rockies: The Photographs of Byron Harmon 1906-1934*, Oxford University Press, Toronto, 1978.

HAYNES, F. JAY
See Minnesota.

HAYNES, GEORGE
Photographic printer active in Brandon, Manitoba, 1884.

HENRY, E. E.
Operated a studio in Kansas; may have been active in Manitoba, pre-1860.

HIME, HUMPHREY LLOYD
Born in Moy, Ireland, September 17, 1833; died in Toronto, October 31, 1903. Migrated to England in 1853, to Canada in 1854, and in 1855 was working as a surveyor at the Indian Reserve of Owen Sound and Sangen. Hime learned photography from his surveying partners, William Armstrong and Daniel Beere, and became the official photographer on the Assiniboine and Saskatchewan Exploring Expedition of 1858. Using the wet-collodion process, he produced the earliest photographs of the Canadian interior. In 1861 he left the survey firm, apparently abandoned photography, and became a successful financier.
    Richard J. Huyda, *Camera in the Interior: 1858, H. L. Hime, Photographer*, Coach House Press, Totonto, 1975.

JACKSON, G. J.
Active in Nelson, Manitoba, 1884.

JAMES, AMY (MRS.)

JEFFERSON, WILLIAM
Active in Stonewall, Manitoba, 1882, 1884.

JOHNSTON & BENNETT
Partnership of William Johnston and Israel Benetto in Winnipeg, Manitoba, 1882, with studio at 360 Main Street.

JOHNSTON & HALL
Partnership of William Johnston and J. D. or J. W. Hall, active in Winnipeg, Manitoba, 497 Main Street, 1882.

JOHNSTON, JAMES
Active in Emerson, Manitoba, 1882.

JOHNSTON, WILLIAM
Active in Winnipeg, Manitoba, 1882-83. Partner in Johnston & Hall, 497 Main Street, and at 95 Princess Street, 1882. Also listed as partner in Johnston & Bennett at 360 Main Street, 1882. Active in Emerson, Manitoba, on Winnipeg Street, 1882; in Selkirk, Manitoba, 1884.

JONES, THOMAS M.
Active in Winnipeg, Manitoba, 1883-85. Possibly a partner of G. W. Searl.

KERFOOT, D. (MISS)
Photographer in Emerson, Manitoba, 1882.

KERFOOT, M.
Active in Emerson, Manitoba, 1880-82. Located at Dominion Street, 1882.

LOWE, S.
Partner in Hall & Lowe in Winnipeg, Manitoba, 499 Main Street, 1883-85.

MARTEL, W. A.
Operating on the corner of Euclid and Main, c. 1900+.

McCALL, J. A.
Active in Winnipeg, Manitoba, 1882, on McDermott Street.

McGINN, CHARLES
Active in Winnipeg, Manitoba, 1885, at 436 Main Street.

McPHERSON, W.
Active in Winnipeg, Manitoba, 1876-77, on Arthur Street.

MONA GALLERY
Owned by Haines & Grindley, photographic artists active in Calgary, Alberta, on Atlantic Avenue opposite C.P.R. Station, 1885. Also spelled Gridley.

MOORE
Active in Emerson, Manitoba, on Winnipeg Street, 1882.

MORRIS, E.
Active in Winnipeg, Manitoba, 1883. Residence listing at 23 Fonseca Street.

NICHOLLS & PARKIN
Partnership of J. W. Nicholls and Fred W. Parkin, "artistic" photographers, proprietors of Popular Photographic Parlor in Winnipeg, Manitoba, 434 Main Street, 1883-85.

NICHOLLS, J. W.
See Nicholls & Parkin.

NIXON & BEST
Studio active in Winnipeg, Manitoba, 229 Main Street, 1882, with partners Thomas Nixon, Jr. and John Best. Also known as Winnipeg Art Gallery.

NIXON, THOMAS, JR.
Active in St. Boniface West, Manitoba, 1880; in Winnipeg, Manitoba, as Nixon & Best and Winnipeg Art Gallery, 1882, at 229 Main Street opposite Notre Dame Street E.

PAGE, E.
Active in Prince Albert, Saskatchewan, 1884.

PARKIN & COMPANY
Partnership of Fred W. Parkin and J. W. Nicholls, operating the Popular Photographic Parlor in Winnipeg, Manitoba, 1883-85, at 436 Main Street.

PARKIN, FRED W.
Active in Winnipeg, Manitoba with partner J. W. Nicholls at 436 Main Street, 1883-85. Operated the Popular Photographic Parlor.

PENROSE, JAMES
Active in Winnipeg, Manitoba, 1876-82. Studio located at Main Street South and Main Street West, 1876-77; McDermott Street, 1877-78, 1882; 24 Annie Street, 1880, 1882.

PITLADO, C. B.
Active in Winnipeg, Manitoba, at 94 Princess Street, 1882.

POPULAR PHOTOGRAPHIC PARLOR
Studio operated by J. W. Nicholls and Fred W. Parkin, Winnipeg, Manitoba, 1883-85. Also known as Parkin & Company and Nicholls & Parkin.

PULLAR, WILLIAM
Active in Winnipeg, Manitoba, McWilliam Street West, south side, 1885.

PYMAN, H.
Active in Winnipeg, Manitoba, McWilliam Street West near Main Street, 1884.

ROSS, A. J.
See Ross, Best & Company.

ROSS, BEST & COMPANY
Studio in Winnipeg, Manitoba, operated by partners John Ross, A. J. Ross, John Best, and A. J. Best, 1882-85. Located at 1 and 7 McWilliam Street West.

ROSS, JOHN
Partner in Ross, Best & Company, in Winnipeg, Manitoba, 1883-85.

ROWE, J. F.
Active in Portage La Prairie, on Main Street, 1884.

SALTER, J. KERR
Active in Rat Portage, Manitoba (province uncertain - mention of Keewatin District), 1880, 1882. Also listed as J. R.

SCHAEFFER, MARY T. SHARPLES
Born in West Chester, Pennsylvania, October 4, 1861; died in Banff, Januar 23, 1939. Married to Dr. Charles Schaeffer in 1889, whom she met on an excursion to the mountains of Alberta. Beginning in 1891, the Schaeffers traveled often to the Canadian Rockies where they studied the mountain flora which Mary painted, drew and photographed. After the death of her husband in 1903, she continued excursions into the mountains and completed an important study which was published as *Alpine Flora of the Canadian Rocky Mountians* in 1907. Schaeffer continued her trips, writing and photographing, publishing Old Indian Trails of the Canadian Rockies in 1911. She married her Banff mountian guide, Billy Warren, in 1915. She moved to Banff, where she lived with her husband, who became a successful businessman.

SEARL & COMPANY
Partnership in Winnipeg, Manitoba, 42 Dagmar Street, 1882; 574 ½ Main Street, 1884-85. Possibly George W. Searl and Jones.

SEARL & JONES
Studio in Winnipeg, Manitoba, 2 James Street East, 1884.

SEARL, GEORGE W.
Possibly a partner in Searl & Company, American Art Gallery, and Searl & Jones. Active in Winnipeg, Manitoba, as George W. Searl, Ellen Street, 1882.

SHAKESPEARE, NOAH
Operated Gentile's Photographic Studio, Victoria, British Columbia, 1868.

SMITH & COMPANY, S. A.
Active in Minnedosa, Manitoba, 1884.

SMYTHE, SIDNEY ALFRED
S. A. and his brother, A. J. Smythe, settled in Minnedosa, Manitoba, c. 1883, and became itinerant photographers, 1884. They moved to Calgary, 1885, and by 1887, S. A. Smythe was taking all of the photos. He opened a studio in Banff, 1889, but returned to Calgary in the early 1890s. See British Columbia.

SOULE, CORNELIUS J.
Active in Calgary, Alberta, 1884.

ST. JOHN, W. B.
Active in Minnedosa and Neepawa, c. 1895.

WEIDMAN, JAMES
Active in Rat Portage, Manitoba (province uncertain - mention of Keewatin District noted in another listing), 1882-84. Also spelled Weiman.

WELBERG, GODFREY M.
Active in Stonewall, Manitoba, 1884.

WILLIAMS, SAMUEL
Active in Midnapore (Fish Creek), Alberta, 1884.

WINNIPEG ART GALLERY
Operated by partners Thomas Nixon, Jr. and John Best in Winnipeg, Manitoba, 1882, at 229 Main Street opposite Notre Dame Street E.

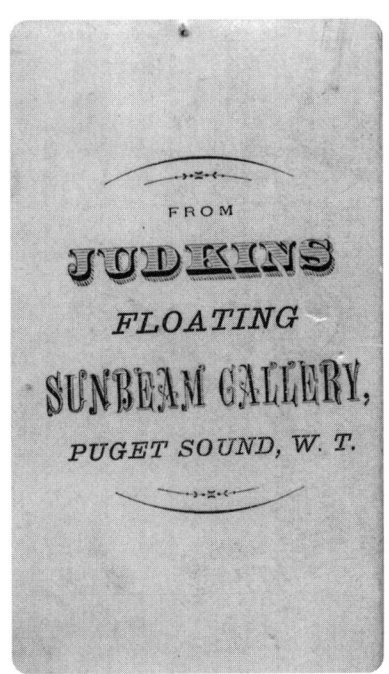

Much of the the information in this section was provided by Michael Cirelli.

AABERG, J. P.
Operated the Palace in Tacoma, 1890.

ALBRECHT, A. A.
Born c. 1864; died in Bellingham, Washington, 1951. Primarily a traveling photographer; itinerant in the Seattle area, 1918, his last active year. See British Columbia.

ALVERSON
Photographer in Seattle; produced Indian portraits and landscapes, now scarce.

AMRHEIN, JOSEPH
Born in Switzerland, 1880. Stereo photographer in Francis, 1910-20; issued views of logging, lumber mills, railroads and towns.

ANDERSON & HAMACHER
Studio in Ellensburg, Washington Territory, 1885; partnership of Hilda Anderson and E. J. Hamacher.

ANDERSON, HILDA
Partner with E. J. Hamacher in Ellensburg, Washington Territory, 1885, operating as Anderson & Hamacher.

ARMSTRONG & LUNN
Operated the Elite in Seattle, 1885. Partnership of John F. Armstrong and Axel M. Lunn, 1516 ½ Front Street, 1891-92.

ARMSTRONG, J. F.
Partner in Armstrong & Lunn, 1885.

ARMSTRONG, J. N.
Active in Vancouver, 1880.

ARTHUR, JOHN
Active in Castle Rock, 1890.

AYP EXPOSITION SERIES
Seattle company issuing views of Alaska-Yukon-Pacific exposition, c. 1909; unknown photographer.

BAILEY, A. C.
Active in Spokane, 1880-95. Listed by the National Stereoscopic Society as F. C. Bailey.

BALL & SONS
Studio in Seattle, 1892-1900.

BALL, J. P.
Died in Hawaii, c. 1904. Came to Seattle from Montana, early 1890s; may be the black daguerreotypist in Cincinnati, Ohio, 1850s.

BARNES
Active in Waterville, 1890.

BARNES, LAFE W.
Died in Oroville, California, December 5, 1951. Photographer in Snohomish, 1890.

BARRON, CHARLES A.
Active in Snohomish, 1907.

BARROWS, I. D.
Stereo photographer in Tacoma.

BART, COLE W.
Active in Puyallup, advertising "All Branches of Photography First Grade Work." Reportedly issued rare stereos.

BECHTEL, G. W.
Active in Colfax, 1886; also in Spokane.

BEERS, J. W.
Stereo photographer active in Walla Walla.

BENNET
Stereo photographer in Fort Flagler.

BERTRAND, E. E.
Stereo photographer in Spokane.

BILLINGHURST, JOHN H.
Photographer and publisher of stereoviews in Anacortes.

BLOME, JOHN HENRY
Active in Everett, 1893. See British Columbia and California.

BLOSSER, J. A.
Stereo photographer active in Snohomish, producing "Views of Cascade Mountains, Puget Sound, and the Pacific Northwest," c. 1905-06; also known as Blosser Scenic Art Company.

BONNELL, FREDERICK
Stereo photographer in Puyallup.

BONNER, A. G.
Stereo photographer in Tacoma.

BOOEN, J. O.
Active Snohomish County, Washington, 1895. See British Columbia.

BOYD & BRAAS
Partnership of William F. Boyd and George H. Braas in Seattle, 614 Front Street, 1890-93.

BOYD, WILLIAM F.
Partner in Boyd & Braas, Seattle, 1890-93, with George H. Braas, operating as. Operated alone at 713 First Avenue, c. 1900.

BRAAS, GEORGE H.
Active in Seattle with partner William F. Boyd, operating as Boyd & Braas, 1890-93.

BRADLEY & BRADLEY
Operated the Hart Studio in Seattle.

BRADLEY, LEVI
Partner in Monnet & Bradley with Orrin E. Monnett in Fairhaven, 1890.

BRITAIN, P. L.
Active in eastern Washington, 1895.

BRODECK, HENRY H.
Died in Walla Walla, 1886. Operated as Brodeck & Company, a prominent portrait gallery in Walla Walla, 1880; "Photographed for the Northwest Trading Co."

BRYANT, ARCHIE
Active in Floyd.

BUSHNELL, CORRY A.
Active in Ellensburg, Washington Territory, 1891-95.

CALDWELL, IRA
Billed as a "Scenic Photographer," Seattle, c. 1895.

CANARIS, CATHERINE
Active in Vancouver and Portland, Oregon.

CANARIS, FRANK H.
Active in Portland, Oregon, and Long Beach, Washington.

CARPENTER, A. L.
Active in Tacoma.

CARRATT
Partner in Miller & Carrat, Goldendale, 1895; also active in Oregon.

CATTON, C. W.
Stereo photographer active in Tacoma, 1891.

CAWTHORN
Active in Kelso.

CAWTHORN, J. B.
Active in Palouse, 1895.

CHURCHLEY, A. G.
Active in Kelso, 1890.

CLARK, EDWARD A.
Born in Pennsylvania; died in Port Madison, 1860. He moved to California, 1850; to Seattle, 1852, and served as Justice of the Peace and auditor; operated a daguerreotype studio, c. 1854-60.

CLARK, L. WILSON
Active in Olympia, 1881-87. Also active in Albany, Oregon, c. 1887-89.

COOMBS & COMPANY, H. F.
Active in North Yakima, 1895.

CRITTENDEN, B. B.
"Landscape and Architectural Photographer" active in Tacoma.

CROWELL, GEORGE W.
One of the proprietors of the Elite Photo Studio in Tacoma, 1884-90, partner with his brother, J. L, operating as Crowell Brothers.

CROWELL, J. LEONARD
Partner in Crowell Brothers with G. W., operating the Elite Photo Studio in Tacoma, 1884-90.

CURTIS, ASAHEL
Born in Le Sueur County, Minnesota, 1874; died in Seattle, 1941. Asahel moved to Port Orchard, 1888, at age 13; he joined his brother, Edward S. Curtis, 1895, learning photography and photo engraving. Edward sent Asahel to the Klondike to photograph the gold rush, 1897; a dispute over proper credits on Asahel's images led to a break between the brothers. Asahel worked for Seattle newspapers, 1900; partner with William P. Romans and later with Walter Miller. He began the Asahel Curtis Photo Company, 1920. Imogen Cunningham worked in his lab, developing prints for brother Edward, by whom she was employed. Asahel was active in civic affairs and was an avid mountain climber; he recorded a broad range of life in Washington, particularly the Puget Sound region, and was known for producing fine hand tinted landscapes of Mount Rainier and other Washington scenes.

Archie Satterfield, *An Asahel Curtis Portfolio*, Seattle, Chronicle Books, San Francisco, California, 1985.

Richard Frederick and Jeanne Engerman, *Asahel Curtis, Photographs of the Great Northwest*, Washington State Historical Society, Tacoma, Washington, 1983.

David Sucher, ed., *The Asahel Curtis Sampler: Photographs of Puget Sound Past*, Puget Sound Access, Seattle, 1973.

CURTIS, EDWARD S.

Born in Wisconsin, 1868; died in Los Angeles, California, October 19, 1952. Older brother of Asahel Curtis. Edward moved to the Puget Sound area with his ailing father, 1887, and built a cabin in Port Orchard. He formed a photography partnership with Rasmus Rothi in Seattle, 1891; partner with Thomas Guptill, 1892-97. Curtis photographed Princess Angeline, daughter of Chief Seattle (namesake of Washington's metropolis and the leader of the Suquamish Indians of the Puget Sound area), 1895 or 1896. Thus began Curtis' fascination and later obsession with photographing Native Americans. Curtis befriended such notables as C. Hart Merriam, George Bird Grinell, Gifford Pinchot and John Muir. Theodore Roosevelt and J. P. Morgan, were his patrons, the former supporting and the latter financing Curtis' monumental work, *The North American Indian*. The set of twenty volumes and accompanying portfolios were illustrated with beautiful gravures on three kinds of paper; Japanese tissue, vellum and Holland. Adolf Muhr managed Curtis' studio during his frequent and lengthy trips throughout the West to photograph Indians. Muhr sold large numbers of Curtis' work to keep the cash flowing and the family alive. Imogen Cunningham was one of Curtis' technicians. When Muhr died in 1913, management of the studio passed to Ella McBride and Curtis' daughter, Beth. Edwin Johanson was the chief studio photographer and the studio began selling "Curt-tones," also known as goldtones or orotones, stunning images with gold highlights. In 1916, Curtis' wife divorced him and was awarded nearly all their property. Curtis made films, produced books and continued work on *The North American Indian*, completing it in 1930. He was exhausted and went into seclusion to regain his health. After a long rest in Denver, Colorado and Los Angeles, Curtis began mining, and eventually settled with his daughter, Beth, in Whittier, California.

Christopher Cardoza, Ed., *Native Nations: First Americans as Seen by Edward S. Curtis*, Callaway Editions/ Bullfinch Press /Little Brown and Company, Boston, New York, Toronto, London, 1993.

Barry Pritzker, *Edward S. Curtis*, Brompton Books, Greenwich, Connecticut, 1993.

Barbara A. Davis, Edward S. Curtis, *The Life and Times of a Shadow Catcher*, Chronicle Books, San Francisco, California, 1985.

Christopher M. Lyman, *The Vanishing Race and Other Illusions: Photographs of Indians by Edward S. Curtis*, Pantheon Books, New York, in association with the Smithsonian Institution, 1982.

Florence Curtis Graybill and Victor Boesen, *Edward Sheriff Curtis, Visions of a Vanishing Race*, American Legacy Press, New York, 1981.

A. D. Coleman and T. C. McLuhan, *Portraits from North American Indian Life*, Outerbridge & Lazard, Inc. in association with the American Museum of Natural History, New York, 1972.

Joseph Epes Brown, *The North American Indians, Photographs by Edward S. Curtis*, Aperture Books, Millerton, New York, 1972.

T. C. McLuhan, *Touch the Earth: A Self-Portrait of Indian Existence*, Outerbridge & Dienstfrey, New York, 1971.

Ralph W. Andrews, *Curtis' Western Indians*, Superior Publishing Company, Seattle, Washington, 1961.

Edward S. Curtis, *Indian Days of the Long Ago*, World Book Company, Yonkers-on-Hudson, New York, 1927.

DANIHY, BARTHOLOMEW

Born in Ireland, August 15, 1847; died in Vader, Washington, March 4, 1930. His family settled in Missouri after coming to the U.S. when he was a small boy. Moved to Washington Territory with his wife, 1880; fished with the Indians and marketed their catches. Active in Toledo, c. 1900. Close friend of Buffalo Bill who visited Danihy while he was in nearby Centralia for a show. Danihy moved to Vader, 1919, operating a photography shop.

DAVIDSON, ISAAC GRUNDY
Active in Tacoma, 1890. See Oregon.

DAVIS, WALTER
Active in Seattle, 1888. See British Columbia.

DAVIS, WILLIAM H.
Active in Bellingham, early 1870s; New Westminster and Victoria, British Columbia, 1875; Sehome, 1876-77; Nanaimo, 1877+.

DEMOREST
Active in Garfield, c. 1895.

DENNIE, OLIVER
Active in Tacoma and Olympia, Washington, 1873. Also known as O. Denny. See Oregon and California.

DIXON PORTRAIT GALLERY
Active in Colfax, 1885.

DOBBS, B. B.
Died in Seattle, December 30, 1937. Active in New Whatcom, 1895.

DOLLARHIDE, E. F.
Studio at the corner of Commercial and Washington Streets, Seattle, c. 1880.

DORSEZ, F. H.
Originally from San Francisco, California. Operated the Souvenir Art Studio in Seattle with E. Schwerin, 1883-86.

DOWNEY, B. A.
Active in Chehalis, 1890.

DUCKERING, WILLIAM
Died in Seattle, March 26, 1933. Active in Olympia, 1895. Manager of Wilse's Seattle Photographic Company, 1900-13; located in the McDonald Building at 811 Second Avenue.

DUVALL, C. M.
Active in Goldendale, 1890.

EASTMAN, FARNHAM, J.
Active in Cheney, 1884.

EATON, NATHAN
Died in Elma, March 9, 1883. Active in Chambers Prairie near Olympia, 1865.

ELDER, ARTIST
Active in Dayton, 1892.

ELITE PHOTO STUDIO
Active in Tacoma, 1884-90, operated by George W. and J. Leonard Crowell; also known as Crowell Brothers.

ELITE STUDIO
Active in Spokane, 1890.

EMERY, WILLIAM G.
Studio in Pullman, 1895; Vancouver, 1907-13. See Oregon and Idaho.

ENTERPRISE PHOTO STUDIO
Operated by S. C. Smith in North Yakima, 1904-07; produced views of scenery, San Francisco fire and Yosemite.

EVINROOD, E. W.
Amateur stereo photographer in Seattle, 1910.

EWING, D. B.
Stereo photographer in Everett.

FERGUSON, RICHARD M.
Studio in Tacoma, 1903.

FORD, GILES WHEELER
Died in Steilacoom, May 17, 1871. Daguerreotypist and ambrotypist operating in Steilacoom next to Wilson & Dunlap's on Main Street, summer 1858; in Olympia opposite J. B. Webber & Company, 1858. He left for Semiahmoo and Victoria, British Columbia, September 1858. Partner with E. A. Light in Steilacoom, 1859; operated Ford's studio located in the rear of Mr. Williamson's store, 1860. Later worked as a real estate agent.

FOSLIDE, JOHN
Stereo photographer in Buckley.

FOX & SON, A. D.
Studio in Pomeroy, 1890.

FRANK, CHARLES E.
Active in Whatcom, 1883; Snohomish, 1876.

FRENCH, A.
Partner in La Roche & French, Tacoma, 1891.

FRYE & COMPANY, H. H.
Gallery in Woodland, 1875. See Hiram Hamilton Frye in California.

FULTON & McMURRY
Studio in Port Townsend, 1895; A. S. Fulton and J. M. McMurry.

GLYFE, ALEX.
Active in South Bend, c. 1895.

GODARD'S STUDIO
Active in Dayton, 1895.

GOODWIN, HOZA L.
Published stereoviews in Pullman.

GRAHAM, JOHN W.
Published stereoviews in Spokane.

GROSSMANN & OWINGS
Gallery in Spokane at 245 Riverside Avenue, c. 1890.

HADLEY, U. P. & HATTIE
U. P. died in Bellingham, October 15, 1912; Hattie died in Greys Harbor County, May 24, 1918. Operated studio in Tacoma, 1890s.

HAMACHER & LORING
E. J. Hamacher and Henry K. Loring in Walla Walla, c. 1870s.

HAMACHER, E. J.
Active in Ellensburg, Washington Territory, 1885, operating as Anderson & Hamacher with Hilda Anderson; operated alone, 1888.

HANSEN, ANDREW
Active in Tacoma, 1891-99; also known as Andrew Hansen & Son. Produced stereoviews.

HANSEN, C. W.
Active in Pomeroy, 1895.

HARGRAVE, J. R.
Active in Kelso, 1900.

HARMON
Active in Goldendale, Washington Territory, 1890.

HARMON, BYRON
Studio in Tacoma, mid-1890s. He was an itinerant toward the end of the century, traveling through the southwest, to the east and returning west through Canada. Based in Banff, Alberta, early 1900s. See Western Canada.

HARVEY BROTHERS
Partnership active in Blaine, c. 1880.

HARWOOD, FRANK
Stereo photographer in Seattle, c. 1906-20s; produced views of steamboat, Alaska-Yukon Exposition grounds, water tower, Courthouse, children at play, view of UPRR tunnel.

HASTINGS, OREGON COLUMBUS
Died in Victoria, British Columbia, August 5, 1912. Active in Port Townsend, 1883. See British Columbia.

HEGG, E. A.
Born in Bollnas, Sweden, September 17, 1867; died in San Diego, California, December 13, 1948. The Hegg family moved to Wisconsin, 1870. After training in art and photography, Hegg opened a studio in Washburn, Wisconsin, 1882, at age fifteen. Moved to the Puget Sound area, 1888; opened a studio in Sehome (New Whatcom), 1888; a second studio at Fairhaven, 1889 or 1890. He photographed the Lummi Indians, fishing around Bellingham Bay and logging, and made portraits of the local citizens. Hegg traveled to the Klondike, 1897, and took a large number of views of the miners during the gold rush and scenes of Alaska and the Yukon. He operated several studios in the North, and a studio in Bellingham at Elk and Holly Streets after his Klondike adventures. He sold the Bellingham studio, 1946. Hegg also traveled to Hawaii on assignment for a San Francisco newspaper, and may have operated a studio in Fresno, California for several years. See Alaska.

HEGG, PETER L.
Died in Bellingham, August 3, 1942. Operated studio with his brother, E. A. Hegg in New Whatcom, 1890.

HERRIN, DAVID C.
See Oregon.

HESTER, ERNST
Brother of Wilhelm Hester; active in Seattle, 1893.

HESTER, ROBERT M.
Active in Dayton, 1890.

HESTER, WILHELM
Born in Oldenburg, Germany, October 13, 1872; died in Seattle, February 25, 1947. Arrived in the U.S. with his brother Ernst, 1890, and settled in Montana for three years. The brothers arrived in Seattle, 1893, where Willhelm was listed as an artist and Ernst as photographer. Wilhelm photographed Puget Sound shipping, 1893-98. The brothers went to Alaska and successfully mined gold; Ernst started a brewery. Wilhelm returned to Seattle, 1898, and continued his commercial maritime photography business until at least 1915.
   Robert A. Weinstein, *Tall Ships on Puget Sound, The Marine Photographs of Wilhelm Hester, University of Washington Press, 1978.*

HICKS
Active in New Tacoma, Washington Territory, 1885.

HOBBS, I. N.
Stereo photographer active in Tacoma at 226 South 26th, c. 1890.

HOFSTEATER & COMPANY
Operated the Floating Gallery in Vancouver, 1886.

HOFSTEATER, O. M.
Active in Vancouver, 1885.

HOLMES, SAMUEL
Died in Olympia, November 5, 1873. Active in Olympia, 1854.

HORTON, G. D.
Active in Tacoma and Snohomish areas, operating the Palace Floating Gallery.

HOUGHTON, THOMAS A.
Traveling photographer in Washington Territory, 1885. See Oregon.

HOVER
Partner with William in Ives & Hover, Tacoma, c. 1895, 98, operating the Lick Gallery.

HOYT, HIRAM
Stereo photographer in Seattle.

HUDSON & MARTINSON
Partnership active in Tacoma at 1138 Railroad, 1891.

HUNTINGTON BROTHERS
Partnership active in Olympia, 1878.

HUNTINGTON, CHARLES J.
Died in LaConnor, Washington, November 1, 1878. Operated as Huntington Brothers in Olympia, 1878.

IMPERIAL PHOTOGRAPH COMPANY
Issued stereoviews in Seattle.

IVES & HOVER
Operated the Lick Gallery in Tacoma, 1895-98; William Ives.

JACKSON, ALBERT L.
Active in Tacoma. See Oregon.

JACKSON, WILLIAM P.
Active in Tacoma, Washington Territory, 1885.

JONES, JAMES
Publisher of views and "Dealer in all Kinds of stationery, Notions, Indian Curios, Groceries, Liquors and Cigars" in Port Townsend. Reportedly issued rare views of local scenery.

JUDKINS, DAVID ROBY
Born in Chesterville, Maine, January 17, 1836; died in Santa Maria, California, December 11, 1909. Brother of J. C. and Lorenzo; probably learned the daguerreian art from Lorenzo; apprenticed with W. H. Lane of Fitchburg, Massachusetts, and succeeded him in the studio, 1868. Opened a studio in Logansport, Indiana, 1877; moved to Seattle, 1879, and operated in five locations around Puget Sound, including his famous Floating Sunbeam Gallery. He was known for his outdoor views of life, industry and maritime activities. He sold the floating gallery, 1884, and opened a portrait studio at Second and Columbia Streets. Later was located at 522 Depot; Second and Marion Streets; 100 Ash; and 22 Depot. He went to the Yukon gold fields for a short time, 1895; in San Francisco, 1903-06; Santa Maria, 1906-09. See Oregon and California.

JUDKINS, E. G.
Died in Santa Maria, California, May 22, 1912. Nephew of D. R. and J. C. Judkins. See Oregon.

JUDKINS FLOATING SUNBEAM GALLERY
Operated by D. R. Judkins in Puget Sound, 1880. The gallery was on a barge that was towed to various locations. See British Columbia.

JUDKINS, J. C.
Died in Yuma, Arizona, August 7, 1906. Active in Seattle, 1890-1901. Brother of D. R. Judkins. See Oregon.

KAUTZ, IRA A.
Active in Seattle.

KELLY, MILLARD F.
Born in Ohio, 1857; died in Yakima, January 13, 1911. Active in Tacoma, 1885.

KELSO, T. M.
Amateur stereo photographer in Reynolds.

KINCADE, JOSEPH C.
Stereo photographer in Tacoma; studio located at 905 E Street, 1890; 212 South 11th Street, 1891-92; 1118 11th Street, 1893-94. Reportedly issued rare views of local scenery.

KING, C. E. & HATTIE
Active in Tacoma, 1890-1901.

KINSEY, CLARENCE
Kinsey was reared in Snoqualmie and learned photography from brothers Clarke and Darius. Partner with brother Clarke in Kinsey & Kinsey, studio in Grand Forks, Alaska.
> Norm Bolotin, *Klondike Lost, A Decade of Photographs by Kinsey & Kinsey*, Alaska Northwest Publishing Company, Anchorage, Alaska, 1980.

KINSEY, CLARKE
Born 1877. Partner with brother Darius in Snoqualmie and Seattle, 1895-98. Established a mining claim in Grand Forks, Alaska with his brother Clarence during the gold rush, 1898. They operated the Kinsey & Kinsey Studio for many years, capturing numerous images of Klondike life.
> Norm Bolotin, *Klondike Lost, A Decade of Photographs by Kinsey & Kinsey*, Alaska Northwest Publishing Company, 1980.

KINSEY, DARIUS
Born in Maryville, Missouri, July 23, 1869; died May 13, 1945. Arrived in Snoqualmie, 1889. Began photography, 1890, and was a partner with brother Clark by 1895, making logging and scenic photographs and portraits. Kinsey was making stereoviews, c. 1897, and by 1900, the 11 x 14 inch prints that made him famous. Married Tabitha Pritts, 1896, and she became the manager of production and darkroom throughout Kinsey's fifty year career. The couple moved to Woolley (later Sedro-Woolley), operated a portrait studio and created a large number of photographs of the Northwest timber industry. Kinsey made stereoviews of Yellowstone, 1904. Moved to 1607 East Alder Street in Seattle, 1906; 5811 Greenwood Avenue, 1918; studio was known as Timber Views Company after 1919. Kinsey also made panoramas and lantern slides.
> David Bohn and Rudolfo Petschek, *Kinsey Photographer*, Scrimshaw Press, 1978, Chronicle Books, San Francisco, California, two volumes in one, 1982.
> David Bohn and Rudolfo Petschek, *Kinsey Photographer, The Locomotive Portraits*, Chronicle Books, San Francisco, California, 1984.

KINSEY, TABITHA PRITTS
Born 1875; died November 23, 1963. Married to Darius Kinsey, 1896. She was the manager of the Kinsey studio and darkroom, processing an enormous number of prints from glass, and later, film negatives.

KIRK, DANIEL W.
Opened a studio in partnership with Anders Beers Wilse, 1897; sold out to Wilse after six months.

LA ROCHE & FRENCH
Partnership of Frank La Roche and A. French in Tacoma at 501 California Block, 1891. Offered "Free Hand Crayons and Water Colors. Artistic Lighting and Posing."

LA ROCHE, FRANK
Born in Philadelphia, Pennsylvania, June 20, 1853; died in Sedro Wooley, Washington, April 15, 1934. Active in Seattle, 1890; Sedro-Woolley; Alaska and Yukon, 1897. Partner in La Roche & French, 1891. See Alaska and British Columbia.

LANTERMAN, F. P.
Talented amateur stereo photographer in North Yakima.

LARSON, LOUIS
Stereo photographer in Tacoma at 1322 fi Pacific Avenue, 1896.

LEY, THOMAS A.
Active in Dayton, Washington Territory, 1885.

LICK GALLERY
Operated by Ives & Hover in Tacoma, 1895-98.

LINDAHL, CON.
Active in Tacoma, 1895.

LORAIN, LORENZO
Active in Fort Walla Walla, 1850s. See Oregon.

LORING, HENRY K.
Partners in Hamacher & Loring, active in Walla Walla, c. 1870s; also worked alone.

LORYEA, ARCHIBALD
Died in Spokane, November 26, 1900. Active in Spokane, 1897-1900. Brother of Milton Loryea. See California.

LORYEA, MILTON
Active in Spokane, 1890s; brother of Archie Loryea. See California.

LOUNDAGIN, JAMES O.
Died near Myncaster, British Columbia, April 30, 1912. Active in Waitsburg, 1900.

LUDDEN, A.
Stereo photographer active in Tacoma, c. 1898.

LUNN, AXEL M.
Born in Sweden, February 6, 1867; died in Bremerton, June 1947. Partner in Armstrong & Lunn.

LYNN, ELLISON A.
Died in Tacoma, June 10, 1923. Active in Seattle and Tacoma. Successor to Davidson at 1108 Pacific Avenue, Bernice Building, Tacoma, c. 1895.

MARGO & WUNDERLICH
Partnership operating gallery in Spokane Falls, 1886.

MARGO, J. C.
Active in Sprague, 1886.

MARKELL, J. W.
Active in Colfax, Washington Territory, 1885.

MARSH, DANIEL
Active in Colfax, 1885; Sedro-Woolley, 1907.

MARTENSEN, EMBERT
Stereo photographer in Tacoma, 1892.

MARTINSON
Partner in Hudson & Martinson at 1138 Railroad in Tacoma, 1891.

MATSURA, FRANK
Born in Japan, 1874; died in Okanogan, June 1913. Matsura arrived in Okanogan from Seattle, 1903; operated photography studio, 1904-12; known for portraits and landscapes.
    JoAnn Roe, *Frank Matsura, Frontier Photographer*, Madrona Publishers, 1981.

MATZGER, W. O.
Died in Dayton, June 28, 1917. Active in Dayton, 1880-83.

MAXWELL BROTHERS
Studio in Spokane Falls, 1886; Charles Thomas Maxwell and Joseph D. Maxwell. See Idaho.

MAXWELL, CHARLES THOMAS
Born in Piney, Tennessee, May 20, 1865; died 1914. One of ten children and connected to the Greer family of Pennsylvania who fought in the Revolutionary War. He moved to Walla Walla, Washington Territory, 1883, joining his brother Joseph D. Maxwell in his studio. The Maxwell brothers opened another gallery in Spokane Falls, 1884, and with two more brothers, G. Y. and W. W., established a third gallery in Dayton. The three studios continued operating until c. 1900.

MAXWELL, GRAYSON Y.
Operated Maxwell Brothers studio in Dayton with W. W. Maxwell; associated with brothers C. T. and J. D. Maxwell.

MAXWELL, JOSEPH D.
Opened a studio in Walla Walla, 1875; joined by his brother, C. T., 1878; opened a branch gallery in Spokane Falls, 1884. With two additional brothers, G. Y. and W. W., opened another gallery in Dayton; the three galleries operated until c. 1900.

MAXWELL, W. W.
Operated the Maxwell Brothers studio in Dayton with G. Y. Maxwell; associated with brothers C. T. and J. D. Maxwell.

McCLAIRE, M. S.
Died in Seattle, March 3, 1917. Active in Seattle, 1885.

McINNIS, HECTOR C.
Active in Ellensburg, 1895.

McKINNEY BROTHERS
Partnership active in Walla Walla, 1890.

McKNIGHT BROTHERS
Samuel F. and John C. McKnight in Seattle, 1887.

McMURRY, J. M.
Died in Yuba City, California, July 23, 1944. Active in Port Townsend, 1886.

MERTINS, HUGO H.
Born in Essen, Germany, c. 1859; died in Olympia, Washington, 1948. Active in Waterbury, Connecticut, 1881; Tacoma, Washington, 1889; Sheridan, Oregon, 1901-03; Orting, Washington, early 1900s; Centralia and Orting, c. 1908; Centralia, 1931.

MILLER & CARRATT
Partnership active in Goldendale, 1895.

MONNET & BRADLEY
Studio in Fairhaven, 1890; Orrin E. Monnet and Levi Bradley.

MONTGOMERY, J. H.
Active in Walla Walla, 1873. See Oregon and Idaho.

MOORE, GEORGE
Active in Seattle, 1870-97.

MORFORD, CHARLES H.
Died in Seattle, October 13, 1953. Active in Seattle, 1885-89.

MORSE, SAMUEL GAY
Born in northern California, 1859; died in Port Angeles, 1921. Arrived in Port Angeles as a boy, 1863. Sheriff of Clallam County, Indian agent and later superintendent of the training school at Neah Bay, known to the natives as "Chief Morses." He had a store at Taholah on the Quinault Reservation; as an avid amateur photographer, he recorded the life of the Makah, Quileute and Klallam Indians.

> Carolyn Marr, *Portrait in Time: Photographs of the Makah by Samuel G. Morse, 1896-1903*, Makah Cultural and Research Center, Seattle, Washington, 1987.

MUELLER
Stereo photographer in Ellensburg.

MUGFORD, J. P.
Amateur stereo photographer active in Elma.

MUHR, ADOLPH
Died 1913. Manager of the studio of Edward S. Curtis for many years when Curtis was absent on lengthy field trips.

MUIRHEAD, LEWIS POTTER, JR.
Active in Seattle. See British Columbia.

MUTH & COMPANY, L.
Active in Walla Walla.

NORTHWEST TRADING COMPANY
Operated by Henry H. Brodeck in Walla Walla, c. 1880. Views marked "Photographed for the Northwest Trading Co." Also known as Brodeck & Company.

NOWELL, FRANK A.
Studio in Seattle and official photographer of the Alaska-Yukon-Pacific Exposition, 1909. See Alaska.

OAKES
Partner in Tennant & Oakes, Seattle. A photographer named Omega Oakes worked in Oregon, 1870s-80s.

OSBORN, J. Q.
Active in Walla Walla, 1880.

OWINGS
Partner in Willis & Owings operating in Colfax, 1890.

PACIFIC PHOTOGRAPHIC VIEW COMPANY
Stereoview company based in Seattle and Tacoma. Issued series of views of Mt. Tacoma, Rainier National Park, hikers, climbers traversing rock outcroppings and snow scenes, c. 1905.

PALACE
Studio in Tacoma, 1890, operated by J. P. Aaberg.

PALMER, FRANK
Died in Spokane, June 28, 1920. Active in Spokane, c. 1898-1920.

PAUTZKE, OTTO W.
Died in Ellensburg, November 24, 1918. Active in Ellensburg.

PEISER, THEODORE E.
Died in San Francisco, February 11, 1922. Arrived in Seattle from San Francisco, California, 1883; active as a photographer, 1885.

PERKINS, WILLIAM S.
Stereo photographer active in Colfax.

PETERSON & BROTHER
Active in Seattle, c. 1875-83, partnership of Louis and Henry Peterson. Operated the Seattle Art Gallery on Front Street. A cabinet card without location identified in the imprint, depicts gold panning paraphernalia, suggesting L. E. Peterson worked at the time of the Alaskan gold rush, c. 1898. Published stereoviews of early street scenes of Seattle.

PETERSON, HENRY
One of the Peterson brothers in Seattle.

PETERSON, LOUIS
Born in Norway, c. 1847; died in Seattle, 1934. Arrived in Seattle from Chicago, 1876. One of the Peterson brothers. First name also spelled Lewis. See British Columbia.

PETERSON'S PHOTO GALLERY
Studio in New Whatcom, c. 1880.

PIERCE, WESLEY C.
Operated as Webster & Pierce in Whatcom and Blaine, 1891, with partner Leonard A. Webster.

PLUMMER, F. C.
Died in Seattle, August 29, 1931. Photographer in Seattle and Tacoma.

PRATSCH, C. R.
Active in Aberdeen, 1890.

RAINIER STUDIO
Gallery in Seattle, 1885.

RALSTON, J. E.
Worked for Edward S. Curtis in Seattle, 1906.

REED, WILLIAM H.
Partner with McKenney in Tacoma, c. 1870s-80s; worked alone, 1893-94.

ROBERTSON & HASTINGS
Studio at Port Townsend, 1873. Photographed Haida artifacts.

ROBERTSON, WILLIAM FRANCIS
Active in Seattle, 1870; Tacoma, 1880-83. Recorded Catholic missionary and Indians at Tulalip, 1865. See British Columbia.

ROGERS, A. D.
Died in Olympia, June 5, 1917. Active in Olympia, 1895.

ROMINGER, G. T.
Stereo photographer in Spokane.

ROSENKRANZ, HELEN (MISS)
Active in Spokane Falls, 1890.

ROTHI, R. P.
Assistant to James H. Crockwell in Utah, c. 1887. Active in Seattle, 1890-1910. Early partner of Edward S. Curtis.

ROYAL ENGINEERS
With the British Boundary Commission around Fort Colville in 1860-61, they worked as far south as Fort Vancouver and The Dalles; made albumen prints of the Columbia River and a few portraits of Indians including Spokan Garry.

RUTTER, THOMAS H.
Died in Port Orchard, August 21, 1925. Active in Tacoma, 1888.

SAMMIS, EDWARD M.
Operated a studio in Olympia, 1860-61, on Fourth Street near Main. Traveled to Lewiston, Idaho, where he photographed a panorama of the city and Columbia River, 1862. Moved to Seattle and operated a gallery until c. 1866. Partner in Sammis & Hills, 14 Second Street, San Francisco, California, 1867; partner in Kiefer & Sammis, Visalia; listed in Contra Costa County, 1867-73. He made the famous carte-de-visite of Chief Sealth (Seattle) of the Suquamish, 1861.

SCHUMACHER, LEO J.
Active in Walla Walla, c. 1878. Also spelled Schumaker. See California, Nevada and Oregon.

SCHWERIN, E.
Originally from San Francisco, California. Operated the Souvenir Art Studio in Seattle with F. H. Dorsez, 1883-86.

SCOTFORD, J. H.
Active in Michigan, Missouri and Oregon, c. 1870s; in Tacoma, Washington at 915 and 917 C Street, c. 1885. Produced stereoviews. See Oregon.

SHAW, DAVID C.
Born in Iowa, 1857. Arrived in Lynden, 1883; engaged in photography business, 1883-1892, then moved to Elkhart, Wisconsin.

SHEANE, ROBERT
Active in Chehalis, 1889-91; operated in Shelton with his son Robert R. using the name Robert Sheane & Son, 1901-05; listed alone in Montesano, 1909-11. See Oregon.

SHIVELEY, E. W.
Died in Spokane, January 3, 1932. Active in Spokane, 1890.

SHUSTER, H. S.
Active in Aberdeen, Washington, 1889.

SIEWERT, HERMAN
Active in Puyallup, 1890s. Also spelled Siwert.

SMITH, C. S.
Active in Seattle and Port Townsend, Washington, 1881. See Oregon.

SMITH, FRANCIS A.
Born in Ohio, July 1830; died in Tacoma, November 30, 1903. Active in Walla Walla County, 1887; Waitsburgh, 1888-89; Wilbur, 1891; Tacoma, 1900-03. See Oregon.

SMITH, IDA B.
Born 1857; Died in Olympia, October 3, 1923. Photographer in Olympia c. early 1900s; traveled to the Tonopah and Goldfields mining districts, 1905.

SMITH, L. E.
Stereo photographer in Cheney.

SMITH, LLOYD E.
Manufacturer and publisher of stereoviews in North Yakima; issued stereoviews of expositions and fairs, including Washington State Fair, 1902; also produced views of San Francisco and earthquake aftermath. Possibly the same as L. E. Smith.

SMITH, S. C.
Operated the Enterprise Photo Studio in North Yakima, producing views of scenery, San Francisco fire, Yosemite, 1904-07.

SORENSEN, H. C.
Stereo photographer in Blanchard.

SOULE, JOHN P.
Died in Seattle, November 27, 1904. Active in Seattle, 1889.

SOUVENIR ART STUDIO
Gallery active in Seattle 1883-86, operated by F. H. Dorsez & E. Schwerin, originally from San Francisco, California.

SPAULDING
Partner in Browne & Spaulding.

SQUIRE & CROWELL
Partnership active in Tacoma, c. 1890s, producing stereoviews.

STAMPFLER VIEW COMPANY
Operated by Jules H. Stampfler in Ashford, c. 1909. Produced views of Rainier National Park, Washington state scenery and exceptional studies of Mt. Tacoma and environs, published by H. L. Toles of Seattle. Successor to Whiting.

STANLEY, JOHN MIX
An artist with the 1853 Stevens Expedition who took daguerreotypes of landscapes to assist in completing drawings and paintings. Daguerreotypes of natives were taken, but none are known to have survived.

STEPHENS, S. S. (MRS.)
Active in Seattle, 1882; Walla Walla, 1883.

STEVENS
Partner in Webster & Stevens, Seattle, 1902-60.

STEVENS, B. F.
Stereo photographer active in Washington.

SUMMERS, WALTER
Stereo photographer in Orting.

TALIAFERO, B. W.
Active in Walla Walla, 1879. See Oregon.

TAYLOR, LACHLAN
Died in Seattle, April 29, 1915. Active in Pullman, 1885; Seattle, 1901.

TENNANT & OAKES
Partnership active in Seattle. See Oakes.

THOMAS, JESSE E.
Died in Port Angeles, March 23, 1928. Active in Port Angeles, 1890.

TOLES, HERBERT L.
Active in Seattle, 1907-14.

TOLLMAN & PRESTON
Partnership active in Long Beach, 1885.

TOLLMAN, JOHN W.
Active in Olympia, Long Beach, South Bend and Aberdeen, 1887; Vancouver, 1903-05. See Oregon.

TOLLMAN, THOMAS W.
See Oregon.

WAGGENER, JAMES, JR.
Died in Vancouver, June 24, 1933. Active in Vancouver, 1885.

WAGNESS, JOHN T.
Died in Stanwood, May 30, 1936. Active in Tacoma, 1888.

WALLACE, GEORGE R.
Active in Snohomish, 1895.

WATSON, O. W.
Active in Spokane, 1900.

WEBSTER & PIERCE
Studio in Whatcom and Blaine operated by Leonard A. Webster and Wesley C. Pierce, 1891.

WEBSTER & STEVENS
Partnership active in Seattle, 1902-60s.

WEBSTER, LEONARD A.
Operated with partner Wesley C. Pierce as Webster & Pierce in Whatcom and Blaine, 1891.

WHEELER APPLIED ARTS COMPANY
Published stereoviews in Seattle.

WIGHTMAN, CHARLES E.
Operated the Palace Floating Gallery.

WILBURN, JAMES A.
Active in Colville, 1896.

WILLIAMS, F. R.
Active in Centralia, 1885.

WILLIS & OWINGS
Active in Colfax, 1890.

WILSE, ANDERS BEERS
Born in Flekkefjord, Norway, 1865; died in Oslo, Norway, February 21, 1949. Moved to Minneapolis, Minnesota, 1884, where he worked as a surveyor and acquired his first camera. Moved to Seattle to work as a railroad surveyor and engineer, 1890. Documented the construction of the Great Northern Railroad line over the Cascade Mountains, 1892-93. Images often signed "A. B. W." Opened his first studio with Daniel W. Kirk, 1897, but took full control after six months. Wilse documented prospectors going to the Klondike, soldiers embarking for the Spanish-American War and Makah Indians; he was billed as a "scenic fotografer." He worked as cartographer and photographer on a mineral expedition to the Granite Mountain Range in Montana, 1898. By 1900, Wilse's studio was known as the Seattle Photographic Company, located in the McDonald Building at 811 Second Avenue. Wilse left for a visit in Norway, 1900, but never returned; William Duckering managed the company, 1900-13. Wilse established a studio in Kristiania (Oslo) and worked the tourist ships plying the fjords; he published two autobiographies: *En Emigrants Ungdomserindringer (An Emigrant's Memories of His Youth),* Oslo, 1936, and later, *Norsk Landscap og Norske Men.*
    Carolyn J. Marr, "Anders Beer Wilse: Photographer of the Pacific Northwest and Norway," *Columbia Magazine,* summer 1994.

WINCHESTER, F. E.
Died in Seattle, 1914. Active in Walla Walla, 1886.

WINDELL
Stereo photographer in Dayton.

WINGREN, O. J.
Stereo photographer active in La Conner.

WOLFE, G. M.
Active in Quiniualt and member of the International Photographic Association; in Woodburn, Oregon, c. 1912.

WOOD, T. M.
Active in Walla Walla, 1866. See Oregon and Idaho.

WOODARD, A. B.
Died in Olympia, February 24, 1918. Active in Tumwater, 1867; Olympia, 1868-80. Became a prominent dentist in Olympia. Leased his Olympia studio to Oliver Dennie, 1873; sold the studio to L. W. Clark, 1881. See Oregon.

WOODARD, A. E.
Active in Olympia, Washington Territory, 1875. Brother of A. B. Woodard.

WORTHINGTON, W. T.
Active in New Tacoma, 1883.

WUNDERLICH
Partner in Margo & Wunderlich, Spokane Falls, 1886.

YANTIS, JOHN V.
Born in Sweet Spring, Missouri, January 16, 1845; died in Olympia, July 16, 1925. Crossed the plains with his family at age six, 1852, settling in Thurston County. Member of the Washington Territory legislature, and city clerk in Olympia. Ambrotypist in Olympia, 1865, in the rooms formerly occupied by W. J. Yeager and E. M. Sammis on Fourth Street near Main.

YEAGER, W. J.
Ambrotypist in Olympia, 1861-65; studio on Fourth Street, near Main, formerly used by E. M. Sammis.

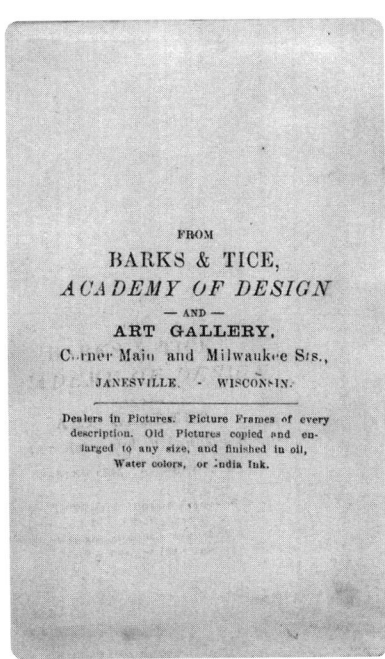

FROM
BARKS & TICE,
ACADEMY OF DESIGN
— AND —
ART GALLERY,
Corner Main and Milwaukee Sts.,
JANESVILLE. - WISCONSIN.

Dealers in Pictures. Picture Frames of every
description. Old Pictures copied and en-
larged to any size, and finished in oil,
Water colors, or India Ink.

A substantial amount of the information in this section was provided by John Graf.

ACADEMY OF DESIGN
Partnership of J. F. Barks and J. A. Tice, operating in Janesville, 1862, corner of Main and Milwaukee Streets; also known as Barks & Tice.

ADLINGTON & FAVOR
Partnership with studios in Viroqua, Mt. Sterling, Soldier's Grove and Cashton, 1890.

ALBERT, A.
Daguerreotypist active in Madison, 1860.

ALLEN, P.
Daguerreotypist active in Lock Haven, 1857.

ALLEN, W. H.
Active at Chippewa Falls c. 1885.

ALVORD, D. M.
Active at Kenosha, 1860.

ALVORD, DAVID N.
Daguerreotypist active in Kenosha, 1857.

ALVORD, JERUSHA E. (MRS.)
Daguerreotypist originally from New York, active in Kenosha, 1857-c.1860.

AMERICAN VIEW COMPANY
Publisher of stereoviews for their own imprint, also for Eastman Brothers of Oshkosh, who were booksellers; located in Neenah.

ANDERSON, E. J.
Active in Edgerton.

ANDERSON, J. S.
Studio on Sixth Street, Racine, 1860.

ANDREWS, A. F.
Active in North LaCrosse, c. 1890.

ANGER, W.
"Optician & Maker of Stereoscopic Views," at 97 Wisconsin Street in Milwaukee.

ANSCHUETZ
Active in Boscobel, 1880.

ARMOR, A. H.
Active in Portage, 1870.

ARMSTRONG
Operated the Broadway Gallery in Milwaukee, 1890, at 389 Broadway.

ART UNION GALLERY
Daguerreian gallery active in Ripon, 1885 (possibly 1857-85); operated by Joshua H. Wyckoff.

ASPINALL, ALFRED
Daguerreotypist active in Kaukauna, 1857.

ATCHINSON
Stereo photographer in Stoughton.

BABCOCK, WARREN D.
Daguerreotypist originally from Vermont, active in Beaver Dam, 1857-60; Columbus, 1857.

BACHELDER, C.
Daguerreotypist from New Hampshire, active in Fond du Lac, 1848.

BACHELDER, WILLIAM L.
Went to Crawford County, Iowa to study photography with his brother, 1866; moved to Durand, Wisconsin, and opened his own studio, 1871.

BAER, ALFRED
Active in Baraboo, 1880.

BAGLEY, WILBUR F.
Daguerreotypist active in Milwaukee, 1858-60.

BAILEY, F.
Daguerreotypist active in Milwaukee, 1859-60.

BAILEY'S STUDIO
Active in Ashland, 1900.

BALDWIN, A. A.
Stereo photographer in Ludlow, 1873.

BALDWIN, WILL D.
Stereo photographer active in Superior City.

BANGS & ENO
Active in Milwaukee, 1870.

BANGS, E. D.
Active in Clinton, Whitewater and Milwaukee, 1860-80; West Bend, 1875, operating as Goetz & Bangs.

BANNISTER
Active in New Richmond, 1890.

BARDELL, F.
Stereo photographer in Albany.

BARKER
Active in Milwaukee, 1900.

BARKS & TICE
Partnership of J. F. Barks and J. A. Tice in Janesville, operating Academy of Design, corner of Main and Milwaukee Streets, 1862.

BARKS, J. F.
Operated an Academy of Design and Art Gallery, corner of Main and Milwaukee Streets, Janesville, 1862. Stereo photographer; active later in Texas.

BARLOW, R. H.
Active in Elkhorn, 1880.

BARNARD, L. O.
Daguerreotypist active in Neenah, 1856-57, operating Wheeler & Barnard Daguerrean Gallery with Samuel Wheeler in Shoemaker and Verbeck's Building.

BARNES
Active in Winona, 1875-90.

BARNES, MARCELLA W.
Daguerreotypist active in New York and Michigan, 1853, before operating a gallery in Elkhorn, 1857.

BARON, JOHN A.
Stereo photographer in Superior.

BARROWS
Daguerreotypist in Janesville listed as Ogilvie & Barrows-Suppliers, 1857.

BATES, ELLEN A. (MRS.)
Daguerreotypist active in Waukesha, 1857-58, on Main Street.

BATES, JAMES B.
Daguerreotypist active in Waukesha, 1855-58, on Main Street.

BAUDER GEORGE W.
Active in Marinette, 1880.

BAYLEY & PATTERSON
Active in Milwaukee, 1860; possibly Charles H. Bayley.

BAYLEY, CHARLES H.
Active in LaCrosse, 1860.

BEACH & JOHNSON
Studio in LaCrosse, 1867, corner of Front and Main Streets.

BEACH, E. A.
Active in LaCrosse, 1860; partner in Beach & Johnson, 1867.

BECKER
Active in Sauk City, 1895.

BENNETT, BENJAMIN S.
Daguerreotypist active in Milwaukee, 1858-59, operating as Truscott & Bennett.

BENNETT, H. H.
Major studio photographer and producer of stereoviews; main studio at Kilbourn City, another in Milwaukee, 1875-1900. Produced a multitude of stereoviews of scenes in and around the Wisconsin Dells, an important series on the Winnebago Indians, an interesting series of rafting down the Mississippi, and others. Published the series "A Summer in Japan" by stereographer William H. Metcalf. Bennett's photography business was conducted by his family for several generations in Kilbourn City after his death.

BENNETT, S. N.
Stereo photographer active in Oconomoc and Milwaukee.

BENTLEY, BETHUEL
Daguerreotypist and ambrotypist active in Plainfield, 1857.

BEVERAGE, M. C.
Stereo photographer in Oconto.

BILLING, EDWARD
Produced stereoviews of Racine and vicinity; also spelled Billings.

BINGHAM, T. P.
Issued rare "Wisconsin Illustrated" stereoviews; no studio location given, but active in Appleton.

BINTLE, M. M.
Stereo photographer in Madison.

BISH
Active in Chippewa Falls, 1885-95.

BISHOP
Partner in Davids & Bishop, billed as "Artists & Stereographers" in Hudson.

BISHOP & SON, F.
Active in Waterton, 1860.

BISHOP, FRANK, JR.
Gallery at 97 and 99 Wisconsin Street, Milwaukee, c. 1875; Chippewa Falls, c. 1885, at the Metropolitan Block.

BIXBY, HENRY P.
Daguerreotypist originally from New York, active in Neenah, 1850.

BJOERK, N. F.
Daguerreotypist active in Oshkosh, 1860.

BLACK & COMPANY, L.
Active in Milwaukee, 1860s.

BLACK & SMALL
Operating in Milwaukee c. 1885.

BLACKLEDGE, W. R.
"Artist, Photographer" in LaCrosse.

BLAKE, EDGAR
Daguerreotypist active in Delton, 1857.

BLATCHLEY, W. S.
Stereo photographer in Kilbourn.

BODTKER, JAMES FRANK
Studio in Madison, 1867, over the post office.

BODTKIN, JAMES
Daguerreotypist active in South Grove, 1857.

BOETCHER & LEE
Studio at 106 Bridge Street in Chippewa Falls, c. 1885.

BOGRAND, PETER
Active in Marshfield, 1880.

BONELL, F.
Active in Eau Claire and Chippewa Falls, 1875-90. Also spelled Bonnell.

BOVER BROTHERS
Partnership in West Superior, 1895.

BOWRING, R. D.
Active in De Pere, 1875-90. Also listed as T. D.

BOYCOTT, JAMES
Daguerreotypist originally from England; studio in LaCrosse, 1856-80, at Third Street, operating as Boycott, Summerhayes & Company.

BOYCOTT, SUMMERHAYES & COMPANY
Studio in LaCrosse, 1856-80, at Third Street; James Boycott.

BOYD
Active in Sextonville, 1870.

BOYER BROTHERS
Studio at the corner of 5th Street and Ogden Avenue, West Superior, 1890; 428 Ogden Avenue, c. 1895.

BRADLEY, G. W.
Active in Menasha, 1885.

BRAITHWAITE, JOHN
Active in Neenah, 1860s-70s.

BRANDON, DANIEL F.
Daguerreotypist active in Beloit, 1855-57, operating Brandon's Picture Gallery.

BRAUN, J.
Stereo photographer active in Two Rivers.

BREWSTER, E. F.
Daguerreotypist active in Geneva, 1857.

BRIDER, J. A.
Operated the Glass Gallery in Racine; made stereoviews.

BROCKWAY, S. B.
Daguerrean artist active in Green Bay and De Pere, 1855.

BROICH & KREMER
Active in Milwaukee, 1880; Hugo Broich and F. Kremer.

BROICH, HUGO
Gallery in Milwaukee, at 365 West Water Street, corner of Chestnut, c. 1865. Later operated also at 116 and 118 Spring Street, opposite Plankinton House, Milwaukee, 1880. Incorporated F. Kremer's studio at some point. Also known as Hugo Von Broich.

BROWN, CHARLES H.
Active in Delavan, 1870.

BROWN, D. H.
Active at Chippewa Falls, c. 1895.

BROWN, GEORGE
Stereo photographer active in Wisconsin; details unknown.

BROWN, H. P.
Daguerreotypist active in Cascade, 1857.

BROWN, HENRY S.
Daguerreotypist originally from Vermont, active in Milwaukee, 1846-70, c. 1880. Studio at 201 East Water Street, 1860-70; Cogswell's Block, 89 Wisconsin Street, c. 1880. Studio known as H. S. Brown's Daguerreian Gallery.

BROWN, O. B.
Active in Kenosha.

BUGBEE, VAN H.
Active in Waukesha, c. 1870s, partner in Toley & Bugbee; partner in Tyler & Bugbee, 1881.

BULLARD, O. C.
Daguerreotypist active in Menasha, 1856, located in Bishop's Hall.

BULLOCK
Active in Geneva Lake, 1880, operating the Gallery of Art.

BUNCE
Active in Mondovi.

BURDICK, E. H.
Active in Milton, c. 1860.

BURGHARD, C. F.
Daguerreotypist in Cedarburg, 1857.

BURKE, WILLIAM B.
Daguerreotypist originally from Virginia, operating in Platteville, 1860.

BURNHAM, ASA M.
Daguerreotypist originally from Maine, active in Newport, 1860.

BURNICK, E. H.
Active in Palmyra Springs.

BURNS, M. W.
Operated the Eau Claire Picture Emporium in Eau Claire, 1875-90. A carte-de-viste imprint, c. 1880, advertises the "Gallery of Art opposite the post office."

BURPEE, C. L.
Operated the Fine Art Gallery, formerly Union Gallery, in Beloit, 1863-70.

BURRITT, E. H.
Possibly a partner with F. Pease in St. Paul, 1870s-80s; also active in Milton.

BURTON, E. K.
Stereo photographer in Appleton.

BUTLER
Stereo photographer in West Superior.

BUTTERFIELD, L. T.
Active in Prarie du Chein, 1870.

BYAM, J. W.
Active in Fond du Lac, 1870.

CALLENDER & PATTERSON
Active in Ripon, 1857-66, west side public square; John H. Calender.

CALLENDER, JOHN H.
Daguerreotypist and dentist originally from New Jersey, active in Ripon, 1857-66, partner in Calender & Patterson.

CANFIELD, E. H.
Studio in Milwaukee, 1885, at 224 and 226 Spring Street.

CARL, BARNARD
Daguerreotypist originally from Ireland, active in Neenah, 1850.

CARLETON, G. C.
Active in Waukesha, 1860.

CARLSON & FRANS
Studio at 1509 Fifth Street, West Superior, c. 1895.

CARMODY, J. D.
Active in Madison, 1860.

CARPENTER (MISS)
Daguerreotypist active in Kenosha, 1852-53; Racine, 1853, operating with partner as Mrs. Fulkerson & Miss Carpenter.

CARPENTER, C. C.
Stereo photographer active in Racine.

CASE & JANES
Daguerreotypists active in New Lisbon, 1857.

CASS, WILLIAM
Daguerreotypist originally from New York, active in Horicon, 1857; Hubbard, 1860.

CAUFIELD
Active in Fond du Lac, 1870.

CENTURY PHOTO NOVELTY COMPANY
Operated by R. J. Miller in Milwaukee, at 278 West Water Street. Issued rare stereoviews of statuary and buildings.

CHAMBERLAIN, H. B.
Active in Shullsburg, 1870-90.

CHANDLER
Partner in Wilkins & Chandler, Oshkosh, 1860.

CHARBOURNE
Studio in Milwaukee, 1880, at 224 and 226 Grand Avenue.

CHASE
Stereo photographer active in Cassville.

CHILDS, H. A.
Stereo photographer active in New Richmond.

CITY PHOTOGRAPH GALLERY
Studio in Waupaca, 1870; proprietor and operator, T. Rich, at corner of Main and Granite Streets.

CLAIBOURNE
Active in Fond du Lac, 1890.

CLARK
Active in Janesville, 1860.

CLARK, HIRAM S.
Daguerreotypist active in Neenah, 1857; Green Bay, 1860-68, operating the New Art Gallery.

CLARK, (MR.)
Daguerreotypist active in Southport, 1850; also operated as Mr. Clark & Lady.

CLARKE, A. B.
Active in Milton.

CLEGG, MARY A.
Active in Darlington, 1870.

CLEMENTS, MICHEL
Active in Sheboygan, 1870.

CLIFFORD & GIBSON
Art Studio in Milwaukee, 1860, at the corner of Wisconsin and Milwaukee Streets; J. S. Gibson & R. A. Clifford.

CLIFFORD, R. A.
Operated the Photographic and Fine Art Gallery in Milwaukee, 1850-66, located at one time at 171 East Water Street. Partner in Clifford & Gibson, 1860.

CLIZBE, CARRIE (MISS)
Active in Elroy, c. 1895.

CODDING, E.
Stereo photographer in Knoxville and Rocklake.

COLE, G. H.
Daguerreotypist in Appleton, 1855.

COLLETT, J. E.
Active in Chippewa Falls, 1870-90.

COLWARD, B.
Stereo photographer in Oostbury.

COLWELL
Daguerreotypist active in Madison, 1857, operating Colwell & Company-Suppliers.

COMEE, S. S.
Active in Jefferson, 1875-90.

CONNOR
Daguerreotypist in Racine, 1857, operating as Walker & Connor.

COOK
Stereo photographer in Delton.

COOLEY, C. E.
Daguerreotypist in Watertown, 1857.

CORNISH, J. J.
Active in Dodgeville, 1865.

COTTRELL & RICHARDSON
Partnership operating studio in Sparta, 1875.

COULEY, C. R.
Daguerreotypist originally from Ohio, active in Madison, 1860; worked for E. R. Curtiss.

COURTEAU
Partner in Kertson & Courteau, active in Sauk Center, c. 1886.

CRAMTON, H. L.
Daguerreotypist active in Oshkosh, 1857.

CRANDALL BROTHERS
Operated a studio in Milton Junction, c. 1890.

CROSS, D. H.
Daguerreotypist in Waterloo, 1857.

CROSS, E. B.
Daguerreotypist active in Waterloo, 1857.

CROWNS, J. H.
Daguerreotypist originally from New York, active in Fox Lake, 1860-66.

CULBERTSON, R. W.
Daguerreotypist active in Dunnville, 1857.

CULBERTSON, W. R.
Daguerreotypist in North Pepin, 1857.

CUNNINGHAM, HENRY
Daguerreotypist from New York, active in Williamstown, 1850.

CUNNINGHAM, J. H.
Daguerreotypist active in Kenosha, 1851.

CURTIS, E. H.
Daguerreotypist in Ogden, 1857.

CURTISS, EDWARD R.
Born in 1836. Daguerreotypist originally from Connecticut, active in Madison, 1859-90, "Ambrotype, Daguerreotype and Photographic Artist." Operated the Photographic Art Palace; studio was destroyed by fire, 1891. Issued "The Beauties of the City of the Lakes" stereoviews. Also spelled Curtis.

CURTISS, N. S.
Active in Watertown, 1870.

DABB, JASON V.
Stereo photographer in Mineral Point.

DAHL, A. L.
Active in Madison, 1870.

DAILEY
Active in Beloit, 1880.

DAKE
Stereo photographer in Plainfield.

DARE, G. F.
Stereo photographer in Melrose.

DAVIDS & BISHOP
"Artists & Stereographers" in Hudson; Davids later worked alone.

DAVIS, E. M.
Stereo photographer active in Oconto.

DEARBORN, C. A.
Issued "Devil's Lake Views" in Baraboo, c. 1900; possibly an amateur.

DEGUIRE
Studio at 820 College Avenue, Appleton, c. 1885.

DELAM, H.
Daguerreotypist in Fort Atkinson, 1857.

DELANO, E. E.
Stereo photographer active in Waterloo.

DEVOE, A. J.
Active in Sextonville, 1870-90.

DILLEY, STEPHEN B.
Daguerreotypist originally from Pennsylvania, active in Eau Claire, 1860.

DILLON, JOHN W.
Active in Fond du Lac, 1870.

DOANE, H. R.
Active in Delavan, 1860-80.

DORWARD, W. J.
Active in Madison, 1880-1900.

DOTY, G. N.
Daguerreotypist active in Stevens Point, 1857-65.

DOUGLASS, DAVID A.
Daguerreotypist from New York, operating in Prarie du Chien, 1860.

DRESSER, WILLIAM
Daguerreotypist active in Madison, 1847.

DUFRESNE, E.
Active in Watertown, 1880.

DUNSHEE, H. S.
Active in Beloit, 1860.

DUNTON & JOURDAN
Daguerreotypists operating in Plover, 1857.

DURKEE, HENRY
Daguerreotypist active in Mackford, 1857.

DWIGHT, T., JR.
Active in Beloit, 1860.

EASLEY, D. N.
Daguerreotypist active in Mayville, 1857.

EASTMAN BROTHERS
Booksellers in Oshkosh who also sold stereoviews published by the American View Company of Neenah.

EASTMAN, THOMAS
Daguerreotypist operating the Floating Daguerrean Palace in LaCrosse, 1859.

EAU CLAIRE PICTURE EMPORIUM
Gallery in Eau Claire, 1875-90, operated by M. W. Burns. A carte-de-visite imprint c. 1880 advertises the "Gallery of Art opposite the post office."

ELY, COOK
Active in Oshkosh and Racine, 1870-90s, partner in Lockwood & Ely.

ENNOR & SKEWIS
Partnership active in Richland Center, 1880.

ENO
Active in Milwaukee, 1870, operating as Bangs & Eno.

ESKIL, JORGEN J.
"Portrait & Landscape Photographer" in Florence.

ESSOX, JOHN B
Daguerreotypist originally from New York, active in Leroy, 1860.

EVERLY, FRANCIS
Daguerreotypist in West Bend, 1857.

EVERSON, E. H.
Stereo photographer in Monroe.

FAIR, J.
Daguerreotypist active in Oshkosh, 1853-55, operating as J. Fair & Son.

FARR & GOODMAN
Active in Prarie du Chien, 1870; H. R. Farr.

FARR, FOSTER
Daguerreotypist originally from New York, active in Ashippun, 1860.

FARR, H. R.
Active in Minneapolis and Prarie du Chien, 1870-90; partner in Farr & Goodman, 1870.

FARRINGTON, C.
Daguerreotypist active in Otterville, 1857.

FAULKNER, F. D.
Active in Chippewa Falls, 1870.

FAVOR
Partner in Adlington & Favor with studios in Viroqua, Mt. Sterling, Soldier's Grove and Cashton, 1890.

FAY, ALMERON
Daguerreotypist originally from New York, active in Haney, 1860.

FERMANN, W. A.
Active in Stoughton, 1870-80.

FIELD, JULIAN HERMAN
Born in Waupun, Wisconsin, February 19,1869; died in Fayetteville, Arkansas, January 14,1936. First studio in Berlin; married to his assistant, Minnie Bell Dies. Moved to Fayetteville, 1913, where he opened a portrait studio. He was also known for pictorialist art images and some were published in nationally circulating periodicals. Field produced book illustrations and did extensive work depicting life at the Univeristy of Arkansas and around Fayetteville.

FIELD, MINNIE BELL DIES
Born March 16, 1879; died in Fayetteville, 1962. Wife of Julian Herman Field, she served as his assistant at his studio in Waupun, Wisconsin, before and after their marriage. She continued her work as a lab technician and retoucher at their Fayetteville studio, and after his death in 1936, she continued to sell from the studio's inventory of photographs.

FISH PHOTO
Active in Readstown, c. 1900.

FISHER, J. A.
Stereo photographer active in Jefferson.

FISK, BERT
Photographer in North Freedom; produced rare comic stereoviews, such as a man riding bicycle in his sleep, and a man washing clothes while a woman reads magazine and others.

FLEMING, E. G.
Active in Merrill, 1895.

FLOATING DAGUERREAN PALACE
Operated by Thomas Eastman in LaCrosse, 1859.

FORDINCK, G.
Stereo photographer in Carling.

FOWLER & HORN
Studio in Milwaukee, 1856-60; operated by W. Elbert Fowler and Edward W. Horn.

FOWLER, ELBERT W.
Daguerreotypist active in Milwaukee, 1856-60, with Edward W. Horn, operating as Fowler & Horn.

FOWLER, F. M.
Active in Madison, 1860. Possibly same as J. M. Fowler.

FOX LAKE VIEW COMPANY
Issued rare stereoviews, copies of Anthony images of Niagara; located in Fox Lake.

FRANS
Partner in Carlson & Frans, 1509 Fifth Street, West Superior, c. 1895.

FRISSELL, E. C. (MRS.)
Active in Jefferson, 1860; Fort Atkinson, c. 1870.

FULKERSON (MRS.)
Daguerreotypist active in Kenosha, 1852-53; partner in Mrs. Fulkerson & Miss Carpenter in Racine, 1853.

FULKERSON (MRS.) & CARPENTER (MISS)
Active in Kenosha, 1852-53; in Racine, 1853.

FULLER, JOHN S.
Daguerreotypist from Vermont, active in Madison, 1855-65; operated Fuller's Temple of Art & Stereoscopic Gallery, c. 1860-65.

GALLAHER, J. B.
Operated the Star Gallery in Chippewa Falls and Neillsville offering "Views of Chippewa Falls & Vicinity." Also spelled Gallagher.

GARRISON, D. H.
Daguerreotypist active in Berlin, 1857.

GATES, LEROY
Daguerreotypist in Kilbourn City, 1860-65, operating Gates Picture Gallery.

GAULT, J. A.
Partner in Gault & Lind, Marinette, c. 1885.

GESELL, GERHARD
Active in Alma, 1860-65.

GIBBS, J. J.
Daguerreotypist active in Sheboygan, 1854.

GIBBS, J. R.
Daguerreotypist active in Gibbville, 1857.

GIBSON & GILLETT
Daguerreotypists in Fond du Lac, 1856; J. S. Gibson and A. H. Gillett, also known as J. S. Gibson's & Company.

GIBSON, J. S.
Daguerreotypist active in Appleton, 1854; partner with A. H. Gillett operating as Gibson & Gillett in Fond Du Lac, 1854-56; with C. T. Ripley as Ripley & Gibson, 1854-56; as J. S. Gibson & Company in Green Bay, 1856; Wautoma, 1857; Milwaukee, 1860, partner in Clifford & Gibson.

GILLETT, A. H.
Daguerreotypist in Fond du Lac, 1856, with J. S. Gibson, operating as Gibson & Gillett.

GLASS, C. F. & H. B.
Daguerreotypists in Janesville, 1870-90.

GOETZ & BANGS
Daguerreotypists active in West Bend, 1875; E. D. Bangs.

GOFF, O. S.
See Dakota.

GOINES, JOSEPH A.
Daguerreotypist originally from Virginia, active in Oshkosh, 1860.

GOODMAN
Partner in Farr & Goodman, Prarie du Chien, 1870.

GOODMAN, H. P.
Active in Whitewater, c. 1885.

GRAHAM VIEW & COPYING HOUSE
Active in Beaver Dam.

GRAMM, A. F.
"Artist & Photographer" in Mt. Haber.

GRAVES
Partner in Mcpherson, Roloson & Graves.

GREAT CENTRAL DAGUERREAN GALLERY
Active in Milwaukee, 1857, operated by Charles M. Seeley.

GREEN & WHEELER
Active in Racine, 1860; possibly D. W. Wheeler.

GREEN, G. B.
Daguerreotypist originally from New York, active in Fond du Lac, 1857, operating Green's Gallery of Arts.

GREENE, B. F.
Active in Janesville, 1870.

GROH & BROTHER, G. M.
Active in Sheboygan, 1870-90.

GUILD, GEORGE
Daguerreotypist active in Osceola Mills, 1857.

HAGENDORFF, LOUIS
Active in Milwaukee, 1870-90.

HALE, CHARLES E.
Daguerreotypist in Mazomanie, 1857.

HALL & RUDD
Active in Green Bay, 1870.

HALL, O. J.
Daguerreotypist originally from New York, active in Neenah, 1850.

HALLETT, G. M.
Stereo photographer active in Corbie.

HALLICK, E. S. (MISS)
Daguerreotypist originally from New York, operating in Palmyra, 1860.

HAND, ORVILLE
Daguerreotypist active in Janesville, 1855.

HAND, W. A.
Active in Janesville, 1875-90.

HARDY, W. H.
Daguerreotypist active in Genesee, 1857.

HARMON, HENRY S.
Daguerreotypist operating studio in Sheboygan, 1857-71.

HARRIS, H.
Active in Chetek, 1880.

HARRISON, JAMES F.
Daguerreotypist originally from England, active in Oshkosh, 1854-57.

HASKELL, HIRAM, H.
Daguerreotypist active in Grand Rapids, 1857; Sun Prarie, 1860. Possibly the same as Hiram M. Haskell.

HASKINS
Daguerreotypist active in Waukesha, 1855, operating Haskins Daguerrean Rooms.

HAWLEY, J. P.
Daguerreotypist originally from England, operating in Appleton, 1852-66.

HAYDEN, JAMES
Daguerreotypist active in Attica, 1857.

HEATH & MOSS
Brief partnership in LaCrosse; H. C. Heath and possibly T. F. Moss.

HEATH, HENRY C.
Daguerreotypist from New York, active in LaCrosse, 1858-1900.

HEBERT, J. O.
Stereo photographer in Fond du Lac and Grand Rapids.

HEEB, ADAM
Active in Milwaukee, 1880.

HEGG, E. A.
Studio in Washburn, 1883-88. See Washington.

HELSOM, R. O.
Active in Menomonie, c. 1885.

HENTSCHER, H.
Active in Manitowoc, 1870.

HERRICK, E. L.
Daguerreotypist active in Beloit, 1853.

HESLER, ALEXANDER
Daguerreotypist originally from Canada, active in Madison, 1847-48; Southport, 1849.

HICKOX, M. A. (MRS.)
Daguerreotypist originally from Ohio, active in Koshkonong, 1860.

HILLMAN, W. J.
Active in Richland Center, 1875.

HILTON, W. H.
Active in Omro, c. 1880.

HOADLEY, JAMES H.
Daguerreotypist active in Sheboygan, 1857.

HOFFERT, H. C.
Amateur stereo photographer in Racine; member of the Stereoscopic Society, 1939.

HOLLY, M. S.
Photographer in Berline, active c. 1870s; reportedly made stereoviews.

HOOK, W. E.
Active in Neenah, 1870.

HORN, EDWARD
Daguerreotypist active in Milwaukee, 1856-60, operating as Fowler & Horn with Elbert W. Fowler.

HORTON, G. W.
Possibly a partner with Spink in Oshkosh, 1870s-80s; also active in Beaver Dam.

HOSKEN, W. K.
Active in Oconomowoc, 1860.

HOSKING, J. E.
Active in Mineral Point, 1880.

HOUGHTON, GEORGE HARPER
Daguerreotypist originally from Vermont, active in Kilbourn City, 1857-59, operating Houghton's Gallery.

HOWARD
Active in Oconomowoc, 1870.

HOYT, MARY S.
Born in Connecticut. Daguerreotypist who attended the first convention of the New York State Daguerrean Association, 1851, while living in Syracuse. Active in Portage City, Wisconsin, 1860.

HUFF, EARL F.
Daguerreotypist originally from New York, active in Kenosha, 1850.

HUGGINS, JAMES H.
Daguerreotypist active in Milwaukee, 1857.

HUGHES, FREDERICK N.
Daguerreotypist in Sheboygan and Southport, 1849.

HUTCHINSON & SON
Stereo photographer active in Appleton.

ISAAC'S STUDIO
Active in Eau Claire.

ISAACS, A. C.
Active in Madison, 1880.

IVERSON & COMPANY, J. C.
Located at 425 and 427 Water Street in Milwaukee, 1915-58; published stereoviews by H. H. Bennett and William P. Vollert.

IVES, STARR M.
Daguerreotypist originally from New York, active in Horicon, 1857; Centre, 1860.

JAMES, D.
Active in Marshfield, 1880. See Traveling.

JANES
Daguerreotypist in New Lisbon, 1857, operating as Case & Janes.

JANSSEN, E.
Active in Beloit, 1880.

JELLY, D.
Stereo photographer in Minerva Point.

JENKINS, D.
Active in Mineral Point, 1880.

JOB, CHARLES
Daguerreotypist active in Mukwonago, 1857.

JOHNSON
Partner in Beach & Johnson, corner of Front and Main Streets in LaCrosse, 1867.

JOHNSON, ALFRED S.
Daguerreotypist originally from England, active in White Creek, 1860.

JOHNSON, C. A.
Daguerreotypist active in Madison, 1854-57.

JOHNSON, WILLIAM
Daguerreotypist originally from New York, active in Janesville, 1850.

JOHNSTON, DAVID
Daguerreotypist active in Waukesha, 1857.

JOHNSTON, J. W.
Daguerreotypist active in Whitewater, 1857.

JOLLEY, JOHN
Daguerreotypist originally from Ireland, active in Portage City, 1870.

JONES
Studio at 13 West Main Street, Madison, c. 1885. Possibly N. P. Jones.

JONES, DANIEL
Daguerreotypist active in Kenosha, 1857, operating as Monfoet & Jones with H. A. Monfoet.

JONES, JEREMIAH
Daguerreotypist originally from Ohio, active in Janesville, 1850.

JONES, MANNING
Daguerreotypist active in Beloit, 1857, operating with Andrew W. Peters as Jones' Photographic Picture Gallery, or Peters & Jones Picture Gallery.

JONES, N. P.
Active in Madison, 1870.

JOSLYN, JAMES H.
Daguerreotypist originally from New York, active in Beloit and Plover, 1857; Kenosha, 1860-67.

JOURDAN
Daguerreotypist active in Plover, 1857, operating as Dunton & Jourdan.

JOURDAN, GEORGE E.
Daguerreotypist and ambrotypist active in Green Bay, 1855-57; active in Neenah, 1858, with E. W. Peets operating as Jourdan & Peets Ambrotype Gallery.

JUDD, SARAH LOUISE
Born in Farmington, Hartford County, Connecticut, June 26, 1806; died in Stillwater, Minnesota, October 12, 1886. Daguerreotypist active in Stillwater, Wisconsin Territory, 1848-50.

JUNE, T. O.
Active in Necedah, c. 1895. Name may be F. O. June.

KELLOGG, D. W.
Daguerreotypist active in Jefferson, 1857.

KELLOGG, E. S.
Daguerreotypist active in Beaver Dam, 1857-67.

KELLOGG, J. D.
Active in Watertown, 1860.

KELLOGG, MARK H.
Daguerreotypist originally from Canada, active in LaCrosse, 1860.

KELLOGG, W. F.
Active in River Falls, 1875-90.

KELSEY
Daguerreotypist active in Stevens Point, 1857.

KELSEY, A.
Daguerreotypist active in Delavan, 1857-60.

KELSEY, J. F.
Daguerreotypist active in Hortonville, 1857.

KENDALL, FERNANDO C.
Daguerreotypist originally from Canada, active in Springvale, 1860.

KENDALL, RICHARD
Daguerreotypist from Wisconsin, active in Mineral Point, 1860.

KENNAN, THOMAS L.
Daguerreotypist originally from New York, active in Oshkosh, 1849, operating Miniature Rooms.

KERTSON & COURTEAU
Partnership in Sauk Center, c. 1886; issued stereoviews of St. Cloud cyclone, 1886.

KESLER, R. E.
Active in Burlington, 1860.

KESSLAR, J. J.
Daguerreotypist active in Grafton, 1857.

KING, GEORGE P.
Daguerreotypist active in Green Bay, 1858-59.

KIRCHOFF, OTTO E.
Active in Milwaukee, 1880.

KLINGHOLZ, HUGO
Active in Manitowoc, 1875-90.

KLUTCSCH, JOHN
Daguerreotypist active in Sauk City, 1857.

KNAPP, H. C.
Daguerreotypist active in Geneva Bay, 1857.

KNIGHT, W. M.
Daguerreotypist active in Racine, 1851.

KREMER, F.
Daguerreotypist active in Milwaukee, 1880, operating as Broich & Kremer with Hugo Broich. Also be spelled Kramer.

KUHN, FREDERICK
Partner with George Trager in Mazomanie, 1888. See Nebraska.

LACY, EUGENE O.
Daguerreotypist from New York, active in Prarie du Chien, 1860.

LAMARSH
Partner in Truesdall & LaMarsh, Kenosha, c. 1870s.

LAMB, W. H.
Active in Glidden, 1880.

LAMB, W. W.
Active in Medford, 1870.

LAND, J. C.
Stereo photographer active in Waukesha; issued stereoviews "In and About the Dells of the Wisconsin River."

LANE, W. H.
"Photo. Artist & Dealer in Albums, Stereoscopes" in Monfort and Hazel Green; issued "European views."

LANGWORTHY, BENJAMIN F.
Daguerreotypist originally from Ohio, active in Oshkosh, 1853, with A. B. Parsons operating as Parsons & Langworthy.

LATHROP, W. H.
Active in LaCrosse, 1875-90.

LATIMER, K.
Daguerreotypist active in Fairwater, 1857.

LAW, G.
Active in Burlington, 1860.

LEA, GEORGE
Photographer in Tomah; made stereoviews of Wisconsin scenery, Chicago, and North Western Railroad.

LECHER
Active in Milwaukee, 1880.

LEE
Partner in Boetcher & Lee, 106 Bridge Street in Chippewa Falls, c. 1885.

LEWIS, HARRY
Stereo photographer in Milwaukee at 104 and 106 Wisconsin Street.

LIND, G. A.
Partner in Gault & Lind, Marinette, c. 1885; also active in Fond du Lac.

LOCKWOOD & ELY
Partnership active in Racine, c. 1870s-90s; Cook Ely.

LOCKWOOD, E. N. (MRS.)
Photographer in Ripon, c. 1870; probably the wife of W. M. Lock-wood.

LOCKWOOD, W. M. & MRS.
Photographers and publishers in Green Lake and Ripon c. 1870. Mrs. W. M. may be the same as Mrs. E. N.

LOCKWOOD, WILLIAM M.
Daguerreotypist originally from New York, with studios located in Waupun, 1853-56; Oshkosh, 1856-57; Ripon, 1857-89. Probably the same as W. M. Lockwood.

LONG, J. T., JR.
Active in Menomonie, 1880.

LOOFBOROUGH & RAITT
Partnership active in Wisconsin, details unknown. Possibly T. G. Raitt who also worked alone in Ashland at some point.

LOOMIS, J. C.
Daguerreotypist active in Ozaukee, 1857.

LOOPS, CHARLES
Active in Milwaukee, 1875-90.

LOUDEN, GAVIS
Daguerreotypist active in Janesville as Thompson & Louden, 1856-57; in Port Hope, 1857.

LOVE, J. W.
Active in Portage City, 1860-80.

LOWMILLER, F.
Studio and landscape photographer in Milwaukee.

LUCAS, C. W.
Active in Broadhead, 1880.

LUCK, T.
Active in Racine, 1875-90.

LUTSEY, H. G.
Photographer in New London; issued rare "Views of Keshena."

LYDSTON, A. F.
Active in Milwaukee, 1860.

MACADAM, T. T.
Stereo photographer in Galesville.

MACK, WILLIAM H.
Daguerreotypist active in Viola, 1857.

MANN, W. G.
Active in Waukesha, 1875-90.

MANVILLE & MALLORY
Partnership in Sheboygan, 1870.

MANVILLE, C. B.
Active in Green Bay, 1870.

MANVILLE, FAYETTE W.
Daguerreotypist and photographer in Sheboygan, 1859-91.

MANZER
Active in Oshkosh, 1890.

MARQUIS, A., JR.
Active in Milwaukee, 1860.

MARSH, E. N.
Daguerreotypist active in Baraboo, 1857.

MARSH, HIRAM
Daguerreotypist originally from New York, active in Sheboygan, 1854.

MARSH, JAMES D.
Daguerreotypist originally from New York, Active in Sheboygan (Falls), 1850.

MARTIN
Daguerreotypist active in Berlin, 1857.

MARTIN, A. S.
Daguerreotypist active in Stevens Point, 1857.

MARTIN, H. B.
Daguerreotypist active in Stevens Point, 1857.

MARTIN, T. W.
Active in Shullsburg, 1870.

MATHIEU
Active in Watertown, 1880.

MAXWELL, DAVID
Daguerreotypist from Pennsylvania, active in Jamestown, 1860.

McCARTY, AUGUSTUS
Daguerreotypist active in Sheboygan, 1849.

McCOLLISTER, E. R.
Active in Baraboo, 1880.

McEWEN, THEODORE
Daguerreotypist originally from Ohio, active in Portage City, 1860.

McGARY
Active in Norwalk, 1870-90.

McHENRY, JOHN A.
Daguerreotypist active in Racine, 1857.

McINTYRE, W. M.
Studio on Franklin Street, Port Washington, c. 1862.

McKENNEY, DAVIS
Daguerreotypist active in Berlin, 1857.

McPHERSON & ROLOSON
Active in Darien, 1870; W. H. Roloson.

McPHERSON & SONS
Stereo photographer in Delavan.

McPHERSON, ROLOSON, & GRAVES
Partnership active in Delava; W. H. Roloson.

McSCHOOLER, L. W.
Daguerreotypist active in Berlin, 1857.

McSPADDEN, GEORGE
Daguerreotypist originally from Ireland, active in Neenah, 1850.

MEASON, L. E.
Active in LaCrosse, 1875.

MEDLAR, J. B.
Active in Jefferson, 1870.

MENZEL
Active in Grand Rapids, c. 1895.

MERRIMAN, O. G.
Active in Eau Claire, 1880.

MERRITON, H.
Daguerreotypist active in Marquette, 1857.

METCALF, WILLIAM H.
Born in New York, 1821; died in Milwaukee, 1892. Amateur in Milwaukee who began studying with H. H. Bennett of Kilbourn City and became an accomplished photographer, although he was a partner in a Milwaukee shoe factory by trade. Metcalf traveled to Japan, c. 1877, and made fine series of stereoviews, "A Summer in Japan," published by Bennett and credited to "W. H. M." A few rare stereoviews are known with a W. H. Metcalf blind-stamp. Provided Bennett with considerably financial support over 20 year period and gave him a studio. No connection with W. H. Metcalf of Texas.

MILLER
Active in Ashland, 1885.

MILLER, DAVIS
Daguerreotypist originally from Vermont, active in Princeton, 1860.

MILLER, HERMAN N.
Photographer in Milwaukee, successor to Miller Brothers.

MILLER, J. C.
Active in Green Bay, 1875-90.

MILLER, J. D.
Partner in Schroeder & Miller, Green Bay, c. 1877.

MILLER, JOHN C.
Daguerreotypist originally from Germany, active in Waukesha, 1858-62.

MILLER, WILLIAM
Active in West Bend, c. 1868.

MOECKLI
Gallery at 1111 North 8th Street, Sheboygen, c. 1900.

MOFFETT, C. R.
Daguerreotypist originally from Kentucky, active in Mineral Point, 1860.

MOHR, JAMES
Daguerreotypist originally from Pennsylvania, active in LaCrosse, 1853.

MONFOET & JONES
Partnership of H. A. Monfoet and Daniel Jones, operating in Kenosha, 1857.

MONFOET, H. A.
Daguerreotypist active in Kenosha, 1857, with Daniel Jones, operating as Monfoet & Jones.

MONROE, C. J.
Stereo photographer in Dallas and Hawkins, c. 1900-08; produced stereoviews of hunting, fishing and logging.

MONROE, A. L. (MRS)
Active in Thorp, 1880.

MOORES
Daguerreotypist active in Kewaunee, 1857, operating as Moores & Company.

MORGAN, GEORGE
Stereo photographer in Viroqua.

MORGANEIER, J. H.
Active in Sheboygan, 1870.

MORSE
Daguerreotypist active in Montello, 1857.

MOSELEY BROTHERS
Active in Janesville, 1870.

MOSS, T. F.
Active in Hudson, 1880; possibly a partner in Heath & Moss, LaCrosse.

MOULD, F. W.
Studio at 413 South 3rd Street, LaCrosse, c. 1890.

MOULD, M.
Active in Baraboo and Devil's Lake, 1860-80.

MOULD, SIM
Active in Baraboo, 1880.

MOULTON, L. V.
Active in Beaver Dam, 1870.

MUNGER, D. G.
Active in Oconomowoc, 1870-90.

MYERS, E. M.
Active in LaCrosse, 1880.

NEVEL
Active in Baldwin, c. 1895.

NIAS, RAYMOND
Photographer and publisher of stereoviews located in Sparta; issued stereoviews of Medicinal Artesian Springs, Sparta, Indians, teepees, meat slaughter and other local scenes.

NIELSON
Active in Madison, 1880.

NORTH-WESTERN VIEW COMPANY
Active in Baraboo, 1900.

NOYES & BENNETT
Partnership in Oconomowoc, 1880.

NOYES, J. B.
Active in Lake Geneva, 1880.

NUSS, W. H.
Studio at 215 North Washington Street, c. 1890.

NYE, JAMES L.
Active in Platteville, 1880.

O'BRIEN
Active in Waukesha.

OCCIDENTAL VIEW COMPANY
Seller for American Stereoscopic Company in Stoughton.

OGILVIE & BARROWS
Daguerreotypists in Janesville, 1857.

ORDEMANN, T.
Active in Menomonie, 1875-90.

OTIS, O. C.
Daguerreotypist in Oconomowoc, 1855, operating O. C. Otis Picture Gallery.

OWEN, W. H.
Active in Evansville, 1860.

PALMER (MR. & MRS.)
Active in Tomah, 1880.

PARIS, JAMES
Active in Fond du Lac, 1860-75.

PARISH, DANIEL
Daguerreotypist originally from New York, active in Adams, 1850.

PARKER, GEORGE F.
Daguerreotypist active in Milwaukee, 1850.

PARKINSON, LEROY
Active in Fox Lake; published "Fox Lake Scenery."

PARRHISUS, A.
Daguerreotypist originally from Prussia, active in Lowell, 1860.

PARRHISUS, H.
Daguerreotypist originally from Prussia, in Lowell, 1860.

PARSONS & LANGWORTHY
Daguerreotypists active in Oshkosh, 1853, operated by Benjamin F. Langworthy and A. B. Parsons.

PARSONS, A. B.
Daguerreotypist active in Oshkosh, 1853, operating as Parsons & Langworthy with Benjamin F. Langworthy.

PATRICK, W. W.
Daguerreotypist active in Portland, 1857.

PATTEN, J. S.
Daguerreotypist active in LaCrosse, 1854-58.

PATTERSON
Partner with John Callender in Ripon, operating as Callender & Patterson at west side public square, 1857; operating as Bayley & Patterson, Milwaukee, 1860.

PATTERSON, ABRAM C.
Daguerreotypist originally from New York, active in Green Bay, 1847-49.

PATTERSON, R.
Daguerreotypist active in Wisconsin, c. 1857.

PATTON, H. F.
Active in Appleton, 1860.

PAYNE, F. E.
Stereo photographer in Elroy, 1884.

PEASE, F.
Possibly in partnership with E. H. Burrit in St. Paul, 1870s-80s.

PEASE, HORACE
Daguerreotypist originally from Connecticut, active in Milwaukee, 1850.

PECK, HENRY S.
Active in Racine; issued views of Yale. See G. C. Thomas.

PECK, JULIA S.
Daguerreotypist active in Beloit, 1860.

PEETS, E .W.
Daguerreotypist and ambrotypist active in Neenah, 1858, with George E. Jourdan operating Jourdan & Peets Ambrotype Gallery.

PENDERGAST, WILSON & COMPANY
Daguerreotypists active in Milwaukee, 1855.

PERKINS, C. D.
Daguerreotypist active in Janesville, 1856.

PERKINS, H. J.
Active in Waupaca, c. 1880s. Produced stereviews.

PERKINS PHOTOGRAPH & AMBROTYPE CAR
Active in Oshkosh, 1860.

PERKINS, T. K.
Stereo photographer active in Dale.

PETERS & JONES PICTURE GALLERY
Daguerreian gallery in Beloit, 1857, operated by Andrew W. Peters and Manning Jones.

PETERS, A. M.
Active in Beloit, 1860.

PETERS, ANDREW W.
Daguerreotypist operating the Peters & Jones Picture Gallery in Beloit, 1857, with Manning Jones.

PETERSON, CHARLES T.
Photographer or publisher of rare stereoviews; located in Milwaukee.

PETRI, WILLIAM M. (MRS.)
Daguerreotypist active in Sheboygan, 1854-88.

PHILLIPS
Active in Argyle, 1875-85.

PHOTOGRAPHIC ART PALACE
Operated by Edward R. Curtiss in Madison, 1859-90.

PHRENNY, JOHN
Daguerreotypist originally from Pennsylvania, active in Fountain Prairie, 1860.

PIPER, H.
Active in Black Earth, 1865.

PIPER, W. S.
Active in Portage City, 1900.

PLANK, FRED A.
Daguerreotypist originally from New York, active in Wilmont, 1857; Randall, 1860.

PLUMB, S. L.
Stereo photographer in Portage.

PODOLL, G.
Active in Cedarburg, 1875.

PORTER, J. R.
Stereo photographer active in Jacsville.

POTTER, A. J.
Daguerreotypist active in Waukesha, 1850-51.

POTTER, J .O.
Daguerreotypist active in Waukesha, 1850-51.

POWERS, J. E.
Daguerreotypist originally from New York, active in Janesville, 1853-57; Christiania, 1860.

POWERS, STEWART
Daguerreotypist in Janesville, 1857.

PREBENSEN
Active in Neenah, c. 1875.

PRESTON, N. A.
Daguerreotypist operating as Richardson & Preston in Monroe, 1857.

PRYOR, W. A.
Studio at 121 North Fourth Street, LaCrosse, c. 1890.

PUTNAM, CHARLES W.
Daguerreotypist active in Oconomowoc, 1860.

RAINHELD, H. E. (MRS.)
Active in Ft. Atkinson, 1860.

RAITT, T. G.
Photographer and publisher of "Lake Superior and North Wisconsin Views" from studio in Ashland. Also photographed the Chippewa Reservation, Apostle Islands, Washburn and vicinity. Possibly a partner in Loofborough & Raitt.

RAUCH, THEODORE
Daguerreotypist active in Ashford, 1857.

RAWIES, CASPAR
Daguerreotypist originally from Prussia, active in Watertown, 1860.

RAWSON, CHARLES S.
Daguerreotypist in Milwaukee, 1860.

RAYMOND
Active in LaCrosse, 1870.

RENYON, O. A.
Daguerreotypist active in Black Earth, 1857.

RICH, T.
Operator and proprietor of City Photograph Gallery in Waupaca, 1870, at corner of Main and Granite Streets.

RICHARDSON & PRESTON
Partnership of James Richardson and N. A. Preston, daguerreotypists in Monroe, 1857-60.

RICHARDSON BROTHERS
Active in Sparta, 1880-1900; F. Richardson.

RICHARDSON, F.
Partner in Cottrell & Richardson, Sparta, 1875; operating as Richardson Brothers, 1880.

RICHARDSON, G. W.
Daguerreotypist active in Napasha, 1857.

RICHARDSON, JAMES
Daguerreotypist originally from New York, active in Monroe, 1857-60, operating Richardson & Preston.

RICHARDSON, WILLIAM F.
Daguerreotypist in Fox Lake, 1857.

RICHMOND, GEORGE N.
Daguerreotypist originally from New York, active in Milwaukee, 1850.

RIDGEWAY, I. A.
Stereo photographer in Portage.

RIPLEY & GIBSON
Daguerreotypists C. T. Ripley and J. S. Gibson, active in Fond du Lac, 1854-57.

RIPLEY, C. T.
Daguerreotypist active in Fond du Lac, 1854-57, operating as Ripley & Gibson with J. S. Gibson.

ROBERTS & WHITING
Active in Madison, 1865.

ROBERTS, H. N.
Active in Madison, 1860.

ROBERTS, NAOMA E.
Born in New York, c. 1840. Daguerreotypist and ambrotypist active in Fox Lake, 1860.

ROBINSON, H. M.
Active in Green Bay, 1850-51, with S. N. Robinson, operating as Robinson Brothers, Daguerreians.

ROBINSON, HENRY
Daguerreotypist originally from New York, active in Rochester, 1850.

ROBINSON, N. H.
Daguerreotypist active in Sheboygan, 1856.

ROBINSON, NEWELL
Daguerreotypist originally from Vermont, active in Rochester, 1850.

ROBINSON, S. N.
Active in Green Bay, 1850-51, operating Robinson Brothers, Daguerreians with H. M. Robinson.

ROBINSON, W.
Daguerreotypist originally from New York, active in Milwaukee, 1850.

ROBINSON, W. H. H.
Active in Oshkosh, 1870.

ROCHWITE, SETON
Designer of the most successful stereo camera of all time, the Realist. He also designed and produced the Kindar and Hyponar stereo attachments for the Exacta. Member of Stereoscopic Society, 1930s; active in Wauwatosa.

ROCKSTEAD, S. N.
Stereo photographer in Durand and Blanchardville.

ROGAN
Issued rare stereoviews of Arcadia; active in Whitehall.

ROLOSON, W. H.
Active in Darien, 1870, operating as McPherson & Roloson and McPherson, Roloson & Graves in Delavan.

ROSS
Active in Appleton, 1895.

ROUSENVELL, WILLIAM
Daguerreotypist active in Winooskie, 1857.

RUDD
Partner in Hall & Rudd, Green Bay, 1870.

RUNDLETT, CHARLES W.
Active in Watertown, 1870, operating as Rundlett Brothers.

SANFORD, W. H.
Daguerreotypist active in Kenosha, 1856, operating "Daguerrean & Ambrotype Rooms."

SCHADDE, P. JOSEPH
"Photographer, Artist, & Inventor of the Repeating Camera," active in Sauk City.

SCHNEIDER
Studio on Washington Street, Green Bay, c. 1890.

SCHNEIDER, A.
Active in Milwaukee, 1870-90.

SCHROEDER & MILLER
Partnership of G. F. Schroeder and J. D. Miller in Green Bay, c. 1877.

SCHROEDER, C. F.
Active in Green Bay, 1895. Probably the same as G. F. Schroeder.

SCIDMORE, A.
Active in Appleton, 1870.

SEELEY, CHARLES M.
Daguerreotypist active in Milwaukee, 1857, operating the Great Central Daguerrean Gallery.

SENNETT, E. C.
Active in Grand Rapids and Stevens Point, 1870.

SEVERANS
Partner in Sprague & Severans operating in Mauston, 1860.

SHAKER
Active in Eau Claire, 1900.

SHERMAN, C. V.
Daguerreotypist active in New London, 1857.

SHERMAN, W. H.
Daguerreotypist originally from Vermont, active in Beloit, 1855-60; Milwaukee, 1860-80.

SILSBEE
Partner in Truesdell & Silsbee, Kenosha, 1870.

SIMPSON (MISS)
Operated as daguerreotypist with her brother, Lewry, in Kenosha, 1857.

SIMPSON, LEWRY
Daguerreotypist active in Kenosha, 1857, operating as Lewry Simpson & Sister.

SKEWIS
Partner in Ennor & Skewis, active in Richland Center, 1880.

SLATER, E. P.
Active in Black River Falls, 1870.

SLAYTON, CURTIS H.
Daguerreotypist originally from New York, active in Westfield, 1857; Harris, 1860.

SMALL
Partner in Black & Small operating in Milwaukee c. 1885.

SMITH & TAYLOR
Studio in Augusta, c. 1885.

SMITH, C. M.
Daguerreotypist active in Oconomoc, 1860-62.

SMITH, G. W.
Daguerreotypist active in Green Bay, 1852-53; Appleton, 1853, operating the Daguerrean Gallery.

SMITH, GEORGE M.
Daguerreotypist active in Beloit, 1852.

SMITH, H. N.
Stereo photographer active in Lake Keuka.

SPENCER, WILLIAM
Daguerreotypist originally from New York, active in Dunkirk, 1860.

SPETTEL BROTHERS
Gallery in North LaCrosse, c. 1890, at 806 Caledonia Street.

SPICER, C. A.
Active in Clintonville, 1875-85.

SPINK & HORTON
Partnership active in Oshkosh, c. 1880s; possibly G. W. Horton.

SPRAGUE & SEVERANS
Partnership in Mauston, 1860.

SPRING, A.
Daguerreotypist active in Sheboygan, 1849, operating as W. G. & A. Spring.

SPRING, W. G.
Daguerreotypist active in Sheboygan, 1849, operating as W. G. & A. Spring.

SPRING, W. G. & A.
Partnership in Sheboygan, 1849..

STAINS, JOSEPH
Daguerreotypist active in South Grove, 1857.

STAMM
Daguerreotypist active in Milwaukee, 1851, operating as Stamm & Upman with D. Upman.

STANLEY, A. R.
Daguerreotypist active in Schullsburgh, 1857.

STAPLES, D. B.
Daguerreotypist active in Dodgeville, 1857.

STAR GALLERY
Operated by J. B. Gallaher in Chippewa Falls and Neillsville.

STARK, WILLIAM
Daguerreotypist active in Manitowoc, 1857.

STEIN, W. L.
Active in Milwaukee, 1880, 1900.

STEINBORN, F. J.
Active in Hustisford, 1880.

STEPHENSON, JOHN
Daguerreotypist originally from New York, active in Leeds, 1860.

STEVENS, GEORGE
Daguerreotypist active in Harmony, 1857.

STIMSON
Active in South Superior, 1890; Appleton, c. 1900.

STOKES, A.
Daguerreotypist active in Chippewa, 1857.

STREIT, F. W.
Stereo photographer active in Milwaukee.

STROUD, W. L.
Daguerreotypist active in Oshkosh, 1856-60, operating Stroud's New Daguerreian Gallery.

STYLES (MRS.)
Daguerreotypist active in Mifflin, 1857-58.

SUMMERHAYES
Daguerreotypist active in LaCrosse, 1856-60, operating Boycott, Summerhayes & Company.

SUNDERLAND, W. F.
Active in Nhosho, 1880.

SUTTER
Located at 128 Wisconsin Street, Milwaukee, 1875-90.

TANNER, CHARLES F.
Stereo photographer active in Janesville, c. 1880s.

TAYLOR
Partner in Smith & Taylor, active in Augusta, c. 1885.

TAYLOR, A. E.
Active in Clinton, 1875-90.

TAYLOR, M. F.
Active in Rochester, 1870.

TAYLOR, S. M.
Stereo photographer active in Berlin.

TEBO
Stereo photographer active in Eau Claire, 1870s.

TEN EYCK (MRS.)
Active in Milwaukee, 1860.

TERRY, M.
Daguerreotypist active in Racine, 1857.

TERWILLERGER, W.
Daguerreotypist in Pardeeville, 1857.

THOMAS & WHEELER
Partnership of G. C. Thomas and possibly D. W. Wheeler in Racine, c. 1870s.

THOMAS, G. C.
Successor to Henry S. Peck at same address in Racine; at least two stereoviews of Yale issued under this label were originally by Peck, so he may have purchased entire stock. Active c. 1880s.

THOMAS, H. W.
Active in Hartford, 1860.

THOMPSON & LOUDEN
Daguerreotypists active in Janesville, 1856-57; Gavin Louden and Samuel F. Thompson.

THOMPSON, SAMUEL F.
Daguerreotypist active in Janesville, 1856-66, with Jacob A. Tice in Thompson & Tice.

THUEMMLER, PH. E.
Active in Milwaukee, 1870-90.

TICE, JACOB A.
Daguerreotypist active in Janesville, 1857-70. Partner in Barks & Tice with J. A. Tice, operating Academy of Design, corner of Main and Milwaukee Streets, 1862; with Samuel F. Thompson, 1856-66, in Thompson & Tice.

TOLEY & BUGBEE
Partnership of Van H. Bugbee and Toley in Waukesha, c. 1870s.

TRAGER, GEORGE
Active in Whitewater and Mazomanie, c. 1888. Also known as Gus. See Nebraska.

TRIMBLE, N.
Daguerreotypist active in Madison, 1857.

TRIPP, JAMES
Active in Berlin, 1860.

TRISTS (MISSES)
Daguerreotypists, possibly sisters, active in Edgerton, 1857.

TRUESDALL & LAMARSH
Partnership of S. W. Truesdall and LaMarsh in Kenosha, c. 1870s. Issued rare stereoviews.

TRUESDELL & SILSBEE
Active in Kenosha, 1870.

TRUESDELL, S. W.
Daguerreotypist originally from New York, active in Kenosha, 1860-85; partner in Truesdell & Silsbee, 1870.

TRUSCOTT & BENNETT
Active in Milwaukee, 1858-59; Benjamin S. Bennett.

TURNER, CHARLES F.
Stereo photographer in Janesville.

TUTTLE
Daguerreotypist active in Janesville, 1854, operating Tuttle & Son.

TUTTLE, H.
Daguerreotypist originally from Michigan, active in Sheboygan, 1854; Columbus, 1860.

TUTTLE, T.
Daguerreotypist active in Palmyra, 1857.

TWIST, JULIA S.
Photographer in Beloit, c. 1860; traveled to California in search of her husband, 1861.

TYLER & BUGBEE
Partnership of Van H. Bugbee and Tyler, operating in Waukesha, c. 1881.

TYLER, O. E. & H. C.
Active in Waukesha, 1860-80.

UNION GALLERY
Operated in Beloit before 1863; known as the Fine Art Gallery owned by C. L. Burpee, 1863-70.

UPMAN, D.
Daguerreotypist originally from Germany, operating as Stamm & Upman in Milwaukee, 1850-51.

UTLEY, WILLIAM L.
Daguerreotypist originally from Ohio, active in Racine, 1850.

VAN DE WALL & SON, F.
Active in Lancaster, 1870-85.

VAN DE WALL, W. B.
Active in Lancaster, 1880.

VAUGHN, CORNEL
Daguerreotypist originally from Vermont, active in Berlin and Portage City, 1857; Oshkosh, 1860.

VEDDER, JOHN H.
Daguerreotypist active in Oxford, 1857.

VIKING VIEW COMPANY
Active in Edgerton, 1900.

VOLLERT, WILLIAM P.
Active in Milwaukee, c. 1900s; made stereoviews published by J. C. Iverson.

VOLQUARTS
Active in Plymouth, 1875.

VON BROICH, HUGO
Daguerreotypist originally from Germany, active in Milwaukee, 1857-80. Also known as Hugo Broich.

WAGNER, J. A.
Active in Burlington, 1880.

WAKEFIELD, LELAND HOWARD
Born in Cornish, New Hampshire, July 9, 1823. Daguerreotypist active in Boston, Massachusetts, 1845-47. Moved to Kenosha, Wisconsin, 1847-52, operating Daguerreotype Rooms. Moved to Oregon, continuing in photography in Portland and Oregon City, 1852-53. Eventually moved to California. See Oregon.

WALCOTT
Active in Berlin.

WALDERON, J. C.
Daguerreotypist originally from Canada, active in Mt. Pleasant, 1860.

WALDO, DAVID H.
Daguerreotypist active in Milwaukee, 1854.

WALKER
Partner in Webster & Walker active in Janesville and Oshkosh, 1860.

WALKER & CONNOR
Daguerreotypists active in Racine, 1857.

WALKER, HENRY J.
Daguerreotypist originally from England, active in Wingville, 1860.

WARREN, S. K.
Stereo photographer in Geneva.

WATERMAN, IRA
Daguerreotypist active in Plainfield, 1857.

WEAVER, O. F.
Active in Beaver Dam.

WEBB, D. W.
Daguerreotypist active in Mineral Point, 1845.

WEBSTER
Active in Oshkosh, 1895.

WEBSTER
Active in Horicon, 1860.

WEBSTER & WALKER
Partnership in Janesville and Oshkosh, 1860.

WEBSTER, W. F.
Active in Oshkosh, 1880.

WELPER, HENRY
Stereo photographer active in West Eau Claire.

WEST, H. T.
Daguerreotypist active in Kenosha, 1856.

WHEELER & BARNARD DAGUERREAN GALLERY
Operated by L. O. Barnard and Samuel Wheeler in Neenah, 1856-57, in Shoemaker and Verbeck's Building.

WHEELER, A. H.
Issued stereoviews of "Wauwatosa Scenery."

WHEELER, D. W.
Possibly a partner in Green & Wheeler, Racine, 1860; possibly with G. C. Thomas, c. 1870s; also active in Milwaukee.

WHEELER, SAMUEL
Daguerreotypist active in Neenah, 1856-57, operating Wheeler & Barnard Daguerrean Gallery with L. O. Barnard; also known as S. Wheeler Daguerrean Gallery in Shoemaker and Verbeck's Building.

WHIPPLE, JOHN P.
Daguerreotypist originally from Maine. Active in Sheboygan, 1854-57; Green Bay, 1860; operated the Daguerrean Gallery in De Pere, 1861; Whitewater, 1870.

WHITE, H. G.
Active in Milwaukee, 1870.

WHITESIDES, WILLIAM
Active in Ashland, 1870.

WHITING
Partner in Roberts & Whiting active in Madison, 1865.

WHITNEY, WILLIAM S.
Daguerreotypist in Madison, 1855.

WIGGINS, SILAS T.
Daguerreotypist active in Waneka, 1857.

WILCOX, AUGUSTUS
Daguerreotypist active in LaCrosse, 1853.

WILKINS & CHANDLER
Studio in Oshkosh, 1860.

WILKINS & COMPANY
Oshkosh, 1860.

WILKINS, C. E.
Stereo photographer in Delavan; active in Fond du Lac, 1870.

WILKINS, IRA
Daguerreotypist active in Viroqua, 1857.

WILKINS, J.
Daguerreotypist active in Sparta, 1857.

WILKINS, ORSELL E.
Daguerreotypist active in Fond du Lac, 1860-66.

WILKINSON, A. C.
Daguerreotypist originally from New Hampshire, active in Beloit, 1850.

WILLIAMS
Active in Medford, c. 1895

WILLIAMS, D. C.
Daguerreotypist in Chippewa, 1857.

WILLIAMS, F. J.
Active in Platteville, 1870.

WILSON
Daguerreotypist operating Pendergast, Wilson & Company in Milwaukee, 1855.

WILSON, A. T.
Daguerreotypist active in Sheboygan, 1853.

WILSON, JOHN
Daguerreotypist originally from Ohio, active in Platteville, 1860.

WINCHESTER, D. D.
Daguerreotypist in Southport, 1847.

WINKLE, J.
Active in Wild Rose, 1875-90.

WISE, GEORGE W.
Active in Janesville.

WOOD, E. B.
Daguerreotypist originally from New York, active in Albion, 1860.

WOOD, GEORGE C.
Daguerreotypist operating the Daguerreotype & Phrenological Room in Milwaukee, 1847.

WOOD, I. N.
Daguerreotypist active in Rural, 1857.

WOOD, SYDNEY A.
Daguerreotypist in Madison, 1857.

WORTHEN, E. B.
Daguerreotypist originally from Massachusetts, active in Stevens Point, 1857; Lisbon, 1860.

WRIGHT, HENRY U.
Daguerreotypist active in Potosi, 1857.

WRIGHT, O. B.
Daguerreotypist in Oakfield, 1857.

WRIGHT, W. J.
Active in Fennimore, 1880.

WYCKOFF, JOSHUA H.
Daguerreotypist originally from New York, active in Ripon, 1857-85. Operated Wycoff & Company, 1860; Art Union Gallery, 1885 (possibly 1857-85). Also spelled Wycoff.

YOUNG, V. H.
Active in Platteville, 1880.

ZIERER, JOHN
Active in Oostburg and St. Nazianz, 1900.

ZIVNEY, F.
Stereo photographer in Milwaukee.

SAWYER & BEAUCAIRE,
ARTISTS,
CHEYENNE, WY. TER.

Special thanks to Loren Jost for his substantial contribution to this section.

ALLEN, ARLAND T.
Active in Buffalo, 1880.

ALTER, C. F.
Active in Cheyenne, 1870-75. First name may have been Charles.

ARNOLD
Partner in Masters & Arnold, active in Cheyenne, 1875.

ASCH, JULIUS
Active in Cheyenne, 1884, in the Whipple and Hay Block.

BAKER
Active in Carbon, c. 1880.

BAKER & JOHNSTON
Active in Evanston and Rock Springs, 1885. Photographed the Shoshoni Indians on the reservation. Also spelled Johnson.

BALLHAM, G. T.
Amateur stereo photographer active in Cheyenne.

BARBER
Partner in Weyle & Barber, Laramie, 1895.

BEAMAN, E. O.
Photographer with the Powell Survey, 1871. See Arizona.

BEAUCAIRE
Partner in Sawyer & Beaucaire, Cheyenne, 1880.

BIERSTADT, ALBERT
Traveling photographer on expedition in Wyoming, 1859, accompanied by assistant F. S. Frost. Famous Hudson River School artist and brother of Boston photographer, Charles Bierstadt.

BISHOP, CHARLES W.
Active in Laramie City, 1870.

BROWN, A. A.
Active in Rawlins, 1890-1900.

BUFFUM, B. C.
Stereo photographer in Laramie.

CALFEE, H. B.
Stereo photographer in Wyoming offering views of "The Enchanted Land or Wonders of The Yellowstone National Park." Also photographed Indians; partner with Catlin in Bozeman, Montana, 1880s. See Montana.

CARPENTER, LOUIS
Active in Fort Laramie, 1870.

COLORADO VIEW COMPANY
Cheyenne company publishing the Wyoming stereoviews of photographers Ed Tangen and George H. Hall. Also had offices in Boulder, Colorado; may be the same as Colorado Stereograph Company .

COUCH, J. A. (MRS.)
Active in Lander, 1895-1900.

CRISSMAN, J.
Active in Laramie, late 1860s, 1878, 1880. First name may be Joshua.

DALGLEISH
Active in Buffalo, 1895.

DARE, DANIEL D.
Studio in Cheyenne, 1875, 1878; on Ferguson between 16th and 17th, 1878.

DWIGHT, FRANCIS E.
Active in Casper, 1900.

EDIGTON, CHARLES
Active in Bessemer, 1900. Name may be Edington.

FRANKLAND, MARGERY
Active in Cheyenne, 1900.

FROST, S. F.
Assistant to Bierstadt on expedition in Wyoming, 1859.

GEIGER, EARL R.
Stereo photographer in Kemmerer; made view of staged holdup in store.

GLOVER, RIDGWAY
Active in Fort Laramie, 1866.

GRABILL, JOHN C. H.
Active in Sturgis, Dakota Territory, c. 1886; in Deadwood, Lead and Hot Springs, c. 1890. Photographed the scene after the Wounded Knee massacre. Details of Wyoming work unknown.

HALL, GEORGE H.
Stereo photographer; views of Wyoming cowboys, buildings and local people were published by Colorado View Company of Cheyenne.

HARRIS
Traveling photographers operating as Harris & Company in Rock Springs and Lander, 1898.

HARTWELL & SON, SILAS M.
Active in Laramie in 1878, 1884-85, 1890.

HAYNES, F. JAY.
Active in Yellowstone National Park, 1883-1916. Traveling photographer with President Chester A. Arthur during trip, 1883. Photographed park in winter, 1887, 1894. Official park photographer, 1884-1916. See Dakota.

HEYN, L.
Active in Laramie on Third Street, c. 1890.

HINES, T. J.
Photographer with the J. W. Barlow Expedition in Wyoming, 1871.

HOT SPRINGS ART COMPANY
Issued stereoviews of Big Horn Springs, c. 1900.

HOUGHTON, MERRITT DANA
Active in Rawlins and Laramie, 1880-84.

HOWARD
Active in Fort Bridger, Wyoming Territory, 1875.

HULL, ARUNDEL C.
See Nebraska.

HUNT
Active in Newcastle, 1890.

JACKSON, WILLIAM H.
Photographer for the Hayden Survey and Hayden's Yellowstone expedition, 1870. Toured Wyoming, 1892, producing photographs for the Wyoming exhibit at Chicago's 1893 Columbian Exposition. See Nebraska.

JENKINS BROTHERS
Partnership of William I., Frank A. and John B. Jenkins in Cheyenne, 1884.

JENKINS, FRANK A.
Active in Cheyenne at 318 Hill, 1884. Operated as Jenkins Brothers with brothers William I. and John B. Jenkins.

JENKINS, JOHN B.
Operated as Jenkins Brothers in Cheyenne, 1884, at 318 Hill, with brothers Frank A. and William I. Jenkins.

JENKINS, WILLIAM I.
Active in Cheyenne with brothers Frank A. and John B. Jenkins, 1884.

JOHNSON, ELI
Active in Evanston, 1880. May have been a partner in Baker & Johnson.

JOHNSTON, W. J.
Active in Green River, 1880.

KIRKLAND BROTHERS
Charles D. and George W. Kirkland based in Cheyenne, 1874-75; also operated in Colorado and Wyoming, and worked independently, 1870s-80s.

KIRKLAND, CHARLES .D.
Opened a studio in Denver, 1874. Active in Cheyenne, 1880, 1884; located at 298 Ferguson, 1884. He augmented his photography with the manufacture of lithium printing-out paper under the label Kirkland Lithium Paper Company, and moved the company to Denver, 1894. See Colorado.

KIRKLAND, GEORGE W.
He and his brother, Charles D., worked for William Chamberlain in Denver, c. 1868. Active in Cheyenne, c. 1875. See Colorado.

LEMON, F. J.
Traveling photographer in Lander, 1899, as representative of Slawter & Walker of Salt Lake City.

MASTERS & ARNOLD
Active in Cheyenne, 1875.

MASTERS & COMPANY
Partnership in Cheyenne, 1885.

MASTERS, W. H.
Partner in Masters & Arnold and Masters & Company in Cheyenne on 16th between Ferguson and Eddy; 1878.

McFADDEN, GEORGE. M.
Active in Laramie City, c. 1870, 1875, 1878. May be George W.

McHENRY, JOHN A.
Active in Hartville, 1900. Brother of William F. McHenry.

McHENRY, WILLIAM F.
Active in Hartville, 1900.

MEAD, ALBERT G.
Active in Cheyenne, 1870.

MILLER, L. B.
Active in Sundance, 1885.

MITCHELL, DANIEL S.
Active in Cheyenne on Eddy between 16th and 17th streets, 1878.
See Nebraska.

MONROE, CHARLES
Active in Cheyenne, 1900.

MOORE, ERNEST
Active in Cheyenne, 1900.

PIERSON, SIMON
Active in Fort Bridger, 1870.

RINEHARD, F. A.
Photographed Indians in Wyoming, late 1890s. Probably Frank A.
Rinehart. See Colorado.

ROBERTS
Partner in Ross & Roberts, Buffalo, 1890.

ROSS & ROBERTS
Active in Buffalo, 1890.

SAWYER & BEAUCAIRE
Active in Cheyenne, 1880

SCOTT, GEORGE W.
Active in Lander, 1890s.

SKOLDS, C. T.
Gallery in Cheyenne at 1717 Capital Avenue, c. 1890.

SPRING, PEARL
Active in Cheyenne, 1900.

STACY, GEORGE
Active in Cheyenne, 1900.

STIMSON, JOSEPH E.
Official photographer for Union Pacific Railroad in Cheyenne, 1889-
1903; also photographer for the Bureau of Reclamation. Active in
the Lander area, 1903; Riverton area, 1910, 1929.

TANGEN, ED
Stereo photographer; views of Wyoming cowboys, buildings and local
people were published by Colorado View Company of Cheyenne.

THAYER
Active in Rock Springs and South Pass areas, 1899.

VAN WERT, PAUL
Active in Cheyenne, 1900.

WALKER, L. S.
Active in Cheyenne.

WALLACE, CHARLES (MRS.)
Active in Lander, 1895-99.

WALLACE, THOMAS J.
Assisted his sister-in-law, Mrs. Charles Wallace in Lander, 1898.

WALTERS, CHARLES
Active in Cheyenne, 1900; brother of William Walters.

WALTERS, WILLIAM
Active in Cheyenne, 1900.

WEBSTER
Active in Laramie, 1890.

WEYLE & BARBER
Partnership active in Laramie, 1895.

WITHS, GEORGE B.
Active in Fort Laramie, 1868.

WRIGHT, WILLIAM
Active in Cheyenne, 1880.

YOUNG, C. T.
Active in Laramie, 1880.

INDEX OF PHOTOGRAPHERS

A

A & A Lightning Viewing Company . . .California
Aaberg, J. P. .Washington
Aaron, Sidney D. . . . . .Arkansas, Texas
Abbot, John . . . . .West Canada
Abbott, C. L. . . . . .Colorado, New Mexico
Abbott, Theo. (Miss) . . . . .California
Abbott, Warren D. . . . . .Nebraska
Abel, Dola (Mrs.) . . . . .Colorado
Abell . . . . .California
Abell & Priest . . . . .California, Oregon
Abell & Son, Frank G. . . . . .Oregon
Abell & Welsh . . . . .California, Oregon
Abell, Frank George . . . . .California, Oregon
Abell, George L. . . . . .Oregon, Traveling
Abell's Art Gallery . . . . .California
Abell's Art-Studio Car . . . . . . .California, Traveling
Abell–Herrin Company . . . . .Oregon
Aberdeen, Lady Ishbel Maria . . . .British Columbia
Abernathy . . . . .Texas
Abernathy, M. L. .Texas
Abraham & Isaacs . . . . .Colorado
Abraham, A. . . . . .Texas
Abrams, James L. . . . . .Oregon
Academy of Art .Texas
Academy of Design . . . . .Wisconsin
Acadia Studio .Oregon
Ace & Aebischer . . . . .Utah
Achleitner, Otto . . . . .Colorado
Acker, G. C. . . . . .Iowa
Acker, G. G. . . . . .Kansas
Acme Gallery . . . . .Colorado
Acme Photograph Studios . . . . .California
Acme Studio . . . . .Texas
Acme View & Advertising
    Company . . . . .Oregon
Acme View Company . . . . .Nebraska
Actino Photograph Car . . . . .Traveling
Adams . . . . .New Mexico, Texas
Adams & Company . . . . .Alaska
Adams & Hill . . . . .Texas
Adams & Larkin . . . . .Alaska
Adams & Larson . . . . .Iowa
Adams & Martin . . . . .Oregon
Adams & Pierce . . . . .British Columbia
Adams & Shear .Iowa
Adams & Skeels . . . . .Kansas
Adams & Thomson's . . . . .Kansas
Adams, A. W. . . . . .Iowa, Kansas
Adams Brothers .Utah
Adams Brothers & Company . . . . .Colorado
Adams, E. . . . . .Colorado
Adams, E. (Mrs.) . . . . .Iowa
Adams, E. C. . . . . .British Columbia
Adams, E. W. . . . . .California
Adams, Earnest .Texas
Adams, Elias L. .Texas
Adams, F. S. . . . . .Colorado, New Mexico
Adams, Frederick V. . . . . .California
Adams, G. H. . . . . .Iowa
Adams, J. O. . . . . .Kansas
Adams, Laura May . . . . .California
Adams, Luella M. . . . . .Oregon
Adams, O. E. . . . . .Iowa
Adams, O. R. . . . . .Iowa
Adams, R. F. .Missouri
Adams, S. M. . . . . .California
Adams, W. G. . . . . .Iowa
Adams, William H. . . . . .Texas
Adamson, Otis & Ella E. . . . . .Arkansas
Addis & Koch . . . . .California
Addis & Noel .Kansas
Addis & Porter . . . . .Arizona

Addis, Alfred S. . . . . . . .Arizona, California, Iowa,
    Kansas, New Mexico
Addis, Robert W. . . . . .California
Addison, A. S. . . . . .California
Addison, George A. . . . . .Oklahoma, Texas
Adgate, Theodore . . . . .Texas
Adkins & Harrison . . . . .Arizona
Adkins, Nellie S. . . . . .Texas
Adkins, Wesley C. . . . . .Arizona
Adlington & Favor . . . . .Wisconsin
Admire, C. A. . . . . .Nebraska
Adrien, J. . . . . .Nebraska
Advance Portrait House . . . . .Oregon
Aebischer . . . . .Utah
Aerne & Nordstorm . . . . .Oregon
Aerne, Christopher, Jr. . . . . .Oregon
Aerne, Robert .Oregon
Agner, Charles . . . . .California
Agnew, E. W. . . . . .Nebraska
Agnew, J. E. . . . . .Iowa
Agnew, William Burl . . . . .British Columbia
Agramonte . . . . .Utah
Ah Hee . . . . .Hawaii
Ahashi, Karou . . . . .California
Ahlman, H. . . . . .California
Ahlmnann, W. C. . . . . .Nebraska
Ahlstrom, Charles . . . . .Kansas
Ah–Sing, Fong . . . . .California
Aichberg, Christian . . . . .California
Aiken, F. J. . . . . .Traveling
Aikers, William F. . . . . .Texas
Ainsworth . . . . .Missouri
Ainsworth, Maud . . . . .Oregon
Akers, E. M. . . . . .Oregon
Alameda Photograph Company . . . . . . .California
Alaska View & Photo Company . . . . .Alaska
Albee, E. S. . . . . .Nebraska
Albert, A. . . . . .Texas, Wisconsin
Alberta Photographic Company . . . .West Canada
Albertson . . . . .Arkansas
Albertstone, R. . . . . .Alaska
Albrecht, A. A. . . . . .British Columbia,
    Traveling, Washington
Albrecht, Hugo . . . . .Kansas
Albrecht, Oliver . . . . .California
Albright Art Parlors . . . . .New Mexico
Albright, Franc Luse (Mrs.) . . . . .New Mexico
Albright, G. J. . . . . .Texas
Albright, M. (Miss) . . . . .Oregon
Alden, D. R. . . . . .Kansas
Alder Cottage Studio . . . . .British Columbia
Aldin, D. R. . . . . .Kansas
Aldine Photo–Villa . . . . .Kansas
Aldrich, Clarence Ulysses . . . . .California
Aldrich, Frank C. . . . . .Oregon
Aldridge, George . . . . .Kansas
Alexander . . . . .Colorado
Alexander & Green . . . . . . .New Mexico, Texas
Alexander, A. D. . . . . .Nebraska
Alexander, C. G. . . . . .Nebraska
Alexander, E. R. . . . . .Texas
Alexander, J. A. . . . . .Texas
Alexander, J. M. L. . . . . .British Columbia
Alexander, Jim A. . . . . .New Mexico, Texas
Alexander, Pinckney C. . . . . .Texas
Alexander, William . . . . .Texas
Alger, James .California
Alisky, Charles . . . . .California
Alison, John . . . . .New Mexico, Texas
Alkire, A. S. .California
Allatt . . . . .Oregon
Allen . .California, Iowa, Nebraska, Traveling, Utah
Allen & Company . . . . .California
Allen & Hay .California

Allen & Whitfield . . . . .Texas
Allen, A. H. . . . . .Iowa
Allen, A. W. .Nebraska
Allen, Arland T. . . . . .Wyoming
Allen, Arthur W. . . . . .Nebraska
Allen, Bennett G. . . . . .California
Allen, C. F. . . . . .Colorado, Iowa
Allen, C. P. . . . . .New Mexico
Allen, Charles R. . . . . .Arizona
Allen, Edward P. . . . . .British Columbia
Allen, Edwin K. . . . . .Texas
Allen, Edwin S. . . . . .Colorado
Allen, Fletcher .Texas
Allen, Frank . . . . .Kansas
Allen, Frederick C. . . . . .Oregon
Allen, George R. . . . . .Texas
Allen, Henry R. .Texas
Allen, Ida . . . . .California
Allen, Increase . . . . .Colorado
Allen, J. H. . . . . .Kansas
Allen, James A. . . . . .Idaho
Allen, Laura T. . . . . .California
Allen, O. G. . . . . .Oregon
Allen, P. . . . . .Wisconsin
Allen, Rata (Miss) . . . . .Oregon
Allen, Thomas . . . . .Kansas
Allen, W. H. . . . . .Arizona, Wisconsin
Allen, W. T. . . . . .Idaho
Allen, William Russell . . . . .British Columbia
Allhands, A. J. . . . . .California
Allin, R. . . . . .Texas
Allison . . . . .Idaho
Allison, J. L. . . . . .Idaho, Montana,
    New Mexico, Texas, Traveling
Allison, W. C. . . . . .Dakota
Allman, Louis P. . . . . .Arkansas
Allsworth, Samuel . . . . .Idaho
Allyn, Mark .Colorado
Allyna Studio .Oregon
Alma Art Gallery . . . . .Kansas
Almond, Kate . . . . .California
Aloha Gallery .Hawaii
Alred, Jake . . . . .Texas
Alta Studios .California
Altenburgh, William . . . . .Arizona
Alter, C. F. . . . . .Colorado, Wyoming
Altine . . . . .Nebraska
Altpeter & Anderson . . . . .California
Altpeter, Louis P. . . . . .California
Alverson . . . . .Arkansas, Washington
Alverson, Frank . . . . .California, Oregon
Alvord . . . . .Nebraska
Alvord, Charles A. . . . . .Oregon
Alvord, D. M. . . . . .Wisconsin
Alvord, David N. . . . . .Wisconsin
Alvord, E. D. .Missouri
Alvord, Jerusha E. (Mrs.) . . . . .Wisconsin
Alworth & Pierce Photos . . . . .California
Alworth, N. B. . . . . .California
Amaya, K. . . . . .Hawaii
Ambrose, Thomas . . . . .Oregon
Amen, M. . . . . .Texas
Ameniya, R. .California
American Art Gallery . . . . .West Canada
American Art Studio . . . . .California
American Portrait Company . . . . .Oregon
American Stereoscopic Company . . . . . . .Arizona
American View Company . . . .California, Dakota,
    Oregon, Wisconsin
American Viewing Company . . . . .Nebraska
Amermon, Ada (Mrs.) . . . . .Nebraska
Ames Brothers . . . . .Oklahoma
Ames, F. A. . . . . .Arizona
Ames, N. F. . . . . .Kansas

Ames, W. P. ....Nebraska
Amian, Brother ....New Mexico
Amos, Leah ....Idaho
Amrhein, Joseph ....Washington
Amsden ....California
Amsden & Dutkewich ......California, Traveling
Amsden, William Oscar ....California
Analytis, James ....Oregon
Anaya, Charles ....California
Anderson ....Dakota, Minnesota,
New Mexico, Texas
Anderson & Bennett ....Texas
Anderson & Bickel ....Texas
Anderson & Blessing ....Texas
Anderson & Company, C. B. ....Texas
Anderson & Company, Charles W. .....Colorado
Anderson & Crandall ....Utah
Anderson & Hamacher ....Washington
Anderson & Leon ....Colorado
Anderson & Peterson ....Minnesota
Anderson & Pollock ....California
Anderson, A. E. ....Nebraska
Anderson, A. T. ....Nebraska
Anderson, Adam ....Utah
Anderson, Addison ....Utah
Anderson, Alfred ....Oregon
Anderson, Barbara ....California
Anderson Brothers ....Nebraska, Texas
Anderson, C. ....Nebraska
Anderson, C. J. ....Idaho, Nebraska
Anderson, C. M. ....Iowa
Anderson, C. R. ....Texas
Anderson, C. W. ....Oregon, Traveling
Anderson, Charles B. ....Texas
Anderson, E. ....Minnesota
Anderson, E. C. ....Nebraska
Anderson, E. H. ....Oregon
Anderson, E. J. ....Wisconsin
Anderson, E. M. ....California
Anderson, E. W. ....Colorado
Anderson, Edward ....Texas
Anderson, Eliza ....California
Anderson, George ....West Canada
Anderson, George Edward ....Traveling, Utah
Anderson, H. A. ....Iowa, Minnesota
Anderson, Henry ....British Columbia
Anderson, Hilda ....Washington
Anderson, Hugh ....California
Anderson, J. August ....Colorado
Anderson, J. B. ....Oregon
Anderson, J. H. ....Nebraska
Anderson, J. S. ....Wisconsin
Anderson, J. Stanley ......Idaho, Traveling, Utah
Anderson, John ....Texas
Anderson, John A. ......Dakota, Nebraska
Anderson, L. E. ....Oregon
Anderson, L. M. ....Oregon
Anderson, Louis ....Texas
Anderson, Mary E. ....Idaho
Anderson, N. J. ....Nebraska
Anderson, Ole ....Minnesota
Anderson, P. ....Kansas
Anderson, P. G. ....Dakota
Anderson, Peter ....Iowa
Anderson, Robert W. ....British Columbia
Anderson, Samuel ....Texas
Anderson, Stanley L. ....Idaho
Anderson, Thomas ....Kansas
Anderson, Thomas B. ....Texas
Anderson, W. C. ....Iowa
Anderson, W. F. ....Nebraska
Anderson, William H. ....Texas
Andreas, P. M. (Mrs.) ....Idaho
Andresen, J. M. ....Nebraska
Andrews & Company, E. ....New Mexico
Andrews & Lange ....California
Andrews & McKenzie ....New Mexico
Andrews, A. (Miss) ....Oregon

Andrews, A. F. ....Wisconsin
Andrews, Byron ....Oregon
Andrews, C. B. ....Hawaii
Andrews, Dr. Enos ....New Mexico
Andrews, E. B. ....California, Traveling
Andrews, Edwin Steck ....New Mexico
Andrews, George ....Nebraska
Andrews, Howard L. ....Nebraska
Andrews, J. A. ....Missouri
Andrews, Thomas P. ....California
Angell & Weeks ....Minnesota
Angell, C. L. ....Minnesota
Angell, James ....Nebraska
Angell's Art Gallery, C. L. ....Minnesota
Angelus Studio ....California, Oregon
Anger, W. ....Wisconsin
Ankenman & Butler ....Texas
Ankenman, Nicholas ....Texas
Ann Ting Gock & Company ....California
Anonymous ....California, Traveling
Anschuetz ....Iowa, Wisconsin
Anselberg & Booth ....Arkansas
Anselberg, David W. ....Arkansas
Ansley & Tinkel ....Texas
Ansley, B. S. ....California
Ansley, Cary D. ....Texas
Ansley, Robert ....Texas
Ansley, W. T. ....New Mexico, Texas
Ansley, William ....Texas
Anthony & Hill ....Texas
Anthony, F. ....Arizona
Anthony, Milton M. ....Texas
Antrim & Powers ....California
Antrim, B. Jay ....California, Hawaii
Apel, Edward ....Texas
Apfel, Henry ....Iowa
Aplin & Williamson ....Iowa
Aplin, H. N. ....Iowa
Appel, Gustave R. ....Colorado
Applegate, J. W. ....California, Oregon, Traveling
Appleton & Company, D. E. ....California
APV & P Company ....Arizona
Araah, Professor A. ....Iowa
Arai ....California
Archer & Company ....Texas
Archer, John R. ....Texas
Archer, John W. ....California
Ard, John W. ....Texas
Areldson Photo ....Arizona
Arey, Herbert L. ....Oregon
Arganbright, Charles ....Iowa
Argenbright, Alva L. (Mrs.) ....New Mexico
Aristo Studio ....New Mexico
Arizona Gallery ....Arizona
Arizona Photo Company ....Arizona
Arizona Photo Gallery ....Arizona
Arizona Photograph Company, Inc. ....Arizona
Arizona Souvenir Picture Company .....Arizona
Arizona Tent Gallery ....Arizona
Arkna, Alford ....Texas
Arlaud, Adolph A. ....Kansas
Arleta Studio ....Oregon
Arlington & Dana ....Oklahoma
Arlington & Reed ....California
Armanntrout, M. J. ....Colorado
Armantrout, M. I. ....Kansas
Armatage (Mrs.) ....Oregon
Armer, Laura Adams ....California
Armington, W. R. ....Colorado
Armitage, Percival ....Arizona
Armor, A. H. ....Wisconsin
Armstead & Son ....Nebraska
Armstrong ....New Mexico, Wisconsin
Armstrong & Dean ....Oregon
Armstrong & Lunn ....Washington
Armstrong, A. (Miss) ....Colorado
Armstrong, A. J. ....Oregon
Armstrong, C. M. ....Iowa

Armstrong, Charles B. ....Idaho
Armstrong, Charles L. ....West Canada
Armstrong, Cyrus M. ....California
Armstrong, J. A. ....Iowa
Armstrong, J. F. ....Washington
Armstrong, J. N. ....Oregon, Washington
Armstrong, Martin ....Oklahoma, Texas
Armstrong, S. ....Iowa
Arnest, John M. ....California
Arnold ....California, Dakota, Wyoming
Arnold, Amelia ....California
Arnold, Benjamin D. ....Oregon
Arnold, E. F. ....Iowa
Arnold, Hosmer K. ....Oregon
Arnold, Richard J. ....California
Arnold, William P. ....California
Arnold, William T. ....California
Arrington, Ed. ....Colorado
Arriola, Edward F. ....California
Arrowsmith Photo Studio ....California
Arrowsmith, W. H. ....California, Traveling
Art Gallery ....Texas
Art Saloon ....Texas
Art Studio ....Idaho, Minnesota
Art Union Gallery ....Wisconsin
Artcliff Photo Studio ....Oregon
Artcraft ....Oregon
Arthur, H. D. ....Texas
Arthur, John ....Washington
Arts Shop ....New Mexico
Artz ....Traveling
Arvin & Wright ....Texas
Arvin, James A. ....Texas
Asbeck, August ....California
Asberry, C. ....Texas
Asch, Julius ....Wyoming
Ash, Ormsby M. ....Oregon
Ashbury, Steve ....Texas
Ashby, E. (Mrs.) ....Nevada
Asher, J. W. ....Nebraska
Asher, Julius ....California
Ashford, Francis ....Oregon
Ashford, Penny M. ....Texas
Ashford, Theodicia ....Texas
Ashley, A. O. ....Nebraska
Ashley, Blanche ....California
Ashley, Thomas ....Texas
Ashley's City Gallery ....Texas
Ashman, William ....British Columbia
Ashton, George ....Iowa
Askew & Glenn ....Texas
Askew, Samuel R. ....Texas
Askren ....Iowa
Askren & Baldwin ....Iowa, Traveling
Askren, I. M. ....Traveling
Aspinall, Alfred ....Wisconsin
Asplund, Theodore Carl ....New Mexico
Atcherson, C. E. ....Kansas
Atchinson ....Wisconsin
Atchinson, A. W. ....Texas
Atchison Portrait Company ....Kansas
Atencio, J. M. ....New Mexico
Atherton, A. C. ....Iowa
Atherton, H. M. ....Kansas
Atkeson, Laura ....Oregon
Atkeson, William T. ....Oregon
Atkins ....Kansas
Atkins, A. S. ....Arkansas
Atkins, Massard & Company ....Colorado
Atkinson ....Kansas
Atkinson, C. A. ....Iowa
Atkinson, C. W. ....Traveling
Atkinson, Charles W. ....Kansas
Atkinson, G. W. ....Texas
Atkinson, George W. ....Texas
Atkinson, J. B. ....British Columbia
Atkinson, S. P. (Mrs.) ....Iowa
Atkinson's Railroad Gallery ....Traveling

INDEX OF PHOTOGRAPHERS 529

Atkisson, W. Russell . . . . .New Mexico
Atlantic & Pacific View Portrait
Company .New Mexico
Atlantic Pacific View & Portrait
Company . . . . .Arizona
Atlantic Photo–View & Advertising
Company . . . . .Oregon, Traveling
Attwater's Photo Studio . . . . .Arkansas
Attwood, Myrtle (Miss) . . . . . .New Mexico, Texas
Atwater & Garrison . . . . .California
Atwell, Elizabeth . . . . .California
Atwood & Marshall .Iowa
Atwood, B. L. .California
Atwood, H. A. (Mrs.) . . . . .Oregon
Aubrey, Charles . . . . .Texas
Auerbach, R. . . . . .Texas
Aufrecht, Gustav . . . . .California
Auger, Lina . . . . .California
Augustine, G. W. . . . . .Colorado
Augustine, William R. . . . . .Colorado
Aulls & Cannon . . . . .Colorado
Aultman, O. E. . . . . .Colorado, New Mexico
Aultman, Otis A. . . . . .New Mexico, Texas
Aune, Aasta (Miss) . . . . .Oregon
Aune, Amante . . . . .Oregon
Aune Brothers . . . . .Oregon
Aune, Peter O. . . . . .Oregon
Aune, Struck . . . . .Oregon
Aune–Ball, Inc. . . . . .Oregon
Austin . . . . .Texas, Traveling
Austin & Company . . . . .California
Austin, A. H. . . . . .Arizona
Austin, Clyde B. . . . . .California
Austin, D. . . . . .Nebraska
Austin, Daniel . . . . .Nebraska
Austin, Hugh A. . . . . .Texas
Austin, J. . . . . .Minnesota
Austin, J. V. . . . . .Texas
Austin, Jay . . . . .California
Austin, John O. . . . . .Texas
Austin Photograph Company . . . . .Texas
Autrey, G. D. . . . . .Texas
Autrey, L. M. (Mrs.) . . . . .New Mexico
Aveldson . . . . .Arizona
Avery, C. D. . . . . .Kansas
Avery, D. A. . . . . .Oregon
Avery, J. C. . . . . .Colorado, Kansas
Avery, J. W. . . . . .California
Avery, Julian M. . . . . .Colorado
Avery, R. S. . . . . .Traveling
Avery, William L. .Oregon
Ax Brothers . . . . .Traveling
Ax, H. . . . . .Traveling
Ayers . . . . .Nebraska
Ayers, Elizabeth N. . . . . .California
Ayers, Ellis . . . . .Minnesota
Ayers, Perry . . . . .Iowa
Ayers, W. G. (Mr. & Mrs.) . . . . .Iowa
Aylsworth & Loomis . . . . .Traveling
Aylsworth, J. H. .Traveling
AYP Exposition Series . . . . .Washington
Ayres . . . . .Montana
Ayres, E. . . . . .Iowa
Ayres, Milton A. . . . . .California

B

Babberger, William .Kansas
Babbitt & Howard . . . . .Colorado
Babbitt & Shannon . . . . .Missouri
Babbitt, J. P. . . . . .Colorado, Kansas
Babbitt's, C. W. .Traveling
Babcock, Charles . . . . .Iowa
Babcock, Charles F. . . . . .California
Babcock, W. D. . . . . .Iowa
Babcock, Warren D. . . . . .Wisconsin
Bachelder, C. . . . . .Wisconsin
Bachelder, William L. . . . . .Wisconsin
Bachman, John .California
Backer, L. J. . . . . .Oregon
Backstrom, Alexander D. . . . . .Texas
Backus, E. . . . . .Nebraska
Backus, Morgan . . . . .Oregon
Bacon . . . . .Minnesota, Nebraska
Bacon & Company, J. H. . . . . .Texas
Bacon Brothers .California
Bacon, Edward .California
Bacon, F. C. . . . . .Iowa
Bacon, Frank W. . . . . .California
Bacon, George . . . . .Iowa
Bacon, J. Ed. . . . . .California
Bacon, James H. . . . . .Texas
Bacon, Max E. . . . . .New Mexico, Traveling
Bade, J. . . . . .Texas
Badger . . . . .Oregon
Baechle, Oscar H. . . . . .Kansas
Baechler & Company, C. . . . . .Oregon
Baechler & Wagner Brothers . . . . .Oregon
Baechler, Charles . . . . .Oregon
Baecker, Julius . . . . .New Mexico, Texas
Baer, Alfred . . . . .Wisconsin
Baer, Erwin . . . . .Arizona
Baer, Reverend Walter Wesley . . .British Columbia
Bagley, H. T. (Mrs.) . . . . .Oregon
Bagley, Joe . . . . .Utah
Bagley, Newton .California
Bagley, Wilbur F. . . . . .Wisconsin
Bagnasco, Peter .California
Bagnasco, Policarpo . . . . .Arizona, California, New Mexico, Oregon, Traveling
Bagne . . . . .Minnesota
Bailey . . . . .California, Kansas
Bailey & Company, C. S. . . . . . .British Columbia
Bailey & Cramer . . . . .California
Bailey & Hand . . . . .Texas
Bailey & Neelands . . . . .British Columbia
Bailey & Pickett .California
Bailey & Terry . . . . .Texas
Bailey, A. C. . . . . .Washington
Bailey, A. P. . . . . .California
Bailey, Arlie A., Jr. .Oregon
Bailey Brothers . . . . . .British Columbia, California
Bailey, C. H. . . . . .California
Bailey, Charles S. . . . . .British Columbia
Bailey, Dix & Mead . . . . .Dakota
Bailey, E. N. . . . . .Texas
Bailey, E. P. (Miss) . . . . .California
Bailey, F. . . . . .Wisconsin
Bailey, F. S. . . . . .Idaho
Bailey, Frank B. . . . . .Texas
Bailey, J. (Mrs.) . . . . .California
Bailey, J. L. . . . . .Oregon
Bailey, M. W. . . . . .Kansas
Bailey, Morris . . . . .California
Bailey, W. . . . . .Arizona
Bailey, William . . . . .British Columbia
Bailey's Studio . . . . .Wisconsin
Baillie, W. L. . . . . .Nebraska
Bailor, J. M. . . . . .Nebraska
Bain, J. . . . . .Texas
Baines, W. L. . . . . .Minnesota
Bair, John . . . . .Texas
Baird . . . . .California
Baird & Twiford . . . . .Iowa
Baird, C. W. . . . . .Texas
Baird, J. A. . . . . .Kansas
Baird, Willis . . . . .Oregon
Baker . . . . . .British Columbia, Oregon, Wyoming
Baker (Mrs.) . . . . .Texas
Baker & Cathcart . . . . .California
Baker & Cornell . . . . .New Mexico
Baker & Cushman . . . . .California
Baker & Johnston . . . . .Traveling, Wyoming
Baker & Kinson . . . . .Oregon
Baker & Koehler . . . . .Oregon
Baker & Leach . . . . .Texas, New Mexico
Baker & Raymond . . . . .Texas
Baker, C. O. . . . . .Nebraska
Baker, Carl R. . . . . .Oregon
Baker, Charles Leverett . . . . .California
Baker, Charles S. . . . . .California
Baker, E. W. . . . . .Arizona, Idaho, Nevada, New Mexico
Baker, Edward W. . . . . .California
Baker, Ellis W. . . . . .Colorado
Baker, Ellis William . . . . .California
Baker, F. E. . . . . .Colorado
Baker, F. N. . . . . .California
Baker, G. G. . . . . .Colorado
Baker, G. W. . . . . .California
Baker, H. H. . . . . .Oregon
Baker, Isaac Wallace . . . . .California, Traveling
Baker, J. G. . . . . .Iowa
Baker, J. H. . . . . .Idaho
Baker, J. W. . . . . .Arkansas
Baker, James H. . . . . .California, Oregon
Baker, Jesse H. . . . . .California
Baker, John William . . . . .California
Baker, Josiah C. .Colorado
Baker, Lawson . . . . .Texas
Baker, Mineola . . . . .California
Baker Portrait Company, H. H. . . . . .Oregon
Baker, Ray Jerome .Hawaii
Baker, Raymond . . . . .Texas
Baker, S. F. . . . . .California
Baker, W. . . . . .Iowa
Baker, W. A. . . . . .Texas
Baker, W. H. . . . . .Texas
Baker, Walter T. .California
Baker, William C. . . . . .Texas
Baker, William Peacock . . . . .British Columbia
Bakowski, B. B. . . . . .Oregon
Balard, Unis K. . . . . .Arkansas
Balberger . . . . .Kansas
Baldry, A. S. . . . . .Nebraska
Baldwin . . . . .Indian Territory, Iowa, Traveling
Baldwin & Betancue . . . . .California
Baldwin & Blondal . . . . .Western Canada
Baldwin & Clements . . . . .California
Baldwin & Daugherty . . . . .Iowa
Baldwin & Ostergren . . . . .Kansas
Baldwin & Snodgrass . . . . .Texas
Baldwin & Son . . . . .Kansas
Baldwin, A. A. . . . . .Wisconsin
Baldwin, C. F. . . . . .Iowa
Baldwin, C. M. . . . . .Iowa
Baldwin, E. A. . . . . .Traveling
Baldwin, F. C. . . . . .Kansas
Baldwin, George .Colorado
Baldwin, H. O. . . . . .Iowa
Baldwin, James R. .Oregon
Baldwin, John E. D. . . . . .California
Baldwin, Maude E. . . . . .Oregon
Baldwin, Nereus . . . . .Kansas
Baldwin Photo Company . . . . .California
Baldwin, S. S. . . . . .Colorado
Baldwin, Will D. . . . . .Wisconsin
Baldwin's Art Gallery . . . . .Kansas
Balfrey . . . . .California
Ball . . . . .Dakota, Oregon
Ball & Rindahl . . . . .Dakota
Ball & Son, J. P. .Montana
Ball & Sons . . . . .Washington
Ball & Souby . . . . .Texas
Ball, Dix & Mead . . . . .Dakota
Ball, George . . . . .California
Ball, J. P. . . . . .Oregon, Washington
Ball Studios . . . . .Oregon
Ballard, C. . . . . .British Columbia
Ballard, C. B. . . . . .Texas
Ballham, G. T. . . . . .Wyoming
Ballinger, L. A. . . . . .Arizona
Ballough, Monte George . . . . .Colorado
Ballow, Roy F. . . . . .California
Ballweg, Phillip . . . . .Oregon

Baloun, Edmund ... California
Balster, F. S. ... Colorado
Baltzly, Benjamin ... British Columbia
Ban-Ap Photo ... Arizona
Banbrock, William E. ... California, Nevada, Traveling
Bancroft ... Minnesota
Bancroft, C. D. ... Iowa
Bancroft, Eddy ... Texas
Bangley, C. W. ... Colorado
Bangs & Eno ... Wisconsin
Bangs, D. ... Minnesota
Bangs, E. D. ... Wisconsin
Bangs, Henry ... Nebraska
Banks ... Nebraska
Banks Brothers ... Minnesota
Banks, E. J. ... Kansas
Banks, J. C. ... Oregon
Banks, Thomas ... Texas
Bankston, Andrew J. ... Texas
Bankston, Emmet C. ... Texas
Banner Photo Car ... Traveling
Banner, Roliene E. ... Arizona, New Mexico, Traveling
Bannifer, W. H. ... Texas
Banning, Garnett (Mrs.) ... Nebraska
Bannister ... Wisconsin
Banta ... Texas
Barbe, C. G. ... Texas
Barbe, C. L. ... Nebraska
Barber ... Wyoming
Barber, Andy ... Nebraska
Barber, Harry ... West Canada
Barber, John F. ... Colorado
Barber, W. B. ... Kansas
Barbour (Mrs.) ... California
Barcafer ... Missouri
Barclay, C. Edwin ... Oregon
Bardell, F. ... Wisconsin
Bardin, G. M. ... Texas
Bardwell, B. ... Arkansas
Bardwell, Carey L. ... Arkansas
Barenstecher, (Mrs.) ... Oregon
Barke ... Iowa
Barker ... Kansas, Wisconsin
Barker & Gatch ... Colorado
Barker & Gregg ... Kansas
Barker & Mellen ... Colorado
Barker, A. W. ... Colorado
Barker, Albert W. ... Arkansas
Barker, Cornelia ... Texas
Barker, E. S. ... New Mexico
Barker, Edward W. ... Oregon
Barker, G. V. ... Montana
Barker, George V. ... Idaho
Barker, M. W. ... Texas
Barkhuff, John ... Iowa
Barks ... Iowa
Barks & Tice ... Wisconsin
Barks, J. F. ... Texas, Wisconsin
Barley & Vila ... Colorado
Barley, H. C. ... Alaska
Barling, M. (Mrs.) ... Nebraska
Barlow, Henry ... Iowa
Barlow, R. H. ... Wisconsin
Barnard ... Iowa
Barnard & Johnson ... Kansas
Barnard, Hugh F. ... Oregon
Barnard, L. O. ... Wisconsin
Barnard, Paul ... Idaho
Barnard, Thomas Nathan ... Idaho
Barnes ... Arkansas, Washington, Wisconsin
Barnes & Kennedy ... Iowa
Barnes, J. E. ... New Mexico
Barnes, J. H. ... Minnesota
Barnes, James ... Idaho
Barnes, John ... California
Barnes, Lafe W. ... Washington
Barnes, Marcella W. ... Wisconsin
Barnes, Peter Benjamin ... Texas
Barnes, W. L. ... Minnesota
Barnes, Will Croft ... Arizona, New Mexico, Traveling
Barnett, Charles W. ... Arizona
Barnett, Ed. Z. ... California
Barnett, Edward E. ... Oregon
Barnett, L. M. G. ... Iowa
Barney & Crist ... Oregon
Barney, B. F. ... Colorado
Barney, Lewis N. ... California
Barney, Mary S. ... California
Barnhart ... Colorado
Barnhart, J. S. ... Traveling
Barnhouse & Wheeler ... Colorado
Barnhouse, T. E. ... Colorado
Barnkisel, H. ... California
Barnum & Campbell ... Oregon
Barnum & Ridgeway ... Missouri
Barnum, Charles ... New Mexico
Barnum, John T. ... Oregon
Barnum, P. C. ... Texas
Baron, John A. ... Wisconsin
Barr & Wright ... Texas
Barr, David P. ... Texas
Barr, John M. ... Kansas
Barraclough, W. H. ... British Columbia
Barrett (Mrs.) ... Colorado
Barrett & Anderson ... Texas
Barrett & Hart ... Nebraska
Barrett, A. E. ... Nebraska
Barrett Brothers ... Traveling
Barrett, Clara M. ... Texas
Barrett, Jack ... New Mexico
Barrett, John H. ... Texas
Barrett, Thomas ... Traveling
Barrett, Thomas K. ... Texas
Barron, Charles A. ... Washington
Barron, Russell J. ... Texas
Barrows ... Wisconsin
Barrows, I. D. ... Washington
Barrows, Tina Hamblock ... Oregon
Barry, A. ... Texas
Barry, D. F. ... Colorado, Dakota, Montana, Traveling
Barsantee & Duggan ... Texas
Bart, C. W. ... British Columbia, Washington
Bartels, Harry F. ... Oregon
Bartels, K. L. ... Missouri
Bartels, Otis T. ... Oregon
Barter, E. E. ... Idaho
Barthelmess & Schofield ... New Mexico
Barthelmess, Christian ... Arizona, Colorado, Montana, New Mexico
Barthold, A. ... Texas
Barthole, W. ... British Columbia
Bartlett & Hooker ... Texas
Bartlett, Frederick W. ... Texas
Bartlett, Jesse C. ... Texas
Bartlett, K. P. L. ... Texas
Bartlett, L. B. (Mrs.) ... British Columbia
Bartlett, Orville O. ... Idaho
Bartley & Fell's ... California
Bartley, F. H. ... California
Barton, M. B. ... Dakota, Iowa
Barton, W. E. ... Texas
Bartram ... Minnesota
Bartram & Taylor ... Minnesota
Bartram, Robert ... Missouri
Basey, Charles E. ... Oregon
Bass ... Colorado
Bass, Albert A. ... Texas
Bass, Edwin A. ... New Mexico
Bass, Lawrence P. ... Colorado
Bass, Thomas ... California
Bassett & Whaite ... Oregon
Bassett, Frank T. ... Oregon
Bassett, John E. ... Oregon
Bassett, William P. ... British Columbia
Bastian, Thomas H. ... Colorado
Baston, J. A. ... Colorado
Batchelder ... Minnesota
Batchelder, B. P. (Mrs.) ... California
Batchelder, Benjamin Pierce ... California
Batchelder, J. C. ... Traveling
Batchelder, Perez M. ... California, Traveling
Batcheller & Wallbaum ... Nebraska
Bate, Tom H. ... Arizona
Bateman & Company, Guy L. ... California
Bates (Miss) ... Nebraska
Bates & Hawley ... Nebraska
Bates & Muhr ... Colorado
Bates & Nye ... Colorado
Bates & Webb ... Colorado
Bates, Ellen A. (Mrs.) ... Wisconsin
Bates, G. A. ... Iowa
Bates, James B. ... Wisconsin
Bates, James E. ... Idaho
Bates, John S. ... Texas
Bates, O. B. ... Iowa
Bates, Phillip ... Oregon
Bates, William L. ... Colorado
Bath, William ... Texas
Batters, W. F. ... Texas
Bauder, George W. ... Wisconsin
Baudressu & Company, A. ... Texas
Bauer & Son, S. ... Kansas
Bauer, C. ... Texas
Bauer, Charles A. ... Oregon
Bauer, Mary (Miss) ... Kansas
Bauer, P. H. ... Kansas
Bauer, Sebastian ... Kansas
Baugen, Simon ... British Columbia
Baughman, H. F. ... Oregon
Baum, Dr. Henry Mason ... New Mexico
Baum, George C. ... Texas
Baum's Art Studio ... Kansas
Bauman ... Nebraska
Bauman, G. C. ... Iowa
Bauman, Jules ... Arizona
Bauman, Pheobe (Mrs.) ... Kansas
Baumann, G. J. ... Nebraska
Baumann, H. ... Nebraska
Baumgardt Publishing Company ... California
Baumwart, B. M. ... Iowa
Bauslaugh, A. ... West Canada
Bawden, J. ... California
Baxter & Blank ... California
Baxter & Company ... Texas
Baxter, Henry G. ... Texas
Baxter, S. D. ... Texas
Baxter, William ... Texas
Bay & Wright ... Texas
Bayley & Cramer ... California
Bayley & Cuinter ... California
Bayley & O'Hara ... California
Bayley & Patterson ... Wisconsin
Bayley, Charles H. ... Wisconsin
Bayley, Merrill F. ... California
Bayley, N. J. ... California
Bayley, W. F. ... California
Bayley, Wilbur Fisk ... California
Bayley, William F. ... California
Bayley's Photograph Gallery ... California
Baylis, G. E. (Mrs.) ... California
Bayou City Ambrotype Rooms ... Texas
Bays, Beach & Meek ... Texas
Bays, Davis Henry ... Traveling
Beach & Johnson ... Wisconsin
Beach, A. W. ... Iowa
Beach, Albert L. ... Texas
Beach, E. A. ... Minnesota, Wisconsin
Beach, Frank E. ... Texas
Beach, George ... Texas
Beachle, Charles F. ... Kansas

Burns & Ohsfeldt . . . Oregon
Burns & Raymond . . . Idaho
Burns Brothers . . . Idaho, Oregon
Burns, Bruce . . . Idaho
Burns, Emily E. . . . California
Burns, Ida A. . . . Idaho
Burns, James Grover . . . Idaho
Burns, K. (Miss) . . . Oregon
Burns, M. Bruce . . . Oregon
Burns, M. W. . . . Wisconsin
Burns, Owen Spencer . . . Oregon
Burns, Robert . . . Idaho, Oregon
Burns, W. K. . . . Missouri
Burns, Warren . . . Texas
Burns, William J. . . . Oregon
Burnside . . . Iowa
Burpee, C. L. . . . Wisconsin
Burr, H. C. . . . Dakota
Burrall . . . New Mexico
Burrall, Arthur . . . Texas
Burrell, J. B. . . . Oregon
Burridge, Charles . . . Nebraska
Burris, Mathew . . . California
Burritt & Pease . . . Minnesota
Burritt, E. H. . . . Minnesota, Wisconsin
Burroughs, E. R. . . . Idaho
Burrows, H. G. . . . Nebraska
Burt, Charles S. . . . Arizona
Burt, George . . . Kansas
Burt, I. K. E. . . . Minnesota
Burt, L. S. (Mrs.) . . . California
Burtis, George . . . Arizona
Burtis, George (Mrs.) . . . Arizona
Burtness, Conner C. . . . New Mexico
Burton . . . Oregon
Burton, C. . . . Texas
Burton, Dorothy M. . . . Oregon
Burton, E. K. . . . Wisconsin
Burton, George . . . Idaho
Burton, Matthew C. . . . Texas
Burton, W. C. . . . Texas
Burton, Walter Francis . . . British Columbia
Busby, Edward Scott . . . Alaska, British Columbia
Buser & Son . . . Iowa
Buser, Henry R. . . . Iowa
Buser, J. S. . . . Iowa
Bush, C. T. . . . Iowa
Bush, E. E. . . . California
Bush, Effie A. . . . Texas
Bush, Henry . . . British Columbia, California
Bush, J. E. . . . Kansas
Bush, James . . . Oregon
Bush, James Lafayette . . . California
Bushby & Company . . . Oregon
Bushby, Asa C. . . . Oregon
Bushman & Company . . . Arizona
Bushnell, Corry A. . . . Oregon, Washington
Bushnell, E. P. . . . Missouri
Bushnell, Frank P. . . . Oregon
Bushnell, Frederick H. . . . California
Bushnell, G. R. . . . California
Bushnell Photo . . . California
Bushnell Photo Company . . . California
Bushnell–Langford Photo Company . . . Oregon
Bushong & Feldman . . . New Mexico, Texas
Bushong, John C. . . . New Mexico, Texas
Busse, Robert . . . Nebraska
Butcher & Company . . . British Columbia
Butcher, Arthur . . . British Columbia
Butcher, Solomon D. . . . Nebraska, Traveling
Butler . . . California, Wisconsin
Butler & Dorsez . . . California
Butler & Franks . . . Oregon
Butler, A. H. . . . Texas
Butler, Benjamin D. . . . Oregon
Butler, C. W. . . . Texas
Butler, Charles A. . . . California
Butler, Cook . . . California
Butler, E. P. . . . Nevada
Butler, Edward P. . . . California, Traveling
Butler, G. R. . . . California
Butler, H. . . . Dakota, Nebraska
Butler, J. E. (Mrs.) . . . Texas
Butler, J. Frederick . . . New Mexico
Butler, M. L. . . . Texas
Butler, Professor Gilbert . . . Idaho
Butler, R. S. . . . Kansas
Butler Studio . . . Iowa
Butler, T. A. . . . California
Butler, W. E. . . . Minnesota
Butman, W. C. . . . New Mexico
Butman, W. W. . . . New Mexico
Butterfield & Ralston . . . Dakota
Butterfield, L. T. . . . Wisconsin
Butterfield, S. H. . . . California
Butters, William . . . Iowa
Butterworth, Charles . . . Oregon
Button & Higgins . . . California
Button & Hogan's Photographic Art Gallery . . . California
Button, Charles Gilbert . . . California, Oregon
Buttree . . . Colorado
Buxton, Bertram H. . . . British Columbia
Buys, William . . . Utah
Byam, J. W. . . . Wisconsin
Bybee . . . Oregon
Bybee & Cannon . . . Oregon
Byerly, Orison . . . Iowa
Byers, Bernard L. . . . Oregon
Byles, C. W. . . . Colorado
Byram, W. B. . . . California
Byrd, David . . . California
Byrd, W. . . . Texas
Byrd, William . . . California
Byrnes, J. C. . . . Iowa
Byrns, Thomas . . . California

C

C & S Studio . . . Kansas
C. C. M. Company . . . Oregon
Cable, R. E. . . . Colorado, New Mexico
Caboni, Efisio . . . California
Cade, H. C. . . . Nevada
Caderan, A. W. . . . Texas
Cadman, A. N. . . . Texas
Cadman, Albert W. . . . Arkansas
Cadwell, Aaron W. . . . Texas
Cadwell, Fred B. . . . Texas
Cadwell, M. & A. W. . . . Texas
Cadwell, Moses . . . Texas
Cady, George B. . . . California
Cady, H. C. . . . California
Caesar & Company, Charles . . . Nebraska
Cahn, (Miss) . . . California
Calahan Brothers . . . Arkansas
Calahan, Dennis . . . Arkansas
Calahan, George R. . . . Arkansas
Calahan, H. C. . . . Texas
Calaway, C. N. . . . Texas
Caldwell & Spagliam . . . Texas
Caldwell, Charles H. . . . Texas
Caldwell, Chester M. . . . Oregon
Caldwell, Ira . . . Washington
Caldwell, J. R. . . . Texas
Caldwell, John . . . Oregon
Caldwell, W. M. . . . Arkansas
Caldwell, W. T. . . . Nebraska
Caldwell, William M. . . . Texas
Caleson's Gallery . . . Minnesota
Calfee & Catlin . . . Montana
Calfee, H. B. . . . Montana, Wyoming
Calhoun . . . Colorado
Calhoun, J. M. . . . Nebraska
California Art Company . . . California
California Art Gallery . . . Arizona
California Art Photo Company . . . California
California Gallery . . . California, Iowa, Oregon
California Photo Tent . . . California, Traveling
California Photographic Gallery . . . California
California Studio . . . Oregon
Calkins, F. C. . . . Idaho
Calkins, J. T. . . . Iowa
Callaghan . . . Oregon
Callahan, T. M. . . . Indian Territory
Callarman, F. A. . . . Alaska
Callaway & Peterson . . . Texas
Callaway, Alonzo Newell . . . Texas
Callender & Patterson . . . Wisconsin
Callender, John H. . . . Wisconsin
Calohan, C. W. . . . Missouri
Calvar, Frank . . . New Mexico, Texas
Calvarusso, Francisco . . . New Mexico
Calvert, Alvida . . . Oregon
Calvert, Charles E. . . . Oregon
Calvert, Grace E. . . . Oregon
Calvert, Harry . . . Oregon
Calvert, J. . . . British Columbia
Calvert's Studio . . . Oregon
Calvery, Thomas . . . California
Calvin, J. P. . . . Iowa
Calvin, Robert . . . Texas
Calvin, William T. . . . Idaho
Cameron, Agnes Deans . . . British Columbia
Cameron, Evelyn Jephson . . . Montana
Cameron, J. D. . . . California
Cammack . . . Iowa
Cammack & Johnson . . . Oregon
Cammack, Fred M. . . . Oregon
Cammel, R. H. . . . Texas
Cammel, W. M. . . . Texas
Cammert, Edmund R. . . . California
Camp, C. D. . . . Nebraska
Camp, G. A. . . . Nebraska
Campbell . . . British Columbia, Oregon
Campbell & Company, Robert . . . Utah
Campbell & Edwards . . . Oklahoma
Campbell, A. D. . . . California
Campbell, A. R. . . . Nebraska
Campbell, Charles . . . Colorado
Campbell, Charles Alexander . . . California
Campbell, Hamilton . . . Oregon, Traveling
Campbell, J. F. . . . British Columbia
Campbell, James . . . California
Campbell, John . . . Oregon
Campbell, John P. . . . Texas
Campbell, M. L. . . . Kansas
Campbell, Martha . . . Iowa
Campbell, S. S. . . . California
Campbell, W. H. . . . Nebraska
Camps & Oltman . . . California
Camps, Frank L. . . . California, Oregon
Canaday, H. . . . Oregon
Canaris, Catherine . . . Oregon, Washington
Canaris, Frank H. . . . Oregon, Washington
Cander, John . . . Texas
Candlin, L. M. (Mrs.) . . . Oregon
Canfield, E. H. . . . Texas, Wisconsin
Canfield, Francis Orra . . . British Columbia
Cann . . . Nevada, Oregon
Cann, Dell . . . California
Cannell, M. J. . . . Nebraska
Canning & Rust . . . Minnesota
Canning, Arthur A. . . . British Columbia
Canning, M. A. (Mrs.) . . . Minnesota
Cannon . . . Oregon
Cannon, Eron . . . California
Cannon, Marsena . . . California, Utah
Cannon, O. C. . . . Colorado
Cannon, Othniel R. . . . Colorado
Cannon, W. A. . . . Colorado
Cannon, William C. . . . California
Canova . . . Idaho
Canova Gallery . . . Idaho
Cantwell, George C. . . . Alaska

Chamberlain, Mary L. . . . . .Kansas
Chamberlain, Walter A. . . . . .Colorado
Chamberlain, William G. . . . . .Colorado
Chambers, Arthur . . . . .Nebraska
Chambers, Arthur Hyde . . . . . . .British Columbia
Chambers, J. B. . . . . .Texas
Chambers, James .Texas
Chambers, John . . . . .Texas
Chan, Isabelle May (Mrs.) . . . . .California
Chan, K. S. . . . . .California
Chan, Leo . . . . .California
Chanay, E. C. . . . . .Texas
Chanay, Ella . . . . .Texas
Chandlee & Chandlee . . . . .Arkansas
Chandlee, Marietta . . . . .Kansas
Chandler . . . . .Wisconsin
Chandler, Dell . . . . .New Mexico
Chandler, Gerald A. . . . . .Idaho
Chandler, Jesse W. . . . . .California
Chandler, William M. . . . . .Texas
Channel, Elias . . . . .Kansas
Chapman . . . . .Texas
Chapman & Company . . . . .Arkansas
Chapman & Roloson . . . . .Nebraska
Chapman & Williams . . . . .Texas
Chapman, A. . . . . .Iowa, Nebraska
Chapman, Andrew . . . . .Texas
Chapman, C. C. .Idaho
Chapman, C. G. . . . . .Kansas
Chapman, E. V. .Texas
Chapman, Frank .Texas
Chapman, J. E. H. . . . . .Texas
Chapman, J. G. . . . . .Colorado
Chapman, J. P. . . . . .Nebraska
Chapman, John H. . . . . .Texas
Chapman, John Howard
    Arthur . . . . .British Columbia
Chapman, W. . . . . .British Columbia
Charbourne . . . . .Wisconsin
Charles, A. (Miss) . . . . .Kansas
Charles, James C. . . . . .Texas
Chase . .Arizona, Colorado, Minnesota, Wisconsin
Chase & Egbert . . . . .Iowa
Chase & Lewis .Colorado
Chase & Swanson . . . . .Colorado
Chase & Wolcott . . . . .Colorado
Chase, A. W. . . . . .California
Chase, B. B. (Mrs.) . . . . .Colorado
Chase, C. B. . . . . .Minnesota
Chase, C. W. . . . . .Iowa
Chase, Dana B. . . . . .Colorado, New Mexico
Chase, E. S. . . . . .Colorado
Chase, E. T. . . . . .Oregon
Chase, F. R. . . . . .Nebraska
Chase, H. L. . . . . .Colorado
Chase, Henry L. .Hawaii
Chase, J. W. . . . . .California
Chase, John A. . . . . .Colorado, Kansas
Chase, Lorenzo G. . . . . .California
Chase, Morton E. . . . . .Colorado
Chase, N. W. . . . . .New Mexico
Chase's Photo Gallery . . . . .Colorado
Chatfield & Allen . . . . .Iowa
Chatham, Perry .Texas
Chatterton & Son . . . . .Iowa
Chatterton, F. C. .Iowa
Chatterton, H. D. . . . . .Iowa
Chatterton, M. (Miss) . . . . .Oregon
Chau, Ka . . . . .California
Chaudet Art Company Railway
    Photo Car . . . . .Traveling
Chenault . . . . .Texas
Cheney & Grimm . . . . .Oregon
Cheney, B. F. . . . . .Idaho
Cheney, Edith C. . . . . .Oregon
Cheney, Eston S. . . . . .Oregon
Cheney, Ethel .Oregon
Cheney, Willie Tuttle . . . . .Idaho

Cheney's Art Gallery . . . . .Oregon
Chenhall, John . . . . .California
Chenoweth, D. W. . . . . .Nebraska
Cherrington Brothers . . . . .Oregon
Cherrington, Thomas J. . . . . .Oregon
Cherrington, William M. . . . . .Oregon
Cherry & Weatherington . . . . .Texas
Cherry, Charles W. . . . . .Texas
Cherry, Edgar .California
Cherry, George R. . . . . .Texas
Chesebro, Edward C. . . . . .California
Chesley, G. W. . . . . .Minnesota
Chessel, Made . . . . .Texas
Chester, Benjamin . . . . .Colorado
Chew & Jandus . . . . .Colorado
Chew, Ah . . . . .California
Chew, N. I. . . . . .Colorado
Chicago Art Gallery . . . . . . .Arkansas, California
Chicago Gallery . . . . .Nebraska
Chicago Viewing Company . . . . .New Mexico
Chico Art Gallery . . . . .California
Chidister, B. F. .Kansas
Child, Arthur . . . . .Iowa
Child, L. C. . . . . .Hawaii
Children's Art Gallery Company . . . . . . .Oregon
Childres, B. L. . . . . .Colorado
Childress, Guildford B. . . . . .Texas
Childress, Willie .Texas
Childs, Alfred R. . . . . .Colorado
Childs, H. A. .Wisconsin
Chin, Lin . . . . .California
Ching Chow . . . . .Hawaii
Chinlund, Elmer A. . . . . .Oregon
Chinlund, Frantz William . . . . .Oregon
Chinn & Sowby .Texas
Chinn, George W. . . . . .Idaho
Chinnery, J. H. .Oregon
Chio, Ming Hin . . . . .California
Chipman, Alice L. . . . . .Texas
Chipman, Uva . . . . .Texas
Chisholm, C. P. .Texas
Choate, W. W. . . . . .Missouri
Choicen . . . . .Nebraska
Choicener, J. F. . . . . .Nebraska
Christensen, D. E. . . . . .Colorado
Christensen, H. P. . . . . .Nebraska
Christensen, Peter C. . . . . .Arizona
Christian, Willie .Texas
Christiani, Charles O. . . . . .Oregon
Christiansen . . . . .Nebraska
Christiansen, Karl Brink . . . . . .British Columbia
Christman, E. J. . . . . .Minnesota
Christopher & Company, E. . . . . .Colorado
Christopher, J. D. . . . . .Texas
Christy & Son .Colorado
Christy, Isaac Marshall . . . . .Arizona
Christy Studio .Oregon
Chukinger, Willy . . . . .Texas
Chung, Sim . . . . .California
Church, Alena .Kansas
Church, Clifton .Texas
Churchill . . . . .Texas
Churchill (Mrs.) .Texas
Churchill & Company . . . . .Nebraska
Churchill & West . . . . .Texas
Churchill, D. J. .Kansas
Churchill, George O. . . . . .Nebraska
Churchill, W. D. . . . . .Colorado
Churchley & Hargrave . . . . .Oregon
Churchley, A. G. . . . . .Washington
Churchley, Amy G. . . . . .Oregon
Churchley, Arthur G. . . . . .Oregon
Churchman . . . . .California
Churchman Brothers . . . . .California
Churchman, J. W. . . . . .California
Churchman, S. E. . . . . .California
Ciliaz, Herman .Texas
Cimarron Gallery . . . . .Oklahoma

Cirrk's Photo Company . . . . .Kansas
City Art Gallery . . . . .Missouri
City Fine Art Gallery . . . . .Kansas
City Gallery . . . . .Dakota, Iowa
City Mart . . . . .California
City Photo Gallery . . . . .California
City Photograph Gallery . . . . . . .Iowa, Montana,
                                        Nevada, Wisconsin
City Picture Rooms . . . . .Nebraska
Claiborne, C. E. . . . . .New Mexico
Claibourne . . . . .Wisconsin
Clampet, Jo W. .Texas
Clancy, Andrew . . . . .California
Clapman, J. . . . . .Texas
Clapp & Pratt .Oregon
Clark . . . . .Kansas, Oregon, Texas, Wisconsin
Clark (Mr.) . . . . .Wisconsin
Clark & Barker .Texas
Clark & Clark .Oregon
Clark & Erdlen . . . . .Colorado
Clark & Heyde . . . . .Nebraska
Clark & Johnston . . . . .California
Clark & Wood .Oregon
Clark, A. . . . . .Arkansas
Clark, A. G. . . . . .California
Clark, A. M. . . . . .Nebraska
Clark Brothers .Oregon
Clark, C. C. . . . . .Nebraska
Clark, C. E. . . . . .Nebraska
Clark, C. F. . . . . .Kansas
Clark, C. H. . . . . .Colorado
Clark, Charles .Arizona
Clark, Charles B. . . . . .Colorado
Clark, Charles W. . . . . .Oregon
Clark, D. G. . . . . .Colorado, Nebraska
Clark, E. A. . . . . .Traveling
Clark, E. L. . . . . .California
Clark, Edward A. . . . . .Washington
Clark, Ellen E. (Mrs.) . . . . .Texas
Clark, F. M. . . . . .Texas
Clark, F. Melvin . . . . .Oregon
Clark, F. W. . . . . .Iowa
Clark, Frank E. . . . . .Colorado
Clark, Fred A. .Oregon
Clark, George .Oregon
Clark, George P. . . . . .California
Clark, Hiram S. . . . . .Wisconsin
Clark, J. C. . . . . .California
Clark, J. H. . . . . .British Columbia, Oregon
Clark, John C. .Oregon
Clark, John F. .Colorado
Clark, L. . . . . .Iowa
Clark, L. Wilson . . . . .Oregon, Washington
Clark, M. L. (Mrs.) . . . . .Minnesota
Clark, May (Miss) . . . . .New Mexico
Clark Photos .California
Clark, R. H. . . . . .Arizona
Clark, Robert .Arizona
Clark, Robert A. (Mrs.) . . . . .Colorado
Clark, W. B. . . . . .Texas
Clark, W. L. . . . . .California
Clark, William F. . . . . .Nebraska
Clark, William J. . . . . .Arkansas
Clark's Fine Art Studio . . . . .Nebraska
Clark's Photo Company . . . . . . .California, Kansas
Clark's Studio .Oregon
Clarke, A. B. .Wisconsin
Clarke, Edwin R. . . . . .Colorado
Clarke, J. F. . . . . .Oregon
Clarke, W. .West Canada
Clary & Root . . . . .Texas
Claudet, Francis George . . . . . .British Columbia
Clausen, A. J. . . . . .Iowa
Clausen, C. H. (Mrs.) . . . . .Arizona
Clausen, C. H. . . . . .Arizona, California
Clausen, C. M. . . . . .Iowa
Clausen, Elfred . . . . .Iowa
Claussenius, Herman . . . . .Oregon

D

D'heureuse, Rudolph ....Arizona
D'ole, S. ....Kansas
D'ole, T. W. ....Kansas
Da Lee, A. G. ....Kansas
Dabb, J. V. ....Iowa
Dabb, Jason V. ....Wisconsin
Dabb, R. I. ....Iowa
Dabbs, J. V. ....Kansas
Daft ....Iowa
Dagger, O. P. ....Iowa
Daggett, Frances (Mrs.) ....Colorado
Daguerre Atelier Photographique .....California
Dahl & Halvorsen ....Nebraska
Dahl, A. L. ....Wisconsin
Dahl, Louis ....Texas
Dahlgren, John ....Oregon
Dahlquist, W. A. ....Idaho
Dahms, Gustav ....Iowa
Dailey ....Wisconsin
Dailey, Jonas ....Oregon
Dailey, Mary (Mrs.) ....Oregon
Dailey, R. ....California
Daily, John William ....California
Daisy Car ....Traveling
Daivson, C. K. ....Oregon
Dake ....Oklahoma, Wisconsin
Dale, C. S. ....Texas
Dales, G. S. ....Colorado
Dalgleish ....Wyoming
Dalgleish, George ....Colorado
Dalgleish, Gilbert ....Oregon
Dalgleish, Thomas ....Texas
Dall, J. H. ....California
Dallas Copying & Enlarging Company .....Texas
Dallas Copying House ....Texas
Dally, Frederick ....British Columbia
Dalton, Frank ....Oregon
Dalton, Samuel ....Texas
Dalton, William Tinniswood ...British Columbia
Damand ....Texas
Dames & Butler ....California
Dames & Hayes ....California
Dames & Keil ....California
Dames & Williams ....California
Dames, Delia C. ....California
Dames, William W. ....California
Dammand, R. P. ....Iowa
Dammond, R. P. ....California
Damon, Marshall ....California
Damron, V. C. ....California
Dana ....Oklahoma, Oregon
Dando, Farnham C. ....California
Daniel, Arthur ....Texas
Daniel, Joseph E. ....Texas
Daniels & Conkling ....Utah
Daniels & Hafen ....Utah
Daniels, Craig F. ....Minnesota
Daniels, J. L. ....Traveling
Daniels, M. T. ....Iowa
Daniels, Orson A. ....Utah
Daniels Studio ....Utah
Daniels, Thomas E., Jr. ....Utah
Danielson, Frank M. ....Colorado
Danihy, Bartholomew ....Washington
Danner, Theodore D. ....Oregon
Darbyshire ....California
Darden, George A. ....Texas
Dare & Collins Art Store ....Texas
Dare, D. D. ....Colorado, Wyoming
Dare, G. F. ....Wisconsin
Daring, O. H. ....Nebraska
Darling & Ingersoll ....Oregon
Darling, Belle ....Oregon
Darlington, Charles A. ....California
Darms, H. A. ....Alaska
Darragh & Godfrey ....California

Darragh, Dr. J. C. ....California
Darrah, Hugh ....Iowa
Dart ....Traveling
Darton, Nelson Horatio ....New Mexico
Dassonville, William E. ....California
Datesman, P. ....Iowa
Datesman, Peter ....California
Datesman, Peter P. ....Oregon
Datsman, P. ....Nebraska
Daugherty ....Iowa, Oklahoma
Daugherty, C. ....Texas
Daugherty, Charles J. ....California
Daugherty, Mary A. ....California
Daughtery, S. ....Kansas
Davenport, C. F. ....Kansas
Davenport, James ....Minnesota
Davenport, Lizzie (Mrs.) ....Oregon
Davenport, M. L. ....Arizona
Davenport, Perry F. ....Texas
Davey, Frank ....Hawaii
David, Edmund ....Texas
David, V. E. ....Colorado
Davids & Bishop ....Wisconsin
Davidson .....California, Dakota, Iowa, Traveling
Davidson, Arthur H. ....Arizona
Davidson, C. M. ....California
Davidson, D. A. ....Oregon
Davidson, E. M. ....California
Davidson, Edgar L. ....Oregon
Davidson, Eva J. (Mrs.) ....California
Davidson, George W. ....Texas
Davidson, H. & R. ....California
Davidson, I. G. ....Oregon, Washington
Davidson, J. ....Oregon
Davidson, John S. ....Oregon
Davidson, L. S. ....California
Davidson, Le Roy ....Oregon
Davidson, Norvalle Rice .....California, Traveling
Davidson, T. M. ....Nebraska
Davies ....Nebraska
Davies, George W. ....Oregon
Davies, John ....Nebraska
Daviess ....Missouri
Davis ....California, Missouri, Nebraska
Davis (Mrs.) ....Texas
Davis & Garrett ....Nebraska
Davis & Tull ....Oregon
Davis, A. Leaman ....Oregon
Davis, Arthur ....Texas
Davis, Benjamin F. ....New Mexico
Davis Brothers ....California, Idaho
Davis, C. A. ....Texas
Davis, C. H. ....Nebraska
Davis, C. L. ....Colorado
Davis, Calvin Lee ....Oklahoma
Davis, Charles ....Idaho
Davis, E. G. ....Traveling
Davis, E. M. ....Wisconsin
Davis, Florence N. (Mrs.) ....California
Davis, George A. ....Texas
Davis, H. A. ....Idaho
Davis Henry ....Texas
Davis, Hugh C. ....Oregon
Davis, J. F. ....Iowa
Davis, J. P. ....Texas
Davis, J. W. ....Texas
Davis, James A. ....Texas
Davis, James M. ....Missouri
Davis, James R. ....Texas
Davis, John ....Idaho
Davis, Joseph ....British Columbia
Davis, L. M. ....Oregon
Davis, Lewis G. Brewster ....Idaho
Davis, M. C. ....Texas
Davis, Marion T. ....Idaho
Davis, Marshall P. ....Oregon
Davis, O. A. ....Missouri

Davis, O. T. ....Colorado, New Mexico
Davis Photo ....California
Davis Photography Studio ....California
Davis, R. C. ....New Mexico
Davis, Robert M. ....Colorado
Davis, S. (Miss) ....British Columbia
Davis, S. P. ....Oregon, Traveling
Davis, W. B. ....Oregon
Davis, W. H. ....Iowa, West Canada
Davis, W. L. ....Nebraska
Davis, W. W. ....Oregon
Davis, Walter .....British Columbia, Washington
Davis, Walter Alfred ....California
Davis, Walter Austin ....California
Davis, William ....Minnesota, Oregon
Davis, William H. ....British Columbia,
                                Washington
Davison, John M. ....Texas
Davy ....Minnesota
Dawson ....Kansas
Dawson, C. B. ....Oregon
Dawson, Everett ....Texas
Dawson, F. E. ....Iowa
Dawson, George Mercer ....Alaska,
                          British Columbia
Dawson Mammoth Art Gallery ....Traveling
Dawson, R. W. ....Arkansas
Day ....Oregon
Day & Lyon ....Oregon
Day, E. ....Traveling
Day, E. M. ....Nebraska
Day, E. M. (Mrs.) ....Nebraska
Day, Ernest ....Idaho
Day, Lewis L. ....Oregon
Day, M. A. ....Nebraska
Day, Madge (Miss) ....British Columbia
Day, S. C. ....Nebraska
Day, Sarah E. (Mrs.) ....Oregon
Day, T. J. ....Nebraska
Day, Thomas P. ....Texas
Daylight Studio ....Kansas
Dayton, M. ....Colorado
Dayton Studio ....Iowa
De Buhr, Joseph ....California
De Graff, W. H. ....Dakota
De Groff, Edward ....Alaska
De Groot & Kellog ....California
De Groot, Harry ....California
De Groot, Henry, Jr. ....California
De Guire, L. J. ....Minnesota
De Hart ....Missouri
De Lano, Frank H. ....Iowa
De Long, C. A. ....Minnesota
De Long, O. V. ....New Mexico, Texas
De Mello, John, Sr. ....Hawaii
De Monbrum, David ....Oregon
De Vergilio, Samuel ....California
De Wert, Mae M. (Miss) ....Oregon
Deady, William G. ....California, Nevada
Deakins, E. D. ....New Mexico
Dealey Brothers ....California
Dealey, Charles Allen ....California, Oregon
Dean ....Oregon, Texas, Traveling
Dean & Gray ....California
Dean, Frank E. ....Colorado
Dean, George E. ....California
Dean, J. K. ....California
Dean, James ....California, Oregon
Dean, Orie Snyder ....California
Dean, Robert D. ....Texas
Deane ....Oregon
Deane & Morgan ....Texas
Deane Brothers ....Missouri
Deane, Clarence C. ....Texas
Deane, E. B. ....British Columbia
Deane, Granville M. ....Texas
Deane, Jervis C. ....Texas
Deane, M. O. (Mrs.) ....Texas

Douglass, John H., Jr. ....Oregon
Douglass, John H., Sr. ....Oregon
Douglass, T. C. ....Texas
Douglass Traveling Car ....Traveling
Douglass, Walter ....Texas
Douning & Evans ....California
Douthitt, Ada ....Kansas
Douthitt, Laura ....Kansas
Douthitt, Louise ....Kansas
Dove ....California
Dowdy, Jesse L. ....Texas
Dowe ....California, Traveling
Dowe & Murphy ....California
Dowe & Pickett ....California
Dowe, Arthur W. ..California, New Mexico, Texas
Dowe Brothers ....California
Dowe, D. W. ....Arizona
Dowe, Duane W. ....California
Dowe, Lewis ....California
Dowe, O. L. ....New Mexico
Dowe, Oscar S. ......California, Idaho, Nevada,
                            Oregon, Traveling
Dowell, Alex ....Oregon
Downey ....California, Traveling
Downey & Son, W. M. ....California
Downey, B. A. ....Washington
Downing ....Indian Territory, Texas
Downing & Bates ....Texas
Downing & Evans ....California
Downing & Smith ....California
Downing Brothers ....California
Downing, D. Owen ....California
Downing, Eugene ....California
Downing, George ....Kansas
Downing, J. C. ....Missouri
Downing, J. H. ....California
Downing, Jesse C. ....Texas
Downing, Mortimer A. ....New Mexico
Downing, Rea & Rauscher ....California
Downing, William C. ....Texas
Downs, Edson J. ....Kansas
Doyle, Samuel ....California
Drake ....Colorado, Oklahoma
Drake, Charles L. ....Arizona
Drake, Emery R. ....Oregon
Drake, H. J. ....Texas
Drake, H. S. ....Traveling
Drake, June D. ....Oregon
Drane, Edward ....Texas
Draper, Edgar ....Nebraska
Draper, Herbert ....Alaska
Draper, William G. ....Oregon
Draper, Z. T. ....Utah
Drenkel, D. R. ....Colorado
Drenkhahn (Mrs.) ....California
Dressel ....California
Dressel, G. A. ....Minnesota
Dresser ....Kansas
Dresser, Alfred Woodroffe .....British Columbia
Dresser, George H. ....Kansas
Dresser, William ....Wisconsin
Drew, Addie ....California
Drewery, H. ....Utah
Drewery, Harry ....Idaho
Dreyling, Gustav ....Texas
Driver, Doug Otis ....Texas
Driver, Joseph M. ....Texas
Drum, O. ....Indian Territory, Kansas, Oklahoma
Drum Railroad Photo Car ....Traveling
Drumfield ....Colorado
Drummond, Arthur ....British Columbia
Dryden, R. H. ....Texas
Duben, C. ....California
Dubois, T. N. ....Texas
Duckering, William ....Washington
Duclos ....Alaska
Dudley, E. T. ....Texas
Dudley, George ....Kansas

Dudley, M. ....Colorado
Duer, Stump & Company ....Texas
Duer, W. T. ....Texas
Duff, N. Frank ....Texas
Duffield, John D. ....Texas
Duffin ....Dakota
Duffin & Company ....West Canada
Duffin, Simon ....West Canada
Dufrene ....Oregon
Dufresne, E. ....Wisconsin
Dufresne, Joseph Z. ....Oregon
Duganne ....Dakota
Dugen, Bassantect ....Texas
Duggan ....Texas
Duhem Brothers ....Colorado
Duhem, Constant ....California, Colorado
Duhem, Harold ....California
Duhem, Julia (Mrs.) ....California
Duhem, Victor H. ....California
Duhem, Victor L. ....California
Duhem, Victor M. ....California, Colorado
Duhling ....Nebraska
Duis, B. R. ....Nebraska
Dulaney, J. E. ....Texas
Dulchan, William ....Texas
Dummermuth, Frank E. ....Oregon
Dunbar, Charles Trott ....British Columbia
Duncan ....Texas
Duncan, A. B. ....Traveling
Duncan, E. ....Texas
Duncan, Francis K. ....Texas
Duncan, Frank ....Oregon
Duncan, Minnie ....Nebraska
Duncan, W. A. ....Iowa, Missouri
Duncan, William ....British Columbia
Dunham ....Iowa, Traveling
Dunham & Bluett ....California
Dunham & Cook ....California
Dunham & Kelsey ....California, Nevada
Dunham & Lathrop ....California, Nevada
Dunham, Allen Murry ....California
Dunham, Ephraim G. ....California
Dunham, F. ....Iowa
Dunham, Orley Wyatt ....California
Dunham, R. M. ....Oregon
Dunk, D. T. ....Texas
Dunlap Brothers ....Arkansas
Dunlap, Charles L. ....Arkansas
Dunlap, Craig ....Texas
Dunlap, J. F. ....Idaho
Dunlap, J. H. ....Iowa
Dunlap, Knight (Mrs.) ....California
Dunlap, Robert H. ....Oregon
Dunlap, T. A. ....Iowa
Dunlap, W. ....Missouri
Dunlap, W. L. ....Nebraska
Dunlap, W. T. ....Texas
Dunlap, William W. ....Arkansas
Dunleavy, J. E. ....Texas
Dunn ....Missouri
Dunn & Easton ....Dakota
Dunn & Payne ....Texas
Dunn, A. S. W. ....Texas
Dunn, Carrie E. (Mrs.) ....Oregon
Dunn, Courtney E. ....California
Dunn, G. W. ....Texas
Dunn, Ivo M. ....Kansas
Dunn, Thomas C. ....Kansas
Dunn, William, Sr. ....Texas
Dunnaway, Andrew ....Texas
Dunshee, H. S. ....Wisconsin
Dunsmuir Studio ....California
Dunton & Jourdan ....Wisconsin
Dunton, Oscar E. ....Colorado
Durand, E. D. ....Hawaii
Durant, G. S. ....Missouri
Duray, J. H. ....Idaho
Durgan, Frank ....California

Durham, George C. ....Oregon
Durkee, B. S. ....Oregon
Durkee, Henry ....Wisconsin
Durland & Company ....Kansas
Durocher, C. G. ....West Canada
Durose ....California
Durrant, Walter H. ....Idaho
Durston, Glenn A. ....Oregon
Duryea Photo Company ......British Columbia
Duryea, William C. ....British Columbia
Dusseau, A. J. ....Montana
Dusterhoeft, William ....British Columbia
Dusy, Frank ....California
Dutcher, Edwin M. ....California
Dutcher, Moses ....California
Dutcher, Sarah (Miss) ....California
Dutkewich ....California, Traveling
Dutler, D. S. ....Kansas
Dutro & Reed ....Montana
Dutro, Dan ....Montana
Dutton, S. ....California
Duvall, C. M. ....Washington
Duvall, Clarke ....Oregon
Duvall, J. H. ....Missouri
Duzenberry, Huron ....Kansas
Dwight, D. W. ....Nebraska
Dwight, F. E. ....Iowa, Nebraska
Dwight, Francis E. ....Wyoming
Dwight, Joseph F. ....Iowa
Dwight, T., Jr. ....Wisconsin
Dwyer, Dennis J. ....Oregon
Dyall, H. C. ....Iowa
Dyall, T. W. ....Iowa
Dye, D. S. ....Nebraska
Dyer ....Kansas
Dyer & Luders ....California
Dyer, John W. ....Colorado
Dyer, Joseph M. ....Texas
Dyer, William Denny ....California

E

Eader, G. A. ....Nebraska
Eagle Clift Studio ....California
Eagle Gallery ....California
Eagle Studio ....Iowa
Eakin, J. S. ....Texas
Eames & Elliott ....Missouri
Eames, Charles ....California
Eames, Elizabeth J. (Mrs.) ....California
Eanes, Frank ....Texas
Eanes, John ....Texas
Eanes, Perry ....Texas
Earl, J. P. ....Iowa
Earl, Miles W. ....Oregon
Earle, M. R. ....Traveling
Easley, D. N. ....Wisconsin
Eason Brothers ....Nebraska
Eason, D. ....New Mexico
Eason, E. ....Nebraska
East Oakland Gallery ....California
East Side Photo Studio ....Oregon
East, Thomas ....Nebraska
Eastburn, F. P. ....Traveling
Eastburn, Frank P. ....California
Easterly, Thomas ....Missouri
Easthope & Company ....British Columbia
Easthope, E. Frederick ....British Columbia
Eastman ....Arizona
Eastman Brothers ....Wisconsin
Eastman, C. H. ....Colorado
Eastman, E. A. (Mrs.) ....California
Eastman, Emily R. (Mrs.) ....California
Eastman, Farnham, J. ....Washington
Eastman, Frank P. ....California
Eastman, G. L. ....Colorado
Eastman, Gilman L. ....Idaho, Oregon
Eastman, J. H. ....Oregon
Eastman, Jervie H. ....California

Forsdahl, M. . . . . .Colorado
Forsyth, N. A. . . . . .Montana
Fort Worth Art Gallery . . . . .Texas
Fortin, J. . . . . .California, New Mexico
Fortin, Jasper . . . . .Arizona
Fortin, Joseph . . . . .Idaho, Oregon
Fortune, E. W. .California
Forzell, C. . . . . .California
Foslide, John . . . . .Washington
Fosnot & Hunter . . . . .Iowa
Fosnot, L. C. . . . . .Iowa
Foss & Halsey .California
Foss & Hickox . . . . .California
Foss, Oscar . . . . .California
Foster . . . . .California, Oregon
Foster, Charles E. . . . . .Missouri, Texas
Foster, E. H. . . . . .Dakota
Foster, H. W. . . . . .Nebraska
Foster, J. C. . . . . .Nebraska
Foster, J. L. . . . . .California
Foster, Laura H. . . . . .Oregon
Foster, Perry . . . . .Oregon
Foster, R. M. . . . . .Kansas
Foster, W. M. . . . . .Texas
Fouch, John H. . . . . .Minnesota, Montana
Fouchek, S. A. . . . . .Iowa
Fougner, Iver . . . . .British Columbia
Foulkes, David .Oregon
Fouzer, C. L. (Mrs.) . . . . .Texas
Fowler . . . . .Indian Territory, Kansas
Fowler & Horn . . . . .Wisconsin
Fowler, D. D. . . . . .Oregon
Fowler, Elbert W. . . . . .Wisconsin
Fowler, F. M. .Wisconsin
Fowler, George H. . . . . .Oregon
Fowler, N. G. . . . . .Texas
Fowler, S. T. . . . . .Texas
Fowler, William B. . . . . .Idaho
Fowler, William Howard . . . . .Arkansas
Fowler, William R. . . . . .Texas
Fowzer . . . . .California
Fowzer & Hayes . . . . .California
Fowzer & Samuels . . . . .California
Fowzer, George J. . . . . .California
Fowzer, Jacob .California
Fox & Son, A. D. . . . . .Washington
Fox & Symons . . . . .Utah
Fox & Wiltse . . . . .Dakota
Fox, A. J. . . . . .Missouri
Fox, Alexander . . . . .California, Utah
Fox, G. A. . . . . .Iowa
Fox, G. W. . . . . .Dakota
Fox, H. . . . . .Colorado
Fox, John . . . . .Arkansas
Fox Lake View Company . . . . .Wisconsin
Fox, Lauretta . . . . .Kansas
Fox, W. W. . . . . .British Columbia
Fraesdorf, William . . . . .Arizona
Francis & Griffin . . . . .Colorado
Francis, E. K. . . . . .British Columbia
Francis, G. D. .Traveling
Francis, Helen . . . . .Kansas
Frank .Missouri, Texas
Frank, Charles E. . . . . .Washington
Frankland, Margery . . . . .Wyoming
Franklin & Company, W. S. . . . . .Texas
Franklin & Darlington . . . . .California
Franklin & Howell . . . . .California
Franklin & Leschinsky . . . . .Nebraska
Franklin & Son, D. . . . . .Traveling
Franklin & White . . . . .California
Franklin, E. B. . . . . .Traveling
Franklin, John C. . . . . .California
Franklin, Lena . . . . .California
Franklin, Maurice A. . . . . .California
Franklyn, F. J. .Nebraska
Franks & Butler . . . . .Oregon
Franks, F. D. . . . . .Oregon

Franks, Mary E. (Miss) . . . . .Texas
Frans . . . . .Wisconsin
Frantz, A. L. . . . . .Iowa
Frary, Emery . . . . .Nebraska
Fraser, Charles .Oregon
Fraser, W. C. . . . . .Colorado
Fraser, William A. . . . . .Kansas
Frasier, F. K. . . . . .Traveling
Frauenholz, Eleanor . . . . .California
Frazer (Mrs.) .Missouri
Frazer & Simpson . . . . .Missouri
Frazer, D. H. (Miss) . . . . .California
Frazier . . . . .Arkansas
Frazier, J. Frank . . . . .Nebraska
Frederick & Daniel . . . . .Texas
Frederick, D. A. .Kansas
Frederick, E. K. . . . . .British Columbia
Frederickson, G. A. . . . . .Iowa
Fredlund . . . . .Iowa
Freeborn, L. H. . . . . .Iowa
Freedman & Company, T. . . . . .Colorado
Freehafer, F. . . . . .Traveling
Freeman, Alfred . . . . .Colorado, Texas
Freeman, Barnabas Courtland . . .British Columbia
Freeman, D. G. .Kansas
Freeman, Edmund R. . . . . .California
Freeman, Elijah M. . . . . .Texas
Freeman, Emma B. . . . . .California
Freeman, Eva P. . . . . .California
Freeman, Gamiel C. . . . . .Texas
Freeman, J. B. .Colorado
Freeman, L. H. . . . . .Texas
Freeman, S. A. .Oregon
Freeman, W. E. . . . . .Colorado
Freese & Fetrow . . . . .California
French, A. . . . . .Washington
French, Arthur . . . . .Colorado
French, F. . . . . .Kansas
French, F. A. (Mrs.) . . . . .Oregon
French, Fred A. . . . . .Oregon
French, H. A. . . . . .Oregon
French, Ira G. .California
French, James A. . . . . .California
French, Julia A. (Mrs.) . . . . .California
French, May (Miss) . . . . .British Columbia
French, R. G. . . . . .Texas
French, Theodore D. . . . . .Idaho
French, W. J. . . . . .British Columbia
French's Stereoscopic Views . . . .Kansas, Missouri
Freund . . . . .Iowa
Frey, E. S. . . . . .Iowa
Frey, Emil . . . . .Texas
Frey, William . . . . .Texas
Frichot, Brutus .Kansas
Frick, R. N. . . . . .California
Fricke & Company . . . . .Colorado
Friden, E. H. . . . . .Missouri
Frieman, A. . . . . .Texas
Friend, A. O. .California
Friend, Herve .California
Frisby, Edwin . . . . .Texas
Frissell, E. C. (Mrs.) . . . . .Wisconsin
Fritts, C. . . . . .Missouri
Fritz & Clark . . . . .Oregon
Fritz & Crosley .Oregon
Fritz & Good .Nebraska
Fritz & Malnight . . . . .Dakota
Fritz, Charles . . . . .Oregon
Fritz, Frank Z. . . . . .Traveling
Fritz, J. . . . . .Traveling
Fritz, J. H. . . . . .Iowa
Fritz, Ralph . . . . .Iowa
Fritz, T. . . . . .Iowa
Fritz, W. P. . . . . .Nebraska
Fritz, William . . . . .Texas
Froebe, Theodore W. . . . . .Hawaii
Froelich, Gus . . . . .Texas
From & Company . . . . .Nebraska

Frost & Conner .Oregon
Frost, Addie (Mrs.) . . . . .Colorado
Frost Brothers .Colorado
Frost, C. B. F. . . . . .New Mexico
Frost, Charles . . . . .Iowa
Frost, Edward Sands . . . . .California
Frost, Fannie L. (Miss) . . . . .Texas
Frost, Frank . . . . .New Mexico
Frost, Garner B. . . . . .Oregon
Frost, George A. .Idaho
Frost, George B. . . . . .Oregon
Frost, George Henry . . . . .California
Frost, S. F. . . . . .Colorado, Utah, Wyoming
Frosts . . . . .Oregon
Frovarp, C. R. .Dakota
Frush, Mabel . . . . .Iowa
Fruzenlicker . . . . .Oregon
Fry . . . . .Iowa
Fry, Leslie H. .Oregon
Fry, W. D. . . . . .Iowa
Frye & Company, H. H. . . . . .Washington
Frye & Jenkins . . . . .California
Frye Brothers . . . . .California
Frye, Hiram Hamilton . . . . .California
Fryett, Frank C. . . . . .California, New Mexico
Fryklund, Oscar . . . . .Dakota
Fuerman, Henry . . . . .Arizona
Fuhrman, R. H. . . . . .California
Fujii, M. . . . . .California
Fulk . . . . .Iowa
Fulkerson (Mrs.) . . . . .Wisconsin
Fulkerson (Mrs.) & Carpenter (Miss) . .Wisconsin
Fullard, William . . . . .California
Fuller & Williams . . . . .California
Fuller, A. W. .California
Fuller, C. (Mrs.) . . . . .California
Fuller, J. A. . . . . .Minnesota, Texas
Fuller, John S. . . . . .Wisconsin
Fuller, William H. . . . . .California
Fuller's Temple of Art & Stereoscopic
   Gallery . . . . .Wisconsin
Fullerton Photo Company . . . . .California
Fullerton, Samuel J. . . . . .California
Fullilore, H. . . . . .Colorado
Fulsom . . . . .Oregon
Fulsom, L. A. . . . . .Texas
Fulton & McMurry . . . . .Washington
Fulton, Christopher . . . . .British Columbia
Fults . . . . .Missouri
Funk, John R. .Oregon
Furcht, Delia E. .Idaho
Furguson, Katie . . . . .Arkansas
Furl, J. Frank .Arizona
Furlong & Company . . . . .Missouri
Furlong & Crispell . . . . .New Mexico
Furlong, James N. . . . . .New Mexico
Furman, R. H. . . . . .Colorado
Furneux, Charles . . . . .Hawaii
Fyler & Chandlee . . . . .Arkansas
Fyler, F. F. . . . . .Arkansas
Fyock, D. E. . . . . .Nebraska

G

Gaddis, Floe . . . . .Oregon
Gadion, D. . . . . .California
Gaetz, Ella . . . . .Idaho
Gage, Edward F. . . . . .California
Gage, H. K. . . . . .California, Nevada
Gage, M. D. (Mrs.) . . . . .California, Nevada
Gagne, Ed. . . . . .California
Gaige, George A. . . . . .New Mexico
Gaige, J. G. . . . . . .Arizona, New Mexico, Texas,
                                                    Traveling
Gailbraith, Roy L. . . . . .Arizona
Gaines . . . . .California
Gaines, A. F. .California
Gaines, Flane Henry H. . . . . .California
Galbraith & Company, Harvey . . . . . . .Colorado

Glaiser, Thomas .... California
Glanville, George W. .... Idaho
Glascock .... New Mexico, Texas
Glaser, Adolph .... New Mexico
Glass, C. F. & H. B. .... Wisconsin
Glass, C. G. .... Kansas
Glau, E. F. .... Iowa
Glavind .... Dakota
Gleason, L. .... Oregon
Glendening .... Kansas
Glendenning, M. W. .... Oregon
Glendenny, N. .... Missouri
Glendinen & Faul .... Colorado
Glendinen, John Y. .... Colorado
Glenn .... Colorado
Glenn & Company, J. H. .... Texas
Glenn, B. H. .... Texas
Glenn, Benjamin .... Oregon
Glenn, E. T. .... Oregon
Glenn, T. H. .... Texas
Glenum .... Dakota
Glew, Eugene E. .... Colorado
Glidden, G. D. .... Oregon
Globe Photo Company .... Colorado
Globe Photographic Company .... Arizona
Globe Studio .... Kansas
Glock, Albert .... Texas
Glover, Ridgway .... Colorado, Wyoming
Glyfe, Alex .... Washington
Goben, Edgar L. .... Texas
Goben, James L. .... Texas
Goben, Perry F. .... Texas
Gobin, G. L. .... Texas
Gock & Company, Ann Ting .... California
Gock, Hen Yen .... California
Godard's Studio .... Washington
Godeus, John David .... California
Godeus, Mary Anna Clifton .... California
Godeus, Mary Clara .... California
Godfrey, H. J. .... California
Godfrey, P. .... Missouri
Godfrey, Professor .... California
Godfrey, William M. .... California
Godkin, W. R. .... Nebraska
Godrey, W. .... British Columbia
Goebel, R. .... Missouri
Goehner & Company .... Colorado
Goehner, Gustave A. (Mrs.) .... Colorado
Goehner, Gustave A. .... Colorado
Goehner, H. .... Colorado
Goerke & Son, Paul .... Colorado
Goeser, Antony .... Iowa
Goethe, M. A. .... Oregon
Goetz & Bangs .... Wisconsin
Goetz, H. .... California
Goetzman .... Alaska
Goff, Edmond .... Kansas
Goff, O. S. .... Colorado, Dakota, Montana, Traveling, Wisconsin
Gohner .... Colorado
Goines, Joseph A. .... Wisconsin
Goins, James .... Colorado
Gold, J. .... New Mexico
Golden State Photographic Gallery ..... California
Goldman, Henry .... Texas
Goldsberry & Briggs .... Iowa
Goldsberry & Company .... Colorado
Goldsberry, B. E. .... Iowa
Goldsmith, Hugo B. .... Oregon
Goldsmith, Louis J. .... Oregon
Goldsmith, M. A. (Mrs.) .... Nebraska
Goldsmith, Milton P. .... Oregon
Goldson, L. .... Oregon
Goldthone, O. M. .... Texas
Golsh, A. C. .... California
Goltra, Edward B. .... California
Gomez & Villalobos .... New Mexico, Texas
Gomez, J. Luz .... New Mexico, Texas
Gomez, M. F. .... New Mexico, Texas
Gommel, G. Edward .... Arizona
Gomond, Joseph W. .... Idaho
Gonner & Hurd .... Colorado
Gonner, Frank .... Colorado
Gonsalves, Joaquin Augusto .... Hawaii
Gonzales, G. .... New Mexico
Gonzales, Leonardo .... Arizona
Good .... Nebraska
Good Gallery .... California
Good, H. L. .... British Columbia
Goodale, C. M. .... New Mexico
Goodall, H. S. .... Iowa
Goodenough & Company .... California
Goodenough, Otis .... Iowa
Goodfellow, Stephen .... Hawaii
Goodholm, F. .... Kansas
Goodhue, Ira D. .... Idaho
Goodie .... British Columbia
Goodloe, Guy .... New Mexico, Texas
Goodman .... Wisconsin
Goodman & Brothers .... Colorado
Goodman, C. .... California
Goodman, Charles .... New Mexico
Goodman, Charles H. .... Colorado
Goodman, Charles M. .... Utah
Goodman, H. P. .... Wisconsin
Goodmurphy, Herbert Fuller .. British Columbia
Goodnight's Studio .... Kansas
Goodnow & Son, A. H. .... Iowa
Goodrich & Lewis .... Nebraska
Goodrich, P. (Miss) .... Kansas
Goodwin .... Utah
Goodwin, Hoza L. .... Washington
Goodwin, James H. .... Missouri
Goodwin, Julius .... Texas
Goodwin, Louise S. .... California
Goodwin, Olive .... Minnesota
Goodwin, T. J. .... Texas
Goodyear, Charles Eugene .... California
Goranson, Frank .... Iowa
Gordon .... Texas
Gordon, G. W. .... Oregon
Gordon, Pete .... California
Gordon Portrait Company .... Idaho
Gordon, William A. .... Oregon
Gore .... Colorado
Gore, Thomas Sinclair .... British Columbia
Goren, L. F. .... Texas
Gorman, G. S. .... Texas
Gormer, Frank .... Colorado
Gorr, Frances E. (Mrs.) .... California
Gorsuch, Nicholas B. .... Texas
Gosha & Company, C. E. .... Colorado
Gosling .... Iowa
Gosper, Ethel .... New Mexico
Goss, Albert .... Nebraska
Gosting, George G. .... Iowa
Gottleib, Harry Joseph Arizona, New Mexico, Texas, Traveling
Gottula, L. .... Nebraska
Gouhenant, Adolphe F. .... Texas
Gould .... California, Iowa
Gould, A. .... Traveling
Gould, Gilbert E. .... California
Gould, J. W. .... California
Gould, W. J. .... British Columbia
Goulty, Earl D. .... Oregon
Gourley, George S. .... Oregon
Gove & Allen .... California
Gove, O. M. .... California
Gove, William S. .... Texas
Graack, N. P. .... Iowa
Grabill, Burch Enos .... Arkansas
Grabill, J. C. H. .... Colorado, Dakota, Nebraska, Wyoming
Grachy, J. G. .... Oregon
Gradt, L. W. .... Texas
Graff, Mamie (Miss) .... California
Grafton, Eliza C. .... California
Graham .... Montana
Graham, A. E. .... Arkansas
Graham, Clara (Miss) .... California
Graham, Donald .... Texas
Graham, E. D. .... Missouri
Graham, Ella (Miss) .... Kansas
Graham, Emma .... California
Graham, Fred S. .... Dakota
Graham, H. M. .... Kansas
Graham, Horton N. .... Oregon
Graham, J. W. .... Missouri
Graham, James B. .... Colorado
Graham, John W. .... Washington
Graham, L. A. .... California
Graham, Lavinia J. .... Idaho
Graham, S. B. .... Colorado
Graham, Samuel B. .... Oregon
Graham, Thomas J. .... West Canada
Graham View & Copying House ...... Wisconsin
Graham, W. A. .... Texas
Graham, W. M. .... California
Graham, Walter T. .... Nebraska
Graham's Art Gallery .... Missouri
Graham's City Gallery .... Missouri
Grahm, J. William .... Kansas
Gramm, A. F. .... Wisconsin
Grand Art Photograph Gallery .... California
Grand Central Gallery .... Nebraska
Granger, D. .... Colorado
Grant .... California
Grant, C. M. .... Kansas
Grant, J. W. .... Texas
Grant, Martin Howe .... California
Grant, U. S. .... Nebraska
Grant, W. Wallace .... Missouri
Grasett, E. H. .... California
Graslett, Dan .... Texas
Gravenslund & Jackson .... Iowa
Graves .... Wisconsin
Graves, Clarence E. .... Oregon
Graves, E. A. .... Iowa
Graves, G. A. .... Arizona
Graves, Hubert D. .... Oregon
Graves, Lemuel C. .... Colorado
Graves, Sewell F. .... California
Graves, Timothy L. .... Idaho, Oregon
Gray & Cromwell .... Oregon
Gray & Dohse .... Oregon
Gray, Andrew .... British Columbia
Gray Brothers .... Arkansas
Gray Brothers Parlor Gallery .... Kansas
Gray, Charles J. .... Oregon
Gray, Grace (Miss) .... Kansas
Gray, H. .... California
Gray, H. B. .... Texas
Gray, Howard E. .... Nebraska
Gray, J. F. .... Texas
Gray, James L. .... Texas
Gray, Lucien .... Arkansas
Gray, Mary .... Texas
Gray, S. E. .... Oregon
Gray, Thomas J. .... Texas
Gray, W. L. .... New Mexico
Gray, W. M. .... New Mexico
Graybiel, Edwin .... California
Gray–Button Photo Parlors .... Texas
Great Celebrated Centennial Flying Photograph Gallery .... Traveling
Great Central Daguerrean Gallery ..... Wisconsin
Great Eastern Photographic & Advertising Company .... British Columbia, California, Oregon, Traveling
Great Western Photo Publishing Company .... Nebraska
Great Western View Company .... Arizona
Green .... California, New Mexico, Texas

Hall & Rudd ....Wisconsin
Hall, Ada A. ....California
Hall, Aribert F. ....Oregon
Hall, B. ....Arkansas
Hall, C. ....Colorado
Hall, C. I. ....Nebraska
Hall, Charles A. B. ....California
Hall, Charles F. ....Texas
Hall, E. W. ....California
Hall, F. M. ....Texas, Traveling
Hall, G. B. ....California
Hall, George H. ....Colorado, Wyoming
Hall, George P. ....Missouri
Hall, H. G. ....Nebraska
Hall, Ichabod Nelson ....Texas
Hall, J. ....Traveling
Hall, J. D. ....West Canada
Hall, J. P. ....Iowa
Hall, J. R. ....Iowa
Hall, James Deakin ....British Columbia
Hall, James J. ....Oregon
Hall, John W. ....Idaho
Hall, Julius ....Traveling
Hall, Lillie E. ....California
Hall, Lindsley ....Oregon
Hall, Lottie C. (Mrs.) ....Oregon
Hall, Mida ....Iowa
Hall, N. N. ....Texas
Hall, O. J. ....Wisconsin
Hall, Peter J. ....Idaho
Hall, W. Maurice ....Oregon
Hall, W. R. ....Kansas
Hall, William ....British Columbia, Oregon
Hall, William E. ....Kansas
Hall, William M. ....Oregon
Hall, William N. ....Idaho
Halladay ....Kansas
Hallberg's Art Studio ....Indian Territory
Haller, Charles ....Texas
Haller, Charles M. ....Oregon
Haller, Ruth ....Oregon
Hallett, G. M. ....Wisconsin
Hallick, E. S. (Miss) ....Wisconsin
Halliday, John ....Nebraska
Halliday, William May ....British Columbia
Hallifax, B. E. ....Dakota
Hallopeter, C. S. ....Iowa
Halloran, J. J. ....Nebraska
Hallwig & Company ....Missouri
Hallwig, G. O. ....Missouri
Hally, W. H. ....Arkansas
Halsey & Coffin ....California
Halsey & Scripture ....California
Halsey, Henry H. ....California
Halsey, Hiram H. ....California
Halsey, I. S. ....California
Halsted & Kehm ....Dakota
Halvorsen ....Nebraska
Halvorsen, J. R. ....Iowa
Hamacher & Loring ....Washington
Hamacher, E. J. .....Alaska, Oregon, Washington
Hamada, M. ....Oregon
Hamamura, N. ....British Columbia
Hamann, William ....Nebraska
Hamel ....Dakota
Hamel & Brooks ....Dakota
Hamel, E. H. ....Nebraska
Hamill, A. S. ....Oregon
Hamilron & Kendrick ....Colorado
Hamilton ....California, Kansas, Oklahoma
Hamilton & Davidson ....Dakota
Hamilton & Hoyt ....Iowa
Hamilton & Jackson ....California
Hamilton & Kellog ....California
Hamilton & Kodylek ....Iowa
Hamilton & Rockafellow ....Dakota
Hamilton & Shew ....California
Hamilton & Taylor ....Nebraska

Hamilton & Tidball ....California
Hamilton, A. C. ....Kansas
Hamilton, Albert E. ....Oregon
Hamilton, C. L. ....Dakota
Hamilton, Charles A. ....California
Hamilton, Charles F. ....California
Hamilton, Grant C. ....Nebraska
Hamilton, I. B. ....Iowa
Hamilton, J. ....Nebraska
Hamilton, J. H. ....Iowa
Hamilton, James W. M. ....Idaho
Hamilton, Lauchlan Alexander ..British Columbia
Hamilton Produce Company ....Texas
Hamilton, Rose ....Oregon
Hamilton, S. C. R. ....Montana
Hamilton, Thomas K. ....Texas
Hamilton's Gallery ....California
Hamley, Emily ....Idaho
Hamlin, J. R. ....Dakota
Hamly ....Indian Territory
Hammaker, H. C. ....Arizona
Hammaker, H. L. ....Arizona
Hammel ....Nebraska
Hammer, L. F. ....Missouri
Hammer, Laurence ....Texas
Hammer, Richard W. ....Arizona
Hammersley, Charles V. ....Missouri
Hammersmith, John E. ....California
Hammerton, Charles Henry ....California
Hammoch, John G. ....Texas
Hammon, John ....Iowa
Hammond, Amelia F. (Mrs.) ....Oregon
Hammond, Harry ....Iowa
Hammond, Harry E. ....Oregon
Hammond, Henry ....British Columbia
Hammond, John ....British Columbia
Hammond, S. G. ....Nebraska
Hammond, Thomas ....British Columbia
Hammond, W. A. ....Nebraska
Hammor ....California
Hampton & Gamble ....Iowa
Hamrich, Wesley ....Iowa
Hanaway, Daniel ....California
Hance & Mast ....New Mexico
Hance, G. W. ....New Mexico
Hancock, Edward S. ....Idaho
Hand, Hiram ....Texas
Hand, Orville ....Wisconsin
Hand, W. A. ....Wisconsin
Handley ....Oregon
Handley, J. C. ....California
Handy & Waldon ....New Mexico
Hanes, S. A. (Mrs.) ....Iowa
Haney, Ada ....Texas
Haney, J. W. ....Kansas
Hangroug & Son ....Oklahoma
Hanks, O. T. ....Texas
Hanna ....Colorado
Hanna, A. J. ....Colorado, Texas
Hanna, Forman ....Arizona
Hanna, O. R. ....Colorado
Hanna, Robert M. ....Texas
Hannig, Ida (Miss) ....Texas
Hannig, Julius ....Texas
Hansard ....Texas
Hansard & Howerton ....Arkansas
Hansard & Larrick ....Arkansas
Hansard & Osborn ....Arkansas
Hansard, Arthur ....Arkansas
Hansard, J. W. ....Missouri
Hansard, John W. ....Arkansas
Hansard, Raphael W. ....Arkansas
Hansbrook, W. A. ....Kansas
Hansbrough ....Kansas
Hanscom, Adelaide Marquand ....California
Hanscom, Moses ....California
Hansen, Andrew ....Washington
Hansen, Axel ....Idaho

Hansen, C. ....Nebraska
Hansen, C. W. ....Washington
Hansen, Carl ....California
Hansen, Charles ....California
Hansen, Flora ....California
Hansen, H. B. ....Arizona
Hansen, H. T. ....Dakota
Hansen, J. John ....Oregon
Hansen, Jacob ....California
Hansen, Neil ....Iowa
Hansley, J. K. ....Texas
Hansmans ....Colorado
Hanson ....California
Hanson & Davidson ....Oregon
Hanson & Erichson ....Idaho
Hanson, Barraud ....Texas
Hanson, Charles W. ....Idaho
Hanson, Frederick ....Idaho
Hanson, H. P. ....Nebraska
Hanson, J. A. ....California
Hanson, Jacob ....Oregon
Hanson, John ....California
Hanson, John A. ....Idaho, Oregon
Hanson, V. C. ....California, Oregon
Hanzal, Franz ....Texas
Hanzolsh, Sam ....Texas
Hapgood, C. (Miss) ....Kansas
Happy Hollow ....Arkansas
Harada, T. ....California
Haran, James A. ....Oregon
Harbin ....Texas
Harbschen ....Texas
Hard, E. ....Texas
Hard, J. ....Texas
Harden, Homer T. ....Kansas
Harden, J. J. ....Oregon
Hardesty & Armstrong ....California
Hardesty & Brown ....Missouri
Hardesty & Dean ....Missouri
Hardesty, Frank ....California, Texas
Hardesty, J. ....Texas
Hardgraves, James D. ....Texas
Hardin, Ambrose ....Texas
Harding, C. C. ....Colorado
Harding, Frederick ....Kansas
Hardy & Denison ....Minnesota
Hardy, Alma ....Utah
Hardy, Denison & Robertson ....Minnesota
Hardy, Edna ....California
Hardy, John ....California, Minnesota
Hardy, John (Mrs.) ....California
Hardy, W. H. ......California, Oregon, Traveling,
                                          Wisconsin
Hare, Alice A. ....California
Hare, G. B. ....Nebraska
Harford, George G. ....Traveling
Hargen & Skatrud ....Idaho
Hargen, Elias B. ....Idaho
Harger ....Iowa
Hargrave, J. R. ....Washington
Hargrave, Richard M. ....Arizona
Hargrove, C. R. (Mrs.) ....Texas
Hargrove, J. G. ....Texas
Hargroves, J. J. ....Colorado
Harker, A. ....California
Harker, W. T. ....California
Harkey, W. ....Texas
Harkey, Willie ....Texas
Harkness, F. M. ....California
Harkullas, S. (Mrs.) ....Colorado
Harlacher & Melendy ....Iowa
Harlacher, G. H. ....Iowa
Harlan & Glenn ....Colorado
Harlan & Glew ....Colorado
Harlan & Gregg ....Colorado
Harlan, Andrew James ....Colorado
Harlan, D. M. ....California
Harlbog, Charles ....California

Hayes & Short . . . . .Oregon
Hayes & Stenmark .Idaho
Hayes, Amelia . . . . .Oregon
Hayes, C. W. . . . . .Idaho
Hayes, Dr. J. J. . . . . .Oklahoma
Hayes, Harry C. .Oregon
Hayes, Henry C. . . . . .California
Hayes, John W. . . . . .Texas
Hayes, T. J. . . . . .Oregon
Haymaker, H. L. .Arizona
Haynes .British Columbia
Haynes, F. E. . . . . .Minnesota
Haynes, F. Jay . . . . .Colorado, Dakota, Idaho, Minnesota, Montana, Traveling, West Canada, Wyoming
Haynes, Fred E. . . . . .Dakota
Haynes, George . . . . .West Canada
Haynes, Hannie . . . . .Kansas
Haynes, Thomas . . . . .California
Haynes, Willis P. .Arizona
Hays . . . . .California
Hays, E. S. . . . . .California
Hays, George . . . . .Kansas
Hays, J. . . . . .Kansas
Hays, L. (Miss) . . . . .Kansas
Hays, R. H. . . . . .Missouri
Hayter, C. H. . . . . .Colorado
Hayward & Muzzall . . . . .California
Hayward, E. J. .California
Haywood, J. D. . . . . .California
Haywood, M. C. . . . . .Kansas, New Mexico
Haywood, S. J. . . . . .California
Hayworth, J. P. . . . . .Texas
Hazelhurst, Emma V. . . . . .California
Hazeltine & Son, L. S. . . . . .California
Hazeltine, George Irving . . . . . .California, Oregon
Hazeltine, Leland S. . . . . .Idaho, Montana
Hazeltine, Martin Mason . . . . . .California, Idaho, Nevada, Oregon, Traveling
Hazlett, J. W. . . . . .California
Hdrdlicka, Ales . . . . .Arizona
Head, Edward J. .Colorado
Head, J. G. . . . . .Missouri
Head, T. D. . . . . .California
Headley & Austin . . . . .Traveling
Headley & Morgan . . . . .Colorado
Headley, E. B. . . . . .Colorado, New Mexico
Heald & Stiff . . . . .Missouri
Heald, D. M. . . . . .Iowa
Healy, Addie G. . . . . .California
Healy, Edwin Ruthven . . . . .California
Heanes, E. A. . . . . .Texas
Hearn, Thomas . . . . .Texas
Heath & Bailey .California
Heath & Moss .Wisconsin
Heath, Charles E. .Arizona
Heath, Henry C. . . . . .Wisconsin
Heath, James . . . . .California
Heath Studio . . . . .Arizona
Heath Studios . . . . .Arizona
Heaton, James R. .Oregon
Hebard & Sons, E. A. . . . . .Nebraska
Hebard, C. E. . . . . .Nebraska
Hebard, F. L. . . . . .Nebraska
Heber, H. Thomas . . . . .Utah
Hebert, J. O. . . . . .Wisconsin
Heck, R. W. . . . . .Oregon
Heckart, W. P. . . . . .Iowa
Hecker, A. E. . . . . .Nebraska
Hecker, Alice . . . . .California
Heckley, Albert . . . . .British Columbia
Heckley, Joseph Woodward . . . . .British Columbia
Heckman, Daniel G. . . . . .Kansas
Heckman, Joseph William . . . . . .British Columbia
Hecox . . . . .New Mexico
Hecox, F. C. . . . . .Texas
Hedemann, Christian Jacob . . . . .Hawaii
Hedge, Frederick A. . . . . .California
Hedlund, A. . . . . .Oregon
Hedum & Bishop . . . . .California, Idaho
Hedum, Charles C. .Idaho
Heeb, Adam . . . . .Wisconsin
Heering, John H. . . . . .California
Heffner, H. C. . . . . .Nebraska
Hefner, Claude S. . . . . .Texas
Hegeman, Elizabeth Compton . . . . .Arizona
Hegg, Eric A. . . . . .Alaska, British Columbia, Washington, Wisconsin
Hegg, Peter L. .Washington
Heidrick, A. C. .California
Heighstedt, A. W. . . . . .Minnesota
Heim, J. G. . . . . .Iowa
Hein Brothers . . . . .Colorado
Heine, Hannah (Mrs.) . . . . .Kansas
Heinen, Henry . . . . .Minnesota
Heiney, Albert . . . . .Oregon
Heiney, Arthur . . . . .Oregon
Heinninger, C. P. . . . . .California
Heins, Otto . . . . .Oregon
Heiron & Schlute . . . . .Texas
Heiron, H. B. . . . . .Texas
Heiss, W. H. . . . . .Traveling
Heister, Henry T. . . . . .Arizona, New Mexico
Held, George C. . . . . .Oregon
Held, J. . . . . .Oregon
Heldinger, Henry . . . . .Texas
Helio–Art Studio . . . . .California
Helios . . . . .California
Hellen, Lottie M. (Mrs.) . . . . .California
Heller, Louis . . . . .California, Oregon
Hellin & Westrup . . . . .Texas
Helling, James . . . . .Minnesota
Helliwell, Clara L. .Oregon
Helliwell, Florence Edith . . . . .Oregon
Helliwell, Louise C. . . . . .Oregon
Helm & Amos . . . . .Idaho
Helm, Daniel . . . . .Idaho
Helm, Milton H. . . . . .Idaho
Helme, William . . . . .Colorado
Helmerick, Philip . . . . .Nebraska
Helsom, Edwin . . . . .Idaho
Helsom, R. O. . . . . .Wisconsin
Hemenway . . . . .Colorado
Hemenway, Oscar E. . . . . .Oregon
Hemingway & Holmes . . . . .California
Hemingway's Art Gallery . . . . .Missouri
Hemming, Edward . . . . .Texas
Hemminger, C. B. . . . . .California
Henausin, W. F. E. C. . . . . .Texas
Hendee & Haynes . . . . .British Columbia
Hendee, Denny H. . .California, Oregon, Traveling
Hendee, Edwin . . . . .British Columbia
Hendee, Edwin B. . . . . .California
Hendee, Edwin L. . . . . .Oregon
Hendee, Otho S. . . . . .Oregon
Hendee Photo Company . . . . . . .British Columbia
Hendee, Samuel L. .Oregon
Hendeman, John . . . . .Texas
Henderson, Alexander . . . . .British Columbia
Henderson, C. G. . . . . .Nebraska
Henderson, E. N. . . . . .Traveling
Henderson, H. A. E. .Texas
Henderson, Harold Morton . . . .British Columbia
Henderson, J. F. . . . . .Texas
Henderson, L. D. . . . . .Texas
Henderson, Lincoln . . . . .California
Henderson, William .Texas
Hendrick, H. G. . . . . .New Mexico
Hendrick, James . . . . .Texas
Hendricks . . . . .Texas
Hendricks, Horace Gates . . . . .California
Hendricks, William F. . . . . .Oregon
Hendson, William . . . . .Texas
Heneks, William C. . . . . .Iowa
Henfield, John . . . . .California
Heninger, W. J. . . . . .Nebraska
Henley, G. A. . . . . .Idaho
Henline, Archie C. .Oregon
Hennepin Studio . . . . .Minnesota
Hennessy, F. . . . . .British Columbia
Hennessy, Fred W. . . . . .California
Henrichsen, Lars C. . . . . .Oregon
Henry Brothers . . . . .New Mexico
Henry, E. E. . . . . .Kansas, West Canada
Henry Erichson . . . . .Oregon
Henry, J. W. . . . . .Nebraska
Henry, Johnson . . . . .Texas
Henry, Levi . . . . .Iowa, Missouri
Henry, R. H. . . . . .Kansas
Henry, Thomas E. B. . . . . .British Columbia
Henry, V. H. . . . . .Oregon
Henry, William Alexander . . . . .California
Henshaw, H. W. . . . . .California, Hawaii
Hentig, Arthur S. .Colorado
Hentschell, Gustave .Texas
Hentscher, H. . . . . .Wisconsin
Hepburn . . . . .Nevada
Hepburn, Maude M. . . . . .Oregon
Hepp, G. W. . . . . .Texas
Herera, G. . . . . .Texas
Heringa, Edward . . . . .New Mexico
Heringer . . . . .Oklahoma
Herman, F. P. . . . . .Oregon
Heroy, W. B. . . . . .Idaho
Herrick, E. L. . . . . .Wisconsin
Herrick, M. . . . . .Oregon
Herrick, W. A. . . . . .California
Herrin, David C. . .Oregon, Traveling, Washington
Herrin, Margaret E. (Mrs.) . . . . .Oregon, Traveling
Hersckfeld, Walter . . . . .British Columbia
Hersom, C. E. . . . . .Colorado
Hertzman, J. A. . . . . .Oregon
Herum, J. . . . . .Dakota
Herwick, J. T. . . . . .Texas
Hesler, Alexander . . . . .Iowa, Wisconsin
Heslop, E. . . . . .Oregon
Hess & Company . . . . .New Mexico
Hester, Ernst . . . . .Washington
Hester, Robert M. . . . . .Washington
Hester, Wilhelm . . . . .Washington
Heston, W. . . . . .Missouri
Hetherington, G. H. . . . . .Colorado
Hetrick, Alice . . . . .Oregon
Heusler, Frank . . . . .Oregon
Heuthen . . . . .Arizona
Hewitt, D. F. . . . . .Idaho
Hewitt, Frederick Horace . . . . .California
Hewitt, H. A. . . . . .Nebraska
Hewitt, James (Mrs.) . . . . .Oregon
Heyde . . . . .Nebraska
Heyland, Herman . . . . .Texas
Heyn & Company, S. . . . . .Nebraska
Heyn, G. (Mrs.) . . . . .Nebraska
Heyn, George . . . . .Nebraska
Heyn, Herman . . . . .Nebraska
Heyn, L. . . . . .Wyoming
Heyn Photo Supply . . . . .Nebraska
Heyn, S. . . . . .Nebraska
Heyn Studio . . . . .Nebraska
Heywood, S. J. . . . . .California
Hibbs . . . . .Traveling
Hickam, William P. . . . . .Oregon
Hickerson, Harold J. . . . . .Oregon
Hickethier, Augustus . . . . .Oregon, Traveling
Hickey, Mallie B. . . . . .Oregon
Hickey, Margaret F. . . . . .Oregon
Hickman, Herman . . . . .Texas
Hickox & Company . . . . .Iowa, Minnesota
Hickox & Douglass . . . . .Iowa
Hickox, A. A. . . . . .California
Hickox, L. P. . . . . .California
Hickox, M. A. (Mrs.) . . . . .Wisconsin
Hickox, R. A. . . . . .Kansas
Hicks . . . . .Oregon, Washington

Holt, Jesse W. . . . . Oregon
Holt, N. N. . . . . Texas
Holt, Robert . . . . Texas
Holt, W. U. . . . . Texas
Holtz, P. . . . . Oregon
Homan, Charles A. . . . . Alaska, British Columbia
Home Gallery . . . . California
Home Studio . . . . California, Texas
Homer, John A. . . . . Idaho
Honey, D. A. . . . . Nebraska
Honey, J. W. . . . . Kansas
Hongell, A. . . . . Montana
Honn, Bessie . . . . California
Honolulu Ambrotype Rooms . . . . Hawaii
Hoobs, I. N. . . . . Kansas
Hood, J. R. . . . . Texas
Hood, John . . . . British Columbia
Hood River Studio . . . . Oregon
Hood, William . . . . . British Columbia, California
Hook, W. E. . . . . Colorado, Wisconsin
Hook, William E. . . . . New Mexico
Hook, William M. . . . . Kansas
Hooker, A. E. . . . . Minnesota
Hooker, Caddie G. . . . . Oregon
Hooker, F. S. . . . . Texas
Hoop, S. W. . . . . Kansas
Hooper . . . . Kansas
Hooper, C. N. . . . . Alaska
Hooper, R. B. . . . . Oregon
Hoopes, H. E. . . . . Arizona, California
Hoot . . . . Iowa
Hoot & Read . . . . Iowa
Hoover, D. F. . . . . Kansas
Hoover, Hattie . . . . California
Hoover, W. M. . . . . Nebraska
Hoper, J. D. . . . . Texas
Hopfield, Leonard S. . . . . Oregon
Hopkins & Holcomb . . . . Kansas
Hopkins & Reed . . . . Colorado
Hopkins, Benjamin S. . . . . Colorado, New Mexico
Hopkins, F. H. (Mrs.) . . . . Oregon
Hopkins, Francis M. . . . . Kansas
Hopkins, George B. . . . . Kansas
Hopkins, Helen R. (Miss) . . . . California
Hopkins, Jessie (Miss) . . . . California
Hopkins, Professor F. Loosehimself . . New Mexico
Hopkins, S. D. . . . . Colorado, Kansas
Hopkins, T. E. . . . . Colorado
Hopkins, Thaddeus E. . . . . Colorado
Hoppe, E. L. . . . . Kansas
Hopper, E. A. . . . . Oregon
Hopperstad, Carrie . . . . California
Hopping, Charlie H. . . . . Colorado
Horacek, William . . . . Kansas
Hord, J. R. . . . . California
Horetzky, Charles George . . . . . . British Columbia
Horkmans, D. M. . . . . Kansas
Horn . . . . Texas
Horn, Edward . . . . Wisconsin
Horn, John Patrick . . . . California
Horn, John W. . . . . Texas
Horner . . . . Nebraska, New Mexico
Horner, Harry H. . . . . Arizona
Horning, A. . . . . Dakota
Horrup, C. A. . . . . Kansas
Horswill, A. J. . . . . Dakota
Horton & Company . . . . Iowa
Horton, G. D. . . . . Washington
Horton, G. W. . . . . Wisconsin
Horton, Gilbert D. . . . . Oregon
Horton, J. . . . . Arizona
Horton, J. A. . . . . New Mexico
Horton, King . . . . Texas
Hose, Orville L. . . . . Colorado
Hosford, C. H. (Mrs.) . . . . Colorado
Hosier & Bass . . . . Colorado
Hosier & Calhoun . . . . Colorado
Hosier, F. H. . . . . Colorado
Hosken, W. K. . . . . Wisconsin
Hosking, J. E. . . . . Wisconsin
Hosner, Y. P. . . . . Oklahoma
Hossack, Hugh Moule Alexander . . . . . . California
Hot Springs Art Company . . . . Wyoming
Houck, Hamilton . . . . Texas
Hough . . . . Montana
Hough & Son . . . . Nebraska
Hough, E. H. . . . . Nebraska
Hough, Elizabeth . . . . California
Hough, R. S. . . . . Texas
Hough, Reverend J. W. . . . . California
Hough, Walter . . . . Arizona
Hought, H. H. . . . . Oregon
Houghtaling, Abraham J. . . . . California
Houghtaylen, S. A. (Mrs.) . . . . Nebraska
Houghton & Powell . . . . Iowa
Houghton, A. A. . . . . Iowa
Houghton, A. S. . . . . Colorado
Houghton, Albert S. . . . . Oregon
Houghton, George Harper . . . . Wisconsin
Houghton, Merritt Dana . . . . Wyoming
Houghton, Thomas A. . . . . . . Oregon, Traveling, Washington
Houguard, John G. . . . . Utah
House, E. . . . . Kansas
House, Emmett . . . . Texas
House, H. L. . . . . Iowa
Houseworth, Thomas . . . . Arizona, California
Housghen, J. A. . . . . Texas
Houston City Gallery . . . . Texas
Houston Daguerreian Gallery . . . . Texas
Houston, Forbes . . . . Texas
Houston, Frank K. . . . . Traveling
Houston, H. H. . . . . California
Houston Sky-Light Ambrotype Gallery . . . . Texas
Hover . . . . Iowa, Washington
Hover & Brother . . . . Iowa
Hover & Shaw . . . . Nebraska
Hover & Wyer . . . . Iowa
Hover Brothers . . . . Colorado
Hover, J. W. . . . . Kansas
Hover, William M. . . . . Nebraska
Hovey, Guy Carleton . . . . California
Howard . . Colorado, Kansas, Wisconsin, Wyoming
Howard, C. H. . . . . Kansas
Howard, E. A. . . . . Colorado
Howard, F. L. . . . . Nebraska
Howard, George . . . . Kansas
Howard, J. . . . . British Columbia
Howard, J. B. . . . . Nebraska
Howard, James Soloman . . . . California
Howard, M. B. . . . . Colorado, New Mexico
Howard, N. W. . . . . Kansas
Howard, P. J. . . . . Texas
Howard, William L. . . . . Arkansas, Traveling
Howarth . . . . Utah
Howe . . . . Colorado
Howe, Ithamar . . . . California, Traveling
Howe, John Milton . . . . California
Howe, William H. . . . . Texas
Howel, John . . . . Texas
Howell, Bertram Archer . . . . British Columbia
Howell, Edgar Wade . . . . California
Howell, Herman . . . . Texas
Howell, John A. . . . . Texas
Howell, Kathleen Gertrude (Lena) . . . . British Columbia
Howell, L. R. . . . . Idaho
Howell, T. L. . . . . Texas
Hower, Atlin B. . . . . Idaho, Montana, Oregon
Howerton, J. R. . . . . Arkansas
Howes, M. A. . . . . Colorado
Howes, Samuel P. . . . . California
Howison, J. W. . . . . British Columbia
Howitt, C. (Miss) . . . . Minnesota
Howland . . . . California
Howland & Chadwick . . . . California
Howland & Dewey . . . . California
Howland & Fagersteen . . . . California
Howland & Peters . . . . California
Howland & Vasconcelles . . . . California
Howland, Benjamin Franklin . . . . California
Howland, Clarence A. . . . . California
Howland, Frederick T. . . . . California
Howland, H. A. . . . . California
Howland, James F. S. . . . . California
Howland, M. F. R. . . . . California
Howland, R. P. . . . . California
Howland, W. F. . . . . Hawaii
Hoy & Ellis . . . . Texas
Hoy, Lilian G. . . . . Oregon
Hoy, Wood & Company . . . . Texas
Hoyer, F. M. . . . . Nebraska
Hoyt . . . . British Columbia
Hoyt, B. F. . . . . Iowa
Hoyt, E. E. . . . . Texas
Hoyt, Elmer . . . . Texas
Hoyt, Fannie (Mrs.) . . . . Utah
Hoyt, George W. . . . . Oregon
Hoyt, H. . . . . New Mexico
Hoyt, Hiram . . . . . . California, Texas, Washington
Hoyt, Mary S. . . . . Wisconsin
Hoyt, Robert W. . . . . Oregon
Hoyt, William R. . . . . Oregon
Hubbard & East . . . . Oregon
Hubbard, E. W. . . . . Colorado
Hubbard, W. H. . . . . Nebraska
Hubbell (Miss) . . . . California
Hubbell, J. Albert . . . . Colorado
Hubbell, Royal . . . . Colorado, New Mexico
Hubbell, Viola T. . . . . California
Hubert . . . . Texas
Hubley, Grace . . . . California
Hubner, Gerhardt Robert . . . . Oregon
Hubscham, Lewis . . . . Texas
Hucks, George A. . . . . California
Hucks, J. George . . . . California
Huckwate, I. . . . . Texas
Huddleston, Lola L. . . . . California
Hudnall . . . . Oregon
Hudson . . . . California
Hudson (Miss) . . . . California
Hudson & Martinson . . . . Washington
Hudson, Arthur . . . . Idaho
Hudson, C. H. . . . . Minnesota
Hudson, Charles W. . . . . Oregon
Hudson, Ed . . . . Texas
Hudson, Frank . . . . Texas
Hudson, J. L. . . . . Iowa
Hudson, Joseph L. . . . . Colorado
Hudson, William . . . . Texas
Huebinger Brothers . . . . Iowa
Huested, R. W. . . . . Traveling
Huey's Art Gallery . . . . Kansas
Huff . . . . Indian Territory, Oklahoma, Texas
Huff, Earl F. . . . . Wisconsin
Huff, John B. . . . . Texas
Huff Sisters . . . . Missouri
Huffman & Barnard . . . . Iowa
Huffman, C. M. (Mrs.) . . . . Iowa
Huffman, Charles . . . . Oregon
Huffman, L. A. . . . . Minnesota
Huffman, Laton A. . . . . Montana
Huffman, P. C. . . . . Iowa
Hug, Eugene F. . . . . Oregon
Hug, Henry H. . . . . Oregon
Huggins, James H. . . . . Wisconsin
Hugh & McClane . . . . Texas
Hughes . . . . . Indian Territory, Nebraska, Oregon, Traveling
Hughes & Allen . . . . Nebraska
Hughes & Alvord . . . . Nebraska
Hughes & Company . . . . Nebraska
Hughes & Poe . . . . Nebraska
Hughes & Sandberg . . . . Nebraska

558 BIOGRAPHIES OF WESTERN PHOTOGRAPHERS

Jackson, Frank A. .Oregon
Jackson, Frederick D. . . . . .Colorado
Jackson, G. J. . . . . .West Canada
Jackson, Gus B. . . . . .Texas
Jackson, Isaac . . . . .Texas
Jackson, J. L. . . . . .Texas
Jackson, J. N. . . . . .Texas
Jackson, John . . . . . . .British Columbia, California
Jackson, Joseph . . . . .California
Jackson, W. B. . . . . .Texas
Jackson, W. D. . . . . .Texas
Jackson, William D., Sr. . . . . .Texas
Jackson, William D., Jr. . . . . .Texas
Jackson, William H. . . .Arizona, Colorado, Idaho, Nebraska, New Mexico, Traveling, Wyoming
Jackson, William P. . . . . .Washington
Jackson–Smith Photo Company . . . . . . .Colorado
Jacobi . . . . .Texas
Jacobs, A. L. . . . . .Colorado, Oregon
Jacobs, Benjamin F. . . . . .California
Jacobs, James Monroe . . . . .California
Jacobs, Samuel E. . . . . .Texas
Jacobs, W. E. . . . . .Nebraska
Jacobs, W. H. . . . . .Iowa
Jacobs, W. L. . . . . .Nebraska
Jacobsen, C. . . . . .California
Jacobsen, J. . . . . .Nebraska
Jacobsen, S. E. . . . . .Texas
Jacobson, Mary E. (Mrs.) . . . . .Texas
Jacobson, O. B. . . . . .British Columbia
Jacobson, Philip . . . . .Idaho
Jacobson, Samuel E. . . . . .Texas
Jacoby & Son . . . . .Minnesota
Jacoby, Charles L. . . . . .Minnesota
Jacoby, F. C. . . . . .Iowa
Jacoby, Hiram J. . . . . .Minnesota
Jacoby, J. F. . . . . .Iowa, Traveling
Jacoby, William H. . . . . .Minnesota
Jacoby's Art Gallery . . . . .Minnesota
Jacoby's Photographic Art Palace . . . . . .Minnesota
Jagger, Thomas Augustus . . . . .Hawaii
Jamerson & Townsend . . . . .Colorado
James & Company . . . . .Iowa, Nebraska
James & Maull . . . . .Colorado
James & Pratt . . . . .Iowa
James & Son . . . . .Colorado, Iowa
James & Sturtevant . . . . .Colorado
James, Amy (Mrs.) . . . . .West Canada
James, C. (John) (William H.) . . . . .Colorado
James, C. C. . . . . .Colorado
James, D. . . . . .Traveling, Wisconsin
James, David E. . . . . .Iowa
James, George Wharton . . . . . .Arizona, California, New Mexico
James, J. . . . . .Texas
James, J. William . . . . .Texas
James, N. W. (Mrs.) . . . . .Iowa
James, T., Jr. . . . . .Missouri
James, Tom . . . . .Iowa
James, William B. .Oregon
James, William E. . . . . .California
Jameson, Arthur E. .Kansas
Jandus, William .Colorado
Janes . . . . .Wisconsin
Janes & Banta . . . . .Texas
Janes & May . . . . .Texas
Janousek, L. . . . . .Dakota, Nebraska
Janson, Fred M. . . . . .Texas
Janssen, E. . . . . .Wisconsin
Jarman, I. N. . . . . .Texas
Jarvis . . . . .Nebraska, Oregon
Jarvis, B. . . . . .Iowa
Jarvis, Benjamin .California
Jarvis, Charles . . . . .Arizona
Jarvis, Lucien Emerson . . . . .California
Jarvis White Art Company . . . . .Iowa
Jarvis, William H. . . . . .Minnesota
Jaycox, D. L. . . . . .California
Jaycox, P. L. . . . . .Kansas
Jaycox, W. . . . . .Traveling
Jaynes & Jolly . . . . .Texas
Jeancon, Jean Allard . . . . .New Mexico
Jefferies, H. L. . . . . .Texas
Jeffers, Wells & Kipps . . . . .California
Jeffers, William H. . . . . .California
Jefferson, William . . . . .West Canada
Jeffery, H. M. . . . . .Nebraska
Jeffryes, F. H. . . . . .Nebraska
Jelgerhuis, John . . . . .Iowa
Jellum, H. Lee . . . . .California
Jellum, Herbert Lee . . . . .Idaho
Jelly, D. . . . . .Wisconsin
Jenison, E. P. . . . . .Iowa
Jenkin, William P. . . . . .British Columbia
Jenkins . . . . .Indian Territory
Jenkins & Son . . . . .Nebraska
Jenkins Brothers . . . . .Wyoming
Jenkins, Charles . . . . .Kansas
Jenkins, D. . . . . .Wisconsin
Jenkins, Frank A. .Wyoming
Jenkins, J. C. . . . . .California
Jenkins, John B. . . . . .Wyoming
Jenkins, John E. . . . . .Kansas
Jenkins, S. P. . . . . .Arizona
Jenkins, William I. . . . . .Wyoming
Jenks, E. L. . . . . .Oregon
Jenks, Joel Alonzo . . . . .Idaho
Jenks, Nellie F. (Miss) . . . . .California
Jennings . . . . .Arizona
Jennings & Russell . . . . .Colorado
Jennings, C. P. . . . . .Utah
Jennings, Charles H. . . . . .Colorado
Jennings, E. M. . . . . .Arizona
Jennings, J. . . . . .Oregon
Jennings, Joseph . . . . .Kansas
Jennings, R. P. . . . . .Texas
Jennings, T. J. . . . . .Nebraska
Jennings, William H. . . . . .Oregon
Jenny, Joseph . . . . .Oregon
Jensen . . . . .Dakota, Iowa
Jensen & Peterson . . . . .Iowa
Jensen, Andrew . . . . .Oregon
Jensen Brothers .Minnesota
Jensen, M. . . . . .Utah
Jensen's Studio . . . . .Oregon
Jenson, A. M. . . . . .Colorado
Jepson . . . . .Kansas
Jerabek, J. V. . . . . .Texas
Jernigan, Martin . . . . .Texas
Jerome . . . . .California
Jerrel & Motz . . . . .Colorado
Jerrell, W. L. . . . . .New Mexico, Traveling
Jerrold, Douglas E. . . . . .Texas
Jesse, Maximilian T. .Texas
Jessup . . . . .Iowa
Jetzler, Carl Lucas . . . . .California
Jewel, Izetta (Miss) . . . . .Oregon
Jewell, Flora . . . . .Nebraska
Jewell, George . . . . .Nebraska
Jewett . . . . .Missouri
Jewett, E. C. (Mrs.) . . . . .Iowa
Jipson, F. B. (Miss) .Kansas
Job, Charles . . . . .Wisconsin
Joe's Gallery . . . . .Texas
Johannes & Lum . . . . .Oregon
Johannes, John G. . . . . .Oregon
Johns, C. C. . . . . .Nebraska
Johns, W. C. . . . . .Texas
Johns, William F. . . . . .California
Johnson . . . . .Alaska, California, Kansas, New Mexico, Wisconsin
Johnson & Company, L. H. . . . . .Texas
Johnson & Company, G. W. . . . . .Iowa
Johnson & Hanson .Oregon
Johnson & Montgomery . . . . .Iowa
Johnson & Son . . . . .Idaho
Johnson & Stamps . . . . .Texas
Johnson & Sullivan . . . . .California
Johnson & Sullivan's Portable Gallery . . .Traveling
Johnson & Woodring . . . . .Colorado
Johnson, A. D. . . . . .Colorado
Johnson, A. M. . . . . .California
Johnson, A. P. . . . . .California, Colorado
Johnson, Adolph R. . . . . .Colorado
Johnson, Albert J. . . . . .Alaska
Johnson, Alfred S. . . . . .Wisconsin
Johnson, Allie (Mrs.) . . . . .Oregon
Johnson, Andrew . . . . .British Columbia
Johnson, Ansgar E. . . . . .Idaho
Johnson, B. R. . . . . .California
Johnson Brothers . . . . .California
Johnson, C. (Mrs.) . . . . .British Columbia
Johnson, C. A. . . . . .Wisconsin
Johnson, C. E. . . . . .California
Johnson, C. H. (Mrs.) . . . . .Colorado
Johnson, C. J. . . . . .Nebraska
Johnson, C. O. . . . . .Iowa
Johnson, C. W. . . . . .Dakota
Johnson, Charles .Colorado
Johnson, Charles Ellis .Utah
Johnson, Charles F. . . . . .Minnesota
Johnson, Charles Granville . . . . .Arizona
Johnson, Charles M. . . . . .California
Johnson, Charles Wallace Jacob . . . . . . .California
Johnson, Clinton . . . . .California, Traveling
Johnson, E. G. . . . . .Idaho
Johnson, E. W. . . . . .Iowa
Johnson, Edward . . . . .Texas
Johnson, Edward E. . . . . .California
Johnson, Eli . . . . .Wyoming
Johnson, F. . . . . .Nebraska
Johnson, F. O. . . . . .Iowa
Johnson, G. F. . . . . .Iowa
Johnson, G. G. . . . . .Iowa
Johnson, G. W. . . . . .Iowa
Johnson, George .California
Johnson, George E. . . . . .Nebraska
Johnson, George H. . . . . .California, Nevada
Johnson, Glen . . . . .Oregon
Johnson, I. M. . . . . .Colorado
Johnson, Ira T. . . . . .Nebraska
Johnson, J. B. . . . . .California
Johnson, J. C. . . . . .Nebraska
Johnson, J. E. . . . . .Iowa, Minnesota, Oregon
Johnson, J. H. (Mrs.) .Texas
Johnson, J. H. . . . . .Texas
Johnson, J. W. . . . . .Oregon
Johnson, John . . . . .Dakota
Johnson, John F. . . . . .Oregon
Johnson, John P. . . . . .Colorado, Idaho
Johnson, Joseph . . . . .Texas
Johnson, Josie . . . . .Minnesota
Johnson, K. M. . . . . .Arizona
Johnson, L. Y. . . . . .Oregon
Johnson, Louis . . . . .Texas
Johnson, Luther C. . . . . .Texas
Johnson, Lynnette (Mrs.) . . . . .California
Johnson, Mollie . . . . .Oregon
Johnson, N. E. . . . . .Arizona
Johnson, O. F. . . . . .Minnesota
Johnson, O. R. . . . . .Arkansas, Oregon
Johnson, P. . . . . .Iowa
Johnson Photo Company . . . . .California
Johnson, R. . . . . .Nebraska
Johnson, Rankin M. . . . . .Oregon
Johnson, Richard T. . . . . .California
Johnson, Ross . . . . .Oregon
Johnson, S. E. . . . . .Texas
Johnson, Samuel . . . . .Kansas
Johnson, Selma . . . . .Kansas
Johnson, T. R. (Mrs.) .Idaho
Johnson, Thomas H. .Texas
Johnson, Tom . . . . .California

Kelley, Roy F. . . . . .Arizona
Kelliher's Photograph Gallery . . . . .Colorado
Kellner, Anthony . . . . .Kansas
Kellog . . . . .California
Kellog, Andrew J. . . . . .California
Kellog, B. F. . . . . .Oregon
Kellog, G. P. . . . . .California
Kellogg, C. R. (Miss) . . . . .New Mexico
Kellogg, D. W. .Wisconsin
Kellogg, E. S. . . . . .Wisconsin
Kellogg, J. D. . . . . .Minnesota, Wisconsin
Kellogg, Mark H. . . . . .Wisconsin
Kellogg, Ruby (Miss) . . . . .Oregon
Kellogg, W. F. . . . . .Wisconsin
Kellogsol, L. W. . . . . .Texas
Kellum & Bradley . . . . .Colorado
Kelly . . . . .Dakota, Indian Territory
Kelly & McDonough . . . . . . .California, Montana
Kelly & Odell . . . . .Dakota
Kelly & Runnels . . . . .California
Kelly & Sobieski . . . . .California
Kelly & Taylor . . . . .Nebraska
Kelly, Colum . . . . .Texas
Kelly, Frederick .California
Kelly, G. . . . . .California
Kelly, George . . . . .California
Kelly, James A. . . . . .Texas
Kelly, James S. . . . . .Oregon
Kelly, Millard F. . . .British Columbia, Washington
Kelly, Peter . . . . .Kansas
Kelly, R. L. . . . . .Dakota
Kelly, R. P. . . . . .Texas
Kelsey . . . . .Wisconsin
Kelsey, A. . . . . .Wisconsin
Kelsey, C. C. . . . . .California
Kelsey, J. F. . . . . .Wisconsin
Kelsey, Thomas . . . . .Hawaii
Kelso . . . . .Nebraska
Kelso, T. M. . . . . .Oregon, Washington
Kelteringham, C. B. .Texas
Kelton, Charles H. . . . . .California
Kem, S. A. . . . . New Mexico, Oklahoma
Kemble, Charles M. .Idaho
Kemerer, George . . . . .New Mexico
Kemmerer . . . . .New Mexico
Kemp & Coleman . . . . .Arizona, California
Kemp & Kluit . . . . .Arizona, California, Traveling
Kemp & Vance .California
Kemp, Edward H. . . . . .Arizona
Kemp, H. . . . . .Traveling
Kemp, Henry . . . . .California
Kemp, J. C. . . . . .California, Traveling
Kemp Van Ee, Henry . . . . .California
Kemp, William .California
Kemper, Morris . . . . .Kansas
Kempton, R. John . . . . .Texas
Kendall & Clinch . . . . .California
Kendall, Fernando C. . . . . .Wisconsin
Kendall, R. A. . . . . .California
Kendall, Richard . . . . .Wisconsin
Kendall, William . . . . .Texas
Kendel, W. . . . . .Texas
Kenderdine, Francon C. . . . . .Kansas
Kendig . . . . .Missouri
Kendig & Son, C. . . . . .Missouri
Kendrick . . . . .Idaho
Kendrick, H. A. .California
Kendricks . . . . .Oregon
Kenemedy, J. F. .Nebraska
Kennady, M. A. .Colorado
Kennan, George W. . . . . .Arkansas
Kennan, Thomas L. . . . . .Wisconsin
Kennat . . . . .Arizona
Kennedy . . . . .Iowa
Kennedy & Clark . . . . .Nebraska
Kennedy & Company, M. A. . . . . .Kansas
Kennedy & Pinkerton . . . . .Texas
Kennedy, Amelia G. . . . . .California
Kennedy, I. F. . . . . .Nebraska
Kennedy, J. F. . . . . .Arkansas
Kennedy, L. G. . . . . .Kansas
Kennedy Noble Studio . . . . .Nebraska
Kennedy, Walter B. . . . . .Texas
Kennett & Jones . . . . .California
Kennett, Luther W. . . . . .California
Kennett, R. . . . . .Colorado
Kent & Bailey . . . . .Kansas
Kent, I. N. . . . . .Kansas
Kent Stereoscopic View Company . . . . .Oklahoma
Kent, Violet . . . . .Oregon
Kenyon, Wily . . . . .Oregon
Kepler, V. M. (Mrs.) . . . . .Colorado
Keppingham, Captain . . . . .Texas
Kerfoot, D. (Miss) . . . . .West Canada
Kerfoot, M. . . . . .West Canada
Kerim . . . . .Nebraska
Kerlin, Theodore J. . . . . .California
Kerr . . . . .Colorado
Kerr, Byron N. . . . . .British Columbia
Kerr, M. T. . . . . .Texas
Kerr, S. C. . . . . .Oregon
Kersting, F. W. . . . . .Texas
Kertson & Courteau . . . . .Wisconsin
Kertz Brothers . . . . .Utah
Kertz, Jacob . . . . .Utah
Kerwin & Gross .Colorado
Kerwin, Rose . . . . .California
Kesler, R. E. . . . . .Wisconsin
Kesslar, J. J. . . . . .Wisconsin
Kesten & Company, William . . . . .Iowa
Kester, Charles M. .Oregon
Ketchum, W. G. . . . . .Missouri
Kettering's Studio . . . . .Arkansas
Keuler, William . . . . .Texas
Keuritz, Otto . . . . .Texas
Key & Teisman . . . . .Arizona
Key, W. H. . . . . .Arizona
Key, W. M. . . . . .Texas
Keyes, William M. . . . . .Iowa
Keys, M. . . . . .Texas
Keys Photo Studio .Arizona
Keyser & Brinkley . . . . .Iowa
Keystone Traveling Gallery . . . . .Traveling
Keystone View Company . . . . . . .Kansas, Oregon
Kibbe . . . . .Nebraska
Kibbe, Edwin T. . . . . .Texas
Kidd, James P. . . . . .Oregon
Kiddoo, E. E. . . . . .Iowa
Kiefer & Sammis . . . . .California
Kiernan, Annie S. . . . . .Kansas
Kies & Brian . . . . .California
Kies, Harry . . . . .California
Kilborn & Gilbert . . . . .Nebraska
Kilborn & Rifenburg .Iowa
Kilborn, W. D. . . . . .Nebraska
Kilborn, W. F. . . . . .Iowa, Nebraska
Kilbourn, Myron J. . . . . .Arkansas
Kilbourne, J. F. . . . . .Iowa
Kilcoyne, J. A. (Mrs.) . . . . .Oregon
Kildare & Company, E. L. . . . . .California
Kildare & Thwaites . . . . .California
Kildare, E. J. . . . . .California
Kildare, E. S. . . . . .California
Kilgore, Will A. .Colorado
Kimball, Howard A. . . . . .Kansas
Kimball, R. H. . . . . .Kansas
Kimble, Clare . . . . .Oregon
Kimble, E. R. . . . . .Oregon
Kincade, Charles . . . . .Texas
Kincade, Joseph C. . . . . .Washington
Kincaid, J. C. . . . . .Arkansas
Kincaid, J. H. . . . . .Oregon
Kincaid, J. T. . . . . .California
King & Glavind . . . . .Dakota
King & Heiss . . . . .Traveling
King Brothers . . . . .California
King, C. E. & Hattie . . . . .Washington
King, Charles C. . . . . .Oregon
King, George P. .Wisconsin
King, J. . . . . .Iowa
King, J. B. . . . . .Utah
King, J. L. . . . . .California
King, J. P. . . . . .Iowa
King, J. R. . . . . .Kansas
King, John H. . . . . .Colorado
King, John Howard Havelock . . .British Columbia
King, Joseph W. . . . . .California, Hawaii
King, M. L. . . . . .Iowa
King, W. W. . . . . .Nebraska
King, William S. .Colorado
Kingham, J. B. . . . . .Oklahoma
Kingsley, Charles R. . . . . .Idaho, Oregon
Kingsley, John L. . . . . .California
Kingsley, John L. (Mrs.) . . . . .California
Kingtgen . . . . .Dakota
Kinkead Brothers . . . . .Nebraska
Kinnaird, W. W. .Missouri
Kinnard, J. A. . . . . .Texas
Kinne & Downing . . . . .Texas
Kinne, Walter O. . . . . .Texas
Kinney . . . . .Arizona
Kinney & Tooley . . . . .Kansas
Kinney, John . . . . .Kansas
Kinsey & Kinsey . . . . .Alaska
Kinsey, Clarence . . . . .Alaska, Washington
Kinsey, Clarke . . . . .Alaska, Washington
Kinsey, Darius . . . . .Montana, Washington
Kinsey, Tabitha Pritts . . . . .Washington
Kinson . . . . .Oregon
Kint, C. . . . . .California
Kipling, Thomas . . . . .British Columbia
Kippenbrock, O. C. . . . . .Iowa
Kipps, Alfred K. .California
Kirby & Company, L. . . . . .Iowa
Kirby & Guyer . . . . .Traveling
Kirby, F. . . . . .Iowa
Kirby, J. Martin . . . . .Colorado
Kirby, O. A. . . . . .Idaho
Kirby, Orrin A. . . . . .Oregon
Kirchoff, Otto E. .Wisconsin
Kirk, Daniel W. . . . . .Washington
Kirk, G. W. . . . . .Oregon
Kirk, H. P. . . . . .Iowa
Kirkham, John . . . . .Texas
Kirkham, John W. . . . . .Kansas
Kirkland Brothers . . . . .Colorado, Wyoming
Kirkland, Charles D. . . . . . . .Colorado, Wyoming
Kirkland, George W. . . . . . . .Colorado, Wyoming
Kirkland, P. G. . . . . .Colorado
Kirkpatrick . . . . .Missouri
Kirkpatrick, A. W. . . . . .Texas
Kirmeyer, Joseph . . . . .Kansas
Kiser, Frederick H. .Oregon
Kiser, Oscar H. . . . . .Oregon
Kissel, E. L. . . . . .New Mexico, Traveling
Kissel, S. W. . . . . .Kansas
Kitchen, Joseph . . . . .Iowa
Kite, John . . . . .Texas
Kiteringham, C. B. . . . . .Texas
Klain, Nathan M. . . . . .California
Kleckner & Snyder .Kansas
Kleckner, M. A. . . . . .Kansas, Traveling
Kleckner, Warren . . . . .California
Klein . . . . .Kansas
Kleinhammer, Ida M. (Miss) . . . . .California
Kleinhans, C. F. .Nebraska
Klench, Flora . . . . .California
Klenze, H. G. . . . . .Dakota
Klepfer, G. W. . . . . .Oklahoma
Klindt, Charles . . . . .California
Kline, Charles W. . . . . .California
Kline, J. W. . . . . .Arizona
Kline, Joseph L. . . . . .Colorado
Kline, Myrtle . . . . .Texas

Larson . . . . Iowa, Nevada, Oregon
Larson, Anton . . . . Minnesota
Larson, Charles . . . . Utah
Larson, Louis . . . . Washington
Larson, Olaf P. . . . . Arizona, Idaho
Larson, Selma . . . . California
Larson, Thomas Christian . . . . Utah
Larss & Duclos . . . . Alaska
Larss & Pierce . . . . British Columbia
Larss, Per Edward . . . . . Alaska, British Columbia
Larue, E. C. . . . . California
Las Cruces Art Gallery . . . . New Mexico
Las Cruces Photograph Gallery . . . . . New Mexico
Lasby, Dr. William F. . . . . Minnesota
Lasley, Margaret Rose . . . . California
Lasmoth, J. M. . . . . Nebraska
Lassensen & Hilstad . . . . Dakota
Lassesen, P. E. . . . . Dakota
Lassiter, J. W. . . . . Texas
Lassonde, Paul H. . . . . British Columbia
Latham, N. G. Mrs.) . . . . Nebraska
Lathrop . . . . California
Lathrop, W. H. Wisconsin
Latimer, K. . . . . Wisconsin
Latour, Ira Hinsdale . . . . Missouri
Latour, Lionel L. Missouri
Latour, William . . . . Missouri
Latour's Photographic Gallery & Studio of Portrait Painting . . . . Missouri
Lau, J. F. . . . . Oregon
Laughling, Sadie . . . . California
Laurens . . . . Montana
Laurens, A. . . . . Montana
Laurent, C. M. . . . . Kansas
Laurie, Robert H. F. . . . . Oregon, Traveling
Laurl . . . . Oregon
Laursen, Vigo . . . . British Columbia
Lauskin, Marie . . . . California
Lavalleur, Eugene Everett . . . . Oregon
Lavering, E. C. . . . . Idaho
Lavigne . . . . Traveling
Law & Miller . . . . Idaho
Law, D. J. . . . . Idaho
Law, Frederick . . . . Colorado
Law, G. . . . . Wisconsin
Law, John . . . . Idaho
Lawhon, John P. . . . . Texas
Lawhun & Zwerner . . . . California
Lawhun, Marion (Miss) . . . . California
Lawhun, Samuel . . . . California
Lawless, E. J. . . . . California
Lawn Studio . . . . California
Lawrence & Company, George R. . . . . Idaho
Lawrence & Company, W. H. . . . . Colorado
Lawrence & Houseworth . . . . California
Lawrence & O'Connor . . . . Iowa
Lawrence & Son . . . . California
Lawrence, A. J. . . . . Colorado
Lawrence, Alfred . . . . Kansas
Lawrence, C. A. Traveling
Lawrence, C. S. Colorado
Lawrence, D. H. . . . . Texas
Lawrence, George E. . . . . California
Lawrence, George S. . . . . California
Lawrence, H. F. California
Lawrence, O. J. . . . . Texas
Lawrence, William . . . . California, Nebraska
Lawrence, William H. . . . . California
Lawrence, William R. . . . . Oregon
Lawson . . . . Montana
Lawson, B. . . . . Nebraska
Lawson, Benjamin W. . . . . California
Lawson, Tom . . . . Arizona
Lawson, W. H. . . . . Texas
Lawton, Lena W. . . . . California
Laycock, F. M. . . . . Colorado
Laycock, Henry E. . . . . Colorado
Laycox, Alice . . . . Oregon
Layer, Agnes . . . . Oregon
Layton, F. J. . . . . Oregon
Layton, J. M. . . . . Texas
Le Fevre, W. L. . . . . Iowa
Le Forge, F. M. California
Le Munyon, C. E. . . . . British Columbia, Montana
Le Plongeon, Augustus . . . . California
Lea, George . . . . Wisconsin
Leach . . . . Texas
Leach & Hanna . . . . Texas
Leach & Randolph . . . . Texas
Leach, Don M. . . . . New Mexico, Texas, Traveling
Leach, Ed. A. . . . . Nebraska
Leach, F. M. . . . . Iowa
Leach, J. A. . . . . Colorado
Leach, Joe A. . . . . Texas
Leadville Photo & View Company . . . . . Colorado
Lean & Company, J. . . . . Kansas
Lean & Company, Mrs. E. L. . . . . Kansas
Lear & Cotton . . . . Nebraska
Learned . . . . California
Leas, J. A. . . . . Oregon
Leavenworth, John Randolph . . . . California
Leavenworth, Stone & Company . . . . . . California
Leavitt, Diana S. . . . . California
Leavitt, F. L. . . . . California
Lebleux, Ferdinand . . . . Hawaii
Lebo . . . . California
Lecher . . . . Wisconsin
Leckenby, A. B. . . . . Oregon
Leckie–Ewing, R. . . . . British Columbia
Ledbetter, Abner B. . . . . Texas
Leder, Charles . . . . Oregon
Ledgerwood, Edward . . . . Oregon
Lee . . . . Indian Territory, Oregon, Wisconsin
Lee & Company, J. B. . . . . Kansas
Lee, Alice I. . . . . Idaho
Lee, Anton . . . . Idaho
Lee Brothers . . . . Minnesota
Lee, C. J. . . . . Dakota, Traveling
Lee, Ellen (Miss) . . . . Texas
Lee, Emmet . . . . Arkansas
Lee, F. J. . . . . Dakota
Lee, Frederick . . . . Kansas
Lee, H. V. . . . . Idaho
Lee, Le Roy . . . . California
Lee, T. H. . . . . Kansas
Lee, W. L. . . . . Nebraska
Lee, W. Thomas . . . . California, Nevada
Lee Wah . . . . British Columbia
Lee, Willard Malcomb . . . . California
Lee, William . . . . Texas
Lee, William A. . . . . New Mexico
Lee's Photo Car . . . . Traveling
Leek, Nellie M. . . . . Kansas
Leek, Norman . . . . Idaho
Leeland Art & Manufacturing Company . . Dakota
Leeper, George W. Oregon
Leeper's Art Studio . . . . Indian Territory
Leeson, Benjamin W. . . . . British Columbia
Leeson, Harry O. . . . . Texas
Leeson, William H. . . . . Texas
Leffler, Frank B. . . . . Texas
Leftwich Brothers . . . . Missouri
Leftwich, John Warwick . . . . California
Leftwich, Mary F. . . . . California
Leganer, E. R. . . . . Texas
Legerton, John S. . . . . Traveling
Legislative Gallery . . . . Nebraska
Legreed & Floe . . . . Iowa
Legrud . . . . Dakota
Legterton, John . . . . Texas
Lehman . . . . Colorado
Lehman, Bertie . . . . British Columbia
Lehman, H. . . . . Nebraska
Lehmer, C. I. (Mrs.) . . . . Nebraska
Lehr, O. . . . . California
Leifs, Ernst . . . . Texas
Leighton, M. O. . . . . Idaho
Leimgruber, F. . . . . Texas
Leinery & Parker . . . . Texas
Leisenring . . . . Iowa
Leisenring Brothers . . . . Iowa
Leisenring, J. . . . . Iowa
Leisenring, K. . . . . Iowa
Leister, H. . . . . Texas
Leman, Charles H. . . . . Texas
Lemley, George W. Kansas
Lemmon, Mark J. . . . . New Mexico, Texas
Lemon, F. J. . . . . Traveling, Wyoming
Lemon, F. L. . . . . British Columbia
Lemone & Testasudz . . . . Texas
Lemos, W. . . . . California
Lempriere, Arthur Reid . . . . British Columbia
Lenard . . . . Colorado
Lenmons, C. F. . . . . Texas
Lennox . . . . Texas
Lenny, William J. . . . . Texas
Lenox & Hart . . . . Idaho
Lenox, Harry H. . . . . Idaho
Lenox, John W. . . . . Texas
Lentz, William H. . . . . California
Lenz Brothers . . . . Iowa
Lenz, J. M. . . . . California, Iowa
Leon . . . . Oregon
Leon & Anderson . . . . Colorado
Leon & Chapman . . . . Nebraska
Leon & Johnston . . . . Nebraska
Leon, D. L. . . . . Nebraska
Leon, John J. . . . . Nebraska
Leon, T. J. . . . . Colorado
Leon's Studio . . . . Oregon
Leonard . . . . Idaho, Texas
Leonard & Haywood . . . . New Mexico
Leonard & Martin . . . . Kansas
Leonard, Carl . . . . Nebraska
Leonard, Ella . . . . Kansas
Leonard, I. . . . . Kansas
Leonard, J. H. . . . . Kansas, New Mexico
Leonard, Joe . . . . Idaho
Leonard, John Edson . . . . Oregon
Leonard, Joseph D. . . . . Oregon
Leonard, P. F. . . . . Missouri
Leonard, V. V. . . . . Nebraska
Leonhard, Frank O. Kansas
Leopold . . . . Oregon
Leppert, E. D. . . . . Oregon
Lerne, Palmer . . . . Texas
Lerosin, David . . . . Texas
Leroy, Arvid L. . . . . Oregon
Leroy, Robert . . . . Kansas
Leschinsky, Julius . . . . Nebraska
Leschinsky, Max . . . . Nebraska
Leseur, J. H. . . . . Kansas
Lesher, Charles . . . . California
Leslie, Hiram E. . . . . Idaho, Nevada
Lesmeister, Cecelia (Mrs.) . . . . Oregon
Lesmeister, Frederick W. . . . . Oregon
Lester, D. Curtis . . . . Idaho
Lesure & Scovells Portable Picture Palace . . . . Traveling
Letellier, Thomas R. . . . . Colorado
Lettle, E. . . . . Colorado
Letton's Art Studio . . . . Missouri
Letz, Jaques . . . . Oregon
Leupton, O. L. . . . . Iowa
Levi, H. (Mrs.) . . . . Kansas
Levi, I. G. . . . . California
Levi, Laura . . . . Kansas
Levy, H. M. . . . . Colorado
Levy, Leah A. . . . . California
Levy, Mary Clara . . . . California
Leweis, Fred . . . . Idaho
Lewin, Otto . . . . California
Lewis . . . . Nebraska
Lewis & Allen . . . . Utah

568 BIOGRAPHIES OF WESTERN PHOTOGRAPHERS

Miller, Max . . . . . Texas
Miller, N. B. . . . . . British Columbia
Miller, Peter . . . . . Iowa
Miller Post Card Company . . . . . Oregon
Miller, R. . . . . . California
Miller, R. B. (Mr. & Mrs.) . . . . . Colorado
Miller, R. H. . . . . . Dakota
Miller, Reverend . . . . . British Columbia
Miller, Ruth . . . . . Oregon
Miller, Sarah Eloise . . . . . California
Miller, T. . . . . . British Columbia
Miller, T. C. . . . . . Colorado
Miller, Victor . . . . . Arizona
Miller, W. E. . . . . . Iowa
Miller, William . . . . . Iowa, Wisconsin
Miller, William W. . . . . . Texas
Miller's Photograph Car, S. R. . . . . . Traveling
Millett, E. M. . . . . . New Mexico
Millett, Ida (Mrs.) . . . . . New Mexico
Millholin & Dodds . . . . . Texas
Millholin, James M. . . . . . Texas
Milln, Ralph S. . . . . . Oregon
Millon, G. . . . . . Colorado
Mills & Son, E. L. . . . . . Arkansas
Mills, C. B. . . . . . Iowa
Mills, C. C. . . . . . Utah
Mills, C. H. . . . . . California
Mills, Charles H. . . . . . Colorado
Mills, Frank C. . . . . . Texas
Mills, M. E. . . . . . Colorado
Mills, N. A. . . . . . Iowa
Mills, Richard I. . . . . . Idaho
Mills, Thomas . . . . . British Columbia
Mills, William . . . . . Texas
Mills, William Allison Blair . . . . . California
Milne, A. . . . . . British Columbia
Milne, Charles . . . . . California
Milner . . . . . Colorado
Milo . . . . . Arizona
Milross & Wren . . . . . British Columbia
Milross, William Thomas . . . . . British Columbia
Miltz & Overton . . . . . California
Miltz & Swart . . . . . California
Miltz, Theodore G. . . . . . California
Mims & Rafferty . . . . . Texas
Mims, Edward Wellington . . . . . Texas
Minard, Thaddeus M. . . . . . Oregon
Mindell, S. D. . . . . . Texas
Miner, Nettie M. . . . . . Nebraska
Miner's Photographing Company . . . . . Colorado
Minne Ha Ha Gallery . . . . . Minnesota
Minnich, Ira . . . . . Kansas
Minor, Robert . . . . . California
Minshift, C. G. . . . . . Texas
Minshull, Charles . . . . . Texas
Minto, Lady Mary Caroline . . . . . Alaska, British Columbia
Minton & Trask . . . . . Colorado
Minturn, John . . . . . Kansas
Miser, W. L. . . . . . Oregon
Mishler & Walker . . . . . New Mexico
Mishler, Calvin S. . . . . . New Mexico
Mishler, M. M. . . . . . Kansas
Misner, H. E. . . . . . Oregon
Mission Studios . . . . . Arizona
Mitchell & Baer . . . . . Arizona
Mitchell & Labadie . . . . . Texas
Mitchell, A. M. . . . . . Colorado
Mitchell, A. W. . . . . . Colorado
Mitchell, Alfred A. A. . . . . . Hawaii
Mitchell, Carrie M. (Miss) . . . . . Kansas
Mitchell, D. S. . . . . . Kansas
Mitchell, Daniel Francis . . . . . Arizona
Mitchell, Daniel S. . . . . . Nebraska, Wyoming
Mitchell, Gertrude F. . . . . . Minnesota
Mitchell, Lillie L. (Mrs.) . . . . . Colorado
Mitchell, Maybelle G. . . . . . California
Mitchell, McGowan & Company . . . . . Nebraska
Mitchell, Roy . . . . . Texas
Mitchell, T. E. . . . . . Texas
Mitchell, T. L. . . . . . Missouri
Mitchell, Thomas E. . . . . . Texas
Mitchell, Walter . . . . . Missouri
Mitchell's Ground Floor Gallery . . . . . Missouri
Mith, G. B. (Mrs.) . . . . . California
Mizuno, S. . . . . . Oregon
Moberly, L. . . . . . Missouri
Moberly, Louis . . . . . Texas
Mobley, Professor Robert . . . . . Idaho
Model Photo Gallery . . . . . Arizona
Model Studio . . . . . Kansas
Moe & Lee . . . . . Dakota
Moe, O. J. . . . . . Dakota
Moeckli . . . . . Wisconsin
Moehring, Clara (Miss) . . . . . Texas
Moehring, Clara (Mrs.) . . . . . Texas
Moehring, Herman . . . . . Texas
Moelk, Charles F. . . . . . Texas
Moeller, J. R. . . . . . Nebraska
Moeller, John R. . . . . . California
Moffett, C. R. . . . . . Wisconsin
Moffitt, David J. . . . . . Texas
Moffitt, John H. . . . . . Oregon
Mohler & Company . . . . . Kansas
Mohler & Parks . . . . . Texas
Mohler & Rush . . . . . Texas
Mohler, Conrad . . . . . Texas
Mohler, J. A. . . . . . Texas
Mohler, J. W. . . . . . Kansas
Mohr, James . . . . . Wisconsin
Moir, Thomas . . . . . Texas
Mojonier, A. Louis . . . . . California
Mollenhauer, Edward . . . . . Texas
Mona Gallery . . . . . West Canada
Monaco, John B. . . . . . California
Monaco, Liberta . . . . . California
Monaco, Louis . . . . . California, Nevada
Monaco, Louis P. . . . . . California
Monaco, Marino . . . . . California
Monahan, William . . . . . California
Monell, John . . . . . Minnesota
Monfoet & Jones . . . . . Wisconsin
Monfoet, H. A. . . . . . Wisconsin
Monfort & Hill . . . . . Iowa
Mongold, Mae (Mrs.) . . . . . Oregon
Monk, J. R. . . . . . Texas
Monk, T. R. (Mrs.) . . . . . Oregon
Monmonier, William B. . . . . . California
Monmonier, William D. . . . . . California
Monnet & Bradley . . . . . Washington
Monotti, Giuseppe . . . . . California
Monroe, A. L. . . . . . Oregon
Monroe, A. L. (Mrs.) . . . . . Wisconsin
Monroe, C. J. . . . . . Wisconsin
Monroe, C. R. . . . . . Traveling
Monroe, Charles . . . . . Wyoming
Monroe, E. B. . . . . . California
Monroe, James . . . . . Texas
Monroe, W. H. . . . . . Iowa
Monroe–Thompson Photograph Company . . . . . Colorado
Monsen, Frederick . . . . . California
Monson, F. I. . . . . . Utah
Montag, William J. . . . . . Oregon
Montana View Company . . . . . Montana
Montano, Andreas Avelino . . . . . Hawaii
Montee, Frank A. . . . . . Oregon
Montee, James W. . . . . . Oregon
Monteitn, W. W. . . . . . Kansas
Montezuma View Company . . . . . New Mexico
Montfort, E. . . . . . Arizona, New Mexico
Montgomery . . . . . Iowa
Montgomery & Tarkington . . . . . Nebraska
Montgomery, C. E. . . . . . Oregon
Montgomery, J. H. . . . Idaho, Oregon, Washington
Montgomery, James F. . . . . . Texas
Moodmorth . . . . . Texas
Moody & Campbell . . . . . Nebraska
Moody, H. W. . . . . . California
Mooers & Plummer . . . . . Minnesota
Mooers, J. L. . . . . . California
Mooers, W. A. . . . . . Oregon
Moon . . . . . California
Moon, Carl . . . . . California, Oklahoma
Moon, Carl E. . . . . . New Mexico
Moon, F. W. . . . . . Arizona
Moon, H. C. . . . . . Oregon
Moon, Karl E. . . . . . Arizona
Moon, Leroy . . . . . Texas
Moon, Uletus . . . . . Texas
Mooney . . . . . Iowa
Mooney, James . . . . . Arizona, New Mexico
Mooney, Margaret . . . . . Texas
Moon–Keleher Studio . . . . . New Mexico
Moore . . . . . . British Columbia, California, Texas, West Canada
Moore & Bethane . . . . . Dakota
Moore & Christiansen . . . . . Nebraska
Moore & Mayers . . . . . Texas
Moore & Patterson . . . . . Texas
Moore & Skelton . . . . . California
Moore & Williams . . . . . Texas
Moore, A. R. . . . . . California
Moore, Blanche McNamer (Mrs.) . . . . . Oregon
Moore, C. . . . . . Dakota
Moore, Charles . . . . . Oregon
Moore, Charles C. . . . . . Texas
Moore, Elbridge W. . . . . . Oregon
Moore, Ella M. . . . . . Texas
Moore, Emmet B. . . . . . Texas
Moore, Ernest . . . . . Wyoming
Moore, Francis . . . . . Idaho
Moore, Frank . . . . . Oregon
Moore, G. E. . . . . . California
Moore, G. H. . . . . . Nebraska
Moore, G. L. . . . . . Colorado
Moore, G. W. . . . . . Colorado
Moore, George . . . . . California, Washington
Moore, George L. . . . . . Texas
Moore, George W. . . . . . Texas
Moore, H. C. . . . . . Colorado
Moore, Harry G. . . . . . Colorado
Moore, J. F. . . . . . Texas
Moore, J. P. . . . . . Texas
Moore, J. S. . . . . . Iowa
Moore, Leroy F. . . . . . Texas
Moore, M. E. . . . . . Oregon
Moore, R. E. . . . . . Texas
Moore, Robert . . . . . Texas
Moore, Robert E. . . . . . Texas
Moore, S. E. . . . . . New Mexico
Moore, S. E. L. . . . . . Iowa
Moore, Samuel . . . . . Arizona
Moore, Solon . . . . . Texas
Moore, Thomas Henry . . . . . British Columbia
Moore, Thomas V. . . . . . Alaska
Moore, W. D. . . . . . Oregon
Moore, W. P. . . . . . Arkansas
Moore, William . . . . . Kansas
Moorehead, T. P. . . . . . Nebraska
Moores . . . . . Wisconsin
Moorhouse, Lee . . . . . Oregon
Moosbauer, L. . . . . . Alaska
Mora, Joseph . . . . . Arizona
Moran, Edgar . . . . . Iowa
Moran, Nelly (Miss) . . . . . Oregon
Morde . . . . . British Columbia
Mordoff, Nelle L. (Mrs.) . . . . . California
More & Hager . . . . . Minnesota
More, A. R., Jr. . . . . . Minnesota
Morehead, James Franklin . . . . . California
Moreland, A. W. . . . . . California
Moreledge, Clarence Grant . . . . . Nebraska
Morey, Oliver L. . . . . . Texas

National Copying Company ....Texas
National Photo View & Copying
  Company ....California
Native American Photo Company ......Arizona
Nau ....Nebraska
Nau, H. ....Nebraska
Naughton & Conklin ....Kansas
Naumann & Melander ....Minnesota
Nauschuetz, Bruno ....Texas
Neal (Miss) ....California
Neal & Simmons ....Minnesota
Neal, A. ....Colorado
Neal, B. F. ....Texas
Neal, Charles B. ....Texas
Neal, E. E. ....Iowa
Neamis, R. P. ....Texas
Needham, J. H. ....Iowa
Needles & Addis ....Kansas
Needles & Company, John T. ....Colorado
Needles & Nast ....Colorado
Needles, John T. ....Colorado, Kansas
Neel Brothers ....Colorado
Neel Brothers & Gregory ....Colorado
Neel, J. W. ....Colorado
Neelands Brothers ....British Columbia
Neelands, Hamilton George ...British Columbia
Neelands, James F. ....British Columbia
Neelands, Samuel ....British Columbia
Neff ....Iowa
Neff, Charles ....Iowa, Texas
Neff, Harry L. ....New Mexico
Neff, W. E. ....Oregon
Neiburg, A. ....Nebraska
Neicken, L. M. (Mrs.) ....Oregon
Neihart, A. W. ....Nebraska
Neihart, M. W. ....Nebraska
Neil, G. R. ....Iowa
Neil, T. J. ....Iowa
Neill, George W. ....British Columbia
Neis, Coral Mae (Mrs.) ....New Mexico
Neiswanger, Charles G. ....Kansas
Nelcke, Theresa ....California
Neligh, V. ....Nebraska
Nelkin, J. ....British Columbia
Nelles, W. A. ....Colorado
Nelson & Bailey ....California
Nelson, A. A. (Mrs.) ....California
Nelson, Aaron ....Colorado
Nelson, Alfred N. ....Texas
Nelson, B. H. ....Arkansas
Nelson, B. S. ....Idaho
Nelson, C. C. ....Minnesota
Nelson, Christopher A. ....California
Nelson, Etta B. ....California
Nelson, F. A. ....Minnesota
Nelson, J. D. ....Texas
Nelson, J. H. ....Idaho
Nelson, James ....Nebraska, Traveling
Nelson, John ....Nebraska
Nelson, L. E. ....Colorado
Nelson, N. A. ....Iowa
Nelson, Nels ....Idaho
Nelson, O. A. ....Colorado
Nelson, O. R. ....Nebraska
Nelson Studio ....California
Nelson, T. K. ....Nebraska
Nelson, Velman ....Texas
Nelson's Photographic Studio ....Minnesota
Nemeck, Louis A. ....Arizona
Nemyre, Lena M. ....Oregon
Nenow ....Nebraska
Nephew, J. ....Arizona
Nereus, Baldwin ....Kansas
Nesbitt ....Montana
Nesbitt, A. F. ....Minnesota
Nesemann, Enno ....California
Ness, James Harry ....Oregon
Ness, Joseph ....California

Ness, N. T. ....Texas
Neto, J. B. ....New Mexico
Neuman, William J. ....Arizona
Nevel ....Wisconsin
Neville, David S. ....Colorado
Nevins, George O. ....Colorado
New Era Portrait Company ....California
New Photograph Rooms ....Colorado
New, Sylva ....New Mexico
New York Art Company ....Missouri
New York Art Gallery ....Iowa
New York Gallery ....Arizona, California,
                            Missouri, Oregon
New York Photo Studio ....Arizona
New York Photograph Gallery ..Colorado, Kansas
New York Photographic Company ....Texas
New York Traveling Studio ....Traveling
Newark Gallery ....California
Newberg, P. A. ....Kansas
Newbury, C. S. ....Iowa
Newby & Company, L. C. ....Colorado
Newby & Wilson ....Colorado
Newby, M. W. (Mrs.) ....Colorado
Newby, S. ....Kansas
Newcomb ....Idaho
Newcomb, Alta ....Oregon
Newcomb, Ida ....Oregon
Newcomb, J. F. ....Nebraska
Newcomb, J. L. ....Iowa
Newcomb, M. W. ....Kansas
Newcomb, Marion W. ....Oregon
Newcomb, R. W. ....Utah
Newcomb, T. ....Texas
Newcomb, T. J. ....California, Nebraska, Utah
Newcomb, William ....Utah
Newcombe Brothers ....Utah
Newcombe, C. H. ....Dakota
Newcombe, Charles Frederick ...British Columbia
Newdick, Alfred P. ....California
Newell, Mabelle ....Idaho
Newman, Almeron ....British Columbia,
                              New Mexico
Newman, E. (Mrs.) ....Oregon
Newman, William J. ....Arizona
Newport, F. T. ....Arizona
Newt, A. F. ....Minnesota
Newth, Ernest W. ....California
Newton & Clark ....Texas
Newton, Howell Dewitt ....Colorado
Newton, J. J. ....Iowa
Newton, Lutie T. ....Texas
Newton, W. L. ....California
Newton, William H. ....Texas
Newville, C. H. (Mrs.) ....Iowa
Nias, Raymond ....Wisconsin
Nichel, H. T. ....California
Nichol, W. H. ....Arkansas
Nicholas, J. K. ....Nebraska
Nicholas, James A. ....Kansas
Nicholls & Parkin ....West Canada
Nicholls, J. W. ....West Canada
Nichols ....Iowa
Nichols & Brother's ....Missouri
Nichols & Weddington ....Texas
Nichols, A. C. ....Kansas
Nichols, A. E. ....California
Nichols, A. W. ....Iowa
Nichols, Arthur A. ....Texas
Nichols, C. D. ....Kansas
Nichols, Clyde B. ....Oregon
Nichols, E. P. ....Nebraska
Nichols, G. C. ....Nebraska
Nichols, George B. ....Colorado
Nichols, H. C. ....Kansas
Nichols, Jacob ....Texas
Nichols, L. M. (Miss) ....California
Nichols Norton & Company ....California
Nichols, Sheldon K. ....California

Nichols, William H. ....Arkansas
Nicholson, James ....Texas
Nick & Knecht ....Traveling
Nick, William ....Traveling
Nicka, Allen A. ....Texas
Nicka, Eliga A. ....Texas
Nickas, Christ ....Oregon
Nicklas, W. H. ....New Mexico
Nickols, C. O. ....Iowa
Nickson, Ralph ....British Columbia
Nicolai, H. T. ....Oregon
Nicoulin, J. F. ....Iowa
Nielsen, A. P. ....New Mexico
Nielsen, Carl ....Texas
Nielsen, L. ....Nebraska
Nielson ....Wisconsin
Nielson & Company ....Nebraska
Nielson Brothers ....Texas
Nieson, Carrie (Miss) ....California
Nighswander, Jasper Merle ....Oregon
Nilson, Carl ....Colorado
Nims & Company ....Colorado
Nims, F. A. .....Arizona, Colorado, New Mexico
Nitchy, F. A. (Mrs.) ....Oregon
Nix, E. E. ....Texas
Nixon & Best ....West Canada
Nixon Art Studio ....Iowa
Nixon, Thomas, Jr. ....West Canada
Noble & Company, Jay ....Kansas
Noble & Fell ....California
Noble, C. B. (Mrs.) ....Kansas
Noble, H. E. ....Nebraska
Noble, John ....Nebraska
Noble, Oliver D. ....Colorado
Noble, P. W. ....Nebraska
Noble, Ralph Kendal ....New Mexico
Noble, Skelton Stanford .....California, Traveling
Noble's Gallery ....Kansas
Noble's Photography & Chromotype
  Gallery ....Kansas
Nock, G. R. ....Idaho
Nockin, Edward ....Colorado
Noe ....Kansas
Noe & Lee ....Nevada
Noe & Wirth ....Oregon
Noe, Charles B. ....California
Noe, John S. ....Nevada
Noe, Miguel, Jr. ....California
Noel, C. ....Kansas
Nofts, Robert W. ....Colorado
Nolan, Adam ....Iowa
Nolestein, W. R. ....Nebraska
Nolte, Joseph ....Kansas
Nonpareil Portrait & Publishing
  Company ....Colorado
Norcott, C. K. ....Dakota, Oregon
Norcross & Higinbotham ....California
Norcross, Oliver H. P. ....California
Nordstrom, Carl H. ....Oregon
Norelious, Efron ....Texas
Norman, C. A. (Mrs.) ....Texas
Norman, Henry ....British Columbia
Norris ....Texas
Norris, J. E. ....California, Oregon
Norsworthy, L. F. ....Texas
North & Huff ....Texas
North & Lenny ....Texas
North Beach Gallery ....California
North, I. E. ....Nebraska
North, J. E. ....Nebraska
North, Jerry E. ....Texas
North Omaha Photograph Gallery .....Nebraska
North Pacific Photographic Printing & Engraving
  House ....Oregon
North Photographic Gallery ....Nebraska
North-Western View Company ......Wisconsin
Northcraft & Company, C. E. ....Kansas
Northern, Joe T. ....Texas

Photo Parlor on Wheels . . . Traveling
Photochrome Company . . . California
Photographer's Palace . . . Iowa
Photographic & Fine Art Gallery . . . Iowa
Photographic Art Palace . . . Wisconsin
Photographic Artist Old Gallery . . . Arizona
Photographic Company . . . Oregon
Photographic Parlors . . . California
Photographic Publishing Company . . . California
Phrenny, John . . . Wisconsin
Piatt, C. E. . . . California
Pickard, Howard S. . . . Kansas
Pickard, William . . . Texas
Pickel, Elsworth . . . Oregon
Pickel, Lewis G. . . . Oregon
Pickel, William M. . . . Oregon
Pickels & Pattison . . . Nebraska
Pickels, J. . . . Nebraska
Pickerill & Catterlin . . . Oregon
Pickerill, Frank A. . . . Oregon
Pickerill, P. G. . . . Arkansas
Pickett & Carter . . . Montana
Pickett & Everett . . . California
Pickett, Edward . . . Idaho
Pickett, H. W. . . . Texas
Pickett, J. M. . . . Montana, Nevada
Pickett, John M. . . . California
Pickett, W. B. . . . New Mexico
Pickles, J. W. . . . Nebraska
Pierce . . . California, Iowa
Pierce & Blanchard . . . California
Pierce & Potter . . . Dakota
Pierce, Charles C. . . . California
Pierce, E. W. . . . California
Pierce, G. A. . . . California
Pierce, Harry C. . . . Iowa
Pierce, John B. . . . Texas
Pierce, K. A. . . . Oregon
Pierce, N. E. . . . Iowa
Pierce, Nathan Parda . . . Arizona
Pierce, W. . . . California
Pierce, Wesley C. . . . British Columbia, California, Washington
Pierce, William . . . California
Piercy, Frederick C. . . . Utah
Pierie, W. . . . British Columbia
Pierrot, Eugene . . . Texas
Pierson & Gosling . . . Iowa
Pierson, John . . . Kansas
Pierson, Simon . . . Wyoming
Pietz, Henry . . . Nebraska
Piggott & Shaw . . . California
Piggott, James K. . . . California
Pike & Markham Company . . . Oregon
Pike & O'Neill Company . . . Oregon
Pike & Perrin . . . Oregon
Pike, J. W. . . . Dakota, Nebraska
Pike, Nelson G. . . . Oregon
Pike, Warburton Mayer . . Alaska, British Columbia
Pilliner . . . Montana
Pilliner Daguerrean Gallery . . . California
Pilliner, Frederick J. . . . Idaho
Pilliner, William H. . . . California, Idaho, Nevada
Pillsbury, A. C. . . . Alaska, British Columbia, California
Pimental, J. M. . . . California
Pinckney, J. W. . . . Iowa
Pindell, S. . . . California
Pine Street Gallery . . . Missouri
Pingrey, R. H. . . . Minnesota
Pinkerton . . . Texas
Pinkerton & Smith . . . Texas
Pioneer Gallery . . . Dakota, Nevada
Pioneer Photograph Gallery . . . California
Pioneer Photographic House . . . Nebraska
Piper . . . Texas
Piper, Albert . . . Texas
Piper, Charles James . . . British Columbia
Piper, Charles Thomas Wood . . . British Columbia
Piper, H. . . . Wisconsin
Piper, W. S. . . . Wisconsin
Piser, Thomas E. . . . California
Pitchford, Emily . . . California
Pitlado, C. B. . . . West Canada
Pitman, General John T. . . . Dakota
Pittenger, William . . . Idaho
Pittman (Miss) . . . Oregon
Pittman & Griffith . . . Texas
Pitts & Tucker . . . Texas
Pixley, S. E. . . . Dakota
Place, S. . . . Traveling
Plagemann, John P. . . . Oregon
Plaisted, Jessie C. . . . Kansas
Plank, Fred A. . . . Wisconsin
Plaster, Oscar L. . . . Arkansas
Platt, Thomas C. (Mrs.) . . . British Columbia
Plaza Art Studio . . . New Mexico
Plaza Photo Gallery . . . California
Pleasants, Joseph B. . . . California
Plecker, A. H. . . . Traveling
Ploetz & Haag . . . Kansas
Ploetz, J. . . . Missouri
Plukton & Smith . . . Texas
Plumb, S. L. . . . Wisconsin
Plummer . . . Minnesota
Plummer & Haelsig . . . California
Plummer, F. C. . . . Washington
Plummer, Harry W. . . . California
Plummer, Helen . . . Oregon
Plummer, M. V. (Mrs.) . . . California
Plummer, Margaret V. . . . California
Plummer, Oakes M. . . . Oregon
Plunkett, L. S. . . . Texas
Podoll, G. . . . Wisconsin
Poe . . . Nebraska
Poe & Woods . . . Nebraska
Poe & Wright . . . Texas
Poe, John T. . . . Texas
Poe, P. E. . . . Nebraska
Pokorney, Ludwig L. . . . California, Oregon
Poland, J. W. . . . Kansas
Poldeman, William F. . . . Oregon
Poley & Company, Horace S. . . . Colorado
Poley, Horace Swartley . . . New Mexico
Poling, William . . . Texas
Pollard & Nelles . . . Colorado
Pollard, L. L. . . . Traveling
Pollen, C. A. . . . Colorado
Pollock & Boyden . . . Dakota
Pollock & Duganne . . . Dakota
Pollock, A. . . . Dakota
Pollock, A. M. . . . California
Pollock, James T. . . . California
Pollock, Jeanette . . . Arizona
Pollock, Ralph F. . . . New Mexico
Pollock, Thomas . . . Oregon
Pomeroy, Charles T. . . . Kansas
Pomeroy, Edgar . . . California
Ponch, Adelia . . . Texas
Ponch, M. G. . . . Texas
Pond, Charles L. . . . California, Utah
Pond, Percy E. . . . Alaska
Ponizzardi, L. C. . . . Kansas
Pook, C. . . . Iowa
Pool & Barnes . . . New Mexico
Pool & Butler . . . New Mexico
Pool, Frank P. . . . New Mexico
Pool, J. F. P. . . . Texas
Poore . . . Dakota
Poore, H. R. . . . New Mexico
Pope & Hoffman . . . Oregon
Pope, A. N. . . . Texas
Pope, Oliver M. . . . Oregon
Pope, Seth L. . . . Oregon
Popular Photo Parlour . . . British Columbia
Popular Photographic Parlor . . . West Canada
Portable Photo Parlor . . . Traveling
Portable Photographic Studio . . . Oregon
Portable Picture Palace . . . Traveling
Porter . . . Arizona, Iowa
Porter & Cort . . . New Mexico
Porter & Neff . . . New Mexico
Porter & Son, R. . . . Iowa
Porter, C. Y. . . . Colorado
Porter, D. A. . . . California
Porter, George . . . Colorado
Porter, J. H. . . . Colorado
Porter, J. R. . . . Wisconsin
Porter, Milton E. . . . New Mexico
Porter, Nathaniel Joseph . . . British Columbia
Portillo, Jesus . . . Arizona
Portland Camera Exchange . . . Oregon
Portland Finishing Company . . . Oregon
Portland Gallery . . . Oregon
Portland Portrait Company . . . Oregon
Portland Studio . . . Oregon
Portland Viewing Company . . . Oregon
Posack, A. . . . New Mexico
Posada, Jose . . . New Mexico
Posse, Charles A. . . . Texas
Post, A. B. . . . California, Iowa
Post, Frederick E. . . . Colorado
Post Office Tin Type Gallery . . . Oregon
Postal Shop . . . Oregon
Postles, Anna B. (Mrs.) . . . Oregon
Postles, William F. . . . Oregon
Postlethwaite, Benjamin P. . . . Oregon
Potash, Moses L. . . . Texas
Potter . . . California, Kansas, Oregon, Texas
Potter, A. J. . . . Wisconsin
Potter, C. T. . . . Colorado
Potter, Florence E. (Miss) . . . New Mexico, Texas
Potter, G. W. . . . California, Montana
Potter, H. N. . . . California, Oregon
Potter, J .O. . . . Wisconsin
Potter, J. C. . . . Idaho, Nevada
Potter, J. J. . . . Oregon
Potter, J. W. A. . . . California
Potter, John S. . . . Oregon
Potter, L. A. . . . Texas
Potter, Sadie (Miss) . . . New Mexico
Powe, T. H. . . . Nebraska
Powel, Ellimare . . . Texas
Powell . . . Iowa, Kansas
Powell, Clement . . . Arizona, Colorado
Powell, H. E. . . . Oregon
Powell, J. F. . . . Dakota
Powell, L. T. . . . Texas
Powell, M. (Miss) . . . Kansas
Powell, Nettie M. (Miss) . . . Kansas
Powell Photo . . . Arkansas
Powell, W. A. . . . Colorado, Nebraska
Power . . . Minnesota
Power, Eustace B. . . . Colorado
Power, G. T. . . . Texas
Power, William . . . British Columbia
Powers . . . California, Missouri
Powers, D. R. . . . Nebraska
Powers, J. E. . . . Wisconsin
Powers, Josephine C. . . . California
Powers, N. B. . . . California
Powers, Stewart . . . Wisconsin
Powers, W. C. . . . Colorado
Prater, W. J. . . . Idaho, Utah
Prather . . . Alaska
Prather, E. . . . California
Prather, F. O. . . . Texas
Prather, Thomas O. . . . Texas
Pratsch, C. R. . . . California, Washington
Pratt . . . California, Iowa, Nebraska
Pratt & Green . . . California
Pratt, George H. . . . Texas
Pratt, Guy A. . . . Oregon
Pratt, Love . . . Oregon

INDEX OF PHOTOGRAPHERS 575

Pray, Fred H. ....California
Praytor, William B. ....Texas
Prealinouz, C. ....Texas
Prebensen ....Wisconsin
Preble, Edward W. ....Oregon
Predick, J. B. ....Texas
Premium Art Gallery ....Iowa
Premium Photographic Studio ....Iowa
Prendergast & Freund ....Iowa
Prentice & Hart ....California
Prentice, Helen M. ....California
Prentice, Sergeant Royal ....New Mexico
Prentiss, Arthur ....Oregon
Prentzel, W. R. ....Oregon
Prescott, Arthur ....Texas
Prescott, J. J. ....Idaho, Minnesota
Prescott, Rose Mable ....Kansas
Prescott Studio ....Arizona
Prest & Company ....British Columbia
Prest, William Archie ....British Columbia
Preston ....Washington
Preston, George ....British Columbia
Preston, H. C. ....Nebraska
Preston, John C. ....Arizona
Preston, N. A. ....Wisconsin
Prettyman & Cornish ....Kansas
Prettyman, W. S. ....Kansas, Oklahoma, Traveling
Pretz, J. C. ....California
Preuss Drug Company ....Oregon
Preusser, George ....Texas
Preusuer, Frank ....Texas
Prevot, Anthony ....Texas
Prewitt, W. L. ....Nebraska
Prey ....Nebraska
Prezeau & Tougas ....California
Price ....Minnesota
Price & Sours ....Missouri
Price & Voelker ....California
Price, Andrew ....California, Traveling
Price, C. C. ....Texas
Price, Carl E. ....Texas
Price, D. ....Idaho
Price, D. A. ....Missouri
Price, James M. ....Texas
Price, John ....Texas
Price, L. R. ....Oregon
Price, N. B. ....Colorado
Price, Robert C. ....New Mexico
Price, Thomas ....California
Price, William V. ....Oregon
Priday, E. A. ....Oregon
Prier, Richard ....Oregon
Priest ....Oregon
Priest, Charles F. ....California
Priestly, P. ....Texas
Primik, Frank I. ....Nebraska
Prince, H. ....California
Prince, J. K. ....California
Prindle, Benjamin A. ....California
Prindle, M. M. (Mrs.) ....Minnesota
Pringle, Joseph ....Oregon
Prior, N. W. ....Arizona
Pritchard ....Missouri
Pritchard, Nora B. ....Oregon
Proctor Brothers ....Nebraska
Proctor, Edward L. ....Nebraska
Proctor, J. H. ......Kansas, Minnesota, Nebraska
Proctor, Jefferson ....Iowa
Proctor, Jessie ....Kansas
Progressive Art Company ....California
Prothrow, Sanders C. ....Texas
Proud, John ....Minnesota
Provins ....Nebraska
Pruden ....Colorado
Pryor, W. A. ....Wisconsin
Pryse & Ewing ....Nebraska
Pugh, John W. ....Texas
Pullar, William ....West Canada
Pullen & Wagner ....Texas
Purcell ....Kansas
Purcell, C. E. ....Colorado
Purcell, I. D. ....Kansas
Purdy, J. M. ....Texas
Purey & Company, H. F. ....Texas
Purnelle, H. J. ....Oklahoma, Traveling
Purser, Spencer ....California
Pursley, J. J. ....Kansas, Nebraska
Putnam ....Oregon
Putnam & Snyder ....Nebraska
Putnam & Valentine ....Arizona, California
Putnam, Arion ....California
Putnam, Charles W. ....Wisconsin
Putnam, Clyde A., Sr. ....Oregon
Putnam, John R. ....California
Putnam, S. A. ....Traveling
Putney & Henry ....Kansas
Putney, Harrison ....Kansas
Putty, Edward ....Texas
Putty, G. ....Texas
Putty, G. & E. ....Texas
Putzien, Herman ....Oregon
Pyfer ....Idaho
Pyman, H. ......British Columbia, West Canada
Pywell & Sterzing ....Texas
Pywell, William R. ....Dakota, Texas

Q

Quackenbush, E. H. ....Oregon
Quackenbush, Richard M. ....Colorado
Quant, Blanche ....Oregon
Quant, Dora ....Oregon
Quant, Sumner ....Oregon
Quartermass, C. W. ....Oregon
Queen Art Photo Studio ....British Columbia
Queen Studio ....Arizona
Queensbury ....Texas
Quick Finish Kodak Company ....Arizona
Quiggle & Johnson ....Dakota
Quiggle, H. F. ....Dakota
Quigley Photo ....California
Quin & Lane ....Missouri
Quinn, C. W. ....Texas
Quint, Roy T. ....Arizona
Quirk & Bowden ....California
Quirk & Halsey ....California
Quirk, James ....California, Texas

R

R.T.R. Company ....Oregon
Raba, Ernst ....Texas
Rabe, John A. G. ....Texas
Rader, J. E. ....Arkansas
Rader, R. F. ....California
Raeder, Barbetta E. (Mrs.) ....Oregon
Raenhart ....California
Rafferty, Frank Ernest ....Texas
Ragan & Munn ....Kansas
Ragan & Shannon ....Kansas
Ragan & Winans ....Missouri
Ragan, G. C. ....Nebraska, Oregon
Ragan, George C. ....New Mexico
Ragan, H. D. ....Nebraska
Ragan's Photograph Rooms ....Missouri
Ragland, J. B. ....Texas
Ragsdale & Brother ....Texas
Ragsdale & Wilson ....Texas
Ragsdale, McArthur Cullen ......Texas, Traveling
Ragsdale, Robert B. ....Texas
Rahmeyer, B. H. ....Oregon
Railroad Palace Photo Car ....Traveling
Railroad Photo Car ....Traveling
Rainey ....Texas
Rainier Studio ....Washington
Rainheld, H. E. (Mrs.) ....Wisconsin
Rains, Carver W. ....Texas
Rainwater, Terrel ....Texas
Raisor & Pennell ....Arkansas
Raisor & Werts ....Arkansas
Raitt, T. G. ....Wisconsin
Ralph & Fredlund ....Iowa
Ralston ....Dakota
Ralston, J. E. ....Washington
Ralston, John E. ....Idaho
Ramey & Company, R. A. ....Kansas
Ramos, Maria J. ....Hawaii
Ramsdale, George ....California
Ramsdell, G. H. ....California, Oregon, Traveling
Ramsey, O. ....Texas
Ramsour & Pennell ....Kansas
Ramsour, L. A. ....Kansas
Rance & Company, F. G. ....Utah
Rand, C. A. ....Texas
Rand, L. O., Jr. ....Texas
Randall ....Minnesota
Randall, A. F. ...Arizona, Colorado, New Mexico, Texas, Traveling
Randall, Fred ....Kansas
Randall, Lillian M. ....Oregon
Randall, Stephen ....California
Randall, William G. ....Oregon
Randau, Oswald ....Texas
Randebaugh, J. D. ....Arizona
Randolph ....Texas
Randolph, John P. ....Texas
Rankin ....Kansas, Traveling
Rankin & Company ....Colorado
Rankin, Charles Augusta ....Texas
Rankin, F. S. ....Oregon
Rankin, Frank A. ....Oregon
Rankin, George W. ....California
Rankin, Paris & Allyn ....Colorado
Rankin, William Wesley ....Texas
Ranney, R. H. ....Texas
Ransford, Arthur L. ....Oregon
Ransom, J. G. ....Idaho
Ransom, R. W. ....Minnesota
Ransome, F. L. ....Idaho
Rapin, A. ....Colorado
Rappertie, Arthur S. ....British Columbia
Rasch, Fred A. ....Oregon
Rasmussen, J. Charles ....California
Rasmussen, N. F. ....California
Ratcliff, C. E. ....Arizona
Ratcliffe & Lee ....Texas
Rath, Frank ....California
Rattenbury, Francis Mawson ....Alaska, British Columbia
Rau, Carl ....Dakota
Rau, J. P. ....Texas
Rauch, Theodore ....Wisconsin
Raudeleagh, Oliver B. ....Arizona
Rauscher, H. ....California
Rauthrauff, A. T. ....California
Rawies, Caspar ....Wisconsin
Rawlins, W. J. ....Texas
Rawls, William J. ....Texas
Rawson, Charles S. ....Wisconsin
Ray & Hinson ....New Mexico
Ray, Afflect Archie ....California
Ray, F. L. ....Colorado
Ray, T. J. ....New Mexico
Ray, W. R. ....Texas
Rayburn ....Texas
Raymond ....California, Idaho, Oregon, Texas, Wisconsin
Raymond, Will ....Oregon
Rea, Josie H. (Miss) ....Oregon
Rea, Thomas L. ....California
Rea, W. J. ....California, Missouri
Read ....Iowa
Read & Postlethwaite ....Oregon
Read & Reed ....Colorado
Read, Benjamin F. ....Idaho, Oregon
Read, G. W. ....California

Rose, A. A. .New Mexico
Rose, C. A. .New Mexico
Rose, Chalmers . . . . .Texas
Rose, Charles A. . . . . .New Mexico, Texas
Rose, Charles E. . . . . .Colorado
Rose City Photo Studio . . . . .Oregon
Rose City Studio . . . . .Oregon
Rose, Clarence . . . . .Iowa
Rose, George L. . . . . .Arizona, California
Rose, H. W. . . . . .Kansas
Rose, J. . . . . .Nebraska
Rose, John K. . . . . .Colorado, New Mexico
Rose, Josephine (Mrs.) . . . . .Idaho
Rose, Noah Hamilton . . . . .Texas
Rose, Philip H. . . . . .Texas
Rose Studio . . . . .Oregon
Rosengrant, Dan L. . . . . .Idaho
Rosenkranz, Helen (Miss) . . . . .Washington
Rosenzweig .Nebraska
Roshon & Greene . . . . .Traveling
Roshon's Photographic Car . . . . .Traveling
Rosiger, F. . . . . .Oregon
Roskruge, George . . . . .Arizona
Ross . . . . .Wisconsin
Ross & Ifland . . . . .Kansas
Ross & Ormsby . . . . .California
Ross & Roberts . . . . .Wyoming
Ross, A. J. . . . . .British Columbia, Nebraska,
                                     West Canada
Ross, Best & Company . . . . .West Canada
Ross Brothers . . . . .Nebraska
Ross, Daniel W. . . . . .Idaho
Ross, David W. . . . . .Oregon
Ross, Eddie (Miss) . . . . .New Mexico
Ross, Edward . . . . .Nebraska
Ross, George . . . . .California
Ross, H. E. .Colorado
Ross, H. R. . . . . .Nebraska, Oregon
Ross, Helen (Miss) . . . . .British Columbia
Ross, J. B. .Missouri
Ross, J. Leaske . . . . .Colorado
Ross, J. W. . . . . .Texas
Ross, Jack . . . . .Oregon
Ross, John . . . . .Colorado, West Canada
Ross, P. F. .Missouri
Ross, William . . . . .California
Rosser & Martin . . . . .Arkansas
Rosser, Benjamin L. . . . . .Arkansas
Rosser, J. A. (Mrs.) . . . . .Texas
Rossiter, J. E. .Iowa
Roswall, Fred A. . . . . .Missouri
Roth . . . . .Missouri
Roth, E. H. . . . . .Iowa
Roth, Hermina . . . . .California
Rothberg, H. .Texas
Rothberger, Henry . . . . .Colorado
Rothery, Garrity (Mrs.) . . . . .California
Rothi, R. P. . . . . .Utah, Washington
Rothrock & Barnett . . . . .Arizona
Rothrock & Catton . . . . .Arizona
Rothrock, G. H. . . . . .Arizona, California
Rothwell, E. L. . . . . .British Columbia
Rothwell, Isaac N. . . . . .Texas
Rotnor, George H. . . . . .Oregon
Rouff, Henry . . . . .Colorado
Rough, Charles . . . . .Idaho
Rounds, A. A. . . . . .Dakota
Rounds, Lock & McBride . . . . .Dakota
Rouse, Charles . . . . .California
Rousenvell, William . . . . .Wisconsin
Roush, Ada A. (Miss) . . . . .Oregon
Roussel & Palmer . . . . .California
Roussel, George Onezime . . . . .California
Routledge, Fred A. . . . . .Oregon
Rowe, G. W. .Iowa
Rowe, J. F. . . . . .West Canada
Rowel, William . . . . .Nebraska
Rowgles, Alley . . . . .Texas

Rowin, George . . . . .Oregon
Rowland, Cain . . . . .Texas
Rowland, Pearl . . . . .Texas
Rowlett, E. .Nebraska
Rowlett, J. W. . . . . .Nebraska
Rowley . . . . .Nebraska
Rowley Brothers . . . . .Nebraska
Rowley, E. A. . . . . .Nebraska
Rowley, M. V. . . . . .Colorado
Rowntree, W. A. . . . . .Arizona
Royal Engineers . . .British Columbia, Washington
Royal, Osman (Mrs.) . . . . .Oregon
Royal, Dr. Osman . . . . .Oregon
Royal Studio . . . . .Arizona, British Columbia
Royce, L. M. .Idaho
Royce, Orlen . . . . .Oregon
Royer & Moore . . . . .Colorado
Ruck, D. R. . . . . .Texas
Rudasill, H. M. . . . . .Colorado
Rudd . . . . .Wisconsin
Rudd & Runyan . . . . .Kansas
Ruddell, John B. . . . . .Texas
Rudiger & Company, J. . . . . .Kansas
Rudolph, A. E. . . . . .Texas
Rudolph, H. W. . . . . .Kansas
Rudolph, Julia F. (Mrs.) . . . . .California
Rudy & Clinton . . . . .Colorado
Rudy, W. Ira . . . . .Colorado, New Mexico
Rue, Lewis M. . . . . .California
Rugg, A. B. . . . . .Minnesota
Rugg, D. B. . . . . .Arkansas, Missouri
Rugg, Elliott S. . . . . .Iowa
Ruh, O. L. . . . . .Dakota, Minnesota
Ruins . . . . .Texas
Ruitz, H. . . . . .New Mexico
Rule & Edwards . . . . .California
Rule, Eugene L. . . . . .California
Rulofson, William Henry . . . . .California
Rummelin, P. (Miss) . . . . .Oregon
Rumsey (Mrs.) . . . . .Oregon
Rundle & Fults . . . . .Missouri
Rundle, William . . . . .Idaho
Rundlett, Charles W. . . . . .Wisconsin
Runkle, Maud (Miss) . . . . .Colorado
Runnels, Benjamin F. . . . . .California
Runyan . . . . .Kansas
Rush . . . . .Texas
Rush, C. A. . . . . .Texas
Rush, Charles .Idaho
Rush, John . . . . .Texas
Rush, William B. . . . . .Oregon
Rushing, G. B. D. . . . . .Texas
Rushville Art Gallery & Copying
     Company . . . . .Nebraska
Russ, E. R. .Oregon
Russ, Mary A. (Mrs.) . . . . .Oregon
Russel, A. J. . . . . .Nebraska
Russell . . . . .Oklahoma, Oregon
Russell & Luke . . . . .Colorado
Russell & Vaughn . . . . .Montana
Russell, Andrew J. . . . . .Utah
Russell Brothers . . . . .Colorado
Russell, C. . . . . .Texas
Russell, F. E. (Mrs.) . . . . .Iowa
Russell, Frank . . . . .Arizona
Russell, George . . . . .Montana
Russell, George H. . . . . .California
Russell, I. C. .Idaho
Russell, John . . . . .Oregon, Texas
Russell, John F. . . . . .Texas
Russell, Katherine L. . . . . .California
Russell, R. W. . . . . .New Mexico
Russell, Samuel B. . . . . .Texas
Russell, W. F. . . . . .Kansas
Russell, Warren H. . . . . .Colorado
Russell, William F. . . . . .Arizona
Russell's Studio . . . . .California
Rust . . . . .Minnesota

Ruth, J. . . . . .California
Rutherford, Louisa . . . . .Arkansas
Rutter & Nesbitt . . . . .Montana
Rutter, Thomas H. . . . . . .Montana, Washington
Ryan & Company, T. W. . . . . .Nebraska
Ryan, D. J. .Colorado
Ryan, J. M. . . . . .California
Ryan, W. A. .Dakota
Ryden . . . . .Arizona
Ryden & Westberg . . . . .Arizona
Ryerson, R. D. . . . . .Minnesota
Ryerson, R. D. (Mrs.) . . . . .Minnesota
Ryley . . . . .Nebraska

S

S & Y . . . . .Oregon
Saari, Alfred A. . . . . .Oregon
Sabine, James E. . . . . .Colorado, New Mexico
Sache & Potter . . . . .Texas
Sackrider, Delzie Brown . . . . .California
Sackrider, Henry . . . . .California, Oregon
Sacramento Gallery . . . . .California
Sadler, George . . . . .Arizona
Safford, O. D. . . . . .California
Sage, W. W. . . . . .California
Sainsbury & Johnson . . . . .Utah
Sainsbury, Hyrum . . . . .Utah
Saint, T. G. . . . . .Colorado
Saito, I. . . . . .Oregon
Sakata, Z. .California
Sakurai, S. .California
Salb, A. (Mrs.) . . . . .California
Salb, Albert .Oregon
Sale Brothers . . . . .Traveling
Sale, George E. . . . . .New Mexico
Sale, J. A. . . . . .New Mexico
Salem Art Company . . . . .Oregon
Salmela, H. .Oregon
Salmon Brothers . . . . .Oklahoma
Salmon, William . . . . .California
Salsbury, Frederick Thurston . . . .British Columbia
Salter & Taylor . . . . .Dakota
Salter, J. Kerr . . . . .West Canada
Samain, Charles O. . . . . .Oregon
Samano, Raymond . . . . .Arizona
Samelson & Company . . . . .Colorado
Sammis & Hills . . . . .California
Sammis, Edward M. . . .California, Idaho, Oregon,
                                Traveling, Washington
Sampson & McMillen . . . . .Dakota
Sampson, John Wallace . . . . . . .British Columbia
Samson . . . . .California
Samson & Corning . . . . .Iowa
Samson, Eva (Miss) . . . . .California
Samson, W. H. . . . . .Iowa
Samson, William H. . . . . .Texas
Samuel, Tutley . . . . .Texas
Samuels . . . . .California
Samuels & Forzani . . . . .California
Samuels, Michael A. . . . . .California
Samuelson, C. .Utah
San Francisco Art & Photograph
     Gallery . . . . .California
San Francisco Gallery . . . . . . .California, Oregon
San Francisco Photograph Gallery . .New Mexico
San Francisco Railroad Studio Car . . . . . .Traveling
Sanborn, G. B. . . . . .Colorado
Sanborn, Vail & Company . . . . .Oregon
Sandberg . . . . .Nebraska
Sandeen, William . . . . .Oregon
Sander, Louis . . . . .Idaho
Sanders . . . . .Arizona, California, Iowa
Sanders & Morton . . . . .Oregon
Sanders & Stinson . . . . .California
Sanders, A. M. . . . . .Dakota
Sanders, Boughton E. . . . . .Oregon
Sanders, Dr. .Texas
Sanders, Martin L. . . . . .Texas

Sears, Charles . . . . California
Sears, Charles L. . . . . California
Sears, John . . . . California
Seavy, F. D. . . . . Colorado
Seckner, S. H. . . . . Colorado
Secor, H. H. (Mrs.) . . . . California
Sedgwick, Stephen J. . . . . Utah
Seeley, Charles M. . . . . Wisconsin
Seeley, E. C. . . . . Iowa
Seeley, S. . . . . Nebraska
Segal, A. N. . . . . New Mexico
Segerberg, Bern . . . . California, Colorado
Seibert, J. A. . . . . Missouri
Seideneck, George J. . . . . California
Seifert . . . . California
Seifert & Hudson . . . . California
Seifert, Emil . . . . Oregon
Seigmund Brothers . . . . Oregon
Seiter, E. E. . . . . Minnesota
Seitz, Perry . . . . Colorado
Selby, Belle (Miss) . . . . Kansas
Seldner, Morris . . . . California
Self, Jim . . . . Texas
Seligman, Siegmund . . . . New Mexico
Selkirk, James . . . . Texas
Selkirk, James H. & J. . . . . Texas
Selkirk, James H. . . . . Texas
Sellars, M. J. (Mrs.) . . . . Nebraska
Sellars, M. J. . . . . Nebraska
Selleck & Fisher . . . . California
Selleck, F. L. . . . . Oregon
Selleck, Silas . . . . California
Sellers . . . . Iowa
Sellon & Bennett . . . . Traveling
Sellon, Oscar . . . . Kansas
Sellwood Photo Studio . . . . Oregon
Selring, Julia P. (Mrs.) . . . . Texas
Selvidge, Sol M. . . . . Texas
Selwood, Archibald . . . . British Columbia
Selwyn, Alfred Richard Cecil . . . . British Columbia
Semita . . . . Hawaii
Senbeauber, F. . . . . Texas
Sennett, E. C. . . . . Wisconsin
Senter, William B. . . . . Texas
Sequin, Cevor & Scott . . . . Texas
Serdinko . . . . California
Serdinko, J. . . . . Dakota
Serdinko, John . . . . Texas
Serkinko, Julius . . . . Texas
Seron, Henry M. . . . . California
Sertz, Joseph . . . . Texas
Service, William . . . . Oregon
Sesser, William F. . . . . Hawaii
Sethen, I. J. . . . . Dakota, Idaho
Setzer & Roth . . . . Missouri
Seufert, Arthur . . . . Oregon
Seufert, Frank . . . . Oregon
Severance, Asel E. . . . . Oregon
Severans . . . . Wisconsin
Severin, Frank A. . . . . California
Severin, Theodore P. . . . . Hawaii
Severson, O. . . . . Nebraska
Seveson, George F. . . . . Texas
Sevom, George . . . . Texas
Seward, C. G. . . . . Oregon
Sewell, Daniel . . . . California
Sewell, Edith . . . . California
Sexton, James H. . . . . Arizona
Seymour & Company . . . . Texas
Seymour, H. A. . . . . Iowa
Seymour, James . . . . Colorado
Seymour, N. S. . . . . Iowa
Seymour, Vivus . . . . Oregon
Shafer & Hulse . . . . Oregon
Shafer, John . . . . Kansas
Shafer, Robert A. . . . . Oregon
Shafer, Samuel J. . . . . Oregon
Shaff . . . . Missouri
Shaff, Martin V. . . . . California
Shaffer & Son, S. W. . . . . Iowa
Shaffer, David N. . . . . California
Shaffer, H. W. . . . . Arkansas
Shaffer, S. W. . . . . Iowa
Shaffner & Milner . . . . Colorado
Shaffner, C. H. . . . . Colorado
Shague, H. L. . . . . California
Shaker . . . . Wisconsin
Shakespeare, Noah . . . . British Columbia, West Canada
Shalenberger & Houck . . . . Texas
Shalenberger, O. S. . . . . Texas
Shambeau Studio . . . . Kansas
Shampang, B. A. . . . . Nebraska
Shanafelt . . . . Iowa
Shanafelt, Emma E. . . . . Oregon
Shanafelt, William F. . . . . Oregon
Shanahan & Dufrene . . . . Oregon
Shand, M. E. (Miss) . . . . British Columbia
Shane & Son . . . . Kansas
Shane, J. B. . . . . Kansas, Traveling
Shane, June Belle . . . . Kansas
Shannon . . . . Kansas, Missouri
Shannon & Bird . . . . California
Shannon, John C. . . . . Texas
Shannon, Julia (Mrs.) . . . . California
Shannon, T. E. . . . . Iowa
Sharp & Lair . . . . Iowa
Sharp, W. A. . . . . Kansas
Sharp, W. E. . . . . Texas
Sharp, William . . . . California
Shasta County View Company . . . . California
Shattuck, William H. . . . . California
Shaug, H. L. . . . . California
Shauum & Leach . . . . Texas
Shaver, J. C. . . . . Colorado, Nebraska
Shaver Studio . . . . Oregon
Shaw & Company, J. W. . . . . Texas
Shaw & Lambert . . . . California
Shaw, A. G. . . . . Nebraska
Shaw, C. H. . . . . Arizona
Shaw, C. M. . . . . Nebraska
Shaw, David C. . . . . Washington
Shaw, Douglas . . . . Oregon
Shaw, George M. . . . . New Mexico
Shaw, H. W. . . . . California
Shaw, J. L. . . . . Texas
Shaw, J. W. . . . . Colorado, Texas
Shaw, Seth Louis . . . . California
Shaw, Sophronia Caroline . . . . California
Shaw, William . . . . California
Sheane, Robert . . . . Oregon, Washington
Shear & Parker . . . . Iowa, Traveling
Shear, S. R. . . . . Iowa
Sheek . . . . New Mexico
Sheilds, Hazel . . . . Oregon
Shelby, William . . . . Texas
Sheldon & Roberts . . . . Texas
Sheldon, G. A. . . . . Texas
Sheldon, John Kirk . . . . California
Sheldon Photo Company . . . . Colorado
Shellabarger, G. G. . . . . Kansas
Shelly . . . . Kansas
Shelton, John . . . . Arkansas
Shepard . . . . Indian Territory, Kansas, Minnesota
Shepard & Altine . . . . Nebraska
Shepard & Meyer . . . . Oregon
Shepard, F. . . . . Iowa
Shepard, W. N. P. . . . . Idaho
Shepard, William E. . . . . Nebraska
Sheperd, Frank L. . . . . Kansas
Shephard, W. B. . . . . Kansas
Shepherd . . . . California
Shepherd, George S. . . . . Oregon
Shepherd Photographic Company . . . . Minnesota
Shepherd, R. Harry . . . . Minnesota
Shepherd, William B. . . . . Texas
Sheppard, D. A. . . . . Oregon
Sheppard, Edward . . . . California
Sheppard, George . . . . California
Sheppard, L. T. . . . . California
Sherer, N. D. . . . . Texas
Sherff, L. . . . . Texas
Sherholtz . . . . Colorado
Sherican, C. H. . . . . Iowa
Sheriff, Thomas B. . . . . California
Sherman . . . . Iowa
Sherman & Brown . . . . Oregon
Sherman, C. V. . . . . Wisconsin
Sherman, Clifton G. . . . . Idaho
Sherman, Samuel W. . . . . Texas
Sherman, W. H. . . . . Wisconsin
Sherman, William A. . . . . Oregon
Sherraden . . . . Iowa
Sherraden, C. H. . . . . Iowa
Sherrell & Yates . . . . Texas
Sherriff, John A. . . . . California
Sherriff's Gallery . . . . California
Sherwood, Lou . . . . California
Sherwood, Samuel P. . . . . Oregon
Sheuey, M. . . . . Nebraska
Shew & Bradford . . . . California
Shew, Jacob . . . . California
Shew, Myron . . . . California
Shew, William . . . . California
Sheythe, E. G. . . . . Oregon
Shields, George J. . . . . Texas
Shields, George Oliver . . . . British Columbia
Shiffert, Fred R. . . . . Oklahoma
Shillcock . . . . Arizona
Shimanoto, F. . . . . California
Shipler & Company . . . . Colorado
Shipler & Robinson . . . . Colorado
Shipler & Shew . . . . Colorado
Shipler & Williamson . . . . Colorado
Shipler, Harry . . . . Utah
Shipler, James William . . . . Colorado, Montana, Utah
Shippy . . . . California
Shirey, C. R. . . . . Nebraska
Shirley, George A. . . . . Colorado
Shive, William . . . . Texas
Shiveley, E. W. . . . . Washington
Shockley, J. R. . . . . Missouri
Shogren, Fred A. . . . . Oregon
Shomber, A. Judson . . . . Iowa
Shoot, C. . . . . Kansas
Shore, J. T. . . . . Oklahoma
Short & Stone . . . . Kansas
Short, Charles W. . . . . Oregon
Short, E. B. . . . . Texas
Short, Gordon . . . . Oregon, Traveling
Short, H. N. . . . . California
Short, Harvey N. . . . . Kansas
Short, James H. . . . . Kansas
Short, William . . . . Texas
Shortread . . . . Dakota
Shotwell . . . . Texas
Showell & Kemmerer . . . . New Mexico
Showers, Andrew . . . . California
Shreves & Barron . . . . Texas
Shreves & Murray . . . . Texas
Shreves, William M. . . . . Texas
Shrout . . . . Kansas
Shrun, W. F. . . . . Texas
Shubert, James T. . . . . California
Shuck, Joseph . . . . Nebraska
Shufeldt, Dr. R. W. . . . . New Mexico
Shull, E. D. . . . . California
Shull, Lafayette T. . . . . Texas
Shultz, W. B. . . . . Nebraska
Shumaker, Leo . . . . Oregon
Shun, N. D. . . . . Texas
Shupe, P. T. . . . . Oregon
Shurte, Miles P. . . . . Oregon

Smith, Leila (Mrs.) . . . . . Texas
Smith, Lillian (Mrs.) . . . . . Oregon
Smith, Lloyd E. . . . . . Washington
Smith, Luke . . . . . Nebraska, Traveling
Smith, M. . . . . . Oregon
Smith, M. (Miss) . . . . . British Columbia, Kansas
Smith, M. D. & H. H. . . . . . Texas
Smith, M. L. . . . . . Minnesota
Smith, Matt K. . . . . . Oregon
Smith, Mattie G. . . . . . Idaho
Smith, Minnie (Miss) . . . . . California
Smith, O. C. . . . . . Utah
Smith, P. N. (Mrs.) . . . . . Oregon
Smith, Percy H. (Mrs.) . . . . . Oregon
Smith, R. G. . . . . . Kansas, Nebraska
Smith, R. I. . . . . . Minnesota
Smith, Ray . . . . . Oregon
Smith, Ray S. . . . . . Idaho
Smith, S. C. . . . . . Washington
Smith, S. D. (Mrs.) . . . . . Arizona
Smith, Samuel C. . . . . . Texas
Smith, Sarah (Mrs.) . . . . . Oregon
Smith, Stephen S. . . . . . Colorado
Smith, Sterling C. . . . . . Oregon
Smith, Thompson J. . . . . . Idaho
Smith, Tobe . . . . . Texas
Smith, W. B. . . . . . British Columbia
Smith, W. D. . . . . . Oregon
Smith, W. E. . . . . . Idaho
Smith, W. H. H. . . . . . Iowa
Smith, W. J. . . . . . California
Smith, W. L. . . . . . Oregon
Smith, W. S. . . . . . California
Smith, Wilfrid H. . . . . . New Mexico
Smith, William . . . . . Utah
Smith, William (Mrs.) . . . . . Oregon
Smith, William A. . . . . . New Mexico
Smith, William Alexander . . . . . Iowa
Smith, William B. . . . . . Idaho, Oregon
Smith, William E. . . . . . Texas
Smith's California Photo Car . . . . . California
Smith's California Photograph Car . . . . . Traveling
Smith–Hassell Company . . . . . Colorado
Smrcek, Joseph O. . . . . . Iowa
Smyth, H. S. St. G. . . . . . British Columbia
Smyth, Thomas P. . . . . . California
Smythe, Arthur L. . . . . . California
Smythe, Sidney Alfred . . . . . Alaska, British Columbia, West Canada
Smythe, W. H. . . . . . California
Snead, Frances . . . . . California
Snell & Blackburn . . . . . Texas
Snell & Sargent . . . . . Kansas
Snell & Thompson . . . . . Texas
Snell, A. . . . . . Texas
Snell Brothers . . . . . Texas
Snell, E. B. . . . . . Kansas
Snell, Henry W. . . . . . Texas
Snell, I. B. . . . . . British Columbia
Snell, Jennie B. . . . . . Texas
Snell, Sidney J. . . . . . Texas
Snell, Thomas W. . . . . . Texas
Snell, William H. . . . . . Texas
Snider . . . . . Colorado
Snider & Gordon . . . . . Texas
Snider, W. H. . . . . . Nebraska
Snodgrass . . . . . Texas
Snodgrass, Lucien B. . . . . . Idaho
Snodgrass, Margaret . . . . . Idaho
Snodgrass, Mary . . . . . Idaho
Snodgrass Picture Shop . . . . . Idaho
Snodgrass, William F. . . . . . Oregon
Snook . . . . . Kansas
Snow . . . . . Iowa
Snow & Roos . . . . . California
Snow, C. A. . . . . . Iowa
Snow, H. H. . . . . . Minnesota
Snyder . . . . . Indian Territory, Kansas, Nebraska, Oregon, Texas
Snyder Brothers . . . . . Minnesota
Snyder, Charles E. . . . . . Oregon
Snyder, Charles J. . . . . . Kansas
Snyder, Frank D. . . . . . Oregon
Snyder, Robert . . . . . Kansas
Snyder, Robert R. . . . . . Arkansas
Snyder, Wilson . . . . . Texas
Sobieski, F. C. . . . . . California
Soderberg, Pont . . . . . Colorado, Nebraska
Sohon, G. . . . . . California
Solano Art Gallery . . . . . California
Solberg, O. T. . . . . . Iowa
Solis, Alberto L. . . . . . New Mexico, Texas
Soloman, T. D. . . . . . Texas
Solomon & Holcomb . . . . . Texas
Solomon, R. B. . . . . . Oregon
Solons, Anton . . . . . Colorado
Solsona, Joseph F. . . . . . Texas
Song, W. F. . . . . . California
Sonichseu, N. . . . . . Alaska
Sonnberger . . . . . Colorado
Sonnichsen, Charles . . . . . California
Soo, Ah . . . . . California
Sooy & Company . . . . . California
Sooy & Poley . . . . . Colorado
Sooy, B. F. . . . . . Idaho
Sooy, Benjamin . . . . . Colorado
Sooy, Benton F. . . . . . Utah
Soper, Emma K. . . . . . California
Soper, Roy W. . . . . . Colorado
Sorensen, C. . . . . . Traveling
Sorensen, H. C. . . . . . Washington
Sorensen, J. H. C. . . . . . Oregon
Sorenson . . . . . California
Sorenson, A. . . . . . Oregon
Sorenson, Claus . . . . . Iowa
Souby . . . . . Texas
Soule . . . . . Kansas
Soule & Feather . . . . . Kansas
Soule, Cornelius J. . . . . . West Canada
Soule, Frances . . . . . California
Soule, John P. . . . . . Washington
Soule, W. A. . . . . . Idaho
Soule, William S. . . . . . Indian Territory, Kansas, Oklahoma
Sourisseau, T. . . . . . California
Sours & Company, Charles W. . . . . . Colorado
Sours & Company, Robert S. . . . . . Colorado
Sours Brothers . . . . . Colorado
Sours, Charles W. . . . . . Idaho
Sours, Levi L. . . . . . Oregon
Sours, R. . . . . . Missouri
Sours, R. S. . . . . . Idaho
South Park Photograph Gallery . . . . . California
South Western Publishing Company . . . . . Kansas
Southard, Dr. W. F. . . . . . California
Southerland Sisters . . . . . Idaho
Southern Art Gallery . . . . . Texas
Southern Pacific Railroad Company . . . . California
Southern Photograph Company . . . . . Arkansas
Southwestern Portrait Company . . . . . Texas
Southworth, Albert Sands . . . . . California
Souvenir Photograph Studio . . . . . California
Souvenir Photographic Studio . . . . . California
Souviner Art Studio . . . . . Washington
Sowell, A. D. . . . . . Texas
Sowell, Burrell . . . . . Texas
Sowell, Franklyn S. . . . . . Oregon
Sowell, Joseph Clyde . . . . . Oregon
Spagliam, H. D. . . . . . Texas
Spakes, J. G. . . . . . Nebraska
Spaller, Henry T. . . . . . Kansas
Spang, Amelia . . . . . California
Sparkman, William . . . . . Texas
Sparks, W. A. . . . . . Dakota
Spatz (Mrs.) . . . . . California
Spaugh, Charles H. . . . . . Oregon
Spaulding . . . . . Washington
Spaulding & A. Chalfant . . . . . California
Spaulding Brothers . . . . . Iowa
Spaulding, G. W. . . . . . California
Spaulding, John . . . . . Kansas
Spaulding, W. R. . . . . . Oregon
Speake . . . . . Missouri
Speake & Peirson . . . . . Nebraska
Speake, J. Grant . . . . . Nebraska
Spear, Clara . . . . . California
Spearman, I. . . . . . Texas, Traveling
Specht, J. F. . . . . . Iowa
Speece & Aaron . . . . . Arkansas
Spencer & Hastings . . . . . British Columbia
Spencer, Augustus I. . . . . . Arkansas
Spencer, E. G. M. . . . . . Nebraska
Spencer, F. M . . . . . Idaho
Spencer, Mary (Miss) . . . . . British Columbia
Spencer, Stephen Allen . . . . . British Columbia
Spencer, William . . . . . Wisconsin
Sperry . . . . . Iowa
Sperry, Myra E. (Miss) . . . . . California, Oregon
Spesert, Mary . . . . . California
Spettel Brothers . . . . . Wisconsin
Spicer & Bumbarger . . . . . Kansas
Spicer, C. A. . . . . . Wisconsin
Spiller . . . . . Texas
Spiller & Griffin . . . . . Texas
Spink & Horton . . . . . Wisconsin
Spinks, W. H. . . . . . British Columbia
Spitzey, Edwin . . . . . Kansas
Spitzley, William L. . . . . . New Mexico
Splane, Charles U. . . . . . California
Splitgerben, Julius . . . . . Texas
Sponaugle, M. L. . . . . . New Mexico
Spooner, A. E. (Mrs.) . . . . . Nebraska
Spooner, John Pitcher . . . . . California, Utah
Spooner, Maude . . . . . Iowa
Spooner, Susan M. B. (Miss) . . . . . California
Spotts, J. B. . . . . . Oklahoma
Spracklen & Ghormley . . . . . Colorado
Sprague & Severans . . . . . Wisconsin
Sprague, E. J. (Mrs.) . . . . . Minnesota
Sprague, Lucien A. . . . . . California
Sprague, T. A. . . . . . California
Sprain, John Frederick . . . . . Texas
Spring, A. . . . . . Wisconsin
Spring, Pearl . . . . . Wyoming
Spring, W. G. . . . . . Wisconsin
Spring, W. G. & A. . . . . . Wisconsin
Sprinks, W. . . . . . Texas
Sproul & Sanders . . . . . California
Sproul, James J. . . . . . Texas
Sproul, William C. . . . . . Texas
Spruitt & McCord . . . . . Texas
Spurgeon, John M. . . . . . Oregon
Spurr, E. W. . . . . . Iowa
Squier, E. B. . . . . . Traveling
Squier, L. S. . . . . . Traveling
Squire & Crowell . . . . . Washington
Squire's Traveling Photograph Gallery . . . Traveling
Squires, Con. F. . . . . . Kansas
Srirai . . . . . Hawaii
St. Clair, Alexander . . . . . Kansas
St. Clair, Edward . . . . . Arizona
St. Clair, Fred E. . . . . . Kansas
St. John, W. B. . . . . . West Canada
St. Louis Art Studio . . . . . Oregon
St. Louis Art & Photographic Gallery . . . California
Stacey, C. I. . . . . . Arizona
Stacy, Carrie . . . . . Iowa
Stacy, George . . . . . Wyoming
Stacy, J. W. . . . . . Traveling
Stadden, J. H. . . . . . Oregon
Stadon, J. E. . . . . . Minnesota
Staehr, Anna . . . . . Oregon
Staehr, Emma . . . . . Oregon
Stafford & Company . . . . . Minnesota

Stokes, A. . . . . .Wisconsin
Stokey, David G. . . . . .Texas
Stoll, George . . . . .Colorado
Stoll, Lottie N. (Mrs.) . . . . .Colorado
Stolpe, Herman . . . . .Hawaii
Stolte, E. H. . . . . .Oregon
Stone . . . . .Arizona, California
Stone & Company . . . . .Colorado
Stone & Hansard . . . . .Texas
Stone & Needles . . . . .Colorado
Stone & Reed . . . . .Texas
Stone & Waggoner . . . . .Texas
Stone, A. C. . . . . .Dakota
Stone, Andrew Jackson . . . . . . .British Columbia
Stone, C. B. . . . . .Oregon
Stone, Charles E. . . . . .Traveling
Stone, D. W. . . . . .Kansas
Stone, Dudley . . . . .Arkansas
Stone, E. . . . . .Utah
Stone, E. J. . . . . .Oregon
Stone, Edward . . . . .Texas
Stone, Elmer B. . . . . .Kansas
Stone, Fred L. . . . . .Arizona
Stone, George . . . . .Kansas
Stone, J. .Nebraska
Stone, J. G. . . . . .Missouri
Stone, Robert J. . . . . .Texas
Stone, S. E. . . . . .Oregon
Stonecipher, James A. . . . . .Arkansas
Stonecypher, E. A. . . . . .Nebraska, New Mexico
Stoneman, J. S. . . . . .Colorado
Stoner, Hopewell M. . . . . .Kansas
Stoner, S. B. . . . . .Kansas
Stonestreet, M. . . . . .Iowa
Stonne, H. C. . . . . .Texas
Stoops, L. M. . . . . .Iowa
Stoops, William . . . . .Iowa
Stork, Eugene B. . . . . .Texas
Storke, C. A. . . . . .California
Storm Brothers . . . . .Colorado
Storm, Francis D. . . . . .Colorado
Stormer & Company . . . . .Colorado
Stormer & Nelson . . . . .California
Stormer, H. W. . . . . .Colorado
Stormer, John Benton . . . . .British Columbia,
                                        California
Story, Robert M. . . . . .Texas
Story, W. P. .Texas
Stott, George . . . . .Colorado
Stotz, C. C. . . . . .Arkansas, Oklahoma
Stout . . . . .Missouri
Stout, B. D. . . . . .Nebraska
Stovall & Company . . . . .Texas
Stovall, J. F. . . . . .Texas
Stover . . . . .Texas
Stover, A. C. . . . . .Nebraska
Stover, Alexander . . . . .Texas
Stowe . . . . .Kansas
Stowe, E. G. . . . . .Missouri
Stowe, H. D. . . . . .Kansas
Strader .California
Straffin, Fred D. . . . . .Idaho
Strain . . . . .Kansas
Strain, Fannie . . . . .Texas
Straininger & McKee . . . . .Iowa
Straiton, Thomas Bell . . . . .British Columbia
Strand Studio . . . . .Arizona
Strand, Walter . . . . .Alaska
Strang, Amelia (Mrs.) . . . . .Idaho
Strasburg, Henry . . . . .Nebraska
Stratford . . . . .California
Stratford, J. L. . . . . .Oregon
Stratford, Joseph C. . . . . .Oregon
Strathmann, F. B. . . . . .Kansas
Strathmann, F. J. . . . . .Kansas
Straube, E. . . . . .British Columbia
Straus, Edward . . . . .Oregon
Strauss .Missouri

Strauss, A. C. . . . . .Nebraska
Strauss, B. F. . . . . .Dakota
Strebeck, W. M. . . . . .California
Streeter .Oklahoma
Streeter, G. A. . . . . .California, Kansas
Streeter, J. E. . . . . .Colorado
Streeter, Solomon . . . . .Kansas
Strei, Dora (Miss) . . . . .California
Streit, F. W. . . . . .Wisconsin
Strelow, Serdinko & Company . . . . . . .California
Streuser, M. J. . . . . .Iowa
Strickland, J. . . . . .Texas
Strickland, Mattie (Mrs.) . . . . .Texas
Strickland, T. B. . . . . .Arkansas
Strickrott, John F. . . . . .Kansas
Stridborg, J. A. . . . . .Nebraska, Minnesota
Stright, Charles . . . . .California
Stringer, A. R. . . . . .Oregon
Stringfellow, E. T. & F. . . . . .New Mexico
Stringfellow, F. W. . . . . .Colorado
Stringfield, Alfred Moore . . . . .California
Stringfield, Mina (Mrs.) . . . . .California
Stringham & Howarth . . . . .Utah
Stringham, John . . . . .Utah
Stroinsten, J. M. . . . . .Iowa
Strole, M. A. . . . . .Oregon
Stromston, J. M. . . . . .Nebraska
Strong & Gadion . . . . .California
Strong & Hargroves . . . . .Colorado
Strong, B. F. . . . . .California
Strong, C. C. . . . . .California
Strong, Charles . . . . .California
Strong, George M. . . . . .Oregon
Strong, J. D. . . . . .California
Strong, Joseph D., Jr. . . . . .Hawaii
Strong, Mark Hopkins . . . . .California
Strong, Nathan B. . . . . .California
Strong, Wallace Kealola . . . . .California
Stronsten, Sophia . . . . .Iowa
Stroop, J. F. . . . . .Texas
Stroud . . . . .Kansas
Stroud, W. L. . . . . .Wisconsin
Struble, W. B. . . . . .Oregon
Struckman, Frank . . . . .Idaho, Traveling
Struckmann . . . . .California
Strukman, P. . . . . .Oregon
Strunz & Woodward . . . . .California
Strusser, J. J. . . . . .Iowa
Stryker, C. M. (Mrs.) . . . . .Oregon
Stryker, David S. . . . . .Oregon
Stuart, George E. . . . . .Oregon
Stuart, W. F. . . . . . . .Arizona, New Mexico, Texas
Stuart, William McCorsin . . . . .California
Stubbs & Cammack . . . . .Iowa
Stubbs & Phillips . . . . .California
Stubbs, C. L. . . . . .Arizona, Oregon
Studebaker . . . . .Colorado
Studio De Luxe . . . . .Oregon
Studio Deluxe . . . . .Oregon
Studio Grand . . . . .Kansas
Studio Jackson . . . . .Kansas
Stuehrk, Julius . . . . .Colorado
Stule, F. P. . . . . .Nebraska
Stultz, H. P. . . . . .New Mexico
Stump . . . . .Texas
Stupl, Anton . . . . .Texas
Sturdevant, Eugenio K. . . . . .Texas
Sturdevant, J. B. . . . . .Nebraska
Sturgess, C. & Taylor, G. T. . . . . .Utah
Sturgess, O. G. . . . . .Oregon
Sturtevant & Pruden . . . . .Colorado
Sturtevant, A. . . . . .California, Oregon
Sturtevant, Joseph Bevier . . . . .Colorado
Stutsman, W. G. . . . . .Nebraska
Styles (Mrs.) . . . . .Wisconsin
Suck, Kai . . . . .California
Suden . . . . .Traveling
Sufea, Frank . . . . .Arizona

Sullesbery .Texas
Sullivan .Traveling
Sullivan & Jenkins . . . . .California
Sullivan, Cornelius R. . . . . .Oregon
Sullivan, Mary (Miss) . . . . .Colorado
Sullivan, P. J. . . . . .California
Sullivan, Patrick . . . . .Kansas
Sullivan, Timothy Alfred . . . . .California
Sullivan, William L. . . . . .California
Sumerlin, J. F. . . . . .New Mexico
Sumida . . . . .Hawaii
Summerhayes . . . . .Wisconsin
Summerhays, William . . . . .California
Summers, George . . . . .Kansas
Summers, J. M. W. . . . . .Texas
Summers, Walter . . . . .Washington
Sumner & Bingham . . . . .Minnesota
Sumner, Ira E. . . . . .Minnesota
Sun Pearl Gallery . . . . .Montana
Sun Publishing Company . . . . .Kansas
Sunbeam Gallery . . . . .California, Minnesota,
                                Nebraska, Nevada
Sunbeam Gallery & Studio . . . . .Montana
Sunbeam Photo Studio . . . . . . .British Columbia
Sunbeam Photograph Gallery . . . . .Nevada
Sunbeam Studio . . . . .Arizona
Sunderland, J. C. . . . . .Kansas
Sunderland, W. F. . . . . . . .Minnesota, Wisconsin
Sundy, H. R. . . . . .Nebraska
Sunflower Portrait Gallery . . . . .Kansas
Sunib, A. J. .Iowa
Sunnes, Nels . . . . .Iowa
Sunset Photo Company . . . . .Oregon
Superior Gallery . . . . .Oregon
Suppinger, A. E. . . . . .Arizona, Traveling
Surber, Sylvester A. . . . . .Texas
Susong . . . . .Iowa
Sutphen, Perry D. . . . . .Oregon
Sutter . . . . .Wisconsin
Sutterley & Noe . . . . .Nevada
Sutterley Brothers & Junk . . . . .Idaho
Sutterley, Clement . . . . .Idaho
Sutterley, James Kimball . . . . .Idaho
Sutterly & Dart . . . . .California, Traveling
Sutterly Brothers . . . . . .California, Idaho, Nevada,
                                        Utah
Sutterly, Charles . . . . .California
Sutterly, Clement . . .California, Nevada, Traveling
Sutterly, J. K. . . . . .California, Nevada
Suttle & Rice . . . . .Arkansas
Suttle, Henry J. . . . . .Arkansas
Suttle, Jacob H. . . . . .Arkansas
Sutton .California
Sutton & Cromwell . . . . .California
Sutton, Cora A. . . . . .California, Oregon
Suwa, T. R. . . . . .Hawaii
Suzlem, C. C. . . . . .Texas
Swafford & Swafford . . . . .Texas
Swafford, Adolph . . . . .Texas
Swain . . . . .California
Swain & Simas . . . . .California
Swain & Welsh . . . . .California
Swain, Alice (Miss) . . . . .California
Swain, Allen . . . . .Minnesota
Swain, J. . . . . .Texas
Swain, John J. . . . . .Oregon
Swain, L. A. (Mrs.) . . . . .Minnesota
Swain, Lewis C. . . . . .California
Swain, S. . . . . .Traveling
Swain's Gallery . . . . .Minnesota
Swaine & Mote's Photographic Chariot . .Traveling
Swan & Taylor . . . . .Missouri
Swan, B. P . . . . .Iowa
Swan Brothers . . . . .Colorado
Swan, Carter G. . . . . .Missouri
Swan, Fred W. . . . . .Kansas
Swan, George B. . . . . .Texas
Swan, James C. . . . . .Traveling

Thomas, Joseph J.	Texas
Thomas Manufacturing Company	California
Thomas, P. W.	New Mexico
Thomas, R. F.	Texas
Thomas, W. L.	Nebraska
Thomas, William H.	Texas
Thomas, William W.	Minnesota
Thomas' Photographic Car	Traveling
Thomason	Missouri
Thomason & Leffler	Texas
Thomason, Sophie (Mrs.)	Colorado
Thomberger, Martin	California
Thompson	Colorado, Idaho, Kansas, Missouri, Nebraska, Texas
Thompson & Bovill	British Columbia
Thompson & Company, D. P.	Missouri
Thompson & Louden	Wisconsin
Thompson & Paxton	Oregon
Thompson & Young	Utah
Thompson, Alvah B.	Colorado
Thompson Arts	Missouri
Thompson, B. R.	Oregon
Thompson Brothers	Oregon
Thompson, C. C.	Iowa
Thompson, Charles	Idaho
Thompson, Cornelius	California
Thompson, D.	California
Thompson, D. A. L.	Kansas
Thompson, Dr. Ransom	California
Thompson, E. M. (Miss)	California
Thompson, George	Texas
Thompson, Granville W.	Arkansas
Thompson, Gus S.	Texas
Thompson, H. Lawrence	Colorado
Thompson, Harry	California, Iowa, Oregon
Thompson, Isabella M.	Kansas
Thompson, J. S.	Texas
Thompson, James	Oregon
Thompson, James R.	Texas
Thompson, John E.	British Columbia
Thompson, L. A.	Oregon, Texas
Thompson, P. J.	California
Thompson, Robert M.	Texas
Thompson, Rutha	Texas
Thompson, S. C.	Texas
Thompson, Samuel F.	Wisconsin
Thompson, Stephen Joseph	British Columbia
Thompson Studio	Kansas
Thompson, T. A.	Colorado
Thompson, W.	Texas
Thompson, W. C.	Idaho
Thompson, W. W.	Texas
Thompson, William S.	Texas
Thompson, Z.	Colorado
Thomson & Billington	California
Thomson, D. P.	Missouri
Thorild, Annie	Idaho
Thornblod, Olaf L.	Texas
Thornbrough	California
Thornbrue, G. H.	Iowa
Thorne, H. J.	Oregon
Thorne, H. J. (Mrs.)	Oregon
Thorne, Wayne	Nebraska
Thorne, William E.	Missouri
Thornley	Oklahoma
Thornton, A. C.	Oregon
Thornton, C. F.	Oregon
Thornton Photography	Oregon
Thors, Gertrude M. (Mrs.)	California
Thors, Katherine	California
Thors, Louis	California
Thrall, Samuel A.	Oregon
Thrane & Ringe	Minnesota
Thrane Art Company	Minnesota
Thrane, P. E.	Minnesota
Thrasher, A. F.	California, Idaho, Montana, Traveling
Threshkeld, Harry	Texas
Threshkeld, Mattie	Texas
Throwbeck, Samuel J. O.	Colorado
Thuemmler, Ph. E.	Wisconsin
Thum & Miller	Oregon
Thum, Edward E.	Oregon
Thumann, Henry, Jr.	Oregon
Thune	Minnesota
Thunen, William	California
Thupps, L. A.	Texas
Thurlow, James	Colorado, New Mexico
Thurman, A. M.	Texas
Thurmond, R.	Minnesota
Thwaites & Potter	Oregon
Thwaites, George H.	Arizona
Thwaites, Joseph	California, Oregon
Tibbets, H. C.	Arizona
Tibbs, Nathan J.	Arkansas
Tice, Arthur L.	Kansas
Tice, Jacob A.	Wisconsin
Tidball, Alexander Scott	California
Tidd, A. M. (Miss)	California
Tiderman, B. C.	Kansas
Tidwell, J. E.	Texas
Tieman, C. H.	California, Hawaii
Tierney, H.	Iowa
Tiers, William C.	Texas
Tiesman & Key	Arizona
Tilford, William H.	Missouri
Tillotson & Thompson	Nebraska
Tillotson, F. B.	Iowa
Tillotson, Frank H.	Arizona
Timms, Philip Thomas	British Columbia
Timpe, August	Iowa
Timson, William	Oregon
Tinkel, Frank B.	Texas
Tinkle, F. B.	Oregon
Tisinger, R. M.	Arizona
Titsworth, C. G.	Texas
Tittler, L. L.	Colorado
Titus, T. J.	Nebraska
Tobias	Missouri
Tobias & Company	Missouri
Tobita, U.	Hawaii
Toblar, Louis	Texas
Tobler, S.	Texas
Todd, John A.	California
Toe, Laer	Texas
Tokyokan, Y. Takagi	Oregon
Toles, Herbert L.	Washington
Toley & Bugbee	Wisconsin
Toll, William B.	California
Tollman & Oltman	California
Tollman & Pratsch	California
Tollman & Preston	Washington
Tollman, John W. (Mrs.)	California, Traveling
Tollman, John W.	California, Idaho, Nebraska, Oregon, Traveling, Washington
Tollman, Lulu (Mrs.)	Oregon
Tollman Studio	Oregon
Tollman, Thomas W.	Oregon, Washington
Tolman, T. W.	Iowa, Nebraska
Tomkin, Herbert	California
Tomkins, E. P.	Missouri
Tomlinson Brothers	Missouri
Tomlinson, James A.	New Mexico
Tompsett, William	Nebraska
Tonge	California
Tonkin & Griffin	Idaho
Tonkin, George E.	Idaho
Tooker, Johnathan L.	New Mexico
Tooley	Kansas
Topley, Horatio Nelson	British Columbia
Topping, Ada (Mrs.)	Idaho
Topping, H. H.	Idaho
Tordt, T.	Texas
Torell, S. P.	Nebraska
Torp, A. N.	Iowa
Torres & Brothers	New Mexico
Torres, A. C.	New Mexico
Torres, M.	New Mexico
Tosdal, H. H.	Iowa
Tossell, W. P.	New Mexico
Towne	Oregon
Towne & Moore	Oregon
Towne, B. C.	California
Towne, Bertram C.	Oregon
Towne, C. C.	Oregon
Towne, Lucy A.	Oregon
Towne, Ralph W.	Oregon
Towne, Walter E.	Oregon
Towne, William H.	California, Oregon
Towner, C. S. (Mrs.)	Colorado
Towner, H.	Oregon
Towner, Henry C.	Colorado
Townsend	Colorado
Townsend & Hathaway	Colorado
Townsend, A. C.	Nebraska
Townsend Brothers	Nebraska
Townsend, C. O.	Nebraska
Townsend, George F.	Texas
Townsend, I. L.	Iowa, Nebraska
Townsend, J. A.	Nebraska
Townsend, J. N.	Iowa
Townsend, J. W.	Nebraska
Townsend, L. L.	Kansas
Townsend, L. M.	Iowa
Townsend, Smith Platt	California
Townsend, T. W.	Iowa, Nebraska
Townsend, W. J.	Oregon
Townsley, Isaac M.	Oregon
Toy, Chin K.	California
Toyberg, L. J.	Minnesota
Traber, P. J.	Nebraska
Tracey, F. B.	Oregon
Tracht, William W.	Colorado
Tracie, E. H.	Montana
Tracy	Texas
Trader, F. A.	Kansas
Trader Studio	Kansas
Traeumer, George	Colorado
Trager & Kuhn	Nebraska
Trager & Steadman	Nebraska
Trager, Ernest	Nebraska
Trager, George	Nebraska, Wisconsin
Train & Cromwell	Idaho
Train, Edgar H.	Montana, Traveling
Train, Edgar Henry	California
Train, Edgar Horace	Idaho
Trammell, S. C.	Texas
Transit of Venus Expedition	Hawaii
Trantlow, William C.	Texas
Traphagen, V. C.	Idaho
Trask, Robert T.	Colorado
Trask, S. E.	Oregon
Traulsen Brothers	Nebraska
Traulsen, Peter	Nebraska
Travis & Birkland	Texas
Travis, Fannie B. (Mrs.)	Texas
Travis, W. R.	Colorado
Treat & Grant	California
Treat, A. R.	California, Kansas
Treat, Archibald	California
Tremayne, H. A.	British Columbia
Trendel, John A.	Colorado
Trenham, Newton J.	Minnesota
Tressider, John	California
Tresslar & Gifford	Kansas
Tresslar Brothers	Kansas
Tresslar, Elkanah P.	California, Kansas
Tresslar, Herbert	Kansas
Tresslar, Mable H.	California
Tresslar, S. P.	California, Kansas
Trigg	Kansas
Triloff, William	Nebraska
Trimble	Indian Territory
Trimble & Shepard	Nebraska

Van Winkle, Emma (Miss) . . . . .California
Van Winkle, Isaac L. . . . . .Oregon
Vanadis Expedition . . . . .Hawaii
Vance, E. H. . . . . .California
Vance, George . . . . .Minnesota
Vance, M. C. . . . . .Traveling
Vance, Robert H. . . . . .California
Vance, T. R. . . . . .Texas
Vance, T. William . . . . .California
Vance, William H. . . . . .California
Vancil & McDonald . . . . .Kansas
Vancour . . . . .Arkansas
Vancouver Photo Company . . . .British Columbia
Vandermeulen, G. A. . . . . .Iowa
Vandermier, Abraham . . . . .Texas
Vandermier, Jacob . . . . .Texas
Vanderwarker & Nally . . . . .Minnesota
Vandever . . . . .Arkansas
Vandewall & Company, W. B. . . . . .Nebraska
Vandewall & Viele . . . . .Nebraska
Vandike Brothers . . . . .Nebraska
Vaniman, Melville . . . . .Hawaii
Vankaman, G. W. .Texas
Vankirk, V. . . . . .Arkansas
Vanriper, C. T. . . . . .Texas
Vansant, Joshua, Jr. . . . . .California
Vansant, William Prescott . . . . .California
Varela, A. C. . . . . .California
Varney & McCulloch . . . . .Dakota
Varney, A. K. . . . . .California
Varney, Hiram .Colorado
Varney, J. C. . . . . .Minnesota
Vasconcelles, Joseph J. . . . . .California
Vasquez, Manuel . . . . .New Mexico, Texas
Vassalo, Francis N. . . . . .Texas
Vassar Studio . . . . .Oregon
Vaughan . . . . .California, Utah
Vaughan & Fulton . . . . .British Columbia
Vaughan & Hanson . . . . .Oregon
Vaughan & Keith . . . . .California
Vaughan & Robertson . . . . . . .British Columbia
Vaughan, Emma (Mrs.) . . . . .California
Vaughan, Hector M. . . . . .California
Vaughan, Hector W. . . . . .California
Vaughan, Hiram G. . . . . .California
Vaughan, John . . . . .Oregon
Vaughan, John W. . . . . .British Columbia,
                                    California, Oregon
Vaughan, Rufus K. . . . . .California
Vaughan's First Premium Photograph
    Gallery . . . . .California
Vaughan's Photographic Gallery .British Columbia
Vaughn . . . . .Montana
Vaughn, C. . . . . .Montana
Vaughn, Cornel . . . . .Wisconsin
Vaughn, John W. .Idaho
Vaught, J. M. . . . . .Texas
Vaux Family . . . . .British Columbia
Veatch & Bull . . . . .Iowa
Veatch, A. C. . . . . .Idaho
Vedder, John H. . . . . .Wisconsin
Velarde, Bartholomew . . . .Colorado, New Mexico
Venegas, Alvino . . . . .New Mexico, Texas
Venner, J. F. . . . . .Oregon
Vergee, F. I. . . . . .Oregon
Verkin & Enos . . . . .Texas
Verkin, Paul . . . . .Texas
Verkius, Paul . . . . .Texas
Vernon, William N. . . . . .Idaho
Verser, John H. . . . . .California
Vickers, J. C. . . . . .Texas
Victor, F. F. (Mrs.) . . . . .Oregon
Victor Portrait Company . . . . .New Mexico
Victor Studio . . . . .Oregon
Victoria Theatre Photographic
    Gallery . . . . .British Columbia
Viele . . . . .Nebraska
Vierra, Carlos . . . . .New Mexico

Vieusseux, Charles Edward . . . . .British Columbia
Viking View Company . . . . .Dakota, Minnesota,
                                    Wisconsin
Vila, Joseph . . . . .Colorado
Villalobos . . . . .New Mexico, Texas
Vincent . . . . .Idaho
Vincent, Charles L. . . . . .Texas
Vincent, J. . . . . .California
Vinson, Annie . . . . .Oregon
Vinson, Pheba . . . . .Oregon
Vipond, Arthur . . . . .British Columbia
Vitalini & Bianchi . . . . .California
Vitalini, E. C. .California
Vivier & Fagersteen . . . . .Texas
Vivier, P. . . . . .Texas
Voelker, J. A. . . . . .California
Vogee, Anton . . . . .Alaska, British Columbia
Vogenitz, L. V. . . . . .Kansas
Vogenrt's Art Photos . . . . .Kansas
Voice & Company . . . . .Colorado
Voice & Comstock . . . . .Colorado
Voice & Meile .Colorado
Voice, Ulysses A. . . . . .Colorado
Voight, Leo O. . . . . .Idaho
Vollert, William P. . . . . .Wisconsin
Volquarts . . . . .Wisconsin
Volt & Martell . . . . .Kansas
Volt, J. G. . . . . .Kansas
Von Broich, Hugo . . . . .Wisconsin
Von Falkowsky, Ovan . . . . .California
Von Hasslen . . . . .California
Voorhees, C. M. (Miss) . . . . .Colorado
Voorhees, Frederick W. . . . . .New Mexico
Voorhees, Russell E. . . . . .New Mexico
Voorhies, Amos E. . . . . .Oregon
Voorhies, Edward . . . . .Texas
Voorhies, Frederick W. . . . . .Texas
Voron, F. . . . . .Texas
Vosburgh, M. H. .Iowa
Vreeland . . . . .New Mexico, Traveling
Vreeland Studio . . . . .Oklahoma
Vroman, Adam Clark . . . . .Arizona,
            British Columbia, California, New Mexico
Vullinghs, Adrian John . . . .

W

W & S . . . . .Alaska
Wadds Brothers . . . . .British Columbia
Wadds, David . . . . .British Columbia
Wadds, George Thomas . . . . . .British Columbia
Wade, Madison W. . . . . .Kansas
Wade, Marion A. .Texas
Wade Photo . . . . .Arkansas
Wadell, A. J. V. . . . . .Missouri
Waggener, James, Jr. . . . . .Washington
Waggoner, W. T. .Texas
Wagner .Colorado, Texas
Wagner, Ava (Mrs.) . . . . .California
Wagner, Charles . . . . .Oregon
Wagner, F. S. . . . . .Colorado
Wagner, Frank G. . . . . .Oregon
Wagner, Henry .Oregon
Wagner, J. A. . . . . .Wisconsin
Wagner, James . . . . .Dakota, Nebraska
Wagner, Louis . . . . .Oregon
Wagness, John T. . . . . .Washington
Wagoner, James . . . . .Nebraska
Wagy, J. S. . . . . .Oklahoma
Wahlstrom, Amanda . . . . .Minnesota
Wai Chen Hin .California
Wait . . . . .Iowa, Nebraska
Waite, C. B. . . . . .California, New Mexico
Waite, Medea L. (Mrs.) . . . . .California
Waite Photo Studio, V. H. . . . . .New Mexico
Waite, S. H. . . . . .Kansas
Waite, V. H. . . . . .Kansas
Waitley, E. B. . . . . .Iowa
Wakefield, Leland Howard . . . .Oregon, Wisconsin

Wakeley & Cobb .Texas
Wakeley, George D. . . . . .Colorado, Texas
Wakely & Clements . . . . .Colorado
Wakely, George .Kansas
Wakely, George D. . . . . .Nebraska
Walander & Burkhart . . . . .Montana
Walbridge, Cyrus Edmund . . . . .California
Walbridge, Louie C. . . . . .Kansas
Walcott . . . . .Wisconsin
Walcott, C. D. . . . . .Idaho
Walcott, Frank B. . . . . .Texas
Walderon, J. C. . . . . .Wisconsin
Waldo . . . . .Colorado
Waldo, David H. . . . . .Wisconsin
Waldon . . . . .New Mexico
Waldron . . . . .Nebraska
Waldron & Davies . . . . .Nebraska
Waldron & Wilson . . . . .Iowa
Waldron, May M. (Miss) . . . . .California
Waldter, Louis .Nebraska
Walender & Eitner . . . . .Montana
Wales, C. A. . . . . .Iowa
Wales, H. P. . . . . .Traveling
Wales, T. L. . . . . .Iowa
Walker . . . . . .California, Kansas, Texas, Wisconsin
Walker & Connor . . . . .Wisconsin
Walker & Fagersteen . . . . .California
Walker & Hemenway . . . . .California
Walker Art Company . . . . .Missouri
Walker, C. M. .California
Walker, Charles H. . . . . .California
Walker, Charles L. . . . . .Iowa
Walker, E. S. (Mrs.) . . . . .Texas
Walker, Frederick G. Eyton . . . . .Hawaii
Walker, G. W. .Arkansas
Walker, George H. . . . . .Texas
Walker, Henry J. . . . . .Wisconsin
Walker, Horace H. . . . . .New Mexico
Walker, J. W. . . . . .Colorado
Walker, Jesse M. . . . . .Oregon
Walker, John . . . . .Oregon, Texas
Walker, John A. . . . . .California, Oregon
Walker, L. S. . . . . .Wyoming
Walker, N. P. . . . . .Nebraska
Walker, Ralph C. . . . . .Oregon
Walker, Rol. . . . . .Oregon
Walker, S. C. . . . . .California
Walker, Samuel . . . . .California
Walker, Sidney . . . . .Texas
Walker, Will H. .Oregon
Walker, William H. . . . . .Colorado
Walker, William T. . . . . .Texas
Wall . . . . .Texas
Wall, Cane . . . . .Texas
Wallace . . . . .Nebraska
Wallace & Karnes . . . . .Texas
Wallace, C. W. .Nebraska
Wallace, Charles (Mrs.) . . . . .Wyoming
Wallace, E. E. .Nebraska
Wallace, Elmer E. . . . . .Texas
Wallace, George R. . . . . .Washington
Wallace, J. A. . . . . .California
Wallace, J. L. . . . . .Texas
Wallace, J. M. .California
Wallace, Jean . . . . .Kansas
Wallace, Louis . . . . .Texas
Wallace, Mat S. . . . . .Texas
Wallace, R. W. . . . . .Texas
Wallace, Richard .Texas
Wallace, Thomas J. . . . . .Wyoming
Wallace, W. C. . . . . .Iowa
Wallbaum, C. C. . . . . .Nebraska
Waller, William . . . . .Texas
Wallick, Jodie (Mrs.) . . . . .Oregon
Wallihan, Allen Grant . . . . .Colorado
Wallin, Herman E. . . . . .Oregon
Walline . . . . .Iowa, Traveling
Walline, A. L. . . . . .Iowa

Walline, A. S. ....Iowa
Walling, J. D. ....Oregon
Wallingford, J. L. ....Nebraska
Wallis, R. H. ....Texas
Wallis, W. L. ....Texas
Walsh, Anna M. ....Kansas
Walter & Weidman ....Iowa
Walter Brothers ....Nebraska
Walter, C. P. ....Nebraska
Walter, Eyer Fisher ....Idaho
Walter, H. L. ....Iowa
Walter, Paul A. F. ....New Mexico
Waltermire, C. W. ....Iowa
Waltermire, P. C. ....Iowa, Nebraska
Walters ....Texas
Walters, Charles ....Wyoming
Walters, F. E. ....Nebraska
Walters, J. F. ....Nebraska
Walters, N. ....California
Walters, S. R. ....California
Walters, William ....Wyoming
Waltgenbach, Carl ....Texas
Waltgenbach, Mary ....Texas
Walthall & Hinshaw ....Iowa
Waltmire, N. J. ....Nebraska
Walton ....Oregon
Walton, C. E. ....Arkansas
Walton, Emma F. ....California
Walton, James W. ....California
Walton, William R. ....New Mexico
Walz & Company, W. G. ....Texas
Wamble, R. ....Texas
Wamsley, William ....Kansas
Wanamaker, Rodman ....New Mexico
Wantland ....Oklahoma
Ward ....Colorado, Iowa
Ward, G. R. ....Oklahoma
Ward, Gurney E. ....Texas
Ward, H. ....British Columbia
Ward, H. T. ....Iowa
Ward, Jack ....Texas
Ward, M. T. ....Nebraska
Ward, Mary T. (Mrs.) ....Idaho
Ward, S. A. (Mrs.) ....Texas
Ward, Thomas Chester ....Oregon
Ward's Studio ....New Mexico
Ware ....California
Wareham, C. H. ....Kansas
Warge ....Minnesota
Warner ....California, Utah
Warner & Pierce ....Iowa
Warner, Daniel D. ....Oregon
Warner, F. S. (Mrs.) ....Minnesota
Warner, Henri ....Oregon
Warner, Isaac V. ....Idaho
Warner, J. ....Kansas
Warner, Joseph ....Kansas
Warner, P. H. ....Iowa
Warnky & Abbott ....Colorado, New Mexico
Warnky, F. C. ...Colorado, Missouri, New Mexico
Warnock ....Idaho
Warren ....Oregon
Warren & Son, W. E. ....California
Warren, D. W. ....Iowa
Warren, E. C. ....Oregon
Warren, Emma A. (Mrs.) ....California
Warren, Henry Stephen ....Oregon
Warren, John ....New Mexico
Warren, M. B. ....Iowa
Warren, Manly ....Oregon
Warren, Mary E. ....Texas
Warren, S. K. ....Wisconsin
Warrens, William H. ....Oregon
Warrington, A. W. ....Iowa
Warrington Brothers ....Colorado
Washburn & Bennett ....Minnesota
Washburn, Andrew L. ....Texas

Washburn, W. W. ....Iowa
Wasserman, Frank C. ....Oregon
Wasson, C. L. ....Arizona, Idaho
Wasson, R. M. ....Kansas
Wasson, Sylvester ....Texas
Waston & Simas ....California
Waterhouse & Butler ....Nevada
Waterhouse, George ....California, Nevada
Waterhouse, James ....Oregon
Waterman, George E. ....New Mexico
Waterman, Ira ....Wisconsin
Waterman, Solomon ....Texas
Waters ....California
Waters, F. E. ....Colorado
Waters, Raper James ....California, Nevada
Watkins, Branham W. ....Texas
Watkins Brothers ....Oregon, Texas
Watkins, Carleton E. .Arizona, British Columbia,
     California, Idaho, Nevada, Oregon
Watkins, Everett W. ....Oregon
Watkins, M. ....Minnesota
Watkins, Margaret ....Minnesota
Watkins, Norman R. ....Texas
Watkins, W. W. ....Texas
Watkins, Willis M. ....Texas
Watrous, Stephen W. ....California
Watson ....Oregon
Watson & Dotson ....California
Watson, A. R. ....California
Watson, Charles H. ....British Columbia
Watson, Cornelia A. ....Oregon
Watson, D. D. ....Nebraska
Watson, Guy ....Iowa
Watson, Henry W. ....Colorado
Watson, John W. ....Oregon
Watson, Joseph E. ....Oregon
Watson, Joseph W. ....Texas
Watson, O. T. ....Colorado
Watson, O. W. ...Idaho, Traveling, Washington
Watters, S. E. ....Iowa
Watts, H. Clay ....Arkansas
Watts, John E. ....Oregon
Watts, Joseph ....British Columbia
Watts, Rufus ....Texas
Watts, W. J. ....Texas
Waugh, J. C. ....Texas
Waus, Dan ....Texas
Wax & Tonge ....California
Wax, William ....California
Wear, George R. ....Texas
Weatherington Brothers ....Texas
Weatherington, George R. ....Texas
Weatherington, John W. ....Texas
Weatherly, C. L. & J. A. ....Iowa
Weatherwax, Lulu (Miss) ....California
Weaver, Davidson Roby ....California
Weaver, Hazle Judkins ....California
Weaver, Henry E. ....California
Weaver, J. L. ....Kansas
Weaver, Miles Franklin ....California
Weaver, O. F. ....Wisconsin
Weaver, William S. ....Kansas
Web, Ron ....Texas
Webb ....Indian Territory
Webb, B. F. ....Texas
Webb, D. W. ....Minnesota, Wisconsin
Webb, E. H. ....Texas
Webb, George ....California
Webb, H. & A. ....Oregon
Webb, Helen M. (Mrs.) ....Oregon
Webb, J. F. ....Iowa
Webb, J. T. ....Colorado
Webb, John ....Colorado
Webb, Rufus ....Texas
Webb, Susie E. (Mrs.) ....Oregon
Webb, William E. ....Texas
Webb, William Seward ....British Columbia

Weber ....Kansas
Weber & Klein ....Kansas
Weber, C. C. ....Nebraska
Webster ....Wisconsin, Wyoming
Webster & Pierce ....Washington
Webster & Stevens ....Alaska, Washington
Webster & Walker ....Wisconsin
Webster, A. F. ....Nebraska
Webster, Alfred ....Texas
Webster, B. ....California
Webster Brothers ....Colorado
Webster, F. A. ....California
Webster, F. W. ....Iowa
Webster, Frank H. ....Oregon
Webster, H. D. ....Colorado, Oregon
Webster, John H. ....Texas
Webster, John W. ....Idaho
Webster, Leonard A. ......Arizona, Washington
Webster Stereoscope Company ....Nebraska
Webster, W. F. ....Wisconsin
Weddington ....Texas
Wedekind, Henry ....Oregon
Wedemeyer, William George ....Texas
Wedge ....Texas
Wedmar ....Minnesota
Weed, Charles Leander ....California, Hawaii
Weed, Elizabeth (Miss) ....California
Weed, William L. ....Arizona
Weeks ....Minnesota
Weeks, J. H. ....Kansas
Weeks, R. E. ....Kansas
Weems, J. M. ....Texas
Weenink, H. D. .....Idaho, Montana, Traveling
Wegener, Virginia E. (Miss) ....California
Wegmann & Nau ....Nebraska
Wegmann, J. H. ....Nebraska
Wehe, Lydia E. ....Kansas
Weibling, Harmon G. ....Kansas
Weider ....Iowa
Weider, J. H. (Mrs.) ....Idaho, Oregon
Weidman ....Iowa
Weidman, James ....West Canada
Weidner, Charles ....California
Weigand, E. Maggie (Mrs.) ....Oregon
Weigand, Ernest ....Oregon
Weigel ....Idaho
Weigel, George H. ....Oregon
Weigel, Mary ....Iowa
Weikert, A. N. ....Nebraska
Weile, E. ....California, Oregon
Weinert, J. L. ....Iowa
Weingarth ....California
Weingartle & Burnside ....Iowa
Weintraub & Isaacs ....California
Weister, George ....Oregon
Weister–Meek Company ....Oregon
Weitfle, Charles ....Colorado
Weitfle, Paul L. ....Colorado, New Mexico, Texas
Weitz & Dijeau ....California
Weitz, Hugo ....California
Welberg, Godfrey M. ....West Canada
Welch ....Colorado, Nebraska
Welch & Stephens ....California
Welch, C. A. ....Nebraska
Welch, C. E. ....Dakota
Welch, E. (Mrs.) ....Nebraska
Welch, F. W. ....Idaho
Welch, James ....California
Welch, Jessie (Miss) ....Kansas
Welch, O. D. ....Iowa
Welch, Ruth K. ....Kansas
Welcome Studio ....Oregon
Weld, F. A. ....Nebraska
Weldin & Son ....Nebraska
Welding, Joe ....California
Weller, D. ....California
Weller, L. A. ....Nevada

Wells . . . . .California, Oregon, Missouri
Wells & Dijeau . . . . .California
Wells & Hart . . . . .Oregon
Wells & King .Colorado
Wells & Lady .California
Wells & Sears .California
Wells, Charles H. . . . . .Colorado
Wells, Ebenezer N. . . . . .Oregon
Wells, Frank . . . . .California
Wells, George N. . . . . .California
Wells, Gladys . . . . .Oregon
Wells, H. A. . . . . .Oregon
Wells, J. W. . . . . .Oregon
Wells, L. B. . . . . .Idaho
Wells, N. G. (Mrs.) . . . . .Nebraska
Wells, Thomas . . . . .Nebraska
Wells, Thomas W. . . . . .California
Welper, Henry . . . . .Wisconsin
Welsh . . . . .California
Welsh & Company . . . . .British Columbia
Welsh & Cromwell . . . . .California
Welsh, Delos . . . . .California
Welsh, Howard Milton . . . . . . .British Columbia
Welsh, J. O. . . . . .California, Oregon
Welsh, K. (Miss) . . . . .British Columbia
Welton, Arthur F. . . . . .California
Wendel, James F. . . . . .Idaho
Wendell, Della . . . . .Kansas
Wendell, Frank R. . . . . .New Mexico
Wenderoth, Frederick A. . . . . .California
Wendt, Henry . . . . .California, Oregon, Traveling
Wenfor, George . . . . .Arizona
Weninger, Frank . . . . .Oregon
Wenz, Adolph . . . . .New Mexico
Wenzler, Martha (Miss) . . . . .California
Werner, Fred . . . . .California
Werner, George P. . . . . .Oklahoma
Werts, P. D. . . . . .Iowa
Wertz . . . . .New Mexico
Wertz & Smith . . . . .New Mexico
Wertz, F. B. (Mrs.) . . . . .Oregon
Wertz, J. G. . . . . .Kansas
Wescott, C. H. . . . . .California
Wescott, D. K. . . . . .Nebraska
Wesner Brothers . . . . .Traveling
Wesner, H. B. . . . . .California
Wesner, Michael A. . . . . .California
Wessinger, Paul . . . . .Oregon
Wesson, John A. . . . . .Texas
West . . . . .Oregon
West & Brother, W. W. . . . . .Texas
West, A. M. . . . . .Texas
West, Benjamin . . . . .Texas
West, D. C. . . . . .Texas
West End Studio . . . . .Nebraska
West, H. E. . . . . .Iowa
West, H. T. .Wisconsin
West, John C. . . . . .Texas
West, Minnie . . . . .British Columbia
West, Orvil W. . . . . .Oregon
West, W. W. .Traveling
Westall, E. (Miss) . . . . .California
Westberg & Lind . . . . .Nebraska
Westberg, H. G. . . . . .Nebraska
Westberg, L. E. . . . . .Minnesota
Westberg, W. G. . . . . .Nebraska
Westbrook, J. B. . . . . .Texas
Westbrook, Sarah M. (Mrs.) . . . . .Texas
Westburg, John F. . . . . .Arizona
Westerman, Otto . . . . .Colorado
Western Photo Company . . . . .California
Western Photo Studio . . . . .Oregon
Western Photograph Association . . . . . .Traveling
Western Stereoscopic Company . . . . .New Mexico
Western View Company . . . . .Kansas
Westervelt, E. J. . . . . .New Mexico
Westervelt, James D. . . . . .California
Westgard, A. L. . . . . .Arizona

Westlake, W. J. . . . . .Colorado
Westmann, Orloff . . . . .New Mexico
Weston, E. D. . . . . .Iowa, Oregon
Weston, Edward . . . . .California
Weston, Henry . . . . .California
Weston, Nathaniel . . . . .California
Westphall, George . . . . .Texas
Westrop . . . . .Oregon, Texas, Traveling
Westwood, F. H. . . . . .California
Westwood, Fred . . . . .California
Wetherby . . . . .Iowa
Wetherby & Company . . . . .Iowa
Wetherspoon, J. F. . . . . .Texas
Weyle & Barber . . . . .Wyoming
Weyrich's Studio . . . . .Oregon
Whaite, Rene .Oregon
Whaite, William . . . . .Oregon
Whalen's Portable Gallery . . . . .Traveling
Whaley, G. V. . . . . .Traveling
Wharton–James, George . . . . .New Mexico
Whatley, James B. . . . . .Texas
Whealdon, Joshua . . . . .Texas
Wheat, Harriet E. . . . . .Texas
Wheat, O. H. . . . . .Nebraska
Wheddon & Carpenter . . . . .Texas
Wheeler . . . . .Oregon
Wheeler & Barnard Daguerrean
   Gallery .Wisconsin
Wheeler & Chase . . . . .Colorado
Wheeler & Company . . . . .Colorado
Wheeler & Plecker . . . . .Traveling
Wheeler, A. F. . . . . .Oregon
Wheeler, A. H. . . . . .Wisconsin
Wheeler, Alonzo D. . . . . .Texas
Wheeler Applied Arts Company . . . . .Washington
Wheeler, C. A. . . . . .Nebraska
Wheeler, C. L. . . . . .Colorado
Wheeler, C. M. . . . . .Kansas
Wheeler, Carl S. . . . . .Oregon
Wheeler, D. W. . . . . .Wisconsin
Wheeler, Danforth N. . . . . .Colorado
Wheeler, F. .Nebraska
Wheeler, Frank . . . . .California
Wheeler, Fred . . . . .Kansas
Wheeler, L. G. (Mrs.) . . . . .Minnesota
Wheeler, Louis I. . . . . .Oregon
Wheeler, R. S. .Iowa
Wheeler, S. F. .Iowa
Wheeler, Samuel . . . . .Wisconsin
Wheeler, Una (Miss) . . . . .Colorado
Wheeler, W. D. . . . . .Nebraska
Wheeler, Warren D. . . . . .Oregon
Wheelon, Frank H. . . . . .Oregon
Whelan, William W. . . . . .Oregon
Whelchel, Arthur M. . . . . .Idaho
Whelchel, Walter C. . . . . .Idaho
When . . . . .Missouri
Wherry, W. H. .Texas
Whigham, Richard P. . . . . .California
Whipple, John P. . . . . .Wisconsin
Whisler, H. D. . . . . .California
Whitaker, George C. . . . . .Kansas
Whitaker, W. .Kansas
Whitcomb (Mrs.) . . . . .Minnesota
Whitcomb, D. W. . . . . .Iowa
Whitcombe & Company . . . . .Colorado
White . . . . .California, Iowa, Texas
White (Miss) . . . . .California
White & Colpas . . . . .New Mexico
White & Company, Dr. A. D. . . . . . .New Mexico
White & Demmon . . . . .New Mexico
White & Leach . . . . .New Mexico
White & Underhill . . . . .California
White, A. D. . . . .Colorado, Iowa, Nebraska, Utah
White, A. P. . . . .
White, C. L. .Arizona
White, Charles W. . . . . .Colorado
White, D. P. . . . . .Texas

White, Elizabeth (Miss) . . . . .California
White, G. William (Mrs.) . . . . .California
White, George R. . . . . .California
White, H. G. . . . . .Wisconsin
White, H. J. . . . . .Utah
White, J. . . . . .British Columbia
White, John M. . . . . .British Columbia
White, Joseph L. . . . . .Texas
White, Lily E. . . . . .Oregon
White, Martin . . . . .Colorado
White, Minnie E. . . . . .Kansas
White, P. C. . . . . .California, Colorado
White, Philander Crawford . . . . .California
White, Rufus D. . . . . .California
White, S. G. . . . . .Colorado, Texas
White, T. Brook . . . . .Oregon
White, Thomas J. . . . . . .Idaho, Oregon, Traveling
White, W. A. . . . . .Kansas, Traveling
White, W. S. . . . . .Texas
White, W. W. . . . . .Texas
White, William A. . . . . . .Colorado, New Mexico,
                                    Oklahoma
White, William G. . . . . .California
White's Studio . . . . .British Columbia
White's Young America Picture Gallery . .Traveling
Whiteaker & Hurd . . . . .Oregon
Whiteaker, William H. . . . . .Oregon
Whitefield, Frank . . . . .California
Whiteside, Huldah . . . . .Kansas
Whiteside, Joseph K. . . . . .Kansas
Whitesides, William . . . . .Wisconsin
Whitfield . . . . .Texas
Whitfield, E. P. . . . . .Texas
Whiting . . . . .Wisconsin
Whitley & Walker, S. R. . . . . .Texas
Whitley & Wood . . . . .Texas
Whitley, S. R. .Texas
Whitlock .New Mexico
Whitmore, L. . . . . .Nebraska
Whitney & Roloson . . . . .Colorado
Whitney & Zimmerman . . . . .Minnesota
Whitney, A. C. . . . . .Nebraska
Whitney, Edward B. . . . . .Idaho
Whitney, G. A. (Mrs.) . . . . .Oregon
Whitney, J. . . . . .Idaho
Whitney, Joel Emmons . . . . .Minnesota
Whitney, John M. . . . . .Idaho
Whitney, May (Miss) . . . . .California
Whitney, W. H. . . . . .Colorado
Whitney, William S. . . . . .Wisconsin
Whitson's Palace Railroad Photographic
   Coach . . . . .Traveling
Whittaker & Kennedy . . . . .Texas
Whittemore, F. H. . . . . .Nebraska
Whitten, C. H. . . . . .California
Whitten, S. R. . . . . .Arkansas
Whitter, Jacob . . . . .Colorado
Whittle, J. C. .Texas
Whittlesley . . . . .Dakota
Wholesale View Company . . . . .New Mexico
Whorley's Studio . . . . .New Mexico
Whyman, Robert . . . . .Nebraska
Whyte & Harvey . . . . .Idaho
Whyte, William . . . . .Idaho, Traveling
Wickhorst, E. A. . . . . .Nebraska
Wickiser, S. H. . . . . .Missouri
Wickmiller . . . . .New Mexico
Widder, Frederick O. . . . . .California
Widerberg, Lafayette . . . . .Idaho
Widmer, William W. . . . . .Oregon
Wiggins & Barnes . . . . .Minnesota
Wiggins, Ada M. (Mrs.) . . . . .California
Wiggins, Myra Albert . . . . .Oregon
Wiggins, S. T. . . . . . . .Iowa, Minnesota, Wisconsin
Wight, W. . . . . .Texas
Wightman, Charles E. . . . . .Washington
Wightman, M. (Mrs.) . . . . .California
Wigman . . . . .Iowa

Wingrove, Bessie (Mrs.) ... California
Winkelmann, Fred C. ... Texas
Winkle, J. ... Wisconsin
Winkler, Christian ... Indian Territory, Oklahoma
Winn, J. M. ... Iowa
Winne & Poe ... Texas
Winne, Maggie ... Kansas
Winne, William ... Texas
Winnipeg Art Gallery ... West Canada
Winquist, David ... Oregon
Winslow, L. B. ... Iowa
Winslow, Mary (Miss) ... California, Traveling
Winslow, R. A. (Mrs.) ... Nebraska
Wintemute, George ... British Columbia
Wintemute, J. S. ... California, Oregon
Winter ... Oregon
Winter & Pond ... Alaska
Winter, Clarence L. ... Oregon
Winter, F. ... Missouri
Winter, F. C. ... California
Winter, Frances D. ... Oregon
Winter, John A. ... Oregon
Winter, Lloyd V. ... Alaska
Winter Photo Company ... Oregon
Winter, Robert ... California
Winther & Doerr ... Texas
Winther & Jesse ... Texas
Winther, Nicholas ... Texas
Wintler, Marion A. ... Oregon
Wirh ... Oregon
Wisdom, Charles H. ... Texas
Wise & Prindle ... California
Wise, C. T. ... California
Wise, E. W. ... Missouri
Wise, George W. ... Wisconsin
Wise, James ... California
Wise, S. H. ... Iowa
Wiseman, Rufus Frank ... Texas
Wiseman, Sir William ... British Columbia
Wiseman, William H. ... Texas
Wiskotschill, I. N. ... California
Wismer, Christian ... California
Wisner, Anna (Miss) ... Oregon
Wispa ... Colorado
Withaup, Louis C. ... New Mexico
Wither, Ada (Mrs.) ... Colorado
Withington, Eliza W. (Mrs.) ... California
Withrow, David ... British Columbia
Withs, George B. ... Wyoming
Witt & Young ... California
Wittenberg, Fred P. ... Oregon
Witter, Jacob ... Colorado
Wittick & Bliss ... New Mexico
Wittick & Burge ... Arizona
Wittick & Russell ... New Mexico
Wittick, Archie ... New Mexico
Wittick, George B. ... Arizona, Kansas, New Mexico
Wittick, Thomas ... New Mexico
Witwer, Marie ... Kansas
Witzel, A. W. ... California
Wixon, G. S. ... Traveling
Wohl, William ... Texas
Wohleb, A. (Mrs.) ... California
Wohleb, Henry ... California
Wolcott ... Colorado
Wolcott, H. B. ... Nebraska
Wolf, H. L. ... Kansas
Wolf, J. L. ... Colorado
Wolfe ... Alaska
Wolfe & Kildare ... California
Wolfe, Francis B. ... New Mexico, Texas
Wolfe, G. M. ... Oregon, Washington
Wolfe, H. F. ... California
Wolfe, Joseph M. ... California
Wolfe, Samuel A. ... California
Wolfenstein, Valentine ... California, New Mexico
Wolfgang, L. M. (Miss) ... Iowa
Wolfrom & Emery ... Missouri
Wollett, A. E. ... Iowa
Wolly, A. ... Oregon
Wolpi ... Arizona
Womach, Walter ... Idaho
Womack, J. N. ... Texas
Woman's Art Company ... Oregon
Womble, William ... Texas
Wonfor, George H. ... Arizona, New Mexico, Texas
Wood ... Texas
Wood & Coulter ... Idaho
Wood & Michel ... California
Wood, A. W. ... Missouri
Wood, Ally M. (Miss) ... California
Wood, C. S. ... Iowa
Wood, David H. ... Texas
Wood, E. ... Nebraska
Wood, E. B. ... Wisconsin
Wood, E. H. ... California, Texas
Wood, Frank ... Idaho
Wood, Frank W. ... Oregon
Wood, G. M. ... Colorado
Wood, George C. ... Wisconsin
Wood, H. E. ... Arizona
Wood, I. N. ... Wisconsin
Wood, J. R. ... Arkansas
Wood, J. W. ... Minnesota
Wood, Jessie (Miss) ... British Columbia
Wood, Romanzo E. ... California
Wood, S. W. ... Idaho
Wood, Sydney A. ... Wisconsin
Wood, T. M. ... Oregon, Washington
Wood, T. W. ... California
Wood, Thomas M. ... California, Idaho, Nevada, Traveling
Wood's Art & Photograph Gallery ... California
Wood's Art Gallery ... California
Wood's Gallery ... California
Wood's Photograph Gallery ... California
Wood's Photographic Art Gallery ... California
Woodard & Schelberger ... Texas
Woodard, A. B. ... Idaho, Washington
Woodard, A. E. ... Washington
Woodard, Alonzo Bixby ... Oregon
Woodard, Clark & Company ... Oregon
Woodard, E. A. ... California
Woodbridge's Photo Art Gallery ... Iowa
Woodbury (Mrs.) ... California
Woodbury, C. ... Colorado
Woodbury, I. Dora ... Minnesota
Woodfield, Frank W. ... Oregon
Woodman, Sheldon J. ... Kansas
Woodmansee, Frank ... Utah
Woodruff (Mrs.) ... New Mexico
Woodruff, Charles S. ... Oregon
Woodruff, Samuel ... Texas
Woods ... Nebraska
Woods & Thompson ... California
Woods, Amos ... California
Woods, David Holmes ... California
Woods, Edward L. ... California
Woods, George Reynolds ... California
Woods, J. H. ... Nebraska
Woods, J. M. ... Minnesota
Woods, R. E. ... California
Woodside, Henry Joseph ... Alaska, British Columbia
Woodward ... California
Woodward, George ... New Mexico
Woodward, R. B. ... California
Woodward, W. F. ... Oregon
Woodward, W. H. ... Iowa
Woodworth, H. S. ... Nebraska
Woody, H. C. ... California
Wooley, R. M. ... Texas
Woollett, A. E. ... Iowa
Woolley, S. P. ... Texas
Woolsey & Githens ... Kansas
Woolsey, Frank ... Oregon
Wooster & Elderkin ... New Mexico
Wooster, George N. ... Arizona
Wooten, W. H. ... Texas
Word, Thomas ... New Mexico
Worden, W. E. ... Nebraska
Worden, Willard E. ... California
Worgan, Alfred Dashwood ... British Columbia
Works & Kruger ... Texas
Works, James A. ... Texas
Works, W. R. & J. A. ... Texas
Works, William R. ... Texas
World's Panorama Company ... British Columbia
Wormer ... Traveling
Worrall, Henry ... Kansas
Worsley, B. ... Oregon
Worsley, J. W. ... Oregon
Worth, L. W. ... Arizona
Worthen, E. B. ... Wisconsin
Worthington, James ... Texas
Worthington, W. D. ... California
Worthington, W. T. ... Washington
Worthington, William Thomas ... California
Wortman, Jessie ... Kansas
Wren, J. ... British Columbia
Wren, J. C. ... Texas
Wrenshall Brothers ... Oregon
Wrensted, Benedicte ... Idaho
Wrensted, Ella ... Idaho
Wright ... Minnesota, Texas
Wright & Berkeley ... Texas
Wright & Company, C. H. ... Missouri
Wright & Company ... Texas
Wright & Parker ... New Mexico, Texas
Wright, A. R. ... Utah
Wright Art Studio ... Texas
Wright, Belah ... Kansas
Wright, Burke ... Oregon
Wright, C. J. ... Texas
Wright, Charles ... Texas
Wright, Charles C. ... Colorado
Wright, Charles C. (Mrs.) ... Colorado
Wright, Charles J. ... Texas
Wright, Daniel F. ... California
Wright, E. C. ... California
Wright, E. N. ... Texas
Wright, G. Wallace ... Colorado, Iowa
Wright, H. F. ... Oregon
Wright, Henry U. ... Wisconsin
Wright, James L. ... Texas
Wright, N. J. (Mrs.) ... California
Wright, O. B. ... Wisconsin
Wright, Peter ... California
Wright View Company ... Kansas
Wright, W. J. ... Wisconsin
Wright, W. W. ... Texas
Wright, Wilbur W. ... California
Wright, Willard ... Texas
Wright, William ... Wyoming
Wright, William J. ... Colorado
Wright, Woodward ... Texas
Wulzen, Albert H. ... California, Oregon, Traveling
Wulzen, Otto ... California
Wunderlich ... California, Washington
Wunderlich Brothers ... California
Wuth, Gustav ... California
Wyatt, C. B. ... Kansas
Wyatt, M. J. ... Nebraska
Wyatt, M. J. (Mrs.) ... Nebraska
Wyatt, W. A. ... Nebraska
Wyckoff, Joshua H. ... Wisconsin
Wyer ... Iowa
Wykes, James W. ... Texas
Wylie, E. ... California
Wyllie, E. A. S. ... California
Wyman, F. O. ... California

Abramson, Joan, *Photographers of Old Hawaii,* Island Heritage, Honolulu, 1976.

Alinder, James, ed., with essays by David Featherstone and Russ Anderson, *Carleton E. Watkins, Photographs of the Columbia River and Oregon,* Friends of Photography, in association with the Weston Gallery, 1979.

Andrews, Ralph W., *Curtis' Western Indians: Life and works of Edward S. Curtis,* Superior Publishing, Seattle, 1962.

Andrews, Ralph W., *Photographers of the Frontier West: Their Lives and Their Work,* Superior Publishing Company, Seattle, 1965.

Andrews, Ralph W., *Picture Gallery Pioneers,* Superior Publishing Company, Seattle, 1964.

Becker, Ethel A., *A Treasurey of Alaskana: The Alaska Story,* Superior Publishing Company, Seattle, 1969.

Becker, Ethel A., *Klondike '98: E. A. Hegg Goldrush Album,* Binfords & Mort, Portland, Oregon, 1967.

Belous, Russell E., and Robert E. Weinstein, *Will Soule: Indian Photographer at Ft. Sill, Oklahoma, 1869–74,* Ward Ritchie Press, Los Angeles, 1973.

Bohn, David, and Rudolfo Petschek, *Kinsey Photographer, The Locomotive Portraits,* Chronicle Books, San Francisco, 1984.

Bohn, David, and Rudolfo Petschek, *Kinsey Photographer,* Scrimshaw Press, two volumes, 1978; Chronicle Books, San Francisco, two volumes in one, 1982.

Bolotin, Norm, *Klondike Lost, A Decade of Photographs by Kinsey & Kinsey,* Alaska Northwest Publishing Company, Anchorage, 1980.

Bosak, Jon, "Andrew A. Forbes – Photographs of the Owens Valley Paiute," *Journal of California Anthropology,* Banning, California, summer 1975.

Brigman, Anne, *Songs of a Pagan,* Caxton Printers, Ltd., Caldwell, Idaho, 1949.

Broder, Patrick Janis, *Shadows On Glass: The Indian World of Ben Wittick,* Rowman & Littlefield, 1990.

Brown, Joseph Epes, *The North American Indians, Photographs by Edward S. Curtis,* Aperture Books, New York, 1972.

Brown, Mark H., and W. R. Felton, *Before Barbed Wire: L. A. Huffman, Photographer on Horseback,* Bramwell House, New York, 1956.

Brown, Mark H., and W. R. Felton, *The Frontier Years,* Bramwell House, New York, 1955.

Brust, James S., M.D., "John H. Fouch, First Post Photographer at Fort Keogh," *Montana, the Magazine of Western History,* spring, 1994.

Callarman, Barbara Dye, *Photographers of Nineteenth Century Los Angeles County,* Hacienda Gateway Press, Los Angeles, California, 1993.

Calmenson, Wendy Cunkle, "Likenesses Taken in the Most Approved Style: William Shew, Pioneer Daguerreotypist," *California Historical Quarterly,* San Francisco, spring, 1977.

Cardoza, Christopher, ed., *Native Nations: First Americans as Seen by Edward S. Curtis,* Callaway Editions/ Bullfinch Press /Little Brown and Company, Boston, New York, Toronto, London, 1993.

Carleton E. Watkins, Photographs 1861–74, essay by Peter Palmquist, Fraenkel Gallery, San Francisco, in association with Bedford Arts, 1989.

"Carleton E. Watkins: Pioneer Photographer," *California History,* California Historical Society, San Francisco, fall, 1978.

Coke, Van Deren, *Photography in New Mexico: From the Daguerreotype to the Present,* University of New Mexico Press, Albuquerque, 1979.

Coleman, A. D., and T. C. McLuhan, *Portraits from North American Indian Life,* Outerbridge & Lazard, Inc., in association with the American Museum of Natural History, New York, 1972.

Coulter, Edith M., and Jeanne Van Nostrand, *A Camera In the Gold Rush,* Book Club of California, San Francisco, 1946.

Cunningham, Robert E., *Indian Territory: A Frontier Photographic Record by W. S. Prettyman,* University of Oklahoma Press, 1957.

Current, Karen, *Photography and the Old West,* Abradale Press/Harry N. Abrams, Inc., New York, 1986.

Curtis, Edward S., *Indian Days of the Long Ago,* World Book Company, Yonkers–on–Hudson, New York, 1927.

Davis, Barbara A., *Edward S. Curtis, The Life and Times of a Shadow Catcher,* Chronicle Books, San Francisco, 1985.

Davis, Lynn Ann, with Nelson Foster, *A Photographer in the Kingdom: Christian J. Hedemann's Early Images of Hawai'i,* Bishop Museum Press, 1988.

Davis, Lynn Ann, *Na Pa'i Ki'i,* Bishop Museum Press, Honolulu, 1980.

Dillon, Richard H., *Images of Chinatown: Louis J. Stellman's Chinatown Photographs*, Book Club of California, San Francisco, 1976.

Dillon, Richard H., *The Hatchet Men: The Story of the Tong Wars in San Francisco's Chinatown*, Coward–McCann, Inc., New York, 1962.

Dillon, Richard H., *North Beach: The Italian Heart of San Francisco, Photographs by J. B. Monaco, (1856–1938)*, Presidio Press, Novato, California, 1985.

Dingus, Rick, *The Photographic Artifacts of Timothy O'Sullivan*, University of New Mexico Press, Albuquerque, 1982.

Dornin, George D., *Thirty Years Ago: Gold Rush memories of a Daguerreotype Artist*, Carl Mautz Publishing, Nevada City, 1995.

Driebe, Tom, and Dave Palmiter, *In Search of the Wild Indian: Photographs and Life Works by Carl & Grace Moon*, Maurose Publishing Company, Moscow, Pennsylvania, 1996.

Dunn, James Taylor, "The Diary of Tallmadge Elwell: Pioneer Daguerreotypist, 1852," *The Daguerreian Annual 1992*, The Daguerreian Society, Eureka, California, 1992.

Edward Muybridge: The Stanford Years, 1872–82, Stanford University Catalogue for an exhibition of Muybridge images, Palo Alto, California, 1972.

Elder, Paul, *California the Beautiful: Camera Studies of California Artists, With selections of Prose and Verse from Western Writers*, Paul Elder & Company, San Francisco, 1911.

F. Jay Haynes, Photographer, Montana Historical Society Press, 1981.

Farr, William E., and K. Ross Toole, *Montana: Images of the Past*, Pruett Publishing Company, Boulder, Colorado, 1978.

Fleming, Paul Richardson, and Judith Luskey, *The North American Indians in Early Photographs*, Harper & Rowe, New York, 1986.

Forman Hanna: Pictorial Photographer of the Southwest, Northland Press, Flagstaff, Arizona, 1985.

Fowler, Don D., ed., *"Photographed all the Best Scenery," Jack Hillers' Diary of the Powell Expedition, 1871–1875*, University of Utah Press, Salt Lake City, 1972.

Fowler, Don D., *The Western Photographs of John K. Hillers: "Myself in the Water,"* Smithsonian Institute Press, Washington and London, 1989.

Frederick, Richard, and Jeanne Engerman, *Asahel Curtis, Photographs of the Great Northwest*, Washington State Historical Society, Seattle, 1983.

Frink, Maurice, with Christian Barthlemess, *Photographer on an Army Mule*, University of Oklahoma Press, Norman, 1965.

Genthe, Arnold, *As I Remember*, Reynal & Hitchcock, New York, 1936.

Graybill, Florence Curtis, and Victor Boesen, *Edward Sheriff Curtis: Visions of a Vanishing Race*, American Legacy Press, New York, 1981.

Haas, Robert Bartlett, "William Herman Rulofson, Pioneer Daguerreotypist and Photographic Educator," *California Historical Society Quarterly*, San Francisco, December, 1955, and March, 1956.

Haas, Robert Bartlett, *Muybridge, Man in Motion*, University of California Press, Berkeley, 1976.

Haines, Robert D. Jr., *Carl Moon; Photographer & Illustrator of the American Southwest*, Argonaut Bookshop, San Francisco, 1982.

Hales, Peter B., *William Henry and the Transformation of the American Landscape*, Temple University Press, Philadelphia, 1988.

Hall, Dodds and Triggs, *The World of William Notman*, David R. Godin, Boston, Massachusetts, 1993.

Harrell, Thomas H., Ph.D., *William Henry Jackson, An Annotated Bibliography [1862 to 1995]*, Carl Mautz Publishing, Nevada City, California, 1995.

Hart, Arthur A., *Camera Eye on Idaho: Pioneer Photography 1863–1913*, Caxton Printers, Ltd., Caldwell, Idaho, 1990.

Hayden, F. V., *Sun Pictures of Rocky Mountain Scenery*, Julius Bien, New York, 1870.

Hedren, Paul L., *With Crook in the Black Hills: Stanley J. Morrow's 1876 Photographic Legacy*, Pruett Publishing Company, Boulder, Colorado, 1985.

Heski, Thomas M., *The Little Shadow Catcher: D. F. Barry*, Superior Publishing Company, Seattle, 1978.

Heyman, Therese Thau, *Anne Brigman: Pictorial Photographer/Pagan/Member of the Photo–Secession*, Oakland Museum, Oakland, California, 1974.

Hickman, Paul, and Terence Pitts, *George Fiske, Yosemite Photographer*, Northland Press, Flagstaff, Arizona, 1980.

Hively, William, *Nine Classic California Photographers*, Friends of the Bancroft Library, Berkeley, 1980.

Hoobler, Dorothy, and Thomas Hoobler, *Photographing the Frontier*, G. P. Putnam's Sons, New York, 1980.

Hood, Mary V. Jessup, and Robert Bartlett Haas, "Eadweard Muybridge's Yosemite Valley Photographs, 1867–72," *California Historical Quarterly*, San Francisco, March, 1963.

Horan, James D., *Timothy O'Sullivan, America's Forgotton Photographer*, Bonanza Books, New York, 1966.

Houlihan, Patrick T., and Betsy E. Houlihan, *Lummis in the Pueblos*, Northland Press, Flagstaff, 1986.

Hurt, Wesley R., and William E. Lass, *Frontier Photographer: Stanley J. Morrow's Dakota Years*, University of South Dakota and University of Nebraska Press, 1956.

Huyda, Richard J., *Camera in the Interior: 1858, H. L. Hime, Photographer*, Coach House Press, Totonto, 1975.

Irwin, Will, *Old Chinatown: A Book of Pictures by Arnold Genthe*, Mitchell Kennerley, New York, 1908.

Jackson, Clarence S., *Picture Maker of the Old West; William H. Jackson*, Charles Scribners & Son, New York and London, 1947.

Jackson, William Henry, *Time Exposure; The Autobiography of William Henry Jackson*, G. P. Putman's Sons, New York, 1940.

Jensen, Richard E., R. Eli Paul, and John E. Carter, *Eyewitness at Wounded Knee*, University of Nebraska Press, Omaha, 1991.

Kibbey, Mead B., *The Railroad Photographs of Alfred A. Hart, Artist*, California State Library Foundation, Sacramento, 1995.

Kilgo, Dolores A., *Likeness and Landscape: Thomas M. Easterly and the Art of the Daguerreotype*, Missouri Historical Society Press, St. Louis, 1994.

Kolb, Ellsworth L., *Through the Grand Canyon from Wyoming to Mexico*, Macmillan Company, New York, 1938.

Kombs, Barry B., *Westward to Promontory; Building the Pacific Across the Plains and Mountains*, American West Publishing Company, Palo Alto, California, 1969.

Kraus, George, *High Road to Promontory: Building the Central Pacific Across the High Sierra*, American West Publishing Company, Palo Alto, California, 1969.

Landry, Janet, and Joan Lane, *"Horsethief" Kelley and his Camera*, Estate of A. Bertha Masterson, Aspen, Colorado, 1972.

Latour, Ira H., ed., *Silver Shadows: A Directory and History of Early Photography in Chico and Twelve Counties of Northern California*, Chico Museum Association, Chico, California, 1993.

Lucey, Donna M., *Photographing Montana 1894–1928: The Life and Work of Evelyn Cameron*, Alfred A. Knopf, New York, 1991.

Lyman, Christopher M., *The Vanishing Race and Other Illusions: Photographs of Indians by Edward S. Curtis*, Pantheon Books, New York, in association with the Smithsonian Institution, 1982.

MacDonnell, Kevin, *Eadweard Muybridge: The Man Who Invented the Moving Picture*, Little, Brown & Company, Boston and Toronto, 1972.

Mahood, Ruth I., ed., Beaumont Newhall, introduction, *Photographer of the Southwest: Adam Clark Vroman, 1856–1916*, Ward Ritchie Press, Los Angeles, 1961.

Mangan, Terry Wm., *Colorado on Glass: Colorado's First Half–Century as Seen by the Camera*, Sundance Ltd., Denver, 1975.

Marr, Carolyn, *Portrait in Time: Photographs of the Makah by Samuel G. Morse, 1896–1903*, Makah Cultural and Research Center, Seattle, 1987.

Masayesva, Jr., Victor, and Erin Younger, *Hopi Photographers, Hopi Images*, Sun Tracks & University of Arizona Press, Tucson, 1983.

Mattison, David, *Camera Workers: The British Columbia Photographer's Directory 1858–1900*, Camera Workers Press, Victoria, B. C., 1985.

McLuhan, T. C., *Touch the Earth: A Self-Portrait of Indian Existence*, Outerbridge & Dienstfrey, New York, 1971.

Miller, Allen Clark, *Photographer of a Frontier: The Photographs of Peter Britt*, Interface, Eureka, California, 1976.

Miller, Nina Hull, *Shutters West*, Sage Books, Denver, 1962.

Momaday, N. Scott, *With Eagle Glance: American Indian Photographic Images, 1868–1931*, Museum of the American Indians, New York, 1982.

Montana Historical Society, *F. Jay Haynes, Photographer*, Montana Historical Society Press, 1981.

Moorhouse, Major Lee, *Souvenir Album of Noted Indian Photographs*, Lee Moorhouse, Pendleton, Oregon, 1906.

Morgan, Murray, *One Man's Gold Rush, A Klondike Album, Photographs by E. A. Hegg*, University of Washington Press, Seattle, 1967.

Morieta, Daniela P., ed., *Charles F. Lummis—The Centennial Exhibition Commemorating His Tramp Across the Continent*, Southwest Museum, Pasadena, 1985.

Naef, Weston J., *Era of Exploration: The Rise of Landscape Photography in the American West—1860–1885*, Albright–Knox Art Gallery and Metropolitan Museum of Art, New York, 1975.

Naef, Weston J., *The Rise of Landscape Photography in the American West, 1860–85: Era of Exploration*, Metropolitan Museum of Art, New York, 1977.

Newhall, Beaumont, and Dianna E. Edkins, *William H. Jackson,* Morgan & Morgan, New York, 1974.

O'Connor, Nancy Fields, *Fred E. Miller, Photographer of The Crows,* University of Montana Press, 1985.

Owenulph, "No Trade for Heroes," *The America West,* Palo Alto, California, 1968.

Palmquist, Peter E., *Fine California Views: the Photographs of A. W. Ericson,* Interface California Corporation, 1975.

Palmquist, Peter E., *J. J. Reilly: A Stereoscopic Odyssey 1838–94,* Community Memorial Museum, Yuba City, California, 1989.

Palmquist, Peter E., "Jewish Photographer of the Modoc Indian War," *Western States Jewish History,* Vol. XXII, No. 4, Santa Monica, California, July, 1990.

Palmquist, Peter E., *Carleton E. Watkins, Photographer of the American West,* University of New Mexico Press, Albuquerque, for the Amon Carter Museum, 1983.

Palmquist, Peter E., *The Daguerreian Annual 1990,* The Daguerreian Society, Eureka, California, 1990.

Palmquist, Peter E., "Photographing the Modoc Indian War: Lewis Heller versus Eadweard Muybridge," *History of Photography,* Vol. 2, No. 3, London, July, 1978.

Palmquist, Peter E., "Photography in the West – II," *Journal of the West,* Sunflower University Press, Manhattan, Kansas, 1989.

Palmquist, Peter E., *Pioneer X–Ray Photographer,* Judah L. Magnes Museum, Berkeley, California, 1990.

Palmquist, Peter E., "Raffle Wars: A Chronology of Alphonse J. Liebert in California and France", *The Daguerreian Annual 1992,* The Daguerreian Society,

Palmquist, Peter E., *Redwood & Lumbering in California Forests, A Reconsruction of the Original Edgar Cherry Edition,* Book Club of California, San Francisco, 1983.

Palmquist, Peter E., "Return to El Dorado: A Century of California Stereographs," *California Museum of Photography Bulletin,* Riverside, California, 1986.

Palmquist, Peter E., "William Herman Rulofson: 'The P. T. Barnum of American Photography,'" *The Daguerreian Annual, 1993,* The Daguerreian Society, Green Bay, Wisconsin, 1993.

Palmquist, Peter E., *Lawrence & Houseworth, Thomas Houseworth & Company: A Unique View of the West 1860– 86,* National Stereoscopic Society, Columbus, Ohio, 1980.

Palmquist, Peter E., with Lincoln Kilian, *The Photographers of the Humboldt Bay Region,* Vols. 1–7, Peter E. Palmquist, Arcata, California, 1987.

Palmquist, Peter E., *With Nature's Children: Emma B. Freeman [1880–1928] – Camera and Brush,* Interface California Corporation, Eureka, California, 1976.

"Photographs of the Southwest 1879–1977," *New America,* University of New Mexico, Albuquerque.

Pritzker, Barry, *Edward S. Curtis,* Brompton Books, Greenwich, Connecticut, 1993.

Richards, Bradley W., M.D., *The Savage View: Charles R. Savage, Pioneer Mormon Photographer,* Carl Mautz Publishing, Nevada City, California, 1995.

Richards, Bradley W., M.D., "The Other Promontory Photographer," *Utah historical Quarterly,* Vol. 60, spring, 1992.

Robinson, Bart, *Great Days in the Rockies: The Photographs of Byron Harmon 1906–1934,* Oxford University Press, Toronto, 1978.

Roe, JoAnn, Frank Matsura, *Frontier Photographer,* Madrona Publishers, Seattle, 1981.

Rudisill, Richard, *Directory of Photographers of the New Mexico Territory, 1854–1912,* Museum of New Mexico, Albuquerque, 1973.

Sabers, Mary A., *Charles F. Lummis: A Bibliography,* University of Arizona Library, Tucson, 1977.

San Francisco in the 1850s: Photographic Views by G. R. Fardon, facimile of Fardon's book, *San Francisco Album,* introduction by Robert A. Sobieszek, George Eastman House and Dover Publications, New York, 1977.

Satterfield, Archie, *An Asahel Curtis Portfolio,* Chronicle Books, Seattle, 1985.

Sawyer, Mark, *Forman Hanna: Pictorial Photographer of the Southwest,* Northland Press, Flagstaff, 1985.

Scherer, Joanna Cohan, Editor, *An Idaho photogrpaher In Focus,* Idaho State University Press, Pocatello, Idaho, 1993.

Schwartz, Joan M., "The Past in Focus: Photography & British Columbia, 1858–1914," *B. C. Studies,* University of British Columbia, winter, 1981–82.

Smith, Dwight L., ed., *The Photographer and the River, 1889–90 (Diary of F. A. Nims),* Stagecoach Press, Santa Fe, 1967.

Snyder, Joel, *American Frontiers: The Photographs of Timothy H. O'Sullivan, 1867–1874,* Aperture, New York, 1981.

Solomon Nunes Carvalho: Painter, Photographer and Prophet in Nineteenth Century America, Jewish Historical Society of Maryland, Baltimore, 1989 (various authors, exhibition catalogue).

Street, Richard Steven, *A Kern County Diary, The Forgotten Photographs of Carleton E. Watkins, 1881–88*, Kern County Museum, Bakersfield, 1983.

Sucher, David, ed., *The Asahel Curtis Sampler: Photographs of Puget Sound Past*, Puget Sound Access, Seattle, Washington, 1973.

Sutton, Royal, *The Face of Courage: The Rinehart Collection of Indian Photographs*, Old Army Press, Ft. Collins, 1972.

The Early Pacific Coast Photographs of Carleton E. Watkins, Water Resources Center Archives, Archives Series Report No. 8, University of California, Berkeley, 1960.

Tilden, Freeman, *Following the Frontier with F. Jay Haynes: Pioneer Photographer of the Old West*, Alfred A. Knopf, New York, 1964.

Toedtemeier, Terry, "Oregon Photography: The First Fifty Years," *Oregon Historical Quarterly*, Portland, spring, 1993.

Toedtemeier, Terry, *Wild Beauty: Photography of the Columbia River Gorge, 1865–1915*, Portland Art Museum, Portland.

Traywick, Ben T., *Camillus Sidney Fly, The Man Who Photographed History*, Red Marie's, 1985.

Treadwell, T. K. Tex and William C. Darrah, *Stereophotographers Index*, National Stereoscopic Association, 1993.

Wadsworth, Nelson B., *Set in Stone – Fixed in Glass: The Great Mormon Temple and its Photographers*, Signature Books, Salt Lake City, 1992.

Wadsworth, Nelson B., *Through Camera Eyes*, Brigham Young University Press, Salt Lake City, 1975.

Watkins to Weston: 101 Years of California Photography 1849–1950, Santa Barbara Museum of Art, Roberts Rinehart Publishing, Santa Barbara, 1992.

Webb, William, and Robert A. Weinstein, *Dwellers at the Source: Southwestern Indian Photographs of A. C. Vroman, 1895–1904*, Grossman Publishers, New York, 1973.

Weinstein, Robert A., *Tall Ships on Puget Sound, The Marine Photographs of Wilhelm Hester*, University of Washington Press, Seattle, 1978.

White, Stephen, *Harry Smith: Magic Moments*, Stephen White Editions, Los Angeles, 1981.

Williams, Susan, "The Truth Be Told: The Union Pacific Railroad Photographs of Andrew J. Russell," *View Camera*, Sacramento, California, January/February, 1886.

Wilson, Bonnie G., "Working the Light: Nineteeth Century Professional Photographers in Minnesota," *Minnesota History*, Minnesota Historical Society, St. Paul, summer, 1990.

With New Eyes: Toward an Asian American Art History in the West, San Francisco University, 1985.

Wolf, Daniel, *The American Space: Meaning in Nineteenth Century Landscape Photography*, Wesleyan University Press, Middletown, Connecticut, 1983.

Wright, Barton, Marnie Gaede and Marc Gaede, *The Hopi Photographs of Kate Corey*, Chaco Press, Albuquerque, 1986.

Wright, Robert I., *A Patterson Postcard Checklist/Workbook*, Robert Wright, Ashland, Oregon.

Wyatt, Victoria, *Images from the Inside Passage: An Alaskan Portrait by Winter & Pond*, University of Washington Press, Seattle, in association with the Alaska State Library, 1989.

ALBUMEN PRINT
Positive photographic print made on paper coated with eggwhite and salt solution which is sensitized with silver nitrate solution. Prints were made by exposing the paper to sunlight through a negative.

AMBROTYPE
A glass collodion positive patented in the United States in 1854 by James Cutting.

CABINET CARD
Essentially a larger (4 ½″ x 6 ½″) version of the carte-de-visite, this popular format supplanted the carte-de-visite by the late 1870s, although the first cabinet card photographs appeared in 1866 in England. Primarily a medium for portraiture, the cabinet card dominated commercial photography until the turn-of-the-century.

CALOTYPE (also called TALBOTYPE)
The first successful negative/positive process invented by William Henry Fox Talbot and patented by him in 1841. This process entailed exposing paper sensitized with potassium iodide and silver nitrate in a camera and developing the negative in gallic acid and silver nitrate. Prints were made by the contact method in daylight on paper sensitized with salt and silver nitrate.

CARBON PRINT
Prints produced by exposing a negative against a pigmented gelatin tissue sensitized with potassium bichromate. The surface of the tissue hardens in relation to the amount of light received and when washed, leaves a positive image which is permanent.

CARTE-DE-VISITE
A format developed by Disderi in Paris and patented in 1854 consisting of a 2 ½″ by 4 ½″ mounted photographic print. The primary format for portraiture from the beginning of the Civil War to the late 1870s, the carte-de-visite is referred to often as "cdv" by collectors today. The format continued to be made up to the turn-of-the-century, but was eclipsed in popularity by the larger cabinet card.

COLLODION PROCESS
A process for making negatives involving a glass plate coated with a light sensitive emulsion of gun cotton dissolved in alcohol and ether and mixed with potassium iodide and potassium bromide. Also known as the wet plate collodion process.

CYANOTYPE
A print made with a paper impregnated with iron salts and potassium ferricyanide, creating an image where the darks are blue. Popular paper from the 1890s to WWI.

DAGUERREOTYPE
The first practical photographic process introduced in Paris in 1839 by one of it's inventors, Louis Jaques Mande' Daguerre. The process required a silver coated copper plate which was sensitized with vapors of iodine and developed in mercury fumes after exposure in a camera. The images produced were one-of-a-kind and often beautiful although reflective like a mirror. Being very delicate to touch or the atmosphere, they were sealed and encased in glass, brass mat and leather case.

DRY PLATE
The successor to the wet plate collodion process, dry plates were glass sheets coated with silver halides suspended in gelatin. These pre-prepared negative plates supplanted the wet plate process by the 1880s.

FERROTYPE (also TINTYPE or MELAINOTYPE)
A positive photographic image appearing on a thin sheet of varnished iron which has been sensitized with collodion. A very popular format which competed with the carte-de-visite from the late 1850s through the 1870s, finally becoming a novelty format in use at fairs and amusement parks to the 1930s.

POSTCARD
The photographic postcard became common just after the turn of the century. Beginning in 1902, Eastman Kodak and other manufacturers marketed postcard format photographic paper that was sensitive enough to print under artificial light. This simplified the process of printing photographic negatives and further encouraged both amateur and commercial production of photographic postcards. It was the widespread use of the postcard format in the hands of both professionals and amateurs that continued the visual recording of culture begun by stereoviews.

STEREOVIEW (also STEREOGRAPH)
A pair of views taken at slightly different angles and mounted side by side. Viewed separately by each eye in a stereoviewer, the two images merge to create the illusion of three dimensions. This format was used early in the daguerreotype era and increased in popularity when paper prints became the standard, eventually becoming an item of amusement in virtually every household in America. It is through this format that 19th century culture can be visually witnessed.